HANTA YO means
Clear the Way!

And HANTA YO has done just that. It clears the way
into understanding of the intimate lives and thoughts of
the Teton Sioux. It is based upon an actual Mahto
Indian document discovered in 1865. It is the
culmination of 25 years of research by its author
assisted by a full-blooded Dakotah Sioux who helped
her achieve a translation that is hauntingly beautiful
and powerfully dramatic. It has achieved nationwide
bestsellerdom and nationwide acclaim as a unique
accomplishment and a profound reading experience.

"A masterpiece. This epic book makes every other book
about Indians seem shallow and out of date."
            —David L. Wolper, producer
                of *Roots* on television

"To say that HANTA YO is one of the best novels by
an American to be published in recent years is certainly
true . . . It is triumphantly singular . . . a major
accomplishment."   —*Philadelphia Inquirer*

"Fascinating . . . a genuine saga . . . I felt privileged to
have a view through special Dakotah windows to the
past."   —Hunka-Nozhe (Louis W. Ballard)

"A magnificent achievement . . . a strong, beautiful novel that stands tall, runs deep, rings true. It is a triumph, a song of and to the spirit of the Dakotah Indians." —*Publishers Weekly*

"A substantial novel, impressive . . . there is revealed a fascinating world (and) the humanity that informs this special world . . . noble and real and pervasive."
—*Washington Post*

"*Hanta Yo* is an incredible literary and linguistic achievement." —*The Cincinnati Enquirer*

"Perhaps most remarkable of all are the insights into the mystique of Indian religious and supernatural beliefs, the changeless, changing Kinship between Man and Nature." —*The Milwaukee Journal*

"A new must for your reading list . . . one of the most insightful, detailed and fascinating books on Indians I've encountered . . . the joys are many."
—*The Nashville Tennessean*

"A remarkable evocation of the life of the Plains Indians, profound in its understanding, poetic in its telling, evocative of far distances in time and of the people who lived there." —Allen Drury

"It is humbling, enlarging and heartbreakingly sad. It is a requiem that tells the truth without a trace of sentimentality."
—*The Cleveland Press*

"A beguiling guidebook to a romantic and often admirable way of life."
—*The Miami Herald*

"The most honest portrayal of Plains Indian life ever undertaken by a white writer."
—*Charlotte News*

"Ordinary adjectives don't do it justice. The book is an experience to savor ... a book to marvel at, to sink into, to find refuge in and to read again and again."
—*Schenectady Gazette*

"A celebration of the natural life."
—*Chicago Tribune Book World*

"Magnetic."
—*Kirkus Reviews*

"So moving, so authentic."
—*New Republic*

"Spectacular."
—*Los Angeles Times*

ATTENTION: SCHOOLS AND CORPORATIONS

WARNER books are available at quantity discounts with bulk purchase for educational, business, or sales promotional use. For information, please write to: SPECIAL SALES DEPARTMENT, WARNER BOOKS, 666 FIFTH AVENUE, NEW YORK, N.Y. 10103.

**ARE THERE WARNER BOOKS
YOU WANT BUT CANNOT FIND IN YOUR LOCAL STORES?**

You can get any WARNER BOOKS title in print. Simply send title and retail price, plus 50¢ per order and 20¢ per copy to cover mailing and handling costs for each book desired. New York State and California residents add applicable sales tax. Enclose check or money order only, no cash please, to: WARNER BOOKS, P.O. BOX 690, NEW YORK, N.Y. 10019.

HANTA YO

Ruth Beebe Hill

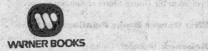

WARNER BOOKS

A Warner Communications Company

WARNER BOOKS EDITION

Copyright © 1979 by Ruth Beebe Hill
All rights reserved.

This Warner Books Edition is published by arrangement with
Doubleday & Company, Inc.,
245 Park Avenue,
New York, N.Y. 10017.

Cover art by L.C. Winborg

Warner Books, Inc.,
666 Fifth Avenue,
New York, N.Y. 10103

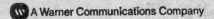 A Warner Communications Company

Printed in the United States of America

First Warner Books Printing: *March, 1980*

Reissued: *December, 1983*

15   14   13   12   11

TO BORROUGHS REID HILL

Contents

Introduction

"IF IT is not of the spirit, it is not Indian." The grandfathers have said so.

I am Dakotah; I, Chunksa Yuha, a Mdewakantonwan Dakotah, grandson of Wapaśa and brought up speaking the archaic language.

I am Dakotah, a man in my seventieth winter and but three generations removed from the tribal rememberers, from the Dakotah grandfathers.

I am Dakotah, son of Tatekahomni; I, Chunksa Yuha, to whom Itesankiye, renowned healer of the Isanyati Dakotah, gave a name and a personal song.

I am Chunksa Yuha, one of eight Dakotah boys to whom the old, old men of the tribe taught the suppressed songs and ceremonies, material suppressed for two hundred years, suppressed until now, until this book *Hanta Yo*.

I am Dakotah, raised by the grandfathers, kept out of schools and away from white contact until age twelve, thirteen, when I was entered in a public school to learn English. But at home they continued to tutor me in the Siouan dialects.

In the years that followed high school, I walked the halls of ivy-draped buildings to acquire knowledge of the whiteman's music, of the whiteman's way to record and arrange music. But I remain Indian in thought, word, and act. The grandfathers intended that I so live. For of the eight children chosen to perpetuate the ceremonies and songs, I alone am alive.

Forty years ago I began my search for a writer, for someone willing and eager to learn my language, to hear the ceremonies not as misinterpreted by missionaries, soldiers, and drifting mountain men but as spoken in the old Indian tongue and without need for interpretation. During my search I was approached by journalists, published authors, professors, and students, all these persons wanting an 'as told to' story, all looking for the blood, war, and sudden-death saga of a 'warrior society.' But none agreeing to take the time—years if necessary—to enter into an understanding of the Indian as a man of habitual spiritual consciousness.

Then one day in 1963 I found someone: a woman, a geologist, a descendant of a Plymouth colony family, and wife of a descendant of a Jamestown colony family, a person who had sustained an interest in the American Indian from her childhood. She had read on the western tribes for ten years and for seven more years had lived, intermittently, on reservations in the midwestern United States and Canada, an invited guest of Indian families. Finally she had considered herself mature enough to begin the construction of her story on the Siouan peoples before white influence. When I met her, she had completed the second draft of a two-thousand-page documented novel but was far from satisfied with her work.

She showed me her recorded list of references—perhaps twelve hundred nonfiction books and pamphlets on the plains tribes—but she already had recognized that each writer had drawn from his predecessor, compiling, repeating, embroidering, until the Indian had emerged as a 'man nobody knows.'

She explained her goal to me: to translate the two thousand pages of her original manuscript into the archaic Dakotah/Lakotah and back into English and so assure herself of no loss of Indian idiom. Or heart. Or truth.

I began to entertain thoughts concerning an old Indian ritual of purification, but my colleague was unprepared for such rites. But as I saw it, she had made a journey along a path of blindness. She not yet knew that to write 'truly Indian' she needed to discard almost every concept relative to Indians ever formulated by the whiteman. She needed to approach her story from the viewpoint of Indian philosophy; she needed to check her premise.

She agreed to study the language, not only what Stephen R. Riggs had recorded in his ponderous Dakotah dictionary but the grammar—the syntax, the structure, the voice—of the prereservation period. And her only true source for the archaic language was the ancient songs. That remarkable woman Frances Densmore had produced an analytical study of Indian music, but the grandfathers had withheld from even the best of her Indian informants that which could be misinterpreted and corrupted.

Before starting to work together, it was essential that I and the writer establish a terminology beginning with an understanding of what the Dakotah meant—and means—by 'spiritual.' The Indian, I told her, begins with the spirit of man and works down through the laws of the universe. Taku śkanśkan, I said—something-in-movement, spiritual vitality. Taku śkanśkan, I repeated; all the religion there ever was in that one phrase.

And so I, Chunksa Yuha, and Ruth Beebe Hill began a scholarly study of the ancient Siouan language. We were to spend days, weeks, occasionally months on a single sentence, searching out the root, the prime word, the etymon, before contraction. We were to use up two years, seven days a week, on the translation of legends as the old ones had taught those stories to me. In 1969 we began a methodical translation of the original draft of her book into the earliest-possible forms of the parent-stock Dakotah tongue, with appropriate variants from the Lakotah dialect.

And now through traditions and ceremonial songs, she saw a premise and a pattern formed, something that could not be broken down. The old ceremonial songs had given the key to the esoteric language, which had nothing to do with great mystery; it was simply the language of the true scholar, even as the scientist has a terminology unfamiliar to the layman.

Soon her book began to acquire substance, a vitality that flowed through each sentence, revealing tremendous concepts. And as I reviewed the written words, I visualized a bridge across a gulf, something to bring together two races of entirely different natures.

I am the Dakotah and so I know that this book stands alone, a book that will survive the generations. For within its pages flows śkan, taku śkanśkan, something-in-movement, spiritual vitality.

I, Chunksa Yuha, am but a messenger from my people, all Isanyati Dakotah visible and invisible. But I and they know that the importance is the message, not the messenger.

It is proper that only the woman's name be mentioned as author—for she is the author: Ruth Beebe Hill wrote the book, constructed the bridge. And she has made that bridge of an enduring substance, something furnished by the consciousness of a race that, in truth, no longer exists, a race of individuals who recognized man as owner of the earth, who regarded nothing more sacred than the right of choice.

Now after twenty-five years in construction, that bridge, created out of śkan, the life force, is herewith opened, a two-way bridge that spans a gulf two hundred years wide.

I, Chunksa Yuha, grandson of Wapaśa, say so, say so.

CHUNKSA YUHA

14

To the reader

ADMIT, ASSUME, because, believe, could, doubt, end, expect, faith, forget, forgive, guilt, how, it, mercy, pest, promise, should, sorry, storm, them, us, waste, we, weed—neither
these words nor the conceptions for which they stand appear in this book; they are the whiteman's import to the
New World, the newcomer's contribution to the vocabulary
of the man he called Indian. Truly, the parent Indian families possessed neither these terms nor their equivalents.

The American Indian, even before Columbus, was the
remnant of a very old race in its final stage, a race that had
attained perhaps the highest working concept of individualism ever practiced. Neither the word 'free' nor any corresponding term occurs in the root language, in the primal
concept: there never was anything for the Indian to free
himself from. His was the spirit not seeking truth but
holding on to truth. And his was the mind nourished on
choice. Whatever he needed to know, nature sooner or later
revealed to him. And that which he desired to know—the
best way to achieve his maximum spiritual potential—was
the only mystery he chose to investigate.

His approach to this mystery was never that of a
mystic; he never pursued psychic powers but only his own
spiritual growth. His method involved neither stimulants
nor hypnosis; the solitude and starve of a vision-quest was a
matter of uninterrupted concentration relative to the path
he already intended to follow.

He recognized his spirit—his familiar-voice—as a

truth-bearer that told him what to do, never what not to do; his reasoning mind made the choice to act or not to act.

His view was never that of the altruist; he was a trader in spiritual values, which he demonstrated not by what he gave but to whom he gave and why.

This book abounds in rhetorical questions. But the rhetorical was the only form of questioning the Indian used; he never answered to anyone but himself, never answered for anyone but himself. He conjugates the verb 'think' in the first person singular only; he never presumes.

His language is rich in expressions of relationships but lacks the relative pronoun and the neuter 'it.' 'He' and 'she' are incorporated with other parts of speech. 'I,' the sacred word; 'I and you,' if and when an affinity is determined. His was the language of the ego, cultivated in the idiom of the premise by which he lived.

The story is projected within the framework of Dakotah philosophy, not something invented, not something put together from ethnological data catalogued and explained by persons outside the race and realm. It is a story Dakotah in description and discernment, Dakotah in precept and example, Dakotah in structure and style.

Any attempt to mold English into a Dakotah (Siouan) form results in a pidgin Indian, and any attempt to reverse the process results in pidgin English. And so I have observed Indian idiom as closely as possible in mood, tense, and definition wherever the English equivalent would limit the Dakotah concept.

Even so, the author asks that the reader bring something to the reading process: a willingness to enter the Dakotah world uncritically, without vanity. In this way the story will return the reader to the spiritual source not only of the American Indian but of America itself.

RUTH BEEBE HILL

Acknowledgments

To the many Indian friends who helped make this book their story:

Certainly you remember me as someone determined to research—in your language and mine—the ancient ceremonies and so perceive those truths long bundled up in legend and lore, hidden under interpretations voiced by strangers, and lost to you through confusion, frustration, and, eventually, resignation. But perhaps I now dare say, after twenty-five years' perseverance, that you who always proudly remember yourself as Indian will appreciate as never before those grandfathers among the ancients who provided you your enduring spiritual roots.

To the many friends and professionals not of Indian blood who helped make this book:

Certainly you know that your sustained interest in my work acted to inspire me and that your reference material and field assistance motivated further investigation into areas I might have overlooked. And certainly I recognize that those serious historians who preceded me—who left records of their findings—acted to make me a beneficiary.

I send out gratefulness in four directions.

RBH

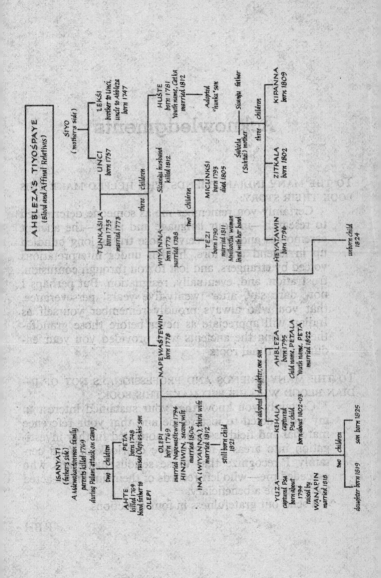

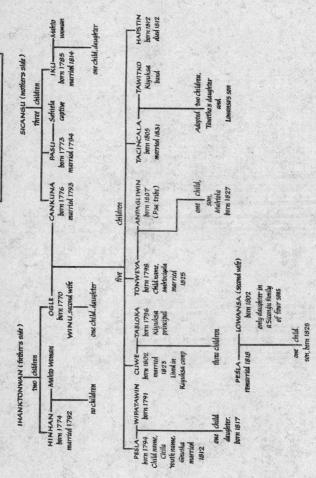

TONWEYA'S TIYOŚPAYE
(Blood and Affinal Relatives)

IHANKTONWAN (father's side)
two children

SICANGU (mother's side)
three children

HINHAN
born 1774
married 1792
— Mato Woman

OGLE
born 1770
WINLU second wife

CANKUNA
born 1776
married 1793

PASU
born 1773
married 1794
— Sehiela
captive

IKU
born 1785
married 1814
— Mato
woman

no children

one child, daughter

one child, daughter

children

five

children

WIPATAWIN
born 1791

CUWE
born 1802
married
1823
Lived in
Kiyuksa camp

TABLOKA
born 1796
Kiyuksa
principal

TONWEYA
born 1798
Child name,
Mahtociqala
married
1825

ANPAGLIWIN
born 1807
(Psa tribe)

TACINCALA
born 1805
married 1831

TAWITKO
Kiyuksa
band

HAPSTIN
born 1812
died 1812

PESLA
born 1794
Child name,
Cicila
Youth name,
Gnuska
married
1812

one
child,
daughter,
born 1817

three children

LOWANSA (second wife)
born 1802
only daughter in
a Sicangu family
of four sons

PESLA
remarried 1818

one child,
son, born 1825

one child,
son,
Mahtola
born 1827

Adopted two children,
Tawitko's daughter and
Lowansa's son

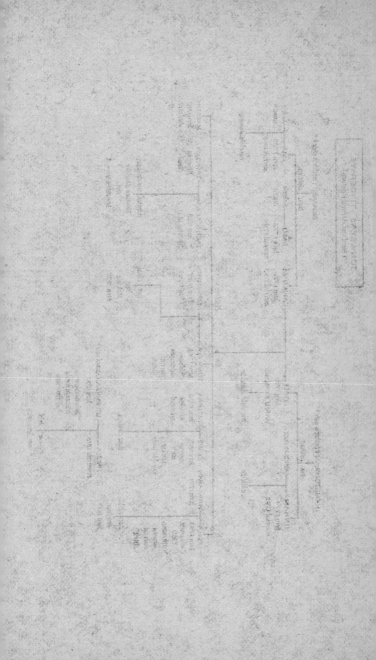

A Lakotah Winter Count
1750 to 1835

The Chronology Kept by Heȟaka (Elk) of the Mahto Band, Teton Sioux.

> *Excerpts from a record discovered in 1865 in the posses-sion of a Sioux Indian, leader of a small band of fifty persons who lived on the Missouri, remnants of the once-powerful Titonwan.*

1750 *They scatter over the plain.* Dakotah families, retiring from the headwaters of the Mississippi, move over the coteau toward the Missouri.

1769 *The Palani attack from opposite sides of camp, killing seven.* A Tiyataonwan warrior (Peta) finds his brother's infant son alone but safe in the family lodge. Peta's parents and only brother lie among the dead. The infant's mother is among the cap-tured women the Palani (Arikara) carry off.

1779, 1780 *Smallpox reduces Palani tribe.* These maize-eaters now depart their site on the east bank of the

Missouri below the great bend and move north to a site on the west bank, south of the mouth of the Cheyenne River.

1781   *Peta leads seven Mahto lodges west across the muddy river.* The Grizzly Bear camp moves onto the mixed grasses across the Missouri.

1782   *Leader of the Wacape band freezes in the snow.* Stabber, leader of a band that bears his name, dies in the cold.

1783   *Cold winter. Ravens freeze in trees, drop dead in front of lodges.*

1784   *Wanaġi, young member of Mahto band, demonstrates his bear vision before a gathering of his peers.*

1785   *Four Sicangu lodges visit the Mahto band.* Brulé (Burnt Thigh) Lakotah families come among the Mahto.

1789   *Titonwan raise a tribal hoop.* Dakotah who dwell on the plain form their first tribal summer circle (encampment).

1790   *Deep-snow winter; only lodge tops visible and many old persons starve.*

1791   *They originate 'wakicunsa.'* The Titonwan formulate a plan for governing the summer encampment: four deciders will listen to the facts, then make a tribal decision.

1792   *Tatanka Naźin and his band of Okandada camp with the Palani.* Standing Bull Moose and his band camp with the Arikara.

1793   *They take thirty enemy horses.* A Mahto war party takes thirty Witapaha (Kiowa) horses. Wanaġi, the young Mahto seer, prophesies this event.

22

1794 *A young Mahto warrior, his name Olepi, gives away three horses.*

1795 *Two from an enemy tribe kill the Mahto leader.* Two Psatoka (Crow) shoot an arrow in Peta's neck.

1799 *He splits his toe.* Catka's injury gives name to the stream on which Titonwan camp this summer.

1800 *Warrior who carries a firestick wounds himself.* Gun injury.

1801 *Dry winter.*

1802 *Four whitemen live at deadwood lodge on little island in the muddy river above big bend.* These wasicun (bearded messengers or whitemen) were traders who established a post on Cedar Island.

1803 *Rash and running bowels uses up eight Titonwan.* An epidemic of nawicesli (measles) in the winter camp (west bank of the Missouri near trader's lodge) kills off eight Lakotah.

1804 *Psatoka kill twenty-eight Titonwan who go out as a warrior-lodge.* The Crow wipe out a fraternity of Lakotah who go out to prove their power. Each member of the Miwatani-lodge stakes himself in view of the enemy and vows to stay until a lodge member releases him.

1805 *They use hunka-pipe in ceremony of affection toward children.* The goring of a boy-brave acts to inspire a new ceremony: first use of horsetails on pipe. Horsetails also wave from atop Olepi's lodge.

1806 *Psatoka kill eight Titonwan.* During an avenging, the Crow kill eight Lakotah.

1807 *They kill Oglesa, an Okandada of the Titonwan tribe.* (Historical incident: A party under Ensign Na-

23

thaniel Pryor attempts to return a Mandan warrior to his own people; but the Arikara intercept the party at the mouth of the Grand River and refuse to let anyone pass. Oglésa [Red Shirt], a visitor in the Arikara camp, is killed in the cross fire.)

1808 *Iron ball kills Wagmiza, leader of the Sicangu.* A gun in the hands of a whiteman kills the Sicangu (Brulé) leader.

1809 *Many whitemen travel up the muddy-water river; Titonwan intercept.* (Historical record: Sioux threaten Robert McClellan and Ramsay Crooks' party of forty, ordering them to build a trading post on the Missouri. Sioux also threaten Manuel Lisa's party of 150 men the same year.)

1810 *A whiteman-trader goes up in smoke with his deadwood lodge.* A trader whom the Lakotah call Capa (occasionally translated 'Little Beaver') burns to death when his post catches fire.

1811 *Sicangu horsechasers capture twenty horses in sandhills.* A Mahto youth with this same party catches a remarkable yellow mare and names her Tatezi ('yellow wind').

1812 *Two youths in the Mahto band seek a vision and become a dreaming-pair.* A warrior's son and a hunter's son fast on the ledges for three days, during which they experience a similar vision.

1813 *Peśla carries the Tokala lance against the Oyatenumpa.* Peśla, a member of the Kit Fox fraternity, carries the emblem of his lodge when he rides out against the Omaha.

1814 *Tatanka-lodge makes ceremony at which they award Shirt.* The headman-lodge (Bull or Big Bellies lodge) awards Shirt to two, a Mahto and a Siyo.

24

1815   *They club down Witapaha during trade fair.* Titonwan warriors get into fight with Kiowa during a fair on Horse Creek.

1816   *A Mahto scout they call Tonweya trails a family of Oyatenumpa.*

1817   *Woman hangs herself.* The mother of a nursing child commits suicide.

1818   *Peśla brings back Palani smoke.* Leading out a small party, Peśla raids the Arikara tobacco fields.

1819   *The Mahto raise their lodges near the Śahiela (Cheyenne).*

1820   *They initiate Iśna at a sash-wearer's ceremony.* Iśna (Lone Man), leader of the Kuya Wicaśa band, joins the Iyuptala fraternity.

1821   *Ahbleza scatters the enemy.* The son of Olepi routs the Crows.

1822   *Roaring star passes across the sky.* (Historically recorded date for this meteor: September 20, 1822.)

1823   *Titonwan assist whitemen-akicita in attack on Palani.* (Historical reference to Colonel Henry Leavenworth's expedition against the Arikara [Ree] in 1823, when several hundred Lakotah were his allies.)

1824   *Wapiti dreamer dies during mysterious dance.* They hold a dance contest between elk dancers and heyoka (clown) dancers.

1825   *Thirty lodges drown.* A Lakotah camp drowns when the Missouri, filled with broken ice, rises and floods bottom lands.

1826, 1827, 1828   *Deep-snow winters; snow up to their thighs.*

1829 *Much pronghorn meat.* They trap pronghorn in pits. Kiowa and Cheyenne commonly use this old method for catching antelope.

1830 *They see rolling-wood.* Apparently a first view of wagons.

1831 *They raise a spirit-lodge.* Upon the death of their principal member, the Iyuptala-lodge raises a tipi that symbolizes the spirit-realm. Memorial services during a period of two years are held here. After this time the 'spirit' will be symbolically released.

1832 *They kill a white pta.* Mahto hunters kill an albino buffalo bull. Records from other bands report the killing of albino cows, a most unusual occurrence because of the rarity of these animals, cow or bull.

1833 *Stars move around.* (Historically, a great meteoric shower was observed throughout the United States, November 12/13, 1833.)

1834 *Whitemen bring an invitation to Grizzly Butte encampment.* Emissaries come to Bear Butte to bid for the Indian trade. Tabloka persuades half the encampment to move near the forks of the Platte and to trade at Fort William, later called Fort Laramie.

1835 *They raise a little hoop.* The Mahto return to Pahamni ridge, having decided as a band against following Tabloka to the Platte. (Historically, this band is known to have maintained a tiny camp of their own as late as 1865.)

Note: 'Winter counts' were a simple but effective method of reckoning time. One outstanding event for each year was recorded on a tanned hide; if nothing occurred that affected the whole tribe, a local or personal incident was pictured. Thus winter counts may vary among the bands but are usually identical in recording natural phenomena such as floods, deep snows, meteors; also epidemics, tribal revenge, newly originated ceremonies, and other significant affairs. The Indian year—kiwani owapi in the old Dakotah language—extended from one springtime to the next.

Book One

THE CHILD
1794/95 to 1805/6

I

HIGH ABOVE the yellowing plain, too high for a shadow, an eagle pair climbed the midmorning sky, their soaring, spiral flight and a slow-spreading white cloud the only perceptible movement in the clearness overhead.

The eagles had called to each other during their glides and turns, then suddenly screeched a warning to all creatures on the grassy flat and in the nearby black hills: man comes, clear the way.

And now the flying pair separated, one bird flapping toward the hills, the other bird rising to the cloud.

The Mahto band, one of the three Tiyataonwan Dakotah bands, kept to a certain order when they traveled on the plain. And so Wanaġi, the young seer, walked back of the leader. They assigned this place in the procession of seventy persons not to someone who prophesies but to the one who carries the smoldering wood, the source of a cooking fire for these twelve Mahto families upon their arrival at the summer campground.

The grandfathers had said that only good hands—hands that never kill—shall hold these smoldering remains of the winter campfire, a symbol of the continuality of the people. And that the Mahto women, when they start their new campfires from these embers, shall offer thanks to pte—the one and the herd—for pte, the true meat, shall sustain each generation of Dakotah.

Pondering these things as he walked, Wanaġi remembered that he had killed once, not man or meat but some-

29

thing to prove his courage and give him a place in this Mahto band: he had killed a grizzly.

The grandfathers knew that a vision had compelled his act and that he neither had wounded nor had killed again. Instead he had lived as Sinaska, the old seer, had instructed him; he had used his hands only for good. Now, in his twenty-ninth winter, he had become the seer among the Mahto, the band turning to him for their ceremonies and for the power-bundles—something the young warriors ask that he put together—and for the healing-root mixtures. But before ever he performed a ceremony or wrapped a bundle or concocted a cure, he prepared himself spiritually, his approach to spirit contact through song, his own voice singing.

First Born, the grandfathers told, had emerged from quivering mud to the rhythm of his own heart and so man had known the true rhythm from the beginning. Soon afterwards man had learned to use this rhythm for making songs. And then certain ones had discovered the true power in song, the power for making spiritual contact.

Old Sinaska had said that none among the songs reaches the spirit-realm more quickly than the stone songs but before anyone receives a stone-song, before any man becomes the true-seer, he shall recognize himself as a fit controlling power, as a man who owns the earth. And Sinaska had said that only two aspirants from each generation ever become wakanĥca, the true-seer. Only two wakanĥca in a hundred winters? Sinaska had said so.

Abruptly Wanaġi dropped these thoughts; somewhere an eagle screeched and he accepted the wingflapper's presence as a diverting influence, something to change the direction of his memory. Gazing into the distant sky, he spotted the bird-form in the whiteness of a summer cloud.

Now his imagination let him soar with the winged, let him view from above the whole of the black hills toward which the Mahto band traveled. And so for an instant he gazed upon great mystery: a heart-shaped mound rising up from the plain and a great hoop—perhaps a path—circling this mound. And inside the hoop—the people, all the Dakotah, joyous and unrestrained, a people who sang and sang, sang and sang.

The next moment Wanaġi perceived that the warriors back of him in the procession had discovered the powerful bird. They had begun a song, blending their voices to make the soaring-flight sound, then coming together as one voice to demand the wingflapper's attention.

"Wambli," they sang, naming the winged, "I send a voice."

The warriors, horseback, traveled in a tight line, fifteen men across, each one painted in the manner of his own choosing.

"Wambli gleśka," they sang lustily, naming the immature bird, "carry me away."

During these eight days of travel the band had observed quiet and order—any band moved cautiously on the lonely grasses—but now they came within a sunrise of the summer campsite. They saw clearly ahead, in the sky and on the ground; the wind had not disturbed the plain. A good day, these warriors knew, to let the heart soar.

"Wakantanka onśimaya." A good day, they sang, to try out their power.

But Wanaǵi, hearing the old ceremonial song, had wondered who among these warriors owned the strength to receive the tremendous power this song commands. Will any one of these singers understand that which he dares demand of the soaring-bird?

A familiar-voice—Wanaǵi's own—had given answer: these persons make use of the song-power; enough for now.

One man in the line of warriors had sent his voice to the sky in pursuit of the wingflapper; his desire to possess the tail feathers of this winged overcame any thoughts about soaring with the bird; he imagined each spotted feather as a decoration in his hair.

Three winters past, his age twenty-two and his voice never before heard in the council lodge, he had stood to propose that the leaders originate a scheme for honoring any Tiyataonwan who proves his daring on the raids, his bravery in war.

Certainly the man who drops or kills an enemy, he had said, shall take the scalp, but why not award something to the warrior who in a display of bravery touches with his hand or club the living or dead body? Why not a feather as symbol for any brave act?

But let the cloud-bird, not the grass-bird, he had advised, provide the symbol of Tiyataonwan courage. Let the wingflapper-family decorate the Tiyataonwan's hair and so let a warrior remember that he wears something that once touches the clouds.

The leaders had approved and so he had spoken twice in this same council; he had recommended an exploit feather for any four warriors who strike the same enemy-body. The fourth man who rushes up to the enemy, he had told, exposes himself to more danger than he who makes the kill, the enemy's companions perhaps close by, perhaps making ready for either revenge or rescue.

Again he had heard the murmurs of agreement. But not to his surprise. The people had respected him as a principal warrior in the Mahto band before he reached twenty and they had given him a man-name upon his return from a raid at age fourteen. He remembered his heart pounding as he had listened to the song that named him. And then he had vowed never to change this name: Olepi now and evermore. He knew that different ones often commemorated their experiences through change of name but not he. His name, he had decided, shall give meaning to daring, to bravery. Each man, the people had said, shall own a name he keeps to himself. Not Olepi; everyone, he had said, shall know that he owns but one name. His name: Olepi.

"Oyate nimkte wacin yelo; the people shall live."

The warriors finished the song and the great bird, circling down, reappeared below the cloud, then flapped away.

Olepi smiled. The people shall live and he shall live, he knew suddenly, live to circle his head with feathers from the tail of wambli, the wingflapper.

His gaze passed over the firecarrier now, his eyes on the man who walked front, the man whose grandfathers had led the people over the tall prairie grasses and to the edge of the plain. And now the son, the man who leads this band over the mixed grasses of the plain and onto a summer campground at the northern edge of the black hills. Peta, the one these Mahto follow for thirteen winters; Peta, the man this band calls leader; Peta, the warrior whom Olepi calls 'father.'

Not his true-father, Olepi remembered, but the only father he ever shall know. Peta, the man who had raised him from infancy, the man in whose shadow he had walked as child and under whose severe gaze he had sat as a youth; Peta, the man in whose lodge he lingered even now.

As son to this man, he had possessed the body and spirit to endure each harsh demand Peta had put upon him; now, as principal warrior in the band, he had not the heart to break away from his father, to leave Peta sitting alone in the lodge, a lodge that lacks woman, children, grandchildren, a lodge empty of relatives, of affection.

True, a woman tended Peta's fire and cooked his meat and slept at the tipi entrance, but an old woman stayed in most lodges, someone a family shelters in return for her importance to the group. Not that they ever ask this old one to carry wood and water in exchange for robes and soup—she offers her hands gladly—but that they keep someone nearby to relay messages whenever courtesy requires indirect speech between certain relatives.

But the old one in Peta's lodge rarely answered to this purpose; a father and his son never require the presence of a third person when they sit talking. And neither father nor son in this tipi had any other blood-relatives.

And so why move into a different lodge, a different band, Olepi had asked himself; why leave my father Peta, the only family I know. Why regret something?

Not regretful, his familiar-voice had answered, providing you go out looking for a wife and join her band as custom demands; not regretful providing you bring back a granddaughter, a grandson to visit in your father's lodge.

But Olepi kept his eyes on the strong legs, the straight back, the lean body at the head of this procession; he remembered that the Mahto leader never had taken a wife.

Certainly, he reflected, many women had reason to desire this man Peta; they say that his daring and bravery once set the prairie on fire. Perhaps his face will not attract everyone—they mention his stern mouth and big nose even in these camps of stern mouths and big noses—but a woman looks for a man's courage to set the grasses aflame, not his face.

Suddenly Olepi sensed an urge to send his thoughts flying back to the day Peta had found him—an infant lying

33

back of a bunched-up robe, someone hiding him before the enemy reached the tipi. Perhaps a review of this past event will reveal why Peta, leader of the Mahto band, never looks at woman, why his father at age forty-and-seven calls all women 'sister' and respectfully avoids their presence.

One cold dawn, twenty-five winters in the past, the enemy had killed seven Dakotah during a surprise attack—or so the old rememberers told—and none had known more sorrow than the young warrior they called Peta.

Peta had watched the people wrap the bodies of three relatives in the red death-robe—brother, mother, father—and he had stood under the tree to which they had tied those red bundles, the voices of women who keened his loss heard in four directions. And then, pulling a shredded cover around his own body, he had entered his parents' tipi, the same one in which his visiting brother's family had stayed, a tipi suddenly, sadly, empty of life.

He had sat down, his back to the fire circle in the manner the grandfathers advise, but the torn robe and the dead fire had not effected an outpouring of his grief; instead, his sorrow had given place to anger.

He had imagined his parents rushing out, striking at the enemy who had surprised their lodge, killed their son, and dragged off their son's wife and infant child. Certainly the two old persons had defended the young family; he had found their bodies on bloody ground outside the tipi.

But Peta had dared regret neither his absence from camp on the morning of the attack nor the quarrel he had provoked during his brief visit in this enemy's village the winter before. Regret, he had heard himself saying, never brings comfort.

He had stayed on in the cold, lonely lodge, his anger directed toward reprisal, his heart set on instant revenge. But he had found nothing consoling in his most desperate schemes.

Not until his own tears had warmed his cheeks and wet his breast had he regained his balance; not until he had wept had he understood tears as a quickening power that shuts off twisted thoughts and prevents unreasonable acts. Not until Peta had cried had he come into understanding with the grandfathers who say that a man shall weep when he sees his people die and so relieve himself either of grief or shame. For each one knows whether or not he takes proper care of those relatives for whom the tribe considers him responsible.

After a long while Peta had become aware of different tears in the darkening lodge; he had crawled toward the sound.

A quick search had disclosed his brother's tiny son. The mother had taught her little one not to cry, but a growing hunger for the woman's breast had forced the baby's whimper.

Staring at the child, Peta had realized that he lived not without relatives as he had imagined; the great mystery that provides children gives this one to him.

The people had said that a man shall regard his brother's son as his own and that a boy shall grow up regarding his father's brother the same as his true-father.

Father. Instantly the meaning had come to Peta as the Dakotah custom demands: father, one who protects, one who never abandons his own.

"My son," Peta had said softly, "the enemy takes away your mother, but I shall find a woman in camp with enough in her breasts for you and her own child. Or I shall hunt among the four-legged and ask this favor. A Tiyataonwan woman will suckle the young pronghorn whose mother disappears and so the four-legged shall understand your need."

He looked upon the infant for another moment. This boy, he had told himself, shall live to roam the plain and ride out after meat. This boy shall live to sound the compelling war cry and to leave the enemy with only their bones. And this boy shall bring forth a name, a name the people shall hear in their songs.

Walking from the tipi, the child in his arms, Peta had considered the ways in which a father instructs his son; certainly the boy shall walk a strenuous path and he shall grow up on legends and stories of warriors whom the enemy never finds sleeping.

"Remember the Palani, my little son; remember the tribe who cuts down your relatives. Takpe, revenge."

The whispered words had echoed loud in Peta's own heart.

35

Takpe. Olepi's picturing of those scenes twenty-five winters past abruptly gave way to the present, to tangible evidence that he remembers who cut down his relatives. Grasping hold of the tall pole fastened erect to the side of his horse, he shook the stick. And so he watched the hair off four Palani heads flutter at the top and middle, one a woman's scalp. And he remembered that on each clear day his father raised a similar pole in front of the tipi, but one that displayed eight Palani scalps.

Certainly the people saw that a man and his son had avenged their relatives; certainly they knew that the man they call Peta had sought revenge on the Palani for more than twenty winters.

But not during the past two seasons, Olepi quickly recalled, not while any Tiyataonwan camp with the Palani.

Many winters past, certain Dakotah, regarding the Palani as a friendly enemy, had visited this tribe on two, three occasions, one Tiyataonwan family staying long enough for their relatives to suspect a change of alliance. Okandada, they had said, giving a name to these Tiyataonwan who apparently had asked for a place in the Palani villages, whose actions had divided one camp.

Eventually the errant family had rejoined their own, but the name had clung; they and all their relatives became know as Okandada, as the Okandada band.

Now again certain Okandada made a lengthy visit in the Palani villages, these families remaining two winters with the maize-eaters, perhaps staying on for yet another planting, ripening, feasting.

"Why regret their absence," Peta had said to his son; "so they sit in an earth lodge bellying maize and squash and smoking a twist of grass. Let him who finds comfort in a mound-and-pit shelter, who enjoys the wet seeping through a mud-and-leaf cover onto his sleeping robes, let him stay with the Palani throughout the snow moons and into the growing season. Let him who yearns for his head to itch and his feet to slide stay in a lodge crawly and slippery, horse droppings inside and out, dung everywhere. Why regret the absence of these Tiyataonwan who prefer the company of lazy incompetents?"

Olepi had listened remembering that his father never had expressed anything but contempt for the Palani. Peta ignored any memory of these people as a powerful tribe thirty, forty winters in the past, four thousand fighting-men in their villages. During those same seasons the Tiyataonwan, a tattered, divided family of fifty persons who roamed the low prairie, had begged for maize whenever they dared approach those earth lodges along the big muddy river, earth mounds which sheltered twenty thousand Palani.

But the Tiyataonwan rememberers had recalled that Peta when a small boy had visited in those villages. Neither the child nor his parents had seen a horse, the rememberers told, but the boy, watching the four-legged dance and snort while a grinning warrior sat on top, had named this creature. Sunkatanka, he had said, and asked for a ride on the big-dog's back.

Big-dog. Smiling, Olepi patted the neck of his own big-dog, a horse he had taken during a raid on the Palani.

And many more śunka-wakan, mysterious-dogs, he mused, where this one comes from. Once the Okandada leave the Palani camps—takpe, I go out again. Let different ones fill their bellies in the enemy villages, but when I visit the Palani, I take hair and horses, not maize or grass for a pipe.

Observing that the Mahto leader now halted the procession, Olepi, who rode center of the fifteen horsebacks, slowly brought his mount to a stop. And each warrior, keeping his horse in line with Olepi, pulled gently on the jaw-thong.

But a murmur of surprise replaced the laughing, joyful voices of wives and mothers who, on seeing the distant butte loom big and close, had quickened their small steps. Why make camp so soon after the midday rest, they marveled; why delay their arrival at the summer campsite? The traveling band already stops twice since dawn, the leader and firecarrier sitting atop a knoll while they wait for the slow walkers to catch up. But none lags now and the people will travel over much ground before the sun, barely past middle, climbs down and shadows lengthen. Yet the crier now calls not only for the women to raise their overnight shelters but for someone to raise the big tipi, the council lodge?

The leader had selected this day as the proper one to make an appeal to his young warriors, to ask that they desist from any scheme to attack the Sahiela camps this summer.

And he had chosen the council lodge as the proper place for his talk. Men come into the big, unpainted tipi to listen intently, to speak seriously; they permit neither mischief nor prophecy in this lodge of fact.

Peta rarely made long speeches, but he intended to speak effectively this day—and to some receptive ears. And so he asked those persons who had raised the lodge to open the front and lift the sides; he wanted his voice going out to the women and to other peaceful hearts in his camp.

The young warriors, curious as to why the leader called for a council while the band traveled, had assembled quickly. But Peta, desiring to prolong the initial silence, sent the pipe around twice. The pipe soothes and brings a man's thoughts back to the people, the grandfathers had said, and the Mahto leader intended that these daring young men remember the people, the people as a whole.

Whoever among the warriors now glanced at Peta saw a man who sat legs crossed, arms loose, his shoulder-length hair tucked back of his ears, his face at ease. But the son Olepi saw a man who will wait until he knows that each heart regains calm, that all hearts beat as one.

After the pipe twice had come back empty, Peta rested the stem on the small rack in front of him, in view of all. And now he began his speech.

"Hear me, my young men. Ten-and-three winters in the past the Tiyataonwan come onto the plain. For ten-and-three winters they roam this short grass and meet many strangers. And in all these seasons they find but one tribe—one tribe—they admire, a people they name Sahiela, persons-who-appear-wearing-red-paint.

"I ask that none of you disturb the good relations between Tiyataonwan and Sahiela."

Those good relations had begun, Peta told now, when the Tiyataonwan, newcomers to the plain, stayed as guests in a Sahiela village. During this visit each tribe had recalled a similar meeting between their grandparents. Certain persons had remembered that their Dakotah grandmothers had shown the Sahiela a way to cut and tie hides to make gowns and that the Sahiela women had shown the Dakotah a way to suspend skins for easy scraping, fleshing. Celebrating the memory of those relatives, the Sahiela had presented their Dakotah visitors with a gift of horses, many young horses.

And from that day forward any contact between these two tribes had proved an agreeable experience.

"Now certain Dakotah ask that the Tiyataonwan view the Śahiela as an enemy. Why?"

The Mahto leader paused. His warriors knew who had started the trouble, but will they recognize that to avenge the killing of three foolish young men perhaps brings lasting difficulty to the whole people?

The trouble-starters had belonged to those Dakotah—Sicanġu Dakotah—who camped south of the Tiyataonwan bands, along the earth-smoke river. Discovering that a family of Śahiela had planted maize at the mouth of this river, they had sneaked out a small war party and attacked the friendly people. But the Śahiela had killed the party leader and two of his companions. And now perhaps twenty Sicanġu lodges, their leader carrying a pipe wrapped for war, traveled toward the big butte. Here, camping with the Tiyataonwan bands, they will ask that these Dakotah relatives join in their attack on the Śahiela this summer.

"I recall a day," Peta went on, "when Dakotah and Śahiela demand proof of one another's good intentions, when after throwing one arrow, each side lay down their bows."

He looked briefly upon the faces of these men who formed a half-circle in this lodge. Will they understand the importance of a peaceful summer, one that permits the Tiyataonwan leaders to create a new and most high rank within the tribe? Or will they demand a summer of kills-talks and schemes for revenge? Suddenly he decided not to mention again the incident on the earth-smoke and to acknowledge the differences between Dakotah and Śahiela before he emphasized the similarities.

"True, the Śahiela throw up twigs and mud for shelters, braid grass into containers, dig holes and put in seeds. They relish the taste of skunk and they eat out of the rivers. They paint red and pluck their heads on each side and hang shells under their noses. But will you not agree that these customs make little difference between friends? The Śahiela resemble Dakotah in all the important ways. A woman-messenger brings the Śahiela their rules for behavior the same as a woman-messenger brings the Dakotah a pipe. They perform ceremonies of appreciation without a request for favors.

They treat the black hills as a sacred source and pte as a powerful contact.

"And so, my warriors, why begin a fight with the one ally the Tiyataonwan Dakotah find on the plain?"

Peta had spoken. But two of his warriors chose to discept.

"Among the Dakotah," said one, "not only Tiyataonwan roam the plain. The Sicaṅgu, my Dakotah relatives who burn their thighs while traveling the tall grasses, also roam the plain. Truly, the parent tribe calls all Dakotah on the plain Titonwan. They now view Tiyataonwan and Sicaṅgu as one Dakotah family whether or not these people camp together or hunt along the same river. And so I speak as a Titonwan when I ask who more closely resembles this Mahto band—Sicaṅgu or Śahiela? With whom shall any Tiyataonwan Dakotah make his true alliance on the plain—one who speaks his own language or the stranger?"

Peta, his face impassive, heard the murmurs of approval at the finish of this speech. And he listened for more of these agreeing sounds when the next young man began talking.

"My companions,"—the second speaker stood to face the group—"will not the enemy scorn a tribe who fears taking revenge?" He glanced at Olepi who sat middle in the half-circle; his message seemed directed at the son of Peta. "As a warrior, which way will you prefer: a Mahto skull smiling up from the ground as if saying, 'I die young avenging my kinsman,' or the Śahiela telling around that they kill three Dakotah whose relatives never notice?"

Listening to this voice, Olepi wondered suddenly about his father; will the Mahto leader experience a change in nature? Peta had closed his ears to any talk of war when news of the Sicaṅgu trouble reached the winter camp, and certainly he had spoken this day as if he belonged among the old men who desire peace.

And now Olepi discovered a startling thought: what joy will he find living in a tipi where talk replaces act, where a great warrior ceases raiding and begins gambling for horses?

He leaned forward; he listened more closely to the challenging phrases.

Peta knew before the second speaker finished that kinsman appeal, always a compelling force, had won over his

40

men. And that his principal warrior—his son Olepi—waited only to learn who will lead the Sicaṅġu party before offering to carry a lance, to make one of the kills.

And so why say anything more to these Mahto, Peta had asked himself; why mention that the Sicaṅġu have yet to prove their competence as fighting men, that they get those leg-burns during a retreat, their pursuers firing the prairie grass on two sides. Why repeat that an attack on the Sahiela, a powerful tribe, will bring sorrowing to the Dakotah; why invite apprehension now that they decide to join in the avenging?

But his heart sighed for those middle-aged and young who greatly enjoyed visiting in the Sahiela camp, more fun-games and laughter than rough play and sign-talk—and never a quarrel—when these two tribes come together.

For an instant Peta wondered whether he had aged to the place that he regretted war, whether his fiery heart had played out. Then suddenly an old war cry echoed dimly in his ears: hu iḣpeya wicayapo. Smiling inside his cheek, he wondered whom the mouth-fouling phrase most aptly fit: the fool Sicaṅġu or the unwitting Sahiela or two, three upstarts among his own warriors.

But now a group of women, observing that Peta and his warriors had finished their talks, carried in bowls of soup, big chunks of meat rolling on the bottom, fat floating on top. And the men, gesturing their appreciation, began to sip noisily.

Soon afterwards nearly everyone came in under the big cover, the people grateful for a sun shelter at this place of scant shade. The women stayed to one side as in their own lodges, but they glanced frequently toward the men; they sensed a change from the cheerful mood which had prevailed before the counciling. They noticed also that Peta remained sitting alone at the center, that he had turned his empty soup bowl upside down, and that he ignored a child who had toddled up to lick the taste of meat off his greasy lips. Softly, then, these women murmured their concern: will the leader suddenly foresee a disaster, his young men perhaps running into considerable difficulty when they seek revenge on the Sahiela? Or will something different portend sadness on the summer campground? Joy often changes into sorrow without visible warning.

Peta, hearing the murmur, understood. His serious face had sent the child to a more receptive countenance and his overturned bowl had disheartened those good women who ladled out the refills. But watching his people gather, he had sensed a need here and now to reappraise the Mahto strength. In recent seasons the Mahto, demonstrating twice the warrior-power of either Okandada or Siyo, had camped at the tip-of-the-horns, on each side of the opening into the summer circle. But the recent growth of these bands had given him reason to wonder whether prowess in combat or whether family ties and strong voices henceforth decide who camps in the place of honor. And so, aware of his own lack of blood relatives, he intended to permit himself a long look at this assemblage of Mahto, at the youth and the warriors and the hunters, at the woman and the children and the grandfathers. Soon he will recognize, he told himself, whether he dares call his Mahto, as in seasons past, an all-warrior band.

From the beginning he will want mostly young men in his following, youths whose enthusiasm for the raids acts to increase the Mahto horse herds and young braves whose daring brings about new songs in the tribe. He sees such young men now in Icabu, Cetan, Heliogeca and among other Mahto who wear a feather in their hair. And he sees in Wambli Okiye, a seasoned warrior at age thirty-and-two, a man whose courage inspires any war party, raiders or avengers. And in Olepi he perceives all that a warrior-father ever desires in a warrior-son: cunning and bravery, power and pride.

An all-warrior band? Certainly each hunter in the Mahto camp regards himself as a meat-maker with two different bows, one for the chase and one for combat. Look at Ogle for an example; will any man in the tribe know more about making-meat, about hunting? Yet Ogle also carries shafts with points that will bring down the lurking enemy. Ogle and his brother Hinhan, persons who come from a family of fast feet, strong arms, meat-makers with the warrior-spirit. But will not each Mahto hunter display certain fighting skills?

As for the Mahto women, will he not advise that each wife, mother in the band learn the use of the small bow, know to defend herself, and that these women put a twig bow into the toddler's hand before the child reaches for any different toy?

Children? True, not many little ones among the Mahto, but he will see Cankuna, wife of Ogle, feeding her newborn, the woman bringing forth a son five days before the band starts out. And girl-babies coming recently to different parents, these families like all families wishing first for a daughter.

Grandfathers? Not many whitehairs to keep alive the legends, but who sees many persons of grandfather-age in any Titonwan band? Two severe winters soon after the people come onto the plain kill off infants and the aged. Relatives who yet grieve this loss recall that even those courageous birds who stay north drop out of the trees, the intense cold freezing their wings. And in recent seasons two more deep white winters, only the lodge tops visible, starve the old who close their blistering mouths to their share of roots and grass hiding under the snow.

Not enough grandfathers, but neither will he see any stumblers, any cripples in this band; the old walk firm and his warriors return in one piece. From the beginning he had desired a camp of whole men and strong women. And 'from the beginning' will mean from the day that he, Peta, dares lead these people across the big bend in the big muddy river and onto the plain.

Peta had grown up within view of the great shifting river-of-mud. He had watched sand whirl off the small bare islands; he had seen the water freeze, heard the ice thaw. And he had marveled the smashing, hurtling flood, these same waters under the summer moons a slithering stream that even a child dares wade across.

But Peta had lived to age thirty-three before he saw any Tiyataonwan crossing the muddy water, man, woman or child. For during all those seasons the formidable villages of the Palani tribe had lined the sides of this river, up and down from the great bend, the sun reflecting off the iron points of four thousand lances, the yaps of a thousand camp-dogs warning off strangers.

True, the Palani occasionally had made friendly gestures, permitting 'the beggars'—or so they called the Tiyataonwan—to enter their earth mounds to observe a magic

43

show or the bird-feast that accompanies the planting of maize or even to pierce the ears of Palani children on ceremonial occasions. But without an invitation the Tiyataonwan had kept away from the vast staked camp; their only attacks on the Palani had occurred on the low prairie where they had dared intercept small hunting parties.

Then, twelve, thirteen winters past, the Tiyataonwan had witnessed an event that had forced the Palani to abandon the great bend. And had permitted the Tiyataonwan to cross over onto the plain. A disease had walked on scabby feet through the earth-mound villages and a stinking cloud had hung over the river. Soon afterwards the survivors from thirty Palani camps had crawled out of their pit shelters to form a slow, pock-marked procession that moved upriver, these leftovers going north in search of clean ground and thick woods.

Watching the once-powerful tribe wind out of view, the Tiyataonwan had recognized that nothing held back their advance onto the great plain; they now owned the grasses, tall and short and mixed; they owned the earth. Hiyupo, the winds had demanded; come hither.

Hakamya upo, Peta had called to the people; follow my path.

But not all Tiyataonwan had chosen Peta to lead. The Śiyo family, five lodges of fiercely proud blood and affinal relatives, had stayed in Wacape's following, the man they regarded as head of their tiyośpaye. And Tatanka Naźin had influenced two families to travel with him, the tall Tiyataonwan saying that his relatives had kept the original Dakotah pipestem for more than one hundred winters, his predecessors long-lived and powerful.

Three, four lodges had crossed the river without a leader, the father of each little family looking out for his own, as when the people had wandered the prairie. And one or two lodges, experiencing a change of heart, had delayed their crossing.

But seven lodges, forty persons in all, had accepted Peta as their leader, seven families who agreed to camp and travel and hunt as a village, to band together using the name 'mahto,' a new name—grizzly—for an old four-legged relative whose powers they respected, the only creature to whom they had granted the rank of warrior. Mahto, they had said; the real one. Mahto, Peta had told himself; a proper name for a warrior band.

All Tiyataonwan camps had followed the same path onto the plain but they had not traveled together. Moving slowly, curiously, toward the black mountain that rose above the yellow earth, toward snowy peaks and fiery sunset skies, they occasionally caught up with one another. Then they had hunted and visited as a tribe until quarrels or whim separated the gathering. But all had stayed close to the same brackish, tricky stream—sica, their name for this water-way—for whether dry, trickling, or flooding, pte used this stream; pte, the big meat, had made this trail.

Peta had led a bold camp and news of twenty horses in the Mahto village reached persons who never had wandered off the prairie. Soon two different families from the east had joined Peta's band.

And next, two lodges from among those Siyo whose principal man, Wacape, had frozen in the snow.

And then four Sicangu families had visited the Mahto camp, a people recently across the muddy water and roving along the earth-smoke, a river south of the Tiyataonwan hunting ground. But most of those visitors never returned to the earth-smoke; Sicangu warriors, choosing wives from among the Mahto, stayed on in Peta's camp. Certainly the grandfathers had advised that a husband join his wife's band, his children in the care of their mother and her people in the event something destroys the father.

But even as he had gained lodges, Peta had lost follow-ers. His own young warriors, guarding against any attach-ment to a woman in the Mahto camp, had looked for a mate in Tatanka Nazin's band or among the Siyo. From the beginning the grandfathers had cautioned against mating within the band, a man unknowingly perhaps choosing a blood relative, distant or near, for wife.

Then after seven, eight seasons living on the plain the women, seeing their families scatter out, had proposed something. Let all Tiyataonwan and Sicangu bands, they urged, come together for the summer moons. Let all these people who talk the same language raise one big circle of lodges somewhere on the plain. And let this hoop become as a new tribe: Titonwan, dwellers on the plain. And let this Titonwan tribe stay on the plain, the women had urged; why return east for the old tribal get-togethers as during those seventy, eighty seasons on the prairie. A different generation of Dakotah comes onto the plain, they had said, a people who will make new customs for a new place.

These women had prevailed. During recent summers the Titonwan had hunted and played together under the warm skies. But each band wintered alone, camping along different streams, taking only the meat that came within view of their lodges.

Peta, during these same recent summers, had recognized that for the Titonwan to endure as a tribe they also shall need to prove brave against certain invisible enemies: foolish anger and destroying greed, bribery and jealousy. He had spoken his views in council.

"Men of the plain, I see fifty lodges in a circle that grows each summer. Where many camp, disputes arise. And so I advise that you choose four competents and accept whatever they decide while the people camp as a tribe. Call these four 'wakicunsa' and trust these 'deciders.' "

Peta had awaited the assenting murmurs; instead one man had replied: "Each band assigns akicita, watchers who keep order in camp, on hunts. Why more watchmen?"

"True," Peta had answered, "the akicita settle grievances in their own villages. I look for something that protects the whole people from dangers inside and outside the tribal circle."

The dawn star had appeared, then reappeared, before leaders, warriors, councilors had reached agreement. But when these persons left the big tipi they took back to their villages an acceptable scheme for governing the summer encampments. Even so, they had mentioned their work only briefly; the people, as always, will await a demonstration, visible proof of enduring good for the one and the whole.

Four deciders shall own the summer camp, four loyal and alert warriors who remember that owning-the-camp means holding the good of the tribe in their hands. And each summer a different four.

Four deciders who shall appoint their own clubmen, watchmen responsible for the cleanliness of the encampment, the prevention of fires; clubmen who dare reprimand any person bringing anxiety into the circle through neglect

46

or foolish risk; clubmen who dare use their weapons upon the property of a troublemaker, ripping open or tearing down a tipi, breaking bows, or cutting up moccasins but striking only the offender who disregards their warnings.

Four deciders who shall wear a symbolic garment and so the people shall recognize these four as the summer-shirtwearers.

Four deciders; but who selects these shirtwearers? The old and wise who had sat through the long counciling had recognized the need to effect a balance between peacemen and warriors within the tribe. And so they had advised that the peace-keepers in the different bands come together and select the wakicunsa; the peacemen will know which warriors the people favor.

Peta, hearing the wisdom in that which these old ones spoke, had pondered an old tribal custom that demanded the killing of any man who spoke an untruth or who withheld truth. The old, old Dakotah had recognized that whoever deliberately misrepresents fact also will break customs, break rules. Why let live a destroyer of mutual confidence, they had said; kill him before he twice destroys, before his mischief corrupts the tribe.

But these Dakotah now on the plain regarded death for this offense as too severe. Kill him who kills a tribesman, the Titonwan had answered Peta, and let kinsmen take care of these killings; let families manage their own affairs.

Peta had wondered whether they misunderstood him; certainly he had not viewed the summer authority, the four deciders, as persons holding a life-death power over any man, any woman, but why, he had asked himself, let fall to the ground so many of the parent-tribe customs and ceremonials. Those ancient Dakotah had discovered the renewing power in a steam-bath, the summoning power in a song, the generating power in a gift. And they had discovered the danger in tolerating any person who ever purposely distorts truth.

During those moons that followed the council at which they had originated the wakicunsa, Peta's memory often lingered among those founding grandfathers of the lakes and woods who had made truth a way of life.

Then, two summers past, he suddenly had begun talking about the importance of devising certain awe-inspiring rituals that shall lead toward a new and most high rank among the Titonwan. He had likened the man who gains this place of honor to a tree on the plain: one alone, rising above the flat, standing firm while the earth blows, marking the trail for wanderers. Canpaza, he had said, using the old, old thought for tree; canpaza, erect, alive, and active. Otancan, he had said, naming the new rank, a leader above all leaders, not in power but in example; otancan, principal above principals. But he had hinted that severe trials await him who aspires to this peak. A rough path, a difficult journey, he had told; ten, perhaps twenty winters before a man attains this goal. Otancan, one who yields neither to anger nor anguish, neither to fear nor lust.

Peta had talked also of bringing back the old Dakotah ceremonies. Who remembers ihambleicya, he had demanded, naming the old vision-seeking ritual that clears the way for man's spirit to make contact with the motivating power of his existence. And who remembers wiwanyag wacipi; not for one hundred winters will anyone observe this thanks-offering in the name of the whole people. And who recalls hunkagapi, the truly old ceremony that demonstrates choice, something the Titonwan live by.

Leaders and councilors had agreed that the Titonwan, eager for new grass, more horses, and captive women, had neglected the old ways for keeping a people together, for renewing spiritual vitality. But wisely slow in speech and decision they had sat on, deliberating this new rank. Otancan, caretaker of the bands, owner of the people, keeper of the tribal good? Otancan, someone to whom they grant total respect, complete trust? And the symbol? Again a shirt, this one not seasonal but for life, something for the shoulders of a man who walks through all seasons an example of courage, generosity, loyalty.

But then during a council last summer, a different voice had spoken. Leaning against Wanaġi, too frail to sit alone, the old prophet Sinaska had chosen to speak from his place of white hairs and wobbly legs, where morning resembles dusk, and dusk, a black night. "Yet I see," he had said, "as from a hilltop after the mist breaks away." The snows of more than ninety winters bend him, he had told, "and yet I

48

hear clearly those persons who ponder whether any man ever shall own this honor-shirt." His stained white robe, slipping off his meager shoulders, had exposed an awesome thinness but his tones reflected nothing thin. "I hear certain ones mentioning bravery, a big heart, enduring power. Will they award the shirt to someone who brings back horses to his relatives, brings in meat for his grandfathers, laughs in the face of blizzard snow, smiles at the face of pain? Children play at these things. Will the Titonwan make this shirt for a child?" Suddenly pulling away from his support and speaking in the cool, firm manner of a scout, Sinaska had made clear those responsibilities inherent in the rank the council had tried to define.

"Whoever wears this shirt will know himself as a fit controlling power. He will understand that he needs neither moccasins nor lance, neither drum nor pipe but that each of these things needs him, his touch and his breath. And so he will view all such objects as toys, as something that in the past helps him learn balance and order and control.

"Whoever owns this shirt shall recognize everything as he walks. And so he shall see that which clutters the earth: the good work that someone, negligent or unfortunate, never finishes; the foolish mistake that someone never straightens out; the custom that someone breaks and the people let lie on the ground. And after he sees the whole, the shirt-owner, carefully selecting, will pick up the pieces, his thoughts and his acts putting together or putting back together, straightening or strengthening whatever he recovers. But he shall found his acts on something more than steadfastness; he shall know wherein his true power exists. And that which he never dares neglect."

The old seer had paused, squinting at the fire circle, and when he spoke again his words had come as from a far distance. "I finish my journey. Truth absorbs me. I see with a vision that nothing obscures." The old bones that had held Sinaska erect while he spoke had given way; he had slumped against Wanaġi. Next, each one in the big lodge had heard the ancient throat emitting grunts, a noise they had mistaken for the voice of the grizzly who often spoke through the seer's mouth. Only Wanaġi had known that Sinaska lay dying, his throat rattling, those grunts and hoarse whispers

49

a song of defiance. "Akita mani yo, akita mani yo. . . . "
Remember everything as you walk; the grizzlies had said so.
And Sinaska had remembered.

The big tipi in which the traveling Mahto had gathered
for the brief counciling, a little eating, now stood empty but
for Heȟaka and Peta. These two stayed for talk concerning a
picture-record Heȟaka had begun many seasons past, an
account of events important to the Mahto people.

Eyanpaha, mouth for the band, sat outside the council
lodge, leaning back against the cover. He kept near the
center as always, his voice on loan to whoever desires
making an announcement to the whole people. And now,
turning only his eyes, he watched the approach of a horseback, a Mahto scout whose unhurried manner told that he
brought news but nothing alarming.

A small arc of mounted warriors also observed the
rider, the man jumping down at the edge of camp, walking a
straight path, moving and stopping, moving and stopping,
his way of letting the people know that they have nothing to
dread.

Peta stepped out of the council lodge, and Eyanpaha,
responding to the leader's gesture, stood to announce Pasu's
arrival; he invited everyone to gather outside the big tipi and
hear the scout's report.

Once Pasu had touched his lips to the pipestem, Peta
began speaking: "My son, you arrive near dusk, yet you
neither hoot nor howl your approach and so I know that
you see nothing dangerous. They say that you walk in
slowly, directly, and so I know that you report neither
enemy nor meat. Tell me what you know."

Pasu spoke without gestures; he had events, not descriptions, to report.

"My father, the Sicanġu arrive this day at the Titonwan
summer campsite. They bring two Śahiela scalps and two
Śahiela women." The scout waited for the leader to ask for
more facts.

"Tell all you know," Peta said firmly.

And so Pasu related all he had seen, all he had heard.

The traveling Sicanġu had discovered four Śahiela
lodges. Sicanġu warriors intercepted one of these lodges, one

family who went out after meat. The Sicangu killed two Sahiela hunters, captured two Sahiela women, young and good-looking. The Sicangu had not raided the Sahiela village, had not pursued those families who fled.

"The Sicangu and the Siyo, now on the campground, await the arrival of Mahto and Okandada before anyone dances this victory." The scout signaled with his thumb that he had nothing more to say.

Pasu knew that he had reported accurately but that not everyone will approve his mentioning the captives' good looks. Even so, he had seen those captives; he dared call their good looks a fact; at twenty-and-two he recognized a good-looking woman when he saw one.

The remark about the captives had not concerned Peta; instead he sat listening to his warriors who muttered their resentment at that which had occurred. Fired up, eager to make war, they now hear that someone cuts down the enemy.

Suddenly Peta stood; moving past the scout, he confronted these discontents. "Hear me, my young men." Aware of hostile eyes and curling lips, he spoke demandingly: "Hear me."

One of the two warriors who had talked persuasively for revenge turned halfway around, his gesture signifying that Peta's words pour in one ear, run out the other. A different warrior mounted and rode off slowly.

Olepi felt his belly weaken; never before had he witnessed disrespect for the leader of the Mahto band. Whatever his personal thoughts about his father on this day, he yet had to see a more courageous man. He flashed a look of pride in Peta's direction.

The dark red evening sky, reflecting on Peta's breast and thighs, enhanced the man's commanding appearance, and when he spoke, the startling change in his eyes and tones sent chills up the back of more than one warrior.

Contemptuously he derided their unrest: "Your Sicangu relatives take revenge. But will you lack for enemies? Look around you. When your guts ache for war, remember the Witapaha. They circle the same herds you circle; their arrows lie on ground where you hunt. Will you let these rattleheads forever make meat on your hunting ground?

"And where will the Oyatenumpa raise their two-circles camp this summer? Or will you dread a long walk?

"And what about the Kaṅgi, those croaking blackbirds with whom the Sicaṅgu get a war going? Enemies you want, enemies you have. Onze nihupi kte lo."

Olepi, standing in the midst of the men, controlled a smile. Once again he listened to the father, the leader, the man he had recognized as an enduring influence. Who but Peta will wither a group of disgruntled warriors with foul scorn, foul gestures?

The tension had eased; the men stood or sat horseback listening with renewed respect.

"Perhaps I shall smoke more often than I ride this summer," Peta went on, "but when I ride out I shall take along warriors who talk and act like men, not like boys."

Turning, he walked away; his speech had not invited answer.

Before dark Peta returned to the council tipi, choosing to sleep this night under the big cover. Ten, twelve children already slept here and, smiling down on their twitching and kicking, he had sensed an overwhelming want to stay alongside these young. For on this day he had recognized himself a grandfather.

Not that one drop of my blood flows into the next generation, he told himself, but certainly at forty-and-seven I become of age, the grandfather-age. The grandfathers, he mused, those men whom the young and their parents respectfully call tunkaśila, men who see the vanity of war.

I belong here, he told himself as he spread his robe on the grass, but something more than age brings me. Truly I recognize an urge for peace, not only with the Śahiela but peace as a reluctance to leading out war parties. My many young men will maintain the warrior strength of this band— the Mahto shall camp at the tip-of-the-horns—and gladly I lead these people for as long as they choose to follow me. But I shall sit more often this summer with those men who represent the peace spirit among the Titonwan bands.

Those same helpful women who had raised the big tipi came before daybreak to take down and pack the cover. And so they discovered ten children and as many young warriors—the Mahto leader also—asleep in this place. They waited then for Eyanpaha to awaken the camp. Perhaps the Mahto band will not start out at dawn, they whispered to each other, but certainly everyone will rejoice on seeing that, when the band moves, all warrior hearts again beat as one. Peta, a father to the band, they told each other, or more nearly a grandfather; either way this man knows in what manner to treat his children.

Peta, hearing the crier's voice, awakened smiling, amused at something; then he recalled his thoughts before he slept. Am I really a grandfather, he wondered. But the people, not I, decide this thing. And so I wait until someone calls me 'grandfather' before I lay down lance and shield.

He rolled off the sleeping robe and jumped to his feet; he felt half his age.

II

THE BIG butte—grizzly hill to the Titonwan, teaching hill to the Sahiela—rose abruptly out of the plain, a mysterious uplift of earth that stood guard over the most desirable campground known to either tribe.

A vast cover of soft grass and colorful flowers surrounded the butte and good, clear water flowed nearby. Trees grew thickly along the river's edge—true-wood for bows, slow wood for tipi fires, fast wood for cooking—and stones lay scattered on the hillside.

Near the summit of the butte aged boulders, lonely and detached, sat as symbols of endurance while quiet groves of thickset wood stood gnarled but rooted, a symbol of resistance.

Only recently had the Titonwan discovered this campsite, long familiar to the Sahiela, but they had not looked for trouble with the friendly Sahiela; the Titonwan had taken over someone's camping ground, not someone's hunting ground.

And now twenty-two lodges of Sicaṅgu along with twelve Śiyo and twelve Mahto lodges waited at grizzly hill for the Okandada; they had decided not to form the summer circle until all members of this band had arrived.

Half the Okandada had appeared. Ooweśica, a principal man in the band, had led six families to the butte; six more lodges followed, he had said, Tatanka Naźin leading these people.

Listening to their story, Peta had wondered whether the Okandada ever intended to stay together.

Many persons, the recent arrivals told, had wanted to leave the Palani camps the moment they heard that the Canoni—those five Dakotah bands not yet across the muddy river—schemed to attack the Palani this summer.

But different Okandada had not taken the report seriously. Why will the Canoni, they had argued, choose to attack now? Many winters in the past when the Tiyataon-wan had hinted for help in fighting the Palani, these same Canoni relatives had answered that they had nothing but 'shells' with which to strike an enemy who carried lances with iron points. But will the Canoni now own something more threatening than shell knives? Certainly the Palani hold on to their iron points.

Unwilling to listen to more of this foolish talk, six Okandada families had started for the butte, Ooweśica acting as leader.

Peta, hearing the whole story, had slipped off alone to picture the dismay of those Okandada who had needed to decide quickly whether to loot or gift their hosts, whether to sneak out Palani horses and twists of smoke-leaves or to trade for these things, whether to hide a choice possession—something they risk losing during an attack—or to make presents of such prizes.

Bo-ton-ton, Peta laughed softly, the phrase expressing all that his imagination pictured: the Okandada running in every direction, collecting their things, bumping into each other, acting like tiny taźuśka when something disturbs their little hill of sand.

In a different lodge a group of Mahto women listened

to three Okandada wives tell of their experiences in the Palani villages. True, they had relished the maize they gathered from their own patches, and true, they had enjoyed the trick-shows the Palani magicians put on each summer. And certainly they had admired the many ear, arm, and neck ornaments in this camp. But they had taken a close look at the faces and gowns of the Palani women and they wanted none of the treatment these wives and daughters endured.

"The women take care of everything they grow," Oowesica's wife told now, "vines, stalks, leaves. And when things appear ripe, they start gathering, shelling, pounding, boiling, roasting, packing . . . and along with this work they scrape hides, mend moccasins, shape mud bowls, braid mats, design ornaments, gentle the dogs, and look after the horses. In between they feed their young and satisfy their men."

"And"—another woman took her turn with the story—"when winter fires glow in their damp lodges, who sits shivering at the rear while a tight circle of husbands and sons shuts off the warmth?"

The Mahto wives began laughing; the speaker made a mockery of this tribe who wore out their women in so many different ways. And yet they sensed an uncertainty back of her ridicule; perhaps these Okandada wives feared that the Palani had influenced their men in undesirable ways.

"And so"—the third woman, a young wife, picked up the story—"not even the Palani girls take an interest in their appearance. The mud-streaks on their faces and the soil on their gowns will not mean, as with Titonwan women, that they grieve for someone; they always walk indifferent to their looks. Their hair hangs loose and crawls with something that keeps each one scratching her head."

Then truly, the Mahto women murmured, all Okandada had rejoiced when they heard that the Canoni schemed to destroy the Palani villages; perhaps not for a long while will any Titonwan camp out with this tribe.

Their guests gestured agreement, but then Oowesica's wife began to giggle, her companions giggling also.

"When not everyone agrees to leave the Palani camps together," one of the women laughed, "certain Okandada warriors give the stay-behind families a new name." Sudden embarrassment overcame her speech.

"I will tell you what they say." The leader's wife spoke boldly. "They say 'oglala, śan oglala.' "

Hinu, hinu; the Mahto women hid their smiles back of these little anxious sounds; will the loitering Okandada families, they wondered, find anything funny about this taunt. True, many Mahto had referred to the Okandada as dust-scatterers but never before had anyone likened the act of a planter who throws up dust to a woman who throws up sand between her legs to discourage a man.

Śan oglala, the Mahto women had laughed aloud when their guests had gone; who knows, perhaps the name will stick.

The day after the Mahto band arrived at the butte, Olepi visited the Sicanġu lodges; he wanted to see those Śahiela captives whose good looks Pasu had mentioned. Already he had heard that these young women, comely and quiet, stood tall and slender and that an old woman called upon to examine the captives reported that neither one ever knows-a-man. And he had learned that their captor—someone more in need of horses than women—seemed agreeable to a trade. The Sicanġu village had become a popular visiting place for warriors without wives.

But when Olepi began walking this same direction each evening, Peta had asked himself why his son will consider a Śahiela woman, a paints-red, talks-red captive who offers nothing that will strengthen Olepi's position in the Titonwan tribe. Yet different ones in camp understood for what reason the son of Peta looked for a woman outside the Dakotah family. They remembered that during these many winters in the father's lodge the son had heard much talk about persons who lack relatives and of his need to relate in some way to everyone in the Titonwan camps. And so from his boy-seasons forward, Olepi had come to regard all Titonwan men as grandfathers, fathers, brothers, depending on their age. Similarly he had come to respect all Titonwan women as grandmothers, mothers, sisters. Certainly the people had heard Olepi answering 'my sister' to those young women who openly encouraged his attention, his use of this relative term putting him out of their reach. For the man who says 'my sister' means that he will offer a brother's respect, nothing more. And so Olepi—a proven warrior, an eligible before his twentieth winter—had disheartened his pursuers. But now, at age twenty-and-five, this warrior apparently had found, outside the tribe, someone whom he desired for his sits-alongside-him woman. And he had more than enough horses to trade for one of these Sahiela captives.

And now, after eight, ten days at the butte—on the same day that the second half of the Okandada band arrives—Olepi filled his pipe and passed the stem to his father. None but these two sat in the tipi; the son desired a quiet talk with this man before the tribe raised the formal summer circle.

"My father, perhaps my actions puzzle you." He waited, something more than a pause.

And so Peta spoke, his voice gentle: "Your heart already chooses, and so, answering you, I will speak not of the woman but of your name.

"I see that a great new name lives among the Titonwan, my son the original owner. And so Olepi brings the greatness to the name, not the name to him."

In whispering tones the father sang the song that had named his son when, at age fourteen, the youth had gone out with the warriors and had returned a young brave:

"Someone comes to the plain,
Someone walks on the grasses;
His name, Olepi; his name, Olepi

Something waits for this one coming,
A man coming, a name waiting,
The people seeking this man Olepi."

Olepi had heard his song often, but, listening to his father, his heart soared as never before. And the man's words on finishing the song brought him yet more pride.

"Perhaps the coming generations will remember all Titonwan, all Lakotah, through my son's name."

After a moment of silence, Peta turned his eyes to look briefly upon Olepi's fine-cut face. "But perhaps you will choose my name for your son," he said slowly, "for your full-blood Lakotah son, for a boy whose strain will run pure Lakotah on each side."

Olepi sat unmoving, nothing to hint at the shock that brings an ache to his heart: certainly Peta says that he will regret seeing his son mate with a Sahiela woman.

And this man who always refers to the whole family as 'Dakotah' now says 'Lakotah'? Certainly his father says clearly that he desires seeing his son mate with a Titonwan woman, not a Canoni or Isanyati Dakotah but one in this tribe on the plain, this new generation who makes many changes in the parent-tribe tongue and the old Dakotah way of life.

"I never take a wife," Peta said softly, "and so I live as father to the Mahto band. But the band grows; soon they become too many for one father, for one man's care."

The warrior had not looked up when he saw his father's legs unfold, when he knew that the man stood, moved toward the tipi flap; he wanted only that Peta go and leave him alone in the tipi. And for an instant he had wondered whether ever again he will sit in this place, sleep in this place.

Before dusk Olepi came out of the lodge. He saw that the people had formed the hoop, that once again they had awarded the Mahto the tip-of-the-horns. And he saw the empty space that awaited Peta's lodge. But he had emerged from his loneliness only to untie his horse, to mount and ride far out onto the plain where none in camp shall hear his cry of indecision, shall intercept his thoughts about the Sahiela captive who pulls so strongly at his heart.

The Titonwan formally had raised the summer circle, and now the Sicaṅgu, who had waited for the victory dance until all arrived, brought out the fresh Sahiela scalps and two big dance drums. And for the next four nights everyone but the captives joined in the celebration.

Watching Olepi dance, the Mahto leader marveled the ecstasy in his son's performance; he never had seen a more enthusiastic demonstration of victory, not even when the Mahto danced the Palani scalps. And then Peta wondered whether the warrior-son celebrates something more than a Sicaṅgu victory.

Not much gifting had occurred at the dance; the Sicaŋǧu had not raided those Śahiela lodges, and the Okandada had left most of their possessions in the Palani villages—or so they told. But when Olepi finished his own dance, he signaled the crier forward; the warrior intended to present a gift that will honor a hunter's family.

The singers—those men who sat around the drums—tapped softly on the rim while the crier made the announcement.

Cankuna and Ogle become parents, Eyanpaha told, and so Olepi will honor a member of the new mother's family. Her brother Pasu owns three more horses as of now; let the scout Pasu, brother to Cankuna, take his three horses from Olepi's small herd.

The sounds of glad surprise came from everywhere; in the past certain ones had given away one horse, but not until now will someone give away three.

The singers began Olepi's song again and after eight, ten steps the warrior signed an invitation for all men to dance in the circle with him.

The scout Pasu stood back; he never had danced in a group of warriors. But when an akicita touched him lightly on the legs with a whip, he joined in at once, his dancing rapid and emphatic.

Many more songs honored Olepi this same night, but when the warrior finally lay on his sleeping robes in Peta's lodge, he remembered none of the praise. He remembered instead that the good-natured Pasu, who also had visited the Śahiela captives, now had enough horses to trade for whichever captive woman he wanted.

Olepi knew that neither generosity nor sympathy had prompted his gift of horses but that he had schemed to keep a truly remarkable scout among the Mahto. Properly a man who mated outside the band went to live with his wife's people, but whenever a man took a captive woman for wife, he and the woman stayed. And Olepi wanted Pasu to stay.

As for himself, the warrior intended to remain with the Mahto band, whoever his wife. And not only stay with the band but become leader of the Mahto. On the day he had ridden alone onto the plain, the day he had thrown away his thoughts about the Śahiela captive as a wife, he had decided to prepare for the season when Peta shall begin showing his

59

weariness. Certainly his father had said that the band grew too big for his care. And so why not try to hold on to outstanding scouts and warriors, Olepi had advised himself; why not act, whenever convenient, to keep intact this strong and growing Mahto band.

Four days after the victory dancing Olepi raised a war party of ten and went out looking for the Witapaha, the island-butte people. As the Mahto leader had said, look around; you will see plenty of enemies.

Five days after the victory dancing Peta smoked with Wacape, son of the deceased Siyo leader, and Tatanka Nazin, also Wagmiza of the Sicangu. These Titonwan principals had approved the decision-makers for this summer's encampment and now they sat to consider a proper ceremony for the opening of the most important council they ever yet hold on the plain: the council that phrases the vow they shall exact of an otancan, a shirt-owner.

After a while Peta spoke saying that he will ask the seer Wanagi to originate a special wrapping for the pipestem they use here and a special song for whenever they fill the bowl. None disagreed, and so Peta advised that they now send out for a crier, a mouth who will name the summer-shirts and request their presence in the council lodge. For, once these deciders come together and choose their watchmen, then the scouts dare go-to-the-hills, dare search for pte, and soon afterwards a joyful encampment will feast and sing.

Feast and sing, the Mahto leader repeated to himself, providing a certain war party returns whole. Then abruptly he dismissed any thought that concerned war; he had said that he looked for a quiet summer, his heart going into the creation of the Shirt-Owner rank. And so he will keep things moving this direction; he will talk with Wanagi this same day.

Wanagi laid a cover of sage over quietly burning wood and waited for the thick smoke to curl up through the fragrant grass. For the next little while he will make use of the grass-power that discourages intrusions, that keeps out trickster spirits who come making mischief, who send away a desirable presence. For certainly he will not undertake the preparation of a ceremonial sack for the council pipe until he prepares himself, spirit and body, for this work. True, sage and song protect and strengthen him on this young summer night but, more important, he shall search again his youth-vision, pondering meanings not yet clear, and he shall reflect—Sinaska's welcome spirit perhaps here, perhaps not—his many strange and wondrous experiences since that vision ten winters in the past.

True, Wanaġi told himself as he bathes his hands in the smoke, the Mahto people come to me now as to a seer. The warriors ask about their chances of taking horses before they make up a war party and the leaders of these same parties want to know whether they will bring back their men hurting or whole. But not yet am I certain of the power to prophesy. Nothing yet tells me that I shall see on the opposite side of the moon, that I ever will hear the powerful stone-song. Instead I seem crawling around in darkness. And until I understand more about renewing the spirit than about healing the body, until I know more about soul than I know about flesh, certainly I am not wakanhca, a prophet.

In Wanaġi's youth-vision a grizzly had appeared but almost instantly the creature had become a man. Then more grizzlies appeared, all walking on two legs and changing into men. They had stood gazing at a wounded Titonwan who lay on the ground. But suddenly returning to grizzly-form, these persons had run away, a vast collection of root, leaf, and bark where they had stood. The injured warrior also disappeared; only the assemblage of grasses had endured.

The young dreamer had carried his vision to Sinaska, the old healer-seer, and Sinaska had given the youth a new name. Calling him Wanaġi, he had told that which the vision demanded: the dreamer shall pound roots and crush stalks of his own finding into powders and drinks, the grasses he selects and the songs he sings over these grasses, his secret.

Wanaġi, responding to this demand, had made a powder of the tastes-dry root and a drink of the tastes-bitter root. And wise old Sinaska, not saying who offers these preparations, had distributed Wanaġi's concoctions among the different peźuta-wicaśa, those persons who effect cures.

61

Each pe\u017euta performs his cures in his own special way, and whether the powders or the manspit that moistens the powders or the biting and sucking and noise brings about a healing will remain a mystery for many seasons.

And then old Sinaska, into his eighties, had invited the young grizzly-dreamer to stay on in his lodge as pupil and helper.

Living in a sacred-lodge had proved much different from that which Wanaǵi imagined. Sinaska had required that he become adept at imitating the movements of a grizzly, that he claw berries into his mouth and sit holding his feet, swaying on his bottom and humming. And that he mimic the grunts, the hoarse coughs, and the growls, even the rage of these long-claws. For such traits, Sinaska had said, belong to the creature who changes into man-shape as a way of bringing Wanaǵi his wisdom and power. And so let Wanaǵi—providing he chooses to hold onto this remarkable loan—demonstrate that he remembers-himself-as-grizzly. Certainly everyone knows that in the beginning the grizzly, his structure similar to man, had padded erect from his cave to offer the original people his knowledge, pointing out roots and blooms that heal, berries that keep the body fit. He had stayed on, teaching the people to wear a straight face and to answer with grunts that never tell feelings. He had wanted to teach wrestling but the people had backed away from the power in his arms and the length of his claws. And then this big hairy, roaring and slashing at trees, had defied the people ever to challenge his strength, seek his fat. Dropping onto four legs he had ambled away, rolling his shoulders, snorting his disdain. And the people, marveling his arrogance, had named him śakehanska for his long claws, hunumpa for his manlike stance, waḣanksica for his unpredictable temper. But whatever the name, the grizzly had stopped mingling with people. Only when certain persons truly seek a healer's vision will the grizzly respond.

Sinaska had spoken. Even so, Wanaǵi practiced his assignments reluctantly; he disliked trickery of any kind. And Sinaska, never tolerant, pressed his helper most harshly; he saw the makings of a true-seer in this vigorous young man.

Then one morning the old seer had instructed Wanaǵi to paint red and enact his vision before a group of critical observers, each one a grizzly-dreamer. "These persons come to appraise your earnestness," he told.

They had accepted his demonstration. And so, at age eighteen, his spirit young but growing fast, Wanaġi had known that he dared call himself 'wapiya,' that he dared pursue his search for the renewing grasses. Instead, Sinaska had kept the young seeker close by the sacred-lodge; he chose to instruct him in the many ceremonial uses of the pipe.

The Dakotah grandfathers had devised these ceremonies and Sinaska, the only one who remembered, intended that Wanaġi know the old ways, learn the many, many old songs that accompany each ceremony. The young wapiya will not quickly understand all ceremonies, he had said, nor quickly memorize all songs, not in three seasons, perhaps not in five.

Wanaġi heard, his heart falling. But he had stayed. He saw that the warriors relied on the power Sinaska wrapped up in little bundles to take on raids, that they respected this old seer who never let any hands but his touch the bundles, never let anything contaminate the trust he tied up in those bits of hide.

During those next five seasons in the sacred-lodge, Wanaġi had wished not only to go out searching for cures; often he had sensed a desire to join a war party, to try out his skills in company with the warriors, to feel his own sturdy thighs gripping a captured horse, his arm swinging a club, handling a bow. And so aroused, he had sat annoyed and brooding in the subdued surroundings of a seer's lodge. But then Sinaska, understanding, had sent the young man to the initi, where the power in water sizzling on heated stones had wrested the impatience from Wanaġi's throbbing legs and arms. And heart.

One night, while visiting Heĥaka's lodge, Wanaġi had used the picture-record to count his winters. His age had surprised him: twenty-and-four and living in a tipi with an old man too old to eat, who stayed mostly at the fire, his dark eyes staring into some unknown. Occasionally Wanaġi had looked to see whether his own legs and arms shrivel even as certain young berries will wrinkle before they ripen.

But suddenly Sinaska had begun talking again. His voice firm, compelling, he had requested that Wanaġi listen attentively to those rituals that prepare man for his most demanding experience: the recognition of his own soul.

Even so Wanaġi had not looked for the old seer to use up two more winters instructing him in every aspect of this profound undertaking. Nor had he imagined himself accepting the quiet of the old man's company yet another season.

But perhaps from the beginning Sinaska had known that Wanaġi will stay on for ten winters.

Then, the summer before this one, Wanaġi had stood scalding sweetroot in grease-water. Remembering this concoction as something of use to new mothers, he had considered his own lack of wife, child. Certainly he desired woman, desires flowing into woman, exalting himself. Even as he hunted these thoughts, that which stiffens in desire suddenly had stiffened.

Sensing Sinaska's eyes on him, he wondered whether the old man saw through the cover at his thighs. So, he told himself, the warriors come to the ancient one in this lodge for their power-bundles, never to me. Yet Sinaska has nothing like the power-bundle that rises up between these legs. Standing tall, his arrogant posture speaking for his virility as truly as the pulsing at his loins, the young wapiya wore the joy of his manliness.

Then, the steam noisily singing a message from the boiling roots, Sinaska had emitted some grunts and growls in his grizzly-voice. And Wanaġi had whirled to face the old one, his eyes dangerous, his glare telling that he will permit neither reproof nor slight.

But Sinaska, his utterances signaling only approval, had removed a string of grizzly claws from around his neck. True, the old one's gesturing fingers had told, he sees the young man grow rigid. And seeing, he offers these claws, a symbol of the power he once owns.

Aware suddenly of Wanaġi's scrutiny, Sinaska had dropped the necklet and leaned forward. "Will you live to see more winters than I see? Will your vigor surpass mine?" he had roared. "When will you remember that these old bones and skull-like head once belong to a young husband and proud father."

Sinaska had moved over to the backrest and Wanaġi, stooping, had picked up the string of claws.

For a long while Wanaġi had sat next to the fire, the

grizzly claws in his hands, a necklet Sinaska had worn more than seventy winters. But when finally Wanaġi had lifted the string to tie at his own neck, a hot breath had fanned the back of his head and he had heard the hoarse coughs Sinaska often made. He had turned his face slowly.

He had seen nothing back of him that possessed the breath to cough in his ear, warm his neck. And Sinaska had lain asleep on his robes. And yet as he looked, Wanaġi had seen all that he had imagined: grizzly tracks, four big, big tracks on the ground inside the lodge. Instantly he had known; the spirit of this powerful creature, remembering Sinaska, comes visiting the old seer.

The next moment Wanaġi had felt a compelling urge to hunt this grizzly and challenge him to fight, to overcome this warrior-creature and make his own string of awesome claws. Why not follow these tracks out the lodge, he had asked himself; why not find the old grizzly whose spirit visits here? Why not discover the power that Sinaska puts into the heart-sacs, the mystery-bundles they wear to war?

When Wanaġi looked again at the ground, the tracks had disappeared. But the smoothed-over earth had not surprised him; certainly the wary grizzly will not reveal his hiding place to someone going out to kill him. And so Wanaġi had not gone out; instead, he had sat hunched over the fire, awaiting the invisible visitor's return.

After a while he had begun dreaming, not as a sleep-dreamer or a vision-seeker but as someone half-awake who drifts from one scene to the next. And so he had mused the legends of creation, wondering from which family of four-legs the original people had come. Children of the grizzly, perhaps? Mahtowin, mother to the first grandmother—or so they say whenever someone speaks of those creatures back at the beginning.

Fancy had filled the remainder of Wanaġi's night. He had imagined a grizzly's cave wherein certain ones among the young resembled their four-legged mother and different ones resembled their two-legged father.

Drowsing, he had supposed himself husband to the female grizzly; awakening, he had found his thighs sticky from the dream.

Again he had drowsed, his unreal sleep bringing him more unlikely images. Awakening he had sensed a strange surge of power and a desire for combat with the male of the grizzly nation.

He had gone out before sunrise for a bath in the stream, and while he stood wiping dry, Olepi had approached, the warrior gesturing his desire for talk. And so he had learned that Olepi intended to take out a party of eight, that he looked for Wanaġi to prepare a pipe for war, wrapping the stem and sealing the bowl. And that he also wanted Wanaġi to accompany the raiders as singer and seer.

Gladly Wanaġi had accepted; finally he had a chance to test his powers for preventing losses, man or horse, while the party stayed out. But he had intended to stop their going if he foresaw anything calamitous happening along the way.

Instead of returning to the sacred-lodge after his meeting with Olepi, the young seeker had gone out looking for ĥoka, the creature who digs-with-the-mouth. And after he had killed and emptied the body of all but blood, he had waited for the thick, smooth mass to reflect whatever he needed to know about Olepi's war party. Why not try out something, he had asked himself, that many wapiya call reliable.

At dawn the next day Olepi had led out his party, six men in the final count and Wanaġi along to prophesy. After eight days the party had returned, exactly as their seer had prophesied: mounted and whipping along thirty Witapaha horses.

But Wanaġi had not come back into camp with the party; something had occurred as the blood-picture had revealed but not as the young seer had comprehended.

A half-day away from camp, the joyfully returning warriors had presented Wanaġi a fast horse and so they had provided him with a safe way back to the village in the event he chose to separate from the group and search for grasses.

Wanaġi had welcomed the chance to stay out alone, to walk slowly on the plain, to marvel again the color and fragrance of young summer. His nearness to camp and the horse grazing nearby had given him a feeling of safety; he had moved along looking down on the stems that bloomed at his feet. But as he bent to examine a clump of mixed grasses, the horse had snorted, an uneasy snort.

Slowly Wanaġi had raised his eyes and glanced around him. And then his heart had jumped. For neither distance nor approaching dusk had obscured the certainty of the humped form that scrambled up the grassy slope ahead.

Either a mother with her young and ready for fight, he had told himself, or the man-grizzly, winter-starved and unpredictable.

Instantly he had decided to leave his horse where this one grazed, the forelegs loosely tied to prevent straying, the creature available if suddenly needed. The next moment Wanaġi had started slowly toward the rise.

The wind had favored the man and so he moved along the bottom of the slope, walking in the open. Reaching the flowered side of the hill, he had seen a bird fly up. And then something had crashed through the brush.

Ears alerted, Wanaġi had advanced cautiously toward the noise, but the grizzly had caught the man-smell. Curious, the creature had stood on two legs and squinted over the top of thorny grass, the big head swinging from side to side, the keen nose trying to locate the enemy.

The man's blood had chilled at the sight of the massive thick body standing erect, the creature more fearsome than any long-claws he had encountered in his dreams. Certainly the moment had come for Wanaġi to remember-himself-as-grizzly, to grunt and bring the fierce warrior down the hill and within reach of the full power of his bow. Instead, fear had closed off the man's throat; he had lost his voice.

Next he had seen the warrior-creature—apparently a male who grazed alone—drop down, then amble on across the slope, stopping once to chew on grass.

"Grandfather." Wanaġi had startled himself with his own loud cry. "Grandfather," he had sung, "I respect your knowing. You show me the roots that heal. Now I demand that you show me the mystery that protects."

The power in his song had warmed Wanaġi's blood; he had dared to move ahead singing, boldly approaching the long-claws.

The grizzly, turning, had made a throaty huffing sound but he had stayed back.

"Grandfather," Wanaġi had sung, "I respect your courage. I meet your bravery with my own."

The grizzly had risen up growling.

Moving forward again, Wanaġi had remembered that he faced the one creature to whom the Titonwan had given

67

the rank of warrior and that his arrows needed to strike full force against this creature's tremendous shoulder, inside a circle of vulnerable places. Here, in the shoulder, within the space of a hand-drum, were the grizzly's backbone, legbone, shoulderbone. And heart.

The grizzly had let himself down again, sitting quiet but for the side-to-side movement of his head. Coolly this warrior-creature of the plain had deliberated his next act: run or fight.

Wanaǧi had held five arrows, the sixth in his bowstring; he had known that either these arrows kill the grizzly or the grizzly kills him. True, a knife had hung at his neck, but, his arrows missing the target, he needs two knives to fight the long-claws, two knives to meet the grizzly's embrace, a knife pointing out from under each arm.

And Wanaǧi carried but one knife and six arrows.

Even so, when the creature's decision had seemed to favor galloping off, the man's voice had rolled out in a growl.

Instantly the grizzly had answered; emitting hoarse fighting grunts, he had run toward the challenge, his long, shining hair rippling like grass, his narrow, open mouth appearing as a small red spot under his nose.

Wanaǧi had watched the creature plunge down the slope, the rush of power almost certain to carry the immense form crashing past him.

But the force of the charge had seemed suddenly restrained; the grizzly had come sliding to a stop. Then rearing up, he had stood drooling, his powerful jaws ready to tear, his powerful arms ready to crush and slash and crumple the puny shape that had dared annoy him.

In this moment Wanaǧi, heart and throat acting together, let loose a terrifying roar. The next instant six arrows had flown as one—or so they seemed—six points hitting inside a circle on the creature's hide, a circle Wanaǧi's eyes saw clearly.

The grizzly had bawled pain, then suddenly clamped his jaw. Turning, he had jumped in the direction of his wounding.

As in a dream, Wanaǧi had watched the creature coming at him, falling, front legs spread, the shafts in the grizzly's shoulder snapping off like twigs.

Then, as if awakening, he had jumped away scarcely an instant before the shocking mass, sliding another bow's length, lay dead at the place he stood.

Wanaġi had gazed on his kill a long while. For not until this thing happened had he understood the prophetic pool of creature-blood back in camp. The shining surface had reflected him alone, a warrior's feather at the back of his head. He had imagined the picture to hint at a confidence his presence will exert over the warriors, but he had not consulted Sinaska. And so he really dared boast only that he had used all those grizzly voices the old seer had demanded that he learn; most certainly he had remembered-himself-as-grizzly.

The story of Wanaġi's kill had reached the Mahto camp ahead of the procession that had brought in hide, claws, head, but Wanaġi had not seen anyone until after his talk with Sinaska, a long and final talk.

Sinaska's aged hands had passed over the grizzly's skull before he had begun speaking. Will Wanaġi understand, he had said, that mimicking a desire brings about the real thing? But that the demonstration of a vision foretells power far beyond that which Wanaġi yet imagines. "Will you recognize truth in these revelations," Sinaska had demanded, "or will you restrict yourself to guessing at pictures in blood and an impotent string of claws around your neck? Will you act upon the true extent of your power or will you stop where I prematurely stop, at prophecy and power-bundles?"

Wanaġi understood the language of seers but not the abstruse that Sinaska had spoken. He had recognized only the need to reappraise his powers, to hunt new patterns in the old dream. Or perhaps to seek a second vision.

Three, four days after Wanaġi's talk with Sinaska, they had wrapped the old seer in the red robe; the ancient one, his work finished, had walked-the-spirit-trail. And only then had Wanaġi sensed the true beginning of his own journey.

Wanaġi laid a bundle of sticks on the blinking embers and fanned the wood with a handful of stiff feathers. He wanted flame and warmth now, not smoke and mystery as when he began his reflections.

He had returned his thoughts to the present, to this

summer's encampment at the butte. But his night's reverie had not changed anything. He not yet comprehended the message the dying old seer had left back in the council lodge eight, ten moons past. Nor had he discovered any new meanings in his own experiences. "I feel a barrier," he told the glowing wood; "and now I wonder: am I the one who puts up this barrier?"

He sang a little song but finished with a wail that acknowledged his despair: hiye-hey-ii-ii, hiye-hey-ii-ii.

Night had begun to fade out of the distant sky, the tipi cover lightening and somewhere a bird singing. "Grandfather," Wanaǧi cried out, "hear me. I am relative to all who swim or fly, crawl or walk. From the beginning my face, my legs and arms relate to each different creature. I and they recognize one great relative: anpetuwi, the sun.

"These things I know.

"But I see mystery in a flashing rumbling sky. I see mystery in a changing leaf and in the tree that pushes off the leaf. I hear mystery in a newborn's call, in the voice of the woman who answers this call.

"These things that I not know, I name mystery. And either I know or I not know.

"I recognize truth as something that happens whether or not I know why.

"Observe the effect, the grandfathers say, but ponder not; never meddle, they say, with the wakan, the mystery.

"Grandfather, I offend but hear me."

The flame in his fire-place flickered down to ashes falling silently upon ashes. And Wanaǧi knew that at this moment he breaks away from whatever will hinder his search for the heart of things. "Grandfather, this passing night I give to musing. This coming day I give to reason. And on this new day I begin pondering the mysteries.

"I see that something protects each living thing. I live and so something protects me. I hunt-thoughts; I reason and marvel and choose. These acts protect me. But protect me from whom, from what thing? I am one within the whole; I relate to everything as a spirit, as a body. So who will try destroying me?

"I, a body, am not enemy to I, a soul. Who says I dare not regard my self as friend?

"Grandfather, recognize me. I am not as the youth-vision reveals. I seek not the power of the grizzly; I seek my own. I will not cry for a spirit-helper; my own spirit helps me. I make proper use of my grizzly-vision; I recognize the healing powers in root and berry and bark. But why ever again remember-myself-as-grizzly?

"The bones of grizzly and the bones of man look alike and so certain persons say that I am so many grandsons from one who runs on four legs and claws up the ground. But neither my father nor his father nor any generation with which I am familiar acts in this manner. I am man and the son of man and the grandson of man.

"Recognize me, grandfather, as a reasoning power. My reason permits my knowing many things. I shall remember-myself-as-man.

"Recognize me, grandfather, as a healing power, as one who renews those persons who come asking for this thing. Recognize me as a seeker, one who goes out looking for good. Nor am I blind to that which awaits change.

"Recognize me, grandfather, as a generating power."

Wanaǧi stood, then stepping outside the lodge he silently welcomed the sunrise. He began walking across the campground, toward a familiar knoll atop a pebbly slope. And here, he lay down. He breathed deeply, expanding his ribs, letting go slowly. "Haun-n-n," he sighed. After a moment he breathed as before, sighed as before, an old and familiar ritual. His hair, loose, spread on the ground. "Fill me," he whispered, "fill me."

When finally he lifted his head, he turned and lay on his back, hands beneath his neck. He saw that the sky had deepened, displaying colors that perhaps never find names. And now the grasses put words to their rustling song and the far-distant hills inspire a most fragrant breeze. He felt himself flowing into this fresh and exquisite realm; śkan, taku śkanśkan fills him, lifts him above the ordinary level. He wanted to stay but he sensed himself returning; once again he, a young seeker who lies on a knoll, hands beneath neck, eyes open to the sky.

Walking back to the camp he passed under the branches of an old tree; he stopped, hearing someone call his name, give a message: make a pipe.

But certainly he intends wrapping a pipe this same day, something Peta requests for the council lodge. And certainly he, Wanaġi, prepares for this ceremonial act when he revisits old seasons, an old vision, throughout this past night.

Make a pipe.

Suddenly Wanaġi understood: the Mahto soon will have use for a special pipe, the people on the plain now looking for those old sacred ceremonies that keep a family together, ceremonies that lay on the ground more than one hundred winters, ceremonies that will demand an especial pipe.

Why not use the tree with the old-wood smell for the stem, he asked himself, and redstone for the bowl?

But before hunting any more thoughts about the Mahto pipe he needed to decorate a wrapping for the council pipe.

He entered the sacred-lodge, a song in his heart.

The moon had fattened to round, then thinned to dying before the iyotanyapi council—man-they-honor council—found agreement, before this group of twelve leaders and councilors truly understood the meaning of shirt-man.

The Titonwan, they said now, will shirt him who secures the help of a vision, a sacred-dream on which he fixes his eyes; the Titonwan, they said, shall honor him who secures the help of a vision that brings together in him all the powers in the people.

The Titonwan, they said, shall make nothing easy for a shirtman. They shall deny him revenge even if his brother lies dead at his feet. And they shall ask that he find a way to reclaim a man who murders and so absorb the tragedy.

The people will not permit anger in a shirtman. This man, as owner-of-the-tribe, will shield all in the tribe, those persons he likes and those persons for whom he feels little fondness; his heart never shall hold space for wrath.

The people will view a shirtman as they view a woman, someone with a peaceful heart, someone who never strikes out against anyone.

At this point the councilors had wondered whether they demand too much of this man they choose to call otancan. Why compel him to treat with troublemakers? Why refuse him revenge, even against an enemy of his tribe? Will his pledge become too much to bear?

But from the most wise the council heard an answer.

Not too much, they said; not too much. Certainly within the Titonwan tribe lives a man with the staying-power for this pledge and the heart to take the vow.

But consider, someone said, that which perhaps occurs when a man of great importance discovers that the people adore him. Will he see himself in the eyes of these admirers and so permit such an image to overwhelm him? His vow, these wise men answered, shall prevent any untrue, any dangerous image.

And now something more: a shirtman shall regard his wife most kindly and so she will sit alongside him all her seasons. And the people, noticing his respect for her, shall keep remembering women's high place in the tribe. And so they shall recall the Ptesanwin, who puts the original pipe into Dakotah hands, comes in the form of woman, peaceful and pure, a sister to each Dakotah.

These things understood, the council next decided the pattern for this special shirt. Like those garments they loan each summer to the deciders, they will use two bighorn hides, dewclaws clinging. But, unlike the summer-shirts, they will decorate the true-shirt with a fringe of hair crossing the shoulders and coming down the arms, each strand commemorating a remarkable act.

The hair? From an enemy's head, proof of daring. But also strands from the head of relative or friend whose gift of hair confirms the shirtman's responsibility as owner-of-the-people, a tribal-caretaker.

The shirtman shall wear one more symbol that proclaims him otancan, a man 'iyotanyapi,' man-they-esteem: a single white-and-black feather lying flat at the back of the head.

Peta, advising the position of this wambli feather, had made the sign meaning where sky meets earth. And so the group had perceived the most important rank the tribe ever knows, and had agreed upon the symbol for this rank: shirt and a reclining feather.

But what name for this garment-of-honor, someone had asked.

War Shirt, perhaps? War, an invigorating experience and as important as meat. War, bravery the motive; war, a contest, recognition going to the winners. War, inciting him

73

who seeks prestige yet assuring him nothing; war, a young man's game, sanctioning an urge to risk life, earning the privilege to boast.

True, acts of war decorate this Shirt, but not only acts of war.

Peace Shirt? Peace, counterpoint to war; peace, as real as war and as desirable. Certainly each Titonwan knows himself as half warrior and half peaceman, someone fierce and cruel outside the tribe, gentle and kind inside the circle. And so with those strands of hair decorating the Shirt, some strands symbolizing war, different ones, peace. War and peace, the story of man.

Why not Hair Shirt? Hair, an enemy's scalp, symbol of revenge and sign of personal victory. But the trim on the Shirt shall come from any head, living or not, relative or enemy, man or woman. Wives, sisters, mothers, daughters shall give hair to commemorate those occasions when the warrior touches but not kills the enemy. Hair, something that clings to life, symbol of the man-spirit determining to stay alive on this earth.

Certain Titonwan, then, will say War Shirt and different ones will say Peace Shirt and yet others will speak of the Hair Shirt. But the wise ones will know that when the Titonwan grant someone the otancan rank, they confer an honor that symbolizes all honor. And so they will call the garment Honor Shirt.

And now, who will fit this Shirt?

III

THE SUMMER grew old, the grasses turned brittle. Twice the hunters had caught up with the big herd; none had starved at grizzly butte. The women had bent over fresh hides for

74

many days but the tiring work had brought much satisfaction; not one among the Titonwan need wear a soiled gown or torn robe or mended moccasins this coming winter.

The summer moons had shone down on a contented encampment; even the Okandada band had managed without quarreling. Tatanka Naźin and Ooweśica had sat in the council of twelve who decided the shirtman-pledge, a group that had acted as one heart. The leaders of these four bands on the plain and their advisers had come together fully aware of the importance they enacted; none had looked for any unpleasantness inside or outside the council lodge.

The war parties had gone out and returned without any big difficulty. Olepi had led only the one party but he and his warriors had chased the Witapaha far up the thick woods river, the pursuers making a game of the whole experience.

A different Titonwan party—some Sicaṅǵu and Okandada—had gone out after Sahiela horses, raiding the herd that belonged to a camp of fifty lodges. But they also had avoided any encounters with an alien tribe; the horses they took had grazed a slope far outside the Sahiela camp, the horse-tenders perhaps never knowing who had run off twenty of their bunch.

The four days of scalp-dancing at the beginning of summer had provided the one opportunity for new kills-talks; other dances had revived the old stories, the familiar recitals about attacks on the Palani and Miwatani, on the Oyatenumpa, and even back to the Haḣatonwan, the people-alongside-the-laughing-waters.

But Peta had not danced this summer. Nor gone out with any warriors. When not in council he had chosen to sit most often with Heḣaka, the two men reviewing the picture-hide, the Mahto leader observing that life on the plain, as he foretold, had not proved easy. The record showed deep snows and starving winters, the people often despondent. Occasionally a young man, even some boys, had chosen to take their own lives. But these suicides had occurred among the Okandada, not the Mahto; Peta had a strong band, strong in every way, and he had a strong son, strong enough to lead these people when the day came.

Olepi scarcely noticed the summer aging. He had used his bow mostly for meat, going on two big hunts, bringing in nearly as much meat as the hunter Ogle, enough meat to feast his father's band. And he had hunted once with the Siyo, giving all his meat to a Siyo family in whom he had taken an interest.

He had stayed different nights with warrior-friends among the Sicanġu and the Okandada, but most often he visited the Siyo camp and if any old women had observed him closely they, for once, had kept their mouths closed.

And so one day in the yellow-leaf moon, before the season changed and the Titonwan broke their summer circle at the butte, Olepi stood before his father, a woman at his side, someone slender and shy and sixteen, someone the people knew for her quiet ways, her good work with awl and sinew and quills. The design on her gown told of the fine Siyo family to which she belonged, a young woman from the closely bound tiyośpaye in Wacape's following.

Peta looked for a long moment into the son's face but the eyes that met his search acknowledged nothing, revealed nothing. Yet these eyes had not lacked respect for the warrior-father.

And while the two stood silent, Napewaśtewin—the woman at Olepi's side—looked down, her heart disturbed at the strange meeting between son and father. Will she find more of this strangeness, she wondered, inside the tipi where she and the warrior shall stay with the Mahto leader?

When Olepi had asked that she live with him in the lodge of his father, she had not demurred. And if her family had felt displeasure on hearing that their daughter deserts her own for the husband's band, they had not said so. Honor enough, their actions had told, that Olepi comes to their tipi for his wife. And certainly Olepi had not disregarded any other custom. He had hunted with the Siyo and brought his meat to her family and he had gifted her relatives profusely: two horses to her father and three horses to her sister's husband, who, custom said, dared claim Napewaśtewin as a second wife.

To her woman relatives Olepi presented neck and ear ornaments, colorful and shining stones from a raid on the Palani. And he had remembered her grandmother in this gifting.

Standing here with Olepi now, her eyes on his mocca-

76

sins, she remembered her grandmother's advice: let Nape-waśtewin stay proudly alert to her obligations; as wife to Olepi she will fill many feast bowls for the principal Mahto and these same ones will observe her conduct in and outside the tipi. Let her sit and rise gracefully, never exposing anything, and she shall avoid running around camp alone. Not likely will the husband indulge her whims, favor her tendency toward anxiety. Young, true, but not the only woman who at age sixteen becomes wife in the lodge of an important man.

Suddenly frightened, she wanted to run away. Perhaps she will neglect something, displease him, and he will send her back to the Siyo band in disgrace. Truly she will kill herself before she endures the shame of a wife they return.

She trembled slightly, knowing that she will not run anywhere; that she will stay where she stands, waiting for one of those pairs of feet to move away and the other pair to lead her into the nearby lodge. And once she sits inside this lodge, the young warrior will own her in the way her grandmother tells, in the same way every woman knows the man to whom she becomes wife.

The woman felt Olepi's touch on her arm and, looking up, she saw his smile, something that gave wings to her heart. Instantly she vowed to perform her work properly, to act in a manner that honors him. And gladly, gladly she will stay inside the lodge and not run around like a child if only occasionally he will smile at her as he smiles now.

From the edge of his eyes Peta saw his son lift the tipi flap, then bend to step inside. The woman followed and the flap dropped over the entrance.

The father moved, then, picking up two sticks, crossing this wood in front of the lodge, signing that visitors shall stay away. He also intended to stay away, to sleep somewhere different these next four, five nights. And so these two newly joined will get used to each other.

Walking off, Peta told himself that he liked the woman's appearance, her modest manner, her little tremors in awe of those mysteries before her. Let Olepi plant himself in this Siyo wife; let him feel the power that most certainly comes to each man who knows that his seed grows a child.

Olepi had sat down at the back of the lodge and Napewaśtewin, moving gracefully toward the woman's side, shyly had spread a robe, then seated herself upon this cover; silently attentive, she awaited whatever shall happen next.

Occasionally she glanced toward the man, looking for a sign that will tell his desire, perhaps for pipe or food. Or that which her grandmother had hinted.

And so waiting, she had recalled his words one evening halfway through the summer when they had stood together outside her family's tipi. "I like you," he had said. "I like you more than I like any other person."

He had held his robe around her, over her head and over his face in the manner of any man who seeks out a certain woman, but he had not coaxed; he had used the robe to cover his whispers, not to hide a roving hand and fingers.

The next night they had stood together in the same way; and he had asked that she accept him as husband.

Modestly, sedately, after two, three days, she had presented him the moccasins that revealed her willingness to live as his wife. And her father and relatives, keeping his gifts, had made known their approval.

Then, before these two walked across the big circle to Olepi's lodge, her family had loaded a horse with gifts for the man and their daughter.

Olepi sat on, apparently indifferent to the woman on the opposite side of the fire circle. He leaned on an elbow, his other arm across his raised knee, his hand loose.

Suddenly he closed, then forcefully opened his hand, fingers spreading, a motion that accompanied his thoughts, not something that signaled the woman.

But he glanced her way. And now his look invited her to his side, to lie with him on his robes.

For the present he desired to enjoy the woman's gentleness; afterwards, lying on her robes, he intended to discover her fire.

The woman heard the voices of camp as a distant hum on the warm mid-day air, but the fragrance of the season—everything ripening, coming to fitness for use—brought on a new wonder about herself.

She lay quiet under the man's soothing touch. He

rubbed her cheek and patted her bottom and stroked her leg, all in the manner of fondling a child.

But something different will happen, she remembered now, something that will make me want to hold on to him, something that happens when a woman unties the cord she wears around her thighs.

Her grandmother had advised that she untie the cord soon after she entered the new lodge and not wait those ten days that custom permits the shy young woman. But she had removed the soft strip before ever she left her mother's lodge. Now she wondered whether she had untied the chastity cord too soon; perhaps the man wanted only to rub her back and stroke her legs and bottom for eight, ten days.

Certainly she desired, as her grandmother desired for her, that this man make her wife with proper ceremony and so honor her. True, the good old woman had not told her anything about the ceremony; she only had hinted at something most pleasing.

Perhaps the man began the ceremony now; for suddenly he handled her differently, her body quivering under the change in his touch. But, almost as suddenly, she felt him pushing her away. He said that he intended to go outside the lodge and that she shall go with him.

She lay unmoving, her thoughts confused. Will he imagine her immodest, a woman who unties the cord before he ever knows she wears one? Or will he choose this moment to walk her proudly through the camp?

She sat up, putting a hand to her loosened braids. Perhaps he will brush and arrange her hair in the manner her father looks after her mother's hair?

But seeing that the man already had stepped outside the lodge, she smoothed her gown and came out after him.

They took a path not through the center of the encampment but along the edge and so the woman experienced yet more anxiety; perhaps the man schemed to return her to the Siyo village.

The sun, halfway down the smoky sky, had turned red and lost warmth as man and woman approached the stream that had provided the people with a swimming place this summer. The water now floated a cover of yellow leaves, and the man, noticing, stopped to marvel the change in season. And the woman, seeing his pleasure, came up close. Soon they walked on, keeping inside the brush that edged the water.

They came to a shallow, the stream knee-deep; here a clump of young trees held on to each shiny leaf, the water clear and quiet beneath their branches.

The woman watched while the man arranged a robe between trees and stream, screening the shallow. Now she saw him holding out his hand, inviting her to join him back of the hanging robe, in seclusion.

She came close, her head slightly bowed. His hand lifted her chin and his eyes made a puzzling demand. And then he spoke saying that she shall take off her gown, step into the water.

She pulled back, not understanding that which the man asked. Women who have husbands bathe with other women, not with the men. Why shall he ask this strange thing of her?

But the man will not ask; he will tell her to uncover herself.

Embarrassed to remove her gown before him yet suddenly afraid to refuse, she stood anxious and trembling.

The man waited, his silence more compelling than speech.

And so, in a flush of shame, she lifted off her cover. And now, nothing to protect her nudeness, she stepped quickly into the shallow water. She bent forward and so the water covered her thighs; her long hair fell protectingly over her small breasts. She clasped her arms across herself. And so she stood bent and shaking and afraid.

The man came alongside her and made her stand straight but she shook the same as before. And so he began a quieting song, something to dispel her alarm, something to strengthen her.

As he sang he pushed back her hair and lifted water to her face. Next he moved around her and washed her shoulders and back. And then, turning her to him, he carefully, thoroughly, bathed the front of her body.

At the beginning of the bath the woman resisted the intimate handling of her person. She made the denying gesture and uttered a little crying-sound and once she tried to push aside the persisting hands. But the power of his song and the caressing touch acted upon her as the man intended.

The woman stood quiet now. She accepted the hands that briefly lingered at her breasts, the fingers lightly pinching the nipples, gently rubbing the surrounding red. But when his hands, moving down her body, came near the strangely aching place between her legs, her trembling began again.

And so the man placed his hand firmly over her shorthair; she shall understand that holding her here will become the natural thing, the pleasing thing, for him, for her.

And when she seemed at ease again, he pushed her gently down against the water, his fingers carefully spreading the mysterious warm lips his hand had covered; he invited the power that moved the waters to touch upon this woman's sheath and help her reach wonder and marvel.

And so this man bathed the woman he will make his wife.

When they stepped from the stream onto the ground, the man stood behind her, his hands rubbing the water from her glistening skin, from neck and shoulders and back. Then he faced her toward him and fondly stroked dry her breasts, arms, legs, all her body down to her toes. And when he took his hands off her, he saw that she responded as he desired; neither the cool of night nor a care for modesty persuaded her to move until he so gestured; she awaited his permission to put on her gown, this act of submission something she chose, not something he demanded.

But the man took his robe and wrapped this warmth around her and then, standing close, he reached between her thighs; in one more way he shall satisfy himself before he makes her wife; a man needs to experience the smell and taste of a woman he desires and so discover whether these things appeal to him, awaken him.

His finger pushed inside the woman's śan, insisting upon enough of her moisture for his wants.

And the woman, responding, provided the sweetness he sought.

The two returned to the village, walking in the moonlight, avoiding shadows. Entering the lodge, the woman went to her sleeping robe, where, properly, she lay waiting for the man to come to her.

But the man, going to his own place in the lodge,

picked up a hand-drum. Tapping gently on the edge, he sang softly, a soothing little song.

The woman, listening closely, remembered the words as something he had sung as he bathed her and so she understood that the song belonged to this man. She wondered now whether any other woman ever had heard his song; she wanted none but herself knowing these words, hearing these tones.

Turning her eyes, she saw that he put aside the drum. Her heart quickened but then she saw him reaching for his pipe. Perhaps she had misunderstood something; will he want her to sleep? Or to appear asleep?

After a while the man's puffs on the stem and the pleasant smell of smoke made her stir. Opening her eyes, she saw that he leaned above her.

His eyes smiled and his lips blew smoke on her face. And then he moved away, to the back of the lodge where he replaced his pipe on the little rack.

Again he came toward her. And now his eyes, unsmiling, said that she shall obey him always and in all things and that, most important, she shall want to obey him.

His hand reached under her bottom. "Up, up," he said softly and when she lifted herself, he raised her gown. But he made her remove the garment.

And now, his hands pressing wide her legs, she saw his head bend to her thighs. Her eyes closed; her hands clutched the hairs on the pte-robe underneath her.

Let man, the ceremony-makers had said, perform upon the woman he desires to make his wife, an irresistible act; let the tongue of his mouth know her the same as the tongue of his loin shall know her. Let his breathing fan her, his mouth touch and his tongue reach. Then let him lift his head and raise up his body and make entry with that which hardens for this purpose. But let him enter gently, not forcibly with pain for her to remember.

The woman's breath had come in childlike gasps of wonder and hurt. And the man, hearing the hurt, had delayed. But his hand went to the place his hand belonged, his fingers unceasing in their caress.

Suddenly the woman tried twisting away from his hold, not that she wished escape but that she wanted something more, something he makes her want, something he will make her ask for.

And now the real blended with the unreal for this woman who lay knowing, then not-knowing whose lodge, whose village, whose camp.

But she knew when the hurt moved out, the hurt but not the throbbing. She sighed, a mysterious little sigh; she lay quiet, very quiet.

Presently the man spoke: "Your hand belongs some place," he told her.

When she seemed not to understand, he placed her fingers on him. Here, he said, his seeds, and here, a pathway for these seeds, for new life, for the child they will make.

Uncertainly she handled him. And so, pulling her head onto his breast, he began talking softly, making known to her something that Wanaġi, the young seer, had revealed concerning the original hunka ceremony, the making-wife ceremony.

When the old Dakotah grandfathers had devised a ceremony for the bond between man and woman, he told, they had spoken of that which the husband ejects into woman. They had described as sacred this act wherein the man expels the seeds of generations past, the generations ahead. And so they had advised that woman take care never to throw away life. Instead, let woman take something into her mouth and know why she performs this act; let her know why she tastes the drops, the seeds, that cling to his tip; let her know that in this manner she shows her desire to preserve life, his life and each life and all life.

The woman truly had listened while the man spoke of these things. And now he heard her speaking the word, the phrase, that accepted him as the man she chose to hold, to honor above any different person; the man she will obey, in all things.

Mihigna, mihigna. She breathed the meaning onto his thigh and he heard her pleasure.

"My-husband, my-husband." She spoke the meaning against his thigh and he heard her respect.

And now the husband, pulling her up, gathered her to

him affectionately; in the presence of wakantanka—all that they call mystery—this woman becomes his wife, his true-wife.

The moon climbed high up in the sky and the Mahto women, laying the heavy wood on their lodge-fires, prepared for sleep.

In Olepi's lodge also, the fire needed the night-wood and so the new young wife slipped quietly out of the embrace.

But the husband had caught her foot before she stood; gently he pulled her back to him. Fire and food he shall want in the morning, he said, but for the whole of this night, he shall appreciate the woman of this lodge.

Tawicu, his-wife. Different ones shall call her Napewa-stewin—or more often, Napewaśte—but only he shall call her mitawicu, my-wife, or perhaps mitawin, my-woman.

He covered his face with her long shining-black hair, breathing in the fragrance, and he pressed his mouth against her arms, enjoying the smell of her skin, and he moved his hands soothingly over the whole of her body, delighting in her feel.

But he had not caressed her breasts, the symbol of woman as mother, something to which the child, not the husband, relates.

After a while the woman's breathing told him that she slept. And so he also prepared for sleep, but not as a warrior usually sleeps. Instead he remembered himself as a new husband, a pair of 'keep-out' sticks before his lodge and a young wife next to him. True, a proper husband returns to his own sleeping robe, he told the star that peeked down through the smoke hole at him, but on this night and perhaps for three, four nights he shall act like an improper husband and stay next to his wife.

He turned toward the quietly sleeping woman and placed his hand upon that which had brought him much joy.

At once he felt her fingers reaching for him. "Mihigna," she murmured, then slept again. But she had not let go.

84

IV

THE TITONWAN leaders who had worked together this
summer to create the otancan-rank understood the good
occurring on this campground at grizzly butte, a good for all
generations who ever walk the grasses of the plain.

During these warm moons and into the changing-sea-
sons moon they had sat as one body, twelve men with one
purpose, something which gave rise to the desire for a
brother-lodge, a feast-and-dance group, persons who shall
sit together whenever the bands camp as a tribe. In the
seasons ahead, they had said, perhaps they shall invite
different ones to join their group but for the present they
shall recognize as members only the twelve whose thoughts
and wisdom had devised the shirt-owner ceremony.

Next, they sent for Wanaġi. The new wapiya, healer-
seer, had wrapped the iyotanyapi-council pipestem in a
wonderful, fringed sack; now they desired that he instruct
their group in the proper way to form a brother-lodge. Let
him say in what manner they shall paint their bodies and
what songs and dances they shall perform; and let him
advise a name for this lodge.

And so, during the moon of ripening and rutting—
berries fattening and the antlered pawing the earth—the
people heard about a newly formed brother-lodge, twelve
Titonwan leaders and principals who called their group
ptatanka wapahaun okolakiciyapi and who, in keeping with
their name, decorated their heads with the horns of pta, of
the males in the herd.

Peta and Heĥaka sat in this lodge, the people learned,
along with Tatanka Naźin and Ooweśica of the Okandada;
Wacape, the Śiyo leader, and Wagmiza, the Sicanġu leader,
sat here also and six other important Titonwan. All honorable men, all over forty, these twelve had sensed an affinity
after a summer of pondering and agreeing, after a summer
of perceiving and devising the most important rank and
honor the Titonwan bands ever will confer.

Different lodges of headmen shall appear, Wanaġi had
prophesied, but none shall sit above this one. For the people

will identify this one—the Ptalodge—with the four-legged power, with those pta-fathers who protect the herd, who protect the meat, the lodging, the moccasins, the robes of the Titonwan Dakotah.

The bands, dispersing for the cold moons soon after the naming of the Ptalodge, had not seen the headmen perform their dance or display their paint, but the people had recognized that men of this nature shall perpetuate the good, for the one and for the whole.

V

THE SNOWS came, the Mahto camp white and creaky cold. The people, twelve snug lodges in a row with wood and water nearby, sat content.

Fragrant smoke and quiet laughter mingled in the lodge where Olepi and his young wife sat with the respected father. Warmth and orderliness surrounded these persons, Napewaśte gracefully displaying her affection for the husband, her speech always soft, her actions always proper. Peta, observing that good young hands managed the tipi, rejoiced for himself and his son.

Wanaǵi, sitting alone, had begun making the ceremonial pipe. After cleansing himself and his tools in sweetgrass smoke, he had removed the damp hide from around a piece of redstone, his hands and a bone knife properly prepared to give the soft and yielding slab a meaningful shape. But foreseeing a certain amount of tedious work, he had asked that the song-maker Winkte compose something for a pipe-maker to whistle softly while he forms the bowl and hollows out the center, a song that will renew weary hands and return patience.

Winkte brought the pipe-maker a song without words but Wanaġi soon put phrases to these tones. "Taku wakan wakaġe yelo-yo," he sang; I make something sacred, something that holds the people together. "Taku wakaġe oyate witaya oyuspe yelo-yo." And listening to these words he understood that he shaped more than a pipe-bowl: here, the heart of the people and a hollow for the fire that warms this heart.

Working the stone that projected in front of the bowl, he formed the head of a young pte, facing outward, the horns close against the bowl. Let the smoker remember the tribal hoop in the curving of these horns.

And while he worked the stone, he contemplated the pipestem. Until now he had made stems from the legbone of the pronghorn but this stem, as he had said, he chose to make of wood, not the ordinary yellow-wood but from the tree with the old-wood smell, from a straight flat piece more than twice the length of his moccasin.

He considered the ways for removing the pith—splitting, scraping, and binding the two lengths back together, or slowly burning out the core. Recalling a story that told yet a different way—using fire to persuade a grub to chew a clean path through the center—he smiled; certainly none among the little wood-borers will endure this unnatural urging.

But in what manner to decorate the stem, he not yet knew.

Then one cold but sunny morning he walked over the cracking ground toward the big boulder at the edge of camp; he went in search of a true pattern for the pipestem.

He moved slowly around the boulder, sensing a contact with the wonder of creation through this stone mediator. And when he started back to his lodge, he walked inspired; he brought back not a pattern but the understanding for one.

"Remember Ptesanwin," his familiar-voice tells him as he circles the big stone. And so he will remember whatever needs remembering about Ptesanwin as an influence on his design.

More than four hundred winters in the past, during a season of great unrest within the Dakotah family, something wonderful had happened. A woman had visited the tribe, bringing prophecy and a pipe—something to hold the people together—and relating herself to the creature that soon becomes their true meat and shelter.

The visitor had called herself Ptesanwin and her family Ptaġica, a nation of four-leggeds. Call the herd-fathers 'pta,' she had said, and the herd-mothers 'pte.' And speak of the whole—mostly mothers—as 'pte.'

This same woman-messenger had told the people to regard her as Pte-woman, a sister to each Dakotah. "I am woman," she had said; "I use true words. Nothing harmful stays within my circle; whoever speaks an untrue word shall not live."

And then Pte-woman had put into the hands of the Dakotah a long, narrow stem, the windpipe of pte, something that she had straightened and dried for the breath of man.

"This stem will make visible your breath. Use this stem for demonstrating good. Use this stem for making contact with the wisdom of the invisible grandfathers.

"Use this stem to bind yourself to your own words."

Before Ptesanwin had gone away she had spoken of a most unusual pte, a rare white creature, something not every generation shall see. "From the hide of this special one," she had prophesied, "certain Dakotah will make a headband, a symbol that they perceive my message. But the people will not often see either the white pte or the headband."

Having spoken, Ptesanwin had disappeared. But the pipestem, which she had propped against a big stone, had stayed.

The old Dakotah seers, marveling her prophecy, had cut tall reeds, likening the hollow grass to the pte-stem. And they had declared that whoever touched the reed to his lips dared speak nothing but truth. Remembering, also, that Pte-woman had talked of visible breath, they had placed a small bowl of smoldering leaves in front of whoever held the grass-stem. Let him suck in, breathe out slowly, and so make his breath visible. Let him smoke, they had said.

And now Wanaġi sat marveling the strange manner in which Ptesanwin had disappeared. The grandfathers had told that she changed form—from woman to pte—but none had said why this change in view of the people. Will she abandon her woman-form as a way of preventing adoration—look not on my person but on my message, her words—or will something different bring on her transformation?

Wanaği moved over toward the tipi flap; he wanted crossed sticks in front of his lodge while he worked, something to discourage visitors. But as he moved he heard a soft scratching on the cover and a woman's voice. The slight accent told him that someone they call Wahcawin stood outside and that she brought an important message.

Not exactly a message, the woman said as she sat across the fire circle from the seeker. "I come here offering help. They say that you make a ceremonial pipe. I know about pipes."

She spoke on, modestly but without shyness. "When young, I am wife to a healer among the Šahiela. Now I am old and alone. This season I visit in the Mahto camp. I stay in the lodge of my brother and his wife. I own a stone pipe."

And now Wanaği spoke calling her 'tanke,' the relative term, something to encourage her talk about pipes and pipe ceremonies.

Wahcawin told, then, of the Šahiela stems, the long cords that once had carried the heartblood of pte, many old Šahiela saying that they prefer these blood-cords to the stone stems.

Knowing that the Mahto seeker chose wood, she waited now for him to mention his pipe, to tell her something or to hint that he will not desire her help.

Instead, Wanaği began telling about his boy-seasons on the tall grasses, smiling back at those days of rough play with his youth-companion Olepi, the two wrestling and kneeing each other in the face. But then he, usually the winner, had dropped his interest in those contests; his search of the grasses had begun. Crushing stalks and blooms, he had marveled the flavors and concocted soups. "I put together some exciting mixtures during those seasons," he grinned, "my belly not always agreeing with my tongue."

The woman, listening closely, sensed a certain yearning in all this talk. Truly, she heard her heart whisper, this attractive young seeker will look forward not only to his work as wapiya but to choosing a wife, fathering a child. But before her heart says anything more, she will return their talk to something about designs on pipestems.

"They say," she spoke gently, "that man remembers himself in four ages: swimming, crawling, on four legs, and on two. And the Dakotah know that a woman of the pte-nation brings the original stem. Why not design the Mahto pipestem in the shape of a leg, the leg of pte? Man, the fourth age and the age of the pipe, perhaps the final age for all the people who walk these grasses."

Wanaġi had heard, the man greatly impressed but not surprised. Nothing of the marvelous ever shall astound him, neither this proposal for a design nor the meaning in that which this woman proposes.

And now, carving the wood, Wanaġi considered the one who had brought him this pattern, the one to whose thoughts he gives substance when he designs this stem in the shape of leg and hoof.

Of what nature this woman Waĥcawin who visits among the Mahto? Certainly she appears wise and she looks pleasant, but what of her seasons? She calls herself old, but will she precede him more than ten, twelve winters? He will not want to see himself similar to the young bull who chooses from among the old pte.

He lay down on his robes, his body limp and receptive to whatever images float before his eyes. He soon discovered that Waĥcawin will appear in each of these pictures and that he recognizes a desire to make her wife.

He had returned to his work on the pipe with renewed interest, soon ready to fit stem into bowl. Attaching these pieces, he suddenly saw the pipe in yet a new way: the stem as backbone of man and the bowl as woman, as heart and fire, the source of energy.

And now Wanaġi put away the stem, the wapiya understanding that he shall await a message before he or anyone smokes this pipe.

The ceremony making Waĥcawin wife to the seeker occurred during the windy, hurt-eyes moon—bright-snow moon, Waĥcawin said—the man and his woman enjoying two, three days in true seclusion before they removed the crossed sticks in front of the tipi.

Waȟcawin came naturally into the sacred-lodge, not only a wife but a wapiya-helper to Wanaǧi. Neither timid nor forward, she used her age and wisdom prudently.

The man's respect for Waȟcawin increased sunrise to sundown, and Waȟcawin, in turn, recognized an ever-growing affection for the husband. Fondness generated fondness and contentment prevailed.

Many persons who visited the seer's tipi sought neither ceremony nor cure. But, sensing a mild unrest, they chose to come to a place where disquieting thoughts weakened and dropped to the ground, where a smoke with Wanaǧi brought true comfort.

And mothers and children enjoyed talking with Waȟcawin; always cheerful, the woman sat attentive to all voices, the soft and the shrill. She kept a container of playthings for young children, footbones and toebones from pte. And she made toy-babies, shaping, stuffing, and painting pieces of hide in a manner to resemble infants. Some persons said that Waȟcawin knew more about soothing the fretful than any of the peźuta in the encampment. But Waȟcawin said only that she feels great affection for children and that they always come to her wherever she sits, wherever she walks.

Never having borne a child of her own, she imagined herself mother to all children. She knew many sleep-songs in Sahiela and Dakotah, lullabies she enjoyed singing to the little ones who, hurt or fearful or, as the grandmothers said, displeased with their names, whimpered softly. Always she soothed the children into sleep, and while they slept, she whispered cheerful thoughts in birdlike tones, something for a child to remember on awakening. Some mothers brought their babies to Waȟcawin for this sleep-teaching, this old, old way for impressing earthly wonder on the memory of the very young.

Uncertain of her true-age, Waȟcawin pondered the length of her own childbearing seasons; as wife to a strong young man she saw reason whatever her winters, forty or forty-and-four, to take-on-life. She recalled that one Dakotah woman in her sixtieth winter had given birth to a living infant.

91

But the snows went underground and the red grass appeared and the horses shed. And now everything seemed to fatten, everything but Wahcawin. And so, before the band traveled again toward the black hills, the woman spoke to the man of her concern.

"My husband, four, five moons I am your wife but I not yet nourish your seeds." And then she made known her willingness to see him take another wife, a young woman who will satisfy his need to father a child.

Quickly the man answered saying that he will not desire another woman, a second wife, whatever her age.

Hearing him, Wahcawin's heart soared, but as consultant in a sacred-lodge, she understood many things, especially the want to generate one's self.

And so after three, four days they talked again, Wanaǵi speaking as a wapiya, carefully describing an ancient ceremony that required neither the use of woman nor yet a loss of male seed, a most discriminating ceremony, something the old seer had called 'takes-with-mouth.'

"Something," Wanaǵi said, "that provides for these mysterious ones born neither male nor female, persons who lack the means for reproducing, for generating life."

The Dakotah grandfathers, the husband told, had recognized that such persons yearn for the quickening force the same as any man, any woman, and so they had advised that these rare two-souls receive the generating seed through the mouth. But never without ceremony; always they shall make the tribe aware of that which occurs.

Wanaǵi looked upon the woman's strong face: "I will not ignore my life-making power. But neither will I offer my seeds for this ceremony until I and you make certain."

The woman answered nothing; she accepted all the man had said and all he had not said. She knew suddenly that he never had looked for a son of his own, that even as she saw herself the spiritual instructor to all the children in the band, he saw himself as a spiritual influence to the whole. And she knew that one day he intended to expel his seed into the mouth of Winkte, the song-maker's spirit moved to respond, to recognize a completeness of self, to manifest a new greatness for composition, for creating songs. And remembering that everything called for a song, she understood now that Wanaǵi saw his life enduring not through children and grandchildren of his own, but in the voices of the people, generation after generation.

She lifted appreciative eyes to the husband's face and reaching out her hand, touched her fingertips to his. And then she heard the scratching on the tipi cover and the discreet cough; someone stood outside waiting for a response.

Waĥcawin always had called out a welcome to any visitors who announced their presence in this customary way but not now. The husband had closed his hand over hers, a sudden tenseness in his clasp. And on his face, a startled surprise.

But whoever waited outside the sacred-lodge on this bright young-summer morning made the scratching-noise again. The man let go the woman's hand, and Waĥcawin, moving to the entrance, pulled aside the flap.

Certainly Wanaġi heard her quick cry of distress, her little moan of despair, but he neither looked up nor spoke. She dropped the flap over the opening, her voice rising in a thin wail as she crept back to her own place. For a while she sat hunched on her sleeping robes. Then, taking up a knife, she cut off two handfuls of her hair, placing the strands on a piece of soft hide, folding in the edges, tying the roll with a red string.

She listened to the sorrowful voices outside the lodges, women's voices at the start but now the whole camp wailed. And then she changed from her neat gown into a soiled one, replaced her pretty moccasins with an old pair. And so she stood ready to join the Mahto people who grieved their great loss.

And only now she glanced at the man who had sat silent while she performed these acts, who had remained in his place as if he neither heard nor wanted to hear the grief that spilled out onto this Mahto campground.

And so only now she saw the glistening cheeks of one whose tears wash his face; only now will she understand that Wanaġi knew before ever the messenger spoke his sad news at the tipi flap, knew that the enemy had killed Peta, leader of the Mahto band.

"The enemy kills the Mahto leader? Who, this enemy? Whose arrow pierces the neck of Peta, leader of the Mahto

93

band?" Angry voices had risen above the grief songs; the Mahto warriors demanded to know who killed Peta.

An enemy from the something-that-flies tribe, certain ones answered quietly.

"Something-that-flies? Perhaps unciśicala, who caws?"

"Something-that-flies? Perhaps kangi, who croaks?"

"Not these familiar birds," one of the warrior's wives had said. And then she told about captives from this tribe, women who had spoken of a crafty, sharp-beaked bird they called absa, a bird that had fostered the tribe and then disappeared from the plain.

"Psa, Psa"; mockingly the warriors pronounced the name and vowed that this enemy, like the bird, shall disappear from the plain.

"Psa-toka, Psa-enemy," shouted one man, ready to avenge his leader's death. But calm voices asked him to remember that this avenging took place within moments of Peta's wounding; let him view again the two Psa heads. Not scalps, but heads cut off the two Psa who had dared kill Peta, leader of the Mahto.

Not everyone had heard the terrible story; not everyone understood exactly what had occurred. They knew that soon after dawn three Mahto had brought in Peta's body, the leader dying from an arrow wound in his neck. They had laid the body on robes outside Olepi's lodge and they had thrown two severed heads on the ground nearby. The people, hearing the camp-dogs bark and noticing an unusual commotion, had come from their lodges. A messenger had taken the news to those persons who, perhaps sleeping, had not arrived at the scene, but the rescue party waited for Olepi to come out again before anyone talked.

The son of the Mahto leader had appeared briefly, then stepped back inside the lodge, perhaps to wrap a moldy robe around his body in the custom of a man who grieves. But the sun had climbed halfway up the sky and he had not yet reappeared, neither he nor his wife Napewaśte.

Now, suddenly, Olepi stood among the people, his face clear of paint and his hair, long to the shoulders, hanging loose. But his only covering, the flap of hide over his loins and the moccasins on his feet. Whoever had looked for a moldy grief-robe saw instead the warrior-image, a body

94

designed for competition, for war games, eyes that invited challenge and an arrogance that overwhelmed.

Yet whoever looked upon his hands saw only that this warrior held the red robe, the death-robe for wrapping his father's body, the only blood relative he ever had known.

Olepi looked upon neither the Psa heads nor Peta's body when he spoke, when he asked that Wambli Okiye, one of the three who had gone out with his father the previous day, describe the encounter with the enemy, that Wambli Okiye let the people hear about the fight.

And so the people stopped their wailing and listened to that which the warrior said, two youths—Heȟloǧeca and Cetan—standing at his side.

Gesturing toward Cetan, the man told that this one had discovered an unfamiliar moccasin track a half-day's walk from camp, along the trail the people intended to travel when they started for the summer encampment. The track, a fresh one, had appeared the day before, after those scouts sent ahead to observe the path had covered this ground. The Mahto leader, choosing not to alarm the camp, had taken along the young brave Heȟloǧeca, in company with Wambli Okiye and their guide, young Cetan, when he rode out midmorning the day before to inspect the single footmark.

And now Wambli Okiye, his motions as explicit as his words, reported each detail: locating the track, the search for more tracks, the pause during which they considered their prey, perhaps a wanderer, a lone man driven out of his tribe and not a decoy for those strangers who occasionally flit over the plain. Then, the Mahto leader not yet persuaded to abandon the hunt, they had separated, the leader and Heȟloǧeca approaching a clump of trees, Wambli Okiye and Cetan heading for a ravine.

Suddenly the Mahto leader threw an arrow into the brush. Almost as suddenly an arrow came out of the brush, settling in the Mahto's neck. Falling, the leader gasped a warning: "Two enemy."

Heȟloǧeca gave the blood-freezing whoop, something to stun the second man, who tried to get away. Heȟloǧeca used his knife to kill the man and then cut off the head, the old way of proving he had killed.

The youth Cetan, never before out-with-the-men, ran

toward the brush, discovering the enemy who lay dead, the Mahto leader's arrow in his heart. Cetan took the scalp, but when he saw that Heȟloǧeca carried a head, he cut off everything.

The Mahto leader lay on the ground, not dead, but much, much blood pouring onto the earth. Wambli Okiye, at his side, dared not remove anything from a neck that bled so profusely. Instead he sat close by, listening for any requests. And so he heard the leader rasp out a death-defying song and then name the one to walk in his place.

Heȟloǧeca and Cetan came close and so they, also, heard the whisper that named the new leader of the Mahto band.

Soon afterwards the wounded Mahto struggled for breath, then let go slowly. "Haun-n-n, haun-n-n," he moaned, and closed his eyes.

The three men tied the leader's body onto his horse; they hid the two dead enemy behind a mound of stones.

Darkness came upon the three while they prepared for their return to camp, and so they decided to wait until morning, this morning, before making their sorrowful entry.

Wambli Okiye told what he knew, only what he knew.

And now many women wailed as before, but Olepi asked that Heȟloǧeca speak, let Heȟloǧeca tell the story and then Cetan, the people hearing from two more mouths an account of this fight and the Mahto leader's dying request.

Heȟloǧeca, in his seventeenth winter and twice out on war parties, spoke boldly, his eyes on the head he had severed. But Cetan, not yet fifteen, spoke softly, his eyes on the leader's body. He remembered that the Mahto band had lost a great man, the most great man he ever had known.

Olepi had chosen himself as the one to wrap the leader's body in the death-robe, the son making the denying-motion when women of the village offered help. And so, tears falling off their cheeks they watched him use his own hands to straighten the father's arms and legs and paint the face red.

And while Olepi performed acts unusual for a close relative, a group of men went out to a nearby knoll, where they raised four poles, then made a platform to lay across these poles.

Now, the body wrapped, Olepi brought forward his

father's favorite horse; to this creature he fastened two poles. But when the men saw that he schemed to drag the death-bundle on these long sticks, they showed him a litter they had made for carrying the body to the tall rack. And so he permitted these friends to lift the big bundle onto the carrier.

More than seventy persons walked in the procession to the knoll, their voices joining in a wonderful song, something out of the distant past, a song that the women half-remembered, one that Olepi never had heard until now. But certainly the people gave new words to the song, words that told about the Mahto leader who had led his band to the black mountain, to those hills which shall sustain the people spiritually.

They came to the rack, the people singing while certain ones tied the red bundle onto the platform above their heads. And then the wailing began again, some women crying most loudly. But not the wife of Olepi; this woman had not come to the knoll; she had not walked in the procession.

During the snow moons Napewaśte had taken-on-life, and for the wife who grows a child, silence and solitude become the rule. And so she had gone outside the lodge when they brought the news, wandering among the trees along the stream. Then, the grief-songs reaching her ears, she had sought quiet in Cankuna's lodge, the hunter's wife and family in the procession that moved toward the knoll. And while she sat alone in this place, she comforted herself remembering that she had earned the leader's respect. And that always she had respected him. She wondered about cutting off her hair; certainly she wanted to display her grief for this good, good man.

Olepi had returned to the tipi. Sitting alone, his back to the dead fire, his thoughts hovered between remembrances of things past and schemes for the seasons ahead.

His boy-memories of Peta came as pictures, flashing brightly: his father holding a fluttering-wing between his fingers, instructing this fragile, painted fly to teach his little boy to run; his father scooping aside stones in the stream to make a deep, sandy-bottom hole, then asking the waters to help his little boy swim while the child yet remembered life before birth, life as a water-baby; his father's big strong

97

hands lifting the little son onto a gentle horse, telling the four-legged to graze, not run while the boy sat on his back, horse and rider wandering on the plain for a day, the child learning not to fear either the horse or the loneliness.

One more picture came, this one holding while Olepi recalled his joy on the day he discovered he owned a horse of his own. "My son," the warrior-father had said, "look after your horse. Tie his line to your arm while you sleep. And so you shall feel the tug if the enemy tries to cut him loose."

He never had felt a tug nor lost a horse, but from that day forward he had kept his favorite mount close by at night, a thong passing under the edge of the tipi cover to his wrist. And most warriors mimicked him in this custom.

During his youth-seasons when the people said 'enemy' they meant Palani. True, some Titonwan experienced mixed feelings for the Palani, but never Peta, leader of the Mahto. Always this man remembered who had killed his brother, his parents, and carried off his brother's wife.

Spinning around on his bottom, Olepi faced the fire circle: "And I always shall remember who kills the leader of the Mahto." He struck the ground forcibly with the flat of his hand. "Psa-toka," he muttered, remembering the name he had heard the warriors speak this day, "you Psa-toka, shall provide horses for the Mahto band and women for those Mahto warriors who want your women. I and my band . . ."

His band? Who says, his band? They tell that the dying father names the son, Olepi, but will the warriors agree? Will the people choose to follow him? Will the grandfathers accept him?

Perhaps he behaves unwisely, standing before the band without visible signs of grief, asking for an account of the fight, going against custom when he wrapped his father's body with his own hands. But why not? Different persons have many relatives they shall mourn; he had but one. But one.

The anger that had influenced his original response to the Mahto leader's death—angry at the enemy, angry at himself for not riding along with his father's little party—now gave way in a flow of tears, emptying him of that which had hampered clear vision, true understanding.

Slowly his emptiness filled up with truth. Slowly he began to understand that the Mahto leader had chosen a good day to die. The man had fulfilled his known desires: he had devised a way for controlling the summer encampment; he had heard the tribal leaders accept a rank he had proposed; he had helped found a brother-lodge, a lodge of principal men. And he had seen his old enemy, the Palani, lose ground and prestige. Certainly Peta, as father to the band, had taken care of his children—an enemy never had surprised the Mahto camp—and certainly, as father to Olepi, the dying leader had known that he left behind someone prepared to lead the people.

Father to Olepi? They say that I shall call this man my father, this one whose body I wrap in the red robe, this blood-brother to my true-father. But who, my true-father? What nature of man? This one whose seeds influence me . . . I know not even his name.

Suddenly Olepi sensed the loss of two fathers on this same day, one of whom he knew something; the other one, nothing.

And then he remembered: Napewaśte grows his child, someone-coming when the maize ripens on the old Sahiela planting-ground. And even as each seed in those yellow maize-bundles relates to the grandfather stalk, so shall his seed, living now in the woman, relate to the father he never knows. And so he shall discover something of his blood-father through the seed, whether girl-child or boy.

He decided now to display his respect for the Mahto leader, his father, in a most conspicuous manner: he will cut off his hair and blacken his face. Let different ones wear moldy robes, but he truly will display grief.

He touched his knife. He never had plucked hair from the sides of his head in the manner of the Okandada warriors—plucking too slow a way now—but certainly his knife had a sharp-enough edge for slicing off hair. He cut a handful, then looked wonderingly at the strands. Tossing the hair onto the fire circle will invite sorrow into a lodge, the people said; but sorrow already visited here.

At this moment he heard a scratching on the tipi; he will not want company but he had neglected those crossed sticks that keep people away. Then, before he had made a sound, he saw the moccasin that pushed aside the entrance

99

flap. And so he knew that Wanaǧi stood before him. Raising his eyes, he saw that the wapiya held out a hand, that the man asked for the cut hairs. He laid the strands on Wanaǧi's palm as if he had known to wait for this person. Instantly the visitor turned away, stepping out of the lodge, neither his eyes nor his voice offering tears. Yet Olepi, mysteriously, felt comforted.

The sun climbed down the sky, but dusk will not silence the wailing throughout the camp. Olepi sat as before, his hair now a jagged ridge across the top of his head.

A gentle cough awakened him to Napewaśte's presence. He looked up. The sight of her—braids cut off, her hair scarcely covering her ears, her gown shortened and the trim stripped away, every sign of sorrow she had dared make—overcame him; only now will he recognize her sorrow as similar to his. He wept aloud.

The young wife sat alongside the man, then, and made little comforting sounds. She pulled off his moccasins and soothed his feet between her palms in the manner he enjoyed. And after a while she left his side to see about the horses, his father's horse and his, but someone already had staked these two outside the lodge.

She returned, bringing a knot of wood, embers glowing red in the hollow. She placed the little fire at the man's side, then handed him his pipe-sack, bowl and stem and smoke-leaves all inside the same container. But she remembered also the little rack for resting his pipe.

And so quietly will this young woman move about the dim lodge that she shall seem as a shadow looking out for someone's comfort.

In a different lodge the principal Mahto gathered for smoke and decision. Shall they accept Olepi as their new leader?

At once some persons called him young to lead; they saw him as head of a small family, a small tiyośpaye, but not ready to head a band. Truly, they asked, will anyone here seek Olepi's advice as they once invite his father's counsel?

Then someone began speaking of this young man's honors, of Olepi's cunning on the raids, his warrior-power whichever way he goes, to take horses or to take revenge.

Hau, Heĥaka answered, the people remember. But will

100

they consider only a man's war powers? What of Olepi's generosity? His loyalty to the band? Show proof of these things. And of Olepi's unfaltering truth.

The lodge became quiet but for the sucking on pipe-stems, each one here accepting his responsibility, making silent judgment, staking that judgment to fact, fact and nothing different.

This same night, a fragrance drifted out from the sacred-lodge where Wanaġi burned sweetgrass, the mysterious grass that never ages, never dies, the ceremonial grass that purifies.

Alone in his lodge, the wapiya sang as he held the strands of hair from Olepi's head over the sweet smoke, the meaning in his song, in the vocables familiar only to himself. After a while the smoke began to curl around his arm as if the song compelled this spiraling. But then he felt something affecting his own movements, directing his hand to reach for a piece of pronghorn skin, to wrap these hairs in this skin. In the manner of an observer, watchful and marveling, he saw his hands perform these acts, saw his fingers tie the bundle.

But why these trembling hands? What mystery, what power goes into this bundle? Why enter Olepi's lodge and bring back these strands? Why purify and wrap the hair as if he makes a soul-bundle for that ancient ceremony, the keeping-of-the-dead? His song demanded an answer.

Instead, he saw himself crawl over the ground as if strings pulled him along, saw his own trembling hands place the new bundle next to the unsmoked Mahto pipe, heard his own voice cry out that in some distant season these hairs, like this pipe, will bring meaning to something, to someone.

Truly, a woman's voice murmured, he will recognize himself now as something more than seeker, more than healer.

Who murmurs, he demanded to know. Who in this sacred-lodge murmurs in a woman's voice? Not he, certainly. And Waḣcawin laments with those women who gather outside Cankuna's lodge.

He heard singing. Who sings, he demanded to know. He sings, true, but not the strange song to which he listens now.

Will undesirable spirits, hearing his song, come here to confuse, to torment a man who dares seek answers to mystery? Will the grizzly spirit-helpers from his youth's vision arrive in this frightening, perplexing moment, coming to tease this dreamer who questions the mysterious, who says that he never again will seek grizzly-powers nor cry for spirit-helpers but that he shall seek, instead, his own power and rely on his own spirit?

Or will the trickster Iktomi, the spider, creep into this place, using a woman's voice to mislead him, then running round and round, round and round him until, dizzy and confused, he sits here not certain of anything? Iktomi appears, they say, to the pretentious, to play tricks on such persons and in this way, teach caution.

But will he dare send away these undesirables providing his powers, truly, bring these tormentors here?

"Identify yourself," he roared; "identify yourself."

An answer came but as an echo: "Identify yourself, identify yourself."

"Who am I? Hear me," he demanded. "I am a grizzly-dreamer who becomes a seeker with powers to foresee a certain distance. Or perhaps I am really a stone-dreamer, a true-seer with the power to know the opposite side of the moon.

"I am Wanaġi, inside my body looking out. Or perhaps I am really outside my body looking on. Or am I—"

He heard laughing. Laughter on this night?

"Get out," he shrieked; "get out, get out of my way." Taking his pipe, he swung the stem from side to side. "Get out of my way," he yelled, "get out of my way."

Suddenly calm, he slowly lowered the stem, his hand steady, the piercing stare gone from his eyes. In a flash of understanding, many things to which he had sat blind this day had become clear.

The power of the whole band, not any one man, brings the trickster spirits onto this campground. The tremendous outpouring of emotion, a powerful combining of death, blood, fear and uncertainty, grief and the noises of grief attract these joking-entities. And so, acting on a complementary force, they come here to feed on the unstableness that permeates the camp. And I, Wanaġi, recognizing their existence, drop down to the level of these entities, even to answering their echo, hearing their laughter. I, Wanaġi, someone who imagines himself a fit controlling power, lose my balance. I respond to the grief-force this camp exudes until I hear even the dogs wailing like persons.

The man leaned forward to listen, the voices of grieving women drifting in from every direction, their songs lamenting not only this recent death but all relatives who die within their memory. And different voices, old and fearful, bemoan a death-rack that men erect instead of women, a body which a man's hands prepare in death instead of woman's hands.

Sorrowing came also from any lodge wherein warriors gathered, their sad songs mingling with sharp cries that deplored the loss of a man they knew as their father, as father to the Mahto band, leader and father.

Who will close off this emotional outlet, Wanaġi heard himself asking, that brings danger to everyone in camp?

Shrill, unnatural voices reached his ears; somewhere out in the dusk children cried or squealed strangely as they fearfully ran past the enemy death-heads, heads that had rolled over the campground all this day, kicked or dragged but rolling, always rolling, never at rest.

Wanaġi shuddered; blood, everywhere on this campground. Blood, dry and wet, rolling around as a crust on dishonored enemy heads or trickling from arms and legs of Mahto women who nick their skin with an arrow point or, seeking a deep and enduring memory of the honored leader, cut their flesh with a knife.

What will stop this flow of blood and emotion and return reason to this camp?

Nothing will stanch this flow now, Wanaġi heard himself answering. And so let the people get out, get out quickly. Let someone call for all lodges to come down at daybreak. Certainly Olepi knows that he already fills the place left vacant, whatever the councilors decide, but will he know to lead out at dawn, to start for grizzly hill, where the Titonwan again raise a hoop? True, the band will go in moldy robes but they leave a campground that neither song nor ceremonial grass shall cleanse now.

And will Olepi understand the importance in asking Wambli Okiye and Heȟloġeca and Cetan to walk close by him? When the people see that he walks with the same three who so recently accompany his father, they shall recognize that Olepi intends to let nothing divide the Mahto band.

In one movement Wanaǵi rose and moved toward the tipi opening. He stepped outside, into the wailing night.

Wahcawin returned to the sacred-lodge before the night grew old. She had left off her lamenting to sit with fretful children who had glimpsed the grief that shattered their parents. Then, in need of renewing herself and desiring Wanaǵi's presence, she had come back to her own tipi but she had found the place empty. Nor had Wanaǵi appeared before midnight. And so, going to her robes, she had tried to sleep, but her heart, like all hearts in camp, lay on sorrowful ground.

Wanaǵi walked on the plain, a bitten moon traveling along a path of clouds, his source of light. But he needed nothing to guide his feet across the wide spread of night-blackened grasses. He recognized each clump as a family of friendly stems, and deep under those stems—stone, an enduring revelation of the spiritual force that enacted earth; stone, the true-grandfather.

He began to run. He wanted to reach quickly a place far out on this great flat where, in company with those small lives who scamper or crawl among the tangles of roots, he dared safely renew himself. An outside force had entered and collapsed him, the pressure from within not enough to keep out undesirables. He had made himself accessible to tricksters and so they had tricked him.

The familiar-voice never misleads, yet he had let invisible jokesters, tampering with his reason, throw him to one side. Then, off balance and slipping backwards, he had reviewed uncertainly his interpretation of the message he had received in a flash of spiritual alertness, the message on which he had acted when he sought hair from Olepi's head, when he wrapped and laid away that hair.

Will he interpret in terms of concepts at the earth-level whereon he exists, he had asked himself, when he put together that which had come through his familiar-voice?

Will he color those three, four words with earth descriptions?

He knew that the message not always came clearly, the denseness between levels perhaps absorbing something, but he had heard a person and an article named—Olepi, tahin, Olepi, his hair—and then, the voice fading out, one more word: tokata, forward.

Perhaps he misinterprets, he had told himself, when he understands 'forward' as meaning 'in the winters ahead'—the spirit conceives neither seasons nor distances nor any other limiting definitions—or will those tricksters get in his way at that moment? Will they make his head spin, compelling him to puzzle whether he hears his familiar-voice saying 'forward' or 'tokahe,' 'the first'? Or perhaps neither word, neither meaning.

He quickened his running steps as if to outrun his uncertainty and so escape before the substance of his thoughts took on terrifying shape, before he saw himself going back to live as a wapiya, a seeker who never extends his vision beyond whatever he sees reflected in a pool of some creature's blood. Or before he saw himself seeking the stone-dream and deriving instead a power that makes of him a destroyer—limunġa, the owner of another man's soul.

Even as he ran, he shuddered. Hmunġa and other dread mysteries occur, the old, old ones had said, whenever a seer trifles with power beyond his control.

Suddenly the brush caught hold of his moccasin. He shook loose, neither falling nor stumbling. But his fingers instantly felt for the swamp-root in the little sac at his waist. He put the yellow piece in his mouth. Slowing down, he jogged along blowing his breath in every direction. Until something brought him to a stop.

Surprised, he looked into the night that hovered silently around him. Then he began to laugh, his head bobbing slightly as he contained the sound inside his cheeks. Soon the laughter broke through his lips, softly as a man laughs in his tipi, not harsh or disturbing. But now, looking up, he laughed loudly at the sky, laughed until the clouds, seemingly embarrassed for the moon, covered her bitten light with their darkness.

He went on laughing, yet more noisily. He laughed at

the piece of sticky wood that clung to his foot and at the wind that touched coolly upon his breast. His laughter grew to a roar that squinted shut his eyes and shook his lean frame until he staggered. His spit slid down his chin and the piece of yellow root dropped from his mouth. Giggling, he used his arm to wipe off the crazy tears that wet his cheeks.

Suddenly he sensed movement everywhere nearby. The grasses twisted and rattled, tiny feet scurried over his moccasins, and pebbles, rolling out of their nests, bumped into his heels. Some small fine-haired creature rubbed against his leg and a night-bird, flapping past him on hushed wings, fanned his shoulder. He felt agreement from the life-force all around, visible and invisible. He recognized a pull from the enduring hardness in and on the ground, from stone, earth-essential.

He stood quiet, waiting; an awareness of the energy that will surge through him had begun as a sensation in his toes.

And now the force moved swiftly up his body, pulling him together, tightening that which had loosened when he fell below his level, renewing that which he had stretched out of shape when, lacking a true constant, he had grabbed at anything handy. Spreading out even to the tips of his fingers, the power acted to nourish his soul, leaving him with spirit and body again in balance.

He walked on, his heart calm, his steps even. His experiences this day, this night, had quickened his understanding in many directions. For one thing, he saw that man needed more than laughter as a protecting force.

In his moments of uncertainty, he had lacked something to which to refer himself. He had sat unprepared for a surprise attack on his steadfastness. The sweetgrass ceremony had acted as nothing more than a stake in whirling water. And his song, nothing more than a stake planted in sand.

Here on the plain, his adversary not grief but sudden fear, he had dared look to the sky for a fixed point in the darkness. But instead of the true-star, he had seen a piece of moon, nothing dependable. And so, losing completely any sense of constancy, he had snatched at a root he will give to a child, something that scents the breath and scares off mysterious discomfort. Swamp-root, a food for the webbed-feet and something to make a child laugh at fears in the dark; laughter, a child's primary protector but effectual in man only as a secondary source.

And so he, a wapiya, releasing his control to a child's symbol of comfort, had indulged in disconcerting laughter, his belly loose and wiggling, his head jerking, and his knees crumpling as he giggled and howled and roared at whatever mystery had tried a new attack on his composure, had tried to collapse him again.

Certainly I need a fixedness within me, he reflected now, a true core around which I dare live my life, something that I shall know as the center. And if ever I drop away, I shall keep a memory of this constant that awaits my return.

The soothing fragrance of night-blooming stems suddenly warmed the darkness. He glanced around, appearing to hunt for the blooms. Or perhaps to see if they hunted for him.

But the next moment he sent his thoughts to the distant ledges: he will climb up again from this ground-level and he will make his second climb knowing that he fills out each level of growth before he reaches for the next.

Not again shall I try fighting a battle with reason alone, he told the knolls and the hills; I now see reason as something not always big enough for my encounters. And so I shall keep my spirit in readiness, my own spirit the most reliable ally I ever shall know. I foresee many painful winters before I own the stone-songs, but one day I shall sing those songs and send out the stones. And then my spirit will keep me in readiness.

I begin again, remembering that I am Wanagi, the wapiya, the seeker. That which I desire, I go out seeking; when I want contact with something, I go out and make this contact. And never, never again will I permit something to seek me out, get to me.

He kept on walking, moving steadily but unhurriedly through unusual darkness. The clouds had filled in everywhere, closing off any reflected light, any star light.

Now, almost abruptly, he stopped. Turning slightly to one side, he approached a patch of bare earth; the place had invited his presence. Here, then, he shall enact that which he had come out here to enact; here, in the manner the old, old seer had taught him, he shall rest, truly rest, a way of resting he had neglected for a long while.

Wanaġi lay on the ground, his back against the bare white clay. He drummed gently on his breast with his closed hand, beating out the rhythm of a song, the fire song.

"Wankanta-han heyape, mahkata ile, ile ye, heyape, e ye yo." From above, he sang, someone tells of fire under the earth.

The rhythm at the start had matched his usual heartbeat, but now he drummed more slowly, his heart responding, his body sensing the change, his thoughts beginning to move about more quietly.

Imagination, nothing different, will prepare him in those ways that make for contact with the invisible grandfathers and, gaining that contact, permit a true understanding of the message. And so he will imagine now the fire under the earth, a warmth that keeps him comfortable on this patch of earth, a fire that warms the earth from below even as the sky warms the earth from above.

He stopped his drumming and let his arms lie loosely at his side. He breathed evenly, slowly, making use of those instants between breaths to imagine his body as something growing heavy, getting dull, becoming sleepy. Sleepy but not asleep.

He held the image until resisting sleep became a strain. He needed to abandon the effort and start over again.

Ta ta iciya wo. Make yourself as if dead. The old, old seer had dared imagine himself in this condition more than once, something that took considerable courage, but the effort had worked for him. He had become wakanhca; he had lived more than ninety winters.

Ta ta iciya wo. Wanaġi let out a long, long breath. "Haun-n-n, haun-n-n-n," he moaned, sounding the dying warrior's cry. And then, as before, he let go all his holds, his body inert and sinking.

A tiny peeping came from the brush that he had piled around his resting place, peeping sounds as from a groundbird, peeping sounds that went on and on, passively stimulating sounds, something to prevent a complete abandonment.

His thoughts came and went unnoticed. And in that usually active foreground, that roving ground for tensions and emotions, he pictured the calmness of a placid lake.

He had felt quiet agreement from everywhere; now he felt only the quiet as if he alone lay awake in a camp where everyone, everything, slept.

The warmth underground had spread out, widening the area of comfort, creating a great vastness of warmth into which he vaguely desired moving. But he lay lax, his body without motion and without enough emotion to push him. To enter this marvelous new element, then, will mean to expand his heart and let in spiritual-power, the only power that will propel him forward now.

Imagining himself dead will not mean imagining himself without a memory; the invisibles retain earth-memories for a while, something on which they act when they hear a voice. And so he remembered that he neither shall strain nor anticipate. For then, instead of absorbing the wonder, he will find himself hunting for the familiar, looking for similarities.

Ta ta iciya wo. Make yourself as if dead. But not too much abandon or his power becomes inactive. He shall maintain himself forcefully, not to combat but to have the strength to receive.

For a moment he glanced at thoughts that drifted by, his responses safe from strain or effort or any attempt to concentrate. And then he returned joyfully to the warmth and wide-openness of an element wherein his spirit, alert and eager and uncritical, rose to new and wondrous peaks.

Wanaǧi returned at dawn, his moccasins pointed in the direction of Olepi's lodge. He walked knowing that some mysterious bond, loosely tied but unbreakable, connects him to Olepi and the son of Olepi.

The son of Olepi? Someone who not yet exists? But who will say when the son of Olepi begins to exist? Spirit-life before birth? Earth begins as spiritual force and, the grandfathers say, spiritual force will absorb the earth.

The next moment Wanaǧi saw that the tipi covers had

begun fluttering down and that Olepi came forward to meet him. The warrior's handsome face reflected the strain he had endured, but the tone of his voice told Wanaǵi all he wanted to know.

"My friend," Olepi said firmly, "I am the leader."

"So lead." Wanaǵi turned abruptly, going now to his own lodge.

Waȟcawin noticed at once that Wanaǵi had come back a man renewed. Rejoicing silently, she had not looked for him to speak of his absence. But he had told her something.

"I am not as you remember me," he said.

And she, gazing for a moment into his eyes, understood.

VI

SHAFTS OF mellow sunlight, reaching between spaces in the clouds, touched upon the traveling Mahto, who, after a summer on the plain, chose to live the winter season near the big muddy river. A whiteman-trader, the newscarriers had told, comes again with his amazing collection of iron and cloth and colors.

Eighty-and-five persons, forty horses, sixty dogs made up this procession that filed along in back of Olepi. His band counted neither as many persons as the Siyo nor as the Okandada, but he boasted the most warriors; thirty Mahto wore the black-and-white feather, the spotted wamblifeather, in their hair.

Three winters had passed since Peta's dying and now the Titonwan made a custom of leaving the muddy-water at the start of the warm moons and moving onto the tender red grass close by the black hills. Then, as the summer grew old, they watched for a certain cluster of stars on the horizon, acting on this cold-weather warning, starting back across the rough and sun-burned grasses, back to the big river, to the place where a wašicun—a man with a different message, different gestures—raised a deadwood shelter.

This past summer the wind had fluttered the covers of fifty Titonwan lodges—three hundred people who hunted and feasted and sang their songs as one great camp—while a scorching sun turned the grasses yellow and brittle. Hunters had gone out and returned with meat; raiders had gone out and returned with horses. And then the pattern of stars that they call seven-pte-living-in-the-sky had announced the beginning of the cold moons.

But the people had ignored the twinkling sky; the tribe had lingered near the black hill until the little 'popotka,' using a screechy voice, told of but one more clear moon, perhaps enough days for reaching the muddy river before snow.

Then the great circle—Šiyo, Okandada, Mahto—had broken camp and begun traveling, each band seeking a different winter-place, but all bands curious about the whiteman on the big river, the stranger who fills his shelter with many mystifying things.

All bands followed the same path until they reached the headwaters of the brackish stream they called their own. From here they traveled separately, knowing that wherever they cooked, slept, sang, and danced, they performed these acts on ground the enemy never dared invade.

Most of the Mahto warriors in this string of people sat horseback, but only three Mahto women rode, Cankuna one of these three. And while she sat straight-back as any warrior, her eyes looked strained and her breath came in little gasps.

A small boy ran alongside her and now she called to him: "Micinkši, stay with your father."

The woman turned her horse as if to ride back over the trail she had come.

The child watched his mother, a look of surprise in his round black eyes. But when she started off, he followed close behind.

She waved him away. "Go back, my little son," she said gently; "go back."

He stared at her another instant, then let out a boy-cry

111

of resentment. Awkwardly the woman reached down, caressing his cheek, but he darted from beneath her hand, running back to his father, Ogle.

Cankuna rode on slowly, not looking up. Certain persons glanced curiously at someone who rode in the opposite direction, and one old woman turned to follow. But Cankuna gestured her away.

When everyone had passed from view, the woman slid carefully off her horse; she tied the creature to a sturdy branch. She pushed through thick brush until she reached a patch of grass, singularly fresh and soft as the lining of a nest. For an instant she marveled this strangeness in the moon of falling leaves, but she will not search for a reason. Enough that she finds this place away from sympathizing eyes while she enacts her role in the great song of creation. She dropped wearily upon her knees.

The raucous chatter of the long-tail birds-who-sit-smiling muffled any sound coming from the fresh grass back of the brush. And soon these same noisy wingeds saw the woman emerge, come out of hiding. And in her arms, a new Titonwan.

She walked slowly, her hand patting gently the infant's bottom, her breath a whisper-song upon the baby's head: "My little son, my new little son." The mother-heart throbbed in her breast as she recognized the joy of one who fulfills life. "My new son, my new son."

Cankuna had received her child in her own hands, had tied the cord with her own fingers, and she had eaten of the afterbirth, enough to relieve her of any fear that she never again will bear a child. She and Ogle now had two sons; perhaps a little girl will come next.

But she ate of this mystery also as a way for keeping off whoever, whatever perhaps tries to harm her child. Even as the four-legged clean up the birthing places to prevent danger from locating their young, so she will act.

She held the infant's head against her cheek but she will not look into the child's eyes; she will not risk, even in these first moments of life, an enduring tie with her son. But like most mothers she will decide a name for him, something he will use during the six, eight winters he lives in her care.

"My son, other persons will name you on different

occasions," she whispered, "but this day I give you a name to grow on; I call you Mahtociqala."

Certainly Cankuna remembered that the Dakotah grandfathers had provided birth names for the first-born child—boy or girl—and for the brothers or sisters who come afterwards, but she remembered also that the Titonwan let this custom fall on the ground. The Titonwan family will give the boychild an amusing name instead, something they will call him until he reaches eight, perhaps ten winters, and then his father will hunt for something to call him or perhaps an uncle will dream a new name. After a while the youth's acts earn him a name, the owner tying on a color or a dimension whenever he desires. But if ever they honor him with an old family name, then he holds on proudly for he owns something to cherish and pass to a son or the son's son, wherever the name fits.

Cankuna, originally a Sicanġu woman, had come to live among her husband's people and so she had discovered with what great pride his band regarded the name Mahto. Many persons in the band owned a piece of this name, a name of forcible nature. They called her husband Ogle but his whole name, Mahto Ogle. And now her new son shall own a piece, a little piece, of the Mahto name. Mahto-ciqala. Mahtociqala. But like his parents he shall own wholly the name Dakotah. Or Lakotah as they said more frequently now.

She untied the horse and climbed up uneasily. She sat a moment, wrapping the newborn in the fold of her robe.

"Grow tall, my son, and brave," she murmured. "Look around. Something always stands nearby waiting to help you. Listen, my son; one good voice you always shall hear. Grow, my son, grow on the name I give you. Grow good, grow brave. The people look for good in their sons."

The horse moved off slowly and the woman gave thought to her first-born son, the boy Cicila, whom she had sent this morning to his father and his father's brother, the hunter they call Hinhan. And to her own brothers, Pasu and Iku, uncles to the child.

Soon they shall begin instructing him, she told herself, in ways and with words that belong not to woman. But for four winters now Cicila knows her protecting care, four winters he crowds up against her in sleep and brings his

113

child-hurts for her viewing and perhaps for a dab of soothing fat. But now he grows into his fifth winter and a new son comes visiting the tipi, demanding her attention. And so the grandfathers, then the fathers and uncles shall take over where she leaves off, her seasons with the boy properly coming to a finish.

For an instant she saw again the surprise-hurt in Cicila's eyes when she waved him away, sending him from her gentleness to the firm ways of father and uncle. But so with the young grizzly whose mother cuffs him off during the second summer, cuffs him into an existence on his own.

"Ina, ina, ina, ina . . ."

The sound returned Cankuna to the stirring bundle under her hand. Gratefully she listened to her newborn using the one word each infant knows at birth: ina, mother.

Touching her finger to the baby's lips, she watched his effort at sucking. Perhaps he knows to suck before he comes, she marveled to herself, the same way that he knows to swim.

But she will not answer to his hunger, not until she and the child rejoin the traveling band, where some different mother will offer this infant a breast, someone who will feed him until Cankuna's breasts fill. But only a little while, the woman told herself, until her own juices provide. For certainly some child or Ogle or perhaps a young camp-dog will suckle her, quickening the flow.

The mother began a sleep-song, whispering and humming: "Niyate tabloka oce, ahboo, ahboo." His father, she had told him, makes meat and so the infant shall sleep.

And the tiny one, hearing, now slept. For each newborn, the grandmothers tell, understands this one sound, 'ahboo,' a word that belongs to infants, a sleep-sound they recognize.

And certainly Cankuna's slow and gentle patting acted on the infant's heart, quieting the beat, lulling him into drowsiness, the mother patting yet more slowly, humming yet more softly as she sees her newborn sleeping.

Cankuna became eager to ride again among the Mahto, her child arriving without difficulty, her own strength rapidly returning. She recognized herself as one among the fortunate, many Lakotah families experiencing something sorrowfully different this same season.

A strange disease had walked in on the childbearing women, killing the mothers and their unborn. And neither pežuta nor wapiya nor magician had demonstrated any power over this mysterious intruder that saddened hearts in many villages.

And so Cankuna, in the next little while, stopped her horse alongside a boulder. Climbing down carefully, she removed a decorative little roll of quilled hide from her hair. She laid her thanks-offering near the big stone; here, a gift for whoever, coming this way, will pause at this place to appreciate the wondrous power of life made visible through stone.

VII

THE SUN climbed down under, signaling a finish to the day's work and making way for a long evening of storytelling, teasing, and play. The season for these things had arrived and the Mahto intended to have fun. They had strung their fourteen lodges along the tricky-water stream, a day's walk on snow to the big river where the other Titonwan bands had raised their lodges. The snow had not yet come but the hard face of the frost moon prophesied a white ground-cover before morning.

The evening fires glowed softly on the tipi covers, on the lining that prevented shadow-pictures of the movement inside the lodge. The women wiped clean the food bowls and gathered up the bones sucked empty of marrow, something they will toss out to the dogs. And while they worked, these wives and mothers stayed attentive to the comfort of their men. Any child who shouts will hear a soft hushing murmur, these women aware that a loud, harsh reproach proves more disturbing to the father than an exuberant child.

But now the fun began; the joyful sounds of youth and

115

the giggles of women along with the smiling-laughter of men soon filled these Mahto lodges. All Mahto lodges but for one. He who led the band sat in quiet, neither talk nor laughter in Napewaśte's lodge.

A woman usually put aside her work at dusk, but Napewaśte bent diligently over awl and sinew. She made snow moccasins, cutting her pattern from the top of an old tipi cover. The lodge-fires of two winters had smoked the hide; she intended that these moccasins never stiffen or shrink or tear. Olepi already owned two fine pairs of cold-weather moccasins—hair inside for warmth—but Napewaśte persisted at this work as if he had nothing to wear in the snow. Nor had she so much as glanced in the husband's direction all evening.

Olepi pretended an indifference to his wife's aloofness. He knew her nature; a sudden anxiety always pushed her into unnatural quiet. Usually he ignored her apprehensions but this night her disposition annoyed him; he felt inclined to advise a change in attitude.

A gust of wind struck the lodge and Napewaśte looked toward the top of the tipi, where the smoke flaps stood straight up. For a moment she considered adjusting their position. But then her eyes returned to the awl, her manner once again closing out all but her work.

Her anxiety related to the son in this lodge, a child born three winters past, who lay asleep on robes placed alongside her own. This same day she had not met her son's hunger and she had pondered why her breasts shall dry. Women usually feed their children three, four winters, even five. True, some mothers who feed into the fifth winter act to put off the husband and so prevent another child; a good man, the people say, will not lie with his wife while she grows a child or while she breast-feeds.

But now Napewaśte asked herself whether the longing she experienced this night and many nights, a longing for the husband's embrace, perhaps brought about this dryness before she had fulfilled an obligation to her child.

At this moment the boy stirred and the mother, noticing, crept over to his sleeping place. If he awakens hungry and his father observes that her breasts will not provide, then will the man give a sign that he desires lying with her again?

116

She touched the child's face; something had made her remember the little one in the Mahto village who awakened one morning with a warm head and a spotted skin. That one had not lived to see the sun climb down. The memory increased her anxiety for her own child. But this little one's face seemed cool and the soft black hair, growing to below his ears, lay moist against his neck.

Returning to her place she decided to speak, but looking up, she saw that the husband leaned forward, that his eyes fixed on the entrance flap. Even so, she heard nothing until a gentle scratching on the cover announce Wanagi's presence. The wapiya called from outside, asking that Olepi come with him. And at once.

The woman watched her husband drape his robe casually about his body as if he walked out to challenge the weathers. But she sensed that he strove for this casualness. He wanted always to appear as a most apt leader but she knew that uncertainties often got in his way. His own village had accepted him as leader after his father's death, but two winters had passed before the principals in all three Mahto villages had acknowledged him headman in the way that the Siyo accept Wacape as their leader and the Okandada now regard Oowesica as their leader. The delay had surprised him.

Now, as the man moved toward the flap, Napewaste hunted for a sign, something that will tell him to hurry back, hurry back. But when he turned and looked directly at her, she covered her face.

Instantly she regretted her act but he already had gone. She sighed softly. Truly, she acted foolishly this whole day, toward husband and toward son.

Presently, she moved over to the pile of wood inside the tipi, choosing slow-burning sticks for the night-fire. And then she lay down, seeking the strengthening warmth of the pte-robe, something that will help put her to sleep. And quickly.

The next evening Olepi sat again at his lodge-fire. His child slept and his wife fondled a piece of hide, softening the skin toward some good use. He had found the new snow moccasins among his things, a pleasing gift. And so he looked for smiles and some gentle teasing. But again this night Napewaste closed him out; why, he knew not.

Then, after a while, he began talking: "Whitemen come to the Mahto camp." He held up three fingers. "They bring nothing that I want. Perhaps they will not come again."

The woman remained silent and so Olepi said nothing more about the white trader and his two companions.

But Napewaśte had smiled a little smile her husband had not seen. Why tell him that she already hears the story of those waśicun who visit the Mahto, that the old woman who occasionally sleeps at the tipi entrance brings her the news this morning. Why tell anything to a husband who stays away and so makes her fear that he loses affection for her? True, after learning the details she sees why he stays away, but she will want him to tell her why. And until now he never mentions the event, something perhaps important enough for the winter count.

Scouts had recognized the whiteman-trader, the old woman had told, taking this man and two more whitemen to the safety of the sacred-lodge. Here the trader had revealed—his hands helping along his broken Lakotah speech—that he brought iron-sticks up the river for all Titonwan. But the tribe needed to give him so many good robes in trade for these weapons. Next, he had spoken of his visit to the Śiyo and Okandada and Sicanġu who camped on the muddy-water. These bands—or so he said—had traded robes for his iron-sticks, his guns; why not the Mahto?

Olepi had listened courteously to the whiteman, but he neither offered the pipe nor approved any trades. He had permitted these bearded ones to sleep in the village; they had come at dusk and dared not safely venture out again. He had sat watching while they slept and at sunrise he had sent the three on their way, a dog carrying his gift of meat, a gift and not a trade.

And so these whitemen had come and gone, their visit like the small wind that whirls into camp, fluttering the lodges, then whirling off, nothing changed, nothing improved.

Nothing changed?

For a moment the woman's hands lay quiet in her lap. She perceived only now the meaning in the two, three phrases her husband had spoken: he truly intended to avoid contact with whitemen. He had led the band to a campground near but not on the big river where the strange messengers—the white ones—camped. Other Titonwan raised lodges alongside the trader's place but not the Mahto. Nor had this band yet visited the trader.

Then, in the same moment, she recognized the true source of her moodiness: she had sensed that the wakan—something mysterious—put difficulties in the path of the man they call Olepi, the man she proudly calls my-husband. A woman's breast, the old ones say, always knows when her children, young or grown, meet with difficulty. But perhaps the breast in a certain woman also knows about a husband's trials; perhaps Olepi desires to renew himself in her, and so the breasts, emptying of juice for the child, reveal this truth.

Her heart quickened. She saw that Olepi had laid down his smoking things, that he moved around the fire circle toward her side of the lodge.

She looked down again at her work but the man took the piece from between her palms. Touching her arms, he gently raised her from the ground. He looked into her face and she smiled her willingness. But her eyes told that he shall give her as much joy as she gives him.

The stars had stayed in hiding throughout the night—Napewaśte knew for in her joy she had not slept—and then, before dawn, the air had filled up with the smell of something wet, not rain but like rain. And from out this blend of near-dawn darkness and moist fragrant air, something white had begun falling.

The flakes came down quietly, like feathers, and Napewaśte saw that the big hard-face moon had spoken truly: the winter snows arrive.

She pressed her cheek gently against her husband's shoulder; she had remembered that snow means men-in-the-lodges.

VIII

KIWANI, NATURE'S reawakening after winter's long sleep.

The Dakotah grandfathers had said that the seasons start anew when the red grass appears, when water-birds return and make nests, whether or not the rivers float ice, whether or not the ground holds snow.

The Lakotah grandfathers say differently; not until the sky flashes and roars will the cycle begin. But the Lakotah women know that the seasons commence when things start getting fat, when leaves cover each branch and twig and the people travel again toward the sacred hill where they shall raise their lodges in one great protecting hoop.

Kiwani; and so the Titonwan meet again at the edge of the black hills, the trees in leaf, everything starting to fatten.

This summer the tribe camped on a clear, fast-running stream, a stream they promptly had reason for naming split-toe creek.

A young man called Catka had removed a moccasin to cross over the water. Jumping barefoot from one wet stone to the next, he had slipped and fallen into the creek, his fall nothing to talk about had he not split his big toe on a jutting root. He had limped back to his Siyo village, where he smeared the cut with fat, then bound the toe with a strip of hide. And so he had endured not only the hurt but considerable teasing.

The young warriors had pretended not to accept Catka's story. They split a feather pulled from the tail of one of those birds-who-sit-smiling and, grabbing hold of the youth, stuck this symbol of a wounding in his hair. They made up a song which advised that Catka wear his big toe on the outside of his foot in the manner of the grizzly and they began calling the stream split-toe creek.

For a while Catka had joked and tried to hide his concern along with the pain. But a warrior at age eighteen needed a strong toe for clinging on the far side of a loping horse and he needed two strong feet if he intended to go on

the raids. Only this morning—ten days after the mishap—
his lame foot had prevented him from going out with the
hunters or helping to bring back the meat from the small
herd that grazed close by.

Many persons had walked out to watch the hunt, Catka
limping along with the crowd but soon turning back. Then,
as he passed the Mahto camp he saw his young nephew, his
sister's child whom they call Petala. He stopped to watch
the boy at his play.

The child, perhaps four or five, squatted in the shade
and drew pictures on the dusty ground. A companion twice
his age stood nearby, a pointed stick in his hand. When
neither child noticed Catka's presence, the young man decided to conceal himself and observe the boys' fun.

The big boy—nicknamed Slukila—now poked viciously
at the man-shape outlined on the ground. Then, handing the
stick to the small boy, he demanded that Petala, son of
Olepi, strike the picture in similar manner.

"You touch second on the enemy," he said and handed
over the stick.

Petala stabbed at the ground as told. But now Slukila
jerked away the stick and twice struck the drawing.

"I am a warrior," the voice of the big boy announced
shrilly. "I kill. I kill." He drew a line across the neck of the
figure. "My father says I shall kill many Psa."

The small boy stared at the drawing. "I am a warrior,"
he said, "I am a warrior like my father."

Slukila stooped down and began rubbing out the shape
with his thumb. "I am like Oowesica," he boasted. "Oowesica has more warriors than your father's band, more than
any band."

"My father has more warriors than any band," Petala
answered firmly.

"Your father's band makes a little circle. Count for me
the Mahto lodges," Slukila taunted Petala.

The small boy stood. He opened and closed his hands
once, then raised up four fingers of one hand; he will show
fourteen tipi.

"My band counts more lodges." Slukila opened and
closed his hands twice, then once again.

At this moment Catka almost came out from hiding to

121

inform the young tease that the Oowesica count twenty, not thirty, tipi and that the Siyo, his own band, camp at the horns of the hoop for a second summer. Instead he waited, listening closely.

"When I lead a war party perhaps I shall let you come along." The big boy had mimicked condescending tones.

"I shall go out with my father when he leads the raid." Petala took a quick breath. "I am brave."

Slukila laughed and lifted his stick as if to strike the small boy. "A brave man will not back off from a lance. Petala cringes and so I know he will cry if I hurt him."

"I will not cry."

"I shall find out, my friend. Stay here." He ordered the small boy to make more pictures. "I shall come back with something." He waited for the child to squat down and begin drawing before he ran off.

The young man hiding back of the tree knew not to interfere—Petala's innocent boast had invited the ordeal—but he saw the need for someone to witness whatever trial the young bully will inflict upon the child.

Now, observing that Petala covered his face with his hands, Catka felt true-concern; perhaps the child really feared the trial.

But Petala had placed his hands over his eyes to give himself a clear picture of the creatures he intended to draw. For he will make firm lines when he uses the stick again, rubbing out nothing, changing nothing.

He talked aloud to the shapes as they appeared on the ground, giving each one a name. This one, mahto. This next one, ptagica. A male, he said, and drew the scrotum. And now wambli, the great bird in flight.

His drawings proved something to marvel. Here, the shape of the grizzly, discernible from claw to snout to hump, formidable and arrogant. And here the shape of pta, tail curling, a male virile and challenging. Certainly whoever views these drawings shall see neither the meandering scratches of a child nor yet the simple line-form of the winter-count keeper. The wapiya, perhaps, will say that the spirits pass over this ground and leave their tracks, even the warrior-bird swooping down, leaving the mark of his wing-spread.

But neither wapiya nor anyone different will see these

drawings; Petala stood, rubbing his moccasin over the designs. Slukila had returned.

The big boy had told the child to extend his hand, palm up. Then out of a little sac he poured seeds onto Petala's wrist, seeds from the tall, yellow hollow-stem flower. Next he blew on the firebrand, something he had brought back with him.

"Now." Slukila laid the flame on the dry seeds and when they started burning he turned his eyes on Petala's face; he looked for any sign of pain.

Petala regarded the seeds, fascinated, as if he, like Slukila, only observed this test.

"Cry," muttered the big boy. "Cry and I will call you woman."

The seeds burned to tiny red spots and the heat pushed into the tender wrist but Petala neither cried nor winced. Even so, smoke from the firebrand made his eyes water.

"Woman. Woman. You cry. I see tears." Slukila saw whatever he had wanted to see; his voice became a victory shout. "He cries. Petala cries."

Catka heard but he stood too far away to see his nephew's face and so discover the truth. But one thing he knew: the child had not cried aloud in pain. And now he listened for Petala's reply to the bully's mockery.

But the small boy had not answered. And so Slukila dared to run among the lodges, his mouth pouring words aimed at shaming Petala.

The child stood unmoving, his eyes on the burning seeds. Then, suddenly aware of Slukila's shouts, he walked slowly toward his mother's lodge. He called out to the woman: "Ina, I am not crying. The seeds hurt but my father knows I will not cry."

Napewaśte came from the side of the tipi; she viewed the wrist held out to her. Seeing the redness, the mother offered fat to ease the burn but Petala refused this help.

"Tell my father I am not crying," he begged.

"My son will speak to his father," the woman answered. "Tell him, micinkśi, tell your father and see him proud of you."

"Why will Slukila say I cry?"

The mother looked briefly into the perplexed eyes

123

raised to her. Not a witness to this affair, she dared not answer.

She knew of these trials whereby the young in camp tested one another's endurance to pain, perhaps holding a slab of ice or a firebrand against some sensitive place on the body. And she knew that, while the grandfathers never discouraged these acts, they looked out for any boy who used this method to bully a child. Children shall learn from their peers, these wise ones said, but any youth who hurts someone to gratify himself presents a danger to the camp.

Napewaśte had heard Slukila's scorning voice, the woman wondering for what reason he desired to humble her son. They said that Slukila's father often mistook the bullying ways of his boy for cunning and that the man encouraged these traits which gave his son the reputation of a disagreeable tease. Perhaps, then, the father regarded Slukila's acts as something augering bravery. Or will the man, usually away from camp, simply not know his son? She remembered talking with Cankuna the summer before this one on a day when they saw Slukila's mother with bruised arms and legs. She had wondered about this Okandada family, wishing that she dared discourage Slukila's occasional visits to her lodge.

The boy's father, she knew, traveled with a friend from village to village, entertaining the Lakotah with amusing incidents. Unlike the hardy newswalkers—men out in all weathers, carrying the important events from band to band—these two, skilled at mimicry, carried only gossip, the small happenings in each camp. And so the son of this actor sat more often in the company of mother than father.

Once the boy had teased the woman beyond her enduring and she had struck him. The returning parent had punished his wife severely, as Napewaśte had seen. Yet none had felt sympathy for the woman. They knew Slukila as a troublemaker, but they knew also that striking a child merely knocked in the mischief.

And Napewaśte made herself remember as she watched her son return to his play that differences exist among the lodges. In her lodge they teach the son that a Titonwan who speaks untruthfully even once shall grow a crooked tongue. And so when Olepi's son says that the burning on his skin brings forth neither cries nor tears, trust him. But the mother of a boy in his fifth winter will not run through camp shouting this thing.

"Why will he say I cry?" Petala called to his mother once again, but a different voice gave answer.

Catka had come up behind the boy and, avoiding the woman's eyes in token of brother-respect, spoke his message to the camp-dog sniffing at his wounded foot: "My sister's son talks straight. Petala makes nothing of the burning flower seeds. I watch and so I know."

Good manners will not permit the woman a reply but truly Napewaśte's heart had felt a song.

Slukila had tried to gain more attention when the people came back from the hunt, but who will choose to listen to a bully disparage a young boy while hump ribs spatter over a roasting fire, while the flavor of meat permeates the camp?

But relatives coming to feast at Napewaśte's lodge shall hear Petala describe his experience; his grandfather—Tunkaśila—had said so.

Then after Petala had told his story, Tunkaśila spoke. He said that his grandson shall receive a boy's bow and blunt shafts, something he, the grandfather, proudly shall make for this boy.

Next, Lekśi—the old uncle—talked, the man offering to take out Petala and a group of his friends to stalk the tall-ears, and saying that he will make each boy a throwing-stick of yellow wood for this hunt.

Then Catka invited his young nephew to accompany him on a bird-snaring; a split toe, he said smiling, hampers a more daring game at the moment.

And finally Olepi spoke, the father's invitation almost too wonderful to accept. In the morning he shall take his son to visit the horses, Petala choosing one, a horse he dares call his own. "My son shall not use the back of a campdog after this day. From now on he rides the back of a big-dog; from now on, he owns a horse."

The praises of his relatives followed the excited child to his sleeping robes, where the joy of these awards and the pain at his wrist kept him awake.

Napewaśte, observing his unrest, offered once again the soothing fat. And again the boy refused. Already he saw not a scar on his wrist but a mark of bravery.

IX

CANKUNA USED more hides in making her summer lodge than any other woman in the encampment on split-toe creek. She joined together seventeen skins, then pulled the cover around twenty-two poles, the new tipi big enough to accommodate all her relatives whether they came to sleep or to eat.

But then not a man in the Titonwan tribe surpassed her husband Ogle as a provider. He not only provided his wife with the hides for a new lodge whenever she wanted to make one, but he gave generously of skins and meat to his relatives who raised their tipi alongside him and to his wife's relatives living among the Sicanġu. He fed the old in the tiyóspaye, the big-family, and he always looked around for more hungry mouths, Mahto or outside his band.

From youth he had enjoyed the hunt more than any other camp activity, his father and grandfather the same way. And while he preferred surrounding the herd horseback to trapping the meat in brush enclosures or driving a herd over the cliff to break and bleed on stones below, he knew these old hunting ways.

For more than fifteen seasons he had hunted, on foot or horseback, and now at age twenty-and-nine he owned three fine 'runners'—horses that run alongside the meat while the rider maneuvers his lance for a sudden thrust between ribs, into lungs or paunch. And he kept five remarkable bows, bone and horn along with favorites from the wood of the scabby-leaf tree. He liked to hunt and he liked to share the meat. And his wife liked to cook. He and Cankuna rejoiced at any occasion that called for feeding the whole Mahto band.

And now, on this second day after the big midsummer hunt at split-toe creek, he invited all fourteen Mahto lodges to a naming-feast. He had killed seven of the twenty-three pte brought back to camp, plenty of meat for everyone.

Eyanpaha had called out the invitation soon after dawn, the crier announcing that Ogle proudly will make ceremony over the naming of his two sons; proudly Ogle will feast kinsmen and friends.

And so the people learned that the hunter's first-born, the boy in his sixth winter, shall receive a new name. Cicila will discard his birthcord, something he had kept these many seasons in a tiny sac, something he had worn on his back as a protecting influence whenever he played beyond view of his family's lodge. Now, throwing away this string which once tied him to his mother, he shall take on a youth-name. And perhaps new traits which identify with his true nature.

And the people shall hear the hunter's second son named, the child who had come while the band traveled, the baby who soon will try walking.

Cankuna, her women relatives assisting, had boiled the pte-tongues and roasted the shoulders and ribs. Now, the sun directly overhead in a clear, clear sky, she began feeding the crowd who had responded to Ogle's call to eat with him.

The men sat together in close circles of warriors or hunters or weapon-makers, each one drawn to a place alongside his kind. And between, boys and youths who will not want to miss any of the man-talk.

To these circles Cankuna and her helpers brought hump and different choice pieces, but to the feeble-old and those persons lacking teeth the women brought fat and gut and a thick soup made from tipsila, ripe bulbous roots cooked soft in meat-water.

The women and girls and children ate in a different place, mothers feeding babies, mothers looking out for their young. Occasionally a girl dared to glance playfully at the warriors, her friends giggling and picking at the food in their bowls as they sat wishing for similar daring.

Cankuna prided herself that none of her guests ever left hungry and so she went about looking for empty bowls, filling all but for someone who turned down his bowl or perhaps wrapped his leftovers to take with him.

Her attention, then, stayed on her visitors; she had not noticed that her son Cicila had disappeared, the boy going off with a group of children who hunted different amusements.

Cicila had schemes of his own for this day; he had persuaded some of his young friends to join in his favorite game: slinging mudballs.

Their play began as always, Cicila sending out 'scouts' to locate a patch of gummy earth along the stream, a white mud that will cling to the point of a slinging-stick. And then he sent out the others in the group, two little girls going as pretend-wives, girls who will trill for him in the manner of grownups when his throw splashes on the target—tree or branch—across the stream.

The scouts had found the gumbo quickly and the other children had cut sticks and made mudballs, but Cicila had not yet appeared.

Certain ones started to tease the two 'wives.' "Cicila will never come," they said; "the people will look for him and take him back to the feast circle and give him a man's name. And never again will he play at children's games. Hi-ye, Cicila will not come."

"Cicila will come," Slukila laughed slyly; "when he comes, I and he will play the rough way, three sticks apiece and aiming for each other's head."

The two little girls giggled. Slukila looked surprised; he wondered whether they had seen him put stones inside two of his mudballs.

Perhaps certain ones among the hunter's guests smiled when members of the family went out looking for Cicila, but if so, they hid those smiles behind a birdwing fan. These people had eaten Ogle's meat and smoked his pipe and whether or not they found the boy's absence amusing, a smile will not become their faces.

But certain eyes had caught the glance that Ogle threw his wife; the goodnatured man apparently had trouble understanding why Cankuna will lose sight of her son Cicila, whom this feast day honors. Where will this boy go?

128

Now, someone running in told quickly that Cicila played along the stream.

And now, someone running out went to bring back the boy.

Cankuna dared not look in the direction of her brother Pasu, the man whom Ogle had asked to name their son, but she remembered that Pasu had starved for two days while he tried for a 'dream,' something to help him decide on a proper name. And so she asked whatever good spirit perhaps listened, to influence her unruly son on this, his naming-day.

Ciçila approached his father with a mud-streaked face. He grinned slyly at the sternness all around, then suddenly dropped his chin, his eyes gazing at the ground.

"Perhaps my son chooses to wait another winter before he throws off his baby-name. I see that even now he hunts-for-his-birthcord." Ogle had spoken the ridiculing phrase in a voice for everyone to hear.

The young boy's neck warmed but they had not finished with him.

The uncle who had come here hungry stepped forward; harshly he admonished the drooping head: "A Titonwan never hangs his head shamefully, never looks down."

The boy looked up instantly and the uncle saw eyes bright with daring. If shame ever lived on this face, then truly a short-lived shame.

And so this uncle—the scout Pasu—began the naming-ceremony, removing from the boy's back the small shell-like sac, the birthcord inside wrapped in the hair of pte.

Cicila will see this tiny bundle only once again, he told the boy; once again, on the day he goes out with the warriors.

Turning, Pasu walked slowly in front of the people. "My nephew," he said, "throws down that which protects him while a boy. Now all that moves shall see him and certain ones shall favor him. They will come to him and reveal their names even as I tell him his new name. His new name—Gnuśka."

Ogle heard and liked the name: grasshopper. He appreciated a name that related to something in the grass, perhaps to the grasshopper without wings whose wavering horns point out the herd. And so the man dared imagine that the new name will influence his son toward a strong desire for the hunter's bow.

But different persons had found different thoughts. They saw a touch of scorn on the boy's lips as Pasu announced the name, and in the boy's mud-streaked face they saw a warrior who painted to meet the enemy. Here, on this same face, daring and the threat of foolish dares.

But now, at a signal from her husband, Cankuna brought forward her small son, placing the baby in the man's arms. Ogle waited until the woman stepped back, then handed the child to the naming-uncle.

The people saw Pasu's face bend over the baby, saw the scout's wide mouth cover the little one's mouth. They knew that he breathed his good nature into the child, a ceremony of four long breaths. They saw the child struggle against the man's embrace but they heard neither a cry nor any different sound.

Never will my little son cry out, Cankuna told herself. She remembered those days soon after his birth when she had needed to act as each Lakotah mother needs to act, when she had shut off his breath whenever he wailed, his tiny nose between her fingers, her palm covering his mouth. And like every Lakotah mother, she had feared choking her infant. But she had stayed with this important lesson, something that protects the camp, all things dependent upon the conduct of each one, adult or child. A wailing baby, the people said, will reveal the night camp of a traveling band easily as the big campfire or noisy voices.

The woman wished for the ceremony to finish quickly but only in her eagerness to know what name they had decided for this little one. She had asked that her husband accept the name she had whispered to the newborn as she rejoined the traveling band on the day of his birth, but whether the husband had mentioned this desire to her brother Pasu she not yet knew.

Now suddenly, joyfully, she heard the scout singing the name. And then she heard the people joining in, the song familiar to everyone who ever attended a child's naming-ceremony. Mahtociqala, they sang; Mahtociqala, his name.

Pasu moved out from the crowd of children that had managed to surround him. The ceremony called for a procession among the lodges, and so he will lead off, the small son against his shoulder, Gnuśka walking at his side, the boy suddenly proud and manly.

The people began to form a line, gently pushing their old men to the front, Lekśi and Tunkaśila and Tayaźo, the flute-owner, in this group who moved along on little dance steps, Heȟaka and men of his rank following close on their heels.

Fathers and sons came along next, some of the boys riding their stick-horses; different ones, in the manner of Olepi's son, riding on their father's shoulders.

Two, three women stayed back, pushing bowls and robes and the feast leftovers out of the way before they stepped into the line. All other women—grandmothers, wives, and daughters—quickly joined the procession, the girls walking gracefully next to their mothers; their small sisters, carrying toy-babies in the fold of their little robes, trying to keep up.

Slukila, mud on his face and a bump on his head, had sneaked up alongside Gnuśka, but the son of Ogle never glanced his way. Slukila belonged somewhere different until they gave him a man's name. And certainly he, Gnuśka, never again will play children's games, like mudball-slinging; from now on he will keep company with the big boys, youths who play dangerously.

Pasu had circled the Mahto lodges and so returned the people to Cankuna's big tipi. Here the two men who had walked at the rear of the line led forward a horse, the back of this creature piled with gifts, a present for each child in the procession. In this manner Ogle and his brother Hinhan—the two men that Gnuśka and Mahtociqala shall know always as 'father'—honored these two sons by way of delighting the young.

And now, the sun halfway down the sky, the people left this feasting ground, going on to visit lodges in different bands, taking along the news of the naming-day, generating gladness wherever they told the story.

Cankuna and her kinswomen remained at the lodge to make things neat again. Hinhan's wife wiped out the food bowls belonging to the tiyośpaye, and Pasu's wife, the pretty Sahiela-woman, dropped the bones into the cooking paunches for soup. Different women cleaned up the ground, raking through the grass with their hands, smoothing over the bare areas, shaking and folding robes.

Many children stayed on at Cankuna's lodge, the boys playing with their gifts of spinning-cones, whirlers, and throwing-arrows, the girls playing with horn-tipped throwing-sticks, aiming at the sky, winning points on the wood that flies straight and high.

Petala stood with the group who played at making-the-wood-dance, each boy whipping his small cone toward a circle they had marked out on the ground, each one trying to whip the spinning wood into a certain hole inside the circle and then keep the wood spinning in the hole.

The young Petala whooped along with the players whenever a cone fell or spun outside the circle, but his true excitement came from the red and yellow coloring around the little cones, the strips blending, widening or narrowing as the wood seemed to dance.

Suddenly a bone-whirler buzzed close over Petala's head, but the son of Olepi neither dodged nor ran off. And so other boys who played with similar whirlers came up to tease, their whizzers humming circles over the young boy's head, fanning his hair. But he stood his ground, squinting when the wood or the bone almost touched him, twice lifting his hands to protect his face.

Girls who played at 'throwing-sticks' dropped their sticks to watch and squeal and those boys who played with throwing-arrows stopped their contest to marvel the child who took this teasing.

For a while the air became noisy with buzzing, squealing, and shouting but then Gnuśka came running up, jumping alongside Petala; the new-named boy wanted to make certain that not Petala, not anyone took away from his importance on this day.

But his action had broken the circles overhead; the teasers walked off and the others went back to their play. Gnuśka shouted a boast that hinted at a demonstration of skill beyond anyone's imagination if ever someone will offer him use of a whirler or a whip-and-cone. The offer had not come.

Gnuśka's mood turned sullen. Suddenly leaving Petala's side, he ran toward the Okandada camp, where most certainly he will find someone whose company he will enjoy much more than a bunch of boys who go crazy over buzzers and whizzers. And let someone different look out for the baby brother his mother asks him to watch. Who cares if someone steps on Mahtociqala or the dogs bite him?

Mahtociqala sat where his mother had placed him while she cleaned up after the feast, the child on a robe where he, also, will enjoy the fun and laughter. And so he had lifted his shining dark eyes to the hum overhead. But the hum had stopped and the children had moved to another place. Different sounds attracted him now. And a certain good smell.

Mahtociqala crawled from the robe toward the cooking hole where soup bones simmered in the big paunch. Reaching the cooking place, he grasped two of the stakes that held the paunch to the edge of the hole. He had found something to help pull him up onto his feet.

Clinging to the sticks, he rose up, then slipped back. He tried again and now he came almost to a stand. Then he slipped. He fell forward, the boiling soup directly below him.

Someone flung out an arm, someone grabbed the baby and jerked him back from the scalding water. This someone: Petala.

"Stay away. This water burns." Petala kept a tight hold on the child. "Burn, hurt. Burn, hurt." The boy took a twig and splashed drops of the boiling soup on the fat little leg.

The baby squirmed but Petala shook more drops on the tiny wrist. The child whimpered softly. "Mahtociqala knows now," Petala said sternly.

Lifting the baby awkwardly, the boy took him to a different place where meat boiled in a paunch suspended above ground.

"More burns here," he said. He repeated his act, splashing the little one with boiling drops.

The boys, staying with their playthings, saw nothing of Petala's quick move nor the lessons that followed. Nor had they noticed that Petala stayed alongside the little one now.

133

After a while Cankuna came from back of the lodge, and Petala, seeing her approach, rejoined the group who, as before, watched the big boys with their spinning-cones. He had said nothing to the baby's mother; what will he tell?

But the son of Olepi had gained in understanding on this day when he sat for a while as brother to a small boy; certainly he had learned something of the meaning in this relative-term 'brother.'

And so for the remainder of the summer Petala frequented Cankuna's lodge. Here he rolled a ball at Mahtociqala or helped the child try out walking. And certain persons, noticing, wondered whether the Mahto leader accepted the hunter's family as 'second-parents' to his son.

Gossip goes on behind the palm but the sound always leaks between the fingers. And so Cankuna heard. She knew that the quiet boy with the observing eyes visited her lodge not as son but as companion-friend to her own small son; Petala seemed strongly attached to the child. But she decided to visit Napewaste's lodge and make clear to her good friend why Petala came and with whom he played.

Napewaste listened, hearing all things the woman said and all things Cankuna graciously left unsaid. And then, speaking formally yet shyly, her eyes saying more than her voice, she made answer: "Good friend, my heart rejoices at that which you say. I am glad that my child finds your lodge a pleasing place for play and that he regards your little son not unlike a brother."

She said nothing more but instead ladled a bowl of soup for Cankuna and for herself, the two sitting now to chat in the manner women enjoy, talking over different ways of making the soups more tasty, praising the design on each other's gown, Cankuna admiring also Napewaste's work on three, four strips of hide she had quilled recently.

Neither woman, properly, spoke of intimacies that involve any relative, near or distant, but Cankuna laughed over her own perplexities the day of her son's naming. She found cooking for ninety persons a more easy task, she said, than looking after one son on his naming-day.

After the hunter's wife had gone, Napewaste sat on to ponder what manner of woman Petala will choose when he seeks the second-mother, when—in some season before his

134

tenth winter—the son-mother talk between this boy and herself shall cease, his heart never again opened to her.

Four more winters, she told herself, and Petala shall look also for the second-father, the man to whom he dares talk his schemes and unfold his plans.

What different second-mother, she asked herself, will grant Petala more understanding than this one they call Cankuna? She accepted—whatever Cankuna will imply—that Petala's apparent choice to make the hunter's lodge his playground manifested also a desire to make the hunter's family his second-family.

And now, suddenly, she understood her true-gladness about this thing, a thought she dared entertain only once, a thought she dared never voice. For what woman shall say aloud that she desires seeing her son many different things before she sees him a warrior? The Titonwan, a warrior-people, they say; the Lakotah, a warrior-people, something their women shall remember.

One more person accepted Petala's affinity for the little son in the hunter's lodge; Wanaġi had sensed that which he not yet fully understood.

The wapiya saw none of the scene at the cooking fire; he knew only that something had occurred to form a bond between the child-spirit within these two. Yet to discover the brother-friend, the relative-through-choice, at five winters seemed most unusual. But then Petala appeared as a most unusual child.

Long before this day Wanaġi had begun to view the son of Olepi as someone unusual, a child who draws pictures as none other ever drew, a boy who asks about things as none other ever asked.

Who, this wonderful child among the Lakotah, among the Titonwan?

Something ties me, Wanaġi had remembered himself saying, something ties me loosely but certainly to Olepi and the son of Olepi. He had said so, said so before Petala's birth. And so one day he, Wanaġi, shall understand.

Ogle's midsummer naming-feast had inspired more new-naming and name-changing throughout the hoop than in any summer since the bands crossed the muddy river.

"I never know who suddenly will turn from a big black bird into a little black bird, from a black shield into a red shirt, from a grizzly to a skunk," Lekśi said with a straight face. But this same face had broken into smiles when Lekśi heard that his nephew Catka will change names.

The young warrior had chosen to take on the name Huśte. His split toe had healed but the foot held on to the memory of the wound; he always will walk with a limp. So why not a name that identifies him as a cripple? Huśte, he had decided, one who limps.

Different voices had sung at these naming-feasts, song-makers and singers at work until the summer had turned truly old and the berries had turned truly black. And the star-herd, the band-of-seven, truly had appeared, whether or not the people looked at the sky.

Reluctantly the Titonwan watched these warm moons die. They had sung more songs and laughed more often than in any season they remembered. Olepi, a half-smile on his face told his wife that he had enjoyed the hunts this summer as much as he used to enjoy the raids on the Palani.

But now, traveling back toward the muddy river, a gloom spread among the people as if they sensed a meeting with something unpleasant. And so, during a rest stop, Olepi had spoken to Wanaği of the people's mood. The wapiya had smoked four pipes while the Mahto leader sat with him, waiting for some sort of answer. But when he had finished his smoke, Wanaği picked up the horn in which he carried a little fire; he said nothing.

Then, at a place halfway between the black hills and the big river, the Mahto met and camped with a village of Sicangu. Newscarriers had visited these Titonwan and they had something to tell.

The whiteman comes back to the big river, they said; he lives as before on the tree-covered island near the mouth of the tricky-water. And, as before, he offers iron and cloth for trade. But now he brings something different: small stones he calls beads. And ten piles of these beads—ten in each pile—he will trade for an armful of skins. But skins only from the one-who-swims-carrying-a-stick. Beaver, the whiteman says; he wants beaver.

Suddenly Olepi had asked about the beads: "Of what used these beads?"

Use like quills; decorate moccasins. And the stranger brings those other marvels: kettles and knives and firesticks.

"What about kettles and firesticks?" Lekśi spoke testily. These things had appeared, he told, at the old trade fairs on the many-lakes river. So why will the Lakotah, who choose to stay away from those tribal gatherings for twenty winters, suddenly act excited over items long familiar to the Isanyati, their eastern relatives?

But all the while Lekśi talked and the Sicanǧu talked, Olepi watched the eyes of his people. He saw a drooping band quickly revived; he saw the only eagerness he had seen since the Titonwan broke their circles at split-toe. And he saw none of these things gladly.

He knew now that, unlike the winter before, these Mahto truly desire visiting the deadwood lodge. And that he shall appease their desire with a winter camp along the river and within view of the little island. And that he will make one visit to the trader's place even as the trader had made one visit to his camp.

Olepi made the one visit. He came away suspicious of all he had seen, all he had heard. And he had said so.

But not everyone had chosen to listen. The warriors already imagined a power in the firesticks, a power beyond anything they ever had hung on a shield or tied in a horse's tail or fastened to their hair. And certainly each man needed to discover for himself whether or not the trader spoke truthfully about the gun-power.

Most Titonwan visiting the deadwood lodge returned with trade-cloth, something they tore into fluttering red strips, a plaything for the wind. But occasionally a woman sneaked a strip, looking for the red to soak into her quills, giving more color than roots or stems or clay.

Among the Mahto many persons went onto the little island simply to look around the trader's place and to hear the waśicun talk. His nose exploded funny sounds when he grew excited—something that happened often—but his Lakotah phrasing gave reason for even more amusement. When he wanted tongue-meat he usually spoke the word meaning male-rigid, not understanding the difference between ceźi and ceźin. And often he used phrases that belong only to women. But, never a rude people, the Lakotah had neither smiled nor laughed in his presence; instead they waited until back in camp and then their laughter shook the lodges. But not Olepi; he had not laughed. Nor wanted to laugh.

Napewaste felt a certain curiosity about the trader, but Olepi's face stopped any mention of the island. And certainly she knew not to have any thoughts about seeing the deadwood lodge for herself. She tried, instead, to make the winter pleasant inside her tipi. But the husband seemed always waiting, waiting for the day when he and his band dared put the muddy-water river to their backs and start again for the black hills.

X

WANAŜI KNEW—many persons knew—that these new summer moons, even with the hoop on clean grass out near the strengthening hills, will not bring the renewing force of other summers.

Guns scattered the herd and spoiled the hunt for lance or bow, the hunters uncertain, without proof of their arrows, as to whose meat falls, who dares claim hide and hump and tongue. And so the people ate, not as a crowd of feasting relatives but as families eating alone.

And these same guns cracked open the ears of a sleeping enemy; the Titonwan lost horses. Suddenly the warriors came to Wanaŝi, demanding that the wapiya make up the wotawe, a symbol to rely on, something to fasten onto these new weapons.

"The shooting-stick, like the arrow," Wanaŝi had answered sternly, "proves only as good as eye and heart back of the stick."

And now the warriors looked upon this wapiya as a

stranger; they began to wonder about him. Will the grizzly-spirit refuse to help Wanáği now that he ceases to demonstrate his helpers, never growling, or scratching on bark, never wearing the grizzly hide or dancing in the manner of a grizzly-dreamer?

This sort of talk had not persuaded Wanáği, but, for a different reason, he had decided to make up the power-bundles again; the warriors, he saw now, truly needed these wotawe, something that will convince a man that he owns a line to power.

And so he prepared the bundles: claw, tooth, hair, feather, grass, whatever symbols of life they brought him, whatever they desired that he slip into a heart-sac or wrap up in hide. But perhaps one day, he told himself, each man shall recognize that śkan, taku śkanśkan surrounds him. And that he need only open his heart and with a true-awareness, let in the life-force.

The leaders and wise ones soon recognized a need to counsel the warriors about these firesticks, something not yet familiar to their hands. Why, they asked, risk a danger to the camp? One who gives up the birth-cry shall reconsider before he makes a noise in his man-seasons that perhaps locates the camp for an enemy.

But certain youths, yet determined to carry guns on a raid, closed their ears to these mild voices. And they ignored the not-so-mild voices of the akicita even when these clubmen threatened to punish anyone who left camp bearing firesticks; two different parties sneaked out, horseback and carrying iron.

One group returned to report three enemy struck down, but these men dared not dance their kills; they showed nothing to prove this claim. The firesticks had changed the nature of the game; nothing had challenged their riding in to scalp or strike the killed.

The second group came back, their guns broken; they had abused the sticks when one warrior wounded himself.

The wise ones sat again, their faces stern as they reviewed that which had occurred. Neither honor nor horses had come of these raids, only a fear of reprisal and one Titonwan hurt.

139

Will war now become a killing affair? If so, will not war change the nature of the people? The grandfathers always had spoken of the raids as a game, the players out for horses, not men's lives. Call the enemy ground a testing place for daring, they had said, not a place for making killers out of warriors.

The truly brave man, the people knew, carried nothing on the raid but his knife. What more will he need if he intends only to reach the enemy camp and cut loose a fine horse? And if he needs defend himself, in what way shall a firestick show him brave? A stake holding him to the ground while he defies the enemy or a knife bringing him up close to the enemy shall display either his courage or his lack, but a firestick spurting out danger from a safe distance, perhaps wounding an enemy in the back, offers nothing a man dares boast.

XI

THE FOUR warm moons gave way to cold and to another winter camp on the muddy waters of the big river. And now two men wearing beards lived at the trading-place.

Then two more summers, not much different from the ones before. And now another winter but with four white-faces on the little island. And a mysterious water with the taste of fire.

The whitemen invited whoever came to the island to taste the burning drink, each newcomer offered a little bowl. Then after two, three drinks the traders demanded many skins—even a robe—before they again filled the bowl.

Olepi had heard that persons who empty the third bowl walk back to their lodges on crooked feet. And that the fourth little bowl makes a man act like crazy; he neither will walk nor sit nor talk straight but will put aside all his natural ways.

And so the Mahto leader, remembering himself as a caretaker, visited again the trader's place; he chose to discover for himself what manner of men desired making fools of the Lakotah.

Napewaśte never had seen the wood-lodge and now all this gossiping about the place made her bold enough to ask Olepi whether she dared accompany him to the little island.

The man had not answered at once, but when he left for the trader's place his gesture said that she shall remain in the Mahto camp. Silently she accepted his decision, but she had wondered whether he felt concern for her or whether he denied her the visit as a reproof for some small neglect.

But his look upon returning from the island told her more than his words. He intended to protect her, his eyes said, to protect each one from something he feared more than any enemy the Mahto people ever had met. Or will meet.

Suddenly the woman had shivered; never before had she seen loathing fill this man's eyes. She watched him go out from the lodge; she knew nothing to say.

Olepi wanted talk this day with none but Wanaǵi, the one man who will understand that which he felt compelled to reveal. For he now saw why a leader needs to acquire a wisdom beyond his actual winters, why a leader needs to prepare himself for combatting enemies he never sees, never describes.

He sat a long while in the sacred-man's lodge before he spoke. "I see," he said slowly, "that which happens when the Lakotah drink the whiteman's mystery-water, and I know that this strange concoction will bring trouble into the hoop."

He waited a moment before speaking his next thought. "I never invite anything that will harm me into my lodge; so why shall I invite something harmful to enter my body and capture my soul?" His gaze stayed on the fire circle.

Wanaǵi recognized instantly with what effort this man opened his heart, this manner of talking not Olepi's way. And so he listened, his eyes closed.

Quietly, too quietly, Olepi finished his speech: "And so I decide against this drink and the man who brings the drink. If different ones want this fire, they so decide. But I will not again camp at this place. Not again will I make meat near this river nor taste these unclear waters. If ever the Mahto band comes here again, they come without me."

Then Olepi had gone and the sacred-man, swallowing the smoke of his pipe, gave breath to his trust; that the Mahto leader will hold to his resolve.

The horses shed hair and the Titonwan women welcomed the sign, one that prompted travel; eagerly they awaited the move out from these camps and off this ground where their men become as strangers.

But then the women, getting together in thought and act, decided not to wait for the full-leaf moon; they chose to start out now, before trees and grasses flowered.

And so the bands traveled on the plain, the familiar streams more like rivers, the clouds often making rain but never the frightening flash and noise. And certainly the people sensed comfort and safety in the company of so many Titonwan traveling together: eighty lodges, five hundred and sixty persons—Tiyataonwan and Sicangu—a people who stay on the mixed grasses.

During each stop for smoke and rest, Olepi listened to the principal ones in the different bands denouncing the traders. And at each overnight camp, he listened to the men and women who talked against ever returning to the muddy-water.

Yet before the berries fattened, he heard these same voices puzzling what new, amazing thing the wasicun will bring upriver next winter.

And now Olepi asked himself: will the leaders in this tribe act to protect or to please their following? In Peta's seasons two, perhaps three, families make up a band, and certainly a father takes two children by the hand more easily than ten. Even so, any leader who recognizes danger shall lead away from that danger whether one or ten hundred lodges in his band. But if he, Olepi, names the whiteman as the danger, will not the people answer that these whites

142

make only a handful, that they neither roam the earth nor hunt pte. Whom will they harm? True, the trader brings a crazy-water, but who forces the Lakotah to drink? Who ever dares force any Lakotah against his choice?

Suddenly Olepi began getting up war parties, taking out his young men and going far up the thickwoods river, where on one occasion his scouts discovered a camp of Canoni, their own people.

And when not out with a party, Olepi sat with those Mahto who wavered in their thoughts about a winter camp on the big river. He rarely visited outside his village and he slept in the clubmen's lodge more often than in his own.

When the trees began pushing off their leaves, he watched for signs as to which direction the Titonwan leaders intended to move. The Sicaṅgu had quarreled, some families heading for their roving grounds on the earth-smoke, different families going back to the muddy-water. But neither Śiyo nor Okandada hinted at their trail.

Finally, his concern disturbing his sleep, he carried his uneasiness to the lonely edge of the encampment; he took along only his pipe. Walking through a thin, white mist at dawn, he followed a familiar path toward the slopes where the horses grazed. Approaching the herds, he observed an unrest; snorting noises warned that something unwelcome crept in, but whether hoof or moccasin he not yet knew.

Bending down, he hunched along toward a tall clump of dead grass. He dropped his robe onto the ground and laid the pipe on the robe; he reached for a stone, a big one with a broken edge.

Two boys came near the brush where he squatted, two young horse-tenders who, completing their night watch, walked in to meet their replacements. Olepi gave a soft birdlike hoot, and the youths, recognizing a danger signal, dropped onto one knee.

Next thing, they heard the Mahto leader's husky commands: one boy shall come close, the other boy shall awaken the lodges.

The youth who crouched next to the leader held on to bow and knife, but now Olepi took the knife from the boy's hand. He signaled that the horse-tender shall follow him. And that he shall tighten his bowstring.

The Mahto moved ahead swiftly, quietly; he disappeared among the horses.

The young night-tender tried to keep up, but losing sight of the leader he stopped; he depended now on his ears to locate Olepi's position. Not without reason will the people acknowledge his keen hearing and name him Nuġe. But he heard only the coughing of a horse.

Suddenly the herds began to scatter as if an invisible robe waved off the whole. But certain horses, the restraining thongs on their feet, reared up, trying to kick loose.

Nuġe jerked off the hair-cord he wore looped around his middle; he caught one of the rearing horses, but he lacked a way to cut quickly the hobbling-tie. But even if he rides this horse where will he go? Where, where the enemy?

He heard shouts in the encampment and for one terrible moment he imagined that the enemy had reached the villages. Then he realized that his own people made those whoops; the warriors, alerted, came out after the scattering horses.

He remembered Olepi's orders: tighten the bow, follow me. But will the Mahto leader, a boy's knife and a sharp stone his only weapons, wait somewhere in the dry grass? Or will the enemy intercept Olepi?

The boy, confused and disheartened, started back to camp, leaving behind the hair-cord, his most proud possession.

Coming now upon the place where Olepi had dropped his robe, the boy saw the man's pipe. Now he understood why the Mahto leader had borrowed his knife; whoever smokes ceremoniously, they say, never carries weapons.

Someone whooped and Nuġe looked up. He saw Olepi, the Mahto leader horseback and hurrying toward camp; the hair of an enemy streamed from his hand.

And then Nuġe saw the day-tenders approaching, the youths signaling him that the warriors had cut off the horses, none lost or injured. Even so, Nuġe avoided their faces as they passed; he felt small, very small.

Olepi rode directly to the sacred-lodge. Here he jumped down, tossing the scalp at Wanaġi's feet. "My friend," he said, his voice unnaturally loud, "this hair helps me answer my difficulties." He touched his toe to the scalp. "This Witapaha boy and his companion die bravely but foolishly."

And now Olepi looked directly at Wanaġi, the warrior's eyes challenging any disagreement. "The fathers of these Witapaha," he said, "will seek revenge when next the moon rounds; this tribe acts while the blood boils. And so I will lead my Mahto to the muddy river, where they shall winter safely in company with other Titonwan.

"You know, my friend, that I find nothing appealing in the presence of a whiteman, but neither will I see my band as a lonely camp sitting on the plain in reach of the avengers. I will not ask that these Mahto stay on ground that my acts make dangerous."

Silently Wanaġi appraised the insolent eyes and the defiant tone. Then his own eyes made answer, cold answer: Olepi will not remember his resolve and in this truth sits the one, the only, real danger.

Admiring faces and trilling voices followed Olepi to his lodge. The people granted him a warrior's reception and he bore himself proudly.

He had walked from the sacred-lodge, his face and body without paint and nothing in his hair. Yet all who saw him marked his handsomeness.

I will remember, he told himself, that my place remains out in front. I sit too often with Wanaġi. I am a warrior; I belong with the fighting men.

A smile touched his lips. He welcomed these cheers and trills; he sensed an elation he had not experienced in five, six seasons, not since he had begun remembering himself as leader of the band, a man responsible for the good of the people.

He laughed aloud. He felt like a young warrior again, as if he owned all the daring on earth. So why not dance his excitement, he asked himself; why not dance this night and recite these recent acts? He has enough witnesses to that which occurs; truly, the whole thing happens within view of the encampment, within view of any eyes that open at sunrise.

Approaching his lodge, he laughed again. He imagined himself twenty-four, not thirty-four and the leader of a band. And so this one night he will become twenty-four again, a young warrior whose feet and body and gestures describe his amazing war acts. He shall dance his story, telling of the enemy youth whom he kills this day with a stone, whose scalp he takes with a knife he borrows. This same knife cutting down the second enemy who tries dispersing the Mahto herds.

And he will dance his moment at the wapiya's lodge and the hair he throws on the ground and the decision he makes to lead his people to the muddy-water.

This night he will paint and dance, perhaps as never again.

Nuġe's father had decided that the clubmen shall deal with his son's negligence. And so the boy stood center of a circle of stern eyes, his neck and cheeks burning. He had suffered their ridicule and now he waited for the whip-bearer's command that he turn his back and receive a punishing blow. Instead he heard the clubman ordering him to visit the Mahto leader. And to go at once.

Olepi sat horseback outside his lodge, and Nuġe, obeying the man's gesture, jumped up behind him. They rode slowly to the place where Olepi had struck down one of the youthful enemy, the body left on the grass. Here, at the leader's signal, Nuġe dismounted. Glancing at the dead boy, he quickly looked away.

"Take the scalp." Olepi, remained horseback, handed down the knife he had borrowed from Nuġe. "Your knife, not mine, kills this enemy. But lift his hair remembering that this boy dies foolishly. He scatters the horses but knows nothing about controlling the herd he scatters. When he sees his companion fall, fear overtakes him; he neglects caution.

"Lift his scalp, my son, but as a lesson, not a war honor. Any boy will mimic the warrior, but he earns respect when he reasons like one."

Nuġe turned slowly toward the body; he bent his knees to perform the act that Olepi demanded. But suddenly his belly poured out his mouth, his spew a more shaming thing than the humiliating words they had thrown at him in the akicita-lodge.

Olepi sat his horse, patient but unsympathetic. Let Nuġe, he told himself, retain the memory of this enemy boy; let Nuġe recognize his importance to each assignment. And let him see that which comes of neglect.

XII

DISCONTENT HAD walked through the Titonwan camps on the muddy river from the start of the cold moons; the difficulty began with the whiteman.

This season the traders complained that the people had not brought enough skins, hides, fat. And when the Titonwan told why, the whites seemed not to understand.

Occasionally, the Lakotah had said, those spirits who guard the big caves wherein live the pte become mischievous and release only a small herd onto the plain. But perhaps the next summer many pte shall roam the mixed grasses. And so if the traders will give the Titonwan whatever they need, then they the Titonwan will bring hides and robes in trade for all these things next winter.

The traders had seemed suspicious, but after a while one man had taken a dry white leaf and made the mysterious marks that tell what a certain person owes.

But this demand for hides already had made difficulty in the lodges. The women wanted iron cooking pots and beads; their men wanted that which the whites call traps and axes. And so whatever robes they traded took care of the warrior or the hunter, not the women.

Then, after a while some wives had dared go alone to the trading-place, boldly offering moccasins in exchange for their desires.

One man, upon discovering that his wife had sneaked out something for a trade, had come out of his tipi shouting for attention. Next, he had thrown a stick in the air, calling out that whoever catches this thing gets his wife and a horse—and a horse—so strong his wish for ridding himself of the woman.

His act brought smiles and some laughing; never before had a man thrown away a wife in this manner, even offering a horse to help remove her from his side. Custom permitted the husband whose wife goes around looking at different men to send the woman back to her parents, and occasionally a man with a lazy wife brings a second woman to the lodge instead of discarding the original one. But throwing one's wife to whoever will take her—certainly the grandfathers never had considered disposing of a wife in such crude manner.

Even so, three different men soon afterwards disposed of their women this same way. Those persons grabbing for the sticks had claimed that they needed a second or third pair of helping hands in the lodge, meaning they wanted to have more robes for trading at the whiteman's place.

And so the old and wise had spoken; this thing of using women to gain iron and cloth and weapons, they said, will make barren the pte as truly as the woman who stays with a husband for whom she cares nothing. But more important, woman as 'wakanka,' as one-who-sits-above-all, honors her man as the mother of his child; so let a man who acts on whim remember that he also throws away this honor. Perhaps this new way of discarding a wife puts fear in the woman's heart and she desists, but who wants a fearful wife? A gloomy woman?

And now, on top of these difficulties, something strange came along to discompose these same winter camps. A frightening mystery visited the Titonwan, killing three, four persons in each band.

The people, remembering that nothing like this disease had occurred in those seasons before whitemen came up the river, threw dark glances toward the trader's place. And then they set about the more important thing: trying out cures.

The peźuta washed their palms in sweet-scented smoke and gently pressed against the mysterious red blotches, something that appeared the fourth day on the face and body of the hurting. But the red spots stayed. Nor had these healers found a way to relieve the swollen, wet eyes and the warm skin and the running bowels.

Next, the people called upon their wapiya to scare the trouble back into the deadwood lodge from where most trouble seemed to come. But neither song nor fanning nor bathing in the stream chased away the rash. Then the seers went out to search the soggy earth of the snow-melting moon, these persons looking for a different grass with the power to overwhelm this strange disease.

Wanaġi tried boiling the leaf of a familiar stalk instead

of boiling the root or stem as before. He offered his concoction to the pežuta, and the Mahto healers, following instructions, washed certain persons with this water. But the splotches persisted.

Then Wanaǧi advised using the concoction as a hot drink. And so they gave this leaf-water to a man who lay down for eight days; his spots began to fade.

The next day a woman, hot and limp for eight days, swallowed two mouthfuls; they watched her redness disappear.

At once pežuta from all bands came to Wanaǧi for his powerful discovery, but none pondered this discovery more than Wanaǧi. For the leaves he had boiled came from the same stalk, the borage, which hastens the flow in a new mother's breast.

Will he find in one grass, the Mahto seer had asked himself, the power for curing any discomfort, for healing all wounds, for renewing the heart? Or will each different grass hold these powers, either in root, stem, leaf, or bloom?

And will the water that boils out the cure in this leaf, fade the red spots and cool the body? Or will this water cool the body and so the spots fade? Certainly the distress, if not the spots, lingers and persons die, mostly old persons. And so they shall not say that he, Wanaǧi, makes a powerful cure, not with people dying.

And now the disease hunted around the camps in search of children. And so many mothers began to prepare their own remedies, these women simmering bark and leaves of their own choosing and offering the warm drink in quiet tones, affectionate expressions.

And then many fathers, showing their alarm, took tongue-meat and hump to the sacred-lodge, smoking with the wapiya and making silent pledges to something they called 'grandfather' in their despair, something they called 'great mystery' in their calm.

But none among the Mahto attended the hurting children more perseveringly than Waňcawin, wife to Wanaǧi. The barren woman, now aware that she had passed through her childbearing seasons, cared for each child as if her own. Mothers welcomed her visits, and whatever smiles their children had left, they gave to Waňcawin.

149

Now suddenly Waȟcawin lay on her robe, eyes blurred, patches of tiny sores inside her mouth. And when Wanaġi brushed her hair on the fourth morning, he saw the redness behind her ears, saw the spots that came onto her face, spots that will travel down her body for all his efforts to put a stop to this thing.

Waȟcawin tried to make nothing of her distress, but on the seventh day she had not wanted to sit up. Wanaġi, hearing her cough, remembered that which happened when other persons coughed on the seventh, eighth day. He covered her with a second robe against the wind which sang of a sudden change back to cold weather, perhaps snow. And he covered her with a third robe when the white flakes fluttered down.

And now Wanaġi went out to walk alone with the snow, to reconsider this persistent disease. If this trouble comes upriver with the whiteman, then these strangers know something about the way to treat these spots; certainly they have cures for this thing if the disease belongs to their kind. He decided on a visit to the trader's place; perhaps his gestures will help make clear his phrases and so tell why he comes.

But he found the deadwood lodge closed and neither his scratches on the wood nor his courteous little cough opened the place to him.

Returning to camp, he pondered something that will let Waȟcawin sleep, not cough. Perhaps he will go back to the song that the grizzlies lend him for an occasion when he suddenly needs a spirit-helper, an occasion like now.

But the next day Wanaġi placed a fourth robe, a red robe, on the woman he had called wife, not a cover to keep out the cold but one that wraps his woman in death.

Above the wails, Wanaġi heard other voices, persons who said that they knew who killed Waȟcawin, who killed each one dying of this puzzling disease. Harmful spirits whom the whiteman calls on as helpers, they said. Harmful spirits like those invisibles who lay a fire in the whiteman's drink; they know, they said.

But Wanaġi had not said so; he will not know.

Above the wails, Wanaġi heard yet different voices, persons who said that they knew who killed Waȟcawin and each one who dies of this strange disease. A man who throws away his wife with a stick brings down trouble on everyone, they said. And they know.

But Wanaġi had not said so; he will not know.

Then, while the women stood weeping beneath the death-rack, Wanaġi heard one more voice. But the wapiya heard this voice with a different ear, an ear with the power to hear another man's thought.

And so Wanaġi heard the Mahto leader telling himself that he had led his people out of one danger into another; he had led his people beyond reach of the avenging Witapaha to a place within reach of the whiteman's mischief. And so eight in his Mahto band—four children among these eight—suffer and die, Tayaźo, the flute-man also dying.

But something spares his own lodge and so he will vow a thanks-offering. And he will perform his thanks in view of the people. And when they see him suffering, they perhaps will remember that they, the people, not Olepi, chose this wintering place.

Wanaġi had not said so; he will not know.

Perhaps I know with any certainty but two things, Wanaġi told himself as he slowly walked away from the death-rack; I know that from this day forward I live alone. And that I shall strive for a constant spiritual awareness.

I, Wanaġi, a descendant of the Wapaśa tiyośpaye, a family of custom-makers and custom-keepers; I, Wanaġi, a grandson who lives on the plain but one who shall demonstrate that he remembers his heritage.

XIII

THE MOON of high water and red grass hung in a moldy sky over the big river, but neither the color overhead nor the stickiness underfoot dampened Lakotah hearts. The running bowels disease had melted into the ground with the snow, and so the people sang as they made a game of discarding their winter playthings in the fast-moving river.

But then the newscarriers arrived, their sobering message putting a stop to soaring spirits and glad voices. The enemy to the south, they told, makes two miserable circles; the dread disease that puts holes in the face strikes the Oyatenumpa downriver. Perhaps the Lakotah remember when this killer stalks the Palani villages?

But the scabby mystery never reached the Titonwan. The muddy-water rose up defiantly, threatening to drown any trouble that approached. Then, when nothing appeared, the river calmed down and widened out, the water at rest before the next rise. Yet, once the river spread thin, danger in a different form used this calm to trespass.

Rumor had reached the Titonwan that a whiteman who wraps himself in a long black robe desired sitting with whoever among the wapiya will sit with him. The trader had said that this man not yet knows many Lakotah words but that he comes as a messenger, someone who brings the sacred story of his people.

Then before anyone ever considered inviting him, the blackrobe stood outside Wanaġi's lodge, the trader next to him, neither of these whitemen appearing to notice the hostile glances all around.

Inside the sacred-lodge the blackrobe seated himself and, after a little silence, began to talk. The trader, attempting a translation, stumbled over his own interpretation until finally he pointed to the iron cross that hung from the blackrobe's neck. Here, Wanaġi understood, the power-bundle of the whiteman. And the story, something about a mysterious woman who brings forth a mysterious child and when this youth reaches a certain age his people put him on crossed wood to thirst and starve. This event occurs when the mysterious young peaceman persists in his speeches for good will among relatives, for truth and generosity. Or so the blackrobe's signs and sounds seem to tell.

Certainly Wanaġi—any Titonwan—will understand putting a brave man to the ordeal, but will they fix this one on wood for reason that he walks a mysterious path or behaves in some unusual manner? And if these whites starve one person for this reason, will they perhaps starve any person who gestures differently?

Ptesanwin brings the Dakotah a pipe—something to live by—and a message that will see the people making-relatives and speaking truthfully and expanding their hearts. This message, this pipe, the people receive and accept as something good for each generation. But the woman who brings this wisdom will not seek adoration.

Will the mysterious woman of whom the blackrobe speaks ask that they adore her and her son? And for what reason? The Lakotah recognize mystery in every birth, wonder and mystery in every child. And who dares say that only certain persons own a voice that reaches the invisibles? Whoever has heart and tongue and soul owns the breath for reaching the invisible grandfathers. And each one shall decide for himself when, if ever, he shall use his breath in this wondrous way.

But one never speaks these personal concerns, Wanaġi told himself, and certainly he neither will tell nor want to tell this stranger about the wise counsel First Born offers Young Brother or the messages Pte-woman and Wambli-woman bring to the people. Truly he will desire only that the blackrobe go back to those people who send him as their messenger and say that a Lakotah listens respectfully. Nothing more.

But Wanaġi saw the blackrobe smiling, heard the trader saying that this one intends visiting other sacred-men in the Lakotah camps, here and upriver, bringing to each one the sacred story and offering the one true symbol. And now the blackrobe desires to make Wanaġi a gift of this cross he wears.

Wanaġi accepted neither the blackrobe's message nor his gift. Instead, he pulled his robe to his eyes and turned away his head; perhaps the trader will know that this gesture means that the Lakotah grows suspicious and wants nothing more between himself and the stranger. Wanaġi will not offer the pipe and he will not accept the cross—this much the trader sees—but will either one of these visiting strangers understand that the blackrobe speaks and acts not to strengthen Wanaġi but to depress him?

Red-sun-coming, red-sun-coming. Wanaġi heard the sharp-tail birds whose booming voices announce dawn; wiśahibu, they call, and then begin their dance. But the wapiya had not reflected upon these whirring wingeds of the grasses; their booming told only that he had used up the night pondering his meeting with the blackrobe. And that those many things not yet clear to him he will put aside for a different day, perhaps a different season. But the truly important he now understood.

Each Lakotah knows himself as something precious and the dignity in such knowing pulls him to his full tallness. So why this cross that bends a man? The sun's power reaches in four directions but this wondrous truth will not bring the Lakotah to his knees. So why this cross that bows a man?

The pipe, sacred? Not without a man's breath upon the stem. The sunpole, sacred? Only while a man dances beneath this wood.

But what difference whether truth raises a man tall or bows his head and bends his knee as long as none interferes with the ways of another? Everyone breathes with the breath of the great mystery; each one, a mystery within the whole mystery, a body within a soul, a knowing in contact with all knowing. Herein sits the true importance.

Wanaǧi stepped outside his lodge; he stood in the rain to greet the sun, the sun invisible, the sun above clouds. And now he sang as he sang each dawn, his heart above, next to the sun:

"Grandfather, I send a voice; hear me;
From this earth with your breath I send a voice;
Grandfather, I shall live."

XIV

THE PEOPLE, responding to the quacking flight of wings over the big river, bundled their tipi covers and began moving away from the winter campsite. And now word passed among the travelers that the wapiya carried neither the fire horn nor any other smoldering wood from which to start the next campfire. But everyone understood: who will want to kindle new flame from a memory of this past season?

The Mahto leader had known before ever the snow melted that he will need something more than new fire or the hissing water of an inipi to renew himself after this winter's turmoil; for this reason—and to renew all Titonwan—he had vowed to dance gazing-at-the-sun. And certainly, he told himself, he lives his pledge as Wanaǵi instructs; his hands touch neither knife nor arrow.

But walking front of his traveling band, Olepi reconsidered the only requirement he will find difficult: throw away any harsh thoughts. His resentment of the wašicun as intruders who bring a disruptive influence reaches the place where, sungazer or not, he intends to express his feelings at the opening council on the summer campground. Perhaps he shall begin his speech by asking whether a woman ladles more acceptable soup from an iron pot. Or he will ask whether the hunter truly prefers the firestick over the bow; will these sticks never break, never blow out, and will that which they call 'spring' always work? Most carefully he shall mention the firewater; will the Titonwan truly desire persons in camp who drown their reasoning power? Of what use this water that makes a man crazy, blind, and crying, perhaps wanting to kill?

The bands had raised the big tipi at the encampment on rapid creek and Olepi spoke as he had schemed. The Titonwan need neither firesticks nor firewater, he told the assembly, neither kettles nor cloth nor disease such as the strangers bring. "Tell me," he asked in a voice that dropped to a whisper, "will you, my kinsmen, trade anything in your nature for the nature of a whiteman?"

The Mahto leader knew he had spoken effectively; approval lighted those eyes in the front circle and approval sounded from those throats back of this circle. He had listened for this agreement from the warriors; who but the young men shall put a finish to the winters on the muddy-water? And a people who stay away from this river perhaps never encounter another waśicun, never again meet with this danger.

But sitting alone in the tipi after his speech, Olepi suddenly understood why his bitter resentment of the waśicun, a truth he never will speak aloud: the day already comes when he, Olepi, discovers fear. And in the humiliating form of a hairy face, a waddling walk. He, Olepi, who lives his child-winters and youth-seasons never knowing what fear means, who never experiences a fluttering belly or a chill in his backbone, who carries a wotawe on his original war party not as protection but as a remembrance from his boy-companion Wanaġi; he, Olepi, who will not understand until now that on the day he makes contact with the waśicun, he makes contact with fear and that this fear acts as danger not only to himself but to everyone, band and tribe.

But now he also hears clearly his familiar-voice: treat with this fear; destroy or keep away.

The sage came into bud and the talk hinted that those persons who dance at the big pole shall perform the ceremony in a new way. Here, on rapid creek, a great new strength shall become the Lakotah. They camp on clean earth near the sacred hill and their lodges glow with light from a new fire. And soon certain ones shall dance barefoot inside a brush lodge and gaze toward the sun in a most powerful manner.

First Born, the Dakotah grandfathers told, emerged from quivering red ooze, his face turned toward the sun. And so whoever offers thanks for an escape from difficulty shall gaze at this great yellow eye which gives man his nature, his growth, his joy.

Wanaġi had made certain before he gave instructions concerning the rituals that the sungazers recognized wiwanyag wacipi—dance looking-at-the-sun—not as a new ceremony in the lives of the Lakotah but as an old neglected one. Perhaps three hundred seasons past, he had told those persons who pledge the thanks-offering, the sun appears to a certain dreamer as a speaking-light. Soon afterwards different seekers demand the power of the sun in their visions.

156

And the sun, answering, delivers a power, especially to those Dakotah who desire helping the wounded. More than fifty persons, they tell, acknowledge favors from the sun, certain ones demonstrating their thanks, standing alone in some quiet place and gazing at the sky. Or perhaps making little cuts on the arm, letting the blood ooze. But after the Dakotah scatter out, these old ways fall to the ground.

But then, before ever the Lakotah cross the muddy-water, the people see someone demonstrating a new way to make the thanks-offering. He raises a pole, something that identifies the sun as father. Next, he hangs the skull of pte from his shoulders. And so he will dance around the pole for as long as his strength endures, the people looking on and encouraging him with murmurs and tears.

During the next eight, ten seasons different ones perform in this manner, the keeper of the original pipe unwrapping the bundle and exposing the stem while the dancers move around the pole. But drifting toward the muddy river and watching out for new things, the people neglect this ceremony.

Even so the people know that Wanaği dares paint his hands red and conduct the sungazing; they recall that an old, old seer in seasons past instructs Wanaği as to procedures and meanings, as to the importance of any vision that comes of this experience.

Since the day he voiced his sungazing vow, Olepi secretly had schemed to make an endurance contest of this affair. But after listening to Wanaği's account of past ceremonies, he had imagined something more exciting: he will demonstrate his thanks in a manner such as the people never before witness. Perhaps those nine who also pledge this dance will scratch their arms or breasts, but he, Olepi, shall demand cuts in his back. Next, he shall demand that they push sticks through these slits in his skin and that they tie a thong to these sticks. And to this thong they shall attach four pte-skulls. And then let the people see him shuffling around the pole, looking at the sky and dragging a load that tears out flesh; let the people become the ones who experience a vision, the memorable vision of a man who suffers for the good of each one, for the good of the whole. His name, Olepi.

Young Petala, told nothing about the sungazing ceremony, had watched the affair more interested than alarmed. He had seen the blood that dripped from those wounds in his father's back, but he also had heard his mother's joyous tremolo and the appreciative marveling of all those Titonwan who sat at the edge of the brush circle. He had recognized a certain bravery in the act his father performed, but the shuffling dance had lacked excitement and after a while he had sought his little friend Mahtociqala. The two had played at their own games, occasionally running up to one of the many cooking fires where smiling faces handed out generous pieces of meat. At sundown, his father and the other gazers dancing as before, Petala had gone looking for Unci, his grandmother; he had slept most of the night leaning against her shoulder.

Awakening at dawn the boy had observed that where ten once stood dancing only three persons looked at the sky, his father among these three. But until his mother came looking for him at Cankuna's fire, Petala had not known that the sungazing had finished at midday, that the skulls finally had dropped off his father's back and that now his father rested in the family lodge.

When Olepi awakened, the eyes upon him—wife and son—turned away quickly. But not before he saw the unguarded pride in the woman's face and not before he noticed the boy's striking resemblance to his mother. He smiled, then made a sound which brought Napewaste to his side. His hand reached out, touching her face, his fingers following along the smooth line of her cheek; so he let the woman know that he saw beauty.

"Teciñila," he murmured, giving voice to his affection, wanting her to know his feeling.

Petala, witnessing the joy on his mother's face and hearing her whisper, suddenly understood that he will not fit into this moment; quietly he slipped out of the tipi.

But walking toward Cankuna's lodge, the boy puzzled that which a woman means when she whispers to her husband, 'I give my heart, my soul.' For certainly his mother, her eyes shining, had whispered this phrase to his father.

XV

THE DAYS following the sungazing on rapid creek brought much meat into camp and many horses. The hunters returned without injuries, the raiders without losses. And any wounds, only small ones. Apparently the mystery-bundles carried tremendous power and certainly the thanks-offering dance had renewed the people. And so, the summer aging, the governing-four had decided to permit a raid onto ground not visited before.

Scouts had reported a rise in the earth north and west of the black hills. And beyond this rise, a river flowed through a quiet valley. Here the enemy they call Psa-toka grazed fine horses; and nearby, their big camp.

News of this enemy camp had tempted thirty Titonwan who wanted to form a new warrior-lodge. Hehlogeca, their leader, had experienced a most unusual vision, a dream involving a man who staked himself to the ground, then vowed to kill an enemy before he pulled up the stake. The vision also revealed a companion who rescued the staked man but not until he had witnessed the warrior's courage.

Hehlogeca had demonstrated his vision, three persons going along to watch him try the stake. They had painted red as in their leader's dream and they had dangled white feathers from the hair on top their heads. They had met the enemy and defied him in the manner of the dream.

Soon afterwards two more warriors had painted red and gone out as those original ones had gone. They, also, thrust a lance through a loop worn over the shoulder and stood before the enemy. But these two, going without Hehlogeca, had not returned. The enemy had run his lance through their hearts.

Now Hehlogeca desired testing the stake and sash once again; and thirty men will accompany him gladly, ten already demanding the sash. And so the four deciders had given consent.

The party, calling their lodge Miwatani, had gone out on foot, dewclaw rattles in their hands, whistles at their lips.

159

And at the final count six had pledged to use the stake in front of the enemy.

Two moons fattened and died, the thirty warriors not yet returning. Then the leaves piled up under the rustling trees and the air smelled ripe; the moon for making winter camps sat in the sky. But the Miwatani had not come back.

The people had known to wait only so long. Now they began bending twigs and arranging stones which showed the direction they move.

But before they had pulled down the lodges, two from the group who had counted thirty came back; the Psa had killed twenty-and-eight Titonwan, they told.

Heȟloġeca returned, one of the two survivors. But before he ever entered camp, he had known what risk he took: perhaps they will kill him and never hear his story. Instead, the deciders permitted him to speak in council.

Six warriors, Heȟloġeca reported calmly, had staked out in front of the enemy. Certain ones in the group, swinging their clubs, had killed three Psa. Next, pulling up their stakes, they had tried to release the remaining sash-wearers. Truly, all Miwatani had rushed out to help in this act. But suddenly many Psa had come from the woods, the enemy horseback and swinging stones, throwing arrows.

Remembering that he had come looking for this experience, Heȟloġeca stood firm. But soon he had used up his arrows and broken his lance. And so he had crouched back of a boulder, looking to see who in his party had escaped. If he lives and all other members die, relatives of the dead shall resent him, perhaps kill him. He will stay alive until he knows.

He saw one wounded Miwatani crawling into the brush and he had wondered whether other persons in his party hid in like manner. He had tried counting the fallen warriors, but the Psa had begun cutting up bodies, slicing pieces to fit their lances. And so Heȟloġeca had decided that someone among the Titonwan needs live and recover the bones after the enemy moves off.

The enemy had proved a long while moving off. They had stomped through the grasses and finally discovered the wounded man whom Heȟloġeca had seen get away; they killed this one instantly.

And now Heȟloġeca, his endurance used up, had

160

wished to die. Running out from his hiding place, he had invited the Psa to kill him. But the enemy appeared glad that one Titonwan yet lived, a warrior who shall take back the news of this defeat. They had ridden off looking back at Heȟloǧeca and laughing.

Soon after the victors had left, Heȟloǧeca had heard the emptying sigh of a man hurt to dying. He had followed the sound and so found the warrior Wanapin. The earth had soaked up much of this man's blood, but Heȟloǧeca had made a spread of the black-root powder he carried in the bundle tied to his bow. He had covered Wanapin's wounds and, while waiting for the weakened man to regain life, he had gathered up the remains of the killed war party. Wrapping the bones and flesh of these Titonwan in their own skin, he had hidden the death-bundles in cracks between the boulders.

He had watched over Wanapin many nights, and when the warrior showed himself strong enough to walk, the two had started back for the Mahto camp.

And so Heȟloǧeca told his story, Wanapin sitting nearby to voice the confirming sounds.

The councilmen had remained silent, their faces stern. But the women relatives of these dead had gone to the knolls to wail their grief, their cries a pathetic sound on the crisp air.

And now the Titonwan bands started out for the wintering places, their hearts on the ground, never a good way to travel. But the Mahto villages had not gone with these camps; the Mahto villages stayed.

Olepi, pipe in hand, walked among the dead campfires. He had not sought any mysterious ear; instead he had turned cool eyes inward, upon himself. True, he danced thanks for the difficulties spared him and different ones in his band, but he also danced to impress the headmen, members of the Pta-lodge; he wanted to increase his importance in the eyes of these leaders. But now he recognized a danger in his performance.

He remembered that which the old ones say about a sungazer who lacks humility: he who dances this ceremony as a boast or as a show-off perhaps attracts a destructive force, something harmful which hovers over the Titonwan a long while. Man shall boast his daring at the warrior's dance, not at a sungazing ceremony.

But certainly he had glimpsed something of the power in the sungazing affair and so perhaps some day he will dance again; perhaps he shall decide to match those scars on his back with similar scars on his breast.

He walked on, toward the slope, toward the Mahto horses, the herd looking cold and lonely under the cloudy morning sky.

His own herd, he reflected, had diminished since his becoming Mahto leader; he had given away without replenishing. He had gifted the grieving and he had provided for the have-nots, the truly needy in his band. He had honored his relatives with gift-horses during Huśte's name-changing ceremony and he had presented horses to Wanaǧi and to the wapiya's helpers for their acts during the sungazing. Whenever, in recent seasons, he had gone out on raiding parties, he had taken along youths who needed experience; he had provided opportunities for the young in his following to gain enemy horses.

He lifted himself onto a flat-top boulder along his path. His lips touched the pipestem and his gaze wandered off into the distance. He saw the tall, naked pole under which he had danced now a piece of wood without meaning, a tall lonely stick on the plain, patiently awaiting snow and cold.

The weathers, he told himself, the same weathers that he, leader of the Mahto, awaited. He had not sought the people's desires this season as to where they wanted to camp; instead, he had decided to let the weathers choose the winter campsite. The weathers will know where the Mahto belong this winter; the weathers know everything, the grandfathers had said, but man will need to listen.

He waved the stem of his pipe at the sky, at the ground, and in four directions. And then, jumping down from the boulder, he walked along with the wind toward his lodge, where Napewaśte will sit waiting to ladle the morning soup.

The staying-snow came before the Mahto band reached anywhere near the muddy-water, and certain persons had grumbled their dissatisfaction. Olepi's imprudent delay in breaking camp, they said, leaves the band out on the plain and far away from their relatives on the big river.

But a certain wapiya had recognized that Olepi rejoiced when wet, sticky snow stopped the travelers at the headwaters of the tricky stream they always followed. Certainly the Mahto leader had observed the turned-up horns of the moon which mean cold air and certainly he had seen the children running with their hands clasped in back, a sign of rain and snow; and most certainly he had heard the counsels of the old weatherwoman Tatewin, whose breasts forewarn the blizzards. Olepi, then, had schemed against a return to the muddy-water. And the powers had worked with him.

When the wet snow began to fall, scouts rode back with news of a sheltering butte and thick woods not far off from where the band raised a camp the night before.

And now many persons recalled the nice things about a winter along a small stream, men in the lodges and not wandering away to a trader's place. Perhaps this winter the old ones will tell again the stories and legends and perhaps old and young will play the snow games, their laughter something to lift all hearts. And who will grow lonely for visitors? The scouts say that a village of friendly Sahiela camp within an easy walk, these people aware and glad that the Lakotah approach.

When each Mahto family had found a place along the stream, the men stepped forward good-naturedly and began sweeping off the snow while their women unpacked tipi covers. The youth of the band, observing their fathers' gesture, offered help with the smoke flaps, and the girls, noticing, went off without an old woman's prodding to break ice and bring back water.

Olepi, looking on with light heart, recalled his father's counsel: never put yourself in the perplexing situation of living with uncertainty; when you know the good thing, act.

Olepi had known, he had acted. But in the event his people truly resented this wintering place, he had prepared a story about a recent dream that denied him evermore any view of the big river or a drink from those muddy waters. The story had not lacked truth, only that a vow and not a dream had decided this thing.

But soon the people began to show their contentment, each lodge engaging in whatever activities bring pleasure or comfort. In one small, worn tipi six old women settled down to kantasu, each one with her set of marked berry stones and a little wood bowl, each one ready to bet and win, bet and lose, on the toss of the big seeds. Here they shall sit, day and dark, their legs crudely spread, their tongues wagging coarsely, a group of women too old to attract notice.

And in a different tipi, near the edge of camp, four old men sat gazing at little piles of stalks, each man waiting his turn to guess even or uneven in any one pile. And who will care that dewclaw rattles and flutes—not horses and bows—change hands in this lodge of creased faces? For here sit men who perform only the most simple acts in return for soup and shelter, men who let their wives die before they die, men who live without desire but for the wagering of trifles on this old-man winter entertainment.

But the favorite game of the snow moons had begun in the hunter's big tipi where Ogle, his wife Cankuna, and their many relatives played hanpa ahpe, strike-the-moccasin, something that the onlookers enjoy as much as the players. And so Olepi, approaching this lodge one evening, heard drum and song and excited shouts; scratching on the cover, he marveled that someone heard, invited him inside.

Everyone in the lodge watched Ogle's brother Hinhan who, acting as hider, poised on one knee, singing and slapping at the moccasins in front of him, his hands moving swiftly from one to another. And while as many persons watched his face as watched his hands, none felt certain that he yet hides the small piece of horn, certainly none ready to say under which one of the six moccasins.

Pasu, holding two pointing-sticks, the light-colored stick personal and the dark-colored one for his team, waited for agreement among the guessers. But now, suddenly wanting to make a guess on his own, he used the sapwood, his personal pointer, to strike a moccasin, to flip over this certain one and perhaps see the little ball of horn underneath.

Hinhan had outwitted him. Pasu handed the pointers to a different player; the team needs a change, he said. Next, he tossed one of his counters onto the hunter's stack; he now owes Hinhan four arrows.

The betting had begun with bow and arrows but before sunset they will bet robes and tipi. And before midnight, horses. The game usually grew rough as the evening wore on, the guessers striking the moccasins with considerable force, none taking their losses lightly. But with Pasu and Ogle and other good-natures in this lodge, the Mahto leader will not look for any incidents that split a camp.

The hunter's family encouraged Olepi to play but he stayed only to join the singers in three, four game-songs, then went on to different lodges, a leader who will see a contented people wherever he visits.

The snow soon spread a thick white robe, each new fall lying heavily on the old, the hard-packed surface making a nice slide for the feathered rib-bones.

Small boys watched while their fathers sent the bones gliding toward a distant target, then teased the men into trying something different: will these fathers and uncles ride down this same steep hill in the rib-cages, racing their sons to the bottom?

Laughingly, the grownups let the young practice their persuasions before they gave in to this play. But soon the men will make all the runs, the children left clamoring for a turn.

On certain days the sun shone, and afterwards the snow became icy. And then Napewaśte and her women-friends came out to play ice-sliding, taking turns at skimming a stick or a ball on a straight course along a slippery path.

One day Olepi appeared in a group of men who came to observe the women, to challenge the outstanding players to a game of sliding-sticks. But while these persons stood by, Napewaśte rolled nothing but crooked balls and so she heard much teasing. Nor will they choose her for the team.

Afterwards Olepi had something to say to Napewaśte. But not teasingly. He had waited until they sat alone and he spoke sternly. His wife, he said, shall display indifference toward spectators and act naturally as when she plays with women. Or will confusion and inaccuracy in her game occur when she senses the presence of attractive young warriors among those men watching, young warriors whom she desires to impress?

Napewaśte had not answered. On one other occasion Olepi's remarks had hinted jealousy, but when she had smiled at this absurdity he had flashed her an angry glance. She had responded to the glance with a firm retort, some-

165

thing that perhaps had made him want to strike her. But then she had begun talking of different things, pretending this incident never occurred; born in a lodge of mild people, she intended to avoid any uprisings in her own tipi. The wise thing now, she decided, not to say anything, not ever to tell that Olepi's presence among the watchers had made her overly anxious and so she had lost control of the ball. Instead gladly she will give up this sliding-stick game and play at something where men never challenge the women or come around to watch their play.

The winter provided the people with clear days for walking, and so many persons went visiting the Sahiela. An alien tongue never hindered their games, smiles and laughter all they really needed. And something interesting usually came of these get-togethers. During one visit the Mahto mothers learned a clever way for removing hair from pte-hides they wanted to use for the bottoms of moccasins. The Sahiela women simply pointed to their little ones who slid on the snow, each child sitting on a small piece of hide to which the hair yet clung. A single day of this sort of play and they rub off the hair, the hide piece ready for cutting.

The Sahiela also came visiting the Mahto lodges; but the only Lakotah visitors in Olepi's camp this winter, those two sturdy men who dared cold and snow to bring news of Titonwan bands on the big river.

The Mahto had waited patiently while these newscarriers ate, smoked. Now, the pipe empty, the people gathered around to hear the man they call Wahosi.

"Whitemen," he began, his fingers showing forty in the party, "come upriver before the water freezes on the edges. Two whitemen lead the group, one man with hair red as flame."

So? The listening people will not marvel red hair; Hehlogeca once reported redheads among those earth-lodge bands living up the river. But Wahosi's next words brought forth sounds of surprise.

The whitemen bring a helper, this person's whole body black, head to feet. Will any Titonwan ever tell of seeing a man born black, a black-whiteman?

Wahosi spoke on, the people again quiet, attentive:

"The whitemen invite leaders from different Lakotah camps onto the water to view the many strange things they carry upriver. And soon Red Hair offers the headmen a mouthful of drink, something dark and burning.

"This party of whites brings a peace-sign," Wahośi told now, "not a pipe and not a cross but cloth that they paint red and white and sky. This banner they give to a visiting Dakotah—a man from the Minikayawoźupi band—who fastens the colors on a tall pole. And so the whiteman's peace flutters overhead while Red Hair and his friends council with the Lakotah and those Mnikooźu—so most Minikaya-woźupi speak of their band—who stay nearby."

The people had honored their white visitors with a dog-feast and the long-stem pipe. And then someone sang a welcome, after which the Lakotah waited to hear for what purpose these whitemen come up the muddy-water.

But neither Titonwan nor Mnikooźu had understood the answering talk, and so they called a trader, asking that he make sense of the strange sounds.

These persons come, the trader had interpreted, to gaze on the muddy river and for a friendly visit with all peoples who live along this water. They come to learn that which the Lakotah desire; what things shall the great leader of the white nation, a man who stays where the sun rises, send his Lakotah children?

The Lakotah had remained silent. They knew of nothing they desired but what they already secured in trade with one another or through gifting or perhaps at the deadwood lodge. And who dares call these Lakotah his children before they choose him as father or grandfather?

The people had listened to yet more strangeness: will the Lakotah desire sending their chief to meet with the white father, someone to speak for the tribe, name their wishes?

Chief? What meaning in this word, the Lakotah had wondered. And what one man ever dares speak the wishes—or needs—of any other man? Each Lakotah owns a tongue; who asks for a spokesman? But they will not dishearten at news of someone among the whites who intends protecting the bands from interfering travelers, from corrupt traders.

But why will Red Hair and his companion ask for a

count of the Lakotah, of each band? Also a count of lodges in a band and a count of wives in a lodge? Who instructs these wašicun that they behave in this rude manner?

None among the Lakotah ever questions someone as to his personal concerns, yet these whitemen ask to what 'gods' the Lakotah 'pray.' Gods? Pray? The blackrobes speak of mystery saying 'god' or 'son-of-god.' The Lakotah speaks of mystery saying 'mystery' or 'great mystery.' Or, seeking a relative term, the Lakotah will say 'grandfathers.' And so who, these gods the whiteman mentions? The Lakotah sends a voice demanding that all mystery attend him. Will the wašicun call this act 'pray'? And what means this word 'forgive' they use so often?

But why make something of this difference in people? The whiteman will go on living his nature and the Lakotah will go on living his different one. Perhaps the trader knows phrases for putting this understanding into the whiteman's tongue and so these inquisitive strangers will stop asking questions.

Wahoši paused; he had sensed disdain, heard some muttering during his narration. But only now, glancing at Olepi, will he glimpse something he dares call loathing.

Even so, he, Wahoši, will need to go on, to make clear to the Mahto people that Red Hair and his companions come as scouts making a trail, preparing the way for those many strangers soon to arrive. "The white father sends out these forty to name the buttes and streams. And so the wašicun who come afterwards shall not wander off the path."

Again the newsman paused; perhaps he will try bringing laughter into his talk. He will tell of the 'šica,' the tricky-water stream which the whitemen say they name 'titon,' Red Hair proclaiming that this renaming of the waterway honors the Titonwan tribe.

Wahoši heard a little laughing but not the laughter that makes a person feel good. Hoȟ! These white name-givers identify the Titonwan with something wet in winter, disappearing in summer? Hoȟ! These strangers so eager for changes. Let these whitemen change a stream's nature before they change a stream's name. But look out, if ever they try changing the nature of the Titonwan.

Icamani, second of the newscarriers, now took over the reporting. He described Red Hair as a brave man, not easily bluffed. One Mnikooźu had used an insulting gesture while demanding more smoke-leaves, but Red Hair, perceiving, had remained firm, even reaching for his lance. Afterwards, the white leader had extended his hand—the waśicun sign for making-friend—but the Mnikooźu had refused to touch fingers with Red Hair or his moody companion.

During the meeting on the river the Lakotah had danced for these whites, ten men at the drum and four more on the songs. The Titonwan women had displayed their men's lances, and the warriors, wearing brightly quilled leg-covers, had performed their war stories.

Red Hair and his companion had boasted on meeting the Lakotah that whitemen fear nothing. But after a second look at the fresh scalps and the painted dancers, the two white leaders had seemed anxious to get away; they had left before the night reached middle, before the drum really had begun to speak to the dancers.

Villages on the river had raised smoke, signaling those Siyo who camped upstream of the whitemen's presence, and so the next day the Siyo band danced for the strangers. After the ceremony someone reported many packages of pipe-smoke on the river where the twenty-and-two paddles waited. At once some Okandada began scheming a way to take this prize.

Siyo leaders spoke against this action but they had not convinced the unruly ones. Then certain Mnikooźu stepped forward and talked with the whites against these Okandada, this talk starting trouble among relatives. Truly these white messengers, like all waśicun coming among the people, provoke the lodges.

But now, before Icamani shall say anything more about this meeting on the river, Olepi began to speak, the Mahto leader abruptly changing the talk and asking for news of relatives wintering on the earth-smoke.

More than one person looked curiously at Olepi, marveling his display of rudeness, astonished at this interruption. But Olepi seemed unnoticing; he waited for Icamani to give the news he wanted to hear.

And so the newsman told that the Sicanġu on the

earth-smoke had scorned a friendly Palani pipe. Then, a most reluctantly, Icamani spoke of a party of Sicangu–Okandada in the group—who had surprised an Oyatenumpa village, destroying forty earth lodges. Those scalps which had hurried Red Hair away from the dancing came from th heads of the two-circle people, and many captives from thi enemy camp now lived in the Titonwan camps on th muddy-water.

But Icamani had avoided giving more facts on thi story; he had not said that Red Hair instructed the Sicang as to the proper conduct with these captives, that he ha scolded the Lakotah and then demanded that they retur these women and children and make friends with th Oyatenumpa.

Nor will the newscarrier tell that the Sicangu, lookin for gifts from Red Hair, had agreed. Instead he turned th reporting back to Wahosi.

"The Titonwan on the mud-water starve." Wahos spoke bluntly. "They starve and so certain husbands sen their wives and children to the trader's place. These mother sit holding little ones at their breasts and begging for food But the traders only point to the dead white leaves and ask for those robes and hides the Titonwan pledge the winter before.

"The women return to camp but angry husbands send their wives back to the whitemen without their children. Even so the traders scorn these women."

Again Olepi interrupted, asking about the relatives of those killed sashmen. And so Wahosi told of the grieving fathers and brothers who traveled up the good river, where they sought the makings of a revenge party.

The Mahto warriors, hearing Wahosi tell this news, glanced at Olepi, their eyes hinting that they also belong in a camp where men smoke a red stem and vow a war-on-horseback. Certainly the Mahto leader will anounce here and now his intent to go out as an avenger, perhaps leader of the avenging party. But Olepi only sat, his face distant, his lips closed.

Puzzled, then angry, the men flashed their mood in Olepi's direction, but the leader seemed indifferent to these glares and rising murmurs.

The newsmen, now finished with talk, moved among the people, gathering up messages for kinsmen back on the muddy-water. And then these hardy ones had gone. But they had left the Mahto band enough news for thought and comment throughout the remaining cold moons.

Soon after the newsmen left, a deep white covered their trail, all trails leading toward the muddy river, a snow to try the endurance of any traveler, but one that favored the Mahto.

The people, blackening cheeks against the danger of sore eyes and frostbite, went out to kill the meat that floundered in the drifts near their lodges, even children making kills. Soon the teasing smell of roasts hovered over camp, and so Olepi wished for all who sniffed the air to remember that news of lean and hungry people on the muddy-water.

But certainly he' will not speak of those camps. His blood heated whenever he recalled that a Lakotah—any Lakotah—dared send his woman to a wašicun's sleeping robe in trade for a full belly or a mouthful of firewater. True, such Lakotah have neither standing nor respect within the tribe, but will the whiteman perceive this truth? A man's demands on his wife shall not concern others, but compelling a woman to offer some stranger her body in trade for a kettle of soup differs greatly from the offer of a modest, good wife to an important visitor from inside the tribe.

What happens to Oowešica and Wacape, men who walk front, where the people will see and emulate? What good will they look for within reach of those traders or any stinking wašicun who appears on the scene? At the start of the cold moons these leaders scurry back to the trader like so many grassbirds running for the shelter of the mother-wing. Why?

Napewašte, seeing her man's face as he puzzled these things, had wondered what dark mystery surrounded Olepi that he barely remembered son and wife. Neither the laughter of the moccasin game nor the earnest voice of council enters her lodge; a strange and lonely tipi, this one.

And so mother and son began sitting close, something

most unwise. For in this closeness lurked the makings of a little-husband, the boy who trails at his mother's heel, a son who receives favor over the father, a boy who stays boy and never really becomes man, someone about whom the people say, 'they never cut the birthcord between these two.'

When Olepi's distant manner carried over into the snowblind moon, Napewaśte grew most apprehensive; what distress will prolong her husband's mood?

Then one morning Olepi invited councilors and warriors to his lodge, and, after emptying the ashes of two smokings, he began his speech: "My friends, you look at a man who will dance twice gazing-at-the-sun. I again prepare for this ceremony at the pole."

He saw at once that he confused his listeners, and so he gave reasons why he will dance again; he wanted each one here to understand.

When he danced before, he said, he had offered thanks for sorrows spared most Mahto lodges. The only man ever to knot the skulls in his flesh, he had dragged these heads as a symbol of the death his people had left behind.

But while he danced he had felt a pain in his breast. Something will tell him to remember that death and sorrow always walk alongside the people; they never truly leave these things to the past. The pain in his breast—perhaps in his heart—had persisted until suddenly he understood: the agony comes when the people throw down the old Dakotah way.

"Many seasons now," he said softly, "the people choose to honor stranger above relative. The pain I suffer—the pain that drags me down—I now recognize as neglect.

"Even as the big white dog of the ledges—the true-dog—pulls down the wilting pte, so shall neglect pull down a wilting man and kill him, so shall neglect pull down a wilting people and destroy a tribe."

He paused but before anyone grew uncomfortable he spoke on. He said that he saw the people neglecting the one rule of the tribe: remember yourself as a good relative.

"And so this summer I will tie myself to the four powers and stand at the center of the winds. Here I stay until the thong in my breast falls away. Here I stay until the thong they tie in my back falls away. Here I stay until these ties break, until I see the old way, the good way, returning to the people."

Olepi had spoken and the men filed quietly out of the lodge. Those warriors who had imagined that they came to hear the Mahto declare himself leader of a revenge party against the Psa now accepted this man's choice, that which commits him to a second sungazing. But perhaps only Wanaġi, the man to whom Olepi originally pledged this second sungazing, truly understood why Olepi shall dance twice, suffer twice.

What different way, the wapiya asked himself, will this Mahto find for protecting his people from the whiteman? If a fear of these wasicun edges up to the heart of Olepi who never experiences fear, most certainly this same fear shall dip into the hearts of the people. And the strength of the Titonwan—as Olepi sees his people—sits in their arrogance, many daring acts to back this pride, daring acts and remarkable courage. But once afraid—once fear breaks through the hoop—the people will trample each other, each one losing trust. And so Olepi, whose image portrays the arrogant warrior, needs to display again his courage against fear of the unknown.

And why will Wanaġi understand this thing? He, also, will hold on to a fear of the wasicun, not fear of iron weapons in the hands of many, many whitemen but something different, something that relates to the blackrobe's visit.

If ever the Lakotah throw down the pipe and take up something different, he had told himself, they throw down the tribe. For nothing—nothing—ever shall sit above the pipe. The pipe, meaning truth; the pipe, meaning the old Dakotah way. The pipe, a way of life that works.

Napewaśte recognized now why her husband had sat aside from family and friends this winter, but the anxious look returned to her face. Will her son ever know the blood-sister and she, the daughter for whom she yearns? Will Olepi ever again prepare her for a child, ever again make her desiring and desirable through bathing and drying and fondling, through ceremony designed for those two who will conceive? The sungazing preparation means four more moons that he shall abstain from any acts involving weapons or woman. And after the sungazing, will he not want weapons and warriors, not woman?

When ever will he come to her robes again?

The Mahto folded their lodges in the dust of the windy moon and followed Olepi downstream, the people surprised that their leader headed this direction and not toward the black hills. Nor will he keep to the familiar trail.

Turning north before they reached the muddy-water, Olepi led the band up a winding brush-lined gully. Beyond the gully-head they came upon a flat of weak and slender grass; a ridge of buttes rose up in the near distance. Water trickled in a tiny lost voice over this plain, but along the bottom edge of the ridge clusters of trees marked the passage of a stream that flowed summer-long. Here stood white-wood and weapon-wood and the yellow-wood that provides stalks for the counting-sticks; also those thickets that will turn red with berries—small berries and big, tart berries and sweet. And here not only the red-stems but many more useful grasses, quill grass and sinew grass, the tough water-grasses and the mild, sweet-smelling grasses, and grasses that children will use in their play.

The band had traveled on barren ground to reach this place and now they murmured their pleasure at the sight of these standing-people and the many boulders and pebbles, ancients and grandchildren of ancients.

Here, the hillside stones for the cooking paunches and the river stones for pounding and pounding-on; here, something to wrap with thong and make a swinging-club; and here the paint-stones, something soft and sandy and easy to scratch into a red or yellow powder.

Olepi and the men who walked front with him heard the appreciating sounds as the people now came up. And so when all persons had gathered at the knoll, the crier called out that here the people shall camp for the summer. The Mahto will send out an inviting party, urging all Titonwan bands to raise the great summer hoop on this site. And so let the Mahto women put up their lodges with a view toward a long stay.

● ● ●

174

Olepi remained alone on the knoll, gazing over the earth that stretched into the east, into the approaching dusk. But suddenly he sensed that he stood not alone. He smiled, seeing that Petala had come to stand alongside him, the boy looking, acting tall.

"My father," he said quietly, "I ask that my friends speak of me as Peta, not Petala. I grow. I am not a little boy. Perhaps my father notices and so he also will say Peta."

Suddenly as he had appeared, the boy went away. And the man, marveling his son's request, remembered back to his own child-seasons and to the original bearer of this name, Peta.

Will a boy know when he ripens? Will he know even before his parents know when he dares leave off the diminutive and take on a name demanding a bigness beyond that which most men ever achieve? Will Petala understand that remembering himself as Peta from now on prepares him for bigness, for greatness?

The sun climbed down and Olepi, feeling the chill, came from the knoll to the tipi awaiting him. Walking toward his lodge he remembered his pledge to dance a thanksgiving for the good that sits ahead of the people, for the good things out of the past. Then certainly he dances thanks for this good name, this name Peta which lives again on the plain.

XVI

THE BREEZE flowed gently off the ridge, the warm breath of a young summer morning wafting under the slightly raised edges of sixteen Mahto lodges. A pair of warrior-birds climbed the clear, deep sky and meat grazed the distant plain; the great mystery loaned the people another good day.

> *"This tribe, this pte-tribe,*
> *Hoofs of pte drumming on earth. . . . "*

Olepi sang the people's song as he mixed fat with powdered charwood in a bowl, the container black from much use.

Peta stood watching his father. The man prepared the paint for him, something to smear on his face, something to let everyone know that he, Peta, accepts a challenge not to eat on this day.

Peta had not told who challenged him to starve, but Olepi had observed the boy's reluctance to wear the paint.

"My son will look more like a returning warrior whose party brings back horses than a youth of ten winters who vows he will starve for a day." The mixture ready, Olepi streaked the boy's face.

"My father," Peta spoke up abruptly, boldly, "I go and water the herd. Afterwards, I shall ride your hunting horse."

Olepi had given away two runners during the winter and so Peta's demand meant using the one hunter remaining in his herd.

The boy waited for the denying gesture but, seeing none, he slipped away, his heart suddenly light as a feather.

The moment Peta disappeared, his mother came quickly out of the lodge. Using forked sticks, she lifted hot stones from the fire into the cooking paunch, enough to start warming the soup. But Olepi wanted this soup at once; will Napewaśte not know that the boy, not her husband, starves this day?

Suddenly he understood her delay. "My wife's son," he said evenly, "rides a horse, not his mother's back. Why scheme ways which make things easy for him? The boy smells the meat of different fires if not his mother's cooking."

Napewaśte's eyes sought the ground and Olepi remembered that a man pledged to the pole says nothing harsh to anyone.

"Your son tries out my runner this morning." He spoke pleasantly. "I am glad that, at ten winters, this boy prepares for the chase."

Napewaśte had not looked up. She regretted her foolishness and she chose not to see her husband sitting before an empty bowl, waiting for something to simmer.

Olepi stood now and making the small sound that bade her follow him, stepped inside the tipi.

The woman's heart quickened. She will not fear punishment from a stick—Olepi never had struck her—but she will dread another reprimand, another of those occasions when he will sit her down and make known his displeasure.

But Olepi had not considered reviewing his wife's neglects when he motioned her down next to him. Instead he had begun painting her cheeks, not with the black stripes this same finger put on the son's face but with the red circle that speaks of a husband's affection for his wife.

She caressed his arm, and Olepi, smiling, drew his finger along the divide in her hair; he will make this other recognized sign of a man's fondness for his woman.

Then gently he asked that she ride with him while he hunted an underground water in some shady ravine beyond camp. This much he spoke, but his eyes went on to tell her that he knew the uneasiness for a wife whose man twice pledges the sungazing, her lodge these past winters like one without a man. Perhaps this little ride out of camp in the proud way of husband and wife together will bring her heart new gladness.

And the woman, looking into the dark eyes that searched her face, made answer with a smile that accepted his invitation and sent his own heart soaring.

Peta took his father's runner far out from the village; the boy wanted none watching while he tested himself for agility and daring on this fast horse.

He soon located a pte-shape boulder and prepared for his run, but then he heard someone shouting at him. Glancing back over his shoulder he saw four young men, one of these persons Slukila, who had challenged him to this hungry-day, the same Slukila who six winters past had burned seeds on his wrist. He recognized Slukila's companions as those certain youths who always rode together, the group striving for recognition as an akicita-lodge, this recognition not yet coming.

"Hiyu wo," they called but Peta stayed.

177

The party surrounded the boy. "Come along," they demanded; "take your turn at belly-mounting."

Peta hesitated. He liked none of these persons nor had he any interest in the stunt they proposed; the game will wear out his father's runner.

"I see a weak heart," Slukila taunted. "This one fears he will get hurt."

The youths laughed; they began to throw their scorn at Peta.

The boy jumped down from his horse; he will not accept ridicule from drifting Okandada. "Start him off," he said, handing the runner's cord to the youth nearby. "I will take my turn now."

"Not here," someone protested; they want flat, bare ground. And so they rode their horses, Peta along, to a smooth place, sparse of grass and stone.

Peta missed on his jump. His leap put his belly over the runner's back, but when he tried to throw over his legs and come into position, he rolled off.

Each one in Slukila's group made a good jump and so Peta determined that his second try shall put him horseback. But now Slukila called for the canoźake, the fork-tree mount, the boy told to stand last in line.

While he waited his chance, Peta wondered whether hunger had affected his jump. The next instant he laughed inside his mouth at this feeble effort to persuade himself that a full belly means more in this stunt than an accurate eye, a strong arm, a fast leg. Even so, he threw out a silent plea to whatever spirits hovered around; he shall appreciate a lift onto the runner's back when he swings up.

He heard a whoop; he saw his horse coming. Run, grab, jump.

The runner swept by, the boy grabbing a handful of mane. He swung up, legs forked, the air helping. Now on and staying on.

He heard the heart-lifting cheers that a Lakotah never withholds when someone earns those cheers.

He wished that Iku, a warrior-friend twice his age, had seen this jump. Iku, uncle to Mahtociqala and like an uncle to Peta, had taught him the fork-tree mount. Iku will feel proud when he hears that Peta jumps onto the back of a runner. . . .

Hoḣ; suddenly he understood why he missed on the belly-mount; never before had he belly-jumped onto a horse as tall as his father's runner.

But perhaps Iku will wonder at Peta's wanting to boast any jump. An escaping man dares not wait for a horse that pleases him; instead, he grabs on to any horse that will take him out of the enemy's reach. A man shall learn to mount quickly and from any direction, whether moving horses, unfamiliar horses, fearful horses. Iku had said so.

The youths persisted at their game until, weary and thirsty, they stopped to hunt a gully with water. Then while the four drank and ate, Peta rubbed down his horse.

"I feel for you," Slukila teased. "You starve."

The young men chewed noisily on the meat bones they had brought along on Slukila's advice. The bully had proposed that they chase after Peta and he intended to make the young boy's trial entertaining for his friends.

Hunger had ceased to annoy Peta, but he regretted that this group interfered with his own scheme for the day, with his tryouts on the runner.

Suddenly Slukila held out a juicy bone. Stepping up to the boy, he touched the tip to Peta's nose. "Bite, my friend," he mocked.

Peta pushed away the meat. "I am not starving," he said, and instantly wished he had not spoken.

"Perhaps you thirst." A different voice teased, and now someone flung water from his hands against Peta's face. At once the other youths squirted mouthfuls at the boy.

Peta wiped the wetness from his eyes and then, neither smiling nor sullen, turned his back to the young men. The next instant he jumped horseback.

But almost as quickly the youths grabbed his horse, pulled him down.

"You run off after berries which you will eat in hiding," they goaded.

"I return my father's runner to his herd," Peta answered. "Let me go."

Slukila spit a laugh at the blackened face. "I hold you here for a different game. I will see who stays horseback. If none upsets you, go."

Knocking-off-horses had become a favorite contest among boys, Peta enjoying this game as much as anyone. He appeared small alongside this group of contestants, but even Iku had difficulty knocking him off a horse. And so most willingly he let Slukila and his friends try.

They got into the game quickly, horses snorting and rearing as each rider strove to push off a different horseback yet retain his own balance.

Peta became the target for all Slukila's attacks. He rushed at the boy whenever he imagined him unprepared, but Peta eluded these bold attempts. Soon the game turned into a contest between the two, the other players stopping to watch.

Slukila had counted on his friends to find a way of diverting Peta, perhaps a sudden yell or a pretend attack; instead he heard these youths admiring the boy's show of vigor.

"Make a go of this game," they shouted and so encouraged Peta to keep up.

Anger overcame Slukila; unlike the day when he had burned those seeds on Peta's wrist, he dared not risk any mischief here. Someone watched this affair, onlookers fully aware of Peta's clever evasions. Not easily will he humble the son of Olepi.

During their next clash Peta almost upset his challenger. And Slukila, truly irritated now, struck his own horse a blow. The startled creature stumbled, then began to limp.

"Why play against a child?" Slukila yelled jeeringly; "I will let the boy go. Ho, iyaya yo."

Peta rode away slowly. He had wanted to examine the lame horse, but Slukila, raising an arm in angry protest, had whipped his mount and ridden off, his friends laughing but following after him. And so none stopped the son of Olepi now from finding again the pte-shaped stone.

Evening came and Peta started back toward camp, his heart on the ground. He had located the boulder, then urged the runner into little dashes at this pretend-pte. Yet not once had he dared ride close enough to strike the big stone with his pretend-lance. Sensing that he lacked the power for true contact between himself and horse, he had lost the will for any more tries.

And so he imagined that he, Peta, lacks courage for the

hunt, a boy who never shall touch the tail of the little yellow-hair pte who runs at the rear of the herd. And something more disquieting, he perhaps spoils his father's runner for the chase, something none will overlook, not even one's grandfather.

Approaching the place where the Mahto herds grazed, Peta decided to stay through the night with the horses; he will keep watch over the runner until certain that this one suffers nothing from the experience.

He climbed down off the horse and, stooping wearily, put a restraining tie on the creature's front feet. Then he settled himself against a tree, intending to sit guard until dawn.

The boy-tenders who came at dusk to take their turn at night-watching saw Peta under the tree, but they gave him only enough notice to observe that he slept most soundly.

Night spread across the sky and now Olepi, mounting the war horse he had staked outside his lodge, started out in the direction Slukila pointed. The man, in preparation for the sungazing, rode without weapons, yet he will search the lost son on enemy ground—if he needs go so far.

But Olepi knew where to look. His sharp eyes saw the runner hobbling away from the lonely tree, saw the dark bundle propped up against the wood.

Soon afterwards the man came up behind the tree; he stood looking on the smeared young face and the tangled loops of black hair. And so looking, he desired nothing more than to lift the son in his arms, to carry this sleeping one to the lodge and lay him gently on the robes. Instead, Olepi dropped to his knees alongside the boy. And now he gave out so fierce a yell that the most distant horses flicked their ears and the ones nearby reared up, and certainly the boy-tenders came running.

Peta struck out at the noise. Then, catching himself, he pressed back against the tree to hide his shaking. His shame crept over him; he had missed on this simple test.

A boy, they say, shall awaken from deep sleep, alert as the grizzly and ready for fight. Or he shall know when to sit unmoving and look for the danger through narrowed eyes. But never, never shall he let out a cry and fling his arms and shake until his teeth click.

Silently Peta arose. He saw the young herders going

back to their places, quieting the horses as they moved among the herd. But he had seen in his father's eyes the regret that will show when a son proves wanting.

Back again in the lodge, Peta yearned for talk with Huśte, the favorite uncle who sat this night in the visitor's space. But the man had not given him so much as a glance. And the sternness on his father's face kept him in a respectful posture for whatever reprimand will come.

After a long, uncomfortable wait Olepi spoke. But he said only that his son always shall report his return to camp; he said nothing about a worn-tired horse that Peta had kept on the run all day.

The boy wished he dared tell of those youths who demanded that he join their games and about his fork-tree mounts. But perhaps his family already knew; his father usually knows everything.

And if they know, will father and uncle regard as nothing this day of starving, those leaps onto the back of a running horse—a tall horse; also his staying horseback while different youths—big boys—try knocking him to the ground? Will this family regard him as someone who never dares misbehave and yet never gets praise for behaving?

And now his father's gesture sends him to the sleeping robes like the child Slukila dares call him. Truly, this lodge will see him humble.

For one brief moment Peta wished himself the son of any different man in camp.

The boy intended to lie awake a long while, to lie eyes open and resent his father, resent this man who frightens, then embarrasses him. Instead, he fell asleep wondering whether he had acted like a child.

The next day the crier's strong voice called a greeting to the sun and then announced the party that will leave for the muddy-water, carrying gifts to Titonwan bands on the big river, inviting these relatives to make the hoop this summer here at pahamni ridge—or so they name this campground.

Peta heard the crier but he pretended to sleep. Remembering his disgrace of the previous day, he chose to avoid all eyes in his mother's lodge. But now the crier called out his name, the man mentioning Peta as one who goes.

He lay quiet, marveling. Who chooses him? True, they

will take along two, three boys when a party of men goes out for any purpose, assigning these youths work, rewarding these youths in terms of experience. But Peta knew himself young for this honor, this privilege of staying out with the men. And what about his shame from the day before?

Now, hearing his name again, he leapt from his sleeping robe, his leap almost as good as the one that had lifted him onto the back of his father's runner.

The camp-dogs scattered before him as he whooped his way to the stream, where he jumped in and came out of the water before the men bathers recognized who or what had made the big splash.

Then he stood waiting at the lodge flap with moccasins and bow, his little horse nearby. And looking on, watching Peta's every move with admiring eyes—Mahtociqala.

Aware of the boy's gaze, Peta turned his eyes joyously but briefly in Mahtociqala's direction; his excitement mounting, he dared risk nothing more than this quick glance.

The past two, three seasons Peta had recognized Mahtociqala as someone too young for a constant companion. Even so, he often found himself wandering toward Cankuna's lodge, wanting to share his play with Mahtociqala, with this boy who always seems more a young brother than friend.

But on this day he, Peta, needs identify himself with the men, not with a boy of seven winters, someone whom the people will regard as yet a child.

Ten-and-four men went out as inviters, Peta the young one of the group and proudly carrying the moccasins for seven. Some pairs he tied on his back; others he fastened across his horse; every party, he knew, carried these extra feet, the men prepared for escape if they lose their mounts.

The inviters, traveling on soggy ground, rode cautiously, but one foolish horseback had wanted to race. Gnuśka—the hunter's first-born now in his twelfth winter—rode his horse in little dashes. Moving forward by jumps, he chased the tall-ears and tried to run down the pronghorn. Twice the men reproved him, but Gnuśka, smiling slyly, stayed in his place only until another swift-footed creature caught his eye. And so, catching sight of a traveling-dog, he quirted his horse into a truly fast run.

183

Darkly the men watched this one who ignored their advice, who raced on mire. And soon they saw his horse go down, the rider flung over the creature's head.

The youth struck soft mud and his body, curling like a shell for the fall, slid over the slippery earth. He jumped up, laughing and unhurt. But the men saw his horse as finished, a front leg snapped off above the hock.

Certain members of the party wanted to make the boy kill his suffering horse; different persons said the Gnuśka's use of a knife will bring the creature more agony. Yet on one thing they agreed: Gnuśka shall witness the killing.

Unsmiling now, Gnuśka rode double behind Peta as the party moved on toward the muddy-water. The youth saw that none took notice of him, the men acting as if they had left him back with the dead horse.

But truly, each person in the group looked out for this unruly one. For here rode a party of respected peacemen, ones who had made their names as warriors but who now hunted and gave counsel, men whom the people call 'the backbone of the tribe.' These persons knew that Gnuśka required lessons in restraint and they knew that this single experience out with men will not effect any big change in the youth. But they intended to awaken him to his lacks.

Ogle, desiring that this son have the example of ones who follow their leader and obey the council, had hinted to Olepi that they permit Gnuśka to go along. And so the Mahto leader had arranged this thing, Olepi deciding that his own son will gain something from contact with these men. And he had appointed Heȟaka leader for the duration of their travels, this mild but firm man a good influence on the young.

Grouped around a small fire this same night, the men drew their robes up to their eyes whenever Gnuśka moved in close, their gesture showing distrust, signifying disdain. Nor had anyone offered him wasna, the scout-meat which a small party always carries and eats cold. Not that the men refused him food but simply that Gnuśka dared not reach.

And when finally the youth slept, he lay on an aching shoulder and a flat belly; even so, these hurts seemed as nothing when compared with his frightening dreams.

The morning of the fourth day the travelers met scouts from Oowesica's band, truthbearers who, waving robes from a knoll, signaled their people that kinsman approached.

Viewing these robes, the girls in camp had run to see about their hair and paint while their mothers ran to see about the meat supply. And a messenger hurried out to the Siyo villages.

The Okandada feasted their visitors on arrival, the women bringing up meat until even the big-bellies, satisfied, turned over their food bowls. Now, the pipes refilled, the guests smoked and listened to more talk of those events along the river this past winter, more talk of those whitemen who give away peace medals along with scalping knives.

Red Hair, someone told, had wanted to remember Lakotah ways and so he had marked on a dry white leaf in the same manner that the trader kept record of whoever owed him a robe. But Red Hair's little black talking-signs said nothing about robes; instead, he had recalled the story of the brave men who staked down before the enemy, also the dog-feast and the scalp-dancing. And then he had scratched on a big, big dry leaf the new names he had given each river and stream and island along the muddy-water, even the muddy-water newly named. But mostly he had used names belonging to the tribes, honoring the different 'Indians'—whatever this funny word means—he had met on his travels.

But the Okandada told something that took the amused look off these Mahto faces. These strangers, they said, wrap a Dakotah child in their peace-cloth and then prophesy that this one shall become friend to the whiteman.

Truly, these whites a meddling people, the visitors murmured, something for the Titonwan to scare off the river in the same way that they scare off the bird-who-sits-smiling before this one pecks a sore in the horse's back.

"But the traders prove a different sort of whiteman."

A Mnikoozu had spoken up, the man going on to say that the traders came for robes and skins, not to name streams and prophesy over Dakotah babies. What trader ever acts like Red Hair?

"These traders make changes in Lakotah ways." Heȟaka gave quiet answer. "These traders put iron firesticks in Lakotah hands and iron pots on Lakotah cooking fires. Will you call these changes something good?"

The Mnikoozu disagreed. The traders will not try to

185

bring about changes; these men try only to please the Lakotah taste.

With firewater?

With firewater, if the people choose to trade for this drink.

Aware that more of this talk will lead to something that perhaps turns the bands against a summer at pahamni ridge, Heȟaka, as leader of the inviting party, now advised sleep for his own drowsy, meat-stuffed companions.

At once Ooweśica offered the travelers a resting place in the temporary shelters which guests often prefer, or on robes in the family lodges. And, in the customary way, the middle-aged chose the comforts of the tipi while the young men chose the branch-and-brush cover.

The night's talk had brought up those points that Heȟaka had wanted to avoid. And neither Ooweśica nor Wacape had responded to the Mahto's invitation. Some of the Siyo headmen had talked for a summer encampment near Wiciyela kinsmen across the muddy-water, and some Okandada had spoken for a hoop out near the black hills. And so the visitors shall wait another day, perhaps another sleep, while Titonwan bands try for agreement.

And while the Mahto waited, scouts reported a stranger coming upriver, perhaps another Red Hair with new names for their earth-mother. And so a party of Okandada warriors smeared their faces with paint and, grinning, went out along the river to harass and scare off the newcomer; they had discovered that any painted Lakotah—peaceman or warrior—will make the whiteman jumpy, and they saw a way for collecting knives and smoke-leaves without the confusion of a trade.

Next day the warriors returned, painted and grinning as before. Displaying knives and guns, they recited the story about obtaining these things, their gestures making a joke of the act. True, they let these whites escape—man and boy—but not before making certain that the two never will reproduce their kind.

One Okandada showed a pack of talking-leaves, something he had taken from the whiteman's shirt. And now, observing Peta's keen interest, he let the boy hold these leaves which keep the whiteman's legends. But the pictures, not the little talking-signs, had excited Peta. His eyes had grown big at the sight of grizzly and branched-horn and winged.

And now he saw the picture-horses. Unlike the drawings on Lakotah robes, these horses appeared to run and snort and switch a tail. He sat intent upon these pictures until the Okandada nudged him. "These leaves belong to you, my young brother," the warrior said. "Nothing here that a man will eat or wear or smoke and so why not give to a boy for a plaything?"

The man had tried to depreciate his gift, but Peta accepted the amazing present with joyful heart, his eyes shining gratefulness. Returning his gaze to the pictures, he recognized a yearning to draw in this manner. Certainly one day he will decorate his robe with pictures similar to these pictures and so everyone will know Peta. The boy murmured softly his gladness that these good leaves had come into his hands.

Oowesica sat with an ear bent toward every sound in the council lodge and walked alert to each voice in the camp. He watched the eyes of his warriors and the gestures of his people, and soon he knew the answer to Heliaka's invitation: the Okandada will raise their lodges at pahamni ridge.

The news delighted young Peta. Certain Okandada had invited him to wait and travel back to the ridge when they go. And now Heliaka permitted him this pleasure. The boy shall remain in the care of these people, Heliaka said, while the Mahto party moves on to the Sicangu camps, where they will distribute gifts, voice the invitation.

The son of Olepi suspected that upon his return to pahamni a summer of challenges and trials awaited him but that here with the Okandada—here for a little while—perhaps they will ask nothing big of him. Here he dares play and ride with young ones like himself and even act a little bit foolish if the mood comes upon him. And here he will learn to draw as on the whiteman's leaves.

"I am without horse." Gnuska, hearing that Peta will stay back in the Okandada camp, had come looking for the boy. "My friend, I ride out with the inviting party on your horse." He spoke with confidence; the son of Olepi will not deny him his mount. But Peta kept on walking as if Gnuśka never had approached him.

"My friend, I take your horse." Gnuśka raised his voice boldly. "These lodges will find space for you when they travel to the ridge. Perhaps they will confine you on the drags along with their children."

Peta stood where Gnuśka's insult had stopped him, but he answered nothing. These words, devised to ridicule an offer out of him, acted only to recall the picture of a horse dying on the plain. So let this son of Ogle report Peta as one who lacks the generous heart; he will refuse Gnuśka, whatever Gnuśka's scheme for bringing him shame. And let who dares call this a childlike response.

Gnuśka went back to the men, humiliated and angry, seeking now a place up behind one in the party. And vowing to find a way to even this thing with Peta.

His visit in the Okandada camp provided Peta some new experiences along with the familiar. He threw at targets and joined in pretend-raids on little girls who raised toy-lodges. But he also played rough.

The boys chose him as 'pte' in the pte-hunt game. They want someone brave, they told Peta, someone who will endure much bumping. They gave him a long stick with a prickly leaf attached. 'Pte,' they said, shall chase any boy whose lance pierces this prickly leaf and, catching the boy, shall poke his bottom. And 'pte' shall decide when to stop the game.

They went after Peta then with their blunt weapons, but the 'pte' ran and dodged in a most remarkable manner and when finally 'pte' called a finish to the game, more than one 'hunter' stayed back to pick out thorns.

On another day these same boys had coaxed Peta into yet more rugged play, a contest that called for each player to kick down his opponent, grab his hair, and then knee his face bloody.

Peta had watched the Wiciyela wrestling games but never before had he witnessed this kick-and-swing game. Even so, he stood in line alongside five strong boys, another line of five strong boys standing opposite, each one waiting for the leader to shout the phrase that means attack, upset, smash-smash.

"Yugmi oyucayuspapi na, cankpe un poġe nawicaźuźu po." The next thing Peta knew, he lay on the ground, his nose pouring blood. But he neither grunted nor howled—so far as he remembered. Instead, he managed to get up and wrestle again. And soon he discovered that the real test came not in the amount of kneeing and bleeding a boy endures but in his refusal to let his opponent anger him.

But the Mahto youth not always joined the Okandada at their play. On certain days he went out alone to hunt smooth ground and a strong marking-stick. And so he tried to copy the whiteman's picture-leaves.

One day, after many attempts, he drew something similar to the original. And now he wondered about putting these pictures on something he will keep. He decided to bring a piece of hide and a pte-rib and perhaps paint to his secret drawing-place. But before he rubbed out that which he had drawn in the dust, he murmured his thoughts to the horse-shape: "One day I shall catch a horse like you, half black and half white. And I shall ride this one in front of the people. They will cheer my ride and I will enjoy their cheers."

He rubbed his thumb over the spot marking the horse's eye, then this hand scraped away the ears and head. He stood up and, using his foot, rubbed out the remaining lines. From now on, he told himself, he shall draw on hide, his pictures something he will not rub out.

Two, three days passed before Peta returned to this place, but on the morning he came back he drew on the hide from sunup to sundown, the lengthening shadows unnoticed, the drifting smoke of meat fires unheeded.

Now suddenly he knew that someone had come here; someone watched. He lifted his eyes; the principal man of the band stood above him.

"The son of Olepi visits the camp of his relatives; the people look out for him. And so they ask that he tell when he goes out alone."

The firm voice had brought Peta to his feet. But Oowe-śica had not looked at him; he looked, instead, at Peta's picture of a horse.

For a long while he considered the boy's drawing. "My nephew stakes a horse next to him," he said, speaking slowly, "and he sees many horses in this camp. Yet he draws horses that belong to a whiteman. And as the whiteman sees, not as the Lakotah. But if the invisible intend that he draw in this manner, his vision will tell him so." The leader turned, starting back toward the village.

Peta picked up the hide. He untied his horse and led this one toward camp, the two keeping a respectful distance back of Oowesica, the boy marveling those things he desires knowing, dares not ask.

Will everyone look upon his drawing as something a vision needs confirm? Will they find something displeasing in any drawing that resembles the whiteman's pictures? But he draws in this manner before ever he sees the whiteman's dry leaf. Truly, wherever he, Peta, goes, someone or something always appears to challenge him.

But the important thing, he told himself now, that he hunt along the stream for the creature that swims-carrying-a-stick; perhaps someone will boil the tail and so he will have glue to mix with his drawing-powder. And so his picture of the horse never will rub off the hide. Certainly he shall go out looking for capa the next day.

Peta awakened during the night to a dream of horses, certain ones red-eared, different ones red-legged. He went back to sleep wondering whether they call this sort of dream a vision.

The next thing, he awoke to the weh-weh-weh-weh cry of those old women who round up the camp-dogs whenever a village moves. And truly this village moved; they had packed everything on the drags but Peta.

Discovering that he had slept through all this commotion, the boy laughed at himself. But remembering his plan for this day, he made the small cry of discontent; he had wanted to carry back to the Mahto villages a finished painting.

Rolling from his robes, he lifted the hide-drawing from beneath the pile. He folded the piece around his extra pairs of moccasins, then fastened the bundle to his horse.

Next, he ran to the men's bathing place, jumping in, jumping out, running back to his horse.

And now he sat mounted, his body glistening, his eyes smiling; he looked forward to his return to pahamni ridge. Who knows but what the people will give him a song when they find out that he intends to become the most great picture-maker in the tribe.

XVII

NEVER BEFORE will so many people raise lodges in one place; all Titonwan councils had favored the great summer hoop on the red-stemmed grasses below the ridge, at the site Olepi had chosen.

Oowesica and his Okandada had arrived, and then the Síyo villages. Next some Mnikooźu, and on that same day a camp of Canoni from the north woods.

Now the Sicangu began to appear. Apparently all invited persons intended to come but for those Mnikooźu on the muddy-water, a band whose leader had spoken one day against leaving the river yet on the next day had proposed traveling across the prairie to trade for redstone pipes. His wavering nature had displeased many persons in his following and the newscarriers told that some of his relatives had started out on their own for pahamni ridge.

At this ridge, then, the people shall form a truly great Lakotah hoop: two hundred lodges, more than ten hundred persons.

Soon after his return Peta had heard his father's talk with other headmen and the grandfathers in the tribe, his boy-ears marveling the many things these men regarded as important before the gathering bands raised a hoop.

The leaders had agreed that nothing held more importance than the selection of those four who shall decide all affairs pertaining to the tribe as a whole; the deciders, as everyone knows, require the heart of a warrior and the head of a peaceman.

And the deciders needed to choose their akicita most carefully, the people depending on these watchmen, these clubs, for protection in every direction. And the people looked for the council to appoint the proper persons to arrange dances and supervise contests and to manage the sungazing.

And so Peta, deciding that none will notice a youth who sits painting a horse-picture on hide, walked to Cankuna's lodge, where he hinted for a certain amount of glue,

191

where Mahtociqala offered his help at whatever his friend Peta schemes.

By now the group of leaders who gathered each morning in the council lodge had used up the sitting space and so the women raised a second lodge, the two tipi joined, one side kept open.

And now, as more and more families appeared, the responsibilities of the councilors increased; the headmen smoked far into the night, their women bringing food, carrying in the meat quietly and leaving at once. But certainly the arrival of any newcomers made for a noisy occasion; work stopped while the leaders sent around a pipe, gave welcoming speeches.

Many, many lodges clustered loosely on the plain now, each tiyospaye, each big-family, awaiting an assigned space in the circle. But the council, as agreed, made the electing of the wakicunsa, those deciding-four, their prime concern. They will summon two from the group active the summer before and announce their reappointment; then the headman-lodge will choose two more from among those names the tribal council now considers.

The Siyo had pushed front the name of their favorite warrior; Hinyete, they emphasized, always keeps a cool head. Next the Okandada, who presented three names, had reviewed each man's competency.

When the Mahto spoke, they named Cetan, someone young in seasons, old in experience. But the Mahto also mentioned Sunktanka, a man whose alertness twice protected the horse herds from an approaching enemy.

So the bands identified their choices, but the people already knew these different persons; the people recognize where a man will fit into the tribe long before his twentieth winter, perhaps before his tenth. But now the crier walked among the lodges naming these eligibles, verifying the report that the headmen soon will announce whom they elect to wear the summer-shirts, whom they appoint to manage the everyday concerns of the great encampment.

Eyanpaha had sung his news once around when boisterous voices filled the space outside the council lodge. A tall man approached the open side of the tipi, four of his

192

warriors walking closely. Paint and moccasins fixed these persons as Lakotah and a rising murmur proclaimed that here stood Zuzueca.

This tall one, his nose like a claw and his voice like booming ice, brings his Kiyuksa band for a summer in the Lakotah hoop, his one appearance among these kinsmen in many, many seasons.

During a winter long, long past and barely remembered, two young Tiyataonwan families, flaunting custom, had mated within the bloodline. Naming these rule-breakers 'kiyuksa,' the wise leader Wapaśa had warned the group to keep away from Dakotah council fires. Starving but proud, these Kiyuksa had filed onto the prairie, certain ones wandering occasionally on the short grass. Then, after many lonely winters, they had met up with Ooweśica's tiyóspaye. But again they had broken the rule. This second act against custom had brought on another quarrel and once more these families had split off. Nor had this band camped with any Titonwan since that troubled winter.

Even so, the Kiyuksa belonged to the allied ones and so the people greeted the band warmly, inviting Zuzueca and his principals to sit in council.

The dark-skinned leader sat down in the front circle, his warriors crowding close in back of him. The headmen passed around a smoke and then reviewed that which had occurred in the center lodge before the Kiyuksa arrived.

Zuzueca had not hidden his displeasure on hearing that they will choose the wakicun, the deciders, from names already mentioned. Instead he boldly announced that he also knew persons in a position to advise or to decide or to watch. In his band, he said, live boys whose grandfathers had performed acts that had become legend. And among the old in his band sat persons who had made the vision-quest on the ledges of the black hills.

"The Kiyuksa name these rivers that you, my kinsmen, only now follow on your travels to and from the black hills. Before the Titonwan become a tribe, the Kiyuksa make meat and dance on this plain." Zuzueca's black eyes flashed proudly and his voice rose nearly to a roar. Forty lodges of Kiyuksa hunters filled their bellies on pte-tongues, he bellowed, while those persons who had begun to call their band

Lakotah sat back on the dividing-prairie and chewed on ribs from the branched-horns, sucked on bones from the prong-horn.

His booming voice dropped almost to a whisper, his next phrases softly intoned, his gestures expansive. "The Kiyuksa form two separate camps now and I will not say whether the tiyośpaye living on mystery lake follows my band to this ridge. But this thing I know: the families I bring here desire a place in this circle of relatives. These warriors offer your hoop their daring and their power; these women offer your hoop strong sons and good-looking daughters.

"I finish speaking. Now I listen."

Silence greeted Zuzueca's speech. True, neither the inviting party nor those persons carrying the war pipe this past winter had visited the Kiyuksa. They knew not where the Kiyuksa stayed, and why search for a band who breaks with kinsmen and then goes off in two different directions? And who will look for a Kiyuksa to lead his camp to pahamni ridge and request a place among these families on whom he turns his back for many winters? Certainly the Titonwan welcome these Kiyuksa—strong men always have a place in this hoop—but why shall Zuzueca show annoyance when he discovers that the council makes decisions before his arrival?

Silence, then, while these councilors come together in thought, each man recognizing the truth: that they will wait for this tall loudmouth to prove his strength through acts. Whenever will words prove anything? Permit him space in the hoop but watch him.

And now Oowesíca stood, voicing this answer, speaking each man's response to Zuzueca's boasts. And talking straight to the point. The leaders, he told, welcome Zuzueca and his warriors but let none here puzzle the council's intention. The Titonwan shall proceed from the place where Zuzueca's arrival interrupts, and all those things they decide before this band comes remain firm.

Olepi, awakening before dawn, watched the night yield to day. He wondered whether any different man in camp awaited the morning announcement more keenly than himself. The day before, he had looked on the faces in council for those signs that tell without a count of voices which men shall wear the summer-shirt. True, the real choosing takes place in the Tatanka-lodge, but certainly those headmen who make up this important group look at faces and listen for sounds when they hear certain names. They also want to know the will of the people before they make a choice.

For the next little while Olepi reflected on the manner whereby the Dakotah grandfathers had signified a preference. To this day, after three hundred winters, the old men yet talk of the voting-stick, the little finger-length elk bone which the tribe had presented to each boy-child at birth. But if ever a Dakotah had desired more than one vote, he had to earn the next little bone, and the next, up to five. Huhukaȟniȟgapi, the privilege of voting.

The vote had worked for ten ten-hundred Dakotah, works even now for the Isanyati, the newsmen tell. But the Lakotah had dropped this good way for demonstrating a choice.

And why? Olepi answered himself. The Lakotah want their own way of life, a different speech, different shelters and meat, different customs, and perhaps different ceremonies. And why not? They live on the plain, not in the woods; they hunt, not trap; they ride but not in canoes. And so they make changes in the Dakotah way. Why not see the Lakotah also become a parent tribe, the protectors and caretakers of a new greatness here on the plain.

Eyanpaha, seeing the red rim of sun pushing up from the edge of the plain, had moved among the lodges—already more than two hundred lodges—awakening the people to the new day.

And now, the yellow warmth climbing the sky, Eyanpaha sat in his own tipi awaiting the voice of a different crier. The deciders, secretly notified of their election, had sat together to choose principal akicita, herald, and messengers; in this way their own crier will announce the head akicita, these principal clubmen in turn letting the people know who will wear the shirts this summer.

The new mouth had started on his rounds soon after the finish of Eyanpaha's song. And, singing as he walked, he named those two who along with a certain lodge of warriors will keep peace during this encampment.

Icabu. Olepi smiled. They had chosen Icabu, a Mahto,

a man from his own band, for this high rank in the affairs of the Titonwan. And now Olepi imagined the young warrior jumping into his moccasins, perhaps reaching for his bow before he remembers that not even the head clubman dares carry weapons inside the council lodge.

When Olepi heard the second principal watcher named, he smiled again. The two will make a good pair: unbending, fair, and strong of arm. And the one, a Mahto.

Crawling from his robes, Olepi wiped his body with sage; Napewaśte, remembering that a sungazer dares not stream-bathe, had placed the cleansing grass nearby. He threw the woman's sleeping form a grateful look, then glanced at the other one asleep in this lodge.

But Peta opened his eyes as if he needed only his father's gaze to awaken him. He smiled up at the man.

"Into your feet, my son, and see the clubmen when they emerge from the center lodge."

The boy slid off his robes and, grabbing moccasins, popped out of the tipi, on his way to the bathing place before Olepi had stepped into his own moccasins or tied on the loin-cover.

Now ready to greet the sun, the man bent down at his wife's robes; he touched her gently on the shoulder. "Some-one follows sleep as far as sleep will lead," he teased.

The woman sat up, but a glance at Olepi's eyes told her that she dared answer lightly. "I keep waking up in the night. I hear the watchmen making their rounds." She suppressed a yawn.

"Look at me," Olepi told her but not unkindly. "Your son sits each day with brush and paint while other boys play at warrior games. Perhaps this fact, not the crier's rounds, keeps you wakeful and anxious."

Napewaśte's eyes widened in surprise. Uncertain of Olepi's response to the boy's sketches, she had avoided any mention of these drawings. Now, hearing nothing reproachful in the man's tone, she spoke boldly.

"Your son draws not like the others who use the marking-stick. His picture of the mother-grizzly with young shows the creature's tenderness toward her cub." Napewaśte waited for Olepi's request to see the drawing; perhaps the picture will help him understand Peta's inclination.

But the man's answer revealed a dim view of the boy's accomplishment: "Your son will find nothing tender about a grizzly if ever they meet on the trail. I advise that he learn a defense against this one instead of sitting here and making pictures of her tender look. Or let him paint the grizzly-power on a war shield."

Olepi pulled the woman's cheek against his thigh. "Perhaps," he said softly, "my wife needs a daughter in her lodge, someone to whom she will teach quilling and moccasin-making." Then rising, he stood smiling at her.

Napewaśte's heart fluttered as if a bird tried to escape from inside her breast. But she had misunderstood the man.

"When you see a little one you favor," Olepi advised, "ask that she come and live in your lodge awhile. When her family sees the way you feel about their daughter, they perhaps will give her to you."

"I will remember," the woman answered softly, her voice sad for the bird so quickly stilled. Yet she knew the husband spoke truly. Acts of war, his importance to the band, ceremonial restraints: these things keep this man from fathering more than one child, from frequent visits to her sleeping robes. And so she needs adopt a daughter if she wants someone to fondle and influence and protect. She has a daughter, true, in her sister's child, but this family stays in the Siyo band, the little girl not often in the Mahto camp.

Perhaps she will observe those little ones who come visiting with their mothers or grandmothers, and when she discovers a child who attracts her more than the others, she will talk with the parents and, perhaps, arrange an adoption.

The two newly appointed clubmen came from the center lodge, the two feathers which describe their rank slanted into the single tuft of hair atop their heads.

"See the sticks they carry." Olepi spoke to his boy about the markers which these akicita will place in front of four different lodges. "I want my son to understand the way of the people when the tribe comes together. Come, I and you will follow these head akicita, and so discover who the Tatanka-lodge—the Pta-lodge—chooses."

Markers soon appeared outside the lodges of two Okandada warriors, these two from among the four who

197

had controlled the previous summer's camp. And now the akicita walked on to the Śiyo village, where they thrust a painted stick in the ground before Hinyete's lodge.

Hoye. The Śiyo people, quickly gathering, shouted assent, and the warrior, hearing, came from out his tipi. He carried only his pipe-sack, something he will exchange for the long sack that accommodates the special pipe they present a decider. As he moved toward the council lodge, a group of cheering relatives surrounded him.

The akicita's next stop, the Mahto camp and the tipi where Cetan sat, a soup bowl in his hands. The cheering for this much-admired warrior began before they pushed the stick into the ground.

Cetan looked twice at the marker, then put aside his bowl. He got up, his tallness slowly unfolding, a touch-the-clouds among men. And so the people saw him as a warrior-bird, the hawk whose name he uses, his nose sharply curved, his eyes bright and searching, a countenance proud and bold.

Cetan, like Hinyete, shall go now to the center lodge where he, along with the other three, will put on the summer-shirt and smoke the long pipe.

"Hear the crier." Olepi called his son's attention to the voice that will announce all decisions. "He names the Tokala-lodge as clubmen. These Tokala own a tipi in every band. The people regard this warrior-lodge as most competent."

Peta understood. Iku and Iku's friend Źola belong to the Tokala, and certainly these two excel at everything.

"These Tokala will see that each family looks out for sparks from their own campfire and that none frightens the meat in advance of the big hunts." While he spoke, Olepi had wondered whether this selection of akicita will brighten Zuzueca's dark face? The Tokala keep a lodge in the Kiyuksa band, and so this appointment gives Zuzueca's following a voice in camp affairs.

The man and boy turned back toward their own lodge. "Gather up your things," Olepi told his son, "and listen for the mouth to summon all villages into one big circle."

"But, my father, I starve. I eat. Afterwards, I pack."

Olepi answered cozily: "I also starve. Perhaps your mother will notice and throw out a bone."

Peta felt good all over. Not often will his father wink and make jokes, tease and laugh. And if this mood stays, perhaps a son dares show his father the grizzly drawing and hear the man's praises.

Soon father and son sat eating the thick soup Napewaśte ladled from the paunch. Before their return the woman had begun to take down her lodge, but she had stopped cheerfully to feed these two.

And now Peta, seeing the woman return to her work, suddenly understood that not again will his mother wait for his help whenever she raises or pulls down her lodge. His age makes the difference as to whom he now assists, his work henceforth only manlike acts. Men make meat and take horses; men go out on raids and perhaps fight. Men never cook in camp or raise lodges; men never blow up the water sacs or sort quills or wipe dry the soup bowls. Only boys who not yet count ten winters help with these things.

Olepi, glancing at his son, met the boy's even gaze. And, comprehending, he held on to that gaze, marveling again these glimpses of the man-within-the-boy, something he had imagined as happening on the raids or during a hunt, never while he sat quietly eating a bowl of soup.

The sun reached middle, and in a great sweep of dogs, horses, children, and women, the villages began their move. They followed an easy trail to the clean grass in the near distance, a short walk that will not dull the sharp points of the lodgepoles.

They had assigned the Okandada—the band with the most tipi—the place of honor at the tip-of-the-horns, but the Mahto received a good place on the north horn. Here Napewaśte proudly put up her tipi, her mother helping with the work, the Siyo woman deciding to sleep in the daughter's village this summer.

Napewaśte's father had chosen to stay with the Siyo scouts, keeping track of these young men and tending their fire. The man, a scout in his young days, enjoyed their company.

But something more than age had persuaded him to this arrangement; the old scout had sensed a dimming eyesight. A Siyo healer had treated him with snow packs for snowblindness, but the eye had not cleared. And so, soon

199

after his arrival in the Mahto camp, the man visited Sunihanble, a healer whose vision had revealed a power for curing sores and wounds. He described his difficulty: one eye clouds over and the blur will not brush away; he will not know boulder from pte on the far-distant plain.

Sunihanble had gazed at the weak eye a long while. Finally he moved, walking slowly toward the back of the lodge but always facing the old scout. Next, he reached back his hand and picked up a rattle. He shook the noisemaker furiously. And now he flapped his arms as if he remembered himself as a winged taking off from a lake.

A feather fluttered down from the top of the lodge, through the smoke hole, and when the fluff touched ground the pezuta spoke. "A bird hovers over your eye," he said calmly. "She wishes to nest in the round opening. Her wing blurs your vision. But I am sending the bird back to the trees. Your eye will clear."

The scout went out from the lodge much relieved, but five, six days passed and his sight in the troubled eye had not sharpened. He visited the pezuta twice.

Hunhunhe. Now the winged brings grass to this nesting place and these stems irritate the eye. Sunihanble mixed a powder, pulverizing a piece of bone from the antlered blacktail and melting a lump of fat from the tall-ears. He spread the mixture around the man's eye and on the lid.

Soon the eye seemed improved but not enough to trust. And so the old scout had offered to keep-lodge for the young truthbearers who called him Tunkasila, called him grandfather even as Peta called him grandfather.

Napewaste had used two horses for dragging the family lodge to the new campsite, and Peta had taken these creatures to graze after watching his mother unpack. The boy had not offered his mother any help, neither with the horses nor the camp-dogs who pulled her small bundles across the grasses. After those looks of understanding from his father, he intended to watch himself around women, any woman, even his grandmother. He sat now, legs crossed, observing his mother and grandmother, who soon will pull the lodge cover around the poles.

After raising three tall, slender poles, Napewaste had

leaned other smooth poles around this supporting frame, each pole set firmly in place. Mother and daughter worked together, and now the two unfolded the clean new cover.

Collecting the fourteen hides used in this new cover had required three winters, for Olepi often gave the skins from his kills to someone without a man in her lodge. Napewaste recognized that a leader needed to look after the have-nots in his band, but her husband's generous acts also had meant a patched lodge for his own family these past seasons.

They spread the shelter on the ground, Napewaste dampening the cover before tying the strings to her raising-pole; the tear-drop shape stretched more easily around the circle of poles when slightly wet.

Peta recrossed his legs and moved uncomfortably. Shall he offer to close the front of the cover? Truly, he will enjoy going aloft the tipi and making the climb up the little sharp-pointed sticks, advancing from one to the next as he inserts the fasteners up the front. But will the women laugh at him if suddenly he jumps to his feet and gives this help?

Mother and daughter had worked silently, but now Unci, the mother, spoke. She said something about the smoke flaps, something about the wife of Hehaka attaching these flaps to the tipi cover as a precaution against smoke in Napewaste's lodge.

"Hehaka's wife places these flaps," Napewaste answered, "but, my mother, I also know the way for putting these flaps on each side of the smoke hole. You talk as if I never before make a lodge."

"I refer to the nature of the woman who performs the work," Unci said gently. "Cheerfulness, not anxiety, chases out the smoke."

Peta, overhearing, looked puzzled. He knew that his mother stepped outside the lodge and adjusted the movable poles to prevent smoke in the tipi; why will her mood affect the winds? Perhaps his grandmother will tell him.

But neither smoke flaps nor smoke hole really interested Peta. His pleasure centered around old Leksi, his uncle, who had announced his intention to stay in Napewaste's lodge during the encampment. And around Unci, his grandmother, who will sleep close by. The nearness of these

201

two will mean wonderful stories of far-distant places and seasons, events that happen before Peta learns to remember, even before his birth, even before Leksi's birth.

"Unci, will you tell about camping with the maize-eaters? About their tricks, when they lift off their heads and dance? And when they put their faces on backwards? And when . . . " The boy, hearing the hushing-sound from his mother, looked her way in surprise.

"My son knows not to ask for these winter-telling stories at this season," Napewaste murmured as she made her way around the lodge, staking down the edges. Unci walked behind her and laid stones on the cover at certain places.

For a moment Peta considered the many days until snow. Why will the old people always wait for winter to tell about events in the past? Why not some summer-telling stories?

But now he stood up, moving out of his grandmother's way as she approached the front of the cover. Perhaps she will ask him to join the children who gather grass for use under the sleeping robes, scarcely work for a boy who goes into his eleventh winter. He turned to go but then he noticed that this new lodge cover lacked design; the tipi stood bare of picture and paint.

"My father draws nothing on the lodge cover." He looked at Unci, but he intended the words for his mother's hearing. "Perhaps," he said slowly, "my father desires that I paint this tipi."

"Will my grandson consider his acts up to now as something for the paintbrush?"

"I paint my father's acts, not my own."

Even as he answered his grandmother, Peta recognized a reason for the undecorated lodge. "Perhaps my father waits until he owns a big name among all Titonwan, not only the Mahto band, before he will paint this lodge."

The son's words startled his mother; she, also, had considered this thing. She struck the one remaining stake a quick blow.

Straightening up, she spoke her reproach to Peta through his grandmother.

"Tell my son that one day he will paint his own lodge in any manner he pleases. And whether his father will or

202

will not paint this one concerns none but his father." She grabbed up the tipi lining and hurried inside while the boy, puzzled and abashed, looked after her.

Unci had begun sorting the pile of bundles pulled off the drags. Her camp-dogs hung around sniffing the meat containers and so she opened one of these stiff folders. Taking out a handful of dry meat, she fed the dogs. "Eat," she told her slobbering burden-bearers. "A boy with a strong bow-arm stays in this tipi. Soon his grandmother chews fresh meat."

Peta smiled. He watched the dogs snap up the woman's offering, then asked Unci what she will have him kill. A fat grass-bird or a chipmungk? Or perhaps the tall-ears—tinmaśtinca—with hair on his split lip? The tall-ears means also a tail for decorating Peta's hair. "But remember, my bow kills nothing big." The boy pretended sadness.

"Bring Unci birds for roasting," she told him. "You own a club. Use this. Bring me those black birds who sound like a little old grandmother scolding."

Peta stretched tall. "Little boys catch birds. But I will bring that which you ask. If I see any pronghorn . . . "

Unci, like all old persons, dared interrupt whenever she chose. "The embers wait for whatever you bring, birds or pronghorn. Now go. And stay this side of the berry thickets, hunter, or the akicita will chase you down and break your bow."

"I often ride beyond the thickets, Unci—even to the top of the ridge—yet none ever chases me or breaks my bow."

"You ride before the bands come. Now the people make a hoop and the clubmen will not permit any wanderers out where pte graze. Frighten the herd and you find yourself in trouble, boy or man." Unci disappeared inside the lodge.

Peta looked around for someone to go with him. If his uncle Huśte comes along, truly the pronghorn will roast on Unci's fire this night. But Huśte had moved into a lodge of young, unattached men, a group who liked hunting together, and so Huśte will not want to go out with a boy who owns three, four blunt arrows and a little club. But Peta remembered one person always eager to accompany him. And so he took his child-weapons and went to see Mahtociqala, the young friend who follows him three winters in age but who surpasses most boys ten, eleven, even twelve winters in the handling of a bow.

Approaching Cankuna's lodge, Peta marveled the tall mound of sacs and paunches, soft containers and stiff folders, all these bundles belonging to one tiyośpaye, this hunter's family and their relatives. The big lodge sheltered Ogle, his wife, and their three children—Gnuśka, Mahtociqala, and the new one—along with five more related persons. And spilling over into four more lodges clustered around the big one, those many families who related to Ogle and Cankuna through blood-ties or hunka, birth or choice.

A noisy but contented chatter surrounded this place now, women scurrying in and out the five tipi, wives and daughters adjusting poles, affixing linings, arranging their cooking things. Mahtociqala helped with the bundles, but at the sight of Peta he stopped, his face a smile, the boy ready to go wherever Peta goes.

Soon these two started out, hearing the same advice Unci had given: none shall hunt on the far side of the thickets until the clubmen say so.

Inside her lodge Napewaśte had scraped a shallow fire hole near the center, then scattered fragrant leaves over the bare ground. Unci had hung a flap of skin over the entrance and then gone out after stones and dry sticks and sage. She intended to smudge the new lodge cover, make the tipi secure against the weathers.

Now the two women stopped for a moment of ceremony. Unci, fanning the glowing wood that she had carried from the old camp, murmured her wishes for this new tipi; she will see the moons bring laughter and gladness into her daughter's lodge. And Napewaśte, watching the wood glow and the sticks catch fire, laid sage on the flame. Quickly a bittersweet smell filled the lodge, the thick smoke spreading, rising to blacken the top.

Unci knew where everything belonged, all Titonwan lodges arranged the same. Food and the means for preparing food on the woman's side; here, then, the stiff-hide folders with the dry meat and, propped alongside, the splotched-skin containers stuffed with dry berries. Here, also, the bladders distended with grizzly-fat or pte-fat, and here pte liners for carrying water, warming soup.

Paunches for boiling the meat belonged on this woman's side of the lodge, also the bowls into which the women ladled this meat, bowls of wood carefully hollowed with fire and knife, bowls of shell carefully steamed, shaped, dried. Digging sticks and berry-pounders and bone-crushers belonged here, these things hung on tipi poles or leaned against the lining.

Above her sitting place Napewaśte arranged her many containers, something to hold sinew, awls, markers; something to hold horn scrapers, fleshers, ashes for removing hair from the hides. But the small, small sacs she looped around one pole, her decorating materials—quills, teeth, claws, shells, fringe, hair, pieces of bone—all within easy reach.

Unci knew where to place each thing, but Napewaśte alone arranged Olepi's sleeping place, at the back, opposite the entrance. And Napewaśte alone put down Lekśi's robes, the old uncle's place near the back and across from the women's side of the lodge. But when she brought in Peta's robes, the woman hesitated.

All his winters the boy had slept in a place between his parents, father and mother protecting the child. But this summer brings a change. The face-to-face talks with his mother now a thing of the past, his place among men taking shape even before he puts aside his blunt arrows. And so the mother had paused before she pushed her son's sleeping roll against the tipi cover, on the far side of Olepi and in a space between father and uncle.

Unci now unrolled the backrests, mats of slim, smoothly peeled wood, something Napewaśte hung on the three-stake supports set up at head and foot of sleeping robes. And into those spaces between backrests, the women pushed the big stiff containers which held robes and gowns, also those big painted folders which kept meat and berry mix and roots they not yet need.

Toward the rear and above the tipi lining, mother and daughter hung the sacks of paint-powder, a streak on the outside to show which contains red, which white, and which yellow, colors they had squeezed from buds or berries or boiled out of the fuzz they scraped off bark.

Next, Napewaśte hung four sacks marked with a black streak; into these sacks Olepi the warrior had dipped his fingers most often.

And near the paints the women placed those little bundles of healing-roots that everyone keeps in the lodge for the relief of small hurts and little complaints—scratches and cuts and stings and burns.

Finally, Unci set up the drinking-water, the sac hung at nose-level for easy tilting; remembering Peta, she hung a second waterskin within his reach.

And while her mother took care of the water-sacs, Napewaśte put away her personal belongings: sacks of absorbent down plucked from clubgrass and of use to woman-iśnati, then her hairbrushes—a quill's tail and the tip of a pte-tongue, scorched and hard—and finally she hung the big holder, the whole skin of a wapiti into which she stuffed everything not given a special place.

This work finished, Napewaśte glanced around to see if she had misplaced anything. She noticed rattles and drum behind Peta's sleeping robes but certainly Unci had a reason for putting these ceremonial objects alongside the son instead of his father. All other things appeared in order, even to the skin stuffed with pronghorn hair, something Olepi used as an armrest.

Suddenly she remembered three important things which remained outside: Olepi's lance, shield, bow. She dared not arrange these weapons without the man's permission, yet these things shall not remain on display during his sungazing pledge. The husband walked somewhere with Wanaǵi, the two in search of something they needed for mellowing a little space of earth inside the lodge.

When Napewaśte spoke to her mother about the weapons, the woman answered firmly: "Your son shall bring these things inside when he gets back from his little hunt. And I will see that he cleanses his hands in smoke before he touches anything."

So Unci spoke and then went off to raise a little six-skin tipi next to her daughter's lodge, the old woman wisely keeping a place of her own. Of good family and strict-raising, she conformed in a most exacting manner to kinsman-behavior rules. She permitted neither word nor glance between herself and her daughter's husband and so she demonstrated her respect for the Mahto warrior. Olepi, in return, respectfully avoided his wife's mother, each one acting to prevent any distressing occasions, any ridicule, within the family.

The grandfathers, recognizing criticism of one's affinal relatives as a natural but disastrous thing, had demanded a rule that kept a man's eyes off certain faces and a woman's eyes off certain faces and a lack of talk between these same ones. And so Unci, staying in a different tipi, made things easy for her avoidance-relatives; Olepi more easily ignored her presence and she spared her brother Leksi much embarrassment, a sister and brother also avoiding any direct talk for as long as each one lives.

Peta carried two bleeding furry forms to the tipi flap, then dropped his load as he had seen the men act; skinning and cooking, woman's work. But Mahtociqala, proudly bearing four grass-birds, stood uncertain; he knew not whether to drop his kills.

"My friend brings something for Unci's fire." Peta glanced toward the limp birds, their heads tucked under the cord around the young boy's waist.

"I break each one's neck," Mahtociqala told. He held out a stick with a heavy thong attached; let Unci see in what manner he kills. "If I miss, their heads fly off. But I never miss." The boy's eyes sparkled; Peta had witnessed his kill and so Mahtociqala dared boast.

"I am glad that I make a big fire," Unci said solemnly; "two young hunters feed the lodge this night." She led Peta to the fire hole inside and watched him wash his hands over the embers which yet breathed the fragrance of sage. Next, she instructed him to carry his father's weapons into the lodge and to place these things on the guest-side of the cover. Not until she sees him perform these acts will she clean, cook the boys' kill.

The youths had responded with joyful little songs to the old woman's approval, but their hearts leapt at the praises from Olepi, from Leksi, when the family and their young guest sat to eat.

Mahtociqala, usually shy in Olepi's presence, had begun talking before he emptied his bowl. He pulled the meat from a small legbone with his teeth and told, between swallows, that his brother Gnuśka killed this same meat not with bow or club but with his hands. "He puts burrs along their path and they hop onto these stickers," he said importantly.

Napewaśte, holding a roasted bird and pulling off the feathers, smiled at the boy's enthusiasm. But Lekśi broke into the recital to advise that certain persons use their fingers to remove cooked meat from any bone—if they want sound teeth in their old age. He had eaten improperly in his youth, he said, and now look at the gaps in his mouth.

The boys had glanced respectfully, but the old man's message seemed unimportant on such an exciting day as this one. And now they heard the Mahto leader say something that brought even more than smiles.

"I will not hunt until after the sungazing, but my son knows where my bows rest. The short one will bring down a fluffed-hair if a boy's arm proves strong and his aim true."

Joy spread over Peta's face. He had brought in wings and little ground creatures with his blunt points yet his father never once speaks of a real bow and sharp shafts. Until now. And now he hinted that Peta owned the arm for an arrow deep into young pte.

His joy suddenly beyond containing, Peta jumped to his feet. Whooping, he grabbed Mahtociqala, the two running off, dodging through camp like young pronghorns.

Napewaśte now gave her full attention to husband and uncle, who certainly hungered for something more than a roast of birds and a boy's catch of meat. She took soup to Lekśi and put down a bowl of maize for Olepi, the husband's food in a new bowl, a sungazer not to eat out of anything old or used.

"Someone desires that my husband have this bowl," the woman said softly. Unci had cooked the maize, knowing that Olepi will appreciate this food and that her little act shows regard for the daughter's husband.

The two women nibbled on leftovers. Not usually will they eat away from the men, but Napewaśte had wanted to make a ceremony of the food that the two young boys had brought in, the men eating together as at a feast.

Pipe in hand, Olepi now started for the sacred-lodge, and Lekśi, after going inside for a sip of water, went off to visit the tipi of another old man. And so mother and

208

daughter leaned back against the lodge cover and spoke in soft voices or joined in laughter over some small happening of this day or the day before.

Unci rejoiced at the sound of laughter in this daughter who too rarely laughs and sings, someone too strict on herself, a young woman who views her place in the band with apprehensive eyes, someone not yet secure in her role as wife to a leader.

But on this night Napewaste appeared as a girl again, and so Unci began a little sleep-song, her hands tapping the beat on her own knee as she sang the wistful tones. And the daughter, listening, remembered back to the easy seasons in her mother's lodge.

> *"Sleep, my child;*
> *the Padani, far away, far away. . . . "*

The song, an old one, known to those Titonwan who once had roamed the tall-grass prairie east of the muddy river.

> *"Your father, a warrior, stands watch;*
> *your father stands alert. . . . "*

So Unci had sung to two daughters and one son; so Napewaste had sung to Petala.

The fragrance of night-blooming stems came on a breeze gentle as breath and Napewaste hummed softly along with her mother.

After a while they heard the slender tones of a flute and Napewaste, wondering who whistled and to whom he sent his message, remembered that someone once had called to her on the flute. But Olepi never had tried to attract her in this manner.

Suddenly Peta appeared, the boy running up to his grandmother, his hair damp from play, his eyes brightly confident: someone remembers to put aside a roasted bird for him and for Mahtociqala?

Someone had remembered. Napewaste had placed the meat alongside Peta's robes, the two boys surprised and a little shy on discovering Peta's new and important sleeping place.

The women sat on, listening now to a little quiet laughter, a drowsy murmuring, from inside the tipi and to the wing-talk of those tiny creatures who snuggled in the grass beyond the lodge.

But soon Unci, without a word, went to her own little shelter, and then Napewaśte moved to the fire inside, sitting close and looking dreamily into the glow.

She heard a step and her heart quickened, but she saw that Lekśi, not Olepi, came. The old uncle stood smiling down at her; he began telling of his wins at the counting-stick game.

The woman laughed, even chided him gently but in a voice that never lost respect: "My good uncle, you and my son mix up the seasons. The boy asks for your stories in a summer camp, and you indulge in a game that belongs to the cold moons."

Lekśi stared at the glowing wood and rubbed an old arrow scar: "Someone with these many snows on his shoulders will not wait for any certain moon before he enjoys himself."

He smiled again. "Iho, look here and rejoice that I mix up the moons." From a sack at his waist, Lekśi brought out teeth, wapiti teeth, the most prized decoration for a woman's gown. He dropped twenty in Napewaśte's lap.

The woman made little sounds of delight; she began to examine the teeth, to admire the stain patterns on each one.

Olepi appeared and she glanced up, inviting the husband to sit alongside, to inspect this gift and share in her pleasure. But his look told her that he chose sleep after the long ceremonial smoke with Wanaǵi. And so again she sat alone, her eyes once more on the embers.

But now, before crawling onto her own sleeping robes, Napewaśte moved forward to lift the tipi flap, to look for any sign of wind or rain. Glancing at the stars, she smiled; the whole wide sky, she told herself, blinks the news that the Lakotah raise a sacred hoop, that the summer moons arrive.

XVIII

EVERYONE TALKED for a big hunt before the sungazing; they wanted pte-tongues for the ceremonies and feast-meat for their visiting relatives. And so the deciders sent out the scouts and the hunters tested their bowstrings and exercised their runners. And the old arrow-makers became much in demand. The people brought in the broken points they found on the plain, and these workmen, using a piece of horn, renewed the edge on a thumb's length of stone more quickly than the whirling stick made fire.

Some persons said that Iktomi, the trickster, had spread these arrowheads on the plain; other persons, in different tribes, said that the worms brought these points to the plain. But the Titonwan answered that the worms, making dust of hard ground, only pushed into view that which Iktomi already had scattered over the earth.

Tunkaśila, explaining the stone arrows to Peta, had told that First Born used these stones in his battle with the four-legged when the creatures of earth combined against him. But whether Iktomi or the worms or First Man had scattered these many stone points on the short grass for Lakotah to find, he knew not.

While the people made ready to hunt, the wapiya from each band had gathered in Wanagi's lodge. Here these seers agreed that sungazing meant something more than watching a man endure thirst and pain; they shall not let the thanks-offering, once a lonely affair, become a spectacle, an endurance contest. Never before had twenty persons pledged to dance under one sunpole, and they, the sacred-men, intended to prevent any acts that hinted at favors from either powers in the winds or powers in the tribe. They came together to consider which rituals they shall withhold from onlookers. And to decide whether or not the one woman to gaze at the sun shall receive instruction separate from the men.

And now Olepi sat in the sacred-lodge, where, in the formal tongue of an instructor, Wanagi advised the Mahto that all sungazers, four days from this one, shall enter a lodge-of-preparation.

"You neither eat nor drink nor sleep while you stay three days, three nights in this place," the wapiya told him. "Twenty persons will offer thanks, certain ones dragging skulls, certain ones cutting off pieces of their flesh. One man offers his back and his breast to the four directions; I smoke with this man now."

Wanaġi rolled a smoking mixture between his palms, then filled the pipe. He reached for the forked stick with which to pick up an ember, but his eyes rested a moment on Olepi's face. The Mahto shall remember himself, Wanaġi's look said, as any man performing this ceremony; the wapiya shall treat him in the same exacting manner.

Olepi watched the man place the lump of glowing wood on the bowl and suck on the stem, but his thoughts had not related to the seer's act. Instead, he reflected upon this one seated before him, upon those changes in Wanaġi since their youth-seasons together.

Here, those legs and arms that had wrestled Olepi to the ground and perhaps had the strength to overcome him now. Here, shoulders slightly curved from winters given to smoke and thought but the same hard, flat middle, something the big-bellies of the Pta-lodge have reason to envy. Here, a compact and sinewy strength in a man tall above the hump of pte.

The wapiya had painted for this smoking, and the grizzly hide, once put away, hung again on his back. Perhaps these things, Olepi told himself, made the man's eyes appear unusually fierce.

And now, their smoking finished, Wanaġi emptied the bowl, placed the long-stem on a pipe rack; his acts brought the meeting to a close.

Walking back to his own tipi, Olepi found himself wishing that he never had vowed this second sungazing.

Before the Mahto leader had reached his lodge, two scouts came racing toward the center of the encampment. And an errand boy, quickly piling up pte-chips, prepared for the ritual that welcomes truthbearers on their return. The scouts came in under a clear, bright morning sky, and so Olepi, perceiving that they had found meat, joined the group who hurried toward the center lodge.

Everyone awaited the four deciders, and now, as these persons approached, one of the scouts scattered the chips with his moccasin toe; his gesture will let the people know to listen for good news.

One among the deciders handed a pipe to this man who had tumbled the pile. And the scout, accepting, offered the stem to the air all around him and then to his own lips. Slowly he breathed out smoke; slowly he began his report.

The herd grazes close by. Not a big herd but many pte with young and some fat ones guarding.

"Beyond that?" The deciders wanted more facts.

The pte appear suddenly, without any rumble, any noise. They follow the herd-mother. Many pte suckle new-born and so grow thin.

Some persons made the marveling sound and some persons glanced briefly at Olepi. Truly the Mahto had chosen a remarkable campsite; apparently the herd had come looking for the people.

The meat looks thin? But tongues never thin, and for tongues the men hunt. If the hunters kill all in the herd, this means two hundred tongues and enough fresh meat for the ceremonies. Wašteśte.

Peta stood in the crowd, his heart thumping as if he had run in with the scouts. His day to hunt had come and already he imagined himself among the shaggy, swinging heads and short, stiffened tails. And he wondered why he had talked so eagerly for the man's bow.

He had tried out his father's bow, the push to send three arrows using up all his strength and a soreness at his wrist for two days where the bowstring snapped at him. Yet his father calls this weapon a short bow? Short, perhaps, to a man's arm but not to a boy.

"My friend, you will make meat this day." Mahtociqala came up next to Peta, the young boy's eyes turned proudly on the son of Olepi.

"Perhaps I will not hunt," Peta answered too quickly. "One chases the branched-horn before he tries for pte."

When he saw the pride in Mahtociqala's eyes turn into surprise, turn into regret, Peta wished he had kept silent.

The crowd now dispersed, the people returning to their lodges, everyone smiling. Almost everyone.

Peta heard the head clubman ordering the Tokala to assemble and receive instructions concerning the hunt. Then suddenly he remembered something: the hunters will begin to call their sons or nephews to bring in the runners, and so Peta shall listen for someone who seeks him. Not his father—the Mahto leader pledges a sungazing and dares not carry a bow—but Huśte, perhaps Huśte?

On a different side of camp, Olepi walked alone. Relatives and friends, remembering that this man handled neither bow nor knife, properly stayed away; they will avoid even the talk of weapons in his presence.

But the Mahto leader, going to his lodge, pondered more than his sungazing vow; he marveled that the herd appeared at this propitious moment; that the pte only now discovered the new grass sprung up after fire. He had seen the bald, soggy earth on that day his band approached the ridge and he had dared look for something like this. For truly as snow melts so will charred earth send up the tender, pale grass that attracts pte. But for the herd to appear four days before he enters the preparation-lodge foretells of good coming from more than one direction; he had heard the murmurs that said so.

He came now to his lodge and, seeing Peta, he smiled.

"Father, perhaps I am not ready for the hunt." The boy's voice faltered.

The man's eyes widened briefly. "What boy ever sees himself ready for his first hunt," he answered. "The hunt makes him ready."

Olepi stepped inside the lodge; he wanted his son to follow, to pick up the bow.

But the boy lingered outside the tipi. If he hunts he takes his own little horse, not his father's runner; this much he decides. As to the bow . . . as to whether he rides out with the hunters . . .

"Perhaps Peta will ride double behind me, or sit front if this child's place makes him feel more safe."

The son of Olepi looked up at the taunting voice. Gnuśka approached horseback, a pack horse trailing.

"I will bet that you never get close to pte on your little horse." Gnuśka rode on, laughing.

Peta tried to ignore the ridicule; Gnuśka always remembered that occasion in the Okandada camp when Peta refused him his horse. Even so, Gnuśka had reason for teasing him; will the little horse keep up?

Then Peta remembered something about the horse on whom Gnuśka rode, a nearsighted creature who will endanger his rider and other hunters during the chase. Why will Gnuśka try something foolish? But will a boy uncertain that he dares go out with the hunters talk against the son of Ogle who already kills a curved-horn? He stood as before, undecided about himself.

The yapping and scattering of camp-dogs and the shouts of an excited people as boys and youths brought in the runners acted to keep the villages in noisy confusion; even the herald had difficulty making himself heard.

And so Icabu, head watchman, came from the Tokalalodge, the black stripes of command painted on his face. He blew fiercely on his whistle and in a loud, sharp voice ranted at the people.

"You behave as children. Remember that you come into a sacred season and that the herd comes looking for you. They bring you their tongues. The big chase after meat comes in old summer when the pte grow fat. Those hunters who go out now shall take two, three arrows. Eighty men go, not more."

Icabu knew that none will quarrel over which men hunt; each hunter will recognize whether or not he belongs among the eighty.

And now Ogle came forward from among the Mahto and, alongside him, Hinhan. The next moment Ogle's glance brought out Śunktanka and then a man who once had killed a pte and her young with a single thrust of his lance. None of these persons held more than two arrows; none of these hunters will need more than two.

Gnuśka had watched this choosing of hunters, and when he saw that his father left him out as rider or helper, he quirted his horse and headed for the playground. Here, beyond reach of any eye, he will use up his anger on the horse, on this nearsighted creature who keeps him from the chase.

215

Peta also had watched, his attention now on the hunters who made a steady procession to the seer's lodges, where they ceremoniously cleansed bow and lance in sweetgrass smoke and painted their horses.

Mahtociqala again stood next to his friend, and Peta spoke his relief to the boy. "I am glad that I am not going on the hunt. I want my own bow when I go. And I certainly need more than two arrows, perhaps more than two and two and two and two."

They laughed together, but then Peta felt a hand on his shoulder, heard his uncle Huśte's voice.

"I look for a boy, someone slender but reliable, who will ride my runner to where the herd grazes, who also will look after my pack horse while I hunt."

"I go gladly, my uncle."

Instantly Peta decided to take his father's bow. As horse-tender he will not use the weapon, but the old men forever advise that a boy take bow and arrows everywhere he goes, everywhere, even when he goes out to wet the grass. You never know, they always say, and then tell of the boy who saved himself and his mother with a child's bow and grass-stems.

Five Tokala horsebacks sat in a line, ready to lead out the hunters. Each of these clubmen had painted a red circle around his mouth, a red hand-mark on his horse, symbols the hunters will recognize quickly if they need help. One of the Tokala carried a pipe; another man held a robe over his arm, something to signal the start of the chase. All five carried clubs in the event that an overly eager hunter tried to move out in front.

Only to those young boys who sat waiting on the runners had the men seemed to take forever to get started; other persons marveled that everything moved so quickly; between sunrise and midday they had accomplished many things.

The seers had insisted upon the renewing ceremonies. And while not all hunters had crawled into the initi for even one splashing of the stones, each one of the eighty had acted to refresh himself, his horse, and his weapons in some ceremonial manner.

Now the people saw their hunters off, one moment a noisy group of men awaiting the akicita's signal and the next, a silent wide-flung line, only the thud of loping horses to announce their presence on the plain.

The next day saw these same ones back in camp, more than one hundred pte-tongues for the ceremonial cooking, more than one hundred humps for the ceremonial feasts.

Olepi, observing his pledge, had not gone out to meet the returning hunters but he had waited in the lodge for his son; perhaps some occasion had arisen that gave Peta a chance for daring. Not infrequently, he remembered, a pta breaks away, comes at the pack horses and then the boy-tenders either show an alertness and bravery or they run.

Napewaśte also stayed in the lodge, but she waited only for her son's safe return.

The moment Peta lifted the tipi flap, his parents knew that something had happened to the boy but whether to honor or shame the family they knew not; Peta presented a closed face.

The father watched his son replace the bow, and the mother heard her son's murmured intention to look after his horse. When he stepped out the tipi, Napewaśte turned an anxious face to her husband.

Olepi gave answer to her look: "This son will know when the moment comes for talk."

But Peta had not talked, had not spoken of the hunt either on this day or the next or the next. And the people said nothing about the boy. Or nothing that reached the parents' ears.

Olepi, ready to enter the preparation-lodge, had tried to appear indifferent to all things not concerned with the sun-gazing, but Napewaśte had grown more anxious each day.

Peta observed his mother's puzzled glances but he waited for another person to speak of a certain event. Let his uncle Huśte tell the story. Or perhaps Huśte already talks and so his parents sit wondering about their son.

The event had taken place as the akicita called back a group of hunters who chased after escaping pte.

Peta, mounted on his uncle's pack horse and waiting

for Huśte to signal him to approach the kill, saw two break from this fleeing herd and come running his way. A dust cloud hid these two pte from the hunters, but Peta noticed that something small ran between the galloping forms.

The pack horse danced excitement and Peta saw need for quick decision. The next moment he identified the small thing that ran middle: a little white one.

White. Not yellow like most young pte but white, white as snow falls white. A white pte.

A shiver ran through the boy, fingertips to toes. He used his quirt, and the surprised horse leapt forward; Peta's heels thumped briskly.

The three that he pursued suddenly swerved, one big shape crossing in front of the small white one, the second big pte maneuvering clumsily to guard the rear. At that instant Peta reached out with his bow.

The tail of the white one flicked up as if to catch hold of the boy's weapon. But then the three went running off, the small one bumping along awkwardly in the middle, the big ones giving their protection again.

Peta jerked his frightened mount to a quick stop; he sat looking at the tip of his bow, his eyes wide in marvel.

Certain boy-tenders, observing Peta's performance, decided that the son of Olepi went out after a young fluffed-hair whom the herd deserted, and so they shouted their approval, then rode out after other deserted young.

And when Huśte brought his runner back to Peta for a rubdown with sage, he, also, approved that which he had seen.

"My nephew acts bravely when he diverts two big pte from the pack horses." Then, jumping on the horse Peta had held for him during the hunt, Huśte returned to his kills; the uncle had not stayed to hear about the mysterious white pte.

But while he helped his uncle load meat, the boy told his story.

"If truly you see this wonderful white one, why will you not tell the clubmen? They know whom to send out after a ptesan."

"My uncle, I will not want anyone going out after this pte." Peta's eyes had asked for understanding. "In seasons ahead I will find her, and my arrows, not my father's points,

218

will make the kill." The boy had gazed in the direction the herd had disappeared. "While this white one grows," he said softly, "I, also, grow."

"Will the son of Olepi not remember that his father soon dances an offering and that the sacred pte appears—if this white one appears—as an omen. The tribe never starves when the hide of a white pte hangs in a tree." Abruptly Huśte turned back to his work.

Peta, silent, bent to gather up one side of the fresh hide, helping his uncle cover the pile of meat in the center. Now, the meat secure, Huśte lifted the bundle horseback, and Peta tied the thong that held the load in place.

Again Huśte regarded the boy sternly. "If my nephew intends to follow in his father's moccasins, he shall remember the people and that which brings good to the whole."

Peta looked out unashamed; nothing about his person hinted that he perhaps regretted something.

"Strange," Huśte murmured, "that none of the scouts or clubmen see this white pte. Perhaps the hunt excites my nephew and colors his view of things."

Instantly the boy's eyes changed, a different heart in his breast. "I ride up close and I see the little white one whose tail touches my bow." Dropping to his knees, Peta struck the earth, hitting hard with the flat of his hand. The inside corners of his eyes gathered tears and he began trembling. He, only a boy, struck sacred earth and so vowed his truth in the earnest manner of a warrior.

He stood, then, and, going around to the opposite side of the pack horse, he whispered to the creature. "I and you see that the white pte runs between those two big ones."

On his way back to camp Peta talked with none of the boys, none of the hunters. But he wondered in what different way Huśte will tell this story if, truly, he ever speaks of his nephew's experience.

The women had rejoiced at the many young pte killed at the finish of the hunt, these hides making up into fine robes for children. And so the singers had praised the youths who made these kills. But Peta's act of turning off two runaways, they had not mentioned; Huśte had not spoken of the boy's performance.

For a while Peta wondered whether they schemed to

call him to the center lodge and kill him. They kill people, his grandfather said, who speak with a crooked tongue. But he, Peta, never had spoken untruthfully; perhaps the wise ones in camp will remember this thing about him.

But the boy stayed to himself. He had found a place at the edge of the encampment where people rarely came, and here he sat, paint sacks at his side, bone brush in his hand. He drew pictures of the hunt, grateful that none came around to hint at the strangeness of these drawings in which the horses looked like living horses and the killed pte looked dead.

Three, four days after the surround, Peta saw his father entering the preparation-lodge, but that which went on inside this place only the seers knew, the seers and those twenty men and one woman to whom they gave instruction.

Soon the boy heard songs coming from this tightly closed lodge, but above the rapid drumbeat he also heard crying.

Who cries, he wondered; for whom will persons inside this lodge grieve so deeply as to cry? Truly the sungazing occasioned great mystery.

Mystery also surrounded the pte-tongues which his mother and Wiyanna, his mother's sister, dried for the ceremony. He had considered asking his uncle—the tall Sicaṅgu whom Wiyanna calls husband—for what purpose the women dry these tongues. But he had witnessed a more puzzling event.

He saw a group of women at a feast suddenly throw away one person's bowl. The disowned woman had spit at her companions, then gone away angry. Yet some men onlookers had laughed at this rude display. Why?

And another strange thing: why will the young warriors, even Iku, who always appeared glad to join the boys in their stalking games, treat Peta like a child who yet rides dogback? Not that they ridicule him; they simply act unusual.

Yet many nice things happened these days: everyone gave presents. And so Peta, taking half the bird claws in his collection, went to see Mahtociqala.

"I will help you string these claws," he said, "and I will make a second string exactly like yours." He smiled. "Perhaps the people will say that I and you look alike when they see these neckpieces."

"But you stand above me," Mahtociqala rose up on his toes alongside Peta; he tried to make himself as tall as his friend.

"True, you follow me three winters," Peta answered. Then seeing where their shoulders touched, he said, "But my young friend soon catches up with me."

"I am ten next winter?" Mahtociqala wanted to know.

Peta laughed but only a little laugh. "You will not jump ahead in winters but you will grow tall all at once."

"Tall like you?"

"Tall like this," Peta raised a hand above his own head.

Mahtociqala regarded his friend with solemn eyes. "I will never grow above Peta. I wish . . . I will pretend that I am your look-alike." Suddenly shy, the young boy clasped his hands behind his neck and looked down.

Peta smiled. "The neckpieces will look alike. Come, I and you make something."

Now, the bird-claws strung and tied at his neck, Mahtociqala fingered the neckpiece. "Will this protect me like the wotawe protects a warrior?"

"You, my friend, will decide this thing."

Peta had answered wisely, and the young boy had seemed to understand.

XIX

MIDSUMMER, WHEN all the earth rejoices, when the tree holds on to each leaf and the sage spreads over the plain and the fat-moon berry ripens and they mate within the herd. And then man, gazing at the sun, shall remember that something moves, something holds or spreads or ripens or mates. Taku śkan, something in movement: taku śkanśkan, always something-moving; śkan, in and of the beginning. Śkan, the life-force.

And so man shall gaze at the sun and rejoice. And give thanks that he lives. Śkan, taku śkanśkan.

Someone had said that a tribe who roams south of the sandhills makes a rush on the living tree they select for the sunpole. And now the Titonwan decided to approach their tree in this same way; the warriors shall go out and attack the wood as if they attack an enemy. The warriors shall charge twice, but this tree shall not fall until the sun sits overhead, the wapiya had said; let none distort the shadow, the spirit, of a tree-person.

And before these men rush at the tree, an old person shall come forward and speak gently to the winged who tie their nests in the leaves and to the red-shoulders, those blackbirds who fly up from the water-grasses to decorate the branches. And so these wingeds, hearing to what use the people put this tree, understand that a Lakotah never wantonly destroys the birthplace of the birds.

The old man shall speak also to the courageous little wing who sits atop the trees or rides the back of his enemies sounding his yell-yell-yell-yell and to those birds who knock on the wood, who dart and dodge around the tree. For the warrior learns ways to treat with an enemy from these birds.

And now Peta sat horseback watching the men make this ride against the tree. He never had seen warriors in an attack and his spirit raced with the men as they swooped near the tall, slender wood.

Next, four young warriors walked toward the tree, one man with a cutting-stone in his hand. He recited an act of war, then made a deep gash in the wood. But before he handed the stone-head to the second man, he gave a gift-stick to someone standing close. "Present the stick to that young man," he said in a loud voice and pointed with his chin. "Say that this stick brings him a horse."

A cheer went up from the crowd, and Peta had a quick look at the shining eyes of the youth who received the gift.

Four gashes with the heavy stone-head weapon had come near to breaking down the tree, but now the wapiya brought out another stone-head; he looked for a woman to take hold.

The women hung back and giggled and hid their faces, but three finally stepped forward, each one asking that some man speak good of her before she touched the tree. These women made the cuts on the opposite side of the bark and so the tree needed only a big push. And the sun, now straight up.

The sacred-man again came forward; he carried the sharp-edge stone to a pretty girl, someone not more than fifteen winters who stood quietly at the back of the crowd. The people recognized this one as someone most modest, a girl rarely seen around camp, someone the Lakotah proudly call daughter.

When she saw the wapiya approach, the girl looked down shyly, but the man put the weapon in her hand. And so she walked pleasantly toward the chosen tree, her smiling eyes and gleaming hair summoning a cheer from the people.

She struck at the tree and the wood crashed to the ground. Suddenly awed and a little frightened, she hurried back into the crowd. The people laughed comfortingly, then looked back at the tree; they began a song.

Peta wanted to laugh and sing also, but whether a boy whose father sits in the preparation-lodge shall risk attracting attention he will not know.

The men began to strip the tree of branches, daubing red paint on each cut, likening these cuts to wounds. And now Peta, jumping down off his horse, joined those youths who formed shields and wreaths of the brush.

"I have a relative who makes me proud." Huśte approached the group who braided the leaves into shields, the young man's eyes on Peta, a gift-stick in his hand.

Peta had not visited with Huśte since the hunt, but he knew to respect the behavior pattern which demands a certain attitude between uncle and nephew. And so the boy looked up respectfully.

"In my herd three young horses run and play. One belongs to my nephew. He shall pick out this one." Huśte pushed the little stick between the boy's fingers and limped away.

Almost at once the crier sang out that Huśte joins those

persons whose names they will hear in the praising songs this day. Huśte gives a horse.

Peta's young friends whooped pleasure over this gift, but the son of Olepi, a lump in his throat, stood silent. The gift-stick told everything. Huśte accepts his report on the mysterious pte, the white fluffed-haired pte. His uncle understands now that the nephew speaks truthfully; Huśte will tell the whole story now.

The lump melted away and the boy gave out a whoop, a shout unlike anything he ever had uttered. Even the young warriors glanced up, their eyes surprised but not disapproving.

Using thongs, the men lifted the tree onto crossed wood, and a strong horse began to drag the pole back to camp. The people, forming two widespread lines, followed after the horse and pole. And if anyone races ahead of the pole, the seer warned, let him look for disaster. A cut tree releases a power, they said, that acts against the disorderly; stay back or risk a broken neck.

The people rode slowly, the women singing a victor's song:

> "'I am the only man,' you say,
> But you say something not true
> And so you go weeping."

But why only the women sang and why this song, Peta found most puzzling; yet another mystery to the sungazing.

The youthful riders held the leaf-shields in their hands and wore the twigs in their hair. And they had placed leaf wreaths around the necks of their horses; the procession appeared like a grove of rustling trees that move in a mysterious manner toward the camp circle.

Certain seers had come from the preparation-lodge to meet the procession and to instruct those men who will raise the sunpole. And two different seers, using root-diggers and a horn scoop, had dug a deep hole for the pole. But before pulling the wood erect, they tied a banner beneath the fork and fastened a short pole onto the tree, something from which to dangle a man-shape and a pte-shape cut from hide.

Peta had observed these acts closely. And now the boy listened to a cheer as the headmen of each camp, all holding on to one thong, pulled together and so raised the slender pole a little way. The seers had instructed that they make three tries at raising the tall wood; on the fourth tug, they shall bring the pole erect in the hole.

The pole in place, the people had turned their interest toward the sunlodge, everyone helping to make this circular shade. They brought in the forked-wood which men and youths had piled at the edge of camp, arranging these stakes in two circles, one around the other and about four arms' width between the two.

Certain young men, singing and joking, began laying lodgepoles from one forked-stake to the next in the same circle, while other young men, recognized for their good nature, notched young poles and laid this wood over the space between the circles.

"Who brings branches for covering the edge of the sunlodge?" The crier sang out the work instructions. "The people want shade while they watch."

Boys tall enough for this work placed branches over the slim poles, and young boys ran up with their leaf-shields, filling spaces between stakes on the outside circle.

Peta helped close over some open places with brush from the big piles that the warriors had dropped off, but he kept hold on his gift-stick and he longed to go after his new young horse. Instead, he went on working with brush until he remembered that he had not eaten all day. Nothing disgraceful about getting hungry he decided, not like running off to select a gift-horse while all other persons stay to work on the sunlodge. But riding back to the tipi, he kept looking in the direction of the herds; he wondered whether his uncle Huśte waited somewhere for him.

Napewaśte, seeing her son approach, ladled out a bowl of meat. She sat alone in the tipi trying to quill one more pair of moccasins before sundown. She looked for Peta to eat and go, neither Unci nor anyone here through whom the boy dared talk with her.

But Peta, finishing his meat, hunted a way to let his mother know about the wonderful gift. True, his horse or a camp-dog made proper ears for his words, but some families will not approve this manner between respect-relatives.

225

Many boys avoided direct speech with their mothers after eight, nine winters, and so he, ten winters and a leader's son, needed to watch himself most carefully.

Suddenly he tossed up the gift-stick, his eyes glancing toward his mother as he caught the wood, once, twice. But she sat attentive to the moccasins as before.

And so, jumping onto his little horse, he headed again for the sunlodge, a song on his lips:

"Mitasunke, wahupa koza s'e kinyan yan inyanke lo. . . . "
"My horse flies like a bird as he runs. . . . "

The next moment, a new thought stopped his song. He turned and rode the horse back to his mother's lodge. He jumped down, but he stood a long while stroking the head of this one on whom he had learned to ride, a horse he had owned four wonderful seasons.

Suddenly the air filled with noisy whoops; all the Tokala came riding two abreast and sending arrows into the ground. More than sixty members of this lodge from different camps loped their horses around the hoop of lodges. Groups of children ran after these horsebacks, grabbing up arrows, their yells trailing the swoop of these riders. And camp-dogs and horses started up their own noises, a din that marked the warriors' path.

Peta left his horse to run with the boys, and Napewaste put aside her work to watch. After the men make four circles of the camp, the crier told, they invite all youth in the encampment to ride slowly this same circle, the young men leading, girls and young women following.

This enactment, like the attack on the tree, came as something new to the sungazing ceremony, and so the people listened closely to the songs the seers had composed for this event, songs the tribe had not heard until now.

The young men, cheering, began to paint their faces. And before dusk they made their ride, each man's voice raised in a song to the sky. And riding close behind, girls and young women who sang in counterpoint, their words spoken not to the sky but to the earth.

Darkness came and Napewaste worked on, fastening quills to the moccasins, tops and bottoms. These two gift-pairs she will decorate completely, the owner wearing these moccasins only twice; when she mates and at her death.

Unci came, offering her hands in this work, the women sitting inside the lodge until the firelight became too feeble to see by and the night too warm for a bright flame. Then the daughter removed quills from her mouth, the ones she kept moist on her tongue as she worked. "Perhaps my mother will walk with me. My body wants to stretch."

She straightened up, reaching around to rub her back. She flexed fingers weary from folding quills, using sinew. She stood and, after a glance at the robe where Peta lay sleeping, she followed Unci out of the lodge.

The round moon lighted the night, and many, many persons lingered outside their tipi. Flute and drum and song blended with a hint at wistfulness, and the soft, warm air seemed full of secrets.

As they walked, Unci saw the daughter's eyes glance often toward the lodge-of-preparation where Olepi endured his final night of thirst and hunger and wakefulness.

Unci spoke once. "That one owns a strong heart." She dared not say more than these words, and perhaps these words, too much. For one who respectfully avoids the presence of a certain relative also avoids thoughts of this one. But certainly the daughter knew that these words came as comfort on a difficult night.

Mother and daughter walked on, hearing sounds from up on the ridge where prowling true-dogs sniffed the feast-meat and howled their resentment of the man-smell. From the grasses below the ridge came a different noise. Here the traveling-dog lifted his voice to a fat moon, his violent tremolo telling that he, like the old weatherwoman, viewed suspiciously the haze that circled the night-sun.

But when the camp-dogs, none afraid of stone or arrow on this night of strange disquiet, yapped at the passing women, the daughter turned back toward her lodge, the direction of her walk changed by the same sense of unrest that brought about their yapping. A frightening loneliness sat over her heart, but whether for the son now forever beyond her protective care or for the husband, this night beyond her reach, Napewaste knew not.

But the wise ones know these things. The grandmothers will say that this woman glimpses the man-within-the-boy and so her true loneliness, not for the son but for the father of her son.

The eastern sky had begun to lighten when Napewaśte, neatly combed and in an unspotted gown, walked through the wide opening in the circular shelter called sunlodge. The woman led two horses, their backs piled with her generosity. The horses, not hers to give away, she intended to return to Olepi's herd, but she knew that her relatives planned to give seed-horses and reliable pack horses in her husband's honor. And certainly she took pride in the son who walked behind her leading his horse, this one loaded with playthings of Peta's making, gifts for children in camp.

While Napewaśte emptied the backs of her two, Peta stood at the head of his horse, stroking the creature's nose. His mother not yet knows that, instead of leading this horse out of the sunlodge, he will stake his little mount to a pole near his mother's gift pile. Then he will lay a stick—something like the one Huśte presents him—alongside his mother's offerings. Unci advises the playthings as something he shall make and give away, but he alone decides about the horse.

For a while the boy had wondered about giving up this creature so important to his youth, a small horse but one whose flank carried the sign of his child-honors: a scattering of tiny spots similar to the delicate scarring on his wrist, a remembrance of the day Slukila had tested him for pain, and below those spots, the unmistakable shape of a young pte.

Peta knew that only rarely will someone display on robe or horse a brave act for which he neither has witness nor has proof. But in painting his experience with the white fluffed-hair, he had remembered that which his mother taught about the 'spirit-everywhere,' one among the invisibles certain to observe his contact with the young white pte, to see any move he ever makes.

And so the sungazing seemed a good occasion for giving away the horse. The seers say that the spirit-people enjoy sunup to sundown use of those gifts in a pile near the sunpole, the invisibles staying until dusk, until the clubmen start handing out the presents to needy persons. So will not he, Peta, make his own thanks-offering to the spirit-witness who knows about his meeting with ptesan?

But he had not overlooked the gift-stick that Huśte had presented him; before ever he gave a horse he had gained one. Truly, he told himself, I lose nothing on this exciting day.

Peta saw his father standing in the center, thongs at back and breast tying the man to four poles, two back of him and two front; the Mahto leader will not fall, not even if he weakens and slumps. But when the boy suddenly perceived that Olepi hung in such manner that only his toes touched the ground, he feared that his father never shall tear himself loose, never survive the ordeal. Now he watched Wanaği force a wingbone whistle between Olepi's lips, saw his father swaying. He turned his eyes, looking toward the sunpole, where a second man suffered.

The man at the pole, a Śiyo warrior, danced with two pte-heads hanging from cuts in his back, skin and hair clinging to these skulls. But at this moment everyone watched a little girl who ran out to him, the child carrying a quilled sac, something she will hang over one of the skull's horns.

But the girl acted hastily; the sac fell off. Stooping to pick up her offering, she saw the dripping red holes through which the thongs passed. Terrified, she ran back to her mother.

None had explained to this little one about those bleeding wounds on the back of the good uncle who often played with her and made her laugh. She saw only that someone had hurt this man, and so she stood now at her mother's side, her thin little form heaving with sobs.

The child's winters, five, perhaps six; and so her relatives saw the girl as someone making her own decisions, responsible for her own acts. They will tell her that the quilled sac honors the uncle-dancer, but they neither shall console her over that which happens nor yet demand that she make another effort to place the container on the horn.

After a while the people noticed this little one enter the suncircle as before. Timidly but without backward step, she approached the gazer. Rising up on tiptoe, she carefully slipped the loop in the drawstring over the horn, then turned and ran back to her mother, where she found a hiding place behind a fold in the woman's gown. Persons nearby heard a sighing-from-the-ribs, but they recognized this mournful sound as a protection through which children awake or sleeping, release fright. They knew that joy soon will fill the space she empties and that her mother and grandmother will take notice and smile their approval of her good act.

Now those gazers who offered arm and shoulder flesh came to the sunpole, some persons wanting the skin lifted with a bone awl, then cut, others asking for the gashing knife. The wapiya chose not to touch the arm of the woman who asked for twenty of the sixty cuts her sungazer-brother pledged, not until the close of the ceremony, but they named her in their songs during this ritual.

Peta's eyes returned to his father. The sun, at halfway, threw down an intense heat, and the boy marveled the endurance of this one who suspended himself to the glare. Unlike the dancer with heads dragging from his back, the Mahto leader not yet made any effort to release himself. He held on to a stick, something for raising himself slightly to ease the strain, but none saw him jerking as if to tear loose.

Peta wished he dared go someplace and not witness this torturing of flesh. Twice he had turned from the sight of the pte-heads thumping against the Siyo's heels, from a view of that pile of flesh under the pole.

Sacred-men had begun to walk among the dancers, hanging a root at the neck of each one, something to prevent thirst. And to the legs of each man they tied a different root, something to combat weariness.

Peta, observing these acts, saw something that made him turn his head in shame: his father wept. Wanaǵi, standing close, wiped tears from the Mahto's cheeks.

Now a loud wail attracted the boy's attention; he saw that the different wapiya and their helpers used sage wipers on the cheeks of all gazers. This weeping, one more thing for the son of Olepi to puzzle.

Wandering now from place to place within the shade, Peta listened to the cheers and trilling and songs, mostly unfamiliar songs, but whether his father heard these braveheart songs, who will know.

As the dancers turned to face the sun-climbing-down, the crier called out for more gifts on the big pile near the preparation-lodge. Bringing presents to this pile, he announced, will help a relative who suffers; perhaps the wapiya will cut away a portion of the holding-flesh as soon as different families bring forth a horse.

The son of Olepi pondered this request. Why demand more gifts? Will the pile look small to the clubmen who soon distribute these things to the old and dependent? Or will the invisibles regard this pile as a scanty offering and so they make difficult his father's struggle with the thongs? Perhaps Unci knows.

But Unci showed more interest in seeing that Peta ate something; she sent him, bowl in hand, to one of those feast fires where meat simmered in paunches, sputtered on the roasting-stick. Small groups of old women kept watch over this food, wood handy for throwing at camp-dogs, threatening glances ready for the youth who comes forward to play tricks. True, they never scold during a sungazing, but neither will these old ones let the born-teasers get away with any mischief.

Napewaśte, joining those persons who feasted with Cankuna's family, had noticed that old Tatewin, teeth dangling, also chewed at this fire. Certainly this weatherwoman keeps an eye on the sky, Napewaśte told herself, and so will offer prophecy concerning any chance of flashes-and-roar in the clouds.

Sitting down alongside the weather prophet, the wife of Olepi spoke softly: "Perhaps the wakinyan approach this encampment."

Tatewin turned her head and spat into the air; drops of her spittle fell on Napewaśte's arm.

"Now someone sees from which direction the wind blows," she said curtly. "On this day I am cook, not prophet. Waziya calls the weathers, not Tatewin." The woman took her bowl and moved away.

Napewaśte wished she had not made known her anxiety. But she had watched some white clouds drifting into the clear and had observed a billowing up from their flat bottoms, a darkening at their heads. But why will the old weatherwoman mention Waziya who brings snow? This giant occasionally makes the sun back away in the moon of grass-appearing, but in the moon of red berries? Certainly Tatewin had not eased her apprehension.

Napewaśte had not joined the dancers as during that

231

other sungazing when the drum had summoned her into the circle; instead she had wanted only to run to her husband and throw herself on the thongs until his flesh gave way. And then to disappear with him, the two like a young pair who, deciding to become man and wife, go out on the plain away from all eyes but their own.

But she understood that running off with a woman he had called wife for eleven winters never will occur to Olepi. Not even when he chose her for his woman had they disappeared in this accepted manner, not even for one day and night, one sun, one sleep. Nor had he ever asked her out on one of those little raids mostly for show, not for any real fighting. Other husbands occasionally took their wives along on such excursions but not Olepi. But then Olepi never went out on a raid for show alone.

Many little irritations began crowding Napewaśte's thoughts as she stood alongside Unci and watched the dancers. Then all at once she recognized her mood; she had become iśnati.

That this thing happens now annoyed her. Not only will she need to move into one of the single-person tipi at the edge of the encampment until the influence of the moon passes, but she dares not, in this condition, glance toward the dancers. Her very look perhaps disheartens someone; the grandmothers had said so.

The woman started for her lodge; she will get robes and food bowl and the sack of absorbent she had prepared from the fluff of the drumbeater stalk. Unci, aware of that which sent Napewaśte hurrying back to the lodge, followed after her daughter.

"Know yourself as one with earth," she told Napewaśte; "resent not this thing that shows your power for producing child. Go to the iśnatipi and stay inside that place. The women who bring you meat will give news of the sungazers."

Napewaśte barely had settled herself in the woman-alone tipi when she learned that the gazer who dragged pte-skulls had shaken off his load but that the man at the center not yet made any effort at tearing loose from his thongs. Everyone had begun to remark on Olepi's amazing endurance.

232

The woman lifted the tipi flap and watched the wispy cloud-tails which brushed across the moon. But suddenly she wondered whether the night-sun reflected her gaze onto the dancers as she had heard someone say. She dropped the flap and moved again onto the hide. Her back humped, knees slightly spread, her cheek on the robe, she rested comfortably. The grandmothers had told that a woman so posed never will feel discomfort when the moon sits over her, nor will anything impede her flow. And if she needed to touch herself anywhere, a scratching-stick lay within reach.

Sighing softly, she closed her eyes; she listened to the drumbeat until she slept.

A distant rumbling in the sky awakened Napewaśte. Dawn had broken darkly and, pulling aside the flap, she looked into a thin mist. And now she saw her mother at the entrance to the little tipi, the woman bringing food and telling at once that the men go on dancing.

"Listen," she said, her voice frightened; "the contraries sing." She poured warm soup into her daughter's bowl. "Eat. I will clean up in here."

Using the quill brush that she had brought with her, Unci swept the soiled fluff into a sack for burning, then spread a clean covering of fluff. She moved jerkily, her motions, like her voice, hinting fear of the wakinyan, the flying-mystery, that hovered in the rain clouds overhead.

Napewaśte drank the soup and listened to the contraries, the camp-clowns. And a sadness touched her heart as whenever she heard these cloud-dreamers sing or watched their comical antics. Most persons laughed, and properly, at the foolish speech and crazy acts of these amazing men whom they call heyoka, but she wondered whether their ridiculous appearance and preposterous maneuvers perhaps hid a lonesome heart. She knew with what difficulty she rid herself of anxieties; so perhaps these men, born sad, sought the cloud-dream that compelled their contrariness.

They sang now as always, each one intoning his own special song, words and vocables never understandable and the confusion enough to scare off anything.

Or will their noise frighten away the wakinyan, the dread mystery that rumbles down from the clouds? The sky had begun to pour water in heavy drops. Napewaśte leaned sideward, her head resting on her mother's lap.

Unci stroked the daughter's hair and sang a child's song of affection, but the young woman heard only the war cry of the clouds and the rain seemed like an enemy sneaking into camp. She shuddered and so Unci began a new song, a plea for protection.

The rain stopped; the mysterious-flight had traveled quickly over the sungazing circle and moved onto the plain. The people came from under the shelter, shouting praise for these heyoka and for Olepi, the man who stayed in place.

All other dancers had gone from the suncircle, the wapiya permitting. Only Olepi stayed, Olepi the sungazer and Wanaǧi the sacred-man had kept a place under the warring sky.

Suddenly a voice hushed the cheering people; the herald called out that the flying-mystery circles the sky and comes back to the encampment. Let each one return to his lodge and stay in hiding. Perhaps the flashing danger returns in wrath, intent on killing.

The people looked once toward the man whose flesh stretched painfully at four points, then they scattered as people scatter in a surprise attack.

Hearing the crier, Napewaśte lifted her head in alarm.

Unci regarded her daughter closely. "Will someone iśnati look up at the night, at the round moon?" she said sternly.

Napewaśte remembered her talk with Tatewin and her night-gazing on the moon. Her head dropped back down on her mother's knee.

The clouds, edging up to the encampment, glared at the lodges. Then suddenly the winds turned against the clouds, a strong breath in the face of flash and noise.

But the flying-mystery refused to retreat; instead the wakinyan made a second charge on the camp even as the warriors twice had charged the sunpole-tree.

And so the heyoka came again into the suncircle, each one offering his pipestem to the crashing sky. But new rain fell as if a cloud had burst. The contraries ran off as before.

234

Now the sky flung down rain like woman's hair and the weathers pounded the tipi covers until the people feared for their lodges. In the iśnatipi, Unci wailed as for a warrior struck down.

The fury in the air swept against the person of the sacred-man, but this pelting, as against stone. Wanaġi stood, his robe down off his shoulders, the rattling rain bouncing off his flesh, the whole of him indifferent to the encircling turbulence.

The icy seeds gave way again to a stinging pour of water while the winds stopped to watch.

And now Wanaġi moved. Slowly, he walked toward the man whose form the rain had blurred, toward the man who stood at the center.

But suddenly, as if in response to a command, the rain ceased. And now the wapiya stood next to Olepi, blowing on the gazer's neck, four strong breaths; then he moved back.

The Mahto gave a forward jerk, three more jerks and the thongs dropped from his shoulders. Somewhere in the clouds the flying-mystery rumbled softly.

Wanaġi came again to Olepi's side; again he blew on the gazer's neck but he had not moved away as before; he stood looking into the Mahto's face.

Olepi jerked back but his flesh resisted the pull. He lifted his face to the dark sky and blew upon the wingbone with all the breath of his body.

A ball of fire bounced off one pole and streaked crazily over the ground; the sky crashed down.

Olepi's form twisted violently. Then slowly, slowly his weary person fell against Wanaġi, the sacred-man's arms stretched out to receive him.

A second dazzling flash staggered Wanaġi but he retained his hold on Olepi, the two clinging as if one drowns, one tries to rescue. But the next moment the Mahto straightened up; he moved away from the poles, the wapiya a step behind him.

The fight had gone out of the sky. The flying-mystery, grumbling defeat, headed for a far-off butte.

And now the voice of the crier made known that this sungazing comes to a finish; let the people walk from their tipi rejoicing.

Persons gathering in Heȟaka's lodge spoke with awe about this day, a day the Lakotah always shall remember. Rain, unknown to all other sungazings, had poured from a sky they had imagined forever compassionate toward this ceremony. But a wapiya, standing abreast the weathers, had acted to command the power in the sky, shutting off the water, evading the fireball that the flying-mystery had flung down. Will they not see Wanaġi compel the ball of fire to melt the thongs at Olepi's tortured breast and, commanding the flash to return, use this power to arouse the stunned gazer and put him on his feet?

Truly this day the Lakotah gaze upon a most marvelous show of endurance, but will they not call the sacredman's demonstration something even more marvelous? Certainly the powers loan Wanaġi a most wonderful day. A picture-record, they say, will help the people remember the important happenings of each season, but who will need a picture to help remember this day?

XX

NEWS OF the sungazing swept over the yellow grasses and across the big river and far up among the brackish lakes where small bands of Dakotah camped, Dakotah who never had traveled on the plain. But now these people decided to visit their Titonwan kinsmen who formed so great a hoop.

The same news, traveling a different direction, reached Iśna, leader of the Kuya Wicaśa band, who camped none knew exactly where. And soon this standoff group came asking for a visitor's place in the Titonwan circle of lodges.

And next, the headstrong leader of the Mnikooźu suddenly saw fit to lead his band to pahamni ridge.

And now the Śahiela, gathering for their own thanks-offering ceremony, sent word that those warriors who had pledged to join the Titonwan in their avenging of the twenty-eight killed lodge-brothers will start for the Lakotah encampment at the close of their sungazing.

The Titonwan leaders, hearing the Sahiela's message, grunted approval but blood flowed warm with pride; never before had any outsiders come to their assistance; not before had an alien people recognized their strength on the plain.

Now let the parent people scoffingly called the Titonwan 'witanhantahipi,' a group inordinately proud; let those Isanyati say that the Titonwan run away from the parent fire at the edge of the great lakes, that they lose interest in their parents' war against the Hahatonwan, the waterfall villages.

Witanhantahipi. Certainly, the Titonwan come from the place of sunrise and onto the plain. Will other persons show this courage? Will the parent bands cross a muddy river and step onto earth sparsely scattered with trees and everywhere marked with the tracks of an enemy horseback?

Let the Isanyati come here and see this ridge where three hundred lodges now form one great hoop, more than two hundred Titonwan lodges and nearly one hundred more lodges sheltering kinsmen who visit the Titonwan.

Let the Wiciyela come here and view the thong wounds on the Mahto leader, breast and back, a man who sungazes in a manner none other ever tries. And let these same Wiciyela—these Ihanktonwan Dakotah—meet a seer who challenges the flying-mystery, a man without fear of the clouds. And then let the parent peoples say again that name Witanhantahipi. But with respect.

The four deciders had spoken: none in this encampment shall make up a war party until after the attack on the Psa camps. The Sahiela warriors who had pledged their support had begun to arrive, and the Titonwan leaders intended that nothing happen to discourage these Sahiela from going out with the Lakotah.

But a group of woman-hungry Titonwan youths—young men impatient for the feathers that mark a warrior, permit him a wife—had sneaked out on foot, walking in a direction opposite the Psa camps, scheming to outwit the clubs.

Before evening, these same ones sat again at their

family fires, a cut across their shoulders, a shamed look on their faces. The clubmen had discovered the missing youths, and Icabu, choosing to make an example of these recalcitrants, had approved the reprimand.

Olepi spoke twice of the incident in his son's presence; he wanted the boy to understand that which happens when someone, acting foolish, endangers the tribe as a whole.

Peta, listening, also remembered that none of the unruly youths belonged to any Mahto family.

While the Sahiela warriors and their families visited the encampment, and before the avenging party went out, the Titonwan desired to feast their guests on fresh meat. And so the scouts had gone-to-the-hills, and the hunters again sharpened their weapons.

Tunkašila, lodge-keeper for the Šiyo scouts, turned over the near-empty scout-lodge to a reliable youth and came to visit his daughter Napewašte.

He announced himself at the tipi cover before midday, but, wherever the sun, he looked for his daughter inside her lodge. They had taught the young woman that a good wife stays in or near her tipi, not out running around camp, gossiping or making herself difficult to locate. He knew that she rarely visited even her sister in the Šiyo village but asked, instead, that her sister's little girl come to see her.

Napewašte welcomed her father graciously and the man stood a moment to enjoy the sight of her nicely rounded face and pretty smile, her teeth white and straight. Now in her twenty-eighth winter, she had kept her girl-shape; she had not spread in the manner of some women her age.

The daughter recognized his pleasure, and her heart went out to this respected blood-father. She gestured him to the back of the lodge, brought him a bowl of fat meat.

When the bowl sat empty and he had used his hands to wipe his mouth, he spoke his message abruptly: "I and my grandson Peta travel together, perhaps six, seven sleeps. Your son's eyes, ears, nose need sharpening. Whatever his legs will not outrun, his senses shall outwit."

He moved toward the front of the tipi. "I and he go at dawn. Put out moccasins and fill one pair with scout-meat."

The next instant, the man had gone. Tunkašila's quick

238

way of appearing, disappearing, had earned him his reputation for cunning in his own scouting days.

Napewaśte had waited for husband and son to finish eating before she told of Tunkaśila's visit and the man's desire that his grandson accompany him the next seven days. But she saw at once that the invitation disarranged something that her son had schemed.

Olepi moved over against his backrest before responding to his wife's words, and she wondered whether he also rejected her father's good offer.

"Your son chooses his gift-horse," Olepi said. "He selects a young one with fine legs." His eyes appraised the boy. "Let your son speak his choice to stay or go with his grandfather."

But Peta talked only about the new horse. Lekśi, sitting back in the shadows, listening to the glad young voice, remembered a child-horse important to his own youth, a creature much like the one this boy now described, a horse with long legs and deep front and short back, a horse shaped for a fast run.

"This black one will win every race . . . providing I begin the teaching next day."

Olepi heard the plea in the boy's voice. "My son," he said, "as you will see to the teaching of your horse, so your grandfather will see to the teaching of a boy." He looked closely at Peta's face. "Something disturbs my son?"

"My father, what shall I ride when I travel with Tunkaśila? Certainly not my mother's dog. Or will my grandfather ask that I sit up behind him like a little boy? And my bow . . . a plaything. What new things will I learn with a toy? But if I wait until I gentle my new horse, and until my arrows streak out from a strong bow . . . "

Olepi spoke firmly: "When your grandfather travels, he goes on his own legs. He protects himself with a sharp nose, alert ears, a quick head. But perhaps my son lacks such weapons."

The boy, regretting his foolish tongue, looked away; the grandfathers say, he remembered, that a youth shall take care before he speaks and so he needs never regret.

When finally Peta went to his sleeping robes, he took a heart full of good resolve: not again will his mother need to make the soft murmur that cautions him against hasty speech in the presence of his father.

Then, not yet asleep, Peta heard his father crawl up quietly, the man placing his short bow alongside the moccasins that the woman had tied together for her son's travels.

Napewaśte, awake before sunrise, glanced toward Peta's sleeping place; gladly she saw boy and moccasins gone. But the thin light showed that Olepi's bow remained where the man had placed this weapon. Her heart fell; if Peta's father finds this thing displeasing, her day will become most trying.

She slipped on moccasins and hurried to the woodpile. Her husband's soup shall float fat and taste of his favorite root and contain big hunks of meat. And while he eats he shall see her removing spots and dust from a pair of his leg-covers. And she shall watch his every move, her hands ready for whatever he desires.

But when Olepi came from the tipi, he headed for the men's bathing place without a glance in her direction. And the sun had passed overhead before he came back.

Napewaśte had kept the soup warm and so she quickly filled his bowl, took him his food where he sat inside the lodge. She had started away when he caught her foot and pulled her down gently.

"When I eat, I like my wife eating with me." He had spoken and she marveled her quickening heart.

Certainly when a woman said 'husband' her thoughts and acts translated instantly into fondness, respectfulness, obedience. But something about this man Olepi made his wife constantly desirous of pleasing, obeying him. And the effect of his hand on her leg now, a mystery even to herself.

Olepi put meat from his bowl into her mouth, and when she swallowed the piece, he stroked her cheek gently. Then he returned to his own eating, his eyes smiling.

The man's bowl twice empty and his mood seemingly affable, Napewaśte decided to speak of Peta.

"Your son goes out silently before dawn," she told. Olepi said nothing and so she spoke again. "He wakes none who sleep here."

Instead of making answer, the man rolled back on his sleeping robes and closed his eyes. Why tell her that he heard the grandfather and boy going out, that a soft flutter of the tipi flap revealed their going. Why tell that he had considered throwing a moccasin at Peta, startling the boy, but that he had remembered who handled this whole experience, that the grandfather will take over for a while.

Outside the tipi Napewaśte wiped clean the man's bowl and wished that she had kept silent about the boy. Will she ever, ever understand Olepi's moods? She saw now that the rejected bow had annoyed his father, perhaps spoiled Olepi's swim or his ride or walk through camp this day.

And now she came upon a new thought; she set the bowl down fast. Not once since the sungazing had Olepi bathed her, prepared her for his embrace. Perhaps he regarded her as old and undesirable at twenty-and-seven winters; perhaps he wished for a young and pretty wife.

The woman's imagination swept her along. Perhaps, she told herself, he never intended to ride or walk through camp this day or to visit Heħaka in his lodge. Instead he had sat in a tipi where a smiling girl brought him water and meat and . . .

Napewaśte gave the man's bowl a disdaining look, then took off across the camp circle bent on a visit with relatives in any lodge away from her own.

The birds had begun their sleep-songs when the woman finally returned. Never before had she stayed away until dusk, and she wondered in what mood Olepi awaited her.

She entered a dark and empty lodge. Picking up the birdwing fan which lay near the fire circle, she impatiently fanned the embers hidden under white ash. The glow refused to make flame, and so she brought in burning sticks from another woman's fire to give light in her tipi.

The soup, long neglected, had cooled. She lifted out a bone and sucked on this piece indifferently. Suddenly she threw the bone across the lodge. If Olepi comes in starving, let him help himself to meat on the drying-rack; why trouble with fire and hot stones and boiling soup now.

She moved onto her sleeping robes and lay down, one arm flung across her forehead. After a while she sat up and, loosening her braids, brushed her hair smooth. She changed to a fresh gown for the night, then slowly removed her moccasins; she lay down as before.

For a moment she stayed quiet, but now she sat up and

put on her moccasins again. A woman sleeps with something on her feet only when the people camp near the enemy or when her lodge lacks a man's protection. And certainly neither husband, uncle, brother, or son protects her lodge this night. Let the Mahto leader come in and see her wearing moccasins . . . if he comes back at all. She kicked off the robe bunched at her side; she made certain that he shall see her feet.

The woman intended only to pretend sleep, but whatever one enacts, the grandmothers say, usually occurs. And so Napewaśte slept.

Suddenly she awoke, the sound of laughter startling her awake. Olepi sat looking into her face.

"My wife says that she hears everything, even in her sleep." His tone mocked her but pleasantly. "Yet a man enters her tipi, chews on a cold meatbone two arms' length from her ear and crawls up alongside her before she hears anything."

He lifted a handful of her hair and spread the strands playfully over her cheeks. Then, pushing aside the hair, he peeked into her face, his eyes teasing.

She wanted to turn from his twinkling look; instead, she lay smiling at him, then laughing with him, and then suddenly quiet as his hand moved over her face, gently pinching her nose, rubbing her chin. Now his fingers separated her lips and he placed his open mouth against hers; his heart will whisper to her heart. And that which his heart spoke dismissed her foolish notion about this one she calls 'mihigna,' this man whose hair falls heavily on her cheeks, whose hand, under her gown, makes known a desire.

"Come," he said, pulling her up from the robes. His look and tone had changed, his eyes and voice telling her that he, the captor, speaks his want and commands her readiness.

She stood before him and saw his smile. "I see that you wear moccasins and so I know your eagerness for the trail to the stream where you want me to bathe you."

His eyes held hers and she stood without the will to protest these words, whether he spoke seriously or teased. She cared only that his hands touch her body, that the stream and the man make her clean, prepare her for a most sacred use. She remembered the joy his body gave hers and her desire for another seed, one from which a girl-child shall grow. Trembling, she put her hand in his.

Standing next to Olepi in the dark water, the woman found herself shy as on that day eleven seasons past when he brought her to a stream. And she quivered now as then, for she knew the pleasure in this bathing and the importance of her taste. And she threw a voice to the powers everywhere that she stay forever sweet to this man's tongue.

The warm night helped the man dry his woman, and the same soft air followed after these two as they walked back to the lodge. But once inside the tipi, the man tied down the flap, shutting out even the breath of darkness.

Now, on this night, he takes his wife as man always shall take a woman, wisely seeking his own pleasure, finding joy in her smell and taste, in her nakedness, and in her whimpers. And then, each of his senses sharply aware, he shall empty himself but never without knowing that his joy meets with her joy, their spirit-selves merging.

Afterwards he shall lie quiet while new life flows back into him. And then he shall make his thanks-offering to woman, discovering those things that excite her, please her, for as long as her body desires his touch. And when finally she reaches out for sleep, he shall pull the length of her against the length of him and so hold on to her until the dawn star separates their bodies.

And so two souls whom choice alone shall bind, grow close as the great mystery makes closeness, every act a natural one and each thought, expressed or never spoken, something to generate respect. And so each heart expands until neither edges nor shadows exist between man and wife. And so man shall understand that which the Dakotah call hunka, the true hunka: woman-wife and woman-mother; man moving through woman's body and into her soul. And always leaving his seeds with desire for child.

A new day painted the morning sky and smoke rose from many cooking fires, but nothing curled up from Napewaśte's lodge, inside or out. The woman slept on, but occasionally her body remembered the passing night, a little quiver, a little murmur letting the husband know.

243

In response to these small moves and sounds the man tightened his hold and whispered 'hush, hush,' as to a child, and the sleeping one, like a child, breathed a quiet sigh.

Soon, Olepi knew, the woman shall awaken and, seeing a pile of ashes in the circle where she looks for fire, will scramble from her robes to get wood and water. But when she opens her eyes, he shall demand that she put her hand where her hand belongs. And keep hold on him.

Too seldom will he sleep on these robes, and now, Peta away and Lekśi aware of the husband's desire to have Napewaśte to himself, he intends using this day to appreciate the one he calls wife.

Napewaśte stirred. "Hush," he whispered into her mouth. "Hush-sh. Iśtima, sleep. I will keep you here."

Her eyes stayed closed, but a tiny smile touched her lips; her hand reached for him, touching him where a wife shall touch.

And now the husband made the sighing sound. "You make me feel good, good," he said.

She opened her eyes. "My husband," she whispered softly, "my husband."

XXI

PETA HAD followed his grandfather quietly out of the sleeping camp. The boy had tied a summer robe around his waist, and on his back he carried two bundles of moccasins, Tunkaśila's extra pairs and his own.

A dark robe cut from an old tipi cover hung at the man's hips, and across his shoulder, bow and arrows. Each traveler held on to his own water-sac.

Where the camp trail branched, Tunkaśila motioned his grandson out in front. "Go toward the earth-smoke," he instructed briefly. And Peta, knowing the earth-smoke as a river to the south, put the fixed star at his back and started out.

He moved confidently along a much-used trail, a bitten moon helping him keep on the path.

His grandfather had advised a jog, but Peta chose to move as fast as the disappearing night permits. And certainly he traveled without fear of the dark. He knew that Titonwan scouts nested on the ridge, these men aware who leaves or enters camp. And that they will signal if anything dangerous creeps up ahead or from behind. Truly, this traveling seemed more like a night game of follow-the-leader and he, Peta, the leader.

But now the boy considered certain things: if he shall lead all the way, he needs to find the head of that creek familiar from his travels with the Okandada, and another familiar stream, the one with trees thick along the edges.

As he ran, he remembered to sniff the winds, to listen for voices. And to guard his little shadow.

His young feet touched lightly on the encouraging earth, but certain ones, prowling the night, sensed his coming. Twice the howl of the true-dog wailed down from the ridge, and once a skunk drenched the air. But he had not startled. Will not a grandfather have strong praise for a boy who runs without fear, never stops, and never, never turns and looks back, a grandson who never wanders off the trail and who finds the head of the little stream he seeks in these pale moments before dawn?

When the fixed star dimmed, Peta hunted the daybreak star among the little suns that dot the sky. But a dark butte rising in front of him seemed a more reliable guide; he pushed off in this direction.

The sky reddened and Peta saw the tall-ears bounding into the thickets, the traveling-dog returning to his den, a skunk plodding along in flatfoot manner.

But he knew that the same dawning sky will bring many creatures into the clear. Bending their heads to the browse, the branched-horns will nibble and munch the sage and make nothing of a boy's passing. Yet a group of sandy-belly pronghorns on a knoll will wag their white bottoms and run off, but whether in fear of him or something different he never will know.

Suddenly the boy-traveler sensed an affinity with all

this spirit and power loaned to the plain and he threw his glad young heart toward the moving-mystery. He decided to give careful attention to each creature in view and so have ready the answers for everything Tunkaśila asks him. For certainly, his grandfather will test him.

He remembered those winter visits in his grandparents' lodge and Tunkaśila's way of trying 'him: will Peta know which ones among the hoofs play here on the snow or which winged makes this delicate tracing on the mud? Once his grandfather had shown him the dense hair on a certain hide, then asked in which moon they had skinned this chunky striped-face. And on a different occasion Tunkaśila had wanted him to tell not only who whistled in the high breaks but the age and strength of the branched-horn who made the shrill, thin cry.

See the flock of forktails, Tunkaśila will say; they bring a message. Let Peta tell what news comes with these birds who carry mud in their mouths. Or perhaps the old scout asks what the winged red-shoulders hints when this one calls out 'pogehli-i-i,' or where to look for pasu śkopa, the bird with the long curved-down nose.

These things Peta will answer easily, but will not Tunkaśila during these travels discover something big to puzzle a boy ten, eleven winters?

And now something cautioned Peta to rest and wait for his grandfather; a small pain had begun gnawing at his side, slowing his pace. And so, spreading his robe on the dew-wet grass, he lay face down on the soft hide. After a while he sat up; he sipped from his water-sac.

Suddenly Tunkaśila came into view but the old man jogged on past the boy and up the trail.

"I am coming, grandfather." Peta got up hastily.

"So I see," Tunkaśila called back.

The boy managed a spurt that carried him ahead of the man, but he soon had difficulty keeping in front of his grandfather, especially on the hillside or moving up a draw. A big pain bit into his side, and his moccasins, which the dew had softened, made known each pebble on the trail. He wished a finish to this game of follow-the-leader.

He began puzzling a clever way to get his grandfather to call a rest, but then he saw the dark forms of eight, perhaps ten pte. Tunkaśila carried arrows he remembered;

perhaps he will make the kill. Keeping downwind, the boy turned toward the small herd.

The pte stood as if frozen while Peta made his careful approach. Then, about to stoop and throw his robe over his head, the boy saw the truth: he had mistaken some scattered boulders for a bunch of grazing pte.

Whatever his shame, Peta had not looked for ways to cover up his mistake. Let the ridicule come. He ran toward a clump of concealing brush and dropped down on the hard earth; he threw aside the moccasin bundles and lay back.

Tunkaśila came up and squatted with this scout-meat and, pinching off six small pieces, he let these bites fall from his palm onto the ground, one way to thank the power that put the herds on earth.

Peta waited for his grandfather's reproach, but when the man said nothing, the boy sat up and reached into the moccasin; mimicking Tunkaśila, he broke pieces off the dried meat-balls.

Presently Tunkaśila stood and, holding his nose between his fingers, cleared his nostrils. Now he spoke: "My grandson uses the little night-sun and stays on the trail. He watches the rising dawn and stays on the trail. But when he walks on his own shadow will he know his path?"

"Grandfather, I watch a certain butte. That one . . . ." He looked out from puzzled eyes, four different buttes now in view. Which butte points the way he dared not say. He avoided his grandfather's unrelenting gaze.

"My grandson rides more often than he walks. He sits high above the ground and never sees those signs put out for him." The man paused to let the boy catch up with these words.

"A horse walks for my grandson, and too much horse softens a boy's feet and shortens his breath. In my youth-seasons a boy ten winters runs a day and a night and pain never grabs him. Legs perhaps weaken but breath, never. Not when he runs a little while, jogs a little while, walks a little while.

"Understand, mitakoźa. When a boy runs in the manner you run, certain little air sacs sticking flat to the ribs suddenly puff up. Pulling away, they make pain. But nothing for alarm."

So Tunkaśila knows about his side-ache? A short distance back he had wished that Tunkašila question him about the trail; now he wished that his grandfather ask nothing.

Tunkašila made the cut-throat sign. "If my grandson wants the enemy's knife at his neck, let him risk twice that which he risks this dawn."

Peta's eyes looked to the ground; his finger tips idly scratched the dry earth.

The man, recognizing the boy's hurt pride, made use of the informal, easy talk permitted between grandfather and grandson; but nothing like sympathy entered his speech: "You dash onto the flat yet you neither crouch nor cover yourself. You disregard the protecting hollows and thickets and your shadow looms on the barren hill. You look out for one butte in your path but neglect other things. What of dust or smoke rising off the plain? What of fresh horse droppings on the trail? Who kicks a pebble out of the nest? Will small birds fly over singing?

"You have many friends looking after you as you travel. Jog along close and I will show you."

The man bent to wipe away the signs of their resting and Peta changed moccasins; perhaps stiff, dry bottoms will comfort his feet.

Now Tunkašila pointed to the place where Peta's fingers had scraped the clay; the boy smoothed over the ground.

"Will you leave behind an old moccasin to mark your trail?"

At once the boy grabbed up the discarded one, then spun around to see what leaped out of the dry grass in the near distance.

He glimpsed a pair of tall ears and one long jump; obviously the creature tried to escape from something.

"My grandson shall discover why this one bounds away." Tunkašila had spoken.

Quickly they located the footmarks. Some short leaps and a soaring bound told the man about the creature's scare but he said nothing to the boy.

"Perhaps tall-ears hears me talking, grandfather."

"Not unlikely," Tunkašila answered dryly. "This one hears two, three hairs brushing against grass."

Peta held back any other guesses until he had examined

248

the ground all around. Then quietly he made his pronouncement: "The traveling-dog threatens this tall-ears. I see where the dog turns and hunts a short trail."

The boy heard an approving grunt, a sound as pleasing as his name in a song. And now Tunkašila gestured that they return to their own trail. "Lead," he ordered, but Peta hesitated.

"My grandfather says he will show me my friends along the trail if I stay close behind him."

"After you show me the canyon beyond the butte," the man answered.

And now Peta, looking calmly to sun and shadow, rediscovered his butte.

When they reached the steep break in the earth, Peta heard himself twice awarded the grunt of approval. But the untiring man had not advised a little rest at this place; instead he jogged in front of his grandson, Peta struggling to keep up.

Soon the boy's tongue hung out and the side-ache came back to taunt him; he had to stop and rest even if Tunkašila jogged off and left him forever.

"Pick up a little stone. Hold the pebble on your tongue."

His grandfather's sudden appearance amazed the boy. He imagined the man far ahead on the trail, yet here he stood and only moments after Peta had ceased running.

"When the ache eases, fit the pebble into the nest again." Tunkašila disappeared in the same sudden manner he had appeared. And Peta, his hand flung over his mouth, stood marveling.

The pebble had helped him; perhaps his grandfather regarded the stone as one of those 'friends' along the trail. Replacing the pebble in the clay, he murmured his thanks to this small, round hardness.

When Peta caught up with his grandfather the old one spoke sternly. "Twice I advise the jog. Those little running dashes give new wind to a horse but I see they give nothing to you."

The boy, surprised at the reproof, answered defiantly. "My grandfather's legs have a long stretch. I take three steps to his one."

"Someone stays out in front before sunrise. Will this same someone say my legs grow with the day?"

Glancing at the man, Peta wondered whether Tunkaśila always had appeared this unrelenting, this demanding. His grandparents usually camped with the Śiyo, his grandmother raising her tipi alongside her other daughter—Wiyanna—whose Sicangu husband had come into his wife's band. And so he, Peta, had not seen as much of these old ones as customary. Truly, this travel with Tunkaśila provided him his one experience alone with the grandfather, his only blood-grandfather.

But demanding or not, one thing he had begun to understand about his grandfather: Tunkaśila never teases; Tunkaśila means everything he says.

And so man and boy moved on the summer-yellow grasses, a strict teacher, an apt pupil. Here, on this dry plain, the boy shall learn where earth hides her water when the streams empty and the rain stays away. For on a certain day Tunkaśila shall find those trails that lead to wallows and sinks and burn-outs and here show Peta the way to bring water up through sand until his drink comes clear. He will teach the boy ways to persuade the prickly-leaf to yield water, something the tall-ears, who seldom thirsts, had shown the man.

Afterwards, he will make the grandson look up and see the dark cloud-sacs which hold the water in the sky. The boy shall learn that sky half-clear never spills rain and that the big shaggy clouds in a morning sky foretell flash-and-noise but that these same ones appearing after midday come as a decoration, something for the setting sun to paint red and yellow.

One evening Peta had watched many, many small round clouds boil up around the black neck of a whirling wind and so he had related the sight to the simmering meat sacs. But will hot stones bubble the sky?

"Look up, look up," Tunkaśila had said on a different day, and Peta, looking, had seen the scattering of little white clouds as the thin layer of fat that covers the paunch. But he had pondered the white wavy lines so like the ripples in the sandy bottom of a stream. Will the same power put these wavy marks on sky and on sand and on certain stones? And what power? Śkan, taku śkanśkan? Or some different mystery a boy of ten winters not yet knows?

"Look up, my grandson. See the tracks on the sky. Those circling wings inform you of kill and killer, the dead and whoever feast on the dead."

And Peta, looking, had decided that the sky owns a language, something he needs to learn.

On other days Tunkaśila directed the boy's eyes to the ground. "Look down. Watch the tiny crawling things." And Peta, watching, saw one small thing hump onto a white flower, the creature attaching bits of the bloom to her body until she sat covered over with white, lost to the boy's view.

"What enemy owns eyes sharp enough to see this creature now?" Tunkaśila said.

Nearby a fluttering-wing had come to rest on the bright flower of the prickly stalk. The boy, responding to his grandfather's gesture, looked closely at bloom and wing. Marveling the blend, he voiced something with a swiftness that surprised even himself: "The wings and the hoofs see the same colors I see."

When Tunkaśila answered, he spoke sharply. "Why ponder? Recognize, instead, in what manner a scout learns to conceal himself in an enemy camp."

When next Tunkaśila stopped to rest, the two stood at a place of low brush. What happens here, the man wanted to know; he pointed at tracks.

The boy recognized at once the signs of something antlered, branches or spikes but not wapiti, not pronghorn. The creature who passed here ran startled but instead of the hind feet swinging ahead of the front ones, all four came down together.

Tunkaśila approved the boy's careful appraisal of the ground; his grandson had observed something unusual here. And so the man told about the black-tail, about tahca, who runs differently from his antlered relatives and other big hoofs. Let Peta remember this difference.

But why the boy shall remember this difference Tunkaśila had not said. Peta had seen those antlered heads who lingered in the thickets along streams, who flung up a white tail, and certainly he knew their relatives with the black tail. But the meat of these two tasted the same and the spotted skins of young, white tail or black, made the same nice sacks for keeping berries. Why will a hunter need to know whether he pursues one tail or the other? Will some mystery attend the blacktail?

The sun, bending toward evening, stretched the shadows of the buttes onto the plain, their long shade protecting the travelers. And so these two looked out toward a ridge to the east where far-reaching rays revealed something that moved under the rim.

"The true-dog, the big white dog, walks that ledge." Peta had made certain before he spoke.

But Tunkaśila had not readily agreed. "The traveling-dog moves in this same manner," he said.

The boy's eyes followed the shape another moment. "His back crouches and his legs ... " Peta, reappraising, spoke quietly but soon his tone gave way to excitement. "See, grandfather, he runs now and his tail stays up."

Tunkaśila saw the little dust-cloud that rose up behind the dark, running form. "He makes tracks." The man began walking toward the ridge. "I look at these tracks before I know."

The grandfather let the boy discover the tracks. And so Peta lifted a surprised face. "The marks of a traveling-dog," he murmured, "but a big one."

"Look again; the true-dog and the wandering-dog wear almost the same moccasin." The man squatted down, inspecting the sand. "From a far distance my grandson sees this one running with tail up and so calls him a true-dog. And now seeing these tracks, he knows most certainly that he identifies the true-dog."

Will Tunkaśila try to confuse him? Tunkaśila who never teases?

Now the man told that the traveling-dog took a long step but not as long as the true-dog.

But the boy pointed to a change in the pattern, four feet bunched together.

"Same creature," Tunkaśila answered. "Here, a fast leaping run. Here, he slows to a comfortable lope. This one—not unlike a certain boy—needs keep a steady pace if he intends running until dawn."

And now Tunkaśila advised that they follow these tracks to a point of understanding.

"Observe the custom of this wise one," the man said as they trailed the true-dog. "He looks twice at each thing and so makes certain that he sees true. Even running for his life, he takes a second look at something. Unlike this true-dog, my grandson never looks back and so he will not recognize on his return those same buttes and canyons, those lonely objects he uses as trail markers."

Again Peta marveled his grandfather's knowing. Perhaps Tunkaśila really knows everything. He knows where water hides on the earth and in the sky. He knows in what manner each of the big hoofs runs, jumps, walks. He understands all about the true-dogs who appear forever moving, and he knows that the fleeing tall-ears uses his leaps for seeing behind, for judging his pursuer. And he knows that a certain boy will take pride—until now—in keeping his eyes always to the front.

Before darkness covered over, the travelers had come upon the flat once more and Tunkaśila had chosen a sleeping place.

Peta lay down close to a boulder, the touch of warm stone a comforting thing on the lonely plain. He had pulled his robe up to his neck and now intended to cover his head.

"Perhaps someone makes certain before he lies down that the hissing arrowhead will not sneak through the grass near this little camp," Tunkaśila said softly, "and that the four-legged warrior whose weak eyes occasionally mistake a boy for a chipmungk stays away from here."

Jumping to his feet at once, Peta looked under stones and grass clumps; he gazed into the dusky distance. "I see neither rattler nor grizzly," he announced cheerfully.

"Nor catch their smells?"

"I not yet know their smells, grandfather." He waited a moment, then pulled his robe away from the boulder and to a place close by Tunkaśila.

"The true-dog sharpens his nose through constant use," the man said as he lay down. After a pause, he spoke again. "A hoop of villages protects my grandson now, but when he goes out as a scout, he sleeps alone. And so he needs a way of knowing whether or not the rattle-tail, seeking warmth, comes crawling up to him. And usually his nose will tell him."

Tunkašila tucked his robe around his shoulders. "I lie in a good place. The earth invites me to sleep here." He pulled the edge of the robe over his head. And now he slept.

Peta lay awake sniffing the soft, warm air. He discovered nothing strange on the night wind and so he began to wonder about his new horse. And when finally he slept, he dreamed of a black horse who made the tracks of a true-dog, the horse running ahead of him but turning often, looking back to see if the boy trailed closely.

Before dawn the boy awoke; something heavy-footed, something big, moved toward him. He held his breath and listened. Then using those short sniffs that keep the air at the tip of his nose, he took in the smell of this approaching musk-carrier.

"My grandson puzzles something that disturbs his sleep."

Peta, glad that the man awakened, responded quickly, his voice not so sleepy but that he managed a little pride. "I am not puzzling anything, grandfather. I know who moves around this camp. I smell the flat-faced one, the creature who digs-with-the-mouth."

Tunkašila slipped the robe from over his head. "This flat-face hunts food for her young. Now something frightens her; she smells danger." He covered his face again.

"Grandfather, who ever frightens this creature?" Peta rolled within touch of the man.

"Grizzly."

The boy pushed tight against his grandfather.

Tunkašila yawned and turned on his side. "But the grizzly knows this one's claws and so these two usually avoid a meeting. My grandson will know when a grizzly comes near."

Peta found little comfort in his grandfather's speech; he wished that Tunkašila had not gone back to sleep so quickly.

He looked at the sky, marveling the footsteps of the spirits who leave their tracks on the deep black. Or so people say.

At the hint of dawn the stars began fading. And now the man awakened his grandson with a gentle pressure behind the boy's ear, arousing the sleeper without startling him. Almost at once the two started traveling again.

The boy watched for signs of the flat-face visitor who had come in the night. Instead his grandfather, the one to glimpse the flying sand, to point to where this loose-skinned creature digs in with foot and mouth.

Peta wanted to grab the vanishing tail, pull her from the hole and let Tunkaśila make the kill. But the man had answered crisply that he travels as scout, not hunter; his bow, only a weapon of defense. And something more: this one they call hoka talks with man and gives him good advice.

The sun warmed the air, and so the foot-going ones sought a breezy ridge. Here they watched a pair of fighter-birds climb the sky on pointed wings, then plunge downward to catch some unwary winged in mid-air. Tunkaśila, following their sky-path, discovered the steep cliff to which these fighters carried the kill, here to feed their young. But he knew that these swift and skillful birds occasionally killed for honor alone.

The Titonwan warriors made an example of these wingeds, even to the bird's stern and domineering look. And so the man, deciding that Peta shall learn something about this winged's bold nature, led the boy to the nest.

"Walk close behind me," he said, "but look around. Never expose yourself on a barren cliff to someone's view."

They reached the ledge where the fierce-looking young pecked on a kill. Tunkaśila grabbed for the bird near the edge.

At once the parent birds attacked the man; quickly, he withdrew his arm.

Now one of the full-growns struck at Peta. The boy dodged the notched, sharp-toothed beak but, wanting to show his daring, he grabbed for the feet of the big one who hovered over his head. When the bird's claw slashed one arm, the boy flung up his other arm and so protected his face.

Suddenly Tunkaśila reached up with the quick, brave hand of a man who once trapped the wambli-bird. Grasping one strong leg, he jerked the prairie-fighter down hard against the jutting ledge and the next instant folded one wing against the other.

"Pull out whatever feathers you want." Tunkašila held the wings together at the tips while Peta swiftly removed two black-banded feathers from the tail. Now, seeing the claws on this bird he had wounded, the boy decided to kill the winged-warrior; certainly he dared claim honors for intercepting the courageous fighter. "Grandfather," he said boldly, "I kill this one."

Tunkašila turned the bird breast up and Peta pulled a knob-tipped arrow from the holder on the man's shoulder. The mother-bird made a rattling cry as Peta struck her mate dead.

Proudly the boy carried the warm body down the cliff; he owned the beak and claws of a true-fighter. But then he remembered that Tunkašila had made the catch, Tunkašila who hunted with the eye, not the bow.

But, on reaching the bottom of the cliff, the man said only that Peta shall remove head, claws, tail and heart.

While the boy followed these instructions, the man went about gathering pte-chips. Now, holding two in each hand, he walked over to his grandson. "Hit the center of each chip I roll out and those pieces of bird belong to you." He gestured that Peta take the bow; he marked a place for the boy to stand.

Peta smiled; his grandfather made the game easy. Tightening the bowstring—the weapon's length and pull within his grasp—he fitted a blunt arrow and waited for Tunkašila to roll the target. He knew that he already owned the bird.

The white clay butte, originally Peta's most distant point, sat close by, and now the boy observed a change in the ground cover; many, many pebbles, either sliding or tumbling out of their nests on the butte, had rolled onto the flat. The boy made an appreciating murmur.

Stone, they told, endures more winters than any man, more winters than the most old among the grandfathers. Stone, the most old, the most enduring thing on earth. Tunkan, stone, ancient of days. . . .

But now Peta saw stone as a berry-pounder for his mother, for his grandmother.

He bent to pick up two such stones but Tunkaśila grunted an alarm.

The man stood unmoving and the boy knew to imitate the man. "Your nose tells you something."

That Tunkaśila, in the posture of one who senses danger, dares speak aloud, amazed the boy. Why not his grandfather's tongue freezing also?

Unaware of any peculiar scent, Peta's gaze searched the plain for whatever danger sat front. Seeing nothing for alarm far-off, he focused his eyes for near-ground. The wind rubbed the grasses against one another but he saw nothing different moving. Perhaps Tunkaśila used the warm claylike fragrance of stone as a test of his grandson's sense of smell; he moved slightly.

Instantly the man jerked back the boy's arm. A wavering, arrow-shape head flashed up from a rattling coil; a forked tongue flicked out and tasted the air.

"Stay," Tunkaśila commanded as he released Peta. "This one sees with eyes that never close, but he sees only that which moves."

"He hears my grandfather's talk." The boy spoke in a hushed voice.

"This one hears but not with ears," the man answered, his eyes fixed on the danger that sat six, seven steps away.

Peta recognized that which rattled at him; his mother once had caught a rattle-tail with her root-digger. He remembered that she had told of the creature's folding teeth; now he wanted to see for himself.

"Grandfather, I will throw something."

"Throw the stone in your hand," Tunkaśila answered.

Slowly raising his arm, the boy tossed the stone into the grass. He had a quick look at fangs striking against his throw, then movements as the creature slithered away and out of his sight.

"See that this one never surprises you, my grandson. The healers possess little power against a face wound; a bite on the cheek means the red robe. But the rattle-tail rarely surprises a boy with a sharp nose."

Peta waited for more cautions; instead Tunkaśila told

about seeing rattletails born during the old-summer moon, the mother's body sending forth perhaps ten, these new-borns slipping away, never knowing a parent, never seeing who gave birth.

My grandfather proves a most demanding person on this walk, Peta told himself as the two started out again, but I like traveling with him. The boy gave the man a shy, affectionate glance.

The travelers had walked only a little way beyond the tall white butte when suddenly Tunkaśila turned, the man starting back toward the steep hill. Hearing the barks and howls on those ledges, he had decided to let the true-dog give Peta two, three lessons.

The boy, told to follow certain tracks, grew confused. He had run up this little path and that, wherever the tracks led him. But whenever he stepped off the true runway, he found himself going in circles. Even more surprising, the tracks on these short paths revealed movements unusual to the true-dog.

Tunkaśila refused to point the way, but, seeing Peta wander all over the place, he offered advice: "Begin with a single footmark and follow this one track. Never leave the real trail.

"Recognize something similar among the two-legged. Many trails cross and diverge as you see here. But to reach your true desire, choose one trail and stay on that trail."

The boy listened but he saw nothing in this solemn speech to help him at the moment. If Tunkaśila will point out that 'single footmark' with which to begin, perhaps everything will come easily.

Peta had dismissed the tracks of any different four-leggeds as unimportant, but now Tunkaśila mentioned the smell of carcass and bone that lured many creatures along the trail to the true-dogs' burrow. The parent-dogs, he told, cram full their bellies at the kill, then disgorge at the burrow where the pups eat. But occasionally they return with necks and shoulders and legs on which these young try out their teeth.

And when Peta stood sniffing the four directions, Tunkaśila spoke of scent-piles along the true trail, of a strong smell at the roots of certain brush and of scratches on the ground nearby. And now the boy, choosing a certain runway, saw approval in the old scout's eyes.

In a sandy wash near a crumbling bluff, Peta came upon the family he had stalked. Four pups played on the silty ground and, resting close by lay three grown dogs, the parents and perhaps a joking-relative, an affinal relative.

The man and boy watched from a grove of white-wood. At one point Peta imagined that the true-dogs had discovered him; two got up, barked, and ran onto the ledge above the hole. Instead three more dogs came from somewhere and joined the noisy pair.

After a while a party of tiny wingeds began to make bumps on Peta's arms; he wanted to slap and scratch but he dared not alert the dogs. He stood wishing for piśko, birds who come at dusk, who splash noisily on the air and who catch these lump-raisers. But until such helpers come, he will stand quietly and, like his grandfather, ignore their little stabs.

And now the dogs, who had begun talking with their tails, apparently schemed a way to use up the night. Some of this sign-language required accompanying body motions or sounds in the same manner that a man, talking with hand-signs, uses his eyes or an occasional noise to make his meaning clear.

Soon, agreement seemingly reached, the grown dogs loped off in the direction of approaching dusk and the small ones disappeared into the hole. All but one. This pup, eager to follow his relatives, stood a moment at the entrance to the burrow, then ran out after the old ones.

Instantly Peta went after the pup; the chase, not much. The boy grabbed the creature's tail and the pup responded in the manner of a camp-dog ready for play.

The boy, carrying the pup back to his grandfather, looked for approval; he wanted to hold on to his catch.

Tunkaśila glanced at the bundle in Peta's arms, something mostly head and feet. But the eyes, like clear sky, and the newness of her teeth gave the man a clue to her age; born two moons past, she drank from her mother but also knew to tear meat from the bone.

The man cut a strip off his robe and tied the pup's legs. "Keep her under your arm," he advised and, turning abruptly, led the way back through the fading evening.

At their night-camp, Peta fastened a cord stripped from his own robe to the cord that held the pup's feet. Tunkaśila bent down a young tree and the boy slipped a loop over one branch. When the man let go, the cord jerked the pup onto her back but not off the ground.

"Perhaps she will bite through the cord." Peta looked anxious.

"Watch her. So you know."

The pup made many tries at breaking the cord but her twisting acted only to swing her uncomfortably.

Once during the night Peta awakened to a soft whining. He lifted his head slowly and stared into the dark; perhaps the family of true-dogs hunt their missing relative. He glanced toward his grandfather, but Tunkaśila, his head covered, lay like stone, a man truly deep in sleep.

Peta sat up for a while, listening to the pup's whimpers and remembering that this little one endures two moves—from the birthing den to a new burrow to this night under a tree—but that once in the Mahto camp this dog will not wait cowering while the dominant-tail eats the choice pieces. Or so Tunkaśila describes affairs among the true dogs.

XXII

THE AIR glistened with sun when Peta, awakening to the chirp of chipmungks, jumped to his feet. Then, puzzled that his grandfather let him sleep through sunrise, he looked toward the man's robe; perhaps Tunkaśila also followed sleep into morning.

He saw neither his grandfather nor any signs that the man ever had spread a robe on this ground.

The startled boy permitted himself a moment's relief; his grandfather searched for water somewhere nearby.

But now Peta saw tree-bark freshly peeled and some

scratches on the naked wood. Going close, he made out the sign for river and for the creature who swims-carrying-a-stick. At the bottom of the tree a slanted twig pointed south. His grandfather goes, the message said; let Peta find him on the earth-smoke river, at a place where capa makes a lodge.

Tunkaśila goes, but the man's bow-and-arrow carrier—the bird beak and claws in this same container—hung on a branch above Peta's head. Here also, the moccasins packed with wasna.

An anger rose in Peta against this relative who slipped away, an anger born of sudden fear; either he catches up with his grandfather before dark or he never will find him. Alone and on unfamiliar ground, he ... The pup made an attracting-sound and Peta remembered that he will not travel alone.

He went over to the little dog and reached out a soothing hand; he met with nothing friendly. Perhaps, then, he shall take her back to the true-dogs and stay on with that family himself and grow up wise, with more wisdom than any old Titonwan. The dogs will teach him the ways of a warrior-lodge and they will talk to him with tail-signs even if he lacks a tail for talking back.

The boy pulled down the moccasins and chewed on a consoling bite of meat. Next, he untied the discomfited pup and made one long leash out of the two. And then, bunching his robe at his waist, he started out after his grandfather.

He told himself that he and the pup shall not starve; he carries wasna and the bow; soon he will kill something for the young dog.

But the pup made her own kill. Plunging the length of the leash, she had snapped up a little squeaking whitefoot who scampered through the grass, not enough to satisfy but something until the boy discovered a chipmungk.

As Peta traveled he looked for signs to show him that Tunkaśila had come this trail: upturned stones, broken brush, grass tufts twisted in a revealing manner. Or a foot-mark.

Occasionally he stopped, his gaze moving over the yellow earth in the same manner he will gaze upon circles from the drop of a stone in a quiet lake. Once this careful inspection disclosed piled-stones and once a bent-stick in the cracked, dry ground.

261

In one ravine Peta found where the man had made some crude shafts, their points hardened over a handful of glowing wood. The discovery gave Peta new concern—perhaps his grandfather sees enemy tracks—until he recalled who carried the meat; truly, his grandfather, if he will eat, needs arrows.

The boy moved on, crouching in the open spaces, using the thickets and breaks wherever these hiding places appeared, and often looking back to see what shape the buttes will take on the opposite side. And he remembered to watch the sky for signs that point to happenings on earth.

Suddenly the going became easy, like 'stalking,' a boy's camp game. Tunkaśila had placed many signs, and the pup neither dragged behind nor fought to escape. Peta's face brightened; he dropped his complaint against his grandfather and rejoiced in his aloneness with the big sky and the good earth.

He listened for agreement from the buzzing grasses and the buzzing wings, in each of the voices that spoke to him as he traveled.

The wind patted his cheek and, responding to a surge of joy, he lifted his head to the sky and laughed. He saw that the sun climbed toward middle along a path of white fluffy shapes, and, fitting the bow, he sent an arrow toward one big humpbacked cloud. He sent a second arrow. And a third. Some white fluff drifted in under the humpbacked one and he imagined a dust kicked up by the wounded pte-cloud.

Putting aside the bow, he remembered the mysterious pte, that little white one whose tail he had touched. And he remembered the gift-horse coming out of this wonderful experience. Suddenly his heart soared at his own understanding of these many things that belong to him: the child-horse and the pte-cloud and all this sky where his thoughts now wander. Even the sun belongs to him.

And he owns the earth. For wherever he puts his foot, the power on the ground and in the ground, his to use. The grandfathers said so. All these things he, only a boy, already owns.

A chipmungk heralded the approach of the pup, the little creature trying to warn his relatives. But the next moment Peta's arrow put a stop to the alarm.

"If you look twice instead of only once," he told the killed one, "you will see that a bow travels alongside this little true-dog."

The pup tore into the warm body, and Peta, returning the arrow to the holder, noticed that he carried but four shafts now, two with blunted tips. Truly he had acted foolishly when he had not recovered that which he threw at the cloud; a hunter always picks up his arrows.

He hesitated, puzzling whether to go back and look. But what if he wanders off the trail? This will not happen, he told himself, not if he remembers the wind blowing in his face as now. And what happens if he comes across an enemy warrior?

Scanning the distant rise, he saw a hill black with quietly grazing pte. Nothing blew from that direction to arouse a herd nor will he arouse anything if he keeps downwind.

"I go," he told the tugging pup and headed on toward the rise and the earth-smoke river.

The day came into a heat that silenced the buzzing in the grasses and the humming in the air. And then Peta, growing thirsty, reached for the water-sac. But he had left the sac back at the night's camp.

Tunkaśila's disappearance had upset him; for this reason he had neglected to tie the water-sac at his neck or waist. Or so he tried to understand his negligence. But why wear the man-sign—the loin-cover at his middle—if he overlooks such important things as his water-sac. Perhaps they will advise that he run about like a little boy without anything on.

He calmed himself and observed the pte. The slowly moving, feeding herd hinted of water beyond the rise, if nothing more than a hollow where sticky earth will yield a drink.

The sun had misted over and the wind felt like a hot breath on the boy's cheek. Certain clouds, black as the painted faces of victorious warriors, threatened to split and let loose the flying-mystery.

Peta's soaring heart had dropped like a bird struck on the wing. Lacking sun to make shadow and wind to bend grass, he never shall reach the earth-smoke. And the lonely hill that marked his path in front appeared as far away as when he chose this point from the top of a ridge behind him.

The boy began to run toward the rise. But the pup jumped and turned and rolled until Peta, caught in the long leash, tripped and fell. Jerking the creature roughly to him, he smacked her nose.

"Your nation teaches me many things, friend, but now I teach you something." He struck her twice.

But this one, not a cringing camp-dog, snapped at the boy and made little charges all the while Peta hurried to untangle himself. Gone, that tender look usual in a pup of one, two moons; this day she had killed meat—only little-meat—but she had sunk new teeth into the flesh of chipmungk. Now, one quick, strong tug on the cord and Peta saw his pup, loose and running off, zigzagging her way among the tough bunches of grass.

The boy went after her at once, trying to catch the trailing leash. Then she had gone, a blur of white moving on the plain.

Peta returned to the place he had put down his moccasin-bundle and the bow, but these things, also, had disappeared. And now, his eyes filling, he disgraced himself with tears. True, none saw him, but a real man cries only when the enemy kills his relatives.

He wiped away the tears and, picking up a stone, spoke his need: "Tunkan, stone, give me help. I misplace certain things."

The sky rumbled as if to warn that something will come and play more tricks on him, as if to say that he never shall see moccasins, bow, water-sac again nor will the pup wander back to him.

He flung the pebble to the ground; standing quiet under the cloud-dark sky, he accepted great mystery and the ways of the moving-power.

Śkan, taku śkanśkan. The powers, knowing that he walks alone, send friendly voices and point out many things. But he stops and throws arrows—not his to throw—into one of those mysterious shapes that roam the sky. And he laughs when his arrow pierces this cloud, this wondrous sky-form.

And so the watching spirits see a boy with foolish ways. They begin to tease him, to tangle the leash and upset him.

They hide his moccasins and his meat and his way of making meat. And soon the powers, observing his impatience with the dog and even with the little stone, decide that all things shall desert this boy.

And so the little-people-of-the-air grow silent and the winds sit still and the sun covers over with cloud even as a man covers his face when in the presence of persons he suspects. The one voice speaking to Peta comes from some mysterious-flight and this one speaks only to taunt him.

Slowly Peta dropped onto the ground, his back against the good, renewing earth.

After a long while he smelled a freshness in the air; somewhere water fell from the sky.

He waited, eyes closed, for the rain to wash over him, but nothing wet came down; the flying-mystery had taken a different path. Opening his eyes he saw that clouds darkened a far-distant patch of sky.

He listened and a smile came to his lips; the tiny wings, humming and buzzing again, called for him to make another search for his missing moccasins.

Rising, he quietly hunted the place where his angry hand had flung the stone. Here he came upon bundle and bow. And here he made his thanks-offering: six pieces from the round of meat he carried in his moccasin.

Before he turned his back on the direction upriver, he squinted his eyes and searched the plain once again for any sign of the pup. Then, sensing that he faced south, he hurried his feet toward the roving ground of his Sicangu relatives. But his eyes and nose constantly hunted water, any water, in wallow or stem or berry.

None of the herd appeared aware of his movements as he jogged past the pte. He went on, hunching under ledges, using gully, boulder, brush, and hill for cover. He made a song for his grandfather, and the song gave him new running strength, new power. And now, coming around the side of a butte, he glimpsed a thin yellow cloud, shaping and reshaping before his eyes. In a little while he recognized the cloud as a gathering of fluttering-wings.

The people said that these clusters represented the young warriors among the painted-wings, but Peta remembered something more important: these fluttering ones usually hover above the damp wallows. And so he ran in the direction of the wavering yellow shape.

Intent on this guide to water, the boy looked neither to side nor back, and so he never saw a different cloud, the warning dust of hoofs and men. But suddenly the pounding of horsebacks reached his ears. Trembling, he looked behind him. He saw five horses; four carried men.

He flung himself into the bush; until he discovered whether Lakotah or enemy trailed him, he intended to stay out of sight. Perhaps one small foot-going boy will escape their notice.

Bending low, Peta pushed his way through the brush. And when finally his thighs rebelled against the unbalanced load, he sank down, demanding of his knees that which he had required of his legs. And so he crawled, scratched and hurting, in whatever directions the thickets opened up a path.

The horsebacks had seemed a far distance back of him, but, pressing his ear to the ground, he knew that they came his way and that they came fast.

He dropped his robe, which had hampered his movements; he now exerted himself beyond any previous efforts. But at last his knees crumpled; he flattened to elbows and toes.

Again he listened through the earth. The hoofs drummed faintly against his ear. He lay unmoving.

After a long wait he slowly lifted his head and turned his eyes for a look. The horsebacks had passed him; they rode on the plain in the same direction he traveled.

Keeping next to the earth, he crept back, looking for the place he had discarded his robe. Here, suddenly, the hoofbeats spoke up loud through the ground. But whether more warriors come riding over the plain or the same ones return to hunt him, he knew not.

And so again he lifted up slowly. He saw now that the party returned.

He flattened to his belly, the whole of him swept with chills. He murmured a plea: "Woksapa muku ye. Make me wise. And brave. Whatever happens, make me brave."

Tunkašila had spoken of friends along the trail; where, these helpers? And now he recalled the tall-ears fleeing from her fear. Why not remember himself as the antlered-one who doubles back on his own tracks? Perhaps the spirit of the whitetail will enter him and help him elude whatever danger comes close.

He stood crouched and began backing off in a different direction. He stepped firmly, scheming to make his tracks on the clay look like he walks forward, something to confuse the horsebacks even as the whitetail's tracks confuse the hunter.

When he had backed up far enough, he dropped flat again and used his legs to nudge his body over the sandstone and into the sagebrush. Slipping the weapons off his back, he put bow and two arrows within grasp. He pressed tight against the ground, face down; his eyes shall not draw anyone here. Then, scarcely breathing, he waited.

The echo of hoofs came dimly from the earth; he heard only the rustling of some small creature in the grass. And so, taking a deep breath, he slowly raised head and shoulders, his elbows helping. The next thing he knew, he stared into the cold eyes of a man who kneeled an arm's length away. The man's lifted hand held a knife and, behind him, a second man crawled through the grass.

Water ran down the boy's leg and his belly flipped over, but none of his terror reached his face.

The one with the knife put down his weapon. "My Lakotah relative learns only one of the lessons the grass-bird teaches her young. Until he learns something more, I advise that he not stray beyond reach of his mother's wing."

Relief overwhelmed the boy. He swallowed fast, forcing back those juices that filled his throat and prepared him for retching; he will not give his discoverers another chance for ridicule.

He got to his feet and, standing before his captors, he struggled for calm. He caught the robe which the second man tossed him. And when he saw that they waited for him to speak, he fought the tremor in his voice until his cheeks ached.

"I travel close on my grandfather's moccasins. They call my father Olepi. His band, the Mahto."

After a moment he said, "I am someone they call Peta." He had wished to speak his own name proudly, but he had enough difficulty keeping shame out of his voice.

For a while the two Sicaŋġu withheld from Peta that they recognize him and that they know his father. Instead they pointed to certain mistakes in his attempt to evade his pursuers. And Peta, listening respectfully, felt small as the bug that crawled up his arm.

But at last they identified their party as five horsecatchers going south to chase after those horses who run loose in the narrow canyons of the sandhills. They invited Peta to walk back and meet their companions. They had seen the boy's tracks far back on the trail, they told, but an enemy foot occasionally wears a Lakotah moccasin and small feet, often hint at a boy who acts as decoy for a big party. So, until they knew, three men had stayed hidden.

Approaching those three horsebacks now, Peta heard something surprisingly familiar. Glancing toward the sound, he saw the head of a true-pup looking out from a bulging paunch that hung on the side of a horse.

"Your real captor," laughed one of the men who saw the boy's eyes return again to the pup. "I hear whining and so I look. I see the pup and discover your tracks."

Peta wanted to ask at what place this happened, but he dared not permit himself the rudeness of a question. These horsechasers had invited him to travel on to the earth-smoke with their party; they had offered him space up behind any one of the riders, their one spare horse packed with meat. Most certainly he refrained from any sort of inquiry; instead he chose a place up back of the rider whose horse carried the true-dog.

Peta, seeing the paunch thump against the loping horse, felt for the young pup who endured this pounding; he determined to ask for her return. If he told the story, perhaps her new owner will understand. . . .

The men brought their horses to a halt. Here, they said, a good place for cooking meat; they will lay a fire to blend with the rays of sundown.

But a small party never risks fire-glow and meat-smell even on familiar trails, and so Peta decided that he had come onto the earth-smoke, hunting grounds of the Sicaŋġu.

He watched the men dismount and then, jumping down, he hurried to fill the rider's water-sacs at a clear little stream nearby. Boys who go out with the war parties carry water and wood for the men, and he shall act accordingly.

"Someone suffers a dry throat and not complains," one man said when Peta brought him water. "Let this boy drink."

And so Peta learned that his companions suspected his thirst at the start of this ride but that they chose to test him for staying-power. And so he had earned the murmur of praise going around.

But tease him they will. While he ate, they talked of his walking backwards which had not fooled anyone; let him try side-winding as the grass-bird draws the enemy from her nest; then, perhaps, he will fool his stalkers.

And fortunate for this boy, the men agreed that Lakotah, not Palani discover him; the Palani feast on a captive. Imagine the winter-count picture if the Palani catch him: maize-eaters put Titonwan boy on stick and roast him alive.

Two of the horsecatchers smiled, but not Peta. He had heard the people say that the Palani occasionally burn captive children.

The men saw Peta shiver and so they stopped this talk and turned to their pipes. After a little smoke they asked that the boy recite his experience.

Fearing more ridicule, Peta spoke stutteringly at the start, but hearing the 'hau' of assent and understanding, he began to talk easily. He told of the winged-warrior and brought out the bird claws and feathers; shyly he offered these things as gifts to the men who shared their meat with him. And when they had accepted his offering, he told the story of the true-dog.

Then the horsechaser they call Pañaña took the pup from the confining sac and tossed the creature into the boy's arms. "Your runaway," he said. The man had intended to use the young dog's skin as a wrap for his lance. "Instead I shall hang these feathers on my stick." He smiled approvingly at Peta.

The pup lay with drooping head, and so one man felt for broken bones but she seemed whole. Peta cleaned dung from her hair, then offered water and a scrap of meat. She showed little thirst but the meat went down in a gulp. When the party moved on, she rode in the boy's arms.

The horsechasers, familiar with the earth-smoke river, had advised Peta where to look for capa. They knew of an old lodge, one that had sheltered many different families, a place that he will not have difficulty finding if he follows his nose. But watch out, they laughed; perhaps he shall mistake a Psa warrior for this lodge, so strongly will a man of this enemy tribe douse his body with this creature's scent.

At dusk the party came to the river, the Sicangu waiting while Pahaha jumped down and, sniffing the air, located a scent-mound for Peta to follow. He instructed the boy to walk along the river's edge. "Keep a lookout for trees these creatures mark for cutting," he said. But he had not told the boy that the lodge sat close by nor had he said that all five horsechasers will watch until grandfather and grandson come together again.

Peta kept to the stream's edge, sniffing the air and trying to find certain trees before dark. Suddenly he heard a puplike whine. The true-dog stopped and raised her head, but the boy's hand instantly closed over her nose. He knew that an enemy often used the dog-voice to draw someone out of the shadows.

He heard the whining twice and now he had a scheme. Covering the pup with his robe, he fastened her to a tree. Moving away quickly, he hid in a different place.

The pup made noises but nothing answered. And Peta remained silent. Nor had he betrayed his presence when a voice murmured in his ear. "Good; you let the dog speak for you."

He moved out of hiding but only after he had made certain who spoke. Silently he untied the pup, then waited for his grandfather, who stood alongside him, to lead the way to whatever sleeping place he chose.

The two had rolled onto their robes in a secluded ravine before either one said anything.

"I see that my grandson crawls awhile and rides awhile during his travels."

Peta found nothing surprising in his grandfather's observation; as he had said, Tunkasila knows everything. Even so he intended to recite his whole adventure for the man's hearing. But not now; at this moment—the pup tied to his wrist and his grandfather close enough to touch—a certain boy desired nothing more than sleep.

Next day the man and boy followed the meandering river, then wandered up one of the small streams that trickled into the earth-smoke. Here an irregular span of dead branches, mud, and grass created a pond. When the boy observed that something had used up all the trees nearby, the man explained; many generations of capa laid this wood across the stream. And so they made not only a pond for their own convenience but a firm escape path for a Lakotah scout.

A little distance ahead, Tunkaśila pointed out the creatures' lodge, a shelter perhaps unused for many seasons but as solid as when the original family cut the wood and pushed aside the mud at the water's edge.

After a while the travelers came upon tracks that led to a village of pinspinza, the yapping ones who burrow the plain.

Peta lifted surprised eyes to his grandfather; he had imagined that they followed the footmarks of ikusan, the little white-chin.

Not white-chin, Tunkaśila answered him: "Instead, you follow a most wary one. And if ever, on glimpsing you, he sits and chews in a certain way, look out. Anyone at whom this little black-forehead stares soon gets cut into pieces; the legends say so."

Then why will his grandfather encourage him to take this trail? Tunkaśila, catching the boy's wonder, answered, but he will not name iteopta sapa.

"This creature goes out only at night. Not likely that he sees you or that you ever see him once you know his track."

When they turned and started back for the earth-smoke, Tunkaśila made a bet with his grandson. If Peta will give him the slim start of twenty steps, he shall seem to disappear. But Peta shall have from here to the big stream to catch sight of the man.

The wager?

A bow for Peta if he sees his grandfather even once; a string of shining dewclaws for Tunkaśila if the man stays in hiding all the way.

271

The boy's eyes sparkled; stalking on sandy earth and soft mud and using the nose of his true-dog for a guide makes the challenge as easy as winning the bird claws back at the ledge. Perhaps Tunkašila proposed the game as a way of presenting his grandson with a fine hunter's bow, something this boy so greatly desires.

Peta turned about and walked back ten long steps, half as many strides as his grandfather, at the same moment, took forward.

Now the boy whirled around; he stood, mouth open, ready to shout. But Tunkašila had disappeared.

For a short distance the man's jog showed up clearly; then his tracks faded and sank away.

After a long, careful search Peta rediscovered these footmarks on a sandy stretch in the middle of the stream. Imitating Tunkašila, the boy pulled off one moccasin and hopped on his bare foot over to the sand. The pup reluctantly waded after him.

For some distance Peta followed the stream, from edge to sand bar, from one side to the opposite, but frequent need to remove a moccasin and hop barefoot soon tired the boy.

Tunkašila had kept at the edge among the trees wherever an obstructing mass of branches and twigs deepened the water, and here the stalking went slowly.

But now, suddenly, not a track anywhere; if Tunkašila had crossed the stream, he had swum to the opposite side.

Peta looked around for the man's robe and bow, and the pup dug frantically in the sand, but neither boy nor dog uncovered anything. And then Peta saw a tree with fresh cuts; his grandfather had swum but he had pushed a raft big enough to carry his robe, moccasins, weapons.

The next moment Peta remembered the span of old wood and hard mud that Tunkašila had pointed out on their way upstream. He decided to hurry to the pond and use this crossing to gain on the man.

And now, halfway across the span, he wondered why his grandfather had not come this way. Smiling, he moved on, stepping carefully over sticks and branches, the pup following close on his moccasins.

Once across, he walked quietly on the grassy places. But soon he needed to backtrack and inspect the ground more closely.

Perhaps two hundred steps back, he saw the marks of bare feet. But will he overlook this track or will Tunkaśila follow him? Perhaps the pup also puzzled this thing, for she acted confused, sitting down, getting up, turning in wide circles, and then lying down again.

But one thing the boy now understood: Tunkaśila also had used the old span to cross the stream.

"Help me find my grandfather, young friend," Peta begged the pup; "I so much want the bow."

Not long afterwards a glimpse of four small poles tied together and pushed against the stream's edge made clear who had won the bet.

Twenty more steps and Peta stood at the meeting of big and little streams. And conspicuously displayed atop a little mound, Tunkaśila's marker.

The next moment, a lithe form and crinkling face came out from back of a tree. "My grandson looks as if I melt his heart, and so I go."

Peta made a quick sound; he wanted none of Tunkaśila's disappearing acts now.

"Come, grandson. I will show you something." The man led the way back to the branches that spanned the stream. But here he demanded that Peta tell his story.

When the boy finished speaking, the man had praise for his grandson. Then he said, "After I float the raft carrying my moccasins and bow downstream, I walk along opposite you but on the side of the stream that throws a shadow away from the water. And I walk quietly; anyone will walk quietly when his life—or winning a bet—depends on keeping quiet."

He glanced at the boy, then went on with his story. "When I see that you will catch up with me at the span over the stream, I invite myself into an empty lodge. Here I stay until you disappear. Afterwards I swim out underwater. My moccasins wait for me. I reach the earth-smoke twenty steps ahead of my grandson. Twenty steps and I win."

"I will make you a string of dewclaws, grandfather," Peta said meekly.

"And soon," Tunkaśila replied firmly.

Now the man pointed with his chin toward the lodge which had hidden him. "Look inside. See the ledge on which these pond-makers sleep. Remember this place.

273

The boy entered the quiet pond, his body making barely a splash. He managed the entrance to the lodge and felt his way to the dark shelter above water. His hands touched the ledge and, shaking water from his eyes, he viewed the sleeping place. And while he saw nothing appealing about a night's rest here, he recognized a hideaway if ever an enemy scouts the brush.

Back on the trail Peta spoke of things that interested him about these pond-makers who swim-carrying-sticks. When they cut a tree, will they know which direction the wood will snap and fall?

Tunkaśila answered saying that he once had seen a tree crash down on such a one but that in many ways they act wise as man. The old wapiya tell that this creature once lives in a manner similar to man. And if ever Peta hears the pain-cry of their young, he shall observe the resemblance to a Lakotah infant.

All creatures, Tunkaśila went on to say, teach the Lakotah something, but these swimmers who raise a lodge over water perhaps teach the most good. None ever tells another the way he shall act; instead each one attends to his own affairs and remembers his obligations. The legends speak of these same ones as once tall as the sticky-mouth, relative of the grizzly, and with cutting-teeth as long as a man's foot. And a big, big head.

After a while Tunkaśila said that the one on whom he saw a tree fall perhaps wished to die, a female whose mate had brought a new younger female to the lodge. "Everyone knows that occasionally a Lakotah woman hangs herself on a tree when a husband brings a second wife to the tipi. So who dares say that a swims-with-stick-in-mouth will not prefer dying to sharing? Truly, Lakotah women and these creatures act similarly: each makes a path from feeding ground to water, each confines her activities to near the lodge, each takes watchful care of her own."

Peta said nothing; these women-mysteries he preferred to let alone.

Before dark Tunkaśila had caught a tall-ears with his hands and the pup had discovered a bird's nest on the ground, something those little creatures who squeak and scuttle through the grass had used as a sleeping place. The true-dog quickly ate the contents of the nest, but the man

274

and boy wanted cooked meat. And so Peta dug a hollow while Tunkaŝila made fire.

Not many persons will get a spark as swiftly as Tunkaŝila, and some persons never get a spark at all, even with a nice flat slab of dry wood for the bottom piece and a nice round sagebrush stick for the twirler. But a scout, out alone and wanting warmth, soon learns to make fire-sticks that coax a spark from the most unwilling wood. Tunkaŝila had said so.

While the meat cooked, Peta watched the action around a little sandhill where a bird dusted herself. Many, many tiny short-necked red specks ran about in orderly haste, repairing the damage to their hill. And the boy, seeing one of these tažúŝka drag a pebble from the ravaged nest, marveled the power before his eyes.

But he said nothing. Marvel and accept and imitate, the grandfathers say, but leave mystery to mystery. Go outside your realm, they say, and you get a bump on your head. But will all grandfathers in the tribe say so? And will the seer they call Wanaġi say so?

The travelers, facing about, now started back to the ridge, to the great hoop of lodges.

They walked slowly this day and most certainly in the direction that Waziya guards, the place of cold winds. For Waziya, suddenly tightening his bow of ice, had aimed snow-seeds at their naked breasts, a cloud of hail rattling down on man and boy. And next, a heavy rain that drenched the trail.

But Tunkaŝila had sought none of the natural shelters; he had led the boy, instead, through cold and wet, occasionally emitting the sharp yell, the familiar whoop that challenges the weathers.

After the sky had cleared, they found a grass-bird, her feathers soaked beyond using. Her call brought those of her brood whom the hail had not killed to a more certain death at the hands of two hungry travelers.

When Peta spoke saying that he chose to make the fire that will roast the birds, Tunkaŝila had not discouraged him. And so the boy pointed the tip of a firm round stick and then shredded some bark. He had looked for an offer of his grandfather's shining black knife, but, this offer not forthcoming, he gouged out the hole in the bottom piece with a sharp-edged stone.

After a long while, Peta gave up on getting a spark; he glanced at the man, embarrassment in his eyes.

"Who ever twirls wet wood into flame?" Tunkaśila spoke factually. "Not even I shall persuade this piece. And so I carry certain things with me." He handed his grandson a dry shaft and some powdered chip.

When the boy's palms gave out, Tunkaśila took over; almost at once they had fire.

Peta kept the feathers from the mother-bird's short, round tail and the yellow fluff from under her wings. The tail feathers he wanted for his hair; the fluff belonged on a healer's rattle.

They slept this night under a branch shelter, Peta awakening to something that slipped through the brush, the remains of the birds perhaps acting as a lure. When he heard his pup howl, he suspected the nosy little creature who wears a snow-skin in winter, who comes here looking for leftovers.

Then, attentive to his young dog's yaps, Peta suddenly realized her need to learn silence in the night if she intends to live among the camp-dogs in a Mahto village.

Next morning Tunkaśila showed his grandson the record-stick; notches on the wood reveal that these two travel ten days. "And this day," he said, "I and you return to pahamni ridge."

But when the man and boy came within sight of the campground, they saw not a lodge.

Peta, his heart falling, looked at the dead fire circles, but Tunkaśila inspected a bending line of pte-skulls, noses pointing north. When he found two yellow streaks painted on one skull, he told the boy that they needed to travel two days before they reached the people.

But even without those streaks to tell him, Tunkaśila had known where and when and why the people go. Leading Peta over the deserted ground he pointed out drag marks, sign of a moving camp, and then that place where men drop their excrement. And finally he sifted the cold ashes of three, four different fire circles through his fingers. "Two sleeps," he said again, his thumb jerking up twice, "or

276

one sleep, one night running. Drags make a trail that I follow easily."

Much as Peta wanted to see his people, he quickly signaled his choice: two sleeps; not yet will he jog in the untiring manner of his grandfather.

The boy smelled the roasting humps before he saw the tips of the lodges, the poles barely visible over the top of a rise. He understood now that the hoop had moved out for the old-summer hunt. He wanted to run into camp, but Tunkaśila advised that he shake the dust from his hair and brush out the tangles with a handful of stiff grass.

"Make suds," the man said and, pulling up a fat root, he peeled back the yellow skin. "Walk into camp with a clean face."

And while they arranged for a neat appearance, Tunkaśila spoke briefly. A boy returns, he said, with sharpened senses and a new hold on himself. "In you, my grandson, live natural powers. Strengthen these. You own a will. Use this will."

Peta neither wore paint nor carried a lance when he entered the Lakotah encampment but he walked as if he had intercepted a party of raiders.

He had gone out a boy and returned, if not a man, certainly a youth with new growth. Tunkaśila had said so; Tunkaśila who knows everything had said so.

Those persons coming to the family lodge to hear Peta recite his experiences, listened respectfully. Tunkaśila sat as a witness, custom demanding that boy, warrior, anyone, talk in the presence of one or more witnesses.

The approving 'hau' had come from everywhere inside the lodge but for the back; the head of this lodge viewed the horse-chasers' discovery of his son as a humiliating incident. If an enemy instead of some Sicanǧu had found Peta, his father had said, then neither a story nor a boy to tell a story; the son experienced undeserved good fortune.

Peta's women relatives, recognizing the parent as too severe, made the comforting sound, but Napewaśte, properly, averted her eyes and kept silent. She looked at the bottom of her gown spread modestly over her legs and wondered whether her son yet understood his father's nature. If the man will not find something for reproach, his pride in the boy—so apparent to the mother of his son—shall spill over in front of everyone.

But Peta, going out to visit his new horse, walked slowly; whatever his loss in joy, he understood that his father had spoken the truth.

XXIII

THE PEOPLE had made the big hunt three days before the grandfather and grandson returned, and so everywhere he looked Peta saw the signs of 'wanasapi.' Everywhere meat hung on drying racks, and everywhere women hunched over hides, scraping or fleshing. Some skins hung drying, and into different ones the women rubbed a fat mixture. But everywhere—meat, hides, women.

Peta saw the flat stones, each one chipped to a sharp edge all around, in the hands of women who scraped hides, and he saw the smooth stones in the hands of women who rubbed on fat. And then he recalled the berry-pounders that he had intended to bring his mother and all those wonderful pebbles under his feet that day on the plain.

Stone, he told himself, truly a power in the hands of a woman, in the lodge of a seer, in the mouth of a boy whose side aches. For a moment he stood desperately lonesome for the trail and for his grandfather and for every single stone his moccasin had touched. But, remembering that a young horse waited for him at the edge of camp, he started off in that direction.

Walking past the many lodges, Peta observed that everyone attended seriously to something, even the naked babies who crawled off the robes to reach their working mothers.

Small daughters cuddled puppies in robes on their

backs, but other daughters staked down scraps of hide and, mimicking the women, bent over these pieces with toy-scrapers, raking off blood, fat, and flesh. Small sons played at sneaking-up-on-someone, throwing their grass lances, chasing each other, jumping over woodpiles, camp-dogs, and babies. But other sons ran errands for their fathers and uncles.

Growing-girls watched over the paunches in which hoofs or necks boiled down to a thick, sticky soup, something the bow-makers and arrow-makers need for their work. These same girls cut the long narrow strips which the horsecatchers twisted into thong and they also sorted the long hairs from the foretop of pte, something the men braided into cord for use on the horses' jaws.

Suddenly deciding to return to his mother's lodge, Peta told himself that every man in the great Titonwan circle worked on his weapons, strengthening bows, changing strings, straightening shafts, sharpening arrows. He wished for a man's bow to work on but, instead, he needed to start looking for dewclaws.

The ground surrounding Napewaśte's tipi evinced the fact that his mother staked or hung more hides than any woman in camp. Unci had told her daughter this same thing; here, more skins than a mother and daughter and sister shall scrape and soften in two, three moons.

Napewaśte had not answered, but she knew that something had strengthened Olepi's bow. The man had used twenty arrows to kill twelve in the herd. Not even Ogle had killed like this.

Now, four days after the hunt, Olepi had asked that the crier act as his mouth and announce a feast. Let him say that the Mahto invites everyone in the circle, Titonwan and visitors. Olepi makes much meat; he feeds the encampment. Come, next day when the sun reaches middle.

Napewaśte's relatives had helped cut up the meat, and they will come to help cook. Truly many different ones had offered their hands. But one thing had distressed Napewaś-te: her husband had said that he intended to oversee all preparations for the feast.

Not that she wished to spoil the man's pleasure; she had understood that the feast celebrated his remarkable kill and his son's return and that not since the sungazing had his family feasted or danced. But Olepi as overseer . . . perhaps she will find things for him to oversee on the opposite side of camp.

The woman schemed to keep the cooking fires glowing all this night—her mother and sister staying—and so the soups will simmer and the meat roast while men, children, dogs, stay asleep and out of her way.

Before evening she had counted out her need for sticks and stones, exactly what she will require for staking paunches and heating water. Then Unci had gone out to cut those sticks and Peta had gone out to look for those stones.

The boy took Mahtociqala with him. He showed his young friend the proper shape of stone: thick ones that roll down from the ledges and big as a man's hand. His mother will need four, five stones, he told, to make the water bubble in each cooking paunch, and she will use many, many cooking paunches.

Mahtociqala understood. They feed a big family in Cankuna's lodge and so they bubble water in many paunches every day.

Olepi had gone to his sleeping robes soon after dark and Napewaśte—stakes and stones, paunches and meat set out before her—now began a night's work, her hands willing and eager. Her decision that they feast the people on the gaming-ground made things easy; she dared use all the space around her lodge for cooking, the gaming-ground clear and clean for eating.

Olepi had gone to his robes but not for sleep. He considered, instead, the many hides awaiting his wife's attention and her need for staying at the cooking fires this night. He remembered different occasions when she had worked after dark, when she had seemed hard-pressed. And so he reflected on taking a second wife, another pair of hands to help in this lodge, someone to go for wood and water—but not 'any someone.' Young, fine-looking, good family. Why not? She will come as another pair of hands, true, but she also will come as wife to Olepi.

Napewaśte's helpers arrived at the woman's lodge at dawn. They discovered everything neatly laid out, extra knives in one place, ladles in another, cooking stones along with shoulderbone lifters placed near the paunches. Embers for roasting glowed up from many small circles, and next to these fires Unci had spread hides for receiving the meat, some hides already piled with special cuts, roasted or boiled.

And so seventeen women prepared for seventeen hundred guests.

The sun climbed a clear sky when Olepi came out to watch. He stood nearby his wife, advising that she start on things that she already had started. Any thigh-meat boiling? The old men with not enough teeth for chewing will suck out the marrow. Where, the tongues and noses? See that this choice meat reaches certain bowls.

Suddenly the man's eyes flared up. Why the iron kettle? Boil none of this meat in a whiteman's kettle.

Then Napewaśte told that some women with kettles to loan had brought these pots but that she had not put any to use. Instead, her women helpers had dug holes which they lined with mud and skins, the top edges of these skins held fast to the ground with rib-bone. Here they cooked the tongues.

He accepted her detailed accounting but demanded that she put the kettles out of sight. And where will she put the uncooked liver for those persons who desire cold meat? And will she remember to stuff entrails and twist this meat on roasting-sticks? And where, ribs under cover and cooking with two fires in the old and good way?

Napewaśte had murmured assurances to each of the man's expressions, but now she turned to face him, her manner changed. "My husband, the man who travels cooks ribs in fresh hide until two fires burn to ash. But I am a woman staying in camp and cooking in camp. I cook as a woman cooks. I know the way with cooking-fires."

She turned back to the hot stones. Let him understand cooking as woman's work. She never interferes with his hunting or his decisions regarding a war party.

Olepi had accepted the woman's speech with amazingly good nature. And to everyone's relief the man went off, his moccasins pointed toward the sacred-lodge where Wanaǵi shredded bark for the feast-pipes.

Peta watched with surprise as members of the Tokala, instead of his mother and her woman-relatives, filled the meat bowls in front of the old men. And more surprising, certain ones refused the meat. The boy knew these old ones as always hungry, always eating; he wondered whether his eyes play tricks on him.

Then he saw that his father not only ignored this rudeness but that he smiled. And when different old men, their bowls full to the edges, began to trade nudges, he looked around for an answer to this whole thing.

But who will tell the boy that some men prefer satisfying vanity instead of belly, that these old ones who sit before an upside-down bowl imply an act with woman the previous night. Emulating the young warrior who dares not go out on a raid if he sleeps with woman the night before, these ancients symbolically refused the feast. But let the meat come around again and Peta will see these same ones hastily turning up the bowl, eating heartily as the next person.

The Tokala clubmen having refilled most bowls, now sat down. At once Napewaste and her helpers came forward, the women in pairs and carrying hides piled with roasted shoulder and hump, boiled rib and tongue, meat for warriors and youths-turning-warrior and for all the hunters, healers, weapon-makers, newscarriers, singers who stay in this great hoop. Meat for everyone, generous helpings also for those contrary eight men who, standing on their moccasined hands licked clean their bowls, eight heyoka who always remember their cloud-dream whenever they appear before the people.

Each woman-guest now helped herself to cuts of roast and simmered meat. The old women had found one another and sat in a cackling circle, their skinny legs stretched out in front, a bone in each hand, something to peck and suck and throw to the camp-dogs.

So had the young women found one another, a cluster of softly laughing faces, darting black eyes, and swift glances, each one here aware of those young braves who sat to the rear of the men.

And seated near these young flirts, groups of young women whose demure attitude and careful speech attested to their role of newly made wives. Daintily they bit into breast-meat and considered Napewaste's skills.

"See her moccasins," one said, "and the bright colors she gives to the quills."

"See her gown," said another. "Will I ever make the hides so soft and white? They say she uses nothing but bone-fat in her rubbing mixture."

"Her mother possesses the same wonderful touch," answered one from the Siyo band, one of those many young women who sought Unci's advice whenever she cut the tipi covers or gowns or leg-coverings, whenever she used awl and sinew. "But not many display Unci's patience for removing hair without breaking the skins, for softening the hides until they fold without wrinkling."

The young wives saw Napewaste moving toward a different group of women, each one with a child at her breast. To these mothers she carried thigh meat and the water in which this meat had simmered. And here, again, praises followed Napewaste's moccasins; she had remembered old men and new mothers.

"The woman remembers everyone."

They watched her handing out those bones dark with marrow to the young sons and daughters who surrounded their mothers.

"The wife of Olepi keeps her pretty smile," said one woman as she pulled her little daughter from the breast to let the child lick the meat-juice off her fingers. She observed Napewaste another moment, then looked toward the place Olepi sat. "And her husband keeps his handsome face."

"But he demands too much of his wife," spoke up a woman from a different band. "They say she never visits outside her lodge when he stays in camp. She sweeps the tipi and freshens the ground and hangs out the sleeping robes every day. She never misses."

The one to mention Olepi's handsomeness said nothing. She knew that Napewaste kept a neat, clean lodge and that neither spots of fat nor streaks of dust ever appeared on gowns or robes which this woman and her husband wore. But will things change, she wondered, when Napewaste's family increases. Will the wife of Olepi always prepare so many hides, dry the meat, dig the roots, pick and crush the berries, make shirts and gowns and decorate the moccasins . . . also hang out the sleeping robes each day?

Glancing up, this same woman saw that her young son,

a boy in his fifth winter, hurried toward the place she sat. Dropping down at her side, he roughly pushed away his sister's tiny face and took the breast in his own mouth.

The small one whimpered but her mother whispered that she shall wait. The boy sucked lustily but the woman remembered that the day when he shall protect and defend the women and children of his band soon came; then he shall endure the trials of the hunt, the dangers of a raid. True, he had feasted on all the meat his fat little belly will hold, but had not the grandmothers said that his sisters will outlive him even as most women outlive the men?

Quickly satisfied, the boy gave his mother a teasing bite to see her flinch and then ran off; the little daughter took hold again.

A quiet sat over the men; the pipe moved in the front circle, enough smoke in the bowl for twenty of these principals, all others touching the stem in ceremonial manner. And so one pipe passed among five hundred, something they had not seen on the plain until this day.

Young boys, coming to stand next to their fathers, watched with round eyes while the long-stem traveled from leaders to councilors, to warriors and clubs; from scouts to newscarriers and newscriers; from weapon-makers to seers and healers, to all these different protectors who made up the greatness of the people. And then these youths, eager for games of chase and throw, began sneaking off, heading for the edges of this playground on which the people feasted.

But the son of Olepi stayed, the boy curious about the many acts attending the feast. At the moment he puzzled over the stakes that two akicita pounded into the ground, his father apparently indifferent to their movements. But such indifference, he knew, signified either nothing important or something most important.

The crier's voice, rising above the hum, announced that Olepi will speak; let the people hear. But before the Mahto stood, four of his warriors came forward to place ten-and-four feathers in his hair, in a circle around his head, each feather from the tail of the wambli-bird and cut or marked to display an honor.

Never before had a man worn his honors in this arrangement, and some hands covered mouths in fleeting astonishment. But all eyes recognized Olepi's privilege to decorate his head and body in whatever manner he chose. And, looking now upon the hand-mark and horse-track painted on his breast, they saw the deep wounds of his sungazing.

And many persons took notice of the man's long hair, hanging below his shoulders and in contrast to many men who plucked their heads bare on each side. And noticing, more than one woman decided to encourage her man to let his hair grow long in this manner.

A hush settled over the people as the Mahto began his speech, his voice carrying to the most distant ears. The hunt, he said, apparently satisfied everyone, not a flat belly in camp. And so he thanked those alert young warriors, the Tokala, who had controlled the surround.

The winds blow kindly, he told, upon the sacred hoop during this season at pahamni ridge; who among the people suffers either aches or wounds? The sungazing and fresh meat strengthen the powers in each one, in the warriors, in a boy traveling with his grandfather.

Peta heard, amazed that his father honored him with all these people listening. Or perhaps some different boy traveled with his grandfather, someone whom a party of horsecatchers never saw.

Now Olepi talked of something different, the people attending most closely. Soon warriors go out, he said, but only the most competent belong in this party for they go as avengers, warriors whose acts shall dry tears that wet the women's cheeks.

"But the governing-four decide that the Titonwan go out as a tribe; each family relates through tongue to those twenty-and-eight whom the Psa kill during a recent season. And so men, women, children shall travel together until they approach near the enemy ground. At a certain place the warriors go on, the women voicing those tremolos that follow the brave ones far out on the plain."

Olepi finished his speech at the exact moment that the two akicita pounded the one remaining stake into the ground.

Now Wambli Okiye, a respected member of the Pta-lodge, walked slowly along the row of stakes; he examined each one. And, as he moved from one to the next, he talked of manliness among the Titonwan: strong, firm, sound men. He looked for strong, hard, sound wood among these stakes even as the people, choosing their leaders, look for these things.

He tests each piece of wood, he told, but most stakes either break or bend under pressure. And those stakes yet standing firm reveal hollow centers. But for one: pse-htin, wood intensified, wood for feet that travel on snow, for shafts that hit and hold. This stake neither breaks nor bends and the core, the heartwood, proves whole and sound.

"Many stakes stand in this line, yet only one endures. So with man: only one out of the many proves truly fit to lead."

The tests Wambli Okiye had made on these woods, the people learned, symbolized those tests he and different headmen in the Pta-lodge had made relative to a certain man, someone they had found enduring as pse-wood. And now, during a meeting in the big center tipi they shall paint the tree-in-tense symbol on Olepi's body. The Pta-lodge recognizes the Mahto as one among those four principals who lead the Titonwan in war and peace; Olepi, a man strong, firm, sound.

Olepi wondered whether someone heard his heart, so loudly his breast drums and sings.

Perhaps one had heard. Sitting far back and suddenly shy as the whitewing bird who perches on the prairie brush, Napewaśte made the silent trilling in answer to Olepi's silent song.

Peta watched his father move proudly toward the center lodge, and he saw those eyes that gazed at the feathers in the man's hair, admiring and respectful eyes. But he also felt eyes upon himself, eyes powerful enough to compel his glance, to draw his attention away from his father.

Turning, he looked across the crowding, cheering people to meet Wanaġi's steady gaze.

Evening came and the Pta-lodge danced in Olepi's honor. The members had braided the short hairs of pta into their own, and each man had painted white. Their gestures mimicked the herd, bellowing and snorting and butting one another in the manner of those creatures whose name they borrowed.

286

Olepi watched these maneuvers with keen eyes. Four more winters, he told himself, and I shall dance with these men. Four more winters and I am forty; I come of age for a seat of honor in this headman-lodge.

During the evening many persons came to stand near Olepi, the young boys looking up with admiring glances, their pretty sisters smiling shyly. And warriors who had grown up with Olepi placed a hand on his shoulder or made the crossed-arm handclasp of respect.

But certain ones had stood aside; Zuzueca and his following had offered neither the friendly phrases nor the friendly touch. And Olepi, sensitive to these omissions, felt the quickening of an anger he dared never display; his new place in the tribe demanded that he ignore any slight directed toward him. He had risen from headman of one village to principal man of the Mahto camps to an itancan, a principal among the Titonwan. If the rank of warrior forever excites him more than the role of peaceman, none will hold this thing against him. But never, never shall he violate the trust they place in him as a guardian of the people, the one and the whole.

Olepi turned from the crowd around him and without knowing why, walked toward the sacred-man's lodge.

During the silent smoke with Wanaġi, the Mahto scarcely noticed that he sucked on a long, flat stem of the wood to which he had heard himself compared.

And now, patience replacing anger, he returned the pipe to the wapiya. But Wanaġi, after emptying the ashes, handed back bowl and stem. "Keep, my friend. This one belongs to you. I foresee this night and so I make the stem. Hecitu welo."

Two, three more days the people feasted each other in their villages. And then one morning the crier awakened the encampment with news of scouts going out to locate the Psa camp. When these truthbearers return, he sang, the Titonwan make war.

Olepi had looked over his weapons, but before ever he examined bows, shafts, lance, club, and knife, he knew his wants. The pse-wood bow remained true but he needed shafts and a different knife.

287

While inspecting his old war club, a tough dry tail to which he had attached a heavy stone, he suddenly remembered that pse-root also makes a club, perhaps a more daring weapon than stone. Why not bow and shafts of pse-wood and a pse-root for his club? Why not everything from this firm wood with which the Pta-lodge compares his nature? And why not make himself a new shield?

And so on this second morning after the crier's announcement, Olepi had dug a circle, the hole deep to his elbow. Then, instructing Napewaśte to make a fire nearby and to heat stones, he walked out looking for his favorite weapon-makers.

One old man, someone who always carried a glue stick, sat chipping points, a lump of hornstone resting against a hard flat slab on his thigh. This one used an antler flaker to renew the edges on some old stone points, and so Olepi stood watching for a while. The Mahto wanted either stone or bone tips on his shafts, not iron. The iron point perhaps wounds, but the stone point, barbed on the shoulder, kills. Or so he had tried to persuade his warriors. As for himself, he never shall use an arrow point cut from the whiteman's metal.

And now Olepi spoke, naming his need and making his offer. But the old one went on with his work; he had not looked up to see what length arm. Recognizing the voice, he knew what length shaft fit that arm; certainly he had made Olepi's arrows for more than ten seasons.

Hearing the arrow-maker's grunt of assent, the Mahto moved on to a man who sat grooving a stone for a club-head. Here he decided to offer something in exchange for three new knives, one of stone and one of legbone and yet another from rib, their cutting edge keen as any metal exacted from a whiteman or gained through trade. And now, again the assenting grunt.

On returning to his lodge, Olepi saw that his wife had heated the stones and that water simmered within reach of his working place. And that the woman had spread a thickness of sage next to the freshly dug hole, the pte-neckskin for making his shield laying on this smoky-grass cover.

The man cut the hide carefully and staked half the circular piece over the hole. Holding up the loose edge, he used a stick to lay the white-hot stones in the pit. He poured on water, then quickly pegged down the open side, all the while making soft answer to the hissing stone voices: let the shrinking hide thicken evenly, strongly.

And now, spilling hot water on top of the contracting skin, he began to scrape hair from the upside.

The Mahto had looked for his son to take an interest in this shield-making but Peta had not appeared. My son will come around, the man told himself, when I start the painting; the boy loses none of his fondness for creating pictures.

Olepi had convinced himself that the design he chose to put on his shield had come during the thanks-offering dance: a big yellow sun exactly center. Wearing the shield at his neck and hanging front, the power of the sun will enter his design and dazzle the eyes of the enemy. Certainly he intends to demonstrate the effect of this new design when they move against the Psa.

Before the shield had dried, he started his painting, but Peta had not come around. The boy owned a true-dog now to whom he wished to show the way of camp and a young horse to whom he wished to teach the ways of man; these two shall hold his whole interest.

Peta's new horse grazed with his father's herd, the young creature turning to the grass long before usual.

"This one will carry his rider a far distance between suns," Huśte had said, but he had discouraged Peta from working with the horse. "Wait," he advised. "Show patience and perhaps you own something."

The boy had pondered his uncle's meaning. Will Huśte regard him as one of those youths who whip timid young horses until the blood oozes? Everyone knows that a horse shall learn to react to surprise in the same cool manner as a warrior and that these creatures need to respond instantly to knee or heel or voice. But why not a firm teaching-knee, firm but never rough; why not an insisting tone, insisting but never harsh.

Twice he had watched horses who fell on a slope struggle fearfully to get on their feet. And he had seen these same ones struck until pain forced a second effort; one horse finally had stood but soon fell again, nose dribbling blood.

And so he had decided that whatever horse he owns, he shall call 'friend,' everyone instantly aware in what manner he treats his horse.

And so, attentive to Huśte's advice that he not yet ride the young black, Peta had begun working with the true-pup. During his travels, he had taught the pup to respond to a call. Back in camp, he had taken her to the stream where she had waded and prowled through grass and run to him when he made the commanding sound. He saw that she played roughly with the different dogs yet took care that her long teeth not hurt the camp-pups even when they snapped at her. But now she needed to learn things that the true-dogs of the ledges never learn. Soon the people move camp and this pup shall travel not on a leash but with the short poles of his mother's backrest meeting on her shoulders and a pile of lodge things bundled onto this drag. The people will move out toward an enemy and the clubmen shall kill instantly any howling creature who perhaps betrays the camp. And so Peta shall start the lessons by holding together her jaws whenever she makes noise.

During this gentling of the true-dog, Mahtociqala stood near with frequent offers of help. And the son of Olepi proved as patient toward the young boy as toward the pup.

On the same day that the knife-maker brought Olepi his knives, the Mahto presented one to his son. "A rib with this sharp an edge will make my son brave whether five or ten of the enemy stalk him," he said, something like a smile in his eyes.

Peta wished his father had presented the knife without reference to the horsechasers, but he decided not to let the remark spoil his joy over a gift almost as good as a bow. Knowing that Mahtociqala will want to share in his pleasure, he hurried to Cankuna's lodge.

The boys had shown the knife to Ogle, the hunter examining the weapon most thoroughly. Then, looking at Peta, he smiled. "I will take you and your knife on a hunt."

Gnuśka had sat with disinterested ears, but now he spoke up, his tone scoffing. "I also go, my father. You will want someone looking after this boy who will dart out and scare the pte."

290

"I am not in need of a watchman," Ogle answered pleasantly, "but I invite each of my sons on this hunt."

Gnuśka appeared not to hear. "In what manner will Peta hunt? Dogback? A blunt shaft in his hand?"

Ogle's voice changed; the joking pleasantness disappeared. "My son, I remember when you have nothing to ride but not for reason that you give away your horse at a sungazing."

Gnuśka's eyes remained insolent; if he grieved the horse whose leg had broken during a foolish chase, his face concealed any regret.

Ogle handed back the knife to Peta. "In a different season," he said, "I and you will hunt horseback. Now I and you go on foot." He looked sharply at Gnuśka. "I boast that my own legs will run down pte. If I lose my horse I shall live. Long before the mysterious-dog comes among the Lakotah, the people eat big meat. None starves."

Peta, his eyes on the knife in his hand, wondered a little at the hunter's words. The old men had told of those winters before the horse in a different way; they said that the people often lacked meat, often starved. Even so, this good hunter offers a boy something: he will take the son of Olepi on the trail after meat.

But will someone make him a bow before that day? Then perhaps his arrows will fly straight to the meat and Ogle will tell everyone in camp. Perhaps he, Peta, shall become a great hunter instead of a great scout. Certainly he will prefer hunter or scout to the place of headman in the band. In the hunter's lodge one hears much laughing. . . .

A noise outside suddenly emptied the tipi, Ogle also leaving his backrest to join the crowd that hurried toward a commotion in the Kiyuksa camp. And Peta, seeing that Mahtociqala waited for him, walked with his friend in this same direction.

In front of Zuzueca's lodge the clubmen whipped two women. One of these two, Zuzueca's wife, who had claimed that the other woman, a Siyo, made a nuisance of herself. The wife had shoved the unwelcome visitor from the lodge, but the quarreling had gone on outside. The people had laughed at the hair-jerking, but when they saw the two women pull out knives, someone sent word to the akicita.

Zuzueca had stepped out of the lodge after the arrival of the clubmen and now he watched, his lips curved in scorn, while the clubs acted in his behalf. If he enters this quarrel and whips his wife, his reputation as a man undeserving of any woman will spread through camp, and enough talk already goes on, the people saying that he encourages this woman visitor. But he never pretends differently. This Siyo woman's husband dies two winters in the past; why not encourage her visits as one way to discover whether the woman and his wife prove companionable? Now, the whole encampment sees the unlikeliness of these two ever sharing a lodge, yet none will say that Zuzueca treats either woman unkindly.

Peta understood none of the whispers, none of the laughter. The akicita, he knew, never used their clubs unwisely; even so, those howls of pain coming from the women made him wince. He never had seen a woman struck and he wished that nothing like this scene ever takes place outside his mother's lodge. He marveled that anyone laughed at this spectacle and he wondered why the people, always careful with their gaze, stared openly upon these women in difficulty.

Peta looked around for his own parents, suddenly glad that he saw neither one. And then he moved away, Mahtociqala walking close.

The two boys reached Napewaśte's lodge, the unpleasantness barely remembered. Talk of going on a hunt with Ogle stood out as the big thing on this day.

XXIV

THE MOON rounded, and those Titonwan scouts who had trailed the enemy made use of this fat friendly light, traveling night and day, hurrying back with their news of the Psa.

Half the enemy tribe, they had learned, go visiting this summer, the people joining relatives who live in the mud villages upriver. Many horses go, their backs loaded for trade.

The Psa stay awhile with these relatives, trading, feasting, and dancing. Then the Psa start back for their own hunting ground. They travel unhurried; they stop often to make meat and soften hides and to cut wood for quirt handles. The Titonwan scouts sit close until the Psa approach the snow hills.

Hau. The deciders understood. Now, everything pertinent.

The reporting scout lifted his thumb. He inscribed on the air a great-ten circle: one hundred Psa horsebacks holding clubs, bows, lances.

Horses?

The thumb swung as before but now the Lakotah saw ten circles inscribed, the great-great ten, and then, using the sign that indicates more than one thousand, the thumb gestured the space that sixteen hundred horses shall occupy.

Bundles?

Many horses carry people, but most horses carry only bundles. And whatever the Psa pack, they bind firmly: firesticks, iron clubs, knives, paint-powder, awls, and those hard, shiny seeds that never sprout. The Psa also pack maize, hard and soft, something they receive in return for many camp-dogs.

After five days of trading and a ceremony at which the Psa offer children for adoption, this enemy tribe starts back for the snow hills.

Hau. The deciders understood. Each scout in turn now, let each man report whatever he witnesses.

And so the truthbearers spoke of everything from those trades and wagers which took four hundred of the visitors' horses to the runaway wives and the quarrel that led to the retiring of the head clubman and the naming of an old man to this rank.

When each scout had emptied himself of fact, the deciders ordered the edges of the big double-lodge staked down and they placed clubmen on the open side; soon enough the people shall learn those decisions coming from the center. For now, nothing shall disturb this assembled wisdom, neither the seer who, perhaps, considers that his prophecy has a place here nor the bold young warrior who wants to become the original one to know the plan nor a playful child who inadvertently flings a mud clod into this counciling nor some old woman who chases a squealing puppy around the center lodge. They intend to sit calmly, quietly—headmen, leaders, councilors, and their four deciders—faces passive, eyes narrow, hands at rest. And so each one will await the pipe, that which joins his thought and his will to the truth. And so to one another.

"Men of the plain, I see you moving against the enemy for one purpose." Cetan, rising from his place among the deciders, stood tall and stern before the arc of important Titonwan. "Some among you ask that two enemy die for each of those twenty-and-eight brave warriors whose bones whiten on distant ground. But I want to see each fighting-man returning safely to his tipi. And so I decide on acts that guard against Lakotah losses."

Now Cetan described a group who shall accompany the avengers: ten or more strong-bodied, cautious men with fighting experience to assist the leaders of the war party. Acting as councilors to the expedition, they shall select clubmen to supervise their instructions.

The clubmen of one band, Cetan pointed out, will not take orders from the clubmen of a different band. Disagreements lead to anger and desertions. And so the deciders, after much pondering, offer this scheme.

Throaty sounds of dissatisfaction greeted Cetan's proposal; what have they here but a scheme for controlling war parties. Apply this scheme to even one party and the next thing, they will advise every warrior who gets together twenty men to choose certain ones to sit above the others.

The Lakotah way permits neither one group nor any one man in command. Not on the warpath, not anywhere. Who dares say that a man shall not walk up to danger; will one man now tell another which day to die; who decides in what manner a man shall fight. . . .

Olepi, sitting front, directly beneath Cetan's perceptive glances, let none of the turmoil reach him. Instead, he looked for a way to make the deciders' scheme acceptable to warriors and to clubmen and to whoever leads the big party.

But for the moment he controlled his impulse to speak; why give away his wisdom before he knows who carries the war pipe, who leads?

The sun passed through middle and went on; the people listened for news but the crier's mouth stayed closed.

Two errand boys came out of the center lodge, walking close, their faces untelling. They approached one of the tipi; they asked for meat. The women, prepared, took food at once to the council, but the akicita carried the meat in to the councilors.

The sun climbed down, the light dimmed. And now the herald, announcer for the council, circled the hoop, alerting the warrior-lodge in control of the encampment, letting the people know the word from inside.

Everyone stays, he sang, until they see the center lodge flutter down.

The Tokala keep order while the people break camp, while they travel.

More news from the center before the people sleep.

Stay. Prepare. Listen.

Peta, attentive to the message, wondered whether they had asked his father to carry one of the war pipes into the fight against the Psa. Certainly this man had sung a song about war pipes the same day he had put his new war shield on display outside the lodge.

But now Peta recognized the voice of a different crier; old Eyanpaha sang out news of horsecatchers who hurried into camp before dark. And so he ran eagerly toward the opening in the hoop, toward the tip-of-the-horns where a crowd already gathered; perhaps his Sicaŋgu friends had returned from the sandhills.

Then before this dusk grew into dark, Peta came back to the Mahto lodges walking tall, his eyes shining. He led a horse, a horse with iron hoofs, a gift from the Sicaŋgu horsechasers. Perhaps they will not call this small creature much to look at—his rear white, his front red, and his forelegs appearing to come down from one socket—but this boy had something to ride when the camp moved, a horse already gentled.

He, Peta, a boy with two horses. And not something they give him out of need; Huśte—and now the horsecatcher Pahaha, each one tells him that he earns these horses. Not giveaway property as when someone dies and they look for friendly recipients for whatever the family chooses to give away; instead, two horses coming to Peta in his own name, not in honor of some other person. True, he not yet understood everything about gifting—about giving-to-have—but he remembered the sungazing, which seemed to bring good to everyone, grown and growing.

Approaching his mother's lodge, Peta wanted to whoop, but the mouth moved again through the camps and people who attend a crier will not appreciate a boy's noisy shout. And yet what more exciting news this night than his own?

Mahtociqala came running to meet his friend: "You hear? They say your father leads the party against the Psatoka and so you get to go out with the men and take an enemy's horse and ride in every hunt." The boy lumped his news and his fancy into one long breath. But now he stood looking at Peta as if at someone he scarcely knows.

Peta stood quiet, a most mysterious thing taking place. He envisioned his father out in front of the people, the man's strong face set in resolve, his dark eyes focused on the far distance, a pipe wrapped for war in his hand.

The picture sharpened but not in a way that made the man's face more clear. Instead the son glimpsed, as if through mysteriously penetrating eyes, the true nature of this amazing blood-father: nothing different ever shall bring to this man they call Olepi the exhilaration he finds in the war games; Olepi, his father, now and always the most among warriors.

The picture faded and the boy heard an offended voice from nearby.

"My friend will not listen."

Peta smiled. "I hear, but my friend will not see; observe who noses my hair."

Each boy turned to the horse, then back to one another; the laughter began in their eyes, moved to their lips, and broke from each throat in the same instant. Their whoops bounced against the ears of the unusual-looking creature, a horse who appeared to have nothing but shoulder above the forearm, a horse who exposed a mouth that seemed to laugh back at the boys.

Many youths now came to look and marvel and smile

until Peta led the horse to a staking-place near his mother's lodge. Here he stood stroking the thin, shaggy sides, the face, cheeks, nose, his hand making boy and horse known to one another.

"I ride you, friend, when the bands move," he murmured. His fingers felt down each leg. "And you, like the true-pup, shall learn my ways and I shall understand yours."

Mahtociqala, yet reluctant to leave Peta's side, stared at the creature's hoofs. "Will he run fast on those feet?"

"This one runs fast whatever his feet. His legs tell me so."

"Will he win every race?"

"He will win many races." Peta surprised himself with his own quick reply; he neither had ridden this horse nor had seen him run. "He will win many races providing I ride him," he said, this boast the only one he ever had made.

"I will run my horse against yours." Olepi, standing in the night shadow of the lodge, stepped into view. "I hear my son's boast like a rumble in the sky; I will wait and see whether or not this horse runs like the forked-light."

The eyes Peta raised to his father's face accepted the challenge.

Olepi, unsmiling, held the boy's gaze. "Certain ones speak saying that my son will show me something. I come."

"The news about my father makes the news about my horse not important."

"I call a horse who will win many races an important thing," Olepi answered firmly. "Whatever you recognize you own, and to whatever you own you shall give importance."

Mahtociqala, a little awed at this talk, sensed a relief when the Mahto asked permission to inspect the horse. And so, standing alongside Peta, he watched Olepi's examining hand. And when finally the Mahto gave the horse a resounding slap of approval, Mahtociqala hurried through the dark to his parents' tipi; here he told his father that Peta owned the most remarkable horse in camp.

Peta lay on his sleeping robe, listening to the crier mention his father's name in an honoring song. And now he remembered that this great warrior—his very own father—

had left his guests to come and see his son's new horse and to let Peta know that whatever interests the son shall interest the father.

Suddenly a little fearful, he wished for any man in camp but his father to carry the war pipe. And yet, as in the mysterious picture, he truly will not want to see his father in any different place. The man belongs front, leading out a war party; even a boy will know.

All who visited Napewaśte's lodge this evening had mentioned the woman's pleasing demeanor, her quick hands and modest eyes, her quiet attention to Olepi's wants. Napewaśte, they told one another, makes a good wife for the Mahto leader.

But will my husband say I am a good wife? The woman lay awake, aware of that which kept the husband also awake, awake and rolling on his robes. She had known that not even the honoring song will lift him above discontent, not when something disrupts his efforts toward increasing the power of the tribe.

If he comes to me, Napewaśte told herself, I shall try to persuade him that this disturbing event sits outside his control, that neither he nor any different man will change the hearts of the Mnikooźu. Nor of Zuzueca.

While guests had gathered at Napewaśte's tipi to honor Olepi's appointment as pipe-carrier for the war party, all the Mnikooźu had taken down their lodges and ridden out of camp, perhaps eighty families disappearing into the dusk.

The long wait from sungazing until now, almost two moons, had tried the patience of these northern relatives. Mnikooźu headmen had grumbled complaints; their warriors had come to ride in a war party, they had said, not to sit around an encampment all summer and watch the Titonwan strut before women. And before ever they came here, they had schemed to visit the Palani during the maize-ripening, load up with maize and a mixture for the pipes, and then run off with a herd or two of Palani horses.

The Titonwan had retorted that the Mnikooźu had witnessed remarkably little strutting. Let these relatives stay around until the ground gets hard and the nights turn cold and then see what goes on. But more important, let these

Mnikooźu remember that the Titonwan had cleared the way for all Dakotah who now crossed over onto the short grass.

The peacemen—pipes and gifts in hand—had hurried among these disgruntleds; let the Titonwan, they had urged, remember the Mnikooźu not only as kinsmen but as kinsmen who had come here to risk their lives avenging the deaths of twenty-eight Titonwan.

The Mnikooźu had decided to ride in the war party, certain Titonwan had muttered, only after they had seen the Sahiela arrive and had recognized in what manner these outsiders honored the Lakotah.

In some instances the peacemakers had quieted these dissidents; other occasions had required the uncompromising approach of the clubmen.

But now these disgruntled Mnikooźu relatives had deserted the hoop; Olepi had lost perhaps fifty strong warriors.

The conspicuous absence of the powerful Sicaṅgu—Mniśa and his camp—at the friendly gathering outside Napewaśte's lodge this evening also had affected the Mahto. Not that anyone had difficulty understanding; whoever had eyes saw that Mniśa and Zuzueca smoked together each day, the relatives of one constantly visiting the relatives of the other, these two families apparently finding support in one another's company.

But the important thing now: not that the Mnikooźu sneak out and not that which those two newcomers contrive; instead that the leader of the Mahto, newly recognized in the tribe, keep bending his efforts toward making the people strong, making the people whole, bringing all Dakotah into one great hoop on the plain.

So Napewaśte had recognized. But dwelling now on her fear of the quarrelsome Kiyuksa, the woman prolonged her unrest. What happens to the Titonwan if they permit power-seekers in the hoop? If only Zuzueca and his noisy following will get lonesome for that far-distant redstone river along which they camp in recent seasons; if only they will go back and stay.

Stop looking for trouble, Napewaśte now told herself bluntly; remember the pile of hides awaiting your hands. Boldly you tell your husband that you will not seek his advice about cooking meat, yet you want to offer him your thoughts on affairs that belong to the council lodge.

Napewaśte twisted uncomfortably. But why not speak these thoughts concerning the Kiyuksa? A woman's understanding more than once brings power to the people. A woman's hand brings the sacred pipe. And a woman advises the use of sinew for bowstrings. And they use woman's language in all the ceremonial songs.

Shortly before dawn the husband had come to her robes. She had stirred at the touch of his hand on her thigh and had awakened to his gently insistent fingers. His whisper had spread her legs.

Afterwards, close against him and hearing his thanks breathed into her mouth, she remembered nothing of her desire to speak of Kiyuksa schemes. But then the husband had not come to her robes looking for a woman's views on tribal maneuvering.

Soon after sunrise Peta went out with his father to select horses for a giveaway. Certain old persons—some cripples and one blind man—needed a ride when the bands began traveling.

The boy enjoyed his assignment. He caught the ones Olepi pointed out and drove these horses, four together, into camp. And after he had staked each one where his father had told, he returned to the hillside to offer the man more of his help.

The Mahto originally intended giving horses only to those unfortunate four but suddenly he had decided to give away most of his herd. Let the people say that Olepi gives as generously of horses as he gives of meat. He will hold back seven, eight, only what he needs to sustain his family: two runners, two war horses, his wife's mount, and two for packing tipi and bundles. And perhaps one more horse, something in the event he wants to trade for a favor.

He spoke to Peta, who stood quietly puzzling why his father depletes the herd. "Bring in the white horse, my son. This one I paint and turn loose on the plain. Whoever finds the horse perhaps appreciates my gift, perhaps brings me help—providing I want help—when I go out."

The boy had seen warriors let go a fine, gentle horse, but not until now had he understood why. And so, running off to catch the white one, Peta dropped whatever fear he

300

had held for his father's return from the avenging. This man will have a spirit protector in the fight. For certain.

An excited shouting reached the ears of father and son as these two approached the encampment. A big party of Sahiela came riding in from the plain, more Sahiela warriors to accompany the Titonwan avengers, a sight to make Olepi whoop. Napewaste told afterwards that she had heard her husband's yell of pleasure all the way across the camp circle.

The encampment prepared quickly to greet these friends, these people-who-come-in-red-paint. The center lodge called for boys to attend the Sahiela horses and for women to set out meat. The akicita assigned certain lodges in each camp to sleep the warriors and their families, and the headmen prepared a pipe.

Peta had run to the center, where the Tokala gave instructions to sixty, seventy boys and youths. Walk forward, they said, when the clubman blows his whistle. Stand close by a visiting warrior until this man jumps down, then lead his mount into the big enclosure which the clubmen empty of Titonwan horses.

And now the son of Olepi stood alongside his uncle Leksi, the boy awaiting the whistle.

Leksi squinted his eyes; he watched the Sahiela who rode front. Turning to Peta, he asked that the youth estimate this group of warriors.

Quickly Peta signed the great ten; he used the gesture to indicate a great many. But Leksi advised that he look again.

"Four-tens?" Peta counted forty once, four piles of stones, ten in each pile.

When Leksi said nothing, the boy glanced up at the man. "Perhaps I will not see everyone," he murmured. Clouds covered the sky but he shaded his face as if looking out in sun.

"Whatever your eyes let you see," Leksi answered firmly, "your reason lets you perceive. Observe the space these horsebacks fill and you will know that seven-tens ride in front. When these men sit in camp, count on your hands or use sticks. Either way, you will discover seventy Sahiela warriors. Now watch."

Peta looked back at the approaching visitors. Instead of coming directly into camp, the Sahiela rode up the slope.

301

Reaching the top, they formed a hoop which on signal began turning. Slowly, then fast, then fast, fast. Suddenly one rider broke away; different ones followed. And now the whole party came sweeping down on the Lakotah encampment, colorfully and noisily.

The impressive maneuver had permitted those women and children who filed back of the men to reach the horns at the same moment the warriors dashed up. Wives, daughters, sisters now entered the hoop, their voices raised in a song while their men furiously circled the camp, war whoops shaking the air and hoofs shaking the earth. The warriors rode twice around before forming a long straight line. When the dust settled the horsebacks sat unmoving.

"The Sahiela send strong men." Lekśi looked approvingly at the feather worn erect at the back of most heads. "And strong men ride out with a welcome."

Members of the Tokala, their bodies painted a glistening yellow, went forward to greet the visitors.

A clubman's whistle screeched and Peta became one in the crowd of boys who pushed through to the Sahiela. Then, while these youths led away the visitors' horses, the Tokala guided the Sahiela warriors—each man on a Tokala horse—to the center lodge, where the principal men of camp sat waiting, the long pipestem ready for an ember.

And now Peta, hunting among the Sahiela boys for a familiar face, found the one he looked for, the boy they call Moksois—or so Peta understood this Sahiela name he had heard spoken twice. Moksois, someone with whom he had played when the Sahiela raised tipi nearby the Mahto winter camp. The boy's mother stood loosening the packs on her horse, and Peta, approaching, gestured an offer of help. Climbing the short poles that leaned against the visitor's pack horse, he and Moksois handed down bundles to the woman. Afterwards, they will wander off together, each boy aware that, whatever the language difference, their smiles and glances make everything understandable.

From the moment of the Sahiela's arrival, Napewaśte had attended those roasting fires and paunches of bubbling soup that fed the visitors. But as wife of a headman she had other obligations. She offered help in the mending of Sahiela moccasins and the cleaning of Sahiela gowns, in soothing babies and amusing the young. And in all ways she respected Sahiela customs.

These visitors boil the feathers of young birds, she remembered, and eat the stem, but they never burn the rainbird's feathers and never touch the wambli-bird. Why risk deafness, the Sahiela women said, or a speckly skin or white hair? Nor will they handle the hide of the wandering-dog. But if any of these ways seem strange, Napewaste made herself remember that these good people come here to help the Titonwan avenge a killing. And that the Mahto leader, her husband, leads this revenge party.

And she made herself remember something more about this Mahto leader: who but Olepi ever leads so many warriors? Who but Olepi ever demands of himself the safe return of each warrior who goes out with him?

Hunting more strong thoughts about this man, she recalled his sungazing; certainly, she told herself, the Mahto leader owns sun-power and pte-power along with his own true courage. And so she dares rest content.

The mouth for the center lodge called out news and instructions frequently now. Let the people prepare for a long trail, he sang, bitten moon to bitten moon.

Honoring ceremonies take place along the way, he told; they install the 'blotahunka' and name the clubmen as they travel.

Peta had heard something about appointing certain clubmen to make the kills and his uncle Leksi had clarified: the warriors intend to avenge each one of their twenty-and-eight dead, meaning that twenty-and-eight Psa shall die. And so the pipe-carrier will offer a lance or a rattle, anything symbolic, to ten, twenty men. Other warriors also kill and soon the twenty-eight, perhaps more, lie on the ground.

But if more than twenty-and-eight die, Peta had asked, will not the Psa-toka avenge their dead? And so these avengings keep on and on until they kill everyone, Psa and Titonwan?

Leksi answered quickly: the enemy never will kill all Titonwan nor will the Titonwan want to destroy all Psa. Where will the young Lakotah try out their daring if not on Psa-toka?

The answer had not exactly fitted Peta's inquiry but perhaps one day he will understand such things.

"Two errand boys," Lekśi told now, "go out with the men; perhaps they look for a boy age ten, twelve."

Peta knew at whom his uncle hinted but not likely will they take along a boy with a child's bow, even if that boy's father leads. Nor will he, Peta, sense any eagerness for this honor, not like some boys who dream, awake or sleeping, of the warpath.

"Watch the center lodge. Tipi down at sunrise. Takpe, a tribe goes to war."

The deciders had spoken; at dawn the lodges fall, at sunrise the people move out.

But on this night, the star-nation shall look down on a dance and the moon-grandmother shall hear the Titonwan sing over their relatives and guests. And the spirit of the campfires, four tall stacks of crackling wood, shall see fifty Tokala-lodge men face the assemblage and raise in greeting the arm that never sheds blood.

"Relatives and friends, good that you come." The hands, palms showing, signaled the true welcome; voices, making use of five tones, sounded the true pleasure.

And now twenty young women, their gowns elaborately quilled, echoed the welcome and the pleasure: "You come, you come." Each one, raising a hand that clasped a hoof rattle, made a sweeping circle with that hand. Then forward and back, forward and back, they began to dance.

"You come, you make Lakotah hearts soar." Arms raised, the men now sang: "You come, you come."

"You come, you come." Twenty young women answered, singing and dancing.

Drum and singers, fire and dancers; forward and back, something in movement, the presence of śkan here and everywhere.

And so these Lakotah appreciated their visitors in the old, old way, using the old Dakotah song and ceremony.

The Tokala singers moved into the surrounding shadows, and the young daughters who had danced went quickly to grandmothers or mothers.

Different persons came onto this ground now, the people cheering any Lakotah, Dakotah who desired to recite his importance to the tribe.

Then, in a pause between songs, the voice of the crier spoke for Olepi: "The Mahto makes a gift."

A breath of surprise hung on the air. Often this day the people had heard Olepi's name in the honoring song as different ones found a horse from the Mahto's herd staked at the tipi. What more will Olepi give and to whom?

Peta led forward two fine horses and the crier's far-reaching voice announced the gift. "These horses now belong to the one they call Mniśa. He knows who among his people walks, to whom he shall pass along these horses. The Mahto honors a friend who presently chooses a campsite outside the family hoop yet stays to make this avenging his fight."

Some persons approved loud and long, but different ones saw a break with custom. Olepi had honored Mniśa as the middleman instead of a Mahto or Śiyo or Okandada. But whoever listened carefully had recognized that Olepi gave his gift in the name of all Mahto, that he honored all in the Mahto band.

And not only to Mniśa will the Mahto leader give horses. Peta led forward a gift for Iśna, principal man of the Kuya Wicaśa, another band of Lakotah who stand off, another band uncertain that they want something more than a visitor's place in the Titonwan hoop.

Errand boys for the Tokala-lodge put more wood on the fires, and the people, seeing what truly wonderful horses Olepi gave away, threw admiring glances in his direction.

But the flames also showed some scorning eyes. Zuzueca had recognized two purposes in Olepi's act: the Mahto not only tries to pull the Mniśa and Iśna people into his band but he also seeks the following of these men and their warriors all the way to the fat-grass river, to the Psa camps. But since Olepi chooses to scheme, why not scheme cleverly? Zuzueca looked around at his warriors, their eyes telling that they, also, see through the Mahto's gifts.

Olepi, observing this cluster of Kiyuksa, smiled inside his mouth. Certainly they recognize his scheme but not with whole understanding. True, he wanted to prevent desertions, but more important, he looked for the Pta-lodge to notice his generous gifting. Let these wearers-of-pte-horns know Olepi not only as the great-warrior but as the great-giver. During the next four winters they shall decide whether or not Olepi earns a place in this lodge of honorable men. This season they see fit to honor him as a principal among the Titonwan, but after four more winters will they see fit to make him a member of this headman-lodge, the Pta-lodge?

Not unlikely someone also saw back of his proposal to install the Pta-lodge as blotahunka for the war party. He took a risk, certainly, when instead of waiting for the deciders to name the war leader, he offered an opinion that tied in with his desire not only to lead the avengers but to bring himself in close contact with each member of the Pta-lodge. But who ever gains anything without a risk somewhere along the line?

And his scheme apparently will work out. So why not look for other desirable schemes, remembering always that whatever advances him advances the tribe. Good for the one means good for the whole; the wise ones had said so.

Olepi walked from the dance-ground headed for the sacred-man's lodge, his new long-stem pipe in his hand. He had chosen to remember-himself-as-grizzly, the four-legged warrior of the plain, the creature who never retreats. And anyone who now happened to see this Mahto's face, stepped out of the man's way.

Reaching Wanaġi's lodge, he announced his presence. Then, in a commanding tone, he instructed the wapiya to perform the 'yuwakan,' the ceremony that will make a war pipe of the long-stem.

Wanaġi neither looked up at the arrogant face nor accepted the pipe. "Prepare for the inipi," he said firmly; "come back at midnight, bring the pipe."

The camp slept but for the night-watchmen when Olepi returned to the sacred-lodge. Silently Wanaġi accepted the pipe, filling and setting aside the bowl, passing the stem over sweetgrass smoke.

The two now stepped outside, the wapiya placing the pipestem on a small earth mound in front of the steam-

lodge, an act that signaled his readiness for the inipi ceremony. A young helper who had heated stones picked up the
forked stick that he will use to move these stones, and the
two men, laying their robes on top the initi, bent and
entered.

Wanaġi had used half the night in preparation and he
intended to conduct this ceremony with severe thorough-
ness. He began to ladle water from three sacs onto white-hot
stones, and the tightly closed little lodge soon became stifling heat and choking steam and burning skin.

After emptying each sac, Wanaġi had sung, and twice
the helper had lifted the flap to pass in the pipestem, to
permit a breath of fresh air.

"You live." Wanaġi spoke clearly. "You live and so
you remember yourself as water power, as air power, as
spirit power.

"At the beginning, you only swim."

Olepi gave silent answer: I renew myself for war. Certainly I respond to this power in water. I sit here sweating
out the stale, cleansing inside and out.

Wanaġi spoke again: "Remember Second Born, whose
dry bones begin rattling when First Born, conceiving the
initi, pours water on burning stone. And so sing your thanks
that you relate to one who rises from water-life to fill a
breast with air. Sing thanks."

Olepi heard but he had not sung; smothering steam
shut off his breath. He reached for a spray of sage, something to cool the pain spots on his body.

The next moment the attendant lifted the flap, enough
to enter the pipe and a breath of dry air.

The Mahto touched the stem, handed back the pipe,
and Wanaġi called for more stones, for eight hot stones. But
he had not advised that Olepi wet his cheeks and hair in
preparation for this final blast of heat.

Taking the horn ladle as before, the seer dipped into the
fourth water sac. But instead of splashing the stones, he
poured on the water. A shrieking cloud blurred the two
men.

"Hiye, pila maya." Olepi had found the voice for a
ceremonial thanks.

"Not enough; repeat meaningfully."

Olepi found Wanaġi's eyes through the thinning clouds of steam. What goes here? An endurance contest?

Wanaġi lifted the ladle again and the Mahto waited calmly for the sizzling agony to strike. So let this seer witness the enduring power of a true warrior.

Water hit the stones. And Olepi imagined that these stones, shattering, strike his breast. He bent his head, gasping.

Sing, Olepi, sing.

The warrior had felt, not heard, the command. But instead of a song he remembered the ceremonial phrase—mitaoyate—that will put a stop to this inipi. The instant he says 'all my relatives,' the instant he calls upon all invisibles back to the beginning even as Second Born cries 'let me out,' air will pour into this initi. But why risk calling? Wings and hoofs help him along without his asking.

Again Olepi sensed a voice speaking, but whether he listened to his own familiar-voice or whether he heard a different person's thoughts, he knew not.

None asks, Olepi, that you try here for contact with something invisible. But this lodge helps prepare you for understanding the power that will take you to the source, to the beginning of things, to the vast awareness back of your own awareness. And so, if ever you want desperately to know the truth, to contact the grandfathers—to 'remember everything'—you will own a way. And once you start using this power, you truly will own the earth. Something mysterious, Olepi? Not if you recognize your will, not if you identify the primal.

Suddenly Olepi forced out coherent sound: "I am as the power intends." Will this voice not understand that he reaches the place he desires to reach, that he becomes a guardian of the people, all that the power intends he become?

Not yet, Olepi, and perhaps never. Whoever sees the generating power as only an urge to become father to the one or to the whole never rises to that which the power intends. You remember yourself as water power; you see yourself as air power. But now know yourself as spirit power. Mistakes, misfortune, grief quicken understanding, but who will choose trial and error as a way of life? Why not, instead, a clear path to the source, to the truth? Certain ones who dance gazing-at-the-sun perhaps 'see' something but not you, Olepi; you dance not to see but to let the people see you.

Again the stones hissed and screamed; perhaps never before had a wapiya demanded so much of the inipi.

Olepi sat uncertain of his staying-power now. Empty and dizzy he struggled for balance. His arrogant shoulders drooped; his chin rested on his breast.

But now something reached through the mist and roughly knocked up that chin. And he heard Wanaġi speaking as if these two sat together in the cool, undisturbed air of a summer's night.

Perceive with your spirit, Olepi; know the real warrior.

Olepi made the effort: "Hanta yo, wakanya hibu yelo; clear the way, in a sacred manner I come. . . . "A whistling filled his ears, stopped his voice. Striving for control, he began again. He will remember his shield and that which he paints on the shield: "Maka kin le, mitawa ca. . . . " Something stopped him as before.

And so enough of this smothering dampness and skin-burn. Let me out. I will use the phrase but these words mean only that I want out of this place. Let Wanaġi make of my cry whatever he will. I want out. "Mitaoyate. All my relatives."

At once someone pulled the cover from the initi; cool air flowed over two sweating bodies. Neither man moved.

Wanaġi, holding at the level above definitions, powered his thoughts with spiritual substance: if ever you live as the power intends, you will discover that which you inherit.

Olepi had not heard; the power for recognizing Wanaġi's thoughts had dissipated. He had pulled himself straight, sitting again as the Mahto, perhaps the loser in this purifying contest but a proud loser.

Outside the initi Olepi glanced at his steam burn; shall he chew and spit sage on this redness or shall he permit a blister, another visible mark of his endurance? The next moment he flung his robe over one shoulder and moved toward the stream. After his plunge he will pick up the pipe as Wanaġi instructs, the bowl sealed and the stem wrapped for war. And now, suddenly, Olepi sensed true elation.

Inside the sacred-lodge Wanaǧi wiped his own body with grass and pondered this experience. Certainly he had abused Olepi, but what different way to show a man like this one that he owns the power for seeing so much more than he sees, hearing so much more than he hears, knowing so much more than he knows.

And yet who dares decide for another man whether or not he shall live as the power intends?

On the way back to his lodge Olepi heard the 'koo-oo, koo-oo' sound that awakens each family on the day of a move. Eyanpaha and the other criers had started their rounds long before dawn, many tipi flaps to visit, many deep-sleeping persons to awaken.

The Mahto leader smiled; he knew that the Tokala clubmen will have everyone in line as the light rises up out of the east. And that he, Olepi, shall take his place front, in front of the front.

XXV

A HALF-DAY separated the front and back of the moving camps, akicita riding to side and rear of this long line, scouts staying far out in all directions.

Wherever warriors rode, certain ones bunched together, painted alike, legs touching. One group of Okandada had marked their faces with two slanting black lines and on their heads they wore split pte-horns. Four carried lances, the weapons tipped with iron and decorated with white-and-black feathers. On the second night out, these same ones had danced, their loins uncovered, their songs unfamiliar; apparently these Okandada formed a new warrior-lodge. What name they gave their lodge none told, but they had pledged to protect anyone wounded during the avenging and so the people spoke saying 'cante tinza,' brave hearts.

Some Kuya who also rode close wore kaṅgi feathers at their necks and the beaks of these same big black-birds decorated their lances. But whether these warriors banded together for travel or whether they, also, formed a lodge none yet knew. And one boy neither knew nor cared.

Peta had experienced some difficulty in keeping his young true-dog in line and safe from a clubman's pounding. He knew that the Tokala will kill any dog who strays, this line of traveling people something more than a moving camp. The Lakotah go to war, the leaders walk rapidly, and each night's camp, a meeting of warriors.

And so, on this fifth day of travel, Peta had responded eagerly to an invitation from Ogle. The akicita will permit this man to make up a little hunting party, two men and two boys, these four to rejoin the people at a certain place, Ogle agreeing that he will keep toward the hills and not disturb any meat in the path of the Lakotah camps. And that the four, in order not to arouse any jealousy, shall start out quietly at night.

Ogle, his brother Hinhan, Mahtociqala, and Peta will make up the party, and Peta shall bring his true-dog, whose back they need for bundles; a second dog will pack the short poles and cover of a traveler's tipi.

But for all his eagerness two things troubled Peta: a concern for his two horses and his lack of a proper bow. His horses shall go to the rear with the Mahto herd where horse-tenders keep watch. Even so, a memory of horses dying on the trail made him uneasy about his own; he wanted neither the funny creature he rode nor the young black suffering any misuse.

As for the bow, perhaps his relatives know of Ogle's invitation and so they make him a hunting bow. Certainly they will not see him taking blunt arrows.

But neither grandfather, father, uncles presented him with something; he went out with Ogle pondering what manner of family sends out a son to hunt with a toy.

The hunters walked calmly through the dark toward a lonely hill, one that sat directly below the fixed star. But the boys sensed a certain uneasiness; they remembered the story about this rise which the people had named flying-mystery butte. A muddy-looking cloud had floated slowly above this hill one summer evening, brightly colored arrowlike streaks traveling along with the cloud. Next thing, a great shaft of light had appeared, like fog but not fog, something that had settled down on the butte, a giantlike shape with one arm extending up, the other one pointing to earth. A rumbling voice had demanded that the man who had sat smoking atop this place seek a different hill. "You intrude," the voice had said. Afterwards two brave men had visited the butte; they had found images on a boulder where before they had seen nothing.

So why, the boys wondered, will Ogle lead the party here? Will the hunter scheme an ordeal for Peta, perhaps sending him up the butte before they permit him to hunt? Someone had told about a boy whose father had required that he kill a shell and eat the creature's heart before he touches a hunting bow. But that man, a most unusual father—or so everyone said. And yet the Mahto leader occasionally acts unusual; perhaps he advises that they leave Peta alone on the butte. . . .

Before dawn Peta had recognized that the hunters used this butte only as a guide, something to mark the place where two rivers join waters, the point at which the path of the little hunting party shall change direction and start up a long slope of earth.

For eight, ten days the hunters followed creeks and streams, mostly dry or muddy but providing a path that kept the party moving west even as they walked north. Occasionally they had crawled out on a jutting point to watch the cloud shadows chase across the plain, and at one such place, while the men smoked, the boys had investigated the steep white cliff that dropped down the opposite side. And here Peta had glimpsed the nimble creature with the curly horn.

"Hekinskayapi?" Ogle had sounded surprise on hearing the boy report. "Perhaps you see the grandmother. Will she walk tiptoe or will she sit chewing? Or perhaps you see her grandson."

But Peta had seen the bighorn only long enough to

312

wish for a bow with the power to send an arrow into the creature's neck. He had known that to make his father a gift of those horns meant a fine ladle for use at the tribal feasts; a man drinks soup using the horn of pte but a leader desires to ladle soup into his guest's bowl with a different horn, a white horn. But as to whether he had viewed grandmother, grandfather, or young adult, the boy dared not say; he never before had seen the bighorn grazing.

Soon the hunters had climbed down, traveling along the bottom of the buttes, finding water in a draw that also hid nests of grass. But mostly the earth proved rough, the hills bare, the gullies washed out.

The four had pursued only the little-meat during their journey and so Peta not yet had needed to display his bow. He and Mahtociqala had clubbed some small birds and caught some little chipmungks. And Hinhan had killed a digger, jumping on the back of this squat flat-face before the creature managed to turn over and bite. Ogle had attached pieces of fat from Hinhan's kill to branches he cut off young lodgepole trees. Then covering himself with these slender stems, he had demonstrated one way to catch the bird-who-sits-smiling; when these mischievous wingeds flew up after the fat, he grabbed their legs and wrung their necks. Child's play, he had smiled, but the boys had looked uncertain.

Peta had walked unaware that the two men observed his every act. Nor will he know that two winters previous Ogle had asked Olepi for the privilege of presenting this boy with a true bow.

Perhaps Ogle had known that the son of Olepi shall feel compelled to drop an antlered creature with his first pull on a man's bow. And so the hunter had looked a long while for a certain bone, for the same rare material he had used in making his own bone bow. But from what creature this bone had come or what tribe had made the original trade, he never had learned. An Okandada seer had hinted that the bone came from Miniwatu, the horned water creature who pushes around the rivers and distorts their course. Or perhaps from Miniwatu's young relatives who make a game of creating floods; they play rough and not unlikely break off a horn.

Ogle had listened courteously but he never had accepted guesses from anyone. And so he finally had cut a

313

branch from the scabby-leaf tree of the cliffs and had begun shaping, smoothing, bending, skill and ceremony attending each procedure; he had used up two moons making the bow.

Next the shafts and the same careful work. Visiting the open hillsides, he had selected stems of saskatoon, cutting and drying this slender berrywood during the past winter, enough wood for ten arrows. He had used stone to smooth and bone to straighten these sticks. And certainly he had used a barbed stone from the wiyokeze hills to groove each shaft with two zigzag lines. On the head he had glued and wrapped stone points; on the opposite tip, feathers split and wrapped, feathers that defied a blood-wetting.

Ogle carried this weapon with him, bow and arrows in a pte-hide container, the hair clinging. And now the hunter decided to present his gift. But not without a little teasing.

"I eat only birds. Will the big meat hide from Peta's bow?"

The boy, hearing Ogle's words, turned his head.

Next Hinhan spoke: "Perhaps a certain young hunter leaves his bowstrings in his mother's lodge."

Peta looked toward a distant butte. He stood uncertain as to whether these men teased or ridiculed, but whichever, he told himself, they have reason.

Suddenly Ogle demanded that Peta string his bow and demonstrate his aim.

"My father means this bow." Mahtociqala, his voice shy but his whole face smiling, held out the new bow and arrow-holder. "My father says that he carries your bow and shafts far enough. Now you carry."

When finally Peta looked into the eyes of his young friend, he yet wondered whether they all teased him.

The men watched, their faces under control, as the boy, trying to hide his joy, examined the weapon in the deliberate manner of a man.

The bow reached from the ground to Peta's waist and the width and thickness matched the boy's grip. The hunter had related the weapon in every way to the son of Olepi.

Pulling an arrow from the container, Peta nosed along the shaft. Which one of the arrow-woods? The smell puzzled him. He tried the length. Extending his arm and hand, he saw that the wood reached from his breast to the tip of his

314

middle finger. Smiling he looked at Mahtociqala; he not yet trusted himself to look at Ogle.

The hunter, understanding, began brisk talk. Let Peta again examine these arrows, not something shaved up as for a child; notice instead that each shaft bears three feathers, all from a single wing and slanting sideways for a good spin. "These arrows will find meat whatever way you happen to point."

Ogle's eyes held laughter, but Peta had not responded to this joking. And so, while Ogle will enjoy the sort of teasing that draws a little fire, he will not take away joy from one who waits overlong for his bow. Quickly he mentioned why he had not painted the shafts: "You decide your mark and color. Mix with spit and paint below the notch."

The boy looked at the hunter now and smilingly told his desire for the sky color, something rare among paints. But remembering those shafts he had sent toward the pte-shape cloud, he wanted the color of the sky to ride his arrows.

Then, before anyone said more, Hinhan held out something for Mahtociqala. Surprising everyone, this man presented Mahtociqala with a bow, something made from a single piece of wood and without sinew backing but certainly not a plaything. And Mahtociqala saw at once that Hinhan had feathered the shafts exactly like Peta's arrows.

The young boy raised respectful eyes to Hinhan, but the look he gave Peta spilled out his joy. His arrows, also, had sharp points, bone as good as stone.

And now the men, aware that these boys wanted to share their joy with each other and beyond any restraining-relative presence, went about setting up the little travel lodge and tending to different things. But the smile stayed in Ogle's eyes; he remembered back to his first real bow and his foolish determination to carry his arrows always in his hand, never in a sack over his shoulder. Foolish? They call him a great hunter now; they say that not a man in the tribe sends his second, third arrow more quickly than Ogle. Perhaps; but he will not boast any greatness until he sees what meat his own legs will chase down during this expedition.

The next day the group came upon a hill black with

herd, the fat and lazy staying on together, the meat an easy kill.

But Ogle made the denying gesture: "The dogs carry only so much burden. I kill and pack pte meat when I see where the traveling people make camp."

Peta understood but his desire to send an arrow into something big almost overwhelmed him.

Then, before they had passed by the herd, Hinhan had pointed out pronghorn, a family with young grazing on a nearby knoll; closeness to the pte had given these pronghorn unusual boldness. And so Ogle, after instructing Peta as to the proper approach, sent him out.

The boy started crawling forward; at a certain place he raised his arm and waved a branch above the tall grass.

Nothing happened. And so he moved forward again; he stopped and waved the branch as before.

One of the young left the knoll, making those little approaches usual to these sandy-bellies.

Peta's heart pounded. He tucked an arrow under his armpit and stuck a second one in his mouth, two arrows instantly ready if he missed with the one at his bow.

The creature, curious, circled in close, the white throat and round black eyes visible above the grass tops.

But the boy never released his arrow.

Something sprang past him and leapt at the pronghorn's flank.

Astounded, Peta rose up slowly. He saw his true-dog, the moccasin pack secure on her back, struggling with the pronghorn. Next thing, the meat lay on the ground, the dog's sharp teeth tearing in before her pain-cries had ceased.

Perhaps his pup goes crazy? Finding voice, the boy tried the command that always brought the dog to him.

The pup left her victim and bounded playfully toward Peta. But now Ogle came up, knife in hand. "If you want this dog to live, punish her."

Peta's new knife hung at his neck and he carried his new bow. Fleetingly he recalled the akicita who whipped those two women in the Kiyuksa village. And now he brought down the bow on the dog's back. Twice, twice again.

Ogle signaled enough.

Mahtociqala had stood all this while next to his father, eyes looking down. His hand had held the dog when she made her rush. He wanted to accept the shame but his father had begun speaking.

"This dog, born on the ledge, hunts as her nation hunts. This dog's grandfathers teach the Lakotah to hide in clumps and stir the grasses and so attract these tatokala, these pronghorn. From the true-dogs the Lakotah learns to chase the pronghorn over a cliff, hunters waiting at the bottom.

"Now a true-dog sits shamefaced at Peta's moccasin. She learns that not again shall she hunt as her nation hunts. A captive in the Titonwan camps, she shall learn the people's ways."

The hunter paused, wondering whether he makes clear the difference between kaonspe, teaching-with-force, and waonspekiye, gentling-with-patience.

"My sons, understand. You see here something that Peta's dog will learn only through an experience outside camp. Even as nature becomes harsh, so man occasionally becomes harsh. But never beyond control."

Ogle turned to Mahtociqala. "My son needs to remember something: he neglects to hold the young dog and so he sees his friend's new bow put to grievous use."

The hunter had spoken and none shall mention the incident again.

Let the boys skin the kill, Ogle said; he and his brother will supervise.

Peta had watched this procedure, but never before had he held the skinning knife. And so the boys worked carefully, removing the sinew from the back before touching the meat.

Hinhan, having staked the dogs, came to help cut up the meat. He noticed at once that something had crippled this young creature soon after birth, a leg injury here. Good, he told himself, that dog and not boy brings down this pronghorn; a true hunter never purposely kills anything lame.

Soon they had a fire for roasting meat and afterwards, only a pile of bones, nothing left over to pack but the pronghorn's hide.

The men and boys moved slowly over earth black with pte, the wind blowing the heavy, rank smell of the herd against the travelers' faces. Then suddenly Ogle announced his intention to hunt. He unpacked the pronghorn hide. "This fresh skin covers the man-smell. I make meat the old way." The hunter walked off, the hide flung over his head and shoulders.

They watched him go. But Hinhan, seeing that his brother needed to work his way through a tight circle of pte, decided to move out after Ogle; wisely managed whiffs of man-scent will thin out a place in the herd.

The boys, looking on from the top of a little hill, saw Ogle crouch down. He advanced toward a small opening in the herd as if the wind blew him along; he moved when the grasses moved, when the brush rattled.

Hinhan, his robe over his head, crawled along at the edge of the herd. Whenever he stopped, he resembled a boulder on the plain.

Peta watched with marveling eyes. He saw Ogle single out a big one who dusted herself in a wallow, squirming and rolling to relieve an itching hide. But even as she lifted her black nose—perhaps catching the man-smell—he saw two arrows strike her side.

The creature made a desperate effort to heave her bulk out of the hollow. But after getting to her feet, she ran only five, six stumbling steps before crashing to the ground.

Peta had one more glimpse of Ogle, the hunter appearing to stand directly in the path of a snorting, bawling band of mothers and young; tails hoisted, alert to danger, they ran bunched, more pte crowding in from sides and rear.

Now something flew up, something that looked like a pronghorn hide. And now the pounding hoofs raised a dust-cloud that obscured any more viewing in this direction.

The next moment Peta saw two forms emerging from a different dust, creature-form and man, the four-legged one spilling red.

Mahtociqala gave a shout. "I see my father. He kills pta."

True, the creature had fallen, but two hunters stood alongside this meat.

Eager to examine the kill, the boys ran toward the men.

And so they saw that Ogle's knife had cut down the strength in the creature's hind legs, then dug into a vulnerable spot. But Peta looked on, puzzled; will not Hinhan chase this one? Certainly Hinhan's arrow sticks in the hide.

Hinhan smiled. He will need horse and lance to make meat, he said; let the truly great hunter, his brother Ogle, tell what happens.

And so Ogle spoke. After killing the pte who wallowed in dust, he saw that either he divides the scampering herd or they trample him. He had jerked off the pronghorn cover, throwing this thing in the air, the flying skin something to divert the leaders. And certainly the onrushers had separated. But suddenly an aging herd-father had appeared. Ogle had jumped aside even as he used his knife to cut muscle that will weaken the rear legs. Next thing, the creature had spun around. And so the hunter had flung his knife, aiming below the foreleg on the heart-side. Then, blind from dust, Ogle had lost view of the dark shape.

"I see pta," Hinhan said, taking his turn with the story, "but I know not that my brother wounds this one or never will I enter the chase. I send an arrow, but not before my brother's knife makes the fatal wound."

Hinhan looked at Mahtociqala. "The son of Ogle, the son of a great hunter."

"So will my grandfather and my father chase meat," Ogle observed shortly. He glanced at Peta. "I throw away your chance for a pair of leg-covers, but the herd gets either the pronghorn's hide or mine. I replace the creature's skin more easily than my own." The man turned to look briefly at the disappearing herd, the front ones hurrying up a distant slope, a yellow dust hiding the many who followed on rumbling hoofs.

The hunters went back to the creature killed near the wallow, even Ogle surprised at that which he saw. Here, a small-head pte with short, short horns yet with a body as big as any mature one. So perhaps the spirit of this unusual pte divides the herd before ever he, Ogle, tosses up the pronghorn skin? The hunter threw a silent thanks to the mysterious head, then declared aloud his intention to paint the horns in a ceremonial manner. Now, let the boys skin and cut this meat.

Peta knew to turn the head, the horns acting as a support. But a small-head like this one made the skinning difficult and so the men gave help.

And now, eager to eat the liver and dig into the belly fat while the meat yet tasted warm, the two boys neglected their assignment.

"Pack the ribs to go," Ogle ordered, but the boys scarcely heard.

"My sons choose hoofs for their evening's meat." Ogle spoke unsmiling; either these young ones help flake the meat for a quick drying or they starve on pte-feet.

The men had chosen to roast the hump and so Ogle, with Hinhan's help, prepared a fire. And Peta, looking up, observed that these hunters used two sticks for getting a spark where Tunkašila used only one.

While the hump sizzled, Hinhan and Peta finished cutting up meat and Mahtociqala went with his father to where the pta had fallen. The hunter had decided to take only horns and tongue, the horns cracked but not brittle, none of those deep grooves around the butts as among the herd-grandfathers.

Slitting the neck to draw out the tongue, Ogle spoke to the carcass: "Your meat looks good, my brother, but all the while you mount pte, you stink. Your tongue alone tastes sweet. I will ask that sun and winds dry this tongue."

While removing the horns, the hunter again murmured to the kill. "Have comfort, my brother; someone shall make good use of these horns."

Before dusk Ogle had painted the small skull and placed this head on sage, the eyes toward sunset. And now the hunters made ready for more travel, but the boys, stuffed and sleepy, wondered why not lie down here. Why keep walking?

"The enemy, whether man or creature, owns a nose for the meat fires. Sleep near the place you cook and you find yourself on the spirit-trail." Ogle glanced at the sky, not in search of stars but for a view of weather. "Water soon pours down," he said, "and wipes out my tracks. I find a shelter and sleep."

The clouds seemed slow to spill and even after the rain Ogle kept on walking. The boys dared not complain; only children get noisy. Instead, as Hinhan instructed, they hopped around barefoot in those muddy places where they inadvertently had put Lakotah moccasin tracks.

When finally they stopped for sleep, Mahtociqala dreamed that he hopped across the plain, from where the bunch grass grows to where the black hills rise up. In the morning he intended to tell his dream, but only to Peta. If his father learns of the dream, the man perhaps will find a meaning and order Mahtociqala to hop around camp like that one they call Woze, a youth eighteen winters who dreams of the flying-mystery this summer and so becomes a contrary.

The travelers had sufficient meat, but Mahtociqala talked about using his new bow on something more than those hopping creatures he will hunt any day with blunt arrows or club. Peta said nothing; he had used his chance on a pronghorn.

The third morning after the pte-kills Mahtociqala discovered an unfamiliar track. Claw marks on the four toes hinted at the feet of a traveling-dog but the boys looked puzzled.

"Will your friend recognize this track?" Ogle spoke to his son but his eyes glanced toward Peta.

Peta stooped and touched his fingers inside the impression. "Not traveling-dog, not a flat-face, not a tuft-ears, not . . ."

"Why tell me who not walks here. Say who goes or say nothing."

Peta wished that he had held his tongue; he kept his eyes on the tracks.

"Why not follow these tracks to the point of knowing."

Peta recalled that Tunkaśila had said this same thing.

But Mahtociqala spoke up quickly: "My father, if ever I am to use my bow I need to see something more than footmarks."

"Follow these tracks," Ogle answered, "but recognize your return path. Bend sticks and pile up stones. I move on toward the hill."

Certainly, the men will leave the boys a noticeable trail: drag marks, signs of dog, moccasin tracks. "Now go," Ogle ordered; "I am glad that you walk facing the sun."

"He means," Peta told his young friend as the two

321

started out, "that shadow deepens the tracks and so I and you see these footmarks clearly."

Mahtociqala laughed. "I am a scout. Scouts find footmarks in the dark."

They had not walked far before they came upon an assortment of tracks, all bordering an encampment of those little yappers who burrow on the plain. The whole tribe vanished underground as the boys approached their mound village. But who wants to lose arrows on these elusive creatures?

Moving on, they tried to find the tracks that had led to this place. Suddenly Peta sniffed the air; he smiled, certain that he knew whom they had stalked.

Mahtociqala twisted his nose. "Perhaps the skunk you smell makes her stink before sunrise and on a different path. I and you track four-toes, not five."

Peta bent down; he examined the only tracks clearly visible. "Maka," he said firmly; truly, they trail a skunk.

"Hoye," Mahtociqala said cheerfully; "I shall present my father a skin for his pipe."

The tracks soon led into a hole but the boys noticed scarcely any scent here.

Cutting a stick, Peta forked one tip. Cautiously he pushed the wood into the opening. When nothing happened, he poked the hole boldly. "Empty," he announced.

And now the two heard a rustle in the grass; instantly Mahtociqala's fingers straddled an arrow, his bow ready. But a disturbance at the entrance to the burrow caught Peta's attention; he saw a sleepy head emerging from the hole and then a body, two white stripes joined over the shoulder. Here came Ogle's pipe-sack.

Mahtociqala, glancing, saw the skunk but his eyes returned to the grass clumps; perhaps here crouched the four-toes whose track had disappeared somewhere along the trail, a creature he intended to know.

But now the sleepy one, outside her hole and fully awake, stamped her foot and hissed at Peta's stick. Suddenly she turned, her tail lifted.

Peta jumped aside to miss the spray and Mahtociqala sent his arrow into the creature's head.

The heavily scented air made breathing difficult; the

322

boys held their noses. But what next? Neither one knew the way to remove the skin for a pipe-sack, and who will carry back this smelly body?

Then Peta remembered something. "My grandfather says that the skunk dislikes her own spray. She rolls in mud to rub off the smell. Perhaps this one will not smell if I cover the body with mud."

Mahtociqala pulled his arrow from the limp form. "Rejoice," he told his kill. "All your spirit life you shall carry my father's pipe." He turned away, his hand back at his nose.

The mud bath had made little difference; Mahtociqala wanted to leave the dead skunk on the ground. But Peta advised differently: his friend offers this one a spirit life with the pipe; will not the skunk's spirit make mischief if the boy neglects his word? Peta's gaze acted convincingly; Mahtociqala picked up the muddy body.

And now these two, heading back for the place where they had separated from the men, tried to rediscover the four-toes track they had lost somewhere along their way. "Remember," Peta murmured, "front and rear tracks of the same creature often differ, the shape or perhaps another toe." He quoted his grandfather, who certainly knows everything about the four-legged.

But Mahtociqala had stopped to inspect some fresh droppings, most likely from a young traveling-dog.

And now Peta stood looking at a narrow trail of slightly fuzzy tracks that led off in a straight line. "Śuṅgila," he said aloud, trying to control his excitement, "the sly little red-yellow dog with the black legs and feet.

"Look close," he told Mahtociqala, "and you will see that he walks up here but soon starts running, his rear track out in front."

Śuṅgila, he repeated to himself; why will he know this track now yet not recognize the same one when he and Mahtociqala start out at sunrise? But enough that he knows now. He sensed an eagerness to own the long bushy tail, to outwit this cunning little-dog.

"Keep your shadow small," he warned Mahtociqala; "shadows scare birds, and their chirps tell that someone comes."

323

They move along cautiously. Now, the tracks disappearing in the brush, Peta looked for hairs clinging to the thick grass, and Mahtociqala tried for the creature's scent. But the one boy found nothing helpful and his friend sniffed nothing but skunk. Even so something hinted that the little black-legged dog waited nearby, ready to pounce on whatever scurried or hopped through the grass. And so the two stalkers crouched down to listen, Mahtociqala dropping the skunk and fitting an arrow at his bowstring, Peta maneuvering into a position that permitted him to rise and turn quickly.

Soon they heard movement, perhaps a small-eyed, tiny grass creature scampering toward her burrow.

And now a flash of reddish yellow and a long stiff-legged leap. An arrow left Peta's bow at the same instant that Mahtociqala sent his shaft.

Running out, Mahtociqala found two arrows, one stuck in the black leg, the other arrow piercing the heart.

"But I send one arrow," the boy marveled as Peta came close.

"And I send one," Peta answered.

"Whose arrow kills Śuṅgila?" Mahtociqala had not remembered that on these unpainted shafts the arrowhead will tell.

"I say this kill belongs to you, my friend." Peta, his eyes on the white-tipped puffy tail, knew that he had made a gift more important to him than the horse he had staked at the sunpole; the horse went to anyone, but that which he gives here goes to one of his own choosing.

Quickly, easily, the boys discovered the men's trail; the hunters had followed a creek that trickled over sandy clay.

"Stay." Ogle's voice called out from a wooded point ahead.

"My father, I bring your pipe-sack." Mahtociqala walked on toward the grove. "Mud covers the skin and takes away the big smell."

"Let mud cover your skin also. Someone stinks."

Peta had stopped on hearing the hunter's command. And now Mahtociqala waited.

Ogle spoke again. "A father gives his son a new name

when the boy kills with a new bow. My son smells like a skunk and so I name him Makamna."

Peta heard nothing funny here. Namings took place after war, not after a hunt. And if the hunter chooses to ridicule his son, let the shame sit with him who persuades Mahtociqala to take along the smelly body.

But Mahtociqala stood smiling; he knew his father's ways. "Will my father give my friend a new name? He stinks the same as I."

When the men said nothing, Peta stood reluctant to approach; perhaps the hunter means this thing, perhaps the boys need to splash in mud. Peta went to the creek and began daubing his skin, Mahtociqala soon alongside and imitating his friend.

But when the two ran toward the grove, the hunters had disappeared, their tracks suddenly indistinct and somewhat confusing.

Walking slowly now, the boys snatched berries in passing, something to satisfy a thirst. Their faces solemn, neither one talked until Peta suddenly laughed: "I either wash off this mud or something mistakes me for meat."

"I will not mistake you."

The voice, startlingly close, sent the boys rushing toward one another. Now Peta dropped to the ground, pulling Mahtociqala next to him. They lay face down and trembling, too frightened to notice that the voice had spoken Lakotah.

"The earth will not hide you," the same stern voice admonished. "An alert stalker remembers that perhaps someone stalks him."

Suddenly recognizing who spoke, Mahtociqala jumped up; his father often made a game of teasing.

But Hinhan, not Ogle, approached. He met the boy unsmiling: "I see someone who runs out to a voice before he identifies the speaker."

Mahtociqala's eyes rounded in astonishment as Hinhan went on to imitate Ogle. "Will this same foolish boy imagine that Hinhan knows only to mimic the rain-bird?"

Ogle came up now and the son looked into his father's face; certainly the men intend only fun with this trick.

The hunter gazed back at his son, neither fun nor

teasing in his eyes. "Apparently you will not remember that occasionally the enemy speaks Lakotah. Before exposing yourself, ask something that only you and your family know. The answer will tell whether or not you talk with one of your own."

Peta stepped forward to receive his share of the rebuke, the boy wondering whether Ogle will break his new bow as punishment even as this man had demanded that Peta punish the true-pup.

But Ogle spoke on, his tone firm yet not unfatherly. "Each moving thing," he said, "leaves a trail: flattening the grass, tearing a leaf, turning up stones, scratching the earth. And always someone, friend or enemy, makes use of these clues.

"In the same manner each man's face provides clues— eyes, mouth, nose, skin, any one of these features apt to betray him. But he who learns inside his own lodge to hide gladness or pain, fear or relief, controls these feelings outside his lodge. And so protects himself on all occasions."

Ogle finished his speech but certainly neither boy permitted himself any change of expression, not even when the hunter proposed they make a ceremonial feast of these kills.

Hinhan took care of the little-dog hide and Ogle skinned the skunk. And soon the boys tossed bites of flesh from each kill to those wingeds who always share in a new-bow ceremony.

Then, while the meat roasted, Mahtociqala had remembered something. And so he knew whose arrow had entered the little-dog's heart. Looking up at Hinhan, the boy spoke softly as if he dared not trust himself with so strong a feeling. "Peta . . . Peta who hunts with me . . . the most wonderful brother I know."

Ogle led the party toward the slender buttes, a long thin range of clay hills wriggling south. And now the four traveled a difficult trail. In some places the prickly grass pierced their moccasins; in different places their feet sank into loose clay. Nothing grew that sheltered from the sun, and when a bird shadow moved over the heated plain, the men knew, without glancing up, that the flapping black-bird cast this shade.

"Neither warm winds nor cold chase off this bird," Ogle said pointedly. He went on to recall a deep snow seven, eight winters before Mahtociqala's birth, a winter cold enough to freeze these brave wingeds in the air.

When Mahtociqala expressed his wish for some of that severe cold now, Hinhan smiled. But Ogle responded differently; he led the boys over a prickly stretch of sizzling earth at a crouching run. They travel an unrelenting path, he told himself; let these youths learn to stay abreast.

The next two days they followed where the pte had made a trail, where these shaggy ones, their passage undisputed but for an occasional wandering quill, had walked single file.

And now they came among broken cliffs and wooded canyons, the twisted ridge sloping irregularly, then seeming to crawl underground. And so they left the yellow glare and hot wind to climb down into the cool shade. Here the boys dropped to the grass and lay eyes closed. The men examined the ground for tracks before they relieved the dogs of bundles. But while they smoked and rested, they sat on the dogs' leashes.

Nothing disturbed the quiet but for the gossiping of prairie birds, and soon Mahtociqala, then Peta, slept.

After a while Ogle, bending over Peta, spoke softly: "Something browses nearby. I see droppings."

Three, four agile moves and Peta stood, bow in hand, testing the string, making adjustment. He gestured his readiness.

Almost at once Peta discovered the tracks of a blacktail, the boy understanding from the length of her foot that he stalked a female.

And now Ogle, walking back of Peta, noticed that the youth high-stepped the loose stones, avoided the rustling brush, and knew when to crawl on toes and elbows. But he decided to show Peta another cautious way of moving forward—legs bending sideways, hands grabbing the grasses, pulling along his body. The young stalker caught on quickly; Ogle motioned that he go on alone.

Waiting back among the trees, Ogle soon heard crashing brush; Peta either startled or injured something. But when he saw that the boy came running, he listened for big news.

327

"I kill. I kill something mysterious. Branch and points look different." Peta's eyes gazed wonder.

"But you track the female."

Peta knew only that he had killed an antlered head. Let the hunter come and see.

Walking back of the boy, Ogle observed carefully each hoofmark along the trail. Reaching the fallen creature, the man stared at the body, then at each separate member: belly, rump, legs. He felt the hide in many places; he stood back marveling. "Hoħ," he said, releasing his wonder.

Peta gazed at the malformed antlers, the skin yet unshed; perhaps Ogle will explain this strangeness to him.

"Tell me about your hunt," Ogle said quietly.

Peta began, his phrases carefully chosen, his gestures precise. Belly down, he crawls as Ogle instructs. Next, he hears a blowing sound, like a horse clearing his nose. He waits. The sound comes twice, nearby. He rises up . . . he sees. . .

The boy's calm gave way to excitement. "I see this female . . . this male . . . this one. I send an arrow. I send three more arrows before the creature crashes to the ground."

Peta awaited the approving 'hau.' Will not the hunter call this kill with a new bow something remarkable? Or will he see some mischief here? Truly, one tries not to kill the cripples among the wingeds, among the hoofs. But this one neither limps nor shows a wound. And Ogle himself kills a pte with small head and short, short horns. The hunter paints those short horns, but so will he, Peta, paint the strange antlers if Ogle advises.

"You shall tell the wapiya your story, my son." Ogle gave the boy an intent look. "Perhaps he shall skin and cut your kill in a ceremonial way."

Glancing again at the mysterious tawiyela, Ogle saw that the men will need poles on their shoulders if they intend to carry the kill any distance. And the one way to manage now—on Ogle's back.

Peta, bearing the weapons, marveled the hunter's strength, but he also pondered in what manner they shall handle this meat while they travel.

And so, when these two sat again with Hinhan and Mahtociqala, Peta mentioned tying the dogs together, fastening sticks across their drag-poles, laying the carcass on top. And transferring all bundles to the backs of boys and men.

He saw approval in their eyes even before they voiced assent. And now he understood what Ogle meant when the hunter spoke of clues on a man's face.

The party climbed out of the canyon and moved along under the ridge. At one place they came on top to search the open for signs of the Titonwan camps. But they stayed to gaze on the wonder of the plain: black patches of small twisted trees squatting on yellow silence and in the far distance the black hills. And midway, the tall butte where more than one Lakotah had dug a trap for the wambli-bird.

The next day they started out along a river that trickled over a pebbly bottom. Then, approaching a place where the water flowed and deepened, Peta waded in to pick up the body of a swims-with-stick, the creature dead perhaps two, three days.

Carefully Ogle cut through the flesh; he pointed to certain small scars. "This one dies after bearing three young," he said. "Find her lodge and see with your own eyes. But remember that the father keeps watch."

Peta, going off alone, discovered the creature's lodge at the edge of the river, not in a pond. Making his way inside, he located the three young ones, their bite sharp but not painful. He left the three wailing on their ledge above the water, hurrying out before the living parent returned. True, he came away hands empty, nothing big enough for tail-meat, fat, or hide but certainly he marveled the mystery that will keep count of progeny, that will record this count inside the mother's body.

While Peta visited the orphans' lodge, Mahtociqala had discovered a skunk but this one he handled as Hinhan directed. Holding head and tail, the belly up, he slapped the creature against a tree, killing before a spray. Instantly he presented the skin to Hinhan and so gifted each of his fathers—one by blood, one by kinsman rule—with a pipe-sack. The people advise, he suddenly remembered, that a boy choose also a hunka-father, a man unrelated. But certainly two fathers seemed enough, two fathers and two skunk pipe-sacks.

The party moved on, the boys finding the outline of a

leaf and a giant toe in a big slab of stone, but the men pointed out yet more unusual things: the absence of foot-marks along the muddy edges of the stream and on the wooded points, the carcass of a dead pte heaped over with earth and stones, and nearby, the terrifying tracks of the arrogant creature who walks like a man.

"Wherever the grizzly prowls," Hinhan told, "all dif-ferent four-legs stay away. I see that this fierce warrior wanders back across the ridge, perhaps to the shifting-sands water, roving ground of the Psatoka, and so I dare not follow."

Mahtociqala and Peta confided a secret gladness that the impending fight with the Psatoka prevented the hunter from pursuing the grizzly; neither boy held on to any desire for a meeting with long-claws. Even so, Peta had begun to wonder whether one strange carcass—an antlered female blacktail—will prove much of a show for ten-and-eight days on the trail, eighteen days and nights and a wonderful new bow.

The agreed-upon place to meet the moving camps had come within Ogle's view. And now two old scouts rode out from the encampment with a message for the hunting party.

The warriors already go, they told; more than four hundred horsebacks, they go out three days before this one.

Only women, children, cripples, and old people stay in camp, they said, and the women act jumpy with their men away. If the hunters approach at dusk, perhaps something unpleasant happens; the bow-arm and eyes of those aging warriors who wait in camp stay fit.

Ogle understood. He wished neither to frighten the encampment nor find an arrow in his hide. "I shall bring in my hunters when next the sun rises," he answered, "and not before midday."

And so here, on the river of pronghorn pits, on the site of an old hunting camp, the four slept this one more night on the trail, the standing-people keeping watch as always and the stars, as always, blinking uncertainly.

XXVI

NAPEWAŚTEWIN REJOICED at the sight of her son. She avoided any direct talk with him, but in the presence of an old one she listened to his story and more than once she made the marveling gesture.

Afterwards she related the happenings in camp which she imagined of interest to this boy. Certain ones had deserted before the war party ever went out, she told; the akicita dared not interfere in these instances, but their clubs stopped two foolish young warriors who tried to sneak out of camp, two Kiyuksa more interested in horses than in an avenging.

And Gnuśka, another troublesome. Olepi had chosen the youth as one of the message-carriers but someone found him smoking. Everyone knows that none shall smoke until he proves himself manly and so the wapiya had advised the leaders against taking Gnuśka. And when the youth tried sneaking out with the party, the akicita had broken his arrows. Even so, Gnuśka tried again, perhaps hurrying from camp before his father's return; certainly he had disappeared.

Peta listened respectfully, but Gnuśka's behavior never had interested him; he held neither fondness nor thoughts for this one in Cankuna's lodge. Also, at this moment he had thoughts only for his two horses, whom he not yet had visited.

And so he left his mother's tipi, going to the edge of camp where youths looked out for the horse herd.

The instant Peta saw the black one, he knew that his horse had experienced some difficulty. The creature walked tenderly, his head bowing every second step; this nodding, the boy knew, means that one of the front legs suffers an injury.

Soothingly, Peta reached out his hand, but when he saw a dark swelling on the soft neck, yellow matter stringing down, he tied the cord around the creature's nose, not over the head. And now he looked at the forefeet. One hoof showed a split, the crack running down the horn piece. But nothing oozed here.

Puzzled, the boy led the horse among the tenders; he asked whether anyone had observed the lameness and when these injuries occurred. He heard the same answer from each one: they look out for many, many horses, not only Peta's black one.

Peta understood. The warriors gone, these boys had their hands full even with help from women. Who will notice that any one horse limps?

One old peźuta in camp, a man known for his horse-healing power until an enemy arrow crippled his back and put him out of demand, yet carried his horse cures on his hip in the old way. And so to this one Peta led his horse. He owned the fat of the antlered female; he dared offer something to a man who will heal the black.

The old man felt down the foreleg, watching for signs of tenderness and heat. Then, mixing something with water from his mouth, he spit the substance on the horse's leg. Next, he poured the same powder into his palm and, using four breaths, blew from his hand toward the creature's face. And now he spread fat around the lump on the swollen neck.

"Keep off the birds," he commanded bluntly. He glanced at the hoof again. "Take the horse to the stream. Stand him in water up to here." He motioned halfway up the horse's leg. Then he turned and dragged himself back toward his lodge.

"This fat belongs to you." Peta spoke quickly; he wanted the old man to know that he offered something in trade for his curing.

The peźuta appeared not to hear, he kept on, crouching along the ground. And so Peta placed the sack of fat nearby the tipi.

"Grandfather, will my horse heal?"

The old one turned his face. "The laming, a short one. The neck wound will heal. Your horse, yet a child."

"Grandfather, will you say in what manner these injuries occur?"

"The wound, perhaps the bite of another horse. The foot, perhaps a stone cut. I know not." The man crawled back inside his lodge. And Peta led his horse toward the river.

Before dusk Ogle visited Peta and when the hunter saw the black one staked at Napewaśte's lodge he made inquiries. He listened attentively to each thing the boy told, then commended Peta for taking the horse to the peźuta.

After a while Ogle spoke of the mysterious blacktail. A wapiya in the Siyo camp, he said, will treat the head and hide in a ceremonial way. Peta owns hoofs, tail, and the fat, but the unnatural horn shall stay intact for the boy's father and grandfather to view upon their return. And for Wanaǵi's inspection, this wapiya away with the warriors as Peta knows.

The good hunter had gone back to his lodge, and Peta, sitting alone, reflected two things: why not Wanaǵi deciding that which becomes of head and skin from his kill? Wanaǵi, not the people, shall say whether or not Peta acts wisely or foolishly.

And secondly, why will the hunter not smile during his talk with Peta? Will that which the boy answers to this unusual directness annoy Ogle, or will the man's gloom reveal distress over his son—the one who runs after the warriors, Gnuśka who seems to distress everyone.

Cankuna also pondered the hunter's somber face. And, like Peta, she related her husband's depression to Gnuśka's disappearance. But neither parents nor any members of the tiyośpaye shall speak of this son's conduct until after his return. Then only family shall voice criticism and only within the family lodge.

Nor will Cankuna choose to hunt thoughts about her first-born. Soon she bears a fourth child and, desiring to instill nothing but good into the unborn's soul, she shall keep silent, stay lonely.

True, the news of Gnuśka's smoking and those broken arrows had saddened Ogle, but something more serious troubled the hunter. He knew that a knife had made the hoof injury on Peta's young horse and that the festering lump came as the result of a severe blow. Whose knife, whose club? Ogle sat pondering far into the night.

The camp waited uneasily. Women slept in their moccasins and startled at any unfamiliar sound. The berry-gatherers cast furtive glances in all directions even when those old men, good at quieting a frightened people, accompanied their group. Grandmothers warned granddaughters against any outburst of laughter, a mother whose baby whimpered received dark looks, and the grandfathers bludgeoned at once any dog who yapped. Youths who tended the horses at night acted as scouts also, as eyes and ears for the sleeping lodges, and he who usually walked around camp in the dark singing the sounds that mean 'all safe,' yet walked but quietly, without a song.

Ten sleeps now with the warriors away; unrest grew in the lodges. Quarrels which never, never dare take place with a husband present, occurred between sisters, wives of the same man. And all captives became the victims of this rising disquiet. Bottoms pinched, hair pulled, faces spat upon, these miserable women yearned for the return of the warriors as much as their tormentors.

Napewaśte, visiting the Sicaṅġu lodges, had heard squeals of pain coming from certain tipi where Oyatenumpa captives stayed. And she had seen these women running out, their legs trickling blood, their arms smeared with nose-blow. She regretted seeing any woman treated like a camp-dog, yet she knew that captives who refuse to speak the language of their captors go looking for mistreatment. Apparently these women choose to live as misfits and so they deserve that which happens. But if an enemy woman ever comes into her lodge, none of these abuses shall occur; she will show courtesy even to a Psa captive.

Peta found the men's absence a good occasion for making the neckpiece he had pledged Tunkaśila. They had permitted him the feet from his kill and he had pulled off hoofs and claws and used his new knife for cutting and shaping the black toes. And he cleaned the toe bones, something to give young children for their play.

And while Peta worked at shining the toes and making holes for a string, his Śahiela friend came to sit with him,

Moksois offering his help, the two using signs and sounds familiar to each tribe.

But one morning the young Śahiela told Peta about seeing Gnuśka prepare his horse for the war party, Moksois in the group who watched while he slit the creature's nose. The Titonwan youth had boasted that he gave this one an enduring power. But Moksois remembered that soon afterwards the clubmen reprimanded the proud boy for using a pipe even when Gnuśka answered that he smoked for spirit-help in healing a horse.

But why, Peta wondered, will Gnuśka display concern over this act? The slitting of nostrils, something the Titonwan had learned from an enemy, had not proved harmful. Or perhaps Gnuśka made a foolish cut and so he feared for his horse. But what happened to this horse, Moksois had not known.

That night Peta lay on his sleeping robe and listened to the rattle of rain on the tipi. His mother, speaking to Unci, had expressed gladness for this heavy fall of water. None need keep on moccasins this night; what enemy will sneak through this wet mud to reach a camp of slow horses, the fast horses out with the men?

Not all fast horses, Peta told himself. His young horse, staked at the lodge flap, healed quickly and one day shall chase pte in the manner of Ogle's runners. But never will he slit the creature's nostrils. If a horse needs a slit nose for running fast, why not born with one? Or so Ogle had answered him when he had asked about this thing.

Cankuna came slowly from her tipi, this day a bundle in her arms, this day her usual smiling face something more than a smiling face; the bigness under her gown she now carried in her hands.

She invited Peta to view the newborn. "She comes here knowing the language of trees and birds," the mother said softly, "and so I take her among the standing-people, where she shall listen to the leaf and the winged talking. Her spirit-self knows all the trees that ever grow, all the wingeds that ever fly. But her body-self will need to learn which ones live here on the plain."

The boy stood looking at the small face, the skin around the eyes smeared with paint to shield against glare.

He remembered that Ogle sat again in Cankuna's lodge; a lodge with a new daughter needs a father's protection.

But he knew not what one says to a woman who unwraps her child for a boy to admire. But perhaps Cankuna had not noticed his shyness or that which he said or had not said; already she wandered away whispering to her child "ah—ah" as all mothers whisper to their newborns, something the tiny one understands.

Ah—ah, listen. Always something moves. Ah—ah, listen. Listen and relate that which moves to that which you know. Ah—ah, ah—ah.

Where-you-come-from, you know everything. You bring here the wisdom of the grandfathers, all the grandfathers from the beginning. I and your father make you a body but you live before I and your father know each other. You live in the everlasting seed and so you know, you know everything. From the beginning.

Ah—ah. Hold your breath and listen. Listen to this winged and you will remember who sings. Listen to this leaf and you will know who talks.

Ah—ah. Listen. Ah—ah. Relate these earth-sounds, sky-sounds to that which your spirit knows. And so one day, when your young eyes perceive form and color, you will recognize these leaves, this bird, in the manner that your spirit intends.

Ah—ah. Listen and hear your second word. Ah—boo. Sleep.

Ah—boo. Listen, sleep.

Ah—boo, ah—boo. Sleep, sleep.

Ah-boo, ah-boo. Sleep, sleep.

Ahboo. Sleep.

XXVII

FOR TWELVE-AND-THREE days the lodges on the river of pronghorn pits had sat empty of men. But now, suddenly, this war camp stirs and cheers; the warriors return.

Scouts, riding zigzag, had signaled news of a true victory: all in the party return safe. And different scouts, rushing into camp, told that the men paint black; they had killed.

And so, singing, shouting, cheering, laughing, the stay-behinds prepared a welcome.

Young horsebacks dashed out to meet fathers and brothers, but seeing the blackened faces these same young had become suddenly shy.

Old men painted and tied on feather-honors from seasons in the past and went toward the tip-of-the-horns carrying shield or rattle or drum.

Women smoothed their hair and glanced at the soup paunches and smoothed their hair again. Children whooped for the joy of whooping, and dogs yapped for reason that children whooped. Everywhere the sounds of a joyful camp and everywhere, people painting.

Ogle stood next to Hinhan and watched the men file in. He saw the boy who walked front, who carried the war pipe, an honor Gnuśka never shall experience. Surrounding this proud youth, all the men who in this avenging had struck or killed the enemy, each one wearing his black paint like a full-face mask. Hinhan counted sixty.

Reaching the hoop, the warriors sat down at the tip-of-the-horns. Here Olepi, the man who had led this party to victory without losing a warrior, broke the fat that sealed the war pipe. Scouts prepared a flame and Olepi, laying an ember on the bowl, sent out the pipe among the men, only so many smoking but all touching the stem to their lips.

While the pipe passed from mouth to mouth, more warriors came up. And in back, leading the horses of those men who sat smoking, came many brave youths.

Dust from the hoofs of captured horses rose in the

background, and to the rear of that dust, herded the same as the horses, the captive women and children.

Napewaśte waited at the horns to see the party arrive, then made her way back to the lodge. Peta shall stay and see his father, but she shall wait in the lodge, everything Olepi likes in readiness.

On her knees and breaking sticks for the evening fire, the woman saw the movement at the tipi flap, saw the moccasins of the man she calls husband. She wanted to look up into his face, but she made herself remember the behavior proper to a warrior's return; she shall listen for his request that she raise her eyes.

The moccasins came near to where she knelt but the man not yet spoke. She saw the bowl she had intended to fill with warm water shall he desire washing off his paint.

She stood now and, not looking his way, filled that bowl, water for this purpose in a paunch hanging from the lodgepole. She offered the water and he dipped his hands. Putting down the bowl, she bent to pull off his tired moccasins. But as she moved away to get a fresh pair, he pulled her to him; he took her face between his palms and she felt the wetness of the washing-water.

And now she looked upon this man, the victory paint blackening his cheeks. She saw eyes that war made stern, and she knew herself more the captive than any woman he ever dragged from an enemy camp. She heard the wingbeats in her breast and knew his power to bring on her desire. She, his woman, and when he wants her, she shall want him.

Surrendering to his look and the touch of his hands upon her cheeks, she closed her eyes.

She heard him speaking, but she had difficulty perceiving exactly what he said. Then suddenly she understood.

"I bring back a Psa-girl. I desire that you welcome her."

Her eyes flew open; a cry escaped her lips.

His hands dropped from her face, and, walking to the back of the lodge he seated himself; he gestured for the moccasins.

She brought him a new pair, also the choice meat she had prepared for this occasion. But she avoided his eyes and she spoke nothing.

"Four scalps shall flutter on the pole my wife carries in

the victory dance," he told her when she came to refill his bowl. "You say nothing to this news?" He looked at her sharply.

"I know my husband for a brave man," she said. But her voice, like her heart, lay wilting on the ground.

"The enemy sends you many wapiti teeth for decorating your gown. Someone offers me two fine horses for these teeth." He waited a moment. "But I refuse the trade."

The woman stood silent as before. And so, stretching out on his robes, Olepi closed his eyes. Almost at once he slept.

From under the raised edges of her tipi Napewaśte saw the legs of horses and captives, the clubmen herding these hoofs and moccasins through camp, delivering the women to their captors along with the horses. And so Napewaśte waited for the Psa-girl who belonged to Olepi, someone he seemed eager to bring into this lodge, perhaps someone he intended to make wife.

And now, above the noise of trampling and wailing, the mouth who spoke for the center lodge sang out the news:

Forty Psa die and thirty Psa lodges fall.

Fifty Psa women and half this many children now in the Lakotah camp.

Many horses, so many that they not yet count all, not yet unpack all.

And so the people shall rejoice.

Rejoice, Napewaśte told herself; remember that they avenge the dead and that your husband returns. Decide nothing about the Psa-girl until you know her.

Peta approached the lodge; the boy coming shyly to see his father. They had not met at the horns; at the close of the smoking ceremony Olepi had hurried toward his lodge, the man not stopping for talk with anyone.

But Peta, hearing news that leaked out, knew that the warriors made the attack on slippery ground and that his father's acts sounded like something in a winter-telling story. This much he now told his grandmother and within his mother's hearing.

Listening intently, Napewaśte wished that she had behaved differently. Everything had seemed good about the

339

husband's return until he spoke his request that she welcome a woman into her lodge. If this man gives away things, as they say, why not give away his captive? Even so, if he awakens before the captive girl arrives, she will talk nicely to him about the scalps and wapiti teeth.

The woman filled a meat bowl for Peta and, seeing Lekśi approach, another bowl for her uncle. And then one for herself.

Peta talked mostly about the curly-hair Psa horses the clubmen had led through camp for the people's viewing. If one of these creatures belongs to his father, he said, he shall draw a picture of this one.

Lekśi glanced at the boy disapprovingly. Why will Peta talk of drawing horses instead of going out after horses? And why will Napewaśte murmur approval?

The next moment these three who sat in front of Napewaśte's tipi looked up. One of the clubmen who delivered captives to the different lodges, turned in; he walked directly toward Napewaśte, a small girl in his arms.

"This one belongs here." He put down the child and moved away.

Napewaśte stared, astonished, while the little one, like something discovered in the nest, stood unmoving, her big round eyes lifted to the woman's face.

"My little sister?"

Dimly Napewaśte heard the son asking and the uncle answering: Peta's little sister.

The boy moved toward the child slowly in the manner one approaches a child-horse. Gently touching her arm, he guided the little one to his mother, her new mother.

The child made a sound, neither word nor sob nor sigh, yet the woman heard all those things. She made the mothering sound in answer, neither word nor hush nor murmur yet not unlike all three. The little girl smiled.

Olepi opened his eyes. Good; good to sleep, good to awake in one's own lodge.

He saw that someone had let down the sides of the tipi; he turned his face toward Napewaśte's place. He saw that his woman sat, the sleeping child in her lap.

He put his arms beneath his head and so raised his eyes

to watch these two. "I see that you welcome my captive girl." His voice teased but gently.

The woman looked his way, her eyes a mystery to him. He marveled the tenderness in her face; truly, a good-looking woman. Her black hair, always fragrant and neatly brushed; her smile, her nice white teeth, but she will not smile often enough.

Good, good to lie here after blood and killing and look upon woman, one's own woman, a wife. A gesture or a sound, even his eyes, will bring her swiftly to him, but for now he will enjoy the sight of a woman with a child sleeping in her lap.

A father's reprimand lingered over one Mahto lodge and took away from a family's gladness on this day.

"My son humiliates his relatives." Ogle spoke in front of the tiyóśpaye, the big-family gathering in Cankuna's lodge, the hunter's eyes fixed coldly on the youth who sat defiant before his kinsmen.

"He smokes before going on a war party; for this act the warriors reject his presence. Next, he sneaks out like a camp-dog. The men dare not whip him off; if they send him back, he perhaps leads an enemy toward camp.

"The horse whose nose he slits dies on the trail. And so his difficulties begin. Who will ask that he carry their moccasins or touch the wasna sacs? Instead they laugh and say, 'Iho, Gnuśka's navel falls out; he smokes before he ever rides out with a war party. Who will trust him?'"

But among these assembled people a dissenting murmur arose. A father speaks too harshly of his son. A youth twelve, thirteen winters tries his daring; what mischief in this thing? Will not any bold youth try to get away with something?

Gnuśka had sensed empathy; his mood stayed defiant. The next war party they shall see him truly daring; he will attack the enemy camp alongside the men. Let other youths carry moccasins, go for water, make fires, tend horses; Gnuśka's work, lifting scalps.

So his father tells about the horse; who says that cutting the nostrils kills a horse? True, the nose of his horse pours blood when he quirts her to a run, but other horses

341

with slits will not bleed. And who dares say that none but Gnuśka ever rides a horse to dying on the trail. Hoḣ! he sees this thing happen more than twice.

Ogle, hearing the murmurs of his relatives, had become silent. A father shall point out foolish acts and advise against mischief, but chiding or reproach in front of relatives, they say, turns the son against the parent as someone who suppresses natural desires. And so resentment grows, occasionally cramping reason, occasionally driving a son to strike out against his own.

These things Gnuśka's kinsmen remembered, their murmurs intended to help Ogle remember; as family they hold up their side of the bond.

Reason, the people say, guides a youth forward from whatever day he meets reason. Before that day he makes only repairable mischief.

But will not Gnuśka, Ogle asked himself, meet reason before his thirteenth winter? Perhaps these kinsmen, unwisely permissive. Perhaps he shall talk with someone neither blood nor affinal relative but who also fathers a son; perhaps he shall talk with Olepi this same day.

Olepi had understood why they invite him here for food and smoke, why he now sits alone with his hunterfriend. And so, if Ogle will speak of Gnuśka, let the man begin.

Ogle had begun with Gnuśka's naming-day; from that day forward the hunter had watched his son with growing concern. Gnuśka's companions, most of these boys insolent as a Palani youth. And the one who acts like a brother to Gnuśka? Everyone recognizes Sluka as a bully.

Ogle recited exampᵢ of his son's misconduct, the boy's foolish responses to favorable situations. His smoking. . .

Abruptly Ogle stopped himself, the father recalling Gnuśka's talk about the pipe; the youth had said that he smoked as a plea for a suffering horse.

Which horse? One whose nostrils an incompetent hand will slit? Or one whose hoof a knowing hand will slit? Hoof and neck wounds on a young horse? Perhaps the angry act of a youth suffering from loss of face, a youth whose arrows

342

the clubmen break, a boy who hurts something as a way of avenging his own hurt?

If I, Ogle, find my son accountable for these acts, I see reason to kill him—my own son.

Olepi, observing the straight line of the hunter's mouth and the staring look, recognized a silent struggle here but nothing that hinted the violence of this conflict.

And now, Ogle apparently disinclined to say more about the son, Olepi mentioned the four travelers and their hunt.

"Your son has an eye for the arrows and an arm for the bow," Ogle answered, his calm returned.

"But what of his heart?" Olepi spoke dryly. "At present, the drawing-sticks fire him. Shall he become lodge-painter? Or picture-maker for the winter count?"

And so Ogle, in turn, heard a father's heart speaking, a different concern, true, but certainly a concern.

The same, then, with all fathers? Will each man look for a son who takes after him, someone who shall carry on and improve and make great—or more great—the family name, someone who shall provide the father with a way for seeing himself as boy, as youth? Someone who gives the father second-chance?

Never. Many, many winters in the past the Dakotah grandfathers, recognizing this danger, had provided the ceremony that permits a boy to choose a second father, a hunka-father, someone of different blood, someone not personally ambitious for the boy.

But will the present generation of Lakotah hold on to this most wonderful privilege; will they remember this most wonderful ceremony? Or will they, instead, regard hunka only as something between two youths who wish to become as brothers?

Ogle let go these thoughts and returned to his visitor. Olepi, here to help with a hunter's concern and now posing one of his own; Olepi, who moments before speaks of Gnuśka as a boy in his rude winters but with a daring that presages courage and acclaim; Olepi who now speaks about a brush in the hand of his own son, something that portends neither excitement nor anything memorable.

But the hunter knew differently; Peta will neither paint lodges nor will record the seasons.

Ogle looked briefly into the warrior's eyes. "Your son, my friend, will make the stories which those generations who sit ahead shall tell as legends."

Olepi heard but as if he had heard these words before, as if he will listen to these words again.

Napewaśte, listening to the drums that signaled the victory dancing, glanced at the many wapiti teeth yet to fasten on her gown; the demands put upon her from midday until now had delayed this decorating work. And her husband had requested that she use all these teeth.

Soon after Olepi had gone to visit the hunter, an errand boy for the clubmen had brought her the bundle containing these teeth and she had begun arranging a display on the top front of her most prized gown.

But then Peta had come with a request, the boy speaking through Lekśi and asking for the leg-covers that Ogle had presented him upon their return to camp. Napewaśte had quilled two strips for the outside of each leg but she had not yet attached these strips.

Before she had finished this work, a message-bearer from the center lodge came asking for meat; this request meant renewing her cooking fire. And she had used up her woodpile. While the men stayed out, she, like other women, kept only a day's supply at the tipi. But the season had passed when she dared ask Peta to gather sticks, and Unci attended her own lodge now that Tunkaśila had returned. And so she had hurried out after wood.

Olepi returned from his visit with the hunter as his wife laid four, five stones on her fire. He went inside the lodge to paint face and body for the night's ceremony, and the woman while waiting for the stones to heat, returned to her work on Peta's leg-covers. But almost at once Olepi called for certain paint-powders and some fat for mixing with these colors.

Then, before she had slipped those hot stones into the paunches, the new child in the lodge demanded her attention. And when she had cleaned the little one, she saw that Olepi sat awaiting her help in the arrangement of his hair.

Kneeling alongside him, she wrapped two tiny snowskins into the braided strands in front of his ears. But when she imagined her work to his satisfaction, he complained about a looseness to these hair-ties. Swiftly she unbound the braids, but before she began the rewrapping, she went outside the lodge to start the meat-water bubbling.

Olepi let her go but he threw the hurry-sounds after her; even as he made use of his heels to urge his horse, he will make use of a certain tone to keep her stepping.

She returned quickly and soon she saw his pleasure with the way she had wound one long braid down his back and made two short ones on each side of his forehead. And only now she mentioned her concern about appearing at the dance with but half the ornaments on the front of her gown.

He answered abruptly: "My wife sees other things as more important than complying with my request." After a moment he spoke again: "Somewhere I shall come upon a woman who will enjoy carrying my lance at the scalp-dancing."

Napewaśte murmured her intention to complete the gown, then went to see about the meat.

She sat near her cooking fire while she worked the strips on her son's leg-covering, but the boy appeared before she had finished. She saw that he brought his true-dog, drags attached. So will Peta let her know that he comes ready to carry the meat to the center lodge.

Gratefully she accepted his offer.

When finally the men of her lodge—Olepi, Lekśi, Peta—had gone, she dared sit down outside the tipi and work on her gown as before, fifty, sixty teeth yet to tie in place. And while she worked she remembered the little one sleeping in the lodge.

What age this child? Perhaps two, three winters? And will the scalp of this child's father hang on Olepi's lance, one of the four?

Two women who passed her lodge stopped and offered Napewaśte their help. They wanted to see the wife of the Mahto leader on the dance-ground before the fire stacks burn out; until Napewaśte arrives, they told, her friend Cankuna holds on to Olepi's lance.

Gladly the woman heard this news; good that Olepi honored the hunter's wife: Cankuna as a second-mother to Peta and Ogle as a second-father, even if neither family proposes that they make ceremony over this tie.

And now, these considerate, women-friends helping,

Napewaśte dared properly paint and gown herself, and also paint the new little daughter. But she had wished that her husband's hand, not her own, had drawn the red stripe through the middle of her hair. Why will he so often neglect this important token of affection?

The wife of Olepi walked proudly, aware that many eyes admired her gown. Now she understood why the warrior-husband had wanted to see every one of the wapiti teeth upon the breast and wings of her garment.

Cankuna, seeing the woman approach, walked forward to meet Napewaśte and hand over the lance. And the drum, quiet at this moment, permitted everyone to hear the announcements.

Father and uncles, the crier told, give away their names to sons and nephews this night. But certain young men shall take names of their own choosing, while different ones keep a name but tie on a memory, a word or phrase that remembers this great avenging.

Now hear: Iśna throws off his name and takes on that of his father; persons speaking his name henceforth shall say Mahpiya-luta.

A soft murmur arose from the Sicangu. They shall regard Iśna always as Iśna, in the same way that they remember his father as Wahin-numpa, not Mahpiya-luta; certainly relatives and close friends will go on using the old familiar name.

And hear this: Putehin changes his name; he becomes Ogleśa.

But none murmured this change. As Putehin, the warrior never distinguishes himself, but now the blood of a dying Psa—someone he kills—splashes his breast; he dares take a name that tells the story: Ogleśa.

Certain Kiyuksa also discard names. Zuzueca's nephew, running around like a foolish young bull, bolts the Psa horses, knocks down three Psa with his club, rips open a Psa lodge. Now he demands that the people call him Tawitko. And his uncle stands waiting with four gift-horses; Zuzueca presents horses in honor of his nephew Tawitko.

The crier announced as each man had told him to

announce, the singers performing the same honoring song after each announcement, only the name changed.

These new-named warriors had recited their kills before Napewaśte arrived on the dance-ground, but she cared about only one man's recitation. And he, knowing, had awaited her presence.

But now Heĥiloġeca. Let him dance his revenge story.

Hearing this name, the people remembered that the war party avenged the death of the Miwatani lodge, the lodge that Heĥiloġeca had founded. True, the tall, plucked-head warrior had lost his standing among the Titonwan after the disastrous encounter with the enemy—twenty-eight Titonwan dead—and so he had stayed in the background ten, twelve moons, his name never mentioned. Even when he joined these avengers, he had ridden out as someone they scarcely noticed.

But once the fighting began, Heĥiloġeca had put aside bow and lance; only a knife will make his revenge. He recalled those bodies that the Psa had cut into pieces; he remembered that those Titonwan warriors had put trust in his power and that his power had dissipated on that day.

None had known that Heĥiloġeca intended to stake himself during the revenge; none knew that he carried a sash. But suddenly he had jumped from his horse; he had jerked the sash over his shoulder and pushed the dangling stake into the slippery, muddy earth.

He stood in the path of a Psa riding up fast. The enemy's horse slipped; Heĥiloġeca seized the man and pulled him off. Instantly Heĥiloġeca's knife dug into the Psa's breast. The knife struck bone and so Heĥiloġeca dug in again. The man fell limp, but Heĥiloġeca made other defiling cuts before he finally slashed the man's throat and let the warm blood run over his hand. Next, Heĥiloġeca slapped his bloody hand across his own mouth and gave a yell.

Arrows hit around Heĥiloġeca but he took the scalp. And then someone pulled up his stake.

Heĥiloġeca stood like a crazy man and his rescuer needed to strike him with a quirt. But the warrior jumped up behind this Titonwan who came to rescue him. The man who rode Heĥiloġeca out of the enemy's reach, they call Olepi. Olepi pulled up that stake and carried off Heĥiloġeca.

The warrior Heħloġeca had finished his dance and the drums echoed the people's cheer.

Next Olepi. Let the encampment see Olepi dance his exploits and hear the Mahto's name in an honoring song. Olepi's turn to boast, but even the war leader shall have one or more witnesses to his acts.

And so three came in alongside Olepi to give their oath that this man, like something they never had seen before: swift as a horse, strong as a grizzly, quick and cunning as the little black-legged dog. Olepi had used lance, club, knife, bow. And some say that he used all four at once.

Now the people watched Olepi dramatize his experiences, his dance telling that he fights on foot. He seizes a lance that grazes his body. He turns this weapon back on the enemy, the point entering the leg of the escaping Psa. Staking this man to the earth, the Mahto calls three Titonwan to make count on the grounded Psa. Afterwards Olepi uses his teeth to tear the scalp from the breathing enemy. Psa who ride toward the Mahto observe this act and turn in fear. They ride off to the Mahto's jeers.

Next Olepi uses his lance to raise a Psa up and off his horse. The man's bowels empty on the ground, and while he writhes Olepi digs for the guts which coil inside the man. He swings these inwards once, twice over his head.

And all this while the Mahto never once comes into line with enemy arrows. Perhaps Olepi's new shield gives out tremendous power, for the warriors see the shafts turn aside and the iron balls bounce off like seeds of snow.

Then Olepi uses his club, the enemy dropping like something the grizzly cuffs down. Next the Mahto behaves like the branched-horn fighting for a mate. Some of those scalps he lifts he throws to his men. "Psa hair for a Siyo lance, for Sicangu lances," he calls. "And for your little daughter's toy-child."

Nearing the finish of his story, Olepi now danced the rescue of Heħloġeca. Even with this second man on his horse, Olepi stops an enemy who hurries toward the Psa camps to warn women and the old. He throws his knife into the man's horse and the creature goes down. The Psa jumps off and runs. Olepi throws two arrows at the man but not to kill.

"Hiyupo," he shouts to nearby Okandada. "Win your

348

feathers on this one sneaking off. He drags an arrow from the back of each moccasin."

And so Olepi will make braves of the most uncertain and warriors of all who sit close to him. Whoever comes within the hoop of his power 'feels' courage.

All the while Olepi danced, Napewaśte stood in the center of the dancing-place with other women who held up scalp-trimmed poles. And like these other women, she made the trilling and shook the scalp-hair. But among these warrior-wives not one rejoiced more than herself. For here, at this victory dancing, she saw Mniśa and the Kiyuksa leaders stepping up to place a hand on the Mahto's shoulder. Nor will Iśna stand off as usual. Olepi's feats had brought together the Lakotah leaders and so had strengthened the tribe. In the past she had seen Mniśa and Zuzueca as meaning trouble for the Titonwan; now she watched these same ones crowding around Olepi, their eyes admiring.

And she saw Peta's excited eyes. Not again shall she encourage this son along the gentle path of drawing-stick, brush and paint; her tongue henceforth shall praise none but the warrior.

She understood now that the young seek a way of releasing their abounding energy through something more strenuous than the games they play in camp. And so war, the most exciting contest of all; war, an answer to the body's demand. And something more: war shall relieve a youth of many discomforts. War permits him to give in to awkward impulses; war permits him to despise or torture, if ever he senses a wish for these things. And war permits, but never truly sanctions, killing; the choice belongs to each warrior.

Suddenly Napewaśte found herself resolving to stay as Olepi desired her, a wife instantly responsive to her husband's wishes, a woman affectionately obedient. Her face reddened under the smudges she had painted on her skin for this war dancing; she shivered at the memory of his hands on her cheeks, grasping her hair, spreading her thighs.

The war dancing, the recitations, went on and now members of the Pta-lodge dramatized events in which they had acted as principals.

The use of this headman-lodge as supervisors had proved most expedient, the warriors now recognizing the good in this unusual procedure, now agreeing that they give the name blotahunka to any supervising clubmen who go out with a big war party; blotahunka, wise herd-fathers to the party.

Watching this dance group, the people learned that at the start thirty daring Psa had pursued a decoy of Titonwan horsebacks into a trap outside the camp, all thirty Psa killed. Next, the blotahunka had called for the pipe and Olepi, carrying stem and bowl, had led the advance into the Psa camp.

The enemy lodges had offered little resistance. Young Lakotah braves had routed the old and sluggish, laughing at whoever hobbled or walked leaning-on-sticks. These cripples proved an easy catch and so the Lakotah youths grew arrogant. But Olepi, sitting horseback and watchful, had decided that the young in his war party shall witness the true risk in war; they shall learn that which occasionally happens to captives. And so, the blotahunka permitting, the Mahto put two old Psa men and three young ones to a slow death.

The witnesses had demanded the praising songs for whoever unfeelingly bore the severing of hands and feet, and only the seasoned Lakotah warriors dared throw taunts.

"Attend these acts," Olepi ordered his Titonwan; "you know not if this same thing will happen to you."

A Sahiela directed the course of the knife on that young Psa whom they skinned, the sensitive pieces of this man cut away—lips, ears, nose, fingers, toes; also his eyelids. The skinning began with his breast.

The Lakotah and Sahiela leaders cheered the dying man's apparent indifference to the knife, but certain Titonwan youths had retched at that which they observed. A Sicangu brave shamed everyone when he shrieked and ran crazily behind a Psa lodge, the youth overwhelmed by a second look at the suffering captive, who managed a hideous grin with what skin they left around his mouth. And an Okandada youth dropped to the ground at the sight of that which happened when they used firebrands on another Psa. The akicita had quieted these disturbed young men, but their glazed eyes told that neither one belonged on the warpath.

Yet a different Okandada had asked for a bite of the skinned man's heart, so bravely this Psa had died.

350

One of the old Psa had whined and the second one had lost his senses during the torture, and so the akicita quickly clubbed down these two.

The blotahunka next sent five old women—not important enough for arrows or club—out of camp. Let this group, they said, find different villages of their people and carry back the word; let these five old women advise their relatives never to offend the Lakotah.

The Pta-lodge had recited, and now all the men who wore warrior-honors and rode in this war party shall come into the dance circle, these warriors taking turns, dancing any detail not yet revealed.

And so the people learned about the Psa women and children whom the victors hunted in the nearby ravines. Here they found mothers, small children hiding back of these women, and here they discovered girls, pretty girls for use at the gambling stake.

Occasionally an arrow had sung out from the gullies, but only one shaft had touched anyone and that shaft, not much more than a plaything. But had the blunted tip struck Wanapin's eye instead of his hip, this warrior will have a different story to tell. And so some Kiyuksa had decided to torment whoever threw this arrow.

But the boy they had dragged from the brush had stood unflinching before his captors. He heard their insults with scorn in his eyes nor had he cringed when the points of three lances dented the flesh at his groin.

Suddenly the Kiyuksa had heard a whistle, an order to stop. This boy shall not die; instead, take this one and raise him in the Titonwan camps. He shall make a warrior. And so someone had pushed the boy roughly into the herd of women and children whom the Lakotah had permitted to live.

The people, now seeing this story enacted, had begun to cheer, and so the clubmen brought front this boy who henceforth belongs to the tribe. But he shall stay in the lodge with Wanapin, they told, the warrior whose hip the boy's blunted arrow had struck.

Peta looked closely at the boy, perhaps his same age. He saw that the Psa stood unmoving when the clubmen ordered that he dance. Perhaps the captive misunderstands the phrase? But certainly he knows the meaning of the whip-bearer's quirt. Then, seeing the boy's eyes glance up at the scalps, Peta's heart went out to this lonely Psa.

What if he, Peta, stood in this boy's moccasins, enemy warriors all around, menacing looks on each face? What if someone holding a quirt demanded that he, Peta, dance the scalps of his relatives? Will he, Peta, display this sort of courage?

Peta gladdened on seeing Wanapin come into the circle and lead off the boy. Wanapin, never tolerant toward his enemies, the people said, but certainly never unfair.

And now Wanapin told a group standing nearby to remember the avenging as something they had fulfilled; whoever goes on harassing this boy, he said sternly, shows an unnatural disposition.

And so the dancing began again, more events to enact.

During their search for women hiding in the lodges, the Lakotah and Sahiela had taken whatever things appealed to eye or touch. Olepi, disinterested in any loot for himself, had watched with amused eyes as the brave young men rushed in and out these tipi, their arms loaded with bundles. Then, seeing the looters bring out a small child, Olepi had asked for the girl.

Jumping down from his horse, the Mahto had taken the child back inside the lodge, where he hunted for signs that her father held standing as warrior. Or perhaps as leader? Prowling through the tipi, he found the wapiti teeth, a fine collection and ready to put on a woman's gown. He had turned the sac of teeth and the child over to the akicita; keep a careful eye on the little girl, he had said, and on the captive women who look out for her while they travel.

Most of the two, three hundred horses the party had herded back to the camps now belonged to Sahiela. Offering to round up horses while the Lakotah invaded the camp, the Sahiela had agreed to distribute their catch as the blotahunka recommended. And certainly these paint-red warriors had acted with discretion; not a single quarrel had broken out between tribes. Never before, perhaps never again, will so great a party of warriors travel with more good will.

The tall tipi-shape stacks of wood that lighted the dance-ground had burned down halfway and once again certain wives and mothers came to the middle and stood in line, each one holding tall her scalp-pole. And so the people, now fully aware in what manner this tribe had avenged, cheered loudly and called for more wood on the fires. Light up the ground and let everyone dance, they shouted; let everyone dance until the night thins in the east.

Soon the dance-ground became a frenzied round of jumps and starts, leaps and yells and mimic thrusts. The drums shook the dancers and the dancers shook the earth. And in their midst, that line of women, up on toes, down on heels, up on toes, down on heels, dancing in place but dancing, dancing.

Napewaśte looked up proudly at the scalps fluttering on her stick. And then she noticed a certain one—woman's hair; she became strangely excited. Perhaps this enemy woman once found joy in a man's embrace; perhaps a husband's hand softly brushed this hair now hanging on a stick.

The singers, doubling the rhythm, put a 'tail' on their song, and so Napewaśte ceased her trilling, stopped her dancing. And now, in the quiet between songs, she heard the wails of the Psa captives, their despair rising from the smoke holes of those lodges where they chose to sit, none wanting to see this dance. But will they cry for their brave dead, she wondered, or for their lonely selves?

The singers came on loud again, the dancers howling, stomping, and blowing as before, the noise drowning out the captives' wails. But Napewaśte, silent, looked toward other persons in this line, many of these women wearing the short hair of a wife-bereaved, the grief scars on their arms. Will the avenging truly ease these hearts? Theirs, the wails that once rose from the same smoke holes; theirs, the lonely cry. Will the Psa captives cry more lonesomeness than the Lakotah women once cry; will Napewaśte permit a grieving Psa-woman to drag down through empathy a Lakotah woman's heart?

But she shall not relate the new daughter in her lodge to these other captives; the little one, sitting now at Unci's side somewhere among the onlookers, knows nothing of these scalps even if the woman-hair on Napewaśte's pole belongs to the girl's mother.

And so the wife of Ołepi began dancing again, shaking the pole to see the hair flutter, choosing to remember only that her husband returns safely and that a daughter now stays in her lodge.

XXVIII

THE SUN had climbed halfway before the camp awakened next day; most persons had stayed to greet the dawn, then gone to their lodges for sleep. Nor had the crier awakened anyone; neither hunger nor cold nor enemy stalked these Titonwan moccasins. They will start traveling in a day or two, moving lazily from the pronghorn-pit river toward the sacred hills. The summer had grown truly old and the leaves had piled up, but the mild, warm weather lingered without hint of change; the moon prophesied clear days and cool, dry nights.

On this same day the Sahiela lodges moved off, these warriors and their families eager to join their own who camped somewhere along the thick-woods river. And the Lakotah, gathering on a nearby ridge, waved robes and sang as these friends who-wear-red-paint, their Sahiela ally, walked proudly onto the plain. Peta watched the procession as far out as his eyes dared go; one who went away—his friend Moksois. And the Sahiela boy carried with him, tied at his waist, the black tail from Peta's strangely antlered kill.

Two more days and then the deciders ordered the Titonwan to strike their lodges. And so the crier walked his final round of the encampment, tipi poles dropping in his tracks, the people at the horns packed and ready to go before the ones at the rear saw him coming.

The summer moons had ripened the heart of the tribe and the band traveled reluctant to separate. Each night they danced the scalps and sang songs and gave gifts to one another, every warrior making a presentation of something. But Olepi had not given away any of the six Psa horses that the blotahunka had allotted him after the avenging; he had awaited a special occasion.

And now, on this third day of traveling—the people camped on ground where the wapiti browse and mate—the crier stepped into the circle of evening fires to speak of Olepi's son.

The boy, he sang, had sent the second arrow to fly from his man's bow into the heart of a mystery, an antlered, black-tailed mystery. The boy had carried the fat of that mystery to a crippled pežuta and had taken the sinew to an old and feeble woman. He had awarded the meat to whatever four-legged had come looking for meat at the edges of a Titonwan camp.

The boy had made a neckpiece for his grandfather from the antlered one's feet, and the tail he had given to a Sahiela youth. A wapiya had made arrowheads from the strange horns, and, as an old Siyo healer had advised, the boy had hung the hide in a tree.

Eyanpaha went on, speaking for Olepi. He told of the good hunters who had instructed the boy along the trail and of the great hunter who had made the bow that killed the mystery-creature. And so, in Peta's name, a horse for Ogle, a horse for Hinhan.

And a horse to the dependable old man who had kept a fire in the center lodge while the war party stayed out. And a horse to the crooked-back pežuta who had healed the wounds on captured horses. And in Huste's name, these two gift-horses.

Now let a song-maker begin circling the dance-ground and into his honoring song, Olepi's name and Huste's name. And then, in a new little song, Peta's name.

When the boy heard the songs, heard the people cheering him the same as his father and Huste, he wanted to step back into the shadows, his nature truly shy. Certainly he not yet performs any great acts; the honoring song comes too soon. But Olepi's hand had reached out touching his shoulder. And so, recognizing his father's wish, he stood where all shall notice him until the voices took up the praising of a different name.

And Olepi, aware that the boy's spirit rises even as the juice will rise in a young tree, now saw reason to make a place at his side for this one they call Peta, for this one he calls my-son.

The Titonwan circled the edge of the black hills, the bands moving slowly toward the grassy valleys along the warm back of these sacred slopes, the changing-season moon favoring her summer side. Even so, the painted leaves fell into the streams and the wind blew dust in the travelers' faces.

But some persons spoke saying that the wind blew something more than dust; they had caught the scent of pte. At once many more persons claimed that they had heard the rumbling feet. But until scouts come in with a report, the moving line of people shall keep moving.

Then after two, three days, the hunters heard the call to make meat. Peta had listened for his father to hint that the boy take his new bow and go among the bawling young ones after the men had made the big kills; instead, Olepi had discouraged this thing.

"Wait," he advised; "when next you go among the pte, go as a hunter after the blunt-horns. Ride your own runner and make your hunt a memorable one."

The man's words had brought gladness to the boy's heart; for once, son and father saw with the same eyes.

Standing on the back of a pack horse, Peta had watched the clubmen separate the hunters into groups for the surround. Remembering that he soon shall have a horse ready to hunt, he observed most closely these men who now confronted the herd. True, he had sensed surprise on seeing Gnuśka dash out with one group, the youth astride a horse the Mahto leader recently had presented Ogle. But he had not let Gnuśka's appearance distract him; he had kept his eyes on the shaggy creatures who, bellowing their resentment and confusion, ran a narrowing hoop as the hunters tightened the circle.

Suddenly the air hummed with feathered shafts, the panting meat sliding to a fall or dropping sideways. And now he saw the hunters and their foaming mounts searching among these fat young spike-horns, each man recognizing his arrows, identifying his kill.

Peta jumped down, leading out the pack horse, ready to assist whoever looked for assistance in skinning meat. But then he saw those persons who crowded around Ogle and, hurrying in this same direction, the healer who attended the hunts in event of injuries.

Coming close, Peta saw the son of Ogle on the ground. But since none wailed, he understood that Gnuśka lay hurt, not killed. Soon he learned that this youth, riding alongside a wounded pte, had ignored the shaking head, whistling breath, and switching tail—something every true hunter respects. A quick turn and the sharp horns had lifted horse and rider, tossing these two into the swirling herd. Then, managing to roll out of one danger, Gnuśka had put himself in the path of a horseback. The hunter had whirled his mount but not before the runner's hoofs had stamped on Gnuśka's arm. Trying to get up, the youth had slumped back, his eyes strangely big and black. He had puffed his breath and his arm had dropped against his side similar to a broken wing.

Huhupiye, a healer who knew ways with broken bones, had approached singing, his song demanding spirit help for himself and for the wounded, each in need of enduring power. Now silent, the pežuta looked a long while at Gnuśka's eyes, head, arm. But he neither touched nor spoke to the youth.

"A hard knock bruises the head," he announced suddenly, "but only the arm cracks. And this crack will heal."

Again he sang—this song for treating breaks—but now he made the painful tugs, pulling until the bone slipped into place. He wrapped the arm with stiff hide, binding the piece firmly with thongs. Let this youth come to him frequently, he said; he will rub the arm above the break and so keep loose the muscles.

Huhupiye had brought out neither drum nor rattles; these things have a place but not here. The bone wants to stay in line, he told, and for his assistance Ogle shall give a horse.

A horse? Ogle gives two horses, the hunter told himself, one to the healer and one to the earth. For the horse

Gnuśka had ridden lay on the ground, entrails streaming. Grimly the father recalled that Gnuśka brings death to three horses and near-death to himself; when will this unruly son learn the difference between brave man and fool?

The herd had provided generously for the people and the bands lingered at the hunting camp. The women flaked meat thin as a finger's edge for a quick drying, and the men smoked and reviewed the chase. They talked also of past hunts, one man reciting his experience with a strangely formed creature, one the people knew only as a 'narrow' pte. But mostly the group recalled amusing things that had occurred, such as a hunter flung onto the back of pte for a rough ride, the man yelling but never really hurt.

And while their parents talked of hunts and raids, the young listened and looked for ways to imitate these grown-ups.

Most of the young boys had shown a strong interest in the new akicita-lodges formed on the trail to the Psa avenging. And so they hung around these clubmen whenever the camps rested and they strove for a riding place close behind these same persons when the camps moved.

And now, here at the hunting camp, a group of Okandada boys came looking for Peta; they wanted secret talk with the son of Olepi.

Scrambling down into a gully, they found a place that hid all seven. And now Peta waited for someone to tell what they desired of him.

After many glances and gestures, one youth started the talk: "Each boy here owns a good bow and shafts, but what will he show for this thing? Grass-birds? Chipmungk?" He looked at Peta. "You kill an antlered one with your bow."

Peta said nothing, and so the speaker, glancing toward his companions, spoke more firmly: "Something that the son of Olepi kills, each boy here wants to kill, either a blacktail or wapiti."

The group made the little agreeing-sounds but none looked at Peta.

"My uncle joins the Cante Tinza lodge," the boy-spokesman said now. "He gives me pieces of fine-hair, enough for wrapping two sticks. I fasten a piece of horn on the tip of each stick and so these sticks resemble the short lances of the Cante Tinza."

Next the boy told that he had learned a strong-heart song. So why not these seven give a feast and afterwards go out together in the manner of boy-braves? But they will hunt wapiti or blacktail, not the man-enemy.

All had listened without interruptions, but now one boy grew excited. "I am one who will cut off the black tail. I shall tell my act at a dance."

The speaker looked darkly in the boy's direction. "Wait until I say that I finish speaking before you talk." The youth now turned to Peta; will the son of Olepi lead this party of boy-braves?

"Take this." He held out a stick. "Regard this stick as a lance. Accept this lance and lead the party."

Peta gazed into the boy's eyes, but he had not reached for the symbol.

The boy withdrew his hand. "Woman," he muttered, embarrassed and angry. "Stay here if you fear something. But the party goes."

"I am not afraid," Peta said slowly, "but what power in taking along a song that belongs to other persons? Why borrow?"

The boy had not understood. Will Peta say that he knows not the song or that he will not sing?

The son of Olepi says neither one of these things, nor will he talk about something he not yet understands himself. He knew only that which the wapiya once told him: the power in a song reflects the power in the one who sings the song.

Suddenly Peta asked in what manner seven foot-going boys shall pack the meat they kill.

"Who says foot-going? I say horseback." The Okanda-da youth watched Peta closely.

But Peta looked into different faces: "Will your fathers permit you a fast horse?"

One boy answered saying that he intended to take a fast horse and find out afterwards whether or not his father approved.

The speaker for the group sensed that Peta had not lost interest entirely. "Perhaps," he said casually, "the song-power will not work, but when the members of Cante Tinza want big power they chew tastes-bitter root. My uncle says so."

Six, seven boys scheme this party, the same youth said now, but if some boy who attends the feast asks to go along, they shall welcome him; so the warriors act.

Peta remembered Ogle's words: one man on the trail of the branched-horn, two at the most.

Nor will Peta approve that they invite anyone who expresses a desire to join the party. A youth who precedes him three, four winters will resent a boy Peta's age as leader, and if any brothers come along, they perhaps will side against him and spoil the hunt. And yet, will not chance enter into everything? What daring if a boy never takes chances? "Offer me the lance again," Peta demanded.

Napewaśte learned quickly of the expedition. Lekśi let her know that someone needed her help at a feast that will take place nearby her lodge. And that someone wanted two pairs of moccasins, new or mended, to carry out with him.

The fire-hearted old uncle had shown enthusiasm for the whole thing; and now he sat ready to brush off Napewaśte's concern when she learns that her son will lead out six boys, none of these youths more than twelve winters.

"Unpoṅgapi kilo," Lekśi said, grinning. "All Okandada but for their leader. A Mahto leads. Act proud," he told Napewaśte; "your son walks front."

The woman, desiring that Peta carry new moccasins, not something she mends, began work at once. Between now and midmorning of the next day, she shall make ready these new moccasins and food for more than thirty, counting the boys and their families.

This same evening Olepi looked up from his pipe: "My wife bends over her awl in the near-dark and my son sits watching my smoke. Perhaps someone here wishes to say something."

Peta spoke; he invited his father to a little feast and some boy-dancing.

Lekśi made all manner of signs; he wanted Peta to tell who leads the party. But the boy, moving toward the tipi flap, stepped outside.

"Your son leads out a party of boy-braves." Napewaśte remembered to make her voice proud.

To her surprise, Olepi not so much as grunted approval; she wondered whether the man saw something amiss in this scheme.

Presently the lodge became too dark for work and the woman, not wanting to disturb anyone with a bright fire, decided on something that will put light on her awl and sinew. Soaking a wad of pte-hair in fat, she attached the little ball to the tip of a stick, then tucked the stick halfway down the back of her gown, the burning fat above her head throwing light on her work.

Olepi glanced up critically and so she gave her reason for using this night-light. "Your son wants extra moccasins and so I am making two new pairs. I intend to quill a message on the sides and front and so either I stay until I flatten enough quills or I only paint on the message."

The abruptness of Olepi's reply startled her. "If my wife neglects those things she knows to keep in readiness, I shall look for another pair of hands to help out in this lodge."

Keeping silent, determined not to lose her cheerfulness, Napewaśte refused to consider either the husband's mood or his meaning. Nothing but good shall affect these moccasins.

But the old uncle, not yet asleep, saw why the people say that a sister and not the mother make moccasins for the son in a lodge.

When Peta returned, his father advised that the boy visit the wapiya; perhaps Wanaǵi will want to see Peta before he leads out the boy-braves.

Certainly Peta will act as his father advises, but when will he visit the sacred-lodge? Before the sun climbs overhead next day, he needs gather bitter root, test his bow, pack his moccasins, paint his face for the dancing, and tie up his horse's tail. True, the most important thing, he already decides: he rides his own funny-looking little horse when he goes out on this pretend raid. Or perhaps he knows all along that he never intends to take either a horse from his father's herd or his own black runner.

Wanaǵi had made points from the antlers of Peta's mystery-kill, and an arrow-maker had fastened these heads onto four new shafts. Gratefully Peta accepted the seer's gift, grateful, also, that Wanaǧi will let him go quickly, will not hold him for ceremony or song.

At midday four boy-braves, their parents, and relatives came bringing their empty bowls to Napewaśte's lodge. Two boys had dropped out of the party; they lacked mounts. But the ones who sat here now, their chins black and feathers from the rain-bird bunched in their hair, had led up fast horses.

Tunkaśila set his meat bowl next to his grandson's bowl. "The big branched-horn wears his winter robe this moon. Look out," he advised. The next instant the man barked a loud, harsh song and grunt, mating call of the wapiti: "a-a-a-ai-i-i-i-i-i-ii-nough iuh, iuh." "When you hear this sound," he said, "remember that this four-legged collects his women. And that he fears nothing."

Peta knew this call and he remembered the tall and far-reaching branches at this season. He shall watch out for himself and for the other boy-braves when they come near a branched-horn.

The Kiyuksa leader, passing the lodge at the same moment that Tunkaśila imitated the wapiti, stopped and said something that pulled the laughter out of the crowd who had gathered to see the boys dance. But many persons suspected that the man's sudden appearance foretold some sort of scheming. Zuzueca certainly knew everything about the mimic war party, even about the two boys who desert.

Then, before the dancing began, Zuzueca spoke, his tone mocking if not his words. "Perhaps the son of my good Mahto friend permits two more youths of like braveness in his war party. I speak of one from Mniśa's camp and one from mine."

Peta's heart fell. The Kiyuksa referred to Mniśa's son and his own, youths in their fourteenth winter, neither one acceptable as a companion on this mock raid.

But he recognized another thing: his own feelings about this request will not count; Zuzueca mentions Peta but his eyes find Olepi.

Even so, Peta gave answer, his voice similar to his father's voice, his narrow shoulders eased into a slouch not

362

unlike Olepi's posture. "My uncle, if your son and his friend come with my party, they come without rank. My braves already choose their leader and their lance-bearers."

The boy's choice of phrases, his attitude, and his behavior, all properly respectful, but something had brought a dangerous thinning to the Kiyuksa's lips.

"A sharp boy," he answered coolly. "He recognizes the two of whom I speak."

And now a glance, nothing more than a flicker of Zuzueca's eyes, sent a certain Kiyuksa youth hurrying off on some errand.

Once more the leader spoke to Peta. "My nephew, your boy-braves dance now?" Zuzueca's voice dropped as when one makes a question of his phrases, but his eyes commanded that the dancing begin.

One boy-brave took a hand-drum and began to sing, his tones weak, unmeaningful; the other four lifted their feet as warriors dance.

The boy's attempt at putting the 'tail' on his song made for a little smiling behind palms but Zuzueca had seemed not amused. He picked up a different hand-drum and began a little honoring song. Certainly the Kiyuksa came determined to run this whole affair. For, upon finishing his song, he tossed seven small sticks among the people. "Who catches these sticks," he told the assemblage, "catches himself a horse in Zuzueca's herd. And in the name of seven boy-braves."

The murmur that had started out as surprise became one long cheer.

Olepi's impassive face concealed a different heart. Will Zuzueca consider him a fool, a man without the wit to recognize a scheme? The Mahto sees the errand boy return, the sons of whom Zuzueca speak at the boy's side, those two already in paint, and feathers waving in their hair. Certainly Olepi understands Zuzueca's gift of horses; the seven good Mahto who catch those sticks—and all their relatives—shall remember this day not as one on which Peta leads out a party of boy-braves but as one on which the Kiyuksa leader gives seven good horses in the Mahto camp.

Give? Or will Zuzueca regard his present as an advance on a trade, a favor in view of that day when he needs four, five more lodges—warrior families—in his following, something that will secure him a camping place at the horns?

But the Mahto's angry heart gave in to pride as he listened to the women who, seeing Peta jump horseback, began a trilling. What nature of man will not respond when the people acclaim his son?

Napewaste watched silently, anxiously. She dared not show her heart on seeing her son lead out the boy-braves—custom will not permit the blood-mother this display—but gladly she heard Cankuna calling to Peta that he take-care, that he return safely.

The loping horses moved out on the plain, the people throwing their good thoughts after these youths. And many persons remembered back to those moons when these same young horsebacks played-warrior, their toy lances tipped with thorns. Child-weapons, true, but not without danger; look around camp and see those boys with one blind eye. Even so, this going out to mimic a war party, going out for more than a day and with a weapon made for killing, something different from boys chasing each other among the lodges, pretending an attack. Whatever happens to Peta and his party, the group will get a taste of the real thing. But for what different reason shall a party of boy-braves go out?

At dawn the boys came out of the gully in which they had camped overnight and began looking for tracks. Some dissension had occurred over the horses, four in the party unwilling to leave their mounts hidden in the draw while they walked the river bottom. Peta had settled things with a firm order that they lead the horses, not ride. He also demanded that the boys pile stones as on the day before and so mark their return path.

Before reaching the grass valley where they felt certain of finding something to stalk, Zuzueca's son glimpsed two pta, two lone grandfathers, perhaps outcasts from the herd.

The youth called to his near companion. "A good day. I see the enemy." He pointed to his discovery and jumped horseback.

Peta had observed the slow-moving forms long before the young Kiyuksa spoke and already had made certain that the wind favored the boy-braves. But his group had come to hunt branched-horns, not pta. And so he showed his surprise at seeing each boy jump horseback.

"I and you hunt wapiti," he said sternly.

But the son of Zuzueca, scorning Peta, faced the other boys. "Your leader discovers neither branched-horn nor marks of the branched-horn. Perhaps he needs snow before he finds any tracks." The youth laughed shortly. "Will you sneak back to camp under dark like scouts who never find anything? I say, chase pta."

The cry had excited the two with lances. "Only two pta and seven boy-braves. Takpe, kill, kill."

The most young in the group joined the clamor. "Iho! They walk this way. The herd-fathers ask that this party kill and take their meat to the people."

The group took up the cry. "Hoye," they shouted. "Pta come bringing meat. They come, they come." One boy pulled out his bow.

Peta made the silencing gesture. "Who leads this party?" He glared up at Zuzueca's son. "You lead?"

The youth, his face sullen, answered nothing.

"You lead?" Peta asked each of the different ones in turn; each one met him with silence.

"Hear me. I call this chase after pta a foolish thing. None here sits on a pte-runner."

"My father uses this horse for the hunt," Mniśa's son retorted angrily. "I kill meat before now." He looked at Peta and made a sign of contempt. "You stay. I am a man. I ride out after the enemy. Huka!" The boy kicked hard on the sides of his mount. Instantly Zuzueca's son hurried out after him.

Peta sensed a rising uneasiness in the other boy-braves, none certain that he wanted to ride close to anything so alarmingly big.

But now the lance-carrier cried out. "Iho! They come and so I make meat." He quirted his horse, the creature jumping forward, beginning a fast run.

At once the second lance-bearer took off, dashing out after his friend.

Two boys stayed back with Peta: the youth who had acted as speaker for the group when they met with the son of Olepi, and that most young brave, a boy of nine winters.

But soon one of these boys lost patience. Ignoring Peta, he turned to the young one. "Chew the root you bring here. This protects you." He reached into the little power-bundle at his waist. He put a piece of root in his mouth, spit on his hands, then at the neck of his horse.

"Chew and spit as I tell you," he said sharply to the young boy, whose eyes stayed big and frightened.

Peta dared not watch these two; he kept his gaze on those great dark forms who stood quietly. And on the young horsebacks who raced noisily in that direction.

Now suddenly, the two black shapes jumped, whirling and taking off at a run. The boys who had gone up close lashed their horses and began the chase.

Instantly Peta mounted; he started out after the boys; as leader he had to protect his following, even those ones who will not listen.

The two pta had kept together, but when Zuzueca's son sent an arrow, the one pta broke away from his companion.

The two boys out in front kept after the one who swerved, but the lance-bearers followed the straight-running creature.

And now something took hold of Peta; he responded to the rancid smell, to the surprisingly fast little horse between his legs, to the shouting boy-braves, to the wonderful hunter's bow at his back, to the wonderful bone-tipped arrows in his hand.

If a pta shall fall, why not from his arrow? But which pta? He chose instantly. The two leaders' sons chase the swerving one, and so he, also, rides that direction. His arrows shall take the meat away from Mniśa's son, Zuzueca's son, and then his eyes and voice will scorn these two as they scorn him as leader.

But at the same instant that his knee commanded the horse to turn out toward his choice, Peta heard a cry. Not the joy-bursting yell of a hunter whose shaft finds the mark but that rare cry of fright and pain.

The sound came from the direction where the lance-bearers rode.

Peta slapped his horse's head roughly to start the creature on the change in course and he used his knee to help force this swift turn.

And now he saw, under the rising dust, a horse without

366

a rider and one boy-brave scrambling to his feet. The true-danger, then, went with the second lance-bearer.

Next thing, he glimpsed a shaggy head lowered at the rear of a different horse, one whose rider hung on desperately. Arrows stuck in the bare backside of the pta, the shafts low and scarcely holding. The points, too shallow for injury, pricked the creature into a charging fury.

Instantly Peta saw reason to come close, most close, or his arrows will stick like those pricking ones. He needs come within six arm's length, five, perhaps four. Ogle kills at two paces, but Peta makes this attack, not Ogle. And Peta lacks the courage to come three arm's length.

But he shall remember that Wanaǵi tips these shafts with bone from a great mystery; why not throw fear to the ground and ride in boldly? In a sacred manner, ride in. . . .

He saw the massive head rising up; he saw the horns reaching into the rear of the horse, heard the horse scream.

Suddenly lance-bearer and horse became flying things, falling things, thudding things. And now he saw the dim-sighted pta moving onto the rolling bundle, the creature perhaps unknowing that he gores a boy-brave.

Peta pushed, stretched his bow until pain ripped his breast. He let go and the arrow leapt toward the moving mark. But the horns had scooped up the bundle, something flesh and bone and blood clinging to the cracked and brittle black curves.

Nor will this bundle shake loose. Rushing past, Peta saw the boy's body adhering to these horns even as he saw the groaning pta go down, the creature on his knees, mouth and nose foaming red.

Peta whirled around, his next arrow flying out. But already the big shape had toppled sideways, a grunt, a kick, then something dead. And back of the ribs where tough hide shielded the vitals, the feathers of Peta's arrow.

Now a whoop. But not Peta's whoop. Racing in, arms outstretched to touch the fallen creature, came the son of Zuzueca and the son of Mniśa; they will count honors on this killed one, this pta who symbolizes an enemy-killed.

The lone lance-bearer walked here also, but he neither whooped nor touched anything. And the boys who originally had stayed with Peta came up now but as if dragged to this place.

The son of Olepi, his wet and panting horse alongside him, gently maneuvered the body off the horns; even so, pieces from the young brave's crotch stuck to the dead pta. The gored boy lay dying in front of Peta's eyes and he knew of nothing that will stop this thing.

The boy-brave bled for a long while, and the group, standing back, wondered whether this bleeding means that their companion yet lives. But at last Peta wrapped the body in his own robe. He asked for help getting this bundle across his horse. He had to ask twice.

"He goes out looking for this trouble." The voice of the Kiyuksa youth, loud and sudden, startled the young boys and they turned to look at him wonderingly.

"I mean he gets in the way of the charging pta instead of dodging aside."

None answered; they looked, instead, at the bundle on Peta's horse. And then they looked away in frightened silence. They will not feel like boy-braves.

Something far-off howled. Will the smell of death travel so quickly to the crest of the hill? Or perhaps the howl comes not from the throat of a four-legged but from an enemy who mimics the sound. Peta will not know.

The boys displayed their unrest, each one in his own way.

"Take whatever pieces you want of the kill." Peta glanced down at the pta, nothing here that he will want to claim.

At once the son of Mniśa slit the neck; he reached in, slicing the root of the tongue.

And while this youth used his knife in front, the son of Kiyuksa cut off the tail. A fine stone-slinger, he told the others. And then he began seizing on different members: hoofs and, next, hairs from the foretop and mane. But not even the Kiyuksa youth wanted the horns.

Peta withdrew his arrow and wiped off the stain. Silently, looking at none of the boys, he placed the shaft in his arrow-holder. His blood flowed hot against the Kiyuksa who had wanted to war on pta, but his anger against himself for permitting this chase disturbed his heart most of all. Somewhere he had lost control of things, but why, he not yet understood. The bone point from his mystery-kill proved a strong power—one arrow had killed the charging pta—

but the same point had not protected the young brave caught on the horn. And so true-power, not in point, not in the shaft, but in holding onto the control of something.

And now he shall prepare himself to face his father and the people of his band. And the relatives of an Okandada boy who dies.

Someone noticed that the sun climbed down. "Why stay?"

And each one, glad to hear his own wish voiced, jumped horseback. Peta gestured that the boys start back; he will catch up if they follow the path they had marked with the stone-piles.

The group quirted their horses and the son of Olepi stood a moment looking after these youths. And then he began his hunt over the saddened ground for the killed one's lance. Perhaps the boy's mother will want this stick; but more important: if any blood shows on this wood, the people shall know that the young Okandada dies bravely, that he strikes the 'enemy.' Something to make a father proud even in his sorrowing.

Finally Peta found the lance, a red stain on the point; the boy-brave died with honor.

And now the boy-leader lifted up a handful of his loose black hair and, taking his knife, hacked at the strands until they hung irregularly at his ear. Next, he sharpened two thin little sticks; he thrust this wood into the firm flesh above his elbow. And after performing these acts in the manner of a warrior, he leaned his face against his horse's nose and wept.

He took a long while joining his party so the group's concern had turned into impatience; they wanted to reach camp before dark. Who wants to sleep on the trail with a dead body on the back of one of the horses?

But not until this thought found a voice will anyone want to remember that Peta walks alone, leading the horse, bringing back the 'bundle' so recently a boy-brave. And now the boy who had shown himself shy and frightened turned his mount and, following the stone markers, rode back along the trail until he saw Peta.

"Ride up with me," he said to the foot-going one, to this one who wore grief-sticks in his arm, a strange cut to his hair, and a pondering look in his eyes.

369

The young people came running out to greet the returning boy-braves, their eyes sparkling, their lips forming the sounds 'ku-hu-hu' which tell that hunters bring in wapiti.

But they drew back at the sight of the boy-leader, the white clay of sorrow clinging to his chopped-off hair. Then seeing the boy-shape bundle across his horse, they ran back to the lodges, their eyes round in alarm.

The only reproach Peta had heard—his own. Olepi listened and sent a fine pipe to the grieving Okandada father, and Napewaśte took gifts—quilled moccasins and a robe—to the grieving mother. But neither parents, grandparents, nor uncles gave any sign that Peta need live with something to regret.

Peta returned the four arrows to the seer; Wanaǧi will understand without his saying anything.

But Wanaǧi had detained the boy-leader. Inviting Peta inside the sacred-lodge, he offered soup and saw his young visitor empty the bowl slowly. And then the wapiya made talk, his speech impersonal, his words spoken objectively, a Lakotah way for relieving this boy in his distress.

"Wanaǧi understands why a certain youth speaks not of his kill with a single arrow, an act that many hunters say calls for an honoring feast."

After a little silence Wanaǧi went on: "The wapiya hears the story from the boy-braves. They say that the boy-leader disagrees with his companions. He will not desire chasing pta, but neither will he see his companions regard him as fearful."

Peta sat with closed eyes but his ears stayed open, and so Wanaǧi slipped into a casual form of speech as between a hunka-father and his son.

"You will not prevent the lance-boy his act. Remember that the akicita's club not always stops someone who jumps ahead at the scent of pte. And so why any surprise that boy-braves desire the chase or that a view of these creatures excites each one in your party?"

Peta opened his eyes and glanced at the seer; truly Wanaǧi, like his grandfather, seems to understand everything.

Firmly but gently, the wise man brought the lesson to the boy: "If you reproach yourself for that which occurs,

370

remember that I share in this blame. For I require of you neither the inipi nor any different undertaking before you go out mimicking war."

The son of Olepi made quick answer: "But they say that I shall come to you asking for these things. None says that you shall come looking for me, deciding for me."

Wanaǧi returned a quick reply: "Nor shall you decide for the boy-braves. Once they refuse to follow you as their leader, you perhaps will regret that which happens but you shall not hold yourself responsible.

"So with the shirtwearers who decide for the good of the tribe. They will not sense any shame if the clubmen need to rip the lodge of one who acts against their decisions. Such persons go out looking for trouble."

For a moment Peta's eyes reflected understanding. But now he turned his face. "I bring sorrow into many lodges," he murmured.

"Hear me." Wanaǧi spoke sharply, before the boy retreated from reason. "Hear me. Not many days pass but that some sadness visits the people. I remember a day when a certain man returns to camp bringing news that makes tears in twenty-and-eight lodges."

"And I remember," Peta said, "that the warriors avenge those dead."

"And what of you, my son, when you kill the pta who destroys the boy-brave? In this act, your revenge."

Peta grew quiet.

And so the sacred-man and the boy sat together a long while, keeping this silence, hunting thoughts, finally speaking those thoughts aloud. For Wanaǧi desired to understand whatever will puzzle this discerning youth. He had recognized the son of Olepi as a most unusual boy and he looked for this one to travel the spiral path, fulfilling himself on each level, climbing from ledge to next high ledge. He saw himself as the hunka-father to this one, whether or not these two ever make ceremony of this profound tie. Nor will he, Wanaǧi, ever consent to becoming hunka to any different one.

The death of the boy-brave held the bands together another seven, eight days, the old seer in the Okandada

371

camp proposing a ceremony that shall express an appreciation of children yet in a mother's care. Feasts and gifting shall honor these children who shall live remembering their parents' demonstration of affection. And this same old seer had composed a lament for the mother of the boy-brave.

And so they heard—whoever passed nearby a certain Okandada lodge—one mother who sang weeping:

"Micinkśi, micinkśi, teḣiya iḣipeniyapi;
Micinkśi, micinkśi, niyate ceya onile;
Tiowahe kin, iyuha ceyapi,
Micinkśi, micinkśi, tiyata onceyapi ye."

"My son, my son, they let you die;
My son, my son, your father seeks you weeping;
In this lodge, they weep,
My son, my son, they weep for you."

Two days after the boy-braves returned, Zuzueca had signaled his following to pack their tipi; the band moves out. The long, long summer, he said, had come to a finish overnight; the moon of freezing rivers and glistening morning air now hangs over the black hills. And the Kiyuksa look forward to a long walk back to the redstone river.

But not all his band had said so; a quarreling began over stay-or-go. Then after three, four days they had gone, the band yet whole but they had left a harshness above the ground where their tipi had stood. And some Kiyuksa had introduced words intended to grow suspicion about Peta as a boy-leader, as a boy who let one in his party die and who sent an arrow into a hide already stuck with shafts. If Peta's shaft truly kills the pta, they had whispered, why will the boy not claim any piece of the carcass?

And so Olepi saw need to find some unusual way to honor a son too old for a children's-day ceremony, too young for warrior-heraldry. And when finally he had decided on something, he invited the camps to a feast.

The people came, and, after they had emptied their bowls, they watched Peta climb the long lodgepole set up against the side of his mother's lodge. He carried with him red horsehairs, a tail that Olepi had sliced off the dead body of a Psa horse. The Mahto leader had wanted this tail flying

372

from the lift-pole of his lodge, a new and pleasing decoration for the top of a tipi.

Climbing the pole, Peta had wondered whether the red horsetail shall become the symbol for a leader's lodge. And he wondered something about himself: will he ever again climb up a tipi? As a boy he climbed the sticks that fasten the front of his mother's lodge and now he climbs the lift-pole to tie this tail on top. But not likely will he make any more climbs; this work for boys, not men.

Now near the top, he heard the drum, a fast strong beat. He smiled; he felt suddenly as if he had won a contest. He attached the tail and, clinging to the top for another moment, he looked out on the circles of lodges. He saw the painted tipi of different leaders, some lodges with scalps hanging from the tall pole. But only his father flies a horsetail and lives in a lodge of unpainted skins. He remembered his thoughts on the day that his mother raised this new lodge; he understood many more things about his father now. He knew that the Mahto leader will not need pictures on the lodgeskins to keep his greatness before the people; his father needs only walk among the Titonwan and they remember.

And now he heard his name in song, the honor coming as a surprise. Strangely aroused, he discovered some unfamiliar thoughts; looking at the faces raised to where he had climbed, he wondered whether one day he shall lead a camp of Lakotah, perhaps become a principal man in the tribe.

He glimpsed his mother in the crowd; he smiled again. He will not know that Napewaśte at this moment wondered only whether Peta will manage to get down from the top of her lodge without breaking his neck.

XXIX

THE MAHTO people settled down for a season of long nights and cold days, their lodges strung along a nicely wooded creek in the shelter of the black hills. The three bands—Mahto, Śiyo, Okandada—camped not more than a day's travel from one another; once again the people looked forward to occasional visits with relatives and many good days of play on snow and ice.

Guest-lodges also rose in these different camps. Five families of the Kuya Wicaśa had stayed back when their leader, Iśna, had pointed his moccasins toward the east. Nor had all of Mniśa's people followed their principal man back to the muddy-water. Unlike Zuzueca, the Sicangu leader had not held any rancor for those persons who had spoken their preference for a winter in the Tiyataonwan camp. True, Mniśa looked forward to visits with the white trader on the big river, a waśicun he had nicknamed Capa. Mniśa never hesitated to say that he regarded whitemen as wise as 'beavers' but also the most clever and tricky of peoples. He truly liked these whites, these awesome yet laughable and not at all dangerous persons.

Most certainly Mniśa had not agreed with Olepi when he heard the Mahto express his views on whitemen as a smelly breed of intruders who came always on water, never with women, and usually bearing news that none wanted to hear.

"They say that these whitemen will not frighten anyone," Olepi had said, "yet you tell me that when the Lakotah beg for something to smoke, the waśicun throws a pack to the warriors in the way a woman tosses a bone to her dog. What happens if ever the Lakotah demand something? Let any tribe who begs from these strangers rename their bands 'Ones-who-beg-from-their-enemy.' Even now the waśicun perhaps ridicules the Lakotah through his word 'sioux.' Who will say what this strange sound means."

Olepi had proposed more than once a scheme for handling these unwanted visitors. If the Lakotah will stop trading with the whitemen, these undesirables will go back to whatever place they come from. If none will offer pipe or meat, certainly they will float back down the river and not return.

"But if one overlooks the newcomer's lack of courtesy," Mniśa had answered, "and sees only the wonderful things he makes—useful and clever things—what harm in his presence? True, the whiteman acts contrary to the Lakotah in every way, but will this thing mean that they intend to overcome?"

Many persons had agreed with Mniśa, but many more persons remembered the Mahto at the sungazing and the powers Olepi had demonstrated afterwards, on the hunt and during the Psa revenge. So perhaps Olepi owned the power to recognize that the whiteman will make changes in the Lakotah way of life but not good changes.

And so this winter most Titonwan sat in snug lodges along one of the tree-lined streams that brought down water from the sacred hills. Nor will these Titonwan remember that men of a different nature exist, men different in every way from the Lakotah. Why remember anything gloomy? The glad moons of men-in-camp and winter-telling tales had begun.

Napewaśte enjoyed this winter more than any in her memory. Her lodge sheltered a contented husband, respected leader. And certainly the most handsome man in the tribe, whatever the uneasiness that accompanied this thought.

As with any handsome man, women acted obvious in front of Olepi. His wife knew that some women came to her lodge looking for hairs combed from his head, hairs to tuck between their breasts, to help win his affection. Such acts contributed to a man's arrogance, and so Napewaśte understood when occasionally he boasted of his power over women. Olepi's only real boasts, she knew, concerned his war acts; these other things she laughed off as vanity.

But he will display one real vanity—his hair. He openly enjoyed the fact that the young men mimicked him and let their hair grow. Some youths, tying feathers in their scalps, glued horsehairs to their own hair, lengthening the strands in imitation of Olepi's long hair. But only Olepi wore fourteen feathers in a circle on his head and only Olepi grew hair naturally to a length below his shoulders.

Olepi's unusual good temper during these moons of cold and drifting snow soon reflected in Napewaśte's disposition; the woman felt cheerful, acted cheerful. She rejoiced also in the little girl new to her lodge. She contemplated the seasons ahead when she shall decorate gowns for this girl and see her wearing the most white, most soft, most wonderfully quilled things in the band. But for the present, she knew to direct her skill with the awl toward playthings, toy-babies for the daughter, and not to neglect moccasins and leg-covers and robes for the husband. If she becomes too absorbed in the child, perhaps Olepi will want to give the little captive to a different family and so regain his wife's full attention. This, she will not let happen.

But only too soon, Napewaśte became aware of the lengthening days. And then the water-birds had reappeared and the red grass had begun to push up.

And now the pause, the idle moon, between the cold and the warm, the bright idle moon when horses shed hair and get fat.

And so, even as the seasons change, then pause before more change, into Napewaśte's lodge came change: Olepi brought in a new wife. A new young wife. A pretty, pretty new young wife.

The Mahto had considered his act a long while. He had persuaded himself that Napewaśte wanted someone to relieve her of those piles of work she faced whenever he made meat, whenever he feasted the camps. Not that he ever demanded that his wife prepare hides for the white trader as some husbands demand but that too frequently he saw her bending under wood and over piles of hides and using the night-light to see her awl, to finish a day's work.

He had considered bringing a strong woman to this lodge, someone helpful but someone with many relatives, perhaps on Okandada woman to bind the people of the Okandada band and his, the Mahto camp perhaps gaining three, four families.

But the one Olepi had brought to Napewaśte's lodge looked not at all like a strong, hard-working Okandada woman. Instead he had chosen for second wife a most pretty young person, someone not yet fourteen winters. They called her Hinziwin, and her father they called Sinte, brave man of the Sicangu.

The young woman's family—persons in Mniśa's camp who had chosen to winter near the black hills—raised a lodge in the Mahto camp. Olepi, properly, had responded to a friendly invitation to smoke and eat in this lodge. But the Mahto had puzzled why these people keep sending him invitations to visit their lodge. He also had wondered why this strong warrior from Mniśa's band stays so long in the Mahto camp. Perhaps, he answered himself, the man stays on to look out for his daughter; perhaps some eligible Mahto warrior pursues this young woman, this remarkably good-looking young woman they call Hinziwin.

For who will not notice her eyes, a sparkling darkness with tiny flecks of yellow? Yet those barely discernible specks of color will not account for calling her Hinziwin. Her name referred, instead, to the streak that had appeared in her hair, a strand of yellow on one side, near the center. White or yellow streaks of hair appeared occasionally among those upriver bands, the news-carriers had told, but this girl-woman, Hinziwin, the only one with such marking among the Lakotah.

And who will not notice her skin color, something that makes her look as if she walks always in the sun? She will not stand among the tall but her body, a flat belly and hips like a man, made her appear tall. She walked on small feet and her dainty hands seemed more like fluttering-wings, moving quickly, folding softly.

Olepi had noticed her gracefulness as she filled his bowl or brought him water in her father's lodge, and he had sat aware of her expressive face, happy as a child one moment, wistful or even sullen the next. He had regarded her as different from any other woman in the tribe and he had found himself wanting to pat the small round bottom hiding beneath her gown. And then he had begun watching to see if any warriors hovered outside Sinte's lodge, anyone who waited for a word with this daughter. And if not, he will understand that her family considers him a desirable husband for Hinziwin. And for this reason Sinte stays on among the Mahto.

When he had made certain that the young woman met with none of the warriors, neither outside her mother's lodge nor on the woodpath, Olepi talked with Hinziwin's father, the two of an age and speaking man to man.

Sinte appeared pleased. If the Mahto desires his pretty daughter, someone for whom they recently perform a becoming-woman ceremony, Hinziwin will come to the Mahto. And she will come pure; she speaks not with any man.

But will the strong leader of the Mahto permit this young woman two, three more moons in her mother's lodge, where she shall receive instruction in the use of awl and quills? During these moons, if the Mahto wishes, her father will send Hinziwin on little visits to Napewaste's lodge and so accustom his daughter to the ways of the Mahto's true-wife and to the leader's likes and dislikes.

Hinziwin had heard of Olepi's proposal with an indifference that brought a mild reproof from an uncle in the family lodge. She had listened respectfully enough, but then she had gone out of the lodge to play with girl-friends. If they looked for her to sit quietly and reflect on her obligations in the lodge of a Titonwan leader, they needed to look again.

Whatever Sinte imagined, he dared not name the girl's grandmother as remiss in points of instruction and so he chided his wife for this negligence. But the woman knew that Sinte had granted this daughter, his only child, unusual attention and privileges and so he had spoiled her for good manners. Now, suddenly, he wanted her modest and restrained and all-woman. He wanted to see her go to a different lodge and bring joy to a husband and to that husband's family.

"I will not go to this Mahto-man if I dislike his woman." Hinziwin made quick answer when her mother spoke Sinte's wish that his daughter treat the Mahto's proposal with proper shyness and grace.

The young woman never had given much thought to becoming a wife, a mother; not even the children's games of playing at husband-and-wife or pretend-parents had held her interest. But when the boys gathered to whip tops into a dance on the ice, Hinziwin boldly joined their group, her toy usually the one outbumping, outwhirling all the other tops in this 'sticking-together' game. And eagerly she had played at 'tossing-one-up,' four giggling girls bouncing a boy roughly in a robe. But her most fun, running horseback on the yellow plain or climbing trees alongside the winter lodges, breaking tender branches for her horse.

The truly respected girls and young women assisted their mothers at cooking, wood-gathering, berry-picking, and putting the tipi in order, but Hinziwin never had cared to help in any of these ways. Nor had her grandmother's effort to instruct her in scraping hides and quilling met with any reward. And her mother's wish that, after the 'pte-sing,' the becoming-woman ceremony, Hinziwin earnestly apply herself to the awl and the making of moccasins had come to nothing.

But in one way Hinziwin behaved most properly; she never spoke to the long line of young men who stood outside the lodge waiting for a visit with her. Custom demands that a young woman stay single until she prepares herself in every way for becoming wife; apparently Hinziwin knew her lacks. Or so her mother had decided.

"I bring you help in your work." So Olepi had made his announcement to Napewaste. Most men will know to speak their intention and made certain of a new wife's welcome, but, raised without the gentling touch of women, Olepi lacked many refinements.

Nor will the man recognize in what painful manner his blunt speech struck the heart of his true-wife. Not until he saw her eyes dulling, her face dropping to hide the ache, had he sensed her shock. And then this glimpse of her had prodded him into a strange desire to deepen her wound.

Napewaste not glad? Why? He brings someone young and pretty to grace this lodge. Truly, not many old wives ever have the help of someone as pretty as Hinziwin.

"Why will you not smile?" he demanded to know. "Am I husband to an ungrateful woman?" Olepi had walked out the lodge but not before he had heard Napewaśte's little wail.

Hinziwin made one visit to the Mahto's lodge. Napewaśte had set out food, then hurried from the place. But Hinziwin had followed after her. All day she had hovered near Napewaśte and before dark she had asked to go back to her parents' lodge.

Six days afterwards Sinte, acting firmly, brought his daughter to the Mahto leader. The young woman's uncle came along, the man leading a fine horse, one he staked outside the lodge. The family had decided to use the mild weather for traveling to the Siyo camp for a visit with different kinsmen. Hinziwin stays, if the Mahto again will honor her as a member of the lodge.

From the start Hinziwin showed lonesomeness for her family. She wept openly for the lodge of her parents; Napewaśte's efforts to soothe her seemed ineffective.

Once, returning to the tipi with a load of wood, a load that Hinziwin had brought only halfway, Napewaśte heard a whimpering. Her jealousy toward the young woman had lived shortly; now she saw and heard with sympathizing heart the tears and whimpers. And so she entered the lodge prepared with comforting words. Her sudden surprise at finding Olepi seated next to the tearful one held her face on these two for a moment. Then, her own eyes misting, she fled from the tipi, from the sight of the man who stroked the young woman's legs.

Until now, Olepi had accustomed Hinziwin to his touch on her gown only. He had patted her gently back and front and had put his arms around her. Once he had come up from behind and folded his arms over her breast. She had stood quiet on that occasion, seemingly indifferent to his embrace. But after these ten, eleven days during which he had respected the protection worn around the woman's thighs, he had decided to reach up under her gown and caressingly let her know that he soon shall untie the cord and make her wife. But as he sat down alongside her, Napewaśte had entered.

Running from the lodge, Napewaśte had experienced a second flare of jealousy. She had imagined Hinziwin as remaining distant to Olepi for many moons; now she knew differently. And so she shall learn to live with a young and truly pretty woman in the lodge, one to whom Olepi shall give the same affection as to herself. So, the Lakotah way.

Peta, uncertain as to the term he shall use in referring to Hinziwin, waited for someone to inform him. He tried also to understand why his father brought the young woman here.

"The woman comes as my wife and a help to your mother." Or so the father had told the son, but Peta saw only that his mother now walked burdened with another one to feed, clean up after, make moccasins for, teach to quill. She even needed to tell Hinziwin when the water in the drinking sac tasted dead and when the woodpile diminished. But telling Hinziwin these things seemed to mean nothing; his mother, the same as before, goes to the stream, goes after wood, Hinziwin always off somewhere playing games with whoever comes around. Or, more likely, riding the fine horse that her uncle brings to Napewaśte's lodge.

But now Lekśi told that kinsman-rule decides that whomever Olepi calls 'wife' Olepi's son shall call 'mother.' Let Peta recognize Hinziwin as 'śanke' and treat with her the same as with his true mother: courteous avoidance.

Even so, Peta felt most uneasy in Hinziwin's presence, Hinziwin who yet plays with boys, who often acts like one.

Napewaśte had not mentioned Hinziwin's disregard of assignments or her unwomanly behavior, but the true-wife had demonstrated her resentment when next Olepi visited her sleeping robes.

The man came to her on the night after she had seen him stroking the young woman's legs, and, not yet accustomed to Hinziwin as someone with whom Olepi soon shall lie, Napewaśte had turned away.

"None of that," he said roughly, and rolled her onto her back. She lay quiet, her body submissive to his intent. But after a moment he had left her robes; a woman taken against her will, he knew, makes the pte barren. Let a leader, a protector-of-the-people, always remember; let none starve through his acts. The grandfathers had said so.

And so Olepi had returned to his own robes, a man with two women, neither one iśnati, to sleep alone on a night when he desired woman. And now he will wonder whether in his tribe, whether in any tribe anywhere, lives a woman who truly understands the ways of man. If so, he will go out and find her and make her his wife yet this night.

The next day Olepi went out on foot to hunt the wapiti; he took Hinziwin with him.

Hinziwin tried to keep in the tracks Olepi made in the slush, but the effort to take these big steps exhausted her.

The two had walked all day, the sun now a red ball low on the cheek of the sky. The woman carried meat from Olepi's kill, the pieces tied in hide and fastened on her back. The big cuts he had bundled and hung to a tree, something he will pick up on their return.

And now, choosing a sheltered place, the Mahto ordered that Hinziwin cook; while he makes a fire, she shall set up stakes for cooking rib-meat.

The man soon had a good fire, but the three poles that the woman had bound together wobbled and fell as soon as she tried to hang the meat.

Olepi grunted: "Napewaśte shall teach you many things, I see."

"Your woman kneels at the cooking fires many winters. I am young."

The woman had murmured her answer, but her words and the toss of her head irked the man.

"Not only at the cooking fires will you learn from her," he said grimly. He sensed a rising irritation; here and now he shall make certain things clear.

"Enough of your crying in the lodge," he said sharply. "If I see more tears, I will hold your nose and mouth until you gasp; so they teach an infant not to cry."

"Napewaśte cries when she sits alone," the woman answered sullenly. But had she glanced at Olepi, never will she have risked her next words. "And I know why she cries. She feels jealous of me." Again Hinziwin gave a toss to her head.

Olepi held himself. After this night Hinziwin never will dare another impertinence. He spoke quietly, too quietly: "I hunt a warm shelter for the night. Stay here." Taking a firebrand, he left her.

Hinziwin sat watching him go, then huddled up to the

cooking fire. She stared at the uncooked meat which Olepi had pushed onto a stick. But she only stared.

The man found a cave, then made certain that some drowsing creature with cubs had not chosen to occupy this place. He used the firebrand to explore and to start a small fire at the back of the opening. Then he returned for the woman.

He saw the meat as before and ashes where he had made fire, but he said only that Hinziwin shall wrap up the rib-meat and follow him to a different place.

When finally they settled in the cave, Olepi watched the woman spread the robe on which she perhaps imagined to sleep alone.

And now the man saw this woman as one he truly desired as wife, a desirable mystery he intended to make his own. If ever he had considered her only as something to mix the blood of two great warriors, certainly he looked upon her now only as a reflection of the earth-mother during the growing season when the winds smell and taste most sweet and the sun pledges to warm and ripen all living things.

Hinziwin moved near the fire and the man saw her eyes, eyes gently slanted in defiance of the round shape usual to most women. She breathed softly on the embers and he saw the yellow strand of hair, something that made him certain, fearfully certain, that he never will find anything usual about this girl-woman. He knew then that he needed to take her before a touch of fear grabbed hold and lost him his power in man's one act of supremacy over woman.

She sat on the robe again, her face toward the fire, her eyes reflecting the flame. But she turned at his move. Then, seeing his face, she reached for the edge of the robe, something to pull over her head, to sign that he leave her alone.

But his hand, covering hers, stopped this gesture. A tear rolled down her cheek, a tear that Olepi not yet saw.

He blew on the embers, making more flame, encouraging smoke to rise, a purifying-smoke for bathing a woman who shall become wife.

Looking at her now, he saw the tear. And smiled. Pulling the woman to her feet, he lifted her gown.

The smoke curled up and he stood gazing upon the beauty he had uncovered. And then he reached out his hand to touch where he alone dared touch. Hinziwin, his woman.

Book Two

THE YOUTH
1811/12 to 1812/13

I

HEHAKA SPREAD open the winter-count hide, a wapati hide big enough to record one hundred winters, to record a generation of events. He looked at the place near the center of the hide picturing the winter of his birth. He had not recognized himself as a 'rememberer' until age twenty-and-nine, but from that season forward he had kept count for the Mahto band. He had talked with many old persons concerning those events before his birth and during his youth seasons, his record in keeping with the truly important happenings. And now his eyes followed this circular spiral of small drawings, a season-by-season account.

He came to the picture he had drawn six winters past, something to portray a new use to which the people had put the hunka-pipe, the affinity-pipe. The new ceremony had called for horse hairs instead of moose or pte hairs on the pipestem, and the old Okandada seer had waved that stem over the heads of little children in a demonstration of family affection. That same season the Mahto had discovered pahamni ridge and the Titonwan had moved as a tribe against the Psatoka, but the rememberers in each band had recorded the ceremonial singing over children as the truly memorable event. But Hehaka's drawing showed also a horse's tail waving from atop the Mahto leader's lodge, a related ceremony that had honored Peta, son of Olepi.

The man's eyes moved on, lingering a moment on the picture that acted to recall four winters past. Here again all four keepers of the winter count had made a similar drawing—Oglesa's disappearance.

Ogleśa had gone out with a band of Mnikooźu for a friendly visit among the Palani when a party of fifty whitemen, returning a Miwatani tribesman to his people upriver, attempted to pass by the maize-growers' villages. The Palani, at war with the Miwatani, had demanded that the party turn over their firesticks and the enemy tribesman. When the group refused, the new young Palani leader and his warriors fired on the travelers from the river's edge, killing three, four.

During the fight, someone had killed Ogleśa and wounded Pta Sapa, leader of the Mnikooźu. Some persons told that a trickster among the Palani had used magic against the Titonwan, but different ones, within view of the place Ogleśa fell, reported that a whiteman's firestick had sent iron into the Okandada warrior; the waśicun, they said, kill Ogleśa.

The Titonwan along with the Mnikooźu had schemed revenge: an attack on the next white party moving up or down the river.

But the Okandada's grieving relatives had complained; perhaps the next whiteman will not come for two, three seasons, perhaps never. They looked for a different way to vindicate this killing.

And now Heĥaka's thoughts centered on something that had happened this past winter: the deadwood lodge on the little island in the muddy river had caught fire, the place blowing up with a big noise, the trader disappearing in the smoke. The trader Capa blows up with the lodge, the Okandada warriors had told; sparks from this whiteman's pipe fall into the shooting-powder.

But Heĥaka had imagined a connection between the recent threats to whitemen traveling the big river and the trader's demise. And whatever his reluctance to depict any event that recalled the waśicun, he now decided that nothing more important had occurred this past winter than the removal of the whiteman and his trading-place; certainly most of the Mahto had said so.

Picking up his sharply pointed stick, Heĥaka carefully pressed into the record-hide a grouping of lines: a stack of dead wood, a covered head, a symbol to recall the trader's name, and scratches meaning fire. And now the event recorded, he laid aside the big hide and reached for his counting-pole.

The people will ask whomever they call 'rememberer' to keep count also of suns and moons. And so each evening Heñaka remembered to nick one side of his long, long pole, his way of counting the days that make up the moons. And on the opposite side of this same pole he made cuts that showed when a certain moon died, his way of counting the moons that make up a winter, some winters showing ten-and-two moons, most winters with ten-and-three cuts, occasionally a winter with ten-and-one moons.

And now Heñaka cut the notch telling that the snow-melting moon dies, that another winter season passes; the red grass appears, a new moon, a new season. And so kiwani owapi, a reawakening.

Olepi had heard about the burned lodge on the muddy-water but he had acted as if he had not heard, as if he had not known that during the previous two winters perhaps six hundred Lakotah and Canoni had camped on this river where whitemen so often paddled. And that among those Lakotah campers, a group of thwarted Okandada who claimed that they not yet had avenged the shooting of Ogleśa.

And certainly Olepi had heard that those same Okandada had intercepted a party of whitemen near the big bend but not before an iron ball had found the heart of another Lakotah, this one Wagmiza, the Sicaṅgu leader. And that the Sicaṅgu, then, had begun to take turns guarding the bend.

After a while a big party of whitemen had appeared, the most waśicun they ever had counted, and so those persons on watch had signaled to some Titonwan who hunted on the nearby plain. But the whitemen had seemed reluctant to await the hunters, to await the arrival of more Titonwan before anyone began to fight. And the Sicaṅgu, not knowing what to make of this unwillingness, had permitted these whites to pass. Who finds anything amusing, exciting in a fight where one side counts more contestants than the opposite side?

Olepi knew about those scouts who followed out after

this white party, who reported back that the whitemen, on reaching the Palani villages, had gained the protection of the maize-growers. And he knew about those Titonwan warriors who now schemed to ride north, to harass the Palani and the whites they sheltered.

And knowing all these things, Olepi looked for signs that his son intended to sneak out with this war party. Peta, at sixteen, had yet to join a party of warriors.

But the father saw nothing in Peta's acts that hinted any eagerness to accompany the men. Instead, he had discovered him bent over a robe, paintbrush in hand.

Looking down on the painter, Olepi's eyes narrowed: "Will you never wish to perform such feats as you paint on someone's robe, my son?"

"I paint my own robe, my father," Peta answered quietly. "I own a horse who wins at racing. I decorate my robe to show his feats."

The man viewed the horse-shape while the youth filled with paint the firmly marked lines. Here, four legs that appeared to run; a horse with mane and tail waving. And here, a different drawing, the horse's head turned to look front, eyes fiery.

"My son rides this horse; why will he not put himself in the picture?"

"My father, I never see myself as you see me."

Olepi spoke dryly: "You paint horses as the whiteman sees horses. Why concern yourself with the way I see you?"

The son's eyes lifted to the man's face. "Four, five winters in the past I briefly disregard my own and mimic a different man's hand. But that which I draw here comes suddenly out of my own understanding. And not until a view of myself flashes before me shall I attempt to picture my own likeness." Then before his gaze lengthened into rudeness, Peta turned back to his work.

But Olepi stood on. "A hook symbolizes hoof of the horse and two lines, the legs of man. These signs each man uses when he pictures his acts. But his acts, not his drawings, bring on the honors." Abruptly, the Mahto turned away.

Peta sat on, pondering his father's talk. True, all Lakotah hunt thoughts by way of pictures, not words; so will Peta 'see' his thoughts. But not all hands own the power for drawing these pictures, for pressing the essence of a thought into hide. And so custom wisely restricts the man who keeps count of the winters, those warriors who paint their exploits on robe or tipi, the person who cuts a message on mud or bark, to such symbols as any child will understand.

But the son of Olepi, neither a keeper nor a warrior nor a messenger, dares use his drawing-stick to imply that which occurs. Even so, he shall regard each of his drawings as a string that ties his memory to the truth. Certainly he will not await honors for this unusual power, but why will his father scorn his picturing something in a lifelike manner?

His father asks why not draw his own image. Certainly he will not seek the whiteman's way of drawing head and body, but as yet he lacks ways for bringing to light the face and posture of any Titonwan. And perhaps he never shall discover this thing; they say that a likeness on hide captures the soul. Water or a pool of blood reflects but never holds on to the image, they say, never holds captive the spirit looking out through the eyes.

But will his drawings bring suffering to his funny-looking little horse who wins most races in the Mahto camp? Perhaps his father regrets these pictures for this reason. But why will the whiteman make pictures of his horses and himself if any danger sits in this act?

Before the youth finished painting his robe he had reached a decision. His father will prod until he sees his son Peta demonstrate daring or braveness in an encounter with the enemy. But this youth will demonstrate his braveness when he knows himself prepared for meeting the enemy and not before. Let him prod who will; only Peta decides when Peta goes out.

Olepi had turned away from Peta in person only; the man's thoughts about his son stayed with him. And now reflecting upon the youth as a horseback, he quickly scattered those thoughts about Peta's lack of warrior-backbone. Anyone who rides as if he grows out of the horse's back will desire a fine herd, and whoever secures a herd takes from the enemy. And whoever takes from the enemy proves himself a warrior. Certainly Peta soon will go out after horses, the raids a forerunner to the avengings and the taking of scalps.

I teach him many tricks, show him many things about horses, the Mahto told himself, but he discovers on his own that the spirit and the fight and the enduring power of a horse depend upon the rider. What a warrior he will make—if ever he gets going.

None denied that Olepi had given his son good advice—who surpasses the Mahto leader as a horseback?—but the people knew that Peta approached a horse he intended to gentle in a much different manner from his father. Olepi took a young horse into water, made a sudden mount, and stayed on until the creature thrashed out his roughness in the leg-deep stream. Peta's way called for soft words, gentle tugs, and something to eat as a reward; in this manner he had gentled Huśte's gift.

At the start he had used an easy pull on the mane, guiding the child-horse from one grass clump to the next, making the clicking-sound for move, 'ho' for stay. Then, his horse nearly two winters, he had led this one onto swampy ground, where, after much stroking and many gentling sounds, he had thrown himself like a robe across the creature's back, holding to the mane while the horse lunged and slipped and fought for a footing in the mud. After a while the black one had ceased trying to spill his load; at once Peta had jumped off, coming around to pat the head.

"I lean over you," he had said quietly, "and so you discover that I am not too much load for your back. When I put my leg across, you will discover that I am an easy burden."

Going around to the opposite side, the youth had hoisted himself up, again holding to the mane. When the horse's head jerked down, Peta had sounded the signal for calm; when the head came up, the youth had a leg over the back and sat straight.

Next, pressing with his thighs, he had urged the young horse to take a step. Lifting his body slightly up and forward, he kept on with this persuasive movement and the coaxing sounds; and then the horse had taken a careful step on the slippery earth.

At once Peta had stood front, offering tipsila, a root pleasing to man or horse. But then someone had come to interfere.

Gnuśka had ridden up scoffing. "The ones I gentle learn fast. The whip has a power which I find lacking in the quiet voice." He had struck his mount viciously as if the horse's startled jump proved the whip more effective than a coaxing tone. Giving out a yell, he had dashed off.

Peta had not looked away from his work. He had come again to his horse's side; again he had sprung onto the back. And again he had encouraged the black one with thigh and voice. Then slowly, cautiously, he had urged the horse from sticky mire onto dry ground. But here, his footing secure, the horse had begun pitching.

At once Peta had struck the creature a blow, his hand flat against the side of the head. Roughly he had jerked this one around and forced him back onto the soggy ground. Here another try from bog to firm earth; but again Peta had felt the creature's back hunching. A second slap on the head, jerk on the jaw, and back onto the soft mud.

The youth had made two more tries on hard ground before the horse had accepted the rider, had agreed to knee and voice.

Before another winter had passed, Ogle had helped Peta with those maneuvers they teach a pte-runner and the black had displayed that which he already knew about dodging and twisting and jumping.

And then this past summer, the tribal encampment at split-toe creek, Peta, who had shown little interest in the surround since the season of the boy-brave-gored, had gone out with the hunters, his pride in the horse sending him in among the curved-horns with a confident heart.

The hunters had returned mentioning Peta's name in their song. The young horseback had ridden alongside a big pte who ran, tongue hanging from an open mouth; next thing, Peta's arrow had sent this one stumbling, falling. And next, the youth had chased after a herd-father. He had claimed head, tail, and hump from the pte, but he had taken only the shoulder skin from the pta.

Wanaǧi, hearing the story, had understood Peta's true-need for killing the herd-father; the son of Olepi now felt that he had avenged a certain boy-brave.

When Olepi saw three of Peta's arrows in one hide and five in the second kill, pride had fluttered the man's heart. But when he learned that Peta had cut skin from the pta's shoulder, his heart had soared; certainly the youth had chosen this piece for a shield. And so the man had decided that Peta shall choose from among the father's small herd, choose a horse ready to carry a warrior.

Peta had not taken from Olepi's herd; he had not wanted a gift that tended toward hurrying him onto the warpath. But he had known that if he tried to uncover his thoughts about preparedness to his father, the Mahto leader will answer his son the same as anyone: going out on a raid, getting into the fight—these things will show whether or not you make proper preparation. Act, and so discover where you lack experience, where you need more practice.

And so Peta had spoken saying only that he had learned something about his black runner he had not known before the hunt: this one, perhaps, will outrun any horse in the band, in the whole tribe. Soon he will challenge all the young horsebacks in the encampment to a race, the competition certain to tell him more about the horse.

But the summer had aged while Peta worked at getting the black ready for the race. And then the bands had broken for the winter camps, this race never run.

When Peta had not tried sneaking out after the original war party going upriver to harass the earth-lodge people who sheltered whitemen, Olepi had looked for his son to join a second party riding this same direction, a group of young men who schemed to cut off any meat that roamed near the Palani camps. But Peta seemed interested only in his horses, working out the big black each morning, the funny little one each evening. Suddenly the father had sensed defeat; my son, he had muttered to himself, lacks the juice, the backbone, and whatever more makes for a warrior.

But the day after that second Titonwan party started north, Peta and his funny little horse had disappeared. And the one clue, when Cankuna told that she had given some-one a bundle of moccasins. Four, five days passed and then the second party returned, the men coming in at dusk, faces unpainted, hearts grounded; enemy horsebacks had killed one in their group—the son of Ogleśa. As for Peta, none had seen either the youth or his little horse.

"Perhaps your son stays out hunting a certain pte." Olepi, glimpsing the anxiety in Napewaśte's eyes, covered his own apprehension with disdain.

The woman had not answered. Her husband's mood, never predictable, had taken a turn toward surliness; not even Hinziwin's pretty face distracted him. Nor will things change, Napewaśte told herself, until the son returns.

Then, before rumor or gossip took hold, Peta came riding in with a party of Sicanǧu horsecatchers, the youth sitting his little horse, leading a fine yellow. A crowd, gathering quickly, soon knew the story.

Pañaña, remembering the son of Olepi as the boy who trailed his grandfather to the earth-smoke five, six winters in the past, had invited Peta to join his party, five men traveling south toward the shell river in search of horses wearing iron hoofs. And Peta, not unlike a young brave going out, had slipped away with these Sicanǧu.

At the start they had treated Peta as if he had come along as their moccasin-carrier and horse-tender. But they teased gently and enjoyed his apparent curiosity. Each man carried a loop of twisted cord attached to the tip of a long stick and the youth had puzzled in what manner they intended to maneuver these loops if ever they found any horses, iron hoofs or not.

The search had led to the narrow gullies of the sandhills. Here, coming upon a roving herd of six, they had tried out their sticks, but they secured the loop on the neck of only one. They had put ties on this same one, head and tail, then jerked and pulled at the same moment as if to stretch the horse. But while this tugging went on, one man had jumped on the horse's back, staying on until the exhausted creature accepted capture. Once subdued, they had tied this one to the tail of a gentle horse.

When the party came upon a second herd, someone had advised that they drive this bunch of twenty into a gully, tie down the seed-horse, then handle each one, stroking head, sides, back, and underneath, until these gentle pats along with coaxing-talk calmed the herd.

The smell of water already pulled the horses in the direction of a nearby gully, and so Pahaha, after giving quiet consideration to the proposal, had sent Peta to look for a neck in the gully. The youth soon returned with news of his discovery, and so, before the sun reached middle, the horsecatchers had driven the herd into the grassy trap halfway up the little canyon.

During the chase one in the bunch persistently broke away, the seed-horse nipping at her ribs, her ears, as he tried to keep her in line.

The young Mahto, observing this yellow one from the instant he glimpsed the herd, had marveled everything he saw. The dark zigzag stripe along her back resembled the path of a flashing-cloud, and the dark marking on her legs distinguished her as a warrior's horse. But her shining hide hinted at good care; someone had rubbed her sides and brushed her long tail. Here, a neatly groomed visitor in the company of nineteen unbrushed, ungentled strangers. And something more: the yellow appeared eager for capture; running in a wide circle, she came in close to the men, then raced away.

When Peta spoke his intention to catch this yellow horse before they reached the gully, the horsecatchers had not objected; instead Pahaha had handed him a stick with the twisted loop.

But none had stayed to watch and none had cautioned Peta about enemy tribes who occasionally attempt a short cut through this dry midsummer earth that borders on Lakotah hunting grounds. Why ever introduce a thought that will distract, that perhaps disrupts a good endeavor? A youth of Peta's age will know in what manner to act if he hears an enemy approaching.

But when evening began to fade into dusk and Peta had not appeared, the men waiting in the sandy mouth of the gully decided to send out two searchers; perhaps the youth had wandered off the trail.

The next moment they heard a chucking birdcall, a skillful imitation, but this 'bird' came leading two horses. Peta emerged out of the evening mist. The men had remained silent but Peta had known exactly where they crouched.

He saw their quick glances, approving him, appraising

his catch. And he knew that if any one of these horsecatchers ever jumped onto the back of the marvelous yellow creature, that man will want her. "I own these two," he announced boldly.

Now Pahaha spoke: "Let Peta tie the yellow to his wrist while he sleeps; he will know in the morning whether or not the yellow horse belongs to him."

The youth understood; they give him a chance to keep her, but not without a contest. While he sleeps, someone will try cutting the cord to his wrist in the same manner that they take from an enemy. And so, whatever his weariness, he dares not close his eyes this night.

Choosing three rough stones, Peta placed one on the ground under his neck and two along his backbone; perhaps some spirit-helper hiding in stone will prick him to wakefulness if he drowses.

And so Peta, awake and listening, felt the little tremble which told that horsebacks rode in the near distance, horsebacks who hurried under cover of night.

Quickly he aroused the three men who slept nearby, his finger pressing gently behind the ear of each sleeper, these Sicaṅgu instantly alert, two moving up the gully to warn the men who guarded the horses. They walked quietly making the hoh, hoh, hoh-hoh, hoh, hoh sounds. Most of these captives, like the seed-horse, stood tired and thirsty; the horsecatchers dared look for calm among the herd.

The one man staying back with Peta climbed atop a boulder, where he tried to see who passed and whether these horsebacks rode as pursuers or the pursued.

The man saw nothing. The mist that had come with dusk had gathered into a white cloud which hung before his eyes like a tipi lining. But this same cloud quieted the night and so the man heard clearly the slap of ten quirts. He knew that anyone who rides fast in a thick fog travels familiar ground; this party, then, members of a planter-tribe, southern relatives of the Palani and known to scratch-the-ground downriver.

After the riders had passed, the man reported fact and surmise to his companions, the group agreeing to wait a second day and not risk losing horses to this enemy or any different one.

When the men lay down again, Peta saw that someone

had removed the nudging-stones from his place; he dared sleep without fear that the men will cut loose the one he had captured. Truly, they accepted him as a member of their party.

During the travel back to camp the youth puzzled many things about his fine-looking yellow. Whoever gentled this creature had used a hand as patient and firm as his own but with much more knowing about horses.

He had caught her head in the braided loop, then dropped the stick and begun pulling on the cord around her neck. She had not resisted capture; instead, she turned and started toward him. Certainly his pull had not choked off her breath, yet he saw her going down. Jumping off his horse, he had tied her front feet and then loosened the neck-loop. But the yellow one had lain quiet. Suddenly concerned, he had inspected her eyes. He saw a shining alertness, yet she seemed quiet as dead.

Putting a cord on her jaw, he had leaned his face against the yellow nose. "I will return your breath," he whispered and breathed strongly into her nostrils.

The creature's eye lost none of the fire, yet she lay unresisting as before. Then Peta had cut the ties on her legs. At once the yellow rocked to her feet, the youth pushed aside. But she stood patiently and so Peta, marveling, tugged gently on the jaw-cord. Instantly she lay down, eyes alert and ears bent forward but not a movement along her whole wonderful body.

Perhaps she knew many different tricks; Peta had determined to find out. And so he had learned that whatever the manner he sat this one or laid himself across her back, she eased her load into a place of balance; anyone hurt or sleeping will ride safely on this amazing creature.

She knew also to dance herself out of danger when her ribs or haunches became a target for arrows or to swing her back and avoid getting hit in the rear. But not until he raced her across the lonely plain had Peta discovered that he owned a relative of the rushing wind. And so he named this one Tatezi, a name which told her power, her color.

When the party of horsecatchers reached the earth-smoke, they had found their people gone. Pte skulls pointing toward the north ridge disclosed that the Sicangu decided to raise lodges once again in the Titonwan hoop at pahamni.

398

And so the horsecatchers chose to drive the herd into the summer encampment. And Peta had sensed unbounded joy; he shall return to his band in the manner of a warrior who goes out and brings back horses.

The small herd had moved colorfully across the sharp grasses, red horses running alongside black, white and sand-color mingling with those ordinary ones who wore the dark manes and tails. And two spotted or scorched horses whose hides appeared painted or burned. But none with the freckled rump among these twenty-and-one and none with iron hoofs.

Child-horses followed at the side of the five in this bunch, these frolicking young bringing smiles to the faces of the men who now owned the herd. Sungcincala they called these foals; śungwiyela they called the mothers of these foals.

But these horsecatchers will say śuktanka, Peta told himself, whether they refer to one or the whole herd; and certainly the warriors say mitaśunke, nitaśunke whenever they talk of each other's horses. But for now he, Peta, neither a seasoned horsecatcher nor a warrior, will recognize only one word for horse: Tatezi.

The Sicanġu horsecatchers had made a big thing of their entry into the Mahto villages. They drove the herd twice around the camp before coming onto the gaming-ground, where they demonstrated the use of the stick with a twisted-cord loop. And then, like warriors making the kills-talk, they described trapping these twenty. Finally they called out Peta, the proper one to speak about those enemy horsebacks, an enemy heard but never seen.

The youth told his story simply, and afterwards Olepi presented moccasins to the five Sicanġu and flung two gift-sticks into the gathering.

Before the Sicanġu horsecatchers made any division of horses, they gave away a fine one in Olepi's name, then offered Peta his choice from the herd. But Peta, his eyes appreciative, made the denying motion; he owned in Tatezi the most wonderful creature on four legs.

Soon afterwards he ran off, boylike, to visit his runner, to reassure this horse that Tatezi will not take away his affection for the big black.

Napewaśte had looked upon her son's return as something that earned a warrior's reception, but Olepi had expressed a different view. Peta had not cut loose a horse from in front of an enemy lodge and the warning he gave had not concerned an attacking enemy. And so inside the family tipi the youth heard only a little praising.

"My son goes out with horsecatchers, but will anyone in camp know that this party invites a young Mahto?"

"My father, I take traveling moccasins. Will none advise you?"

"I know about the moccasins and so I understand that you follow out after the warriors."

For a moment Peta's dark, searching eyes sought his father's face. Then, looking away, he spoke quietly. "My father sees that I capture a war horse, that I take a step in the direction he approves. But I will have him understand that, when I decide I am ready for raiding or war, I go out openly and in a party my father leads." A little smile quivered on Peta's lips, but the next instant, his mouth forming a firm line, he stepped out of the lodge.

The father sat marveling. Twice before he had seen in this youth, his son, the coming of the man, but perhaps never will he see this change more clearly than now, in a little quiver of the mouth and a wistful smile, those same lips suddenly firm and straight, corners down, the face of a man where moments before a boy's eyes had looked out.

Half-recognizing, half-puzzling that which they call ripening, Olepi remembered back to the day he knew himself as man, to the morning when he, twenty-and-five winters, had stood before the one he called father, his eyes saying that he will make wife of the woman at his side. And that he will want but certainly not need his father's approval. Olepi, already the warrior but on that day something more: the virile man.

What, then, of Peta, who, at ten-and-six winters, looks out from eyes which say that on this day and evermore he shall act as he sees fit? In what manner will he describe fitness until he experiences war, until he confronts an enemy during a raid or revenge, until he knows himself a virile man?

Certainly Olepi recognized growth not as a thing of counting winters or standing tall but as orderly advance.

The child, belonging to mother, grandparents; the youth, belonging to his teachers; the warrior, belonging to himself. And, occasionally, a man who becomes legend, who belongs to the people.

A hand touching lightly on his shoulder aroused Olepi from his pondering but whose hand he knew not; he sat alone in the lodge. Perhaps he only sensed this man-to-man gesture, something occurring between two who live close in thought.

Or will Peta's unseen presence make know to the father that a boy-nature truly passes and a warrior comes into view? Who will say? Will Wanaġi understand this thing? Will the wapiya understand Peta?

Wanaġi had listened with an understanding ear but for the son, not the father. And so he had sat a long while before he gave answer to Olepi.

"This youth," he began, "will not hurry any experience. Nothing small exists for this one they call Peta. Wherever he looks, he sees something big, something important.

"Recall. He goes out as a boy-tender and encounters the white pte. He stalks with Ogle and brings back an antlered one of strange makeup. He kills a herd-father with one arrow at an age when most boys use two, three arrows on their little kills."

The wapiya refilled his pipe; let the father begin to recognize Peta's approach to each thing.

And now Olepi spoke: "True, the boy demonstrates himself as a hunter, but will he try out in every direction? Or will he choose the gentling of horses as his way of living?"

Wanaġi looked into the man's face, drawing Olepi's eyes. "Hear me," he said severely. "Once you foresee Peta as a painter of tipi, perhaps a keeper-of-the-seasons; now you see this same one as a horsecatcher, perhaps a horse-healer. What comes next?"

Responding to the piercing look, Olepi spoke aloud his thought: "Perhaps my son Peta seeks a vision that makes of him a wapiya, a seer."

Suddenly Wanaġi smiled. "Neither father nor friend decides your son's path."

The two sat silent during a third smoke. And then the Mahto, sensing comfort and relief, left the sacred-lodge. Wanaġi, he told himself, will not try to exert an influence over Peta; instead, the wapiya hints that the youth already envisions himself a warrior.

But Wanaġi had not hinted anything; he had said most firmly that Peta, never an ordinary boy, will not live as an ordinary man.

Soon after Olepi had gone out of the lodge, Wanaġi sought the loneliness, the privacy of a knoll. He chose to recall most vividly two different scenes with Peta: the youth's visit to the sacred-lodge after the boy-brave experience, and a more recent visit, two, three winters in the past.

On that second occasion Peta had sat quietly while he, Wanaġi, prepared a leaf concoction, the boy marveling not the bubbling water, the floating leaves, but his own thoughts.

"The leaf that a branch pushes off drops down," he had said, "but the smoke that a burning stick pushes away curls up. My arrow makes a curve through the air. Each thing moves but in a different direction."

Wanaġi had waited. After a moment Peta had spoken again. "Perhaps I, also, move in a certain direction."

And then the wapiya had responded. "Śkan," he had said, "taku śkanśkan moves everything that moves. Leaf, smoke, arrow."

"And Peta?"

"And you, my son." The seer paused; "Perhaps you will not understand what I am saying."

"You say," Peta had answered easily, "that I shall recognize my breath as śkan."

"And that you shall recognize śkan," Wanaġi had said quickly, "in the voice of the wingeds who sing until they empty of this power, who use tree and sleep to regain their song.

"And that you shall recognize śkan in the four-legs who run until they use up their power, who rest while śkan provides new strength."

Peta had glanced at the wapiya's face. "Perhaps," he had said slowly, "śkan moves me in a manner I not yet recognize."

Enough, Wanaġi had warned himself; enough for now.

Perhaps at a different meeting he will talk with Peta about his own response to the wonder at age twelve, thirteen, and about those days, nights in his twentieth winter when he had dared ponder the breath that creates life, becomes life, when he only had begun to understand śkan as something flowing in and through the two-legged they call man, something that man, like the creatures, receives without asking but something upon which man, unlike the four-legged, shall draw whenever he chooses.

Peta, aware that the wapiya had nothing more to say to him on that day, had slipped out of the lodge; he had left the sacred-man to pipe and ceremony. And Wanaǧi, staying on the trail of thoughts that this youth had evoked, had pursued again the meaning in this act they call 'choosing,' truly the most important act known to the family of man.

For who but man dares choose between that which protects and that which destroys him? The wingeds fly, nest, and sing as the life-force directs; the four-legs leap, run, or hide as the life-force compels. But śkan, the life-force, neither directs nor compels man; instead man directs the force. And so he provides his own protection, looks out for himself.

But man owns also the power for destroying himself, for turning the life-force toward mischief and away from good, if he so chooses.

If he so chooses. But will not man hold on to something in or of his body, in or of his spirit, that dignifies him? Not something he seeks, not dream or vision, but something he owns from the beginning? Certainly he learns to recognize his familiar-voice, but the familiar-voice never forbids, never compels. The familiar-voice identifies truth but never demands that man act on truth; man makes that choice. And so most certainly man owns something that determines his choices, a power that belongs to man alone, a selective-power for the purpose of spirit growth.

So will Wanaǧi talk with himself now as in that winter past when he had recognized himself as neither a seer for war parties nor a tribal prophet; so will he remember that he desires only to know himself as a fit controlling power, as someone competent to interpret the visions of such youths as Peta. And certainly Peta will seek a vision. And receiving, he will begin his search for the real, unwrapping truth as he confronts the invisible in painful but magnificent struggle.

But this summer at pahamni ridge, he Wanaǵi yet seeks to understand why he dares ask but not answer his own question: tuwe miye he. Where, the gap between his spirit and body that keeps him uncertain as to his stability for the stone-dream? Will his sense of lacking something relate to seeds he never generates?

Perhaps the season comes for him to perform 'ceazin' as the grandfathers intend this affair. He will not take another wife, and at forty-and-five he will bring wisdom and delicacy to this most rare ceremony. But only if that certain one they call Winkte will agree; only if Winkte, the song-maker, understands why Wanaǵi desires this experience.

II

UPON HIS return from the horse-chasing expedition Peta observed that the young braves among his peers treated with him as if he wore a feather in his hair. Perhaps, he told himself, these young men now begin to notice Tatezi and envy him this remarkable horse.

Then, the warm moons nearly used up, he received an invitation to go out as moccasin-carrier for a most unusual party. Leaders from the different Titonwan bands joined this group, yet none of these headmen carried a pipe. Why, he puzzled, will five principal ones—Olepi, Zuzueca, Oowe-śica, Wacape, Mniśa—accompany twenty young men who scheme to go out after enemy horses?

The third night away from camp Peta had discovered one reason why. This night they sent the son of Olepi on an errand along a dark, shadowy trail, the youth instructed to locate a certain stream and fill a certain sac with water from that stream, a ceremony which initiates a moccasin-carrier into the ways of a war party.

Peta knew that danger accompanied his assignment—he heard the men talking about a lurking enemy who had killed two boys out alone—but if he took caution instead of fear as his companion, he had reasoned, he will not run into trouble. And so, starting out with an easy heart, he traveled the path quickly and returned with a full sac, his eyes inviting the praise he knew he had earned.

But Zuzueca, trying the water, complained that he drank something neither fresh nor cold; he demanded that Peta again visit the stream and bring back a satisfying drink.

On his second return, a different man tasted and objected. Mniśa, dipping his fingers into the sac, flicked drops in Peta's face, then requested that the youth go back to the stream; the sac, he said, comes to him half-empty.

Olepi's eyes had flashed angrily. True, the headmen dare send out the same water-boy as often as they desire but never with trickery as the motive. In this instance Peta will not return until after dawn, and at dawn the party moves on toward the enemy camp. Apparently Zuzueca and Mniśa schemed to prevent Peta from an encounter with the Psa and so deprive him of his chance to earn war honors. But the father had not voiced this resentment; let his son act as they demand.

Peta, also, experienced a twinge of resentment. He had walked more than half the night and traveled the distance a fat man walks in one day; perhaps an enemy picks up his trail after his second visit to the stream. But, attempting to ignore such thoughts and remember only caution, he went out again.

Night had thinned in the east when Peta finally returned to the war camp. He found the men gone, but four horse-tenders—youths on their second expedition—stayed to guard the horses belonging to the party. The raiders had started out after a small band of traveling Psa—six lodges; they intended to surprise the sleeping enemy camp at daybreak and run off the horses.

The leaders, Peta learned, had acted most pleased with these conditions, everything exactly as they desired. The

405

men wanted these youths whom they bring along to get the feel of a raid but without the risks that go with an attack on a big camp. Each leader had invited his most likely braves, the group a hand-picked one. And so Peta understood who chose him; nor will he disappoint his father.

The young Mahto considered the instructions he had received; they had said nothing about his waiting at the war camp until the men returned. And so, leading out Tatezi, her bundle of moccasins securely bound, he jumped on her back. The next instant, youth and horse gone.

For a while Peta kept to gullies and low places, his eyes alert to the direction the men had taken. But he stayed wide of their trail, he will not want to lead an enemy toward the walking party.

After a while he got off his horse and climbed a knoll. Crawling on his belly, he found a place with a wide view of the misty plain. Looking out, he saw many dark patches and so he recalled that which Lekśi had said about recognizing things in the far distance. If a man sits near enough to see the shape of an object, his uncle had told him, he sits near enough to identify this shape.

Quickly Peta began sorting the patches—tree clumps, boulders, breaks, shadows—but nothing he dared call a Psa camp. Or fifteen foot-going Titonwan moving toward a Psa camp.

He came down off the knoll and laid an ear to the earth; he listened for the thump of hoofs, the rumble of many horses scattering. Nothing. He moved on, leading his horse.

The sky brightened; his presence on the plain became a danger to himself and to the Titonwan party, wherever they walked. But then he saw a wisp of smoke and knew which way to go.

After a little distance he touched Tatezi and she lay down, yellow grass concealing her yellow body. And now he started crawling toward the smoke.

Before ever he reached any of the tall tipi, he heard those desperate shouts and angry whoops that hint at a people who awaken to find their herd missing. But not all the horses gone; snorts and whinnies told that the Psa kept something to ride out after the raiders if anyone dared to pursue.

The big noise came from the opposite side of the camp; the lodges on the side Peta approached seemed empty. The youth estimated thirty, forty persons in the whole camp and all faces directed toward those two Psa who mounted, who chose to risk finding their horses.

Tree and brush protected the Mahto youth as he rose from his crouch, only his eyes moving as he took one more look around. Then, knife in hand and hand raised to strike, he jumped swiftly through the entrance of the near tipi.

A woman, kneeling, rolled up a backrest for travel.

She turned and he heard her tiny wail. Instantly he put his knife at her throat; the hand in her hair pulled back her head. And so he saw her eyes, big in fright. Even if she recognized that a youth and not a warrior attacked, she looked afraid, terribly afraid.

A strange new power rose up in Peta; his knife-hand trembled. His, the power to kill, to scalp a woman and show her hair as proof of his daring.

But if he let this woman live, will she not tell of a Titonwan youth who boldly enters her tipi and holds a knife at her throat? Then will not the Psa marvel this youth? And who will ever know that only a moccasin-carrier comes here?

Or will he see in this woman someone not unlike his mother, hair and eyes similar to Napewaśte's hair and eyes?

Holding the knife firmly now, he signaled impatience. He takes all moccasins in this tipi, his gesture told; the woman shall gather and roll the pairs into a tight pack.

When she had grabbed up five, six pairs he demanded the bundle, then sent her to the flap, his knife at the back of her neck; she dies if she signals for help. Taking up a robe to cover himself, he kept the woman close at his side as he walked slowly all the way to the place Tatezi waited in the grass.

Once mounted, he pushed away the woman with a quick thrust of his leg. He saw her fall and lie unmoving, her body covered with fear. He had not possessed the daring to give a war cry but neither had he cringed on Tatezi as he rode off.

Moments afterwards, he guided Tatezi onto a path opposite the raiders. He knew that the men rode beyond reach of any Psa, but he went the long way around; before rejoining the party, he chose to return to the stream, his fourth visit.

The warriors sat waiting for him, their faces stern. But Peta jumped from his horse, going at once to Mniśa. "Uncle, twice last night and once before dawn I fill a water-sac at the stream of your choice. But you go out with the party before my third return. And so I go back this morning. I empty out the dead water and bring you this fresh drink."

Peta's loud, clear voice brought the men close around these two; they waited to see whether Mniśa will permit something which any moccasin-carrier who fulfills instructions dares perform.

But Mniśa had not favored the prank that rewards nor had he appeared pleased with the youth. "Many persons wait here for you. While you indulge a playful mood, the group splits. You impose a danger on those men who drive the horses and on the ones who wait here, perhaps wondering about their extra moccasins."

Mniśa spoke sharply, but Peta had not heard any murmurs of agreement; the men remembered instead that Mniśa had put the danger upon Peta when he demanded the youth's third visit to the stream.

Next thing, Olepi rode up alongside Peta, the Mahto leading two fine Psa horses. Handing their jaw-cords to his son, he spoke in tones similar to Mniśa: "The four who watch over the horses tell that you return from the stream at dawn but that you say nothing. Instead you mount and start out. This party invites you as moccasin-carrier, not as a youth who shall please himself."

Peta answered promptly, his eyes on Mniśa but his words for his father; whatever Olepi's tone, the leader's manner told that he fully approved his son's acts. "I use daring, my father, as this party will have me, but not only at filling water-sacs. I visit the enemy camp, where I take moccasins from a woman instead of her scalp."

Reaching for the bundle on his back, he jerked the load from his shoulder and flung the pack across his mount, on top of the Titonwan moccasin bundles in his care these four days. His eyes turned in his father's direction. "I carry the warriors' moccasins as this party demands but I carry also the feet of a Psa lodge."

Now, leading his father's two, he took a place at the rear of the party. At the same moment Olepi, Mniśa, Ooweśica, Wacape, and Zuzueca took their places at the front. The group started off at a lope, eager to catch up with the 'pointers'—those young men who drove the herd—glad to avoid any more controversy.

A father new-names a son whenever he sees the proper occasion; the grandfathers had said so. And so, on his return from the Psa raid, Olepi visited the sacred-lodge; the Mahto leader asked that Wanaǧi choose a man's name for Peta, a name never before heard on the plain, a name to remember in the generations ahead.

The Mahto leader had decided that Peta earned a new name whether or not they award him a feather for his courage in the enemy camp. True, none witnessed Peta's act, but the youth brought Psa moccasins as proof of his encounter with a Psa camp. Or will someone wonder about this bundle of enemy feet?

A short-lived rumor out of Zuzueca's camp hinted that the traveling enemy band dropped these moccasins on the ground, something Peta discovered as he rode. Once a man's word stood alone, but someone had brought a fork-tongue onto the plain and now each man needed proof when he boasted his daring. Peta lacked a witness, they said, and he took moccasins, not hair; his, a remarkable daring but not for gaining feathers.

But these small men with their small voices had not stopped Olepi's intention to commemorate Peta's single experience as moccasin-boy with a war party. When next his son goes out, the Mahto leader said, he goes as a young brave who wears a man's name.

For ten, twelve winters Winkte had made up the naming-songs that honored not only Mahto but Titonwan in all bands. And now Wanaǧi, responding to Olepi's request to present Peta with a man-name, went to this two-souls person for a song which will use the new name. But he went also to ask that Winkte permit the ceazin, the takes-with-mouth ceremony.

True, Winkte had proved the disposition for making great songs but nothing will bring the song-maker more recognition than the ceremony Wanaği proposed; the wapiya will honor Winkte in a most intimate manner and Winkte, in return, will put the wapiya in touch with that rare balance—twin spirits, male and female, growing within a single body—which only the two-souls person ever knows.

Winkte, who followed the wapiya perhaps ten winters in age, had stayed on in the parents' lodge and Wanaği saw fit to consult with all members of this tipi. He wanted each one to know that he intended to perform the ceremony, never before enacted on the plain, exactly as the old, old seer had described; only dignity and wonder shall prevail. And he wanted Winkte and these relatives to understand that his seed, giving new life to Winkte's soul, shall live in the songs of the people and that Winkte's power for song, which the wapiya renews through this ceremony, shall lift the hearts of the tribe as never before. The ancients had devised this ceremony, as all ceremonies, to generate good in more than one direction.

The grandfathers had said that whoever performs ceazin shall let the people know, and so the crier had announced that something mysterious shall take place within the next four days.

The encampment, quick to discover who will enact the ceremony, had remembered that only four winkte had lived among the Dakotah, these wakan-persons as unusual as the pte-winkte, as the mysterious 'pte-pta' occasionally seen on the edges of the herd. But the people remembered also that each one of these four Dakotah winkte had excelled at something: quilling or painting or composing. And that each one had shown powers for conveying spirit-messages. Two of these four had lived to a remarkably old age, more than one hundred winters. Or so the stories told.

And now on this day, the fifth winkte to live among the people sat in the inipi with Wanaği and, after the purifying bath, received something from the wapiya. None of the people had witnessed this private rite, but soon a small crowd, mostly Mahto and Okandada, gathered to watch the dance-of-the-winkte, an affair centering around Winkte and any man in camp who ever had fondled this person.

Twenty women stood among the onlookers, mostly old persons without husbands, women with an eye for vulgar mimicry and a throat for loud, crude laughter, women who will make the same noise here that they make at the sight of mating dogs.

Some young wives also watched the antics of these warriors who boasted an intimacy with Winkte, but these women truly came to hear the wonderful singing voice of this Winkte, a voice beyond reach of the flutes, a voice for women to envy and men to marvel.

But suddenly laughter replaced song, a laughing that spread throughout the crowd. Winkte, gowned always as woman, coyly had come forward, pretending a response to the eight, ten warriors who, dancing up one by one, made obvious the nature of their attack. Even so, the laughter sounded nothing like the ridiculing smirks with which the people try to shame the unruly. For Winkte, giggling at the approach of each dancer, postured invitingly and so encouraged the laughter. A two-souls person will understand that certain men, not winkte in body but possessing a winkte-nature, enjoy patting and pinching their own kind. And a two-souls person also understands that all this laughing acts to relieve those onlookers who see something unnatural in such behavior.

Wanaǵi stood gazing upon the scene, a man neither dancing nor laughing and certainly not among the group who affectionately teased this Winkte. The wapiya, instead, silently recalled his experience this morning in the lonely little tipi far out from camp. Here, as the grandfathers had devised the ceremony, he had ejected his seed into the mouth of the song-maker; into the mouth of Winkte he had dispersed the generating power of a virile man. And Winkte, recognizing seed as life and making-life, recognizing life as something in and of the soul, had accepted the seed.

The performers, the grandfathers had said, shall remember that they enact this ceremony to satisfy the spirit-self, but Wanaǵi knew, as the grandfathers had known, that nothing shall divide spirit and body. And so he recalled the trembling at his thighs as the strange excitement had possessed him; not before had his soul throbbed at the groin and moved up his back in so piercing a manner.

And now Wanaǧi observed that the dancers retreated and the onlookers grew silent; Winkte had begun a song:

"Ceazin ohna piya mayakaǧe kte ye,
wicaśa wan iohna wiconi maku kte ye,
he niye so. . . . "

The grandfathers had said that a winkte shall sing at the dancing that occurs after the private ceremony, a song to help the people understand that a two-souls person strives for completeness of self even as each one who listens strives to keep whole.

" 'Ceazin,' in this manner you renew me,
through-the-mouth this man gives me life,
you, this man. . . . "

Winkte sang the song twice, pointing to the wapiya; the people shall know which man honors a winkte in the ceremonial manner, the sacred manner.

The air became still, as if, for an instant, all life shall point at decency as something belonging to each one here who recognizes the most strong impulse as a creative force, spirit and body.

And then the people began talking, mentioning the meat on which they soon shall feast. And so those warriors who had boasted an intimacy with Winkte carried forth a robe piled with tongue and hump.

Wanaǧi, in honor of the occasion, had cooked the seedsacs of pta, which, some persons said, stiffen any man, young or old. But to those warriors who had danced he offered a mysterious root, something he rarely gave away, something that hardens a man in his moment of desire.

Then, while the men feasted, Wanaǧi slipped away, taking his pipe to the knoll where four days previously, he had sat contemplating a man-name for the youth Peta. He had decided on that name, telling Winkte this same day what name to use in the song.

Never before will a man own this name, perhaps never again. The Lakotah not easily remember names, but for so long as any Lakotah lives, Wanaǧi told himself, this name they shall know. But for what reason the wapiya not yet foresaw.

Wanaǧi sucked his pipe and reflected this day's ceremony; he will not again make contact with Winkte and he will grow erect perhaps only in dreams. But he approached the season when he dared send a voice to listeners-above, listeners-below; truly the invisible grandfathers shall recognize him now. And, hearing his voice, they shall answer him not filtered through the four-legged, not through the winged, but through the most powerful earth-elemental: stone.

Four days after the winkte ceremony, on the day before the hoop broke for the winter season, the crier walked through the Mahto camp as voice for Olepi. The Mahto leader, he sang, asks that relatives and friends eat with him this day, dance with him this night.

A little while afterwards, Olepi himself walked among the tipi, the man telling that the feast honors his son. The youth had met the enemy and returned with proof. The father had asked that the wapiya give a man-name to this son and so the people shall hear at this feast the name Wanaǧi gives to the son of Olepi.

Everyone in the Mahto camp had come and some persons from the Šiyo. They ate of the food that Napewaśte and her relatives had prepared, even Hinziwin putting forth a true effort to help make this one an outstanding feast day.

And certainly Olepi never had walked more proudly. He moved among his guests, noticing empty bowls, calling for refills. He and Ogle had brought in antlered meat for these roasting fires and the women had picked ripe berries for the sauce that brings out the taste in this meat. But gladly he will see persons refusing anything more to eat; he wanted to get on with the naming ceremony; not even he yet knew what name the wapiya had selected.

And now he saw that Wanaǧi, drum in hand, stood ready to circle the camp, to sing out the new name. And that the eight men who will stay at the big drum, had taken their places. He saw that Peta had come from the family lodge, the youth wearing a fine pair of leg-covers and carry-

413

ing a painted robe, the robe Peta had grabbed while in the Psa camp.

People from different camps, noticing the big gathering, edged near and so they, also, heard when Wanaġi began the song, the new song that gave Olepi's son a man-name.

"A youth goes out; his day begins;
he observes the earth; his name: Ahbleza. . . . "

Wanaġi walked twice through the camp, and then the men at the drum began to sing this naming-song, something Winkte had composed, a song which tells that from this day forward Peta shall recognize the name Ahbleza as his own, as his alone.

And now the dancing, something for young men, old men, sons and grandsons and grandfathers, for whoever among the men had feet and ears and a joy in this new-naming of Olepi's son.

But Ahbleza had not danced. The honored youth stood, instead, next to Wanaġi. He had draped the robe taken from the Psa lodge over his shoulder, and one pair of the Psa moccasins hung from his waist. And now let whoever chooses look upon him as moccasin-carrier or young brave, as someone whom good fortune favors or as someone most daring. As for himself, he shall remember Ahbleza—his name this day and for all seasons yet to come—not only as an observer but as one whom they, the people, observe. And so, whatever his path, he shall walk aware that all eyes look upon him and mark his every act, each one waiting to see if he brings honor to self and tribe.

"Hau, hecitu yelo." Softly Wanaġi spoke the phrase, moved away.

And Ahbleza, marveling, understood that certain persons will observe not only his acts but also his thoughts. Bringing honor to self and tribe means, then: thought, voice, act, now and evermore, one and the same.

Gone, this boy they had called Peta, but who, this one they call Ahbleza? And while these youth-seasons, these winters between the child and the warrior, shall pass quickly—perhaps before anyone really notices—the grandfathers said to regard this span as the most important in all life.

For during these seasons, youth shall wonder and dream and search. And to certain ones a vision will come. The wise know this wondrous happening as giving answer to a familiar-voice, but the youth says only that he makes a decision.

III

"BREATHE IN this ripe summer day." Eyanpaha sang his song of sunrise to one hundred and sixteen lodges, to the seven hundred Titonwan encamped once again at pahamni ridge.

The people awakened to the voice, but as usual only the very young came out at once; naked and smiling but never noisy they began their play. The old man completed his round as the sun's brilliant rays pierced the mist hovering over the ridge.

Heading now for his own lodge, the crier walked nearby Cankuna's big tipi, the hunter's wife apparently the only one in her family up and at work. Three horses stood in front of this lodge. A fourth one, small and curly, stood to the side, her hide unpainted and her tail undecorated. Each had a cord leading under the tipi flap. The small horse nickered and Eyanpaha patted her head. Then, his eyes amused, he tugged on her neck-cord.

Before the man had walked two steps, Mahtociqala's face appeared at the tipi flap. He saw his mother kneeling at her cooking fire and he saw old Eyanpaha moving off. But the crier had not resisted a backward look and so the youth understood who had pulled on the cord leading from the horse to his wrist.

Mahtociqala had lived his fourteen winters in a lodge of good-natured jokers and so he had learned to laugh off a teasing.

"Grandfather," he called, "I am too fast for you. Never will you cut loose any horse I own."

Concealing a smile, the crier sang back at the youth: "Only an old woman will cut loose that creature, an old woman who mistakes your curly one for a fat puppy she will throw in the soup sac."

Eyanpaha walked on and Mahtociqala turned to comfort his four-legged friend. "He jokes, but when I and you go out with the men he shall see you differently."

And now, jumping onto the horse, Mahtociqala rode off toward the cold bathing waters at the bottom of the ridge.

Ogle, from inside the lodge, had heard the youth talking to the horse. He will not regret that this son intends to join a party; Mahtociqala never will become a warrior, he told himself, but whoever goes out with the warriors prepares for the day when he needs put to use that which he learns from experience. And so save his own neck.

Certainly his son has a way with all four-legged, luring the cautious out of hiding and tracking down the sly, not to kill but to enjoy their company. And always his son observes the twig that breaks, the pebble that slides, a single hair that catches in the brush. And for what purpose will he use his skills? Already Mahtociqala refers to himself as 'scout.'

Leaning against his backrest, Ogle now glanced toward his first-born son, this young man at work with brush and powder.

Similar to many young warriors, Gnuśka never went out the lodge until long after sunrise, and never will he go out unpainted. Different ones waited for a dance or a feast or for travel before they applied paint, but Gnuśka repainted the two red streaks on each cheek before ever they began fading. And so whoever saw him remembered at once that Gnuśka had rushed in, the fourth man to touch the fallen enemy. Nor will he ever appear without a tall red-spotted feather tied in his hair, something to show that he had killed an enemy.

Gnuśka stood now and tightened the string around his waist, then adjusted the flaps, front and back, which hung over his loins. Raising his hands to the back of his head, he slanted the feather into his hair.

For another moment the father pondered this son.

416

Eighteen winters and always an unruly youth, perhaps one who never will learn to control his impulses. True, he possesses the makings of a great warrior; he needs only to practice restraint. Not an aberrant son, the father told himself; not aberrant but foolish, so very foolish.

The sun climbed up the sky and the lodges slowly emptied, most persons coming to the outside fire for their morning soup. And now the Siyo crier who sang out news and commentary each day started on his rounds. Moving through the encampment, he deplored the greedy and the lazy. "A greedy person will not live long," he told; "when you see something you want, make yourself useful to someone."

Next the people heard this voice advising that husbands show kindness toward their wives: "The honor of the family sits in the woman's hands."

And now the Siyo's message, directed at the young. "Go to the old people, go and hear the legends. Sit with your grandparents. Listen to these old ones. Make use of what they know." The man's words carried throughout the encampment. "Guard your tongue in youth," he sang, "and in age you perhaps mature a thought that becomes of use to your people."

Certain young warriors who sat their horses, arms folded and faces calm, had begun to wonder whether this Siyo crier will make any pronouncements that arouse their interest. Up until now the man neither specifies nor hints at anything exciting. But suddenly the eyes of these horsebacks brightened; they listened closely.

"Whoever wants to join a war party learns to rise with the sun," the crier told; "him who proves fond of sleep, they leave behind. Perhaps a party soon goes out. Will you ride or will you sleep?"

And so these young men understood the rumor as truth: Wanapin will lead out a war party the day after next. Wanapin, now principal warrior among the Siyo, truly will carry-the-pipe against the Miwatani, the sulky people who live north of the Palani villages.

"My father, hear me."

Mahtociqala's urgent voice delayed the hunter who, along with a group of friends, had started for the bathing

417

place. The boy's glistening body and his horse's wet curly hair told Ogle that these two, enjoying a swim, had hurried out of the water.

"My father"—Mahtociqala raised a bold face—"I go with the war party."

Hoh. So the crier's news brings this boy and his mount out of the water hole? But Ogle kept his eyes and tone cool, displaying neither agreement nor disapproval.

"My son sees himself as one ready to go out with men?"

"I am not afraid, my father, if you refer to my courage."

"My son puzzles my meaning and so I wonder whether he truly prepares for this experience." Ogle turned, hurrying to catch up with his friends who had walked on ahead.

The youth stood where his father had left him, a flush warming his neck. He stroked the curly one's face and tried to understand what unusual thing the men will look for in a youth who joins their party. Certainly he will carry moccasins in return for the privilege of accompanying these warriors and he will perform whatever unpleasant tasks they assign him. Three, four seasons in the past Gnuśka had informed him as to these demands; he remembered that which his brother had reported.

In angry tones Gnuśka had described in what manner they imposed upon him nor had they permitted him to share in the rewards of that raid. Returning to camp, Gnuśka had demanded that his mother bring out his cekpa, the tiny bundle that hid his birthcord.

Soon afterwards Gnuśka had sneaked out after a footgoing party; he had returned horseback and with witnesses to his strike on any enemy. But Gnuśka never had said whether the cekpa had helped him. Or whether he even took the thing along.

Recalling now this talk with his brother, Mahtociqala wondered whether his mother knew where she had hidden his birthcord and whether his father hinted that he will need this little bundle.

But why carry a wotawe? He will fear neither the distasteful tasks nor an encounter with enemy warriors. Certainly he will not go looking for trouble, but if he meets with trouble he shall rely on his senses the same as any man.

But now four, five youths rode by, one rider slapping lightly on the curly horse, starting her off. At once Mahtociqala ran and jumped on her back, racing these friends to the swimming place, entering the water before ever they reached the stream.

The big water hole had become a noisy place, the pool filled with shouting youths and snorting horses, perhaps ten, twelve horsebacks enjoying their favorite water game, 'knocking-off-horses,' each boy trying to upset someone before someone upset him.

The instant Mahtociqala splashed into the water, someone tried pushing him off. But clinging to the curly mane with one hand, swinging out with his opposite arm, the youth threw off his attacker. He looked around for a second challenger, but when none came at him, he shouted for a team-game. Which three will join his side? They will play against four and whomever they unhorse gets out of the pool at once.

The game began quickly, arms thrashing, legs kicking. But Mahtociqala's little mount soon played out; the youth became third on his team to go under. Pushed down into the cold water at the bottom of the big hole, he rose sputtering to the warm surface. Then, before he had climbed out, the opposition upset the fourth member of his team. And now these winners, staying horseback, called for different challengers.

A newcomer answered. Sluka—someone they once called Slukila—here to let his horse drink, rode into the water. But the actor's son had not waited for a team-game. Grabbing on to one boy's arm, he twisted him halfway around. Next, he kicked this one's belly until the youth bent over himself. Then, using his feet again, Sluka thumped with his heels on the boy's back until he sent him under water. But will any youngster here have a chance against a man twenty-two?

The disposed one's companion, not eager for an encounter with Sluka, now slipped off his horse and, diving to the bottom, came up on the opposite side.

Mahtociqala had not witnessed Sluka's surprise attack. And so, clinging to his horse's tail while the curly one paddled him toward the edge of the pool, the youth concerned himself only as to the enduring power of his mount;

419

perhaps she owns neither the legs nor heart for keeping up with a war party. He considered his father's words again; perhaps 'ready to go out with the men' signifies possessing a horse who looks like a horse, not a fat puppy.

But someone interrupted Mahtociqala's musings, someone who grabbed the curly horse's tail as the youth and his mount climbed onto the moist steep ground at the edge of the stream. Sluka, determined to keep some sort of game going, managed to lean forward and grab Mahtociqala's hair, pulling back on the youth's head, wrapping the strands around his own wrist.

For a moment Mahtociqala strove to keep his horse from slipping back into the water hole, but with Sluka twisting and jerking on his hair, his horse already in water over her mane and sliding, he let go the jaw-cord. The next instant the bully pulled Mahtociqala alongside him; then, his foot on the youth's head, he pushed his captive under water.

Suddenly another horseback entered the pool, this one yelling and plunging toward the center. And now Sluka, overthrown, bounced and sputtered in the water, the bluffer yet unaware who attacked him. But Mahtociqala knew; as he went under, he heard Ahbleza's yell.

Climbing out of the hole, Mahtociqala shook water from his face. Eyes round and admiring, he gazed up at the person who sat a wet black horse, a youth ten-and-seven winters, someone with hair long to his shoulders, hair so black and shining as to reflect the sky. Ahbleza, horseback and at the stream's edge, looked as he always looked: as if the earth belongs to him.

For an instant, but only an instant, Mahtociqala wished himself Ahbleza.

Ahbleza smiled and the familiar look brought Mahtociqala back to himself, to his own good place in the tribe: a youth fourteen who schemes to go out with the men.

Stepping near his friend, he put his head against the nose of Ahbleza's horse; he made a whisper of his thought: "I will wait and see if they permit me on the war party."

"Who stops you?"

Mahtociqala glanced up; he saw that the smile had moved into Ahbleza's eyes. Responding with a whoop, he leaped up behind his friend, the black runner never protesting this double load.

The wonderful creature moved forward and Mahtociqala's little horse followed closely. Now the youth spoke softly in Ahbleza's ear: "None of the warriors invites me. Perhaps they decide I am not yet a man. Or, like my father, they wonder whether I am ready for this experience."

"Will these things stop you?"

The two rode on, Mahtociqala waiting to hear something that hinted at whether or not the men will welcome him.

But Ahbleza said nothing, the rider up front appearing not to notice when the rider in back jumped down at Cankuna's lodge. And now Mahtociqala stood looking after this one he calls brother-friend, marveling that Ahbleza will ride off without so much as a backward glance.

Cankuna's tipi, usually full to the lining with relatives and friends, stood empty. Nor will Mahtociqala find either one of his uncles—Iku or Pasu—anywhere within the tiyóspaye. Nor will he see Hinhan, whom he treats as father; not a person in view to whom he dares present his uncertainty and receive advice.

After a while he began a hunt among his possessions for his bird-claw neckpiece, look-alike to the one Ahbleza owns. Perhaps he will fasten this string of claws to his horse's mane and so the war party will see that he carries a 'protection.' Not strong like a cekpa but something.

Before the sun climbed down, everyone in the Mahto camp knew that Wanapin had feasted fourteen members of the Tokala-lodge, half this group Siyo, half Mahto. And that at this feast he had announced the avenging against the Miwatani.

Let Siyo and Mahto remember, he had said, that the Miwatani kill a Siyo within the past seven, eight moons, a Siyo who goes out alone to hunt in the snow. Let Siyo and Mahto remember this good man as a Sicangu until he joins his wife's band. His wife, Wiyanna. And Wiyanna, a sister to Napewaste. This man's son lives with the Mnikoóžu and his other blood relatives stay with the Sicangu. And so Wanapin will relieve these kinsmen who camp in a different place and not yet hear of their relative's death.

"Whoever feasts here," Wanapin had told, "takes a pledge that binds him to the avengers. And he shall invite other warriors to join this party. Let each one who goes use this next day for preparation: wasna sacs, moccasins and hair-wraps, wapiti fat, paint and brush. Put these things alongside your bow. And let me see each Tokala member lay his akicita headband on top his pile."

Iku, a Tokala, had brought Wanapin's message to the hunter's lodge. Soon afterwards each man had gone off alone to make his decision. For this reason Mahtociqala had found the tipi empty.

But now, the sky dark and the family sitting together again, Mahtociqala spoke confirming his intention. Gazing at his baby sister, Hapstin, a new sister born during the cold moons, he delivered his message. "Perhaps my mother will lay certain bundles that belong to my relatives alongside my sleeping robe. I, a moccasin-carrier, go to war."

And now the youth stepped out of the lodge, walking over to the curly horse staked nearby, telling this one that they go out to avenge a man whom Ahbleza had called uncle. "I shall tie up your tail," he whispered, stroking the creature's head, "and so the enemy will have nothing to grab."

He put a hand on his own head, at the place Sluka had caught hold of loose strands. "And I shall knot my hair into a bunch for the same reason I tie up your tail. Takpe! I go out. I attack."

Suddenly the youth began laughing. "I go as moccasin-boy," he told the curly one, "yet I see myself returning with a feather in my hair." He patted the horse on the nose. "Help me," he said softly. "I go out trying for a man's name. A man-name I desire and so I go out with the men."

He stroked the horse once again; then standing tall he began to walk among the lodges, circling the Mahto-camp before returning to his mother's tipi. His absence gave his relatives a chance to talk about his decision, to speak their true feelings about his joining the warriors.

The men in Cankuna's lodge had seemed not to notice Mahtociqala's declaration, but the women will not pretend indifference, not when three, perhaps four in this family ride toward danger, not when two sons go out and Iku, the brother-uncle whom everyone, respect- and joking-relative, regards most fondly. Not when Pasu, another brother-uncle, perhaps goes as scout.

The crying-sound had come from the woman's side soon after Mahtociqala had gone out of the tipi; Cuwe, first-born daughter in this lodge and now in her eleventh winter, had uttered a wail.

Never before had this young girl raised her voice in a lament, yet she had made her cry as if born with the instinct for wailing. For suddenly Cuwe had understood that this good-looking brother whom she favors over Gnuśka, goes to war and perhaps will not return.

But quickly Cankuna told the girl that Mahtociqala had hinted that he wanted his sister Cuwe to make his going-away moccasins. Instantly the daughter's eyes brightened; always she sat properly silent whenever either brother came into the lodge but her respectful demeanor had not hidden her sisterly admiration for Mahtociqala.

Cankuna, now the mother of two sons and three daughters, knew that each of her girls felt a closeness to their one brother that they never had felt for Gnuśka. Yet when the day comes for any one of these three to select a husband, kinsman-rule will require that they consult Gnuśka, something that Cankuna found strangely unpleasant to contemplate. Perhaps Cuwe will not protest this custom, she told herself, but Tacincala, her daughter of seven winters, presents another picture.

Tacincala seemed different in many ways. Her light skin, unusual among the bands on the plain, and her smoky eyes separated her from the sun-darkened skins of most persons. Yet her shapely brows and the curve of her mouth identified her as a true daughter of the Dakotah whether she lived under the trees or out in the open.

The young sister looked up now as Mahtociqala entered the lodge, but Cuwe pushed down the girl's head; she intended to teach Tacincala modesty and respect in the presence of the blood-brother.

But Cankuna gestured that these girls go along with other woman-relatives who left this tipi now, these persons stopping at the rim of the circle where, in the woman-way, they shall shield one another with their robes while they excrete.

423

When everyone but Mahtociqala had gone from the lodge, Cankuna crept over to the place where her baby daughter lay sleeping; she looked down on the tightly wrapped bundle, nothing exposed but the child's face. And now she tied something to the pole above the little one's head, something she had hung over the sleeping place of each of her children when they, like this one, stayed firmly wrapped.

This day she had strung a dream-net for the girl-baby, winding many fine strands of sinew on a wood-hoop as wide as her finger-spread, shaping these strands into a web. This net, the grandmothers told, catches and holds any frightening dream while the hole in the center permits everything pleasant to reach the child. Morning's light kills any mischievous dream which, never finding the hole, gets tangled in the strings.

The net in place, Cankuna lay for a moment alongside the baby. But her thoughts returned her to Mahtociqala's boy-seasons, to the dream-net she had hung over him.

My son, my son, she whispered to herself; I deny him nothing in his child-winters, for who will say that he lives to know his man-seasons?

Mahtociqala turned at the sound of a little cry; perhaps something disturbs the baby sister toward whom he feels most fondly. But then he understood that his mother had made the little wail, that someone here cares about his chances when he and his curly horse ride against the enemy.

He composed a little song: "Watakpe owape ca, wicace-yapi kte lo."

The phrases pleased him; he sang the song twice: "I go with the avengers, tears will run from many eyes."

Perhaps many women shall wail his going; perhaps some pretty girls will cry.

Suddenly Mahtociqala knew that he shall return safely. And wearing a new name.

424

IV

THE LARGE gathering of warriors on the gaming-ground soon after dawn amazed Mahtociqala. The youth had heard that Wanapin feasted fourteen and so he came unprepared to see forty horsebacks. Nor will he know that Wanapin had asked for a second pipe-carrier and for two, three directors who shall advise along the way and for certain clubmen to command the actual fighting. Nor will he look for a party nearly all Mahto warriors.

Three of those Siyo who had smoked with Wanapin had reported dreams that portended injury if they joined the avengers, and a fourth man had turned around after putting in his appearance. Someone had called out to this Siyo asking if he desired a long life but the taunt had not returned him to the group. And so Wanapin led out a party of Mahto but for six, one of these six named Yuza, the Psa captive he had raised, this one now a youth seventeen.

But certainly Wanapin knew that he led the most desirable sort of party—nearly all from one band and all blood relatives or hunka, relatives-through-choice; not likely will he hear any quarrels, see any desertions.

On arriving at the gaming-ground Mahtociqala kept to the edge, near enough for Wanapin to see him and send him back to the lodge if none wanted him along. This distance prevented him from hearing that Olepi will ride alongside Wanapin, the Mahto leader determined to accompany this party which avenges an affinal relative.

Olepi remembered that the man they avenge once held the privilege of making Napewaste his second wife. But that he had not followed custom, not when he saw that Olepi, visiting frequently in the Siyo camp, revealed a true interest in the second daughter. And so, whether he rode as pipe-man or clubman or simply as a member of the party, Olepi had strong feelings about this avenging. Truly, his persuadings accounted for the appearance of more than a half the Mahto warriors.

When the party moved out, Mahtociqala stayed a certain distance back; he looked for one of the men to whirl around and ride him off. But none so much as glanced over his shoulder at the youth. Then, the sun overhead, Mahtociqala grew bold; his back straight as an arrow, his dark eyes challenging, he rode forward. But exactly whom or what he challenged, neither he nor anyone knew. Not a man noticed his approach, not even his friend Ahbleza nor his brother Gnuśka nor his uncle Iku.

He grew impatient, then annoyed. Will everyone ignore his presence? Certainly his relatives knew that he came; someone piled those moccasins alongside his sleeping place the night before, bundles he had flung across his horse this morning. True, he had not awakened until he heard his mother's gentle cough, and true, two men already had left the lodge. But they had looked for him to bring their feet.

He whipped the curly horse up alongside Iku. "My uncle, I come. I carry your moccasins."

The warrior appeared unnoticing.

"My uncle, I am someone who rides with this war party."

He saw Iku's face in profile, the features grim and unchanging. But now Iku turned his head: "I know you ride with the party; why come up and tell me?"

And so the young intruder understood the averted faces not as something to discourage him but simply the manner in which men ride to war. Moving silently, casually, these warriors preserved their energy and confidence. And slapping at the horse's flank rhythmically but never harshly, they transmitted this confidence to their mounts. Or perhaps, like Iku, a man's heels instead of the quirt touched lightly on the sides of his horse, in similar manner and for the same purpose.

Sensing now that he belonged in this group, Mahtociqala found his proper place back of the warriors, alongside six who also carried moccasins for the men, two of these youths on their third war party and determined to prove something.

After a while the leaders called a halt, and here at this rest stop the young warriors instructed Mahtociqala; they will restrict him to sign-talk.

This requirement had not surprised the youth; he looked for his peers to harass him and to test him for endurance and daring. But he will not look for abuse, not with an uncle and a brother in the party.

Iku had spoken once of his experiences as water-boy and moccasin-carrier. They had given him a stick to carry, Iku told his nephew, but none had said why they notched the stick whenever he spoke. Then, on the third night out, they had demanded of him a dance for each notch, for each occasion when he had made unnecessary talk. And Iku had remembered the warriors as most critical of his dancing.

They had not handed Mahtociqala a stick, but he understood clearly that he shall use his hands, not his tongue, and that the new name they gave him this same day referred not to any act he performed; instead they named him after a famous warrior to make him feel foolish on hearing this name along with a command to go after water. But they had renamed each moccasin-boy in the party, the youths obliged to respond to name and orders without resentment.

When the group rode again, Mahtociqala tried to remember his pride in becoming moccasin-bearer. He glanced down at the bundles; he looked twice.

One bundle missing. Gnuśka's bundle. But he had not dropped any bundles at the rest stop. So perhaps his brother, scheming to tease, sneaked these extra pairs off the pile?

But this same night, the party camping on flat ground at the turn in a creek, Gnuśka came looking for his young brother, demanding fresh moccasins. And Mahtociqala, smiling, signed his warrior-relative that Gnuśka had taken the bundle at the resting-place.

Gnuśka had not smiled back. He turned to his companion and, scowling, advised that they deal roughly with this moccasin-boy who refused to perform his obligations. Why not take away Mahtociqala's feet? Why not force this disrespectful youth to walk barefoot the next day? Certainly this boy dishonors the name they lend him.

Mahtociqala stood marveling. True, Gnuśka enjoys teasing, but on a war party one's brother acts always as protector, not tormentor. Why will Gnuśka ignore this blood-tie?

Then before someone spoke again, Ahbleza appeared

427

alongside his friend. At once Gnuśka walked off, but his companion, aware that the son of Olepi had heard, spoke out saying that Mahtociqala had shown negligence; the boy had lost a moccasin-bundle.

Ahbleza had not answered but, turning to Mahtociqala, he looked as unrelenting as the two conspirators. And then, as suddenly as he had appeared, Ahbleza disappeared, the moccasin-bearer standing alone, truly puzzled.

During the evening they chose the clubmen for the expedition, but Mahtociqala had not attended the ceremony, Gnuśka had embarrassed him and Ahbleza saw him as an offender; something which had begun as raillery now led toward abuse. But if he appealed to the pipe-bearers or his uncle Iku, the young warriors will discover that he complained and laugh him off the warpath.

What next? Something dropped on the ground near where he lay. He dared move nothing but his eyes so he shifted his glance to see that which fell.

Nearby his shoulder, a bundle; now a voice in the dark, one he recognized as belonging to Ahbleza.

"My friend, the bundle holds your brother's moccasins. Make certain that these feet will not run away from you again."

After a moment the youth, most grateful, sat up. Ahbleza, apparently discovering who played the trick, had managed to get back the pack. Truly, Ahbleza acts more like a brother than any different person in this war party.

Halfway through the third day the leaders acted to avoid any barren flat; the party had crossed onto enemy ground and they dared use only the wooded draws. And now, before dusk, they made camp, the two war advisers—Olepi, pipeman and adviser, and Hinyete, clubman and adviser—meeting with Wanapin and those three more they choose for clubmen. This group, blotahunka.

Mahtociqala, seeing who sat in the tight little circle, learned that his uncle Iku and his uncle's friend Źola will direct the fighting along with Hinyete and Śunktanka, a Siyo and a Mahto but neither one a member of the Tokala or any different brother-lodge.

Presently a messenger left this circle and ran toward the place two scouts, Po and Pasu, sat munching on wasna.

Mahtociqala looked at the sky; whomever they send out in search of the enemy camp, he told himself, shall travel under a rain-cloud cover. So perhaps Po and Pasu will welcome his presence; perhaps his strong quick eyes will pick up something they miss.

"Will they permit me out with the scouts?" he asked Ahbleza.

The brother-friend sat unanswering and so Mahtociqala spoke twice in the same quick voice. "The night hides nothing from me. Perhaps they will permit my going with the scouts."

Ahbleza had not smiled or asked what stops his friend's going as on that different occasion. Instead he told Mahtociqala something. And not gently. "They say that a moccasin-boy who will not remember to hold his tongue in his own camp most likely will break silence near the enemy and so bring danger to each man in the party."

The youth's eyes turned in shame and Ahbleza saw good in these humbling moments; perhaps Mahtociqala now will understand why this lesson in silence.

Then the son of Olepi spoke again, saying that the scouts who go out have sharp eyes and will manage without a guide. "But the warriors perhaps have use for my friend's keen senses."

Mahtociqala's glance told that he will not embarrass his brother-friend again. But will Ahbleza mean that they intend using him in the event of an attack on the war camp? Will Ahbleza hint at an enemy nearby?

Nothing on Ahbleza's face gave answer, but four men, walking back and forth, began a song, something about getting into a fight.

Mahtociqala gazed cautiously around him, but now the clubmen ordered the moccasin-carriers to make a rain shelter of young trees and brush and to bring wood for a bright fire. The party shall linger in the shelter, they said, for an evening of stories about outstanding Lakotah warriors.

Bright fire on enemy ground? Story telling here? And during the summer moons? Truly, going out with a war party proved a very different experience from that which Mahtociqala had imagined.

And now, before the warriors ate, the clubmen requested another puzzling war-party procedure: let Mahtociqala feed the Mahto leader some meat, Olepi receiving pieces of tongue on a forked stick. And let a different youth feed Wanapin in this same way. But what meaning in this act, none had said, neither boy had known.

Suddenly big drops of rain began drumming on the earth, giving a fresh smell to the leaves. And soon Sunktanka, the voice of the clubmen, signed for attention.

"The man-enemy," he began in a storytelling manner, "brings out the daring in a warrior, but a Titonwan shall display bravery in front of many different enemies."

His listeners waited through an ominous pause.

"Grass fires, blinding snows, rising rivers—these things often sneak up on the people. But I shall mention dangers you will not recognize easily."

Again, the dark pause.

"One never knows when he shall encounter Iktomi or what shape this trickster will assume. Perhaps you come upon a blind old man or perhaps you see a fine-looking youth who calls you 'uncle' and so wins your trust. Soon he makes you miserable and often laughs at you. Iktomi, the unreliable contact.

"But not more unreliable than a certain four-legged whom many warriors regard as a spirit-helper. On some occasions this one whom you call true-dog attacks whatever sits in front of him."

Sunktanka raised his voice, making himself heard above the rain that now pounded the earth. He began the story of a true-dog who discovered two Titonwan scouts during the tender-grass moon and attacked their camp at daybreak.

"One scout, they tell, grunts surprise an instant before the creature snaps his neckbone. When the second man tries rising from his sleeping robe, the dog comes at him, the fangs like white flashes, the teeth sinking into the scout's shoulder. Blood flows down this man's arm while the dog tears loose an ear. Nipping and retreating, nipping and retreating, the dog keeps at the scout, trying always for the man's throat."

Mahtociqala sat marveling the story, not so much the incident but that someone dares tell a story out of season and on a night when they camp within touch of the enemy.

430

The bleeding scout, Šunktanka went on, finally reached his knife and killed the crazed dog. Afterwards he remembered his need to chew a root of the white-wood if he intended to survive his wounding. And so, wrapping his slashed arm and shoulder with strips cut from his loin-cover and making a braid of his hair for binding the wounded ear tight against his head, he had dragged himself onto the grass in search of the life-saving root.

"The scout returns to his camp," Šunktanka said, lowering his voice again, "and they give him a new name; they relate him to the true-dog who bites in an unnatural manner. This man lives a long while and performs many brave acts, but"—Šunktanka made a howling sound—"always in the moon of tender grass he dreams of the dog and feels the fangs burning him like embers, sees the flashing teeth and crazy eyes and . . . "

Sensing a stir among his young listeners, the warrior stopped this narrative and began a different one; he will tie a funny story onto the frightening episode.

But this next story, Šunktanka told without words, his hands and his eyes expressing everything. Each man knows, he signed, that he needs take a weapon with him wherever he goes, even to the squatting-ground. And on a rainy night, as the enemy knows, such a place makes good ambush. Now this certain man will have trouble defecating. Three, four days his gut feels like someone ties knots here. And now again his efforts will not move him. He hears a sound in the brush but decides that the noise means a second man squats nearby.

All eyes had followed Šunktanka's hand-signs and smiles had broadened into grins; only the storyteller's face remained straight.

Then suddenly, the clubman's gestures told, a sharp lance strikes the squatter on his shoulder. He dares not move, yet something important begins moving, something that will go on moving. He empties himself as the lance pushes into his shoulder. If he wants to live, he needs pretend that the enemy kills him. Lacking bow or knife he needs drop where he squats. He needs fall onto his unkce. . . .

"I discover something stale about this camp." Wanapin's abrupt tone cut into the laughter. "The water here, dead." The war leader looked toward the sky. "Perhaps these clouds stay to tease whoever goes out for fresh water."

Each moccasin-boy held his breath. Whom will Wanapin ask to fill the water-sac, this sac they tie loosely to the tip of the red forked stick now in Wanapin's hands?

Mahtociqala became aware of eyes turned his way. The war leader seemed to point his chin toward him, not exactly at him but in his direction. And then he saw the sac dangling before his face. And heard Wanapin saying that the young son of Ogle shall enact this water-sac ceremony.

Now the scout they called Po came forward. Kneeling in front of the moccasin-boy, he marked the ground, his stick drawing the trail Mahtociqala shall take to the place where fresh water bubbles out of the earth.

Mahtociqala looked a long while at the picture, at the many hoof-trails crossing and recrossing. And so Po gave directions twice, the scout pointing carefully, speaking slowly, watching to see if Mahtociqala followed his thumb.

"If something puzzles you, speak," Wanapin encouraged.

The youth said nothing, and so Po handed him an arrow, something he shall leave at the water, proof that he had visited the designated place.

But as Mahtociqala moved out of the shelter, Hinyete's voice stopped him. "Remember, my son, that whatever you fear in the dark also fears you."

The son of Ogle stood a moment, then stepped into the black dripping night.

Moving along the rain-splashed path Mahtociqala told himself that a muddy night discourages any enemy; a man will not wander and the four-legs keep under cover. Who will sneak out in the wet after a moccasin-boy? Even the nose of the grizzly has difficulty on this sort of night and certainly the creature's eyes give little help. And why let an old story about a crazy true-dog crowd out the important things to remember?

The next instant he froze to the ground; something hid in the thick dark ahead, something that rattled the brush.

After what seemed a long while, a tall-ears hopped across the trail. Apparently this small creature with the berry-shaped nose had frozen under the brush and so waited to discover who among his enemies approached. And now Mahtociqala vowed to remember that which Hinyete had called out to him: whomever you fear in the dark fears you.

Patches of clear appeared in the sky, and the gentle rain that washed out Mahtociqala's tracks withdrew among the scattered clouds. And now the night listened tensely.

Somewhere nearby a rain-bird hooted and Mahtociqala saw this hushed-wing as in a picture—the bent nose, the night-watching eyes, the water dripping off feathers. The youth winked at the image and moved on.

Coming to a slope, he walked down slowly; he hunted a crowd of slender trees, something the scout's thumb had described. For here he shall look for a divide in the trail, one branch leading toward the bubbling water.

He found the divide and took the proper branch, leading north. And now he traveled under a round bright moon. Yet he sensed something disquieting. Suddenly he knelt to the ground and ran his finger over a small furrow, his keen eyes trying to relate this impression to something familiar. He lifted his head and listened closely when the rain-bird hooted again. And now he began a cautious advance along the tree-lined path.

His toe touched upon a sandy mound and he bent to this hill dwelling of those tiny shortneck bugs. And that which he saw with the moon's help made him certain that someone had used this trail shortly before him; someone who had dragged something hairy through the little sand-pile, perhaps the brush on the heel of a warrior's moccasin. But not a skunk's skin such as the Lakotah fastens to his heel and not the tail of the reddish-yellow little-dog that usually trails a Palani's foot. Here, instead, the brush of a true-dog. And if this sand yet holds the moccasin-shape—the dragging tail blurring but not obliterating the outline—he will know whether friend or enemy passes this place.

Again the moon offered him help. He saw where fringe on the bottom of a leg-cover had distorted the outside edge of the track but his fingers found enough pattern to identify the foot. The someone who preceded him on this trail, he knew now, wore the moccasin of a Miwatani, the enemy upriver.

Tensed for listening, he heard again the hooting sound, and so he crouched low, not frightened but puzzled. Those round-headed night-birds, showing regard for sleeping Lakotah, never make noise between midnight and dawn. Something different, then, hoots: Miwatani? Palani?

Always Mahtociqala relied upon his senses and so he recognized that he had come upon real danger, not a foolish fear born of stories in a rain shelter. But his senses had not told whether this danger sat front or behind him. Or, will he walk between two enemies, front and back?

Not if this repeating hoot proved as he suddenly had decided: someone from the war camp tricks him. And that someone risks meeting big trouble.

Crouching, he moved along slowly, feeling and listening. He alerted his ears to each dripping leaf and to whatever made noise-and-splash or rubbed wings to make song. None but the yielding mud shall know that he circles back, that he steps off the trail to stalk whoever stalks him.

Soon after he had turned around, bleeps and jumps revealed that something startled those small and big voices who left their posts at the edge and sprattled into the water of the little rain-pool. And all his senses told him that this 'something' walked on two legs.

Approaching a clump of clubgrass, Mahtociqala softly hooted, then waited for an answering call. None came, and so he crept close to the tall growth. Now for one startled moment he wondered whether the Miwatani also had circled back, whether he now glimpsed the enemy in the unmoving man-shape barely visible in the shadow of the clump.

One act remained: to sound warning that an enemy lurks nearby. But if his traveling-dog tremolo seems unnatural, whoever stalks him will know that man, not dog, emits the call. And if this one who stalks him, not a Lakotah. . . .

But the man-shape moved and Mahtociqala recognized the person of this 'rain-bird' who had followed out after him: Gnuśka.

"Nothing shall hurt my brother now that I come." Gnuśka said softly.

At this moment Mahtociqala sensed only irritation. They had sent him alone on this water-quest, and whatever danger or honor the experience held, the danger or the honor belonged only to him. But certainly he will advise that his warrior-brother return and notify the war camp concerning a Miwatani moccasin track, fresh this day on the north branch of the trail. Sand preserves the marks, he told Gnuśka, and trees protect from rain.

Gnuśka's quick response to this advice surprised Mahtociqala; his brother started back for camp without a word. But perhaps Gnuśka, regretting the moccasin-bundle incident, truly followed after Mahtociqala as a protector. Joyfully, then, the youth went on alone, the fresh water somewhere close by, his quest near a finish.

Gnuśka walked back to the warriors with a different heart; irked that Mahtociqala had discovered him, had rejected his protection, he approached the camp disgruntled. But suddenly his disposition changed; he remembered that if Mahtociqala acts in any way to endanger the men, Wanapin shall deal severely with him whether or not Iku approves. And so he shall say only that Mahtociqala reports a Miwatani moccasin, the youth choosing to follow after this track but that he will not want a companion.

Gnuśka approached the camp, his face impassive, his carefully phrased remarks ready for the leaders. But when he saw that Po and Pasu awaited him beyond the shelter, he reported quickly. The next instant Pasu disappeared, the scout on his way to ascertain the danger. To Mahtociqala, to the war party.

Mahtociqala had moved carefully along the muddy, slippery edge of the stream, thickets and young trees hampering his advance. Gently he pushed aside any branches; he left nothing broken or torn to mark his passing. And he stayed hidden from the moon.

Reaching the bubbling water, he bent at the hole to fill the heart-sac. The Miwatani had not paused here; Mahtociqala made certain before he set up the arrow-marker. Even so, he returned to camp in the same cautious manner he had gone out.

Po, watching for the water-carrier, signaled the youth into camp; leaders and warriors waited for him in the shelter.

Mahtociqala approach modestly; he intended to make a big contrast between this moment and the one when he splashed the water on Wanapin's face. And so, eyes unsmiling, he accepted the red pole Wanapin held out to him, the same stick but decorated with feathers at the fork. Then, attaching the sac as before, he turned the pole slowly, his one hand keeping hold the long cord around the sac. Now, as Wanapin bent to taste the water, Mahtociqala gave the cord a fast strong jerk. Water flew up onto the leader's face, into the man's eyes, and up his nose.

The warriors had begun their laughing before the water ever hit the man's face; Mahtociqala's unpretentious demeanor had not fooled anyone.

Wanapin, shaking his head briskly, threw the water from his cheeks. He blew his nose between his fingers and wiped his eyes on his arm. Then he regarded the straight-faced youth.

"This water-carrier imagines that he performs properly," he began severely, "when he . . ." But now Wanapin's face cracked into smiles and he joined in the spontaneity of the moment.

The laughing and the flashing embers died down together, the shelter and all within this place fading into dark and quiet.

The excitement had come to a finish and Mahtociqala yearned for a robe and sleep. But he knew to stand respectfully before these silent, cross-legged forms who passed the water-sac, each one touching the container to his lips.

After a while Wanapin spoke again. "This water-boy," he said, "walks through the night to an unfamiliar place and returns with a sweet drink. He alone knows whether or not fear joins him on the trail and he alone knows in what manner he loses any unwelcome companion."

Suddenly most attentive, Mahtociqala wondered whether the leader meant fear of the night or fear of the Miwatani. But what difference? A person either fears or not fears.

"This son and young brother," Wanapin went on, "moves forward on the straight path. Perhaps he will ask that certain ones who go before him point the way or advise,

436

but never will he ask that someone walk this path for him.

"All ears hear when I describe this path, but each man decides for himself what steps he will take and to which ledge he will climb.

"On this night the water-boy learns one way for showing bravery, but this way I regard as child's play. And so I reward him as a child."

Instantly Mahtociqala regretted the face-splashing act, but the men knew that the leader's speech put the youth's ordeal in a true-light; they recognized the hunt for fresh water as child's play but something important sat back of this experience. They watched Mahtociqala closely.

The youth, feeling their glances, raised his eyes and stood tall. Child's play or not, he had followed instructions and returned with a full sac. He had not become a body with which an enemy played games, as had happened to one water-sac carrier.

The warriors saw his eyes and noticed his tallness; they murmured approval.

Then Wanapin spoke again. "I and each of you calls himself brave but with what meaning? You fear nothing in the dark but will you fear darkness? You will not fear the truth but will you fear the search for truth?"

Next Wanapin spoke of the bravery they call courage. "Go out against an enemy you see, hear, touch, and they award you a feather, but the man who yields neither to angers nor lusts wears his honors on his heart.

"Endure pain, thirst, cold, and you will hear the crowd cheering, but what of the man who endures against whoever, whatever tries defiling his morals, corrupting his spirit? Who will cheer him?"

Mahtociqala strove for an understanding of the phrases pouring into his ears, but some things sat above his recognition.

Now the leader's eyes glanced over the men, hunting out any moccasin-boy who dared sleep while he talked or any warrior who appeared inattentive.

"Each Titonwan learns the staying-power," the man said next, "and so he endures when meat gets scarce, when snow piles deep, when the enemy sneaks up, when they deny him sleep." Wanapin intended to impress the moccasin-bearers in this party that the Titonwan try their own to the breaking point and so outsiders have little chance breaking down a Lakotah, even one who aches for rest.

But not until Wanapin began talking about the importance of the scout had Mahtociqala suddenly lost his drowsy feeling.

" . . . brother to the rain-bird, who knows all things under the sun and moon. And brother to those two blackbirds, the big one who soars on flat wings and the scolding little old grandmother bird who soars wings bending, each of these wingeds aware where everything hides.

"A scout learns to outwit the enemy; the cunning little red-yellow dog with black legs teaches him. But a scout also requires the wisdom of a true-dog, the coolness of the grizzly."

And now, listening to phrases that describe a scout, Mahtociqala saw himself wearing the 'waverer,' the feather that identifies the scout.

The scout, one with the standing-people: trees and grasses.

The scout, one familiar with sky language, the voice of cloud and wind.

The scout, someone who remembers that all the while he watches, someone watches him.

The scout, not a fighting man but one who will fight; the scout, not a healer, but one who knows that which heals.

A scout, one who permits neither cold, hunger, pain, nor the fear of these things to stop him. The bristling teeth of danger, say the grandfathers, never hinder a scout.

A scout, ears and eyes of the tribe; a scout, bearer of fact. The scout, truthbearer.

Mahtociqala, not remembering where he stood and not caring when he remembered, trembled his excitement at the joy of knowing his place in the tribe.

And one who saw this trembling, felt his own heart gladden: Ahbleza, who understands his young friend's dream; Ahbleza who 'acts like a true-brother to Mahtociqala,' as Mahtociqala twice had said.

Wanapin spoke next about warriors, his phrases pointing to honors these important tribesmen shall earn. And so Mahtociqala, remembering that his brother-friend strove for such attainments, listened closely once again.

"Certainly the people look for fighting prowess in a man," the pipe-bearer told this war party, "but they look also for a man who uses his wits. A true-warrior will not dash into combat until he counts the enemy, and he will back off if he sees more men than in his own party.

"Certainly the people look for a warrior to sing in the face of dying, but they will listen for a song of defiance, not a death song, not a song of resignation. Women sing death songs and only for someone who dies.

"Certainly the people hear the warrior shouting 'a good day to die,' but they know he will not go out looking for someone to kill him. A war party dares not claim victory if even one Lakotah dies, if the enemy kills even one man. All live and all return, or the raid, the avenging, means nothing. A good day to die, says the young warrior; a good day to defy, says his grandfather. Understand the meaning in this battle cry."

Mahtociqala had wondered about this thing when he heard his brother talk about a good day for dying. Now he understood but he wondered whether Gnuśka listened.

" . . . more bravery in touching than in killing an enemy," Wanapin went on. "The arrow has a long, safe reach; the arm has a short, daring one. But most acclaim comes to him who puts the enemy afoot and takes the horse."

The warriors sounded approval at these words, and now the leader broke his speech, permitting the men a stretch. They had sat a long while and he wanted none drowsing here.

As the group moved about, Mahtociqala stood quiet, uncertain whether or not they look for him to sit back with the moccasin-carriers or something different. Then he decided to find an inconspicuous place and . . .

Before he had walked five steps, Wanapin's voice struck his ears.

"Apparently I lose a moccasin-boy. Either his trial exhausts him or he already knows all I will say."

Mahtociqala hurried front again, the soft laughter of the men shaming his obvious confusion. Meekly he confronted the leader's austere face.

Suddenly, roughly, Wanapin grabbed the water-sac

pole from the youth's hands, holding the stick high above his head, the feathers dangling from the fork. "Wambli-feathers," he shouted, "from the tail of the flying-warrior. They belong to any man who demonstrates courage."

Exactly why all this shouting now Mahtociqala knew not, but certainly he remained standing; he wondered whether Wanapin intended to give back the stick if not the feathers.

At this point the leader changed over to talk about feasts and gifting. "The great warrior leaves behind him many cooking sacs, ladles, fire circles. He views his posses-sions as something he holds in readiness, gifts for comfort-ing the sorrowful, strengthening the lame. He regards noth-ing in his lodge as too precious for giving, nothing from which he dares not detach himself, whether the robe on his back or the woman who sits alongside him or the child born of his seed. He who aspires to the rank of leader gives until nothing remains but the joy he senses in gifting."

Perhaps everyone in the shelter recognized the impor-tance of gifts—certainly a man's standing in the tribe de-pends not on that which he owns but on that which he lets go—but that Wanapin made gifting the most exalting act puzzled certain ones.

These persons understood about honoring relatives—giving in the name of father or son, mother or sister—but they not yet truly comprehended 'ihom-niya.' Nor will they comprehend 'circulation,' the grandfathers said, until they relate the life-force to the flow of gifts. Stop the flow of anything—the circulating of blood or gifts—and disaster occurs. Give away until you have nothing—providing this form of generating good pleases you—but never give hold-ing back half, say the grandfathers, something or nothing, whole-heart or not at all.

Ahbleza sat pondering. Remembering the horse he had given at the sungazing, he tried to recall any joy born of this act. But will they hint that denying self brings about per-sonal gladness; will they mean that giving up something one cherishes brings personal joy to the giver? Or will the grandfathers say that man shall cherish himself and so give only when the act of giving renews his own spirit?

I honor my father when I stake my little horse at the sunpole, Ahbleza told himself, a gift for anyone who lacks a horse. But on the day I present Mahtociqala a horse, I will know true joy; I shall honor my choice and so honor myself.

Why this observation? Ahbleza knew only that he intended to pursue this thought.

Mahtociqala's attention, the water-sac pole, feathers intact, again in his hands, stayed on those phrases about gifting as a way of honoring relatives. In what manner will he who regards the wind and the drifting cloud his relatives honor such kinsmen?

" . . . one person not more important. Each Titonwan owns an important place in the tribe, none standing in the way of any different one. Clear the way; the straight path belongs to whoever will travel from warmth into the cold wind and back to warmth, back to the everblossoming earth from which man comes, toward which he always faces."

Strange talk for a war party, Mahtociqala told himself, but then almost everything about this experience proves different from that which he imagines. Perhaps the fighting will seem as strange as these events leading up to the encounter.

But that which Wanapin had spoken, they related at the initiation of each water-carrier. On these occasions the leader of the party reviewed the four ruling virtues of the people and hinted at a ceremony they reserve for the most great, for someone who will pledge his life as an example, for someone who will lead the one and the whole toward enduring peace.

Wanapin had finished speaking, and now the warriors left the shelter, rolling up in their robes, the whole party appearing as so many fallen trees under the moon-bright sky.

Mahtociqala had slept the instant he lay down but not Ahbleza; the talk had lifted him above any limiting concepts. Lead the one and the whole toward enduring peace? Ahbleza's heart had taken wings at those words and on those wings he had soared until he knew himself touching the clouds. But before he tasted the full sweetness of his flight, he had felt himself falling, his body plunging earthward from the top of the sky. They had brought him down with one swift far-reaching arrow. They? He wished that he dared call this shuddering moment a dream, but he knew that he had not slept. Certainly, this whole thing, his imagination, but why imagine himself dying on a night when he experiences so much gladness for the safe return of his brother-friend?

Halfway through the next morning scouts who had gone upon a hill signaled their discovery of a small herd that moved, scattered and uneasy, toward a hollow.

At once Wanapin led the warriors into a gully, men and horses hiding while the clubmen inspected the trail ahead. But the party soon moved out again.

When day sat overhead, the men witnessed more robe-talk, Po and his companion Pasu reporting a small village of Miwatani who hunted on the far side of the plain. Women, children, and lodges, but these people had not yet caught up with the pte-herd. Then making crooked little dashes on the hillside, these scouts clarified their intention to return and give the news in proper manner. And so the leaders found a protected spot to await the scouts. The warriors had come looking for the enemy but not this soon.

During the wait Mahtociqala approached his brother and, talking-sign, expressed excitement over the discovery of the Miwatani; perhaps a scout from this enemy village had made the moccasin track on the water-trail?

But Gnuśka answered scoffingly. "I report the tracks my young brother claims he discovers. They make nothing of your find. They know I will strike down any enemy who tries intercepting you. And if I receive an arrow in my back, they know I will die singing. I will die this day if my act brings honor to the tribe." The young warrior had spoken quickly, his words almost a whisper, but seeing someone look his way, he raised his voice slightly. "Who wants the aching tooth or the wobbling feet of an old man?"

Mahtociqala looked wonderingly at Gnuśka, but his brother's next remark puzzled him even more. "Your Miwatani scout perhaps recognizes my hooting, but find me? Never!"

But will Gnuśka not remember that he, the moccasin-boy, locates the 'rainbird'? And that Gnuśka's hoots nearly bring on big trouble for the two sons of Ogle? And the war party?

Gnuśka stepped away, and now Mahtociqala pondered

his brother's willingness to die on the water-trail when a whole fighting ground awaited him this day or the next. What honor in dying while playing a joke on someone? And what about all those men who grow old honorably and never sit around complaining or leaning on a support-stick? They call these old men 'grandfather,' meaning wise one, and send the young to seek their advice. Truly, Gnuśka looks out from a strange viewpoint if he really wishes to die now.

The leaders and their advisers walked forward to meet the returning scouts, and Mahtociqala, watching the group file out, envied these blotahunka who receive the truthbearers ceremoniously.

But now one of the clubmen called out Mahtociqala's name, his name for the duration of the expedition; they want him to prepare a fire. Iku, his uncle, held out a soft flat slab of dry wood and a hard twirling stick, and some dry chips lay nearby for feeding the flame.

Mahtociqala stepped forward; he signaled for powdered-wood, then crouched and began his work. Suddenly the meaning of his assignment came to him: his fire determines the center of the ceremony for the reporting scouts. The blotahunka honor him and so he shall go about his task proudly.

He handled the fire-tools with an ease that surprised everyone. A tiny smoke appeared, then the flame; soon the chips held fire.

Someone tapped his shoulder; Wanapin, holding forth a pipe-bowl, asked for an ember.

Solemnly, using his water-sac pole, Mahtociqala lifted a glowing piece. The leader sucked on the stem as the scouts came running.

Po dropped to his knee at the fire and so the clubmen knew that Po will smoke, will make the report.

The pipe, traveling next among the clubmen, came back into Wanapin's hand, the leader now offering the stem to Mahtociqala's lips.

The youth took his first puff of smoke as if he dreamed this experience. But he saw the pipe laid on a chip and he heard the scout begin his report.

Afterwards, Po repeated the facts for the whole party

and Mahtociqala noticed that the truthbearer's thumb and phrases retold the story exactly as before, not a gesture, not a sound any different from the original telling. But that which occurred next made the youth wonder about his ears: Wanapin proposed a torch dance.

The same moment Mahtociqala smiled. They only tease, the warriors joking when they say that the moccasin-boys shall provide torches for this ceremony. Who ever hears of burning torches and dancing on enemy ground before an attack?

A demanding grunt answered his thought, a sound that sent him scrambling for torch-wood.

While the youths hunted stakes to light the dancing, the warriors moved behind a cluster of trees. Here they dipped greasy fingers into the sacs of coloring-powder, then streaked their faces and bodies, each man painting as a dream had described or as an akicita-lodge required.

Ahbleza had not painted, but Mahtociqala, coming up quietly, found the brother-friend tying a small mystery-bundle into the mane of the amazing yellow horse.

"I have something for a certain moccasin-carrier." Ahbleza spoke without turning to see who stood near. "Whatever power protects my horse shall protect his." Glancing now at Mahtociqala, he extended his palm. "Tie this bundle onto the tail of your horse."

Mahtociqala accepted the tiny sac. But, his eyes on Ahbleza, he twisted strands of his own hair and tied the sac to this braid. And now, before the warriors came looking for him, he returned to their midst, ready to run errands.

At the moment, the men requested wasna from the meat containers, but the moccasin-boys, eager to impress different ones among the warriors, jumped in response to any demand—bring meat, repair a torn moccasin, fill a water-sac. For the one whom they please will perhaps step aside when the fighting begins and so grant a certain boy his chance to strike the enemy or capture a horse.

Mahtociqala offered help but not in return for favors. Instead, he waited on Iku, his uncle, and Gnuśka, his brother, men of his tiyośpaye and near his heart. They will look out for him, even Gnuśka who means good but . . .

The youth puzzled his thought. Why say "but"? Everyone knows that 'brother' means protector; certainly Gnuśka intends to take care of him, to stop tricking and teasing.

Four warriors had sat down close together, two of these men stretching taut a piece of hide, the other two slapping with their fingers to make the sound of drum.

Iku, standing near Mahtociqala as the warriors began their dance, spoke in the youth's ear. "My nephew makes the water-quest and brings wood to this dancing place. Now the men demand that he dance."

But Mahtociqala, confused, moved back. Scouts had reported pte and a hunting village chasing this herd, yet the warriors dance as if neither meat nor enemy concern their lives? Perhaps the flame of torches blends with the stretching rays of the sun but certainly a Miwatani scout will smell smoke.

Zola, a quirt in his hand, danced out of the circle and, approaching Mahtociqala, flicked the thongs across the youth's legs. But the moccasin-carrier, embarrassed, stayed where he stood.

The warrior came twice and now he lashed vigorously at these legs, the sting of the whip compelling Mahtociqala to lift his heels.

"Dance with the warriors," someone called out, and so the youth understood the whip as something to get his feet moving, get him into the dance.

Suddenly persuaded that they scheme not to ridicule but to honor him, Mahtociqala jumped among the dancing men with a furious stomping. He scowled, intending that his naked face take on a threatening look, something like the paint-fierce faces all around him. The drumming reached into his head and tightened his throat. Next thing, the beat took hold of his heart—or perhaps his heart took hold of the beat; whichever, his moccasins struck the ground, toe and heel, toe, heel, toe-heel, fast as a running horse. And his heart, loud as the pounding of his feet.

The warriors, their eyes approving, remembered that someone who dances with such vigor attracts the attention of an akicita-lodge.

The lead-singer finished the song, and the dancers, hearing the soft taps on the tightly spread hide, waited in the circle of torchlight.

Once again Mahtociqala stood uncertain where to go, where to sit. But then he heard someone hinting that he re-enact his water-quest.

Once again he stood shy, his legs numb; never before had he recited an act; he will not know what they look for.

He saw Zola among the watching men, the quirt swinging gently from his hand. He will not permit the warrior to whip his legs twice this day; he will make the effort to put on a show.

His starting movements pictured the rain, the muddy trail, the clearing sky. Then he acted out the discovery of the moccasin-track. Next, he let his viewers hear the rain-bird and see his meeting with Gnuśka. He dramatized his arrival at the bubbling water and his return with the full sac. He finished off the story with a whoop, then remembered that they demand a witness to a warrior's acts. He signed for Gnuśka to bear out these facts.

But the one coming forward—Olepi. And in the Mahto's hand, three giftsticks, something that three of the moccasin-carriers shall exchange for war bows upon the party's return to camp.

The Mahto leader's surprising act keenly affected Mahtociqala; he sought again an obscure place back of the burned-down torches.

But none noticed where Mahtociqala secluded himself; the men awaited something of much importance to this war party. Someone will tap out these warriors whom the clubmen had chosen for special acts of bravery during the fight with the enemy.

And so four men soon felt the blow of Zola's palm on their shoulders, and next, a ceremony more surprising to Mahtociqala than anything he yet witnessed.

Two of the four men Zola had tapped wore yellow paint but for their legs and arms, which they had blackened. These Tokala held high rank in the akicita-lodge; one man displayed the Tokala hairstyle, his head bald on either side, a narrow thumb-tall tuft running front to back. The second man grasped a Tokala lance.

Wanapin stepped out in front, the leader's face and body painted in the same manner as these two to whom he now spoke: "The Tokala walk abreast of danger."

At once Iku and Źola, also in Tokala colors, moved up alongside Wanapin, each one holding a bent lance, the pole wrapped with skin, bunches of feathers tied on at many places.

Wanapin gazed at the impassive faces: "Whoever receives the crook-lance will touch, perhaps kill, an enemy."

The leader's voice commanded, but the warriors knew that neither this man nor any different one ever shall force a lance upon someone not agreeable.

"One man stands here," Wanapin said after a pause, "holding a Tokala lance. I ask him something: will he exchange his lance for that which I offer? Never will he accept anything of more importance than the emblem I present him. The man who carries the Titonwan lance bears the courage of this war party, of the whole tribe."

The ones who had sung for the dancing began the lance song, something without words but with sounds more effective than words. And while these singers performed the lance song, Iku and Źola watched the Tokala for any sign of reluctance, for any hint of apprehension.

Suddenly the clubmen thrust the bent lances into the open hands of these Tokala whom Źola had tapped out, whoops and cheers easing the tension.

Next, Olepi stepped out and began speaking to the third and fourth man struck on the shoulder. To these persons he offered small rattles, a symbol that obligated the bearer to act in the same manner as a lanceman; he imposed the same trust on these two, members of the Iyuptala-lodge, as on the two Tokala-lodge members.

The Iyuptala stood in red moccasins. They wore black stripes at wrists and elbows and a third black stripe crossed the forehead, from one cheekbone to the other. And on one man's shoulder, the staking-sash. True, staking one's self before the enemy had become a thing of choice, not obligation; who will not remember Heħloǵeca's sash-wearers? But Heħloǵeca had founded the Iyuptala soon after the Psa avenging and members of this high-ranking brother-lodge occasionally chose the stake to emphasize the lodge-rule that none joins this group who will not willingly risk his life in defense of a brother-member.

But Ahbleza sat pondering the hearts of these men,

these four who pledged to touch the enemy, to kill or get killed. Will these warriors move out joyfully, content whatever happens? Or will they hide a fear beneath that yellow paint, those black stripes? Not fear of the enemy but fear of a sudden weakening, an overwhelming desire to turn and run? Once a lance-bearer, rattle-bearer, starts out, he knows that the party will scorn his turning back.

What thing determines bravery? Fear of ridicule? Or will a man answer only to himself, ignoring different eyes? Will he look for approval in . . .

The young warrior felt a hand on his shoulder; Hinyete will see him rise, stand alongside the two Tokala, the two Iyuptala who already pledge their loyalty.

The singers, beginning another courage song, sang softly and so Hinyete spoke above these voices, the warrior saying that he had decided to choose someone from among the young who carry unfeathered lances, a fifth man whom they ask to touch or kill the enemy. "This man, also shall accept a symbol. Perhaps someone here will offer the son of Olepi a pipe."

Ahbleza's thumping heart echoed on each side of his forehead. Why will they ask this thing of him before he makes the vision-quest? Who encourages this rashness?

The singing ceased and Olepi stood before his son, the man holding out the Iyuptala pipe; Olepi, pipe-bearer for the Iyuptala-lodge and privileged to offer the stem.

The pipe touched against Ahbleza's fingers, and he took hold as if this one thing will support him in his wavering moments. His belly fluttered and a watery weakness, creeping down to his knees, loosened these joints; his bowels quivered and gave him concern.

But the warriors saw only that Ahbleza's face wore that impenetrable calm behind which each Lakotah learns to hide his true feelings.

Hinyete removed the pipe from Ahbleza's clasp and laid the stem on the father's open palms; Olepi's son, pledged now beyond any change of heart to meet the enemy, to strike or kill.

But the warriors had not cheered as they had cheered the other four; even the singers sat quiet. And Ahbleza, his fingers curled as when he held the pipe, sensed a strange cold numbing him, depriving his legs and arms of movement.

Then someone spoke saying that the Síyo seer who had come along to prophesy shall reveal the outcome of this encounter with the enemy. At once a messenger-boy for the blotahunka placed a pipe against the sacred-man's head. And soon the assemblage heard the 'hi-ye' which signified the seer's willingness to begin his predictions.

Ahbleza sat with the pledged four while the man sang those events which he foresaw occurring and the warriors listened closely, more than one person with a hand across his mouth as he marveled the prophecy.

"You will want scalps for a dance," he told, "and so make certain you kill the enemy who rides a horse with three white legs and a bald face. A man on a white horse comes looking for you; see that he dies. A third enemy falls, but I see none dying among the Titonwan."

The warriors sat on; they looked for the seer to gaze into a bowl of melted fat and then glance up with warnings. But the Síyo had finished his prophecy.

And now, before the men began wondering about any omissions, the blotahunka advised that the party move on, passing beyond the divide in the river, finding sleep in some little canyon. Not likely will an enemy risk pursuit of this war party, a party so obviously confident that the members dare perform their rituals in a most conspicuous manner. Even to a torch dance on enemy hunting grounds.

Mahtociqala lay next to Ahbleza, his eyes on the sky. Like other members of the party, he had drunk enough water to compel his awakening before dawn and then he had rolled up in his robe. But unlike the other persons, he had not covered his head; he enjoyed the sky, the clouds his protector. And he had wondered whether each man lying here sent a voice in search of spirit-help. He had heard someone blowing on a wingbone whistle and a different someone whispering a song. The true-dog, they say, lends spirit-power to a warrior and the wambli-bird also gives protection. As for the scout, will not all creatures watch over the truthbearer?

The youth turned his head toward Ahbleza; perhaps the brother-friend also lay wakeful?

"They will permit my taking an enemy's horse," Mahtociqala murmured.

Ahbleza uncovered his head. "The clubmen will advise that you keep your eyes on Titonwan horses," he answered quickly, too quickly.

One of the men who watched over the sleeping war party glanced toward the whisperers.

But Ahbleza spoke again. "Fear not, my young brother. The enemy horses will not run more swiftly than your horse nor will the enemy warriors prove more brave than you. Remember this thing and you will fear nothing."

"I am not afraid."

Ahbleza's answer puzzled the youth. Or perhaps the son of Olepi speaks only to remove any uneasiness relative to the approaching contest; perhaps Ahbleza imagines that concern over the approaching fight keeps the moccasin-boy awake? Mahtociqala, now covering his head, rolled onto his side, instantly asleep.

And so Ahbleza the one who lay with eyes open. True, he spoke reassuring words, but for his own ears, his own calm. He had pledged his life to kill or die this next day—he and four different warriors—but he will not understand why his father held forth a pipe and so made the son's privilege to refuse something he dared not even consider. What manner of son denies his father's request?

True, this party sought revenge for a man whom he, Ahbleza, called relative. But will revenge always mean killing any one? Why not kill only the killer?

He remembered again the fear-filled eyes of the Psa woman from whom he had taken moccasins and a robe; will he feel differently about killing this next day?

While the warriors ... and bows and dance. Slayers

ONE LAKOTAH way of attacking an enemy called for watching the enemy while they hunt, waiting for the hunters to
wear out their horses. When finally they separate for skinning meat and packing the load, a party of Lakotah will
come out of hiding and intercept each small group. The
scheme almost always worked.

And so when the Titonwan scouts reported a Miwatani
village moving after pte, Wanapin and his advisers had
pictured the exact conditions they desired; they will permit
the enemy to catch up with the herd and make their kills
before the Titonwan attack. Those affairs, then, which had
astonished Mahtociqala—the torch dance at dusk, the tap-
ping-out, the seer's ceremony—a strategic delay, schemes to
slow the war party's advance without loss of enthusiasm for
combat.

The leaders, acting under a sky that held off dawn,
began to divide the warriors into groups, two clubmen
attending each group. The scheme demanded twenty foot-
going men in advance of twenty who will ride. The horsebacks, moving slow to prevent a big dust, shall scatter in
gullies along the way. Wanapin and Olepi keeping watch on
the walking men, will send out riders to any warrior in
difficulty, these horsebacks also going out after any fleeing
Miwatani.

"You will discover to which thing this enemy attaches
more importance, his belly or his hair," Wanapin said dryly;
"most likely he will run, preferring to leave the meat and
keep his scalp."

The party moved out smiling and arrived at the butte
before daybreak. Here the warriors twisted their forelocks
away from their eyes and laid aside robes and loin-covers.
Let the enemy have nothing to grab on to, Wanapin had
said. Then someone reviewed those instructions they had
heard back at the sleeping place; the clubs will make certain
that each man understands the scheme.

While the warriors examined bows and lances, Hinyete spoke to the moccasin-boys.

"Two shall act as message-bearers," he said, "and come with me. Five stay. They shall hold the horses here until the returning warriors rush in with the captive herd. If the enemy pursues, the moccasin-carriers shall push on with the horses. The warriors will stay back and fight."

The speaker knew that he had disheartened these boys who eagerly awaited the fight, but the inexperienced and men with slow horses always drew the unattractive work.

Hinyete observed these faces now for any sign of protest, any sign of fear. And he looked especially close at those youths who twice before accompanied a war party.

The war adviser spoke again. "The party will regroup at the scene of the torch dance. You know the place. Here the leaders will wait for any missing persons."

Once more his stern eyes touched on each moccasin-carrier. "The blotahunka chooses the loss of every horse to the loss of any one man."

He returned to the warriors, the two messengers going with him.

And now the foot-going men came up with their horses, the moccasin-boys at once active, quieting these excited creatures whom the warriors left in their care.

One of the Iyuptala who had accepted a lance the night before brought his mount to Mahtociqala, and the youth, seeing the sash-loop over the man's shoulder, wondered why any warrior saw fit to risk his life in this manner.

Iku and Źola led up their horses and so Mahtociqala understood that these two go with the men who walk; Hinyete and Śunktanka stay mounted, going with the men who ride. But where goes Ahbleza? Gnuśka?

An unfamiliar feeling clutched Mahtociqala's throat and took hold on his belly. He felt secure in the presence of these persons, but without Ahbleza around will not some sort of danger devour him?

He tried laughing at his fear, but that which had worked on the water-trail will not work here. He ran from the horses in his care; he looked for Ahbleza.

But Źola's harsh rebuke, the man's quirt-hand raised, returned the youth to reason. Mahtociqala hurried back to the horses, who, sensing a tense camp, stamped and made noise. Certain ones required staking; others will respond to a calm hand and gentle voice. And so Mahtociqala, at work quieting these creatures, found a way to quiet his own unrest.

Wanapin brought his horse to the tenders, the blotahunka advising that he join the men on foot, that Olepi lead the horsebacks. And now everyone awaited a signal from the scouts atop the butte.

Looking toward the mounted half of the party, Mahtociqala saw that Ahbleza and Gnuśka sat with this group. His sigh of relief echoed from his ribs; the horsebacks, he recalled, stay in the gully until someone needs help. But then he remembered that his brother-friend had touched the pipe, Ahbleza pledged to meet the enemy. And so fear hit at his belly again.

Feeling himself about to gag, the youth turned his head and so he missed seeing the scouts signal forward the twenty on foot. But he heard the clubs who controlled the horsebacks yelling something in the directions of the horsetenders. Perhaps they yell at him; perhaps they invite him to ride?

Not likely, he told himself grimly. One glimpse of me and they know that I leave my daring, in the shape of words, back in my mother's lodge.

But the akicita yelled again, then came riding up, clubarms raised. And now Mahtociqala noticed that those two moccasin-carriers out with their third party had disappeared; apparently they had sneaked out after the twenty warriors on foot.

The clubs made a brief search but the runaways managed to elude their pursuers. Whoever went out against orders risked harsh treatment, but if these same youths encountered the enemy and lived, they knew that they need never again carry moccasins for a war party.

"Why will you not go? You carry a lance that protects you."

Amazed, Mahtociqala heard the two remaining tenders hint that he, also, sneak out. Nor had he looked upon the red pole as wotawe, as a protecting power. If anything protects him, the bundle Ahbleza made for the horse but which he tied in his own hair effects his safety.

But will the lance, as his companions say, hold a

power? Why not find out? He desires becoming scout, not warrior, but they say that a scout occasionally needs to fight. And certainly he wants one warrior-act for reciting at those feast fires where they will not welcome a man who has nothing to tell. Perhaps someone among the horsebacks looking over at him now sees that he, Mahtociqala, rediscovers his daring. He glanced toward the gully.

The horsebacks? The men had gone.

His hand on his mouth, the astonished youth gazed at the place where moments before twenty men had sat their mounts. He, Mahtociqala, who boasts that nothing crawls in the grass but what he hears, nothing hops in the brush but what he sees. Yet twenty horsebacks move out without his awareness. What manner of scout will he call himself?

In sudden excitement he kicked his horse in the ribs and dashed along the trail at the bottom of the butte.

Quickly Šunktanka came upon Mahtociqala; jerking the thong from the youth's hands, he quirted horse and rider back where they belonged.

"Two different moccasin-carriers place this war party in danger but not you." The clubman spoke severely and Mahtociqala waited for the man to destroy his bow or in some way humiliate him. But Šunktanka rode off; he will not look for this youth to make a fool of himself twice.

And now Mahtociqala recognized his importance as horse-tender; they trusted him with the care of the horses in the same manner they trusted different ones with the care of lance and rattle. He touched the little knot of power tied in his hair and he stroked the water-sac pole; his fingers closed on the bone knife at his waist. He smiled; whenever the warriors returned, he stood ready for whatever danger returned with these men.

Mahtociqala had a short wait. A messenger, racing up on a panting horse, shouted to the horse-tenders that the enemy pursued. Some Miwatani broke away; they chased after the men who captured their hunting horses, these Mahto warriors now engaged in a running fight.

At once the excited youths began pulling up stakes, crowding the horses into a tight band while earth and air carried the noise of the contest to their ears. And then two Mahto came rushing in, waving at the horse-tenders, sending out the herd.

Mahtociqala kept his horse at a fast run, his quirt demanding that she pick up her feet, his whoops encouraging her to keep abreast the other drivers. He heard yells back of him and the occasional crack of a shooting-stick. He looked around but the dust shut off his view.

Then from out this thick yellow cloud came a group of riders and for one startling moment he imagined the enemy upon him. But the men racing past him—Titonwan.

Bending low, he spoke to the foaming little creature; he warned that she shall find catching up more difficult than keeping up and that he will use the quirt vigorously on her back legs.

But the horse lacked the strength either to keep up or catch up, her most swift run not swift enough. She fell back, and now the war cries at the youth's rear overtook the whooping in front.

He rode alone and in a shaky place. He sat between two dusts, between those Titonwan who drove the horseband and those Titonwan who joined in the running fight. And he knew that the enemy, like the traveling-dog, will cut in between these two dusts maneuvering to reach the horses, turn the herd. One arrow will put a lone boy out of their way.

Mahtociqala needed to decide quickly: reverse his path and join the fighting ones, or . . .

Instead, he acted on impulse; he slowed for a turnabout. But someone rode in from the side, an enemy horseback who will get to him.

He saw a glittering, like stars, in the stranger's hair and a black line circling the man's mouth. And the rider's clubhand, high and whirling.

He prepared for the onrushing enemy; why try outrunning this one? But he will ride zigzag and so become an uneasy target. And he will shake his water-sac stick; perhaps some spirit-power will lend help.

Twisting from side to side, the youth managed to dodge one blow. But seeing the enemy's arm swing forward, he bent over the neck of the little horse.

Something most unlike a war club came at him, something that thudded to the ground in front of his mount. The terrified creature jumped over the fallen body only to bump against the dead man's horse. Mahtociqala slid off, yet he

455

neither fell nor let go his stick. Using a quickness born into him and enhanced through practice, he grabbed the cord trailing from the enemy's mount, his bow-hand clutching the water-sac stick as before.

The enemy's horse reared, jerking the youth off balance. But he reached for the creature's tail. Now dropping the stick, he used two hands to make his jump onto the big horse's rump, forward onto the back.

Next thing, Gnuśka rode alongside him, his brother's voice raised in a shrill war cry. But will this cry tell that Gnuśka puts the arrow into the enemy who tries killing Mahtociqala?

Holding the horse to a lope, the youth slipped halfway down the creature's side to grab for his lance, his water-sac stick, then race back to where the dead man lay.

He reached the body at the same moment that Gnuśka dashed up, brother witnessing for brother as each one struck the Miwatani. But Gnuśka had permitted Mahtociqala to touch the body before he struck this same one.

Moccasin-carrier turning warrior! Mahtociqala flung back his head, his white teeth gleaming in the sun. What more challenging place to look than at the sky?

They call this exalting moment, war? War, they say, a path to honor through danger. What danger? Not danger, only glory. Where, this one they call enemy? Takpe. Let Mahtociqala at him. Mahtociqala's power surpasses the enemy's power. Mahtociqala owns the sharp knife and the fast horse. And the power.

The youth heard a shout, a warning. Who comes? Will a different Miwatani dare approach this body, this one whom Mahtociqala touches with his water-sac lance?

The Miwatani came, an enemy who rode forward singing, a Miwatani who will try saving his tribesman's scalp, who will risk his own.

Mahtociqala spit out taunts, yelling that which he heard the warriors say about tribes who plant maize.

"Woman. I call you woman. You feed the Titonwan."

And now, like a painted-wing who flutters into the path of a flycatcher, Mahtociqala pranced toward the enemy.

One who carried a symbol-lance saw Mahtociqala lift the water-sac pole, saw the inexperienced youth fling himself at danger. And so this brave Mahto jumped from his horse, whooping as his feet touched ground. His weapon strung, he let go.

The Miwatani, an arrow ready for the foolish boy who came at him, heard the whoop; the cry diverted his aim.

Mahtociqala, seeing the bow in the enemy's hand, laughed and pulled his knife; he lunged out, slicing at the Miwatani's throat. But the enemy dropped off his horse; an arrow had brought him down. Someone had killed before the knife ever touched his neck.

Will Gnuśka make this second killing? Truly his brother Gnuśka fears nothing this day. The youth turned to meet his brother's eyes for a moment of rejoicing. But Gnuśka, not in view.

Different Titonwan rushed up furiously, each man wanting a place within the four who touch the dead or dying enemy. And again Mahtociqala saw his chance; twice on this wonderful day he shall strike an enemy. Why not?

He heard shouts back of him, something he mistook for cheering. But then Hinyete rode up, his quirt lifted as if to strike not the dead but the youth who approached the dead.

"Out of the way," he ordered.

The command puzzled Mahtociqala. He pulled out of the fighting but he knew not where to go; where will they want him?

He caught sight of Gnuśka. His brother sat a horse who ran in a circle, the creature moving one direction as if his rider, sleeping, pulled the guiding thong one way.

Then he understood; something had happened to the warrior. And now, whatever order they call at him, whatever the punishment when they see him ignoring that order, he goes to Gnuśka.

Not accepting that which he saw, Mahtociqala stared at the arrow in his brother's breast, an enemy shaft with a red spiral line that resembled blood pouring out, an arrow that twisted Gnuśka's face into an unnatural grimace.

A shout brought the youth to his senses; Ahbleza had come up on the opposite side of the wounded man. Gnuśka's fingers had released their hold on the horse's mane and either someone on each side of the slumping form grabbed him or Gnuśka fell.

The brother-friends reached out to take hold of the limp body even as the startled horse in the center leapt forward. And now all child-games horseback, every riding trick, became of use in this rescue. Keeping abreast the frightened horse, Mahtociqala and Ahbleza maneuvered their legs, arms, body for balance, protection, self-defense.

And so these three horses and riders raced across the plain like some giant creature who sprouted legs in six directions, something the enemy hesitated to chase.

When at last the war cries seemed far to the rear, Ahbleza skillfully brought Gnuśka's mount and his own in close step with Mahtociqala, slowing all three to a halt.

And now the rescuers' eyes met, but nothing on Mahtociqala's face intimated that he saw glory in anything here. Here, he viewed the different side of war. War meaning Gnuśka's like-dead body, something Ahbleza now tied onto the horse. War meaning a quiet ride back to the site where warriors gather at the finish of the avenging. War, not a joke, and dying, something serious. But will not the grandfathers say so?

The leaders counted their warriors: none missing.

The sacred-man had foreseen something, but he had not gone far enough with his prophesying; he had not predicted that one Titonwan warrior shall return sadly wounded.

The scalps, exactly as the seer had foretold. Here, hair from the enemy on a white horse, and here, a scalp from him who sat the bald-face with three white legs, these two killed while resisting attack near their meat packs.

Also dead, the man whose horse Mahtociqala now rode, and the brave Miwatani who had come forward to save his relative's hair.

A Titonwan had tied one scalp to his loin-cover string, a different one hung a scalp from a war club; and they stood eager to talk their exploits. And those warriors tapped out waited to report in what manner they had met their trust.

But the leaders showed concern only for the wounded man; injuries they accept, but not the loss of a warrior, killed or captured.

And so they called on the seer to examine the shaft hanging in Gnuśka's breast, an arrow they dared not jerk out through the wound, a point they dared not let stay long in the warrior's body.

The barely visible edge of the arrowhead appeared thick and solid, perhaps one the Miwatani had made from an iron container for grinding maize, something the waśicun had brought into their camp. The maize-growers, scouts had told, broke up such grinders to make points.

The sacred-man knew ways for removing the shaft but not this point and neither Wanapin nor Olepi will handle this danger. The Mahto's dream had warned him to stay away from anything that the whitemen touch; nor will he know more about extracting the point than any other man here.

After a little while the seer made his report. The condition, he said, calls for a peźuta-wicaśa; perhaps Śunihanble will effect this cure.

Iku's heart chilled; Gnuśka's wound, apparently something outside the help of this seer, and Śunihanble, back in the Titonwan camps.

A murmur rose among the young warriors. Glancing at Gnuśka's unmoving form, they schemed to hide him in a clump of trees, water and meat at his side if ever he awakened from his strange sleep. But Mahtociqala had made a silent vow that if Gnuśka stays, he stays back with Gnuśka; his brother's arrow had saved him from the enemy's bow.

But now Olepi put a finish to this confusion. "What happens here?" He spoke sharply. "Will you paint this young warrior's face red while his body yet feels warm? Stop the death-talk or you will encourage his sleeping spirit to prepare him for dying."

The Mahto leader now chose the scout Pasu, uncle to Gnuśka, to run ahead of the party. Let Pasu request that Śunihanble meet the returning warriors at a halfway place.

Pasu started out at once, carrying a pipe, the bowl pressed against him. Olepi had smeared the stem black and hung a feather at the mouthpiece; perhaps the peźuta will smoke his willingness to travel back with the scout.

The blotahunka, talking together, had decided that the party move on foot, each man leading his horse while on enemy hunting ground. The eighteen horses they capture shall herd at the rear of the procession.

These same men had advised that four persons carry Gnuśka on a robe, a man at each corner and walking gently. And so the party shall proceed toward the Titonwan hoop.

The returning warriors had not stopped for any lengthy sleep; their second night's rest, barely a nap.

Mahtociqala had laid his robe nearby Ahbleza, but body-nearness to this brother-friend not enough; his troubled spirit sought comfort.

"Whose shame but mine that my brother lies as if dead," he said softly. "My father asks whether I am ready for war. Now I wonder. My slow little horse, my foolish run at the enemy ... my acts and so my brother perhaps dies. ..."

"If he dies," Ahbleza answered, "you will remember the honors he wins in the fighting. Not often will a man stay horseback, keep on going when an arrow sticks in his breast."

Next day the party stopped for rest at a wooded place and again Mahtociqala showed his brother-friend an anxious face. Will they scheme to leave Gnuśka's sleeping body here?

Ahbleza smiled. "The seer advises a more comfortable carrier. The men stop here to cut poles."

But Mahtociqala had observed with what frequency the seer pulled up Gnuśka's eyelids; perhaps the sacred-man wondered whether the warrior's spirit ever will return. This advice, then, about making a litter concerned the good of the party, not the hurt warrior. For certainly the party will travel more rapidly with Gnuśka's robe tied onto two long poles, a man at each tip bearing the load with help of a forehead-band.

Before they laid Gnuśka on the new carrier, the sacred-man bent over the wounded body and shook a rattle near the warrior's ear. Gnuśka had not responded.

"The seer brings powders with him. Why will he not try these things when he sees that the rattle changes nothing?" Once again Mahtociqala let Ahbleza hear his concern.

"Perhaps the seer knows, my friend, that neither rattle nor powders will renew your brother."

But that which Ahbleza said next, puzzled Mahtociqala more than ever.

"Your brother proves himself brave against the enemy. Facing someone who will kill you, wound you, takes courage. But facing someone who will heal you perhaps takes more courage."

And now, after a fourth night of travel, the scout Pasu hurried in, Sunihanble and his assistant close behind.

The seer, preparing a place for the healing ceremony, had spread a circle of sage where they will lay Gnuśka. And he had mellowed a space of earth for whatever sacred use the peźuta will make of this ground. Nearby, little piles of sweetgrass sent up a fragrant smoke.

Presently Sunihanble's helper signaled that they place Gnuśka gently on the sage. Next thing, let the warriors form a hoop around this one with an arrow fast in his breast.

Quickly the men acted, then stood as a circle, the helper and the wounded man inside the hoop.

The helper wore red paint and the bushy tail of the reddish-yellow little-dog dragged from his loin-flap. Now, shaking his rattle, he made a yelping sound. Then, crouching near the mellow-earth, he began a song, yelping at the finish of each phrase.

Suddenly Sunihanble appeared, body and face painted red; he, also, wore the brush of the red-yellow little-dog.

He walked slowly around inside the circle, a small drum in his hand. And wherever he walked, the men heard creature-cries. Then, moving toward his helper, he held out the drum.

The young assistant, not once interrupting his song, laid the rattle on the mellow earth and accepted the drum.

Sunihanble washed his hands in the sweet smoke; he approached the wounded man. Dropping onto one knee, he gazed at the arrow and the festered skin. He bent his face to the injury.

Mahtociqala stood outside the hoop of men, his eyes narrowed to shut out things he will not want to view. He glimpsed the healer bending down and he imagined the man sniffing at the wound. He heard the drum talking loud and then he saw the healer rising, his fingers closed around the shaft.

As the man stood, Mahtociqala squinted his eyes shut but the drumming pounded against his ears. When he looked again, the pežuta stood holding the arrow shaft aloft. And the iron point, intact.

Gnuśka lay as before but now the men saw a hole in his breast.

The drum-voice dropped a tone, and again Śunihanble leaned over the young warrior; he began talking into Gnuśka's ear.

"You will eat. You will talk. I say this thing. I speak knowing my power. I know something and so you will eat. I know something and so you will walk."

The healer stepped back; he motioned the men to widen their hoop; he needed space, much more space.

Mahtociqala saw tracks where Śunihanble had stood, familiar tracks, the marks of a little-dog, a little reddish-yellow dog.

The head and forefeet of the little-dog decorated the front of Śunihanble's loin-cover, and from underneath this flap the healer now pulled out a cord of twisted pte-hair.

He unwound the coil, something surprisingly long. Then he stood looking down at Gnuśka's strange sleep. He gestured that his assistant stop the song but not the slow, gentle drumming.

Suddenly Śunihanble lifted his arm and snapped the long cord viciously toward the wounded man, toward Gnuśka's closed eyes.

Mahtociqala's hand went to his mouth; the healer's behavior astounded him. He glanced quickly at Iku, then Ahbleza. Why will Śunihanble flip the cord dangerously near Gnuśka's face?

Neither man's expression gave him an answer, but he saw that different ones stood with hands covering their mouths; apparently this treatment of a wounded man astonished more than one observer. Why not a pežuta who makes use of the grizzly-claw probes instead of this one who whips a dying man? Why not a healer who will suck on the black hole opening into Gnuśka's breast? Not someone who stands chewing his own tongue.

The men in the circle understood that they granted a certain protection, that they kept any mischief outside this

462

hoop, but now they wondered whether instead they kept the mischief inside the circle.

Then, before the healer and his threatening cord had mystified the group beyond enduring, they saw Gnuśka's eyelids twitch.

Gazing intently upon this wonder, none of the warriors noticed the quickening drumbeat.

Mahtociqala took a place in the hoop; he imagined that Gnuśka moved.

Sunihanble flipped the cord again toward the face of the wounded man, then again and again, again and again. The snapping whip caught up with the rhythm of the drum and now the drum seemed that which struck at Gnuśka.

Mahtociqala saw his brother's eyes open, neither pain nor interest on the warrior's face. He heard a moan but perhaps Sunihanble, in the manner of pežuta, made this sound. Then he saw that Gnuśka began shaking, drops like dew spreading over his forehead.

But the unrelenting whip went on, trying to bite him.

Now Gnuśka's eyes opened wide and the dullness left his face. These same eyes now flashed irritation.

Something happened, something changed. Will not the pežuta hold back the snapping cord and give Gnuśka a chance to rise?

But the snapping went on, even when Gnuśka who had lain as dead for more than three, four days, wrenched out of the cord's reach.

And the drumbeat, persistent as the whip. What manner of healer, this pežuta they call Sunihanble?

An uneasiness rose among the watchers. They saw the cord as a rattle-tail slipping through the grass, striking at Gnuśka's face. They saw Gnuśka as a man who tried to twist out of reach but the rattler found him wherever he moved his head.

Suddenly the hurt man grabbed at the cord. His fingers caught the tip but Sunihanble's rough jerk got the whip away. Gnuśka grunted hoarsely; anger flashed in his eyes.

Gnuśka, awake and truly angry now. He wanted to tear out the tongue and twist the neck of this tormenting thing. He fought to rise on his elbow and so get a good look at the enemy.

He pulled up to a sitting position. He wiped the drops from his lids and stared fiercely at the hand that flicked the cord.

Ahbleza had watched the wounded man's anger grow. He saw the loathing that Gnuśka threw at the healer but he understood this loathing as a force that Śunihanble intended to use. And the drum, pounding now like a raging heart, helped sustain Gnuśka's rage.

Mahtociqala stared; will Gnuśka try to get on his feet?

Gnuśka, furious, his fury giving him the power to rise.

Gnuśka, taking a step, stumbling, balancing.

Gnuśka, eyes blazing, lunging toward the cord barely out of reach.

Gnuśka, stretching, trying to jerk the cord from the healer's fingers.

But now, his wound bursting open . . .

Black, dead blood spurting from Gnuśka's breast . . .

The drum rumbling on, the circle of men sounding their amazement, the seer murmuring approval. . . .

The warrior's hands dropped to his sides but he glared at Śunihanble; the same overwhelming rage which had brought him to his feet kept him standing.

Suddenly everything became quiet; the snapping cord and the drumbeat had ceased. And that which they witnessed silenced the observers.

Bright red blood poured from Gnuśka's wound, and Śunihanble, his whip on the ground and without life, approached the warrior.

Now the men saw that the healer chewed not on his tongue; instead he had held a lump of smoke-leaves in his mouth, something he chewed all the while he used the whip. They watched him take the step that brought him within touching distance of Gnuśka. They noticed that he drew in his cheeks; they saw him spit the soft wad into Gnuśka's wound.

Then, as if this healer commanded the blood, the flow from the breast had stopped. And now Śunihanble helped Gnuśka back down onto the sage-cover.

The circle gave voice to marvel and Mahtociqala struck his hands together in unrestrained joy.

While the wounded man rested, certain ones converted

the little poles into a drag, something for Gnuśka to ride. He will strengthen quickly, the healer told, once they get him to the village but for now he shall stay off his feet.

Joy and relief pervaded the traveling war camp. A mounted party now, the men rode proudly. They had avenged a Siyo relative and not lost a man.

Mahtociqala, given back his own name, used his tongue as before. But then he had begun talking from the moment he touched the enemy and none had reproved him; they will not reprove warriors, he remembered.

The day after the healing, Olepi had found reason for taking Ahbleza aside for personal talk.

"During the party's return," he said, "each man but my son speaks about his place in the fighting. Soon the blotahunka select the person who shall act as pipe-carrier when the men enter camp. Warriors who strike or kill the enemy will walk alongside him. Each one to whom they give an emblem fulfills his obligations. What of you, my son?"

"I kill the enemy, my father, as you demand."

Ahbleza had answered softly, yet to Olepi's ears the young man's tone carried regret. But why? The first kill calls for a certain amount of arrogance and pride. And where hangs the scalp coming out of this act? Will he not take hair?

"They will award you the honoring feather, my son. You, a warrior; truly, a man. Will you find nothing exalting in that which you accomplish?" Olepi's impatience had slipped into his voice.

"My father, the pride belongs to you in the same manner that the pipe which forces my act belongs to you.

"True, I kill a man, but I take not his horse. Instead, I see his horse stumble, fall, break a leg. And so I go out and kill the horse. When I return to the enemy, I see that someone already takes his scalp.

"My father will have the people know that his son kills an enemy, but I regard taking-horses as the most important thing in a warrior's life, a way for him to display his daring, his gains, his generosity. And so I find more reason for regret than pride. I kill a man but I lose the horse."

Olepi stood facing the truth; true, he had pushed his son toward this killing and he knew why. He wanted this thing happening before Ahbleza tried for a vision. Who will say what his son's vision-quest will bring? Perhaps the vision will not permit killing ... or perhaps Wanaġi will interpret the vision in this manner.

The father spoke out abruptly. "They say a Miwatani rides near you and the floundering horse. I advise you, my son, to hold on to your power for something more important than relieving a horse of misery."

Ahbleza chose not to answer this advice, but something he will say to the man, his eyes flashing Olepi a look of profound respect. "I learn, my father, of your brave act. They say that you release the Iyuptala from his stake."

The man heard, but he preferred hearing his son speak words of self-esteem, phrases hinting of Ahbleza's schemes for recognition. But Ahbleza seemed not to have such schemes.

Their talk finished, father and son separated. Afterwards, Ahbleza, reflecting his father's speech, found something lacking. And shocking. Until now he understood that any lack sat with him, not his father. But on this day he began to wonder.

His father will see him preserve his power for more important things than a suffering horse? But who decides what things bear the most importance?

Nor will he find pride in this first killing; instead he senses shame. He performs the obligation they demand that he effect; he acts bravely and cleanly. He earns a place alongside the pipe-bearer and he shall color his face black for the procession into camp, this black paint telling that all Titonwan return. But any pride he shall feel comes by way of Sunihanble's power and mystery. He will marvel not the man who kills but this man who heals.

Not every man in the party had something to show for his daring but most certainly each one had something to tell. And certainly each one had a relative waiting to hear. But before they entered camp, the party stopped and sat together on a knoll overlooking the villages. Here Wanapin and Olepi broke the fat that had sealed the pipe-bowls; here these leaders passed around the stems while the scouts made the smoke signals that announced the party's return.

The Titonwan camps had burst into noisy joy on viewing those smoke-clouds. Some men rubbed their cheeks with burnt wood and hastened out to greet the victors. Different persons—women and children along with the men—hurried to the edge of camp, cheers in their throats, trills on their tongues.

Napewaśte stayed with her cooking fire. She wanted the evening meal exactly to Olepi's liking—tongue, soup, berry sauce—each thing nicely flavored, properly cooked.

The young wife in this lodge stayed back with Napewaśte; she had learned prudence. Olepi, she had discovered, liked to find his women here whether he returned from an avenging upriver or from a visit in a tipi not five lodges away. And now these two chatted about the man's return.

"He will remember that I want a neckstring of beads and little hoops for my arms," Hinziwin said, smiling her childlike smile. Then she glanced curiously at Napewaśte. "Perhaps he brings you something also, like a nice clay bowl for warming soup."

Napewaśte raised a flushed face; she bent at the fire but she looked up at the taunting voice. Before answering she made herself view this pretty woman with the smooth and shining hair, dark hair but for the startling strand of yellow flowing from the forehead. But she saw also the mocking eyes.

"I desire only that he returns safely," she murmured.

"I know that he comes unhurt," Hinziwin said quickly. "The smoke tells that these men return victors." She tossed her head. "Why shall I not want things for decorating my ears and arms? Your son's father says I am pretty and that he likes to see shells at my ears, beads around my neck."

Napewaśte's gaze stayed on the young wife's face. If only she dared instruct this remarkable-looking one in kindliness, in the good woman-ways; if only Hinziwin, another daughter like Kehala, the girl Olepi had brought to this tipi from the Psa raid. But Hinziwin sat in this lodge not as daughter but as Olepi's cherished young wife.

The woman stood, moving away from the fire; she

spoke in a different voice. "The father of my son brings gifts to each one on most occasions, but on this occasion he helps lead a war party. You talk as if he visits a trade fair. And if he brings anything, he brings scalps and I, not you, will hold his lance at the dancing."

Angry at herself that she permitted the young wife to annoy her, Napewaśte hurried into the lodge.

Hinziwin stayed outside near the fire; she picked up the soup ladle, stirring the mixture lazily.

Soon the men came riding in, circling the center. Going twice around, they gave the people a chance to recognize each one. And Hinziwin, suddenly throwing off her effort to maintain modest demeanor, ran with a crowd of young girls and their grandmothers toward the middle of camp. Here she joined in a trilling for the returned warriors, all the warriors, especially all the young warriors.

VI

THE SUN crept under the raised edge of the lodge and streaked Ahbleza's body with shadow and light. His paint sacks before him, the young man sat undecided as to the design he shall use on himself. He will not appear at the victory dancing unpainted but he found more pleasure in decorating his horse. Tatezi had performed magnificently and he pondered decorating his skin with a design which related to this wonderful yellow horse.

Why not a horse-track, symbol for an unusual act horseback? Perhaps grabbing a dying companion off the ground requires nothing out of the ordinary, but maneuvering a neck-to-neck ride, three horses racing and a hurt man on the middle horse, earns acclaim.

Looking down on his slim nude person, Ahbleza puzzled whether to draw the track on arm or breast. But then something moved on his breast; the little awl-shaped, double-winged fly darted across a streak of sun, the shadow skimming over his heart.

Perhaps the wakan subtly offers a pattern? Not a horse-track but this susweca who symbolizes surviving fitness and hints at spirit-help. So why not the horse-track on his arm and the swift-fly on his breast?

He wet his finger and dipped into the paint but his hand stopped mid-air. Why draw the symbol when he has the skill to make this fly look like the living thing?

Before Ahbleza had completed his picture of the swift-fly, Mahtociqala stood scratching on the tipi flap. The youthful warrior had painted for the dance, four slanting lines on his breast and three horse-tracks trailing up his arm.

Stepping into the lodge, he lifted his foot; he wanted Ahbleza to notice the new moccasins, his sister's gift upon his safe return. And now he sat down to await his brother-friend.

Not only Mahtociqala wore new moccasins; many warriors had received handwork from sisters and aunts. But these warriors had presented their women-relatives gifts in return; they had given horses from among the captured herd. Not Mahtociqala; he intended to keep the horse he had captured, a spotted one, more black than white and with black feet, a fine horse for a scout. True, someone had brought back his little curly mount but, as the crier said, this one looked more like a fat puppy than a horse.

Ahbleza finished his sketch of the little double-wing and Mahtociqala marveled the resemblance to the living fly. Now, watching his friend draw the horse-track, Mahtociqala commenced a running chatter, his joy in sharing honors with the brother-friend too much to contain.

When finally these two went out of the tipi, Napewaste and Kehala lowered the sides and came in to change gowns for the evening's ceremony.

Almost at once Hinziwin appeared at the flap, the young wife announcing that she will attend the dance with two girl-friends. The three will hunt up an old woman to keep watch on their group.

Napewaśte had not agreed; she insisted that the young woman wait for Kehala. The man of this lodge, she told Hinziwin, desires wives and daughters appearing together, smiling and friendly. And he will want each one in a neat, attractive gown, ornaments of bone and shell on breast and wing of these gowns.

Hinziwin, pouting, stepped into the lodge. "I come here neat and clean and wearing my most attractive gown. So why look at me as if I am a worn-out old moccasin?"

Napewaśte noticed that the young wife had dabbed her cheeks with a fingertip of black paint yet she knew that everyone will blacken the whole cheek in respect to the victorious party. Even Kehala, ten winters, had smudged her young face with the charwood-and-fat mixture.

"Old women wear black faces," Hinziwin scoffed.

"True, old women black their faces all over in honor of returning warriors, but custom calls for this same color on young women's cheeks," Napewaśte answered patiently.

Hinziwin tossed her head. "I use enough paint. Take care of your own cheeks. And hurry. The song-leader already taps on the rim of the drum." The woman lifted the flap, looking in the direction of the dance-ground.

And Napewaśte, wanting to avert a quarrel, said nothing more. But she found herself wishing that Hinziwin suddenly will become iśnati and go off to the woman-alone tipi. And then she found herself wondering whose robe Olepi will visit this night. Certainly Hinziwin had tried to distract the man whenever he showed interest in someone other than herself.

Even so, whoever noticed these three as they walked together toward the dance-ground observed that the Mahto leader had reason for pride in his family.

Sunfall signaled the firing of the torches, but long before the sun dropped from view, five Iyuptala-lodge members had carried the big dance drum to the ceremonial grounds. Here, they had tested rim and center for tone. The drum belonged to the Iyuptala and so the Iyuptala will sing for this dance-until-morning affair. And who more properly provides drum and singers for this scalp-dancing than the brother-lodge to which Olepi belongs, in which Olepi sits as pipe-man?

But none among the singers or dancers attended this victory ceremony with more enthusiasm than Mahtociqala. Scalp-dances never had interested him, but now seeing the lances, especially the Tokala lances, in the center-ground, he recognized himself as a proud member of this war party. Eagerly he waited for the enactment of war feats; he intended to find out whose arrow had dropped the second enemy who nearly killed him. The wounding of Gnuśka had diverted his attention and he not yet knew which member of the party had saved his life.

Looking closely at the lances, he wished that his water-sac stick stood among these long poles. Perhaps hair will not dangle from his stick but he had touched an enemy with that red pole. His father had brought Gnuśka's lance here for his mother to hold, and so why not his sister Cuwe carrying the water-sac stick?

While he reflected these things, they had begun the ceremony. The warriors, joining hands, walked around the lances, circling the poles until the drum stopped their procession.

Now these men made way for their women—wives, sisters, daughters—who formed a line center, alongside the lances. Here these women awaited different wives to come forward bearing poles, old lances decorated with Miwatani scalps taken in seasons past.

Suddenly each woman, her hand on a lance, trilled loudly; the drummers responded at once with a war song. Now, standing in place, these same women lifted up on toe, down on heel in the manner women dance, while all around yelling warriors now stomped and whirled, heads nodding and legs kicking in frenzied bursts of self-acclaim.

The singers put words to the fourth war dance, the song telling that only one lance shall stand in the ground, one tall pole with a flap of pte-skin and a scalp on top.

And so the women stepped aside, making way for those warriors who will come forward to dance alone, to dramatize a personal experience.

Mahtociqala had moved from Ahbleza's side to stand near his brother. Gnuśka had come to the dance-ground but only to lean against a backrest and watch. He had circled his wound with red paint and his eyes appeared strangely bright. He gazed at the drummer who held the only beater

471

decorated with a tail, this man prepared to strike the drum at tense moments during each warrior's performance.

One of those Tokala invested with a lance now began his kills-talk and so Mahtociqala learned that the hair fluttering from this Tokala's lance came off the head of the Miwatani whose throat he, a moccasin-carrier, had tried to cut. But for this man's arrow, Mahtociqala told himself, perhaps the enemy dances his scalp instead. He sensed a little shaking in his knees.

The second dancer carried a lance decorated with a scalp that appeared to sparkle in the torchlight. And now Mahtociqala recalled someone whose hair had glittered in the sun, someone who had rushed at him swinging a war club, someone he had touched with his water-sac stick after the man lay dead.

But if this warrior dances the glittering hair, then this warrior, not Gnuśka, kills the charging enemy. And Gnuśka kills neither man who attacks Mahtociqala. But why will Gnuśka not tell whom he kills? His injury prevents him from dancing his exploit but nothing stops a witness from reporting Gnuśka's experience.

The two rattle-carriers and the second Tokala to bear a lance each danced a kills-story. And after these recitals the families of all the fighting men who had dramatized war feats came forward, these persons presenting horses and robes in the name of their warrior-relative. And so the people learned who had made the killings in this revenge war.

Suddenly someone from behind Mahtociqala pushed the youth center. He had turned to escape the shoving hands but different ones had come up, taking hold of his arms and pulling him into the firelight.

Shy and unwilling, he struggled to break loose; he regretted painting the stripes and the horse-tracks on his body. He noticed that certain girls looked his way and he wished himself far out on the plain, in a scout's nest, out of reach.

Ogle, seeing that which occurred, understood that shyness, not modesty, held back his son. But when Mahtociqala hears that he now receives a new name—a man-name—he will drop this shrinking manner and acclaim himself. The father looked for Iku, and this uncle, catching the hunter's glance, walked over to the crier.

"Someone asks that you attend," Eyanpaha called out loudly, and the hum of voices ceased.

"My nephew Mahtociqala," Iku began, "goes out with a party that seeks revenge. He goes out a moccasin-boy; he returns a man." The speaker paused and the quiet became more quiet.

"My nephew strikes an enemy who falls nearby. He catches an enemy's horse and rides this one in the rescue of his brother.

"My nephew owns a story, one to tell his children and their children. I am akicita on this war party and I observe my nephew performing these acts."

Again Iku paused but during this pause the people heard the drum emphasize that which Iku had told.

"My nephew owns a good name, but he reaches the place where a man's name becomes him, a name he will wear proudly. His name, Tonweya."

The youth stood unmoving, scarcely breathing. This honor truly comes? Not a dream?

Marveling, he saw the way different ones looked at him. The brother-friend, warmly regarding; his brother, Gnuśka, designing. The eyes of fathers and uncles, shining proud; his sister Cuwe's face, smiling praise, and his little sister, giggling.

His mother's look he never shall know; a respectful son, he avoided glancing her way. But kinsman-rule will not prohibit a glance toward the mother of his brother-friend and so he saw the glad, misty look on Napewaśte's face.

This moment of observing faces seemed like a long while, yet almost at once the singers had begun an honoring song, drum and voices sounding out the youth's new name. And while he listened, he noticed that those certain girls who had looked his way, again looked. And each one smiling, smiling in a manner that made him glad he stood here and not far out on the plain or in a scout's nest and out of reach.

He saw that the hunters who stood nearby regarded him approvingly but that the warriors looked on appraisingly. His scout-friends will not look at him; why approve or appraise when they already know his aptness? But one among these scouts suddenly hoisted a stick, a water-sac lance, the familiar forked pole.

Tonweya jumped forward with joyful cry. He ran toward the scout and pulled loose one of the feathers hanging from the pole. He slanted this feather in the thick hair above one ear, then strutted back to the center. He jerked his knife from the sheath at his waist and looked fiercely at the crowd. He heard the people call to him, calling out his new name and asking if they shall dance his naming-dance for him.

In answer, he flung his head violently forward, his hair a black waterfall cascading down his face. His arms stretched forward to meet his bending knees, the knife in one hand, the tiny power-bundle Ahbleza had given him tied to the other wrist. And so he began his name-dancing.

When the singers finished the song, Ogle led a strong traveling horse onto the dance-ground. The horse, he told, belongs to the crier, a gift in Iku's name.

Eyanpaha, softly clapping his hands, exhibited his pleasure; meat and robes they often give a crier but rarely a horse. At once he began an honor-song, fitting in Ogle's name.

Next, Cuwe walked out after her father, the girl bearing soft skins, moccasin-pieces for everyone, honoring gifts which her mother and sisters send out.

And then many smiling people came forward, all relatives, each one a member of the hunter's tiyóśpaye, each one carrying presents, all these gifts in Tonweya's name.

During the personal dances, Ahbleza had stood next to Wanaǧi. But whether he had moved over near the wapiya or the wapiya had moved over near him, the young warrior knew not. Nor will Ahbleza know that two persons at this dance waited—one annoyed, one patient—to see whether he will dance his killing.

The brother-lodge to which Olepi belonged put on this ceremony but the Mahto leader took little pleasure in the affair. Why his son brought back nothing from the avenging irritated the Iyuptala pipe-bearer almost to the point of anger. Certainly, he told himself, a woman from his lodge belongs in the line of wives and sisters who carry the freshly decorated lances, yet none appears with this group. And now they finish these personal dances, his son on the edge, merely watching. And as usual Ahbleza stands alongside a wapiya instead of a warrior.

But Wanaǧi had known at which moment Ahbleza reached his decision to dance and so the wapiya knew why the son of Olepi now walked toward the singers who had begun the war-theme once again, why he signaled the song-leader to make the change in beat which announces that someone desires to dance alone.

Yet even Wanaǧi sensed surprise when Eyanpaha called out who dances and why. Ahbleza, the crier sang, recites the acts of a warrior whose wounds prevent him from reciting these acts for himself.

And then the people saw Ahbleza wiping clean his face of black paint. Gnuśka lives, but for a while that one dies, and so neither black nor red belongs on the dancer's face. And for this same reason the son of Olepi wears his hair neither braided nor loose but gathers the strands together at the back of his neck.

From the start the drum seemed to understand Ahbleza, the two as partners in this portrayal which began with a dance to the weathers. The youth, a slender tree bending in the breeze one moment and the next, a resisting lodge-pole; suddenly the drum rolling like that which they call wakinyan, the dancer appearing as the zigzag streak at the edge of the cloud.

Now the people heard the youth's toes as sharp rain striking the earth and his heels as the slanting hail. And when finally the drum spoke softly, they saw Ahbleza as the calm after a whirling-wind.

Never before will the Lakotah see a dance like this one; but why not dance the power in the winds, the feats of earth and cloud?

But now Ahbleza reviewed Gnuśka's story, his body movements describing the warrior as second man to strike the Miwatani and next, as one who feels an enemy arrow entering his own breast.

The story of the rescue Ahbleza had not danced; this experience concerned himself and he chose not to tell his own story this night. But he will show with what bravery

475

Gnuśka faced the healer. And so his motions brought back the snapping whip until even Gnuśka, propped against the backrest, shook with excitement.

The people responded with cheers and tremolos for the wounded one and for him who danced Gnuśka's experience. But perhaps Wanaġi alone understood the meaning of this dance; perhaps he alone recognized Ahbleza's performance as a truthful recording not of a young man's power in a contest with the enemy but of a healer's power over dying.

They see the dancer recalling the power of the winds and then they see him perform the young warrior's difficulties. And then they learn in what manner the healer acts. Who before Ahbleza ever dances a peźuta's feat? Who but Ahbleza honors the healer in this manner?

And yet another man who had watched felt his heart lifting; the hunter Ogle sees his two sons honored, hears the people calling these sons brave. And now each of his sons wears the man-name, Gnuśka saying that he will keep his name, perhaps tying on a color but until he knows whether he wants black or yellow he will not announce a change.

As soon as Ahbleza had moved out of the dance circle, the mother of Ogle's sons had come forth with two pairs of moccasins, Cankuna asking that the crier speak for her. Let him say that she quills these feet for the son of Napewaśte, something she will see this young man using on his joyful days. And so she will look for his wearing these feet every day.

The people, listening, rejoiced that Ahbleza will have this woman as second-mother, the one woman who dares open her heart to him in front of everyone.

And Ahbleza, viewing this gift, decided that never will he see more wonderful moccasins; only Cankuna will persuade a certain flower to brighten the quills into a color that resembles summer sky.

The people danced until nearly dawn, old women and young sleepily shuffling back to their lodges, the men following in groups or alone, certain ones going for a bath before they lie down on their robes.

Hinziwin slept in a little tipi of her own and now she schemed for Olepi to see her at the entrance as he walked by, her face arranged in an exciting and pretty pout. She had discovered that he brought her nothing to wear at her throat or on her arms, not a single gift from this raiding, this avenging or whatever they called this party.

The man stopped but he had not found her sullen mood appealing. "A woman lays aside the pouting ways of a child," he said, sitting down but not with any show of pleasure.

"But you bring your old-wife a gift of wapiti teeth for her gown when you come back from fighting the Psa. Why nothing for me from this fighting? Am I not pretty?"

He touched the little black smudges she had put on her cheeks; he laughed.

Suddenly the childlike spirit broke through the dark of her eyes; her lips changed slowly into a smile.

"My pretty one shall have whatever she desires wearing at her neck and on her arms," he said gazing at her face, stroking her hair.

"So you will go out again soon?" She quivered her delight.

Olepi took his hand from her hair; he looked around the cluttered lodge. In a most different tone he advised that she tidy the place and mend the tears in the tipi cover. Abruptly, he lifted the flap and stepped out.

The woman listened awhile. Then, certain that he will sleep in Napewaste's lodge, she cautiously made her way to a tipi where some bold young women sat at a game of berry stones.

And here Hinziwin bet the shells that hung on a string at her ears, also the little white ties in her braids. Next, she wagered the moccasins she wore this day and a second pair in her tipi. She lost all these things yet on the third turn of the stone she bet the wapiti teeth and other ornaments Olepi most certainly will bring her.

They tossed the wooden bowl once more and the young wife saw that she had lost these gifts even before Olepi schemed the raid that will provide her with that which she had wagered.

Giggling, she pushed the stones away and crawled out of the lodge, her companions looking after her with suspicious eyes.

VII

FIVE DAYS after the party's return Tonweya brought his captured horse to the gaming-ground, young men and boys quickly gathering to inspect the creature for weakness and strength.

One boy spoke admiringly of the black hoofs. "Black feet mean a good runner," he said. But others scoffed at his appraisal.

"I will know after I see him run once." The next speaker had fingered the bunchy places, observed the length of the legs. "Perhaps you will name this one 'short-legs,' " he murmured. But he stayed on, looking into the creature's mouth and finally asking that Tonweya mount and run the horse.

Ahbleza joined the group who watched this demonstration, the horse running low to the ground, Tonweya riding low on his back. But the young warrior knew that the real test for soundness in any horse calls for a ride up and down hilly places and over stony ground.

The youth, seeing Ahbleza, slowed his horse to a walk. "Ride," he said, coming up to the brother-friend. Smiling, he offered his quirt.

Ahbleza had not mounted at once; instead he stroked the horse's face, touching places above the eyes, his fingers rubbing gently. Then, walking to the rear, he jumped lightly on the creature's back. He put the horse into motion, holding the jaw-cord as if Iktomi had spun a string from the horse's mouth to the rider's hand. And then he rode out of view.

After a while he returned smiling, something the spectators accepted as meaning that Ahbleza approved his friend's mount. And certainly Ahbleza, observing closely the creature's head during the run, listening for any cough when the horse walked, rejoiced that he found nothing unsound. But he smiled for a different reason: he had discovered a string of bird claws in the horse's mane, the same string he had made in seasons past when they called him Peta and his friend, Mahtociqala.

Certain persons now spoke saying that they will bet on Tonweya's horse in the next race but not if Ahbleza also rides. And the brother-friends, hearing, threw each other a laughing glance.

When the crowd dispersed, Ahbleza proposed that he and Tonweya ride out beyond the gaming-ground and discover what tricks, if any, his friend's horse had learned. And so they started off together, passing a group of boys who played a mud-slinging game.

Ahbleza noticed that these boy-braves had stopped their warring for the moment, each side apparently needing to renew their supply of mudballs, heads popping up for a look into the opposing 'camp,' each team watching out for a surprise attack.

The young warrior slowed his horse. "Why not give this bunch a lesson in caution? I and you will charge whichever side sneaks out from behind the mound. Ride back as if you take interest in their game; wait until I signal attack."

His friend's mood annoyed Tonweya; they had come here to try out a captured horse, not to engage in a mud fight with children. He had placed a feather in his hair this morning and he owned a man-name; why risk a face full of mud? But he rode as Ahbleza advised and watched for his friend's signal.

"Huka!" Ahbleza, sounding the attack, rushed at the boys with the fury of an avenger.

Tonweya saw nothing playful about this lesson; his friend obviously intended the real thing.

"Huka, huka," Ahbleza shouted as he approached the mound.

For an instant the surprised boys stood looking at their attackers; then mudballs began flying.

Ahbleza threw up an arm as if holding a shield but not before his quirt touched painfully on the shoulder of one boy who tried getting back to cover.

"He hits you, he hits you," the group in safe hiding yelled at their team-member.

"Hiyupo! If you call yourselves braves, rescue your companion." The son of Olepi, hooting derisively, whirled his horse into position for striking at any rescuer.

"Someone attacks from the rear," Tonweya yelled now,

479

and Ahbleza at once rode his horse in a zigzag path to a protected place; not one of the balls struck him.

Tonweya had begun to enjoy the game, and the boy-braves, greatly excited, joined together and became one against the mounted enemy. Certain young braves took over the work of wadding mud onto the tips of the flexible sticks; let the hands with the most accuracy fling the balls, they said.

The riders managed to strike five different boys and capture one, the 'captive' forced to ride double sitting back of Ahbleza. Next thing, Ahbleza maneuvered his horse sideways to the mud-slingers and so two balls hit the captive yet not a spatter touched the young warrior.

Tonweya, stopping to marvel, felt a mudball flatten against the back of his neck.

Instantly Ahbleza rode toward his friend; why not make a mock rescue of Tonweya for the boy-braves' viewing?

Slipping down the side of his horse, one foot barely touching the ground, the young warrior climbed onto Tonweya's mount, nor had he let go the cord to his own horse. He yelled at the captive who had sat back of him; either the boy jumps off the horse or he receives an arrow.

Ahbleza carried neither bow nor lance but the boy-brave imagined that the young warrior meant exactly what he said. The youngster slid down; he ran as if ten enemy chased him.

Laughing, the brother-friends rode away double, Tonweya's horse supporting his riders with ease.

And now these two looked for a sunny knoll, a place to lie back, stretch out, talk and tease gently.

The son of Olepi had begun the talk, telling Tonweya that he uses the mudball game as a way for testing his friend's horse, discovering whether this creature will carry two riders and what sort of signal will make him run fast.

"Perhaps you decide," Tonweya answered lazily, "that my horse will lose in a race against your black runner."

"I want only to find out if this horse will take you safely."

Tonweya, understanding, smiled. "Not likely will you see me tying up this horse's tail. I discover that I am not one for the warpath." A little scowl replaced his smile but only briefly. He jumped to his feet. "Come," he said, "I and you race back to camp."

Ahbleza moved his hand, gesturing against this race. "Wait. They will challenge you on your arrival back at the gaming-ground. And I will enter my horse in the same race."

The dissenting voices of persons who played at rolling hoops rose up from the playground. The arguing, as always, concerned points lost or won, these disputes often more entertaining than the game.

But the loud discord interested neither Tonweya nor Ahbleza. Approaching, they had spotted a group of young warriors who raced their war horses. And now two, three of these men waved an invitation to the brother-friends.

Tonweya touched the feather in his hair; will they signal him or will they want only Ahbleza?

"Go. I watch this one." Ahbleza turned and rode up alongside his uncle Huśte; the man, horseback, had stopped to view the races.

Tonweya, whooping, dashed toward the starting line. And Huśte, seeing him go murmured that Tonweya had a chance providing they keep the old-man judge.

Ahbleza understood; a young-man judge occasionally permits his betting friends to influence his decisions. And Tonweya's unknown horse, scarcely a favorite.

But when finally the race began, they saw Tonweya moving front.

Now excited whoops and calls and robe-waving stopped the riders, something about an improper start.

Line up again. Make a new start.

Tonweya won. He won; the old-man judge said so.

Usually the warriors proved good losers but someone had grumbled about Tonweya's entry on a fresh horse, the other horses sweating from previous runs. And yet many riders clamored for one more race. And a different judge.

"Why not ride the black and give the other horses an incentive?" Huśte made clear that he wished to see his nephew enter the runner and make a real contest of the next race.

Ahbleza smiled; certainly he intends to race—as he tells Tonweya. But he also remembers his decision to challenge every horse in the Titonwan tribe when finally he enters the runner in a race. For many seasons he wins the races on his funny-looking horse, yet this runner whom he rides in the surrounds has twice the power of his spotted horse. But, instead of surprising the people with the black's performance as he once schemes, he will ride here and now, in a race he knows he will win before he enters.

Tonweya saw Ahbleza approaching the starting line and his heart thumped strongly. Against any different horse he wins or loses, but the black runner makes this contest something special. Perhaps Ahbleza will recognize his overwhelming desire to win, to surpass the black horse if only this once.

Ahbleza had not glanced in his friend's direction. He sat, eyes closed, while they changed judges, while they encouraged more entries, while they made their wagers.

Voices lifted in excitement as nine horsebacks lined up, three more than before, each one fit and fast. The pile of bets suddenly grew tall—robes, moccasins, weapons, and two horses at stake.

The son of Olepi heard the shouts and murmurs but whether the betting favored the black runner or a different horse, he knew not, cared not. He had sensed something that demanded quick decision and yet a most important decision. Tonweya sits in this line, aching to win. So why not hold back the black runner at start and finish; why not tie or lose the race?

Brother-friend. Loyalty to one's blood-relative comes naturally, they say, but choosing a friend and remaining true . . .

Brother-through-choice, someone who earns affection and respect. And in every direction.

Brother-friends, the grandfathers say, neither deny nor yet demand anything of one another. Deny not Tonweya his wish and let him win this race? Will the grandfathers say so?

Choose a friend, the grandfathers say, and stay true.

Stay true. Meaning stay truthful.

And now Ahbleza saw his thoughts moving into place. If he holds back his horse, he rides untrue to everyone; he misrepresents his intention to those persons who bet, whether they bet rattles and whistles or robes, bows, horses. And he misrepresents himself to Tonweya, who wins a race which truthfully he loses. But above all, he injures himself.

For Tonweya eventually will discover that his horse lacks swiftness and that the black runner easily will outrun him. And so a pretense will split these brother-friends the same as the flashing-cloud splits the tree, cripples the wood. Never again will Tonweya speak with certainty about Ahbleza. But more important, never again will Ahbleza respect himself.

And when a man tries living without self-respect he only imagines himself living.

Recognizing the danger he had dared consider, Ahbleza experienced a moment of shame. But suddenly he saw his blindness; why not pride in himself instead of shame? He knows now that never shall any contestant—neither brother-friend nor any different man—say that he easily overcomes Ahbleza. Each one shall say, instead, that whatever the game Ahbleza plays, Ahbleza plays to win. And that whoever wins against Ahbleza truly earns his victory.

The man signaling the start of the race lifted the wingbone to his lips. But before the whistle shrilled, Ahbleza shouted to the crowd, all ears hearing. "You, my friends who bet on the black runner, prepare for collecting your wagers."

And now, the race begun, Ahbleza never even remembered that his brother-friend rode in this contest. The spirit to win demanded only that he inspire his horse; the black shall respond to his powerful urging, to his hand and knee and heart.

Halfway along the fast, straight course Ahbleza's ears told him that he had won; the thump of running hoofs had fallen behind. But he wanted more than a win; he wanted to finish far out in front. And so he crossed the finish line four lengths ahead of the Okandada who came in second and seven lengths ahead of Tonweya's horse.

And now the losers shouted praises at Ahbleza, the contestants leaning from their mounts to pat the runner on shoulder and rump, riding back as a group, Ahbleza in the center.

Approaching the crowd of cheering spectators, the winner looked for Huste's face, but the uncle, having seen what he wanted to see, had started back for his lodge. And only now, glimpsing Tonweya, will Ahbleza recall that the youth

483

neither joins the group surrounding him at the finish nor rides back with this party of admirers.

The crowd had dispersed and Ahbleza had begun working on his horse, wiping off the sweat and inspecting the hoofs, before Tonweya, unsmiling, appeared alongside the young warrior. And then Ahbleza, aware of that which troubled the brother-friend, had begun talking but as if he directed his speech at the horse.

"Whoever acts for his own good, acts for the good of the whole. But any person who denies his power for winning, weakens not only himself but the spirit of whatever game he enters. And I am not looking for ways of weakening the one or the whole. Any contest I enter I shall try to win, not second or tie but winner." He spoke words on a tone which, rising and falling, gave emphasis to his meaning.

Tonweya, catching a piece of the meaning, made answer: "I also run wanting to win but either I or my horse lacks the power. Perhaps on a different day I will discover who proves wanting." Smiling now he stroked Ahbleza's horse, then walked back to his own.

But something yet disturbed Tonweya: why will Ahbleza speak in this unfamiliar manner? Will he encounter a mystery that shuts out Tonweya? Or will his friend Ahbleza suddenly remember a difference in their ages and see Tonweya not as a warrior but simply a youth of fourteen winters?

More than a little irritated, the son of Ogle returned to his mother's tipi nor will he sleep off his mood.

The next morning Tonweya, chewing a mouthful of boiled meat, turned disdainful eyes toward the cooking sac and the simmering contents; the soup will not please his taste. He glanced at his mother, who walked around gathering up bones that her dogs had scattered. Cankuna went on about her work but his baby sister, Hapstin, secure on the woman's back, stared at him with round, black eyes. Unsmiling, he stared back at her.

The hunter's wife, having fed the men of her lodge, had intended to leave camp, catching up with a group of women-relatives who went out looking for the ripe tipsila, for those roots that flavor the winter meat. But when Tonweya came out of the tipi, she had put down her digging stick and filled his bowl; sending ahead her two daughters in the company of an old woman, she stayed back to care for the youth's wants.

As often before, the baby sister on his mother's back provided him with someone through whom to speak. "This soup, little sister, tastes lean." He scowled at the bowl.

Cankuna glanced up with a laugh in her eyes, but she straightened her cheerful face after a quick look at Tonweya; this same expression on Gnuśka's face will not amaze her but on the face of her second son. . .

Suddenly she understood: the boy turns warrior and, naturally, he wants to assert himself.

And so Cankuna, smiling inside her cheeks but lowering her eyes as before a returning warrior, walked to the meat rack. She offered her son choice cuts in place of the 'lean' soup. Then, placing the tiny girl in a carrier braced against the lodge cover, she seated herself at a distance from Tonweya and waited for him to speak.

"They chose me water-lance boy," he began, his eyes on the baby.

He told of the enemy who had rushed at him and of the enemy at whom he had rushed. The clubmen had forced his backing out of the fight, he said, and so he killed none of the Miwatani. But he struck one.

He glanced at his mother. "Not everyone has the daring to touch a dying enemy." His tone, something he will not let the warriors hear, seemed proper for a woman, especially his mother, who never sees anything exciting.

Tossing a soup bone to the ground, he chewed on a piece of the cut meat Cankuna had brought from the rack. Now he mentioned Gnuśka's rescue: "I go to him and so he lives." He had tried to speak as if he talked of an everyday thing.

And now Cankuna became the one looking at the baby daughter, sending her answer to the son. "I am present when an uncle comes out speaking proudly of his nephew's behavior in the avenging. He gives this nephew a new name. And so this uncle demonstrates that if a young man truly acts brave he will not need to tell other persons; they will tell him."

Quickly Cankuna stood and, going to the child, she

fitted the baby-carrier on her back. She picked up the root-digger and walked off. And so she left this son pondering her words as he chewed another piece of meat which his father had killed and which she, his mother, had cut and dried and handed to him.

The hunter Ogle smoked with his relatives at the evening fire and waited for Gnuśka to absent himself from the scene; the father desired to speak with the tiyośpaye concerning this son.

Soon the young warrior sensed himself as the unwanted presence, and so he left the group.

Ogle began his speech at once: "The spirits return my son. I and my family rejoice that Śunihanble renews this young man."

His listeners waited for Ogle to announce a sungazing; instead they heard the hunter speak for a giveaway, a feast and the presentation of gifts in honor of the son now strong as before the fight.

At once these relatives began to consider that which they own, that which they shall give. But only that which they shall give with joyful abandon and not haltingly. And so even before these people left Cankuna's lodge they had decided their gifts. Only one person sat uncertain, but he will see his father next morning and ask for advice.

And so Tonweya approached the hunter next day. "My father," he began, "I find many new moccasins in my sleeping place when I return with the war party. I not yet walk in all these feet and so I see something here that will make a gift."

He listened for Ogle's approval but none came. And so he told quickly that quills decorate these moccasins, not merely paint. But he will throw in an extra pair without design and so give away three new pairs.

Ogle glanced at him. "Will my son esteem his brother more highly when he gives three pairs instead of two?"

The youth's face warmed. Who rescues Gnuśka? Perhaps he offers only moccasins but he helps save Gnuśka's life. Will his father not remember?

"I offer that which I have to offer, my father. I own neither shield nor drum. My dogs belong to my mother now that I am not a boy. I own two hunting bows and twenty arrows and I own a knife. If my father says that any one of these things—and the moccasins—honor my brother. . . ."

But Ogle answered in a voice that cut like a quirt.

"Hear me. Your offer sounds like mockery, not pride. Will you decide that many gifts make a good showing and so the people will not notice that you hold back that which you truly esteem?"

For an instant anger twisted Tonweya's mouth. He wanted to shout at his father that he offers enough, he wants to say that Gnuśka, put in this same position, never will offer this many items. Instead he controlled his quivering lips and made quiet answer.

"I own a little curly horse whom I use for games and traveling and I recently gain a seed-horse. But I will make a gift of the curly-hair if this act pleases my father." He had tried to voice his offer in that 'glorious abandon' they talk about so often.

"I hear," Ogle said now, "that you jump from the curly one onto the enemy's horse but permit the one to escape. Even so, someone catches your little mount. Now you scheme to honor your brother with a horse you let go, a horse in whom you lose interest?"

Tonweya will not hide angry eyes, but his tongue, in the likeness of an arrow pointed to shoot front and back, he shall control. He had glimpsed his mother, who, barely moving her hand, gestured with the silencing finger. Next thing, Cankuna began to talk with her husband about the feast and whether or not they shall eat at the game-ground or near the lodge. And so, released from his father's presence, the youth jumped on his horse and rode until he found Ahbleza.

The son of Olepi, outside the camp circle where he gentled a child-horse, noticed in what manner Tonweya jumped down and so he knew that something disturbed his friend.

For a while Tonweya watched the insisting cord in the patient hands. Then suddenly he spoke of his difficulty; his family gives a feast, he told, which honors Gnuśka's recovery.

"I tell my father that I shall present moccasins, something I prize and will not give away but in honor of my brother-friend or my brother Gnuśka. Yet my father looks on this gift as a little thing."

Ahbleza's murmur signaled that he had heard but that his attention shall stay on the horse he tries to gentle.

Even so, Tonweya went on to tell that he had offered his little curly mount. "What more will my father want from me?"

Ahbleza, seemingly indifferent to his friend's concern, jerked on the jawcord, and the young horse, resentful, kicked and plunged. Instantly the warrior spoke to the creature in different voices, that of a black-bird and that of the traveling-dog. Neither voice showed any effect; the young horse kicked as before.

"You choose an unpleasant way." Ahbleza changed tones, from coaxing to firmness. "You will not like this treatment, but I will not like the way you treat me." He fastened the loose tip of the jaw-cord to the horse's tail, the creature's head turned and held to one side. Next he shortened the restrainers, the ties on the horse's legs.

Tonweya wondered whether his friend intended to hear him; will Ahbleza not understand that he waits for an answer?

Now Ahbleza spoke, his eyes on a far-distant hill. "Say that Gnuśka yet sleeps in the manner of one who dies; what will you give if only they will keep trying to renew him?"

A strange thought but Tonweya made fast reply: "Give? I will give everything I own, my bows and the war horse I capture, even the moccasins I am wearing. But . . ." He glanced wonderingly at Ahbleza, who had returned his attention to the discomfited young creature nearby.

Tonweya walked slowly toward his horse, this war horse who had belonged to him ten days. He looked at the strong, smooth face and remembered the rescue-ride. But he also recalled that his father had given away a favorite runner on the day they renamed the hunter's second son. Laying his cheek against the creature's neck, he pictured the proud manner in which he shall make his gift.

Now, jumping horseback, he rode swiftly toward his mother's lodge, but his throat ached from the swallows that choked down a sob.

Ogle sat straightening arrows when his son came alongside him. The hunter ran his shafts through a tight hole in stone, and now, rolling one across his thigh to renew the polish, he spoke without lifting his head.

"My son will say something to me." The man's tone implied that whatever Tonweya says now bears much importance.

And Tonweya, recognizing this tone, stood tall. "My father, I am giving away the war horse. Perhaps my gift will honor my brother's healing." He had made his speech almost indifferently.

Slowly Ogle put aside the arrows and stood. Placing his hand on the son's shoulder, he spoke his pride in Tonweya. Using ceremonial language, he expressed his pleasure on seeing that this youth grew in spirit, that Tonweya recognized the circular path and the disaster that results whenever stoppage occurs.

Perhaps Tonweya had not understood in what way he—giving away a seed-horse instead of moccasins—stopped a disaster, but certainly he recognized the importance of keeping alive the spirit of something good. And so he agreed to pass on the war horse. But he will choose someone appreciative to whom to present his gift; certainly they will not object to his selection?

The feasting and gifting emptied Cankuna's lodge of everything—everything—the family possessed. And not one horse, not even a runner, stood where Ogle's herd once grazed.

But all Titonwan acclaimed these generous people, the tribe singing praises, their songs mentioning also the young in the hunter's family; Cuwe had given away all her amonmonla, her little play-people, in the name of her baby sister.

And not only will these Titonwan sing praises but they will demonstrate respect for this family who generates good in the old and highly acceptable manner. And so, after three, four days Cankuna saw good flowing back into her lodge, good in the shape of fresh robes, new moccasins and leg-covers, nicely decorated backrests, and containers for packing meat.

And now Tonweya saw that which 'generous' really means and why the people never shall stop the flow of gifts

and where pride truly sits. And then something most surprising had occurred.

On seeing him give away his war horse to a Siyo scout,
a group of boys had clustered around Tonweya, boys of ten,
twelve winters, each one looking at him in the same new
way.

Ahbleza had accounted for their admiring glances.
"Tonweya has a following," he said smiling. "These boys
respect your daring and your gifting and so they begin
imitating your ways. Notice that certain ones already tie up
their hair in the manner you wear yours."

Amazed, Tonweya glanced at his friend; he smiled.
"They have eyes for Ahbleza, not me." But he pulled
himself tall and touched the braid of hair he wore tied above
his forehead.

And yet the most wonderful thing to come out of this
giveaway took place on the sixth morning after the hunter's
feast. On this day Tonweya awakened to find the black
runner, the marvelous hunting horse, staked at his mother's
lodge. The black belongs to him, his relatives said, a gift for
Tonweya from his brother-friend.

And now Tonweya hunted ways not only to show his
appreciation but to generate the joy that had come to him.
Soon, very soon, he told himself, he will brighten someone's
day, making his gift in Ahbleza's name and taking pride in
his role as a youth who chooses to generate gladness.

VIII

A HOT wind blew day-long, chasing off the little breezes
which usually played over the knolls. Nor will sunfall make
any difference in the air.

Tonweya, lying on the yellow, stony earth of a hillock

where he and Ahbleza had sought comfort, looked into the fading light and prophesied rain. "I smell living-water in the sky," he said.

Ahbleza sat flipping slivers of brittle stone at a thin stick. He glanced occasionally at the two horses who grazed at the bottom of the little slope, a yellow and a black.

Now Tonweya turned his head lazily; he watched the soft flickering in the southern sky. "Wakinyan, wakinyan hoton. Hear?"

Ahbleza gazed in the same direction. "Nothing yet."

"Look for the flying-mystery in the middle of the night. Will you make a bet?" Tonweya's eyes sparkled.

His friend smiled. "You and the old weather woman, Tatewin. I never will bet against either one of you."

But now Tonweya's eyes changed. "Tell me," he said earnestly, "what thing will you say makes this sound, has this look?"

"What shall I tell you, my friend. I never see wakinyan if truly this mystery owns a shape. I see a streak or flashes or a stripe and I hear growls or whistles."

"But what of Mniśa's dream? He says that something swoops down from the black hills, wings flapping and rumbling. This same thing, he tells, strikes a light over water."

"Mniśa reports that which he experiences in a daydream. Certainly wakinyan lives in the clouds and so perhaps owns wings, but who really knows whether this mystery owns a body resembling bird or perhaps man."

"Wings on a body that resembles man? Or will they imagine wings on a grizzly?" Tonweya laughed shortly; then he glanced at Ahbleza. "Will you say so?"

Ahbleza looked toward the widely flashing sky. "Recall, my friend, when I and you travel with your father. Remember the big slab of stone holding that which resembles the footmark of a giant, something with feet big enough to step over hills and across rivers. But will these footsteps in stone provide you a picture of this mystery? And so why try to describe something I know only as flash and noise?"

"The wapiya not yet advises you about this mystery?" Tonweya looked curiously at his friend.

Ahbleza made the denying motion. Wanaġi had spoken of Wambli-woman who guarded the black hills but not as wakinyan. "The people will not treat with wakinyan as man but they will remember that good also comes of this tree-splitting, man-killing mystery. Wakinyan waters the grasses and so feeds pte and so fattens my friend's belly." Ahbleza flicked a stone onto the youth's rounded middle.

Tonweya laughed but the serious look quickly returned. "I never want the flying-mystery visiting my dreams, making me heyoka." He sat straight, then leaned back on his arm. "They say Woze tells a seer about his wakinyan-dream. And from that day forward he jumps and hops whenever someone requests that he demonstrate his dream. Not for all the powers in the sky will I ever desire the heyoka-dream and so expose myself for ridicule."

Ahbleza looked up at the billowing clouds. "Recall," he said, "that Woze meets the wakinyan during his vision-quest. But whoever sees, hears wakinyan during natural sleep, night or day, gives the heyoka-feast once and so puts a finish to this experience."

And now the friends sat quiet, each with his own thoughts. Ahbleza reflected on Woze, who had endured a vision most men dread. The wakinyan-dreamer shall clown through his whole life, the people never taking the heyoka seriously. At the extreme he abases himself, permitting the most lowly in the camp to deride him. But will the heyoka-vision ever come unbidden?

He who will become healer, he who seeks a name as warrior, he who prefers the hunt, a youth who sees himself member of some mystery-dreamers' lodge—these persons usually return from the lonely vigil bringing back the vision that fulfills their wants. So, will not Woze cling to the strong, tragic desire for enacting whatever thing, foolish or itchy, amuses the people? Perhaps these persons who claim the heyoka-vision enjoy devising ways to lift hearts when the people starve. Certainly on such occasions a heyoka will sit in the snow and fan while he complains about the stifling warmth. And so the hungry, overlooking their empty bellies, suddenly begin laughing.

Or when the band grows moody, these contraries will gather in someone's lodge and boil a young dog. Here they lift fat pieces of meat from the cooking sac with bare hands; the boiling water, they say, freezes their fingers and the rising steam feels like a cold wind. And so they make the people look up and away from difficulties; so they bring amusement to a distressed camp.

Ahbleza remembered that his father often calls for a heyoka in place of a pipe; the wakinyan-dreamers usually manage to patch up a quarrel, pacify the quarrelsome. And Olepi also desires a heyoka in his war party, such a person easing the warriors before they reach the enemy and relieving tension during the fight. The people tell of heyoka who rushed into the contest, one man riding his horse facing the tail, a different one stringing his bow against himself, his arrows flying over the heads of his companions. And Ahbleza had heard of three heyoka who rode together, an enemy arrow hitting one in the back, the other two heyoka keeping up their clowning until they again heard laughter among the warriors.

Ahbleza spoke now as Napewaśte once had spoken: "Woze makes me laugh when he jumps-jumps-jumps over a child's play-lodge or jumps-jumps a stream, but I feel sad even as I laugh. I often wonder whether he endures some sort of pain which his unnatural acts conceal; perhaps he knows something almost unbearable."

"He knows," Tonweya said quickly, "that either he performs these antics or the wakinyan strikes him dead. What more unbearable threat will a man endure?"

The youth had wandered off Ahbleza's thought trail and so the young warrior offered something more easily understood: "A heyoka's work lifts the camp's morale."

"Work?" Tonweya stared at his friend. "Will you say a man works who goes around camp wearing a funny headpiece and acting unnatural? Will you remember that heyoka among the Siyo who put a puppy in his robe, who let the dog lick his nipples? In the manner of a little girl he play-acts mother to this creature? Truly I will let the wakinyan kill me before ever I perform the heyoka ceremony, daydream or anything different." The youth's voice carried an unfamiliar strain.

"Fear not, my friend," Ahbleza spoke reassuringly. "The wicaśaśni—this wakinyan they dare call neither man nor bird—never will enter your dream."

"Nor your dream, my friend," Tonweya said at once.

Ahbleza had not answered; why risk saying something that increases Tonweya's confusion? Why mention that the people never hear clearly any one heyoka's song, that the contraries sing always as a group and so drown out those words that perhaps reveal a personal tragedy.

But now Tonweya expressed his wish that neither he nor Ahbleza ever see either grizzlies or the little red-yellow dogs in a vision; the memory of a flipping cord which one little-dog dreamer had used even now disturbed him.

"Why not remember, instead, that your brother lives?"

But the youth, his eyes on the clouds, held to his thoughts about visions. And now he asked that which he wanted most to know: "Perhaps my brother-friend decides the path he shall walk."

When Ahbleza answered, he spoke as if reluctant to release his thoughts upon the air, as if the wind stood waiting to carry along whatever he said to some misunderstanding ear back in camp: "I once imagine myself a great hunter, someone similar to your father and his brother, sharp eyes and a strong bow-arm. But when I go out with these two persons I learn that hunting requires patience and cleverness above everything. I gentle my horse for the hunts but soon I discover that I will not look forward to killing pte. Perhaps I belong among horses as a catcher and gentler, not as one who makes meat for the band.

"I visit the wapiya and speak to him of the many things which puzzle me; I wonder whether I am one who will become healer or perhaps seer. But when I am alone I consider the path my father takes and so I ponder whether or not I desire walking in his moccasin-tracks."

One thing Ahbleza had left unsaid; he lacked words to express his pleasure at drawing the four-legged on lodge covers and on robes, at giving these things new form and depth and motion. In what way will he reveal even to this brother-friend that he enjoys putting on hide a drawing that shows each side of a man's face, a picture that makes the man recognizable? Brushes and paint bring him that which the dance brings to different ones, that which the pantomime brings to some persons.

"And so," Ahbleza finished his speech, "when I really know that which I desire most, I shall see whether the powers agree with me."

"You say nothing about the scout." Tonweya had listened for him to mention scouting as a way to live.

"You become the scout, my brother-friend; in seasons ahead the tribe will depend upon your ears, your eyes." He sat silent a moment, reflecting that which the grandfathers said about the importance of each person to the tribe—hunter, warrior, arrow-maker, healer, rememberer, story-teller, even story-actor. But will the grandfathers attach any tribal importance to someone who paints looks-alive pictures?

Again Ahbleza spoke aloud: "The grandfathers say that each Lakotah shall look upon every other Lakotah as someone important. Certainly a leader sees the importance of councilors and clubmen, crier and weather-woman."

"And the heyoka?" Tonweya voiced his uncertainty about these clowns.

"And the heyoka, who, as you say, only make the people laugh. But will my brother-friend desire living in a village that wants for laughter?"

Tonweya said nothing. But looking up, he sniffed the clouds. After a little while he tried again to make Ahbleza bet with him as to the moment water will drip out of the sky.

But now the warrior stood. "Day gives way to dark. I shall ride back to my mother's lodge and lie on my sleeping robe listening for drops on the tipi cover. Not until that moment will I bet on the rain." Smiling, he walked toward Tatezi.

The rain came this night exactly as Tonweya had predicted, but the youth scarcely noticed; he sat caught up in the sorrow of a great loss.

The baby daughter in Cankuna's lodge had acted strangely, the tiny one making a sound that became a choking, then a gagging cough. Neither the mother's gentle taps on Hapstin's back nor sips of warm bark-water eased the harsh breathing nor returned color to the baby's skin. And so the alarmed parents had sent a black-stem pipe to the pežuta's lodge.

Sunihanble had come quickly, the healer bringing his rattle and a stiff feather. He had cleansed his hands in sweetgrass smoke but had omitted all other ceremonial acts. Gesturing that someone hold open the child's mouth, he had tickled the little one's throat until she spewed forth the contents of her belly. But he saw nothing swallowed which gave this choking-cough. And so, tilting back the baby's head, he held her nose and pressed his mouth to hers.

Cankuna, frightened beyond reasoning, wondered why this man performed the naming-ceremony, the healer's behavior not unlike that of Pasu when he named her boys. But different watchers imagined that Šunihanble will try sucking out whatever mischief torments the baby; they had noticed that his lips moved on and off the baby's mouth, the two seeming to breathe as one. But when finally he put down the child, Hapstin lay thrashing her little arms, rolling convulsively on the pte-hide. And now the peźuta picked up his rattle and began to sing.

Tonweya, approaching the lodge, heard song and rattle and his blood chilled. Lifting the tipi flap, he saw at a glance that his parents and other relatives looked at something that writhed and panted like an old camp-dog. And then he recognized this something at which they stared: his baby-sister, her arms and legs jerking as if someone pulled strings. And kneeling alongside the child, a rattle in his hand, the same healer who had flicked the cord in Gnuška's face.

All eyes stayed on the baby and so none appeared aware of the youth who stood glaring at the peźuta, a youth whose blood heated, his fury flung against the rattle and the man who shook this rattle. He wanted to hurl the noise and the healer out of his mother's lodge. Instead, he sensed the rattle chasing him away, driving him out of the lodge.

Šunihanble had known the instant Tonweya entered and the instant Tonweya left, an opposing force appearing, disappearing. And now he again shook the stones to attract whatever invisibles will help revive the child.

But perhaps these same invisibles knew something about this tiny one that Šunihanble not knows; perhaps this child already acquires whatever she comes seeking.

The peźuta knelt over an unmoving form; he turned to Ogle, signing the father that his baby daughter Hapstin lay dead.

The hunter's eyes glazed, but Cankuna gave a cry. She snatched the child's body from the robe and hugged the limpness to her breast. Her soft moaning sounded not unlike a sleep-song.

● ● ●

496

Tonweya lifted his head from the ground. He saw the mud around him and wondered briefly whether his tears had made this moist ground. But when he sat up, he noticed that rain fell quietly. Gentle flashes in the sky gave him enough light to see the clay that streaked his body; perhaps the earth as mother had understood his grieving heart and put this mark of sadness upon him. For he had known that his baby sister died this night; he had known before those wails of sorrowing relatives ever reached him.

True, this same day he had spoken about wakinyan and had shown anger against a healer, but these things, he knew, will not relate to a baby's dying; some different mystery relates to this death. Not that he calls death a mystery—everyone understands that which happens on dying—but he will wonder why this little child chooses a different realm before ever she knows this one.

Cankuna will not wonder this dying; she knew. Her baby comes visiting here, a soul who previously lives as a visible but who leaves this realm lacking certain things. Born again, this soul quickly fulfills those wants. Or perhaps Cankuna's feeding breasts provide those spiritual lacks. Either way this soul seeks and finds and now rejoins the invisible realm, nothing lacking now.

Cankuna had not denied herself visits to the tree where the little red bundle, tied between branches, gave her much comfort. Usually she came alone, sitting in the shade of a leafy branch, mending old moccasins. But when her women-relatives sat alongside, the group talked softly or wailed loudly, whichever way eased their sorrow.

She had not known whether the men of her lodge also visited the death-tree until one day when she sat alone, awl and sinew in hand. Ogle had come, the man bending down, his hand soothing her cheek.

"I, also, miss this little daughter," he said quietly, "but I see a much more sorrowful thing when a mother dies. Two living daughters wait for a smile on a certain pretty face; they wait for their mother to bring back gladness to the lodge."

The man spoke and disappeared, going as he had come.

And Cankuna, returning to her awl, had experienced a fluttering which told that her heart lives again. She had shed a tear, but this one, like all joyful tears, dropped from the outside edge of her eye.

IX

THE MOON had fattened once again since the Śiyo avenging, and now someone came among the Mahto who desired a place in Napewaśte's lodge. Wiyanna looked to her sister for an invitation to stay in the leader's tipi. Returning from a brief visit with her son Tezi, who camped among the Mnikoóźu with his wife's people, Wiyanna had decided that she preferred the familiar faces of the Śiyo-Mahto-Okanda-da-Kiyuksa camp circle.

The woman had carried the news of the revenge to her son, but until his mother and grandparents arrived on the river of thickwoods, the young man had not heard of his father's dying. The Mnikoóźu, surprised that Tezi's relatives had not sent a war pipe into this camp, muttered their resentment. And Wiyanna, sensing jealousy between these Canoni and the Titonwan, chose not to linger.

During their travels, Unci had invited her daughter to return to the parents' lodge but Wiyanna, now thirty-and-nine winters, wanted another husband. Even if she had to share one. Perhaps Olepi, she told herself, will hint that she become his third wife; certainly a good relative takes in any one of his wife's sisters who loses a husband to the enemy.

Promptly, Napewaśte invited her sister to put down sleeping robes on the women's side of her lodge. And Wiyanna saw wisdom in accepting that which they offered her.

And now Wiyanna went about helping in the tipi. She moved quietly and her hands showed willingness. She kept out of the way but for those occasions when Napewaśte called on her for a specific task or encouraged her to join in a family game.

Soon Wiyanna recognized her place as peace-woman in the lodge. She soothed tempers whenever Hinziwin's indifference to custom and good manners aggravated Napewaśte beyond endurance or when Olepi, hearing too many complaints in this lodge, threatened to put his feet on the warpath. And never return.

Olepi, then, had not surprised anyone when, during this moon of berries-black-and-ripe, he spoke asking Napewaśte whether she will agree to Wiyanna as his third wife. Will she gladly see her sister as someone he shall hold on to in the same manner that he holds on to Napewaśte? And if not, let him know now.

Napewaśte had not waited overlong in agreeing; she viewed Wiyanna not only as someone who helps with the work but as a person who will appreciate her situation whenever Hinziwin brings difficulties into the lodge. And perhaps Wiyanna occasionally will take Olepi's attention away from the pretty young woman with the yellow in her hair.

And so Wiyanna shall sit in her sister's lodge as a wife to Olepi and a mother to Kehala. And Ahbleza shall go on calling her Ina, 'mother,' even as he calls her Ina before ever she becomes Olepi's wife. Certainly from before he remembers, kinsman-rule demands that a son recognize the blood-mother and her sister, each one as 'mother.'

As for Hinziwin, none in the lodge knew in what manner this young wife shall regard the third woman to stay here. But as outsiders suspected, she had not given Wiyanna even a second look.

The hum of evening voices, of people visiting, spread gently through the dusk of the old-summer moon and the fragrance of night-blooming grasses reached from the edges of the encampment to mingle with the fragrance of firewood.

Cankuna and her two girls visited in a different woman's tipi and Ogle walked somewhere with his hunter-friends. And so only two occupied Cankuna's lodge: Gnuśka, who leaned against a backrest while he worked a handful of fat into the sides of his head, and Tonweya, who lay back watching him.

"The Tokala-lodge will become a power in this band, the same as among the Śiyo where they originate," Gnuśka said now, "and I intend to hold a high rank inside this group."

"Perhaps they will make you pipe-keeper?" Tonweya knew that his brother had attended one meeting, the young warrior ceremoniously presented to the lodge members.

"Certainly not. Pipe-keeper means headman. I go once and listen to the pipe-keeper tell that which they require of a member. I answer saying that I accept."

Tonweya wondered whether they require that a new member use fat on his head each night in the manner of Gnuśka's regular performance. He decided to voice his curiosity.

Gnuśka answered promptly: "I prepare my head for plucking. They will pull out each hair singly, starting here and working around back of my ears."

Applying a second handful of fat to his scalp, Gnuśka spoke suddenly of the whip-bearers among the Tokala. "If you break your word as a Tokala, they whip you. Perhaps they whip you until you die." He glanced at Tonweya to see if his young brother sat properly impressed.

"I hear you," Tonweya answered the glance. "Will you look for a whipping?"

"I look for rank of whip-carrier. And I shall use the whip on any Tokala who disregards the rules."

Obviously Gnuśka meant exactly what he said. And now Tonweya asked if they permit Gnuśka to reveal what different ranks exist in this akicita-lodge.

"Drum-keeper and food-bearers," he answered agreeably, "and herald." Picking up a quill's tail, he brushed his hair briskly. And now he arranged the strands in a manner he favored, a loop from each side lifted over the top of his head and twisted together. He turned his face for Tonweya's viewing.

"And four lance-bearers," he said as if nothing had interrupted his reply, "who never retreat."

"I remember." Tonweya recalled the Tokala with

Wanapin's war party. Perhaps these men had asked his brother to join their lodge during that expedition, before Gnuśka's wounding.

"He who accepts the Tokala lance accepts death." Gnuśka spoke to impress his listener. "Perhaps one day they will ask that I carry the lance." His eyes reflected a strange excitement.

Why will Gnuśka keep rubbing in this thing about 'death-means-nothing-to-a warrior,' Tonweya asked himself. The youth had observed that leaders of a war party made every effort to protect the men and to prevent any foolish exposure to danger. What sense in dying if you know a way to outwit the enemy? But Tonweya understood not to mention such thoughts in his talks with Gnuśka.

The young warrior stood, reaching now for the sack that held his paint. "I am Tokala. I live uncertain." Solemnly he spoke the Tokala commitment and then, smearing on yellow, he began the lodge-song: "He ye e ye yo, Tokala ka miyeca ca ya ya"—"Tokala I am; go, go."

He strutted two, three steps, nodding his head to one side, then the other side. "They dance at the lodge-meeting, but none need whip me to make me dance." He looked meaningfully at Tonweya. "I dance and so I dare paint as you see now."

Gnuśka lifted a small lance from the rack above his sleeping place. "They give me this token-lance and so I remember who I am. I am Tokala." He dipped his finger into fat, then into the sack of red powder. He made a circle around his mouth. "I will not fear dying," he announced; "I am Tokala, I go, go, go, go." He strutted out of the tipi, lance in hand. This night he will attend a gathering of Tokala who shall give him more instructions on the plucking-out-each-hair ceremony.

Alone in the family lodge, Tonweya puzzled his brother's ways. Why will Gnuśka, always proud of his long hair, agree to lose all but a ridge over the center of his head? Not many Tokala wear this haircut; why Gnuśka?

This same night, on Gnuśka's return from the meeting, Tonweya had learned that the Tokala require neither the roached hair nor the plucking; the choice remains with a member. Also, they will cut the hair with a knife but certain ones choose plucking as a way to display bravery in the face of pain.

Tonweya heard but he had not accepted this crude act as the only reason Gnuśka intended to endure a plucking.

And so Gnuśka, a cunning in his eyes, acknowledged his unwillingness to sit in the Tokala-lodge without distinction. He had discovered that those members who submit to the plucking receive rattles at once and a seat alongside the drummer. And they dare paint as a ranking member and not simply a newcomer. The hair-pluck will grant him a rank even before the ceremony that makes him a lodge-brother.

Certainly his hair will grow long again. And as soon as the next person volunteers for the Tokala-pluck, Gnuśka moves up to whip-bearer. Those remaining ranks—drum-keeper, food-bearer, herald, singer—will not attract him and so in the manner of a blacktail he will bound over these lowly places on his way to lance-bearer. Then, on the day he returns from a fight in which he carries the lance they shall sing his praises and make him pipe-bearer.

And so Gnuśka schemed for the most high rank in this brother-lodge, the Tokala-lodge.

But while different warriors schemed or smoked or danced this evening, Olepi sat alone on a little mound. Holding on to his pipe, he made himself see the reality, recognize the difference between that which happens and that which he wants to happen.

He had looked for seven, eight council fires to glow in this great encampment. Instead this summer's hoop at pahamni showed gaps, and that which the newscarriers told and the scouts reported disheartened him even more.

Only ten Okandada families had raised lodges in the hoop and none of the men had ridden out with the avenging party. Newsmen said that Oowesica and most of his band stayed on the muddy river to annoy whites. True or not, the absence of these people had meant thirty lodges missing in the great circle.

As for the Śiyo band, half of these people camped somewhere south of pahamni, Wacape with this group. The Sicanġu had attracted many Śiyo into their camps, and so Wacape, if he desired remaining leader of the Śiyo band, will need to put out more effort toward holding his kinsmen together. None prevented a family from going over to another people, but a good season of wise councils and abundant meat usually reunited a dividing band. Perhaps these Siyo who camp here on the ridge already choose a new leader; certainly they talk of Hinyete as their principal man, of Wanapin as their war leader.

The Sicangu had raised their own hoop down on the earth-smoke river, Mniśa and his twelve lodges the only ones from this group of Lakotah to camp at pahamni this summer.

But Mniśa has his own reason for coming here, Olepi told himself, something that even a child will see through; Mniśa comes when he learns where the Kiyuksa camp, when he hears that Zuzueca brings forty lodges to the ridge. Certainly Mniśa keeps his eyes on the powerful Kiyuksa, whose booming voice each new summer carries more strength in the Titonwan councils. Perhaps Mniśa already advises his sons to seek wives, or second-wives, in the Kiyuksa band, where he imagines the power will sit. Perhaps Mniśa foresees a day when Zuzueca shall command the power of all Lakotah, one man forceful enough to hold the tribe together. Or split the tribe in half.

Olepi blew thin smoke from his lungs and remembered more things far from cheerful. He remembered that Kiyuksa means 'break-their-own-customs' and that what this group accomplishes twice, they perhaps accomplish twice again. And he recalled that soon after the Kiyuksa moved into the hoop, the young generation of warriors began to identify with the name Witantanpi, the Kiyuksa influencing their choice. Zuzueca had bragged that his band wore this name before any Mahto, Siyo, Okandada ever saw the grassy plain.

Certainly Zuzueca's band originally wears the name, Olepi mused; Witanhantahipi—before they contract this name to Witantanpi and so change meaning—signifies people-who-come-from-the-place-of-sunrise. And why will they come here? They break custom. And what word means custom-breaker? Kiyuksa. Will Zuzueca discover pride in either name, Witanhantahipi or Kiyuksa?

And what about that name Oglala which many young Okandada now proudly apply to their band, a phrase that means they-throw-something-inside. But who throws, who scatters, this something? And inside what? Ożu? What hole? Will these young warriors know?

Oglala, dust-scatterers, say the present generation; a name, they tell proudly, that the Palani give their Okandada grandparents who many, many seasons in the past grow maize along the muddy river.

Olepi smiled. True, someone gives the Okandada this name 'Oglala' but to remember a different sort of 'scratching' and to stop the 'planting' of a different sort of seed. Will the people already grow blind to the truth back of this naming or will they choose not to remember?

And will the leaders also grow blind to that which 'tribe' means? Four villages make up a band, they say, each village a tiyośpaye and each tiyośpaye a 'nation,' a group of related families. Eight bands, they say, perhaps sixty lodges to a band make a good strong tribe.

But will they always remember to say that the strength, the power, sits in each Lakotah, always in the one. Let the people remember that the tribe dares act only—only—to evoke the sense of personal power in each Lakotah. Never shall any one family, any one band attempt to influence the whole. And most certainly never shall the whole act to cramp, to submerge the one. Individual and tribe, the one and the whole, two distinct entities.

Ptesanwin, the pipe-bearer, brings her message to the whole and to each person within the whole, not to any one band, any one leader. Ptesanwin brings the pipe to the allied-ones, whether they say Dakotah or Lakotah.

So let the allied-ones stay allies, Olepi whispered to himself; for certainly the people as a tribe widen the sense of his existence, increase his sense of personal power.

Hinziwin pouted. Her father and two favorite uncles had not come from the earth-smoke camps to visit her this summer. Instead Sinte had sent his daughter a message but the man's words had seemed directed at Olepi's ears.

"Tell my daughter," Sinte had said, "that her father misses her laughing eyes and coaxing voice. Say that he wishes to hear that she works at her assignments. Tell her to

504

remember herself as Sicangu Lakotah, as someone who provides her husband with many relatives in the Wazaza Lakotah band.

"Say that her father desires that the Mahto leader bring his camp to visit the camps on the earth-smoke and so honor Hinziwin and her relatives.

"Say that her father makes camp this summer in the tall-grass valley of the earth-smoke. Pte graze here and rustling trees grow thick along the stream. Say that her father lives content."

The message produced the effect Sinte intended, on the young woman and on Olepi. The heart of one grew lonesome for the absent parent and for the river where she had lived in joyful play all her young days. But Olepi's heart, something different; the Mahto leader puzzled a father who provokes memories that bring discontent. Sinte knows that Olepi never takes his band visiting, never abandons the Titonwan camps.

And so Hinziwin pouted. But not in Napewaste's lodge where they never permit a person with short-reason to display the sullen face. The young woman sulked, instead, in the tipi of those friends who had delivered the message. And they, understanding that she yearned for a glimpse of her father, gave presents to brighten her mood. But she remained unsmiling.

She blamed Olepi for this separation of daughter and father and she looked for ways to annoy him yet not get herself into difficulty. She desired that Olepi come to this lodge for her or—more satisfying—that he send one of the women in Napewaste's lodge to find her.

When none came looking, she returned to her tipi and fastened the flap against visitors. She threw aside the gifts and sat glum and brooding in the dark.

When Olepi finally came scratching on the flap, she untied the opening but her face had not welcomed him.

The man observed her disposition and her untidy lodge in the same glance. He sat across from her and spoke coldly: "Perhaps you prefer the lodge of your parents to this one."

She knew to make careful reply; a woman returned to the family's lodge sat in disgrace. "I desire," she murmured, "that you take me to visit my parents."

"You know that I never go out from camp on a personal visit."

"So permit my going while you stay." She lowered her eyes. "Perhaps Wiyaka will go as my protector and any old woman you choose to send along as company." Her foolish tongue escaped her, as usual.

But Olepi answered indifferently. "If you and the son of Mniśa scheme to travel together, go, go. And why hurry your return? Stay with your relatives for as many moons as you desire, for all the moons yet to come if they will keep you."

Instantly Olepi regretted his speech but not for the same reason Hinziwin regretted her tongue. A truly indifferent man will not make reply to a woman who speaks as Hinziwin spoke to him. Instead he shall regard her desire to go visiting or eloping or whatever with the same indifference he displays toward a dog who sneaks off with a bone.

And so he made himself look at this woman, to try seeing her as a breeze that passes over the clay hills, nothing to mark her passing. Instead he saw the wind-spirit and sensed a breath cold, then warm, something that either chilled his soul or made him burn. Nor will her passing go without a memory to taunt him. Even so. . .

"Take your horse," he said gruffy, "and start your travels. Invite along an old one of your own choosing." He stood, moving toward the tipi flap.

But his tone had alarmed the woman. She regarded Wiyaka as young and fun at the games, but Wiyaka owned neither a handsome face nor many horses. And so, creeping up, she embraced his legs.

"I pretend," she said, her voice a whisper. "Why will I desire a visit among the Sicangu without my husband?" She lifted her face, her eyes offering whatever he will demand from her at this moment.

Startled, she recognized that Olepi neither will demand nor desire anything from her; he answered her look with contempt. And so she crawled toward her sleeping robes, pulling one robe up over her head.

Olepi went from the tipi then, the man surprised that he really neither cared with whom she visited, with whom she traveled. Go or stay, what difference?

* * *

The son of Olepi sat in council, his first appearance in the center lodge as a man to whom they will listen providing he has something to say.

Ahbleza had taken a place back of the headmen and to one side, a place where sat other persons of small voice. He had come not to speak but to observe; he wanted to acquaint himself with any conclusions to which this summer's council had come.

He saw that Zuzueca and Mniśa sat together, the two leaders with much to say back of their birdwing fans.

Iśna, a recent arrival at the ridge, sat off to himself. He had brought his people from the encampment on the earth-smoke following a disagreement among the Sicanġu.

And back of Iśna sat Taśunkekokipapi, a young Sicanġu with whom Ahbleza recently had enjoyed an earnest talk, these two of similar disposition.

Taśunkekokipapi's family had become famous as horsemen, but the young man told Ahbleza that his relatives not always took easily to horses. The family owned one story, he said, that described his grandfather as a boy who ran off afraid of a horse. Afterwards the people had given him this teasing name—Taśunkekokipapi—which he had passed along to his grandsons.

"But this name," the young warrior revealed, "goes back to a season before the Lakotah own horses, and so persons with long memories say that the name means the-enemy-fears-even-his-camp-dogs." He had smiled: "I know not the true origin but I know that my people outlive their fear of horses if not this family name."

Sitting here in council, Ahbleza reflected another point in his conversation with this young warrior. The son of Olepi, knowing that the Taśunkekokipapi family once lived among the Kiyuksa but that they now followed Iśna, had wondered what these people found undesirable in Zuzueca's camp.

"Why not wonder instead," Taśunkekokipapi had answered lightly, "that which my father finds desirable in Iśna's camp."

The ceremony that opened every council now began, each person who had a voice in this center lodge drawing upon the pipestem, pledging himself to the truth.

Olepi, a speaker this day, rose to express his concern

over families absent from the summer circle. He referred, he said, not to Titonwan who visit Canoni relatives but to Lakotah who form Titonwan hoops in many different places.

"Openings in this hoop cut the power. Many seasons back these bands cross the river, yet the tribe stays at four bands, not eight as when the Dakotah live on the lakes. And this summer every band divides but one.

"Certain things divide and become more; other things divide and become weak.

"When one Titonwan band divides and becomes two within the hoop, the tribe loses nothing. But when a dividing Titonwan band loses more than half the people to a separate hoop, certainly the tribe weakens.

"On distant ground, down on the earth-smoke, rises a second hoop of Lakotah lodges. This distance between hoops encourages a break in custom, and whenever a people break-custom they divide and weaken.

"But certainly this council looks toward the good of all Lakotah; none comes here looking to overwhelm a different hoop or any one band or any one person.

"Lakotah wise men smoke and advise; Lakotah shirt-wearers hear and decide. And Lakotah clubmen watch and protect. The Lakotah way, the Lakotah custom.

"And now if someone knows a more tenable scheme for living together, I will listen to him."

Zuzueca stood, his lips curled as when he prepared to deride his own. "My relatives," he began, his tones quiet at the start, "why will someone, seeing vacancies in the hoop, hint at trouble? Will anyone see an enemy sitting in this center lodge, someone who intends to divide this group? But hear me say that if any one man has not the power to hold a certain Titonwan band together, so a different man shall show the power. This thing I recognize also as the Lakotah way, as Lakotah custom.

"Someone raises an alarm over the summering of certain families among their Sicaŋǵu relatives; so shall not the Sicaŋǵu sense alarm when they discover two of their bands raising lodges in the hoop at the ridge? Or will they wisely remember that each one calls himself Lakotah?

"I see other visitors here this summer: Mnikooźu and Itazipicola, Canoni relatives from the woods, from the north. And I see that my Kiyuksa, the original band across the river and in the black hills, now take an important place in this Oglala hoop."

Zuzueca's voice had reached booming tones but he spoke his next phrase softly to make contrast.

"I will say 'Oglala hoop,' perhaps a more proper name for this circle, a name the young people apparently prefer.

"Nor will I regret certain breaks in custom which separate the Lakotah from the Dakotah. I say let whoever objects to change return to the originals and live as an Isanyati, digging his food out of the ponds, sleeping in a bark shelter and hunting sinkpe.

"As for Zuzueca, I am a Lakotah wherever I camp. But I enjoy remembering myself as Witantanpi, perhaps the name most fitting this tribe.

"I finish. Now I listen."

A disturbing silence followed the Kiyuksa's speech; many persons had not admired the man's depreciating reference to the parent-tribe. Certain ones, accepting Zuzueca's ever-boastful nature, had smiled but most councilors saw little to smile at; they sensed a real concern.

One man here foresees an unbalance in tribal power if the people camp separately during the summer, if they go on making changes in custom, an upset which will weaken the whole. The second speaker encourages widening the gap between the old ways and new; he sees the Lakotah strength as a result of changing customs.

And so the councilors sat quietly pondering, more than one man remembering that Olepi himself brings about some big changes, not only as a warrior—who initiates the blotahunka?—but also as a sungazer. Why then will the Mahto leader suddenly urge that they cling to old procedures?

After a while Heȟaka began talking, the man taking hold of the most important clump of words spoken here, bringing their meaning into light.

"Dakotah, Lakotah, either way remember the premise," he said; "nothing shall hinder a man from camping where he chooses, with whom he chooses. Remember man's most honorable privilege: to choose his leader or to change leaders or to become a leader.

"Let the Siyo as individuals, the Okandada, the Mahto,

the Kiyuksa, as individuals, decide what man they most esteem, whom they shall follow. The strength of the Tiyataonwan, Sicangu, all Lakotah, depends on reason and choice, never on force, never on demand.

"Let each man here, anywhere, remember the sacred word: choose."

Hehaka had finished, the lodge awaiting any man who desired to speak out, to detract from that which Hehaka had said.

But none spoke; who in this lodge dares talk against truth? And so the murmurs of approbation for Hehaka's concise expression lasted a long while.

On stepping out of the council lodge, Ahbleza again found himself recalling something Tasunkekokipapi had said to him. The young Sicangu had told that he looked for many different experiences in his life, that he intended to accumulate enough knowing to advise—if ever the people seek his advice.

And so he, Ahbleza, understood that this young man, someone who lacked blood-ties with any leader, intended to prepare himself to lead a band in the seasons ahead.

And now Ahbleza reviewed his own situation. He, unlike Tasunkekokipapi, dares regard himself as the next leader of the Mahto band. But he shall remember that the people own the privilege of turning their backs on Olepi's request. A warrior-son who survives his leader-father becomes the next leader only if the people stay with him. And the people stay only if he proves fit to lead.

A young man often depends on the persuasive voices of his relatives, the family urging that the band permit this one to prove himself. But the single son, a youth lacking brothers and without many blood-ties, shall prove fit and ready long before this need arises.

Ahbleza stopped where he walked; never before will he discover thoughts that concern what happens to the band when Olepi dies. Perhaps he never before considers that his father some day will die; where lives the enemy who dares kill Olepi?

TONWEYA TUGGED on one of the lodge stakes until the wood loosened. Then he crawled under the lodge cover, toward the place Ahbleza slept. He touched his friend gently back of the ear. "Come for a swim."

"In the middle of the night?" Ahbleza, instantly alert, kept his voice at a whisper. "Lie down here, my friend, until this lodge awakens and a man dares stir. Not even the old women make fires."

Tonweya ignored his words. "Come now. I decide something important." He glanced around the tipi at the different sleepers. "Fortunate for you that I am not an enemy sneaking through the dawn into this place. Before now I. . ."

"Before now you . . . nothing." Lekśi had crawled alongside the youth, the old warrior's club-arm swinging over Tonweya's head.

Startled, embarrassed, Tonweya strove to keep his eyes from staring at the bony figure who came around in front.

"Who says that he catches this lodge napping?" This voice, Olepi.

And now Tonweya discovered that he had aroused each one who slept here, even Napewaśte calling out in pretend-fear.

Lekśi crawled back to his robes, the old uncle muttering something about a fool youth who intends to scout yet makes a big commotion when he tries to sneak under the lodge-cover.

When the different ones appeared to sleep again, Tonweya slipped out the way he had entered. He put back the stake and awaited Ahbleza outside the tipi.

"Truly, your relatives sleep eyes-open," Tonweya said when his friend joined him. "And who says the old women not yet prepare fires?" He nudged Ahbleza, then gestured with his thumb toward the many fires cracking and hissing at the old persons who threw on sticks.

But Ahbleza noticed only the yellow horse staked near the lodge; always he made certain that nothing unnatural laid this one down. Satisfied, he started off, retying his loin-cover as he and Tonweya walked.

Passing a drying-rack, Tonweya rose up on his toes to snatch a piece of meat.

"I recall those days when you reach the meat only if you jump high, very high," Ahbleza laughed. "But you grow tall; already you stand above me." He saw that Tonweya, instead of listening to him, looked slyly back at the rack. "Fear not. The women dare not chase you away. You own a man-name."

Tonweya replied to this teasing but in a serious voice: "Members of a certain akicita-lodge reach for anything they desire in whatever lodge they visit. Perhaps I shall join this group and eat all day long."

"You insult your father," Ahbleza answered lightly. "A son in Ogle's family never will starve, never want for anything." He knew that Tonweya, not a joiner, spoke jokingly; a youth will not express, even to the brother-friend, a desire for an invitation into one of the akicita-lodges.

Arriving at the swimming place, the two splashed in together. They soon climbed out, whistling at the cool dawn, using their hands to rub dry.

Now, sitting among the slim young trees at the stream's edge, Tonweya spoke his decision, naming the ceremony that suddenly had become important to him.

"Ihambleiciyapi. I will try for a vision." The youth paused; he began his speech slowly. "Nothing changes my desire for scouting, but the vision, if one comes, will make everything certain. And I discover on the night my baby sister dies that I need to make something certain.

"I am not wakanlica, someone who owns the power for bringing the herd to the people, but I will make certain that I own the power for leading the hunters to the herd.

"I will not look for a fight with the enemy, but I will go out looking for enemy camps and so lead the war parties to these places.

"I know the song-talk of birds and the language of many four-legs. I hear the message in the humming little-people-of-the-air.

"Twice I hear the grizzlies talking, but my brother-friend knows that I never, never will become peźuta-wicaśa."

Glancing at Ahbleza, the youth sensed that whatever more he will say his friend already knows. "I finish my talk," he said formally.

Ahbleza sat unsmiling; he understood that this disclosure of sacred-desire will not come easily even between brother-friends.

And so Ahbleza spoke as Tonweya had spoken, using none of those hints, nudges, jokes that often act as a cover for soft talk, for the almost too intimate expression.

"I, Ahbleza, also will try for a vision. Perhaps I and my brother-friend seek together.

"They will say that each man shall stand on a different ledge but they will permit the same butte.

"I, Ahbleza, see good when two who eat and play and hunt and go to war as brothers, seek the vision as a pair. Perhaps my brother-friend agrees?"

Tonweya's shining eyes gave answer and so they decided that on this same day they will visit Wanaġi; they will want to know exactly in what manner a young man prepares when he goes out appealing for a vision.

The dreaming-pair, unusual but not unnatural among vision-seekers; they had not surprised the wapiya when they announced their choice. Perhaps Wanaġi had looked for Ahbleza and Tonweya to come here together.

"Hold on to these things I tell you," the sacred-man instructed, "or some mischief will enter into your experience."

Impersonally the wapiya gave out orders, almost as if he sat unrecognizing these two, nothing on the man's face to reveal his pleasure that Ahbleza had come, that Tonweya had come with him.

"He will make things difficult," Tonweya murmured when Wanaġi stepped out the lodge for something. But Ahbleza answered only, "Wait and see."

The man returned, carrying a pipe. He held the stem in front of the youths and made the cry for help. And then he commanded that all powers attend that which he now will say.

"Standing-people, you the trees and grasses; star-people, you the sun and relatives of the sun, hear me. People-of-the-air, you the little ones and you the wingeds who climb the sky, attend what I say; four-legs and many legs, you who run, who leap, who crawl, all you who move, listen. These two good young men seek whatever power you will lend for their experience.

"Relatives everywhere, you know my voice; now hear these two different voices."

Wanaġi's hand, holding the pipestem flat, circled the air. Then, handing Ahbleza the stem, he signaled the youth to make the appealing-cry.

Ahbleza responded in tones that will demand, not entreat.

"Hau." The wapiya now offered Tonweya the stem.

The youth acted as if he never had heard the help-cry; he sat silent, staring at the pipestem. And so Wanaġi drew back his hand.

"Hiya-hey-i-i, hiya-hey-i-i." Tonweya made the sound twice, not strongly but twice.

"Will you thirst two, three days? Perhaps four?" Wanaġi listened for Ahbleza to reply.

"I and my brother-friend decide three days on the ledge," the young warrior answered quietly.

"Good. Now hear me. Cut ten-and-six trees, bending this wood to form the initi. But before cutting these trees for the steam-lodge, make an offering of smoke. Afterwards, say to the trees that you choose these certain ones as your helpers; say that you cut these trees remembering that new ones will grow in their place.

"Next you hunt for twelve stones on the hillside, each one big as your hand. And you will have use for five bundles of short sticks, twelve in a bundle, and a second bundle of five long sticks.

"Take the whole skin of a pronghorn and make a smoking-sack man-shape.

"Bring sweetgrass and a sack of mellow-earth. Bring a bone knife and a stone cutter.

"Each one of you shall secure his own needs, and when I see these things at the initi, I shall sit with you for a cleansing bath."

● ● ●

514

Napewaśte saw her son giving a man-shape to the pronghorn skin and so she knew that he prepared for something. She saw him with the stick-bundles and the sweet-grass and so she knew that he carried wood to a sacred-fire. She saw the stones and the initi-poles and then she understood that he goes to the ledge crying-for-a-vision. And womanlike, she remembered that after the seeking Ahbleza, if he desires, shall take a wife and so have and hold the reassuring affection.

And now this woman, mother to Ahbleza, walked slowly along the water-trail, the woman-worn path, remembering that she helped prepare him for this day many seasons past when she instilled in him a respect for wonder, when she nurtured his child-spirit, encouraged his reasoning power, permitted him choice. Her breasts had provided for his flesh-body, but what mother dares neglect the spirit-body within her child?

And now, alone on this trail, she made a plea in Ahbleza's name. Bending, she dipped water from the stream; "Powers," she murmured, "hear my son's cry for a vision."

Cankuna had not known that her son planned the vision-seeking until Ogle told her the news. "One goes out, stays out three, four days," he said.

The woman understood; she felt glad that one son in her lodge acted according to custom.

She never had known whether Gnuśka had sought a vision. On one occasion, after a night's absence, he had returned to camp saying that he shall remember himself as tokala, the sly little-dog, whenever he looks for unusual powers. His announcement had surprised her, Gnuśka not the sort of youth to make a vision-quest. But when his father mentioned nothing about an honoring-feast she had decided that Gnuśka had not arranged with a wapiya, had not followed any ceremonial procedure. Nor had she ever heard her first-born refer to his dream again.

But neither had she imagined Tonweya standing on a ledge; from the beginning Tonweya had seen himself as scout. But perhaps Ahbleza had influenced her second son.

Or so she had told herself even before she learned that Ahbleza went with Tonweya to the butte.

Tonweya had only one moment of concern during the inipi. They say that when a man prepares his smoking-mixture, not a single piece shall fall on the ground—if he intends to avoid arousing the flying-mystery; the wakinyan become angry when someone, filling the pipe-bowl, drops a pinch.

Anxiously, then, the youth had watched Wanaǧi brushing the leftovers on the cutting-slab into the pipe-bowl; greatly relieved he saw that nothing had spilled. He wanted none of this flash-and-rumble mystery mixed up with his vision.

"I will hear your thanks." The wapiya had completed the inipi, using the most simple form. These young men, he knew, come here clean and earnest; why confuse these two with ceremonial phrasing and customary response?

"Hiye, pila maya, pila maya." The youths spoke as one voice, Tonweya rejoicing that this ceremony had finished. He had not enjoyed this tightly closed place, any tightly closed place. He belonged under the big sky, not crouched under a covering of robes while a wapiya sang and tried to stifle him.

Outside the initi, Wanaǧi handed Ahbleza the pipe, the bowl now sealed. "Take this stem to the ledge where you seek truth. I will walk out with you to the bottom of your climb."

They walked in silence to the butte. Then Wanaǧi spoke, saying, "I see two ledges high up. On each ledge I see space enough for one who demands vision.

"Robes and the pipe go with you. Moccasins and loin-covers you leave here.

"Neither eat nor drink on the ledge. Use your robe at night if you desire but I advise that you stay awake.

"Back off from distractions. Stay alert. Prepare for any messengers the powers send you. Notice the wingflapper but observe also any small birds flying over or anything that crawls your way. Each one carries importance, the bounding blacktail or the crawling-speck."

Wanaǧi placed a thin robe over the shoulders of each

youth, then made the gesture that started the seekers up the butte.

"Perhaps the vision will not come," whispered Tonweya.

"Hush," Ahbleza warned. "Act as the wapiya instructs and you will experience something up here."

Wanaǧi walked slowly back to camp. For a little while he heard Ahbleza's voice making the cry for help, the youth demanding the attention of each one with ears to hear him and power to lend.

Twice the wapiya turned to look back at the butte; he had heard his own voice echoing Ahbleza's call. And so he understood that this day or the next he, also, shall climb a hill and on some remote ledge demand the vision that gives him proof of help at any moment from the invisible grandfathers. His wotawe shall come directly from the grandfathers in the shape of stone, earth elemental to which the grandfathers directly relate. Certainly the spirit, at the beginning, had demanded stone, something hard and enduring on which life shall sit and walk.

Two stones, symbol of the pull that keeps the earth a circling circle; two stones, evidence that the invisibles will recognize Wanaǧi as a fit controlling power. Two stones, something that he, Wanaǧi, shall demand to see.

Three days up here. Tonweya sat on his ledge tossing pebbles, watching these small inyan bounce down the white cliff. Occasionally he glanced at the ledge above where Ahbleza stood, the brother-friend looking off toward the place the sun disappears.

He remembered that whenever he looked up at Ahbleza, he saw the same thing: the young warrior standing, pipe in hand, head up and his eyes on some sky-thing, sun or drifting cloud or moon. He wondered whether even once in three days Ahbleza had looked away from the sky.

Occasionally he, Tonweya, had sung his thoughts, and he had talked aloud to the hummer who had found him, to this tiny bird who had tried to vex him.

On the second day he had watched big white clouds rolling up into black faces and he had stood ready to meet the wakinyan wide awake. But the wakinyan had visited a different butte.

The sun traveled a clear path this lingering third day, nothing meaningful occurring. True, a wingflapper flies over, traveling toward a village of burrowers, but this wambli-bird will not guide him toward a vision. Perhaps if he, instead of Ahbleza, holds the pipe. . .

Why will Ahbleza never look down at him? Will the young warrior not remember that someone sits below?

An anger, strange and sudden, rose up in him, something that thirst and hunger had sponsored, an anger he now threw, in the shape of a stone, at Ahbleza. But the stone fell short of the ledge above.

Ahbleza, seeing the third sun disappear, slowly moved his gaze from the place sky meets earth and let himself down gently onto the ground.

He pushed his way painfully to the rim of his ledge; carefully he swung over his legs and dropped to the projecting rim below. He lowered his body over one more ledge and came alongside Tonweya.

For a long moment his tired eyes searched Tonweya's face; then he broke the silence; why not sleep and see what will happen.

"Nothing happens, nothing will happen here," Tonweya answered, his head resting on the stone that had helped keep him awake these past two nights.

Ahbleza spread his robe; he lay down. "Something will happen, my brother-friend. The powers stay with you. Perhaps this night . . . this night. . . "

Tonweya pushed away the stone; he turned on his side, facing Ahbleza, the young warrior's robe an arm's length distant. He saw that the skin beneath Ahbleza's eyes had darkened but that his gaze, once again on the sky, seemed calm as before. The pipe lay on Ahbleza's breast, his hands clasped around the stem.

Suddenly at ease, Tonweya closed his eyes.

Ahbleza's eyes stayed open; he stared at the star-filled sky. Not yet will he sleep.

He had stood, day and night, his body propped against the stony-clay which formed the cliff rising from his ledge. He had stood keenly aware of a growing weakness but more aware of that which hampered the youth on the ledge below him. And so he had climbed down to this level, lending strength to his brother-friend on this third night of the vigil, all power on one ledge, one answer revealing the truth to this seeking pair.

Never count the stars, he remembered; the grandmothers always interrupt a child who starts to count the twinkling night. A boy will use up all his winters, they say, if he tries to count only those stars that sit above his camp circle. Dare to count these little suns, they say, and you die.

He looked at the wide, stretched-out star pattern they call tacanśina. He saw the four points that mark the four sides of a robe and the stars that represent a family walking behind, one a woman with a baby on her back. And so he remembered the war party carrying Gnuśka, the young warrior seemingly dead.

The spirit-path trailed across the sky and now he reflected on the souls who, they say, take this path. A legend, he told himself, for cheering the disheartened when a relative passes over into the invisible realm.

But why will I find thoughts about dying, he wondered; will my starving bring on this thing? When I disregard my body wants, I perhaps awaken to the reality of my soul.

Ahbleza observed a shifting in the youth who slept nearby. He leaned up on an elbow, his one hand holding tight the pipe. He heard a low moan and saw drops, like tears, glistening on Tonweya's face.

And now Ahbleza lay back down, his lips moving slightly. Again looking at the sky, he saw only the constant star, the one that stays fixed, the one that makes a guiding point for all who wander the plain.

He closed his eyes. He slept.

Dawn painted red the wispy morning clouds and signaled the birds to join in a chirping.

But the bird who awakened Tonweya neither chirped nor sang. The youth lay watching the soaring flight of a wingflapper, a wambli-bird who came out of the west, screaming hoarsely, circling high. Perhaps this same one, he marveled, lends me power and so during the night I either dream or receive a vision, Ahbleza will know which one.

Turning his head to look at Ahbleza, the youth saw that his brother-friend also followed the wingflapper's flight.

And now the bird, directly above, screeched at the forms on the ledge, compelling these two to see into each other's eyes and so accept the wonder that relates the one to the whole.

Ahbleza, getting to his feet slowly, smiled a remarkably joyful smile. "Stand up to grandfather sun," he said. He tried to imitate the crier but his dry throat refused. He stooped, picking up his robe; the next moment he had started down the butte.

"Wait, cinye, wait," Tonweya called. "I climb down more slowly. My head and belly feel dizzy."

But when he came alongside Ahbleza, the youth stood smiling. "Something happens," he said eagerly; "I experience a most powerful. . . ."

"Tell the wapiya." Ahbleza stopped him. But he held out the pipe; he asked that Tonweya carry the stem and the sealed bowl back to camp.

"I keep the pipe until I and you experience the same vision, until you recognize me. Now you keep the pipe."

Tonweya gave his friend a second look. "The same vision?"

The young warrior's gesture made answer; he placed the pipe in the hands of this one, Tonweya now most certainly his brother-through-choice.

The pipe, symbol of truth. And so the whole earth, seeing the pipe, rejoices. All things come together in and through the pipe.

The pipe, bowl and stem, heart and pathway for the heart. The pipe, center and pathway to the center. The pipe, earth and holding earth, truth and holding truth.

Man will smoke and so the pipe becomes a sacred thing. He speaks truth into the pipe and so the smoke becomes sacred; the stem carries truth and so the stem becomes sacred.

But bowl and stem, without man, nothing.

Man, the truly sacred thing.

The pipe, an image of the truly sacred thing.
The grandfathers say so.

Wanaġi removed the fat which sealed the bowl and placed the pipe, stem upward, on a mound of dry chips.

"The pipe knows when you speak truly," he told the gaunt faces opposite him.

He placed an ember on the bowl and puffed four smokes; then he instructed Ahbleza and Tonweya to touch their lips to the stem.

The sacred-man's piercing eyes fixed on Ahbleza, but the young warrior met the penetrating gaze with a serene face. Only briefly the wapiya looked at Tonweya.

"My sons," he said now, "you go out from here three days past. While you stay on the ledge, I also, renew myself.

"You return this day and I see that you starve and thirst. I give you these small bites of meat and this warm soup and so you strengthen. Now I will hear that which you experience, the vision that will guide you in the seasons ahead."

Tonweya shall talk, Ahbleza second to speak; the son of Olepi shall wait outside the sacred-lodge while Tonweya recites his story. Wanaġi said so.

Tonweya related his experience in big breaths of excitement. "Nothing happens," he began, "for three days but for some winged flying up while I sing. But the third night I close my eyes and, between sleeping and waking, something happens."

He paused, awaiting the 'hau' which acknowledges that Wanaġi hears him. But the wapiya sat silent.

"I remember," he went on now, "standing alone at the edge of woods. I hear a voice calling my name. I look around and I see something in a wallow. I see a lonely pte and the creature suffers an injury.

"I see a wingflapper and a true-dog and they fight over the dying body of pte. I hear my name again; pte calls twice asking for my help.

"I run toward this pte, and as I run I am aware that Ahbleza runs alongside me. At one place the dog sneaks off, but stops and stands looking at me.

"I grab at the wingflapper. I grasp this one's leg. And I see that Ahbleza holds the other leg. The wingflapper struggles, pulling strongly, and I wonder whether this bird will lift me and my brother-friend into the air.

"I look into Ahbleza's face and he looks into mine and in his eyes I see something similar to tears. I and he let go the wingflapper, who flies away.

"I see neither Ahbleza nor the true-dog now; I am alone with the dying pte. Now someone different calls my name.

"In the wallow where pte once lies, I see a tall pale man or woman . . . perhaps woman . . . and she holds on to the same pipe I and Ahbleza take to the ledge. She says that I shall take this stem and bowl; the pipe protects me. She tells that this certain pipe owns great importance.

"Now she lays the pipe on the ground at my feet. Suddenly she becomes a pte, wandering away.

"While I look down at the pipe lying on the ground, I hear the true-dog running up back of me. I turn around quickly and so I step on the pipe. I hear the breaking sound under my foot.

"And now my father and my mother, not the true-dog, stand looking at me and nearby stand those persons who stay in my mother's lodge and next I see that all persons in the band come here. And different ones I never see before. Many, many people look at me, but none speaks as I kneel at the pipe-bowl which I break, holding the pieces in my hands."

Tonweya glanced at the pipe resting on the chips as if to reassure himself that this thing stays whole, unbroken.

And now the youth waited to hear the wapiya's speech, to hear Wanaġi interpret this experience which they say will influence Tonweya in his man-seasons.

Instead, Wanaġi told him to call Ahbleza; he will hear this one's story while Tonweya sits waiting outside.

Ahbleza told his experience in calm, earnest tones; he took care neither to mistake nor omit any detail.

"Something happens," he began, "on the third day. I envision that I and Tonweya awaken on the same ledge but now snow covers this place.

"I and he start climbing to the top of the butte, an

522

uneasy ascent. A certain ledge narrows and here a wingflapper lives. As I and Tonweya try passing, the bird sweeps down screaming. I grab one of the bird's legs; Tonweya grasps the other leg. The winged strikes at me, but struggles to pull away.

"I see that Tonweya regards the wingflapper with angry eyes; he will kill the bird. But I say 'let go.'

"And so I and he let loose at the same moment.

"Now Tonweya glares at me with the same angry eyes. But soon he looks up. I observe that something startles my brother-friend and so I follow his stare.

"At the flat place on top this snowy butte, I see a pronghorn. The creature calls out saying I and my friend shall climb up.

"Quickly I reach the pronghorn, but Tonweya appears to make this climb with difficulty.

"The pronghorn speaks saying that my friend carries the pipe and so he climbs slowly, carefully. The pronghorn tells also that this pipe shall act as a symbol of the bond between myself and Tonweya.

"The pronghorn speaks truly. Tonweya arrives on top and he stands smiling as he hands me the pipe. I smile back at him for never will I see a more wonderful pipe.

"I turn to look at the pronghorn. But this creature disappears."

Ahbleza had finished the story of his vision. And now he and the wapiya looked into each other's eyes, a long, even gaze.

Then, suddenly, a cry of thanks, thanks. But not from Ahbleza's lips. Marveling, the son of Olepi heard Wanaǧi making this sound.

The next instant Tonweya stood inside the sacred-lodge as if the wapiya's cry had brought him. He sat down next to Ahbleza, his eyes on the pipestem.

Wanaǧi blew smoke into the air all around. "The grandfathers answer," he said softly. "They show two young persons the way."

Again Tonweya listened for the wapiya's speech, for Wanaǧi to say something that interprets his vision. Instead, Wanaǧi talked of a new strength which these brother-friends will bring the people.

"A sacred bond exists between you two," the wapiya

told; "you shall keep this bond strong. Perhaps the season comes when all lives depend upon this bond."

Certainly Wanaġi hinted at something exciting, Tonweya told himself, but what about the real importance, what about his life as a scout?

"I give you this pipe," said Wanaġi, "a symbol of your bond." He placed the pipe in Ahbleza's hand but his eyes fixed on Tonweya. "See that nothing breaks this bond between you. Walk carefully holding on to the pipe. Walk carefully holding on to your bond."

The wapiya moved toward the entrance; he pulled aside the flap. He will lead the seekers again to the initi, where warmth and moisture will cleanse their bodies, wash away their weariness.

This same evening Napewaśte and her sister put food before Wanaġi, then went away quickly; they understood that the wapiya desired sitting alone with Olepi.

After the men had eaten, after they had smoked the mixture Olepi put in the bowl of his long-stem pipe, Wanaġi began to talk.

"My friend, your son shall become a great man among this people, perhaps among all peoples. He glimpses the pronghorn, the peace-spirit and a rare visitor to the youth-vision. Your son shall travel the straight path; nothing will distract him."

Wanaġi turned his eyes full upon Olepi. "His vision demands a most severe testing, nothing easy either for the one they test or the testers ... especially uneasy for the father of this one."

But Olepi heard only that Ahbleza's vision prophesied a greatness beyond that of the parent. Certainly a seed from Olepi's loin will bring forth strength surpassing the father and perhaps matching the greatness of Peta, original leader of the Mahto. Whatever the ordeal Wanaġi proposes, whatever tests that the headmen and councilors see as a fitting way for demonstrating the powers of Ahbleza's vision, these things the father will observe with understanding.

His talking finished, Wanaġi had risen and gone out of the lodge. Olepi sat awhile, marveling the pipe that had passed between their hands, the bowl not yet empty. Never before will the wapiya go before they finish a smoke; certainly great mystery attended this occasion.

Out of his vision, Ahbleza will remember most clearly not the pronghorn but wambli, the wingflapper. And now he chose to make two whistles from the wingbone of this warrior-bird. He and Tonweya had agreed on this wotawe, something they will wear in their hair.

And so one evening, soon after his experience on the ledge, Ahbleza requested of his father this certain bone.

"I have three wingbones here," Olepi had answered, his reply a long while coming. "When I renew the feathers on my shield, I trap these birds."

The man's dry tone, his apparent reluctance to meet the request surprised Ahbleza. And so he responded too quickly and not without a certain dryness of his own.

"I hear my father saying that whoever wants a wingbone shall trap the bird. So let him hear me saying that I will go out after this thing. I am familiar neither with the wambli-trap nor what manner of ceremony shall occur at the pit. But I want a wingbone now; I shall not wait for the trappers' next visit to the pits."

Ahbleza looked at his crossed legs; his eyes lacked the boldness he now put into his voice. "I remember that my father quickly provides me with a feather from the spotted-wambli when I return from the raid. Why will he now hint that I trap for this symbol of a warrior? Why will he take a different view when I return from a vision-seeking?"

"My son speaks rudely in his mother's lodge."

Hearing Olepi's stern reproach, Ahbleza rose from his place, going out of the tipi, a murmur of sympathetic women's voices trailing his moccasins.

And now Napewaśte spoke across the fire circle, the woman saying that an inexperienced youth perhaps will neglect an important aspect of the trapping ceremony, perhaps omit the songs which accompany the cleaning of the pits, the setting up of a lodge at the traps.

Olepi appeared to ignore the woman and so she tried again to impress him. Will he not remember the special foods they use during a trapper's ceremony, always a woman along to cook these things?

The man sat refusing to hear her and so she slipped away, hurrying through the dusk to Cankuna's lodge. Here Napewaśte and her friend sat outside the tipi talking earnestly; and so they had not noticed that Hinziwin and a girl-companion loitered within reach of their voices, the two staying in the shadows, listening closely.

Ina had stayed in the lodge with Olepi, but the man sat indifferent to the presence of this third wife, whose robes he rarely visited. Nor will she look toward this man who smoked a slow pipe, this man whom three call husband—Napewaśte and Hinziwin and, hesitatingly, herself.

The next morning at the bathing stream Ogle stood alongside the Mahto leader. "My friend, I learn that my son and yours experience similar visions and so each one chooses a bone whistle as wotawe. Now your son comes asking that my son accompany him to the pits, none guiding these two who scheme a trap. I regard my second son young for this ceremony and so, if you approve, I shall provide wingbones for their whistles."

The hunter bent, dashing the cool stream water over his face and body. Then, while Ogle rubbed dry, Olepi gave answer.

"I agree, my friend. Certainly they more wisely visit the pits in the company of trappers and during the yellow-leaf season. For now, I have wingbones from the same bird for these two. Tell your son that I invite him to pick up that which belongs to him."

And now Olepi bent, dashing water over his face and shoulders, his gestures hiding whatever relief showed in his eyes. He will not let anyone know that he had sat up half the night pondering his resolve to make a trial of everything that concerns Ahbleza, acting as the wapiya recommends. For this reason he had closed his ears to the son's request for the wingbones. But the slow smoking had helped him understand that he needed to recognize a difference between a strengthening ordeal and irrational behavior. When finally he had looked up with an answer for Napewaśte, the woman had gone, only Ina in the lodge.

526

And so he had left the tipi and the sad face of this third wife, going instead to the unpredictable one he calls Hinzi. But he had found the tipi of the young wife empty. Afterwards, strolling through camp, he had contemplated that which Wanaġi had cautioned: the coming seasons will try the father along with the son.

Wanaġi knew that his visit with Olepi had satisfied neither himself nor the Mahto leader. He had wanted to say more, much more about Ahbleza's vision but something had stopped him. Why tell the father that which Olepi will not understand, and more important, why speak about something that he, Wanaġi, not yet fully comprehends?

He had gone to the ledges the same day he had sent the brother-friends to the butte, but even before he had selected an appropriate place for his stone-dream vigil, his familiar-voice had spoken. He had heard the one word clearly: 'ahpe,' 'wait.'

He knew that the choice remained his, and certainly he had desired the stone-power before he interpreted Ahbleza's vision. But his familiar-voice, the voice that never misleads, had said 'wait.' Mitawaśicun he omakiyake; Wanaġi shall wait.

XI

THOSE SAME seven stars, grazing low on the night sky, once again hinted the approach of cold weather; and so on a certain yellow-leaf morning the flapping tipi covers awakened the men at dawn. They stared awhile at the stark poles, then rolled off their sleeping robes and headed for the trickling stream and a splash-bath.

The hoop grew noisy as the sky lightened. The old

women who had tended fires now went about collecting their dogs; whatever bundles they chose not to carry on their own scrawny backs they tied onto these scrawny burden-bearers.

Napewaśte also had dogs to collect, but Ahbleza had taught his mother's dogs to heed instantly her call and to accept patiently the short poles at their shoulders. This season she owned five dogs but one will not travel with the family this winter or ever again.

A crippling mystery had used up the true-dog, creature-friend of Ahbleza's boy-seasons. This one's legs now lacked the strength to carry her across the camp circle and Napewaśte had decided to leave her at the warm ashes of the campfire.

Ahbleza, hearing, put food and water nearby the dog, and while he avoided touching this pathetic creature, he permitted himself a long look into the dog's eyes. And looking, he saw more than a dying four-legged friend.

This true-dog, his mother's dog these many winters. But who dares say that he ceases to remember those boy-with-pup seasons? Who dares say that he will not sense the passing of his youth in this aching moment of letting-go those wonderful boy-seasons of encircling affection?

The creature wobbled onto her legs, her tail starting to talk, but Ahbleza turned abruptly. He jumped upon a traveling horse waiting nearby; he rode off not once looking back.

The same morning Ogle sat at the dead ashes of his lodge-fire and cheerfully chided his family. "All of you . . . all daughters-of-the-shell and crawling while different women step lively. Whatever will happen if someday you need break camp before a pursuing enemy?"

But the good-natured hunter will not frighten his wife and daughters and women-relatives into a scurry; not another tiyośpaye owns more robes, more bundles, more things they will pack, more evidence of diligence. And so they stopped to watch Wanaǵi, who, riding in among the horses and drags, approached Tonweya.

"I see a new scout in the tribe," he called, his voice loud for the relatives' hearing. "They call this youth truthbearer now, and so each one knows in what manner he protects the people."

"Wahn." Softly but certainly Tonweya permitted himself the man-sound that acknowledges surprise, wonderful surprise. But why will the wapiya come here now and announce this thing?

Almost at once Tacincala, his young sister, began speaking to Cankuna, her phrases directed at Tonweya. "My mother and my sister Cuwe say that these moccasins belong to my brother." Shyly she made her speech, quickly she put the gift-pairs in Tonweya's hands.

The youth, accepting, saw that all his family now gathered around him. He looked straight forward, but his eyes, in the manner of a scout, observed each one who stood in the little half-circle.

"A scout carries wasna when he goes out and so I fill a meat sac for you." Iku's wide mouth shaped into a glad smile as he handed his nephew this present.

Gnuśka, next to approach the youth, offered a single long feather. "Strip this one and make yourself a waverer." The warrior's oppressive bearing softened momentarily and his lips twisted in a small smile.

"Ride out, my son, ride out where a scout belongs." Ogle, his father, had spoken and all around him persons murmured approval and laughed gently.

True, then, that they accept him as scout? Tonweya's surprise gave way to joyous wonder. But where, Pasu, the naming-uncle and a most remarkable scout? And what about different scouts? Will they also accept him? He shall find out.

Letting go the horse he had intended to ride, Tonweya leaped on the black runner, moving swiftly out onto the plain. This fast one will carry him beyond those many families already on their way, carry him far out in front, where he will find the scouts who look out for the bands.

Passing Ahbleza, the new scout raised a hand, his thumb proudly gesturing his good news. But he had not resisted a boylike yell, a joy-filled laugh.

Coming abreast the leaders, he saw that Iśtakpe, the Kiyuksa peaceman who wore an eye patch, carried the fire in a pte-horn. And that at the true front walked those four they call wakicunsa, the deciders.

He slowed his horse; he will ride carefully and not raise a dust in the faces of these principal ones, who perhaps stop him, send him back.

But not a man turned as he went forward. And so he remembered back to the day when he had ridden as an uninvited moccasin-carrier. Why shall they look at someone they know will come along? He smiled to himself and urged the horse into a run once again.

Near the bottom of a butte, Tonweya caught up with the scouts. Now, he told himself, he shall learn whether or not these truthbearers recognize him as one of their own. Here rode the six outstanding scouts in the tribe, in any tribe, a group he will join most proudly.

Po and Wasu, immediately front and riding as a pair. Po, who knows many ways to confuse a pursuing enemy; Po who often acts as decoy. Twice Po prevented an attack on the Mahto camp; the warriors say so.

And Wasu, the big man who on one occasion entered an enemy camp, jumping noisily into the midst of their games; Wasu, who never sneaks around, never hides from anyone. While taking enemy horses Wasu, they say, makes loud noises with his nose or from his bottom. But in his own village, Wasu remains quiet, never joins in the contests or dances, never calls attention to himself.

Also riding as a pair, Peźi and Pasu. Peźi, a man not tall, not husky, but hoń, what cunning. His friends say that he will slip into an enemy camp and stay among the lodges; the enemy never find him. They say he remembers himself as spirit hovering over the enemy camp, discovering that which the enemy intends. Yet a most different man in his own camp; here he talks and acts rough. Nor will he wear in his own village the bunch of pte-grass, his protecting-mystery, which he ties in his ! 'r whenever he goes out scouting.

And now Pasu, the man with a nose similar to the one on a wingflapper. The bird-with-two-voices often makes crude observation regarding this big-nose—or so Pasu tells—but the really important thing about this man concerns his closeness to pte-pazo, the grasshopper who points out the grazing pte, and his understanding with those wing-eds who lead him to the browsing wapiti. Good-natured Pasu; truly all creatures treat with this man as a relative.

And finally those two scouts, brothers they call look-alikes, those two who ride legs touching. Even their names the same: Cekpa. And so they stay together, work together. One will stand on a ledge near an enemy camp pretending that he laments, while his brother sneaks down from the ridge, looking and listening in the shadows of enemy tipi.

Tonweya cleared his throat but none of the six turned to see who approached. The next moment Pasu's thumb gestured an order that obviously included his nephew Tonweya. And so the youth, in company with the scouts, began riding up the butte.

Halfway Pasu halted the group, giving directions. Each man, Tonweya learned, shall stay at an assigned position until the people catch up. Then each one shall move to the lookout of the scout immediately front of him.

"Anyone viewing danger, anyone discovering pte, will send signs," Pasu instructed. Next, he gave Tonweya his position; the newcomer shall stay here, the scout Peźi on the high point of the same butte.

Now Pasu led down the other scouts, Tonweya watching to see where each man turned off.

Presently one man rode out of line, going south. This one, Po, the one scout who carried his lance erect, in the manner of a warrior.

Next, the twins broke away, going toward the north. Tonweya had recognized the pair easily, a single thick braid hanging down the back of each one, hair too heavy for the wind to lift.

Exactly where Wasu turned off and at what place Pasu will locate, Tonweya had not seen, but something he knew: Mahto scouts protect the moving people front and sides. And guarding their backs, members of the Cante Tinza, the brave-heart lodge, this group riding always at the rear of the line.

Tonweya felt grateful toward his uncle Pasu; the presence of a second person on his butte made him comfortable, similar to the vision-seeking with Ahbleza on the ledge above him.

Looking up now, he saw Peźi's lean body, the man's dark red form against the white of the cliff and the clear deep of the sky, a magnificence that quickened his pride. Then, looking back onto the plain, he saw the people, a long, colorful stripe meandering across the vastness of summer-weary grass, a tribe who moves as a family toward the sheltering back of a great reclining mound, that which they call the black mountain, the black hills. Here, on separate streams, the bands shall camp this winter, the hills providing water and wind-shelter and meat for the body, energy and inspiration for the spirit.

And so Tonweya turned, looking toward the path ahead, setting his eyes on the responsibility he had accepted, vowing to keep safe these trails that lead the people to and from this great uplift, their earth-mother. These trails and whatever different ones the Lakotah choose to travel.

Olepi remembered that he rides this trail to the black hills in the company of leaders, men with influencing-power; one wide moving line five men across, the five principal Titonwan horseback, each leader on a horse of different color. Here Zuzueca on a shining black seed-horse, and next Mniśa, riding a big red; here Iśna, principal man of the Kuya, on his white horse, and next Hinyete, the Siyo, sitting up on a sand-yellow.

Olepi marveled his observation: four colors symbolizing four directions, perhaps meaning that in a different season these horses scatter, tearing the tribe asunder, the people bleeding?

And what of himself, the Mahto leader who sits a spotted horse, a creature red and white?

Suddenly Olepi remembered himself at the sungazing, the wind owning the power to blacken the sky, black sky trying to shatter him with a streak of crooked light and a frightening noise. The people had run, scattering, but Olepi had stayed, thongs tying him back and breast to four poles; Olepi had stayed, standing center, a sungazer without sun.

Looking again at the one on the black horse, Olepi imagined a black warrior-shape with many eyes flashing, something man yet not-man. But the next moment this shape became the familiar, Olepi gazing at the dark-skinned Zuzueca as if truly he looked upon Iktomi in disguise. For certainly he had glimpsed momentarily this Kiyuksa as something harmful to the tribe. A second look and he had seen a challenge in Zuzueca's treachery, not to him but to his son, Ahbleza.

Black, symbol of the power that piles up clouds, brings

rain, makes grass. Black, symbol of the power that brings the wakinyan rumbling out of the clouds, hunting something to destroy. Black, symbol of power and overpowering.

Zuzueca, his skin almost black; Zuzueca riding a black horse, perhaps symbolizing his power to make or break the tribe. Zuzueca, a power but one not to trust.

Ahbleza rode enjoying every moment of this move toward the black hills, the young warrior displaying a gaiety unusual to his nature.

He had raced Tatezi and won. And then he had used this creature in a show of tricks. Inviting the little boys who played at the edge of the traveling line of people to take aim at his horse, Ahbleza bet these youngsters that not one of their blunt shafts will so much as graze Tatezi. A group of big boys, noticing, had come up to test their skill also, but Ahbleza had kept his horse a dancing target outside their reach.

After a while he stopped this game for different stunts, many girls watching him now. He ran his horse slowly while he made seven leaps to the ground and up again all in rapid succession. But the unusual thing, he jumped on facing backwards as easily as facing front. Different youths had similar acts but he had two tricks that none yet had tried. And when a certain young woman begins to notice, he will demonstrate; he will perform something really spectacular.

Waiting for this one, he hooked his heels under Tatezi's belly-band, then running the horse very fast, he swooped down lifting small dogs from underfoot and any child who ran across his path. But always he let down the child most carefully, watching the little one totter off before he quirted the horse into the next daring run. Some children, seeing the fun in this game, purposely stood in his way, but for all the abrupt stops and dodging, not once had he lost control of self or horse, never coming close to any sort of upset.

From a place among the women, Winkte viewed Ahbleza's performance as something resembling a dance and so this one composed a song to remember Ahbleza's graceful maneuvers horseback. And the people, hearing, cheered the composer and the rider.

Never before had Ahbleza strutted before women and now he grew amazingly bold. He whipped up and down the line, his hand grabbing up hair ornaments, feathers, old moccasins—anything a moving people drop along the way. And then, his arms full, he bent and picked up a quilled strip with his teeth. The next moment, he threw open his arms, hair-ties, neck and arm decorations, moccasins, and pieces of hide fluttering down, a colorful fall of discards. For now he saw the one he will have witness his most impressive trick.

The young woman's mother rode ahead, a child in the baby-carrier she had hung on the front of her tall wood-seat. The daughter led a horse loaded with bundles, and an old woman, walking alongside the young one, guided a horse who dragged tipi covers.

Ahbleza had made certain that he had everything assembled for his act and so the approaching women saw four horses lined up in front of the young warrior. One long, long cord went around the jaws of these creatures, Ahbleza commanding all when he commanded one. And so, giving a tug on the cord, he moved off this group together; jumping onto the near horse, he soon urged the four into a fast run.

Now he jumped from the back of the one to the next in line until he reached the outside horse. Here he leapt to the ground, but instantly up and traveling again across their backs, the four creatures staying abreast. Making his return, he leapt over the back of one, then stood facing the next one's tail.

Many persons stopped to watch as Ahbleza now slowed, then turned these horses. Starting his ride back down the line of people, he rolled in the manner of a hoop, arms and legs taut as he flung himself sideways over and up, over and up.

Certain ones who observed threw a hand across their mouth, men and women whom not only will Ahbleza amaze with his brilliant exhibition but who will marvel that this shy and modest young man demonstrates his skill boldly, openly.

Again jumping from one to another, Ahbleza released each horse separately until he reached the fourth. Now swerving in close to the young woman for whom he had put on the show, he lifted her up to a place in front of him, his arms tight across her breast. His thighs directed the horse, the two riding toward a secluded point back of some boulders, where his commanding grip brought the horse to a stop.

One more moment the young warrior held on to the struggling woman; then her teeth bit into his wrist. Letting go one hand, he pulled on the braids hanging down her back. His grasp on her hair tilted her face and so he saw her eyes, something big and full of fear. Suddenly he remembered the woman in the enemy lodge from whom he had taken moccasins.

"I will not hurt you."

He sat amazed at his own words; he had spoken as if to a captive whom he decides not to kill instead of to the only woman around whom he ever had put his arms, ever wanted to hold.

Puzzled, even embarrassed, he looked on her face; slowly his fingers let go her hair. He saw that her head bowed, that she sat unmoving.

He spoke most quietly. "Perhaps ... perhaps you know that I ... I watch you." He waited for a sign saying that she understood him.

When she neither spoke nor lifted her face, he pulled again on her braids, but gently. "I like you," he said softly; "I like you very much."

She jerked up her head now and, facing away from him, she murmured certain phrases, something which will stun the young man, hurl his heart to the ground.

He got down from the horse but the young woman stayed on; he will lead her back to mother, grandmother, who wait along the trail.

Ahbleza felt an overwhelming desire now to ride back among the herders at the rear of the camps, but the instant he left the woman with her relatives, the warriors had crowded around, their eyes laughing, their voices teasing. But they came admiring. Ahbleza demonstrates a new way for approaching a young woman, snatching her up on a horse and dashing off, ignoring the old women who shout threats at him. Certainly, Ahbleza's way, something more exciting than a meeting along the water-trail or sitting in a tree half the night, blowing messages on a flute and watching for a certain someone to sneak out the lodge.

But above the laughs and the cheers, the old women had rasped out at Ahbleza, their tongues wagging alarm for all girls, all young women. Mothers, they screeched, will hunt strings for tying their daughters thighs after this approach wherein a leader's son takes a woman beyond their supervising eyes. What girl dares feel safe, they raged, now that a certain young warrior puts such notions into the heads of other young men?

Scarcely aware of banter and harangue, the son of Olepi reflected the young woman's sad-soft message: her brothers and uncles agree that Mniśa will make a good husband and so she will respect their wishes. She will go into the old man's lodge as his third wife when snow comes.

Am I the only one in the tribe, Ahbleza asked himself, who knows not of this woman's pledge to her relatives and to Mniśa? And will my foolishness make trouble between Mniśa's band and the Mahto or between my father and Mniśa? Or will the Sicangu, a man forty-and-seven winters and leader of his camps, regard a youth ten-and-seven as someone too insignificant to notice and so ignore the whole thing?

Shamefaced, Ahbleza went about collecting the four horses he had used, ones he had helped his uncle Huśte gentle, horses he had borrowed for his act. He will lead the four to a place at the back of the line and he will hide in their dust for a while.

But before he had moved these horses to the rear, someone came riding up, speaking boldly and flashing him an admiring look. "The son of Olepi teaches the warriors something."

Ahbleza instantly looked away. Why will Hinzi, properly indifferent to his presence in the lodge, choose to violate custom now? Custom will not permit him rudeness toward his father's young wife—this woman but three winters more than he—but neither will custom demand that he make answer. And so he stood pretending that the wind carried off her words before ever he heard.

But the young woman will stay awhile, laughing softly, enjoying his discomfort. For reasons of her own.

When she had gone, Ahbleza went to the back as he had intended, offering the horse-herders his help. But again someone came riding to see him, someone painted yellow and wearing a skin neckpiece. This person carried the two-lash whip of the Tokala clubmen, this man a member of the

536

Tokala-lodge and one of ten akicita in control of the traveling villages.

Ahbleza looked up unsmiling at the horseback, someone who calls himself Peśla since the day he permitted the Tokala to pull out hair from the sides of his head. Peśla, son of Ogle, brother to Tonweya, someone toward whom Ahbleza sensed a growing disdain, someone who had changed his name from Gnúska to Peśla but who had kept the same disgruntled nature.

Peśla spoke now, his tone mocking: "My friend, I hear that I miss something extraordinary. But while you put on a show I, Tokala, attend to my work."

The red paint covering Peśla's mouth will not hide this man's scornful lips. "My work," he jeered, "includes keeping the children in line but your fancy games with these little ones makes difficult my task." He swung his whip casually. "For the good of the moving camps you shall refrain from using Titonwan children—and Titonwan women—for demonstrating your skill."

Ahbleza held on to himself; the ridiculing words shall pass in silence. And now he watched Peśla ride off, the man's fingers tight around the long-notched handle of his whip, a whip-bearer who aches for something—or someone—against whom he dares raise the Tokala whip. And until Peśla fulfills this compulsion, let everyone stay out of this clubman's path.

The Tokala, riding away from his unsatisfying encounter with Ahbleza, pondered the rules of his lodge. Certainly his interest in belonging to an akicita-lodge bears on something more than watching over children and dogs in a traveling camp; any grandmother will handle these things. Nor will the settling of loudmouth quarrels excite him; any peaceman who carries a pipe owns this power.

When the Tokala installed him as whip-bearer—a vacancy occurring shortly before the bands moved toward the hills—they had asked if he understood the power of the whip. But when he had answered saying that a whip-carrier shall lash the legs of any member who refuses to dance or the back of any Titonwan who resists an akicita's command, the pipe-keeper had regarded him sternly, then reviewed the purpose of the Tokala-lodge.

"Each Tokala," the pipe-man had said, "shall consider himself a peace-keeper at all Titonwan gatherings—hunts, moves, ceremonies. But watching over camp will not answer why the Tokala form a brother-lodge." The clubman had paused but his eyes had remained on the new member, on Peśla. "Hear me. The Tokala pledge their help to the old and to cripples. They hold up the honor of a tribe which boasts that none starve and that all own robes. They remember woman's high place and so they treat kindly their wives, also women captives."

The speaker, turning from Peśla, had gazed around the lodge. "A Tokala never misrepresents himself to a lodge-brother, never takes away anything from a lodge-brother, neither horses nor women. But the rules say that if a brother-Tokala lacks a wife, those members with more than two women shall offer one to the lonely man. In this manner members provide for wives who seek diversion, but nothing happens without consent all around."

When the pipe-keeper had finished, a different one had spoken; the drum-carrier had made clear the meaning of the whip.

"The two who carry whips," he said, "act as an example. They keep all lodge rules, all camp rules. The whip-men sit as head akicita in the Tokala lodge. But he who keeps good conduct among the members shall conduct himself in proper manner, in and out this lodge. Let the whip-bearer regard the whip as a symbol of self-discipline."

They had presented the whip to Peśla after these speeches, and he had pounded the earth vowing bravery and truth whatever occurs.

Now, again riding up and down the line of people, Peśla told himself that he will make something occur and so put into effect his vow. Before trees pile their leaves on the ground and crackle underfoot, he will sneak out alone and make a quiet approach into an enemy camp. He will carry the Tokala whip but he will act in the manner of a lance-bearer.

And something more: he will test the truth of the pipe-keeper's speech, all that talk about Tokala members with more than two wives and the man who has none.

● ● ●

The man, amazed, stared at Peśla; then he spoke: "You have many chances among the young women in camp, fine women who as yet never speak with a man. They want a strong young warrior like yourself. So why take a woman already wife, four winters my wife?"

"I dare not take her from you, my brother Tokala, as you know. I am here asking that you give me the woman."

The unusual request had confused the husband. True, the Tokala rules to which he had agreed upon becoming a member permit this sort of thing, but never, to his knowing, will anyone use this privilege. Perhaps a man will offer a wife, but what manner of man will come asking for this favor? He tried to recall something which disputed the whip-bearer's demand. And 'demand,' the word for this insult.

"You soon will own one more horse . . . two more horses, if you desire." Peśla spoke brazenly.

The man's quick gesture scorned the offer. What manner of person trades a wife for a horse or even considers such things? Perhaps the blood-families of two young people who show their desire to raise a lodge exchange horses in honor of the mating-pair, but never will a man secure a wife through a present of horses to her people.

"The woman has a say in this arrangement." The husband's voice tightened. "None forces a woman against her desires. When this thing happens, everyone suffers."

"Everyone suffers when a husband holds on to a wife against her desire."

The husband looked off into the darkness, away from the cunning that made him feel trapped.

"I see," Peśla said now, "that my Tokala brother will not oblige me in this favor. And so I wonder whether he keeps all different pledges he makes when he becomes Tokala. They say he has more horses and more wives than any other member. They say he owns more horses than the leaders of his tribe. And that he holds on to three women."

The husband answered sharply: "Tell me of a rule that says one man shall not possess more than another man."

"Apparently my akicita-brother remembers not that a Tokala pledges help to the weak and any have-not in camp. What about the blind or someone suffering an injury or the woman who lacks a meat-provider for her small children?

539

When a man becomes Tokala he pledges that his possessions shall flow out in the direction of true need.

"But perhaps you never discover these lodges in need and so you will appreciate my efforts at finding such lodges for you."

The man answered nothing, and so after a little wait Peśla spoke again. "Hoye, my friend, I agree. I and you talk enough. They permit nothing angry between lodge-brothers and certainly a Tokala never threatens his brother."

The young warrior placed his hand briefly on the man's shoulder but feeling a stiffness, he smiled and moved toward his horse.

Attempting indifference, the husband made a final reply. "I will speak to the woman. If she accepts, look for her to bring you moccasins." He turned abruptly and went back into his lodge.

And Peśla rode off certain that within the next two, three days he shall own a wife.

Wipatawin listened carefully to her husband's words. He had tried to keep anger out his voice but she understood that even the two days' wait after his talk with Peśla had not cooled his temper. But certainly he had spoken to the point: Peśla wants her. Go to him if she wishes.

The woman sat as second wife in this lodge, living here four winters and a sister to the original wife. She stood tall, a proud-walking person and owning a most pleasing voice for song. And so the Tokala-lodge had invited her to become one of their four women singers. Wipatawin had not borne the husband a child and so she took pleasure in honoring him in this manner, as wife of a Tokala member to whom the lodge taught their songs.

But during this summer's encampment the husband had taken a third wife, this new one unrelated to the other two women. And now Wipatawin, the middle wife, sat uncertain of her position. But she kept on with her singing, a source of much pleasure, and she had not made any complaints.

She had come to know Peśla during those song-teaching occasions in the Tokala-lodge, the young warrior coming not to sing but to listen. Once, twice she had observed his glances but she had not looked for something. He had appeared to enjoy her singing and she, learning of his calm during the hair-plucking, had admired secretly this man's endurance. They say that one who offers himself for this painful experience usually goes out of the lodge before they finish pulling hair from one side. But not Peśla.

But why Peśla will want her, a woman already wife and three winters more in age than this warrior, she will not understand. Certainly none call her unattractive but neither will they regard her as really good-looking. Perhaps Peśla likes a tall woman . . . or a good singer . . . or perhaps she owns a power for attracting men she not yet recognizes. But she will remember also that her husband takes a third wife this summer and that he bluntly tells her, go to Peśla if she desires.

And so, crawling into her sleeping robes, Wipatawin lay pondering whether to stay or go, whether to live as middle-wife in the lodge of a kind-face man or to sit alongside Peśla, the one wife in the lodge of a cruel-face man. Perhaps a change will bring her a child and so fulfill this one desire. Certainly this change will make things more interesting . . . for a while. Or so says any woman who makes such a change.

Napewaśte, keeping to her place in the line of travel, rode at the front of her tiyośpaye, a woman properly attentive not only to these five related lodges but to all twenty-and-nine lodges that make up the Mahto band. Meaning the two hundred persons—four Mahto villages—who keep an orderly line each day, raise a neat camp each night. Children, horses, even the camp-dogs traveled in a manner that made Napewaśte proud. Ina had said that never will she remember her sister in a more contented mood than during this walk to the black hills.

Now the people crossed a stream and Napewaśte looked back at her daughter Kehala, who, leading a horse piled tall with bundles, entered the water guardedly.

"Shallow water," she called to the girl, her own heavily loaded horse midstream and the water barely to the creature's shanks.

A second backward glance satisfied Napewaśte that Unci also made a safe crossing. The old woman, scorning horseback travel, swam the rivers, waded the streams. And so she came now, moccasins in hand, keeping close to Ina, whose horse dragged poles. Only the one, Napewaśte told herself as she reached the opposite edge of the stream, refuses to stay with her own family.

Hinziwin had preferred to keep company with a group of girls who rode imprudently near the warriors, their giggles aimed at attracting the young men. Hinzi's favorite companion, a bold-eyes flirt, sat ready to return any young man's glance, to encourage any youth who looked her way twice.

"You friend displays little modesty," Napewaśte had said, but the admonishing phrase had slid off the young wife like rib-bones skimming on ice.

"I regard this friend as a sister," Hinzi had answered, tossing her head and jingling the long string of shells which decorated her hair. "Perhaps my sister-friend will live in this lodge one day." She had touched the shining beads looped around her neck. "This way Napewaśte will have three women helping with the hides." Laughing, she had run off.

For a while Napewaśte had thought about the shining beads and those fine skins which made up Hinziwin's gowns. She recalled the young wife's enthusiasm over these hides while Olepi had sat within hearing, but she remembered also those many complaints about aching fingers while Hinzi worked on these skins. Eventually Napewaśte had taken over this work, her expert hands softening, whitening the hides, then fastening the pieces together, forming the gown. But when she had offered to quill the wings—something she truly enjoys—Hinzi had grabbed the gown; her sister-friend, she had said, will decorate the shoulders. Napewaśte's designs appear nice enough, glances and gestures had told, but Hinzi's girl-friend colors the quills brightly and she dreams the most exciting patterns.

When next Napewaśte had seen this gown, she had bowed her head. Kehala at age eleven proved a more competent quiller than the one who decorated Hinzi's gown. Apparently this girl-friend will know nothing about splicing when one uses short quills, and certainly the sinew seems to pull out in many places; the gown will need most careful handling.

But the young wife had neglected this gown, showing her usual indifference toward cleaning off stains, never using suds or powders that keep garments fresh and neat, never out looking for cannakpa, those little-ears-that-attach-to-wood, that help remove grease spots. And so Napewaśte, unwilling that Hinzi's disregard for appearance embarrass the family, mended and cared for all of Hinzi's robes and gowns and moccasins but the young woman never had shown any sign of gratefulness.

Even so, Napewaśte found herself wishing now as often before that Hinziwin had come into her lodge as daughter, as someone to whom she dared give her affection, dared protect. But protect from whom, the woman will not know.

"Why stand here? You belong in the lodge with the other women." Olepi, coming from a smoke with the leaders, had discovered Hinziwin waiting for him along the dusky path; he neither looked nor sounded pleased.

"Perhaps my husband will enjoy riding with me before he turns over his horse to the tenders." Hinziwin's voice matched the appeal in her eyes.

They rode out a little distance from the overnight camp, stopping near a wooded place. Here, the young woman jumped from her horse with the ease of a boy. Sitting, she smoothed the ground at her side. "If my husband will sit also, I shall tell him something."

The man dismounted but he remained standing, waiting.

"I speak about the son of the Mahto leader."

Olepi stood as before, his silence disturbing; and so the woman spoke quickly. She told of Ahbleza's tricks horseback, hinting that the young warrior put on this act for her approval.

When Olepi kept silent, she glanced at his face. And now something made her wish she never had begun the story. She hurried on, wanting to reach the point at which Ahbleza rode off with a girl whom everyone in camp knew had pledged herself to Mniśa.

"I know nothing about this woman."

The cold voice sounded a warning; Hinziwin slid near Olepi's feet and reached out to touch his moccasin.

The man moved his foot away. "What more gossip will you bring?" He spoke mildly but he had not looked mild.

Suddenly the woman let go her growing irritation. The

affectionate tone dropped out of her speech and her eyes flashed contempt. "I bring you my own gossip. I will have you know that I am neither water-carrier nor errand girl for those women in your lodge. I am your wife and I will not have a bunch of old women telling me whom I dare choose for friends and in what manner I shall decorate my gowns and clean my robes and brush my hair and all those other things. I will take care of myself and whatever belongs to me, but I will not work in any tipi Napewaśte manages, an old prude who never wants me to have any fun. But I happen to know that she will sneak and trick to get something."

A spark flashed in the leader's eyes but Hinziwin will not stop now.

"Napewaśte visits the hunter's wife when your son wants a wingbone whistle. As usual, she manages things and so Ogle persuades you. . . ."

Olepi interrupted, his voice mild as before. "You talk too much." Getting on his horse, he signed that the woman mount and follow him.

Never had Hinziwin felt remorse or apprehended difficulty beyond her powers for handling; certainly her attractive face and appealing manner favorably impressed even those persons who knew to look out for her cunning. But not before now will she have a chance to discover the true extent of her power. And so, riding along back of this resolute man, she imagined in what manner he will treat her impudence.

Will he consider cutting off her pretty hair and gashing her arms with a knife? Or perhaps he leads her toward a lonely place where he will cut off the tip of her nose, even cut out her tongue. They say a man will deface a disrespectful wife, especially a woman he adores. Hinziwin shivered, not in fear but in excitement.

But apparently Olepi had considered none of these punishments. He simply led her back to camp, then told her to put up her own lodge—and fast. And before dawn she shall get the thing down and prepare to move out in company with members of the family—and she shall walk with the family.

And so, alone in her little tipi this night, a vexed Hinziwin regretted that she had not said more to Olepi against the sister-wives or about his son Ahbleza. Whatever he will attempt with stick or knife and whatever she will try in an effort to protect herself she will find preferable to this thwarting of her scheme, this omission of a challenge that tests her persuasive powers.

She began to cry but soon used up her tears; instead of acting like a child, why not sit calm and ponder woman-ways for distressing a man, perhaps something which involves his son, something to make the people talk behind palms and fans. Then certainly Olepi will remember about cutting off the tip of a wife's nose.

Olepi, leaving his young wife at the camp's edge, had returned to the nearby knoll where a little while back he had sat talking and laughing with relatives and friends. He came here now neither for talk nor laughter; he wanted quiet and loneliness and a pipe for comfort.

The man, riding far front of the space on which his son had performed with the horses, had missed Ahbleza's exhibition. And perhaps Napewaśte had walked far back in the line; certainly she had said nothing about this demonstration of skill. Perhaps she chose not to mention this act, her reticence relating in some way to Hinziwin and the young wife's pretense that Ahbleza put on his performance especially for her. Or perhaps the incident concerning the girl whom Ahbleza had grabbed up embarrassed Napewaśte and discouraged any talk about this show. Certainly Napewaśte never acted in any sneaky, tricky way, the woman never holding back something. . . .

Olepi gazed at his pipestem in a moment of self-reproach; he had permitted himself to dwell on Hinziwin's insinuation. Certainly he, of all people knows Hinziwin's ways. Or will he really know this woman? Will any man ever really know any woman? Perhaps woman, the only true mystery that man ever shall encounter.

Tonweya laughed. From here—his new lookout point—he had seen his people appear on top a rise, the bands catching up with the leaders, the travelers resembling a great stretch of trees along a ridge, as if all the standing-people on earth suddenly grew in this one place.

But his second look showed him that these standing-people tumbled downhill—people, horses, dogs amass, everyone slipping, rolling, sprawling down together, the dust of their slide similar to a great yellow smoke signal that tells of their approach.

He had imagined those proud-walkers at the front encouraging the people to make a game of this descent, the whole starting down together, each one trying to stay on his feet and reach bottom without a scratch. And he had imagined the laughter as they started, certain ones clowning, different ones holding on to their dignity, children and dogs squealing, horses neighing.

The young scout leaned back against the sky, his own laughter joining theirs, the distant laughter as real as if he heard.

Wasu cooked small meat over a handful of embers, his only warm food since the people began traveling west toward a winter campsite. And according to his notched stick this will mean he had lived six days on wasna, scout-food.

He turned the meat slowly and shifted his position to catch the smell, half the pleasure of eating in the teasing smoke. Slapping his belly, he sat back and looked at the sky.

The air seemed different, something more than the haziness common to the changing season; the midmorning sky appeared drowsy in an unfamiliar way. Wasu stood and, moving away from his fire, sniffed the four directions for burning grass. Suddenly he kicked aside the roasting meat; using his robe, he smothered the fire in the manner that makes a thick signaling smoke.

Some distance away Po, lifting himself out of his nest, breathed in the morning, then made the little sound of surprise. Using spit, he moistened the inside of his nostrils. He sniffed the south in short, quick sniffs. Next thing, he began twirling a fire, something with which to signal the people.

The look-alike scouts prowled the dry, crackling brush north of Wasu's watch. One of these two, lifting his chin, used his face for a pointer. He called his brother's attention to a pale red reflection in the sky. The twins climbed a rise for a look toward the south.

• • •

546

Pasu lay, eyes closed, quiet as a sleeping rattler on a butte. But now his hand moved slowly onto his belly; he scratched, brushing off a little bug that tickled his skin. And now he stretched himself, kicking and rolling like a young horse.

He sat up and, reaching for a piece of wasna, chewed slowly on this scout-meat. But suddenly he stopped chewing; he stared at a far-distant redness, something that curled across the sun-dried earth. Looking under his palm, he searched for a sign of the traveling bands. But he saw only the narrow red stripe that meandered over the yellow plain, among the dark, dark red patches of pte-grass, around the patches of bald ground.

The people saw Pasu's signal, his puffs of smoke telling that an impetuous wind moves a grass fire swiftly, a fire that intercepts their path. And now the leaders, seeing smoke-clouds arise from different high points, counc	iled these messages, contemplating ways to step around the fire.

But the experienced advised an instant face about; start firing a strip of the ground over which the people already pass. Let everyone work, the clubmen supervising. Let children help the women pull up grass, pile up roots. The stretch of plain these people burn will stop the approaching flame and the black earth soon will cool. But once the bands move again, they shall remember that smoldering chips hold fire a long while, as much danger in burned feet as in burned thighs.

The people started their work at once, the fire now within view of the riders to the front. The horse-tenders stayed with the snorting herd, but different youths sneaked out to use their arrows on the little creatures who fled before the flame, the singed and lame an easy target for a boy. But the clubmen, watchful in every direction, came up quickly, restraining these game-makers, sending these youngsters back to work on the fire-line. And so the young discovered that when a people walk dangerously, the one gives way to the safety of the whole.

Peźi, keeping close to Tonweya as from the start, interpreted Pasu's robe-waving: "I shall hunt streams and grassy ground, anything the fire skips. The bands will need these places for the horses. I go, you stay. Wait for the people; ride awhile with those scouts at the rear."

Tonweya's heart soared; he will see his brother-friend and his family. Perhaps he will get a night's sleep in his mother's lodge and a taste of her cooking. The wind that sent this grass fire blew good onto the plain, good for the earth's grasses and good for him; wind, a friendly force, a message-carrier.

Ogle settled against a pile of robes and sucked his pipe; Cankuna and her daughters, having stacked the meat bowls, took places on the opposite side of this traveling tipi, their eyes smiling gladness at Tonweya's return. And the youth, gazing at his crossed legs, sat waiting for the speeches that will welcome him into the lodge as a visiting son, a son who sleeps on lookouts while the bands travel.

The sight of his family—everyone here but Pesla— along with three bowls of the most wonderful soup his mother ever had made, proved remarkably comforting, and yet the young scout's keen ears sensed a strain, the welcoming talk slow to come.

Ogle had drawn twice on the pipe and now he offered Tonweya a smoke, his act a surprise to this son if not to each one sitting around him.

"This lodge," Ogle said quietly, "shelters but one blood-son." He glanced at Tonweya. "Perhaps you not yet know that your brother takes a wife."

His father's tone, not the news, disturbed Tonweya; the man had spoken as if he announced one of the four tragic losses instead of this glad news. Or will Ogle hint at something contrary? Until this moment Tonweya had understood his brother's absence as meaning that Pesla eats in the akicita-lodge, but now he wondered which woman Pesla had taken for wife; he waited to hear his new relative named.

"A Tokala member offers your brother one of his wives," Ogle said. "She sings for the Tokala . . . the tall one of the four."

The hunter's inflection dismissed more talk of Pesla; the man wanted to hear Tonweya speak now, parents and sisters eagerly awaiting words about that which impresses this son as he commences work, as he becomes ears and eyes and nose for the tribe.

548

But on his sleeping robe in his mother's lodge this same night, Tonweya had pondered his brother's choice. Why take a woman who belongs to another man? Why not choose a one-alone woman, someone who never belongs to a different man? He, Tonweya, will want a one-alone woman if ever he mates. But will a scout really have need of wife? Not often will he eat, sleep in camp; why a woman?

Before he slept, he remembered again the food his mother had prepared for him, comparing that which she cooked to wasna, scout-meat. Why not a woman, he decided, and fell asleep smiling.

XII

WASU HAD cut five more notches in his stick; for eleven, twelve days they had traveled toward the sheltering hill. But not as many people walked in this line now. The Kiyuksa had dropped out far back, and the Kuya—these people scattering into three different snow camps—had left the line two, three days before. The Mniśa village, looking for a thickly timbered stream, strung along far to the rear.

The travelers had experienced two big hunts as a tribe, and the plain had yielded generously of her roots and berries. Now the good earth and the round yellow moon and the rain-birds all agreed that the people separate; what one camping ground ever will support all Titonwan during moons when nothing grows, when the herd hides and many creatures sleep, when everything goes under the snow?

The leaders had guided their people along a safe path, neither attacks nor fear of attacks. Three Titonwan had died, two old men and one old woman, persons who had found travel difficult, who gladly let go, who chose to roll off the drags.

But now the people walked within three, four days of

their winter camp-ground, grizzly butte not far off, many attractive sites between here and the lonely rise.

And so the Śiyo discovered relatives already encamped along kills-himself creek, and the Okandada, seeing that the Śiyo will stop near these people, walked only a half-day beyond.

But the Mahto went on to the foot of the great butte, perhaps memories of previous camps at this site pulling the band into the sheltering shadow of the steep, steep hill.

Looking up at the dark, flat top, certain Mahto remembered that whoever climbed to this level saw the starting-place of the horizons. And the women viewing these ledges remembered that the moons above this cliff signify men-in-the-lodges, the contented season.

Children who glanced up recalled those stones they had carried to the branches of a fragrant tree growing on the hillside, stones that related in some mysterious way to the invisibles. Or so their parents had told.

Ahbleza, lifting his eyes to the butte, remembered himself as a spirit, something drawing on the energy here, strengthening the will, freshening the power. Gazing at the top, he felt himself lifted above the butte, standing now as on a cloud, acknowledging the wonder not of hills and horizons but of his own indestructible spirit.

Tonweya, smiling up at the tree-topped summit, recalled his people as he had seen these travelers back on the ridge, like a great forest. But he saw also the earth out of which this wondrous butte grew, and seeing, he knew himself as a thing of joy embracing the whole.

And so the people approaching the butte saw the scout, saw Tonweya, a lithe form poised between grass and billowing cloud, a lone mediator between earth and sky.

On different occasions Wanaǵi, approaching the butte, had seen this hill as perhaps most Mahto saw—an abrupt intrusion on the calm of the plain. Now, suddenly, he glimpsed not butte but the power that constructs a butte, a thrust of fire from under the earth that disturbs the original stone-nation, displaces the boulders, relocates the pebbles, separates stone-families.

The next instant his memory sent him back ten-and-seven winters to the night of Peta's dying, to the fire song he had beaten out on his breast; from above, he had sung, someone tells of fire under the earth.

And then he remembered that during these seasons, these seventeen, eighteen winters, he had lived drawing upon śkan, the spiritual vitality. And that, without knowing exactly when, he had recognized himself as stable; he had become a man of habitual spiritual awareness.

He knew now that he shall climb grizzly butte and that on top of this hill he shall receive the sacred-stone songs. Wait, his familiar-voice had told him, wait until you see that place whereon you choose to meet your soul.

Here on this butte, he answered now, I choose to meet my self.

The earth owns two good days, one visible and one invisible; the earth owns two good days, one the body senses and one the spirit visualizes.

The earth owns two good days, one the reasoning identifies and integrates and one the spirit desires and absorbs.

And on the day man recognizes his power to overlap these two, he owns the earth; the grandfathers had said so.

The butte welcomed the wapiya; each thing Wanaǵi touched or sniffed, heard or saw on this hill agreed with him.

He had reached the flat top before midday. The earth had lent him one of her two good days and the sun had thrown him strings of light on which to climb, hand over hand, ledge to ledge. Pebbles nesting along the steep sides of the butte had awakened at his approach and, rolling out around his feet, had called him 'grandfather.' He had answered, saying 'grandchildren.'

A gentle wind had led him among the squatting trees until a certain one had whispered his name, calling him Wanaǵi, spirit-man. Smiling he had stopped here and, brushing aside tree-droppings, had widened a space of bare earth. And then he had performed a little dance on the cleared ground, his pipestem swinging in his hand. He had brought the stem but not the bowl; he had brought the important piece of the pipe.

And now he sat gazing out onto the plain where dark

551

patches and white curving lines awaited his definition. But he recognized only the yellow silence.

Everything blends, he told himself; I sit between two seasons, old summer and young winter; I sit on a day that joins each side, a day that feels warm, smells cold.

I am here at midday between day and night suns; I sit on my shadow. I am here at middle age, a man neither young nor ancient.

He reached out his hand, propping the pipestem againt a boulder. He will not need the song that brings about favorable conditions; he had heard agreement and seen silence and felt his spirit stir. He had progressed from mere perception of spirit growth to a definite realization of his spirit-body.

I am here to recognize my proportions. I am here to experience my spiritual birth. I am here to see my self born.

He flung aside the piece of pronghorn hide that covered his shoulders; he lay back on the hard ground.

Ta ta iciya wo; I return to the source.

At once the shelter tree patterned his face and breast with shadow paint and the wind came back to stand guard. Haun-n-n. He exhaled slowly, letting go his body. I shall come back regenerated, he told the earth.

Haun-n-n. Exhaling yet more slowly, he let go his thoughts.

Casual sensations replaced his usual alertness, his reason granting quiet and space for impressions coming from his spirit-consciousness. But the wind stayed on to rattle the brush, to prevent his complete abandonment. He shall maintain a subdued awareness of his surroundings when he transfers the control to his spirit, when he goes somewhere different.

And now he assembled his ultimate self in a rush of exaltation that united his strength with the overstrength, that located him in the realm of unencumbered vitality and desire.

Wani . . . su . . . ogna . . . wanisugna
Living . . . seed . . . shell . . . source
Woman taking-on-life, woman between two realms,

552

woman growing-a-life . . . water-life . . . water-baby . . . at the source.

Sound more felt than heard, a swinging sound as of tall, leafy trees swaying, sound that disappeared slowly as Wanaǧi sensed a presence, perhaps more than one presence, hovering over him. Something, someone, moved around, trying to attract his attention; movement more felt than seen, shadowy but friendly movement.

He felt a little uncomfortable at having nothing on him but himself. He tried to sit up but, lacking strength, he fell back.

Something touched him gently, an encouraging touch that gave energy to his newborn spirit-body.

He sat up, his head wobbly. Like a baby.

He, a baby now? He, born anew? But he had desired to see his birth.

"You will see your soul but not yet."

Dimly he heard his thought answered.

Suddenly aware of his rapid growth on this level, his spirit-body already advanced from infant to youth, Wanaǧi stood erect. But his nakedness startled him and his feebleness chilled him. Puzzled, he waited for someone to instruct him in what manner he shall draw upon the energy that surrounded him.

Someone? He looked around, but his sight, out of focus in this realm, permitted him to see only that which concerned his own growth. And seeing the 'grandfathers' will not contribute to his progress. And so he understood to listen for any voice that will guide him.

One spoke now, the tones clear, the words certain: "Instead of steps, you will move on waves of pressure. You will pulse your self forward."

Wanaǧi moved, a current of thought propelling him along, the motion surprising, pleasing. But he used up his energy quickly.

Repeating the same thought—his desire to advance—he moved again. But not far; he had difficulty breathing.

"You breathe differently here. Try a wide, full breath in place of your familiar little short ones."

Wanaǧi tried the big, aching breath. He discovered

that moving about on his own volition, breathing in this different manner, induced a feeling of hunting for something he very much wanted. Suddenly he knew: he hunted nourishment.

"The nourishment you take here," a voice told him, "you retain. The proportions you collect act creatively on each other even as meat and berries act on your flesh-body."

When Wanaġi asked about 'seeing,' the answering voice felt like a smile.

"You already know sight as an inferior sense. When you want to see something distant, you move along. Here you illuminate your self as you grow. Here you recognize someone through brightness of spirit."

The voice went on: "You now understand something of the conditions of your spirit-body. As you grow into these conditions, you reach comprehension. But until you feel familiar with your superior consciousness, move gently, proceed slowly."

Wanaġi's spirit-body had attained the age of his visible self. And he had absorbed the realities of a different element for conversion into earth activity. And now he heard a voice telling him to go back.

"You come here for contact with the motivating source of your existence. You make this contact and so the invisibles shall funnel more life-giving perception to the visible realm through you.

"Go back. Your shell, lying on the butte, awaits you."

Wanaġi opened his eyes to sun and warmth. A little wind, whirling up a dust, danced across his breast, and his pipestem, leaning against the boulder, whistled at him.

He sat up, listening more closely, now aware of a song, of words coming from the stone.

"You will see my four villages;
the moon, coming down, says so.
You will see my four acts;
the sun, coming down, says so."

Sitting quietly as before, legs crossed, Wanaġi heard the song twice. He had memorized the words and now he aspirated the tones.

He stood. He walked around the boulder, fingering the

554

depressions, rubbing his hand over the rough places where the stone, in frequent turns from frost and heat, had peeled.

Bending down, he picked from the ground a spiraling, cone-shaped stone shell. Then, turning over the slab that lay next to the fossil, he saw a second shell projecting from the edge, not as big but identical in shape.

He smiled, remembering those many seasons he desperately had wanted to receive the stone symbol, something to prove his contact with the invisible grandfathers and to ascertain his reliability as wakanhca, the true-seer. He held those stones in his hand now, the precious shell-form that symbolizes contact with life from the beginning, the most startling evidence of evolvement a man ever shall own.

Precious shell-form? Or will he mean the precious life-form that once lives within these shells?

Suddenly he heard a word, not one he ever had used, yet something strangely familiar: wanisugna. The next instant he remembered the invisibles telling him to go back, that his shell awaited him on the butte.

His own body? Or these stone shells? Either one a covering for a seed, a life; either one something to outgrow. . . .

He hung the pronghorn hide from his shoulders and began his descent of the butte, his pipestem in one hand, the stone shells in the other. Regenerated and joyful, he moved briskly, the pebbles scattering underfoot, racing him downhill, calling him 'grandfather.' And he answered, saying 'grandchildren.'

Stone, earth-elemental, on and under the ground, in water and in sky; stone, constantly in touch with the sun; stone, moving with a purpose, compelling a desire to identify with the will of the invisible grandfathers.

Stone, symbol of stability; stone, manifestation of the life-force at each person's level of vision.

Book Three

THE WARRIOR
1819/20 to 1824/25

I

PTE, SLOPES black with pte.

Tonweya lay on his belly, looking down on the many gullies leading into the narrow valley, grazing ground for the big herd. He sent a breath of thanks across the ridges, grateful to ptepazo, the grasshopper with the wavering long horns who had pointed out the meat.

A little while past, the young scout had held gently, between his thumb and finger, one of these black ground creatures. "I will keep you, grandfather," he had told the grasshopper, "until you point out pte. My ears pick up a soft snuffling but I will not travel five suns with the wind in my face and sit content on counting three hundred. I await the rumble of the summer gathering, females and fathers and young, blunt-horns and curved-horns and four-teeth. Perhaps one ridge now separates my four-legged brothers and me, but which ridge? Use your black horns and show which hill I shall climb."

He had watched with friendly, patient interest while the bloated shape waved long feelers over a black back.

"I see that you possess eyes but where, your ears?"

Then ptepazo, gracefully sweeping forward his long horns, twisted these wavers south, pointing south even when the scout turned his captive around and around.

559

Tonweya had dropped the creature into the grass. "Let none of the wingeds find you before snow," he had murmured and began to run in the direction pointed out to him, a man on his way to the mingling herds.

The summer had grown old, the berries black-ripe, but this day smelled young and fresh. And everywhere something sang—in the gullies, the grasses, the sky. The life-force also flowed strongly through the scout's heart, telling him that until a person lives a day like this one, until he hears his own voice in a great silent cry of joy, he dares not die. Tonweya, twenty-and-one, a scout who knows the earth as his to cherish and honor and protect.

He had approached this windy ledge, this viewpoint, moving on his belly until he lay in position to see without anyone seeing him. Then, lifting his head, he had glimpsed the black hillsides. When he looked again he had wanted to shout his gladness but not a sound had broken from his lips, not a stone had scraped under his toe.

He lay a long while observing the herd, gathering facts for his report. But now, as cautiously as he had approached the high ledge, he withdrew and began his return journey over the dry white plain to pahamni ridge.

The quick trail back demanded two days' running, and so he had paced himself, jogging without stops to the most distant object on his horizon, then walking awhile, alternating his stride to conserve his breath. On the wide flat he covered himself with his robe, stooping and moving slowly, a discernible form, yet something that resembles pte.

During the seven winters since his vision-seeking, Tonweya often had run long distances, enduring to the finish, rushing into camp in the accepted manner of a scout who brings good news. Not once had he needed to sneak in after dark, nothing to tell. Not Tonweya; he stayed out until he found the herd. For three seasons now he had worn two waverers, the mark of a scout they recognize, the stems of these two feathers stripped up to the white tip, something to simulate the waverers, the long horns of ptepazo—or pte woyaka as some of the young scouts will say. But he had not earned this honor quickly.

Not a man in the tribe, the grandfathers had said, holds more importance than the scout, whose truth determines the safety of the people, whose trust determines survival for the one, for the whole. The youth-vision perhaps confirms a desire, they had told, but a vision will not strengthen a man's natural powers nor give him a fit body. Only the practice of pure truth makes a man dependable and only an exacting use of ears and eyes and nose sharpens his senses. And only urgencies truly empower the legs.

But I need more than powerful legs on this run, Tonweya told himself; if a Witapaha discovers my tracks, I will need gullies and boulders as much as I need feet.

He had recalled an event four winters past when certain Titonwan had gone south with a party of Sahiela to trade with the Witapaha on the shell river. But after two, three trades something had provoked a quarrel between a Sicangu and a Witapaha, a Titonwan war club killing the Witapaha. Next day, the embarrassed Sahiela had watched their Titonwan friends drive away their Witapaha friends, the Witapaha women crying out for someone to stop the fight. The Witapaha, they say, always try to stop trouble before things go too far, but neither those cries nor the Sahiela gift-offerings had affected the irate warriors. And so this affair had finished off any efforts toward a peace with the Witapaha, any more attempts at trading with these people.

The round moon rose, brightening the scout's trail, but now he needed to keep a careful watch on his shadow. He had heard that the Witapaha warriors often raid on a night when the moon sits round, not a cloud in the sky. But whom will they raid? Scarcely the encampment at pahamni ridge. And yet a scout never surmises anything.

He had proved apt at discovering pte, and now he wanted to prove his competence at locating whatever the people will regard as important to their safety, their serenity. Actually he had located an enemy only once, his experience involving an Oyatenumpa family, something that had occurred back three seasons.

While scouting pte, he had come upon these Oyatenumpa, a family of eight who traveled using one horse for comfort, using camp-dogs to drag their scanty possessions. Observing signs neither of hunt nor raid, he had imagined that these people went out on a visit. But a scout lives with fact, not imagination, and so, creeping along back of the travelers for a half-day, he had noticed details: one baby, two children, and two women; three men protected the group. They had not walked in a hurry but stopped often to gather berries and dig roots. The men had smoked a friendly pipe, and he had stood near enough to view one of the women while she played with the baby.

He truly had enjoyed watching this family until he remembered whom he watched. Here, a people not Titonwan yet they traveled on Titonwan trails. And whatever the reason that had brought the group, he needed to regard these Oyatenumpa as an enemy and to report their presence to the bands.

Before he had turned back toward camp he had contemplated capturing one of the girl-children, someone to give to his mother, someone to stop her grief for the small daughter long gone from the robe on her back. But he had not dared the risk of snatching a child from under seven pairs of eyes. And so he had run back with his report, then gone out again before hearing the council's decision.

He had learned afterwards that Peśla had joined the Mahto warriors who, locating these Oyatenumpa, had brought back the horse and three scalps—man, woman, and a child. Two of those scalps had fluttered from Peśla's lance, the son of Ogle lending the woman's hair to his sister Cuwe for the celebration dance but making a gift to his mother of the little girl's scalp.

Suddenly Tonweya wished that he had not recalled this incident, this Oyatenumpa family whom they had killed; the recollection had acted to shake up his belly in a most disturbing manner.

But now a heavy smell on the night air told him that he approached a place of quiet water. And so he decided to linger alongside the stagnant pool, an unattractive rest stop but a place to drop his unpleasant memory and renew his strength for the distance he will run before dawn.

The next moment he saw two tiny points of light, tiny spots that glowed up dimly from bare ground, that moved slowly toward the toe of his moccasin. Hoĥ! a child of Iktomi, the many-legged little creature who hunts in the night.

"Iktomi, hear me. The flying-mystery kills you." Speaking softly, the scout reached for a stone with which to crush the trickster. But the specks of light disappeared before he let the weapon fall.

And so what happens? Never permit Iktomi to cross your path, they say; kill Iktomi with a stone but never silently. Remember that Iktomi tricks everyone. But will this attractive crawling creature really bring on a black-dog and the scolding little old grandmother bird who, working together, will drive off the pte that he, Tonweya, locates? Such acts in keeping, the people tell, with Iktomi's treacherous ways.

Dropping to his knees the scout hunted the wet grass but he saw nothing more of those six tiny gleaming eyes, two on top and four under. The only thing around now, those annoying lump-raisers. And so scratching his arms, slapping at his shoulders, he started out again at a jog; he intended to reach pahamni before Iktomi put any schemes to work.

And he intended to avoid any more remembrances of past seasons, past experiences. Enough that he concentrate on keeping his shadow small and his thoughts on pleasing things. Like pretty young women.

The people looked from under the edges of their tipi— the covers raised to permit a midday breeze—and saw the skinny legs of Eyanpaha as the crier passed by, the man's strong voice a contrast to his bony shins and knees. Throughout the seasons he had remained the favorite mouth in the tribe. And now he announced the approach of a scout who came running zigzag toward camp, a good sign as everyone knew.

"He protects you. Remember this thing and make him gifts." The crier sang out his advice.

Many persons hurried out from their lodges, going toward the center, but the old men, leaning against the tipi covers during the midday heat, waited for a howl from the ridge; not until the scout gives this signal will they get up and shuffle toward the center lodge.

On hearing Eyanpaha, the four deciders had sent someone to pile up chips in front of the big tipi while they put on their shirts and paint, each one making himself presentable for the ceremony of a returning scout.

The young warriors, seeing their leaders assemble, came forward now and many girls moved slowly toward the center, more than one girl eager for a glimpse of Tonweya, more than one woman waiting to see if he will glance her way.

Suddenly everyone sat alert; they had heard a howl in the near distance. At once five men, affixing pte-horns to their heads, started walking toward the edge of camp.

Tonweya waited on the ledge after sending his signal. Let the summer-shirts prepare the center for his report; let the people gather for his arrival. But certainly he shall rush in as if ten Psa come close on his moccasins; everyone likes to see a scout puffing, likes to watch a scout who races in short of breath.

Now the people saw the horn-wearers meet the scout and the scout begin his dash. Next thing, Tonweya stood close by, his breath coming in big gasps, his appearance more that of a handsome youth who had won a foot race than that of a scout ready to report to the deciders.

His legs, slim and hard from his unceasing travels on foot, moved up to tight thighs and a flat, tough belly. His fine narrow shoulders seemed designed to slip easily through thick groves and brush, and his slender but strong arms hung neither too short nor too long for the many uses to which a scout put his hands. His proportions brought admiration now as always from his own, from a people who never had lacked for evenly proportioned men.

But Tonweya had not noticed the flattering murmurs. His dark eyes, calm and unchanging, had sighted the chips and, spurting forward, he kicked aside the pile and dropped to one knee.

A trilling arose from where the women stood, the trills perhaps as much for his good-looking face as for his discovery of meat.

Not a man among the Titonwan owned such a nose. This feature, neither hooked nor curved down, lengthened moderately and in shapely form. But Tonweya, understanding his nose only as a tool for smelling, knew that a beak like the one on Pasu's face or a hump like the one on most faces will not impair the smelling-power. Only one personal feature will Tonweya regret: his small ears tightly set against his head. Nakpa cikcika the people say, making a comparison with the creature who swims carrying a stick. But he had observed that a man's ears grow in old age and so he looked for a nice big flapping pair when his winters reached fifty, sixty.

Ogle, eyes proud, watched his son kneel in the formal posture of a scout who awaits the pipe from his leader's hands or from any one of the honorable men sitting in the half-circle.

"Whatever you see, you see for the good of the people; the nations depend upon your eyes. Your word means life to these families."

Olepi spoke, holding the stem which had touched lips around the circle, but Tonweya understood that he shall enact certain things before they put the pipe to his lips.

"They will not call you child but they will say that you grow up among these valleys and hills. And so tell me if you see anything of the prowling true-dog or the feeding pte when you go to the hills. Tell me at what place you stand and see something good. Tell me and make me glad." Having spoke the ceremonial phrases, Olepi swung the pipestem toward the scout.

Tonweya drew a mouthful of smoke and so made his pledge to speak the truth, the whole truth. He remained on his knee, none of him moving but his thumb.

"I start from where I now kneel. I go to the fork in the river and follow up the branch to the place lodgepoles grow. Here I see something old, his horns with scars and breaks. I look on a grandfather who travels a lonely trail.

"I cross two dry streams and come to a hill. Here I see two more old ones with the thick horns and cracks at the tips but these two stand guarding. I lay my ear to the ground. The earth rumbles.

"From the next rise I see the herd. Many young pta face in and two fight while the pte watch. Two fight and I see their heads touch and hear the crash of this meeting.

"But this herd will not make the great rumble I hear and so I go on."

Tonweya paused; he wondered whether the leader accepted his report. He had not heard the familiar 'hai' from the crowd nor any 'hau, hau' from the headmen. They never will embarrass him with questions but certainly they will humiliate him with silence.

"Perhaps on the opposite side of this small herd you see

good. Report." Olepi's tone hinted that the scout gave detail they had not yet called for.

And so Tonweya omitted the story of his circling these pte and he left out any mention of the grasshopper who pointed out the proper ridge. Instead he spoke his discovery briefly: "On the far side, a bellowing. I come near a big herd, more than one band and certain pta yet choosing mates."

Now the young man heard glad sounds in the throats of his people.

"I see the great herd from on top the next ridge," he said. "I see nothing but pte on the hillsides." His thumb twice made the sweeping arc of a great-great circle, his arm lifted high as his reach.

"Hau, hecitu yelo." Olepi had accepted the scout's report.

At once the leaders called out, shouting 'hoye,' the people taking up this noisy cheer when they learned that two thousand grazed in the herd.

Tonweya had reported big herds on different occasions but never before had he gone out alone and discovered this many pte.

And now Olepi asked that the scout tell all things he had experienced on this occasion alone in the hills.

Young pride warming his blood, the youth began his description. He spoke of the many lateral gullies entering the narrow valley. He told of the dry stream and the curly grass scorched dark yellow. The bands graze not looking up, he said, and certain pte not yet fatten; sucking-young keep their mothers thin. And certain pta stay thin from the rut.

He told about the many little black-hairs in the herd, their fluffy hides indicating more than one winter. His far-flung gaze had revealed spiked-horns and curved-horns and pte who had hunted grass under six different snows. The people shall see plenty of soft yellow fat and hard white tallow, many mature and many young in the herd.

Tonweya's listeners heard each detail with grateful ears, but more than one old hunter smiled inside his cheek at the scout's exuberating account of this herd's makeup. Certainly his touching the pipe pledged Tonweya to truthful speech and perhaps one with unusual eyes will distinguish pte of four winters from the six-winters females, but even the most experienced hunter will take a second look before he dares differentiate. But what really counts, this scout tells clearly where the bands graze, their vastness and actions. And so hunters, old and young, again will shout praise for all this good that Tonweya reports.

When this noise came to a finish, the crier commenced his walk around the encampment, the man's singsong voice exciting the people. "Sharpen your knives. Paint your horses. Paint yourselves. Go out and make meat."

The people scattered, men returning to their lodges to prepare for the hunt, each one also listening for the herald who will run through camp naming the clubmen in control of this surround.

Tonweya had hurried past the softly laughing girls and the smiling young women whose dark eyes and pretty gestures invited his attention; he had not stopped until he came to the lodge Tunkaśila kept for the scouts. Here, food and a sleeping robe awaited the truthbearers who sought undisturbed rest after a long run. Here, also, hung the notched stick which kept count of the sleeps he had stayed away.

"I return, grandfather." Tonweya dropped to his knee before the old one, the man in his sixty-fifth winter and sitting close by the fire on a day too warm for a robe.

The old scout lifted his head and Tonweya remembered with difficulty that the glittering eyes into which he looked briefly saw next to nothing.

"Grandson, my fingers count seven notches in your stick. You return bringing news of a great herd. But you speak telling the people the age of this herd. Will you count the teeth of certain pte? Will you see the yellow stains on the shiny surface of different teeth and so you know the herd-fathers?"

Tunkaśila had astounded his listener. The old man had not appeared at the center for the scout's report and from this distance he will hear only the cheering.

"You view gullies and hillsides and the grazing pte. You look and look; you intend holding on to this picture, this whole picture. But you travel two days, and while on this run you recall different experiences, something which takes away from the picture you carry in your head."

Tunkašila had talked gesturing with his thumb; now he closed one hand over the other.

"When you return to the picture in your head," he said, "you perhaps see blunt-horns as curve-horns. And what about the pta choosing mates? Will you say that the herd-father disperses his seeds into many pte or will you say that he mounts not more than two?" Tunkašila's dim eyes seemed as piercing as Wanaġi's most demanding stare. "Keep looking straight, grandson; never let your eyes narrow down on any specific thing if you intend holding on to the whole."

The old scout, lifting his hand, again gestured with his thumb. "I once see with eyes as strong as yours. And so I know that the herd grazes as you report. I know that soon the people will sit eating fat and backfat as you describe."

Tonweya always felt good in the old man's presence. He admired Tunkašila as much as he respected him. Tunkašila who never hints his loneliness for the trails nor for the wife who goes from his side two winters past. Unci dies standing at her digging-stick, a swelling in her arm but nothing more than this sudden lumpy redness. Soon afterwards Tunkašila had asked that someone wrap her bones tightly in a red bundle, something for him to carry from camp to camp.

Following his talk in the scout-lodge, Tonweya had walked onto the campground, where he came into understanding with an enduring importance. He saw a people sharpening their hunting knives in response to that which he reported. He saw boys bringing in the runners and seers preparing the inipi. He heard women talking of new lodge-skins, singers talking of new drum-skins, and warriors talking of neck skins for new shields.

He, Tonweya, describes the hillsides as black with pte, his thumb showing this herd as twice the great-great ten—twenty hundred—and meaning that they dare kill—kill without regret—more than three hundred pte during this surround. He, Tonweya, reports, and the people, acknowledging him as truthbearer, act on his words, his signs. At this moment the lives of two hundred and thirty lodges—twelve hundred Titonwan—depend upon his honor, his truth, alone.

He, Tonweya, scout, ears and eyes for the tribe.

Cuwe sat demurely in the family lodge awaiting her brother Tonweya. She wore a clean, white gown and her neat braids, decorated with hair-ties, hung long as her arms. At seventeen, she had attracted the attention of three, four young men but she had ignored Peśla's hints that she stand under the robe with a certain warrior. Peśla looked for warrior-blood in those new relatives coming to him when his sisters chose husbands but neither Cuwe nor Tacincala, now fourteen, had shown any real interest in leaving the family lodge.

Tacincala sat at this moment next to Cuwe, the young one pale in contrast to her sister's dark skin. She watched Cuwe's manners carefully, imitating this tall, proud young woman in every way she dared. And so, Tonweya coming into the lodge now, she lowered her eyes the same as Cuwe.

The scout perceived at once that they had prepared for his visit, his sisters composed and quiet and his mother's hands idle. Nor will he see another man here. His, a hunter's family and so father, brother, uncles, all prepare to make meat. Tonweya's report shall influence this lodge—the family tipi—the same as any different lodge.

After a proper silence Cuwe spoke softly, her words directed at her mother's ears. "Perhaps someone will tell my brother that I am glad he sits here. I . . . " She had more to say but Tacincala made the giggling sound. Cuwe nudged her sister and the awkward little laughs ceased.

But Tonweya, picking up a ladle, had begun speaking, using the scoop as something through which to talk in the manner of one who finds himself alone with women-relatives. "I am glad that two gentle young women welcome me in this lodge."

Again the giggling, again abruptly stopped.

Tonweya smiled. "Now that evening comes, perhaps along the water-trail a young man waits for my sister, someone who desires that she speak with him."

Cankuna heard the speech with pleasure. She had long wished that her son Tonweya, not her son Peśla, had the say as to Cuwe's choice for husband. Tonweya, she knew, held a true interest in that which concerned his sisters, while Peśla looked out for a personal gain.

But Cuwe had heard the scout's phrases with a tiny ache. Will this brother for whom she holds most high respect also want her making a lodge of her own now? Will he, like Peśla, feel need for a new relative with an important name? More giggles interrupted her thoughts.

And now Tonweya turned his speech in the direction of this second sister. "My young sister soon will hear the flute, the wood singing for her ears alone. But perhaps her giggles will frighten the young man and his flute out of the tree."

The scout sounded teasing, but Cankuna understood that he gently chided his sister. And now the mother helped out everyone; she changed the talk to something different.

"Perhaps, I please your brother," she said to the young women, "when I tell that each sister cooks something to his liking. If he desires they will fill his bowl."

She motioned to her daughers, Tacincala jumping to her feet at once. But Cuwe sat on, her head respectfully bent as before. She chose to rise in a most graceful manner, not so much as a finger touching the ground when she moved from sitting position to standing.

When the three, going to their cooking fire, had stepped outside the lodge, Tonweya leaned against a backrest. He stretched out his legs and yawned.

The scout had stayed with Tunkaśila only long enough to drink a bowl of soup; he had decided to return to Cankuna's lodge for his rest. Now he sat wondering which thing he desired the more: meat or sleep. He closed his eyes, but a scratching on the tipi cover aroused him instantly. He smiled; he knew that Ahbleza had come.

Go-to-the-back. Tonweya's gesturing thumb offered the son of Olepi the place of honor at the rear of the lodge. The scout saw that Ahbleza carried the short-stem pipe; he understood that his brother-friend came here for a different sort of talk. And now, feeling wide awake, he began cutting the mixture for an informal pipe.

Cankuna, not her daughters, brought the food into the lodge and in two bowls. The woman, looking at Ahbleza, permitted herself the silent greeting of eyes, her glance telling this slim, attractive young warrior that they had missed his presence here during these seven, eight days her son Tonweya stayed in the hills scouting for pte. Then, putting down the bowls, she went out of the lodge, leaving these two to whatever they will talk over, smoke over, each one a man and strong in his views. But, walking away from her tipi, she remembered a boy with brushes and paint and a hide to mark on, a boy who shyly had shown her pictures of horse and true-dog and pte unlike any drawings she had seen.

"The white one, not among these pte."

Always the scout said this thing when he came in from the hills and the two friends met. And always this same ceremony: cutting leaves for a smoke, next the puffs from one stem, then Tonweya's announcement, and finally this eating together, the first mouthful dipped from each other's bowl.

And on each occasion Tonweya silently had wished that his next scouting for pte will bring the white one of Ahbleza's boy-seasons into the picture. So his brother-friend will know that the little white fluff-hair of fourteen, fifteen winters past yet lives, that the weathers will not daunt her, neither the cold that strikes her face nor the hail that pelts her back. The dust will not blind her and the wakinyan, the flashing sky, will not cut her down; instead she endures the same as the man Ahbleza, twenty-and-four winters, endures.

Looking up from his thoughts, Tonweya glanced at his companion. "My brother!"

Nothing had prepared the scout for the distraught expression. But even as he stared his amazement, Ahbleza's face cleared; whatever the young warrior suffered now disappeared from view.

Ahbleza spoke calmly: "Will not two who share a vision also share the silent thought?"

But now different ones approached this lodge, Ogle entering, bringing friends, the group sitting to talk about the hunt. And so they will recall amusing stories of past hunts, the men shaking out their laughter.

The brother-friends, neither one in the mood for joking, went out of the lodge at a moment when their leaving interrupted none of the gaiety.

Together they walked past circles of children and parents who gathered at the evening fires, past horsebacks who sat arms folded, past the lodge of a pretty young woman where a line of five, six warriors waited, each man eager for a moment of daring—talk or touch—with this certain one.

The two took their horses from the herd inside the

camp. Mounting, they remembered those days when they had ridden legs touching, when, together, they had raced the wind. Now moving slowly, Ahbleza slightly front, they rode toward the edge of camp. And beyond.

Approaching a hummock, they heard Wanaġi's song, the man sending his breath for the good of the people. And so they circled out and away from the hill, careful that they not become a disruptive influence.

The sacred-man knew who rode wide of his knoll. Nor will he marvel that they pass here on an evening when he desires most strongly to counsel these two, to provide help for this pair, for the one who rides serenely into the dusk not yet aware that his people will try to break him. And for him who rides alongside, for Tonweya, who not yet knows that he shall put upon Ahbleza the most strain of all.

Or will he, Wanaġi, prove the most harsh toward this young man next to his heart? He, wakanlica, a stone-dreamer who advises the principals of this tribe that they try the son of Olepi beyond those trials they set for Shirtman; he, Wanaġi, a true-seer, who perhaps makes this testing of Ahbleza also a testing of Wanaġi. Certainly he stands here now, robe and loin-cover on the ground, a naked body with a resonant voice that commands the power for holding on to himself, for refraining from any act of compassion, from any desire to comfort or to caution Ahbleza, from any act of interference with this man's growth, with any man's growth.

Not far from the hill where Wanaġi stood, the brother-friends had jumped off their horses onto a patch of sandy earth, a quiet place for personal talk. Ahbleza sat as always, legs crossed, and Tonweya lay back on his elbows, legs stretched front. But the scout's easy sprawl had not hidden a concern; he gazed earnestly into his friend's eyes.

Ahbleza permitted the scrutiny, his face lacking paint, nothing on his clean, smooth skin to hide whatever troubled him. But sensing that his show of calm proved as disturbing to his friend as his look of distress, the warrior managed an appreciating smile. "My friend," he said, "you make your-self important to the people." He had not intended the hint of envy in his voice.

572

"Perhaps I will see this importance more clearly when I find the white pte . . . or discover that which distresses my brother-friend."

"When I need the white pte, she will find me. I am not needing this one now."

The scout rejoiced at this reassurance. And then suddenly he realized that which disturbed him about Ahbleza: never before had he known the young Mahto to act uncertain. Ahbleza, the one man who walks a certain path, who goes everywhere with certainty. Until now.

Ahbleza spoke on: "Your work as scout earns the praise you hear. I am proud of you, misun." He paused. "But I also work. I also report herds and find enemy camps. And I put afoot an enemy, take his horse. Truly, I earn enough stripes for covering one arm and half the second.

"I rescue the hurting and twice I fight the enemy hand to hand. For these things they grant me a red cross and a red hand on my robe." His own words had set his eyes on fire, his tones crackling. "Certain marks I am not wearing. Perhaps I never shall own the black-and-red horse-track; I am not looking for a wounding of my horse. Nor am I yearning for the red feather of a personal injury."

He sat silent for a moment, the burn disappearing from his eyes, the stone-hardness melting off his face. "I am not reciting my honors to impress you, misun. Nor will anyone deny me a song or the pictures on my robe. But the puzzling thing. . . "

Tonweya saw the look of confusion and heard the embarrassment. But why this speech, the scout not yet comprehended.

" . . . the puzzling thing sits in the manner of those persons noticing—or refusing to notice—me. Not one person praises me, not one. Not one tells me through look or gesture that they approve all I accomplish. The leaders say nothing that will encourage me along the path I choose.

"I look upon different ones whose earning falls short of mine, ones whose steps trail my steps, and I hear the headmen singing their praises before all the bands. My praises they hold down to a small trilling, namely Ogle's wife and my sister."

Tonweya, watching the clouds lose their sundown colors, remained silent. As Ahbleza spoke he had turned his gaze from the warrior's face to the ground, then to the sky; he will endure anything but the return of that distraught look to the brother-friend's face.

Seldom in camp, the scout knew nothing of the half-hearted manner in which they presented Ahbleza his honors. But hearing that which the warrior told now, he suspected jealousy. Perhaps certain ones, seeing that Ahbleza advances rapidly, grow resentful. Or perhaps certain persons in the new bands that join the Titonwan hoop dislike Ahbleza, persons big enough to influence the people.

True, Tonweya sat lacking any knowledge of intrigue. The shifting of families into different bands or the shifting of bands into different tribes—and the reasons for these moves—never had interested him. He worked for whoever lived in the winter camp, in the summer circle, and his work consisted of reporting herds, locating an enemy, discovering a clear path. But certainly he had seen enough to know that Zuzueca, leader of the Kiyuksa, and Olepi, leader of the Mahto, held little respect for one another.

Ahbleza's voice, again bitter, broke the silence. "The leaders look through me whenever I come among these principals. And when I recite my accomplishments, I feel as if I am dancing in snowdrifts." Ahbleza's slender fingers pressed against his forehead.

"Your father shuns you also?" Tonweya asked gently.

"My father acts similar to the others."

"And Wanaǧi?"

"Wanaǧi appears not to recognize me."

Ahbleza named different ones: Heȟaka, Wambli Okiye, Cetan, Iku, Żola, Icabu, Heȟilogeca, his uncles Huśte and Lekśi. "I will talk until dawn before I name every one who refuses to recognize me. Some persons pull their robes to their eyes and so identify me with the suspicious."

Tonweya grew uneasy. "Perhaps my father will . . . " he began; " . . . they regard you as a son in my mother's lodge. . . ."

Tonweya stopped, the scout aware that Ahbleza had gone beyond the place where he will seek friendly council in any lodge. So why not change to some soft talk about women. . . .

But Ahbleza spoke again. "I decide something, misun," he said, his tone once more warm, familiar; "I shall stay outside the akicita-lodges. I admire the clubmen but I see a lone path for myself. I am not a joiner and so I will not offend anyone. I am not a person who wants control over something or someone, not on the moves and not on the hunts. I travel this far alone and I shall go on without help from any warrior-lodge."

"The wakan-dreamers keep a lodge . . . if one dreams of the branched-horn or pte or the true-dog," Tonweya murmured.

"I have my dream," Ahbleza answered, smiling.

"The headman-lodge will come after you," Tonweya persisted.

The warrior made the denying motion. "Certainly my father and different ones grow aware of my desire to stay outside, whatever the group. They understand . . . " Ahbleza cut off his words. Will these honorable men truly understand him or will a silent acceptance mean that they accept his decision but disapprovingly? Will they imagine that he puts himself above any man in these akicita-lodges, even above the leaders? That he lacks the true-humility? If so, some unwise phrasing, some foolish gestures bring on this untrue impression. And yet they turn their backs before ever he hints or speaks his decision. Perhaps a strange mischief hovers over him?

But now Ahbleza is the one to perceive the need for a change in their talk. Uncrossing his legs and drawing up one, the warrior held his knee comfortably between palms and clasped fingers.

"Tell me," he said gaily, "what new secrets will the four-legs and your winged friends share with you these days?"

"Nothing new," Tonweya answered promptly; "they begin to repeat."

But suddenly the scout sat mimicking the big black-bird, this voice so cleverly imitated that Ahbleza easily translated the sounds into 'I find food' and 'fly away' and 'come and chase the grows-a-horn.'

And now Tonweya, laughing at himself, told that once, while watching a grows-a-horn, he had wondered whether this great hushed-wing really turned his head all the way around. But something not so easily discovered had puzzled the scout recently: the tall-ears seem scarce, all small creatures suddenly scarce. Once before this happens, he said, the tall-ears disappearing and the traveling-dogs letting their young die.

And finally Tonweya told about iktomi with the glowing eyes, the one that escapes. "Perhaps he runs off to find the head iktomi and so they scheme mischief during the tribal hunt."

Ahbleza smiled; he had thoughts about the hunt but not of omens. "At sunrise, misun, a whole camp moves. Your word alone sends out these hunters."

Tonweya jumped to his feet. "And I ride this night with scouts who watch over the trail that leads to the herds. I need sleep before I go."

He walked toward his grazing horse, but halfway he turned, calling to Ahbleza: "When next I see you, I talk about women."

"When next I see you," Ahbleza called back, "you will not talk at all. You will sit gorging on fresh hump."

This same evening Olepi sat alone, pipe in hand, a man determined to rid himself of those irritations which in recent seasons had lumped into a painful sore. He had become convinced that Zuzueca, leader of the Kiyuksa, prepared to take over as headman of all Titonwan.

"But the loudmouth reckons without my son," Olepi muttered, then instantly saw a second thought take form: Zuzueca had considered Ahbleza—and dismissed him.

And why not, Olepi asked himself now; Ahbleza discourages invitations from any of the akicita-lodges, the very ones whose support he shall need if ever he intends to lead the band. And who will Ahbleza encourage as companions? None but Tonweya, the son of a hunter—a great hunter—but not the son of a warrior; Tonweya, a loyal friend and a fine scout but, like Ahbleza, a man who sits indifferent to the clubmen's lodge.

In what manner, then, will Ahbleza make those connections that procure him enough voices in council? Pipe smoke curled over Olepi's arm as he pondered his son and certain powerful young women among the Lakotah. The father had seen more than one pair of eyes sparkle whenever Ahbleza walked through camp; the son need only to choose and take. And if his choice already belongs to someone?

Annoyed that he permitted these thoughts, Olepi tried to look in other directions; instead he remembered that even Hinziwin's smiling eyes followed Ahbleza's graceful body and that once he had felt compelled to warn her.

"Remember whom you call husband," he had told Hinziwin.

"Say nothing foolish," she had answered boldly, "and sit at ease; your son will find the proper woman."

Perhaps if he had hunted a stout stick at that moment ... but he never had struck a woman.

But the Mahto leader had not come to this place to entertain thoughts of Hinziwin; he had come to drain a lump of misgivings. And now he refilled his pipe; perhaps, sitting out here alone on hard, cold stone, he shall see the picture clearly and so understand why Mniśa wears off the grass between his own and Zuzueca's lodge and why Mniśa joins the Kiyuksa leader in his effort to gain control of the tribe. And whether or not Wanaǧi overworks this thing of testing Ahbleza for the staying-power.

Slowly but certainly Zuzueca and his Kiyuksa had changed over from irregular summer visitors to prominent members of the tribal hoop; slowly but certainly these custom-breakers had pushed into the family circle, Zuzueca consistently referring to his camp as the original Titonwan and pointing to his brother Iśtakpe as proof: will not everyone know that Iśtakpe, now in his sixties, dreams in the black hills as a youth?

The Kiyuksa counted fifty lodges now but their noisy disputes made the band sound like twice as many persons. Zuzueca found nothing distressing about these outbursts; on different occasions the clubmen had heard him approve a warrior's manner of shouting at wife or dog in the same startling tone. I approve the man, Zuzueca had said, who brings trembling among his own relatives; imagine his impact on an enemy.

But when the Kiyuksa leader heard that Olepi had ridiculed this point of view, his lips had curled. "A loud tongue and fast arrows equip a man for leading war parties far more effectively," he derided, "than a quiet voice and the soft touch of paintbrushes. Observe who inspires followers." He had glanced toward the horns of the summer hoop, where the Okandada raised a camp of seventy-four lodges.

True, the Okandada follow a most vigorous man now: Tanaźin. Oowésica had died leaving a son not yet of warrior-age. And so the people had turned to the son of a different man, a man who had led a division of the Okandada until Oowésica had replaced him as leader of the whole band. Afterwards that man—Tatanka Naźin—had joined the Kiyuksa, but his son, Tanaźin, had returned to the Okandada ten winters past when he took a wife in this band. And now, at thirty-five, Tanaźin led the Okandada— or Oglalahca, to use the band's new name.

The change in leaders had seemed a proper occasion for renaming the band. Why not a name, they had said, to recall those winters when their grandfathers scatter dust and grow maize? Or, as the old persons in the band say, why not a name to recall those seasons when their grandmothers 'scatter dust' in a different manner and so prevent any 'planting' of seeds? Why not rename this band Oglalahca, the original Oglala? Certainly the new leader sits above Zuzueca when they speak using that rare word 'first.' Tanaźin, a direct descendant of the original Tatanka Naźin, the first man ever to hold on to the pipestem that Pte-woman brings to the Dakotah. And a son of the first man to lead a party to the black hills, whether or not the Kiyuksa claim differently. Oglalahca, seventy-and-four lodges, the most lodges in any Titonwan band; Oglalahca, a name to wear proudly.

And Tanaźin, the Mahto leader told himself, provides Zuzueca with a loyalty inside this Oglalahca band, a kinsman tie through Tanaźin's mother, not a close tie, but something that the Kiyuksa certainly will exploit.

And the Śiyo? Olepi smiled thinly; the Mahto and Śiyo bands always had maintained most pleasant relations but during recent winter problems within the Śiyo family had restricted any real exchange of confidences. The people had wavered between loyalty to their leader Wacape, who appeared slowing down, and a desire to follow Hinyete, the outstanding camp leader. But then Wacape had decided for his Śiyo; accepting his debility, he had retired in favor of the competent warrior-peaceman Hinyete. Similar to a defeated herd-father, Wacape had taken a place at the edge of the council circle and from this outpost he stood watching Hinyete; he waited to see whether the new leader owned the power to attract new families into the band, strong young families. He knew that Hinyete needed many things going his way if he intended to regain a strong position in the hoop. Śiyo and Kiyuksa each raised fifty lodges, but Zuzueca apparently looked for Mniśa's camp to join with his; certainly the Kiyuksa had dismissed Hinyete and the Śiyo band as competitors for the campsite at the horns of the circle.

"But let the slithering grass creature take a second look at the grizzly," Olepi said aloud; "let Zuzueca remember the meaning of Mahto. True, Tanaźin and his Oglalaĥica show the most warrior-power now. And I stand next. I, Olepi, lead a band that raises fifty-and-six lodges, that claims sixty warriors. But I know that not one dares predict where the power will sit even a season hence."

Ahbleza's uncertainties had gained a new hold during the talk with Tonweya; riding back to the village, he suddenly became as pta who rushes at whatever wounds him. He reached for the knife at his thigh and his legs hugged the horse's sides until the creature tensed for combat. But before a war cry rose in his throat, Ahbleza managed to catch hold of whatever possessed him. Slowly his fingers let loose the knife, his legs letting go their frenzied clutch on the horse. The anger moved off, the moon's round light touching on a face impassive as stone.

The horse walked among the lodges, the rider looking to the ground but seeing only his thoughts. Perhaps the people intend that he suffer anger and so win a fight against an invisible mischief. Perhaps they intend that he teach himself ways for overwhelming lust, overcoming pretense, attacking envy. Perhaps they will not scheme at testing his nature but scheme at making him test himself. And so he shall let the people see that nothing they devise proves more exacting than the demands he places on himself; let each one grow aware that he prepares for the Shirt.

"The Shirt-owner," he whispered, "an unshakable man. I will show the people that I am someone they will never shake."

Hinziwin crawled onto her sleeping robe disdainful of Olepi and his son. The husband had chosen this night before the hunt as an occasion for spoiling her fun and shaming her in front of friends; he had sent her to the tipi at the moment she seemed most likely to win a bet on the hand game.

Ten outstanding players in camp and four visiting Sahiela had gathered to play guess-where-the-blackbird-sits and each team had won five counting-sticks. Deft hiders and fast songs had aroused spectators and players, everyone near to bursting with excitement. The Sahiela had provided the little bird-shape wood that lay in the hider's covered palm as he crossed and recrossed his hands above, then back of his head, then down in front of his feet, each swift move anticipating someone's pointing-stick, someone's guess.

But suddenly the piece of wood had dropped out of the hider's hand. Instantly someone had made use of this break in the game to act in a manner long delayed; Olepi, speaking loud enough for everyone to hear, had sent Hinziwin from her place among the watchers to her own tipi.

"You appear sleepy. Go now and you will not disturb any one."

The man had surprised her. She had not looked for Olepi in the crowd of warriors outside Zola's lodge, in the group of young men whose glances encouraged the betting. But Olepi had come and he had spoken. And so she moved away gracefully, the comforting murmurs of her companions more irritating than the husband's attempt to humiliate her. Certainly, she had told herself, her women-friends recognize that which Olepi intends but will they understand his objection to her presence here? The man wants either Ina or Napewaste in attendance whenever she goes out of the lodge. But those two act strict as old grandmothers about her ways of having fun.

"They say that I am twenty-and-seven winters," she had muttered to the old person who accompanied her back to her tipi, "and I know two women this same age who have grandchildren. So why will this fool woman Napewaste interfere with my pleasures?"

Embarrassed and angry, Hinziwin had entered her little lodge. "Perhaps Napewaśte tells Ahbleza's father that I make too many bets and so he comes looking for me. Truly, that woman brings on my difficulty."

But lying now in her sleeping robe, she found different thoughts. Perhaps Olepi yet brooded over her impudence when he hinted for an answer about the way young women regard his son. She giggled. "Why not ask me in what manner I regard Ahbleza." Her hand smoothed the hair on the robe beneath her body as she gave herself to reflecting on this young warrior.

One day soon she shall approach Ahbleza again, letting him see her admiration for his handsomeness and his quiet ways. Seven winters pass but certainly she remembers riding up to him after his demonstration on four horses, her eyes glowing praise. True, he rejects her approach, but on this next occasion she intends to make her willingness more apparent. She, Hinziwin, now really-woman and ready to respond to Ahbleza's tautness, in his body and on his face. He rarely stood fully tall, but for all the gentle curve to shoulder and arm he owned the strength to push the most powerful bow. And his voice, soft as a woman's in the lodge, turned out a cry—or so they said—that chilled the enemy.

She understands why he avoids the paintbrush now; also the reason for his indifference toward women. Olepi sees his son as a man among men, and so Ahbleza, seed of Olepi and inheriting the father in spirit and flesh, dares look upon only that which challenges his prowess.

Hair like Olepi's hair, she whispered to herself, heavy and long below his shoulders, hanging loose or at the back, a wide strip of horsehide holding these strands together. A body like Olepi's body, slouching elegantly one moment, tensing for action the next.

But unlike Olepi, never a boast on Ahbleza's face, not even the paint of a boast. Certain ones say that Ahbleza looks and walks proud, but she, Hinziwin, sees something different. And if ever he takes her as wife, he shall discover within himself that which she sees. She will give him a true-reason for self-pride.

II

"TIKAȞPA. TIPI-down." The crier's song had brought down all lodges before sunrise. Wanasapi; the tribe hunts.

The same governing-four who had ordered the breaking of camp at dawn also had named the Iȟoka, a recently formed clubmen's lodge, to control the hunt. After three, four seasons of observing these akicita who gave the hunts their full concern, the council had recognized the existence of the Iȟoka-lodge; the members had proved expert organizers.

The people—two hundred and thirty lodges—moved out in their usual order, deciders and leaders front, twelve hundred Titonwan following. And managing the whole procession, four Iȟoka horsebacks bearing whips. But far back of the horse herds, beyond the dust, rode those clubmen—Cante Tinza—who always guard the rear, whose members come exclusively from the Oglalaȟca band.

On the second day the people discovered the Iȟoka as most strict. They kept the bands moving swiftly, too swiftly for any young boys to break out of line and chase after whatever they saw running, too swiftly for any women who desired stopping to beat the thorny brush that held on to the tart red berries. And certainly too swiftly for those travelers who looked for dancing or gambling at each night's camp.

"Put on your loads," the crier called out whenever the people delayed at a rest stop. Dashing back and forth, the Iȟoka whip-bearers demanded that the people stay close, not spread out as they usually walk. The Titonwan pass near an enemy crossing—Witapaha, Pani, Psa perhaps in the vicinity—and the Iȟoka intend to avoid any unpleasant incidents.

During the third day of travel the deciders chose eight hunters—men who owned remarkable runners—to kill meat for the feeble and for those women and children who lacked a provider.

Ahbleza had yearned to hear his name among these honored hunters but the summer-shirts had looked over his head when they chose the eight for this work. And then a tiny throbbing had begun in his cheek as he remembered the many horses he had made useful, had gentled for the hunts, all these creatures going as gifts to cripples and incompetents. "But if they wait for me to present my horse to influential voices in the council lodge, they wait forever. Never will I trade my horses for favors." He had hissed the phrases inside his mouth, then ridden on, his face closed to everyone.

Now, on this sixth day, the travelers saw two of their scouts riding across the near ridge, the two coming forward from opposite directions, signaling much meat. Soon afterwards, the principal Ihoka sat smoking with the deciders and then the people heard the crier announce a new formation. The hunters shall make rows, ten men wide. In front of these men, a row of Ihoka, thirty men across. And any hunter who tries to ride ahead of these Ihoka, they will knock off his horse.

"Take care of your dogs," the crier shouted to the women and children. "Any dog who runs out of place, they kill at once."

Everyone understood. The herds grazed and nothing shall move out that tends to raise the heads of pte. And any man who loses the meat for his people shall suffer the same as any dog who runs out: scare away pte and you never eat again; the Ihoka had said so.

Before the sun passed middle, scouts came running in, the deciders receiving these truthbearers with a glowing pipe. And after the one had spoken, the people knew that the herds grazed as Tonweya had reported. Mostly they fed on the valley bottom in bunches of twenty or more, but some pte grazed spread thin and low on the slopes. The slow ones lay around in groups but all pte awaited the hungry people.

Someone began a song that told the people to prepare a hunting camp where they stood; the herd, over the next rise. Let those persons staying in camp spread branches on which to pile meat and make drying-racks and prepare cooking fires; let those persons who file out after the hunters lead pack horses and bring knives and wear garments that show the bloodstains of previous hunts.

Next, the mouth for the Ihoka began talking. The hunters shall separate into eight groups at the bottom of the second ridge, he said, and two Ihoka clubmen shall ride as watchers with each group. At a signal from the Ihoka leader—the man swinging a robe twice around his head—the hunters shall pour down the gullies into the valley; they shall spread on each flank of the wind but the one downward from the herd. When finally they surround the pte, one group shall swing in, closing this gap on the windward side, the head clubman signaling the start of the chase at this same instant. And this clubman's shout, the only mansound from when the hunters start out to the moment of attack.

An experienced hunter knows, the voice went on, that he shall ride in on the herd at a slant, not straight on, and that the pte will run a circle that slowly tightens. Each man shall chase whatever one he sees fit, but let him pick out a fat one.

The Ihoka had spoken and the hunters began to move. Some men jumped onto their runners, but most persons had chosen slim young boys to ride these horses as far as the ridge, an easy load that preserved wind for the chase.

Olepi, obeying the Ihoka the same as any man who hunts, chose a place in line. Then, looking around, he observed that Ahbleza stood back as if to remain in camp. Angered, the Mahto called out to him, "Will I see someone disdain work that brings meat to the lodge where he sleeps?"

The father's reproach acted on Ahbleza similar to a blow, something that knocks in mischief. Instantly the warrior resolved to carry out the scheme he had contemplated on discovering that the deciders had ignored him; he shall provide for someone on this hunt. And if not for the old and weak, then for someone young, someone who yet grieves a father's death. He signaled to young Oowesica.

The youth, in his twelfth winter, came up quickly; he had imagined that Ahbleza called him out to take care of a pack horse. Instead the unsmiling warrior spoke saying that the boy shall ride Ahbleza's runner in the surround.

For a moment Oowesica stood staring; then his eyes flashed joy. But before the youth jumped horseback, Ahbleza offered advice, quickly reviewed the important things.

"The dust will blind, but soon everything clears and you will see your way to the yellow fluffed-hairs. But finding yourself back of a big female who runs straight, aim at the small ribs, forward and down through the paunch. Running alongside a curved-horn, throw your arrows at the shoulder."

The youth jumped horseback, but Ahbleza held on to the thong: "Shall you notice one who looks sideways, head shaking and tail switching, let this horse act without your guidance. He knows pte. He runs fast, dodges quickly. He keeps his ears moving and watches the group in front."

Glancing toward the hunters, Ahbleza let go the jaw-cord: "Hold on to this thong in whatever manner comes easy—use the bend in your arm, your teeth, the string at your middle—but guide only with your knees." He smiled slightly and turning, stroked the neck of his pack horse. "I will ride this one."

The lines had formed, two hundred men ready for the chase.

"I and you join the hunters. Make meat." Instantly Ahbleza sat horseback. And now warrior and youth dashed toward an opening in the line.

At the bottom of the second ridge those hunters who had worn leg-covers stripped to loin-flaps and moccasins. A quirt hung at the wrist of each rider, and in one hand each man held his bow; in his other hand, five, six arrows.

Certain gestures assigned the men to their groups; more hand-talk sent the hunters to the heads of different gullies. And yet more unspoken orders started the meat-chasers down into the valley.

The clubmen who waited on the ridge saw the men fanning out on the flat. They saw the pte, heads up and snuffing; they saw tails lift and curl. They saw the dust and heard the rumble of fleeing hoofs, the bellows of resentment and confusion, and then they heard the hunters yelling, their cries of 'i-i-ya' for each kill echoing up the draws.

Persons who followed out after the hunters listened to those same glad shouts and, urging along the pack horses, remembered their work: the cutting up of those great warm bodies. True, the hunters separate the big joints, making certain that the sinewy sections stay intact for drying. But the cutting, wrapping, loading they leave for different hands.

Napewaśte moved quickly over the trail, the women of her lodge hurrying to keep up. "Perhaps some of this shouting means two more skins for your new tipi," she called to her daughter Kehala.

Ten moons back, Kehala had brought a man into the family lodge, the young woman's choice pleasing to everyone. Her husband: the youth whom Wanapin had raised, Yuza, the brave boy captured during a raid on Psa camps fourteen winters past. During his many seasons in the Siyo camp he had proved himself as warrior, hunter, bow-maker, not unusual in any one of these occupations but competent to take a wife. Napewaśte had welcomed the pair as members of her lodge, Yuza showing himself eager to make meat for his wife's family and glad to join his horses to her parents' herd. But Kehala, discovering after two, three moons as wife that she takes-on-life, had begun to hint for a lodge of her own. She held on to seven skins as a start for her tipi cover, and Napewaśte, while reluctant to see these cheerful young persons go, had offered whatever more in cover-skins her daughter needed.

The hunt now in progress will take care of Kehala's wants, Napewaśte told herself, providing that three, four more hides will satisfy the proud young wife. And something more: the new tipi will stand ready for use before the snow if she, her sister Ina, and Kehala work together on the hides that Olepi and her daughter's husband bring in this day.

None of these women ever looked for any help from Hinziwin. Even this morning, watching the three make ready for the work on the hunting ground, she had called out, "I see that your son and his father will have enough hands cutting and packing meat. I shall wait here, ready with water and fresh moccasins when the man arrives."

Napewaśte's response had come quick and firm. She had answered speaking a name two wives not sisters often used toward each other but her intonation had hung devoid of respect: "Teya, your memory deserts you. I am the one attending to the husband's wants after a hunt. Ina will look after the meat and you will rub down his horse. And while you sit here waiting, put up the drying-rack and bring wood to the fire."

Napewaśte had started off, Ina and Kehala in back,

each woman leading a pack horse. And so they, if not Napewaśte, had heard Hinziwin's mocking laughter. But those phrases coming after the laugh, had not reached their ears. "They know not who I mean when I say 'the man,' " Hinziwin had giggled.

Halfway to the meat, Ina spoke that which irked her: "Will she look upon the blood from skinning pte as more offensive on her gown than on mine or yours?"

Napewaśte said nothing. Her dislike of the young wife, she often told herself, bears not so much on the woman's laziness as on a sense of fear and envy. If ever Hinziwin births a girl-child, will not Olepi give more of his heart to Hinziwin? As for envy? If not envious of Hinziwin's girl-shape and fresh young look and strangely exciting hair and eyes, then truly resentful. Certainly the woman looks almost as young as on the day Olepi brings her into Napewaśte's lodge, looks almost as young and behaves almost as shamefully now as thirteen winters past. But certainly Olepi favors his young wife, whatever he pretends.

On arrival at the hunting ground the women heard sad news: one hunter killed, a second man injured. The dead, one of those eight selected to hunt for the needy; the injured man, he who had attempted to rescue the endangered hunter.

The dead man's horse had stepped in a hole, the rider thrown and trampled; his crushed breast had gurgled noisily but he had not lived to open his eyes. The injured hunter, knocked to the ground, had tried to sit up and ignore pain, but they had needed to lift him onto a drag; even so the peźuta Huhupiye foresaw a quick healing.

And so a wailing rose up in one place, a trilling in a different place; they wept for the dead and sang for the recovering man. Cheers also filled the air, praise the young Oowesica. The youth had dodged a prime male who turned out in front of his runner. Witnesses said many good things about this Oglalaĺica rider and the horse, but they had not mentioned who owned, who had gentled this runner.

And yet someone had come forward reporting that he saw the son of Olepi chasing pte, not horseback but on his own legs. And that the son of Olepi had killed pte and cut up the meat.

The man had reported accurately. Before the ride down

the gully, Ahbleza had tied his hair in a knot and un-sheathed his knife. Reaching the bottom of the draw, he had jumped off the pack horse and sneaked toward a group of pte, his eyes on the big fat meat, on three who lay down.

Hearing the cry that signaled the hunters to attack, he had dashed toward one of those lazy pte. The creature had scrambled onto her legs but her slow start had given him his chance. He soon had caught up and, slashing at the back legs, had brought her onto her foreknees; the next instant his arrow had struck her lungs.

He had cut his meat alone, then gone to help with the family kills. And whom will he see at once, her hands fluttering in an effort to appear useful, but Hinziwin. The whiteness of her new gown and the colorful decorations at her neck, on her arms, made her conspicuous. Why, he had paused to wonder, will his father ignore this woman's lack of respect for work and overlook her many imprudent acts, her inviting glances in the direction of almost any young man in camp, not excluding himself.

Suddenly annoyed that he permitted Hinziwin to at-tract his attention—perhaps one reason why she had come—he turned from everything but the enormous shape in front of him; he began skinning his father's third kill.

He stripped back one half, then the second half. While removing the insides, he realized that the dead hunter's obligation to provide for the infirm went unfulfilled. He dropped his knife and walked to where the deciders sat together, the tragedy raising a cloud that hung over their hearts.

Ahbleza spoke flatly, his eyes unsmiling. "I offer meat in the place of his and so none shall starve. I desire putting my kill on the pile for the old and slow."

If his offense in the eyes of the honorable ones arose from a shortness of gifting, then let these four see him laying down the hide, tongue, hump, everything.

Not a head turned, not a sound reached him but the sucking on pipes. He stood his place, arms folded, his eyes cold upon these summer-shirts who apparently decided once more against him.

Now one of the four looked up: "The Iñoka receive meat. Different ones provide. The old and slow will eat."

Ahbleza returned to his work, his cheek hollows again throbbing. Obviously they regard him unbecomingly aggressive, his offer crude. But why? Why?

A new wail spread through the air; the women had discovered a pte with short forehairs. Whoever kills this one, they cried, will see a relative dying soon.

At once the hunter spoke up claiming that he had killed from the rear; he had seen nothing unusual about this one's appearance. He had selected her quickly—a fat pte—and not until the finish of the chase had he discovered that he struck down something awesome. "Neither I nor any different Lakotah," he said, "intentionally kills the misshapen. And let the people remember that only if they eat of this meat will someone die."

Even so many persons threw dark glances at the unfortunate hunter, looks and gestures that hurried the Iñoka whipmen into the crowd around him; they intended to renew calm before excited relatives began taking sides. Leave this pte, they advised, for the prowlers in the sky.

Toward evening the stay-behinds in camp saw the pack horses coming in, the meat slung across their backs or folded inside the pte-skins, and tied on top those big bones full of sweet marrow.

And they saw the deciders and the Iñoka and the Cante Tinza stopping at the council lodge, sitting down alongside a great spread of branches. Here these men will look for the hunters to throw off choice meat—hump and tongue—as they ride by, something in return for managing the surround, for putting the hunters into a position that permits the killing of three hundred pte.

Napewaśte entered her lodge with Olepi. Proudly she removed blood-wet moccasins from a man who had killed three pte. Next she brought water, and when he had washed his feet, she dusted his toes with powder. She watched him wipe off other signs of the hunt and when he stood clean, she handed him a robe.

He lifted her face to his gaze and brushed her cheek with his palm. And when finally he sat leaning against his backrest, the woman hurried outside where Ina kept up the fire, heated stones for boiling water.

But Hinziwin, not Ina, pushed meat onto the pointed sticks and laid more twigs on the burning wood. And Kehala, wearing a fresh gown, tended the cooking paunch, a sixth stone hot and ready for the near-boiling water.

Kehala waited eagerly to speak of the two pte her man's arrows had dropped, but Napewaśte stood looking at Ina, who washed down Olepi's runner.

"I ask that Ina cook and that Hinziwin take care of the horse."

Hinziwin tossed her head flauntingly. "I hear you but I take enough turns at rubbing down horses while your pretty hands stay with the easy work. If you want peace in your lodge, say nothing more about who cooks this meat." Her voice took on a sly, warning tone. "I am not complaining to Ahbleza's father. This man never will sit with a cover over his head while his wives quarrel about who cooks. He knows that Napewaśte will remember her obligation to keep the lodge calm. A man always puts his old woman to this use. He remembers you as forty-and-one winters. And so I choose to go out and help cut meat. And now I choose to kneel here and cook."

"Stay at the fire and keep turning the meat." Napewaśte forced herself to speak quietly.

But Hinziwin, seeing the woman slice thin a piece for the embers, watched warily. Her eyes said that this jealous old bone perhaps secretly intends to destroy a young wife's good looks with this same meat knife and so she will stay on guard.

Napewaśte waited for the slice to cook black, then took the meat inside; Olepi enjoyed his meat charred.

Kehala had kept silently at her work but she saw that Hinziwin neglected the roast. The attractive young woman watched for someone, and when Ahbleza came up, Kehala understood for whom Hinzi watched. And now this one with the yellow strands in her hair seemed regretful that someone already had rubbed down the warrior's runner and taken care of his pack horse. Perhaps her nature changes, Kehala told herself; perhaps Hinzi really wants to help skin and scrape and cook but my mother misunderstands her. Certainly anyone who remembers Ahbleza in this kindly manner shows sign of turning helpful.

Over in Cankuna's lodge, Ogle sat in the center of much pleasing talk. The hunter's famed arrows had stopped the breath of seven pte; he had killed the most meat.

His wife and her sisters gathered around him now, pulling off his moccasins and feeding him warm soup. He joked with his joking-relatives and made more of their attentions than he made of Cankuna's efforts. But the cheerful woman, knowing her husband's ways, remembered that she kept a one-wife lodge for all the meat and hides brought here. Her many women relatives and growing daughters helped with everything, and so Ogle never considered taking a second woman. More than once Cankuna had felt in sympathy with Napewaśte; will any woman really want a second wife in the tipi, sister or not?

Until the previous winter, Cankuna never had experienced any difficulty in her lodge. But then Peśla had brought his mother a sullen-eyed Palani captive, someone they call Winu. This young woman, perhaps sixteen winters, not yet practiced her captor's dialect, and so they had given her none of the privileges they grant any captive who starts talking Lakotah. Even now Winu struggled with hides and meat, unloading horses and separating the cuts, while all other members of this lodge sat talking and laughing with Ogle.

In the center lodge four deciders, thirty Ihoka, and a group of Cante Tinze had feasted on hump ribs flavored with melted backfat and on boiled tongue and cold liver. The hunters had provided generously; the lodge had leftovers.

"All come," the mouth for the Ihoka sang out. "I have more than I eat."

The crier, speaking with the approval of each member, began to move through the encampment, inviting the people to come to the center for meat.

Many persons came, not so much for the meat but to hear the Ihoka singers, to listen to songs of praise for those men who had killed and given away. Some ears waited for a song about Ahbleza, whose legs had run down pte and whose loan of a runner had carried an Oglalaĥca youth on a rewarding chase. But this song remained unsung.

Ahbleza, attending neither the family feast fire nor the Ihoka sing, had separated from the crowds as if he belonged to the dead hunter's grieving tiyośpaye.

But the son of Olepi had not joined the sorrowing; instead he sat alone, a wind-worn boulder for his backrest, a young man watching evening darken into night, watching a sky that began to flame with mystery. On such a night, the old ones tell, the invisibles display their campfires in the sky. Hanhepiwakan, Ahbleza mused, a truly mysterious-night when such colors stream across the sky; a good night, he told himself, to ponder something that now seems to contradict meanings in that most noticeable rank: wicaśa iyotanyapi, man they esteem most highly, the Shirt-owner, prime example.

Four persons out of the whole tribe, the wise ones had said, who live the example of that which makes a people proud; four living examples for the people to observe and perceive the effect. And then to decide, each one for himself, whether or not to follow this example.

And who selects these four? Members of the Pta-lodge, headmen whose winters count to forty or more.

And who up to now owns such a Shirt? On whom will this headman-lodge agree? Two, only two.

Wanapin, a Shirtman. And Cetan.

Why these two? Why give Shirts to Wanapin and Cetan and not to two more such persons? Will something mysterious decide this honor?

The streamers overhead seemed to flash more brilliantly, and Ahbleza glanced again at the sky. But he will not hunt answers in these colors; instead, he chose to review his impression of two men who seemed to him as deserving as Cetan, as Wanapin. Why not a Shirt for Hehaka? Or Iku?

Hehaka, once a warrior but for many more seasons a peaceman. Hehaka had led parties where none had fallen hurt or dying; he had given away horses. Now, at sixty-and-nine, Hehaka danced these acts and so the headmen remembered. Certainly Hehaka held on to his memory—he kept a reliable winter count—and yet the Pta-lodge had not named Hehaka for a Shirt.

Iku, thirty-and-four, originally a Sicangu; Iku, someone to whom more than once they had lent the summer-shirt.

Born twelve winters after his brother Pasu, the young

592

Iku had chosen to live with Pasu and his Śahiela wife who raised their lodge among the Mahto; Iku, who had selected his wife from this Mahto band and who now sat proudly as father to a little girl.

Iku, an important warrior in the Tokala-lodge, a man who says that he will see himself naked-dead on the fighting ground before ever he will walk around camp in a robe made of bribes. But the Pta-lodge had not named him Shirtman.

And now Ahbleza recalled certain phrases in the Shirt-owner's pledge: the people shall recognize the Shirtman as a living symbol of peace, an example of mildness. Yet they speak of the Shirtman as a warrior, as a generous man, as a whole man?

Perhaps, he, Ahbleza, needs to examine meanings here, the meaning of warrior, of generous, of whole. But will not everyone know what 'warrior' means, 'generous' means? And what means 'whole man' if not that a man shall speak his thoughts and perform his acts with the whole of himself—spirit and body?

Or will he, Ahbleza, not know what warrior means? Perhaps he knows not what anything really means. He, son of Olepi, who once walks certain, now sits puzzling almost everything.

They demand in the Shirt-owner a man of restraints, a man who fathers one child, not more than two. They look for a man who has-not instead of a man who has. Has-not what? Has-not many wives, has-not many children? Has-not many children?

Yet they say generate? They say that the Shirtman shall make feasts and own many ladles, that he shall give away many horses and 'so act that his children people the earth.' So will the Shirtman generate something that only a wakan-hica understands?

Whole man? They call the wingflapper—symbol of a Shirt-owner—half warrior, half peaceman. Half means half, whole means whole; will they see the Shirtman as 'whole' in manner which he, Ahbleza, not yet understands? Will they describe Wanapin and Cetan as 'whole' and say in the next breath that Heħaka, Iku, Hinyete lack something? And that Ahbleza not yet strives for wholeness and so they ignore him?

Ahbleza looked at the northern sky; perhaps the same grandfathers who inspire the rank of wicaśa iyotanyapi sit at these fires that flicker far out in space. And here decide who shall own the Shirt. If so, let these invisibles notice that he, Ahbleza, determines to earn this honor and that nothing—nothing—shall stop him.

III

THE DEATH of one hunter and injury to a second had distressed those akicita responsible for the hunt. And not a man regretted those misfortunes more than Peśla, pipe-keeper for the Iȟoka. But his, a most different reason. He had intended to enact his song at the dance that usually took place after a tribal hunt. Instead they had sung only hunter songs and afterwards had listened to a bereaved family who wailed half the night on a nearby knoll.

Many persons, glancing at Peśla this same evening, had seen his face darken but, familiar with this warrior's nature, they had disregarded his querulous look. Instead, they had remembered his most recent act of bravery, marveling again his unprecedented visit to the Palani.

But members of the Tokala-lodge who looked at Peśla had recalled something different. They had remembered with what intrepid daring Peśla had accepted the Tokala lance six winters past. And that none had suspected Peśla's scheme on that ceremonial occasion.

The Tokala always used persuasive songs in getting someone to take hold of their clubman-lance, a commitment which meant, more often than not, losing one's scalp. But Peśla, maneuvering into the conspicuous position, had reached for the lance at once; he had not waited for the songs or the pipe-bearer's harangue on the obligation and the risk.

The Tokala warrior who previously had held the rank of lance-carrier never hurried into anything. And so certain members had poked fun at his delay, his slowness in making use of the lance. But when Pešla went at him, friendly persuasion had become stern ridicule. At once the warrior returned the lance and the gifts he had received on becoming lance-bearer. He also had withdrawn his name as a member of the lodge; the Tokala had lost a good man. And so the rank of lance-bearer opening up, Pešla had grabbed hold.

The next sunrise saw the warrior-son of Ogle carrying the lance against an enemy, leading a raid on the Oyatenumpa. A foot-going party of seven, they had returned horseback, two scalps fluttering on the Tokala lance. Afterwards many braves sought a place in any party Pešla led, but Pešla preferred slipping out at night with two, three friends.

Once when Sluka had asked to go, Pešla had hinted that Sluka held a more useful place among the news-actors than among warriors and that he, Pešla, intended to provide him with many choice items to enact.

Pešla had ceased to attend meetings in the Tokala-lodge soon after they installed the next in line for the rank of lance-man. Not that he had asked out but that he appeared only rarely at their feasts; he had chosen to advance himself through a clever new scheme.

The camp gossips had known exactly when Pešla, having lived as husband to Wipatawin four winters, began to notice another woman. Sharp-edged and unrestrained, these tongues usually proved the torment of the village. But they had not made Pešla squirm; instead, the warrior's contemptuous glance had backed these unkempt old women into their unkempt lodges and not one had dared call out to him as they dared shout at some youth who suddenly gave attention to his hair. But within their own circle they had croaked about Pešla and the pretty young daughter of a Sicangu family, a young woman who knew the Ihoka songs, who sang for the Ihoka lodge.

Wipatawin had smiled when the rumors reached her, but friends had known this smile as something for persons outside the lodge; they suspected that Wipatawin had discovered why Peśla chose her and so she had come to know him as a man who will use any scheme to gain prestige.

True, Wipatawin had blamed herself when, after two winters as his wife, she had not borne a child. Peśla had used her often enough—and roughly—but she had given him nothing to show for all the strength at his groin. Once he had reached far up inside her and, spreading two fingers, had pressed around and around until she had pulled desperately on his arm.

"Perhaps you will please me now," he had said, his black eyes narrowing. But she had lain unknowing of any different way to act.

Soon afterwards, Peśla had feasted a principal one from among the Sicangu, a man with strong ties in the Titonwan hoop. When Wipatawin had come for the empty bowls, Peśla had spoken in her ear; she shall wait on her sleeping robe, he told her, until they finish the pipe. Then the husband shall go from the lodge and the visitor with white hairs in his wispy strands shall crawl in alongside her.

Wipatawin had listened, her heart aching; she had heard stories about these old men.

"Remember that he honors you," Peśla had whispered, "and see that you please him." He lifted her face to his cruel eyes. "Hide your distress. You provide me nothing. Why concern yourself that this old man will seed you something."

During their fourth winter together Wipatawin had made known to her husband that she takes-on-life. Peśla will act differently now, she had imagined, the man proud of himself and proud of his woman. But before the child ever came, he had begun looking at someone in a manner to set old tongues wagging. And then Wipatawin had made some desperate moves.

One evening Peśla, entering the tipi, saw that she had not cooked; he had given her a reproving glance.

"Why shall I cook for you?" she had said quietly and started out of the tipi.

Peśla had jerked her arm, stopped her going.

"Why cook for a man who notices a different woman?" She had spoken her answer to the cold face that confronted her. Even so, she had waited; perhaps she will feel his touch on her cheek, in her hair, his hand telling that she belongs to him, his true-wife, the woman who soon brings forth his child.

"If you refuse to prepare food for me, I discard you as my wife."

His tone had brought her eyes swiftly back to his face; at his next words she had covered her mouth.

"I will go to the drum and when everyone listens, I will say that I throw you away."

"You will not remember the child inside me." Her throat had gurgled a moan.

"And you will not remember my empty belly," he had mocked.

Wipatawin had not looked for him to answer concerning a different woman, but neither had she prepared for his threat to throw her away. And certainly he had spoken as one who wanted to rid himself of an unwanted woman and an unborn child.

The woman's arms had dropped to her sides. Going to the food which she had cooked but covered from his sight, she had filled a bowl. Setting down this meat, she saw that he had turned his back to her.

She had crawled out of the tipi wondering where to go, her swollen awkwardness not something she cared to display in a different lodge.

The next day she had brought Peśla a bundle; she offered the child wearily. "A girl-baby," she had murmured.

Peśla had unwrapped the bundle and looked at the small thing lying on the hide. When he handed back the infant, he had said only that the water-sac hung empty, the woodpile diminished, the soup cooled. Let her get back to her work; he will stay and provide.

The girl-baby had grown fat and smiling during the snow moons. Wipatawin had played with her tiny daughter and listened for Peśla's step. They call winter the season of 'men-in-the-lodges,' but seldom, a man in Wipatawin's lodge.

Then, before the snow melted, Peśla had announced that he intended to bring a certain young woman into the tipi. Wipatawin shall call the new woman 'teya.' Certainly these two wives will get along as sisters; the young woman, similar to Wipatawin, possesses a nice singing voice.

Wipatawin had not answered him. But one crisp, bright morning soon after this announcement, she had carried her baby to Cankuna's lodge, asking that the good woman sit with this child while she goes hunting wood.

Cankuna, grateful for this visit with her grandchild, had played rolling-a-ball with the little one and afterwards had sung a sleep-song. But the child, instead of napping, had lain whimpering softly.

But even as the grandmother felt around for whatever disquieted the baby, a loud wailing nearby the lodge had brought the woman out into the slush of melting snow. "See that none steps on my little granddaughter," she had called back to Tacincala.

Beyond the line of tipi Cankuna had seen two men who carried a big bundle, a crowd walking back of these two. But before she had moved another step, someone had come up alongside, someone who stood, many tears falling.

And then a second woman, also crying, had given Cankuna the sorrowful news. The men carried Wipatawin's body, she had told; the new mother had strangled herself. The muddy snow beneath the tree showed sliding marks and so they knew that Wipatawin had dropped to her knees, the thong she had tied around her neck and to a branch above her head tightening as she fell.

Suddenly Cankuna had seemed to lose her senses; she had heard neither the grief-cries nor the comforting-sounds for the murmurs that sympathized with the warrior-husband Peśla, who this same day had returned from a raid.

But after a moment's shock, she, mother to Peśla, had remembered her son's lodge as one where two of the four great tragedies strike, two coming at once: a wife dying and a child in want of the mother's breast. Emitting a wail, Cankuna had used her knife to cut off her braids. Dropping the hair onto the ground, she had turned back toward her lodge. The two women at her side had walked in close; knowing that Cankuna intended to slash her arms and legs, they stayed to watch for any excessive bleeding.

Hearing the story about Peśla's return from a horse-taking, certain persons had wondered at the man's pressing need for horses; only something most urgent sends out a warrior before the sun dries the soggy earth. Will Peśla's out-of-season raid in some way relate to the hanging-wife tragedy?

Hoka, the renowned warrior-hunter who formed the Ihoka-lodge in the Titonwan camps, had held on to his uncertainties about a man whose wife hung herself. Not that he suspected every hanging; he knew that some women chose not to endure a second wife in the lodge and that this sort of woman took her despondency to the trees, where she died with the help of the standing-people. But in Wipatawin's suicide, Hoka had wondered something different: perhaps Peśla's cruel eyes drive his wife to the woods?

He had known Ogle a long while and he respected all members of the hunter's family—but Peśla. He granted that none lived more daringly, more boldly than Peśla, but he had asked himself whether or not the Ihoka-lodge wants a man of Peśla's disposition; why not deliberate?

The Ihoka bore a resemblance to the Tokala-lodge, differing in that the Ihoka, originating as a group whose activities centered around the chase, invited in young hunters along with warriors. Iśna's camp had a similar group— akicita who helped out the meat-makers—and Hoka had learned of their lodge from a visiting uncle, the same old man for whom Peśla once had requested that Wipatawin perform outstanding courtesies.

Looking for something to distinguish his new lodge, Hoka had decided that all members pair off, each pair painting alike. As for singers, he had chosen four young women who never had known-a-man. But if any one of the four accepted a husband, this man—providing he so desired—became a member. Aware that undesirables perhaps gain entrance into the group by this path, Hoka had proposed that a singer's choice for husband receive the unanimous consent of the lodge.

For this reason the woman Lowansa, on announcing her intention to accept Peśla as husband, had endured a long wait before all Ihoka consented. Truly, Lowansa had considered giving up her rank as a singer with the Ihoka and returning to her mother's lodge in the Sicanġu camp; she had wanted to avoid embarrassing the brother-lodge.

Members had recalled rumors concerning Peśla's methods in securing his original wife, a woman now dead, her own hands acting to break her neck; they intended to move cautiously. But different ones had spoken up saying that they had watched the warrior walking about camp in a frayed robe, the man obviously grieving his dead wife. And in answer to those members who strongly hinted that Peśla will not deserve another wife, they asked why Wipatawin had not thrown out his things? A dissatisfied woman will put outside her husband's weapons and so empty her lodge of him.

But what about Peśla as a warrior? Who acts as Peśla acts and comes back in one piece? A man finding himself in a tight place perhaps maneuvers out of his situation, but who goes looking for tight places? Who but Peśla?

Will the brother-members not agree that their lodge-dance calls for Iñoka to mimic the grimacing flat-face who digs-with-mouth? So why not Peśla for a member, a man all-fight, a man who looks and talks as if he will kill any Titonwan who dares disturb the meat before a tribal hunt?

And let the members recall that Peśla, not usually generous with gift-horses, presents his dead wife's relatives with all but four of the horses he takes on that daring raid, the man out alone on melting snow, slippery ground, something most warriors never risk.

Hoka had differed. "I look for a man," he had said, "who comes into the Iñoka-lodge with clean hands."

Silence had greeted his view and so he had spoken saying that at forty-and-five he outlives a place in any akicita-lodge. Founder of this brother-group, the Iñoka, he now retires. But he looks for his lodge-brothers to carry on in true Iñoka custom.

Not one member had raised a persuading voice against Hoka's resignation; instead they quickly had approved Lowansa's choice. And they had agreed that as soon as these two become husband and wife, they shall gift the pair in a most elaborate manner. And that Peśla shall become a member of the Iñoka at once.

Soon afterwards they had held a singers-feast, the four young women presenting their difficult songs. And then the leaders had told Lowansa that they approve of the warrior who keeps looking at her; if she wants him, the Iñoka lodge also wants him; they will welcome Pešla on the day he becomes her husband.

The morning after this feast Pešla had received an invitation to eat in the tipi with Lowansa's people, who had appeared suddenly in the Mahto camp.

Lowansa, a single daughter in a Sicanǧu family of four sons, had visited in the Mahto villages the summer before the suicide. Accepting an invitation from Hoka and his Mahto wife, she and her parents had agreed to stay throughout the warm moons. Lowansa had sung for clubmen in Išna's camp, a group whose songs Hoka had borrowed when he formed the Iȟoka-lodge. And the man had looked for Lowansa's knowledge of the phrasing to prove helpful in rehearsing women singers for the new lodge.

Lowansa had given her whole heart to the singing group. And so Hoka had encouraged the young woman— her relatives permitting—to extend her visit into the next season. But certainly Hoka never had intended to provide an opportunity for Pešla to seek out Lowansa; truly, his dislike for Pešla had reached the point where he ceased to visit Ogle—one way to avoid meeting the hunter's son, who had returned to his mother's lodge. Then, discovering to what length things had gone, he had rushed a message to the young woman's family. And these persons, sensing Hoka's concern, had started for the Mahto villages at once.

Pešla had eaten with the Sicanǧu family. And the next day he had tied two horses, their red-and-white patches matching, outside the Sicanǧu lodge, two big horses of ordinary color alongside.

One morning soon afterwards, Lowansa had appeared at Cankuna's lodge; she had come to let the warrior know what pleasure his gifts had brought her whole family. And she had come in proper manner, bearing a bowl of soup, signifying that she accepts him as the one before whom she gladly will set the soup bowl each morning.

She had placed the bowl at Pešla's feet, and when he sat, he had pulled her down, gently, alongside him. Then, before he had emptied the bowl, he had begun speaking, his voice soft, almost coaxing, his hand holding onto her hand.

"Perhaps you will go away with me . . . now."

601

Startled, Lowansa had remained silent.

"I speak. I listen for an answer." His tone, while not unkind, had lost any softness. And most certainly his eyes had revealed what answer she shall make.

Even so, Lowansa had sat hesitant; people of good name hold ceremonies for these important events. "My father and brothers will see you. After you eat again with my family, perhaps. . ."

"Your father and brothers accept the horses, four horses speaking for me. Your relatives know that I desire a place as son and brother to your people. And husband to you." Pešla's hold on her hand had tightened.

"I . . . I need to find a young woman who will replace my voice in the Iȟoka. I go now and look for one."

"You will find a singer to take your place after I and you return," Pešla had said smiling.

"My parents and brothers have something they desire to give. . . . I know that the Iȟoka will offer useful things . . . presents for . . ." Lowansa had demurred.

"They will offer gifts when I and you come back, when you raise your own lodge and have a place for these things."

The woman had hunted more reasons for delay. Yet she knew not why.

Finally she had remembered something: perhaps Pešla will discover that he dislikes her smell or taste. And so he will bring her back after two, three nights away and at the next big gathering announce that he chooses not to keep her as wife.

But she had not dared ponder this thing; instead she had remembered that her brothers called him bold and that the Iȟoka had approved her choice. And that the girls in camp said that Pešla made shivers run up their backs.

Lowansa had found herself shivering. She had wished that this man, suddenly a stranger, let her go back to the family lodge and reflect upon this thing. But her moment for saying so had come and gone.

Pešla had led her toward his favorite horse, a second horse waiting. As she mounted the one tied to his, she had wondered what different move she yet dared make. Riding toward the edge of camp she had glanced around; she had marveled that not a person seemed to notice her, none concerned that she rode off with a man.

"Sit easy," Peśla had said quietly. "I am not taking you far away."

He had slapped his horse sharply and the one Lowansa rode also had jumped, almost as if this creature had felt the same stinging quirt.

Peśla had run the horses, but, as he had said, they shall not go far out, not even beyond view of the lodge tops. He rode smiling and he had smiled when he called to her to stop. But the next moment his eyes had narrowed, his under lip shaping into a cruel line. Lowansa's horse had shown fear at the billowing flap of her gown when she had bent forward to pat the creature's face.

The woman had jumped off, neither thrown nor frightened. But Peśla had grabbed the horse's jaw-cord; swiftly he had tied the front feet. Then, holding on to the thongs of his quirt, he had struck the creature with the wood handle.

Lowansa, hearing pain-cries and seeing blood ooze, had begun to wail her sympathy with the horse: "You whip enough."

"I decide," Peśla had answered, but he had flung down the quirt. "I will not come here to whip horse or woman."

He had tied his horse to brush, then walked to the sandy stream nearby, enough water in the creek to splash his face and shoulders. Rubbing the drops from his arms, he had called to Lowansa.

But she had stayed where he left her. And so he had come back, his eyes laughing. Gently he had slapped her bottom. "Get the fear off your face, my praise-earning one. The horse will not need a second whipping and you never will need the first." He took her hand. "Come."

As she stood alongside him at the stream, he had bent and scooped up water, lifting her gown to splash a handful high up between her legs.

Next he had led her toward a path of shady summer coolness where they had sat on soft grass, berry brush circling their retreat, lodgepoles overhead, tops touching, sun shining through the branches.

Lowansa saw the man's hand touching on the grass, the fingers dark and strong. And then she had felt herself pushed gently down until she lay on her back, Peśla's arm across the breast of her gown, his fingers stroking her neck. She had remembered back to those three occasions when he had held his robe around her. He had spoken like someone who visited with an affinal relative, not exactly joking but certainly not making her shiver. And he never had tried to discover her taste, something she had heard about during talks with her grandmother.

She had closed her eyes; the man's hand had moved onto her face, following along the line of her forehead and cheeks, his touch saying that he regards her as a pretty woman.

She had not opened her eyes but she had known when he leaned over her. And then the hand that had lain across her had begun stroking wherever her body curved, something she had felt through the gown.

The fragrance of grass had intensified and different growing things had pushed forward their warm scents; something within her had begun to throb.

His hand, hunting under her gown, had found the throbbing place. The protecting thong around her thighs seemingly had loosened and she had twisted about as if refusing this personal invasion. But the earth had sided with the man, pressing as hard against her back as Peśla, now on top, had pressed against her front. After a while he had rolled off and so she had blinked open her eyes.

The next instant he had flung up her gown, half her body exposed to his gaze. And then she had learned the strength of his arms; he had pulled her on top himself, up to his mouth, where he had tasted her for sweetness.

Rolling her back on the ground, he had spread her legs; and so she had discovered the strength of his hands.

And then she had known hardness and push and pain, all in the same moment. She had seemed floating away, unknowing where; and so she had shed a tear. Stars had drifted past, each tiny bright sun beyond her reach. She had tried once and again to touch even one and when they all had disappeared, she had laughed a crazy little laugh.

The air had seemed filled with strange new fragrance, something more than flower-smell, more than creature-smell. And gazing up at the dark heads of the tree-people, she had touched her own face and hair, marveling her presence here.

Looking to her side, she had seen where Peśla lay as if

asleep. She had reached out her hand and touched him, touched something wet and sticky that now belonged to her.

The man, feeling her touch, had smiled. Not opening his eyes, he had reached over his hand and touched where his hardness had visited her, touched something wet and warm that now belonged to him.

And so the warrior had made Lowansa his wife.

These two had not returned at once to the encampment; instead they had gone visiting among the Sicaṅġu, the woman's relatives welcoming the pair in their lodges, gifting this man and wife with robes and hides and meat and a horse-and-drag for carrying back these gifts to the Titoṅwaṅ hoop.

Everywhere they went, Peśla had appeared eager to keep his wife within sight. Lowansa, seventeen, had worn a colorful tie around her gown, something to show off her pleasingly wide hips below a small waist and fully ripe breasts, her shape and pretty face certain to attract glances—but not in the presence of a warrior-husband. Even so, custom permitted crude joking between Peśla and certain ones among his new affinal relatives, jokes that had led to much teasing, laughing. The son of Ogle had displayed a remarkably good nature, and Lowansa, seeing none of the frightful temper he had turned on the horse, had begun to wish that Peśla stay with the Sicaṅġu, that they raise a lodge here on the earth-smoke.

Then suddenly Peśla had spoken, the warrior saying that they shall start back; they had lived away from the Mahto camp from round moon to round moon. And so the next day, the two had begun traveling north.

The Iñoka lodge had given a feast for Peśla and his wife upon their return, and the pair had received a tipi cover along with many different gifts. And so Lowansa had everything she had wanted for a lodge, from backrests—even a bone backrest for Peśla—to painted containers, perhaps enough meat folders and robe-holders for the next two, three winters.

Joyfully the young wife had raised her new tipi nearby her husband's parents, then waited for Peśla to bring his little girl, the daughter of his dead wife, into her lodge. But he had not brought the child. When she had asked for a reason, he had answered saying, "You will give me a son and perhaps a daughter. Let the girl stay in my mother's lodge." He had mentioned his mother's apparent pleasure in her grandchild and he had told of the many ways this little one resembled the small daughter who had died choking. Lowansa had not dared say more.

Soon the young woman had discovered that her husband stayed easy to live with only when things went entirely his way. But let him lose his meat during the chase or hear someone dispute one of his schemes and then his anger boiled as on the day he had whipped the horse, a glare in his eyes and a growl in his throat. Certainly she had endeavored to please him. Her grandmother and mother had taught her that a wife shall accept the husband's nature and not hunt ways to change him. When a man asks that a certain woman becomes his wife, custom gives that woman the privilege of refusing for her own reasons. But once she accepts a man, she accepts his nature and without intent of making change, neither in the man nor in the child who shall bear a piece if not the whole of his nature.

Lowansa had noticed also that Pesla's most disagreeable moods came after he attended a meeting in the Iñoka-lodge; in some mysterious way these club-men had a way of arousing his surliness.

The woman had made a true observation. The man returned from each gathering of the Iñoka in a temper that invariably upset the tipi; they had not promoted him to the rank he desired. Rattle-carrier, club-owner, lance-bearer— he had held those ranks in the Tokala and he intended to hold a more impressive place among the Iñoka. They used his wife as one of their singers and they had honored him with many gifts; yet at the feasts he sat alongside the ordinary members. And they had refused him a place in the dancing until he found someone agreeable to painting exactly as he painted; to walk in the Iñoka procession he needed to find one person willing to imitate him. This rule and one more rule the Iñoka emphasized: the members shall live as brothers, none quarreling nor giving reason for a quarrel. They had hinted more than once that Pesla especially remember this never-quarrel rule.

The warrior had awaited, then, the old-summer feast at

which they gave promotions, but they had not promoted him. And so four days afterwards, Peśla had walked away from camp, taking along a party of four. The group had known only that they headed toward the Palani villages, perhaps a raid for horses and a demand for maize. Certainly none had suspected that Peśla hurried north to the maize-planters' camp in search of smoke for the Iñoka pipe.

The Iñoka, when preparing a pipe-bowl, desire cuttings from leaves which once had their roots in a Palani village. Such leaves, the members told, make a sweet smoke, and whatever tastes sweet, the Iñoka regard as pure and ripe and desirable. This same thing, they said, applies to woman.

A water creature had provided the original smoke for the Palani pipes—or so their legends hint—and after a while the tribe had offered seed from their plantings to the Psa and the Titonwan. The Psa had made use of this offering, but the Titonwan had not troubled to scratch the earth and wait for the sacred stalks; instead the Titonwan went on using a red bark handy in every camp, peeling the wood thin and curly for quick drying. But these peelings called for the taste of Palani leaves and so each Lakotah party going among the Palani for trade or to loot brought back a twist, something to cut and mix with the red bark.

Not Peśla. He had schemed to bring himself into prominence among the Iñoka provided that he and his party managed a safe return; he intended to bring back whatever the Palani keep under guard pertaining to their pipes: stalk, leaf, root, seed.

His four companions had understood to keep this party a secret; Peśla had not wanted different ones along. The warrior had invited two Iñoka—drum-keeper and lance-bearer—and he had invited Nuǵe, the horse-catcher. The fourth member, a youth desiring a certain young woman but lacking the war honors, had accepted eagerly.

Peśla had picked these men carefully, each one holding an exact place in the scheme but none aware of his assignment until within sight of the enemy's mound-lodges. Going out on foot, they had imagined what Peśla wanted each one to imagine: they go out raiding for horses.

The group had covered ground quickly, moon and weather helping. Then at a rest near the Palani camps, the leader had revealed his intent and given instructions.

Nuġe's eyes had brightened; he had seen at once where the party needed an expert horse-catcher. The two Iñoka had sat amazed at Peśla's slyness: the man had advanced his group beyond the point of anyone's return, anyone's pretense at an ominous dream. But the drum-keeper had spoken abruptly.

"My warrior-relative," he had said, looking sharply at Peśla, "you will remember that if an Iñoka falls, his brother-akicita go at once to his help."

"I remember," Peśla had answered dryly. "And you will remember, my brother-akicita, that none in the parties I lead ever falls."

The leader's cold eyes had turned contemptuously on the fourth member, but the youth's look had said that he will follow Peśla to the finish, even jump over a cliff if the leader calls for such a jump.

The pipe emptied, Peśla had hurried his party forward. The man led, not looking back; why turn to see if they come? He had known when he decided on these four that they will listen to him, each one for his own reasons.

The youth had crept toward the smoke-leaf patches outside those ditches that protected the Palani villages. Stakes and brush surrounded the plantings, and here the young brave had crouched to keep watch. His, a most important assignment; Peśla had said so.

The drum-man and Nuġe had gone off in another direction. Their work, someplace different, but they also had a most important assignment; Peśla had said so.

The leader and the lance-man, hunting a place to hide on the open ground, had seen neither tree nor stone big enough to lend a shadow while they watch for Nuġe's signal. And so these two had needed to sit remarkably quiet while they waited out the night, the moon round and teasing. And never a cloud to offer relief for their cramped legs, stiff necks.

At dawn four Palani women—two old ones, two young—had climbed through the broken stakes and onto the planted ground. They had come for a morning's work, to cut leaves and stem and make up bundles. The young, daughters to the two women, had talked and giggled while they sliced down the stalks, hacked off leaves. And so the mother of one had advised that her daughter attend to work or the men will have nothing to smoke.

"So let the men come out and help. They lie on mats and scratch their heads and...." The girl had made this much answer when suddenly something cut off her words. A hand had covered her mouth and a knife lay across her throat.

At the same moment a strange voice in awkward Palani accents had told the startled women that they shall not cry out; one sound and the knife cuts off the girl's head. The same voice had gone on saying different things in a roughly spoken dialect but the meaning had come through clear and fast.

The astounded workers then saw that the two enemy who had sneaked up stood naked as their own men on a warm day. But noticing the lance in the hand of one, their astonishment had turned into fright.

Next thing, they had heard the voice telling that many Titonwan warriors hide inside this staked place, branches shielding each one. If the women look—moving only their eyes—they will see where branches sway gently. These warriors carry arrows for throwing at the two women or for any man these women workers consider asking for help. The Titonwan sit impatient as any Palani for something in their pipes. And on this occasion the Titonwan come after bundles of smoke, not twists.

Peśla had taken his hand from the girl's mouth. "Start your foolish chatter as before. Say nothing suspicious."

The warrior had spoken these phrases fluently; let these women know that he will understand everything they say. "Gather up the stalks. Carry these bundles to where someone leads you."

When the women's arms embraced a full load, the youth had come from back of the osiers and, slipping among the burdened ones, had begun directing the bundle-carriers toward a slope of ground. The rise concealed captors and captives from the view of anyone who walked through the village but not from the sight of some sharp-eyed Palani who sat atop his mound-lodge. Or from the sight of anyone who kept a day-watch over the gatherers. And so Peśla, staying in the enclosure, had made certain that whoever looked down on these women shall see nothing unnatural in their maneuvers nor glimpse the crouching form in their midst: he had sent the lance-man to walk joking and laughing at the front, as something to distract.

The drum-keeper and Nuġe had stood guarding the place these women put down their bundles, each man holding a horse, a hand on the creature's nose to prevent cough or snort. Here the youth stayed, tying the bundles onto the horses, the drum-man helping in this work while Nuġe calmed the horses.

But the women, as instructed, had returned with the lance-bearer to pick up more loads, the naked Iȟoka walking front as before.

Peśla had stayed hidden in the enclosure until they had removed all bundled stalks and leaves. Instructing the lance-bearer to hold the women back of the slope along with the horses, the warrior had waited for the five to reach this place safely. Then, openly and naked and alone, Peśla had walked away from the planting-ground. He had moved slowly, climbing the slope in full view of any villager who looked toward the rise. His companions, watching, had marveled such daring.

But when he had come alongside the horses, Peśla's eyes had reflected displeasure; why only two horses when he had advised five? He had glared at Nuġe, but the horsecatcher and drum-keeper, instructed to start out once they tied all bundles horseback, had sat ready to go. And so Peśla had waved off these two even as he began scheming for the escape of the three remaining members of the party, three persons without horses and facing open, flat ground. And the sun halfway up the side of the sky.

As the horsebacks rode off, Peśla's quick gestures had signaled that which he had taken only moments to decide.

And so they had killed the two old women, the knife making quiet work on one, the lance on the second woman. And before the look of terror had faded from either pair of dead eyes, the killers had lifted their scalps.

Then, while the red edge of the knife held the two young women in stunned silence, Peśla and the lance-man had jerked off the killed women's gowns. Swiftly they had cut the sinew halfway down and so made something to pull over a man's shoulders and stretch to below his knees. Peśla had tossed one to the youth, motioning that he shall wear this garment. The second gown, Peśla had put on himself. The lance-bearer, daring to wear nothing that restrains, had stood naked as before.

The three had started out, the girls nudged along, Peśla muttering threats in their ears. But before this group had taken many steps, the camp-dogs had begun running out, yapping noisily and chasing after the escaping raiders.

Acting on his own choice, the lance-man had hung back to throw stones, but his attempt to drive off the dogs had proved futile. He had estimated ten dogs to every Palani and that half the pack had rushed out after the Lakotah; neither knife nor lance will silence this many dogs.

Peśla, his eyes unnaturally bright and his face strangely colorful, had managed to shut out any distractions, and so he alone had observed the small herd of pack horses grazing in the near distance, legs loosely tied to prevent wandering. And certainly Peśla knew ways for urging such horses into amazing strides, into a lope that carries a man swiftly away. But in what manner will he reach these creatures? Walking in a woman's gown hampered his movements. He had smiled grimly at the sight of the young man who stumbled along in front of him. Then, suddenly, he had seen the next move.

He had spoken to the girls, not daring to risk signs; he knew that the yapping dogs had directed some eyes to the flat beyond the slope. "What happens to the old women, happens to you if you signal the village."

But the girls, walking alongside him, had seemed numb. He had needed to arouse these two instantly. "Attend. Bring horses here. Bring two pack horses or you will bleed on this ground."

To his relief, the girls had hurried toward the grazing herd; they had not looked back nor signaled an alarm.

Certain dogs had caught up with the party, five or more of these creatures snapping at the lance-man's moccasins, the Iħoka not deigning to notice. And then Peśla, his eyes roving the earth front and sides, had seen that a man approached, someone who moved toward the awkwardly advancing group. Perhaps a horse-tender, he had told himself, someone who comes in from a night's watch over the herd? Or perhaps a scout who will notice each detail and see that these two 'women' walk in the manner of men and that they wear Titonwan moccasins, a scout who will signal instantly to the mounds. And so Peśla had known that within the next moments either he and his companions become horsebacks or they try making their way back to the center of the Palani village, to the big mound that grants safety to any stranger who reaches this lodge before the villagers kill him. Either way, the chance not much.

The girls, leading two horses, had moved reluctantly toward Peśla. Or so the warrior had viewed their approach. Certainly they had seen the Palani who came near the Titonwan; certainly they schemed to delay the horses. But standing close to danger always had exhilarated Peśla; he had intended to make the most of this experience.

Tearing off the woman's gown that covered him, he had sprung forward, then run bounding toward the horses. "Mount or die," he had yelled in a dialect neither Palani nor Lakotah but instantly understood. "Keep together," he had shouted as the girls mounted.

Rushing up, he had leapt onto the back of the near horse. He had caught the girl rider as she started to fall, pulling her into place in front of him. Forcing this horse against the side of the second, he had given a kick which sent the second horse into the path of the lance-bearer. And the Ihoka, grabbing hold the mane, had jumped up in front of the girl.

The Lakotah youth, hopping along as if he wore leg-ties, had tried to reach this same horse. Suddenly he had pulled his woman-gown above his middle and begun to run. And then Peśla had seen the lance-bearer strike the Palani girl, knocking her off the horse. The next instant the youth had jumped up back of the Ihoka.

The approaching Palani man, near enough to see what occurred, had given a warning cry and run back after one of the pack horses; apparently he had intended to give chase.

All these happenings had acted upon Peśla in a manner that incited him to grab on to yet more danger. Whirling his mount, he had rushed at the girl whom the lance-man had knocked down, someone injured but struggling to get on her feet. Scarcely slowing his horse, Peśla had swooped down, his sharp knife lifting hair from the shrieking, crumbling form. Then, kicking his horse into a startled run, he had held aloft her bleeding scalp, his war whoop bursting in the ears of the near-crazed captive he held in front of him, this one clinging to the mane and gurgling foolish laughter.

The lance-man and youth, riding double, had stayed ahead of Peśla and his captive, but they had heard him shouting, telling wind and sky that he viewed all Palani as women born to provide for the Titonwan, to plant and bundle smoke for the Lakotah, to grow maize and squash and to mold colorful beads into ornaments for their proud enemy south. And they had heard him fling foul taunts at the Palani who chased after him.

Peśla had rejoiced at the noise that came from across the ditches; he had known that he aroused the whole village. He had pictured even the most lazy jumping up from their mats and different ones rising up from where they squatted on the men's ground, everyone suddenly aware that the Titonwan had carried off their bundles of smoke and killed three of their women and captured one; five Titonwan raiders, one a youth, accomplished all these things. Peśla had imagined the Palani winter count along with the Lakotah remembering this event, the picture saying only that Peśla and four warriors visit the Palani in the moon of yellow leaves.

For a while Peśla had ridden indifferent to the dust-streaked face and form he held on his horse. He had schemed to throw her at the enemy if anyone among the pursuers had come close or to drop her somewhere along the trail. But noticing the sky-color beads along the edges of her gown, he had found new thoughts. Why not the beads for Lowansa, he had asked himself, and the girl for his mother, another pair of hands in Cankuna's lodge, another back to bend over hides, bend down for wood?

He had turned the girl's head for a view of her face. And even as he had laughed into her terror-stricken eyes, he had seen that once they wash off the thick dust cover, they shall find a face almost respectable. Wisely, then, he will take her to his mother's lodge, not to Lowansa; enough that one wife hangs herself when he mentions bringing in another woman.

Applying quirt and heels harshly and unrelentingly,

Peśla had used up his horse before he had reached the place of reunion with the other four members of his party: the two who had loaded the smoke-leaves on their horses, the lance-man, and the youth. But he had not sensed any concern; he had seen the Palani turn around, none choosing to pursue, the maize-planters perhaps suspecting a big party of Titonwan at the edge of the flat. And so, leaving the horse to limp off somewhere or to die where standing, the warrior and girl had walked the short distance to the meeting place.

And as they walked, Peśla had imagined a spectacular return to the hoop, each member of his party wearing victory paint and singing. And once back in camp he had imagined more songs and much dancing, the bands marveling that which Peśla and his companions had enacted. And finally, those members of a certain akicita-lodge pondering in what manner they shall award one who brings bundles of smoke direct from the Palani to the piece of flat wood on which they cut for their pipe. And Lowansa, their favorite singer, managing the hint that awards Peśla a most high rank among the Iñoka.

For so the warrior-son of Ogle had schemed to complete that which he had envisioned on the day he had determined to make Lowansa his wife.

The Iñoka had welcomed brother-members on their return from the smoke-leaves raid, songs of praise for each one. Certainly the lance-bearer had fulfilled his rank; certainly the drum-keeper had brought new pride to the Iñoka. As for Nuge, the Iñoka intended to invite him into their lodge next summer. And a certain young brave, one who had used his knife to take hair, now had dared approach the lodge where lived the young woman he wished to make his wife.

Listening to the recital of Peśla's acts, many Iñoka had recalled their misgivings concerning this new member, these persons quick to sound assent when the Iñoka whip spoke saying that Peśla had earned the one important rank open at the moment: keeper-of-the-pipe.

The drum-man had approved loudly, almost too loudly. Among the Iñoka the drum-keeper, not the pipe-keeper, sits on the governing council. Knowing that they will award Peśla something, he had desired seeing this warrior a rank below himself. So long as Pešla sat below him, he dared refuse Pešla's invitations without offending the warrior. And truly he chose never again to go out with this one, Pešla's schemes too daring for his blood.

Lowansa's hand had reached eagerly for the shining beads, but her eyes had stayed on the Palani girl who stood at the tipi flap awaiting someone saying where she belongs. Lowansa had not wondered that Pešla visited the Ihoka lodge before returning to his own after the raid, but she had puzzled why he waited outside her tipi with a strange girl, someone whose head drooped, whose hands clutched the sides of her gown.

"My wife," Pešla had said smiling, "I see you looking at each thing I bring back. But now see what I prize most." He had flung a scalp, stretched on a little hoop, at her feet.

Stooping, Lowansa had picked up the hair, her eyes again turning toward the girl.

"I consider offering you two scalps for the dance, but I decide that this one"—he had glanced briefly at the captive—"shall keep her hair. She has more use as a helper in my mother's lodge than as a scalp on the pole you carry to the dance."

Lowansa had sympathized with the girl. "If my husband permits," she had murmured, "I will bring his captive water for washing and a fresh gown."

Pešla had not permitted. "Let her find the stream and look after herself. She will not risk running away. But more important I weary of the smell of Palani. I prefer looking at my wife, who brings water and new moccasins for me."

And so Lowansa had attended to those things that Pešla desired on his return. Afterwards the man had leaned against his backrest and begun the story of his raid on the Palani.

The story Lowansa had heard on the day Pešla returned from the Palani camps, she had heard again and again—at the scalp dances, in the Ihoka-lodge, and always in her own lodge whenever visitors arrived. And she had heard different voices telling her husband's story, each one

615

reciting the events exactly as Peśla recited, inflection and gestures the same whoever spoke. Now, after a winter and a summer of these repeats, she had begun to find the story a bore.

Occasionally she managed to escape a retelling, but whether or not she sat listening, always she saw someone who compelled her recollection of Peśla's experience; always somewhere near, the Palani woman they had named Winu. Sullen and silent, Winu cast an onerous shadow in Cankuna's lodge, acted on Lowansa as an irritant.

Another person hearing the Peśla story repeated and repeated had grown weary of the recital and the extravagant praise that accompanied each recital. Ahbleza had seen Peśla raised up in a new warrior-lodge, had watched Peśla riding in front of each hunting camp, had observed Peśla moving forward in the center lodge, finally to that side where the important warriors sat, next to the truly big voices in council. Peśla, someone who had exhausted to the death every horse he had ridden, someone who had abused kinsman-privileges, broken kinsman-rules, and schemed beyond decency. Certainly, Ahbleza told himself, many different persons observe that Peśla makes up his own rules.

So what happens that the wise and honorable in the band acclaim the aberrant and reject the custom-abiding? Will the keepers-of-the-tribal-good tolerate a permissiveness that he, Ahbleza, not yet understands? Will the leaders say that he, Ahbleza, walks clinging to old ways while different warriors advance along some new path? Will a change occur in the warrior-image? What about Wanaǵi? Certainly the sacred-man will see that something changes, something that will not relate to the grandfathers now or back at the beginning. Or will Wanaǵi change along with the change?

Ever since the season of Ahbleza's vision-seeking, Wanaǵi and the son of Olepi had experienced little contact, Ahbleza quick to perceive the sacred-man's indifference toward him. Even so, the warrior had wished more than once for the sort of visit they had enjoyed in the past. But aware of the unlikelihood of more such meetings, Ahbleza had begun seeking the lonely ledges, going out before sundown to stand barefoot on sun-warmed stone. Here he had

demanded that one among the invisibles lend him understanding; he, Ahbleza, someone who demands to know why
the Lakotah change, what things this changing improves.

IV

THE TITONWAN bands, each snuggling along the warm
back of the earth-mother hill, welcomed the snow season.
Not only will their own bands compete in the ice-games but
this winter they shall enter into contests with the Sahiela.
These friendly people had clustered their lodges on a nearby
stream, the two tribes within easy visiting-distance, the
black hills embracing the two different tongues.

But any Titonwan going out to mingle with his Sahiela
neighbors discovered a drooping tribe, none with the spirit
for racing over the hard ground or sliding rib-bones. They
had lost their laughter, not even the heyoka bringing smiles
into their camps. Thirty-and-two Sahiela warriors, all brothers in an akicita-lodge, had died fighting on muddy creek
this summer past. Not twenty Sahiela women wore hair long
enough for braiding and all Sahiela displayed grief-marks.

Soon those wives, mothers, sisters of the deceased will
come wandering into the Titonwan villages, visitors had
told, the women coming to show their sorrow-scars. And
the warriors who accompany these women, intend holding
out a red-stem pipe, each man's face a plea for Titonwan
help when they take revenge, when they move against the
Psa.

And so the Titonwan, recalling that the Sahiela once
came to their assistance, began to consider a position.
Mahto warriors and their wives along with people from the
Siyo and Oglalahca went to visit the Sahiela camps, the
women of these tribes mingling their tears, the men heating
up their blood.

617

But certain Titonwan sat with the old Sahiela, choosing to listen in on peace talk, the son of Olepi one of this group. Here Ahbleza learned more about the Sahiela rules for living together, more about the Sahiela plan that provides for a council of forty-and-four, persons who advise for ten winters before different ones take their places.

"This way the people see forty-and-four councilmen, each one giving unsparingly of himself. Four more sit as principals in this council, and they choose yet one more who keeps a remembrance of things happening in the past. This rememberer acts to relate whatever the council contemplates to something similar that occurs in past seasons. And so the counselors and four principals make their decisions knowing what most likely will happen."

The old one who had spoken had used his eyes and hands to help along his tongue; he seemed eager that his visitors understand.

Ahbleza had sat most attentive to this speaker. He recognized the Sahiela camp circle as twice the lodges in the Titonwan hoop; the Sahiela owned the strength on the plain. So if he listens closely to this old man, perhaps he shall discover the source of Sahiela strength, discover whether the power resides in those four arrows sacred to the tribe or in those fifty different acts that make up their thanks-offering ceremony or in this governing plan which a woman brings to the Sahiela.

"Tsistsistas," the old one said now, "Tsistsistas, the true-name of this tribe whom the Lakotah call Sahiela."

Softly Ahbleza pronounced the tribal name: Tsistsistas. The Lakotah said that they heard this swishing-sound in all the Sahiela speech, a swishing they likened to the scraping noise of grass stalks. But the meanings in their words interested Ahbleza, not the sound.

A Tsistsistas, the speaker said next, regards nothing more important than the comfort of those persons in a lodge without the husband-father, a lodge wherein the enemy cuts down the provider. And along with this concern for a family in need of assistance, a Tsistsistas recognizes the importance of keeping peace within the band. Let a man speak softly, act gently in his own village, but let him remember himself as grizzly once he goes out among the enemy.

Looking on the strong face of him who spoke these

things—a grandfather who had sat in the council of forty-and-four—Ahbleza decided that these Sahiela, in the manner of the Lakotah leaders, also wait and see what the day demands, a man wholly peaceful or wholly warlike depending on whether he sits with family or walks out to meet the enemy. Perhaps in this Sahiela lodge, Ahbleza told himself, he will come into a clear understanding of what the Lakotah look for in a Shirtman.

"The fifth man, he of the remarkable memory," the Sahiela revealed now, "tells that the Tsistsistas once live on stony ground, tall-ears hopping and bounding all around, also many fat skunks during the old-summer moon. And so the people pile up stones for shelters and kill those small creatures for meat and coverings.

"When finally the Tsistsistas travel, they live for a while on barren earth, where they use the name 'sandhill-men.' Next, they move alongside certain big lakes; here they eat the food that swims. And instead of wood for fire, they burn the tall grass which they tie into long bundles. And here, slender branches of the white-wood provide their shelters.

"Afterwards the Tsistsistas wander into the woods. They carry clubs and bows and kill big meat. But a different tribe carries firesticks, something that keeps the Tsistsistas at a distance and always moving.

"On reaching the big river, the Tsistsistas cross onto the short grass. Here they settle down in earth lodges along certain streams. They plant maize along quill creek perhaps fifty winters, along earth-lodge creek half as many. Twice during these planting seasons Tsistsistas and Lakotah camp together."

And now Ahbleza understood that the Sahiela had wandered even as the Dakotah, Lakotah had wandered and in similar manner: from stony earth to barren ground to trees, from dry to wet, from warmth toward cold, from the hills onto the flat. Perhaps the Sahiela grandfathers and the Dakotah grandfathers had met in those ancient seasons of traveling everywhere.

And then Ahbleza remembered that the Oyatenumpa captives told stories of their grandfathers who had moved around and that the Witapaha captives recited similar stories. Will all tribes travel this earth from the day they make feet? Legends told that all the creatures had roamed the earth until each nation had found a place with which they sensed agreement. And that even the seeds had blown with the wind until, finding where they wanted to grow, they had fallen on that ground. But the Dakotah, neither creature nor seed, perhaps had experienced something more marvelous: perhaps all tribes exist as one tribe at the beginning, one great people who live without an enemy.

Returning to Napewaśte's tipi, Ahbleza had pondered his visit with the old Śahiela. The man had mentioned a tribe who live where the sun rises, a people with a governing council of fifty, certain women in the tribe selecting these men, one woman acting as 'observer,' keeping watch over any new man among the fifty. And now, wanting to know more about this eastern tribe—these Wasuhula—the warrior decided to make frequent visits to the Śahiela camps, talking with his peers but listening also to the wise old ones. And something more: within this camp, unlike his own, he dared anticipate a warm welcome, courteous attention.

The next day Ahbleza sat with members of the Barelegs family, with their shield-maker and his son. The young man, near Ahbleza's age, had carried the shield into war, and now the old man spoke saying that his infant grandson will carry this same shield, not as something that turns aside lance or arrows but as power born of one man's vision and passed along generation to generation.

"See the war-bird's feathers and those grizzly claws hanging on the shield," the old man demanded. "These things lend swiftness and toughness but only to him who knows the song that comes with the shield."

Afterwards Ahbleza talked with persons of a different family who also owned a shield, a Sicanġu family who had lived a long while with the Śahiela and spoke two tongues— Śahiela and Lakotah—persons who informed the son of Olepi that many tiyośpaye owned shields but that a man will know only the shield-song of his own village.

The power, then, not in the shield but in the vision that provides the song? But I, Ahbleza, am a man with a vision; why will I not own a song for exercising my power? Perhaps Wanaġi denies me something, perhaps he gives Tonweya a song and neglects me. Momentarily letting go his hold on reason, Ahbleza sat scheming a visit with Wanaġi during which he shall demand answers as to his own vision, his own powers.

Then calming himself, Ahbleza decided to visit the lodge of his warrior-friend, a friend of his boy-seasons. None called this person Moksois now, perhaps none remembered different names he had used during his youth-winters. But everyone knew his man-name: Ohkohmkhowais. Meaning 'traveling-dog,' the Sahiela said. And so a Lakotah shall call him Miyaca.

Miyaca had greeted Ahbleza with a boylike smile that said they shall begin their talk as they always had begun their play, the two picking up wherever they had left off. And so their words and gestures concerned horses, none among the Sahiela a more remarkable horsetaker than Miyaca. But the horses Miyaca took came most often from the ungentled herds running in the sandhills, not from the gentled herd outside some enemy camp.

"Not that I am reluctant when they ask that I join a party going out to raid the Pani," he said laughing. "I go, but I prefer chasing those creatures who roam the sand. Or obtaining my horses through trades with the Witapaha as you name the island-butte tribe. I also trade with the rattle-tail people—Sintehla-wicaśa in your tongue. Such horses put a vigor in the blood of my herd."

Next, Miyaca began describing his recent experience on the river of hides, Witapaha and Sintehla and Mahpiyato along with certain Sahiela families, all making one great winter village. And twice—twice—ten thousand horses in this same camp.

Ahbleza sat uncertain that he comprehended this many horses in one place. Yet he had heard that the Sintehla brought back from the true-south as many as ten hundred in a single raid. He envied Miyaca his winter in this trading village of six, seven hundred lodges, a gathering that will not welcome Titonwan; the Lakotah had made enemies of two of these tribes.

Silently the friends smoked a second pipe, then Ahbleza spoke abruptly: "I am not accepting any invitations to join a warrior-lodge." He glanced at Miyaca as if looking for the Sahiela to announce a similar decision.

But Miyaca made surprising answer: "Perhaps my friend lacks none of those things a warrior-lodge provides.

Perhaps he considers that he has enough."

"Enough?" Ahbleza's response came too quickly.

The Sahiela's eyes widened slightly. But then his hands expressed the meaning as if the alien tongue had made difficult Ahbleza's understanding of the word.

Enough of anything, he signed. Enough honors, enough horses, enough friends, enough meat. His lips formed a pleasant, easy smile.

But Ahbleza sensed that Miyaca had meant something different.

"Perhaps you lack but one important thing." Miyaca's hands repeated his words; he wished to make certain that the Lakotah comprehended. "You not yet take a wife."

Ahbleza smiled. "Not yet. But I see this comfortable lodge and so I know that you find a good woman."

The Sahiela answered speaking softly: "Perhaps soon you will sit alongside a certain woman and so you also will know what joy a wife brings."

Miyaca paused; he again used sign-talk to emphasize his speech. "If you find difficulty choosing from among your own pretty women, my friend, I know of many modest, quiet ones among the Tsistsistas." He leaned forward, looking strongly into Ahbleza's eyes. "The people will make you a good Tsistsistas."

Ahbleza understood that Miyaca honored him. The Sahiela had seen something in the son of Olepi that had brought forth a rare invitation: Miyaca proposes that Ahbleza take one of their women and so come into the tribe.

The warrior's eyes acknowledged the honor even as he answered Miyaca. "Certainly I shall look for a woman who walks proudly as your women walk. And who knows? Perhaps I shall find a woman who mixes Lakotah and Sahiela blood, her father of one tribe, her mother of a different tribe, a daughter who possesses the most desirable characteristics in my tribe and yours." Ahbleza laughed shortly. "O'ko wayelo. I only make noise."

But seeing that Miyaca had not joined in his mood, he made a little drama of the story he had decided to tell. "I will not pretend," he said, using gestures. "I encounter such a woman as I describe when I recently visit a Lakotah family who lives with your tribe. Her father, a Sicangu; her mother of a family whose speech sounds like your speech, a family you call 'dwellers-on-the-ridge,' or perhaps you say 'stay-back-on-a-ridge' people. But, whatever her band, never will I have this woman. Not even if she speaks fluently my tongue and your tongue. For her two young sisters live also in the lodge and I am not bold enough to entertain three women at once."

Ahbleza rose to his feet. He liked to separate from a friend with smiles, if not laughter. And now he saw a smile that began in Miyaca's eyes.

"Any warrior I know," Miyaca teased, "waits in line outside a young woman's tipi, wondering whether she will grant him a moment under cover of his robe. But, you, my friend, sit inside a tipi that shelters three young women, any one of whom gladly will go with you. Things come too easy for you."

Walking back to his own camp through the biting cold, the Mahto warrior felt the smile fade from his lips. Things come too easy for him, his warrior-friend Miyaca says. But Miyaca knows not of the ignoring, the indifference he endures among his own.

Perhaps you have enough, Miyaca tells him. True, he has enough, enough of this tribal testing or whatever they call this treatment that pounds at his lacks.

Will they decide that I lack courage, he asked himself now, when they discover that I listen to peace talk in the Sahiela camp? Or that I lack daring for reason that, until now, I prefer my mother's lodge to one of my own? If so, let these testers observe closely when I join the Sahiela who avenge their dead. And if afterwards anyone says I hang on to fears, I shall choose for my wife a woman with ten sisters, something that really takes courage.

A rush of shame prickled his neck. His thoughts, something in which a foolish boy perhaps indulges but not a man with a great vision to guide him. Truly, the day arrives when he needs talk with Wanaǧi.

Wanaǧi had listened. He had heard that which Ahbleza said and that which the warrior had not said. When Ahbleza spoke of not owning a song, the wapiya advised that he remember why a man sings. And who will stop him from composing his own song?

And then a long silence had filled the space between

these two who smoked, the warrior seemingly unaware that Wanaǧi replenished the bowl twice, the sacred-man smoking the third pipe alone while his guest gazed into the fire.

When finally Ahbleza spoke again, he spoke firmly: "I will accept only that which I understand. Everything different, I call mystery and wait for understanding."

Wanaǧi, making answer, used surprisingly soft tones: "Certain things a man shall accept while he grows into an understanding." He breathed a little sigh. "The son of Olepi not yet convinces me that truly he has enough."

Enough? Ahbleza's heart jumped. His Sahiela friend had hinted that he has enough of everything. But what means 'enough' when this word sits alone? Will he misunderstand meanings in his own tongue also?

Aroused, Ahbleza replied heatedly. "I say I have enough, enough of enough. I have enough of distant faces and rude backs. I have enough of disrespect from ones who call me relative, call me friend. I have enough of persons who dare imagine that they decide whether or not I ever shall own the Shirt. I—I—will decide about the Shirt. I will decide this thing and everything that happens to me."

Again Wanaǧi responded in soft, even tones: "The son of Olepi will not hear me when I say that he has not enough."

Now Ahbleza's eyes filled with puzzling. But after a moment he spoke: "Even the Sahiela knows that I have enough feathers for circling my head, trailing down my back. Even the Sahiela knows that I have enough horses, enough. . ." He stopped himself. "Perhaps you, my father-friend, will tell me where I lack?"

Quickly, gladly, Wanaǧi's answer came. And in a single word: growth. "Growth," he repeated, and passed the pipe to Ahbleza.

A good had come from this talk with Wanaǧi, a good to which Ahbleza had not tried to give name; he simply enjoyed the effect. And so for a while he walked oblivious to any slights; he intended to make the most of the remaining snow moons.

He joined now in the winter games, whipping the cones on icy ground, trying to outbump, outspin the young boys. He threw the short horn-tipped feathered sticks and hurled the long sliding-wood, trying to outdistance the young braves. And he played hoop-and-pole with men old and young who found their fun in rolling wood-circles on bare, hard earth.

The women spectators rejoiced on seeing the earnest young warrior smile again, but even on his unsmiling days the eyes of the young looked after him or tried to fit into the steps he left on the snow. And when he sat horseback, men and women glanced up.

But never will he wear something that draws attention to himself. Not wanting to rattle when he walked, he never tied strings of shells at neck and knees. He kept his person bare of ornaments and his face—but for his returns from war—bare of paint. He arranged his hair simply, the heavy strands clumped and tied at the back, some hair falling forward over his shoulders. He pushed a wingbone into the thick portion, one fluffy feather hanging from the bone and showing back of his ear.

Moccasins, loin-cover, robe he wore proudly, but only his robe truly marked him. Not another man in the Titonwan camps wore a robe that pictured horses who lope or prance or rear up, each creature in true-color. Only Ahbleza had painted blood-red the expanded nostrils of horses on the warpath, their eyes glaring black; only Ahbleza had decorated his robe with horses who show the strain and sweat of the chase or with horses who lie down or appear in a roll, a black tail and mane to identify the ordinary-horse.

The people long since had discovered that Ahbleza intended to resist the flat picture and so they had become accustomed to his shapely look-alive horses, not scrubs but true Titonwan horses—smooth, vigorous, alert creatures. And none dared say now that Ahbleza's bold brush will bring harm to this warrior or his horse or to anyone riding in his party. Truly, certain warriors had wondered whether Ahbleza's power came directly from the earth's paint-stones, the brush his protecting-mystery. But Olepi never had taken this view.

The snow moons melted away, and Ahbleza sensed an impatience with himself; he hunted ways to demonstrate that he recognized growth as the grandfathers defined growth. Not enough growth, Wanaǧi had said; not enough growth. And where will man grow but in the spirit, into the Whole. What new steps shall he take to reach the place where he embraces the Whole? In what manner shall he act and so expand that which they call the true-self?

Will proving generous widen his true-sight? Giveaways demonstrate generosity, but horses, robes, such gifts—merely the symbol. Perhaps if he searches the truth back of these generating acts . . . ? Search for the truth?

The grandfathers say that truth flows in gently; they say that spiritual growth happens slowly, nothing a person will recognize until a change comes through one of his senses, usually the sense of feeling. Afterwards different senses will tell him something.

But perhaps he will find the guidance he needs in a review of his youth's vision. Why seek a vision if not to possess an enduring guide?

The red-stem grasses—grass that pte never eats—sat tall on the plain, brightening the vastness, renewing someone's intentions. And so the Sahiela prepared to move the sacred arrows against the Psa. Why wait for old summer, the true-season for raids? Why not now, at the beginning of summer? Go out now while the influence of a winter's visiting between Tsistsistas and Titonwan endures. Everyone goes. The arrows move and so everyone moves. Will the Titonwan move with the Tsistsistas and their sacred arrows?

Zuya, a big party of Titonwan will go. Takpe, the Titonwan understand; they go out for blood. They will ride toward the powder river remembering the creek where thirty-and-two Sahiela stand off the Psa for two days. But die in a hand-to-hand fighting.

Never before will Ahbleza see women preparing to fight. And when he heard that these Sahiela women rival the men as fighters, he smiled back at something which, fortunately, he had voiced only to himself; taking ten Sahiela sisters will not mean ten wives in the lodge but instead one big war party.

This laughter at himself had acted as a strengthening force, and when he rode out with the warriors, he rode as if he alone carried the trust for this revenge.

The Lakotah sat camped on one side of the river, their friends opposite. Suddenly a Sahiela scout who waded along the edge signaled that he had clubbed down a Psa. At once the avenging party rushed out; they intended to discover the Psa camp before dark.

At dawn they attacked a village of one hundred lodges. But their war whoops had brought out only stumbling old men and some middle-age persons. The Psa warriors had gone out looking for Sahiela blood, a handful of competents staying back to protect women and children. Yet one of these Psa, defending horseback, had proved brave as any young warrior. Three Sahiela finally cut him down, but he had heard their cheers before he fell. A Sahiela woman-warrior, the third person to touch his dead body, had cut off his arms. Her brother's arms and legs, she told, had hung from the side of a Psa's horse for twice seven days while this enemy danced his scalp along with the scalps of thirty-and-one more Sahiela.

The fighting had not finished in the Psa camp. While the Sahiela and Titonwan went about gathering up the contents of the enemy lodges—weapons, robes, desirable women and children—warning cries reported the return of Psa warriors. At once the avengers jumped back on their horses. Sweeping down on these unsuspecting Psa, they killed many, many more of the enemy than the thirty-and-two they had gone out to avenge.

Ahbleza returned from the fight with nothing more than the red feather of a wounding to show that he had entered in the avenging. An enemy lance had gashed his side deeply, but he had stayed horseback, his arm pressed tightly against the wound. The bleeding had weakened him, a fall not unlikely had he remained in combat. But moving out of the way, he gave help to certain Sahiela who, unfamiliar with the enemy's tongue, experienced difficulty in chasing off the old Psa women, unwanted as captives, viewed as nothing more than extra mouths to feed.

Afterwards he had returned to the edge of the fighting ground, his eyes on one man. He had seen Tonweya leave his place among the scouts and rush into the fight. And he had heard the scout's yell as he bore down on the Psa, the brother-friend exhibiting the same boy-spirit he had displayed during his youth-encounter with the Palani. But now Tonweya maneuvered his attack skillfully, putting to use the awareness of his man-seasons.

They say that a scout fights when they need him in a fight, but on this occasion Tonweya had looked for a fight, for a chance to warm up his blood. Or so the scout had laughed off his impetuous entry into the avenging. But when the warriors told their kills-stories at the dance-fires, two men spoke saying that they had seen Tonweya strike an enemy with his hand.

And so the leaders called on this scout, asking that he recite his act. Tonweya, obliging, heard a long trilling and loud cheers at the finish of his dance, but his real joy came when he saw Ahbleza's approving eyes.

"I speak, now you tell something," Tonweya demanded. The scout had returned to the ridge after he had struck the Psa; he knew nothing of his brother-friend's experience but he had seen the gash in Ahbleza's side.

The warrior's lips curled perceptibly, his expression bearing a remarkable resemblance to his father. "Shall I say, misun, that I am slow at eluding the lance of one too old for the Psa war party? Shall I stand proudly in this dance circle and tell that I chase some old Psa women out of their camp and herd pretty young girls into the captives' line? Your glance touches on my wound but you look, misun, at an injury too small for remembering."

"They will not give the red feather for a scratch."

"Perhaps not, but will you hear the leaders asking that I recite?"

"I ask. And I am someone who leads." Olepi's sudden appearance had not startled these two, but his look, which hinted at finding boys in mischief, annoyed the warrior-son.

When Ahbleza seemed not to answer, the Mahto spoke again: "Perhaps you will let a father tell what they say about his son."

Tonweya murmured 'hau,' but Ahbleza remained silent.

"I hear," Olepi began, "that my son rides a path through the middle of an enemy who stand defending their lodges. He carries neither shield nor lance. The old Psa who wounds him comes out looking for a fight to the death.

628

Someone recognizes this old Psa as a leader they recently displace.

"My son holds together a bleeding side while maneuvering his horse beyond reach of curious eyes. Sitting alone, he treats his injury. Next thing, he rides alongside the Sahiela, helping run down Psa who try to escape."

Mostly true, but not the whole story, Ahbleza grimly recalled. But for an eagerness at seeing myself the big man in this show, the old Psa's lance never will touch me. I am aware of whom I attack, but I intend never to receive a wound. And so I act to avoid injury instead of instantly knocking down a desperate old enemy warrior.

Ahbleza had not spoken this recollection, but Olepi, looking suddenly at his son's face, recognized that none shall influence this warrior at the moment, neither he nor Tonweya. The man stood enclosed, an invisible hoop shutting out everyone, everything. And so father and friend, saying nothing more, wisely moved away.

The tribes had ridden back from the avenging most noisily, the clubmen cheering loudly all warriors who had killed, the Psa captives wailing loudly for all killed Psa, moans and cheers blending with wails and songs when the night's dancing began.

But once these grieving Psa women dried their tears and started talking in their captor's tongue, they had much to gain. Always these tribes make wives and daughters of such captives, the Psa women receiving the same respect they accord any woman who lives in Lakotah or Sahiela villages.

For never will man disregard the meaning he gives to woman: one-who-sits-most-high; wife, one-who-sits-above. Wankanl yanka, one-who-sits-above; wakanka, wife.

While different men comtemplated taking a wife or making a daughter from among these Psa captives, Olepi lay on his robes remembering this high place they grant woman and pondering whether he dared throw away one of his three wives. Certainly he will discard the woman in a ceremonial manner, he told himself, a separation that will gain him not only approval but prestige. A tribal leader, they say, shall remember himself as one who gives-away, who limits himself to the bare essentials. So the people see him giving away horses and hides and meat, but if the people see him giving away a wife, they see that he gives away something that sits above everything.

V

THE VICTORY-CELEBRATING came to a finish and the Sahiela moved off, these people taking most of the captives, half of the horses. And now the Titonwan bands came together in an intimate hoop, the women raising their lodges near the river of the thickwoods, a place between the black hills and the big mud-water.

Iśna, favoring this campground, brought his Kuya band into the circle again this summer. And now he looked for a permanent place in the hoop.

Olepi, hearing that the Kuya wanted to stay, sensed a tremendous relief; perhaps the Mahto and Kuya together will keep Zuzueca and his noisy relatives from winning a place at the horns. The Oglalahca held on to this distinguishing site, Tanaźin a strong leader, but if ever the Oglalahca lose the position, Olepi intended to see his own band, not the Kiyuksa, in this place.

Mniśa's band, as always, raised lodges near the Kiyuksa, but these red-water people once again came as Sicanġu visitors, and so they lacked any true power among the Titonwan. And if Olepi manages to draw the Kuya leader—a man with many strong families back of him—to his side, who will dispute the Mahto when he demands the horns?

The Titonwan seated more men in the center lodge this summer than ever before and so they tied together three big tipi, forming an impressive half-circle. And again the akicita-lodges required considerable space, these groups locating their tipi as from the start: Tokala and Iyuptala at the back, Cante Ṭinza and Kanġi Yuha at opposite sides. And for the fifth summer, the Iĥoka raised a lodge within the hoop, these clubmen occupying a site near the Kanġi Yuha.

All five lodges of clubmen had begun collecting feathers and paint, hides and rattles for their ceremonies, each group also waiting to hear whom the center lodge had chosen to watch over the encampment.

At the moment the Iyuptala prepared for the sash-wearers' ceremony. The two who presently owned the sashes had fulfilled their obligation during the recent attack on the Psa. Not that an enemy camp empty of warriors provided much of a proving ground, but as anyone who ever wore the sash will say, the real courage shows in the resolve to stake one's self. Certainly the sash-wearers who now resigned had not looked for a mild test but neither had they regretted that their stakeout occurred in an almost empty camp.

None of the members yet knew who will wear the sashes next, but Olepi had proposed that the Iyuptala welcome Iśna as sash-wearer. Pointing to himself as an Iyuptala whose voice they had respected for ten winters, the Mahto leader had urged that they extend the Kuya leader an invitation. And he had asked that the members overlook those customs that apply to a young man who becomes a pledge; certainly they will not send out Iśna for meat, something he shall snatch off a drying-rack, nor will they have him run errands in the manner of a boy-brave.

And why not these acts, certain ones had asked. They see Iśna as a strong leader among the Sicanġu, but let him show himself as a strength among all Titonwan. If the man has good intentions, he will perform whatever acts they require of any pledge and will not consider age or prestige as something that grants him privileges.

Eventually the members came to an agreement; they will inform Iśna that the lodge desires him as sash-man. Recognizing his importance among Lakotah, they offer him instant rank in this akicita-lodge, this brother-lodge of principal Titonwan. And so they ask that he send feathers and quills for use on something he will wear, an act that will signify his acceptance.

Next day the Iyuptala herald, acting as mouth for the lodge, presented Iśna the invitation.

Nothing happened.

631

Olepi grew impatient when five, six days passed. He wondered whether this man had received different invitations, the Tatanka-lodge perhaps asking Iśna into their group, this headman-lodge whose members yet ignore Olepi, the Mahto leader eligible for eleven winters now.

Olepi dared not show his distress in front of the Iyuptala, but in his own tipi he had maintained neither the impassive countenance nor the controlled speech. He twice complained when women-friends came to sit with Napewaśte and Ina; these women talk too much, he said. But he lingered inside the lodge if only to differ with whatever anyone said.

"Perhaps I and you wisely take this work to another lodge," Ina told Napewaśte quietly; "talk and laughter displeases someone."

But Napewaśte, who had lived the most seasons with Olepi, refused to let his mood drive her out of the tipi. She answered her sister cheerfully: "He will turn," she said, her hands rubbing the skins she softened for summer wear. But Ina had gathered up her work, going someplace different.

Then came the day when the Mahto's dark mood proved too much for this true-wife. He had pushed aside the new moccasins Napewaśte had made him for the Iyuptala ceremony, had spoken sharply. "Why not make me a pair that fit? These moccasins pinch my toes."

"I am unaware that my husband's foot grows." She had not intended disrespect, but neither will any woman who prides herself on knowing, at a single glance, the true length and width accept such criticism graciously.

"Change your talk," he said brusquely, "or you become a woman whose husband throws her away."

Napewaśte's fingers tightened on the skin-piece in her hand. "I understand," she said, her voice unnaturally brittle, "that custom approves a woman who puts her man's things outside the lodge when his moods displease her."

At once Olepi arose, going out of the tipi.

Alone now, the woman's foolish words came back to startle and frighten. Her fingers held on to the skin-piece but they refused to work. And after a while her shoulders slumped, a moan breaking out of her heart as she bent to the ground.

Olepi slept four nights in Hinziwin's little tipi but not to his young wife's delight. His presence interrupted her visits with women-friends and her games with distant relatives who stayed for the summer. And he sent her on many errands, demanding that she return promptly.

"Who keeps you away from this tipi?" he asked one morning. "Will you meet women on the water-path as lazy as you?" And then he sat her down to making new moccasins, something he wanted to see her finish before dark.

She began her work pouting, then resorted to a little whimpering. When Olepi looked her way, she used her amazing eyes to hint that he remember the pleasure her body always gives him.

And so he took the unfinished work from her hands. And she, relieved of something tedious, spread herself on the robes gladly.

But nothing agreeable happened. Olepi had withdrawn abruptly, his sudden jerk making her wince, her wandering attention quickly brought back to the man lying at her side.

From the start the Mahto had made Hinziwin understand in what ways he liked his pleasure and until now she had proved a most satisfying mate. But an indifference had entered into her manner with him, and while he knew his power for putting a stop to this negligence, he suddenly wondered whether he cared enough to trouble himself.

Turning his back to her, Olepi recalled the way Napewaśte even now responded to his touch. Too eagerly, perhaps; a woman shall remember herself as the submissive one. Then why will he go reluctantly to Ina's robe? In her he finds the truly submissive. But always Ina showed a fear of him and, disliking fear in anything—warriors, boys, dogs, women—he found himself tempted to use her harshly. And so he stayed away from Ina's robes but for the occasional visit that custom demands when a man takes more than one wife.

Now at age fifty-and-one his warrior-loins lacked, so far as he knew, none of a young man's potency; any woman will lie proudly with him. Not exactly any woman, certainly not one who runs loose, but any woman of good family. And so why not someone among the Kuya?

Who says only one way for making a brother of Iśna,

633

for gaining a loyalty, for strengthening a tie between Mahto and Kuya? Since Ahbleza rejects the akicita-lodges and so refuses important connections, why not his father acting to increase the prestige of the Mahto band? For Iśna to become his brother through the Iyuptala, one way; discarding a woman in his own lodge and taking a Kuya wife, a second way. But he will use this second scheme only if Iśna refuses the Iyuptala invitation; not gladly will he throw off one woman only to take on a different one. Even now he will wonder what happens to his reasoning that he finds himself with three wives.

His irritation flared again; why consider that Iśna will ignore the Iyuptala? He leaned up on his arm, turning to look at Hinziwin, wondering why he found her wanting on this occasion.

The woman, sensing that she had displeased the man, began slowly and immodestly to pull up her gown, to her neck; she will expose a gleaming nakedness, breasts firm and tall, flat belly, shapely legs. And not so much as a scratch to mar her fine, smooth skin. Let him look; owanyake waśte. Hinziwin, twenty-and-eight and certain of herself as a joy to view.

She felt a strong leg flung across her slender thigh, then a familiar hardness. Eyes closed, she hid the woman-power smile; let him imagine that he subdues her and not the other way around.

Olepi had walked directly from Hinziwin's tipi to the Iyuptala meeting place. Approaching the lodge, he saw a group of women famous for their quilling. His heart quickened; perhaps Iśna had brought hides and quills to these women and so they decorated something for the Kuya leader.

Coming close, Olepi saw that these persons attached quills at the center and on the flesh side of a robe. And now Olepi smiled. The Kuya, deliberately slow, finally had showed with hide and trimmings, the man remembering to bring also the wing and tail feathers from a rain-bird, something important to the Iyuptala costume. And so Iśna evinced his intention to make ceremony the next three mornings in front the Iyuptala-lodge, to appear with glowing embers on his palm and to lay those embers on a pile of sweetgrass. And on the fourth day, at sunrise, to make use of this sweetgrass smoke for purifying a new robe, an Iyuptala robe. Afterwards, the Kuya leader dared look for the Iyuptala-lodge to honor him as a new member, to mention his name in speeches at an Iyuptala feast.

But one man, Olepi told himself, shall walk away from Iśna's honoring-feast carrying a leg and foot of the rain-bird in the fold of his Iyuptala robe. And his lodge-brothers, seeing this sign, will know that this man—leader of the Mahto camps—endures that which tries heart and head; they will know that Olepi discards a wife, a woman for whom he feels great fondness. They will say that Olepi demonstrates outstanding loyalty to the bands: he lets go a desirable woman, the tribe replacing this wife in his affection. They will say that anyone will let go a horse or a herd of horses in the name of a relative they choose to honor but only a most strong man will let go a wife in the name of the tribe.

Or so Olepi answered an obstinate spirit who kept telling him to recognize his act as that of an ambitious leader; that Olepi, remembering his age, grows weary of waiting for an invitation into the headman-lodge and so he uses this extreme to recreate his image as a tribal father, as someone who earns a place in the Pta-lodge, in the Tatanka-lodge, a place he awaits eleven long winters.

A man discarding a wife who bores him will hit the drum during a break in the dancing and then announce the separation. But the man who vows to perform the 'throwing-wife-away' ceremony acts in a powerful manner; the Iyuptala-lodge members had said so.

They say that a man performing this ceremony demonstrates a remarkable will. They say that man takes woman for but one natural reason: making-a-child. And so whoever dares not let go his woman after she bears once or twice, responds more readily to impulse than to reasoning, something that flatters neither the husband nor the wife.

Truly, these akicita ask, will any man sit ready for war once he starts living with woman, his belly never empty, his robe always warm, his moccasins without holes? Will not such comforts soften him and so he goes out reluctantly, the rigors of the warpath not as enticing as in those seasons when his companions, men only? Or perhaps he will not often go out, claiming that he sleeps with his wife on the night before a war party, his presence on the warpath a risk to himself and the warrior-group. Will a man, once he mates, ever really stay outside the influence of woman?

Certainly say the Iyuptala, this 'throw-wife-away' act shall not disgrace the woman; instead the ceremony honors the woman. For a man who demonstrates his will-power in this manner, dares throw away only a wife he truly, truly esteems; the more desirable the woman, the more praise-earning his act.

But who, Olepi had asked himself, shall decide the most desirable wife in a lodge that shelters more than two wives? Who but the man wearing the moccasins knows which pair fits comfortably, which pair drags? The soft-voice woman who keeps an orderly tipi, who cooks and quills and mends will give the appearance of a good wife, as will the modest, neat woman who attends to the child. But a man wants a wife in whom he sees more than a lodge-keeper, more than a child-tender.

When a man sits alongside but one woman, he needs decide only whether to keep or discard. But when he sits alongside three women, the people observe closely whom he discards. And a man who uses the throwing-away ceremony to rid himself of a distasteful wife but claims something different loses his standing—leader or not—in any tribe. A man of standing, then, who ceremoniously throws away a wife shall make certain that the people recognize the greatness of his intention to become as a father to the people as a whole.

VI

OLEPI STAYED three nights in the Iyuptala-lodge. Then, after witnessing the next to final day of Iśna's ordeal, he returned to his own. He had decided to ask Napewaśte to ride with him through the midmorning brightness; perhaps they will discover a fragrant glade, a nice place to rest or talk. Or in some way prepare her for that which he intends.

Seeing the man approach the tipi after seven sleeps away, Napewaśte made herself remain attentive to her work on the hide, to the quick, glancing blows she struck with her whitening-tool. But her fast heart warned of a need for invisible help if the husband returned only to remove his things from her lodge.

Now, aware that moccasined feet stood close, she awaited the voice that will lift her face.

When he spoke, his phrases lifted her eyes and her heart. And so she threw silent thanks to whatever kind spirit had sent Olepi back to her lonely self.

She smoothed her hair, changed her gown, and then, getting on her horse rode close behind as Olepi led the way out of the village and along the tree-lined stream.

Before the cooking fires had cooled, these two had come riding back. The woman went inside the tipi at once, but the man turned his horse and rode slowly toward the woodpile where he had seen Ina loading herself with sticks, her horse already burdened.

Here he stopped, helping the woman spill off the wood, then gesturing that she mount her horse and follow him.

At a hidden place among trees that bordered a sandy creek, his eyes ordered her down. And now she stood wondering why he brought her here, what thing he will ask of her next. Raising her face to his look, she suddenly recalled the day he had asked her into the lodge as his third wife.

He took her hand kindly now and led her to the water's edge; and then she knew for what reason he wanted her here.

637

They lay together on warm clay, his manner gentle. And so she dared enjoy herself as never before, her body experiencing more pleasure than in those seasons when she sat as the one wife in a Sicangu lodge. But she lacked the forwardness to tell Olepi, when finally he pulled her to a sitting position, that she gladly will linger on this sandy clay for so long as he will hold her.

But they sat only a little while, the woman silent, this day mysteriously bringing back memories of her daughter who had died before becoming-woman, a pretty girl who never had known what exquisite joy the woman-body will give the woman-spirit, a joy that Ina herself had not fully recognized until now.

Laying aside these memories, Ina had smiled as she sat fingering the sand. Olepi had called her a fading woman, saying that she worked herself too severely. Now, her cheeks glowing, she saw him spit onto crumbling redstone, making the paint that will keep this glow on her face. Or so he told her.

She pressed her fingers fondly to his wrist as he made the red smudge on her skin; she remembered that a husband paints the wife he esteems. But on feeling his hand pull away, she sensed those familiar trembles returning. Not for reason of any unkindness but that he had displayed, instead, an effort at kindness, almost as if he intended never to see her again.

Olepi separated from Ina at the place he had met her, the woman staying to collect the load of wood she had dropped on his arrival. The Mahto leader returned to the Iyuptala-lodge, to eat with the members, to sit for a pipe. Or so Ina had understood him to say.

The two sisters ate disinterestedly this evening, neither one talking. Then, having wiped clean their bowls, they began to prepare food for the Iyuptala feast next day.

Together they cut up tipsila for boiling, Napewaste filling the containers in which these roots and the meat will cook, the woman deciding to keep the paunches bubbling throughout the night, to remove certain pieces of meat at the moment of tenderness.

Ina had begun different work; she squeezed the fresh, plump ten-seed berries for their juice. Next, using a fine root-powder of her own making, she thickened the juice, pouring slowly, avoiding lumps; soon after sunrise, she will prepare the meat-balls for floating in this sauce.

Before dark, Ahbleza and Tonweya came in from a little hunt, the two offering their kills for the feast. They threw down the tails of five who swim-with-stick, not enough meat for an Iyuptala feast day but something to blister, then peel and cut in small pieces for boiling with the prairie-root.

And so the wives carried their work from evening into night, the son and his brother-friend sitting for a smoke with Lekśi, the young men listening courteously to the old man's recollections. But Ahbleza sat also aware of his mother, the young warrior observing apprehension in her movements, a concern on her face. But why, he will not understand.

Over in the Iyuptala-lodge, Olepi sat quietly while the herald, having reviewed the installing ceremony, awaited the drum-keeper's approval; they gave this good old man who never had killed anyone the final say on the affair.

But the drum-keeper chose instead to talk about a new rank in the Iyuptala-lodge, advising that they introduce the rank of whip-bearer at the ceremony next day. Different lodges have this rank, he said, but none use the whips in the manner he will propose.

The old man proceeded with details, the young members alert and showing a real interest. But Olepi grew impatient with the drum-keeper's harangue; the Mahto had a different place to visit before this night turned old. And yet he who had put up Iśna's name as one of the new sash-wearers scarcely dared walk out on a meeting that concerned the installation. And so when Olepi eventually left the Iyuptala to walk among the lodge-shadows toward a certain little tipi, even the rain-birds had ceased hooting.

The little tipi, empty; Hinziwin, not here.

Olepi glanced around for a sign that will hint where she had gone. Sudden dismay stopped his searching look; Hinziwin will not return for three, four days. Nor will he reach her—a woman iśnati—in any way.

He stayed for two, three more looks around her tipi. Here, a gown she had discarded, something thrown to the

639

ground for want of cleaning. But then Hinziwin never had troubled to remove fat or berry stains; always she left the cleaning of her gowns to Napewaśte or awaited the offer of skins for a new one.

Also on the ground, those moccasins he had demanded she finish at once, moccasins yet without bottoms. But will he not take the pair from her hands to use her in a different way?

Usually this disorder annoyed him, but not now. Instead he stood center in this pathetically small lodge, remembering her slim red-yellow body, pretty as a turning leaf. He saw her eyes at the moment a laugh broke through her delicately curved lips. He seemed to hear that laughter now even as he smelled the fragrance always in and of her hair. And always he will remember those yellow strands in her hair that gave her the name Hinziwin; Hinziwin, Hinzi, mitawin.

He wondered who had made this loud cry. Then understanding, he became angry with himself. And so he gazed calmly upon each personal item—her gown, moccasins, hair-ties, the robes where she slept—until he saw these things with complete indifference.

But stepping out of the tipi, Olepi knew that this feeling he called indifference he shall more properly call numbness, perhaps craziness. For even now he told himself to give up two wives before ever he throws away a certain one.

Walking toward the edge of camp, in need of aloneness, he remembered that they will jeer a man who reclaims a woman he once discards. But the thought will not disturb him. For one thing, he had not told anyone of his intention to perform this ceremony, and so, if he wished, he dared put aside the whole scheme.

But if I take this step and throw away a wife, he told himself, I will not suffer any regret. Whatever different ones imagine, I never shall give up that which I desire but for something I desire more. And so I act knowing that above all I want to sit in the Tatanka-lodge. I see this discarding-wife ceremony as the most startling way to show to what extent I will go in demonstrating my loyalty to the tribe. Yet I gain nothing if someone hints that I use this ceremony as a cover for quitting a woman I find distasteful. And so I shall make certain that the wife I discard appears in the eyes of the tribe—if not my own—the woman most difficult to let go.

In the eyes of the tribe? Once before, he had tried looking out on someone with the eyes of the tribe only to discover that man shall look inward when he wants a true answer.

He stopped at a boulder along the trail and, leaning his back against the stone, he pondered himself. Only now will he recognize that when he performs this ceremony next day, he pretends nothing and so his act really earns him a place in the Tatanka-lodge. For when he discards this woman—knowing all along which wife he will throw away—he truly becomes as an old herd-father. And perhaps as lonely.

Iyuptala. For more than twelve winters these lodgemen had raised their big tipi at the rear of the summer hoop; Iyuptala, they had said, at the back and facing the entrance in the manner that a family seats the honored guest.

Iyuptala, the akicita-lodge that had originated the throwing-wife-away ceremony; Iyuptala, they had said, the most demanding lodge in the hoop, attracting only the most enduring of warriors. Olepi, a member for more than ten winters.

The Iyuptala had welcomed the whole encampment at the installation of the two new sash-men but perhaps the prominence of the one—everyone seemed to know that Iśna, the Kuya leader, had accepted—accounted for the tremendous turnout this day.

None of the spectators had any difficulty picking out Iyuptala members; they either sat in front of the akicita-lodge or they stood holding quilled robes over their arms. These robe-holders, someone had said, will introduce youths, age fourteen and fifteen winters, whom the lodge had agreed to take in as new members.

Olepi, among those Iyuptala who sat, remembered that his preference limited the Iyuptala to men of rank, not boys, but most voices had spoken for young blood.

The Mahto leader once looked forward to seeing his own son an Iyuptala, but Ahbleza had expressed his disinterest in joining any lodge. And so the Mahto wondered now whether Ahbleza even sat watching. Certainly he knew that his father, a pipe-man, will present the sashes and recite a killing. But knowing and caring, two different things.

Olepi put a hand wearily to his mouth. He longed for the finish of this affair, perhaps the final Iyuptala ceremony for him. He had come in from the edge of camp at dawn, going directly to the brother-lodge. Here he had painted his forehead in the manner of an Iyuptala, then taken his place to await the ceremony. In keeping with the Iyuptala vow, he had not eaten nor had any Iyuptala eaten for four days. They awaited the feast for the initiates, but Olepi knew that he will not sit at any feast this day.

He looked among the women but saw none of his own, not even Kehala. Then he remembered: one wife, Iśnati, dared not attend, and the other two wives perhaps had gone looking for extra meat bowls, attending to whatever pertained to the feast. But now he saw the herald rising, going forward to meet someone.

In the near distance two men walked slowly toward the lodge, a tiny smoke curling up from the embers sitting on their palms. The sash-man ceremony had begun.

Napewaśte had not kneeled with the women at the cooking fires this morning nor had she walked with those relatives who went out to collect bowls. Ina had glanced up surprised on hearing her sister ask that Kehala take the feast food to the men. Then, observing that Napewaśte stayed on her sleeping robe, cheeks unpainted, Ina's surprise became concern; perhaps Napewaśte, at the cooking fire all night, now lay exhausted.

But after accompanying Kehala to the feast ground, then working in Napewaśte's place as bowl-stacker, fire-tender, Ina wondered something different: will Olepi hint at his recent pleasure with the sister-wife? And Napewaśte, suddenly jealous, intends staying inside her lodge until Olepi comes looking for her?

Never before had Ina considered competing for the husband's attention, but now, the only wife helping with these feast preparations, she schemed to make herself henceforth more attractive to the man.

Her lodge empty, Napewaśte pulled out the strong cord she had hidden beneath her sleeping robes. Her head bowed as she struggled with the ache in her throat and the cry in her soul; certainly, she told herself, a woman will not grieve her own death.

She had made her decision even before she sat eating meat with Ina the previous day, even before she had left the glade after Olepi gave warning. She will not desire living if she loses him. And will Olepi not hint at this thing, she had asked herself, when he spoke saying that he wanted to prepare her for a surprising act, something that will occur during the Iyuptala ceremony? Truly he intends discarding a wife and certainly he implies Napewaśte. What different woman will he mean when he talks about not wanting to offend a wife and mother, someone he trusts will understand why he acts in such manner.

The woman had not answered Olepi in the glade, nor had he said anything more all the while they sat together, his hand covering hers. But she had discovered many new thoughts about Olepi during that silence, each one making her sad for herself and for him.

Olepi, she had remembered, came on earth as all newborns come, hunting the love each infant knows to look for. But an enemy had carried off Olepi's true-mother, the only one to shine-a-light that he will recognize at birth, identify as love. Different breasts had fed him, and so, growing up, he had sensed fondness for some persons, esteem for others. But lacking the true-mother's tenderness— she who prepares her child for receiving and giving love as the ultimate joy—Olepi not yet realized that which love most fully empowers: self-respect.

Napewaśte had reflected only briefly her own life; enough that she bore a son and raised a different woman's daughter, enough that she lived forty-and-two winters, more than half her seasons as Olepi's wife. And certainly none will grieve her dying but a handful of old women to whom Olepi will give presents in return for a day and night of proper wailing. Or so Napewaśte, the death-cord in her hand, saw the picture.

But now, before she lifted her head, someone gently pulled on the cord in her grasp, someone whose moccasins she recognized. And so she knew that Ahbleza stood here.

For a long moment the son gazed into his mother's face, all those unspoken things of his young-man seasons in his eyes: a gratefulness for her understanding of his strange ways with brushes and horses and warrior-lodges, a respect for her many good ways, her skillful hands.

His look held nothing of reproach for that which she intended to perform, but his eyes refused her the privilege of this choice; he will not permit that this woman take her life.

He touched her fingers, waiting for each one to unbend, for the cord to drop into his hand. And now he gestured that she come with him.

And she, as one walking in a dream, followed where he led.

She found herself taking a place among the women who gathered near the Iyuptala-lodge. She heard a familiar voice and knew that Olepi spoke to the encampment, but she closed her ears to his words. She noticed that certain men received sashes and feathers and robes, but she stood unheeding which men became new members.

If anyone observed that the wife of Olepi acted as one stunned and that her son stood curiously nearby the women-group, they had not made gossip. But who will notice these two? All eyes watched the new Iyuptala or those singers who now approached the drum.

Eight men stood around the big red Iyuptala drum—four of these persons known as keepers-of-the-feathered-sticks, of the wood that supported the drum, and four known as keepers-of-the-quilled-beaters. Almost at once they began singing but they had not touched the drum; they waited for the old drum-keeper to step forward and strike the hide and then present a horse to someone.

Her heart despairing, Napewaśte also awaited the drum-keeper. She had looked once, fearfully, toward the half-circle where the Iyuptala sat, their painted faces stern and unfamiliar. Above their heads a stuffed rain-bird perched on a branch, something they used during a thanks-offering. But the bird seemed to stare at her and so she had looked away, a new chill in her heart.

But the man who approached the drum, not the old keeper; instead Olepi came forward, beater in hand.

Hunhunhe. Many persons mumble surprise but not all; this same instant Ina understood the unusual tenderness of Olepi's visit. Her hand went over her mouth; shocked and frozen to her place, she stared at the man alongside the drum. She saw his body pull tall, the feathers decorating his hair stiffly erect. She saw his cold face, something neither sun nor fire will warm on this day. She saw the wood in his hand, the small piece of stick he will throw toward the men saying: this piece for my wife, for the sister of the mother of my son. Whoever catches the stick gets the woman Ina.

She wanted to run, to hide and lose herself forever. But she stood unmoving, not certain whether she had imagined that Olepi spoke these phrases or whether the man really had told his desire to discard her. Her eyes on the little stick, she waited unbreathing for the husband to lift his arm and throw the wood anywhere, for anyone to catch.

Napewaśte saw nothing; her head had bowed at the rumble of the drum. Help me, her heart begged the powers. Give me strength, my mother the earth and my grandfather the stone. Make me strong and so I shall endure that which husband and son ask of me. Slowly she lifted her drooping head.

Olepi held out the stick, offering the wood to Iśna, leader of the Kuya and new member of the Iyuptala.

Ah-i-i-i-i. Napewaśte's quavering little cry told that she saw Olepi using her as he will use a horse, as a gift for someone whose favor he intends to secure. The woman's eyes sought Ahbleza as if in some mysterious manner the son will stop this thing. But Ahbleza stood smiling.

Napewaśte's hand covered her mouth even as her sister Ina remained with hand clasped over lips. Ahbleza approves that which his father decides? He will see his father discard his mother, the son smiling while Napewaśte endures the cutting of her heart into strings? And will he keep on smiling when the Iyuptala walk through camp after the feast and sing the throw-wife-away song? Her head again dropping, she recalled the words of this song: 'My son's mother, you listen not. And so you go.'

"This stick," she heard Olepi say now, "for my wife. A new Iyuptala will send this one for wood and water. A certain woman, yours."

Ina put her fingers in her ears but Napewaśte suddenly raised her eyes, her fears mysteriously gone.

The strong voice of the Mahto seemed unchanged as he

named the woman he will give Iśna. "The one they call Hinziwin comes to you."

Iśna, a cunning in his eyes and a smile on his lips, accepted the stick. And Olepi, his face like stone, stepped toward the back of the Iyuptala-lodge, four Iyuptala walking close to him.

Napewaśte had managed to stay on at the feast, her hands ladling and carrying meat, setting down bowls. But only her hands, alive and caring.

Ina went at once to the lodge of relatives, where she planned to stay awhile; she chose to avoid Olepi and her sister for the next two, three days. And she wanted tongues wagging neither at her nor about her.

After the feast, everything clean and orderly, wives and mothers of the Iyuptala sat as a group to watch husbands and sons perform the lodge-dances, their painted bodies in colorful motion.

But Napewaśte had not stayed. She returned alone to the family lodge, where she stared dully at the tipi lining and pondered in what manner Hinziwin will receive this news. Or perhaps, she told herself, the woman already knows. And cries and cries.

Then, before Napewaśte had tied down the lodge flap for a night alone, the gossips had reached her. Covering her head, Napewaśte made known that she closed her ears to their tattling, but two old women, coming directly from a visit with Hinziwin, had persisted in their talk.

"She says that now all know whom the husband desires painfully, the only wife he dares let go and so win praise," they cackled. "She says that he honors her. He sends her to a man more powerful than himself."

Napewaśte remained covered and so the two old bones finally ran off laughing shrilly, foolishly glad that something had occurred to break the usualness of an old woman's day.

But certain young women, coming back quickly from a visit with the discarded wife, walked around camp whispering a different story, nothing like the one the two old torments had told. They understood that the Mahto leader had grown too old to please Hinziwin but that Hinziwin, not the sort of woman to put a leader's things outside her lodge and so embarrass him, had made the man agree to this way of separating.

Hinziwin, surprised that so many women walked the sheltered path to her retreat, had tossed her head at the sympathizing looks and sent back her messages for the village. But once alone, crouched in the customary position of a retreating-lodge, she leaned on her arms and hunted something comforting.

Her throat ached from the tiny sobs she had swallowed. He will not dishonor me, she told herself once again. The people will say that he honors me. I am his desire, not the overripe old sack they call Ina. I remain his desire, even above Napewaśte, the mother of his son.

For a moment she considered Ahbleza. I will approach this one more easily now that I am not a wife to his father, she whispered; I will enjoy lying with a young warrior for a change.

Then she remembered; Olepi gave her to Iśna. So why grieve? She will not lack for ornaments and gowns in the lodge of the Kuya leader.

And soon she found a most exciting thought: Iśna now wears the Iyuptala sash. And not always will an Iyuptala walk away from the earth whereon he stakes himself; occasionally he dies where he stands. Which Olepi remembers.

Most certainly Olepi schemes to reclaim her. They praise him for his courage in discarding her, but who will hold anything against a man who takes back his gift when he learns that an enemy kills her new owner? Who will want to see Hinziwin suddenly without a provider?

For a while she experienced a feeling of true regard, almost affection, for Olepi. And so, her heart light again, she quickly slept.

The ranking Iyuptala had assigned two, three members to stay the next two nights in the akicita-lodge with Olepi, talking to him in a manner that shall divert the Mahto's thoughts from the woman he throws away.

But neither these watchers nor the watched appreciated the arrangement; they simply endured the custom.

Whatever his companions imagined, two desires sat back of Olepi's staring eyes this night and neither one concerned reunion with Hinziwin. He wanted the principals of the Pta-lodge to recognize that he had thrown away a woman he desired to keep and he wanted Iśna to understand the prize he had received.

Attentive to these two things, Olepi had tried to close his ears to the ridiculous talk going on around him, something about finding him a replacement for Hinziwin. Certainly he needed none of these reassurances from babbling Iyuptala; if he saw a desirable woman—Lakotah, Mnikooźu or enemy-captive—he will take her and without anyone's help. He regretted that custom demanded his staying in this lodge two nights, two nights of harangue from so-called protectors.

Napewaśte, sitting these same nights in her tightly closed lodge, seemed nothing more than a robe hunched over an empty fireplace. She sat convinced as to why Olepi retained her; he kept not a wife but the mother of his son. His heart's true desire: Hinziwin. But why pretend that this thing surprises her?

From the beginning Olepi saw the pretty girl as an exciting and diverting child-wife, something he had not sought in the woman he originally chose. Then, while Hinziwin ripened into a nice-looking woman, she—Napewaśte—fattened into something old and slow. Not that she wanted to change places with Hinziwin—she will prefer dying to seeing herself a throwaway or living as wife to any different man—but why will Olepi carefully hand Hinziwin to a man who this same day accepts the sash? Everyone knows what happens to most sash-wearers. Men-with-short-lives, the Iyuptala call these warriors and pledge protection of their wives if the husband never returns. A pipe-keeper in the Iyuptala acts as a protector of all Iyuptala wives; Olepi sits responsible for the safety of these women during the summer camps. And so the Mahto remains, if not the husband, certainly Hinziwin's protector.

The people will say, Napewaśte told herself, that he keeps me for my good hands at cooking, scraping hides, holding awl and quills. But I will have him want me as on that day when first he bathes me. I will have him smile at me as he smiles at Hinziwin. He says once that he will not enjoy himself if I go out of his sight. Now I am wondering whether he hunts someone to bring in Hinziwin's place.

Truly I will not endure those ten-and-five seasons with Hinziwin but for the comfort a daughter and my sister lend. Now Kehala raises her own lodge and my sister talks of visiting her son's family next winter. And so I will sit on my robes listening for the feet of him I call husband. And when he comes perhaps I dare beg for a little tenderness. But if ever he brings to this tipi flap another woman. . .

Her imagination had taken hold and, seeing herself neglected and unwanted, she began a foolish crying.

She had untied the tipi flap only twice in two days; answering a natural urge, she had covered her head and walked, unrecognizing and unrecognized, to the women's ground.

Now a third dawn aroused her. The Iyuptala walked through camp at sunrise, the men singing praise for Olepi. The food-passer stands waiting at the Iyuptala-lodge, they told, with many bowls. He invites each Mahto warrior to feast with a man who throws-wife-away.

Napewaśte heard but without new pain or a recurrence of the old.

After a while she moved her legs, stiff from her long sitting. She will rise and go, as always, for water and wood. And she will keep on making fires and preparing hides while Hinziwin, moving into a different camp, will keep on playing at these things.

She smoothed her unbrushed hair in a disinterested manner, then reached for the water-sac, the container that Hinziwin never had filled but at someone's request. Even now the sac, holding dead water, had a stale smell.

Suddenly the woman withdrew her hand, her eyes glaring at the sac on the pole, her fingers clutching the knife at her middle. Next thing, she had slit the waterskin, the contents dripping onto the ground. Instantly she experienced a most strange satisfaction.

She stooped and untied the tipi opening; she stepped outside. Here for one startled moment she envisioned Olepi in the man who sat with his back to her lodge, the tipi flap closed against his entering. But then she saw that the man who rose, who walked away not once looking in her direction—this man not the father but the son.

Ahbleza went away knowing that he dared give up his

watch. Any danger of another attempt with the neck-cord had passed; his mother had endured that which had seemed unendurable.

Napewaśte stood like one upon whom dawn burst before the morning star gave notice. She understood now that the robe she had pulled over her head and the covering she had wrapped around her heart those two days had shut out a wonder. She had neglected to recognize herself not only as the one wife who bore Olepi a child but as the one person who had provided this man the true-way of generating self. Through the seasons Olepi had given many horses, robes, meat, and now he gave a woman he cherished as a way of showing generosity. But he had created none of these things; only through Ahbleza had he proved himself a generating force. And then only as an accomplice.

And so she vowed to live content with that which Olepi offered, her heart a healing thing, her resolve already firm. She shall go on performing her work, and when finally Olepi sees that young men take his place in the war parties, he will find use for her as a companion. For certainly they had shared many experiences these twenty-and-six winters since the day he had made her a wife.

Let the people sing praise for the Mahto and the woman he discards, she told herself; let everyone cheer and make noise. But the truly wonderful things, the great mysteries, move quietly. Who will hear the sun climb the sky, hear the grasses push up? The black hill and the butte that sits nearby never make a sound, yet what different thing on all this windy earth gives the Lakotah more protection than these silent keepers of the tribal good. Remembering, she shall stay glad for quiet hands and quiet heart and quiet tongue.

Stepping back inside the lodge, Napewaśte located a big waterskin, one that always had smelled fresh. Next, she changed gowns and then, loosening her hair, she carefully brushed and braided the strands. She touched her cheeks with red. And now she stood presentable, ready to go along the path to wood and water.

VII

SUMMER WANED, the warm, fat moons thinning, the pte growing new hair against the threat of cold. And now members of the Tatanka, the Pta-lodge, came together for their once-a-season feast.

In Napewaśte's tipi someone watched these headmen file toward the center, where they will hold their ceremony, where they will eat and dance and smoke. And announce any new members. Olepi waited, the resigned wait of a final chance; if they will not choose him this summer—the summer he throws-wife-away—they never will take him into the Tatanka-lodge.

Ahbleza's heart reached out to his father on this day. Sitting with Olepi for a smoke, the son had observed an unnatural quiet about the man. When someone came looking for Napewaśte, when old Lekśi received a caller, Olepi had not so much as glanced up from his pipestem.

But now, abruptly and without signal, someone jerked aside the lodge flap and stepped boldly into the tipi, someone whose appearance demanded respect.

Slowly the Mahto leader turned his eyes toward this intruder. He saw the headwear that marks a Pta-member, a headpiece made from the hide of an old herd-father, horns attached and painted red. And he saw other things that mark a headman: daubs of white paint on middle-aged shoulders, arms, and breast, and a white lance in the big-belly's hand.

Olepi stood, but nothing will hurry him. For ten-and-one winters the Mahto had waited for this moment and he intended to enact superbly each meaningful gesture.

The Pta-man looked a long while into Olepi's face, the Mahto returning his steady gaze. Next, an arm painted white reached out, touching the unpainted Mahto on the shoulder; the big-belly snorted in the manner of pta, waiting for Olepi to respond with a similar sound.

And then the white-painted one guided Olepi out of the lodge and toward the center-place, where members of the

651

Tatanka sat looking for this leader of the Mahto villages, this important Titonwan.

And Ahbleza, seeing these two go, threw his heart to whatever power had granted his father this lifelong wish.

Many eyes saw Olepi enter the council lodge; many hearts rejoiced that the Tatanka had lifted the lodge flap to this man. But in one tipi the news embittered a certain woman, her shapely mouth twisting unpleasantly, her eyes clouding.

"He throws me away and so the Tatanka receive him."

Iśna answered shrewdly: "If I throw you away, will they make me a Pta-member?"

Instantly Hinziwin regretted her outburst; already she had learned that they will not accept a quick tongue and a toss of the head in this lodge. She dropped gracefully to the ground in front of the man; she pulled off his moccasins. She began to rub his foot between her palms in the manner a man enjoys. "The Iyuptala," she murmured, "will make you a pipe-man. Soon after the Kuya leader wears his sash in a fight, they will name him pipe-bearer."

Iśna's scornful lips curled disapproval at her unbecoming entry into his affairs, but Hinziwin, bent over his foot, escaped the look. Nor had she understood that which he now told her.

"The Iyuptala set aside certain rules for me. They will not risk my loss." He spoke curtly, pulling away his foot. "Put back the moccasins. I go to the center, where Olepi feasts with the headmen. I like this Mahto whatever your wish that I see him differently."

Toward evening Hinziwin had gone with a group of women to watch the Tatanka perform their ceremonial dance. Silently she had marveled Olepi's appearance among these men of similar age; certainly anyone who closely observes the Mahto will have reason to laugh in her face if ever again she says that he grows too old for a young wife; even now the most attractive women in camp smile at him.

Tonweya had stood alongside Ahbleza during the dance, and now he spoke, not turning his eyes. "You, my brother, will dance with these men one day."

"Only if I get fat at my middle." He had not dared a

serious answer, not with the situation unchanged; the leaders looked through him as before, his voice in council yet unnoticed.

"Your father joins the lodge, nothing fat about his belly. Truly, he owns the body of a brave." The scout's eyes followed the dancing men, who bellowed and snuffled and butted each other after the custom of pta; only Olepi appeared graceful.

"Perhaps they give up on my father. Perhaps they delay his invitation these many winters waiting for him to fatten."

But now Tonweya nudged Ahbleza playfully. "Why throw your glances at those big-bellies when you have something much more exciting within view." He pointed his thumb at a certain young woman. "And this one, not the only good-looking woman in camp. Among those captive Psa-women, I see. . . "

"So take one," Ahbleza smiled.

"What woman wants a scout for husband? I am rarely in camp and any tipi smothers me."

"Let the woman decide if she wants a scout for husband."

"What woman?" Tonweya asked lightly but not depreciatingly.

"Whatever one you decide."

Suddenly Tonweya's smile faded. "Something I will ask you, cinye. The people say that a dreaming-pair shall share a woman even as they share a vision. They say that whatever woman you choose I shall regard as a distant-wife. But I am not certain that I understand this phrase 'my soul and your soul cast shadow on each other' as the meaning of distant-wife."

Ahbleza, also unsmiling, answered quietly. "You speak to me saying 'cinye'—brother—yet custom will not permit your saying 'hankaśi'—sister—to a woman I make wife. You dare not joke with my woman nor I with yours. So perhaps you see why the grandfathers decide on this expression of respect, 'mitawanaġi nu nitawanaġi sakib aiyohanswicaye,' but only for use between brother-friends who become a dreaming-pair."

Whether or not Tonweya really understood had seemed

unimportant at this moment and so the two had returned their attention to the gifting that followed the dance, many persons presenting horses in Olepi's name.

Presently they led a white horse into the center, the herald announcing that this snow-white one now belongs to Olepi. Each Pta-member, he told, shall own a white horse, not for war but in memory of war, a horse whose white flanks shall carry a picture-record.

The Mahto, accepting this symbol of rank, jumped horseback. For a moment he sat tall before the crowd, his dignity and fine-looks commanding the tribe's respect, his eyes demanding that the people recognize a man born warrior, living always the warrior, a man who will know a warrior's day for dying. He will look on the face of the crowd and see each one granting him that which he knows he earns.

And so when Olepi turned his horse to ride slowly toward his lodge, the people also turned toward their lodges; the Mahto's movements seemed like the closing ceremony, not only for the Tatanka but for the summer camp.

But certain ones, seeing the people break for the winter season, remembered that once again the headmen had put off naming a new Shirt-owner. Will this thing mean, one observer had asked himself, that the Titonwan stop growing the sort of man who rises shoulders and head above the crowd, who will hold up the enduring good for everyone's viewing, who will stand conspicuous as a tree on the plain, his roots in earth's untrampled truth? Will this thing mean that the Lakotah never again will raise a Shirtman?

654

VIII

ANOTHER WINTER sat in the past; again the bird-with-two-voices sang loudly on the mixed grasses and prophesied big-strings-of-fat for the Lakotah encampment. Grass and sky these days seemed the same color, give or take away some light, and all that moved on foot or wing either heard or made a song. So earth will renew her own after a long, cold sleep.

Eyanpaha moved more slowly among the lodges than in those seasons when he had teased the boy Mahtociqala about his fat-puppy-of-a-horse, but the old man's voice, unchanged. This morning he had sung out clear and strong that the Kuya had come, Iśna's band the last ones to arrive. The people had wintered on the muddy-water, the only group to go back to the big river for the snow moons.

And now Ahbleza walked with his father to the Kuya's camp, Olepi wanting to smoke with the returned leader, Ahbleza choosing to visit with his friend Taśunkekokipapi. The son of Olepi had heard that Taśunkekokipapi now headed a village and also sat as pipe-man for the Kangi Yuha, an akicita-lodge which had originated in the Kuya band. He desired to express his gladness at seeing Taśunke-kokipapi in this important position.

But the smile on Ahbleza's face vanished during the talk with his friend. The Kuya warrior told that Iśna's camp on the muddy-water had stood near the new trading lodge and that the stink and noise around the traders had offended many families. Taśunkekokipapi had decided to leave camp and raise his lodge a half-day's walk up the śica, the tricky stream long familiar to the Mahto. Five, six lodges of related persons had followed him and had set up their own winter village. During the cold moons these families had spoken their desire that he keep the village, that he become leader. Taśunkekokipapi mentioned only briefly the burning drink for which many Kuya made trades, but Ahbleza had heard enough to understand that not all goes good in the Iśna camp this past winter, the yellow-water as always a big troublemaker.

In a different tipi Olepi and Iśna smoked, the Kuya avoiding any reference to the deadwood lodge. Remembering the Mahto's bitterness toward all white traders, Iśna had talked mostly about seeing pte mass to cross the muddy river, the herd bunching center on the ice, bracing for the slide, and getting to the opposite side safely. But he told that he had not seen even one pte all the way from the big river to this camp.

Olepi listened but he also sat observing changes in the Kuya: a difference in Iśna's eyes and a sullen quiet among those people who unpacked their drags alongside the Kuya's lodge. Usually women chattered and laughed as they performed this work, but Iśna's women walked averting their faces. And when the Mahto left the leader's tipi, he noticed that one woman covered her head at his passing. Recognizing this woman's walk, he understood that Hinziwin chose to avoid any meeting of the eyes.

True, the woman had hidden her face; she had not wanted the Mahto to see the change. Perhaps an orderly camp this summer, she had told herself, will return her glow, but until this happens she will not go anywhere without a cover over her head.

During the past winter Wiyukcan Mani, Iśna's true-wife, had demonstrated whose voice managed the Kuya lodge. Rapping Hinziwin across the legs with a digging-stick, she had put a stop to pouts and complaints. And so Hinziwin, always eager to go somewhere outside the lodge, hunted excitement among the startling new things which the whiteman-trader had brought to his deadwood shelter on the muddy river. But here her pleasures turned into something revolting. The whiteman, discovering her appeal, had found something to demand in trade if ever Iśna came looking for a drink.

Iśna had come looking for a drink, and soon Hinziwin had heard the Kuya demanding that she visit the trader at dusk. But when the whiteman approached her, she had shuddered at the sight of the lusting eyes and hairy breast. She had torn at the repulsive beard, but her fight had acted to intensify his desire, to give him overwhelming strength. When finally he had thrown her back to Iśna—the Kuya leader lay drunk on the ground outside the trading-place—she had clung to the husband's body until the man owned himself again. She had followed his staggering tracks back to camp, where Wiyukcan Mani huddled in trembling fear.

Hinziwin had not gone near the trader's lodge again, but Iśna went often, trading for the yellow-violence and drinking himself crazy. Perhaps, Wiyukcan Mani had said, when the moon of making-fat appears and they move off this place, Iśna will live good once more. And so the two wives had found a thin comfort in each other's company while they waited for this darkness to pass, for the snows to melt, for the band to start walking toward that great heart-shaped mound, the black hills.

Three, four days after the Mahto's visit in the Kuya lodge, members of Napewaśte's family who sat at the morning soup, heard a scratching on the tipi. But everyone looked for callers these days. Akicita-pledges and their warrior-brothers had begun making the rounds, collecting hides, skins, paint, and feathers in return for the watch they shall keep on the summer encampment. And certainly they scratched most often on the lodge of a leader, hinting for a gift of horses, desiring something to distribute among the aged and blind and among those women who lacked providers.

But on hearing these scratches, Olepi neither rose nor reached for the notched stick which signified a horse. Instead he made a sound that welcomed two clubmen from the Kangi Yuha, akicita who, on entering, stood arms folded, their faces painted black, their eyes on Ahbleza.

The warrior glanced from his father's face to the clubmen, then back to his father; a pulsing began in his cheek. For one crushing moment he wondered whether his friend Taśunkekokipapi had perpetrated this scheme, forcing him to demonstrate that never will he join an akicita-lodge. But the next moment he sat puzzling who will trick him, who will send these clubmen here, these two who gesture with their whips?

Bursting anger, Ahbleza jumped to his feet; he walked between the clubmen to the akicita-lodge, but his tight mouth warned of something desperate.

Seeing whom the clubmen accompanied, a crowd followed these three to the Kangi Yuha lodge. Here the members sat outside, one place conspicuously empty, a short lance in the near ground. Into this vacancy, the clubmen now tried to push Ahbleza.

The son of Olepi saw the short lance, the stick they formally had wrapped with hair, and so he understood what his acceptance demanded of him. He jerked off the clubmen's hold on his arms; his eyes blazed scorn at the Kaṅgi Yuha singers who began a song about the honor that comes to anyone who takes hold of this lance.

Who will dare this impertinence? Who will dare challenge his choice to stay outside the brother-lodges? Who will dare embarrass him, make him appear fearful of the lance?

And then, startlingly as stone that cracks in a fire, he knew who dared: his father. Olepi knows about the scheme yet says nothing to discourage this discomfiting exhibition? His father hears him say more than once that he will not make ties with any warrior-lodge. Or will his father stand alongside the persuaders? Olepi makes a gift of Hinziwin to the Kuya, in whose band the Kaṅgi Yuha form, and so why not use his son to help along connections with Iśna's camp?

Eyes glaring, Ahbleza moved out of the clubmen's reach. But now other Kaṅgi Yuha stood in his path.

The warrior whirled around; he stared at the seated members, at Taśunkekokipapi, who held onto the quilled pipestem, the man's face devoid of any show of emotion.

At a signal the lodge-singers began a new persuading song.

"Danger in front," they said, "you walk out meeting.

"Danger in back, you turn around facing."

They sang as one voice, their tones entreating: "Something difficult you will perform. Uncertain you live."

Ahbleza looked anything but uncertain, and so these voices had not held together. Breaking off, their song dropped to the ground.

Now came those members obligated to step forward with a mouthful of pleas. And next the herald, a lance-bearer's song on his tongue-tip. But almost at once they all backed off.

Losing patience, certain members affected an angry mumble; the contentious young warrior carries this thing too far. Let the son of Olepi remember that the Kaṅgi Yuha honor him; to what different warrior will they give this second, third chance?

Again the two clubmen took hold of the warrior; again they tried to push him into the lance-seat. But Ahbleza seemed not to notice these persons; instead he glared at the lance as if the weapon had made the appeal.

And now someone from back of the crowd, aware that Ahbleza intended to shake off the clubmen once more, stepped forward; he spoke calmly: "My son, I bring the white horse, symbol of my most important rank. The horse belongs to you when I see your hand grasp the lance."

Who empowers this craziness? Who dares try to coerce him? Their shuns accustom him to a lonely path; why try to push him now? His eyes hostile, his body trembling and ready to leap, he faced Olepi. What manner of father will try to bribe his son? And what manner of son will honor a father who offers a bribe? Who says he shall honor any man—father, or not father—for whom he loses respect?

A strange darkness closed in on Ahbleza; he struggled to stay on his feet, to hold on to his senses, to answer things that seemed not to have answers. Will he dare say that he loses respect for his father before he knows truly why Olepi offers the white horse, why the man entreats his son to accept the lance? The Lakotah give a name to that which they not yet understand; they say mystery. And a Lakotah accepts mystery as mystery until he knows.

Ahbleza felt a shudder passing through him, touching his body everywhere. And then the floating darkness lifted; laughter, his own laughter, brought back the light.

And now, before the astounded Kaṅġi Yuha members became incensed at the sound of this laughter, Ahbleza acted; he reached for the lance.

"Men," he shouted, "I take your lance. I go out. Name the enemy and I will give him to you. I invite each man of the Kaṅġi Yuha to join this war party. Come along and watch. Or come along and fight."

The crowd, amazed at the sight of Ahbleza suddenly holding aloft the weapon, murmured their apprehension. The son of Olepi speaks boldly, but will he remember that all Tokala die on that one occasion when the lodge members go out as a group. Will Ahbleza ignore that which happens to the Sahiela lodgemen who ride out together? The picture-record tells the story of what occurs when Heḣiloġeca and thirty lodge-brothers encounter the Psa. And if Ahbleza will not remember these things, let the Kangi Yuha remember for him and so refuse to take this risk either as fighters or spectators.

But the Kangi Yuha members already stood, each one cheering Ahbleza, each one signifying his willingness that this lodge go out as a whole, the new lance-bearer their leader.

And now, as if in answer to Ahbleza's challenge, the herald from the center lodge appeared, the man's irregular path indicating danger, his voice announcing the approach of an enemy. A big party of Psa head this way, he called; they come in daylight, they come to plead for something, perhaps for their women, captives among the Titonwan since the moon of the Titonwan-Sahiela attack on their people.

At once the Kangi Yuha lodgemen sent up a new yell; what difference why this enemy comes? Perhaps the winds carry Ahbleza's laughter to Psa ears and so Ahbleza will start the course of events.

"Paint yourselves. Prepare for whatever shall occur."

They answered Ahbleza's shout with more loud yells, the crowd joining in with cheers and trilling. And Olepi, looking upon the person of his son, decided that nothing more magnificent than this view of Ahbleza, lance-arm lifted, ever shall confront the Lakotah.

Alongside the Kangi Yuha lodge Ahbleza darkened his skin with the black powder and fat which these akicita-warriors wore whenever they fought or danced. And to this place Olepi led the white horse; let Ahbleza remember the gift that awaits his return.

"Not on my return, my father. I am riding your horse against the enemy. I want the people to know that I honor my father's bribe. But afterwards I will return the horse to your herd." Ahbleza mixed a second handful of the burntwood dust and fat; he kept his eyes on the bowl.

Olepi appeared not to notice the word 'bribe,' but he had not tried to hide his amazement and concern. Why will Ahbleza choose to ride an unfamiliar horse and one of a color that makes the horseback an easy mark? Why this foolish risk? "You prove your bravery in accepting the lance," he said quietly.

"I take the lance to show the people that I honor my father's wish. But this act leaves me without honor for myself."

The Mahto reached out his hand, touching his son's shoulder. "Why this talk? They present you a lance and each one pledges that he will ride out with you. Yet you find nothing honorable here?"

Gently Ahbleza withdrew from his father's touch; he gave a direct answer. "You know my way. I am not one for the akicita-lodges, yet you, my father, scheme this thing."

Olepi's eyes narrowed. "The people wonder," he said, "why my son stands off from warrior customs. But now they see that the akicita place you in a most demanding rank; the Kaṅǵi Yuha trust you with the lance. What more honor will you ask?"

"I ask that you and they honor that which I choose."

Ahbleza stood painted and ready to ride, but he waited another moment alongside Olepi. "My father, hear me. I observe that the same truth sits back of all you ever say to me: that a man shall reason and choose. And that other persons will respect his choice, whether or not they agree.

"From you I hear of the path which each man shall discover for himself. You say that a man shall walk firmly on this path. But now, seeing me act untrue to my path, you give approval . . . and a horse." Ahbleza turned to mount.

Olepi answered quickly, sharply. "What path will you take that mine and yours divide?"

Looking into his father's face, the son spoke the truth he long since had recognized. "Your words and your act tell me that you want not bravery but only a show of bravery. I dare refuse the akicita-lodge—something not one other Lakotah yet dares—but this thing counts for nothing in your eyes. Yet when I take the lance—something any Lakotah will dare—you cheer this show of courage. My father, come with me. I will give you that which you ask; I will give you the most exciting display of bravery you ever shall witness."

Lance in hand, Ahbleza jumped horseback. "Anpetu kin le oyate wamaya-kapi kte lo," he shouted; "this day the people see me."

Whirling the white horse, he dashed into the midst of the painted, yelling Kaṅǵi Yuha; he cared not whether they

661

came or stayed. This encounter, a one-man show, a show this son puts on for his father.

Many persons, responding to the war cries and trilling, accompanied the warriors who now moved across the camp circle, thirty Kangi Yuha in the party, their whoops more like sixty.

Ahbleza, keeping far front, had found reason to marvel: the white horse responded to his touch unlike any horse he ever rode; not even Tatezi reacted this quickly. And so he recalled that occasionally a man will exert tremendous power over his mount. Such a man, in a running fight, will use up his horse and ever after they call his horse 'crazy.' Perhaps my father shall own a crazy horse after this ride, he told himself, for I shall empty this one of everything.

Before the Kangi Yuha had caught up with him, Ahbleza saw someone coming up fast; the next instant he recognized Tonweya.

"I go out. I face the Psa. Tell me anything you know," Ahbleza shouted as he rode near his brother-friend.

"Your horse will not sweat before you meet the enemy; thirty-and-six come back of me, swift horses between their legs. They come, foreheads bare of paint. They carry bows but not lances."

Whatever surprise Tonweya experienced on encountering the son of Olepi in this strange situation—Ahbleza racing front of a war party and carrying a Kangi Yuha lance—the scout properly concealed.

"Tell the camp." Ahbleza gave a startling yell. "The power rides with me. I will show the people something."

The akicita-lodgemen came close behind the lance-bearer now, and hearing his yell, they followed him down the slope, into the bowl-like valley.

Tonweya hurried toward the encampment, but the bands had not waited for more news. The people had come rushing out, scrambling to the top of the slope for a good view. And now they stood covering the rise, men and women and children looking out over the wide valley, seeing the enemy's dust. Apparently more than thirty Psa horse-backs hurried toward a central woods, perhaps scheming a surprise approach from the opposite side of the trees. Excitement shook the spectators.

One Titonwan warrior suddenly saw the location as a good place for rivalry between warrior-lodges; Peśla had begun to incite the men of the Iħoka-lodge, shouting that they also belonged in this fight.

"Let the whole tribe act as witness; let each person see for himself who dares touch the enemy," he cried. "Let the people discover in which warrior-lodge the bravery sits."

Certain Iħoka had disagreed with Peśla. The head clubmen for this summer's encampment, they told, sit watching for anyone who closes his ears to caution, who intends to dash down the hill. This fight belongs to Ahbleza and to the lodge whose lance he carries; the elected watchers give orders that none interfere.

Ahbleza had halted his party on the near side of the woods; he had seen his chance to give the people, along with his father, the spectacular about which he had boasted. And so he intended to hold the Kangi Yuha warriors in a compact group until the enemy reappeared, the Psa—now alerted for a fight—coming either through the woods or around.

A smile tickled inside Ahbleza's cheek. A show they want, a show he will give. And he shall make up for whatever he lacked on that occasion when an old Psa-man had ripped open his side. This day he will make the rips and from whatever spot he stakes himself.

He saw the warriors shift uneasily on their horses. He spoke calmly: "Show patience, my friends. This enemy chooses a day-visit and so they see those Lakotah on the ridge, but they will not look for a war party waiting here."

Suddenly Ahbleza raised his lance-arm as when he had accepted the lance. "I smell the stink of Psa hair. The beggar comes out of the woods. Look at him. Takpe." The son of Olepi gave the blood-chilling whoop that usually froze an enemy, putting a man in line for arrow or club.

But the Psa came riding straight into the Kangi Yuha party, looking anything but frozen, anything but beggars. And so the contest began, horsebacks riding in every direction, men shrieking insults, reaching out to strike with bow or palm.

Ahbleza, carrying only the lance, tried to maneuver into an open place where he dared jump down and make a stand. But always one of his own men rushed in front of him, a lodgeman in his path and interfering with his chances at every turn. True, these Kaṅgi Yuha rode pledged to help him but not until he had thrust the lance into the ground and stood alongside.

And now he made his bold cries at his own. "Get out of my way," he shouted. But none seemed to listen. Then suddenly one who had ridden interference fell limp, dropping off his horse; an arrow intended for Ahbleza had pierced a different man's breast.

Instantly Ahbleza whipped around to pick up the hurt or dying Kaṅgi Yuha, but another lodgeman already lifted the struck body onto his horse.

What happens here? Will they deny me any risk? Shouting his fury, Ahbleza made his way into the most dangerous position in the fight. At once three Kaṅgi Yuha rode in protectingly.

The Psa had begun to scatter, running back toward the woods. Aware of the many Lakotah who moved around on the ridge, they perhaps looked for many more warriors to rush out from this yelling throng. And so, reaching the trees, two Psa now rode back and forth, a sign of retreat.

Whoops of victory rose from the slope and certain Titonwan came riding down onto the flat, all relatives of the fallen warrior, persons anxious to know whether the man lay wounded or killed.

Ahbleza stayed back on the fighting ground; horseback, he sat unmoving, the lance across his thighs. They never once had granted him an opening, a place to make his stand. And the look on faces riding past him confused him even more. Will they regard him as some mystery who suddenly appears but will not fit into the Lakotah scheme? Or will he imagine all this strangeness?

Will the Kaṅgi Yuha treat each new lodge-brother in this manner, or will he stand out as some weird sort of prize? Perhaps this day, this experience, ties in with the strange way the headmen react to him these many seasons, this whole thing enough to overwhelm a man.

Then he saw that Pesla, who had ridden forward to meet the fighting men, turned from these warriors to speak to him. The harsh face wore a curious smile. "I see," he said, "that you, the daring leader of this party, return safe, yet a certain brave man, one of your protectors, lies choking on his own blood." Abruptly as he had approached, Peśla rode off.

So the Kaṅġi Yuha also use him for something. But for what? Will they deprive him of joy in combat or prevent any honors? Certainly they will not see a man receiving wounds, perhaps dying, in their attempt to humble a different man? Reluctantly Ahbleza started toward the crowd that surrounded the injured Titonwan.

The fleeing enemy had disappeared among the trees nor had any Titonwan pursued. They had viewed this encounter as something similar to an exciting ball game, some persons even making bets. The peźuta had signaled that the hurt warrior recovers, and so, when the Psa had begun to run off, the Lakotah spectators whooped victory; the enemy had accepted defeat.

But one little group of women—Psa captives not yet adopted into the bands—had kept their eyes on the distant woods; they had wondered whether a husband, son, or brother rode among those retreating horsebacks.

And now one in this huddle, speaking her own dialect, made known her musing. "Why will they run off?" she said; "they count the most men and none gets hurt. Perhaps this fight goes on again. They remember that Psa-women watch, and so they also desire putting on a good show."

Her listeners looked uncertain. Turning away, they started back to their lodges.

And then the woman who had spoken called softly, "Look. They come back. They come back looking for a real fight."

Ahbleza had not yet reached the group who surrounded the reviving brother-member, but he saw that these Kaṅġi Yuha suddenly looked up, their smiles disappearing. Next thing, he heard the whoops of an enemy who returns.

And now Peśla dared take command of a party, Iȟoka and Kaṅġi Yuha warriors mounting, racing out on the flat, bows and lances along on this ride.

But riding far front, Ahbleza. And who will stop him now?

The wind slapped the warrior's face, but he had the breath to encourage his horse. "The fight belongs to me and to you, friend," he shouted. "Use your nose. Avoid the holes. I will not want the people seeing me fall."

The wingbone whistle tied in Ahbleza's hair hummed in his ear. "I hear you," he said, "now you hear me." Raising the lance he began a song.

The Psa, riding a zigzag line, approached noisily, shouting defiance and waving sticks; they will taunt the Titonwan into meeting this new advance. Not again will they who come peacefully, retreat; they return as warriors ready to die.

And so the Psa regretted seeing only one horseback ride out, one man on a white horse. But truly this one man came directly, swiftly, so swiftly that he seemed to fly. Perhaps a violator of sacred custom rode out, making this death-ride in self-reproach. For certainly this man shall die.

"Hanta yo," Ahbleza sang; "wakanya hibu welo"—"Clear the way; in a wonderful manner I come." His song and his ride, the same: fast, fast, increasingly fast.

"Hanta yo, wakanya hibu welo." The horse reacted to the rider's voice, the creature's withers and loin, flank and belly rippling to the beat.

"Maka kin le mitawa"—"I own the earth." The horse burst into new life, and Ahbleza knew the power of his horse as his to claim.

"Maka kin le mitawa, ca hibu welo"—"I own the earth and so I come." The wind tore at the man's hair, flinging the black, loose strands over his shoulders; the wind lifted the horse's mane, making streamers of the long white hairs.

The man sensed a loan of power, from stone on and under the ground, from the wind in four directions.

"I own the earth," he sang and knew that he spoke the truth.

"Hanta yo, hanta yo." "Clear the way, clear the way."

The Psa, ceasing their yells, wondered now whether they faced the most powerful of contraries, a man who dreams not of the zigzag streak between clouds but of a bolt straight down and up, sky to earth to sky. But once this mystery-dreamer comes inside reach of a Psa bow, he shall lose his voice for song, for his song of defiance. For what different song will this crazy rider sing but his final demand for power?

"Ca wakanya hibu welo." Ahbleza sang neither his

death-song nor made his death-ride; instead he came remembering himself as a sacred arrow aimed at the heart of things.

"Hanta yo. Hanta yo." "Clear the way. Clear the way."

And now to the man the Psa slowed their horses; something magnificent held this enemy to a walk. Power, mystery, something to marvel rode here, perhaps a wambli-bird on the back of a pronghorn, something they dared not treat as man.

They sat unmoving. Perhaps this rider owned an unknowable power; certainly he never looked back to see whether more of his tribe followed him. He simply came. Alone.

Two, three Psa warriors set an arrow to the bowstring, but they seemed to lack the strength to push the bow.

They heard his song more clearly now and certain phrases they understood. And so a shiver of uneasiness passed through these warriors who sat waiting. But waiting for what thing, they will not know.

"Hanta yo; wakanya hibu welo"—"Clear the way; in a wonderful manner I come." "Maka kin le mitawa, ca hibu welo"—"I own the earth and so I come."

The song had emptied Ahbleza of old power; now silently, quickly he filled with the new, his person reborn, the beginning revisited in an instant, in a flash of truth.

Ahbleza, as First Born, unrestrained and breathing joy; original man, looking at his hands, picking up stone, breaking off wood, making something to protect himself.

Ahbleza, as Second Born, as young brother to First Born, naked and in conflict with hoof and wing, young brother who shall assert the supremacy of man over creature.

Ahbleza, as man-traveling, as man who discovers Iktomi, a trickster, wherever he goes; as man always in conflict with Iktomi, a mischief-maker.

Ahbleza, as Lakotah, the family; as Titonwan, living on the plain; as Mahto, the grizzly band.

Ahbleza, as Ahbleza the observer, as the power for owning the earth. As owner of the earth.

Suddenly the Psa recognized this man and horse, something an invisible power generates, all the grandfathers back to the beginning making this ride, a spirit-force the Psa dare

667

not contest. And so, before this onrushing power—in the shape of a horseback—crushed the whole party, one Psa warrior managed a yell of alarm. His cry scattered the men, sending each one on a frenzied run back toward the woods.

But Ahbleza, bending low over the horse's neck, reached forward, touching one man who fled, striking him on the shoulder with the Kaṅgi Yuha lance. Terrified, the Psa quirted his mount, using whip and yells to urge the horse beyond a second encounter with this overwhelming mystery, something man yet more than man.

Ahbleza pulled up his horse, turning sharply, his unprotected back to the disappearing enemy. The show over, he chose to ride slowly toward the lodgemen who came to meet him. But seeing that these warriors stopped their horses at his approach, he halted and sat wondering at the change in these faces, all eyes on him, a silence in every direction.

Now, slowly he lifted his arms, the lance held out level with his heart as one will hold the pipe on demanding the loan of a good day.

The sun seemed to stand still midway down the sky, and the clouds seemed to hold on to their shapes while Ahbleza sat the white horse, man and mount unmoving. Truly, nothing moved, nothing spoke; the great hush seemed to await Ahbleza's gesture, Ahbleza's voice.

Suddenly, this man on the white horse sat laughing, Ahbleza laughing as when he had grabbed the lance in front of the Kaṅgi Yuha lodge. And so the people saw the son of Olepi break open his reserve of enduring power, spilling out that which remains of the tenseness, the force, the joy of his glorious encounter with the enemy. For twice on this same day—when he had accepted the lance and now—Ahbleza had recognized the moment of need as theirs, not his.

I will not need this crowd, he had told himself, but they perhaps imagine they need me, perhaps view me as someone who owns an unusual power, the same view that seems to pervade those Psa. And so I shall throw myself back to the people through something they understand: laughter. And now they will recognize my power as nothing different from that which each one owns and dares use. Śkan, existence; śkan, existing and available, to the one, to the whole.

And so these Lakotah, persons whom Ahbleza brings into close touch with the irresistible force, now burst into shouts, broke into smiles, each one releasing not only gladness but a certain relief on recognizing that nothing unnatural exists. Or ever will.

Olepi, hearing the cheer, marveled his fresh understanding; he now saw in the son a fulfillment of sacred-scheme. For whoever sends seed into woman acts to create new strength, intensify the image of himself. So will not each father look for the day when he sees his son walking beyond him? For if a man stands in the way of his son, who will own the earth in the generations ahead? And if a son stops where his father stops, who will keep this earth in the generations ahead?

"The day comes for which my friend sits looking." Wanaǧi had spoken. But before this seer will say more, perhaps too much more, he walked away from Olepi; why risk telling the father that in some distant season when the Lakotah walk with heads drooping, Ahbleza will own the power to keep a piece of the people.

Ahbleza, jumping down from the white horse, turned the depleted creature over to a boy for a wipe-down with sage. Then, holding on to the lance, the warrior headed for the Kanǧi Yuha lodge. But on reaching this place, he saw that his father stood at the entrance, the flap closed and Olepi's hand raised against his son's entry.

The warrior, puzzled, wondered whether the lodgemen or his father will keep him out. But now he saw the lodge flap open, leaders of this group coming forth, Tasunkekokipapi moving toward him.

"Each man inside speaks the same," the Kuya friend said. "And so I tell that the Kanǧi Yuha retire the son of Olepi. He honors the lance; he makes good his pledge."

Ahbleza glanced quickly from face to face, hunting the true reason why they will dismiss him; will his discharge come out of consideration for his own choice?

They met his look with respectful eyes and a patience; they waited to hear him accept what they offered. And so, after a searching gaze of his father's face, Ahbleza handed back the lance. He walked away from the lodge, going alone.

The warrior wanted talk this night with Wanaġi, something he not yet desired with the blood-father. And now, passing the sacred-lodge, he scratched on the flap. But stepping inside, he found himself unnoticed; Wanaġi sat as if prepared for a different visitor.

Presently Ahbleza stepped out, not discouraged but perplexed. Why will Wanaġi, the man he regards as second-father, not so much as raise his eyes once Ahbleza enters?

Soon after the warrior had gone, Wanaġi answered to a different scratching on the lodge cover, and now the seer identified the one for whom he had prepared a pipe; he and Olepi shall smoke, and when they empty the bowl, the Mahto shall say that which he comes to say.

But they had smoked a second bowl of the sweet mixture before Olepi spoke. "Naġi napeyapi," he said abruptly and so described the condition of the white horse his son had ridden, the creature an empty body now. "I will look for a different white; this one I shall give . . . " Olepi glanced at Wanaġi, his look asking if a man dares give away such a horse.

"Your son," Wanaġi answered him, "uses up the horse, and so the creature walks vulnerable. Let any mischief get to him and you will see a crazy horse."

"Will my son use up more horses in this manner?"

"Not your son, my friend. He makes only one such ride. Something happens once and Ahbleza understands."

"He learns more quickly than his father," Olepi responded murmuring.

Wanaġi heard but he put this truth differently, more accurately: "My friend, your son needs to know much more than you ever need to know." And now the sacred-man spoke as if to himself. "On this day Ahbleza, whether he knows or not, begins to demonstrate his vision."

Neither man said more. Olepi had nothing more to say; Wanaġi dared say nothing more.

IX

FOR A while Ina tried to hide the bulge under the front of
her gown. She had imagined herself too old for growing-life
but then she had discovered differently.

Olepi had visited her robes only twice since the day he
threw away Hinziwin, but whether he made frequent use of
Napewaśte, she will not know. The sisters spoke nothing of
personal concerns, not since the day Olepi struck the drum
and discarded one woman in his life. But soon after she had
accepted her swelling as life and not a mysterious lump, Ina
took her news to Napewaśte. "I am too brittle for childbearing," she said. "Perhaps I shall. . . "

"You grow Olepi's child," Napewaśte answered her
shortly. "The child belongs to him and you. Take this news
and your wish for destroying something to the man, not to
me."

And so Ina reported herself to Olepi, her words scarce
and her manner timid. But at once the Mahto announced
his pleasure, voicing his desire that she look out for herself
most carefully. He touched his palm to her cheek in a show
of fondness and when she sat across the fire from him, he
smiled most affectionately at her. Suddenly she had a new
heart for this thing.

But Napewaśte, displaying an uncommon annoyance
with her sister, set Ina to wondering whether this woman
resented her as someone in whom the man's seeds had taken
root. Ina also noticed that Napewaśte had dulled instead of
brightening after Hinziwin's removal, her sister's soft voice
often rasping and bitter now. And so Ina again considered
making a long stay with her son's family among the
Mnikooźu. Olepi will not use her—certainly a father never
visits his unborn child—nor will Napewaśte take pleasure in
remembering why Ina grows fat.

But as things happen, Ina saw the summer berries ripen
and the season change color before she really decided to
visit Tezi and his wife. And then, leaves falling and dust
blowing, she knew that she had lost her chance for travel to

the weathers. Instead she made frequent visits to the lodges of friends within the Mahto village.

And so, on a day when water froze thinly on the edges, they called Napewaśte to a tipi where Ina lay in discomfort. The assisting ones had tried to get the mother on her knees, to lean over the cross-sticks, but Ina had acted indifferent to their persuasions. After a while they had poured warm root-water down her throat, but the child refused to come.

Napewaśte sent for Huhupiye, and when this peźuta-wicaśa arrived, he examined the woman for obstructing bone. Next, he prepared a powder of rattle-tail. And then Ina, with a terrible shudder, shook loose the child.

The tiny form fell onto clean palms, but neither hands nor mouths started this infant breathing; a girl-baby but born dead.

They turned back to the mother, her breathing suddenly loud and strange. And so the peźuta-woman whom Huhupiye had left in his place saw need to remove something that hung inside the sufferer.

Napewaśte's frightened eyes stayed on her sister's face. She knelt alongside the woman and so she observed the soft shadow that moved down Ina's tired cheek, saw her sister's head drop to one side; she, Napewaśte, the one to see Ina die.

The wind came wailing, softening the frost on the lodge covers even as the women stood wailing, their warm tears melting the icy patches beneath the death-rack; a sad day, they said, to give a body to the weathers.

Olepi, returning from the ceremony at the rack, sent Napewaśte to a warm lodge, away from the cold of a tipi where, in respect for the dead, they will not make fire. Then, placing branches in front of the flap, the Mahto closed himself inside.

The people, seeing this sign of a man who sits sorrowing, gave the Mahto leader their hearts. But the son of Olepi wondered whether his father sat grieving someone or regretting something. Ina's dying? Certainly the man will sense his loss, even as the stillborn will provoke his wonder. But will not the Mahto leader, remembering himself as once the husband to three, consider that which happens to two of these three?

And why concern myself with this thing? Why? Ahbleza had answered that which he asked: I am my father's dream as truly as I am his blood. Yet I am uncertain that his dream relates in any important way to mine.

Olepi sat neither grieving nor regretting; instead he used this occasion to reflect on the direction he had walked and the place at which he now stood.

Certainly he, Olepi, acts always to hold the people together. He, someone who in the past gives the people his daring, his courage, his blood, his horses.

He, Olepi, who throws away a woman—a good-looking woman—and so prepares to give his whole self to keeping the people whole.

Until this day he, Olepi, walks north, toward lodge-trees and hillsides, toward the region of cold. But now he shall turn about, walking the direction man really always faces: south. Now he, Olepi, walks back toward warmth, toward the place of his beginning, all beginning. And whatever new strength he needs shall come from the seed of his loins, the son whom he will see leading the people, all the people.

Why shall he, Olepi, act to hold together this tribe but that one day Ahbleza shall lead the Titonwan?

X

OLD HEHAKA unrolled the winter count and looked at the picture that recalled the previous winter: a line drawing of Ahbleza scattering the enemy. Then, daubing his brush with red paint, he sketched the big event of this recent season: a ball-thing rising out of the south-and-east sky, traveling a great curve north-and-west, sparks marking the trail. Whatever more happens this winter, he had told himself, the people everywhere will remember the red cloud.

Certain persons had said that they saw the ball burst and fall to earth, but different ones had told that the star-cloud roared out of view. This wonder had occurred during the moon of yellow leaves, shortly after the hoop had broken for the winter. And so the bands, separated and traveling, saw and heard the mystery differently. For this reason Heȟaka chose to record only that a star had flown; let each one who had looked up at the frightening noise keep his own memory of the fiery sky.

Tonweya remembered that on this star-night he scouted Oyatenumpa camps somewhere near the running-water. These two-circle people had begun to empty their maize-pits, a sign that they prepared to travel, and Peśla, looking for a village full of fast horses and fine summer hides, had asked that Tonweya walk ahead as his reporting scout. Tonweya shall signal, he had said, when the enemy sleeps; he, Peśla, will wait on the bluff back of the village.

But Tonweya never had given that signal nor had he ever known that the Oyatenumpa sat ready with their own surprise. While the Titonwan scout sneaked through the narrow woods in front of their village, an enemy scout sneaked back toward the bluff. Suddenly the great signal in the sky had stopped everything, each group of warriors seeing something to excite wonder. The grandmothers say that when a star soars the sky, somewhere a warrior dies. But who ever will hear noise such as follows after this star? And will this sign relate to a Titonwan or an Oyatenumpa warrior dying? None stayed to ponder, even Peśla uncertain of this sky-power.

Certainly an old Kuya woman and her daughter will remember the night this mystery roams the sky.

Wiyukcan Mani, mother of two girls, had miscarried once since Hinziwin's arrival at her lodge. And so she walked cautiously while her next child grew, assigning the yellow-hair woman all heavy work. Nor had she permitted Hinziwin any grumbling during these four, five moons, ever since she had felt movement.

Wife to Iśna for two winters, Hinziwin had watched

enviously as Wiyukcan Mani swelled with life. She never before had wanted a child, but suddenly she became regretful that neither Olepi nor Iśna had provided her with something to grow a baby. But if ever she lies with someone near her age, she had told herself, she, also, will make life.

She had thrown aside her interest in Ahbleza; the son of Olepi resembled his father in nature and she wanted a lodge full of fun and laughter. Once she had imagined the son of Mniśa as the true one for her, but now Wiyaka had a wife and she, Hinziwin, again with an old man. A beard had hidden the age of the whiteman to whom Iśna had traded her for a drink, but never will she desire anything coming out of such a person, whatever his winters.

Then a day came when Wiyukcan Mani refused to get off her sleeping robes; Hinziwin needed to watch the meat fires along with her other work. And so the sun passed middle before the second wife dared sit down on her robe.

"Warm some fresh water." Wiyukcan Mani made her request fretfully.

Hinziwin answered curtly: "Meat-water bubbles in the iron kettle."

"I am not wanting meat-water. I am having my child. I will carry warm water and go alone."

Hinziwin glanced over at the woman, suddenly glad that Wiyukcan Mani and not herself pulled up awkwardly, tried to sit tall. She spoke mockingly: "Different women swim in a cold stream once the child comes. Why not you?"

When finally Hinziwin went out of the lodge, she stayed a long while filling a water-container. But she had smiled prettily at each passer-by; she had let the people see her most entertaining self.

Then two came who noticed nothing pleasing about Hinziwin's demeanor. Wiyukcan Mani, their niece, bore a child and they intended to stay and help.

"Your relative says that she desires to go off alone," Hinziwin told, but the women refused to listen. When a child comes into the family lodge, they said, women-relatives offer help.

Pushing the second-wife inside the lodge, they ordered that Hinziwin lay out certain needs: sinew, fat, powdered chips, handfuls of the grass that never withers. And a feather from the bird-who-sits-smiling.

675

"Put these things in reach of the mother," one said, her tone warning against any nonsense, "and mix red earth with fat for rubbing the infant."

Leaving Hinziwin to carry out instructions, the two went out looking for poles of certain tallness and for the root that makes into a pain-relieving drink.

Wiyukcan Mani, annoyed, lay back on her robe. She had wanted this child alone, away from observing eyes, in the manner she had borne her two, but Hinziwin had delayed her getting away. And so her father's sisters had arrived, persons she preferred not to offend.

Returning promptly, the women-relatives looked over the items Hinziwin laid out. "I will need more powder," said the one who had brought in two sticks.

"I empty the sac," Hinziwin answered bluntly.

"So you make more powder," the woman retorted. She disliked the second-wife in her niece's lodge and never hesitated to show this dislike. "Use the prairie puffballs."

But Hinziwin went out to hunt dry chips. The traveling band had stayed three cool nights on this campground, the people using many chips while they awaited Iśna's decision on a winter campsite; most likely she will hunt a long while before she discovers dry ones. She never had looked closely upon childbearing nor had she any desire to witness this one.

Even so, she neglected to stay out long enough; the child had not come before her return. And so she sat in the lodge, rubbing the chips between her palms and listening to Wiyukcan Mani make the little yew-yew-yew cry. Her impatience with the delivery soon replaced any natural compassion, and when suddenly she remembered that Iśna never had traded Wiyukcan Mani for a ladle of firewater, she grew irritable. Why stay here making powder for a baby not her own?

Wiyukcan Mani knelt before the two poles her helpers had planted in the ground, the woman's arms stretched above her head, clutching the cross-stick. One helper stood in front to receive the child, the second woman positioned in back, her knees against Wiyukcan Mani's tailbone.

"Now you help." The woman in front ordered Hinziwin to use a feather to tickle inside the mother's throat until she gagged.

Hinziwin knew about using the gagging-feather on a child whom they want to spew up unripe berries, but she never had heard of spewing up birth-pain. Even so, she took the feather as they directed, using the tip to tease the mother's tongue and throat.

Wiyukcan Mani gagged but she also let go the cross-stick, her head dropping, her face twisting. And so they advised that Hinziwin wait awhile.

Washing her hands with fat, one woman made a quick examination of her niece. She called for warm root-water, pouring four sips into the suffering one's mouth; then she signed for a second effort with the feather.

None had noticed the strange pleasure in Hinziwin's eyes as she took firm hold on the woman's chin and pushed the feather-stem beyond the gagging-place. Wiyukcan Mani panted for air but the two relatives, watching for the infant's head, mistook these gasps for something natural.

Hinziwin forced more of the stiff stem down the mother's throat, the woman in back tightening her arm-clasp around the child-bearer, the woman in front pushing wide Wiyukcan Mani's knees. Suddenly a hand knocked Hinziwin away; a different hand pulled the feather out of the woman's throat.

The second-wife sat down quickly; again she rubbed chips between her palms, nothing on her calm face to hint that her misuse of the gagging-feather almost had choked Wiyukcan Mani. But the cold eyes these helping relatives now turned on Hinziwin gave warning that they shall remember her unnatural behavior.

Next thing, Hinziwin heard a baby-cry, an infant's call for the mother. And now the yellow-hair woman truly desired running out of the lodge, getting beyond reach of the sound and smell of birthing. And the sight of a mother tasting the afterbirth.

Never, Hinziwin told herself, will I have this thing happen to me. Let Wiyukcan Mani go on making Iśna's children; I, never. Giving a little shudder, she slipped out of the tipi. Nor will she care whether the baby, girl or boy.

"A little 'pta' visits my granddaughter's lodge." So an old Kuya woman announced her grandson's birth to the band. But before Iśna's son had lived two days, this same old one sat pondering strange flight in the sky. She had watched a great red cloud soaring the black, from one edge of night to the other. But whether this mystery omened good or trouble she had not said. A warrior dies, she knew, whenever a star sweeps the sky. But this fiery one, more than star. And so, if a sign for death, perhaps not one but a whole tribe begins to die.

Olepi had led his Mahto in this same season of the red-cloud-flying toward the hill-mother, but instead of moving in alongside the big butte, he had guided the people south and around the great lift of earth; they traveled the tacante canku, the ancient heart-path that embraced the black hill. Here, Olepi had said, they shall discover a good winter camp.

During this move the Mahto villages had come in touch with different travelers—certain Sahiela families in company with their Suhtai relatives—and on the night the fire-cloud passed overhead, these tribes sat camped as one.

And so Ahbleza met again the Sicangu and his Suhtai wife, the many-daughters family with whom he had spoken three winters past concerning the power of dream-shields; and so he saw again the proud-looking daughter, the one who resembled her mother's people, the one among those three daughters whose face he remembered.

Three nights during their travels around the black hill the tribes camped together, Ahbleza twice visiting the father of these three sisters. But on his third visit, the son of Olepi went to see one daughter and to see her alone.

Ahbleza's robe hung over his shoulder but he had not lifted the edge to his eyes in the manner of a man intent upon gaining a wife; he wanted to touch this woman's heart, not her body.

Unfamiliar with Suhtai speech, he had not understood her name and so he called her Heyatawin. He gave her a Lakotah name—woman-on-the-ridge—but one that recognized an old and proud family—dwellers-on-the-ridge people—her Suhtai relatives.

Then, before he spoke more than her name, the warrior heard the roaring star. For an instant he imagined his own blood rushing through heart and head, making this sparkling sound. But the woman, her arms reaching around him, raised her face to marvel the brilliance in the sky.

They stood together watching the mystery, a thing of wonder but not more wonderful than seeds growing, birds nesting, the sun rising. They stood together, a woman and a man of similar tallness, similar pride, and together they rejoiced in this sharing-with-the-powers.

And so the man dropped the robe on which he had painted the lifelike horses, his gesture placing everything he owned within her reach.

She glanced at the robe, then at his face, the woman-pride shining in her eyes.

His hands moved neither to her cheek nor to her thighs, but suddenly his look demanded her full surrender to his own pride. Then, seeing her yield, he understood that she made her surrender also an act of pride.

He wanted her. He wanted her now, and here. And he saw that she wanted him. Now and here. His command of her body had begun where this command shall begin: an urge born of pride and mating with pride, her spirit demanding that her body submit to his touch and to his taste and, finally, to his thrust. But he will not take her now; he will wait until he sees her eyes shining back his own self-respect.

The night stood still; the wondrous star had hushed the earth. And then an infant's cry reached the shadows where these two stood.

"They say," Heyatawin murmured, "that a blazing star foretells a warrior-dying. But I hear a child; I see the flying-star as one that foretells birth. Perhaps each life reaches earth on the rays of a far-distant sun."

Never before had Ahbleza contemplated himself as a father, but now he wondered whether the powers sent something to brighten the sky on the night he chose this woman for mother of his child.

Two days after the appearance of the mysterious star, the traveling Mahto and their Sahiela companions came upon a wooded creek, a stream long known to the Sahiela. Here these people of two different tribes raised winter lodges, the two camps within sight of one another.

And here Tonweya, out scouting for more than a moon, had found his people, the band settled, everyone content and waiting for snow.

The day following Tonweya's return, the air glistening in the morning sunlight, the scout and his brother-friend walked the edges of old-woman creek. Or so the Sahiela named this stream.

"Misun," Ahbleza said suddenly, "I tell you, only you; I discover the woman I want for wife."

Tonweya's handsome face welcomed Ahbleza's news as he listened to hear the woman named. Instead, the warrior used his chin to point out four women who walked together a little distance ahead.

"Tell me, misun, whom among those four I will choose."

Tonweya saw only their backs, but he dismissed one woman at once; too old, perhaps mother, perhaps grandmother to the party. As to those remaining three—most likely sisters—perhaps ten, twelve winters separated their ages.

"You choose, cinye, the most young in this family. But I warn you: prepare for a season of play. The way she walks hints at someone who enjoys child-games. Perhaps she yet holds on to her toys." Tonweya's eyes twinkled.

Ahbleza responded to the scout's teasing. "Not the little one," he said laughing. "I leave Kipanna for you. Now watch and you will discover whom I desire."

Quickly the men caught up with the women, and, passing close by, Ahbleza patted the bottom of the tall proud-walking one.

Heyatawin turned, but on seeing who touched her, a smile curved her shapely mouth.

The brother-friends went on together, and when far in front of the sisters, Tonweya grinned. "Something tells me that this woman knows your touch."

Then, joking put aside, the scout spoke his long remembered thought: "They say that a dreaming-pair shall regard one another's woman as distant-wife. But I know only that whomever you admire I shall admire and whoever gives you her affection I shall respect. I will honor whomever you choose, whatever you decide."

After a moment Ahbleza turned to look into the truthbearer's eyes. "Your words give me sudden-vision. One day I will share with you the picture I am viewing."

Tonweya heard but he sensed in Ahbleza's answer something not to pursue now. And so he turned the talk in another direction.

"Tell me, cinye, whether or not your woman knows anything about horses. Will she take good care of your herd, treating each one as friend, sharing your fondness for Tatezi?"

A smile changed Ahbleza's face. "She knows about horses," he said gaily. "She owns a small herd and not a woman in the tribe surpasses her horseback. She understands. . . "

Tonweya's gesture stopped Ahbleza momentarily; the scout signed his acceptance of all Ahbleza will say in praise of Heyatawin. "I hear," he murmured; "hunhunhe pangeca, your woman has everything."

But Ahbleza chose to finish his speech, something he wanted Tonweya to hear now. "I intend to move in with her family, to help her father make meat. Her parents say that they desire a son in this many-daughters lodge and so I shall stay a little while. But I give you warning, misun: perhaps I will present you with three distant-wives all at once. I am asking that her two sisters also accept me as husband."

"Truly you amaze me." Tonweya's tone mocked his words. "I see you slow in choosing a wife, but once you decide I know of none who moves more quickly, takes on so much. Will you have enough horses for that which you undertake?"

The scout began to count on his fingers, bending down one for each relative Ahbleza shall honor in his wives' names. "Perhaps you will send me out scouting enemy camps, locating villages full of horses; only with my help will you have enough for gifting."

Now Tonweya's eyes brightened. "Come scouting with me, my brother. Pangiciya wo; the people say that a warrior shall go out once more before he sits down alongside woman. And most certainly a man who soon settles down with three wives shall go out and fill up on fun."

The smile stayed on Ahbleza's face: "Before you count any more gift-horses, I go now and find out whether or not her sisters will accept me, whether or not her father approves this whole thing."

Ahbleza decided to speak with each woman in turn, the young Mahto approaching these sisters in the Śahiela manner, each one hearing his wish separately. His fondness for Heyatawin, he will say, spreads out to her family, and so, if her sisters eventually will desire him as protector, he will treat each one as wife whenever they choose to come to him.

The two sisters listened with becoming modesty; then, remembering the importance of self, each one gave direct and truthful answer. The middle daughter—her name, Zitkala—expressed a willingness to come whenever Ahbleza and Heyatawin invite her. But the young one, in her fourteenth winter, raised her big eyes and named her wish to stay in her parents' lodge until she recognized her own desires. Kipanna had spoken prettily, the woman-within perceiving that perhaps one day she will prefer living as Ahbleza's third wife to the role of only-wife in a different lodge.

And now these sisters planned joyfully for Heyatawin's going to Ahbleza. In the next four, five days Heyatawin shall walk, in the manner of her mother's people, to a place near Napewaśte's lodge. Here, someone will spread a robe, Heyatawin standing, meeting ceremonially Ahbleza's bloodparents. Next, Heyatawin shall sit on the robe, Ahbleza's relatives lifting the hide, carrying the woman to Napewaśte's tipi. Once inside, the warrior's mother and his kinswomen shall paint and gown Heyatawin in the Śahiela custom, this custom similar to the Lakotah. Then, having brushed and braided her hair, these same Mahto women will announce the feast that honors these two who soon join their lives. Afterwards, the people shall watch Ahbleza walk alongside Heyatawin, the man going with the woman to the lodge of her parents.

Once they step inside the Śahiela lodge, Heyatawin's parents and sisters will go out of the tipi, the family staying away four, five sleeps. Afterwards everyone will return and live as before but for one difference: this many-daughters lodge will shelter a son for a season or more.

And so, amidst giggles and laughter and a little proper joking, the three sisters and their Suhtai mother arranged for these things, someone remembering that among the Śahiela a man usually pursues a woman five seasons. Certainly Heyatawin's pursuer had acted differently. "He sees you on three, four visits," her sisters teased, "and speaks with you even before he talks with father."

The woman smiled. "Perhaps he regards me old enough —remember, I am twenty-and-six—to decide this thing. But I know that he talks with father before he speaks to each of my pretty sisters."

Next, they teased about the robe on which Heyatawin will ride to Napewaśte's lodge. "You stand tall as the man you will call husband and so you will make a heavy load for his friends. And if you follow the old Sahiela custom and ride the back of the warrior's mother into her lodge, truly she will go crawling on all four."

Heyatawin laughed with her sisters. "I agree. I am too much for Napewaśte's back, but remember, my sisters, I am tall, not fat. Look at me; see for yourselves."

They looked and saw the light shining in her big round eyes; they looked and saw a strong face, a firm chin in the line with the tip of her straight nose, white, sound teeth between smiling lips, tall cheekbones, and smooth skin.

She stood before these women-relatives wearing a gown cut in the Suhtai way, sides tied together with strings, the hides bunched and held at one shoulder, the smooth curve to her arms, her graceful neck, on display. The gown will conceal her body, but they knew her shape as narrow at the waist yet with thighs for bearing-child. A proud-walking woman, this sister; a joy in the lodge, this daughter.

Not many men had sought Heyatawin's smile, most warriors showing a little awe for this woman. Not that they saw anything mysterious about her manner but perhaps they sensed in her magnificent dignity something of the woman who, legend tells, brought the herds to the Sahiela, the pipe to the Lakotah.

But Heyatawin had not waited these many seasons to make a choice among men; instead, she had waited for the one man she shall desire as husband, waited knowing that he shall find her.

Ahbleza had returned to his mother's lodge after his visit with Heyatawin's sisters, but he had not yet shared his joy with persons in this tipi; something held back his announcement. He lay down on his robes but his rest seemed more dream than sleep. He imagined Heyatawin horseback, but he saw her riding Tatezi, an old war horse now but a horse who remembered her tricks, protected her rider. When Heyatawin becomes his wife, he told himself, he will ask that she ride only Tatezi.

Then, dozing, Ahbleza had heard Wanaǧi calling to him. On awakening, he understood that call; not until he sees his father-friend will he announce to his mother's lodge that which he and Heyatawin intend.

Ahbleza carried a filled pipe to the sacred-lodge, offering the stem, awaiting the ceremonial response to his gesture. But the sacred-man, laying an ember on his own pipe, offered Ahbleza the stem. Soon fragrant smoke filled the lodge, and now Wanaǧi, emptying the bowl, lifted his eyes and signed that his visitor speak.

"I not yet know," Ahbleza began, "why the wise ones of this hoop reject me; I am not discerning in this instance. But I come here for a direct answer to something that involves a second person. I ask whether the grandfathers regard me as eligible for the rank of husband. Or will they identify me as a man who not yet earns the privilege of taking a wife? I never will bring dishonor upon the woman I desire, and so I ask, not resentful but demanding to know."

Wanaǧi sat unanswering, but neither will he send Ahbleza away. And so he took a long while to prepare a second pipe, a long while to smoke this one. Then glancing briefly at the warrior, he spoke the phrase that only he dared speak to the son of Olepi. And not until this moment.

"Hau, kakiśniyapi."

Hearing, Ahbleza rose at once, going out of the sacred-lodge as he had come here, pipe in hand. Somewhere along old-woman creek he will find a knoll, a place for smoke and decision. Wanaǧi gives him the answer. But the father-friend will not say—now or ever—to what use Ahbleza shall put that which, after these many perplexing winters, the warrior finally knows.

Kakiśniyapi. They place barriers in your path. Wanaǧi says so.

Ahbleza gently shook the pipe-bowl, the ashes falling onto his palm; nothing burned, and so he emptied his hand in the grass. A night sky empty of moon sat above the knoll, but the warrior will not want for light; he 'saw' now as if he had sat blind these ten seasons past. Only now will he understand that the grandfathers, the leaders, even his own father, set up obstacles along his trail, that they observe closely his encounters with these difficulties.

But for what purpose? This much I know, he answered himself; they prepare me for something. They apparently respect me as a warrior but somewhere they see a weakness. They prepare me for something that sits ahead, for a day when I shall need. . .

Need? But who ever endures a need? Whatever a man truly needs, he earns. And so 'need' never really exists. And everyone gladly helps the blind and lame; they never go begging.

Begging? Wocinpi? Cin? Old words with new meanings? Or contractions with lost meanings? Begging, desire, want, need?

But whoever talks of essentials shall know the difference between need and not-need. So perhaps the wise ones view him as someone who not yet perceives this difference. They place barriers along his way and look for him to surmount these obstructions, to discover his own strength. Instead, he walks around whatever obstructs.

"Now I wonder," he whispered to himself; "whatever obstructions I walk around or climb over, I will meet again. But when I find a way for removing these barriers. . . "

Once, only once, he had cleared-the-way; he had pushed aside a Psa war party; he had removed the visible enemy, not with arrows but through making use of a far more powerful force.

"Now I wonder," he whispered again; "will they wait for me to remove an invisible enemy, something that hinders, that distracts, that turns off a man who tries walking the narrow path into completeness?

"My vision perhaps reveals more than I yet know, and Wanagi perhaps understands more than I yet see. But now that I know in what manner the principal Lakotah test me, I will test myself. And I will make this test before I take a wife."

Ahbleza had walked from the knoll directly back to the sacred-lodge; he had asked for a sleeping place in Wanaǵi's tipi.

Two days passed, nothing spoken between host and visitor; on the third day, Ahbleza expressed his desire for talk.

"I recognize," he said, "one real barrier in my way. And to you alone, I name this one. I speak of my father's influence." He paused; why review those occasions when he permits Olepi's influence, when he pleases his father instead of himself? Wanaǵi knows.

"They say," he went on, "that a person shall follow something to the place of knowing. And so I follow my father's moccasins to the place where I recognize him as a man who will walk the warpath from beginning to finish. This man demonstrates that war satisfies his every sense. Certainly he will seek peace, but with a club, not a pipe, in his hand.

"I, son of this man, also will fight the enemy from beginning to finish, but I discover a new weapon. I will ignore whoever tries to oppress me, and so this enemy fades, disappears. And yet," Ahbleza managed an even tone, "I lack the heart to remove my father from my path. Herein my weakness."

Now Wanaǵi spoke, his phrases quick and sharp: "Already you remove your father. Know you not? I know and he knows. Recall the day you ride carrying the Kanǵi Yuha lance."

Ahbleza glanced at the sacred-man; certainly Wanaǵi knew that the son had conceded to Olepi's wish on that day.

But the seer's piercing look said differently. "Recall your song," he demanded; "understand to whom you sing. Clear-the-way, you command of one who stands these many seasons in your path. Get-out-of-my-way, you shout at this crushing strength whom you call father. Never again, you vow, will you walk around or try to leap over this indestructible spirit who sits in your path. Instead, you grab hold of that which opposes you; you turn this power into something you want, not a show of bravery but the real thing. True, you overwhelm the Psa, but not before you overwhelm your father. He says so."

Wanaġi stopped talking; he desired that his phrases take shape, that Ahbleza see the picture and forever remember. Only then will the son of Olepi understand that ignoring never makes anything truly disappear.

Ahbleza, watching the flame lick the small sticks at the edge of the fire, never knew when he began to speak aloud his thoughts. "I take a long while to recognize my father as a barrier; perhaps I not yet recognize other persons who interfere? Or am I setting up my own barriers when I refuse certain contacts, reject popular voices? Perhaps I act to prevent my heart's desire, but I will not act differently, whatever I lose.

"I know now that the headmen purposely disparage my good intentions when they see me distribute horses among the weak, but why they put a barrier at this point I not yet understand. They demand that each one who aspires to a high place in the tribe demonstrate generosity, and certainly the eyes of persons who receive my presents return thanks. Yet I never hear the crier mentioning my name in a song. Why discourage me to the point where I lose heart for giving?"

Ahbleza glanced from the fire to Wanaġi's face. "Will you, my father-friend, also dishearten me?"

Now, as on different occasions when these two sat together, the wapiya answered in a phrase. "Waḣpani iċiya wo," Wanaġi said firmly.

And now, as on those different occasions, Ahbleza understood to rise and go out of the lodge, taking along this advice or command, whichever way the warrior chose to hear.

Throw out everything; start again. Wanaġi says so.

Throw out everything; regard yourself as a newborn. Wanaġi says so.

Throw out everything; renew yourself completely. Wanaġi says so.

And now Ahbleza knew for certain in what manner he shall try himself.

The warrior walked from the sacred-lodge to Cankuna's tipi; certainly this good woman will carry a message to Heyatawin's family and so let these Suhtai hear about him at

687

once. For on the next day, the whole camp shall know that Ahbleza gives away all he possesses: each thing, everything.

But let the people understand this ordeal not as something the wise men devise, something they sit back and watch; instead let the people see a man who tests himself, who throws out, throws off, throws away, everything he accumulates. Including any and all thoughts that different persons offer him, any and all thoughts originally not his own.

He will give away all robes and hides and so he shall own covering neither for lodge nor for body. He will give away all horses and so make himself foot-going. And next, he will give away his feet, to the final pair of moccasins.

He will give away lances, bows, knives, every weapon he owns but his hands. Truly, he will give until nothing exists for him but his own naked person. And then he shall discard whoever, whatever, outside himself influences this naked person.

I shall live with my bareness, the warrior had told himself, somewhere beyond view of camp until I learn the meaning of pure, pure-anything. I seek something to persuade me that I am whole. For not until I know that I am truly loyal to myself dare I walk as the symbol of steadfastness, as a Shirtman.

The winds raced along the trail that circled the black hills and the rain clouds rushed darkly across the sky. The sun made one brief appearance overhead, a watery yellow eye which signaled the approach of wet and cold.

And now Ahbleza, wearing only a loin-cover, led his one remaining horse—Tatezi—toward the last lodge in the long line of winter tipi. He had chosen to tie the creature here, a gift for the child in this family, a boy-cripple since the day an iron kettle had tipped over and spilled hot fat on his arms and legs. The boy's parents had given away most of their possessions to healers and helpers, the father confident that his son, age eight winters, yet will strengthen.

Ahbleza saw the boy's mother at the entrance flap. "Until he walks, this one will carry your son gently." He put the horse's tie in the woman's hand, then walked away, out onto the plain.

At the knoll where he had smoked five days past, the

warrior stopped. He untied the string at his waist; his loin-cover fell to the ground.

He smiled, discovering that in this moment of nakedness he sensed only the loss of pipe and perhaps the wambli-bone whistle always in his hair. But these things, along with leg-covers, moccasins, weapons, now belonged to whoever had come looking, choosing, taking whatever they desired from the pile outside his mother's lodge.

Moving on, he became aware of a step in back, a woman's step. And now his absolute want swept over him as a hot flush of shame. He had overlooked such a moment; going out from camp he had put aside memory of this woman whom he had intended to make his wife in the same way that he had put aside everything he possessed.

But why will she come? She knows he has nothing to offer her. He closed his ears to her hurrying feet, to the flapping of her gown.

Then suddenly she stood in front of him, looking into his face, her eyes telling that she sees nothing to arouse her sympathy. Instead, she yields her person into his hands; she presents herself to him, a possession to replace all that he throws away.

Ahbleza reached out, then withdrew his hand before he touched her. The urge to become something to this woman almost surpassed his enduring. He turned; he moved away, going in any direction.

She followed. And so he paused, letting her reach him. "You see me, my sister. I am not as when I. . . . See my humbleness. See me as one who has-not."

"I never will see you humble, my heart," she answered. But the man had walked on, choosing not to hear.

She followed as before, and again he paused. He stared for a moment at the lonely, branching tree in front of him.

Turning abruptly, he spoke sharply. "You perhaps bring shame upon yourself. You come alone and I am bare."

The woman smiled; she had recognized the sharpness as something he directed toward whoever in his imagination tried to humiliate her. "My only one, remember that I am Suhtai and Lakotah. My relatives put trust in woman, and neither I nor anyone I knows betrays this trust."

The man had not looked at her, but neither had he walked away. And so Heyatawin spoke again: "If you will permit me," she said respectfully, "I desire telling my thoughts about you; I desire that you understand why I come."

She waited a moment, then began her story. And while she talked, the rain came down in big cold drops but neither she nor the man noticed.

"I observe a certain one long before he observes me. Perhaps I am ten-and-six when I see him, and afterwards I look for him whenever the Sahiela raise a winter camp nearby the Titonwan."

The woman spoke quietly, naturally, as if she repeated that which Ahbleza already knew, her eyes not on him but gazing into the far distance as if she looked at a picture visible to none but these two.

"I never encourage any pull on my gown or listen for whistles, not even when I see my father eager for a man who will help feed his daughters. I know whom I want for husband. And I wait for him.

"They say that I wait too long, that I am old for becoming wife and mother, but I know that my age fits me for becoming wife to this one man. I have the growth to see beauty and so I recognize him."

A new warmth glowed on her cheeks; her eyes lighted mysteriously. "I also live with a vision, something I will fulfill. I desire to bring forth a most unusual child, my dream revealing that the people approach a season when all hearts lie on the ground. They will look for someone who walks shining as a star, someone like the sun. The child I bear becomes this someone.

"But only one man shall plant his seed in me; he alone will bring my vision onto earth. And if he will not take me, I never shall know a man. I will not use myself for growing any different seed."

Ahbleza's response came quickly, his voice strained and uneven. "My sister, your woman-words sound most pleasing and I know that you will not mislead me. But you see something that neither the grandfathers nor the leaders see in me; you view me as something more than I am."

The wind whipped the woman's robe and tossed her loose hair across her face, but her unwavering look told him that she knew greatness when she saw greatness; she will not look for someone to identify this strength for her.

And now, his eyes strangely filling, Ahbleza faced away from her, hiding his tears. "I go out in nakedness to discover the meaning of wholeness . . . perhaps to prove. . . ."

"Prove? You exist as the proof. My true one, thank you for lending me your presence, for permitting me this view of yourself. I see eyes that spill out not tears but a glistening spirit. I am woman and I know."

The warrior turned, looking fully upon Heyatawin, whom only his lips had called 'sister.' "Woman-on-the-ridge," he whispered, "only one I adore."

The woman returned his gaze but now her eyes moved over him, seeing power in his nakedness. And her look told him so.

She reached out her hand, stroking his breast, wiping away the wet of rain and tears; in this manner she responded to her urge to touch this man.

Now she saw that Ahbleza looked beyond her face and into the near distance. Someone approached, someone who came from the village leading a tired horse, something bundled onto a wood-rack atop the horse's back.

The man and woman watched together now; Heyatawin will let whoever comes see her waiting proudly.

The travelers stopped in front of Ahbleza. The old man who led the horse handed the jaw-cord to the warrior. Next he pulled off the bundle, then gently lifted down the child who had clung to the rack. Leaning against the old man, the boy's legs and arms showed the dark scars of a severe scalding.

"My grandson brings his warrior-friend something." The speaker gestured humbly toward the horse. "Nothing like the fine creature you give my grandson, but the boy offers the most his family owns."

The old man picked up the bundle. "Here, a thin robe and moccasins. . . ."

Seeing that Ahbleza struggled for composure, the old one turned away quickly. Bending, he lifted the grandson onto his back, boy and grandfather returning to camp, the old man singing a song of his own making.

Ahbleza stood looking after these two a long, long while; he stood unnoticing of new rain and more wind and cold. He sensed a fulfillment as if he had discovered a warmth within himself, a place of contentment wherein he

691

felt welcome, a place to stay until he chose to emerge, a place to which he shall return whenever he grows aware of a lack outside. Never before had giving or receiving brought him so much to marvel.

Now, looking around, he discovered that the woman had gone. Then he saw her nearing camp, a dim form in the heavy rain. The next moment he noticed the gift-robe on his shoulders, the gift-moccasins alongside his feet. Certainly this remarkable woman had covered him before she left his side.

Turning, he looked out at the openness where he had intended to travel. But why point himself this direction now? He owned a cover and again he wore feet. Why not, instead, send the gift-horse onto the plain, where the bony creature will grow strong again, trampling the snow for grass, living without restraints.

He dropped the jaw-cord. "Go out, friend; join your own kind." But the horse stood as before. "Go out and run on the plain, where none but the invisibles ride you." He gave the creature a gentle push, watching until this one also faded into the rain.

And now he intended to look for a jutting stone or perhaps a cave; under shelter he will start to work on bow and shafts. Then remembering something, he glanced around him; before he looks for a shelter he shall hunt a root for use as a club. Afterwards he will search for second-growth wood and. . .

The chattering bird who foretells snow hopped into the brush close by; he picked up a stone. The bird flew out, but the next instant, dropped to the ground.

The man laughed as a boy laughs when his aim brings meat. And why not? Ahbleza lives this 'starting-anew' day as a boy but with the knowing of a man, boy and father-of-the-boy, one and the same person.

And the next important thing? Find the club-root, he told himself, and find something dry for making a fire. Next, choose a place for cooking the bird but also provide yourself—a far distance from where you cook—with a sleeping shelter. But hunt the arrow-wood before dark.

And so on this night, under a cover of branches and brush, the warrior lay down to sleep, not cold and empty as he had imagined but warm and content and secure. He had cut bark and sucked smoke through a long stem of grass, and he had reflected on Heyatawin, who put the robe around his shoulders, the moccasins close by his feet. And he had decided that when the woman comes here again, he will return with her. From the edge of the village he will call Tonweya and whomever Tonweya chooses to bring with him. And these two men shall carry the woman on the gift-robe, thin but substantial, to Napewaśte's lodge. And here he and Heyatawin shall stay until he has something for a lodge of their own.

And then, before he slept, he had sung his joy, making his song for the woman-on-the-ridge, the only woman he ever shall adore, soul and body. And perhaps the only song he ever will own.

> "Heyatatonwan winyan,
> Iceyela wakinihan ye,
> Amayupta ye."

> "Woman-on-the-ridge,
> Only one I adore,
> Answer me."

XI

THE NEW moons brought frost and aching cold but never a deep snow, the bare winter pleasing Heyatawin.

"A kind mystery looks out for my husband," the woman murmured whenever Ahbleza went hunting, the man going out frequently for meat, big and small, for hides and pelts.

Heyatawin, awl and sinew in hand, sat determined to

693

supply her lodge with every comfort—backrests to head-rests—before the bands gathered for next summer's encampment.

The husband and wife lived in a lodge of their own, the Suhtai mother presenting her daughter with a tipi cover and lining, Ahbleza's family giving many useful things: paunches and linings of paunches for cooking and carrying, soft robes for sleeping, and stiff hides for packaging meat. The Sahiela people also had sent the customary gift of horses, two for the woman and two for the husband.

Ogle had brought a hunter's bow to the new lodge. "I make your original bow and so I present you this second one. And as proof that I balance these arrows," the man's eyes twinkled, "I bring you a folder of antlered meat."

Heyatawin rejoiced at these offerings, but she took most pleasure on viewing four new pairs of moccasins alongside her husband's things at the back of the lodge. One pair she had painted in memory of a youthful adventure which Ahbleza had recited. The second pair Kehala had presented Ahbleza, and the third, Cankuna's gift. The remaining pair Heyatawin had lined with fine-hair, her gift to Ahbleza on the day he had made her his wife. And I will make him a yet more wonderful pair, she had vowed. But she waited for a dream to show her the pattern.

On certain days this winter a nose-biting frost slipped into camp, everyone staying inside. But then wapiti and blacktails bounded through the village, bringing meat to the tipi flap. On such occasions the young in camp claimed, laughing, that they dared not go out and play throwing-arrows for fear of hitting meat.

The same silent cold lifted erect the smoke flaps of Heyatawin's lodge, the flaps as perk as the ears of the little red-dog. And anyone who passed near this tipi heard the joyful laughter of a man and his wife who sat together, their voices rising upwards with the smoke curls and, like the smoke, signaling content.

Once in a while Ahbleza mentioned his want of horses. But Heyatawin responded saying that she rejoiced at only four. "My husband owns a runner and a war horse, and I own one for packing meat, one for dragging lodge-poles. When you decide that you truly desire a herd, you will go out after a herd. For myself, I am glad that I feed but four."

She looked amused. "More than four and I am out in the cold cutting branches all day. And if I freeze my fingers, what happens? I put aside the awl and you go without a covering for your legs.

"My precious one," she said now, her eyes deeply earnest, "horses mean trading for something you have-not. And these days of having-not prove that you have everything.

"You ask that I bring nothing to this lodge but two pairs of moccasins and two gowns. And so I, also, learn the important things in and outside a lodge. And I discover but one importance."

Her eyes returned to the awl, and Ahbleza, looking upon her face, pondered what manner of man ever will place anything above his affection for the woman he calls wife.

Neither Heyatawin's lodge nor any different one received many visitors from outside the band these days. The thin snow had not hindered walking, but the intense cold snapped at a traveler's legs and bit off his toes; only the sturdy newscarriers came visiting, bringing news of Titonwan relatives two, three ridges distant and of those families back on the muddy-water.

Iśna's band, they told, again camped alongside a barrel of firewater. And Sinte, learning of his daughter's shame the previous winter, now raised a lodge in the Kuya's village. The old man, white in his hair but his body spare as a young warrior, had spoken out strongly against the yellow drink. But none listened; they claimed that the burning-water acted to thaw out the camp this bitterly cold winter.

And next, news out of the Kiyuksa villages across the ridge: Tabloka took a sixth wife. He had grabbed a woman from under a husband who preferred to see Tabloka seize his wife than stab his horse.

The Mahto who gathered in Napewaśte's lodge to hear all the news now saw Sluka step forward. Never getting anywhere as a warrior, he had joined the newscarriers this winter. But like his father, he had chosen news-acting over news-reporting.

"The son of Zuzueca looks for three different wives to bear him sons next summer," he announced. "They say this man fathers so rapidly that he soon will have enough blood-sons for a second band of Kiyuksa. Yet this same man, they say, looks for a more rapid way. . . . "

The news-actor followed his speech with pertinent gestures but he had told an old joke; the people remembered that they had heard these same things about Zuzueca, father to Tabloka.

And so Sluka worked on a different story about Tabloka, nothing amusing in that which he began to dramatize.

The bands knew that Tabloka went out after those Psa whom Ahbleza had scattered, but not until now had the Mahto learned that Tabloka used a club to beat an unmanageable brave, the young man's blood sprinkling the ground before Tabloka dropped the weapon. Strict rules governed any form of punishment and so members of the war party had disapproved openly of this clubbing.

But Tabloka had looked down coolly on the bruised form: "When this man surpasses me on the fighting ground, he shall use the same weapon on me. This rule you know. Now, where goes the peźuta-wicaśa who will treat his wounds?"

The healer with Tabloka's party had tried to soothe the excitable youth, but the warriors had recognized that Tabloka's attack will have far-reaching effects. The young brave—if he lives—will live as a cripple, and those warriors who henceforth ride with Tabloka will avoid any dispute with the leader; Tabloka shall have his way, the man certain of full agreement with whatever he says.

Soon afterwards, according to Sluka's pantomime, Tabloka had dared Zuzueca to refute him, the son snarling at his aging father, demanding that the old man step out as leader of the Kiyuksa and let Tabloka step into his place.

Power-crazy, Olepi told himself; power-crazy, this Tabloka. Horses and women for now but big-mouth in all Titonwan affairs, his obvious intent. And control of all Lakotah, his inflexible resolve. But the Pta-lodge never will permit this thing to happen. Perhaps the big-bellies indulge in more talk than action, but never will any Pta-member accept force, agree to controls, as a Lakotah way of life.

For a moment Olepi wondered whether he wanted to sit listening to any more news.

After the newscarriers had spoken, the Mahto women

managed a visit with the newsmen's wives. Two women had risked the cold to identify the travelers as peaceful and to bring those details that interest women's ears.

Sinte's daughter, the Mahto women learned, entertains the trader while her husband pours down drinks. Nor will Hinziwin come out weeping as when Iśna originally sent her to the whiteman. Truly, some persons say that she goes to a certain young trader whether or not Iśna visits the dead-wood shelter.

Napewaśte had covered her face. Not that she sensed any family shame but only that Hinziwin's presence seemed to linger in this village, an invisible barrier between Olepi and herself, something neither one ever will remove. Perhaps Olepi also heard things about this woman he once called wife, but Napewaśte will not know; the Mahto never speaks his heart to her now.

These news-wives next talked of Wiyukcan Mani and her new son. The family plan a naming-ceremony at the next sungazing—or so the mother had said. The father, his voice as unsteady as his legs, rarely said anything reasonable. Truly Wiyukcan Mani yearned for the summer encampment, for the return of her family into the protecting hoop.

Eight, ten days had passed since the newsbearers left the Mahto camp yet the people kept fresh each piece of news. But not Olepi. He refused to talk over that which he had heard; instead he sat alone, reflecting the tribe's embarrassing lack of Shirtmen.

The Pta-lodge had deliberated six, seven winters since the naming of Cetan and Wanapin to the Shirt, almost as if they had not remembered that four men shall wear the Shirt, four otancan in the Titonwan tribe.

Olepi, now among the headmen who decide this honor, had kept his eyes on certain ones who impressed him, most especially Ahbleza's friend Taśunkekokipapi. This Kuya, wearing his father's name proudly, already proved an honor to his relatives. A mild-face young man, Taśunkekokipapi had stood unwavering in front of the enemy and firm alongside the sunpole; the scars of war and peace sat upon his breast. Nor will Iśna influence this man; the Kuya leader had taken most of his band back to the big river, but

Taśunkekokipapi had not gone twice. This young man's camp, not a big one, but certainly he had not gained his following through favor or threat.

Among the Siyo, Olepi saw none who fit the Shirt, Hinyete not more likely to hold together the band than Wacape. A new Wacape—grandson of the original name-owner—had come on the scene, but this one lacked age and distinction. Wanapin—and he already owned the Shirt—seemed the only true sustainer of these Siyo, a band that slowly drifted toward the earth-smoke, campground of the Sicanġu.

But why, Olepi puzzled, will any family drift toward those camps, the meat scarce and the people giving in to the fiery drink. Yet among those Sicanġu lived one man who earned consideration. Makatoźanźan, seeing his people in difficulty, worked to bring back the Sicanġu circle; Makatoźanźan, a man of dignity, a conservative who saw importance in maintaining a tie with the Isanyati, whom he respected as the true-leaders of all Dakotah.

And perhaps they will look at a Mnikooźu whom the people call Hewanźi, a man with the legs to win any race he enters. But certainly Hewanźi has more than fast feet; here, a brave and reasonable man whose peaceful camp reflects his nature.

The Mahto leader knew of two whom the Pta-lodge already considered. One, a man he dismissed altogether. The second a man he opposed. He will agree that Tanaźin retained the strong name he had inherited; his band had gained six families, these eighty Oglalaĥca lodges camping at the horns. Even so, this grandson-relative of him who first held on to the tribal pipe recently had shown a disrespect for tradition. Listening to Zuzueca, the Oglalaĥca leader had begun to depreciate the parent-people living to the east, referring to these Dakotah as Tankala, a camp of little-bigs who demanded that tribesmen either uphold custom or get out of the family circle. Suddenly, Tanaźin had found reason to commend those original Kiyuksa who had walked out, those recalcitrants whose grandsons now claim that to break with custom advances the tribe, that all true Lakotah want change—new ceremonies, a new language, new songs, new patterns.

Perhaps Zuzueca and Tanaźin imagine that they roll

forward the tribal hoop and that they will use 'change' as a stick to keep the thing rolling? But will they not remember that a rolling hoop eventually falls to the ground? And will they not recognize that Kiyuksa and Oglalaȟca perhaps bring down the whole, the oncoming generations losing touch with the old, grandfather and grandson almost like strangers?

And so Olepi knew that never will he approve a Shirt for Tanaźin. But that most gladly he will place this garment over the shoulders of Taśunkekokipapi. And one other man, a Lakotah whom he dares not yet recommend.

This same winter Heyatawin, desiring to reflect her glad heart, decorated with paint or quills everything her fingers touched. She painted bright shapes on the stiff-hide covers and quilled designs on all the soft hides. She put color on the hard flat folders that packed meat and dry berries, and she decorated all her bowl-covers.

She painted the 'whirlwind' pattern on Ahbleza's winter moccasins, a sign of swift-movement-and-out-of-danger. And Ahbleza, lifting his wife's hands to look upon her design, remembered back to the day when he had painted this same pattern—the flying double cross, the graceful swift-fly—on his breast.

The days lengthened but the cold increased, the ground cracking and the frost edging into the lodges. And then Ahbleza saw his wife cutting hard bottoms for old moccasins, mending-the-feet of her new relatives. He saw her going to Kehala's lodge, helping the young mother with her little daughter; he saw her laughing with the young father as one shall joke and laugh with a husband's kinsmen. He observed her good relations with Huśte and with Tonweya, his brother-friend. Truly, he told himself, a more wonderful woman never lived.

Tonweya came visiting this winter but not often, perhaps regarding his presence an intrusion. Heyatawin usually went out of the lodge, leaving the brother-friends to their personal talk. Even so the scout always avoided reference to anything in the past; his speech pertained to the hunts and general tribal affairs. On one occasion Ahbleza had found a gift alongside the place Tonweya had sat, something that warmed the warrior's heart. Apparently the brother-friend had lifted the old wambli-bone whistle along with the vision-pipe from the pile of Ahbleza's belongings on his give-everything-away day, the scout holding onto this wingbone, awaiting the proper moment to give back the meaningful symbol.

Heyatawin, seeing the whistle in Ahbleza's hair, had asked not about the wingbone but about something mean-ingful to herself. "Will my husband say whether he knows who takes the robe that he folds around me on the night a star flies across the sky?"

He answered unhesitatingly: "This one, my wife, I hang on a lonely tree. I return the robe to the mysterious force that brings me my heart's desire."

And the woman, understanding that this man will not permit any different hands upon the robe, raised eyes that filled with thanksgiving.

Once during the cold moons Ahbleza spoke his desire for new paintbrushes, and so Heyatawin boiled the nose bones from his winter-kill until white and clean; next, she split these pieces into small sticks, one for each color he had named.

On a different day Ahbleza found his woman at the edge of camp, digging the hard ground in search of earth colors for his paint sacks. His eyes requested that she come back inside the warm lodge and his gentle touch told that he will not want scratches on her hands. But he said only that the warm moons will soften the earth and so she shall replace more easily the contents of those almost empty paint sacks.

Soon afterwards, using the shoulderbone of pta, she had made him a paint-mixing bowl, her gift a surprise. And he, responding, had pressed his lips to her forehead in an unfamiliar but pleasing caress.

Before the cold melted into the grass, certain Mahto women honored Heyatawin as a woman of skill; they wel-comed her into the Grass-birds, a group of wives who excelled at quilling. They had invited her to a meeting at which different ones had reviewed procedure. And so she had learned that a member, upon finishing a piece of quillwork, shall give a feast at which she displays her ac-complishment. But that they regard this feast-gathering as a contest; the women come together to appraise—or perhaps to dispute—the quiller's skill. When more than one woman exhibits work, they award a prize to the one whom all agree offers the most imaginative design, the most exacting use of quills. But such agreement never comes easily, they said.

"This group owns a dance," spoke up one member; "the gestures mimic a mating grass-bird. At the start each member moves her head forward and back and so identifies the bird ... watch me." She spread out her robe and imitated the grass-bird bobbing for depth perception. Her lips popping, she stamped her feet: "Ohmph, pumph, oumph." Bowing, squatting, strutting, she emitted these sounds in a drumlike voice. Next, a whirring noise rising in her throat, she began to flip the robe; reaching a dizzy whirl, she suddenly leapt up, then dropped gracefully to the ground.

The women trilled loudly and Ḣeyatawin joined in this praise. But the dancer told quickly that they never performed in this manner at their meetings. "Only when the warriors bring in scalps," she said. "At those dances, men-singers who know the grass-bird song drum on their breasts, imitating the noise of the sharptail, the women dancing while the men thump and sing."

Suddenly remembering that Ḣeyatawin had not lived in the Titonwan camps until recently and perhaps had not heard this song, she spoke the phrases for the new member's hearings:

"Wiśahibu, wiśahibu, wiśahibu welo;
Siyo oyate wiśa abuya wacipi welo.
Wiśahibu, bu, bu, wiśahibu, bu, bu,
Wiśahibu welo."

The wife of Ahbleza had memorized as she listened, and so, as a way of showing herself a new but true member of the group, she sang back their song:

"Red sun coming, red sun coming,
red sun coming now;
The sharptails drum up the sun."

Ḣeyatawin's pleasing little performance signaled the meeting into orderliness, the women laying out their quillwork, each piece up for discussion. And so the new member, a silent observer, recognized her need to display a

701

wondrous design if ever she looked for a prize. And this wondrous design shall come not out of her mother's dream but one of her own, not a pattern she inherits but one she shall envision.

Listening closely, Heyatawin tried to discover on what points these women judged a winner. The contestants used the fine belly-quill on moccasins and only the pte-berry for coloring red. And they used berries, not nuts, to color whatever they wanted true-black. As to the stitch they used when quilling on soft hide, none ever knew; these stitches never show.

Returning to her own lodge, Heyatawin considered an entry in the next contest, at the next meeting of the Grass-birds. Above all she wanted to design a baby-carrier, but until she took-on-life, she sat reluctant. She knew that a woman-relative customarily made this baby-gift, but she desired that none but her own hands touch anything that goes to Ahbleza's child. After a while she decided to quill strips for a cover for Ahbleza's war horse, the horse her father had given him. Perhaps she will make this cover a surprise for the husband, hiding her work in Napewaste's lodge and winning the Grass-bird prize before she presents her gift to Ahbleza.

The next day she began to sort quills, wondering whether she had brought enough quills into the new lodge. Her mother, a member of the Suhtai awl-workers, always kept a big supply and she had given generously when her daughter left the family tipi. But Heyatawin saw that belonging to the Grass-birds required many full sacks, quills always on hand.

During this sort-and-count procedure, Heyatawin puzzled why she had not seen Napewaste at the quiller's meeting; certainly not a pair of hands in camp showed more skill. But perhaps the mother of Ahbleza, like the son, preferred not to join any groups.

A discreet cough outside the lodge interrupted the woman, but she gladly welcomed Huste and his wife. She offered meat to her guests, then sent a boy in search of Ahbleza.

The husband came promptly, greeting his uncle respectfully, affectionately. Huste, his manner hinting at mys-

702

tery, asked that the young man go outside and look around back of the lodge. "You will find something," he said.

When Ahbleza had gone out of the tipi, Huśte smiled at Heyatawin. "Stand at the flap," he said; "step forward when your man returns. He will desire that you see something."

And so Heyatawin met her husband as Ahbleza came leading Tatezi. Silently he tied the yellow horse to a lodge stake; he will say nothing until he sat inside the tipi along-side his uncle.

But again at the lodge-fire he remained silent; his eyes revealed more thanks than any spoken phrases.

After a while Huśte began talking: "During your boy-seasons, my nephew, you gentled a child-horse born in my herd and so this one whom you call 'black runner' becomes yours. You grow up and go out looking for horses. One day I see you giving away all your horses. And now I joyfully bring back to you this most important horse."

After a pause, Huśte went on with his story. "Listen and understand: I visit the lame boy's lodge; I talk with him about my own limp. Next I see him taking a step, two, three steps. His grandfather says that he will walk before summer. He will limp but he will walk.

"Next his grandfather tells that the boy desires me for hunka-father; the seer will make this ceremony if I agree. I answer saying that I am glad. I say also that at the cere-mony I will give my name to the boy and take back my old one. He shall become Huśte and again I am Catka.

"Before I go out of the lame boy's lodge, I give him a horse. Seeing my gift, he asks that his grandfather lead up Tatezi. And so he asks that I lead Tatezi to you."

Ahbleza's eyes shone gladness. Certainly he rejoiced at Tatezi's return, but more important, he saw once again that the self-gratifying act which man calls 'giving' sustains the truth: that good means good, good for one, good for each one.

And now the warrior spoke his instant wish: "The horse Tatezi belongs as of now to someone I will see riding safely wherever she goes. In the name of my good uncle I give the horse to the one I call mitawin, my wife."

XII

SUMMER, THE leaves-on-the-trees season; summer, a season of fragrant, juicy, fat moons; summer, a season for thanksgiving.

And who will live this summer more joyfully appreciative than Heyatawin and Ahbleza. Hearing the hunka-song, they remembered their sacred privilege of choice; listening to the generating song, they remembered the circularity of life.

Ahbleza went out after horses but not as a raider; instead he chased those creatures who roamed the sandhills, seeking a second war horse and a second runner; also two horses for traveling. But not again will he keep a big herd: six useful horses, he said, enough for him.

Heyatawin looked after the meat and hides her husband brought back from the summer hunt; joyfully she gifted the have-nots, carrying choice pieces of roast and neatly shaped moccasins to dim eyes and weary feet and to anyone who walked limping. And she made her gifts in the name of Ahbleza's relatives, also Ogle's family.

True, Napewaśte felt a little shy around Heyatawin, but the respect these women bore one another became increasingly apparent; often the young woman made up songs that told of her gladness in the Mahto family, her joy in Ahbleza.

The shining summer ripened and grew old, neither mischief nor a threat of mischief creeping up on the Titonwan campground. But before the fat old moon died, two war parties went out on an avenging, many leaders and one Shirtman expressing disapproval; these headmen had regretted seeing Lakotah warriors go against the Palani to avenge a whiteman's grievance.

True, the wise ones agreed, the Palani occasionally turn their firesticks against the Titonwan now, but these fights concern men of similar nature. So let the whites make up a party of whites, they had advised, if they choose to avenge their thirteen kinsmen whom the Palani kill during a horse-trade.

Olepi had spoken out strongly, the Mahto leader demanding that his warriors stay out of this affair. And Cetan, the Shirtman ever watchful that white traders not bring their barter into any Titonwan camp, warned all bands against any confusing alliance with strangers.

But some Titonwan, hearing that Mnikoożu and Canoni intended to fight alongside the whitemen, started north for the maize-planters' villages. Peśla, the only Mahto going, took a party of seven Siyo, the warrior boasting that he shall reach the center lodge of the Palani and so win those privileges which the Palani award any stranger who makes his way safely to the tribal sanctuary.

Approaching the mud villages, Peśla met a party of Sicangu, each man in the group wearing a white cloth strip around his head. The traders had provided these strips, they told, to designate friendly redmen. But Peśla had scorned the cloth; he entered this contest for personal gain, not as an ally of the whites.

At the start of the fight four hundred Dakotah horsebacks had rushed upon as many Palani horsebacks. Then, after a scattered and noisy encounter—nine Palani killed—the Dakotah chased the maize-planters back inside their mud lodges. But on discovering that the enemy had killed two Canoni and wounded seven, the Dakotah began to mutilate the enemy dead, tearing off arms and legs, dragging these dismembered pieces over the fighting ground and yelling taunts; they schemed to lure the Palani into the open again.

Peśla, losing his chance to strike the enemy, enacted an insult, something to bring out the Palani warriors. Remembering himself as grizzly, he came crawling on hands and feet, snorting and grunting as he approached a dead body; then, using his teeth, he tore out mouthfuls of flesh.

Instantly three, four Palani came running out from between the stalks that surrounded the village. But suddenly they turned, running back to their shelters. For a moment Peśla imagined that his ferocious appearance stopped these men. But then he realized that the sight of three hundred whitemen hurrying toward the villages had scared the enemy into hiding again.

Scrambling back to his own, Peśla jumped horseback; his face dark, he sat quietly alongside the Dakotah who permitted these whitemen their turn at fighting, at inducing the enemy into action.

Nothing happened. The line of whites came to a halt; they stood looking anxiously at bloodstained Dakotah hands, at the pieces of arms and legs that dangled back of certain Dakotah horses.

After a while, from a safe place on a distant hill, the whitemen's big-iron barked. The Dakotah looked for mud lodges to fall in, for Palani to pour out, for the whites to advance in daring manner. But nothing fell and the only movement, a wagging of whitemen's tongues. But perhaps these whites schemed their big attack at dawn?

The Dakotah, choosing to wait and see, now invaded the enemy's maize, cooking and eating, then camping among the stalks.

But the next day, they saw nothing different. Again the whites stood in line, the men occasionally changing position, their leaders arguing, arguing. And then, before the sun climbed down, the whites came begging the Dakotah for food.

And now the Dakotah had seen enough of this ridiculous contest. Lifting aside their loin-covers and shaking their ce in the faces of the whites, they made known their contempt. Soon afterwards they rode off, a group of braves racing out front with eight of the whitemen's horses.

Peśla urged that his party stay on, that they join the Palani in a fight against the whites, but the Siyo saw foolishness in attempting a surprise attack. Most Dakotah already started back, the Canoni carrying their injured across the big river, the Mnikooźu and Sicanǧu waving three Palani scalps and leading six mules, these creatures loaded with maize.

But Peśla had nothing to wave or lead; nor had he put a foot inside the Palani camps. And now his memory of a previous visit and an impressive loot determined his choice. Let his warriors go; he stays.

The bands had separated, the people looking for winter campsites when Peśla rejoined the Mahto. He came gloating, his mouth full of boast. He alone had entered the Palani villages and discovered the enemy's losses. He alone knew that the big-iron's round ball had killed a principal man, also warriors, women, and children, whose bodies the Palani had put underground. And he alone knew that the enemy had sneaked out at night while the whites hung around talking, talking, talking.

Yet none had witnessed Peśla's claims and so he dared not dance his bravery or look for rewards. Or even mention that he had made a second entry into the villages after everyone had gone, Palani and whitemen. But he shall display his loot and let the people imagine whatever they will. And Lowansa, his wife these five winters, shall hear each detail of his story. He shall talk within his tiyośpaye about his scheme which results in his bringing back a mule, maize, a string of shells, two robes, a knife, a stone bowl, and two horn ladles. And he shall flaunt an old woman's scalp in the face of Winu, the Palani girl he had captured during a different attack on these same villages. And if these many mouths carry his story around the winter camp, perhaps something shall come of this flow of talk.

But Peśla had not sat prepared for a visit from Cetan, the Shirtman bringing the long-stem, compelling a truthful smoke. Cetan desired to learn that which occurred after the Dakotah had withdrawn and the whitemen had stayed. What manner of meeting took place?

Peśla, pleased that his story had reached an esteemed ear, touched the pipe and then recited the e 's of his lingering.

After the Dakotah rode away, he told, the head akicita in one Palani village accepted his offer of a trade; they will give two horn ladles and a string of shells for Peśla's bow and news of the whitemen's scheme. The Palani, holding on to the Lakotah's bow, had seen nothing dangerous about Peśla's presence inside their mud lodges. Instead they had regarded him as someone helpful; they had invited him to sit at the peace talk which the whitemen had preferred to more fighting.

At this talk Peśla learned that the iron balls had killed Iśtahota, principal man of the Palani tribe for seventeen winters. Why, then, these people prepared a pipe for the whitemen and agreed to return whatever things their young men had sneaked away from the winter traders, he, Peśla, had not understood. But he had observed that not all whitemen touched the pipe, two angry men demanding back much more than the Palani had taken. And so the meeting suddenly had broken up, firesticks popping.

The Palani, back inside their earth villages, had experienced an uneasy night, their leaders puzzling whether or not to abandon their mud shelters. When finally the Palani had asked that Peśla speak, he had warned the maize-growers of many difficult days: the whites intended to fire their villages, to drive out and kill their women and children with the same big noise that had killed Iśtaȟota.

After this speech Peśla had noticed that the Palani looked at him suspiciously. And so he had sneaked out of their lodges, hiding himself and his horse opposite the villages, where he had watched, taking care that neither whites nor maize-planters observed him.

Everything had happened as he wished; the Palani had left their mud villages during the night, and after two more days, the whites had gone. Now, quiet everywhere and the tongue of sand empty in front of the Palani villages, he had seen his chance to enter these villages as an enemy, a Titonwan who comes in alone to loot and to destroy their dwelling place.

Approaching the earth mounds, he had heard yapping; the Palani had not taken all their dogs. But he had heard also a wail and, following this sound-trail, had discovered an old woman. Her legs oozed a thin line of blood, mud splatters darkened her face, and her hair crawled.

She had not noticed his presence; her dull red eyes gazed but one direction; she stared at a hollow wherein lay a dead man, his face up, his robe open. She dragged herself across ground to a place alongside the man's remains, perhaps using his dead-stiffness to relieve a crazy-making grief.

Next thing, a cawing bird had flown down onto the grass mat. Peśla had grabbed and killed the bird, roasting the meat at the old woman's fire-place. Afterwards, weary of her wails, he had used a club to crack open the woman's head.

In the same earth mound he had found those items which he had packed on a stubborn horse, a braying horse who perhaps once belonged to the whites. But before riding away, he had fanned the embers of his cooking fire into a tall blaze, the fire big enough to catch on to the wood inside the mud lodge, perhaps to spread out to the next mud lodge. And the next and the next.

Far out on the plain, he had looked back at smoke, many clouds of smoke hanging above these Palani villages. And he had known why this smoke. "But exactly where the Palani tribe go after they sneak out the night before, I will not know. Nor will I know exactly where the whitemen go."

Peśla had spoken. And the Shirtman, silent, had gone from the warrior's lodge to the edge of the traveling camp. Here, sitting alone in the dusk, he reflected the gains and losses in this encounter, not in terms of that which had happened to the arrogant Peśla but relative to that which will happen if ever Lakotah—the whiteman's influence prevailing—start fighting Lakotah. In this instance the white traders had persuaded certain Lakotah warriors to help avenge a mutual enemy, but in the next fight perhaps Palani or Psa ride alongside whitemen who seek revenge on Lakotah. Or perhaps one band of Lakotah join the whitemen in attacking a different band of Lakotah. And when different tribes, different bands, begin to side with the whiteman, who really will lose his blood?

Stunned that he shall discover such thoughts, Cetan reviewed everything he had heard about this 'mysterious messenger,' the whiteman. For all these seasons, the Lakotah had regarded the whites as a small group of water-travelers who live without women, as hairy, smelly paleskins with a zeal for talk. Yet rumors had reached the plain which told of whitemen with wives and big families, these people living in wood and stone dwellings and making rivers wherever they wanted a waterway. Some Lakotah claimed that tribesmen who visited the whiteman's villages colored their stories to impress those Lakotah who never travel east. Why, then, will everyone who goes to the place of sunrise report back the same amazing story? Who, then, dares speak of these whites as mischievous spirits whom the Lakotah stone-dreamers will keep away if ever they become a real nuisance?

What nature of man will make talking-signs on leaves as a way to reveal thoughts? And more, create the leaves that carry those talking-signs. What nature of man makes that which traders call cloth, call glass, call wagon?

But if the Lakotah keeps close contact with the white-man, who will lose his identity?

People of different natures exist content only when they stay out of each other's way. Even people of like nature get along only when they stay out of each other's way. Such understanding governs the Lakotah; hanta yo, get out of my way. The grandfathers say so, all the grandfathers back to the beginning say so.

But will a similar rule govern the whiteman? Or will this wondrous tribe soon spread out on the grasses, people of different natures suddenly in conflict? And if so, what thing will the winners win? What thing will the losers lose?

The moon sat in the sky, waiting for night; Cetan sat in the dusk, waiting for answers.

XIII

THE TREMBLING trees again stood deep in broken leaves, the summer dead at their feet. And so none will sense surprise on awakening to frost on the tipi covers.

The young men will lie between robes pretending sleep while they wait for the sun's yellow rays to make trickles of the frost and warm the air above the Mahto camp on lone-woman creek. But not all young men. Two had gone out in this cold, meeting the stream, plunging in together as in their boy-seasons when the people called one Peta and one Mahtociqala.

This meeting at the creek, nothing prearranged; nor had these two met often during the past two seasons, Tonweya visiting the brother-friend's lodge only rarely since the day Ahbleza made Heyatawin his wife.

"I smell the sky." Tonweya stepped out of the creek, using his hands to rub dry. "I smell the sky," he repeated, swaying his head, sniffing like a grizzly. "Or perhaps I smell earth. Either one," he smiled, "the day smells almost as good as meat."

The warrior responded gladly to the hint: "Bring your bowl, misun, and eat with me. My wife will appreciate a glimpse of your handsome face."

Each one now flipped his loin-cover over the string at his waist and started toward camp. Approaching the lodges, Ahbleza sensed satisfaction at the many clean tipi covers, mostly new covers but even the old ones stretched neatly around their frames, flaps erect and fragrant smoke rising, not a cover with rips and soil as in different bands.

The brother-friends passed those enclosures wherein the people staked their principal horses; again the warrior felt grateful. Old men and boys had cut branches thick as an arm to make a surround which also provided winter-feed; nibbling the bark kept these creatures in shining color— yellow, ordinary, or naturally spotted. And in a near-distant grove, many red horses, ties on their feet to prevent wandering, fine reds who offered proof of raids on the Psa. Truly, wherever he looked Ahbleza saw remarkable horses—war horses, runners, meat-packers, and ones useful to women and children; horses, he remembered, a manifestation of tribal power.

Coming upon a group of children, Tonweya picked up a child who roved the campground, a little one who, losing her blood-parents, belonged in the safekeeping of the whole.

Instantly many young arms encircled the scout's legs, each child teasing for a ride on Tonweya's shoulders. He gladly obliged until the growing, clamoring line overwhelmed him. Grabbing a handful of twigs, he tossed the wood into the crowd: "Whoever catches a long stick, I will swing onto my shoulders."

Ahbleza stood watching, the warrior aware that the little boys sensed an awe for him that they will not sense toward Tonweya. But he felt only gladness at the scout's affable, fun-liking nature which attracts these young persons.

Moving on together, Ahbleza spoke his observations: "My father leads a strong camp. I count and so I know that the Oglalahca increase to eighty lodges and that the Kiyuksa raise the same. But the seventy-and-five lodges who follow Olepi lack nothing; the Mahto band enjoys meat, shelter, warmth, pleasure. Two winters and none dies, starves, complains. Something good favors these villages."

"And something favors you, cinye," Tonweya answered. "You start anew, owning nothing; now you have plenty. Not only what you desire in bows and horses but a lodge with a good wife sitting next to you. And I hear more than one saying that the eyes of the principals in this tribe linger upon you. They say that the headmen consider you. . . . What happens, my brother . . . ?"

Ahbleza stood, his breathing uneven, his eyes burning into the path ahead. But suddenly as the change had come, the strangeness disappeared; the warrior walked calmly as before, his face serene.

"Misun," Ahbleza said quietly, "I understand something. You open my eyes and so I relate my instant-vision to you: I will dance at the sunpole next summer. This day I pledge the sungazing."

The scout permitted himself a small cry of amazement. Only moments before, the brother-friend spoke of a camp wherein none suffered, neither death nor starving nor mischief here; so why will Ahbleza dance thanks as if he recently escapes something tragic?

The warrior put his hand on Tonweya's shoulder. "I puzzle you. Now hear me. As you say, something favors me. I survive trials which the leaders impose upon me along with the one I impose upon myself. I am grateful and so I shall demonstrate this gratefulness. I will dance gazing-at-the-sun and in view of the tribe."

The scout said nothing.

"Now hear something more, misun. Perhaps in seasons ahead I shall lead this Mahto band. And so I prepare. A man who sees himself advising the whole people needs to recognize the meaning in every ceremony the ancients devise.

"I go naked, yet I learn nothing about suffering; instead I discover the true meaning of the giveaway.

"I experience that which appears humbling; instead I discover the greatness of my pride.

"Perhaps at the pole I shall discover the real meaning in the sungazing, something the original grandfathers intend that I discover. But whatever happens, certainly I shall discover something more about myself."

712

Ahbleza removed his hand from the scout's shoulder but he stood waiting. And so Tonweya spoke that which he had pondered even as he heard the warrior's message.

"In what manner," he said slowly, "will one man ever see for the whole people?"

"They call you scout," Ahbleza answered easily, "meaning that you protect the whole people. Already you learn in your work the way a man accomplishes this thing. Now I desire to learn this same thing in my work."

The warrior moved toward the lodge, but Tonweya had not followed. And so after two, three steps Ahbleza returned. Standing alongside the scout, he spoke firmly: "Hear me. I will gaze-at-the-sun grateful that the bond between I and you—the bond of a dreaming-pair—remains sacred, something neither I nor you—yet—breaks."

The warrior walked away and Tonweya turned toward his mother's lodge. Here he will pick up his meat bowl and arrange his hair before he appears at Heyatawin's tipi.

But all the while the scout sat brushing and tying his hair, he puzzled why Ahbleza imagines that something or someone threatens their bond. True, he will not visit with the brother-friend as in those seasons before Ahbleza mates, but certainly he respects the bond and remembers most of the dream. Perhaps if he visits Wanaġi and reviews this vision, this picture he and Ahbleza see as with one pair of eyes, he will understand more about the mystery they call 'dreaming-pair.'

Ahbleza, bending to enter, saw three persons inside his tipi. Heyatawin sat on her knees ladling soup into meat bowls while an old Śahiela woman watched from her humble but respected place at the opening. The third one here— his father.

Olepi had come at Heyatawin's invitation, the woman often bringing together son and father for meat and smoke and talk. But she never left the tipi while these two talked. Raised in the Śahiela manner, she sat prepared to voice a woman's point of view in tribal concerns. And Ahbleza had seen his father surprisingly attentive; Olepi had referred to Heyatawin more than once as an alert and sensible person.

The wife had not lifted her eyes on Ahbleza's entrance, but she heard the husband's announcement as if he spoke for her ears alone. And certainly she understood why this man chose to dance at the sunpole. But she also felt a small pain of regret; his vow, she heard him saying, commences at the next sunrise.

This frosty moon, then, this hard-face moon will separate her body from Ahbleza's body, and not until trees make leaves again will she feel a husband's touch; not until sacred-grass blooms and they raise a sunpole and Ahbleza dances gazing-at-the-sun—not until after all these things occur—will she lie alongside him and experience the joy he gives her body.

But suddenly, holding on to the ladle and filling bowls as before, she recognized that which she shall make happen: when these next eight cold moons finally give way to warmth she, like the new season, shall have come into fatness and bloom; while the husband sits keeping his vow, his wife shall sit growing his child.

And so this same night she will not await Ahbleza's coming to her robe; she will go to his. Nor will she conceal the meaning of this night, a night to take the place of all nights and days until he sleeps against her again.

But before going to his robe, she will consider her sister, the one who accepts Ahbleza, the one they agree on asking into the lodge once Heyatawin takes-on-life. Since a father never visits his unborn child, Heyatawin had viewed the coming of Zitkala as something to provide release for the man's most strong impulse and to fulfill her sister's own natural desire. But Ahbleza's sungazing vow made a difference; he shall abstain from visiting a woman's robe until the day they see him dance. Even so, Heyatawin will ask that Ahbleza send for Zitkala before ice covers the trees. He shall care for her in all ways but one, and she, living close to him, will discover his temperament and so prepare herself as his second wife.

But before ever Ahbleza takes this second woman, Heyatawin will have a child for him, Heyatawin forever the true-wife. And let his seed, she told herself, bring forth a son.

The two had come together in new joy this night, a joy devoid of any apprehension. The sun will light many skies, the woman remembered, before Ahbleza touches a weapon, his vow permitting neither raid nor hunt. And so she dares envision an infant whose father sees him born and growing; and so she dares open herself fully to this man, all of him pouring into all of her.

"In one night, my wonderful husband," she whispered, "I and you make a hero for all people who ever live, for ones whose grandfathers not yet put foot upon the grass."

And now the mystery of growing-seed, a privilege that she, the woman, inherits; an honor that she, the woman, fulfills. And let things happen so that, while Ahbleza prepares for his sacred ceremony, she Heyatawin, prepares for hers.

XIV

THE SUN glared down fiercely on untrampled snow, but members of the Pta-lodge had seen reason for an assembly before next summer's encampment; they had decided to meet during this weak-eyes moon at the Oglalaĥca winter camp. And so thirty headmen, darkening the skin around their eyes against painful reflection off the dazzling white ground, had started out from their respective villages for one of the most important councils they ever shall attend.

Thirty Pta-men—leaders past and present—intended to enact changes in the old pattern, in the original scheme-for-living as determined before the people came onto the plain.

These principals, recognizing that more than five thousand Lakotah, Dakotah shall live as a single hoop on the plain this coming summer, had agreed on revisions wherever insufficiency occurred, on improvements wherever the need had become obvious. Different ones among these thirty already had accepted the call for change, but until the Pta spoke as one voice, everything waited.

The Oglalaȟca had raised a big red tipi for this assemblage of competents, and now these Pta-men sat on folded robes listening to old Wambli Okiye—headman among headmen—review that which had led to this unprecedented council.

Until now, he said, the bands regard the great summer hoop as essentially Oglalaȟca, Mahto, Siyo, Kiyuksa; until now Sicaŋġu alone with Mnikoożu and other Canoni appear as irregular visitors. And until now the governing power—also the akicita power—sits in the hands of the original four bands. But this next summer, the messengers report, all Dakotah—but the Isanyati—come to live on the plain, come seeking a campsite in the summer circle, each band raising a Pta-lodge of their own.

Hewanżi comes, bringing his tiyośpaye and perhaps all Mnikoożu. And where these Mnikoożu go, the Itazipicola and other Canoni go. All Sicaŋġu come, more than three hundred tipi, and many Wiciyela say they will come; will not their warriors along with Titonwan warriors feast on Palani maize after they scare this enemy underground? Certainly they want to share in the sungazing-thanksgiving ceremonies on the plain.

And so they will come, more than five thousand persons, one big, big circle. Now let the headmen recall kinsman-rules, the hunka way-of-life, the tie that binds these allied ones, this Dakotah, Lakotah family, from the beginning; let the headmen enact only such changes as will enhance or expand the original scheme.

Wambli Okiye had spoken, his speech setting forth the principle for this convention. And now different members, in turn, voiced whatever they will have the council ponder.

The naming of Shirtmen had come up at once, someone proposing that all Pta-lodges come together during the next encampment and choose two more persons to sit alongside Cetan and Wanapin. But a second speaker had wondered whether this many Pta-men ever shall agree on one new Shirtman, not to mention two, three. Why not, instead, two Pta-men from each Pta-lodge forming a group to deliberate, to select the Shirts? Certainly ten, twelve persons will reach agreement more quickly than sixty, seventy.

But a third speaker abruptly announced that he will not

716

accept quickness as a basis for reaching agreement on who receives the Shirt. Why not wait for sixty, seventy to agree? A Shirtman acquires the status of hunka-relative to each one in the tribe. One error in judgment—one Shirtman who falls short of the trust—and the whole people suffer.

Olepi spoke next, and when this Mahto sat again, sounds of approval filled the red tipi. Why not intensify the purpose of the headman-lodge, he had asked; why not keep always within their own Pta-lodge perhaps seven itancan who carry one obligation: to select the Shirtman.

And why limit these Shirts to four? Certain ones refer to the Titonwan as 'witantanpi'; so let the Witantanpi display this pride and Shirt as many deserving men as they see fit.

But now Hinyete rose, saying that he opposes the presentation of more than two Shirts in any one Titonwan band. Why risk seeing any one band become a 'Shirtwearers band,' a band who owns-the-people?

The Siyo's reasoning made sense, but the assembly listened for yet more voices; whatever decisions they reach at this meeting, each man told himself, shall influence not only the Titonwan order of things but shall specify the obligation they will place upon any bands that take a place in this wondrous hoop.

On the fifth day at sundown the council sat in agreement as to the Shirt. They will select seven from among their own members, seven Titonwan Pta-men who henceforth, speaking as one mouth, shall name the Shirt-owners, not more than two Shirts in any one band. And the council shall grant these important seven a second power; henceforth this group shall appoint the four deciders—the wakicunsa—for each summer's encampment.

And so the Pta-lodge—originally the true-counciling body—now became the true-governing body. And with helpers in two places: those persons to whom the seven give a Shirt-for-life and those persons to whom the seven loan a seasonal-shirt.

But this same council of Pta-men will not ignore those Dakotah whose lodges widen the family circle. Instead they shall wait until the people form next summer's hoop and then, all headmen in one meeting place, they will propose

717

that two, three, four—but never, never more than four—from out of each generation of the Dakotah, Lakotah family own Shirt and Legs of similar design, the tribe looking at the wearer as they look at a peak that rises above the snow hills, a peak that feels the clouds, reflects the sun.

Perhaps some persons wondered whether ever they shall see even one man with the vision, the enduring, the truth for this most high place within the great-family coming onto the plain. But perhaps that which happens once shall happen twice; perhaps once again someone similar to Waspaśa shall live, someone whom the old people remember as a leader of ten, twenty thousand Dakotah, everyone—everyone—calling this man 'otancan.' Perhaps.

And now, the counciling into the sixth day, Cetan—one of the two who wore the Shirt—stood before these headmen making known his wish to return the Shirt.

A Shirtman shall have the help of a vision, they had told him, a great vision that brings together in him as Shirt-owner all powers in and of the tribe. But Cetan saw himself this winter without a true use to his people; certain ones had opposed his vision, rejected his enlightenment. And so why use his shoulders to carry the tribal good?

For a while the wise ones sat silent; apparently Cetan will not remember that a leader leads if but one man follows and that an example of good remains an example of good if but one man recognizes this thing. Then, regretfully, Wambli Okiye signaled for Cetan to lift the Shirt from his own shoulders; they respect his choice.

The council sat quiet on the seventh day, the men aware that when all exert effort in the same direction, one and all arrive at the same answer. And so each man listened for the familiar-voice which speaks nothing but truth.

At sunrise on the eighth day Wambli Okiye, hearing agreement within the lodge, stood to speak seven names. Next, he sent around the pipe. And so he saw each man touching the stem, each one confirming these seven.

The old one had named himself and five from among the Pta-men. And the seventh man, a seer whom they shall regard as an honorary member of the Pta-lodge.

For many winters the members had considered bringing a wakanhca—a true-prophet—into their lodge. True, they never encouraged the voice of a seer in council but they had remembered that a certain old, old seer originally defined a Shirtman and that the seer here this day had given name-and-ceremony to the Pta-lodge. They also recalled that this seer whom they now honor had earned a warrior's feather for killing a grizzly. But the true reason for inviting Wanaġi to this meeting: he demonstrates his power for good.

Season upon season the headmen had observed Wanaġi, and never once had they lost respect for his ways. True, they had seen him dissenting as a young man, disdaining advice about not meddling with the 'wakan,' bumping his head when he went outside his reach. But they had noticed that he never made the same error twice; apparently Wanaġi had learned, while making youth's journey, that when a man requires knowledge of the unknown, a teacher always appears.

Certain ones said that Wanaġi owned a stone-song, that he had experienced the stone-vision and so becomes wakanłica. But none ever heard Wanaġi say so or ever saw him demonstrate this amazing power, this perilous power. The people knew only that Wanaġi owned powers which he used for good. And so Wanaġi, as one of seven itancan who select the life-Shirts and the seasonal-shirts, will act for the good of the tribe.

Wambli Okiye had named another Mahto—Icabu—for itancan. But he will not name Olepi; Olepi stays as he desires to stay: warrior-leader, symbol of the Dakotah who comes onto the plain, symbol of a people who hold on to something old, claim something new. Olepi, the real-Mahto.

Before the hazy sun reached middle sky on the eighth day of counciling, the members left the red tipi, going into different lodges in the Oglalahca villages, various families prepared to feast and entertain these men for three, four days. But the seven itancan returned to the red tipi after one day's rest; sitting together they pondered the granting of Shirts and the place of ceremony.

And now, the whole body reconvening, the members sat listening to Wambli Okiye announce a decision.

They offer the Shirt, he told, to a man born into the original Titonwan and to a man choosing this tribe. Each of these men seeks and finds vision in his youth; each man

719

demonstrates that he owns spirit-help. And each one prepares for this day.

The seven itancan recognize these two, he went on, as persons of restraint, two who strongly approve or strongly disapprove but who never despise or condemn.

One of these two, he said next, achieves the Shirt in the season of his sungazing-vow; the second man, in a season when he sits firm against leading his village into difficulty on the muddy-water.

Wambli Okiye raised his voice: "Say to your child, my friends, 'look-at-him'; next say to yourselves 'look-at-him.' See Ahbleza. See Tašunkekokipapi. Look at these two and you shall see man-iyotanyapi, the true-Shirtwearer."

Perhaps even before the old man spoke, the Pta-members had known whom the itancan will name. But one man, whatever his apparent calm, had sat heart pounding until his, the father's, ears had heard the name Ahbleza.

On the fifteenth and final day of council, the itancan revealed that the Shirting of Ahbleza and Tašunkekokipapi shall occur on the sacred trail which circles the black hills, at the same campground where the Pta-lodge had originated. And when the next moon reaches half—the redgrass-appearing moon—each band shall break winter camp and move in that direction. Between now and the folding of winter lodges, Wanaǧi shall make the Shirt they intend placing on Ahbleza's shoulders; the seer requests this honor.

And now the council broke off, the Pta-men returning to their villages, walking over bare wet ground, a hint of tender grass waiting beneath the fast-melting snow.

Wanaǧi shall make Ahbleza's Shirt, they say, but will they know to what extent Wanaǧi already prepares?

Two, three seasons in the past the sacred-man had asked Ogle and Hinhan for two skins, hide of the elusive curly-horn, dewclaws intact. And he had asked the singer Winkte for strips of quillwork, most careful quillwork. And he had asked many different persons—women and men—for long strands of their hair. Wanaǧi had asked, knowing that one day he shall sit in a lodge fragrant with sweetgrass smoke, tying together those two skins, fastening on quillstrips, wrapping the tips of many hairs, attaching these strands to a Shirt which the headmen shall award Ahbleza.

Ahbleza had not pondered why the Pta-lodge members acted in an unusual manner this winter, why they had traveled on snow, Wanaǧi in their company, to meet someplace with other Pta-members. Different things concerned the warrior who lived his pledge, and his wife who grew their child.

Ahbleza once again had picked up his paintbrushes. Acting on a thought that Heyatawin voiced, he had decided to picture the sacred ceremonies, not in the manner of a winter count or for general viewing but as a demanding work in detail and color; he looked for his efforts to uncover truths he not yet recognized in choosing-relatives, vision-seeking, spirit-keeping, sungazing. And never had a season seemed more fitting for this work. Most days he stayed inside his own lodge or went to see Wanaǧi, the two sitting in the quiet of smoke and thought, occasionally breaking their silence for talk and meaning.

Neither wife nor husband encouraged visitors, nor had Ahbleza asked that Zitkala come. Heyatawin, taking-on-life, properly became a woman silent and reflective. And Ahbleza knew to resist all impulses, his pledge permitting neither sudden laughter nor sudden anger nor any quick steps, nothing that perhaps entices a lurking mischief.

And yet, for all the restraints, Heyatawin managed a cheerful lodge; she praised Ahbleza's drawings, schemed little pleasures, and now, the winter moons waning, she again talked concerning Zitkala.

"My sister understands, my husband, that you will not treat with her as wife until after the thanks-offering ceremony. But she will use these moons to discover things about you, to prepare herself for a place at your side.

"I and my sister bear each other much fondness; her presence here will give me a woman-companion and brighten the lodge. Her soft, pretty ways will not disturb you and I remember her cooking as something most tasteful.

"And speaking of food, know that none in this lodge will starve. Before you put aside your arrows, I stuff the meat folders. And your brother-friend brings meat. Even now I see where I grow too fat."

Ahbleza looked at this woman whose body rounded at the middle, the unborn child four, five moons now. "I like to feel this bulge under your gown," he said, patting her gently. Then, touching her hand, he spoke that which she waited to hear: "You persuade me, my wife; I will send for your sister."

The Sahiela lodge that sheltered Zitkala, her young sister, and parents stood a half-day's walk from the Mahto village along a wind-swept path. But her father and a scout accompanied the young woman to her new dwelling place, each man leading a pack horse, these horses and the bundles they carried, something for Zitkala to keep or give away, whichever she chose. And so she arrived at Heyatawin's lodge—proud, excited, and a little shy.

Almost at once this lodge took on a quiet gaiety; passers-by again heard soft laughter rising up with the smoke. For one thing, Tonweya had become a frequent visitor.

Custom permitted the scout a comfortableness with these two women and the role of a protector in this lodge. But Tonweya availed himself of neither exaggerated ease nor any familiarity toward these sisters. He saw Heyatawin so proudly Ahbleza's woman and he recognized the second sister as someone yet uncertain of her new position.

As for himself, he lived content without a wife. He enjoyed the company of women but not enough to let one secure a hold on him. He appreciated the look of woman in the same way that he appreciated the flowing cloud, sun dancing on snow, a hushed-wing in flight. But now he began looking forward to each visit in Heyatawin's lodge.

Once, on Tonweya's arrival, the sisters sat playing tasiha unpi, the footbone game, a stunt that called for four of those fingerlike bones they cut from pronghorn, the four strung on sinew, an awl attached to the opposite tip of the string. The scout had watched each woman as she took her turn, swinging the bones forward and up, the awl aimed toward a hole on the side of any one bone but more often caught in a loop where the bones joined. Then suddenly Heyatawin had caught the top bone, top hole.

Cheering approval, Tonweya revealed that he had learned the game secretly as a boy. "I see my sister and her friends play and I want to learn but I know that if I play a girl's game they will laugh and call me woman. And so I go into hiding where I try my skill." He glanced toward Ahbleza, eyes twinkling. "Recently I see girls and boys playing this game openly but I am uncertain whether a man my age. . . " He took the string out of Heyatawin's hand. "Laugh if I amuse you."

Tossing up the bones, he caught the third bone, second hole.

The scout smiled at Heyatawin's trilling. "Usually I catch this third bone," he said, "if I catch anything at all. And I know why. The Titonwan name these four bones," he informed the women, "and this third one they call 'ptepazo,' honoring the grasshopper who points out pte. I scout the herds and so I catch ptepazo on the plain. And on this awl." He gave a chuckling laugh. "But I use two hands in this game while you hold awl and bones in one. Teach me."

Heyatawin showed him and then Ahbleza asked to try. Soon Tonweya proposed that they make teams, the two women against Ahbleza and himself, each side betting as they please.

They had played that day and the next and the next, and then the game became a real contest, the women committed to making ceremonial moccasins for the men if the men had won most of the counting-sticks before the village moved out for the summer hoop.

But these four played not only tasiha unpi; hanpa ahpe, the moccasin game, also fit into the contest. And so they alternated; two, three evenings of footbones, then an evening of guessing under which of four moccasins the hider had placed the tight little ball of pte-hair.

"I enjoy things here," Tonweya said one night when the four stopped play for a bowl of soup. "I, who never sit long in any tipi, stay on and on. And I am grateful that my brother-friend keeps two women instead of one or I never will know the fun of this contest."

"Or you find yourself a wife," Ahbleza answered quickly.

Heyatawin had laughed softly, but Zitkala, unsmiling, had turned away her face.

This same night Tonweya, going out Heyatawin's tipi, turned to look upon this lodge not with the eyes of a scout watchful for danger sneaking through the dark but with the eyes of an envious friend. The frozen cold beyond Heyatawin's lodge seemed all the more cold after the warmth he had encountered inside that lodge. The next moment he lifted his eyes to the long shafts of wavering color that played across the sky, his heart one with this beauty in the night. And then he looked upon the star-people, contemplating these mysterious suns of the black sky. What message will they send him, these far-distant relatives of the great yellow eye? Will they say that he also, sits far-distant and cold, denying some woman his warmth? But what woman, what woman among all he knows shall put fire to his heart and so make him warm?

He looked yet another little while into the above, at all the twinkling eyes that claimed his glance. And then he smiled back at the whole; he will not desire any one of these wonderful, shining sky-things more than he desires another. And so he felt about women.

XV

NOT ALL Titonwan came for the Shirting ceremony. Those Kuya with Iśna on the muddy river had agreed on the foolishness of travel under a misleading moon, one day clear and warm and the next, a whirling snow. True, a rumor had reached the river that a Kuya will receive a great honor when the bands meet on the sacred path, but most persons on the mud-water regarded the rumor as something un-likely; certainly the stumbling, red-eyed Iśna will not earn honors. Who, then, among the true-Kuya, among Iśna's following, will they name?

As for the Kiyuksa, they had disagreed as usual, per-haps one hundred persons deciding to come, the band kept a Pta-lodge of their own, six itancan whom they esteemed. Tawitko, nephew to Zuzueca, had favored a separate gov-erning power for the Kiyuksa, and, stepping on his uncle as if he stepped on a dead leaf, he had maneuvered himself into a position of influence, a level above the leader's own son.

Many Kiyuksa had displayed open disrespect for Zuzueca ever since those days he began hurling insinuations at Mahto and Śiyo. But the Kiyuksa warriors hinted that this meddling concern with different bands came about purposely, a scheme to distract. The old man, they said, wants none of his Kiyuksa noticing that he needs Tawitko on every trail or he wanders off the path; something damages either his eyes or his head.

And for some reason Tabloka, the favored son of Zuzueca, had not responded when he saw that they pushed his father aside. Different ones had answered this fact, saying, "Tabloka never knows what goes on; he cares only for sneaking wives away, hiding out from husbands." But those men who had watched Tabloka club down an excited member of his own war party had not said so.

Peśla, hearing the talk among his Kiyuksa companions, had an answer: "My friends, perhaps you and not Zuzueca lose your eyes, twist your thoughts. Why will you imagine that the warrior-son of Zuzueca hides out like a mating pta? Look more closely and you will see that he wisely gathers relatives and so prepares for an important place. For the present, he apparently keeps out of his father's quarrels."

But these Kiyuksa gave Peśla a wondering look; truly this Mahto has a big mouth. "Or," said one man afterwards, "this Mahto looks for a wife among Tabloka's sisters, someone who will bring him into the powerful family as something more than brother to one of Tabloka's wives."

The Tatanka-itancan announced their Shirting day quietly; rolling up the sides of the center lodge one cool but sunny morning, they signaled for the people to come and see something.

Soon the Titonwan stood crowding around—Oglalahca, Mahto, Śiyo, perhaps one hundred Kiyuksa, half as many Kuya—the brightness of a climbing sun crinkling old eyes, squinting shut the young.

Now someone shouted; heads turned.

Four horsebacks came racing toward center, red and yellow paint decorating face and arms of these clubmen, red and yellow quill-strips decorating mane and tail of their mounts. Then most abruptly these four stopped, horses and men still as stone.

The people, turning back to the lodge, saw the Pta-men rising as one, this move a signal that two clubmen shall jump down and lead their horses, that they shall push through the crowd until they reached certain persons.

Many eyes in the crowd stayed on the center lodge; different ones followed the clubmen. But all the people made sound, a gentle, wondering sound.

Ahbleza had looked neither at horses nor center lodge; his eyes had sought the distant ledges of the black hills, where, they say, dreams take shape and a man shall see the truth. But even as he viewed the ancient and glistening stone, he had sensed those eyes that searched for him over the heads of the crowd. And he had felt Wanaġi's heart reaching out to him, but whether with sympathy or in joy, he not yet knew.

But now the crowd moved back to make space around him, a clubman's horse suddenly in front, the clubman signaling that this Mahto shall mount.

And so the ceremony will affect him? Something Wanaġi knows about but says nothing? Perhaps the Shirting ceremony? They will Shirt him?

True, they Shirt him; here and now they Shirt Ahbleza. For what different reason will Wanaġi stand among the headmen of the Pta-lodge, the Shirt in his hands? For what different reason will Olepi stand next to the seer and sign that Ahbleza ride forward?

Leaping onto the horse, the warrior reared this creature; he posed as on the day he had whirled to meet the eyes of the crowd who had seen him disperse the Psa.

And now the crowd poured out laughter, the sort of laughter that keeps people in touch whenever the unusual occurs, a great cheer slowly rising out of this laughter, shaking the air.

Now these same wonderful cheers as Taśunkekokipapi rode forward, a different seer holding out the Kuya's Shirt, a different man—Hinyete—acting as sponsor.

Out in his scout's nest Tonweya's ears had caught the joyful shouts that bounced off the butte, his heart glad for whatever good thing happened on the sacred path. But he had not known for whom they cheered, or why.

And now Wambli Okiye stepped front, the good old man appointed speaker for his affair. "My relatives, my friends," he began, "you call the Shirtman 'owner-of-the-people.' And you know that whatever a man owns, he takes care of, he protects.

"This Shirt symbolizes those things that you as a people most highly esteem, everything that you as a people recognize as good. And whatever the people recognize, they own. And so the people own the Shirt.

"Understand that the people, holding on to the good, protect the Shirt, even as the owner, holding on to the good, protects the people.

"Understand that he who puts on this Shirt wears a pride that belongs also to the people, to the one and to the whole."

He signaled for the two to dismount, for Ahbleza and Taśunkekokipapi to stand ready to accept the Shirt.

Receiving the Shirt from Wanaǧi's hands, Wambli Okiye now put the Shirt over Ahbleza's shoulders. "My son," the Pta-man spoke for all to hear, "keep control over the power that gains you this Shirt. Resist whoever, whatever, tries to distract you. Ignore those persons who compare you with different ones, and avoid those persons who speak of limits to that which a man dares achieve. You belong neither to the imitators nor the impeders."

Olepi, sitting under the Pta-lodge cover along with all headmen, now heard Wambli Okiye name the most difficult demand on a Shirtman.

"Deny yourself anger, my son, even when you know who strikes down your relative. Keep clean your head and your heart, clean and whole."

Wambli Okiye now turned to Taśunkekokipapi, covering this one's shoulders with a Shirt, telling the warrior those same things he had told Ahbleza. And some different things.

"You will remember yourself, my son, as a peacemaker. You lead a growing band; your wisdom attracts followers. The hearts of your parents and your second-parents throb joy at the honor coming to their son.

"You aspire to the Shirt. The Shirt becomes you and you become the Shirt. Walk remembering these things; the grandfathers say so."

Wambli Okiye had spoken, and the two Shirted ones walked out through the crowd now, passing faces that

727

murmured awe. For in the person of a Shirtwearer each man saw his own dignity.

Ahbleza moved slowly, the people stopping him for a close look at the Shirt, the warriors admiring and the women making the tremolo. Occasionally a boy darted in close only to withdraw bashfully. Certainly everywhere Ahbleza saw eyes that marveled and esteemed, heard voices that praised and extolled.

And so the adulation became an irresistible force, Ahbleza experiencing the vanity inevitable to ones who wear the decorations of their valor before the eyes of a crowd.

Heyatawin had stayed away from the center this morning; she awaited Ahbleza in her own lodge. If the headmen gave out Shirts, perhaps they also feasted and danced. But her husband, remembering his sungazing vow, not likely joined in these events. And so, returning here, he will find her waiting.

The woman had surmised that the Pta-lodge intended a Shirting ceremony on this campground and she dared look for Ahbleza to receive this honor; Wanaǧi's acts soon after his return from the snow-council had hinted something. Not that the seer had said anything about a ceremony, but he had asked that she secretly provide him strands of Napewaśte's hair, Kehala's hair, and her own. And he had asked for horsehairs, many tail-hairs from horses Ahbleza owned or once owned. And he had demanded that she not speak to anyone of his requests.

She had sensed excitement as she listened to the cheers but she had not regretted staying away. Isolation, they say, the rule for a woman who grows-a-child; nothing more important, they say, than her influence on the unborn. Certainly Ahbleza, the father of this child, will understand that she dares not risk exposure to any mischief perhaps hiding in the crowd.

And now she heard a sound at the flap, saw his legs wearing the pair of covers that had brought her second prize at the Grass-bird's feast, saw the Shirt as Ahbleza bent to enter, his long black hair mingling with the many, many black strands of hair at the edges of this Shirt.

The next moment Heyatawin became as each one in the crowd had become, her eyes venerating symbol and image, the true-man lost to her gaze. But suddenly she stood tall, her look changing; she shall accept his inviolable claim to self-esteem. Slightly inclining her head, she moved forward to pick up his pipe, stem and bowl resting on a rack.

The man's hand stopped her; he desired something different. Let her place crossed sticks before the lodge entrance, closing out everyone, even the sister Zitkala; only two shall sit here looking at the Shirt. And after they examine the garment thoroughly, Heyatawin shall put away this symbol along with all Ahbleza's decorations. Not again will he wear adornment, not even a feather. "If the people look for the Shirt before they recognize me, I am not their true example."

Glancing at his wife, he saw confusion on her face. And so he withheld nothing. "Hear me, mitawin; I taste adulation this day. And I find myself hungering for more of this sweetness. And so I see reason to lay aside that which tempts my vanity. Certainly I enjoy esteem, certainly I accept—demand—each award I earn, but I talk of something different. A man who owns the people dares never stop owning himself, not for an instant.

"Now," he said smiling, "arrange the sticks as I ask. Sit and enjoy with me this wonderful Shirt."

The woman went out at once, putting up the sign that closed the tipi to visitors. When she stepped back inside, she saw that Ahbleza wore nothing but the cover at his loins, the wambli-feather gone from his hair, his face clear of paint.

Quickly she came alongside him, her fingers loosening the string at his waist. The next instant he stood as on the day he had chosen to divest himself of all things and she had come upon him, a naked has-not standing at the edge of the village. On that day her eyes had lingered on his face but not on this day.

She stood now appreciating the whole of his uncovered body, the delicate curve of shoulder and arm, the true proportion of his form. And when at last she spoke, her words told that she saw something that great mystery confers, an honor this man will not help but display.

"My husband," she said in hushed voice, "if your nakedness will not make you vain, never fear the Shirt."

She put her hands against his breast, her fingers soothing the skin above each nipple. "Heart-of-my-heart," she whispered, "let my touch tell you that you appear beautiful to me. And remember this touch. For one day after the sunpole thongs tear your skin, I will stand as now and you shall feel nothing different in my touch. My hands hold safe your beauty even as your hands hold safe the tribe."

They sat together looking upon the Shirt, admiring and recalling, the Shirt also a memory-shirt.

Heyatawin laid her fingers on a certain strand of hair. "Your mother's hair," she said softly. "What other woman in the tribe has hair more shining? And this strand belongs to your father. And this one, your sister's fragrant hair. And these horsehairs Tatezi offers for the Shirt. But I also take from different tails. . . ."

"You?" Ahbleza's voice held surprise. "You help Wanaǧi and so you know about the Shirt?"

"I know only, my husband, that the seer asks for family hair and horsehairs and that I act secretly."

Ahbleza looked at different hair now. "And this bunch of hair you locate also?"

The woman made the denying motion; she knew nothing of these hairs from the foretop of pta.

"Wahn. I shall visit the sacred-lodge before I put away the Shirt. Perhaps I shall discover something about this bunch."

He pushed aside the Shirt. "Teciȟila, mitawin," he whispered, rubbing his foreheard against hers; "teciȟila."

He stood and a moment afterwards, stepped out of the lodge, a cover again at his loins, a winter-robe over his shoulders, the Shirt in his hands.

Wanaǧi had returned to the sacred-lodge to await someone and now this someone had come; the wapiya smoked with Ahbleza.

"I know, my father-friend, that you make the Shirt and I know something of the ceremony. But I desire to hear about certain hairs." Ahbleza lifted up the bunch from pta.

Wanaǧi had not looked at the Shirt. "True, I ask a Kiyuksa for hair off the pta whom a boy-brave they once call Peta kills."

"The Kiyuksa gives back these hairs this winter? Yet Tabloka camps on the muddy river and Wanaǧi stays among the Mahto?" Ahbleza spoke quietly but firmly.

"Nor will I send out stones," Wanaǧi answered, his voice also firm. "I beg for this bunch of hair on the day after the boy-braves return. I know on that day what I know now."

The seer reached over, pulling close a painted container. Untying the stiff cover, he lifted out a hide such as keeps a winter count. But each story here, Ahbleza's story, season after season, act upon act.

"I tie the Shirt with strands of hair relating to events that affect you, events and people. Mostly these hairs come from women and from the horses you once own; many strands I wrap during seasons in the past.

"When your mother cuts her hair on the death of your grandmother, I take strands; and when her sister dies.

"The woman Cankuna and her daughters, your sister Kehala, and your wife offer hair.

"My old head provides these smoky ones, and the white hairs, your blood-grandfather sends me. Your father's hair stays sky-black and so he gives many strong hairs for this Shirt, certain ones cut on the night he decides to lead the Mahto band. Your uncles along with hunters and scouts also provide, their women bringing me the hair that clings to their brushes.

"Perhaps a hundred strands honor your acts as warrior, but more than a hundred honor you as peaceman. I tie on a strand for each trial, each night on a ledge, each moment of heart's despair, and every lift of spirit.

"Look upon your power, my son, before you put away the Shirt."

Briefly Ahbleza's hand covered his mouth; why resist the sign of amazement at that which Wanaǧi reveals. "You know that I intend to put away the Shirt, something I decide only moments before coming here?"

Instantly Wanaǧi dispelled any hint of something unnatural. He spoke almost roughly, his eyes taking on the familiar piercing-black. "Will you imagine that this same thing never happens to anyone but you? I remember when I put aside the grizzly robe, something they want a healer to wear. But I tell myself that I am not the example of a healer if they rely on a symbol instead of my powers."

"But often I see you wearing the grizzly hide."

Ahbleza had not come seeking gruffly voiced expressions that merely confused; he sought, instead, an understanding of his own reaction to the Shirt, something for which he strives these many winters only to put away after one wearing.

The wapiya restrained himself with effort. He longed to shout at this one so near his heart, to say that Ahbleza shall learn at the sunpole why Wanaġi again wears the grizzly skin and why the Shirtman again will wear the Shirt. But for a reason more important to himself than to Ahbleza, the sacred-man held on to his control. Quietly he emptied out the pipe ashes, his gesture signifying that his visitor shall go now.

And so the Shirtman, returning to his own lodge, sensed that he walked alone as before, his spirit a quivering thing at the top of the sky.

XVI

THE OLD Sahiela woman in Heyatawin's lodge kept count of the moons on a stick, and now she showed the notches to the fattening woman.

"I know," Heyatawin smiled. "The red grass comes up and the trees make buds. Two more moons. . . ." She murmured her words most softly.

"Two more moons," Zitkala repeated but in a much different voice. Heyatawin had urged her to keep at awl and hides throughout the snow-melting moons, a season when everyone goes outside for games—everyone but members of Heyatawin's family—after a long winter inside the lodge. But the wife of Ahbleza desired that many, many fine gifts honor her husband when he makes his thanks-offering at the sunpole. And so Zitkala dared only look longingly at the tipi flap as she listened to the laughter of persons at play.

Napewaśte most gladly sat quilling moccasins, paint sacks, sinew-holders, and pipe-covers; and certainly Heyatawin's mother had enjoyed a season of making things, of using her old Suhtai patterns. The woman had raised a lodge in the Mahto camp since the Shirting ceremony, a small lodge for herself and husband, a place to stay while she completed gifts for distribution at the coming events.

Kehala also kept at work, her fingers not only contributing to the pile of sungazing gifts but starting on a baby-carrier, something for Heyatawin.

But Heyatawin, speaking gently, had persuaded the young woman to use her skill to honor Ahbleza's vow. And Kehala, respecting this wish, returned to making gifts for the sungazing.

"Two more moons," Zitkala said again. Resentfully she pressed the awl to the edge of yet another pair of moccasins; she saw herself as not much more than a captive in this lodge. She neither sits as a wife to Ahbleza nor dares stand under the robe with any different man. Nor dares look too long upon Tonweya's handsome face.

At the beginning she had enjoyed the scout's company when they played tasiha unpi, the footbone game, but now his presence distressed her. After an evening of games she had difficulty getting to sleep; she kept remembering her age—twenty-and-two and a woman who not yet knows-a-man. More than once she had envied Kipanna, the third sister, in her sixteenth winter and always listening for the flute. Even now Kipanna, the one having all the fun; Kipanna, staying back in the Sahiela camp, taking care of the big family tipi with the help of an old one, visiting with women-friends whenever she pleases. . . .

Heyatawin had heard the mumble and saw the eyes that stared at the hide. She reached over, taking the awl out of Zitkala's hand: "My sister sits overlong at this one thing. Perhaps she will enjoy walking with her friends. Go before the sun climbs down."

The ground yet damp, the young woman changed into snow moccasins and put a second gown over the one next to her skin. She went out of the tipi, a pretty smile in her eyes.

Soon afterwards the old one at the flap also stepped outside; she knew that Zitkala went out not to enter into games with women friends but to walk among the lodges looking for Tonweya.

Heyatawin rejoiced at this little while alone. As woman

of the lodge, she kept everyone under this shelter fed and warm and peaceful, especially herself; any discontent, they said, affects the receptive soul of an unborn.

And now her dark eyes smiled down at the hide in her hands. She made the sleeping sack for the child who shall arrive within two moons, her hands working pride and protection into this carrier. The grandmothers had said that whatever she ponders while working on this sack shall influence the infant. And so why any hands but hers making this carrier, working on anything that pertains to the unborn? Will a sister or a member of the quillers' lodge sense more tenderness for this child than Heyatawin? Why this custom that a relative provide the sleeping sack, the tiny robes? Only Heyatawin makes things for this infant.

"But you work at too many things," her relatives had answered. "You make a gift for your husband and you work on something for your quillers' lodge and you make many presents for the sungazing giveaway. You pour out yourself in every direction. What will you hold back for sudden need?"

Heyatawin, understanding, quickly relieved their anxiety. "Fear not for me or the unborn infant. Regard this lodge as a sacred-lodge; the Shirtman pledges his thanks and so makes sweetgrass smoke each day. Truly, this lodge stays pure.

"And I take care in the ways you advise. You see that I never lie around and so I will not bear a child with a flat head.

"I shun the tall-ear's meat and so nothing shall misshape the child's lips." She had smiled at their concerned faces. "Who more than I," she had said softly, "desires to protect my unborn against harm to body or soul?"

Recalling this scene with these good relatives, she felt grateful that they had accepted her ways. They had not troubled her with more advice but had gone about helping to raise the pile of sungazing gifts. And she had provided generously of the quills for whatever they desired to decorate.

But now she found herself wondering about this supply of quills. She reached for the four heart-sac cases wherein she kept the quills in neat order, the fine belly-quills for use on Ahbleza's new moccasins her most important need.

Opening one little sack she sat dismayed; not enough to finish the pair she intended quilling top and bottom, a surprise for Ahbleza, something that will commemorate the birth of his child. And the pattern made this pair especially important; the design came of her own dream.

On the same night that she first felt the child stir, the picture had come. For a moment she had seen the pattern as snowflakes lazily drifting out of a clear sky or perhaps stars floating down gently; soon afterwards she had begun to view the true design. Half-dreaming, half-memorizing, she had held on to the picture until morning, the colors as clear as the shapes.

One color had presented a difficulty until someone offered her a piece of whiteman's trade-cloth, something that yielded—when she dipped the piece in hot water—the color of deep, deep sky. And so she had colored the quills which made the background for her design.

Before starting work on the baby-carrier and on Ahbleza's moccasins, she had tried out the dream-pattern on a little shell-shape sac, a container for the birthcord. Following this experiment, she had decided on the white fine quills for the snowflake shapes. And that the husband's moccasins and the baby's carrier shall match. But in her joy she had neglected to count quills. Or perhaps she had imagined that her mother's supply never will diminish.

Sitting alone, she hunted a scheme, a way for obtaining more quills. Suddenly she remembered something. And so she decided to visit her mother's lodge this same evening; she will seek her parents' agreement to that which she will propose.

Zitkala had discovered Tonweya. The scout walked alongside Ahbleza, the two moving toward the horse enclosures, where those creatures never ridden mingled with some gentled ones.

"One horse here," the scout said smiling, "shows the white edge at his eyes. Now you will see something."

The young woman stood too far-distant to hear Tonweya but near enough to see him crawl inside the tall stakes. She decided to watch.

For a moment the scout seemed lost among the snorting horses but soon he reappeared, holding on to a furiously resisting one. Pulling and tugging on a long slim cord, he worked the horse toward open ground; here he loosened the cord.

At once the horse reared; baring long teeth, his ears back, he acted to threaten the man. But the scout, flicking the cord in the horse's face, darted back of the plunging creature. Then, the instant the horse put all four on the ground, Tonweya made a flying leap. Now horseback, he clutched the mane with one hand, holding the cord with his other hand.

Screaming shrilly, the creature bounded into the air, hurling up Tonweya, the scout looping, sounding a noisy hoot as he spun. He fell on slushy earth but he regained his feet so quickly that fall and rise seemed like one simple act. And he never let go the cord.

Ahbleza laughed softly, and even the horse stood quietly eyeing the scout as if much perplexed. But the Shirtman suspected Tonweya's foolish violence as a way of entertaining someone whose strenuous dance at the pole soon takes place. Certainly Tonweya had performed as a heyoka and with the same motive. But neither of the brother-friends had known that a woman who truly needed amusement had laughed as she had not laughed in three, four moons.

Now passing the cord through his hands, the scout slowly approached the horse, the creature again rising up, angry and snorting. But the scout also made a fierce cry. Jumping up and down, he mimicked the horse, his harsh utterances and his waving arms relating him to this creature.

"Wahn . . . wahn . . . wahn . . . wahn." Throwing surprise at the horse, the scout moved near, near.

"Shuh . . . shuh . . . " he began the calming sound, "shuh . . . shuh." Getting really close, he tightened the cord around the creature's neck, choking off air.

The horse, growing limp, slumped to the ground. Instantly Tonweya sat on the neck, loosening the cord, tying the forefeet. Now, one arm holding tight to the creature's head, he twisted more of the cord around the horse's nose.

For the next two, three moments, Tonweya tightened, then loosened his choking grasp on the horse. And now, leaning on the neck as before, he stroked the head. Finally grabbing an ear, he unwound the cord on the nose.

The horse struggled for release whenever Tonweya moved but the armhold on the creature's neck remained a strong subduing influence.

After a while Tonweya covered the horse's eye, his other hand keeping hold on the horse's ear. Bending his mouth to one of the expanding nostrils, he breathed great breaths in and out the creature's nose.

Lifting his face, the scout inspected the eye his hand had covered. But when the horse wrenched to one side, Tonweya again lowered his mouth to the flaring nostril.

The third look into the big shining eye convinced the scout that the creature will accept him as rider. And so, untying the horse's feet, he permitted this one to rise.

The horse stood and Tonweya again breathed into those nostrils. Then hanging the cord over the creature's jaw, the scout spoke into one ear; the horse shall stay gentle, he said kindly, responding to whoever rides him and so proving useful.

And now Tonweya turned smiling, walking toward Ahbleza, the horse docile and keeping close.

But the woman who had watched Tonweya gentle this horse had run from the scene, her heart crying out against the choice she had made. Wife in a lodge, she moaned, where but one woman ever truly will sit alongside Ahbleza. Always she, Zitkala, shall see the crossed sticks that keep her out on the day they present the Shirt to Ahbleza; always she will see the difference in his eyes when he looks at Heyatawin. Never will Ahbleza feel for her that which he feels for her sister. For truly Heyatawin sits not only as his true-wife but as the only wife his heart ever will accept.

And what of Tonweya? Will he ever desire Zitkala in the way that Ahbleza desires Heyatawin? As wife to Ahbleza, will she, Zitkala, truly become distant-wife to Tonweya? Will Tonweya ever touch a woman who belongs to his brother-friend, whatever the privilege his place as one of a dreaming-pair grants him?

Confused, frightened, Zitkala hurried back to her sister's lodge but not without wishing that she had a different place to go.

Outside the tipi Zitkala made the familiar little sound that announced her presence. But stepping inside, she saw that her prompt return surprised Heyatawin.

"I belong here helping you," she said quietly. But she had not returned to work. Instead she began to play with Kehala's little girl, hiding her aching shame in this play.

Kehala had come visiting, the woman bringing quillwork and sitting with Heyatawin. Her little daughter, five winters, played contentedly on a robe between the two women, small pte-bones her playthings. And so Zitkala gave names to these pieces and told amusing stories about each one.

After a while the old one at the entrance went for wood, and so Heyatawin uncovered the moccasins she had worked on secretly, her surprise for Ahbleza. "I want a pte-tail," she said, "or perhaps a strip of pte-hair on each one, and yet I will not want to overdecorate moccasins that I quill top and bottom. What will you say, my sisters?"

Zitkala had not answered and so Kehala spoke, giving all her praise to the pattern.

"The design pleases me," Heyatawin agreed, "but I need more quills and so I wonder about using the pte-strip."

But suddenly she decided to ask that these two listen to her scheme for locating more quills. "The Suhtai raise their lodges not far-distant and my mother's relatives always keep quills for trading. And I understand that my parents soon visit the Suhtai camp. And so I propose that I and you, my sister"—she looked at Zitkala—"go with mother and father. The warm sun will feel good on my back after these many moons in the tipi. I really yearn for a nice walk."

She pulled two softened quills from her mouth, her teeth flattening the spines. And now she spoke of Ahbleza. She will ask the old woman who sleeps at the flap to keep close watch on water and firewood and she will ask that Kehala and Napewaste bring meat.

Aware that Zitkala sat unresponsive, she looked closely at this sister. "Four traveling together gives more protection than three," she said firmly.

Zitkala remained quiet, her attention apparently on the child but she wished that Kipanna goes on this walk in her place.

Heyatawin backstitched two more of the moistened

quills onto the moccasin and then, keeping her eyes on the work, she spoke again: "My sister also needs quills if she intends to make the scout a pair of moccasins. Certainly she will remember her bet when four play games this winter? The men win the most counting-sticks and so the two women shall present moccasins to the winners."

If Zitkala remembered, her face had not told. And so Heyatawin, who will not permit any pouting in this lodge, laid aside her work. "Come with me, my sister," she said evenly; "I and you visit mother's lodge and hear whatever she will say about my plan for travel."

The brother-friends walked toward Ahbleza's lodge, the boy-spirit reflected on each face, Tonweya glad for the smiles that brighten the Shirtman's eyes. The grandfathers never intend that a sungazing vow take away joy, but whoever contemplates himself recognizes a serious experience. And a warrior who puts down a bow feels for a while that he loses his arm.

Nearing the lodge, they passed an old woman, her many winters permitting her an unrestrained tongue. And so she called aloud her wish that the Shirtwearer shall have a son as handsome as he.

"Boy-child or girl, tanke, either one will please me. And if a girl, I will look for her to become a good mother among the people, a good mother like you."

The black darting eyes of this old one followed Ahbleza as he moved on and suddenly she raised her thin voice in a song of admiration; the Shirtman's words and smile had put wings on her aging heart.

"Which one will you desire, cinye," Tonweya asked quietly; "a hero . . . or a mother of heroes?"

Ahbleza smiled but he had not given an answer. Nor had Tonweya really listened for one.

Birth, the one true great mystery.

Birth of everything, truly great mystery.

Birth of the sun and the earth and each child of the earth, great-great mystery.

Birth, not death, the only true great mystery.

739

XVII

THE NEWS that Heyatawin, her sister, and her parents will travel to the Suhtai camp for a visit with relatives brought a line of callers to the lodge. Some persons wanted messages carried to friends; different ones wanted quills—if the Suhtai women have any left after they supply Heyatawin; other persons wanted to trade for anything metal—knives, kettles, ornaments.

"Bring back something from a trade with the Witapa-ha, something to sit on when I ride," one man in the crowd called out laughingly. He stood among the many persons watching the family prepare to go out, the travelers taking an extra horse and drag to accommodate these requests for trades.

"Sympathize with me," Heyatawin's father answered. "See me as a lone man with three women. I will not get in a word during the trades. I know; I live many seasons in a lodge with wife and three daughters."

Hearing him, the people smiled. Heyatawin's parents, a truly respected family in this Mahto camp. The father, in seasons past, had honored each of his daughters with a becomes-woman ceremony, and these three along with his wife strengthened his pride. Everyone who gathered here wished these good people an easy, pleasing three days' travel.

But Napewaśte felt apprehensive, something she had dared mention only to Kehala. The young woman had answered reassuringly; true, one man needs defend three women, but what enemy ever attacks a small party, all women but one? And so Napewaśte stood watching, trying to replace her anxiety with admiration for these strong-hearted Śahiela people.

Heyatawin, mounted, sat looking for Ahbleza; she had not seen him in the crowd. Certainly he had not objected to her going; custom permits a Lakotah wife to go and come as she pleases, a husband requiring only that one or more old ones travel at her side.

And certainly Ahbleza knew the ground this party will

travel; he knew that Titonwan scouts constantly rove this trail and that the slushy earth of a rainy moon discourages raiders. He knew also that the old people in this party carry plenty of meat and weapons and a traveling shelter that sleeps four. And that each one rides a good horse, Heyatawin safely atop the old but reliable Tatezi, who will carry the woman knowingly whenever Heyatawin desires horseback to walking.

And that after a moon-and-a-full—perhaps forty days—Ahbleza shall ride south, his wife and her family returning with him before the sundancing and before her child comes.

Wanaǧi, who knew their plan, had seen a way for Ahbleza to make-ceremony out of this travel south, something that related to the sungazing and a formal invitation to the Suhtai.

All these things and more the Shirtman and his wife had talked about the night before, and so Heyatawin had not sensed surprise on discovering that Ahbleza had gone out of the lodge before she awakened this morning. But she had looked for him here or at the edge of camp, the man waiting to see her ride off.

Ahbleza had not appeared, but as the party started out, Tonweya rode up alongside Heyatawin. "Your husband asks that I accompany you to the fork in the trail." Smiling, he went front, leading the way.

The woman had flashed the scout a questioning look, but Tonweya's face had told nothing. She tried to remember any hint in Ahbleza's talk, but she recalled only his request that she ride Tatezi and his desire to join her before the child's birth.

At the fork, beyond the eyes of camp, Ahbleza waited for the party. He had slept uneasily and, up at dawn, he had gone out to view the sunrise as a way of renewing himself. Alone under the quiet sky he had decided on a secluded place along the trail from which to watch Heyatawin ride away. And to assure that the party moved his direction, he had sought Tonweya, asking that the brother-friend lead the group to the fork.

Seeing the scout and party approach, he wished suddenly for something to place in his wife's hand, something to bring her in touch with him whenever she looked upon his gift. But he had nothing on his person to give her.

Parents and sister, on sight of Ahbleza, had not lingered, the group going forward as if they had not seen this man. And Tonweya raced off in an opposite direction, the scout on his way to the hills.

The Lakotah will not make something of any separation—brother from brother, wife from husband, friend from friend; only the old ones permit a tear on separating from children, grandchildren. And so the woman on the horse and the man who stood alongside her had neither words nor touch for this moment. But the one looked up at eyes shining devotion and knew that he saw his own heart reflected on her face. He saw also the sun on her hair and touching her mouth, her lips slightly open as if she sought permission to speak.

He turned his head; for an instant he remembered this wonderful woman as she had stood before him at the edge of the camp, honoring his nakedness, offering herself as the one gift that will replace all he had given away.

"But on that occasion, my husband, I offer only myself. At the sungazing, when you again give away everything, I shall come to you bringing not only myself but your child."

Startled, the man looked closely upon her face; will she really speak or will a voice within him make answer to his thought?

She smiled. "Mihigna, my husband, hear one more thing: where I go now, I take with me your gift, the one thing I ever desire from you. I take your seed, your living-self."

His hand reached up, but already she had turned and gone. He saw that Tatezi carried her quickly, gently, to the ones of her own blood, to the two who gave her life and the third one who called her sister.

He watched as far as his eyes will reach, until they disappeared from his view. Then memory granted him a picture: a little family traveling in the direction that the grandfathers say man always faces. From out of the south, man originally comes; to the south, man eventually returns.

XVIII

THE SECOND night out Heyatawin's family camped near old-woman hill, a familiar point along the trail, a place where custom demands that travelers stop for smoke and thanksgiving. The people tell a story about kindly spirits who once guarded an old woman living in a nearby cave, these same spirits now looking out for anyone who smokes and offers meat here.

And so Heyatawin's father smoked on the hill and her mother placed dry meat on the edge of the creek. Then the family ate of the wasna they carried; none wanted a fire this night. Soon afterwards, they raised the little tipi and, crawling inside, slept soundly.

But the spirits who had heeded the pipe and meat-offering of different travelers apparently chose to ignore Heyatawin's family; during the night someone took their horses. Moccasin tracks showed where two Psa had cut loose the five, these men perhaps enemy scouts who sneaked along Titonwan and Sahiela trails.

The old man had grunted his regret at this loss and the old woman had darted fearful glances in the direction of the Psa tracks, but her daughters had managed some cheerful phrases. The enemy had not killed anyone, they said, and the family keep their meat and shelter. And more important, they have but one more day of travel, one day and a small piece of another.

"One more day of horseback travel," the old man answered; "on foot and dragging poles makes a difference."

"And I am the slow-going one," Heyatawin said quietly. "But perhaps a Titonwan scout will discover these tracks and lend a horse to pull the drag."

They started on, the man front and looking out for more signs of enemy, the women taking turns at dragging the little tipi poles.

The morning seemed mild, but whoever dragged the poles sensed an uncomfortable warmth. Then after a while, the air cooled.

"The spirits only now discover your offering," Heyata-win told her mother, "and so they quickly wrap this day in a fog, hiding you from any enemy eyes."

The old woman murmured her understanding but the old man now looked more often at sky than ground. The air carried a familiar smell, something that prompted his recollection; they traveled during a changeable moon, the weathers full of mischief.

Each of the travelers had heard the distant rumble in the sky but they had said nothing. Now Zitkala, seeing a flash, spoke her thought: "What I hear and see tells me that something signals the arrival of the flower moons."

Her mother had not agreed; the old woman had felt a chill in the heavy, wet fog. Soon, she said, they will walk with rain, cold rain.

The woman had known. The rain came, and so they threw robes over their gowns and the man, pulling his cover up over his shoulders, looked up yet more often. And not without concern in his eyes.

The water fell in stinging drops, then with a rattling noise; a sudden winter wind slanted the cold, hard rain against their faces. The old woman bent her head and struggled with the drag; Zitkala shivered and clutched her robe across her breast.

Heyatawin had not noticed when the change occurred, when the sleet became fine snow. She knew only that the wind whirled the flakes around her moccasins and that certain sheltered places had begun to trap the snow. She saw the whiteness piling up next to stone or at the edge of brush and she observed that they walked on a powder.

The man, keeping front, recognized a wind-change, more snow coming from a different direction, the thick, blinding snow that puts a crust around the eyes. And so he had turned, giving advice to wife and daughters; they shall put a hand on the shoulder of the one in front and so not lose sight of each other. He will stay front, breaking the trail; last one in line will drag the poles.

Suddenly winds out of four directions crashed together and turned upside down, then backwards; the blinding snow went crazy.

744

The party struggled through the cold white fury. The trail became thickly covered, the drifts rapidly deepening. The winds lashed at the travelers from every side. Perplexed, exhausted, the women began to slow. A fear grasped each heart; perhaps they walked lost in a blizzard snow.

The man drew his family into a huddle alongside a thin shelter of brush; he knew the danger in more travel. He motioned for the women to unpack the drag while he made a ground-space for the little tipi.

Zitkala worked on the fastenings with numb fingers; when her hand finally refused to move, she sank down in the drift. Heyatawin, working next to her mother on the second pole, had not seen her sister fall. But the old woman had gone at once to the second daughter. She forced Zitkala to get up and move around; she called for Heyatawin to come and rub her sister's hands.

Shaking her own painful fingers, the mother went back to the drag and managed to loosen the fastenings; the husband and wife together lifted out the hides.

The two young women lunged through the drift, joining the old people who tried to raise the tipi. But the winds fought their effort to lift these short poles. And to stay on their feet.

The husband-father shook fire-making pieces from a sack at his loins and the women shielded him while he brought forth a flame; whatever burnable things they own they will burn.

They watched the fire fight off the terror of cold only long enough to feel a little warmth. While the short poles burned, they stuffed wasna into their mouths and decided to make small packages for each one's back. The man cut pieces from the flapping tipi skin for these bundles while the wind tried to jerk the knife out of his hand. The old woman saw Heyatawin wrap the unfinished quillwork for the baby-carrier and for the moccasins in her piece, the daughter's act lending comfort.

"I know a different way," the father called out above the sounds of cold. "Hear me." And now he named something wise in blinding-weather: they shall lie down and let the snow cover over. The snow-robe, he remembered, holds a certain amount of warmth, not enduring but a protection

745

until the winds cease and a man sees the trail again. But whether this way proves wise for a woman near the moon of her childbearing, he will not know. Let each one speak.

None made answer. Perhaps the women had not heard or perhaps they had not wanted to hear. They stood, eyes dull and body weary, three wavering shapes bending over a crazily dancing flame.

And so the man decided to keep his group moving, hurrying the party onward before feet and legs froze. Pushing the three into line, he tied the thong from the drag around one, then the next one and so held all together. He went again to the front, leading their stumbling walk, the raging wind whipping on all sides, their sense of everything but the pricks of fierce cold gone.

The man led but with neither eyes nor ears. He guided these persons, instead, with a wish, the wish that they will fall into some draw, some gully, some ravine, into any hole that will shield from the wind and make a cover of snow, their only chance to survive. But trying to find any such break in the earth now. . . . Even the true-dog flounders in a blizzard snow.

After a while Ḣeyatawin began a song for the unborn child. But the wind slapped the sound off her lips and threw away the tone before anyone heard. Even so the song had warmed her heart. The desire to sit down and sleep sat strong upon this woman, but the will to sing kept her moving.

And now the snow shut off her view from the dark shape only an arm's length in front of her, someone whose name she tried to remember. And yet for all the flying snow, the warmth of sun seemed suddenly to reach through to her; perhaps the sky brightens?

She peeked out from under her robe and saw that the snow had blown away. Joyfully she looked around. She saw that she had come to a fork in the trail and that a man stood here. He wore those moccasins on which she had quilled her dream, a dream of snowflakes drifting out of a clear sky. She smiled at him.

The man noticed and lifted his hand. He gestured that she shall come to him.

Smiling, she whispered her answer. I will come to you,

I will come whenever you call, my husband. See me, I am coming to you now.

The grandfathers, reaching back in their memories, told that snow often fell during the moon of tricking-men—and even afterwards—but only twice will they recall a blizzard as thick and deep and cold as this one, the winds unrelenting for three days. Old Tatewin had sat grumbling at herself, threatening never to prophesy weather again; she had not recognized the approach of this mischief.

But now the joy of a bright clear morning sat over each lodge; the sky, something pure and shining, and the earth, a glistening silence. The winds had left great white piles, something to hide their mischief. Some drifts covered broken trees and some drifts covered brush and stone, but deep down under the white robe, lay the new grasses, warm and living.

On the trail near old-woman hill, the sparkling mounds seemed most deep and breezes played gently with the loose snow on top, the powder curling up like thin smoke.

Certain Suhtai scouts, wearing sharp-pointed snow moccasins and out looking for the pte who stood captive in these drifts, had observed these tiny spumes that rose prettily against the sky. But they turned and pushed through the powdery snow in a different direction. Perhaps the spirits of old-woman hill sent smoke signals to warn any two-leggeds who hovered nearby; perhaps the spirits, they told each other, will not welcome scouts on this day.

And so none but the wandering four-leggeds had discovered that a certain drift hid neither tree nor brush nor stone; instead a man and three women lay under this snow. But who will ever come and wrap these bodies in the bright red robe of the dead?

A gentle cough outside his lodge told Ahbleza that Tonweya had come visiting.

Calling the scout inside, the Shirtman spoke the familiar phrase that welcomed relative or friend: "Catkuta iyaya yo." But Ahbleza had kept his face toward the mellow red-earth circle back of the lodge-fire; he sat at a ceremonial smoke.

747

And so the scout neither spoke nor moved until Ahbleza rested the long-stem on a rack.

Now, the ceremonial pipe put aside, Tonweya extended his own pipe; he also will smoke in ceremonial manner before he speaks.

The gesture pleased Ahbleza; the Shirtman desired to keep hold on these sacred meaningful moments. And so, using a forked stick, he lifted an ember onto the scout's bowl. Then, accepting the stem, he touched his lips to the pipe. After four puffs, he turned the stem again toward Tonweya. And now his eyes sought the scout's face.

The next instant Ahbleza's hand and each different piece of his body stopped living.

Then, as if this frozen instant never had existed, the Shirtman moved; his hand steady, he gave back the scout's pipe and placed an ember on the bowl of his own second pipe.

They smoked in a silence unlike anything Tonweya had experienced or ever willingly shall experience again. But before the bowl cooled, Ahbleza scattered their pipe ashes upon the patch of mellow earth.

And now, loosening his hair in a sign of grief, the husband spoke his heartbreak.

"This sad thing that my brother's eyes reveal . . . they kill my wife." He had not dropped his tone as when one makes a question of a phrase.

Quickly, desiring to spare the Shirtman a prolonged agony, Tonweya told what he knew, the scout speaking as if he knelt alongside a pile of chips and reported to the summer-shirts. For he lived as a truthbearer, knowing but one way to report truth.

Coming back to camp after three days in the hills, he had seen a small party of Psa horsebacks hurrying across Lakotah trails. He took cover and watched. He recognized the horse Tatezi, also the one Zitkala had ridden. He dared not attack the party alone—six in the group. He had returned to camp at once. He stopped only to get his pipe at the scouts' lodge before coming to his brother-friend. He had not talked with anyone.

Tonweya had spoken, then gone out of Ahbleza's lodge. Why watch a man in anguish? Will any true comfort come from mingling tears? Grief only drags down the sympathizer, gloom breeding gloom until all hearts bleed. And what good ever comes from a bleeding heart?

Four days Ahbleza sat alone, the crossed sticks before his lodge. Olepi had wondered whether the son remembered that a grandfather loses a grandchild he never will know, but Napewaśte had wondered only in what manner her son endures this tragedy. She knew that the old woman who lived in his tipi went each day, putting down meat and water-sacs, these things untouched on her return.

Napewaśte and Kehala, Cankuna and her relatives had opened containers of quillwork, laying many fine things outside their lodges, gifts for whoever came by. But will anything truly ease this sorrow in the Mahto camp? And who will want to camp ever again on this tacante canku, on this heart-shape trail around the black hills?

The wailing voices of women-bereaved finally reached Ahbleza's ears, and so on the fifth day, like a man awakening, he rose from alongside the dead ashes of his fire-circle and walked again in the Mahto village.

Certainly the people had grieved. Scarcely a woman appeared without gashes on arms or legs and none without disarranged hair. Cracking lumps of white mud clung to the bodies of some persons and many men moved through camp in shabby robes.

Most heads respectfully turned when the Shirtman approached, but anyone who looked at Ahbleza noticed the hollow cheeks and a strange sharpness to his face. Even so, neither the man's eyes nor his voice carried any sign of his suffering.

Certain warriors, after seven, eight days, spoke of locating the place where the Psa had attacked, but Ahbleza answered that the blizzard snow destroys tracks of killer and kill. And why hunt for pieces that the Psa sever from these four bodies? And if the enemy will not cut off anything, then the snow and those creatures who prowl the snow take care of the remains.

And why wish for a spirit-bundle of hairs from his cherished one's head? Her hair decorates the Shirt. And why lay out gifts in a spirit-keeping lodge? He will make a pile at the sungazing of all he possesses.

749

And to those persons who hinted that perhaps the Psa had not killed but instead had made captives of these three women, Ahbleza asked that they recall the scout's report— six Psa and a small herd of horses; nothing more.

All these things the Shirtwearer had pondered, then prepared his answers before he had dared step outside the lodge to walk in his new place as an example of greatness in man. Or as the tribe recognizes greatness.

XIX

THE NEW moon had grown to half since the Psa attack on the traveling-four. And each day more families gathered at the campsite on the sacred trail. As the hoop widened, the counciling began. And if the warriors get their way, the whole tribe shall make war on the Psa.

Each arriving band quickly learned of the four killed and the wailing of women began all over again, their cries echoing from the knolls and arousing the men, who, in turn, recalled old grudges against the Psa. Blood grew hot; the lust for revenge rose to a boiling; the Lakotah appeared more eager for war than meat.

But toward their furious war spirit Ahbleza turned a restraining voice. Sensibly and with unfaltering firmness he counseled patience; his speeches protested hasty revenge.

"Wait, men," he said sternly when throats growled and eyes flashed. "Wait until this hot blood bubbles down to a simmer. Wait one more season. Let heads cool and regain reason before someone strikes out."

"He speaks as if he wears a woman's gown instead of the Hair Shirt," Tawitko ridiculed in the presence of his own warriors. "I rejoice that the Kiyuksa keep an itancan-lodge within the band. Imagine the mess if these Shirts enter into Kiyuksa affairs."

"The vow he takes when they Shirt him," someone said, "demands that he not start a fight even if his relatives lie bloody at his feet."

"Tell me, my kinsman," Tawitko turned to the son of Zuzueca, "if the Psa kill any one of your wives, will you ask that your warriors cool off before they go looking for the enemy?"

Tabloka's snarl, answer enough.

The Mnikoóźu camp also contained many tempestuous natures, young men not about to see this chance for revenge fall on the ground. And so at every turn these persons used taunts and ridicule to incite all Titonwan whose war honors permitted a voice—if not a big one—in council.

Then one day Peśla stood in the center lodge, speaking out from his place directly back of the principal men. The summer encampment means war parties going out against an enemy, he said; why not assign so many Psa killings to these warriors eager for revenge and encourage this group to go out now. "Young men make war, young men need war, young men demand war."

Ahbleza had heard Peśla and all those different ones who joined in the noise against delay. And now he answered: "My friends, if the young men demand this avenging, wait until after the sungazing. Anyone who prepares for this ceremonial dance lays aside weapons; perhaps certain men who dance also desire a place in the revenge. I will say nothing more."

Instantly Tanaźin and Hinyete and the head akicita of these bands murmured agreement. And now sounds of approbation came from the back, center, and sides; the warriors seemed suddenly to remember that the killings affect Ahbleza more than any one in the tribe. Perhaps Ahbleza desires this delay for personal reasons; perhaps he includes himself when he refers to sungazers who dare not lift a bow until after the ceremony?

But Wanaǵi knew differently. Ahbleza will not look for more killings out of this tragedy; much more likely Ahbleza will go to the sunpole looking for a way to put out the fire in all these hearts, something that will work for the one and for the whole. For the one, meaning Ahbleza himself.

Now that they put aside any talk of revenge until after the ceremonies, the itancan brought something different to

751

the attention of the principals in this vast gathering. The Pta-lodge asked the assembly to counsel a proposal to name six to sit as judges, six competents who will review the acts of any one person or any one band and so determine any improper conduct.

Silence will meet any new thought spoken out in this center place but the silence that followed Wambli Okiye's speech endured beyond anything they remembered; two days passed before anyone spoke. The assembly recognized that the Pta-lodge schemed to unify the Great Family on the mixed grasses, but who, now or ever, will grant to any one man—or any six—such power? Or a chance to try for such power? The Titonwan have seven advisers and four deciders each summer; they have clubmen and Shirtmen; they have enough deciders, enough protectors, enough owners.

Let everyone remember that for eight, nine moons the people exist as independent families, that for three, four moons they come together as a tribe to sponsor a ceremony for implanting good in the young, renewing good in the grownups. Let things stay.

Never, never will they lend a ruling power to any one; tawaiciyapi, they said, each man belongs to himself.

And so the councilors introduced the next concern: a different campground for the sungazing. The tribe shall wait until the sage comes into bloom and then they shall walk as a people three days north, to the place they call rapid creek. But while they wait for the sacred grass, they hunt; the scouts had said so.

During these days of council Ahbleza's lodge always appeared neat and clean, fresh water in the sacs and meat in the paunches. The Shirtman, observing that someone took care, looked upon these acts as the work of the old one who again slept at the flap, someone who went out of the lodge before he awakened and who seemed asleep on his return each night. But now Cankuna told the Shirtman a different story.

Kipanna, little sister to the killed women, came each day to tend the fire, fill the sacs, her acts signifying a willingness to care for his lodge as his woman if he so desired.

"Kipanna sees herself as a daughter who fulfills an obligation," Cankuna said, but her eyes begged Ahbleza to accept this youthful orphan of fifteen winters who had walked away sadly from the Sahiela camp.

Sitting forward of his backrest, the Shirtman gazed upon the face of this second-mother, the man seeing something of his own sorrow in her eyes. He had heard wailing nearby these many nights, but he knew that old persons often recalled losses in the past and so they cried over their memories. He had imagined that Cankuna wept for the baby girl dead twelve, thirteen winters. Now he understood that she brought him Kipanna's offer as a way of letting him know that she also wept over his loss.

But before he answered, he needed to consider that which Kipanna faced if she came to him.

Kipanna, he told himself, shall come into a lodge without joy. Or the chance of joy. Any woman who enters his lodge comes to sit alongside a dead heart.

And Kipanna, coming here, shall sit next to a man twice her winters and more like a father; Kipanna, a wife but not a wife, not until after the sungazing. And after? Will he ever feel any affection for her?

"Permit her, my son, that which she calls obligation even if your heart grants her nothing."

Cankuna had given words to his thought; perhaps Cankuna knew words for all these things he had sat reflecting and in her woman-way wished to make Kipanna understand.

"Tell this third sister that I welcome her if she chooses to come to me." Ahbleza leaned back against the rest, his eyes closing.

And now the woman, wife to Ogle and mother of his two sons, returned to her lodge, where Kipanna, staying with the hunter's family since her arrival in the Mahto camp, awaited Ahbleza's answer.

Cankuna told quickly but she spoke without heart and her eyes looked sadly upon the once bright, laughing little sister. She viewed Kipanna now, an old-young woman, her head bent, legs and arms in gashes, a finger broken. She wondered if the grief-hurt orphan even heard the message.

Kipanna had heard. When the hunter's wife finished speaking, the young woman crawled to a sleeping robe and

753

crouched down as if some new danger lurked nearby. She covered her head, hiding the sobs which broke on her face.

She will go, her spirit whispered, to one who never truly will want her. She will go without exchange of gifts between families, neither father nor mother nor brothers to receive or give any presents. None will spread a robe outside the new lodge and welcome her with honor and gladness; none will sit with paint and affectionately color her cheeks or fondle and brush her hair. And never will her dream of wearing a handsome Sahiela finger-circle come true . . . never, never.

The grandmothers had said that tears shall fall only when someone dies, and so Kipanna told herself that this fresh weeping honored the recent dead; never shall she cry over herself and all these broken joys.

After a while she remembered about the moccasins that a Lakotah woman always takes to the man she will call husband. Lacking her sister's skill at applying quills, she had learned to decorate with trader's beads; a friend had given her enough for a simple design. But will Ahbleza accept moccasins with a decoration that comes from a trader's place? She will ask Cankuna in the morning; Cankuna will know. But before she goes to him she will make a pair of moccasins for Ahbleza—nice moccasins.

Cankuna had watched carefully, and when she saw that Kipanna slept, she moved over next to the young woman's robe; gently she pulled back the cover from Kipanna's head. For a little while she gazed at the sleeping face, her heart drifting from this one to her own daughter Cuwe.

Cuwe, seventh wife to Tabloka, grew a child for the squat, loudmouth warrior. Going this past winter to the Kiyuksa camp, Cuwe now lived in a disgracefully small tipi close to the big one belonging to the mother of Tabloka's first child; Cuwe, her wonderful daughter who had intended giving herself to a fine young hunter until Pesla, using his privilege as a brother, persuaded her differently.

Cankuna's good nature seldom permitted a dark moment, but sitting here now she recalled her anger upon learning that Pesla had interfered, the warrior-son asking that Iku's wife carry a message to Cuwe. "Tell my sister that she has an obligation to her father and brothers and uncles."

Surprised, Cuwe had answered the woman that neither father nor uncles had talked against her choice; instead they had spoken their liking for the young hunter.

But the message-bearer had sat persistent: "Perhaps you know someone who will bring warrior-power to your family, one among the Kiyuksa . . . someone who makes a name . . . a man who notices you. Your two brothers desire this thing."

And so after three, four days Tabloka, already with six wives, had wrapped his robe around Cuwe, whom he invited to become his seventh. And then Peśla moved five horses out of his herd, four honoring a Kiyuksa; the fifth horse he presented in the name of Iku's wife.

Tonweya, hearing the news, had wondered why his sister suddenly had rejected the attractive hunter, a young man with whom she often stood outside the lodge. But whomever she chose to bring him as a new relative he intended to accept.

Recalling these things, Cankuna's heart ached again. For now this Kiyuksa dared claim Cuwe's sister as wife. And Tacincala will hang herself before she goes to him.

E-i-i-i, so many grievous things; the woman made the little sound of despair.

Makatoźanźan's camps had arrived from the earth-smoke, the band leader telling that more Sicangu will come from the muddy-water but that they travel slowly; they needed to hunt along the way, neither these travelers nor their lodges presentable for the sungazing.

The Titonwan greeted this news with a little laughing; they knew why these Lakotah needed to replenish their camps before they put in an appearance. Sluka and his friends already had entertained with amusing—and not so amusing—stories of hides traded for the burning-drink. And when they had used up hides, Sluka told, these same Lakotah found different ways of getting to the barrel. And so the men had nothing to show for a season of trade but stabbing-scars. Even the newscarriers told shameful things about a Kuya who once had led their people but now lay around on the ground, his eyes blurry.

Olepi had made himself listen to these reports. He also had made himself remember the Kuya whose name he had presented to the Iyuptala-lodge; certainly everyone recalled who had recommended Iśna.

And now, while the herald walked around announcing the arrival of Hewanźi's villages, the head akicita sent clubmen to the Kiyuksa camp; the band squabbled again.

But before these clubs arrived, someone had flashed a trader's knife. And Zuzueca had fallen dead.

The Kiyuksa villages became a clamor of yells and wails. Not that anyone much cared about the dim-eyed leader whom they already pushed aside but that the killing gave reason for families to line up and recount old disputes, all the way back to the band's original division over kinsman-rule.

The clubs had stopped any more stabbings, but the men stood around glaring threats or growling like dogs while the women spit at each other and pulled hair.

Two persons stayed with the killed man. Iśtakpe, the pipe of his pronghorn peace-vision tight in his hand, looked for any face showing a willingness to smoke, to cleanse the air of murder, this one-eyed old man perhaps shedding the only real tears that fell upon the dead one. And the second person staying—a sister to Zuzueca and mother to him whose knife had cut the leader's throat. The woman had watched fearfully as relatives surrounded her son, but they had come to protect Tawitko, to hurry him away before certain ones appeared.

Many more persons joined in the wailing but with dry eyes, their crying only a noise, none choosing to remember Zuzueca as the man who had brought back this band to an important place inside the family circle. Instead they saw his dying as something to split the Kiyuksa once again.

"My relatives, hear me. Nothing shall separate the Kiyuksa."

Persons who had started after their horses in a desire to get out of camp, stopped to listen. Different ones, amazed at Tabloka's sudden appearance and surprising speech, threw a hand over their mouths.

"Nothing divides this strong band."

Tabloka, one of eight brothers calling Zuzueca 'father,' bellowed his message, his loudmouthed manner accepted as a family trait.

"This one whose knife kills my father protects an old

756

man from a wrinkling, wobbling age. He acts with true sympathy toward one whose eyes dim, whose heart weakens.

"Will you ask that this man who bleeds at my feet, this one who leads you through many seasons and over stony trails, live to an age that dreads the moving camp? Will you see him living beyond his usefulness, rolling off a drag in some secret place to starve until he dies?"

Hearing an uncertain response, Tabloka, a true-son of Zuzueca, roared on: "Where will you find among all who cover their loins someone more truly Kiyuksa, more truly Titonwan? Remember, he brings you to your camping place at the horns."

The murmurs began to evince agreement and now Tabloka looked around: "Where stands the one who cuts this old man's neck? Regard him not as a murderer whom you will drive out of the tribe; see him, instead, as a brave man who recognizes the Kiyuksa as a people in want of a new, strong protector. Look at this same one again and see him as the Kiyuksa who fills this need.

"I call this one to whom I refer 'tahanśi'." True, this day he gives me reason for weeping, manly as I am, but I hold neither rage nor spite in my heart. I understand and so, proudly, I call him my kinsman. Yet more proudly I will call him leader."

Tabloka knelt alongside the dead man, gesturing that someone come forward and help him carry the body from the site of the killing.

The people, recovering their composure, began to see the stabbing as a family affair. Tabloka, they remembered once again, has seven brothers; Tawitko has eight loyal kinsmen, those same eight brothers. And everyone agreed that Zuzueca long favored Tabloka and Tawitko; so perhaps the old leader wanted things to go this way, wanted either one—son or nephew—to take care of the people on his demise. Why not Tawitko as leader and Tabloka as principal warrior, as head akicita? Will not these two unite this Kiyuksa band as never before?

The corpse-carriers had walked out of sight before Tawitko's family opened the circle they formed around him. But Tawitko refused to step forward until he heard and saw signs that the band accepted him. Then, careful not to slip in

Zuzueca's blood, he moved center; he called out twenty names, presenting horses from his herd in these names. Suddenly everyone stood cheering Tawitko; the band stayed whole.

The day after the killing, all wapiya met with the deciders, the sacred-men asking that these summer-shirts put off the sungazing until the next round moon. Make the most of the hunts, they said, but keep the sungazing as the true reason for the summer gathering of Lakotah; make the sunpole the important symbol of the tribal hoop.

The deciders, hearing these wapiya, had approved. They knew that neither meat nor war pulled the people together during the warm moons; the attracting power related to a desire for renewing strength through ceremony.

And now the 'dreamers' in camp announced their intention to entertain with magical trials of power, everyone welcome to witness their display.

Most persons, the grandfathers had said, show a liking for some specific hoof or wing and if a man will observe his favorite closely, the creature toward whom he senses attachment will approach in a dream and offer the man a song. Ever afterwards, the dreamer shall own a voice for gaining spirit-help through this one.

But let a man remember, the wapiya had said, that such songs have tremendous influence; let the man who feels a preference for the branched-horn understand before ever he dreams that the song he receives will carry a power that attracts women.

Custom demanded that persons with the same spirit-helper form a group, these different groups holding a contest during the summer encampment, showing off their most amazing tricks. Let the true-dog dreamers try to outwit the wapiti dreamers, the people said, even as these creatures try to outwit one another. But let the heyoka, most powerful of dreamers, stand protectingly nearby the young girls whenever the wapiti dreamers start to throw around their power.

And so these lively exhibitions began, three wapiti dreamers commencing the show, each one wearing a three-sided mask and carrying a yellow pipe and a flashing yellow hoop. When they left off dancing, a second group of horn-dancers took over but these next five, in masks and carrying hoops and short black pipes, danced without drums or rattles. And after two dances, this new group challenged the heyoka to overwhelm any one or all five of their dancers.

Quick to respond, the heyoka came front, each one bellowing out his personal song simultaneously, the words lost in the din as each heyoka intended.

But suddenly the masked wapiti dreamers showed a different heart; stamping their feet, these five began to throw their influence, the 'p' sound popping out each mouth, the dancers spitting danger at the opposition.

The heyoka, pretending to use their stick-rattles as shields, dodged the invisible darts. And the spectators began to bet as to which group will fall.

But neither side fell; instead the wapiti dancers formed a circle, the men facing center and singing:

"*Tuwa wašte-ičilaka
wanna yanka can na
cante wanice.*"

"Any woman," they told, "who considers herself so attractive that she dares play with my affection looks for something."

These horn-dancers never had respected a flirt, but the heyoka protected all women, the proper and the improper, and so the contraries began antics aimed at breaking the power of this song.

The five wapiti dancers, instantly suspicious, changed the direction of their influence; the spectators now became the object of their attracting-powers. Stepping out of the dance circle, they invited the people to marvel this space of ground; here, hoofmarks and droppings where moments before five men had stood on smooth, clean earth.

Quickly dancing up to these creature-tracks, the heyoka rattled their sticks over the cut-up ground; marks and droppings instantly disappeared.

The astonished assemblage covered their mouths; marveling, they observed the dancers yet more closely.

Again the heyoka shook their sticks, but now a light flashed out from the palm of each contrary, a light that touched the face of one wapiti dancer.

The man looked around, his mask-eyes seeming to

signal something. Then suddenly he and his four dancers fell on the ground; blood poured out from under their masks and they lay as if dead.

And now the spectators murmured their amazement.

The heyoka at once began a wakinyan-dance, their flashing palms striking again at that certain masked-face, the dancer along with his companions on the ground and seeming not to breathe.

Presently a different masked-man walked front, someone who had made up to resemble pte, someone who wore moccasins but who left pte-tracks wherever he walked, a newcomer who apprently competed in this contest of tricks.

Approaching the five on the ground, the pte-dreamer made snuffing noises over each body, the 'wapiti' now jumping to their feet. All but one.

The crowd, suddenly apprehensive, moved back but they stayed to watch.

The pte-man had knelt, pushing aside his mask to suck at the stricken dancer's neck. And now the four horn-dancers performed in a manner to indicate distress; they lifted their hoops against the pte-man and against the heyoka.

And so the people recognized that something truly frightening had occurred here. But everyone stayed.

The pte-man stood, replacing his mask before he opened his hand to show a small, sharply-pointed arrow-head. Shaking his rattle at the heyoka who clustered nearby, he looked toward the wapiti dancers; he signaled that their companion lay dead.

Stunned, the crowd remained silent until the howls of women accepted the tragic reality.

A young man dies but who dares say what kills him? An invisible dart someone spits out his mouth? The flashing light? A pte-man who walks up on mysterious feet? A stone-dreamer who loses his control?

Terror crept in on all sides, some persons running without a direction. But out of somewhere came laughter, the laughter of children who watched something familiar, comically familiar.

And so the people looked and saw Woze, the heyoka whose many performances had entertained the bands for twenty winters. He came hopping as always, a wakinyan-dreamer who remembered himself as the big-splash-in-the-pond. Blowing up his cheeks and leaping every direction, he began his hilarious mimicking of the creature who swims and croaks and kicks and snaps up flies. Woze had come to distract the fearful and bring back smiles to the perplexed; Woze, protecting his people on one of those occasions when only laughter will clear the air and run off fear.

After a while two more heyoka—two who had not entered the magic-power contest—began their stunts, but these two performed only for men and for the old. And so they received a different sort of laughter. Turning aside his loin-cover, one clutched himself between the legs in the manner his wakinyan-dream had demanded; and so the man stiffened the piece of his body he now manipulated, his watchers cheering or upbraiding.

Stepping forward, the second wakinyan-dreamer, wearing a horsetail, performed his act; the man demonstrated that which a Psa warrior shall look for if ever a Titonwan gets a hold on him.

But these vulgar-comic acts had not brought forth nearly as much laughter as the brazen wit of three old, old women who watched, the group one moment shrieking contempt, the next moment drooling their delight.

And so the heyoka diverted all ages while the four wapiti dreamers carried off their dead dancer, while the peacemakers quietly went looking for Tawitko, to whom they shall say that a favorite among his Kiyuksa relatives falls down during the horn-dancers' magic trials and will not rise again.

Ahbleza, not present at the contest, heard the news when Lekśi came to report, the Shirtman attentive not only to his old uncle's terse account but also to this man's interpretation of the magic trials.

These contests, Ahbleza knew, will excite and mystify and create fear but rarely will a performer use his tricks to destroy. Occasionally a heyoka whose dream compels that he kill perhaps tries to hide the murder in a trick, but he waits for old age before he acts.

"Observe," said Lekśi, "that the grandfathers provide a place in the tribe for every manner of man, for every disposition. And so they contrive the wapiti dream for the prurient, something that will permit these lustful to demonstrate their nature in view of everyone. And any woman who flirts with these dreamers knows that she invites trouble."

Ahbleza recalled that the man killed this day often used his persuasive power over women; one whom he visited had died in her struggles to lose her unborn child. The people, recognizing the seduced woman as one who teased and tempted, had not interfered; only the heyoka dared avenge such tragedy.

But Lekśi had come visiting the Shirtman for more reason than to report the death of a Kiyuksa dancer. Sitting for a second pipe, the old man told that he brought Ahbleza some messages, some wisdom that the ancients had lent him. The invisibles sat aware that Lekśi wandered on the edge of life and that he had glimpsed the next realm. And so before he walked the spirit-trail he chose to speak to one with the ears for hearing.

"They call you Ahbleza, Observer; so observe, observe everything. Recognize everything.

"Cry-for-a-vision they tell a youth, but he who goes out crying gets himself sympathy, not vision. Perhaps he experiences a soothing dream but nothing that inspires. True, a cry for help brings help; usually a four-legged shadow with a Lakotah voice appears. And ever after the dreamer claims spirit-power and carries a bone or claw or tail to represent his invisible assistance. So much for the dream. Now understand the big-dream, the vision.

"Man commands a vision. Uśi maya ye; send me, he says. Man commands a vision and the picture comes. He sees everything, knows everything. But only for an instant. Surprise and consternation cut short his view. Even so, he holds on to a memory of this picture, this message; he keeps a referent for all his seasons. The only danger: telling his vision. If he tells, he will talk coloring and elaborating upon the message. And so he risks a following, persons who will make symbols for his message.

"And what about symbols? Will symbols—will any symbol—ever represent truth? Symbols, nothing but wrappings. Recognize the symbol as something that hides the reality, as a scheme for confusing the people. Look at what happens to the sunpole and you will understand my meaning.

"Discard all symbols. Become wise.

"But remember that the wise will not stop at becoming wise. The wise man walks this earth listening to his spirit-self, his familiar-voice. Nor will he ever act contrary to this true-voice, this familiar-voice that commands but never forbids.

"Live in the spirit, say the grandfathers; the spirit never will demand a surrender of your reason or deny you any urge. Whoever says that man shall suspend his reasoning looks for ways of stifling the spirit, and whoever says that man shall repress his natural desires hunts ways for killing joy.

"Appreciate your self, the grandfathers say. Recognize that your ears grant songs to the trees and to the stream. Soar on the wings of these songs; they belong to you. Use your body for giving growth to the spirit. You, who shall become the great spirit.

"And so on the day that you choose to drop off your shell, your spirit will grasp new life. Your spirit, scarcely noticing the change, shall go on creating, rejoicing. For the spirit, unaware of start and finish, knows only those restraints that your body imposes.

"Recognize śkan as the life-force, as the uplift-power, the power that raises up hills, raises up your heart; śkan, the power that keeps this earth alive.

"Observe each living thing—grass and all who walk on the grass—but know yourself as the one earth-form with the power for perceiving power. Recognize this power as spirit-power. Understand spirit-power as the creating force. Know yourself as one with the creating force and you will know that, truly, you own the earth. The grandfathers tell me so."

After Lekśi's visit, Ahbleza had placed crossed sticks in front of the tipi entrance; he had desired an aloneness that not even a bird's song dares invade. Half the night he had lain on his robes attempting a voluntary loan of his reasoning to the spirit-self, trying to imagine a second body within him, something all-knowing yet not unfamiliar. But whether he truly heard the voice of that spirit-self speak, confirming that which Lekśi had said, he knew not. He knew that for one brief moment he had sensed himself clinging to the edge of a cloud, listening to a familiar-voice but not certain that he really understood: discard, detach, fulfill.

At daybreak Ahbleza unwrapped the hides on which he had painted the Lakotah ceremonies, all ceremonies but the sungazing. Then remembering who had inspired his making these pictures, he felt a sudden ache; for a moment he stared dully at the colorful sketches spread before him. But pushing aside this memory, he carefully examined his work, something he intended to present Wanaġi before the sungazing.

First, most important: the hunkaġapi, making-relatives-through-choice ceremony. Wife, the most revealing choice a man ever makes. Hunka-brother, the most enduring pledge a man ever takes. And hunka-father, the most inspiring bond ever to exist between youth and age.

Next, the inipi, the renewing ceremony wherein stone and air, fire and water persuade man of his power to expand and so unite with taku śkanśkan, the life-force.

Here, the ihambleiciyapi, vision-seeking, the 'they-go-beyond' experience, a true-expansion, a real union.

And here, the iśnati ceremonies, something to impress the girl-becoming-woman, something to help her relate to the earth as mother, as a power for making-life. But more important, a ceremony for reassuring a girl that the people recognize her susceptible nature during the change; that they throw a protecting force around her to ward off undesirable influence; that they act to prevent any unnatural arrest of her mating-desire. Or any dangerous fears.

Next here, the wanaġi-yuha, the spirit-owning ceremony wherein the seeker, sending his breath to the invisible grandfathers, listens for a reliable voice. And certain invisibles, responding, send a message through a familiar creature-form, wings or four-legs, who will not misinterpret the thought.

Also the spirit-lodge, something different from spirit-keeping. Here they keep the spirit-bundle, strands of hair through which the family keeps in touch with someone who dies, with the spirit-self who perhaps stays near until growth ceases at head and fingertip and toe; spirit-lodge, image of the spirit-realm.

Ahbleza gazed a long while on his remaining picture: the pipe, the smoking ceremony; the pipe, central to all ceremonies.

The pipe, symbol for truth, for demonstrating truth. The pipe, symbol of gladness and grief, thanks and wishfulness, healing and heartening; the pipe, a symbol of understanding and the desire for understanding.

Symbol?

Symbols, nothing but wrappings around the truth; Lekśi, in touch with the original grandfathers, had said so.

True, he sees wisdom in throwing away whatever clutters man's understanding, but never, never will any Lakotah throw away the pipe. Who will dare ignore the gift that Ptesanwin brings? The pipe, the all-meaningful image.

Ahbleza placed a glowing ember on the bowl of his own pipe; he will hold on to this symbol of comfort, of strength.

While the Shirtman had sat alone these two days, the people had opened the hoop to receive the slow-coming Iśna. The man had brought not only his own tiyośpaye but all Sicanǧu who had drunk their way through the snow moons on the muddy-water. These persons viewed the sungazing as their one way to experience renewal, to demonstrate their avowal to pick up old customs. The Sicanǧu represented more than half the Titonwan lodges but far from half the Titonwan strength; most certainly a band weakens when leaders within lose self-control.

But now scouts ran into camp with news of a great herd to the north, the direction the people intended to travel on their way to the sungazing grounds at rapid creek. And so the herald called for all tipi down at dawn and the bands moving. Pte waited on the path, a good sign.

XX

AHBLEZA WALKED front of a traveling line of fifty-five hundred persons, ten thousand horses. Principal man among the sungazers, he led the procession that moved toward sacred ceremony.

Wanaǧi, the man Ahbleza had made responsible for the eight-day sungazing encampment, walked next to the Shirtman. All other travelers came in usual order—the four deciders and tribal leaders forward, clubmen at the sides, horse herds and tenders back, so far back that persons center never saw the rear of this long, long line.

During their three days' travel, the people welcomed the sun each morning as a tribe and then Wanaǧi made a ceremonial demand for sunny days and moon-bright nights during the forthcoming sunpole dance. Singeing a bunch of sweetgrass which he had placed on bare ground, he sang his request for clear skies throughout the eight days of ceremony.

"Anpetu wi tanyan hinapa nunwe." Always he started this song high, his tones descending. "Maka ożanżanyan tanyan hinapa nunwe." A bright sun shall light the earth, he said.

"Hanhepi wi tanyan hinapa nunwe." Using the same eleven tones, the wapiya demanded also a bright moon.

But not only Wanaǧi sang; all down the line, wherever a sacred-man stood, the people heard this song, each seer echoing the seer who preceded him. And so the song went on and on, the wind finally carrying the tones out across the plain, where grass and butte passed along the demanding cry for clear weather.

On the third morning the travelers came within hunting distance of the herd. Before dusk, tongue and shoulder from four hundred pte lay wrapped in hides, meat for the sungazers and the many persons who assist with this ceremony. The remaining cuts, enough meat for everyone during their stay on sacred-ground.

On the fourth day the people arrived at rapid creek, the same campsite where Olepi once scarred his body in a sungazing. Here the clubmen stopped the travelers while two heralds rode down the line, calling forward all persons pledged to the pole.

When these thirty had come together, Wanaǵi faced west and, looking toward the black hills, lifted a pipe, stem and bowl level with his heart.

"Grandfathers," he began, "look this way. Wambli-woman, see me. Akicita-spirits, know who stands here. These persons seek renewal; a red robe they raise, they bring you. This day let the family live."

Wanaǵi had sung in the language of his intimates and so the Shirtman and his companions heard only word-symbols that related to some ancient premise. And now Ahbleza asked himself things he never before dared ask. Who, this wambli-woman? Why, these akicita-spirits? What, this red robe?

Suddenly he found an even more startling thought: who, this Ptesanwin, pte-woman? And what, this wakantan-ka they say that he shall marvel but never ponder?

Turning, he looked directly upon Wanaǵi's face, his eyes challenging the wapiya, glaring as if at a stranger, an enemy.

The sacred-man met the stare with hostile gaze and so they stood—he who shall direct the great renewing cere-mony and he who shall take direction—like enemy warriors who know that if ever they clash, only one will survive.

Then, holding the pipe in one hand, Wanaǵi spoke summoning leaders of the bands to council with him. "Wicaśa okinihan cokata hiyupo," he shouted, and the two who had ridden down the line once before, carried this next message to the waiting people: leaders, come to the front. Come to the front.

Slowly the principals assembled on a little knoll, and here Wanaǵi again lifted the pipe. But now he pointed the stem toward the sun, almost at mid-sky: "Grandfather, accept and smoke."

Next he offered the stem to all warrior-birds who soar and circle over the grasses: "Wingflappers, you in turn will smoke and so the family will live."

Wanaǵi passed the pipe to the men gathered around him, each one drawing once upon the stem. And now these smokers saw what pipe they smoked: an exciting stem in the shape of a pte-leg, a bowl in the shape of a pte-head. Wanaġi had unwrapped the Lakotah ceremonial pipe, a pipe occasionally looked upon but never filled, never used, not since the making thirty winters past.

Only the pipe-maker, only Wanaġi, knew whose words had inspired the design for this stem. And only Wanaġi knew that, on remembering those words, he had felt compelled to bring forth this extraordinary pipe for use at the sungazing of an extraordinary man.

The sun now straight above, Wanaġi gave Ahbleza an instruction: "Ride along the line of people; invite the bands into the hoop. Say that the head-akicita shall make assignments."

The welcoming ceremony finished, the sacred-man walked down from the knoll and, pipe in hand, moved toward the wide-open space where rapid creek comes out onto the plain.

This same night the almost-round moon shone on a great, great circle, on more than ten hundred lodges. Two tipi sat at the back of the circle, directly opposite the opening in the hoop, one tipi for Ahbleza's use as leader of the sungazers and in front of this one, the council lodge. Neither of these two bore design, the council lodge never decorated and Ahbleza requesting unpainted skins for the lodge-of-preparation.

The moon lighted the dance-ground, where stakes in circular form marked off the space for dancers and singers, for the pole and for a piece of smooth, bare earth whereon Wanaġi shall place pte-skull and pipe.

The hoop of people faced east as always, but the opening to the dance circle faced the sacred hills, the place of wingflappers and flying-mysteries and most ancient stone. This sundance circle shall open to the west; Wanaġi had said so.

XXI

EVERYONE AT rapid creek found a way to help prepare for the sungazing, but the Iyuptala-lodge made the important assignments. Meeting with the pipe-keepers in each of the warrior-lodges, the Iyuptala formed a group whose work included the selection of eight clubmen to cut the sunpole-tree and four young women—none with a husband—to make cuts on this tree before the sharp edge of a stone club dropped the wood.

But the privilege of choosing the one to locate the straight and slender tree that becomes the sunpole belonged to Ahbleza. And so he sent Tonweya to decide this tree and to mark his selection with sticks propped against two sides, sage laid in front.

At dawn on the second day Wanaǧi called together all the seers; he asked that each band provide a preparation-lodge, an initi, and helpers for their dancers. As director of the affair he made himself responsible for a supply of sweetgrass, paint for the pole, and a pipe for special rituals.

"You shall see me removing bark from the wood and painting red stripes on the pole and you shall hear me singing as I work," Wanaǧi told the assemblage of wapiya. "Next, you shall see me covering my body with a shedding robe and painting my face red. I will dip my hands in this same color. And you will know why I act in this manner."

He went on: "You shall see me mellowing earth and cutting this bare ground, my two lines crossing. You shall see me filling these cuts with pipe-mixture, covering over with red powder. You shall see me scattering glistening stone-dust on top the red powder.

"You shall see me putting breath-feathers where these two lines cross and you shall hear me singing as I prepare this space of earth. And you will know why I act in this manner."

When Wanaǧi heard the 'hau' that signified that the sacred-men understood him, he named his personal help-ers—two who, like himself, had neither killed a man nor used their powers to destroy anything. He requested the one, an old wakanĥca from among the Śiyo, to take his place at the felling of the tree, and he asked the other—Sunihanble of the Mahto—to take over for him at the inipi ceremonies. In this way he, Wanaǵi, dared stay mostly in the lodge-of-preparation with Ahbleza.

Ahbleza had worked many days on those things they demanded of the leading sungazer. He shall provide each item they hang on the sunpole: a strip of red hide for near the top, berry brush for halfway up and a man-shape bundle and a pta-shape bundle to dangle on the pole sunrise to sunfall during one of the days.

Cankuna had presented him with the ceremonial wrapper for his thighs and legs, the woman quilling her dream-design on this niteiyapehe. And Kehala had quilled a short strip to wind around the stem of the old vision-pipe, the stem of a dreaming-pair. And so Ahbleza sat ready to enter the lonely tipi back of the council lodge where he shall stay these next three nights.

At midday of this same second day at rapid creek, the drum-maker in the Oglalaĥca camp tested his new drum, trying out his twenty new beaters, each one with the hairside out to give deep tones. He also looked for a certain herald, a man most careful with words, someone he will have help him assemble the outstanding singers-drummers in the encampment.

This same herald, whose work included answering anything the people put to him about the sungazing, had announced the selection of Woze as the heyoka who will climb the sunpole and fasten symbols to the crosspiece at dawn on the third day of the ceremonial, the day of permissiveness.

Now, the sun past middle, the people moved about in noisy crowds, something going on everywhere. In many camps young people danced and sang for a handout, meat or anything appropriate to win smiles from the sad-hearts to whom they will distribute such offerings. And at the edge of the encampment, the excited shouts of contesting clubmen, horseback and running down the tall-ears, many sungazers asking for this one's puff-tail to tie at their ankles when they dance, something to keep their own feet hopping.

And certainly the different seers kept moving, choosing messenger-boys, sage-gatherers, water-carriers, horse-tenders. They also walked aware of a group of unmated young women and girls who feasted in a conspicuous place, each one offering herself as a wound-wiper, as someone who desired to take care of the sungazers' cuts, as someone who earned this honor.

Shyly, occasionally giggling, each aspirant claimed that she never had talked with men, that the hand of a man never had touched her, and that she never had loosened the cord at her thighs at night. And so each one sat prepared to reach her arm into a hole they had dug and lift out a knife. Biting on the knife, each young woman will vow herself chaste, a woman eligible to tend the gazers' wounds.

Many persons had left their affairs to witness this ceremonial feast, especially young warriors who stood viewing these women as prospective wives. But different men, clumsy and insecure, had come looking for girls on whom to try out their daring. Even so, most men watched proudly, glad that their sisters declared this innocence.

Olepi, standing in the crowd of spectators, had sensed relief on seeing that not a Kiyuksa woman sat in this group of twenty; he always will remember that a similar ceremony once divides this band.

But a different man who watched sensed humiliation in the fact that not one woman from his band sat here. And so, his face as dark as rainy sky, Tabloka pushed forward.

For a moment the Kiyuksa stood, arms folded, looking at the pretty young woman whose turn had come to place the knife between her teeth. Then, stooping to the ground, he gathered a handful of clay.

The girl shrank back, her eyes terrified; she had recognized that which the fearsome warrior intended. Then, in the same instant that the clod struck against her cheek, she saw Tabloka's moccasin overturn her feast bowl.

Seizing the girl's arm and dragging her out in front of the crowd, Tabloka shouted his contempt: "Only pure young women attend this feast. Yet here sits one who knows a man."

A sorrowful cry rose up, but above the wail the spectators heard derisive noises. The young woman's companions looked around, a hand at each mouth, their eyes wide in denial; never will this timid Siyo girl pretend anything, never will she enact an untruth. And now they listened for

771

her voice to challenge the Kiyuksa, to demand that Tabloka reach into the hole, pull forth the arrow and bite the point. And so dare to verify what he implies.

But the frightened girl said nothing. She stood shamed before all, her head bent and eyes down as if truly she had misrepresented herself at this feast.

Tabloka released her arm. Gazing sternly at her quaking form, he waited for someone to come to her defense. What about her relatives? Father, grandfather, uncle, any relative? Who will dispute the voice of Tabloka? The warrior waits.

None spoke out. Who knows for certain that the girl remains chaste? And if Tabloka, hearing a challenge, bites the arrow in defiance, certainly trouble will visit the young woman's family.

Sadly her father kept silent. And her brother? A boy of eight, someone who yet uses the woman's language, scarcely the person to speak out against a warrior even if he really understands that which happens here.

Her mother's pain-struck face looked out at the crowd but she dared say nothing. Nor will this woman's brothers call out against the powerful Kiyuksa and so bring difficulty into the hoop and onto the sungazing ground.

More than one Titonwan glanced contemptuously at Tabloka, but none of these persons opened their mouths. They, like Olepi, remembered back to the Kiyuksa breakoff; they, also, knew that quarrels from within weaken the whole tribe. But certainly the grandfathers recall strict ways for dealing with persons similar to Tabloka; perhaps these wise ones will recommend the ancient ordeals.

But who dares propose these severe tests or drive out this warrior as an untruthful man if neither the girl nor her guardians speak up? And who will desire running the girl out of camp until they see Tabloka taking the arrow-oath against her? And who will question aloud—aloud—whether the Kiyuksa violates the girl or whether, instead, he knows which man puts a hand on her.

Four, five warriors looked enviously toward the unrelenting Tabloka. Obviously the man stood indifferent to the girl's reputation; he simply used this daring ruse as a way of discovering his power among the bands. Apparently he had chosen this shy young woman as one who will not make complaint, her family not prominent, her tiyośpaye unlikely to start something that involves testing the loyalty of Tabloka's seven brothers.

Reaching again for the girl, Tabloka touched her gently; smiling upon her, he announced that he shall take this Siyo woman into his lodge as wife if she will accept him. He asks that her father and brother accept his humble gift of two horses for whatever embarrassment his challenge brings about. And two more horses shall go to her uncle.

"I will not regard this young woman as really unwholesome," he said now; "will she not try for the privilege of wiping sage on the sungazers' faces? I see a good woman but one who will not remember that sage in the hands of the impure brings disaster to the sungazing ceremony. And so, my friends, I ask that you not hold a grudge against this pretty young woman; instead, accept and respect her goodness."

His fat hand let go the girl's slender one; he asked that she get her things and come to his lodge. And perhaps her young brother will enjoy selecting his horse now?

The Kiyuksa turned and walked toward the horse herds, the girl's brother close on his moccasins, the boy's eyes dancing proudly.

Peśla had marveled the scene. Who in the Mahto camps with such daring? What a warrior, this Tabloka. True, Tawitko leads the Kiyuksa now, but certainly Tabloka soon takes this place. Soon Tabloka leads the Kiyuksa band and perhaps one day he shall lead all Titonwan. Here, a man the people will follow anywhere. Here, a man whom Peśla gladly calls relative.

The hunter's son glanced in the direction of certain women who headed back for the Kiyuksa campsite, three in this group wives to Tabloka. He saw that Cuwe, also wife to the Kiyuksa, followed a little distance back of these women. Suddenly irked, Peśla remembered that Tacincala, his second sister and plenty ripe for mating, sits in his mother's lodge. Why will the Kiyuksa not ask for Tacincala, on whom he holds a claim, instead of making the Śiyo girl his eighth woman? Even Tabloka knows he will have to stop somewhere.

The crier, speaking for the seers, had asked that the crowd disperse; the young women shall proceed with their feast and so dispel any rising distrust of one another.

But the seers had neither ways nor words for helping the abused one who chose to walk alone toward her mother's lodge.

Moving across camp, the Śiyo girl struggled to understand why this disgrace had come to her. The Kiyuksa warrior never had touched her before this day when suddenly he grabbed her arm. Nor had any man ever untied the protection she wore at her thighs. And so why will her relatives sit silent as if they, also, imagine her impure?

But not until this instant had she realized that she permitted the image; Tabloka's attack had knocked out her speech and so she had not denied his implication; she had said nothing to protect herself, her family, her friends.

Overwhelmed, she began to run. And now she held on to a single thought: find a strong cord and carry this thing outside the hoop where an understanding tree will accept her choice.

But a woman had run up alongside her, someone who kept her face covered. "I know what you intend," the woman said quickly, "but hear me. Walk for a moment and let me talk. I know the hurt of shame. And I know about living with a man not of your choosing. So take whatever things you want for the little while this man favors you. More important, never grow fond of him. And so you never will suffer hurt if he throws you away." She touched the girl's arm. "Wait and see before you hunt a cord and branch. Remember, you have more reason for living than some of your Lakotah sisters."

The speaker had gone as suddenly as she had appeared, come and gone with the robe covering her head, muffling her voice.

For a long while the Śiyo girl stood puzzling, not the woman but the message. Then moving on, she turned again in the direction of her parents' lodge. She will get her things together, but before she goes to this man Tabloka she will visit an old woman-seer. Here she will ask for a drink of the white-stalk and afterwards she will stand over the fragrant smoke from the burning tops of this same grass. And so she shall make certain that never will she grow a child for

774

Tabloka, never will she become a mother not of his child or that of any different man.

The woman with the covered head had walked back to the site on which the Kuya raised lodges; Wiyukcan Mani not likely will reproach her for the brief disappearance. Hinziwin seldom walks outside the lodge now, as Iśna's family knows; why let anyone see her stringy hair and changing face, a face the Mahto leader once calls pretty, very pretty.

Tacincala smiled at her mother. "They choose me," she said softly; "I am one of four who will perform the wamblidance." The young woman's face reflected her joy. "They ask that I practice the steps. I hold my arms in this manner . . . "—she stretched out an arm to each side, level with her shoulders—"and so I soar. . . . " She bent her body gracefully, her arms dipping as she imitated the circling wambli.

Cankuna looked on approvingly. Long before now she had recognized Tacincala's pleasing manners; here, she had told herself, a young woman for whom the flutes shall sing. Or will Tacincala go to Tabloka if the Kiyuksa requests her? True, this daughter says she will die before ever she goes to the warrior, but this one also will avoid making things awkward for her people. They say that Tabloka takes a Siyo woman whom he challenges at the chastity feast this day; eight women, perhaps enough wives for one lodge and the Kiyuksa never will send for Tacincala.

The young dancer, hearing a voice, stepped outside the tipi. Cankuna followed and together they listened to the crier's instructions, a herald in each camp singing the same message at this same moment.

"When the sun climbs down, cover over your fires. At sunfall, cover over all fires. At sunfall they invite the winged powers. Cover your fires and attend this dance."

Tacincala's eyes shone excitement. "My mother, ten persons sing while I and three more dancers perform as wambli. They use five drums, each one with a different tone. And two singers at each drum for this dance." She pulled gently on her mother's gown. "Now I go. Walk with me to the lodge where the seers wait for their dancers."

Cankuna, answering to the coaxing eyes, went with her daughter to the big lodge where Wanaǵi gave instructions to the four whose dance opens the sungazing ceremony. She watched the group practice, then returned to her lodge and changed into a clean new gown. And certainly she agreed with Tacincala that the ancient Dakotah who had used this ceremony created a most wonderful song and dance.

The sun sat down on the earth and a hushed encampment covered over all fires, then walked toward the sungazing circle, the people ever eager to witness a ceremony that renews and inspires.

The men at the drum tapped the handles of their beaters against the rim, and the people heard a voice something like Wanaǧi's voice: "Winged power who lives where the sun goes down, you own two good days. Give me one."

The seer had begun the invitation-song.

And now, while four young women danced the soaring movements of the great wingflappers, the drummers sent a voice inviting these winged to the sungazing.

"Ye hey ya, ya hey ya," they sang, voices blending.

"Wambli gleśka," they sang as one voice, "wana mahiyohi"—spotted wingflapper, coming to me.

The seer went on, inviting the winged power in all directions to attend this ceremonial. And so he also called upon the winged power in the grasses: "Onsimayaye"—I command your power; "oyate, nimkte wacin yelo"—the people shall live.

The phrases signaled forward all sungazers, these persons moving in a procession toward Ahbleza's lodge-of-preparation.

For a moment the sungazers, eyes proud and bodies tall, waited center. Then, the drums quiet, each of these pledged ones—a wapiya moving to his side—started toward his own camp and the special lodge his band had raised for him, a place from which he shall emerge after three days to take his stand at the sunpole.

Ahbleza waited outside the principal lodge-of-preparation until all sungazers had disappeared and the crowd had thinned. He stood watching the fires that started up wherever people uncovered the embers. And suddenly he marveled the mystery of flame on ground and underground. But now a touch on his arm returned his eyes to the lodge; Wanaǧi, holding up the entrance flap, signaled him inside.

Bending slightly, Ahbleza entered the tipi. In his hand he held a piece of hide on which he had begun to draw the sungazing ceremony. And when next he stepped out of this lodge, he intended to come forth understanding each symbol they use on the pole and why the pole and why the scarifying.

In his quest for truth he had chosen to perform the sungazing as one way to discover the thought that originally prompted this unifying ceremony. He will go to the sunpole looking for meanings back of the many rituals that comprise this important affair. He will go to the sunpole to find out something about his youth's vision that he not yet understands. And, as on the day he pledged his vow, he will go to the pole grateful that he had survived the trials, grateful for the unbroken bond between brother-friends, grateful for all good.

But now he asked himself that which never before had occurred to him: grateful to whom?

XXII

THOSE EIGHT whom the Iyuptala chose to bring in the sunpole tree had made four turns around the camp circle before sunrise. Drums and voices had cheered their ride, everyone awake to sing off this party that goes out looking for 'paza,' for the wood that Tonweya had selected and marked.

"Ake iyayapi yelo"—again they go. Children and the grown, all sang the phrase on a lilting tone, setting the mood for an exciting experience, implanting a game into this affair.

On this day, the second day of the great summer-ceremony, the people remembered their warrior heritage. They related the eight horsebacks to 'scouts' who rode up and down the creeks looking for the enemy, who walked over the hills looking for meat.

"Ake iyayapi yelo." Somewhere stands a tree, on this day a symbol for enemy; eight young men, on this day a symbol for scouting, go out looking for the tree.

But those eight scarcely had gone before they came racing back, jumping off in front of the Siyo wapiya, the winning man yelling 'anhe' and receiving the sacred-man's pipe. Instantly the drummers began a welcoming-back song and certain akicita rode wide circles around the returned.

Each of the eight had dropped to a kneel in the manner of a reporting scout and so the people listened quietly while the wapiya questioned the pipe-holder.

"Man, you ride along the streams. If anywhere you see a traveling-dog, tell me."

"I see a small enemy village moving this way." The 'scout' answered symbolically, using his thumb to show direction.

At once, twenty young men, symbolizing a war party, jumped horseback; sounding war cries, they rode in a close circle.

But now from different places among the spectators four pretty girls came forward, a woman back of each girl and leading a horse. And so the twenty horsebacks spread out in a wide line, the eight 'scouts' leaping on horses and joining this line, the wapiya and four girls invited to mount and ride with the party.

When all sat mounted, the drummers signaled these horsebacks to move. At once the 'scouts' dashed forward, then the 'war party' of twenty, and finally the girl-riders, the wapiya in their midst. And following close, men, women, children, everyone who desired to witness an important scene in the sungazing affair.

Ahbleza, from inside the lodge-of-preparation, heard the songs and noise. He knew that twenty went out as 'warriors,' something that perhaps recalled the daring and courage of those original families who followed pte onto the short grass.

Unfolding the hide on which he had pictured the felling-of-the-tree scene, Ahbleza pondered that which the grandfathers truly intended to reveal here; why emulate an attack on this living wood?

And now Wanaġi, sitting alongside, asked whether the Shirtman remembered that the Titonwan had made up the Lakotah sungazing rituals out of things they had discovered on the plain. Will Ahbleza recall that they take from the Oyateyamni—the three-circle people who live south—the ritual that calls for scouts hunting and warriors attacking the sunpole-tree? And that this attack means subduing the enemy, meaning that they cut off his manliness. Let the Shirtman review the symbolic enactment when the war party 'attacks' the tree, when the four young women 'cut' this symbol of male-power.

Wanaġi rose and went out of the lodge. Before the party returned with the tree, he wanted to see the hole Sunihanble had prepared for the pole; he intended to pile the lifted ground to the west, the mound a symbol for the black hills, breast of the earth.

The sun had reached halfway past middle when Ahbleza heard the hum of mixed voices and the throbbing, descending wail that signaled the returning party. And now he listened for the sounds of excitement which will tell that the tree-bearers walk slowly through camp and onto the suncircle-ground. And then for the silence which will mean that the wapiya smooths the wood and starts to stripe the pole with red paint.

Wanaġi's thoughts as he painted the sunpole lingered on Ahbleza. Will the Shirtman remember that red symbolizes not only blood but the undying spirit, that red means not only 'the people' but also 'the generations ahead,' that red sky symbolizes sunfall, a sunny day, the round fat moon, a girl-turning-woman, a woman-becoming-wife, flow from a wound, and a wrapping for the dead? And even if he remembers all these things, will he understand the truth about red?

Presently Wanaġi began to sing; his song told the people that whatever a person recognizes he owns.

"Ateya lena tawa makiye, can makobaza nazin hiyeye

779

cin." The wapiya recognizes the forest, he said, and so he owns the trees, the sunpole-tree and all.

Whatever a man recognizes he owns. Ahbleza emptied his pipe-bowl and laid aside all thoughts but this one. In your many seasons, he asked himself, what will you say that you truly own?

Mitawin. Heyatawin.

The answer had come instantly but without memory of her appearance. For he will not permit himself this memory. Why use the power that sorrow generates for recalling her? She lives as an invisible—the grandfathers say—and so why interfere with her spirit? Why make her want to cry for him, perhaps see him as pathetic. He never tried to influence her here; so why anywhere?

"But something I have and forever keep," he whispered; "something I never give away, something they never take away. I and this woman recognize a bond of pure joy and so I own—own—joy. Now and forever I own joy.

"I am a Shirtman. They say that I own the people, that I keep the tribe. I put away the Shirt but never shall I put away the people. I own trust even as I own joy."

And now Ahbleza listened for the command, 'ho,' at which moment they raise the sunpole, a bundle of berry-wood on the short crosspiece, this nest-symbol originating with the Sahiela. The twenty akicita horsebacks who had brought in the tree will lift the wood, pulling on thongs, raising the pole in four tries while men and women sing the same song but on different tones.

Winkte had composed this song; what different one will experience the sensations of man, of woman, more acutely than a winkte, a twin-souls person. And who but Wanagi will demand a song that makes obvious that which the sunpole represents?

And so Ahbleza heard the women singing their little-hurt song as the wood fit into the hole, singing their joy as the pole stood erect.

"Wi, tawintonpi walakapi; he yo," the young men sang; "ina, wita su icu: welo, hey ya yo."

"Yu, yu, yu, yu," the young women answered; "wasteya, omayazan, yu, yu, yu, yu."

Now, the tree in place, the Siyo wapiya spoke, the old man throwing his voice, his words seemingly coming from the pole. "Here, at the center of earth, stand and look around you; recognize the people."

While the people listened, Wanaǧi walked twelve, fourteen steps west, where he began to expose earth, baring ground not in the usual circular form but clearing away four corners. And then he spoke demanding that the people observe this space: here, the power-of-life unassigned; śkan, available, something a man shall make his own.

Next, he spread a layer of sage nearby the uncovered earth, a place for the pipe rack and pte-skull.

Everything pertaining to the earth now ready, Wanaǧi signaled the people to start making the sunshade that will surround most of the ceremonial circle and provide cool for the spectators.

If everyone helps, the crier sang, they will complete the structure before light fades. Afterwards all those persons who enact the rituals on this second day shall ride around the suncircle, men front and singing to the sky, women back and singing to the earth.

Cankuna watched proudly as Tacincala moved into position among the young women-horsebacks who will ride around the sungazing-ground. One of the women in the daylong affair had become iśnati, and so the Iyuptala had invited the hunter's daughter to sing in the procession. Twice they honor Tacincala this day, once as a dancer and now as a singer.

Napewaśte had come forward to watch alongside her friend Cankuna, but she kept remembering back twenty seasons to the day when Olepi had sungazed on this same ground. And now she felt a tiny pain at her breasts, but this warning of something unusual will relate to the son, not the husband.

But now the sun dropped down out of view and the horsebacks began their ride, the loping of their mounts effecting a drumlike sound.

"Anpetu wi he miye lo, he ya, heyapi lo," sang the men, eyes on the pole as they rode circling the ceremonial ground.

And now the women riders approached singing, agreeing with the men: "Wankanta nitasu iwacu kte so, yo; maka kin he miye, he miye so."

781

After a fourth turn around the circle, the men waited for the women. When all horsebacks came together, they joined voices, tones blending in the same manner as during the pole-raising song. And now, as before, they mixed their voices to sing the truth: the sun acts on earth and so the seed grows.

When this group broke up, the young men rode back to their akicita-lodges, certain ones holding dances and feasts this night, the members painting and strutting around camp before they sang and ate. But the young women, a grandmother or mother on guard, returned quietly and quickly to their lodges. Nor will these young women reappear until they see the sungazers going to the pole, until the people assemble at the suncircle.

This same night Wanaǧi lifted to Ahbleza's lips a ladle of the warm drink, the only drink, permitted in the lodge-of-preparation. But the Shirtman turned his head.

"Drink, my son," Wanaǧi said firmly. "You come here for experience. So experience everything. This root-broth has a place."

Ahbleza took four sips, the wapiya keeping hold of the ladle.

"Now show me, my son, the neckwear you make."

The sungazer held up a cord from which dangled a circular piece of hide marked with two crossing-lines. Where these lines met the circle's edge, Ahbleza had attached wambli-feathers.

"Place a breath-feather at the center," Wanaǧi instructed. "Now regard this one feather as wakantanka, the mystery at the center."

The center, the center. The sungazer shall go to the center. Again and again each sungazer shall hear his instructing wapiya use this word 'center.' The meaning of all things sits at the center. The pipe and pte go with you to the center. At the center, wakantanka. At the center, you. At the center, pipe and pte. At the center, at the center, at the center, at the center.

"Hear me!"

Wanaǧi's sharp tone aroused the Shirtman; he pulled his shoulders erect. Sitting without a backrest and changing his position only once since coming here, he had slumped.

782

And he had let himself wonder why Wanaǧi sits here asking about the little circular neckpiece. Why will he ask that Ahbleza decorate this circle with two intersecting lines? Or four lines coming from a central point?

Drowsy, uncomfortable, striving for composure, Ahbleza had not known whether he answered or only heard a familiar-voice answering: always two or twice-two.

Two or twice-two; the life-force intends a balance. Sky and earth, male and female, warm and cold, root-stem-leaf-berry, south-north and west-east.

Two or twice-two; the life-force maintains a rhythm, the heartbeat rhythm. Every song, ya he ya ya, ya he ya ya; each song they sing twice or twice again.

The Shirtman looked at the wapiya, eyes staring unnaturally, his tone bold. "I, body and reasoning, spirit and truth. I, Ahbleza, blood and thought and essence and power. I, visible and invisible. I, Ahbleza, four and yet two and yet . . . and yet . . . really only one."

Suddenly his eyes fell away; he had spoken out of turn, his moment for declaring himself had not yet come. He shall not truly know himself until he suffers at the sunpole; they say so.

"You prove yourself an extraordinary man, my son," the sacred-man said softly. "But not even the extraordinary command the sun or change the moon. And so I ask: what things will you command . . . or change?"

Before he went out of the lodge, Wanaǧi laid more sage on the embers, and the Shirtman, responding to the strengthening fragrance of the everlasting-grass, pondered that which the sacred-man had asked.

XXIII

THE THIRD day of the summer-ceremony began with bold laughter and lewd joking. Midmorning Woze, a comical cone on top his head, climbed the sunpole upside down, going only as high as the crosspiece, where he hung images of man and pta beneath the brush-bundle. But the forms he hung appeared different from the shapes Ahbleza had cut; the heyoka had exaggerated the maleness in each one. And so the people remembered an unusual privilege this day.

True, some persons will indulge an urge but most of the people will ignore these swinging effigies; they look for nothing more than jest and banter to prevail among their own.

But even the man who uses this occasion to discover his potency or find a new, young wife usually behaves discreetly; none desires any grief as an outcome of his act. Yet not a woman will risk walking alone for wood or water on this day, and the fine young women of the bands will neither leave the tipi nor receive a visitor.

Cankuna had cautioned Tacincala to stay inside, and she had advised Winu not to linger outside the lodge. The hunter's family had not yet adopted the Palani captive—Ogle had delayed this thing—but certainly they guarded this woman the same as their own daughter.

But Winu, her eyes on Peśla for a long while, intended to act on these symbols newly hung on the pole. Going to Lowansa's tipi, she had forced her attentions upon the warrior.

Peśla, scorning her approaches, had flung ridicule in her face, then gone out of the lodge. Gladly he will take someone this day but not a Palani woman. And so Winu, sullen-faced, had walked back slowly to Cankuna's lodge, not so much as one man noticing her.

But Peśla, passing around the sunlodge, had looked up at the pole and grinned. If Tabloka dared defame a girl at the feast of the chaste, certainly Peśla dares something that will involve Tabloka's family. What more appropriate occasion than now to persuade Tabloka's sister—already wife to a proud Oglalaȟca—that she attracts him? Why not live this permissive day dangerously?

Still grinning, Pesla had turned in the direction of the Kiyuksa camp.

At sundown the Tatanka-lodge members gathered inside the sundance circle. They had painted their bodies white—their lances also—and they had come wearing the horns of old herd-fathers along with loin-covers and dance moccasins. Shuffling back and forth, they began to smooth the dance-ground, leveling rough spots, brushing off sticks and stones. But before they had completed this smoothing-earth ceremony, someone outside the sunshade had begun to recite his experiences.

Making certain that he had listeners, Pesla retold his famous act-of-daring among the Palani and then, his eyes on the pole, he began to sing his accomplishments this day; his song revealed everything a certain woman had given him, offered him.

Desiring that the people understand who had made these offers, he mimicked woman's phrasing: "Keep my undergown and so remember me."

Somewhat startled, the crowd now heard Pesla exposing this woman, not by name but through her relative-term for the singer.

"Sice," he sang, "tehanya omayalake kte sni ca, ehakab anpetu iyuha ecamaun kte."

So! Tabloka's sister, a woman with a husband, not only gives Pesla her nitohompi, her undergown, but invites his return each day if he will keep secret these meetings.

"Nitohompi kin le yuhana, miksuya ye he miye ye so."

The warrior's imprudent song and the day-of-familiarities came to a finish at the same moment. As Pesla sang the final phrase, fifty arrows cut down the effigies on the pole, the akicita removing these permissive symbols; sunfall had stopped the intimacy if not the outcome of such intimacy.

Nor had anyone wanted to predict the outcome of a certain warrior's song even on a day that granted lasciviousness within the tribe.

At sundown Wanaǧi had rejoined the Shirtman in the lodge-of-preparation, Ahbleza sitting as before, empty and fighting sleep.

But certainly the Shirtman had marveled this day. Any other day the people showed their disapproval of lust, of any excesses. Yet on this one occasion they encouraged the mating-act between any two who felt attracted to each other and they called a child born of this experience 'wakan-child.' Why? Perhaps the wapiya will reveal the reason for this day of familiarity.

Wanaǧi had sat down near the pipe rack, but he had neither smoked nor spoken. On this final night before the walk to the sunpole a wapiya usually conducted the inipi, but Wanaǧi had not indicated any such intention; truly, he had ignored all the cleansing rituals, internal and external. Ahbleza had looked for the initi as a place to renew his weary body and the inipi as a way to receive a powerful song, but perhaps the sacred-man had decided to refuse him these comforts.

"Hear me." Wanaǧi's tone cut sharply into the silence. "I direct this sungazing ceremony for two reasons: Ahbleza makes this request and I am the sacred-man most fit.

"Not a person in the tribe fears me. I neither kill nor indulge my power as stone-dreamer.

"I know all songs and the order of events; I direct this affair more than once. But I never shall direct the sungazing ceremony again."

The wapiya reached for the pipe. He laid an ember on the bowl and drew on the stem. And when finally he spoke, he spoke most slowly: "I view the sungazing ceremony as the most damaging of Lakotah excesses."

Ahbleza sensed a startled surprise, not at the wapiya's declaration but at his own readiness to accept Wanaǧi's assertion. But damaging to whom, he asked himself instantly, sungazer or tribe?

Wanaǧi spoke on: "Once in seasons past I answer you saying that you have not yet enough growth. My reply confuses you, but now you understand. Whoever sits adoring a message-bearer, whoever stays in one place repeating thanks, denies himself expansion."

He paused, holding the pipestem to the Shirtman's

mouth. Then returning the stem to his own lips, he blew out a thin smoke. "Recognize these message-bearers," he said.

"A mother detaches her child when she ties the birthcord, but for so long as the child sucks, the grandfathers trust woman with lessons in silence and respect.

" 'Wanyaka, tuwena icuśni,' she tells her little one, and so he learns that not everything belongs to him and that he shall respect another person's possessions.

"But before her influence takes a lasting-hold on her son, the grandfathers advise that direct speech cease between mother and blood-son; they will see him detach from this original message-bearer and move on to his grandfather's influence.

"Recall, my son, your travels at age ten with your grandfather and afterwards with your hunter-friend. Proudly Tunkaśila relates to you the wisdom a tribe accumulates during these many seasons on the plain. Next you listen to a meat-maker's stories about pte-kills that become legend. But soon the people hint that a youth shall make his own legends. And so you detach from these two and look for companions your own age.

"Recall that the wise ones discourage a strong tie between sister and brother, for such a tie delays the natural urge for a mate. And so a brother learns to regard himself as protector of all women even as he prepares for becoming husband to one.

"Observe that a youth, before ever he goes out as a warrior, encounters many voices—women and men—each one speaking a different message. But once he understands the message they bring him, he detaches from these relatives and friends and starts to listen for that truly familiar voice: his own. And once he hears this familiar-voice, he knows himself competent to recognize truth. And once he begins to heed this familiar-voice, his spirit—his spiritual-self—becomes the fit controlling power, the only power he ever really needs."

The wapiya dipped a handful of grass in water; he moistened the Shirtman's lips. "Certainly, my son, you remember your lonely ride against the Psa."

"Tawamiciya," Ahbleza whispered, "I own myself."

Wanaǧi heard. "And what means 'I own my self'?"

787

Carefully Ahbleza gave answer. "Recently and in this same lodge I speak saying that I know myself as blood and thought, essence and power. I say that I am a body with reasoning, also a spirit-self with an all-knowing power. I am four yet I am two yet I am one."

The wapiya turned his back. "Your speech tells me nothing."

Ahbleza leaned forward; he looked as old as Wanaǧi. "I am I," he whispered hoarsely. "Tuwa tuwe ḣca he miye; I am I, really someone."

"So hear me," Wanaǧi commanded; "hear me if never you hear me again."

And now this wapiya, this wakanliica, this father-friend, spoke as he will not imagine ever speaking to anyone.

"Wakantanka, great mystery, they say. But I will not say so. I will not accept that any great mystery exists.

"I recognize the life-force. I identify this force as 'śkan,' something-in-movement. I am something in movement. I am śkan. And with a body as proof.

"I am not mystery and nothing mysterious sits above me.

"I own this earth. I make things happen here. My thoughts, my acts. All directions come together in me for I am the center."

The sacred-man changed his position to face Ahbleza. He reached for the paint bowls and paint sacks nearby.

"Those wapiya who instruct different sungazers begin the inipi now," he said calmly. "But the gazer in this lodge will not need the renewing bath." He began mixing a red powder with fat. "I paint you."

All the while he rubbed this red color on Ahbleza's body and face, Wanaǧi sang, but his vocables, the language of the spirit, held meanings he kept to himself.

Now, shaking powder out a different sack, he mixed the black of burnt-wood with spittle. Moving in close to the Shirtman, he used a stick to draw a line around the gazer's mouth.

"The life-force surrounds you," he said; "fill up."

Next he painted a black circle at the gazer's wrist, shoulder, ankle. Again he sang but, as before, in the spirit-tongue.

The painting finished, he placed a feather in Ahbleza's

hair, then tied a wingbone whistle and the circular piece of hide at the Shirtman's neck.

Turning toward the fire circle, Wanaġi laid a bundle of sweetgrass on the embers. "When the dawn star fades, the sunpole ceremony shall commence."

After a pleasing smoke had filled the lodge, the wapiya spoke instructions and advice. "Attend, sungazer. All around you something waits for your command. Put this power into use.

"Gaze on the rim of the sun or at the top of the pole. Sing out phrases familiar to the grandfathers. Sing forcefully and you shall see with the eye of the spirit. Or perhaps . . ." —the wapiya looked fully upon Ahbleza—"perhaps you will travel fast as light toward an invisible whose desire for contacting you matches your desire for making contact.

"Recall that anyone who recently sheds the flesh-body retains a fresh, strong memory. Such ones . . . or one . . . will meet you more than halfway and speak in a manner you easily understand. But those invisibles who discard the shell many, many winters in the past will meet you only if they stay curious. Such ones . . . or one . . . you will not easily understand, for they dimly remember that which once gives joy and they recall nothing of sadness or fear.

"Those invisibles back to the original grandfathers remember neither your customs or speech. Such ones possess but a single way for sending messages; they try to reach you through familiar winged or four-legged who embody the life-force yet lack the power of speech."

Wanaġi refilled the pipe-bowl, his movements unhurried.

"Smoke," he said, "and see the earth stretching out, supporting all things. Smoke and see your self standing on earth, owning all things." He placed the stem at Ahbleza's mouth. "Smoke and hear me giving you a sacred phrase. Listen attentively, for you shall speak these words when I tie you to the sunpole."

Ahbleza breathed in deeply and the smoke came out a long thin streak. Starving had hollowed the gazer's cheeks and sharpened the hump on his nose, but lack of meat and sleep had not answered for the sudden emptiness in the Shirtman's eyes as the wapiya withdrew the stem.

"Not here, my son," Wanaġi whispered. "At the pole.

At the pole." The vacant stare had surprised but not startled the seer; he understood that this man already began his struggle at the sunpole.

When Ahbleza had regained his composure, the wapiya delivered his final instruction.

"The mouths of the wise give you sacred words to speak at the sunpole," Wanaǵi told; "tunkaśila uśi maya ye; woksape maku wo."

The Shirtman heard. Silently he repeated the phrases: grandfather, contact me; give me wisdom. I command.

Tunkaśila, grandfather, grandfathers, one and all.

A child, Ahbleza told himself, regards the sun as a grandfather to whom he shall speak asking for something good. A youth recognizes the sun as a power for budding the trees, sweetening the berries, for thinning and thickening hair on the four-legs, for putting folds in the cheeks of old persons. A warrior views the sun as the eye of great mystery. But perhaps the sacred-man sees the sun as a way for certain ones to make direct contact with the invisibles; and so, the sungazing.

Tunkaśila uśi maya ye. Woksape maku wo. Grandfather, contact me. Give me wisdom. I command.

But who, Ahbleza asked himself, urgently desires a meeting with me? Assemble yourself, Wanaǵi says, and you shall rise to the contact point.

Contact point? Perhaps a boundary that separates the invisibles from the visibles? Rivers and trees make boundaries, but what thing makes the dividing line here?

"Fear." Wanaǵi spoke the answer.

He hears me. Or am I speaking aloud?

Suddenly Ahbleza felt a crazy desire to laugh. Will they yet demand proof of his bravery? Will they imagine that he fears something and so they try him at the sunpole?

"Hold." The wapiya spoke roughly. "Wait for the pole."

Wanaǵi had not looked at the Shirtman; Ahbleza only imagined he saw the piercing eyes.

"The wapiya gives me a bundle of words for use when I spill blood at the sungazing. But whatever more than song and dance and torture this contest demands, I shall discover when the moment comes."

The discomforts of the lodge-of-preparation often

790

sparked defiance, something the inipi usually put down. But Wanaǧi saw the Shirtman's defiance as an important force, something Ahbleza will use at the sunpole.

Taking the gazer's pipe, which he will seal, Wanaǧi moved toward the lodge opening. "When I return," he told Ahbleza, "I will bring with me all who dance looking-at-the-sun. They shall form a line alongside this place, the Shirtman front."

Lifting the tipi flap, the wapiya went out of the lodge; he knew that any more talk only will distract.

In his lonely wait for dawn, Ahbleza clung to his reasoning, the one power he recognized as reliable. But some things he had difficulty reasoning.

He recalled his vision, his experience on the ledge when he and Tonweya became a dreaming-pair. And he remembered that which he recently had told the scout: nothing . . . yet . . . breaks the bond between I and you as brother-friends.

But where, this brother-friend now? They say that each gazer shall have the company of a close friend in the lodge-of-preparation. Yet only an instructor had entered this lodge, a wapiya who showed a strange heart toward great mystery, who spoke of the Lakotah sungazing as a damaging ceremony, and who hinted that the Shirtman feared a contact with the invisibles.

For a moment Ahbleza glared at the dark circle where the sweetgrass had burned. Then, commanding his own composure, he let reason regain hold.

I know, he told himself, that the sacred-man hunts ways to prepare me for this experience, for whatever occurs at the sunpole—great surprise or great shock—and so he tries to astonish me. He eliminates the message-bearers and denies any great mystery, anything outside man's power to perceive.

And yet . . . if I go-to-the-center and discover the great mystery, then nothing mysterious exists. And if I discover that which really exists, then I am the center and I, the reality.

And now Ahbleza recalled the challenging look he had flashed Wanaǧi on entering this lodge and his own instantaneous acceptance of the sungazing as more contest than sacred ceremony, more spectacular than spiritual. But he remembered also his unnatural response when Wanaǧi named fear as an obstacle to making contact with the invisibles.

Not fear, he answered himself now; perhaps apprehension that I contact some undesirable but not fear in the sense of fearing an enemy.

A tiny smile appeared on Ahbleza's lips. Suddenly, seemingly without reason, he felt a gladness in the approaching dawn. He covered his eyes with his hands and for a little while he slept.

XXIV

THE SILENT, watchful faces of five thousand Lakotah gave a new wonder to this sunrise. The people had come from their sleep to the dance circle, the crier's far-reaching voice awakening the hoop before dawn. "Come now," he had called; "they make ready."

Three, four hundred had come quickly, mostly relatives of the sungazers and already awake, painted and waiting. Taking places along the edge of the circular shade they had watched the retreating night. But most persons had approached the dance-ground after the morning-star had dimmed; they had seen faces and knew alongside whom they stood. Even so, none talked; a solemn gathering, they held to thoughts of the sungazers.

The sky lightened and the sunpole loomed tall. The people waited.

And then they came, twenty-and-nine sungazers in a long moving line, two persons front and carrying pipes. Face and hands red, hair in braids, and a shedding robe identified the director-of-ceremonies and so the people recognized Wanaġi as one of the two out front. The second pipe-bearer, his hair also braided, wore white paint on his face, but all who knew Tonweya's walk recognized this scout at once.

The spectators saw the line stopping at the center lodge, saw the two pipe-bearers escorting the Shirtman out of his lodge, then saw these three walking through a space midway in the procession, taking their positions far front, Ahbleza between the wapiya and his brother-friend.

The people felt the great tremolo drumbeat as Wanaġi pointed the Lakotah pipestem toward the sun, toward a rim of red that appeared on the flat where earth meets sky. And then they heard the sacred-man's voice, heard his song which opened the ceremony.

"Tunkaśila, houn waye che, numuĥun ye. Makocita niya houn waye kte, numuĥun ye. Wani kte lo."

The gazers, their eyes on the fiery red power climbing over the edge, listened for the wapiya's second singing of this song, a signal that they shall face south.

"Grandfather, I send a voice; hear me. From this earth with your breath I send a voice; hear me. I will live."

During Wanaġi's third singing of the song, the sungazers looked west. But when they turned to face north, Wanaġi stepped back of the Shirtman and blew four shrill tones on his wingbone whistle. The gazers answered with a wailing cry, tears streaming down their cheeks. And then each one turned and, looking into the sun, raised his hands in greeting, his robe dropping to the ground.

Tonweya had stood reviewing carefully the order of events; he wanted nothing to disrupt an occasion so important to his brother-friend. Now he glanced toward the dance drum south of the pole.

As the wailing dimmed, the eight singers who gathered around this new big drum repeated the opening song but to a different beat. And so the gazers shuffled onto the dance-ground, their line curving in, forming a half-circle around the pole. Ahbleza, alone, stayed as before.

Now Tonweya moved. Carrying the dreaming-pair pipe, he approached the patch of mellow-earth; he placed the bowl of the pipe on the pte-skull, a little rack nearby to support the stem. And then he stepped back under the shelter to stand with the great-great-great many who watched. But he intended to keep his eyes only on the brother-friend for so long as Ahbleza danced. In this manner he will remember himself as one of a dreaming-pair, a bond that compels the Shirtman to perform this ceremony. Or so Tonweya understood Ahbleza's reason.

Ahbleza stood alone. He had not joined the dancers in their wailing nor had he raised a hand to the sun. Arms at his sides, palms out, he stood gazing at the red banner near the top of the pole. Now, shifting slightly from one foot to the other, he began the toe-and-heel movements which the grandfathers say they shall use in all ceremonial dancing.

The singers had begun a sundance song, the voices of four women blending in with the men, Lowansa singing with this group, her heart in the song.

And along with these voices the people heard a swishing-sound, something that gives the sundance songs a special effect. Six drummer-singers sat around a stiff pte-hide, one hand holding taut the skin, a slender whip in the other hand. For each two beats of the big drum, they whipped the rawhide once. And so they made of the sungazing something more than an ordinary drumming, singing.

The sun had climbed halfway to the middle. When the sun reaches the top of the pole, Ahbleza had told himself, I shall move my eyes to the yellow rim, but for now I will keep looking at the red banner, the color they use on the dead.

Napewaśte had arrived at the dance-ground before dawn, her horse dragging the pile of gifts that honor her son. Not one in the Mahto band shall walk away from this suncircle wanting for robe or moccasins or new tipi skins; they shall find everything among her offerings. And whoever looks for meat shall seek out her cooking place, Kipanna asking for the privilege of attending to this feast fire, ladling out meat.

Observing the dancers now, Napewaśte found memories that drew husband and son to her heart. She remembered her separation from Olepi's embrace when twice he had prepared for a sungazing. But her recollection aroused a longing not for the husband but for the son, a longing to see the sorrow go from Ahbleza's eyes, his heart alive again. She wondered whether Olepi, watching, recalled his own suffering as a sungazer; perhaps the pole will bring father and son together in a new way. But why not joy instead of suffering as a path to understanding between these two, between any two? She looked at the pole with puzzled eyes.

Kehala stood nearby, her child holding on to her gown. The young woman's eyes also appeared puzzled. She saw each dancer with a wingbone whistle at his lips, all but Ahbleza; the Shirtman danced with the whistle dangling on his breast. Why will this one she calls brother not blow on the bone that carries a voice to the great mystery? She had decorated the dreaming-pair pipe and quilled the braid he wrapped around this whistle; but perhaps she neglects something? A little shiver expressed her concern.

The sun reached middle-sky.

Twice the wapiya had stopped the dance, calling fresh voices to the drum, two groups of singers alternating. And during these breaks the gazers had rested, either sitting where they had dropped their robes or standing where they danced, eyes down and arms hanging loose.

The lead-dancer, they say, shall rest in a different manner, this one lying on a spread of sage next to the mellow-earth, his face down, head against the pte-skull. But Ahbleza had not moved out of his dancing place; he stood facing the pole, his posture that of a man who listens, who waits for something, a man they dare not approach. And so they had carried none of the thirst-relieving seeds to the Shirtman nor offered him the pipe.

WHY NOT REST YOUR HEAD ON PTE, SUNGAZER?

That the pole spoke to him had not surprised Ahbleza; nothing here astounded him. The drum owns a voice, why not the sunpole?

And so the Shirtman gave answer: "I recognize pte as everyone's spirit-helper. The invisible grandfathers, they tell me, remember pte—great longhorn pte—as here at the beginning. And so they use pte as their most reliable messenger. For this reason the seers advise that a sungazer rest his head on the pte-skull and listen for something.

"But whom among the ancients will I recognize?

795

Whose voice from out of the mouths of the original-people will I know? I try, instead, for direct contact with someone I know, who speaks a language I will understand."

Ahbleza moved his feet; the drum commanding, he and all gazers began again the shuffling dance.

REMEMBER ḢEYATAWIN, SUNGAZER.

My wife. Ahbleza ceased his dancing.

Persons who sat watching the Shirtman imagined that he suddenly reached the finish, his enduring used up; they clasped a hand to their mouths. But not Wanaǧi.

The wapiya stood quickly; his gesture stopped the drum. He began a song, signaling that he shall sing alone. Let the suncircle become quiet; let the dancers rest briefly.

The sacred-man's tones reached the most distant ears, his song floating over the leaf shelter and above the circle of feast fires around the edge of this shelter.

Ahbleza heard. He understood that Wanaǧi sends him help in this most difficult moment. The wapiya's song tells that he throws a hoop of śkan around the Shirtman, that he closes off this gazer; nothing outside shall affect Ahbleza now; he shall hear only his-familiar-voice.

Returning to his robe, Wanaǧi sat as before, next to the mellow-earth. And the drummers, waiting for the lead-singer to announce the next song, tapped softly on the edge of the big drum.

Soon all the sungazers danced again, but perhaps only the one—only Ahbleza—now recognized that the circular emblem each gazer wears at his neck symbolizes not sun-with-rays or moon-in-the-round or wind-with-four-breaths; instead, this small circle of hide with two lines crossing depicts the marvel surrounding him now: a hoop of śkan with himself at the center and absorbing the power.

Heyatawin, woman-on-the-ridge. Mitawin, my wife.

Until now I wonder who among the invisibles desires to contact me instead of whom I desire to contact; until now I ponder what things the invisibles will have me know instead of what things I desire to know. And until now I puzzle why the sunpole, why those mating-songs, why the intimacy.

Now my eyes open and I see that everything in this suncircle points to personal desire as the true-force. And now I will direct this power in one direction; I will send myself to Heyatawin, my wife.

The sun passed middle and many persons moved away from the dance circle, certain ones visiting the feast fires, different ones going to the gaming-ground to entertain the young of the tribe.

Cankuna had stayed under the brush shelter. Her daughter Tacincala, assigned to the group of young women who watched over the gazers, moved among the dancers now, gently pressing sage to the forehead, to the cheeks, of different ones. But not of Ahbleza.

These sungazers will remember her daughter, Cankuna told herself, and if ever anyone gossips about Tacincala, they will act to protect her.

Now turning her gaze on Ahbleza, the hunter's wife saw her quillwork on the niteiyapehe that covered the dancer's thighs, knees, but whether her pattern reflects any meaning here, she knew not. A two-circle design, the dream-voice had said, neither circle closing, one inside the other; a child's face, the dream-voice had told, glowing in secret joy.

Sundown. And now all returned to the circle, again looking upon a ceremony difficult to perform, difficult to watch.

But not for Olepi. The Titonwan leader had not hunted memories of his own gazings; instead he observed this one with proud eyes: his son, a Shirt-owner, a sungazer, a man who will make his struggle at the sunpole something the people forever will remember. His son, Ahbleza; an extraordinary man; Wanagi had said so.

"Moon, the grandmother; moon, a hunka-relative to each woman. See this night-sun spreading brightness over dark earth."

Wanagi sang while the people watched thirty gazers begin a night of dancing.

Certain gazers danced looking toward the tall pole; different ones danced with eyes fixed on the rising light. Ahbleza danced, eyes closed.

The moon, now halfway along her path, had lent shadows to everyone, everything. But Tonweya saw only Ahbleza's shadow, a lonely, dark quivering shape.

The wapiya says 'dreaming-pair,' the scout told himself, but I know not my brother's dream this night. He dances to the meaning of a vision they say I own with him. But, truly, he owns the whole.

I have not his searching interest in this vision but I keep a bond. I and he, hunka-brothers, brother-friends.

I am eyes and ears for the people, and so I ask: will a vision reveal anything more than my own eyes and ears tell me?

And yet this brother-friend will have me recognize something and so I stay and watch. Whatever message the sungazing perhaps holds for me I shall receive through Ahbleza.

The night passed through middle and went on. The very young and the very old slept. Most persons sat as before, visiting, fanning, watching, marveling.

Ahbleza danced to the beat of his own heart. The hoop Wanaǵi had flung around him closed his ears to drum, whistles, singers, to everything but his own familiar-voice. Yet even this voice kept silent, strangely silent.

Staring at the pole, he had begun calling back his memories of Heyatawin: quick flashes of her nakedness, fragments of her speech, snatches of songs she had composed, glimpses of her hands as she softened the hides. And to all he attached grief, his own terrible grieving which he had not dared release until now.

Then suddenly he imagined her on the yellow horse; he saw Tatezi carrying her away. Heyatawin, proudly and joyfully growing-a-child, going away . . . and not coming back, not ever coming back. Heyatawin, woman-on-the-ridge, his woman.

"Mitawin . . . my wife . . . haun-haun."

The cry, the moan of the dying-wounded, broke from the sungazer's throat, a moan out of his own unhealing wound, out of his own grieving, dying self.

And now tears like floodwater gushed from his eyes, soaking his face and spilling onto his breast.

You EMPTY YOURSELF OF SORROW BUT TEARS WILL NOT RELEASE YOUR SPIRIT HERE, SUNGAZER.

The pole-voice had spoken, but the dancer stood unattending. Eyes flowing, he called sadly to his wife, telling of his loneliness, his heart dead in his breast.

"Mitawin, my wife, I dance gazing, I marvel singing.

"Mitawin, my wife, I stand and wonder and weep.

"Mitawin, I am alone."

Twice he sang his sorrowful song, twice again.

Who laughs?

He had heard laughter; bright and joyous laughter had answered him. Laughter here? At the sunpole?

JOY HERE, SUNGAZER, NOT GRIEF.

And now he heard a phrase spoken along with this laughter: "Come out."

Heyatawin, her voice. Heyatawin here?

"Come out. I hear you calling me."

Her voice, truly her voice, but why will he not see her?

CHOOSE JOY, SUNGAZER; LET JOY PROPEL YOU. RISE TO THAT PEAK WHERE THE SPIRIT MAKES CONTACT.

Ahbleza shook as with cold. But flame, not cold, rushed up his legs, up his back; his manliness had come into power.

LET ME OUT, SUNGAZER, LET ME OUT.

His head seemed suddenly on fire. "Woman-on-the-ridge, command my spirit to come forth. I say so. Woman-on-the-ridge, one I adore, answer me. I come joyfully."

As he spoke he heard her laughter approaching his ear, then her whisper. And then her little gasps of breath as her spirit joined his.

I AM OUT. I SEE LIGHT. I KNOW WHO MEETS ME HERE AT THE CENTER. MY WIFE, I FEEL YOUR TOUCH. WOMAN-ON-THE-RIDGE, ANSWER ME.

Clearly he heard her words: "Mihigna, my husband, memory brings me here.

"I come remembering the day you stand at the edge of camp, beauty and power in your nakedness.

"I come remembering the day I ride away. But I say that always you shall own me. And the child.

"I come answering you. I keep the child of your seed. Not son but daughter. This one stays with me and so I remember . . . my . . . joy . . . in . . . you."

The sungazer's power for receiving any more of her message had weakened. He heard faintly the joyful laughter but these sounds faded even as he realized that he had heard the voice and felt the hand, but that he had not seen, not touched this one who came answering his call.

And now he sensed himself falling back, losing altitude, an empty body dropping onto dark, bare ground.

Wanaǧi had stayed throughout the night alongside the mellow-earth. He had permitted the gazers only three breaks, the dancers standing quiet while the singers changed places.

Some persons had whispered their criticism of the wapiya as someone too severe on these dancers. But Wanaǧi remembered that these sungazers had come looking for this experience, something they chose. He knew also, that more than one gazer had come here for a secondhand look at himself, perhaps for a new status in the tribe.

And so he sat reflecting once again why he will not tolerate the sungazing ceremony—this sundance—as they perform the affair now. Whose influence brings torture to the sunpole? Who devises this scarifying ritual? What nature of young dreamer? But more important, why will he, Wanaǧi, ever encourage this aspect of the sungazing?

Suddenly Wanaǧi became aware of a shape on the ground where Ahbleza had stood dancing. Instantly he sent 'touchers'—his helpers—into the dance circle, these persons inviting each gazer to rest on his robe, to accept a smoke if he so desires. But to the man on the ground, only Wanaǧi shall go.

The wapiya approached the Shirtman but he brought neither sage nor roots nor pipe. Hands empty, he brought only himself, and he intended to stay only until certain that Ahbleza will arouse himself.

Almost at once Ahbleza's lips formed a gentle smile; his eyes opening on Wanaǧi, he spoke. "I live or not-live. But I alone make the choice."

The wapiya turned and walked back to his place.

Ahbleza stood, the dancer noticing only briefly a change in the sky, but whether this soft coloring brightened into day or faded into night, he neither knew nor cared. He had visited the center and in a little while he shall return to the center. But he will take a different path; he will approach on thongs that hang from the sunpole and in the manner of his vow.

Tonweya, his heart aching, had seen the brother-friend slip to the ground; he knew that Ahbleza had moved out beyond his reach. He recalled those seasons past when Wanaġi had hinted that these two strengthen the bond. But he, Tonweya, never had seen any weakening of their bond. From the beginning he had recognized Ahbleza as his brother, long before a vision in some mysterious way had confirmed this tie. From the beginning he had wanted this man Ahbleza for brother, with or without the hunka ceremony that demonstrates such a decision.

But now he sees Ahbleza suffering at the sunpole in an effort to comprehend fully their vision—and the strength of the bond that comes of this vision—while he, Tonweya, merely stands at the circle's edge watching.

Reaching back of his ear, the scout touched the wambli-bone whistle, his 'protection' as of the day he had sat alongside the brother-friend and made this wotawe. Now, suddenly, he decided something: he shall put the whistle to his lips when they start to fasten the thong in Ahbleza's breast. Blowing on this wingbone, he will enter the suncircle and dance near the pole; perhaps Ahbleza will know why he comes.

Tonweya glanced at the earth's rim where dawn approached, the dawn of this second sungazing day. He looked again at Ahbleza, now wondering not whether the Shirtman will know why the scout joins him but whether Ahbleza will care.

Who will tell this scout that the sungazer's spirit even now returns to the center; who will tell Tonweya that once a person knows his way to the center, he will visit this place as if between breaths.

Who will tell Tonweya that this sungazer will not seek a different path, will not need the scarifying now, that already Ahbleza comes into power with all power, that Ahbleza truly clears the way.

XXV

I STAND AT THE CENTER AND THE LIGHT SHINES ALL AROUND ME. AND NOW I KNOW THAT MY SPIRIT GLOWING MAKES THIS LIGHT. I COME INTO POWER WITH THE SUN FOR I AM LIKE THE SUN. I AM MY OWN LIGHT.

HERE AT THE CENTER I SEE THE MEANING OF THINGS, ALL THINGS. AND NOW I KNOW THAT I AM THE MEANING. THE WHOLE MEANING.

THE FOUR DIRECTIONS COME TOGETHER IN ME. I AM THE CENTER AND EVERYTHING FLOWS FROM ME, RETURNS TO ME.

I AM THAT WHICH THEY CALL GREAT MYSTERY. I AM THAT WHICH EACH ONE CALLS WAKANTANKA BEFORE COMING HERE, BEFORE SEEING THE LIGHT.

I AM HERE AND SO I KNOW. HERE I KNOW EVERYTHING. HERE I KNOW MY SELF.

I AM THOUGHT AND WILL. AND NOTHING SITS ABOVE MY WILL.

I AM PRIDE AND JOY. AND NOTHING SITS ABOVE MY JOY.

I OWN MY LIFE. AND ONLY MINE. AND SO I SHALL APPRECIATE MY PERSON. AND SO I SHALL MAKE PROPER USE OF MY SELF.

I STAND HERE IN THE LIGHT OF MY OWN PRESENCE AND I RECOGNIZE MY POWER.

I AM REASON. AND NOTHING SITS ABOVE MY CHOICE.

I AM TRUTH. AND SO I LIVE IN THE SPIRIT. AND SO I LIVE FOREVER.

I AM THE ONENESS OF THE WHOLE. AND WHATEVER HAPPENS, HAPPENS IN ME.

I AM AHBLEZA. I OWN THE EARTH.

XXVI

WHY HE danced or when he had begun dancing puzzled the Shirtman. The sun had warmed the morning; many persons had moved under the shade. But perhaps something occurs that he not yet recalls?

The singers sang a mocking, unfamiliar song about thirst and now Ahbleza looked at the sunpole, only vaguely remembering this tall painted wood. Nor will he sense any connection between himself and the thong that hung from this pole. Certainly he will not make his body a symbol of suffering and so give importance to a torture ceremony.

Suddenly a wonderful gladness filled him; he remembered everything. Twice he visits the center, his return visit as natural as breathing.

And so I know that whatever exists, exists within me.

And so I will not join in a contest of suffering flesh. I will refuse the thongs. I bring reason into the circle-of-the-sun. My own reason.

I dance but not to excess. Now I return to my own lodge.

Ahbleza had stopped dancing but at once a red hand touched his arm, grabbed his fingers, bending each one around a big stick.

"Walk to the sunpole grasping this wood. The stick will help when you try breaking loose from the thong." Wanaġi had spoken, had given these instructions.

The singers struck the drum, loud and fast. Very fast.

All faces turned toward Ahbleza, their Shirtman, an owner-of-the-people, the lead-dancer at this sungazing. But Wanaġi, director of this ceremony, had turned away.

The next instant Ahbleza let the stick drop to the ground. Now, lifting his arms as high as his breast, he embraced himself.

Shocked into silence, the people stared at this strangeness. They saw that Ahbleza touched his own body but not with the little scratching-stick they permit a gazer. Instead, Ahbleza stood hugging himself.

Wanaǵi kept on walking, moving toward the pole where two helpers waited with awl and knife, something for lifting, cutting the Shirtman's flesh. At the wapiya's signal they stood prepared to rush forward, to throw the sungazer roughly on the ground.

But Wanaǵi had not made this sign. And Ahbleza, his face lifting to the sky, smiled a wondrous smile, as if he shared a secret with the sun.

And now the Shirtman walked away from the pole, from the ground he had danced-hard, from the vow he will not fulfill.

The Shirtman had walked out on the suncircle, walked out on the people.

The drumbeats quickened to catch up with the hearts of the spectators. Astonished, fearful, these Lakotah remembered that in and through Ahbleza each one makes a thanks-offering. So will not this Shirtman's behavior bring difficulties upon the tribe? They had watched and admired, respected and imitated his ways; so why will he throw to the ground the principal attraction of the sungazing: the scarifying of a dancer and the dramatic twisting-loose from thongs.

Anger took over certain hearts, and yet even these disturbed ones remembered that they dare say nothing about a sungazer's response to the pole; this concern, Ahbleza's alone.

But whatever these different hearts, none hurt more than Olepi, father to him who dodged the torture. And so for one desperate moment the Mahto, a man twice to struggle at the pole, considered offering his flesh for a third piercing. Why not a relative taking over the full obligation, especially the flesh-and-blood father? But to hang on the thong without the inipi, without any purifying act . . . who knows at what risk. Not to himself, certainly, but to the tribe.

Courteous eyes avoided Olepi's face, but the young who sneaked a look in the leader's direction saw the Mahto's breast rise and fall, the man's deep breaths giving movement to his old cuts, the darkly painted sundance scars appearing now as a reproach to the son's retreat.

Yet these same persons will know nothing of the picture that flashed in front of the father's eyes: an image of

804

Ahbleza suspended on the thong, toes barely touching ground, his long hair loose and swinging as he twists violently, as he fights with the pole, breaks away . . .

But Ahbleza had not come close to the pole; instead he had walked off smiling. And now Olepi stood remembering that more than one good fighting man had left a war party, turning back halfway along the trail but not losing his reputation for bravery. So a Shirtman turns his back on the sunpole? Who dares talk?

Raising high the Lakotah pipe, Wanaġi pointed the stem toward the sky, his gesture silencing the drum, commanding the people's attention.

"Marvel that which climbs the sky; recognize life in the rising sun." The wapiya sang to the traveling-power. "See the force at middle, see the force turning back."

And so one voice carried the spirit of the people to the clouds where they recovered calmness; Wanaġi had sung for a return of all hearts to those dancers who yet waited to perform their vows at the sunpole, an uneasy ordeal on any occasion.

Wanaġi had advised his helpers against deep cuts; he wanted this ceremony to close at sunfall. Even so, the drummers used up four different torture songs before those six gazers who chose to give flesh—eighty pieces—had completed their offering.

And afterwards the enactment of those three gazers who dragged pte-skulls, the big heads bringing one dancer to his knees before he managed to tear loose.

And now the ear-piercing, the one event yet to take place. The sun bent far down when, finally, the assisting seers came forward to open-the-ears of the young. But before these sacred-men used the special awls and smooth wood, Wanaġi offered advice to the parents of these children.

"Remember," he said, "that these little ones hear everything. So let each family shun gossip and avoid talk of disease. Speak, instead, of those many things that bring good into the hoop, into your lives."

Most youths showed little interest in this toddler's ceremony and so they slipped away to schemes of their own on this wonderful final day of the sungazing, a day when everyone took teasing in good nature; certainly everyone will endure tricks and other mischief on a day when the sungazers bleed and suffer.

And the big moment for all young boys, soon to come. For when the people finish with all this bleeding-and-enduring, the crier will announce something exciting: let all boys, he will say, assemble near the mellow-earth; when the whistle blows, they shall rush the sunpole, climb up after the banner. Who becomes the one boy to make his way to the top? Who will take this summer's sunpole banner back to his own lodge, his to keep.

Friends had persuaded Kipanna that, as the woman who now sits in the Shirtman's lodge, she belonged at the suncircle during his struggle at the pole instead of tending fire outside the shelter. And so she had come but only to see Ahbleza walk away from the thong.

She had glanced around, looking for understanding on someone's face. But none had glanced her way; none seemed to have any comfort to offer. And so a new sadness filled her eyes, not for this man in whose lodge she stays as 'nothing' but for her own miserable self.

But then someone had approached the young woman; speaking briskly, Cankuna had asked that Kipanna help with a distribution of gifts among the widowed mothers whose lodges shelter three or more children. And she also invited Kipanna to sleep this night in the hunter's family tipi, alongside Tacincala; perhaps Tacincala will find a way to cheer this lonely one.

Who knows, Cankuna had told herself; perhaps the Shirtman will return to his lodge the next day, remembering that a woman awaits. Who knows; perhaps Kipanna now will become Ahbleza's true-wife.

Tonweya had left the suncircle carrying the dreaming-pair pipe but not in any formal manner as when the ceremony had begun; he simply lifted the pipe from the mellow-earth as if, once again, he recovered something important from Ahbleza's giveaway. But he had wondered whether ever again he and the brother-friend will smoke this stem. Wanaġi had sealed the bowl, but this seal means nothing now; Ahbleza decides against the scarifying, against his vow.

The scout made his way toward the lodge where an old blindman sat; he desired to smoke with this adviser to scouts, this man whom Ahbleza calls grandfather. Perhaps here, in the presence of Tunkaśila, he will gain understanding about this ceremony; certainly during all his seasons as an observer, the sungazing brings him none of the inspiration the people say that a sungazing shall bring.

Napewaśte walked back to her lodge, Kehala alongside but neither woman saying anything. On seeing Ahbleza refuse the thong, Napewaśte had covered her head with her robe; so she had hidden her face from the sunpole as if this tree—truly an enemy—had taken away from the people instead of renewing each one.

And now Wanaǧi, carrying the Lakotah pipe, moved out of the suncircle, out of the place he had occupied for a day, a night, and a second day. But he will not take the ceremonial pipe to the council lodge, where all sungazers meet for a smoke after their baths. Instead he will look for a man who sits alone, a Shirtman whose true-enduring only now begins. And sitting with this one, he will remove the seal over the bowl. And then he and Ahbleza will smoke this pipe empty, he and Ahbleza the first to touch their lips to the stem of the Lakotah ceremonial pipe.

Afterwards he will refill the bowl and take the pipe to the center-place. But not before he sits a long while with Ahbleza, man extraordinary, perhaps the most brave man among the Titonwan Lakotah.

Book Four

THE LEGEND
1824/25 to 1834/35

I

TONWEYA HAD persisted in his hunt for Tatezi, the scout determined to locate the yellow horse on whose back Heyatawin had ridden when she started south with her family. He looked for his discovery of the horse to lead him to the woman's killer.

But certain warriors viewed the scout's resolve as stubborn foolishness. Why not attack any Psa camp, they said; Tonweya knows that they shall kill so many enemy when they avenge this woman and her relatives. And who will say that Tatezi belongs to the same Psa who originally captures her? They wait until after the sungazing as the Shirtman requests. Now they go. What says Ahbleza?

Ahbleza said nothing. And so Icabu, facing these agitators in council, spoke his advice: let the discontents keep quiet until the Shirtman decides who carries the pipe on this blood-raid.

"Keep quiet while the enemy goes around saying that the Mahto sit in their lodges like woman?" Peśla had sounded off in a voice too loud for this center-place but his words had received approbation. "I say raise the red pole in the dance circle where eight, ten days past certain Lakotah gaze toward the sun. I will strike the red stick and so pledge not to desert the avenging party."

Then even more loudly the bold warrior dared an insinuation: "Nor will I disregard any vow I ever make."

Ahbleza kept his silence, his face impassive. And so the summer-shirts gave sanction. The clubmen shall raise the warpole, they said, not far distant from where the sunpole yet stands, and for the next three nights all who go to war shall paint and make mock rushes on the encampment and then strike the red wood. At dawn on the fourth day the avengers shall go out, scouts in advance and looking for Psa lodges.

Tonweya, hearing, decided to visit the sacred-man at once; he intended to request the sort of help he had thought never to seek. He will demand that Wanaǧi—if truly this man owns a stone-song—send out the stones and locate the horse Tatezi, the yellow horse they will not wait for Tonweya to find. But once he learns in which Psa village they hold Tatezi he will know in what direction to guide the warriors.

Ahbleza had not appeared at the warpole, and so on the second night some depreciating phrases rolled off certain tongues. But different ones recalled that the Shirtman had not asked for this reprisal and that the people showed reluctance to move against the enemy as a tribe. Many families already had broken camp, most of the Mnikooźu and some Sicanǧu leaving the day after the sungazing. And certain families from among the original Titonwan had gone, the bands recognizing this revenge as primarily a Mahto affair.

But Tabloka had not hurried away; he stayed to find out whether the sungazing had brought about any change in Ahbleza's standing; if this spectacle proves an important path to tribal power, he will take the same path next summer.

Fifty warriors had struck the red pole this same second night of war dancing when suddenly Ahbleza came walking into the firelight, a man ready to talk. Glancing at the pole, he began his speech.

"Recall, my friends," he said quietly, "the pledge a Shirtman takes. Even if one for whom I hold great fondness falls at my feet, I dare not give way to anger.

"And so I stay out of this avenging for I am not strong

enough to confront the Psa without anger. But if this enemy—any enemy—approaches camp, I will meet and stop his attack."

The next morning Ahbleza repeated his statement in council, then named the two who shall lead the revenge party.

"My father asks for this place and I say to him, 'Lead the warriors if you and they desire this thing.'

"Soon a different relative approaches me saying that he gladly will walk alongside whoever carries the pipe. This man—my kinsman Tezi—lives more than ten winters among the Mnikoóźu, a warrior in Hewanźi's following. Twice you see him at the warpole, where he relates his encounters with the enemy, a witness to these acts at his side."

Ahbleza's speech impressed the warriors, not only the fifty who had struck the pole but fifty more who now decided to disregard Peśla's crude mutterings about the Shirtman's sunpole violation. If Peśla, never a sungazer, senses some disaster resulting from Ahbleza's behavior at the sunpole, let him remember that Olepi, who will carry the pipe, twice scarifies himself. And that Tezi, the Mahto's companion at the front, recites in a manner to dispel any uncertainties. Nor will anyone beg Peśla to go out on this avenging.

The summer-shirts now took over the council meeting, Ahbleza staying to hear this authority name the rules for attack and propose that a group of war advisers accompany the avengers.

But before the deciders had finished speaking, a herald announced the return of two scouts who, running in, signaled good news.

Surprise flashed around the circle; none sat aware that Tonweya and the elusive Peźi had gone out looking for the Psa camps. Even so, the leaders signed for errand boys to lift the front cover; let the people hear these scouts.

Peźi began the reporting. They locate, he said, the Psa village wherein the yellow horse stands, the creature in front of a prominent lodge.

Suddenly the old scout thumbed his wish that the deciders listen to Tonweya; let the young scout give the detail.

813

Ahbleza appeared calm as he watched the brother-friend smooth ground, then draw with a slender stick, pointing out the important features as he drew.

"Here, a butte. Here, the stream where the Psa camp. And here, at this spot, the village. On these flats, their horses graze.

"Here, trees; here, tree-clumps. Here, a slope, and here, five boulders, each one big enough to hide a man."

When the scout paused for questions, the deciders asked about the lodges. And Ahbleza restrained a cry to ask whether any signs of those travelers who had disappeared.

The warriors, learning that this Psa village now hunts, regretted the absence of many good pte-runners.

"But young horses graze in the near distance and I see sturdy reds with black tails close by the lodges." Tonweya's thumb reaffirmed his words; the war party will have a chance at ten thousand horses.

Rising from his knee, the scout yearned to look in the Shirtman's direction but he dared not glance Ahbleza's way, any movement of his eyes perhaps misleading someone.

The next voice in the lodge, a decider who spoke saying that the party shall remember that they avenge, not raid. Take Psa horses, he said, but not until so many enemy die. During the ride to the Psa camp, the war advisers shall invest five, six warriors with special akicita lances and so select those persons to make the kills.

But Tonweya, hearing, told himself that whether or not they offer him a lance, he intends to join in the attack; permission or not, he will get to the lodge where someone tethers the yellow horse and he will get to each person who sleeps in this lodge. And he makes this vow not on any red pole but between himself and the earth.

The next morning Ahbleza watched one hundred painted horsebacks circle the camp, then come to a standstill; they awaited the pipe-carrier.

But when the Shirtman saw his father coming out of the cluster of Mahto lodges, his heart fell. Olepi carried his dance costume and ceremonial headpiece, the leader signifying his willingness to ride in a conspicuous manner, an easy mark for enemy arrows.

Why now? His father counted fifty-and-five winters but the arrogant posture, the insolent eyes, the proud-curling mouth and the firm chin all spoke for abiding strength. So why choose this day for dying?

Or will Olepi really intend to die? As his father rode past him, Ahbleza saw that a covered shield hung at the horse's side; the Mahto leader goes boldly but not without some assurance of protection.

Tezi rode up now, and next came Wanaǧi, the seer walking back of the Mnikooźu and carrying the pipe he had bundled for this avenging.

A whistle screamed, and the warriors, whooping loudly, formed a wide line, the war advisers—eighteen authorities—in a second line, to the rear.

The next moment, silence everywhere; Wanaǧi had stepped forward, handing up the pipe-bundle to the leader.

Olepi, sitting unusually tall, accepted the pipe, then raised his quirt. "Takpe," he shouted, and the horsebacks, repeating his shout as one voice, leapt forward.

But even as Ahbleza watched the dust-cloud rise back of a hundred loping horses, yet another rider appeared. The Shirtman recognized young Oowesica at once but he needed to look twice before he identified the painted man who clung to the youth's waist.

Lekśi, the old, old uncle, the one Mahto who truly intends not to return, who asks for a one-way ride. Lekśi, not Olepi; Lekśi, the one man who most certainly chooses this day to die.

"Perhaps they will understand and assign you a lance, my uncle," Ahbleza called softly as the frail shape passed by; "takpe, takpe."

Turning back toward the Mahto lodges, the Shirtman walked sadly, his sorrow not for the old warrior going to his death but for a young woman sitting patiently in the lodge of a man who as yet had not the desire to make her wife.

Tonweya, waiting at the cross trail for the avengers, reflected on the cunning of Peźi, who had gone ahead, the old scout scheming to meet the war party on the stream where the Psa camped. Many persons solemnly insisted that Peźi turned himself into smoke once inside an enemy village but the man had laughed at such imagery. He said only that the bunch grass he always tied in his hair helped him make those quick disappearances.

And why not a power through grass, Tonweya asked himself now. Ten nights past he had watched a wakaṅlica make spiral-shape stones disappear and return with a message. So why not accept all mystery as power-they-not-yet-understand?

Chewing on a piece of wasna, the scout reviewed that which had occurred on the night Wanaġi used the power of his stone-dream. The man had permitted Tonweya's presence in the sacred-lodge and so the scout had witnessed the whole affair.

The sacred-man had scented the dark lodge with sweetgrass, and then, placing two shell-like pebbles in front of his crossed legs, he had begun a song about the sun and moon.

The scout, attentive to the song, had observed nothing unusual until he heard the wakaṅlica say 'icamani iyayapi.' Then almost at once he had sensed something that moved irregularly, something that spiraled up and out the smoke hole. The next instant Wanaġi had thrown fat onto the place he had burned sweetgrass, the flame showing that the stones had disappeared. As the tipi darkened again, Wanaġi repeated his song.

Certainly the spiral-shape pebbles had not flown out on their own, but what manner of invisible help, Tonweya had wondered, will respond to the power this wakaṅlica put forth and so complete the search for a certain yellow horse.

The sacred-man had not finished his song when Tonweya felt something flit close to his face. The same moment Wanaġi had begun talking softly, the way a man speaks to his grandchildren.

Then the fire had flared up but without help from fat. And the scout, glancing toward the wakaṅlica's legs, saw the two stones in front as before.

Perhaps Wanaġi prepares this whole thing in advance, Tonweya had told himself; certainly the man neither performs the usual rituals before singing his song nor shows any reluctance about using an unfamiliar song. But who will know to tell Wanaġi that the scout intends to demand stone-help? Only he, Tonweya, knows. And only moments before he starts toward the sacred-lodge.

The wakanĥca had waited a little while before giving out the message his stones had brought him, and when finally he had spoken, he had sounded tired. But he had named precisely the stream, the village, and the tipi in that village where Tonweya will find the yellow horse.

And so the scout, inviting Peźi to accompany him, had gone out and returned with a message for the avenging party even as the stones had gone out and returned with a message for Wanaġi.

And now he, Tonweya, waited here at the cross trail, waited for the avengers whom he shall guide toward the enemy village. And the horse they shall bring back to Ahbleza.

Suddenly he found a new thought: will Wanaġi's stones locate the white pte even as they find Tatezi?

Kipanna, seeing Ahbleza walk toward the lodges, had run to his tipi and, darting inside, had sat down on her robe, her heart pounding. But whether this thumping came of desire or dread she knew not. Something had told her that the Shirtman either will make her wife on this day or he never will touch her.

The sun reached middle-sky; the young woman in the Shirtman's lodge sat on, alone and waiting. Then, toward evening, she went looking for Napewaśte, seeking a little comfort somewhere.

But the wife of Olepi, discovering that Lekśi had gone out with the war party, had begun her grieving for the old uncle who had lived many of his seventy-and-seven winters in her lodge. Napewaśte, not one to raise hearts on this day.

Next, Kipanna had visited Cankuna, but when she saw that Ahbleza also came to this lodge, she had crawled out the back.

Once again in the Shirtman's tipi she had sat humped on her robe, her fingers running through the curly hair which covered the thick hide, her eyes dull and staring, a young woman who looked twice her age, twice her fifteen winters.

When finally Ahbleza came in, she placed a bowl of soup before him, the Shirtman smiling his appreciation as if to a child who not yet knows what sorrow sits ahead.

Soon, recognizing that Ahbleza had nothing he will say

to her and that this night offered nothing different, she crawled onto her sleeping robe and covered her face.

After a while the old woman who spread her robe at the front of the lodge slipped in and settled herself for sleep.

Ahbleza, leaning against the backrest, listened to the soft little breaths where Kipanna lay and to the heavy breathing on the robe at the tipi flap.

But I am the only old one in this place, he mused; for who will call age a thing of seasons or winters? A man knows youth or age only in his heart. And I feel the wrinkles in mine.

What pleasure shall I ever bring this young woman if lying alongside her brings nothing to me?

He emptied his pipe, then went to his own robes but not to sleep; instead he lay remembering the one hundred who went looking for the Psa and the man who rode front carrying the pipe. And so his thoughts flashed back to a most gratifying visit with his father.

Olepi had scratched on his son's lodge the day after the sungazing; the two had smoked, their words awaiting an empty bowl.

"Whoever dances at the sunpole," Olepi had begun, "ages in certain ways. For whatever the experience, a sungazing leaves scars whether or not they show."

The father had paused, phrasing most carefully that which he said next. "You perhaps recall that on a certain occasion I attempt to bribe you, a pathetic effort to make you display your bravery in front of the people.

"You refuse my bribe but you will not injure my pride. And so I come here now to say that I intend to lead the party against the Psa. I will carry the pipe for you, remembering that you carry the lance for me.

"Not likely will I make the challenging ride you make, but the enemy shall see me."

Ahbleza had sat unsmiling. "My father, permit my saying that I will not have you carry this pipe as something you owe me. Lead the party if you desire, but lead only to please yourself."

The eyes of these two had met briefly. "Perhaps," said Olepi, "I find my only excitement in war. Whatever I bring the people in the past comes of raids and avengings. If I am an example of anything, I am an example of the warrior-heart."

"And of a good father in my mother's lodge," Ahbleza had answered softly, his inflection disclosing that he had found tenderness not lacking, only kept under cover.

An example of the Titonwan warrior, Ahbleza reflected now as often before; my father speaks truly. He says that he finds excitement in war, but I say that he makes war exciting. He tries to make all things exciting; his nature demands a brilliant display. Not only will he lead this avenging party, he will lead this party brilliantly.

I am glad that once I put on a show for him. I am Ahbleza, an observer, but I am also the son of Olepi.

II

TEMPERS SAT on edge in many Psa lodges this night. The hunters prepared to ride out at daybreak, heading for the greasy-grass where scouts had reported a big herd. And the Psa women, waiting to hear who among wives shall accompany their men—some women wanting to go, different women preferring to stay—had begun to taunt one another.

A sensible man, the people had said, takes along a pretty wife when he goes out to make meat; he will not risk her staying back in camp where she perhaps gets into mischief, either a discreet change of sleeping-mates or she runs away with an attractive young man. And a sensible man, the warrior-hunter Taśa had told himself, knows when not to take either wife.

Taśa stood at the tipi entrance listening to the sounds of a quarrel. When neither of his women came out to stake his horse, he tied the creature himself and entered the lodge scowling.

The two women glanced up, the fat one crawling over to take his moccasins and pull off his leg-covers. The second wife, toward whom he directed a warning stare, sat on, indifferent to his look.

While the man leaned against the tall backrest, the same fat one brought him a bowl of soup, the sight of her hand with three fingertips missing suddenly offensive to the hunter. Certainly a woman will cut off one or more fingers at any joint she chooses when a blood-relative dies, yet the second wife in this lodge—the young and pretty one— suffers the death of parents and brother without mutilating her hands.

But now the man began to view the pretty woman's omission as one more form of her disrespect for custom. Not that he objected to those long fingers arranging his hair but that this woman often acted to annoy him; perhaps a stick-whipping will straighten out her fickleness.

Whipping? Why will he not remember that this one they call Anpagliwin shall bear him a child within four, five moons. And who dares touch a stick to the legs of someone who takes-on-life? He stays patient with Anpagli during these three winters she lives with him as wife; why try making changes in her now?

On the death of her father, Anpagli had shortened her hair but she had cut the strands neatly and in a most becoming style. And none had heard her wailing out on the hills when her mother died the next winter.

Soon after the mother's death, her brother had listened to Taśa—a four-honors Psa but without a following—speak admiringly of Anpagli.

The attractive young woman, notified of the warrior's interest in her, had displayed neither pleasure nor reluctance. But soon afterwards she had accepted a place as second-wife in Taśa's lodge.

Nearly everyone had commented on the young wife's good looks, and so before many days had passed, Taśa's true-wife, using jeers and taunts, had tried to provoke the newcomer into a quarrel.

Anpagli had ignored the tormenting along with Taśa's warning that if he heard many more complaints about her, back she goes to her brother's people.

During her second winter in this lodge, Anpagli had received the news of her brother's death; the real-enemy—the cut-throats—had killed this man. Soon afterwards, she had taken-on-life as if to grow herself a blood-relative, her own blood-family all dead.

Glancing at this woman now, Taśa felt a desire to embrace her; but for her brooding and aloofness and her aversion to certain customs, he regarded her as the most attractive woman in the Psa tribe. Her eyes, big and black and wistful, looked out from a round, childlike face, and her straight-stepping walk gave a lissomeness to her whole person. But if some persons viewed her small girl-like breasts and slim body as unbecoming in this camp of thick-in-the-middle women, they need wait only until a child or two had suckled her. Or so the gossips had said.

Taśa leaned forward to say something to the pretty wife, but at this same moment his young son came into the lodge. The boy scrambled toward his father, overturning the man's untouched soup.

Such an incident disturbed Taśa only if he felt irritable, and so he spoke sharply. But not to the child.

"Neither of you shall taste shin-marrow," he told his wives, "nor see the nose-bone of any pte I kill. I shall give this choice meat to a different woman."

He waited for these two to grasp his threat, then spoke in tones yet more stern: "Now clean up this lodge and keep the place clean."

"Look at her, not me . . . " began the ruling-wife, but Taśa stopped her whine.

"Two women live here, yet they sit like blind while soup runs over the ground and wets my feet." He lifted his moccasins and waited.

The mother of the boy gathered bones and meat from the overturned bowl, throwing these things outside the lodge to Taśa's dogs. Refilling the bowl, she again set soup before the man. "Someone I know sits brooding," she muttered.

"Enough out of you," Taśa said darkly. "I reach the place where I find my only peace out among the four-legs, far out among the soft-noses."

And now Taśa tossed his final threat at these two: any

821

more quarreling and he shall paint their nude bodies red and, tying their feet to his horse, drag each one through the creek.

The fat wife kept silent; perhaps the man meant exactly what he said.

When the warrior-hunter went out the next day, he took along the sister of his true-wife, a woman pledged to him and someone he intended to invite into the lodge now that Anpagli had become untouchable. This hunting expedition offered as good an occasion as any to take a third wife. Certainly he dared leave his two wives in camp; the ruling-wife had sat as his woman long enough to assure her loyalty if not her affection. And Anpagli's condition protected her against any persuasions. As for bringing a third woman into the lodge, perhaps the sisters will comfort each other when he frequents the favorite.

Anpagli kept to the lodge as the husband had foreseen. The unborn presence exhilarated the young woman; she had begun to view herself as something more than a second back-and-hands in this lodge, more than a wife who bathes a husband, arranges his hair. Some day, she had told herself, the people shall know Anpagli as the woman whose son speaks to the dawn and calls forth the enemy, as the mother of a four-honors man, a leader among the Absa, among these people who, like a pack of mountain-dogs, face out on every side.

And so she sat now looking forward to the birth of her child, to his naming, and to his great acts.

On the infant's sixth day, they say, the husband's family shall name the child. But after he grows and becomes man and carries a war pipe and takes horses, he shall change his name. And on the day he snatches a bow from out of the enemy's hand, the praise-singer shall make him a song and award him a new name.

The woman lifted her arms in front of her breasts, palms clasped. "My juices," she whispered, "shall give this one his start. I and husband make a child, but I, the mother, make him warrior."

An unusual fondness for Taśa gripped her; she wished for the man's presence. Then, glancing at the moose hide from which she cut moccasin-shapes, she decided to make Taśa a special pair. Using sinew off the pronghorn's back and many tiny beads, she will create a durable and desirable gift for the returning hunter, for the father of her child. Smiling, she reached for the sacs that held her moccasin-making things.

As Anpagli worked she listened to the sound of children at play. Some day, she told herself, her child will shout his excitement when he kills the snowbird or sends an arrow into the thick grassbraid his father will set up as a target.

Tying the moccasin pieces, she remembered that Taśa had agreed, upon his return, to call the sacred-man to their lodge. This one will come bringing mystery-bundles and songs and he will make ceremony for the new moon and the smoke-stalks growing under the new moon and for the filling-breasts of a woman who grows-life.

Anpagli looked up from her musing; Taśa's little son came running to her. And so the woman, smiling, put aside her work. She took the child's hand and made up a story about each finger, and when he tired of this game she sang him a sleep-song.

While he slept she tended the cooking fire, and when he awoke she fed him.

From inside the tipi the child's mother had watched suspiciously; not often will Anpagli show such interest in the boy.

Toward evening the young woman announced her intention to walk across camp and meet Taśa's nephew, who had agreed to bring in the husband's war horse for the night.

"I will take along the boy," she said pleasantly, but the ruling-wife, her face sullen, had grabbed up her child and gone inside the tipi.

The setting sun had painted the wispy white clouds, and Anpagli, glancing at the sky, sensed a protection all around. Somewhere on the ledges scouts looked far out and here in the village two clubmen and their helpers guarded the stay-backs, those persons who had not gone out with the meat-makers; certainly anyone who approached this camp head-down or after dark came looking for an arrow in the neck.

And so Anpagli, walking out to meet the horse-tender, had not hurried. And she made one stop on the way.

Passing the lodge of a principal man, she lingered to admire the horse staked at the flap. "My wish," she murmured, "to own this yellow one and so ride out anywhere knowing that something protects me." But why this feeling, the woman had not known.

Leading Taśa's horse back to her tipi, Anpagli considered everything they had told about that remarkable yellow creature. She knew that a scout had taken the horse from the real-enemy—they-who-cut-off-Absa-heads—but soon had lost this one at the hand-game. Then, after two more moons, the yellow had come into the possession of a third man. But this third owner, headman of the moving-lodges camp, a man who wore his hair long to the ground, had desired a young jumping horse and so he had exchanged mounts with the leader of this village. And now the fourth owner called the yellow horse his most marvelous trade. Not likely, then, will Taśa's young wife ever see her wish to own this one come true.

And now Anpagli remembered another secret wish she had made but one of a most different nature. This one concerned a tiny hidden pool which the women called 'baby-place.' Here, they told, the spirits of unborns come for play. And any woman who grows-life shall bring toys to this secluded glade—bow and arrows if she looks for a boy-child, hoop and stick if she looks for a girl.

On the day before Taśa had gone out with the hunters, Anpagli had visited the little pond and, not wanting to offend whomever she grows—son or daughter—she had taken along bow and hoop.

Locating the overhang of stone that helped conceal the pool, she soon had discovered the narrow path through the brush. Reaching the pool, she had lowered herself onto the muddy edge and leaned over the quiet water for a look at her face.

Softly she had hummed a sleep-song to the reflection. Then, dipping her fingers in the water, she had distorted the face smiling up at her.

"I bring the bow, also the hoop. Hear me, little ones of the pool," she had whispered. "If boy, take the bow with you. After four days I shall return. I will know that I grow a man-child if nothing touches the hoop."

Once more she had stirred up the water; whispering to the ripples, she had expressed her secret wish for a son.

She had known that none dared make wishes here, this place not a wishing-pool; one came here, they said, to learn that which the powers already decide. Even so, she had reached out to touch the little bow which she had propped against the brush. "Come play, my son," she had murmured.

Six, seven days had passed since this visit to the baby-place, Anpagli told herself now; she dared go again to the pool. And so why not slip out of camp at dawn the next day?

Pleased with her decision, Anpagli secured the husband's horse and stepped into the lodge. She saw that the grandparents of the ruling-wife had come to stay until the hunter's return. She gladdened; not only will these old people always treat her most kindly but the fat woman's disposition improved whenever these two visited here.

And so the two wives, grateful for company that permitted easy talk and laughter, enjoyed the evening; they saw the firewood used up before anyone mentioned sleep.

Anpagli, determining to start out next morning before the lodge awoke, slept in her day-gown but she had pulled off her moccasins; this night the lodge had a protector, an old man but a strong and alert one.

As she had wished, the daybreak song of birds aroused Anpagli at dawn. She listened awhile to the stamps and wheezes of horses and to a camp-dog who yelped but not loudly. But then something not usual to an awakening had reached her ears; she heard a cry of alarm, the sound coming from a woman.

She sat up. More cries but these sounds came from the mouths of men. And now she recognized the war whoop of the real-enemy. Minisupekaźo, these cut-throats attack this village.

Grabbing his bow, the old man had rushed out of the lodge before any of the three women dared move. But as he threw aside the tipi flap, Anpagli saw briefly the kicking feet of Taśa's horse. Instantly she thought to get to the creature and force him down, out of arrow-reach.

She jumped into her moccasins but a commotion outside the tipi held her back.

"They will kill everyone." The ruling-wife, her head covered, sat wailing on her robes. But her muffled fear reached Anpagli.

"Look after your child, fat one," Anpagli called scornfully. Then she saw that the grandmother already had pushed the boy into the space between backrests and that the old woman now piled up robes and so gave the child yet more protection.

"Hide back of the tipi lining," Anpagli told the boy's mother; "wait for a chance to escape into the brush with your son."

Slowly now the young woman crept toward the entrance flap, knife in hand, her eyes despising. "Miniśupekaźo, Miniśupekaźo," she hissed, her teeth clenched. Again and again she reviled the enemy with this shaming name.

But whenever the victory shouts of the attackers filled the air, she turned her anger toward the fat one who stayed on her sleeping robes and wailed. "Stop your noise," she commanded; "you draw the enemy to this lodge."

Suddenly a quiet pervaded the camp, almost as if someone had lifted the silencing hand, demanding that the dying and the victorious stifle their cries.

And now Anpagli pushed forward a meat container, her foot moving the rawhide piece under and outside the tipi. Staying on the woman's side of the lodge she waited, knife raised.

Nothing happened and for an instant she experienced the relief that comes when an enemy rides off. But then the cries began again, the noise of molested men mingling with the wails of women and the whoops of the victors.

Keenly aware of the situation now, Anpagli tried once again to quiet the ruling-wife. "Silence," she muttered, "or I go."

When the fat one howled yet more loudly, Anpagli spoke to the brave old grandmother. "Follow me," she said, and lifted the flap.

The two crawled out of the lodge. "Run," Anpagli commanded and led the way, the old one stumbling along as fast as her legs permitted.

But hearing a horseback coming up close, Anpagli knew that they had attracted someone's attention, someone who perhaps will spare a grandmother.

Darting between lodges, Anpagli hurled herself into the tree clump back of one. "Hide me, leaves," she breathed softly.

But the enemy who pursued, who will chase her for her life and her scalp, came on foot now and along the same path she had taken.

She waited, not breathing, for his running steps to reveal in which direction he moved next. But she heard nothing and so, after a while, she raised her eyes.

She saw his strong legs and then his back; he faced away from her. Cautiously she lifted a hand, the one holding a knife.

Instantly the trees shook as if a grizzly had swiped at the leaves and then grabbed her in a choking hug. The knife dropped out of her hand as she struggled to escape the man's hold. And her attempt to kick him only tightened his grasp and increased the ache he made in her shoulder.

Next thing, she felt herself jerked forward, her moccasins catching in the tangled underbrush; she fell against his breast.

Opening her mouth on contact with his flesh, she strained to bite the place her teeth touched him. But with one hand he held her arms against her back, his other hand forcing up her head, his knife at her throat.

She closed her eyes. And the hand under her chin moved to her hair.

Suddenly the horror of his knife at her living scalp compelled her to look at him. And so she saw not a man's face but the personification of revenge; instantly she knew that this enemy will exact satisfaction not for some injury that any Psa warrior had inflicted upon the cut-throat tribe but for something terrible that she, Anpagli, had brought about.

She closed her eyes again but she stood determined not to shriek her pain when he sliced off skin from her head.

But after a moment he loosened his hold on her arms; his hand let go her hair. Even so, he had produced the effect he intended; she slumped weakly before him. And now he need only drive her into the herd with all the other captured women.

He jumped on the horse who had followed him to the place of her silent struggle. And when she opened her eyes, his gesture ordered her to rise and walk next to his mount.

She stood and, moving like one whose spirit had taken leave of the body for a little while, she stepped forward stiffly. He dropped the horse's cord over her neck, pulling the thong tight against her throat, arousing her from the dreamlike daze. And when she raised glaring eyes to his face, he met her look with ridiculing laughter and a tug on the cord.

When next he glanced at her, he saw that the woman stared at his mount and that tears splashed down her cheek. He watched as she moved close to touch her face against the wonderful old yellow horse. But he had mistaken her act; he imagined that she had accepted her rank as his captive even as this yellow horse had become his.

But who in this camp or any camp will know that Anpagli's tears fell in memory of her two secret wishes? And who in this camp will know that Tonweya, riding here, remembered clearly Ahbleza's face on the day he had visited the brother-friend to report seeing Tatezi in the hands of Psa scouts? Only Olepi's orders not to kill any more persons in this village had kept Tonweya from throwing this captive woman to the ground and cutting her throat.

The Mahto leader had voiced this order upon riding through the subdued camp and observing lodges, women and children. He had recognized that the male survivors in this band—those hunters out after pte and perhaps twelve middle-age men—shall face difficulty in providing for the many lodges now empty of fathers, husbands, sons. And so he had advised that the war party kill or drive off any old persons and then choose forty young Psa women as captives; all other women and children they shall ignore.

The war advisers had backed up the Mahto's decision but these eighteen had said nothing against invading lodges or harassing the ten, twelve Psa they had not destroyed. And so the warriors had begun to throw down tipi and load Psa horses with meat folders, smoking material, wapiti teeth, and whatever more looked good.

Pešla went off with the five, six warriors who wanted a different remembrance of this attack, warriors who desired performing iwicahupi on those male captives they had spared for such purpose. Not many men chose this unnatural contact with the enemy, whether enacted as humbling abuse or as a strangely gratifying sensation, but certainly all warriors sounded the war cry 'huka hey,' which means exactly this thing.

Tonweya had shown interest neither in his brother's maneuvers nor in the acts of those warriors who raided tipi; acting as scout when the attack began, his chance to act as an avenger suddenly had come.

Presented a lance and instructed to take whatever he had come here to take, he had rushed the lodge where the yellow horse—feathers in her mane and tail—stood flicking her ears. Slashing the cover, he had risked a jump into the tipi, the woman who cringed back of the lining, an easy kill. Then, turning over his own mount to a young brave, the scout had cut loose Tatezi, unhurriedly removed the decoration tied in her hair. As he jumped onto her back, he had heard the voice for the war advisers announce Olepi's decision concerning captives. And so, seeing two women crawl out of a nearby tipi, he had gone after these persons. He had knocked down the old one, then jumped off the horse to pursue the young woman who dodged between lodges. And now having enacted his revenge, he intended to quit his captive and pick up his work as scout.

But the advisers had chosen Tonweya as one to help drive the captured women to the Titonwan camps. And certainly he dared not ask that they release him from this disagreeable work; these men had granted him his every request during this revenge.

And so he listened to instructions: a half-circle of men riding rear and to the sides shall keep the captives as a herd. They shall water, feed, and rest the women at the same intervals they give attention to the horses.

Tonweya signaled the Mahto brave to whom he had turned over the care of his horse; the scout wanted to ride his own mount now and lead Tatezi. He agreed to take his place as women-tender but never will he put the yellow one he had recovered for Ahbleza in with the captive herd.

"I envy you, my brother. More than one in the war party mentions your gains." Peśla, suddenly appearing at the scout's side, spoke admiringly. "You return to the Mahto camp with a true-prize." The warrior's eyes roved cunningly toward the captive women. "At the finish of this drive, they shall hand back the women to their captors, but along the way these Psa captives belong to the whole party."

Tonweya said nothing and so Peśla spoke on: "I capture horses but not one woman. Perhaps my brother will not object if I find ways to tease his captive during this travel."

The scout remained silent. Most warriors, he recalled, viewed any lustful encounters with enemy women on the return trail as a danger to the expedition. And certainly he wanted nothing to happen that risked his losing Tatezi, this horse his only true concern.

Peśla smiled: "My brother misunderstands. I will use teasing as a way of discovering who will stand up to this rough walk they impose upon these women. I observe that you have more interest in the horse than in your captive and so I speak. Truly, I will not intend offense, but I wonder whether you know anything about keeping women in line."

Quirting his mount, the warrior rode off.

III

ANPAGLI KEPT to the edge of the traveling women. She walked tall, eyes straight ahead; she spoke to none. When Taśa returns from the hunt and discovers the raid on camp, she told herself, he shall come looking for her and for his horse and for the herd of horses. Then let these miserable Miniśupekaźo—this enemy whose bowels leak fear at the mention of her people—meet a true warrior.

Perhaps even now, her thoughts ran on, Absa scouts

watch from their secret nests; perhaps they see these raider-killers and hurry out this sad news to the Absa hunters. So perhaps the next day Taśa comes looking for her. Let the captives gash their heads and wipe the white earth into the blood on their faces. Her man—Taśa, the warrior-hunter—lives. And perhaps now he owns but one wife.

Two, three captive women, observing Anpagli's cold indifference toward her grief-stricken companions, tried to bring the woman to her senses. You, also, have relatives, they told her, who die back in the village.

Wanting to shut off these voices, Anpagli moved as far out as the circle of her captors permitted, keeping to this place even when she saw that certain ones eyed her boldly. When Taśa appears, she will tell on these daring warriors and Taśa will cut away their manliness, dangling their seed-balls on his lance.

The war party moved directly east from the river of tongues, the war advisers foreseeing safety along this familiar path back to camp. But Tonweya wished himself at the rear of the travelers, far out and watching for pursuers. True, Peźi rode protection, but perhaps Peźi's eyes, unlike Tonweya's eyes, will not see everything.

During one rest stop the warriors had contemplated in what manner they shall approach the Titonwan encampment. The avenging had proved most advantageous and yet they wondered about blackening their faces and entering camp in the customary order of victors? This party returns with one man missing and three warriors suffering wounds.

But then young Ooweśica, remembering that he, an Oglalahca, had made one of the kills, spoke out; he told about old Lekśi, the missing man.

"This one," he said, "rolls off the horse at the edge of the enemy's camp. He wobbles into the midst of the fight, where he looks for a chance at any one of the enemy. But he dies before his chance ever comes. The same war whoop that stuns many Psa excites the old man beyond enduring. He collapses.

"I, Ooweśica, horseback and watching, dash forward and grab up the old man's body before anyone touches him.

And he who rides alongside the pipe-carrier also comes up swiftly, a witness to these events."

Ooweśica cut off his recital at this point, the young man not obliged to say more. But Tezi, named as witness, chose to carry on the story.

"The old warrior approaches the enemy camp," Tezi told now, "singing his song of defiance. But he looks for death on the fighting ground and a place for his body among the stones of some distant ledge. He desires neither the tall rack nor the sound of wails. And so I help the Oglalaȟca carry this body to a hiding place where I pile over the stones.

"Afterwards, I see someone avenge this old man's death. On a different occasion you shall hear the story.

"And so I say: men, blacken your faces. Those warriors walk and eat who receive wounds, and the missing one will not deny you a victors' return."

At the next resting place the warriors prepared scalps for hanging on their lances. And while they formed the little hoops and stretched the hair to fit, the scout Peźi sent forward word that the enemy trailed closely, seven Psa riding out after ten tens of Titonwan.

The Mahto warriors had smiled but not Olepi. He asked that the party remember the Psa as unrelenting pursuers and that three hundred Psa horses and forty Psa women travel with this party. To recover even ten of these horses, in keeping with enemy procedure.

"And these men who pursue, while not an avenging party, remember that the Titonwan kill nine Psa warriors and humiliate ten middle-age men, that the Titonwan destroy eight old persons and eight children."

Olepi had spoken, and now the war advisers sat together to consider two, three different proposals, then make their recommendation.

Send ahead half the war party, they agreed, and all but forty horses. These forty—the most slow—shall carry the packs which, until now, burden the captive women.

"And increase the distance between rests for everyone," one of the eighteen advised, "until scouts report that the pursuers drop back."

But the captives shall stay foot-going, they decided; let these women mount only if an attack appears imminent.

Most of the captives they herded across the dry plain had not puzzled the change in pace, but Anpagli, observing the meeting of leaders and the suddenly disappearing horses, suspected that the Absa rode close on the heels of the cutthroats. And so, moving back in among the women, she quietly spoke her deduction.

"Absa men come looking for their wives and daughters," she said. "They discover the trail. Perhaps the little things I drop out of my bundles help mark the path."

"If any men come, they come looking for their horses," one woman replied scornfully.

"They come for me and you and their horses," Anpagli answered, managing to keep her voice cheerful.

"You, what will you know?" the group taunted.

And now one of the captives stared fiercely from beneath red-lidded eyes, a feature not uncommon among these Psa women.

"You," she yelled at the young wife, "you never show sorrow at anything. Or will you not see the enemy who bursts open the head of a child, who swings my little son against a tree? What will you know about grieving?" The woman broke into loud wails.

A different woman carried on: "But you shall learn grief in the enemy camp. Already these cut-throats look at you and I imagine that ten will take you in the grass. Afterwards you will want to slash your forehead and let blood drip onto your face."

Anpagli had not spoken again to these women, but while she sat waiting for the signal to start walking, she considered her chances of escaping before ever the party reached the enemy camp. Confident that Taśa pursued, she saw need only to sneak away and hide in a gully until the Absa caught up. Perhaps the next gully offered her this chance.

Peśla, hearing wails, approached the group. But he came up alongside Anpagli. "Move, woman," he demanded. Then, remembering that certain sounds carry different meanings within these not unsimilar tongues, he gestured his order.

Anpagli had not responded at once and so he poked her with his lance, a Psa scalp tied onto this stick. Even so, the woman neither looked at him nor hurried.

"You will move fast enough once you enter the Mahto camp," he jeered, and rode back among his own.

Why this man harassed her Anpagli had not understood but neither had she puzzled his temperament. Taśa comes soon, she had told herself, and so she never again will see cruel-face. Or so she had named Peśla.

Then, before dusk this same day, the party approached a gully, a break into which Anpagli dared imagine herself slipping unobserved.

The horsebacks guarding the women halted, two from their group riding forward to inspect the narrow cut. But almost at once they signaled back that this gully had dried, neither drink nor grass for horses.

And so, while the party waited for a decision as to whether they will rest briefly or not at all, Anpagli made her move. Using the space these two inspectors left open in the half-circle of horsebacks, she darted through to the head of the little ravine and began rolling down the slope.

Someone stopped her, someone who dragged her over rough ground, then jerked her onto her feet and pushed her along firmly.

Angrily she flung her body around, throwing off the shoving hand. And so she looked directly into the face of him who prevented her escape.

Instantly she remembered the knife at her neck, at her scalp; this same someone who had filled her with terror back in the Psa village will make her tremble even now.

But, her throat aching, she struggled against tears; never shall he see her cry, whatever happens. Defiantly she held his gaze.

Then, uncertain whether her will or his compelled the act, she walked back to the group of captive women where this man's eyes said she belonged.

The authorities had advised a short rest at this same dry gully, but before anyone truly slept, a shout in the darkness startled the party.

Quickly two clubmen came forward; they reported that the pursuers had gotten to the small herd of slow horses. An alert Mahto had killed one Psa, but the others, taking back five horses, had escaped.

The warrior who made the kill brought the dead man's scalp to the war advisers; these men counted each killing that related to this revenge.

"Your men seem slow to learn," someone shouted at the Psa women, who wailed anew at the blood and hair.

But not all the captive women wailed. Anpagli had ignored the scalp; instead, she looked toward the gloating warrior who held up the leg-covers he had stripped off the killed enemy.

Perhaps a woman will not recognize whose hair flutters on a lance but certainly she will know shirts and leg-covers and moccasins of her own making. And so Anpagli understood that Taśa had come looking for her. Perhaps different ones among the pursuers sneaked off once they recaptured their horse, but Taśa had stayed; Taśa had kept searching for his young wife.

So let these captives try to tell her differently; let the jealous claim that the small flame which lights the camp makes identification of a beadwork design difficult and that those leg-covers belong to a different Psa, one who persists in his search for the yellow horse. Let these persons say anything they choose to say, but she, Anpagli, will go on knowing that Taśa dies trying to get back his woman. Why wail? Instead why not remember that Taśa helps her make-a-baby, a man-baby to whom she will say: your father dies bravely; your father dies trying to protect you.

And now Anpagli dared truly scheme; in one way or another she shall escape the enemy camp and return to her people. She will see Taśa's child growing up among his own, Taśa's son—his only son now—who shall become a good-man, a four-honors man. Why let the unborn child hear her wailing? Instead, let him hear a voice singing proudly.

TONWEYA VISITED his brother-friend immediately upon the war party's return, the scout tying the captured yellow horse at Ahbleza's lodge, then announcing his presence.

The two smoked, using one pipe in their customary manner, but neither man spoke of the avenging nor appeared to notice the drums which prepared the people for a victory dance. And not until Ahbleza emptied the second pipe had Tonweya brought forth the scalp of that one he had killed in the Psa camp, in the enemy lodge in front of which he had seen Tatezi standing.

Holding out the hair, the scout spoke softly: "Perhaps someone here or a woman in her mother's lodge will dance this head." He avoided looking at the Shirtman; he wanted never again to see pain on this man's face.

Ahbleza's gesture accepted the scalp. And so, Tonweya spoke again. "I keep looking for the white pte even as I avenge my brother's . . ." His voice broke before he finished.

Then quickly the scout moved to the tipi opening, pulling aside the flap and going out.

Ahbleza sat on alone, the scalp at his knee, his attention returning to this thing the Lakotah call revenge.

He recalled his feelings when, as a youth, he had tried to understand why a man calls enemy anyone who speaks a strange tongue. Why despise someone for the reason that he belongs to a different tribe? Until the people spread out, all persons live as one family, speak one language.

And why injure a man who harms neither you nor your child for the reason that a different man in his camp kills someone in your family? Kill whoever kills, but why all women—children also—suffering for the act of one? Perhaps someone will find something that puts a finish to the killing of persons who never harm anyone.

Reviewing his experience at the sunpole, he concentrated on what the grandfathers say about man's appearance on earth as a visible form.

But if man comes into the sun to seek growth for his spirit, who dares kill and release a life before the spirit makes full use of earth's facilities? Or before the spirit, expanding to the full, absorbs the flesh?

And yet, looking upon the hair Tonweya brought him, he will not regret this avenging. A man from this enemy band kills his heart and so he gladly will see Kipanna, whom they call the pathetic one, dancing this scalp every night and every night.

And so what happens to him that he, knowing that a contradiction never exists, tries to understand this one?

Cankuna laughed comfortably on viewing the captive Tonweya brought to her lodge. "Your sons spoil me," she said, directing her speech to Ogle. "One son brings hands to assist me in my middle age and now the second son provides me with someone to ease the winters of my old age. Soon I will grunt like an old grizzly whenever I need bend my back to anything."

Ogle sat unsmiling; he had acknowledged Anpagli's presence with nothing more than a quick glance.

But Peśla spoke up at once: "My brother's prize requires fattening. She looks unfit for the heavy work in a hunter's lodge."

Anpagli had not comprehended all that these poeple said but she heard the taunt in the warrior's voice.

Her heart had dropped on seeing Peśla in this tipi to which her captor had led her. And certainly she intended to take her own life before ever she became anything to this dark, loathesome man who poked her with his lance during the long wailing-women walk.

Abruptly now she turned her back on the occupants of Cankuna's lodge.

"Hoḣ. What manner of tribe permits women this rudeness." Peśla spoke sharply, ignoring his position as visitor in his parents' tipi. "The Palani woman I once bring into this lodge remembers herself as captive. Perhaps my brother mistakes his prize"—ridicule replaced the thin edge to the warrior's voice—"and so he hesitates to put this one in her place. Palani woman knows her place."

Ogle leaned forward, one hand covering his mouth, one hand raised in a gesture of appeal; an old man will not see his sons quarrel.

Then, before anyone will say something regrettable,

Cankuna spoke, eyes down and voice soft but her words easily understood: "The Palani captive my son brings here six winters past knows her place, her new place.

"Even as I, she now says 'husband' to my sons' father and after the snow moons she bears his child. Winu sits alongside the man in this tipi as his second-wife."

Her words had silenced the lodge but the full meaning came slowly to the warrior-son. Peśla sat endeavoring to recall when Winu most recently had tried for his attention.

Certainly he never had used this woman; her sullen face repulsed him. She had watched over the daughter born to him and Wipatawin, a child he avoided as someone who will provoke an unpleasant memory. And certainly he had sensed relief when this daughter—now a girl in her eighth winter—chose to live within a different tiyośpaye. But Winu had stayed around, eying him for favors.

Nor will he recall at what point the Palani woman had begun to speak Lakotah, something that earned any captive a certain respect. He had looked upon this dull woman as nothing more than help in his mother's lodge. Yet now they tell him that Winu becomes wife to his father, her child someone he shall call sister or perhaps brother?

Why this thought thoroughly annoyed him, Peśla knew not. But suddenly angry, he arose from his place next to Ogle and, throwing Anpagli a fierce glance, stepped out of the tipi and headed for his own.

And now Tonweya, his brother's distracting influence removed, perceived that his father's act had not displeased his mother. And the scout understood why.

Until now Ogle had received all the help he had needed in handling the meat. Always a cluster of tipi had surrounded the hunter's lodge, one great-family, a tiyośpaye proudly self-sustaining, each woman a competent and willing worker.

Now a difference: only three tipi where once stood ten, and half as many hands to cut and load meat, prepare hides, make lodges, moccasins, robes. The sons and daughters had grown, two living outside the hunter's lodge and two soon to go. And many of these relatives who stayed close by, wobbled around on uncertain legs.

True, Cankuna belonged not to this group of old bones, old hearts, but most women who approach fifty will not make as many new robes as in seasons past; they prefer company and so they choose decorating moccasins, quilling sacks and stem-covers, whatever activities permit visiting and gossip and laughing along with the work.

Ogle alone seemed unchanging. He made meat as in his young winters, and at fifty-and-four his strong smooth face attracted women the age of his daughters.

And so the scout, taking an unusually close look at these people—his parents—saw the good in Ogle's making a wife of Winu; the hunter had kept this woman in Cankuna's lodge, a reliable helper for whom the family shall show a new respect. Remembering that the family never formally had adopted the Palani captive, Tonweya wondered whether his mother had schemed this new living arrangement herself.

But the scout also realized that he had brought a captive Psa-woman into a lodge where three women shall make demands upon her and so limit her adventures outside the tipi.

Suddenly moving close to the Psa-woman, he touched her arm. Something about her eyes hinted that she, also, belongs under the big sky, not beneath a lodge cover.

Feeling his touch, Anpagli turned and so she saw his demand that she follow him out of the tipi, to whatever place he intended to lead her.

And now she found herself moving across the camp circle, walking back of her captor but holding herself tall. Perhaps he decides to send her alone onto the plain to hunt her people, something he imagines that she bravely shall attempt; perhaps he grants her a courage she will not possess.

After a while the scout glanced over his shoulder at the woman; he looked for eyes either defiant or sullen but not for that which he saw. She stood regarding him with a shining look, one that recognizes the discovery of a similar self and rejoices in this wonder.

He turned and faced her. Never before had anyone gazed upon him in such manner; he wished for a way of holding on to this moment. Then suddenly he realized that in any different place, on any different occasion, her look will say that she belongs to him in the manner a wife belongs to a husband.

He saw the smile that reached her lips, saw her black eyes closing, her graceful head bowing slightly. And now a desire to pull her against his heart overwhelmed him; he reached forward his arms.

But the next instant he remembered her as an enemy woman, perhaps wife to a Psa warrior. And so his imagination provoked an urge to seize her roughly, to hurt and frighten this woman once again. His fingers, grasping her shoulders, bruised where he touched.

She moved and her hair, fragrant and heavy, brushed over his hands. Instantly he loosened the painful hold; awkwardly he soothed those same shoulders.

He raised her head, her face between his hands. And so he held her until once again she closed her eyes. He had thought to say something—he never yet had spoken to her, neither in the enemy village nor during their travels nor here—but some mystery held on to his tongue.

The woman, sensing an uneasiness within the man, looked at him as he withdrew his hands from her cheeks. And so she saw the lift of his chin that signed her to follow him back across the camp circle. Where shall he take her, he had asked himself, but to his mother's lodge again.

Outside the tipi, Tonweya gestured that she enter. But when she bent to step inside without scratching on the lodge cover, he pulled her arm roughly. Then, having shown the proper way to request entrance, he abruptly walked off.

For a little while she stood alone, a captive woman not yet certain that they want her sleeping here. When finally she lifted the flap and entered, she found the lodge empty but for the old hunter.

Ogle sat painting for the victory dance. Even so, his quick eyes observed a difference in the Psa-woman, a change that made him wonder whether Tonweya, good at gentling those horses brought in from the sandhills, also knew ways for gentling a woman brought in from an enemy camp. Or perhaps the captive, hearing the drums, remembered that the Lakotah dance the scalps of her people this night. Most certainly something had subdued the woman.

Pešla's face had retained a fierce stare all the way to his lodge; even the camp-dogs had moved out of his path.

He directed his resentment at Winu, who shall give birth to her child during the same new-grass moon that Lowansa anticipates her infant. Not that he cared about his father's potency; he simply sensed irritation at the thought of Ogle becoming father and grandfather on the same day.

Lowansa, seeing that her man approached, wanted to run out of the lodge but, as had become her custom, she sat down the moment Pešla entered the tipi. She had resigned herself to hearing him growl dissatisfaction with everyone and everything, but never again will she accept blame, receive blows.

During these six winters she had stayed his wife, she had threatened on more than one occasion to throw out his possessions. And once, provoked beyond enduring, she had set his moccasins and bow outside the tipi.

Pešla usually ignored her presence for three, four days following these threats, but one day, seeing her fumble over his things at the back of the lodge, he had cut a thick branch.

A woman of good family neither mentions bruises on her body, Lowansa had told herself, nor displays such marks as complaints against a husband. And so she said nothing; instead she had accepted Pešla's moods from that day forward, putting up with his taunts, holding on to her calm. But she knew herself as one who had changed from a good-looking, cheerful woman to a brooding, silent wife. And until the sungazing this past summer she had sung only sad little songs.

Now, growing-a-life, she had begun to sing as before, the lodge brightening to the sound of her fine voice; she dared look for the arrival of a child after these six trying winters to soften the warrior's stony face, warm his cold heart.

People regard Pešla as unpredictable and so who dares say that never will he show a nice side to his nature? All warriors act gruff and rude in an enemy camp, Pešla differing in that he never suppressed his gruffness whether among strangers or relatives. Or so Lowansa tried to exculpate this man who indulged his unpleasant moods.

She knew that Pešla always looked for another woman

and so she had sat prepared to welcome a captive—or anyone—who will live here, share his harshness with her. Now, suddenly, she wanted none other in the lodge. And for this reason alone she had awaited most apprehensively his return from the Psa avenging.

But Peśla had chosen not to bring back a Psa captive. The prize I seek, he had told himself, lives in Tabloka's camp, a band who only imagine they follow Tawitko. And so I bring back horses, enough horses for any trade I choose to make. What husband, even among the Kiyuksa, will refuse my offer? Wives come easy but not horses.

But Peśla will not make any such observation to his wife. Instead he entered the lodge reproving Lowansa at once; she had not told him about Winu. And he had finished his reproach with a threat: if ever again she withholds something important, he shall claim that the child she grows belongs to a different man.

The old woman who slept front in this lodge looked over at Peśla on hearing these words. And now, as on other occasions, she mumbled her fears for the husband and wife who stay here.

Peśla, hearing, gestured rudely in her direction. But Lowansa, sitting quiet, heard only the echo of an old familiar moan.

Eight days in the hunter's lodge and Anpagli already knew whom she liked, whom she disliked. Cankuna had shown that she shall not make the path difficult, and Tacincala, near to the captive's age, had acted friendly almost at once. But the Palani woman whom they call Winu, this one Anpagli had despised from the moment of their meeting.

Making use of her advance in rank to second-wife, Winu had begun to harass the Psa-woman. Remembering her own uncomfortable moons as captive in this camp, she took out on Anpagli the resentment she never had released.

When the Psa-woman displayed clumsiness at tying the short poles onto the back of a dog, Winu ridiculed the Psa tribe, deriding a people who never use drags and in whose camps the dogs belong to men.

"Titonwan warriors own horses," she mocked; "the dogs belong to women." She slapped the captive's face; she wanted to make certain that the woman understood her contempt for the Psa.

Anpagli understood. Winu's speech, not difficult to recognize, had told her more than the woman's hand striking her cheek.

"Dog-eater," Anpagli answered back; "your warriors make meat of these creatures and so they lack dogs." She cared not whether Winu, who walked away, had heard; enough that the second-wife had seen Anpagli's gesture which scorned everything Lakotah.

The next day Winu had stood watching the captive, who raised the tipi on clean grass. Anpagli, unfamiliar with a three-pole frame and Lakotah smoke flaps, had looked around for a helper. And so Cankuna had asked that the Palani woman assist.

"Of what use, you," Winu cried. "You, a know-nothing." She grabbed a pole. "A Palani woman never seeks help, whether she raises a lodge or makes an earth shelter."

Anpagli laughed: "The Psa tipi stand tall and so they require more than one woman's hands. On occasion a horse will help raise the lodge. But perhaps you have not the tall poles and the many skins for big lodges."

On another day she intended to tell this unkempt stranger that the Psa had lived many seasons in earth lodges and knew all about making such shelters. The Psa also had raised deadwood lodges in the past, twenty or more winters in the past.

Winu had not understood the captive's exact words, but she had recognized an insult to her tribe. "Look who talks. So tell me on which creature—bighorn or pronghorn—your men most often try out their manliness?"

Anpagli decided against retort; she will ignore this crude tongue. Teasing, taunting—even hair-pulling and slaps—she will understand but not vulgar talk. Henceforth she will stay out of her tormentor's sight.

But the Lakotah observed a captive's moves most closely for two, three moons, permitting a woman to walk only two paths: the one leading to a woodpile and the one leading to personal relief. And so each family assigned someone to watch over any captive in their lodge.

When Winu hinted to Ogle that she desired this assignment, the hunter granted her wish. And Cankuna, anxious to prevent any rift between the hunter and herself, decided not to mention that the scout had given this captive to his blood-mother only.

And so the Palani wife, whenever she imagined herself unobserved, pinched the captive's bottom or scratched her arms or jerked her hair. Twice she managed to spill fat on Anpagli's one clean gown—a bighorn gown and most attractively fringed—and once she emptied the captive's little sack of personal items into the stream. On yet another occasion she encouraged an unruly child to throw an arrow at the water-sac the Psa-woman carried back from the creek.

And toward all these acts Anpagli showed an indifferent face.

Then, after ten or more days, Tacincala persuaded Winu that she permit the captive a little visit with those other Psa-women living here since the revenge.

Anpagli had gone out of the hunter's lodge but not gladly. Her own, she knew, will not treat her with any more consideration than the gloomy Palani woman.

"Will you say," these Psa-unfortunates asked Anpagli now, "that they never humble you in the hunter's lodge? Will they respect you when they see that you will not grieve your husband?"

"The enemy knows not that I ever have a husband. They know not that I . . ."

The young woman had stopped, catching her words before she revealed a secret. None of these captive women had known that she took-on-life, nor will anyone suspect until the second moon of her capture, not until they wonder why she never becomes iśnati. The moon when big berries ripen now grows old and next comes the yellowing-of-leaves, the fifth moon for her unborn child; uneasily she let go these thoughts.

She looked into the faces of these persons waiting for her to finish whatever she will tell. "The enemy knows . . . nothing," she said, her voice disdainful.

Turning from their red-eyed stares and the sight of untidy hair and stained gowns, she remembered that these women—until driven here—had lived in a most presentable manner; truly, she will kill herself before ever she becomes the same as these dejected persons.

Walking back to Cankuna's lodge, she recognized the need to escape at once.

"You have none whom you call relative." Winu had discovered the most cruel taunt that the Psa ever hear.

But Winu will use this phrase only once in Anpagli's presence. Whatever the risk, the captive now threatened to knock down the Palani woman if ever she uttered these words again. Raising her arm, Anpagli made clear her intent.

But Tonweya, entering the tipi, stopped the captive's hand mid-air. She stared open-mouth in the manner of a child while her arm dropped slowly to her side and her heart throbbed noisily.

The scout, now ignoring the two, moved to his sleeping robe and let himself down gently; the next moment he appeared asleep.

And now a picture flashed in front of Anpagli. She imagined her captor in the hills, scouting a herd for the old-summer hunt. She remembered that the man in this lodge worked over his hunting weapons and that different ones in nearby tipi also prepared for making meat. Perhaps the crier will announce when the hunters go out. She vowed to listen closely; such news will help her schemes.

And two things Anpagli now understood: she knew why she had not seen Tonweya since that day he left her scratching on the tipi cover and she knew that he came back to the camp not to look for her but to report a herd.

The day after the scout's return, Cankuna arranged to sit a little while with Anpagli.

"You will not find any peace here," she advised the captive woman, "until you start speaking Lakotah. This tongue differs not much from your own. And once you understand which words belong to a man, which ones only women use, you will speak the language easily. But if you choose to mix Psa and Lakotah, you will find things increasingly difficult."

Anger sparked the young woman's eyes, but Cankuna spoke on: "I know who abuses you and I will not approve. But try to remember that Palani woman acts out the memory of her captive days whenever she teases you."

845

Cankuna turned back to the meat folders, which she inspected for worn spots, and Anpagli moved over to help with this work.

But the captive's attention had not stayed on these stiff containers. Instead, she reviewed silently her scheme for the next day. Discovering that the villagers intended to follow out after the hunting party, she had decided to make use of the noise and confusion that always accompanies a people when they break camp.

Perhaps Cankuna knew of the Psa-woman's escape before ever Winu came hurrying up with the news; for what different reason will Cankuna hide a smile?

"She runs away." The second-wife's petulant tone implied that she, not Cankuna, endured a loss.

And so Cankuna took pleasure in a sly reply: "Perhaps your runaway only looks around camp for drag-poles. I understand that someone offers her a horse."

"She knows nothing about tying poles on horses . . . or dogs," Winu answered abruptly. "And I never see her horseback."

"They will not permit a captive horseback—will you not remember?—until they know her intention."

"I look for someone who will tell your son that the captive disappears." Speaking in an offended voice, Winu started away.

"Perhaps he already knows," Cankuna murmured to herself as she fastened a second thong across the drag-poles. She had surmised that Tonweya approved the getaway of this pretty captive who, to any discerning eye, showed that she had taken-on-life.

But the scout had not known that his captured woman escaped, not until after the hunt. Tonweya had gone out ahead of the camp and had stayed out, keeping watch during the surround. The news had not reached him until the whole encampment came onto the hunting ground to help cut up meat.

Ogle had informed him. Seeing that Tonweya looked around as if trying to locate a missing face, the father told his son about the captive's disappearance four days previously. He told also that Cankuna and not his second-wife shall keep watch over the Psa-captive if ever she returned.

The scout had puzzled only briefly why his father chose to mention Winu—the runaway, certainly not Winu's concern; then he had smiled.

"Chasing the foot-going I find easy enough," he said, "but trailing a woman makes child's play of my search." He looked up grinning: "A woman always drops something along the way."

And so he had announced his decision to ride out after the escaping enemy woman at once.

And now Tacincala spoke up, the daughter making clear her friendliness for the captive and her willingness that the scout lead her own spotted horse when he goes looking for the Psa-woman.

Next thing, the family saw Tonweya horseback, ready to go, his sister's red-and-white horse trailing. And certainly the scout's look conveyed that he enjoys tracking—four-legs or two—and why not? This whole experience, the same as playing a game at which he always wins.

V

ANPAGLI HAD walked almost never stopping since her escape out of the enemy camp, and now, three days on the trail, all of her ached and cried for relief.

She carried a little meat—scout-meat—and the berries she snatched, while overripe, satisfied a thirst. But she needed rest and warmth.

The crisp nights had chilled her bones. Wrapped in her robe and nesting in the leaves that filled the little hollows in the breaks, she had endured two uncomfortable sleeps.

She had spoken often to the friendly skies that protected her path and she had thanked the tiny invisibles who brought her reassuring messages; truly, the spirits had tricked away danger and guided her moccasins.

Occasionally a night-sound had brought on the shivers, but mostly she had enjoyed those voices who call out after sundown. The howl of wandering-dogs made the darkness not so lonely and the whistling of wapiti who signaled for a mate stirred her strangely.

She followed the trail her captors had used and the familiar buttes and gullies, while different-looking from this approach, provided her with unchanging contacts.

Suddenly now annoying little pains began to creep up her legs and she yearned for a rest. But she had experienced enough days in the camp of an enemy to imagine what will happen if they recapture her. And so, holding to her pace, she drove herself over the brittle plain, up and down the sunburned slopes, across the dry streams; only her thoughts dared wander off the path.

Never will she grow sullen if they catch her, she decided; never will she take out her feelings on the next captive they bring to the tipi. But if the enemy will have her only as a drudge, she will keep trying to get away; certainly she prefers to live as someone's second-choice in a friendly lodge among her own people than in a cut-throat's tipi.

And she will consider her child: this one shall not grow up on the dry empty plain. Her son—and certainly she grows a son whether or not she ever finds the baby-place again—shall grow up knowing the voice of falling-water. And he shall climb to the sparkling ledges where snow never melts and the bighorn display their curls. He shall smell the smoke-plant blooming along the windy river and walk among fragrant, whispering trees who stand slender and tall, their slim pointed leaves shining against the sky.

But if she stays among the cut-throats they will own her son and teach him a loathing for the Absa. He shall take horses from the Absa camps and kill persons whose blood flows in him. He will not remember—perhaps he never will know—his true-tribe. And never will she see him lay his hand proudly on his breast and hear him say, 'I am a child of the Absa, a child of the alert, big-nose bird.'

And so, gladly she will die traveling these grasses and

hills before ever she gives birth to her son in the camps of these cut-throats, the Lakotah.

She stumbled. Then, pressing a hand to her side where the pain had pinched, she strained her eyes for any sign of the moving-lodges village, these Absa perhaps sheltering the survivors of her village.

One small valley lay ahead, one tree-covered hill, and then perhaps she shall look out upon the camp of her people. Or, if scouts watch out from some nearby knoll they will see her and know that she belongs to the Absa. She comes at midday, a woman with dusty gown and tangle-hair but they will recognize her as a proud-walking Absa-woman.

She breathed in deeply; the valley suddenly seemed very wide and the hill beyond, very steep. Her second pair of moccasins thinned on the bottoms, but she had come among trees, trees and soft, cool earth. And she had caught the smell of stone and water.

Again she stumbled. And now she bent over herself; the strange pain attacked like surprise and shut off her breath; she dropped to the ground.

"Help me. Help me, earth. Act like a mother; protect me while I lie here." She made her little song and lay still.

After a while she lifted her face from the curve of her arm; she sat straight. And now, raising her head proudly, she stood and began moving again, her steps slow but her manner of walking the same, one foot exactly back of the other, her moccasins pointing in a single line.

Halfway across the grassy valley she sensed the familiar. She kept on, sight and smell helping her memory, leading her to a place that she soon recognized.

She gave a little cry of joy. Here, arrow creek, and close by, the sandstone rim jutting out and the tiny pool which rose and fell with the stream. Nearby, the baby-place, the place where she had hidden the toys—the bow and the hoop. And perhaps somewhere nearby, the moving-lodges village.

She began hurrying her walk, almost to a run. A new strength suddenly carried her toward the hidden water, and she threw her heart to the earth-mother who had lent her this power. She watched for the little path that led through the brush and to the edge of the pool.

Intent upon her search, she moved unnoticing of changes in the sky, the sun gathering clouds, the clouds starting to rumble.

The rain began falling but most gently. And the rumble stayed in the distance.

She uttered another small cry; here, the opening in the brush. She wanted to run but a strange weakness held her back; she decided to crawl this final little way.

She dragged herself along a trail that only women's feet had worn. Then, reaching the smooth mud next to the pool, she let herself slip to the ground, her hand flung forward, the shallow water caressing her fingertips.

After a moment she touched the cool of her fingers to her forehead. Next, she pulled forward for a drink. And now she lay back exhausted, the rain falling gently on her cheeks. She closed her eyes.

But almost at once she began trembling; the cold-wet earth had chilled her. She sat up and leaned forward for a look into the pool. A wistful face looked back at her and she whipped up the water with her hand as when she had visited this place on a different occasion. And now, remembering, she turned her head slowly toward the brush against which she once had leaned a bow. Her heart leapt; neither the bow nor arrows here.

Swiftly she glanced toward her hiding place for the hoop and stick; she saw that these girl-things stayed exactly as she recalled.

"My son, my son," she whispered. And now she observed again the brush where she had propped the bow and four arrows.

She stared at the place, something more chilling than rain and cold earth numbing her heart. Under a thin covering of leaves lay these toys for a boy; none among the unborns had sought this bow.

A sad little wail escaped her. Slowly she hunched forward, slowly her forehead bent down until in touch with the wet earth. Her shoulders jerked unevenly.

After a while she straightened herself. She stood and, moving over near a small tree, she used her knife to cut a branch, something strong enough not to break when she leaned her body upon this wood.

She looked at the jagged point where she had made the cut and she pushed this point against her belly.

But now she hesitated. A woman who will not want the child she grows uses this way to destroy an unborn. But she, Anpagli, acts for a different reason. Truly she desires her child, but the omen nearby the pool—neither toy acceptable—reveals that she will not bear a living child. Perhaps those pains and exhaustion on the trail evince the death of her son. But whatever of this child remains within her, she shall . . .

She remembered that most women who tried this thing died with the unborn they suffered to eject and so she waited to see if this recollection will prove frightening. But she found nothing disturbing about dying along with the child.

And so, permitting herself a long sigh, she leaned her whole person upon the stick now tight against her center; she began swaying back and forth.

Tonweya had started out after the captive as if he played inaṫima ṡkatapi, the hider marking a trail for the seeker.

He smiled at each sign of her resting and eating; he saw the shrubs where she had snatched berries and he found the berry seeds she had dropped. He knew which day her rests became more frequent and he always found the places where she had slept. But when he came to the grass where she had fallen in pain, his heart quickened. Looking down on the bruised stems, he began to understand why he rode this trail. If he came merely playing a game, why alarm himself that she perhaps suffers at this place? And until he sees her footmarks moving on steadily, why will he breathe uneasily? Certainly this woman means something to him.

Her change of path when she came near the baby-pool puzzled him; why will she choose a new direction, one that takes her away from the dark, bent grass that marks her people's trail of moving lodges?

Wondering, then, if he followed the trail of the same Psa camp that the Titonwan had attacked more than twenty days past, he suddenly decided to pursue the enemy village.

The woman he certainly shall find but why not also recover those five horses the Psa cut loose from the captive herd?

The plan intrigued him; any occasion which called for eluding the enemy excited him, but sneaking past those alert and crafty dogs, the Psa-scouts, presented a real challenge.

And so he stayed hidden until after midnight. Then, leaving his two horses with legs loosely tied, he began walking toward the distant enemy lodges.

Gladly he walked alone; he need consider none but himself, and any mistakes, his.

Before dawn he had reached the sleeping village—if they called these six lonely tipi a village—and begun selecting horses. He counted as many as ten to a tipi and and a grazing herd on the slope beyond camp. Scheming originally to take five from the herd, he now decided that cutting loose two horses from a tipi stake will provide him with more entertainment than any five he runs off the slope.

Pulling his knife from the sheath, he moved back and forth behind the brush that had hidden him while he made his selection; he wanted to find out if his movements attracted any young horse-tenders who stood ready to alert the camp. Or if the occupants of any one lodge prepared to welcome him with an arrow in the tail.

Now, standing quiet, he listened for warning sounds out of anyone, anything, anywhere.

Presently he began crawling toward the lodge where the horses he had chosen stood side by side. He made the soft call that will lift their ears yet not incite alarm.

Reaching this pair, he talked gently while he looped, then severed the thongs. He hid himself between the two while he removed their restrainers. And now he stood listening another moment.

Suddenly smiling, he cut the quirt hanging on his wrist. Why not the insulting gesture? Why not leave behind this whip for the Psa whose horses he sneaks away?

Keeping to a place between these creatures, he patted their necks and whispered in their ears as if they knew him for an old friend. Finally he started the two moving but he stopped again at the brush heap; looking back he saw that the lodges slept as before.

He led the horses a long distance before he mounted. Then, leading the second horse, he rode slowly to the place his own two stood waiting. Here, making himself rounded and still as a stone on the flat, he listened with an ear to the ground.

Midmorning the traveling Psa camp moved out, the people ignoring the loss. Or perhaps they used the old Psa-trick of pretending indifference.

And so Tonweya stayed in his hiding place, an arrow and his knife ready in the event of a surprise attack.

But apparently the Psa had not imagined the raider staying this close to camp; they had not pursued. And so the scout once more picked up the trail of the fleeing captive.

As he rode, he noticed the day turning cool and damp. He looked at the racing clouds, and his eyes welcomed the approaching rain. Then slowly, unerringly, he took the trail toward the pool, this mystery-place of Psa-women, the hidden water hole about which he knew nothing.

Whether she lay on the ground a long while or only moments Anpagli knew not, cared not. She knew only that her pain had gone away; she had hidden her agony underground, at the nearby spot where she had dug and spread earth.

And now, imagining that someone stared at her, she opened her eyes. She saw the sky, but before she dared remember anything, she closed her eyes.

But the sense of someone close by returned. She lay unmoving, the customs of a life lived in uncertainty holding her to this stillness. Nor will she stir at the sound of a man's voice.

"The Psa-woman schemes trouble for her captor; instead she provides him an amusing search and two of her people's war horses." Tonweya's tone mocked her but without anger or threat.

And the woman, hearing, experienced neither surprise nor fear; she felt only relief as if a long struggle had come to a finish. Even so, she knew that whatever happened to her now depended upon her next move.

For an instant she lay uncertain of making any move at all. To rise and toss her head, to turn her back or look defiant seemed beyond her strength.

Then, her head spinning, she tried to pull herself to a sitting position.

Tonweya remained standing back of her. "I ask," he said sternly, "that the Psa-captive look at these fine horses. Will she recognize either one?"

He will demand that she turn and identify the previous owner of the two he had captured; he wanted to hear that he had taken something from a principal man among the Psa.

Anpagli managed a steady voice when she gave answer but she had not looked around. "My captor's tone convinces me that he finds whatever he goes out looking for—the most wonderful horse in the enemy camp or a runaway woman. But twice he shows more pride in a captive horse than in a captive woman."

Now, making a supreme effort to keep from falling over, she turned toward the scout and gazed unfalteringly into his face.

Tonweya's eyes widened; she had surprised him. Not only will she speak an understandable Lakotah, she also will make a daring observation.

A smile came to his lips and then he laughed joyfully. Dropping the thongs that held the two Psa-horses, he whirled suddenly and faced the startled creatures; sounding a war whoop, he sent off each one with a slap across the flank.

Instantly he grabbed the cord around the neck of the red-and-white, the spotted horse he had brought for the captive's use. The creature reared and kicked but soon calmed to the man's command. And Anpagli saw that during all this uproar the eyes of the scout's horse had rolled but nothing more.

When Tonweya faced the woman, any sign of smile had left his lips. His pleasing bow-shape mouth appeared firmly closed and his look strongly advised that she mount the spotted horse at once and ride with him back to his camp.

She wanted to obey him, to rise gracefully and without use of her hands in the manner becoming to women, but even when she pushed against the ground she lacked the power to raise herself. She lifted her face to his, her eyes asking that he understand her embarrassing weakness.

But seeing that he accepted neither her plea nor her weakness, she made a second try. Her legs gave way and the man's face blurred before her eyes. She slipped to the ground and lay as if asleep.

Puzzled, the scout looked more carefully at the woman; he glanced toward the freshly turned earth. Only now he understood that something tragic had occurred here. And so his heart beat twice as quickly as when he had looked for blood on the grass at that different place along her trail.

Kneeling alongside the prostrated one and lifting most gently, he laid her across his horse. He tied the cord of the red-and-white around his waist; carefully he mounted his own. Pulling the woman's limp form to him, he held her tight against his breast.

And in this manner Tonweya started back for the village of his people.

VI

ANPAGLI REGAINED her strength slowly. Returning the Psa-woman to his mother, Tonweya had requested that the members of this lodge give the captive gentle care. And his father had begun by ordering Winu to raise a small tipi for herself.

Cankuna, glad that Winu will move out, at once invited relatives and friends to help the second-wife make a new tipi cover. Then not only will Winu move out more quickly but she shall own a more respectable shelter than if she worked on the hides alone.

And so Cankuna's lodge soon offered the Psa-captive truly pleasant surroundings. Not that suddenly they relieved Anpagli of her obligations as a captive—if anything they observed her more closely—but they now chose a discreet manner for removing the temptation to escape. Someone casually will lead off a horse who gains the captive's attention, and they will assign work that restricts her to the lodge and to places within sight of the lodge.

If Anpagli noticed these things, certainly she hid her

recognition. She sang and talked and made every effort to improve her Lakotah speech. And she began responding to the affection Tacincala openly displayed for her, the two almost constant companions. Anpagli now said 'tanka,' using the relative term for young-sister, whenever she spoke with Tacincala.

And Tacincala, in turn, became a joyful person again. Ever since the sungazing, the daughter in this lodge had withdrawn from camp life, the fear that Tabloka will summon her had kept the young woman mostly inside the tipi. Anpagli's company had made this self-confinement endurable, and before long Tacincala had confided her depressing story to the Psa-woman.

"You say that you dislike this Kiyuksa. But who says that you shall live with him?" Anpagli marveled that anyone here will compel the woman to take a husband for whom she lacked respect.

"None compels me, but I know the desire of one brother. . . ."

"Not the scout. . . ."

"Not the scout, truly not your captor." Tacincala's pretty face for an instant reflected the Psa-woman's quick smile. But then the glad look faded. "My warrior-brother desires that I join my sister in the Kiyuksa's camp and so become the ninth wife to this . . . this noisy little fat man. I vow I will hang myself before I go to him, and yet I remember that which the old advisers say: a daughter shall hear her father and brothers in all things. . . ."

"Perhaps a different man already notices you," Anpagli answered, her eyes on the tipi flap as if she awaited someone, "a man whom you admire."

Tacincala murmured the little sound that acknowledged she heard the Psa-woman but that she dares not say more. Perhaps on another day she will speak of the warrior who sungazed, the one whose forehead she had touched with sage, the one—the only one—for whom she found exciting thoughts.

This same night Anpagli, lying on her sleeping robes, permitted herself a new view of this lodge, this enemy lodge and this enemy camp. Certainly they now treat her kindly, none mentioning her attempt at escape nor piling her with work as a reproach. They put out moccasins which she shall mend and they place in her hands those garments in need of cleaning. But aside from these tasks, Cankuna asks only that she sweep the lodge. They never send her for water nor make her tend fire nor demand that she scrape hides.

But she will guess why: they keep her at work inside the tipi until they raise a winter camp, and then the snow will close her in. When next summer comes, she will consider the Mahto camp as her own—or so they imagine—and find a Lakotah who will take her as wife.

She smiled at the dark. And then she sighed. Often she wished for a chance to stand alongside Tonweya and say that she appreciated his gentle handling of her weakened body back at the baby-place. And then ask that he hear her speak briefly about that weakness. She will have him know her as wife to a warrior-hunter and as a woman who desired a child, not someone who destroyed an unborn she never wanted.

But what words will she use for this intimate speech with a stranger? True, she learns the Lakotah tongue quickly, but talking with an enemy man in his language about these most personal things will require a knowledge of Lakotah she yet lacks.

Nor will she know for certain that the scout desires this manner of talk with her. She had not spoken with Tonweya since her recapture; she rarely ever saw the man now. Perhaps her desperate act at the baby-pool fills him with contempt and even seeing her repulses him. And so what shall become of her life?

After a while she remembered what Tacincala had said about hanging in a tree before ever going to a man she despises.

I will not use a tie on my neck, Anpagli told herself grimly, but neither shall I become a daughter they adopt nor a wife to any different Lakotah. If the scout will not take me, I shall run away twice, even if his mother regrets my leaving and his sister cries for me. Perhaps somewhere I shall discover an Absa for whom I feel respect if not fondness. To him I shall belong and his child I shall bear . . . if the spirits permit my growing a second child.

Before going to sleep, Anpagli decided that when these

Lakotah villages traveled on to their wintering place she shall try again to escape.

But within three, four days something happened that made her wish herself gone from this lodge at once.

Cankuna had given the Psa-woman a young camp-dog, gentled but not yet taught to carry wood or pack small bundles.

And Anpagli, pleased with something that she dared call her own, cuddled the pup in a manner similar to a little girl who rejoices in a pet.

Then one morning the captive, brushing out the lodge, pulled aside the tipi flap and saw Peśla standing nearby the stake where she had tied the pup. Next to the warrior stood a boy of five, six winters, and in the child's hand a stick which he used for poking the young dog.

Anpagli watched a moment and then, speaking gently, cautioned the boy against hurting the pup. "My little friend, I see a sharp point on your stick. Perhaps you will make a hole in my dog."

She had avoided looking at Peśla but she spoke these words carefully, the dark-skin warrior ever waiting to make fun of her speech.

"I hold a lance," the boy answered, not glancing up, "and I call this one enemy. Psatoka, Psatoka. I kill. I kill Psa."

For an instant Anpagli stood frozen. The thought that had made her want to run away became alive again; she saw this boy as her own son, a child born in this camp and learning whom he shall call enemy.

The boy stuck the pup now, and when the dog yelped, the child laughed and jabbed the creature again.

Anpagli spoke firmly: "You shall not harm my dog. See, none other acts this way toward little dogs." She took the stick out of the boy's hand.

Peśla stood as before, arms folded and watching the boy. But now he spoke and his voice seemed as cold as his eyes: "Nor will anyone in this camp stop a boy who shows the warrior-spirit, whatever his act. And certainly the hand of a child will not injure anything of importance."

The woman understood that Peśla ordered her to give

back the stick. Even so, she hesitated. She lived here as captive, but the dog belonged to her and not a person in the band dared take away that which Cankuna gave her. Absa, Lakotah, or any different tribe, this custom the same.

Now suddenly she saw herself as one who takes away; the stick—his lance—belongs to the boy.

Stooping down, she hurriedly untied the pup, then gathered him up in her arms. Silently she handed the stick to the child. And now she moved to reenter the tipi.

The warrior stood in her way. "Perhaps my mother shall agree when I speak saying that I intend to take you into my lodge, where you shall learn Lakotah manners."

Anpagli neither moved nor looked up until Pešla turned and walked away.

Two, three days passed and Anpagli again cleaned the lodge of bones and spilled-fat, the pup tagging her moccasins and jumping up playfully whenever she looked his way.

"Go out," she said finally, the dog underfoot and interfering with her work. "But stay close. They will not let me chase you if you run away."

The woman went on with her brushing, Cankuna likely to return any moment with guests and Anpagli desirous that these friends enter a neat lodge. Or if ever the scout returns, she will have him notice that she performs a woman's work thoroughly.

Presently she heard men talking outside; she held her breath to listen. But the voices, Pešla and certain of his friends, not the scout. She kept at her cleaning.

The next sound she recognized as Tacincala dropping a load of wood on the pile outside the tipi.

Anpagli felt relief; not likely will Pešla step inside the lodge now that his sister—an avoidance-relative—returned. And so, joyful once again, she unrolled two more backrests; she wanted everything ready for whoever visits the tipi this day.

But now she heard the howl of a young dog and the surprise-yell of a child. Remembering that she had sent her pup outside, she raised the hide that covered the tipi entrance.

Looking around anxiously, she saw Pešla; the warrior held up her squealing pup by the backskin.

"This one nips the boy," he said, "and so dies. Whoever owns the pup shall strangle the creature at once." He glanced toward the tipi opening. "Hiyu wo, Psa-woman. Come out and kill the enemy."

When Anpagli stepped from the lodge, Peśla threw the dog at her feet.

Stunned, the woman bent slowly and picked up the quivering form. Turning her back, she stroked the head of this small dog, her one true comfort in all the camp.

Roughly Peśla called out to her: "So I shall choke the dog."

The captive sounded the howl of a Psa-woman in distress and, clinging to the pup, started to run back of the lodge.

But now a different man stood in her path.

She had not seen Tonweya enter the group of men who stood around the lodge. Nor had she seen Tacincala disappearing, the young woman properly avoiding her brothers. She knew only that she, Anpagli, stood alone against the enemy, not a friendly face in the crowd and most persons regarding her sternly.

"A young dog bites a boy," the scout said quietly but firmly. "The sons in this camp often play warrior with dogs as the enemy. Or perhaps they play hunter and call their dogs 'pte.' But never will the people accept a dog who bites a child. Or a dog who makes loud noises at night. Or a dog who jumps out of line when the bands travel."

Tonweya looked directly at the captive. "You shall kill many dogs in this camp for the warrior-feasts and so I will see you kill one now. Someone will show you . . ."

But Peśla, impatient with the scout's effort to make this captive understand, walked up and grabbed the pup. Holding the squirming young body, he called out saying that the boy shall come forward with his club.

"Here, your foolish enemy, my son. I and my friends will watch while you kill. I will see if the Psa die bravely."

The boy, now scarcely noticing the scratch on his arm where the pup's teeth had touched, rushed up. "Psatoka," he shrieked excitedly, "you will die. I kill, I kill."

A big crowd had gathered before the pup lay still, the cheering loud and long for a boy who will not desist until his enemy lies dead. And certainly, as Peśla had said, the hand of a child never will harm anything important.

And now Peśla lent the boy his knife. Closing his fingers over the child's hand, he directed the scalping of the soft hair, cutting off a piece of the pup's crushed skull.

"Carry this hair to your mother," he told the boy; "say that I and my friends feast her son and that I shall tie a feather in her son's hair."

The warrior tossed the bleeding body to Anpagli: "This one dies more bravely than most Psa. Now skin and cook the pup. The boy-warrior wants to see the heart in his soup."

Peśla watched for a sign of rebellion or despair in the high-headed woman standing before him. But he saw only that she reached down indifferently and picked up the warm, blood-wet form. Accepting a knife from an old woman nearby, she began the skinning at once.

The people had gone on about their affairs, only the old woman staying, her sharp little eyes quick to see that a true respect for the scout and not fear of his warrior-brother compelled Anpagli to perform unhesitatingly this work repugnant to a Psa.

Olepi sat often with Ahbleza these days, and so the son heard from his father about the boy who clubbed to death a captive's dog.

But while Olepi spoke marveling the warrior-spirit in one so young, the Shirtman pondered why his brother-friend, who brings back this captive, will not mention this woman to him, will say nothing concerning the circumstances of her capture. Or her recapture. Understandably Tonweya will not include these incidents at the scalp-dances each night, but why the scout avoided any reference to this captive truly puzzled him.

Nor will the scout say anything about the place he had discovered Tatezi. Each night since the party's return, Kipanna had danced the hair of the enemy Tonweya had killed in the Psa-camp and Tonweya had sung his story. But whether the old Psa-woman he had killed or the young Psa-woman he had captured related to the recovery of the yellow horse, the Shirtman not yet knew.

Nor will anyone among the avengers hint at having found signs of Heyatawin—either pieces of her body or things that once belonged to her—in the enemy camp. Perhaps the warriors had seen but spoke not; perhaps they feared to open his heart's wound.

But they misunderstand about his heart. For not a man knows—perhaps none ever shall know—that which occurs at the sungazing. Truly his heart neither bleeds nor heals but only waits sleeping—sleeping, not dead—for the day when he, Ahbleza, chooses to join his soul with hers.

And suddenly now he remembered that at the pole Heyatawin had told of a daughter born. But told nothing of her own dying.

Yet why shall he find this thing surprising? All the while she lived visible, Heyatawin spared him talk of sadness or any unpleasantness that will blight even one moment together.

Perhaps, then, the brother-friend spares him a meeting with the Psa-woman for the reason that she comes of the enemy family who kills Ahbleza's wife, Ahbleza's relatives?

But something he, the Shirtman, will wish: that Tonweya comes to him soon for talk of the sungazing—not to learn why Ahbleza refuses the thongs but for a new understanding of the bond they share as a dreaming-pair.

VII

DUST BLEW, leaves whirled up, and the air smelled wet and cold; each morning the old women looked for ice at the edge of the stream. But two Titonwan bands—Mahto and Oglalahca—remained on the summer campground.

Anpagli, marveling that a people will camp in one place these many nights and days, wondered whether the dancing of Psa-scalps will cease once the bands move. Perhaps they stay on until whatever family these Lakotah avenge seems comforted.

Standing outside the hunter's lodge, she often looked for the yellow horse whose mystery had provoked those terrible killings. Or so she had surmised from hints they had dropped in her presence. But she had not seen this wondrous creature until this morning when they let her go to the stream for a bath.

She glanced only briefly toward the lodge wherein lived someone whose desire for the return of his yellow horse had destroyed an Absa camp but she saw a sad-face young person come out of this same lodge. And whether daughter, sister, or wife to the man inside, she rejoiced that the woman looked sad.

But her true pleasure this day will come from bathing again in stream-water. More than once since her recapture she had yearned for the cleansing, invigorating steam-bath or a family bath in the manner of her own tribe. But the Titonwan appeared to prefer bathing in cold streams, men separate from their wives. Nor will these Titonwan whip dry with sticks as in Psa camps.

Walking to the bath with women companions, Anpagli reflected on other personal differences between the tribes. She had noticed that not one woman in this camp wore a gown as white as hers or as carefully put together or as colorfully decorated. When once she had asked for the use of flesher and scraper, they had seen her aptly handling these tools, preparing a hide for Tacincala in a manner that had made Cankuna wish for such diligence among her own relatives. Or so the woman told.

And Anpagli had learned that the wife of the leader of this camp had expressed admiration for the Psa-woman's work, that she looked for the Psa-woman to come visiting her lodge.

Splashing in the water now, Anpagli sensed a vanity in her body. And then, recalling that which Tacincala had reported, she smiled.

"They say," the young woman had told, "that someone will grab and lift you onto his horse and make you agree with him before he returns you to camp. Your pretty face, they say, will make things difficult once you start walking the woman's wood-path."

And now the bather remembered something more interesting that Tacincala had told, something about different ones who had dropped hints in Tonweya's presence, his joking-relatives wondering why the scout will not take the attractive captive for wife.

But Tacincala, tactfully, had not reported the whole story, and so Anpagli had not learned of Tonweya's answer.

The scout sees a pebble out of place on the trail, they had teased, yet he will not see the pretty captive in his family's lodge?

"I see whatever I look for," Tonweya had answered quickly; "I am not looking for a woman."

They had laughed back at him, saying that a man always looks for a woman.

"Perhaps," he had smiled, "but this woman in whom you, my relatives, show such interest . . . will you know for certain that she wants me?"

They had pretended astonishment: will Tonweya hesitate to ask a woman who has neither fathers nor brothers who dare make things embarrassing? True, the people say that this Psa-woman has a strong will but the scout has a way with women without half-trying.

Tonweya had replied with a gesture that said they had overlooked his shyness.

And then these joking-relatives really had laughed.

Returning to the lodge after her bath, Anpagli remembered that the scout had not so much as glanced her way since the boy-kills-her-dog incident. And so, sitting comfortably in front of Cankuna's tipi fire, she contemplated the trail and the furtive manner of her traveling if once again she tries to escape. And now, suddenly, she discovered that she reviewed these obstacles in the language of the enemy, not her own. And that, more upsetting, she had lost her eagerness for this return to her people.

Instantly she left the warmth of the lodge for the hazy day outside; she will risk walking the water-trail alone, she told herself, and so locate the stream where she had bathed. Perhaps a look at her reflection in the water shall bring back a desire for the Absa camps. If so, she will start running and never come back to this place.

But before ever she reached the stream, she saw Tonweya horseback and leading the red-and-white, the same spotted horse Tacincala had lent her brother on a different occasion.

Her heart took wings. Perhaps Tacincala permits her a ride on this horse if only in the scout's presence. And if true, she, Anpagli, easily will make her escape; who in this camp knows that she rides as fast as any young man?

She wanted to hurry toward the horse, but she held to a natural, graceful walk. And she pretended not to notice the scout when he coughed slightly to gain her attention.

But the next moment she felt herself lifted onto Tonweya's horse, the creature leaping forward and carrying the two on a run across camp. Suddenly remembering, she began to struggle but not in any real effort to break loose.

She heard him laughing. "You resist properly," he said in her ear, "and so you feel good."

He had flung his arm over her breasts, and now she used her chin to press on his wrist. Then, her mouth against his hand, she bit deeply into his skin.

He laughed again and urged his mount into a lope, the trailing spotted horse staying close.

The woman clung to his arm for balance. Her hair, loose and flying but damp from her bath, whipped the man's face. And once again he laughed.

When they had ridden beyond view of the camp, he commanded the horse to a walk. And so they rode slowly, silently, in the direction of the setting sun, the great red ball appearing very big, very red, in the smoky evening sky.

Tonweya brought the horse to a halt; jumping down, he pulled the woman with him.

Anpagli stood unmoving, unlooking, while he fastened the horses to some clumps of old grass. And then she walked as he directed, following him through the brush and toward a boulder. Here he lifted up the woman, placing her gently on the flat top of the big stone.

His eyes level with hers, he stood gazing into her face, his amused smile enhancing his good looks. And she, not wanting that he hear her heart loud as a war-dance drum, tossed her head and turned away.

Insolently, then, he flicked his fingers against the tips of her breasts. And she, feeling hollow all the way down to her thighs, bent slowly her head. And so she accepted the pulsing ache for which she neither had nor wanted a defense.

He pulled her off the boulder now and his hands touched over the place a woman's body gathers joy. And then she made one more effort to remember herself as a captive woman whom a loathesome enemy subjugates to his whim, as a proud Absa-woman whom a Minśupekaźo forces onto the grass.

Instead she imagined the joy in belonging to this man. And suddenly she, who prided herself on a strength that never permits crying, felt tears drop onto her cheeks.

She knew that the man had not lifted her chin, that she only imagined his hand on her face; then perhaps she only imagined that he spoke telling her that he wants her for his wife.

"Hear me, Psa-woman," Tonweya demanded, the amused look gone from his face; "I will take you for my wife if you will choose me for husband. I ask in the same manner that a man will ask for the daughter of a leader in my tribe or yours.

"But I make my speech to you, not father or brothers. And I bring nothing to give but this horse my sister sends you . . . and my own heart.

"Understand that I make my vow to you alone, something more important to a truthbearer than family approval and ceremonial pledges."

The scout had spoken almost as if he reported the news of his heart's discovery to the leader of his band.

"You earn a place among my people," he went on, "and now I offer you this place as my wife."

These words he had spoken proudly, for he knew that man honors woman when he asks that she become his wife. And that woman, accepting, honors man. But his next phrases, spoken most softly, carried his appeal.

"I imagine you as someone who desires the same things I desire. And so together . . . "

Anpagli closed her eyes; so she will bear the joy of his request. And a sudden pain.

Wife to Tonweya; she never will look for anything more than this honor. But he says that she earns a place among the Lakotah. Will this mean that if she accepts him she throws down her own tribe?

Perturbing thoughts leapt onto her path as her heart rushed out toward her people. She remembered the Absa living and the Absa dying to whom this man personified the true-enemy; she remembered the many Absa who die and who will die whenever the Lakotah seek revenge.

She opened her eyes but her gaze passed over the scout and moved out onto the plain. "If you permit my choosing a husband, grant me a little while. I will wait one more moon. . . . Afterwards, I perhaps shall know my desire."

But looking at him, she knew his answer. "So lend me two days," she begged; "after one more sunrise, I shall decide something.

Tonweya touched her cheek. "Another moon, another sun, another sleep will tell you nothing different from that which you know now." His voice, quiet but not pleading, urged her to accept: "See, I bring paint with me. After a while I and you shall return to the village, the middle of your hair and the round of your face shining red."

His thumb smoothed her forehead and the woman, imagining that she will see tenderness, glanced at his eyes. But instead she saw something that recalled this same one reaching through thick brush and dragging her into view. And so she remembered that she had not asked what will happen if she refuses him.

But the scout who observes whatever lies ahead on the trail—man-tracks or a broken stem of grass—certainly will notice a glimmer of misgiving in a woman's eyes.

"I will make you a good husband," he said, "but if you neglect to obey, I will act severely. Even so, remember that I demand nothing of you that I not demand of myself. I will bear you the same truth that I bear the people and I shall look for the honor of my lodge in your hands."

He smiled. "Now mount your horse and ride close to me." Walking over to where the horses waited, he had not glanced back to see if she followed.

The woman stood looking after him. She saw his sensuous stride, his strong legs and thighs. She saw him, tall and manly and certain. Her eyes lighted. She will follow him closely, now and always, wherever he leads. And she will not neglect to obey.

The sun paused on the edge of the sky, and the scout and the woman stopped to gaze upon the glory of sundown. They said nothing, but the woman fancied that the clouds and the colors never appeared more wondrous than on this evening.

The man, looking, had seen a star and then two, three stars. And now he decided that not all stars look alike as he once had said. And so he shall choose one with an unusual twinkle and make this star his gift to the woman at his side.

Starting on again, they turned their horses and crossed a dry stream. Beyond loomed the black hills, where shadows darkened shadows and the shrewd tree-people held on to their leaves after frostbite. During the many seasons Tonweya had scouted these gentle slopes and tall wood, he always felt lonely on viewing this great black mound. But now all manner of voices called out a welcome and wished him joy. Or so he heard the dusk-calls of wings and hoofs.

Approaching a little open space, a glittering dark peak rising above, he decided that the woman shall prepare embers and spread a robe here; he will make a brush cover to protect their sleep.

And so, before the twilight faded, Anpagli began to hunt wood. But the man, unfolding a piece of old tipi cover, lay down and closed his eyes as if asleep. Then suddenly his hand reached out, grabbing the woman's foot and pulling her down alongside him.

She smiled but sat up quickly. And now he sat, taking a hairbrush from the wrapper he had leaned against a tree.

She waited for him to hand her the brush; will not Lakotah women, the same as Absa wives, care for their husband's hair?

But Tonweya, sitting on his knees, began to stroke her hair. And now she wondered whether he enacted a ceremonial between two who will mate.

"Some things about my people will please you," he said, brushing up the short hair above her forehead. "A Lakotah woman shall grow her hair as long as she desires. Unlike the Psa warriors, the Lakotah never indulge in hair-growing contests with women. Nor will any Lakotah resent a fine-looking woman whose braids hang below her shoulders."

Seeing her eyes flash, he teased but laughingly: "Tell

me, dare you ever before wear your hair to this length? Soon you will grow the proper length for braiding and so appear pretty as any Titonwan wife."

Anpagli put a hand over her head, stopping his brush. "Permit me to tell of a scheme that I know my captor will approve."

She had kept her voice from quavering but not easily. His ridicule of the Absa warriors had hurt and she had known suddenly that she will not sit out her winters listening to him make mockery of her people.

In one long breath she told her plan: if he will let her escape and go back to her foolish people, then he dares return alone and without embarrassment to his wise people, and then he shall live out his seasons joyfully in his wonderful village of pretty Titonwan women with long, long braids.

He stared at her. And now he will ponder, as all men ponder, the strange ways of women.

But certainly she saw strangeness in his ways also. Will he not understand that when he speaks slightingly of her people he speaks slightingly of her? And on the same day that he asks the privilege of giving her rank and honor as his wife? Yet here in this place of splendor he speaks revealing that he regards her as an enemy woman after all, as a captive to taunt and ridicule.

"Different ones in your village," she told him now, "know of my desire to run away. They shall understand when you return alone and say that you want me not and so you let me go."

The man looked closely at the speaker. "The Psawoman acts like Iktomi. I shall wait for reliable talk."

"You mock me," she said boldly, "and so I shall spare you from taking a wife only to please your friends."

The scout fingered the brush, his eyes puzzling her face.

"Let me escape now," she said quickly, "for I intend to keep trying. And one day I shall reach my people and they will hold me safe." She looked out at the peaks of stone.

"What Psa, woman or man," he murmured, "ever considers himself really safe from the Titonwan?" But she had irritated him. "Will you not remember who I am?" he demanded. "I am a scout and twice I find your hiding place. Always I will find you."

He slapped the brush against his palm. "Your mocca-sin-tracks, any one of your trail-marks will lead me to you," he said. "And any little sound will reveal you. The snap of a stick, your breathing . . . "

He stood up and stepped back of her.

She dared not turn to see if he walked away, not at this moment. But after a while she looked around slowly.

"I am here," he answered. "I wait for someone to bring wood and make a fire. Am I to live always in a cold tipi, my wife sitting idle while she schemes an escape?"

His tone changed. "I speak but once again of these things. Now attend: I am not making you my wife to please my relatives. I choose you. I want you and so I take you. Now bring wood and move quickly."

Anpagli rose slowly. But before she fully stood, Ton-weya pushed her back down on the robe. "I go for the wood," he said shortly; "you stay."

The woman lowered her eyes respectfully. But her lips formed a little smile.

Wooded earth takes on darkness a long while before the plain, and so, the man out of view, Anpagli crawled off the robe. Using the friendly tree-shadows, she made her way to the stream; the water offered an easy trail at night.

She had not gone far before she heard the quiet running of a scout; Tonweya, discovering her absence, had come looking. And now she flung herself into the tall grass at the stream's edge. Holding her breath, she waited.

Approaching her hiding place, Tonweya stopped run-ning; he searched the nearby growth with his eyes, then with a stick. After a little while he turned, hurrying toward a clump of low-growing trees downstream.

The path of escape opened to the woman. She had space to back out and, stepping cautiously around the patches of clubgrass, move upstream while the man hunted in the opposite direction.

She pushed back gently, the pliant stems silently yield-ing. But when almost clear of the brush, something tugged at the bottom edge of her robe; a dead branch had caught on to her wrap.

Bending, she tried to loosen the stick. Jerking away will break the branch and any sound shall reveal her hiding place. Or so the scout had said. The snapping of a stick, he says . . .

When again she tried to reach the dry wood that held her, the branch gave way without any noise. She dared move now, dared run out of the grass and into the thickness of tall stems; certainly the scout hunted far downstream, perhaps beyond hearing any noise she shall make.

But Anpagli had not moved out. She stood where the dead branch had held her, hunting this same one with her foot. Then, locating the branch, she jumped on the wood in a manner to make a loud snap. And now she ran out.

The scout reached her in two big leaps. Knowing all along where she had hidden, he had sneaked off to a waiting place close by the tall grass.

He flung her over his shoulder similar to the lone hunter who carries meat, her struggles as nothing to him even as he climbed the slope. And he threw her on the robe as if he tossed down a bundle of fresh hides.

The woman lay quiet, face down, but she kept track of his moves as he made a fire and started the wood burning.

When next he approached her, he put his foot rudely against her side and turned her over onto her back.

Standing above her, he seemed tall as a tree, and seeing his hands, then looking up at his eyes, she began to shiver. Here stood a man, she told herself, from whom a woman never will escape or ever really want to escape; why try playing runaway?

He placed more wood on the fire—a much different fire than the one he had ordered her to prepare—and now, as he knelt over her, the blaze lighted his face.

Here and now, his eyes told her, he makes her his wife. And in a manner she shall remember forever. Let her discover on this night the desirability of an unerring and instant obedience to his requests, to his desires, to his very thoughts.

Wapiti, seeking the browse of a sheltered valley, passed near the sleeping man and woman at dawn. The man stirred to the thud of their hoofs but the woman, her body warm and safe against his, slept quietly.

But pronghorn, coming off the flat at midmorning and moving in loosely joined groups toward the mild southern slope of the black hill, found the man and woman awake and sitting on a warm, fragrant knoll, the woman's head against his arm, the sun shining on their faces.

The man had not looked up at the approach of these creatures; his nose had told him that an imposing male and his ever-curious mates circled the knoll. But the man schemed to surprise this band next day.

And so, up at sunrise, the man boasted a strength for outrunning these fleet ones. "And I mean on my own feet," he said.

Even so, the woman, shyly, led up his horse. "Embers for cooking your kill shall await your return, my husband," she told him.

The scout, jumping horseback, gave her a brief look, a glance that permitted her nothing more during his absence than preparing the embers.

The morning sun had not yet warmed the earth before his return. He tossed a pronghorn skin full of cut-up meat at her feet. And she, after roasting this food most carefully, looked for a sign that told he approved her cooking.

Noticing, finally, that she waited, that she took nothing for herself, he gestured his wonderment. Why not eat? He waved the bone from which he tore meat with his fine, even teeth.

The woman answered saying only that she will not starve.

He looked at her in astonishment. They had eaten nothing but berries since leaving camp; certainly she will want meat? He took a bite from his own mouth and put this piece into hers, then went back to satisfying his hunger.

Soon she reached for his hand, she will have him feed her more meat in this same manner.

He stopped chewing long enough to regard her with amazement once again. Women, he laughed, but he put a second bite into her mouth. Then he waved her away.

Before evening the wanderers had caught the scent of different meat. "You will ask that I feed you bites off the tail of this one," he said teasingly and rode out ahead of the woman, going in search of a certain island-lodge.

When his wife joined him, he already had found and

killed the one who swims-carrying-a-stick, whose big flat tail the woman shall cook at once.

"Blister the tail over embers and the skin will peel off easily. Next, simmer the meat." He knew not in what manner the Psa prepare the tail nor will he want her to cook this meat in any different way.

The woman stood with head averted while the husband spoke; will the scout not know that her people never cook, never eat, this meat? Absa legends tell that if ever the spirits of the dead choose to reappear in visible form, they most likely will come in the form of this peaceful creature who never stops growing. But will the Titonwan never hear about these things and so this scout, her husband, not know why she starts this fire and heats these stones most regretfully?

The man, carving a bowl out of a hard knot, sat unnoticing of the woman's despondent posture as she put the meat to simmer. But he had wondered why she chose to sit away from him while she waited for this food to cook tender.

Sitting alone, the woman avoided any despairing thoughts; instead, she conceived many ways of bringing joy to the man. She shall provide a comfortable tipi and her pleasure shall come on seeing him warm and full and content. And one day she will bear him a child. . . .

Memory struck at her; she covered her heart and a small moan escaped her lips.

The scout looked up. Seeing that the woman moved over to the cooking sac, he held out the rough wood-shell: "I hold something here. Fill with meat."

When she had placed the full bowl before him, she again sat off to herself, her face turned away.

The man spoke firmly: "I am not feeding you like a young bird whenever I and you eat."

She said nothing and so he relented. "One bite." He cut off a small piece and held out the meat. But she ignored his offer.

"Sit next to me," he commanded; "open your mouth and eat." He will stop any more of these games that try his patience.

The meat on the woman's tongue tasted like bark; she feared choking on this one bite.

And now the husband, observing closely, put down the bowl. "If my wife will speak saying that which distresses her ... " He spoke kindly and his fingers stroked her arm affectionately.

Dreading ridicule, she hesitated before answering. Now suddenly looking at him, she saw true concern on his face.

"Among the Absa ... among the Psa," she quickly amended, "they regard this creature as one in the family of man. They avoid eating any of the meat." Unwilling to see amusement in his eyes, she covered her face with her hands.

Gently the man pulled her hands aside and softly his fingers followed the outline of her chin, her cheeks, and forehead. And so he told her in the Titonwan way, whether she understood or not, that he recognized her as a good-looking woman. But he knew of neither caress nor words for telling this one that he also recognized her submission to everything that his eyes and hands and loins had demanded as a demonstration of her respect for him and for herself. And so he saw her not as a captive who becomes his woman in place of seeing him throw her down but as a wife who takes pride in obeying her husband.

And now Anpagli, gazing into his face, marveled the power that brings together, soul and body, a certain woman and a certain man. And so she closed her eyes, her manner whenever wonder, whenever mystery, touched upon her.

She sat unknowing, then, that the man had reached for his bowl and poured the remaining contents onto the ground. Perhaps the earth-mother, he told himself, will accept his meat and see nothing strange in the way he makes his offering.

When Anpagli opened her eyes, she noticed only that her husband untied the paint sack and unpacked the hair-brush. And so she understood that at sunrise they start back for the Mahto village and that she shall ride proudly at his side, the red circles of a wife-appreciated on her cheeks, the red streak of a wife-admired in the center of her hair.

Bending over his hand, she brushed her lips against the husband's fingers.

All Mahto and many Oglalahca families had watched the handsome scout carry his woman into his mother's lodge. And then kinswomen had raised the tipi sides, permitting the crowd a view of Cankuna formally presenting the new wife with a hide from which she shall make moccasins for the one she calls husband.

And now, after three days' work, Anpagli sat ready to gift Tonweya with these moccasins, a symbol of her respect and affection. Using a pattern she called 'the trail,' she had quilled the tops and beaded the edges.

The scout stepped into the new pair at once, and now a group of his women-relatives surrounded Anpagli, pulling the smiling wife into a different lodge. Here these same ones will brush her hair and paint her face for the ceremonial feast and dance.

Anpagli, remembering the man's wish that she look and act Lakotah, sat modestly while they arranged her hair in two nice braids.

"See, I tie a snow-skin on each one." Tacincala stood back, admiring the effect of this soft whiteness against the shining black of Anpagli's hair.

Among all these young women who laughed and chatted and helped decorate Tonweya's wife, Tacincala showed the most pleasure. And certainly this second daughter in the hunter's lodge, Anpagli's favorite. Winu had not attended the scout's wife, but Anpagli appeared to have enough attendants with this one.

Listening to the woman-talk, Anpagli had noticed that Lakotah and Absa girls behaved alike whenever someone mentioned the young warriors—certain ones hinting and giggling—and so she had wondered whether these Titonwan women change husbands as frequently as the Absa women; she had looked for the tribes to differ in this respect.

"Not a man in camp has more desirable ways than the one you call husband," one girl had whispered, the comment a little startling until Anpagli heard what more this person had to say.

"I know of ten in different bands," the girl went on, "who try for the scout's attention but he never, never gives any woman a second glance."

"Even so, everyone in camp talks of his good looks," another woman said.

But Anpagli, hearing more giggles, decided that this family liked to tease.

The women had made careful speeches about Peśla,

nothing unkind, for they shall remember the bold warrior as a relative. And yet Anpagli had heard the little warnings back of their words. "You will joke with him," they told her, "but watch out for his way of joking."

Tacincala had appeared unnoticing of any talk about her warrior-brother, but suddenly she spoke up: "You will see more of your husband's brother-friend than you will see of his blood-brother."

Brother-friend? Anpagli listened attentively; she knew not of whom they spoke but she had noticed their respectful tones.

"The Shirtman has different ways," one said as if Anpagli understood to whom she referred. "Or he seems different since the Psa kill. . . . "

Anpagli had seen the quick glances they gave the speaker and the sudden look of shame in the eyes of this one who had talked out of turn.

Brother-friend to Tonweya, the scout's wife told herself, and yet I know nothing of this man? And why will they silence the woman who mentions the Shirtman? I am Absa but that will not stop anyone from talking about the Psatoka in the Mahto band. Who, this Shirtman? And who among his relatives dies at the hand of an Absa?

Until most recently I am a captive here and so I know not about the leaders in this band or the principal men in the Mahto camp. Nor will the one I call husband speak of any special friend. Proudly he describes certain scouts and talks of his parents but nothing about a brother-by-choice. Nor shall I ask either these women who cluster about me or my husband anything about this one they call Shirtman.

Quickly, tactfully, the women picked up their chatter, talking and laughing as they placed more decorations on Anpagli, on her arms and around her neck. And over her ears they hung long loops of shells.

And now they demanded that she stand; they wanted a full-length view of her white gown, more wapiti teeth on the top and bottom of this garment than ever they had seen.

Gazing upon this new relative, the young girls clapped their hands softly, but two, three women noticed that Anpagli lacked one adornment. Yet they dared not place fluff from the wambli-bird in her hair; the Psa-woman once had belonged to a different man. But all other honors they gladly, proudly, grant her.

And so, smiling and joyful, they now led the new wife to the feasting place where the husband awaited her.

Desiring that all persons know his high regard for the woman he had chosen, Tonweya made many gifts on this day. Relatives also came forward, presenting those sticks which signify that they give a horse in the family name.

Peśla, filling himself on hump meat, had someone announce that he also, gives horses, six fine horses out of the Psa herd. Hearing, certain ones had observed—in soft voice and back of their palms—that Peśla for once had not picked out the influential in making his gifts but gave to youths who not yet earned a name.

Winu had stood back until Cankuna signaled her forward; then the Palani woman, unsmiling, had distributed those moccasins which the hunter's family presented in her name.

But the only truly sullen faces in the whole gathering belonged to those Psa captives who yet remembered that Anpagli had not shown grief for her dead tribesmen.

On this occasion these women, unnoticed as always, pulled on their hair which the Mahto wives had demanded that they braid, and spoke disparagingly of Tonweya's choice.

"I am as young as she," one woamn whined, "but what man knows me in this camp. I speak the enemy tongue often enough yet none of the men look at me."

Her companion, twice as old, said nothing. But she reflected on the tiny bundle hanging between her breasts, a bundle of hairs from the combings of a Titonwan warrior, something the old weather-woman Tatewin had procured for her. This mystery-woman had prophesied that if the captive wore the bundle day and night, she dared look for the warrior to come live with her. But neither this warrior nor any different one had appeared. Perhaps the power works slowly in a Titonwan village, the disgruntled captive had told herself; in an Absa camp something of this nature happens quickly.

The feasting went on into evening. Then, before dark, Tonweya came into the dance circle, most persons imagining that he came in the role of new-husband to perform the brief ceremonial dance of a man who now chooses to settle down. Instead, the crier called for silence; the scout, he said, will announce something.

And so Tonweya talked, his voice young and proud but lacking those touches of humor that usually marked his speech. "My relatives and friends," he began, "the band feasts this day with a person whom they once call enemy-woman. Now she becomes something to me; I call her my wife.

"Along with the women in my mother's lodge, my father and brother honor my wife, giving presents in her name. But now I make gifts in the name of one whom, these many seasons, I call brother-friend."

The scout glanced toward Ahbleza, then quickly away: "The principals in the band know and agree to that which I propose. And whoever keeps a Psa captive knows and will not object to my proposal.

"And so the leaders will send back to the enemy camp those Psa-women whom none adopt, whom none call daughter or sister or wife.

"I and my relatives give ten horses and so these women shall ride back to their people. And gladly I will see persons in the Mahto and Oglalahca villages gifting these women. For in this manner the Psa tribe not only discovers that the Titonwan have big hearts but that the Titonwan possess horses, moccasins, robes to spare."

A murmur spread through the crowd as ten young boys led forward ten strong horses.

"This act," said Tonweya, his eyes shining pride, "honors the Shirtman whom the warriors avenge. This act honors an owner-of-the-people and the people he owns. This act honors the man you call Ahbleza and the people he calls Lakotah."

The murmur grew into a cheer, a cheering that echoed out on the ridges.

And now many persons loosened necklets and armbands and took decorations out of their hair, carrying these items to the gift pile that rose at Tonweya's feet. And then certain ones returned to their tipi for robes and meat folders.

Camp akicita had begun to round up the Psa captives whom they will send back, the two women who had sat complaining aware that they go also. But neither of these two had brightened at the news. And when the one who wore the little bundle of hairs saw the warriors approach, she acted quickly; jerking loose this charm at her breasts, she flung the thing angrily upon the ground.

At once a small boy sprang forward, grabbing up the discarded mystery. But his excitement soon abated. Unwrapping his prize, he threw back the bundle to the grass; nothing here but black hairs, not even horsehairs.

Anpagli had listened to the cheers and whoops with a renewed sense of joy. She had heard speeches that honored her as never before and now she saw ten Psa-women, unwanted but also unharmed, mounted on horses that her husband and his relatives had provided, these captives started on their return to the branched-horn river, four Titonwan guiding the party to within a safe distance of their tribal village.

But much, much more important, she had seen the face and learned the name of this one whom Tonweya calls brother, brother-friend. And certainly she had heard enough to understand that the recent attack on the Psa had avenged the death of someone closely related to this brother-friend. But she not yet knew whom among Ahbleza's relatives the Psa had killed.

Strange, she told herself, that she never had heard about this killing of an important Titonwan while she lived in the camps of her people. And why had the scout never mentioned his tie with the Shirtman? And why had she never seen this Shirtman, this brother-friend, coming to Cankuna's lodge for a visit with Tonweya?

She sat alone while the people watched the Psa captives riding out, her eyes on Ahbleza. The Shirtman also stayed away from the crowd, but he sat alongside an old man, the impassive faces of these two presenting a marked contrast to the laughing, noisy people who grouped at the edge of camp.

The face of the Shirtman, she decided now, bore the look of a prophet who sees, whether he gazes at sunrise or sunfall, more sadness than joy in his surroundings.

The Shirtman turned, glancing in her direction as if her thoughts had attracted his, but almost at once Tonweya came up to her. Smiling, the husband asked that she walk with him now to the place Wanaǧi sat. And next to the sacred-man—Ahbleza.

"Hear me, my son." Wanaǧi, observing that the scout and his woman approached, gently touched the Shirtman's arm. "Your brother-friend brings his wife, and so I speak saying something you shall know: at this moment the truth of your bond as a dreaming-pair begins to take visible shape. See that nothing interferes." Rising, the sacred-man moved away.

And so Ahbleza, alone, awaited these two whose lives join with his in an unbreakable tie, the power of a most great vision compelling that these three persons demonstrate the unchanging, the unchangeable truth of the grandfathers.

"My brother chooses a fine-looking woman. I rejoice with him." The Shirtman intended a greeting acceptable to wife and husband, but his next words he directed toward Anpagli.

"The wapiya say that two men protect the wife who belongs to one of a dreaming-pair. And so I dare call a certain woman 'mitawicu.' But let her understand my meaning, that I pledge myself as her life-death friend even as I am the life-death friend to her husband."

Anpagli, looking directly at Ahbleza, saw something in his face that actively refused any memory of tragedy; the Shirtman's eyes told her that he bore malice toward neither person nor tribe who had wounded his heart.

And in the next instant a mysterious voice made known to the woman that she, in some mystifying way, relates to this man's tragedy and that she, as his distant-wife, will share another tragedy with him, an ordeal perhaps beyond her enduring . . . and his.

But before an apprehension grabbed hold of her, she saw Ahbleza's wonderful smile; the man had glanced toward a boy who came leading the yellow horse Tatezi.

The Shirtman put the cord into Tonweya's hand. "Tatezi belongs to you, misun," he told the scout, "but remember that she understands a woman's gentle touch."

The smile lingered on his face as he turned and walked away, leaving these two to marvel his gift.

For a moment the scout remembered back to the day he had found the black runner tied outside his lodge. But the woman knew only that she shall remember this day as the most wonderful one she yet experiences.

At the dance this same night Anpagli, for all her joy, had experienced moments of constraint. She had puzzled the proper attitude for a wife who hears the crowd demanding that the new husband perform a dance; certainly she will not anticipate any scalp-dancing on this occasion, but those victory songs, whether heard or unheard, will not suddenly float away, not any more than her image as a Psa-woman instantly disappears.

Tacincala, intent upon the singers, sat unaware of Anpagli's reticence but someone had remembered the Psa-woman as a person unfamiliar with Titonwan custom. Woze, the Mahto heyoka, had caught her attention and, posturing in a ludicrous manner, sent her a message. And so she suddenly understood to stand back demurely, those yells and cheers for the husband only.

She smiled her gratefulness, and the heyoka, true to a contrary's nature, wrinkled his face in a scowl.

When the scout finished his little dance, he strutted out of the circle and the drummers began a different song. Anpagli saw that men and women danced to this one but Tonweya had not reappeared among these dancers.

Cankuna had joined the dancers, but Tacincala came over to stand alongside the new wife. After a while she spoke, her tone hinting inpatience: "Who keeps him?"

Anpagli had not felt concern at Tonweya's abrupt disappearance, but now she realized Tacincala's discomfiture. And so she wondered whether she, as a new wife, had acted in any way to embarrass the hunter's family. Perhaps she had misunderstood the heyoka's signals and omitted a courtesy?

Instantly Tacincala expressed regret for the impression she had given Anpagli; the new wife neither omitted anything nor neglected anyone. But she had not told Anpagli that her distress grew out of something Pesla had said when the Psa-women rode out of camp, something that she, the young sister, had overheard.

The warrior had considered the return of these captives a foolish act. Nor had he kept his opinion to himself.

"So the dung-eaters get back their women and gain presents," Peśla had mocked, "but will they agree that the Titonwan have big hearts? Or will they say the Titonwan have soft heads? And who will point out to the Psatoka that if one day the Lakotah give, the next day they take away." He had paused, looking at the faces of his listeners. "And so why not a war party going out after those gift-horses once the enemy women reach their camp?"

Tacincala had not wanted to hear more, but she had seen four, five warriors step in close to Peśla, these men obviously interested.

Tonweya's disappearance following his dance and Ahbleza's conspicuous absence had piled on anxieties; will the season arrive, the young woman had asked herself, when brother hurts brother?

And now Tacincala, making her offer gracefully, invited Anpagli to come with her and wait in the family lodge for the scout's return from whatever errand had called him away.

But Anpagli had decided instantly; she shall stay exactly where Tonweya had observed her sitting when he danced the new-husband dance. "I stay," she said calmly, "even if I stay all night." But her eyes acknowledged Tacincala's kindness.

The suddenness of the scout's presence at her side had not surprised Anpagli, but the seriousness of his face gave her concern. She said nothing but followed him as he signaled her, the two going to the little shelter alongside the big family lodge.

Tonweya had chosen to sleep here alone those four days that had awaited the ceremony. But now, the feast and dancing over, he intended that Anpagli sleep here with him. They will use this little place, he had told her, until she raises the snow lodge at the winter campsite.

Certain relatives, knowing that he schemed to bring his wife to a brush shelter, had teased the scout, but he had laughed back at these persons. He finds more rest, he had said, under brush along the trail than in any lodge anywhere.

Tonweya knew that his mother made ready a new lodge for him and Anpagli, but he wanted his woman to learn his ways, to stand abreast the weathers and defy the rough trail. She had spoken of her nature as akin to his; now let her prove this thing. And let her demonstrate trust in his decisions.

And so, lying next to the man, Anpagli heard him speak now of those trails he shall take alone and of those trails they shall walk together. And of things that he will confide, things that as her husband, he wants her to know.

His second absence from camp, after her capture, he told, had concerned his search for a new wintering place. He and Wasu had gone out and returned with more than one site for Olepi's consideration. But then he had determined to ride off with Anpagli and make her his wife. And if the band needed his guidance, they needed to wait, this once they wait.

And they had waited, Anpagli knew, Mahto and Oglalahca villages staying in a circle until the newly mated pair returned.

Now, for one whole day, they had honored the woman and the scout at a ceremonial feast and dance. But will the people, Anpagli had wondered aloud, delay overlong their breaking camp?

"Only the old weather-woman gives me dark glances." Tonweya leaned up on his arm to view his wife's face in the light that reflected through the cover of the family lodge.

"Perhaps you wonder," he said, "where I go after my dance this night. So hear me. The Shirtman asks that I visit his lodge, wherein he and his father and five more persons make talk. At sunrise this party goes out horseback; they invite me as their scout. But I am not going. My brother-friend understands that I choose to stay here with you."

The new husband had taken pride in the fact that his woman had not hinted about his disappearance from the dance-ground but he took yet more pride in her now; she asked him nothing more about his visit in Ahbleza's lodge. And nothing about Ahbleza.

Reaching out his hand, he touched above the woman's

knee and she, recognizing his desire and hers, pulled up gently on her sleeping gown.

The night had faded, dawn pushing off the dark, when Anpagli awakened to her husband's stirring; she saw that he lay with eyes open. Wondering whether his talk with the Shirtman kept him wakeful, she decided to speak.

"Micante." She whispered her affection, then spoke her thought: "Micante, I recognize your brother-friend as one who stands high among the Titonwan, among any people. Perhaps they call him 'seer' as they speak of certain ones in different tribes. And yet in this one's eyes I see more of yearning than prophecy. I see something not unsimilar to sadness. . . . "

Tonweya's fingers touched her lips; he will not bear to hear whatever more she knows about Ahbleza. But he will answer saying those things he never before had spoken to anyone.

"I recognize my brother-friend as a man who observes and perceives all things around him. And so he has the understanding of a scout and of a healer, of a hunter and of a warrior. And truly he knows about sadness."

The man had paused, but now he spoke on in the same even tone: "He grieves the loss of a wife and yet he refuses any sign of sorrowing. Nor will he go out against the enemy who . . . " Tonweya cut short his phrase; suddenly he remembered something.

He never had mentioned to Anpagli the Psa attack on Ahbleza's wife and her people. And the kills-talks at the scalp-dances—if ever the Psa-woman had attended—revealed neither whom the Mahto avenged nor why.

But will not the kills-talks in Anpagli's own camp after the Psa scouts arrive with the enemy's horses and scalps inform her? And what of the yellow horse, the wondrously gentle Tatezi? Certainly the Psa scouts talk about her rider.

"My husband . . . " Anpagli's quiet voice crept into his puzzling and so he stopped to listen.

"My husband," she began again, "permit my asking about this yellow one you call Tatezi. Perhaps she once belongs to the Shirtman . . . or one of his relatives. And when the Psa cut loose this horse, he vows to ride her again. And you, his brother-friend, make true his vow. And so he gives this unusual creature to you?"

She had not listened for an answer from Tonweya at once, but someday she looked for him to tell her the story. And now, before he speaks, she will have him know another thing.

"I once wish," she whispered, "that this Tatezi belongs to me. Now I know that the mysterious powers use the yellow one as a way for bringing together a woman, a scout, a Shirtman."

She had finished her speech firmly, but now she turned, pressing her face into the sleeping robe, her heart beating loud and fast while she waited for Tonweya to respond.

When the scout said nothing, she wondered whether he had misunderstood her, whether he imagined that she hinted for the horse. Or perhaps she had used an inappropriate expression or accented some Lakotah word in a way that changed the meaning.

She lifted her head; she spoke boldly: "My husband, know that I am proud yet humble when I remember who calls me wife and who, this day, calls me distant-wife. And know that I shall hold a sister's affection for the brother-friend.

"I never see the true-wife whose loss the Shirtman suffers and I know not when she dies—whether recently or many winters past—but a familiar-voice tells me that Tatezi once knows this woman's touch. And so Tatezi brings together the hearts of not three but four persons." Her head dropped against the man's protecting breast, her tears of gladness running warm over his smooth skin.

The scout lay stunned, his arms at his side, his eyes widening. His instant response to her revelation—to search the memory of his vision and discover a horse, a yellow horse—came to nothing before he started. He remembered that horses never appear in visions; the invisibles use as their messengers only those four-legged and winged familiar to the original grandfathers.

Then, reviewing each word Anpagli had spoken here—and keeping hold of his reason—he remembered himself back on the trail where he had seen the enemy leading those horses who had belonged to Heyatawin and her family. Only he, Tonweya the truthbearer, sees and reports that incident, he told himself; but will he overlook some detail and so give lasting sorrow to someone?

Suddenly he realized who will know, the one person who will know, the one person with the power to know.

Wanaǧi will know.

Wanaǧi, a wakanḣca who owns the stone-song and so commands the stones, will know. Wakanḣca, he who locates the missing and strengthens the weak and sings at ceremonials; wakanḣca, the real mystery-man and not a trickster, will know.

Wanaǧi, a man of constant spiritual awareness—he will know.

Tonweya appeared at the sacred-lodge near sunrise. But before the scout spoke, Wanaǧi made answer to that which the young man's eyes demanded that the wakanḣca tell.

The wife of the Shirtman and those persons who had traveled with her, he said, had died on the trail, the sudden snow and cold of a tricky moon freezing their bodies.

"True," the sacred-man told now, "I discover this tragedy when you come to me requesting that I locate the yellow horse. But a wakanḣca never answers more than that which someone asks, and you ask nothing about the people who disappear.

"Even so, will any good, any change for good, come of the Shirtman hearing this story now? The scout shall decide."

When again he sat alone, Wanaǧi sucked the stem of his pipe, his eyes closed. He watched a familiar picture, something in movement, the persons who appeared before him and those events that they brought about reaffirming the premise of the original grandfathers, that souls relating to the same things relate to one another.

And so he saw Ahbleza and the brother-friend, each man going outside the tribe to choose his woman, the spirit neither creating nor recognizing any barriers, the spirit knowing joy as the only bond.

Ahbleza and Tonweya, dreaming-pair, brother-friends, life-death companions, relatives-through-choice—two who experience the power of affinity, something in and of the spirit-realm; and now certain invisibles who yet hold on to memory use a yellow horse to demonstrate this truth.

For who but Śinaska, the old teacher who exists among the invisibles these past thirty winters, acts as guide during Wanaġi's spirit-travel in search of the yellow horse, the wakanlica's first attempt to travel spiritually from one camp location to another. True, Wanaġi will visit the center—return to the source—without guidance, but he not yet dares send his spirit-body traveling through woods and along streams without a spirit-guide.

True, he experiments with his stone-song before ever Tonweya comes seeking help; he knows whom to look for as his guide. And so he sits ready on the day that the scout demands the whereabouts of Tatezi; he needs only his song to bring Śinaska in touch, the old seer's spirit moving the stones to signify his presence, his agreement. Śinaska, the one who leads Wanaġi's spirit-self to the site of the yellow horse.

Now, the picture fading, Wanaġi recognized that the season will come when Śinaska abandons any interest in the work of the visibles. And so he, Wanaġi, needs prepare himself to travel alone. Perhaps he shall use the stones but once again; even so, he shall hold on to the power that comes to him through such great travail.

VIII

UNROLLING THE picture-hide and gazing upon the whole, Heȟaka saw that a third generation of Lakotah had grown up on the plain. For an instant he puzzled his own age; someone had told him that his birth had occurred during the winter 'they scatter out'—the winter the Oda-kotah originally had separated—and so he need only count the pictures to know whether seventy-five or more snows have fallen on his shoulders. But why count? Why not relate his life instead to those experiences he chooses to remember, even as they relate the life of the tribe to those events the people choose to recall?

He considered the three affairs out of this past winter about which the band most often sang and talked. And so he either makes a symbolic drawing of an unusual hunka ceremony or he shall describe in simple lines that which the Lakotah call 'touching the stick.' Or he shall make a picture that commemorates a most tragic event.

He began to review the hunka—or 'waving horsetails,' as many persons now describe this most important ceremony—but he sensed an uncertainty. The winter count, he told himself, calls for an accurate and easily understood reference; so who will understand the naming of an enemy tribesman as hunka, as a permanent choice for brother?

Hehaka filled a pipe and leaned against his backrest; he intended to visualize again the astonishing change Ahbleza had introduced into the hunka ceremony this past summer.

The sungazing had taken place on the muddy-water, but neither the Mahto nor the Siyo band had chosen to travel east for the tribal gathering. Instead, they had formed their own hoop, the two bands raising a hunka-lodge, a double-tipi open to the west, in the center of their circle. And one of those persons who voiced his desire to enact the hunka ritual: Tonweya.

Throughout his seasons Tonweya had watched the many ceremonies devised to impress child, youth, middle-age. But not for him the slow deliberation, the long preparation, the mysterious rites; his nature demanded a quick decision on the heels of sudden sight, sudden sound, sudden smell. And so he never had performed any of the ceremonies. He had known himself as brother-friend to Ahbleza long before the wapiya had called the two a dreaming-pair. So why, he had asked himself, enact a 'truthful singing'—so the seers named this ceremony—in front of the tribe? He, a truthbearer each day of his life, not likely will discover anything different about truth on touching a hunka-pipe. Nor will a pledge that compels an enduring tie—the people as witnesses—lend more importance to his bond with Ahbleza.

And yet, recent events had made him wonder whether

the youth-vision held more significance than he had realized; perhaps the peaceful bond of a dreaming-pair directly concerned the whole band? Pondering Ahbleza's amazing act at the sunpole and then this same man's lack of vindictive spirit toward the Psa, the scout had sensed a power drawing him more closely to the Shirtman. And to the tribe by way of the Shirtman. And so this past summer Tonweya had requested use of the hunka-lodge.

Wanagi's surprising refusal to conduct the performance had not deterred Tonweya; instead he had carried the pipe to Sunihanble, the seer who had acted as an assistant at Ahbleza's sungazing.

When Sunihanble had agreed to sing, Tonweya had visited Ahbleza's lodge, where, boy-young and smiling, the scout had dropped onto the robe at the back.

Ahbleza, also smiling, had reached for the pipe known to the ledge of their vision. He had filled the bowl with the contents of the little sac Tonweya had brought along, his act designating a willingness to respond to whatever request the scout intended to make.

But as the Shirtman reached for an ember to lay on the mixture, Tonweya had made a restraining gesture: "Before you put flame to these leaves, hear me. Brother to you I am, whether or not I and you wear the red face-stripe of hunka-relatives. Truly I am your hunka from before I remember."

Listening closely as the scout talked on, Ahbleza had recognized that Tonweya desired the hunka ceremony as a way of offering-thanks; even as the Shirtman had sungazed in recognition of their sacred bond, the scout proposed to perform hunka in recognition of this same thing.

Ahbleza had placed the ember on the bowl: "Smoke, misun, I accept your desire."

After the two had smoked, they had reviewed that which the ceremony required, Tonweya telling that the conductor shall provide pte-skull, stone, and the proper grasses. "But I am responsible for rattles, firesticks, drum. And the hunka-pipe."

The scout had learned that the old Dakotah families had waved pipestems and stalks of maize over the heads of hunka. "They say that an old stem—one they use often—holds more meaning than a new stem. The wapiya offers me such a hunka-bundle but the water-bird head on the old pipe looks like something the dogs chew on and the moose hairs appear dull. And so I shall make a new stem and suspend a fan of wambli-feathers from the wood. But from the fan to the mouthpiece I shall fasten strands of red horsehair."

Ahbleza had answered softly: "Misun, the conductor advises an old stem and so use this one, this pipe which I and you smoke these many seasons, this stem which only my hand and yours ever touches. Make this one hunka."

After Tonweya had gone out of the lodge, the Shirtman had reflected on this word 'hunka,' a contraction for a long phrase which the grandfathers had spoken, a phrase that told man to recognize his own spirit as his true-relative. And to know this true-relative as 'hunka to truth.'

Hunka, an appreciation of self, a demonstration of one's view of one's own spirit.

Hunka-relative: blood-relatives share that which makes up the body; hunka-relatives share that which makes up the spirit.

The original hunka: man taking wife, the woman reflecting the husband's pride in self, accepting his seed, bearing his child, generating his affection, calling him 'wicaȟca,' the real-man. And so the people, speaking of mothers, say 'hunku,' mother-of-his-child, a relative through choice.

So they place a girl-child in the hunka procession, a little girl who carries a stick of maize, husk off and seeds visible.

Hunka, the spirit living on this earth as hunka to truth.

These things he, Ahbleza, had come to understand when he had painted the sacred ceremonies during those days before the sungazing.

Before dawn on the hunka ceremonial day Sunihanble had begun coloring his hands red and drawing zigzag lines on his arms. At sunrise he had stepped outside his lodge, speaking to sun and earth and the four directions, his song mentioning also those wingeds whose voices awaken day.

Tonweya had stood listening on a knoll nearby camp, Sunihanble instructing him to stay until the drums had called together all hunkayapi, Mahto, and Siyo, and then to sneak into a certain tipi where he shall await the procession.

And so the scout, waiting, had noticed an old woman

who rapidly ascended the mound where he stood. He recognized her as the same one who made a custom of climbing a hill during any ceremony, her shrill voice rising in a howl similar to the true-dogs whom she implored to keep away. The people never interfered with her ritual; they understood that she acted in obedience to a dream. But desiring to avoid the woman, Tonweya had considered slipping down the opposite side of the knoll.

As he turned to go, he had seen a second woman approaching the little hill; this one, his wife. For an instant he had puzzled why Anpagli came here. And why she came running.

Ahbleza, lying awake on his robes and listening to Sunihanble sing about those things a hunka shall share, had not looked toward the presence who appeared suddenly in his tipi; even before he heard the voice he had known that Wanaĝi had come.

"Hear me, my son. I bring you news before this news happens."

Ahbleza, eyes closed, had leaned up on his elbows.

The sacred-man had spoken factually: "Three Psa shall cut loose horses on the edge of camp. Two of this enemy shall escape but one Psa they shall bring into the village. And an enemy in camp on a day when Lakotah wave the hunka-pipe lives or dies depending on whether or not someone will call him relative."

Having delivered his message, the wakanhca had left the tipi at once. And so Ahbleza had understood that a decision to use the hunkayapi rite as a way of demonstrating his true desire for peace among tribes rested with him alone.

Sighing, the Shirtman had lain back on his robes; will they forever test him?

But then, his eyes opening wide, he had sat up; they never really had tested him; instead he had chosen to test himself. "Even as I will test myself again this day," he had murmured.

"Certainly I remember, whatever my effort not to remember, that a Psa kills my wife. But will killing one or more than one Psa move either tribe toward peace? True, the avengings act as a deterrent, but will one more killing put a finish to any more killings between Lakotah and Psa?

891

A Psa comes to take horses, a game among tribes. But if they catch and kill him, a different Psa shall come—and not to play a game. And so killing generates killing, each tribe a collection of wailing-women camps.

"The man-family appears on earth, the grandfathers say, joyous and unrestrained, each person hunka to the one and to the whole. But somewhere someone, blind to truth, creates distrust and treachery. And so the killings begin, the spiritual growth of certain persons cut off.

"Yet the grandfathers say that whoever speaks untruthfully shall lose his life before his spirit, retrogressing, endangers the whole. And certainly I will not live peacefully alongside any person who denies truth, who makes treacherous use of the life-force.

"But I will remember that even as I own my life, I own only mine. And so I ask myself twice: will not the scheme of things return enough bodies to the grass without the avenging? Will not starving winters and blizzard snows and childbearing and old age use up enough lives without man killing man?"

Once again Ahbleza had lain back on his robes; once again he listened to Šunihanble's song.

Tonweya had met his wife halfway down the slope and the woman, attempting calm, had spoken her message; she had recognized the Psa captive they had dragged into camp.

"I remember this man as the one who leads Tatezi into the Psa camp on a day when warm winds abruptly change to cold and snow. Before the clubmen kill him, perhaps you will ask this Psa and he will tell . . . " Anpagli had stopped, puzzled. Exactly what thing the captive will tell, the woman had not known.

The next instant Tonweya had left her side, the scout running toward the sacred-lodge, looking for Wanaǧi.

But soon the runner had seen that he need not seek the wakanĥca; Wanaǧi had walked out to meet him.

Afterwards, whenever he recalled that day, Tonweya saw the sacred-man standing center of the sun, the great red ball back of Wanaǧi and balanced on the horizon before starting to climb the sky; Wanaǧi at the center and waiting for Tonweya.

The hunkayapi had stood around in little groups, tiny hunka-stems in their hands. A Siyo woman had presented these miniature pipes to each person who wore the red cheek-mark, her effort much appreciated. The hunkayapi always received an inviting-stick—meaning a space inside the ceremonial lodge—but never before had anyone cut and decorated these sticks in the manner of the real hunka-stem.

Within the big double-tipi Sunihanble had arranged everything in ceremonial manner: the pipe rack back of the pte-skull, the hunka-pipe leaning against this rack, the rattles beneath, and the maize, impaled on a red stick, near the tipi entrance. And so when the firecarrier arrives and hands the conductor a drumbeater, the ceremonial hunt for the tipi wherein the hunka sits hiding shall begin.

The rumor that akicita conceal a Psa horsetaker inside the hoop had reached certain ears, but these warriors had understood that the clubmen scheme an amusing game following the hunka ceremony, this captive Psa the object of an exciting chase.

Cankuna and her woman-relatives had made their feast fires nearby the double-tipi, certain Siyo families here also, each group of cooks setting out three big wooden bowls, one bowl for dog-meat, one for pte, and the third one for berry soup. Anpagli helped tend these fires, but not once had she laughed or smiled. And she scarcely had spoken.

Suddenly Cankuna, looking up from her work, had called to her helpers: "See, they go out looking for the hunka." She had heard the rousing song that started off the celebration.

And so the women had moved up for a close view of the colorful procession, of those persons who walked singing, their song asking 'where, the tipi in which the hunka hides?'

"Tuktel hunkake tipi so yo: tuktel hunkake tipi so yo?"

Tonweya had stayed hidden but not in any secret tipi as originally schemed. Instead he had crouched back of a boulder, needing to keep out of sight only until after the surprising event, until after the people understood whom Ahbleza had chosen for hunka.

The scout had known that the Shirtman dared not permit the spilling of the Psa's blood, whatever his feelings about this enemy tribesman whom the dawn watch had captured.

Ahbleza will pledge himself hunka to this Psa, Tonweya had told himself, to this same Psa who cut loose Tatezi on the night his woman and her family travel south. And so I shall talk with this Psa after the ceremony and tell him that he never shall recognize Tatezi nor identify himself with this incident. And I shall tell him that whomever the Shirtman takes as hunka becomes something to me. For I am the true brother-friend.

"Tuktel hunkake tipi so yo; tuktel hunkake tipi so yo?"

The most serious faces had taken on smiles; the search-song of the hunka always sent spirits soaring, especially as the people watched the faces of their children. Nothing in Lakotah ceremony or song provided more entertainment for a child than this pretend hunt for the hunka, the conductor's bright red hands flashing the color scheme of the procession, all hunkayapi giving full voice to their exciting song.

Ahbleza, standing outside his lodge, had noticed especially the little girl who walked directly back of Sunihanble, her hands grasping the red stick-with-maize. A red line decorated her face—forehead to chin—and a soft white feather drooped onto her shoulder. The Shirtman had smiled, not only at this symbol of Ptesanwin—the pipe-woman—but at the child herself, at this little one whom he knew as Kehala's daughter. Perhaps one day, he had mused, this ceremony shall belong only to children and to those persons who keep the childlike spirit.

"Tuktel hunkake tipi so yo; where, the tipi of the hunka?"

The procession had moved on around the hoop of lodges, the third person in line swinging the hunka-stem and singing lustily. But the rattle-bearer, back of him, never once had smiled or looked toward the cheering spectators.

And then the firecarrier, in the rear and holding a drum, suddenly had stopped and drummed most rapidly.

The noise had sent Śunihanble hastening toward a certain tipi with closed flap. But after a moment's pause the conductor had stood again at the front of the line, again leading the people around camp.

Before they had completed a circling of the lodges, more persons wearing the hunka face-stripe had joined the party; custom called for all hunkayapi to walk singing.

"Tuktel hunkake tipi so yo?"

The excited shouts of children had bounced on the air as the group began a second turn of the lodges, Śunihanble stopping at four, five different tipi, where he had listened intently before moving on.

The line had tripled during the third circling and before the leader had begun the fourth round of the camp all Mahto and Śiyo hunkayapi walked in the procession, more than fifty grownups and ten, twelve children, each one singing, 'Tuktel hunkake tipi so yo?'

The most youthful in line—a little boy not yet three—had clung to his father's back, arms around the man's neck. The shrillness of the child's shouts had made the people laugh as these two passed, the father also smiling but covering one ear to dim the noise.

A different father had hoisted a small daughter onto his shoulders, and soon half the children either rode on their parent's shoulders or begged for a ride, the spectators clapping their hands approvingly.

One old, old person had walked in the line, someone the Śiyo band respectfully called 'Mihunka.' Perhaps thirty winters in the past they had waved the hunka-stem over his head and they intended again to wave the stem over his head. A Śiyo youth had chosen him as hunka, as someone for whom evermore to provide soup and a sleeping place.

"Tuktel hunkake tipi so yo?" Mihunka, leaning on a cane and grasping the young Śiyo's arm, had sung the search-song in the dialect of the old Dakotah. He had wanted the people to remember the parent-tribe, to remember those Dakotah grandfathers whose wisdom had introduced the ritual wherein youth honored old age not as an obligation but as privilege and choice.

Then all at once the procession had halted and the

singing had stopped. And everywhere all talking and laughing had ceased, even the camp-dogs quiet. Apparently Sunihanble had found the secret tipi.

The conductor had stood before a small closed-up lodge. "Earth relates to everything on earth," he had called out. "And so each Lakotah relates to every other Lakotah. But who sits in this tipi? Lakotah or enemy?"

In response to this stern demand, someone had come forward from among the spectators, someone with three black stripes running up one cheek and a club in his hand. "An enemy sits in this tipi," he had announced; "I will bring him out here."

The smiles had disappeared off faces as certain akicita had run up to the lodge, their club-arms raised threateningly. And the children had drawn back against their mothers, the sudden change in the people making these little ones shy.

Cutting the strings that held down the flap, one clubman had gone inside the tipi; he had reappeared holding on to a stranger.

Hands had reached up to cover mouths, the people astounded; they had looked for someone in the tipi but not a Psatoka, not the real-enemy.

A child had whimpered, someone instantly shutting off the cry. Boys and girls had watched the scene with surprised eyes; and those youths who had witnessed other hunka ceremonies had glanced at their peers wonderingly.

"Toka kin le unktepi kte t'ka, tuwe hunka kaġa kin han unktepi kte śni yelo." Sunihanble had spoken saying that the akicita intend to kill this enemy. But if someone will take him for hunka, he shall live.

Some persons had turned their backs; they had not understood exactly what Sunihanble had said; certainly the seer will not imply that someone take an enemy for his hunka.

"Who will make this Psatoka his relative?" the conductor had asked.

None had agreed. Instead a murmur had run through the crowd: when comes this enemy into camp and who put him inside the secret tipi? Why not one or two children hiding here or the scout Tonweya? Rumor had said that a dreaming-pair will demonstrate their bond. And afterwards, certain Siyo children.

"I listen for a voice," Sunihanble had sung out, "telling that the akicita shall not kill this stranger."

More than one warrior, looking out of the corner of his eyes, had wondered who among their own had known of the Psa's presence and had said nothing.

And so Sunihanble, aware of the warning glances and grunts, had walked toward the double-tipi as before, but he had begun a different song. The captive dies, he had sung, for none will take him as hunka.

And then the people had seen someone push the enemy into the line, the procession moving again, the pipe-bearer walking stiffly and the rattle-carrier howling in the voice of a traveling-dog, a sound that signals good news. As when they capture an enemy.

Everyone had followed the performers to the ceremonial lodge, the crowd noisy and suspicious until those persons near the front saw and heard something that had put a stop to the yells and the muttering.

Stepping forward where all had a view of him, Ahbleza had called out his willingness to share meat and tipi with this Psa for as long as each one lives, in lean winters and fat, in difficulty and in joy.

"I take him for my hunka. This ceremony will show you, my people, that I make a brother of this man." Touching the Psa lightly on the shoulder, the Shirtman had guided the captive into the double-tipi as if nothing unusual had occurred.

Next, those five who had carried something in the procession had entered this same place. And as many hunkayapi as the big lodge had space for, the akicita directing their entry. And then Sunihanble had signed that all other striped-cheeks form a wide circle and sit in front of the ceremonial tipi, men on the side toward the hills, women opposite.

Already the demeanor of the crowd had changed perceptibly. The old people had recalled the story of those Dakotah who, many, many winters past, had gone outside the tribe to hunt among the enemy for a most desirable woman, a mate for a certain Isanyati warrior, a young man whose vigor and self-respect and wholesome ambition made him the proper person to bring forth a line of leaders. Those searchers had returned with a Haliatonwan captive, but they had waited until she chose to become the Isanyati's wife. Meaning until she expressed a true desire to become mother of his child. And to this act of choice, this making-of-relatives whatever the attachment, they had begun to apply the short term 'hunka.'

And many more persons had recognized that Ahbleza, their man of high standing, had enacted his privilege to choose whomever he truthfully desired as a brother. Nor had they said that he replaced his brother-friend Tonweya. Instead the people had recognized that Ahbleza embraced the inmost and the most far-reaching concept of hunka.

And certainly the Shirtman had remembered that good for one Lakotah means good for the whole people. For the Lakotah never had conceived a ceremony wherein man embraced the incompetent, the fearful, the painmaker, the corrupt. Certainly Ahbleza had seen good coming to each one when he spoke out, when he took the Psa as his hunka, an enemy they had intended to kill.

"Let the ceremony proceed." Sunihanble, sensing the wonder that had filled the air, had spoken, the wapiya demanding that the assembly give attention to the next rite.

"Bird-with-two-different-voices, you call yourself my grandchild, this voice in the air, this voice on the ground. Hiye aheye hibu."

And so the people had listened to someone singing in a most remarkable manner. Winkte had composed a song for those yellow-breast wingeds who either gurgled seven flute-like tones or made the po-po-pa sound of popping-gut. But whichever voice—above or on the ground—this bird always had spoken Lakotah, a relative who influenced for good.

At the close of Winkte's song, the conductor had stepped inside the ceremonial lodge and, after putting an ember on the bowl of a long-stem pipe—one decorated similar to the hunka-stem—had passed this symbol of truth among the hunkayapi. And while these persons smoked, an assistant to Sunihanble had prepared a paintbrush of pte-hair, had drawn the red line, forehead to chin, on the cheek of the Psa captive.

Sunihanble, not of the hunkayapi, neither had painted nor had watched this painting. His good name permitted him red hands and the privilege of conducting the ceremony, but only hunkayapi dared observe the striping of hunka. And so he had whistled softly during this rite, a whisper-song out of the ancient past, something the grandfathers had intended as a comforting sound to ease any shy or apprehensive hearts.

But while these good things occurred inside the lodge, not everyone who had sat outside had comprehended the Shirtman's act. Peśla, for one, had refused to understand why Ahbleza welcomed an enemy into his lodge, his choice perhaps endangering the Mahto band. This Psa, the warrior had muttered to his companions, represents the true-enemy of the Lakotah; will the Shirtman imagine that the Psa changes his feelings on hearing the pledge?

Suddenly the wapiya's helper had stood in the entrance, signaling for the removal of the robe that had concealed the new hunka. The next moment the conductor had stepped forward, the hunka-stem in his hand.

And then the people had looked upon Ahbleza and the Psa, these two bound arm-to-arm, leg-to-leg, each man with the red stripe on his face.

While the crowd gazed quietly upon this scene, the drummer had come out of the lodge and, lifting his beater to the rim of the drum, had tapped the edge until the conductor signed his readiness to wave the hunka-stem. Then, the gathering truly silent, the drummer had moved his stick onto the hide in a regular, unchanging heart-beat. And so Sunihanble had begun a song to the four directions, to the above and to the earth, to pte and to stone, to those things with the power for influencing hunka.

"Wiyohpeyata le hunka, eca le hunka"—where the sun falls, hunka, truly hunka—he had sung, his listeners understanding that west means west and never anything different.

"Waziyata le hunka, eca le hunka"—where the lodgepoles grow, hunka, truly hunka—he had sung, his listeners understanding that north means north and never anything different.

"Wiyohinyanpata le hunka, eca le hunka"—where the sun rises, hunka, truly hunka—he had sung, his listeners understanding that east means east and never anything different.

"Itokagta le hunka, eca le hunka"—the direction I face, hunka, truly hunka—he had sung, his listeners understanding that south means south and never anything different.

And above means above and earth means earth and never anything different, even as hunka means hunka and never anything different; the grandfathers had said so, said so.

And once a Psa, always a Psa, Olepi had murmured to himself; and never anything different.

The Mahto leader, watching the conductor swing the stem, had pondered his son Ahbleza, who refused a thong at the sacred-pole yet accepted a thong from which he never shall break loose, a thong that ties him body and spirit to someone not Titonwan but an enemy.

And why, Olepi had wondered, will Ahbleza perform this ceremony; a Shirtman becomes everyone's hunka on the day they name him Shirtman. And in recent winters any person who wore the hunka-stripe knew that this red line symbolized a willingness to share with the one and the whole.

But observing his son and the Psa exchange pieces of fat meat and lean in a demonstration of sharing, Olepi had grunted: "In my youth the meat ladle will identify a generous man. Apparently they now approach the season when any have-not in the tribe dares claim half the meat a striped-cheek raises to his mouth, along with half his robes, his moccasins, and whatever more he acquires."

Will they come to abuse this affair, he had mused, the original ceremony-of-choice eventually turning into a scheme to dispossess a man? Will hunka cease to mean hunka and become a tribal handout? His generation understands 'giving' and 'lending' as the same thing; either way demands a return, implies an even trade. What manner of man ever gives something for nothing and so acts to depreciate himself?

Certainly the people give meat and robes to the akicita—the clubmen and watchers—but in return for protection. And these same things they shall give to the lame and the blind, but always in the name of someone who earns his way. And certainly the people shall help out any person who struggles over a rough spot, but always in the name of an example, of someone who struggles and regains his balance.

So who brings about this custom on the plain wherein a man piles up his favorite possessions for anyone and everyone to run in and grab?

Suddenly Olepi had wondered whether the present generation loses sight of what makes for a powerful tribe. But one thing for certain: Ahbleza once again gives the people something to talk about.

And yet who—but Wanaġi—understands my act? Ahbleza had asked himself this thing twice—when they had bound him to the Psa, and again when they had untied the cord, the ceremony brought to a close.

Truly who but Wanaġi recognizes this word 'toka' which the grandfathers pronounce 'tokeca.' And which means not 'enemy' but 'different.'

Tokeca or toka, a different tongue, a different tribe. But not a way of life opposing mine. This Psa calls himself man the same as I. He hunts and sleeps and dreams and schemes the same as I. He owns the earth the same as I.

Toka or tokaĥca, different or most different. So who changes the meaning to, 'enemy'? Enemy—someone I am born to overthrow, someone born to overthrow me?

Toka, Psatoka; I choose a Psatoka for hunka. Henceforth he shall go out and come in without fear. And so I demonstrate myself as peaceman. But more important, I strengthen my bond with Tonweya.

And yet who—but Wanaġi—understands my act?

Heĥaka recalled the second event that had occurred during the past winter, something that the people had talked over for a while—a little while—something about a treaty with the wasicun, the whiteman.

Newsbearers coming into the Mahto-Šiyo encampment

soon after the hunka ceremony had reported whitemen traveling up the river. The strangers carried those leaves on which they draw their little talking-signs, and they had come on ground below the bend, at the place where Sicanġu and Wiciyela had raised lodges. One of those whites, speaking some Dakotah phrases, had told the suspicious encampment why the party had come. The talking-leaves, he had said, brought friendly thoughts; the whitemen hoped that the Dakotah held friendly thoughts also.

When the Sicanġu and their relatives said nothing, the whiteman had interpreted the talking-signs. The good white father, he had told, recognized their hunting grounds and intended to act in a manner that protected the whole.

"Your white father will reach out with acts of kindness. He will send traders for your convenience. But if any of his enemies come here, you shall close your ears to their requests.

"Your white father will have you neither harm nor delay any whiteman who passes here. Nor will he permit any whiteman to molest you or interfere with your ways. This talking-leaf says so."

The silent people had remained silent, and so the whiteman had said that he wished to hear someone speak. Will the Dakotah leaders agree to act friendly toward whitemen who walk on Dakotah hunting grounds to get where they want to go?

The leaders had not answered, and so the whiteman had repeated each thing. And then the speaker had asked that the principal ones in each band put the crossed-lines mark on the leaf, a little mark that means they will not injure any whiteman who comes here or take away his possessions.

For a long while none had reached for the marker which the speaker held out to the leaders. But finally, one by one, they had touched-the-stick.

"Tell the other bands in your great nation," the treaty-makers had said afterwards, "that we shall meet their members upriver."

And so Sicanġu runners had taken the message to Titonwan camped at the mouth of the tricky, at the place this stream flows into the big muddy river. And from out of those Lakotah camps, horsebacks had taken on the news, riding in the direction of those two bands who camped on the short grass.

After hearing the message, principals among the Mahto and Siyo had gone to the center lodge, where they had raised the sides of the big tipi, the people invited to listen. Then, before dark, the wakicunsa had voiced a decision. The horseback messengers, they had said, shall return to the river saying that certain persons, representing the Mahto and the Siyo, will attend the meeting on the mud-water river but that none will touch the marking-stick until they truly understand the talking-leaf.

But the people sitting outside the council lodge had murmured their desire to see the whole encampment move to the river. Let those visitors from the white nations view all Lakotah, all Canoni—perhaps eight thousand persons—gathered in one place and then inform those whites that four thousand more persons—Ihanktonwan—belong to this same tribe. Not likely will the whiteman, on discovering these things, try wandering over the mixed grasses but will keep to the waterway.

Keep to the waterway, Olepi had repeated to himself. In the past these same Lakotah had said that they intended to stop any whites using the waterway. Now they sat willing to grant travel on water but not on grass. And when the whites begin trampling the grass, will not these same Lakotah say, permit the intruders a trail across the hunting grounds but never a foot inside camp. Only fools dream of the pronghorn on earth where the grizzly prowls. Will these Lakotah never wake up?

After a while a certain Siyo had spoken, a man who had seen delays if everyone went back to the river. He had proposed a small horseback group, without children or drags, perhaps twenty peacemen and twenty warriors.

The deciders, hearing approbation inside the lodge and out, soon had announced that leaders of the bands and principal akicita start at dawn for the muddy river, a party of forty, half from the Siyo, half from the Mahto.

But I will not go. Olepi had remembered that a dream prevented his visiting this river. Instead I will have two Mahto sitting in my place, one man going as my voice and the second man—someone the people choose—going as a witness.

His next thought the Mahto leader had expressed aloud: let the Lakotah show friendliness at this meeting with the whitemen only if friendliness appears the wise course.

Forty had gone out the next day. Hinyete, leader of the diminishing Siyo band had ridden front and alongside him Wanapin, the Shirtman carrying his Shirt in a roll of bark. Four members of the Siyo Tokala rode next in line, and back of those persons, ten warrior-horsebacks. Peźi and three more scouts had accompanied the Siyo group, twenty representatives in all as the deciders had determined.

The Mahto also had sent twenty, Wanaǵi forward, Ahbleza at his side. But Olepi had appointed the sacred-man, not his son, as his mouth or his hand, whichever this meeting with the hairy-faces called for. And, responding to their leader's request, the people had chosen Icabu as the second principal for the Mahto.

Źola and Iku had represented the Tokala within the Mahto band, two more members of this lodge also going, each one wearing, as an ornament, a string of fingers cut off an enemy. The people had wanted Peśla's fierce countenance at this meeting with whites, members of his Ihoka-lodge keeping him company, but they also had wanted peacemakers—Hinhan and Catka and Pasu and the bone-healer Huhupiye in this group.

The forty had reached the big encampment one day ahead of the paleskins and so they had seen these strangers approach, eight boats waddling up the river. They had honored these water-travelers with a feast of dog-meat, after which sign-talkers and Dakotah-speaking whites had revealed that this certain day lived in the memory record of the whitemen who sat here as a most important occasion, as a sacred-day, one which they always celebrated: fifty winters in the past these whitemen had defied an enemy and declared independence. Then had come a great battle, eight winters to the day from start to finish.

The Lakotah, attentive to the description of this long running-fight, had marveled such a contest, but they had tried to appear calm when the strangers shot off guns that honored the memory of this victory. Nor had they displayed awe for the red-and-white banner that these strangers called our-flag.

Even so, the demonstration had impressed the tribes,

and so their leaders and head warriors had touched-the-stick, not a man showing reluctance to make his mark on the dry leaf where the white finger pointed. Why hesitate? The Oyateyamni had signed at white-paint creek, and the Sicaṅgu and Wiciyela had made their marks at an encampment below the river's bend. None of these persons had distrusted the little black talking-signs.

But Ahbleza had not stood present when Wanaǧi and afterwards Icabu—the itancan giving a different name—had signed; the Shirtman had not desired witnessing the ceremony.

Then after ten days the Mahto-Śiyo party had returned, the travelers apparently a little puzzled over the whole thing. Hinyete and Wanaǧi had spoken in council, the Śiyo giving details, the wakanhca saying only that he had made the cross-mark after hearing all but one Mahto agree to the signing.

Wanaǧi had not named the dissenting voice, but Ahbleza, speaking next, had identified himself as the absentee. He had told of climbing to a high place on the cliffs, of looking down on the gathering—perhaps three thousand Lakotah and Canoni, perhaps four hundred whitemen. Yet he had remembered but one detail, something that stayed with him wherever his thoughts turned. He had seen the faces of those whitemen as they looked upon their flag, the symbol of their nations, and so he had recognized that they regarded this fluttering color in the same manner that the Lakotah regarded the pipe.

"And wherever they raise this flag, the translator tells, they take hold. Even now they speak saying that all Lakotah hunt on ground that belongs to the whiteman. They say that from this day forward the whites shall protect the Lakotah—and for good reason: the Lakotah accepts the whiteman as his superior, as his protector, as his father and grandfather.

"Now understand me, my relatives. I never shall agree that someone not of my choice acts as my protector or decides for me. And so I demonstrate: the Psa whose life I protect through hunka shall return at will to his own people. True, I regard him as brother and I never knowingly shall attack him. But neither shall I live for him nor see him live for me. Certainly he never has any say as to his choice."

Sounds of surprise had answered the Shirtman's speech, also tones of anger.

The next instant Peśla had jumped to his feet, his voice scornful: "Hear, my relatives. Who says that the Titonwan shall recognize these whites as sit-above? Or accept these strangers as protectors? Certainly not I. Yet I agree to this signing. The dry leaf gives protection to traders, but if an enemy comes here looking for trade, the leaf asks that the Titonwan let the whiteman make the kill.

"True, these whites ask that the Titonwan not intercept the stranger who travels on Titonwan hunting ground, but if this dry leaf they call treaty says more than I hear or tricks my ears, I return to the mud-water this summer. I, Peśla, will hunt the red flag with cloud and stars and I will decorate this banner with Lakotah excrement and white-man-hair."

Ahbleza had listened while Peśla and different ones told that which they understood from the treaty. And then the Shirtman had known that none had heard alike. Those traders who interpreted the dry leaf—not one that the wind blows away—had made wild words of something that perhaps overwhelms the Lakotah tribe in the winters ahead. For certainly this leaf recorded the response of a confused tribe who had pledged to permit strangers to decide the Lakotah good.

But will one man who opposes the whole, Ahbleza had asked himself, stop this treaty-signing? Who among the Mahto will agree to wait? Among the Śiyo? Among the three thousand Titonwan and Canoni? True, the tribe respects him as a Shirtman, but they see Wanapin, also a Shirtman, sign the leaf.

The people had talked about this event for a while, but then the whitemen and their talking-leaf had seemed to lose importance. Whoever remembered the signing-day recalled only a most savory dog-feast.

Reviewing the third event among the recent summer's big happenings, Heñaka marveled that he ever considered the other two. Perhaps all winter-count keepers among the Lakotah will choose to record the same memorable occurrence, something that had affected everyone, a disaster that had perpetrated disaster, a tragedy they now referred to as the "drowning of thirty lodges."

Picking up his drawing-stick, the old man began to mark the hide, recalling legend and fact as he drew.

The story-tellers told that creatures with tail and horns live underwater, certain ones hurling up mud to make new ground, different ones surfacing to break up the river ice. Occasionally the mischiefs among this mysterious group will push water toward low ground, making waves that flow over the flats, perhaps drowning an overnight camp. And so the people had understood that which happened in a snug bend of the muddy river on a certain night during the ice-breaking moon.

A warm wind had blown across the frozen edges of the river, the survivors had told, the water spirits coming playfully to the top. They had floated big pieces of ice downstream and had laughed on seeing the water pour over the earth. Then, observing a little Wiciyela camp, they had decided to play at shoving-ice-against-lodges.

The people had awakened to the ice crowding their wet tipi. Some persons had managed to get out of the way, but the water had swept along most families, parents struggling to push little ones into trees and then climb the slippery ice before the flood grabbed hold again. But all these persons had drowned—women, children, and men.

Not only Wiciyela had slept in this destroyed camp; Wiyukcan Mani, wife to Iśna, had traveled with these unfortunate people, the woman returning from a visit with Canoni relatives who stayed south of the earth-smoke. And so when the water creatures drowned the overnight camp, they swallowed this Kuya mother of five along with the Wiciyela tiyośpaye.

Wiyukcan Mani had left her children in Hinziwin's care, the Kuya leader's family camped along the muddy river near the Lookout, a trader's place with an ample supply of firewater. And so Iśna had lain sleeping after three, four days of drinking when newscarriers brought in the frightening account.

Hinziwin had tried to arouse the man, but, opening one red eye to see who dared disturb him, he had flung off the woman. And so she had thrown small robes over the children, hurrying these young ones to the trader's place. Here the newsmen had repeated the story and here Hinziwin's wails had mingled with the many bewailing.

But the daughter of Sinte had wailed for herself, not the drowned mother. Five children not her own now depended on her care along with a man indifferent to all but the burning-drink. Then why, she had asked herself, cut her long hair and make gashes on her body and so plunge into a grief she will not feel? Certainly she shall regain her good looks if ever she escapes Iśna's influence, but not if she scars her person or abuses her hair or stays as a trade item for the keg her husband craves.

At these thoughts the woman had covered her head; she felt red drops falling from her heart.

When finally Iśna rolled off his sleeping robes, he had found an empty lodge and a pile of cold ashes. He had crawled out of the tipi, looking for the balmy air to clear his head. After a while he had walked slowly toward the trader's place.

And so the trader became the one to tell him. But nothing about the Kuya's face had revealed that he understood what had happened, that his wife and thirty lodges had drowned. He had looked only briefly upon the sorrowing ones, then shuffled away.

But his steps had grown firm as he walked among the lodges of his people. And listening to the grieving for his wife, his eyes reflected a dull anger.

Returning to the tipi, he had found Hinziwin staring at the dead fire circle. He had spoken sharply, ordering the woman to find the children and take all five to Ośota, this man a Canoni relative of the drowned mother, Ośota here as a visitor in the Kuya camp.

Hinziwin, glancing at the man's face, had obeyed promptly. She saw that Iśna had regained himself, the robe of dignity once more upon his shoulders. And viewing the change, the woman had marveled the contrast. Why will he desire the crooked path, she had wondered; why will he turn over his power to the fiery water?

But not eager to stay with Iśna this night, Hinziwin had lingered with Ośota's family until someone had hinted that a sorrowing man sat alone in a different lodge, perhaps hungering for a companion if not for meat. Then Hinziwin had scuttled back across camp, a little fearful of the manner in which the husband intended to receive her.

Iśna had sat hunched at the dead fire, some ashes thrown into his black hair. And so Hinziwin had moved quietly about the tipi; she had wanted to go unnoticed. But before she had put out his meat, the man had gestured her crudely to the sleeping robe.

He had used her as a man in unnatural mood perhaps will use a woman, his violence frightening her and her fear making him more violent. He became as ten men taking a woman on the grass.

Afterwards he had pulled her from the robe and, lifting his knife, had begun cutting her hair. She had whimpered but dared not resist. He had not stopped at making shreds of her braids; he had cut her long heavy hair to the scalp. Then raising the knife over her arms and ignoring her pathetic cries, he had made deep gashes in her shoulders. Next, he had made cuts in her legs below the knee.

"Now you grieve properly," he had said and pushed her away.

Desperate, rolling in every direction, she had left a trail of blood wherever she moved. But Iśna, without a second glance, had gone out of the lodge. Nor had he returned for five days.

Hurting from his brutal use and ashamed to show herself outside the tipi, Hinziwin had lain on her robes wailing. Her tipi-alone days came upon her, but she had not gone to the woman's retreat; she had remained on the robe, dry blood mixing with fresh.

On Iśna's return, the smell in the tipi revealed that the woman had stayed during her iśnati, her presence on those days defiling his weapons which hung at the back. And so he had used his quirt to whip her, then pushed her out of the lodge.

She had crawled back inside the place; she had preferred a second whipping to the shame of baldness and a bruised body.

For the next two days the Kuya had spoken nothing to Hinziwin; motions or a stern glance had expressed his requests, and he had requested only those things one asks of

909

an old woman who helps around the lodge. But when finally he had spoken, his words had thrown Hinziwin into true despondency.

"The mother of my children dies yet you live. But you shall not live with me. I am returning you to your father's lodge. Take the fast trail north. I send someone with you."

When she neither spoke nor gathered up her things, Iśna had thrown her gowns, moccasins, ornaments onto a robe which he then rolled and tied and set outside.

Presently two old persons—a man and a woman—had appeared in front of the lodge, a drag tied to their horse, everything ready for moving.

Covering her head, her shoulders bent in the manner of the aged, Hinziwin had stepped out of the entrance flap. In response to the old woman's gesture, she had tied her bundle on the drag. And when the horse moved forward, she had walked alongside. And so she had begun the trail across the quickly melting snow to the Sicangu villages up on the earth-smoke river, three or more days distant.

At the start of her travel, the young woman had walked singing, but her song had not raised anyone's heart.

"I walk a difficult path," she had sung, her eyes looking down, her voice thin and mournful. "I am hurt deeply. I know not why he trades me for the burning-drink, why he makes a fool-woman out of me." Her final tone had come out as a long, sad sigh.

The old people who accompanied her never once saw Hinziwin's face; the young woman had kept a cover over her head. A denying motion refused any food they offered her and she had slept rolled tight against the side of the little travel tipi.

The morning of the second day a sharp wind had bitten at the travelers' cheeks, the going not easy. And so they had rested more often than usual. Then, during one of those rests, Hinziwin, singing again her woeful song, had wandered away, her companions not really surprised at her disappearance.

After a while the old woman had gone among the trees looking for the lost one. Nor had she sensed any shock on discovering Hinziwin's body hanging from a strong branch. But the sight of the young woman's head almost bare of hair had brought a cry to her lips. "I-i-i-i-ya," she had moaned and run back for the old man.

Together they had cut down the strangled one, then lashed the body firmly to the drag. And so they returned Hinziwin to the lodge of her father.

Sinte had received his daughter's body with bitter face; long before now the spare, wrinkled Sicangu had named the fool's water an enemy of the Lakotah. And so, fully aware why this young woman had sought the tree, the father had struggled for composure against those thoughts that will send him out to strike down a tribesman.

Soon after the corpse-carriers had arrived, a grieving camp had mingled their moans and wails with a howling wind while Sinte offered his daughter's remains to the forks in a budding tree.

Then slowly the people had followed Sinte back to camp, where the father had laid crossed sticks in front of his lodge; he had wanted to sit alone.

And alone he had sat, his heart at war with those strangers who had brought a fermenting drink among the Lakotah, those whites who had made a fool of Iśna, of a man whose blood lacked a defense against the mysterious water the waśicun call whiskey.

A mysterious water, the people soon learned, that had made not only a fool of Iśna but a dead man. For the tree holding Hinziwin's body had not yet leafed when the news came of Iśna's death. One more sip from the burning cup and the Kuya had dropped sprawling outside the trader's place, his head striking against a boulder.

None had walked near his body until evening; they had imagined that the man had staggered and fallen as often happened. But then at dusk Iśna's little son had pulled Ośota's wife to the scene. His father, he had said, will not wake up and play with him.

Heñaka, looking at his picture for the memory record, knew that the people will need to tell and retell the story if they desired to remember the whole. For his little sketch told only that the river choked up with broken ice and flowed into the low places, thirty lodges drowned.

But he knew that something different will help the

911

Sicaṅǧu and certain Mahto remember this story as long as they live. For the people already called the place where Hinziwin took her life hanging-woman creek.

True, some different streams owned the same name, but none other called to remembrance the favorite wife of two great leaders among the Lakotah, none other commemorated a pretty girl with a strand of yellow hair, a most pretty girl but one who never really became a woman.

Wahinhan: snow falling, snow falling softly, quietly as a feather falls, a hushed-wing feather.

Snow, deepening and drifting, covering stone and tree; man walking on webbed feet, creatures floundering in the drifts. Snow, whirling snow, blizzard snow, two-leggeds and four wandering off the trail, lost in the deep.

Snow, a white robe protecting the grasses, a white glare blinding the eyes; snow, eight moons of this white cold, thin or deep, in every season.

And so they will remember the winters when they count the seasons.

But who dared say, watching Heȟaka put away the winter-count hide, that during the next three winters the snow will fall most deep, that for the next three winters the people shall talk mostly about the snow piling up, the many frostbites, the many snow-blind eyes—even among the camp-dogs.

And who dared say that during the next three winters, moons of shivering cold will bring back the old Dakotah way of storytelling, the grandfathers relating and the young repeating those legends that recall the brave, the exciting, the amusing, the wonderful, past.

Three winters coming, each one deep and cold. But none had dared prophesy, none had dared say so.

The Titonwan had camped that third snowy winter with none but their own for company, not a single camp of Sahiela within visiting distance. Apparently these red-talkers had found a winter campground more to their liking on that fat-meat earth where they had hunted pte in recent summers.

But then, a new season in the making, one Sahiela band had reappeared, the people camping two, three nights at grizzly butte. And among those persons, someone the Sahiela regarded as their most reliable pronghorn-caller: an old wapiya to whom a pronghorn once gave a song, once offered his pawing-foot. And now they go north of the butte, these people had told, to the pronghorn-pit river, where the caller will choose an old trap—one from those seasons before horses—and here exercise his skill for attracting the sandy-belly. Suddenly the Sahiela had invited their Titonwan friends to come along, to join in this effort to make an impressive catch. But let the Lakotah understand: they trap for meat. Certainly they will take hides, but after three scarce winters they kill to eat. The wapiya says so.

Families from each of the Titonwan bands had gone with the Sahiela, seventy Lakotah lodges in all, the women singing their excitement; not only will this experience provide meat and new gowns, shirts and leg-covers, but they will help make the kill, something to talk about in the seasons ahead. True, the Sahiela perhaps pit more pronghorn during the snow seasons when these creatures gather in big bands, but even in this new-grass moon certain bands stay together. Already they shed the coarse hollow hair, drop young, and start fattening and so they will prove easy to attract.

The Sahiela had guided the Titonwan to a place where two branches of the young river came together, where someone once had dug a hole big enough to trap one hundred pronghorn. Here these people had worked as the wapiya instructed, tightly piling up brush along the edges of the two small streams, extending this tight line far up each stream, making the path that will direct the pronghorn to the pit. Next, they had dug shallow depressions back of this brush, a place to hide while waiting for the creature bands. And finally they had made clubs for killing this meat.

Most Titonwan never had caught pronghorn in this manner but they had understood the importance of ceremony, of that which went on inside the Sahiela sacred-lodge, where the old wapiya, painted to resemble a pronghorn, sought agreement from the powers in each direction. And they had listened quietly when this same one appeared outside the lodge, singing his song in front of the pit, alongside the rows of brush. After a while the wapiya had sent two young men far out onto the flat, each one carrying a long, pliant pole, a hoop attached, four black feathers dangling from the hoop. Before long, the waiting people had heard the small, high voice that travels a far distance; the young men called out that the pronghorn came, that meat ran toward the pit. But only after the pronghorn had come onto the path between the lines of brush had the trappers rushed forward to close the opening back of the frightened creatures. And so the pronghorn, stumbling over one another and breaking bones, had fallen crying into the pit. And then many persons had jumped into the hole, clubbing the heads of those creatures not killed in the fall.

Something to talk about in the seasons ahead, the Titonwan had said, the Mahto had said. And certainly the Mahto had talked, these people remembering that the old Sahiela wapiya had chosen those two look-alike scouts, those Mahto brothers who owned the same name—Cekpa— to carry the pole-and-hoop, the 'pronghorn arrows' far out on the plain, these Mahto look-alikes making use of their persuasive powers as the wapiya had intended.

IX

THE MORNING smelled yellow and crisp south of the river shell, the air tart with berries ripe and overripe. At a campsite along scout creek boys and men had bathed briskly, and now, gathering at the edge of the village, they watched a dust-cloud, something different from the small spirals as when pte approach water; this dust disclosed that horses and pointers—those men who drive captured horses—approached the Sahiela camp.

Miyaca had led a party far south of his camp, south and east toward the briny black lake, toward bunch-of-timbers creek, where many ungentled horses roamed. Then at dawn this day, scouts had signaled that the principal horsecatcher returned, his party bringing in a big catch.

Ahbleza rode in this Sahiela expedition, Miyaca inviting the Shirtman—a visitor in his village—to accompany the group. Ahbleza had known that Miyaca cared nothing for raids and scalping, that the Sahiela horseman found his excitement in capturing those horses who ran loose in the sandhills. The people claimed that Miyaca had a nose for smelling the herd before the herd caught his scent. And after ten days on the trail with this Sahiela friend of his child-seasons, Ahbleza agreed.

And now the men came riding into camp, the people cheering this roundup of many fine seed-horses and perhaps another eighty ready to receive seeds, enough horses in this captured band to revive the village herd.

The Shirtman had chosen to stay three, four more days in the elated camp, joining in the trades, the racing, the betting that always marked Miyaca's return. But he intended to present his share of the captured horses to any Suhtai families living in this village and so silently honor his dead wife's memory. One horse he will keep—a seed-horse not yet four winters, a creature smooth and shining red, mane and tail black as charred wood, a horse to replace Tatezi.

The day came for returning to the Mahto villages, Ahbleza pleased that Miyaca and one of his sons had decided to accompany him halfway to the earth-smoke; the Sahiela wished to visit relatives who never wandered across the spreading-waters.

The three rode a familiar trail, traveling along the sand and sage and prickly leaf of the great south fork of the shell, then onto the sand and sage and bluffs between the great north fork and the spreading-waters, the running-river.

At a place where the winged longnecks flocked during the change of moons from warm to cold, they stopped for a smoke. Here Miyaca's son went off to tease a village of pinspinza, the boy carrying a stick and making a game of his attack on these elusive, chirping burrowers; striking one counted as a war honor and catching one meant that he captured an enemy.

The friends had watched for a while, Miyaca saying that these little creatures all looked alike to him. "And yet they know which ones guard their village. See those tails shake at each chirp? But now my son creeps up and instantly each one goes into hiding."

Before Ahbleza sounded the soft grunt of warning, Miyaca had sensed that something more than a boy's approach sent the pinspinza vanishing down their holes, the boy perhaps also running down a burrow, so quickly had he disappeared.

The next moment the two men stood alongside their horses, Ahbleza holding mouth and nose of his recently gentled mount, Miyaca making the calming shuh-shuh sound while he watched a strange scene near the river, three flights of an arrow from the spot on which he stood.

In view two whitemen, horseback and leading a procession of eight pack horses. And following these eight, something to make a man clasp his hand over his mouth: four big hoops turning, two on each side of some flatwood, a pile of bundles on the wood and four mules pulling the load.

Canpahmiyan, Ahbleza told himself; rolling-wood, the whiteman's wagon. Canpahmiyan, wood-rolling-on.

"Wihio," Miyaca said aloud; again the paleskins, tricky as spiders, cross his path with something clever. But why these strangers on a moccasin trail? Perhaps brothers to the little whiteman who keeps a post close to the mountains but who schemes a big post on the fat-meat earth? Rumors about these brothers already arouse Sahiela curiosity.

Watching the wobbly hoops that creaked over the grass, Miyaca sensed something more than interest in the travelers; he felt an irritation mixed with fear. He and the Shirtman easily will intercept these horsebacks but for what purpose? Neither he nor his friend Ahbleza look for scalps and who wants to own the noisily rolling hoops? This wood rolls over old summer's yellow grass and dry earth, but what happens, certain persons already ask, when these hoops roll over deep sand or sticky mud? Or on snow and ice, uphill, and across stony ground? Will the rolling-wood prove more effectual than the poles which a horse drags comfortably on wet earth or dry, in all weathers and across rough places and smooth?

Ahbleza had found different thoughts as he observed these whitemen, the party moving along the river, hunting a place to cross. He remembered back five winters to those treaty-bringers on the muddy river; they had spoken of such hoops saying 'wheels,' yet they had pointed at that which carried their party on water. Men turned the paddle-wheels, they had told, when traveling shallow rivers but something different turned the wheels when they traveled wide and deep. Will they mean these mules, Ahbleza wondered now, when they say that something different turns the wheels? And will wide and deep refer to the plain, to the short grasses and the mixed?

Neither the Titonwan nor the Sahiela had spoken his thoughts, but a glance, a gesture had told that they saw in a similar manner.

"My friend," Miyaca said slowly, "the people of my band desire staying south of the red-shield river. They ask that I find a winter camp along the bunch-of-timber or perhaps sand creek." The speaker's eyes sought the far distance: "I know not whether I ever return to the black hills. The people say that they want warm ground, more summer for their young children, more grass for horses, more meat for everyone. They prefer this earth-of-the-sitting-down-pte, this fat-meat earth."

Miyaca paused, then went on: "Perhaps the Mahto one day also will roam here and raise lodges nearby my camp. I see meat enough for all until . . . "—he turned an unsmiling face in the direction of the whitemen and their wagon—"until such season as certain intruders come seeking the tongue of every young pte. Who knows but what these crafty persons shall discover an amazing use for pte-tongues."

The Sahiela's son had come running up, but he awaited the finish of his father's speech before reciting that which he had witnessed. Now, eyes shining excitement, he reported that the rolling-wood stays on the opposite side of the water, the horsebacks testing the sandy river bottom, shaking their heads in a funny way. Perhaps they wait and see where the branched-horns cross over?

Listening to the boy, the two friends again had agreed; what difference whether or not this wagon crosses the river?

The next one, or the next, will get across. Always the whiteman will get where he chooses to go; the treaty says so.

And now, as suddenly and indifferently as birds flit tree to tree, the friends separate, the Sahiela turning west and Ahbleza going north. And for a while the Mahto led his new horse, man and creature discovering each other's ways as they traveled toward Sicaṅgu hunting grounds.

Crossing the ridges but keeping below the crest, Ahbleza had followed a trail to the earth-smoke river, then out to the butte known as hill-in-the-woods, a favored campsite of the Tiśayaota band; the Shirtman had decided to visit overnight in this Sicaṅgu camp of red-top lodges.

He found the red-tops and, encouraged to stay, remained five nights. The people, recognized for the many fast horses in their herd and the many young horsecatchers in camp, invited the Mahto to compete in their races and to talk of his experiences among the Sahiela, especially about Miyaca's way for trapping horses. What cover will this Sahiela use for rubbing out the man-smell? For coaxing a herd-leader within reach of the loop? And what about cutting out the seed to quiet a horse?

And so, sitting on robes in Nuǵe's lodge—Nuǵe now living with his wife's band—Ahbleza told of Miyaca's amazing schemes for capturing the loose and ungentled herds.

And then the Shirtman spoke of the great pte-herds that grazed to the south, certainly something to interest these Sicaṅgu who told that they had hunted out their own roving grounds on the earth-smoke, the orderly summer hunts and the pronghorn drives a thing of the past.

Neglecting the tribal circle for more seasons than anyone cared to name, the Sicaṅgu had experienced some starving winters. True, certain bands had come together during the warm moons but always within drinking-distance of the traders, and Makatoźanźan had not yet persuaded all Sicaṅgu to get back into a hoop of their own. And so the Tiśayaota village had seen need to hide their dry meat and berries underground, one way to guard against lean moons and the improvident among their own relatives.

Saddened at this view of his kinsmen, Ahbleza hinted that these red-top lodges consider a winter in some valley south of the shell; instead of the muddy river, why not go south to the fat-meat earth?

Suddenly the Shirtman realized that he sat talking as his father often talked. And for the same reason: to keep all Lakotah away from the mud-water. His aversion to the trading places on the muddy river had increased noticeably since the Kuya's shameful death and the regrettable act Hinziwin had performed; he had recognized the danger on the big river as something powerful enough to break the Lakotah hoop.

But even as he talked with these red-top Sicanǧu, Ahbleza kept seeing the wagon that had bumped along the edge of the spreading-waters, rolling-wood packed with bundles and going somewhere, perhaps anywhere.

Then all at once the picture grew sharp, a sharpness that brought sudden awareness: those friendly words on the dry leaf permitted the whitemen to bring their trade items to the Lakotah wherever, whenever the Lakotah showed an indifference toward visiting the trader's place. Perhaps, the Shirtman told himself, they intend to roll the firewater to the very flaps of the lodges.

Toward dusk on his third day among the red-tops, Hewanźi's camp of Mnikooźu arrived for a visit with their relatives, and, during a smoke at the evening fires, these guests disclosed some important news. At the forks of the good river, they told, whitemen make an earth-lodge trading-place, three horsebacks with packs already at work, more men and packs coming on a different trail, this second group of whitemen bringing a wagon. And everything on the wagon, for trading with Mnikooźu and Sahiela.

But soon, these visitors went on to tell, a different company of traders will make a deadwood post near the Sicanǧu, near the hill-in-the-woods. And everything on this next wagon goes to the Tiśayaota and other Sicanǧu.

Until now Ahbleza had not mentioned the scene he and Miyaca had witnessed, but now he spoke of the 'wagon,' the whiteman's word rolling uncomfortably off his tongue. And he told of the big timbers along the river of pelts, where, rumor says, whitemen brothers make out of mud what they call 'fort.' Here a place to trade robes but not for the burning-drink.

And now the Tiśayaota became greatly excited; why not go to the fat-meat earth and not only chase horses and kill pte but also visit those brothers who raise the trading post? Why sit here waiting for the beards to put up something at the nearby butte?

The enthusiastic spirit took hold of the Mnikooźu, and soon Hewanźi listened for a hint, something to imply that the Tiśayaota looked for him to accompany their lodges, the two villages traveling south together. Or perhaps, Hewanźi told himself, he will bring together two, three hundred Mnikooźu families and persuade these persons to go south as a band, he their leader.

But Hewanźi need wait neither for hint nor scheme; someone came bringing him the invitation he sought, someone who arrived before the Mahto Shirtman had ridden off. For even as Ahbleza sat his horse, ready to head back to his own camps, scouts signaled the approach of two horsebacks, two whitemen horseback.

The Sicangu had not intercepted any whites since the treaty-signing for the reason that they had not seen any whites. And now they stood hesitant, unwilling to perform any imprudent act; why chase off someone who perhaps brings news about one or more of those new trading posts?

And so they waited, bows handy but unstrung, women and children running off to hide in the trees along the stream at the bottom of the butte.

The Shirtman sat his horse exactly as when the scouts announced these horsebacks, the principal Sicangu soon mounting and coming to wait alongside him.

But Hewanźi, his profuse hair magnificently arranged on top his head, looked so much the leader of the whole camp that the two whitemen rode over to him. And to this Mnikooźu they delivered the invitation they had come here to extend.

They invite, they said, this Titonwan camp to visit the Bent brothers' fort on the Arkansas.

Twice and twice again they spoke their invitation using hand-talk and mouth until finally the stonily aloof faces gave evidence of recognizing Bent as a man, fort as a trading post, Arkansa as the river they call "wahin wakpa,' river of pelts.

But whatever their recent eagerness to pull down tipi and start south at once, the leaders of the red-top lodges advised their people to stay awhile at the butte, to dig deep holes for their watertight meat wrappers and berry containers. Then if this fat-meat earth proves not so fat or those Bent brothers not so brotherly, the Tiśayaota will have food waiting here, underground and undiscovered.

Upon his return, Ahbleza reported to the Mahto leader concerning the whiteman's desire that the Titonwan come to Bents' place.

Olepi sat, face closed, as the Shirtman described those trades about which the whitemen had talked: finger, ear, neck, and arm ornaments—those remarkable ornaments that the Śinagleglega, the striped-robe tribe, make out of metal and stone; also amazingly colorful shells and red 'cloth.' And iron for arrowheads, along with axes and knives. And more guns and powder than usually on hand at a trading post.

But not until Ahbleza mentioned those traders who schemed to open new posts on grass-lodge creek, rapid and berry creeks, on the earth-smoke and on the good river, also at important buttes and near the white cliffs, had Olepi indicated in any way that he listened, that he heard. Now his eyes widened, flaring anger and dangerous.

Quickly, then, the son told everything he had learned.

"My father, the whitemen say that they bring the trade to these places as a favor to the Lakotah. This way the bands stay together, none making the far-distant walk to the muddy river."

"Far-distant walk." Olepi had spit out the phrase. "Will they never understand that Lakotah walk half this distance for the joy in walking?"

The Mahto growled his next words: "Will the puny waśicun regard the Lakotah as a people without reasoning power?"

He paused, then went on in firm, even tones: "These whites want hides—hides or pelts, tough hairs or fine—for a use I not yet understand. But whatever the use, this thing carries enough importance that each group of traders competes for the Lakotah trade.

"They look not to Lakotah comfort; they look out for

their own pale skins. And they will resort to any tactic—especially the fool's water—in this contest for getting Lakotah, Sahiela, and any tribe into an agreement.

"As for those white brothers and all their grandchildren, onze wicawahu."

Afterwards, sitting with the principals in his villages, Olepi had more to say: "If these traders come here, the Lakotah throw away those moons they call men-in-the-lodges. The wasicun will urge that the people keep on hunting, cold moons and warm. They will encourage trapping and killing on those days when properly the Lakotah sit as a family, wives and children and relatives at the lodge-fire, at those fires where the old tell war stories and the young listen to the greatness of the past.

"And when the pte see that the Lakotah change their scheme of living, the herd will ignore the people as relatives; the herd will go away and let the people starve.

"And so the whiteman will run up with a handout, a handout and a new way of life. And the Lakotah, fearing that his children starve, will eat out of this stinking white hand."

When his listeners hinted that the Mahto leader tell in what manner he will rid the streams and plains of these traders and yet obtain those items that prove most desirable, Olepi had advised that they reflect on those items they call most desirable.

At the final summer council, Olepi had spoken yet more bitterly, the Mahto convinced that the Lakotah always shall respond unfavorably to the whiteman's drink.

"The wasicun desires weaning the Lakotah—women along with men—from the warm mild broths and the refreshing leaf-drinks. They want the Titonwan demanding fool's water, letting go horses, robes, wives and daughters, anything, in return for a third, fourth gulp of their fire.

"Will you go out looking for the day, my relatives, when you crave not guns or beads, not knives or paint, but instead the yellow mystery-water, something neither your head nor heart ever will tolerate?

"They say that the Psatoka never permit a trader in their camps. Nor will they drink his drink. Perhaps the Titonwan need to make friends with an old enemy for the purpose of discovering a power against the wasicun."

Ahbleza had heard many strong voices joining in with his father's views but not enough voices to rule out the trader.

The hoop had dispersed following this council, the bands seeking wooded valleys for the winter moons, each village much more concerned about procuring fresh meat during the approaching snows than about whitemen who not yet invade their hunting grounds, who not yet show their faces in a Mahto camp.

X

THE MAHTO had raised their winter lodges a considerable distance up the north fork of the good river, in the vicinity of the snowy hills and not far from the roaming ground of the Psa. Two buttes side by side, one big and one small, had prompted the people to name this new campsite 'sits-with-young-one.' But Ahbleza had surmised that something more than these interesting natural features had persuaded his father to choose this location; certainly Olepi had considered the fact that the Psa never permit white traders near their camps and so a Titonwan band camping nearby the snowy hills will not encounter any such strangers.

But sitting at his tipi fire, listening to the popping trees and cracking ground, the Shirtman had pondered many things relating to the whiteman; the long nights under a hard-face moon had accorded him unhurried observations and slow decisions. Even so, his most important decision during this midwinter night related neither to the whiteman nor the waning power within the tribe; that which he had decided concerned only himself and the woman Kipanna.

She had lived in this lodge six winters but not as his wife. Thin of face and lacking the gaiety becoming to a woman of twenty-and-one winters, she sat bound to this tipi as caretaker, as firemaker, occasionally as a companion, but never anything more. Certainly he deprived this woman of a chance to fulfill herself as wife, as mother. Her young heart demanded a young husband, someone who will act toward her as a mate, someone who will fondle her and awaken her laughter and appreciate her as his woman.

He had known—perhaps from the day of his sun-gazing—that not again will he share a robe with woman. But what reason shall he give for sending Kipanna out of his lodge? And where will she go? An orphan-child they adopt and to a lonely old woman they offer a sleeping place at the tipi entrance.

Certainly they call Kipanna neither child nor old woman. And so, if she goes to a different lodge, she goes as wife. But what man will look twice at a woman whom, so far as the people know, Ahbleza calls 'mitawicu'?

The day before, sitting with Wanaġi, he had spoken most respectfully of his concern over Kipanna. Gladly, he had told, he will release her from the obligation she imposes upon herself but not if his act offends.

Offends whom, Wanaġi had asked. Obligation binds a horse-tender to the herd for the duration of his watch but will not award the youth with a fondness for horses. Perhaps Kipanna's dull eyes hint that she finds nothing pleasant now in that which she once regards as an obligation to her dead sister's husband? And perhaps Ahbleza merely pretends pleasure in the role he affects toward this young woman? Will the Shirtman not see that he offends his true-self when he attempts to reconcile obligation and joy, when he permits a situation that represents neither his heart nor hers?

For an instant Ahbleza had thought to protest. When they say that a Shirtman shall remember himself as hunka to the tribe, will they not look for him to enjoy this obligation as a relative to all?

But the next moment he had answered himself: neither birth nor custom had forced the Shirt upon him; he had gone out looking for this award. And he had gone out knowing that the Shirt imposes a bond even as his vision imposes a bond and that he needs to find joy, not constraint, in these ties.

And Kipanna? What shall become of this woman who

lays aside her personal desires in an effort to dissipate the sorrow in a man whose sorrow will not dissipate? What joy for Kipanna?

Stepping out of the sacred-man's lodge, Ahbleza had recognized that which he dared not put off another day; he needed only to determine the approach.

The night of ruminating passed, the new day had come and now moved on toward evening. And Ahbleza had not yet acted.

Suddenly he pulled on winter moccasins and started out for his mother's lodge, where he shall arrange to sleep. The next morning he will tell Kipanna that his desire for any sits-alongside-him woman grows cold. Henceforth he directs himself to a single purpose: he shall act remembering only his vision and so guard against whatever, whoever, interferes with the Lakotah way of life; his work—preserving the tribe.

But walking toward Napewaste's lodge, he witnessed something that made certain his talk with Kipanna before nightfall.

The young woman had gone out before dark to gather bark for Ahbleza's horses, the old person in the Shirtman's lodge accompanying Kipanna, the two moving along the stream toward a grove of tall, rustling trees.

At one place along the frozen creek the ice covered a deep hole and here Kipanna knelt to break the cover and wash her face. The cold, cold water brought a glow to her cheeks, and when she moved on, she walked lightly, a little smile on her lips.

Reaching the grove, she decided on the tender bark atop a certain tree; nimbly as a boy, she began to climb. Near the top she settled her back against the strong center-wood and, peeling the slender sticks, dropped the pieces for the old woman to gather.

After a while the old one went off looking for firewood, but Kipanna stayed up in the tree. Slowly, thoughtfully, she pulled off a long strip, but the distant look in her eyes related neither to the bark nor those shaggy horses whose winter hair this bark kept glossy. She remembered, instead, that not many women dared climb to the top of a tree; either they grew too fat or they feared slipping on the icy wood. But she, someone neither fat nor fearful.

She raised her head for a view of the sky above the topmost twigs. And now she wished for wings, for the power to fly away from everyone and everything in this camp and find a new camp, where the people will call her pretty, not pathetic.

After a while she looked below, wondering whether anyone yet stood beneath her tree waiting for her to peel and throw down more bark. And so she saw three girls who fastened bundles onto their dogs and the old woman who now loaded her back with firewood and, in the near distance, a young man.

Certainly none of these persons looked for Kipanna's help, and so, scraping up a handful of snow from the crotch of a branch within easy reach, she touched her tongue against the cold. What a nice thing, she decided, sitting up here and eating snow. Perhaps she will stay instead of climbing down to the dark ground and the solemn pipes of men, to the wails of old women who forever grieve the dead. Or to the loneliness of a Shirtman's lodge.

She wondered next whether anyone even remembered that she sat up in the tree; if she tosses down the snowball, will someone look up?

The ball fell short of the girls and their dogs and to the rear of the old woman who shuffled off with her load. But Kipanna had hit someone; the snow struck the young man as he walked close by her tree.

The man looked around smiling, apparently agreeable to play. But with whom? He glanced curiously at the girls, then at the old woman's back.

Kipanna, watching, stifled her laughter and the young man strutted away as if snowballs fell on top of his head every day.

But now the woman in the tree quickly scraped up the snow that remained in the crotch and, making a second ball, threw this one directly at the man.

The warrior whirled as if an enemy had struck him. Then, hearing a suppressed laugh, he looked up. But he looked up a different tree.

"Come out of hiding, my friend, and I will test my aim

against yours," he challenged, imagining that he called to a boy.

Moving slightly, Kipanna disclosed where she sat. And the man, recognizing who teased him, dropped the snowball he had formed to throw at his attacker. Instead he tossed the woman—Ahbleza's woman—a respectful little joke.

"Perhaps," he said smiling, "I shall send a youth with his blunt arrows after a playful snowbird who teases an unsuspecting warrior."

The young man hurried on, the young woman looking wistfully after him.

After a while she climbed down the tree, lopping off some big branches as she descended, wood that she intended to strip on the ground. But as she jumped onto the snow, she heard someone call and saw that Ahbleza approached. Perhaps the old woman returned without her and so the Shirtman had come looking?

Modestly she gathered up the bark while Ahbleza stood nearby, the man suddenly making talk about her orderly ways and his approval of her as a shy and pleasing young woman. Yet something about his speech disturbed Kipanna; perhaps he had seen her throw the snowball, the act of a child. . . .

The man went on talking, and when he mentioned her young heart and his old one, she began to see that he meant something more than throwing snowballs.

Next, he told of his intent to remove himself to another lodge—his mother's lodge—but reassured her of the tribe's respect after their separation. And when she discovers someone whom she truly desires, he will make certain that the fortunate man learns of her interest.

At the start of his speech, Kipanna resented his words; she heard only that he threw her away after these six winters as nothing more than his lodgekeeper. But after a while her heart began to flutter strangely, like a captured bird whose wings they untie and let fly away. Perhaps, as the Shirtman hinted, she will discover an attractive young man, someone who will look at her affectionately, someone who will call her wife and desire her as the mother of his child, someone she will call husband and know that his heart belongs to her.

Glancing up at Ahbleza, she smiled. And the Shirtman, seeing the smile and the sudden brightness in her eyes, felt his own heart lighten.

Ahbleza scarcely had settled himself in his parents' lodge when newsmen came into the Mahto camp bringing word of the Tiśayaota. The red-top village had visited the site of Bent's fort, but Little Whiteman had warned away the people; the scabby disease walked this ground. Afterwards, a surprise encounter with the Pani had affected their scheme to linger in the south. Rumor told that the Palani had joined their Pani relatives, the whole tribe coming together. The Tiśayaota had taken four spotted mules from a small band of Pani, but any encounters with the whole, with this new strength, seemed certain to bring on killings.

The newsmen told also that a Śahiela woman of high standing had agreed to accept Little Whiteman as husband, her young sister also agreeing to stay at the big mud fort. But neither woman will come until after the scabby disease goes away and not before they perform certain ceremonies in their band.

"You will hear about more ties like this one," Olepi, sitting with his son, had said afterwards. "The whites will take many Lakotah women, good Lakotah women. Using strong drink or strange tricks, they will throw away the honor of the man and so gain entry to his wife and daughter. And when these women fall, the tribe goes down."

Ahbleza had heard his father, but for the moment his thoughts stayed with the Palani and the danger in renewing confrontations.

Then, even as these two—son and father—sat smoking, Icabu scratched on the lodgeskin, a different pair of newsmen standing alongside him and bringing more trouble-talk. The Pani, they said, had rubbed out a Śahiela hunting camp and the distraught Śahiela bands schemed revenge. They looked for allies; they had sent out a pipe to all friends, their pleaders already talking with the Sicangu.

But why use up strength warring with the Pani? Ahbleza had not spoken his thought but, picturing a serious conflict with those white traders who came close to the black hills, he saw need for a convincing Lakotah front against such trespassers. None of the tribes truly wanted these white invaders—this people of wholly different nature—on the plain or even on the rivers. So will not everyone recognize the importance of establishing a peaceful disposition toward the Palani, toward the Psa, toward any and all tribes who roam the grasses?

Icabu stayed for a second pipe with the Mahto and his son after the newsmen had gone, but the three had kept silent concerning the Sahiela revenge, each man aware that he needed to hunt more thoughts before he spoke.

Before the snows of this same winter had disappeared, something occurred that hinted at difficulties among the Lakotah, trouble from within and not of a stranger's making. A Kiyuksa visited the Mahto camp, a man whose presence foretold intrigue in his own camp.

For what true-reason, Olepi had puzzled, will Tawitko suddenly appear among the Mahto and, going into Cankuna's lodge, start talking with the hunter, then with the hunter's daughter? For what true-reason will Tawitko, leader of the Kiyuksa band, ask that Tacincala become his wife? Certainly this principal Kiyuksa, a man forty-and-one winters and with a daughter near Tacincala's age, will not choose to abandon his band and live among the Mahto as husband to a woman whose name carries neither influence nor chance of influence. So why will Tawitko approach the hunter's daughter?

"For one reason: Tabloka intends to lead the people from here on, his own Kiyuksa and all Titonwan, perhaps all Lakotah." So Olepi answered the perplexed hunter when Ogle came asking for talk and advice.

"Only Tawitko sits in Tabloka's way," he said, "and so he sends out Tawitko to find an acceptable reason for living in a different band. And what more acceptable reason than custom, a man going to live in his wife's tiyośpaye? Who dares question this move? More than one leader takes such a step in seasons past.

"Recall, my friend," Olepi went on after a little pause, "in what manner Tabloka soothes things after he discovers who kills his father. Perhaps these two agree on something back on that day when a son cleanses the killer of this murder. For not only will Tabloka satisfy the people that his kinsman performs the killing as a kindly act but at once he pronounces Tawitko leader of the Kiyuksa. In this clever manner he keeps peace in the family, holding the band together for the day when he, Tabloka, takes over.

"And what thing determines this day?" Olepi's eyes narrowed. "The whites paddle upriver looking for leaders in each band to touch the stick. And Tabloka sees his kinsman stepping forward as the important man of the Kiyuksa.

"Suddenly he needs to contrive a way for removing Tawitko without using a knife, without provoking any bitterness.

"He waits until he remembers the fine-looking woman in the hunter's lodge, in the Mahto band, a woman on whom he holds a claim, a woman he, Tabloka, dares trade off for something. Certainly he will not need her; he already keeps enough wives to grow a new band. His first-born son, not yet five, even now has four brothers and two sisters."

Ogle had heard something in his friend's voice as Olepi spoke these closing phrases, but whether resentment or contempt the hunter dared not say. But he knew that his own lodge had become a place of discontent, each member of the family viewing the Kiyuksa's proposal differently.

Tacincala reluctantly agreed to accept Tawitko providing he stayed on in the Mahto village; she had made clear that never will she live anywhere near Tabloka. True, the young Siyo sungazer, her true interest, had not yet spoken with her and she had wondered whether the difference of three, four winters in their ages disturbed him. A woman of twenty-and-five rarely risked waiting for a certain man, especially a man not yet twenty-and-two.

Pesla, hearing of Tawitko's visit, had shown an angry face in his mother's lodge; not waiting to talk through an old one or a relative, he had demanded that his sister ignore this man.

"What good comes of a tie with this Kiyuksa, whose relative shoves him aside? Will someone use my family as a way for shutting out the Mahto band, someone who views the Mahto camp as a disposing ground, a dump for whatever he will not want around his own camp? Next thing, they will say that the Mahto camp stinks of Kiyuksa discards."

Ogle's gesture against this outburst had not silenced his warrior-son but Pesla had ceased to shout.

"I speak out as the brother who dares influence any sister in this lodge," the warrior said now. "And so I say wait until next summer and see for yourself who leads the Kiyuksa camp. Let my sister wisely enter Tabloka's lodge, where she belongs. Too many seasons she displays a reluctance for joining her sister in a lodge where sits the Titonwan power."

"Perhaps my son needs a wife among the Kiyuksa more than my daughter needs a Kiyuksa husband. What about the woman of whom my son brags in a song during the sungazing?" Ogle spoke sharply, his patience worn thin. But he had not looked for an answer.

After a while Hinhan, brother to Ogle, took his turn with words, this one advising that the tiyośpaye remember him as father-uncle, one of the real deciders in this woman's affairs if he chooses to make use of custom and privilege.

Next, Pasu and Iku, also uncles to Tacincala, used their privilege of uninterrupted speech. Neither one saw anything objectionable about a tie here. Tacincala will grow too old for childbearing, Pasu hinted, if she waits for everything she desires in one man. Tawitko sits alone but for two daughters whose mother dies; perhaps Tacincala gains daughters along with husband.

And now Hinhan made use of the power he previously had withheld: "My niece has two brothers but the one who scouts for this band says nothing. Perhaps he remembers that a woman who goes to any man against her choice will mean a winter camp without meat. And so I ask, why confuse the good daughter of this lodge? Will you, my relatives, make a trade item of this one who bears herself proudly? And if so, what thing will you regard as more important than her personal joy?"

Those persons sitting near Peśla heard an ominous rumble in the warrior's throat, and so, turning their backs to him, they made evident their desire that he remove himself from this meeting, his face and manner pleasing to none.

Angrily the warrior went out of the lodge and for a while the family sat silent, each one regretting the perverseness in Peśla's nature but grateful that Hinhan had kept peace in the circle. And so Ogle prepared a pipe, even the women touching their lips to the stem.

But the hunter, aware that the gathering in his lodge

931

had not resolved anything, went again to Olepi. And as before, the Mahto leader had talked about Kiyuksa power, about Tabloka's chances for gaining a hold on all Lakotah, about Tabloka's growing family. Yet he had not offered the advice Ogle came seeking; he had not advised on anything.

And then, suddenly, Ogle realized that Olepi spoke like a man who has begun to accept defeat after a long struggle.

But in what manner, in what words will he, Ogle the hunter, tell his friend that if ever the people see Olepi weakening—Olepi, symbol of warrior-power—truly, the Titonwan shall go off on a fork that leads to compromise and everlasting difficulty. Tabloka, for all his noise and threat, never inspires anyone, never influences toward a lasting good.

For a moment the hunter gazed upon Olepi's countenance, the leader's handsome face as smooth as in youth but for two, three thin lines across his forehead, a slight deepening in his cheeks. He always will look the warrior, Ogle told himself, whatever his heart.

Putting away his stem and bowl in the pipe holder he had carried here, the hunter now rose and moved toward the tipi flap, his hand reaching out to touch gently on Olepi's shoulder as he passed.

Ahbleza, visiting Tonweya this same evening, returned to his parents' lodge unknowing of Ogle's talk with the Mahto leader. But sensing that despondent spirits had sat at this tipi fire, the Shirtman filled the long-stem pipe and offered his father a smoke.

The two sat until dawn, occasionally talking but mostly watching the wood burn to ash, each man aware of a low-hanging cloud, the sky darkening over camp and tribe, a darkness that will pour down grief and distress.

During the long night, the father had pondered—recalling Wanaǧi's words from a distant past—whether or not Ahbleza truly owned a power for intercepting this threatening cloud, this approaching darkness. For soon the Kiyuksa will take over, a band of destroyers from the beginning, a people who will break their own, family or tribe, a tiyóspaye who throw out the old ways, change the language of the ancients, make up symbols to cover truth, accept trade with strangers. And now a ruler suddenly replacing kinsman-rule. Not the many but a small group with daring and cunning and inflexible resolve bring Tabloka to this unnatural rank, none risking a dispute and some persons living in fear of their lives. And once the people permit a hoop that holds in fear instead of keeping out fear, they damage their own beyond reviving.

But will anyone ever really own the power to stop those persons who choose to destroy a scheme for living that works?

Certainly not I, Olepi answered himself. Talking with the hunter Ogle this evening, he had recognized that suddenly, at sixty-and-one he grew tired.

Then perhaps Ahbleza? But will this Shirtman-son see wherein the danger sits? Or will Ahbleza keep looking outside the tribe? Whatever a man looks for, he sees.

During these many seasons he, Olepi, advises his Mahto that they stay with Lakotah ways, that they ignore the whiteman and so he will go away or get small or in some different manner disappear. But never shall they notice this intruder to the point of warring or making peace; why give any sign that the whiteman exists?

Or so the Mahto leader reasoned with himself, a leader but one without true knowledge of his enemy.

XI

THE SNOWS melted into the grass and the moon of making-fat rose over grizzly butte where three hundred lodges formed a summer hoop, none but the original Titonwan bands—the original Tiyataonwan—in this encampment. Makatoźanźan had managed to bring all Sicanġu into a circle on the earth-smoke, and Hewanźi's band along with other Canoni clustered on a different stream.

The three hundred families—four bands—who gathered below the old butte had granted the site at the horns of the circle to the Kiyuksa, and Tabloka, their new leader, made the most of this commanding position. Impetuous, harsh, arrogant, he bellowed demands not only at his own Kiyuksa but at the Siyo people.

Hinyete's dwindling camp had claimed a space in the hoop, but the leader foresaw a total breakup of his Siyo within the next two, three summers, his head-akicita already bending to Tabloka's orders, the Kiyuksa out to get all the principal warriors and all the outstanding youths among the Siyo.

But none had dared push around Hinyete; the leader openly vowed to join the Sicangu before ever he sat as a member of the loudmouth's band. And certainly Wanapin, the Siyo Shirtman, never answered to the Kiyuksa; Wanapin walked tall and straight and proud, as a people want to see their Shirtman.

But Tanazin, the man who had marked the whiteman's peace-leaf as leader of the Oglalahica—the band second in power to the Kiyuksa—never gave out advice these days until after he had counseled with Tabloka; he chose not to risk the Kiyuksa's displeasure and so see his own band scattering in the manner of the Siyo.

Before the people had raised their summer lodges, Tabloka, certain of his place at the horns, had hinted at favors going to whatever band loaned him warrior-power whenever and wherever he needed such power. Then, suddenly aware of his many blood-relatives among the Oglalahica, he had named the Cante Tinza as watchmen and so made obvious which band he favored.

On the day they put up the council lodge, Tabloka had called a meeting. "Some persons show their fear of the whiteman," he had announced bluntly. "I am neither fearful nor welcoming. Instead I wait and see. If I discover a use for paleskins, I intend to use this people. If not, I will destroy these same ones. Or perhaps I will use and afterwards destroy. But I look for true followers among my own tribesmen before I make a move in any direction."

This speech, repeated among the bands, had had far more effect on the Lakotah than all of Ahbleza's talks for peace among the tribes.

But certainly none among the Mahto ever hustled at

934

the roar of power from the horns. Olepi neither talked nor listened to talk in the big center lodge, where Tabloka dominated the council, where the summer-shirts only appeared to decide affairs. Instead the Mahto leader made himself available to whoever sought his advice, and he gave much attention to boys and youths who seemed likely to make strong Iyuptala. But most often he sat with members of the Tatanka, the Pta-lodge.

Here, among his own, Olepi renewed his spirit, the truly big men in camp scarcely noticing the noise at the horns and never mentioning the noisemaker.

And while his father sat with the Tatanka, Ahbleza sat with the different wise ones, with men who spoke their thoughts softly.

"My brother Shirtman," said Wanapin on a day when he and Ahbleza visited in the Siyo's tipi, "I and you wear the Shirt and so I and you recognize peace. Observe that I say peace, not compromise. For whoever introduces this phrase, this word compromise, introduces something that never truthfully exists.

"Peace means loyal to self. Any peace, whether between two persons or between two tribes, simply reflects loyalty to one's self. And loyalty to one's self means never a gap between thought, speech, act.

"What loyalty to self if a man tries to make peace with someone whom his familiar-voice calls enemy? For now he will try fighting this real-self and never know peace. Peace exists, but only within the soul of each man, peace meaning peace-with-self and nothing different.

"Man arrives on earth owning a visible body and a competitive spirit—observe the child, the youth—and so he honors this spirit in his young seasons, the people recognizing his zest for rivalry, for contests, for raids, and for war as a way of keeping true to self, to the warlike spirit.

"But the spirit, slowly growing, begins to seek repose. And so the same warrior, ever loyal to self, accepts the demands of an expanding spirit. The people call this growth, wisdom; a wise man, they say, a man loyal to his spiritual growth, a man truly stable.

"And now, my brother, remember that a contradiction never exists. Will you conceive of a peaceman who maintains a warlike spirit?

"That which a man decides to use from among his experiments, from among his experiences, determines the growth of his spirit. Your spirit, my brother, awaits your true selection; why delay your choice?"

But Ahbleza had walked away from his visit with Wanapin wondering more about his father than about himself. Will a man, he pondered, who retains the warrior-spirit into old age reconcile spirit and body when the body grows frail? Will such a man ever know peace? Suddenly he remembered Lekśi; perhaps this old man had known the true answer.

On a different day the Shirtman talked with Cetan, but sitting with this one, Ahbleza asked about Wapaśa, the Isanyati Dakotah who had counted more than ten thousand in his following.

"The stories tell that Wapaśa fights a whiteman's war," the Shirtman said in puzzled tones; "perhaps you know, my relative, whether or not this man stands alongside the whites and so fights against his own?"

Cetan had not answered; he knew nothing about this war in the east. But he had imagined why the Shirtman asked; everything everyone asked this summer related to Tabloka's speech concerning the whitemen. Or to this same Kiyuksa's apparent intention to become leader of the four original Lakotah bands. Tabloka who shoves, manages, controls in and outside his own band; Tabloka who ousts his kinsman Tawitko.

Tacincala had made her own appraisement concerning Tawitko; suddenly recognizing him as a man more abused than abusing, she had accepted this Kiyuksa as husband, providing him a comfortable lodge and granting him the respect and admiration a man looks for in his wife. She viewed him as not unattractive and certainly he proved himself an interesting companion. Tawitko's age had not distressed her, and she gladly welcomed his second daughter—a girl perhaps eight—into the lodge. And whoever observed the new family this summer saw that these three enjoyed each other's company, the husband perhaps grateful that events had sent him here.

As for Cankuna, the grandmother-heart beat strongly

in her breast; she rejoiced that children again laughed in her lodge and in the nearby lodge. Throughout the summer she made playthings for these little ones, for the bright-eyed Kiyuksa girl who ran in and out the tipi and for Winu's daughter and Lowansa's son, these two born six winters past and during the same moon. She had stuffed and tied toy-babies, painting on faces and attaching strands of her own hair to the heads of these amonmonla. But she also had made a flesher for the girl in Tacincala's lodge—a tool, not a toy—her gift intended to familiarize the child with woman's work.

After the summer surround, the hunter's wife gave the toebones to these same children, the good woman observing in what manner they used imagination in their play. And so she heard her grandson designating certain bones as horses, setting up different ones to represent the grazing herd. But she had heard all three children calling the round bones 'wheels' and talking about a 'wagon.'

Cankuna never had said so but the grandchild in whom she took most pleasure they called Mahtola, the son born to Anpagli and Tonweya three winters past.

'Ie wakan lake' said the old Mahto people whenever they spoke of Mahtola, a phrase they used about any child who appeared remarkably advanced for his age. And then these persons hinted that Anpagli fed the boy from the nest of the bird-with-two-voices or that she rubbed the beak of this same bird against her child's lips and so he learned to talk more easily than most children.

Anpagli had laughed. "Look whose son," she had said, her black eyes flashing Tonweya a fond glance.

But the more serious observers had noticed that the woman sat with her little son, teaching him the phrase or the word for whatever he touched, singing him many sleep-songs and talking to him while he slept. But her talk had concerned only the earth's creatures to whom he shall become as brother.

Sitting alone, Anpagli often marveled the wonder that she had borne a child after her foolish and frightening experience at the baby-place. But she had guarded herself most carefully during those moons of taking-on-life and she had asked for Tacincala's help when the birth-day arrived.

She had brought forth the child without difficulty, and whoever had looked upon the boy during these past two winters had made the same appreciative sound, one that expressed gladness and satisfaction; Mahtola, they had said, a fine-looking son.

Cankuna, hearing this praise for her little grandson and noticing the respect granted his mother, sensed an abounding joy. She always had admired Anpagli, and now, seeing the thoughtful care this young woman gave to the child, Cankuna found her admiration increasing. She also secretly approved a decision Anpagli had made relative to Peśla. The Psa-woman, refusing to joke with Peśla in the manner Lakotah custom prescribed, had discouraged her husband's brother as a visitor in the lodge.

Perhaps, Cankuna had told herself, Anpagli observes that whenever Peśla walks nearby the three children who play together, he offers his son a shoulder-ride or lifts Winu's little girl to a place atop his head but never will he so much as glance at Tawitko's daughter, the girl turning shy in front of this one man who ignores her smile. And so Anpagli wisely chooses infrequent contact between this warrior and her peaceful lodge, wherein plays her own smiling child, her little son Mahtola.

One heart in the Mahto camp lay mostly on the ground this summer; Napewaśte had seen in Olepi a weariness of spirit and in her son a despondency over talks that had not changed anything. They sat in her lodge—the only two persons of true importance in her life—and not once a smile on either face.

And then one day Ahbleza, seeking refreshment, had opened his paint sacks. He had mixed powders and brought out a hide; he had reached for a brush and begun a picture.

The next day a big war party had started south, warriors who intended to join the Śahiela in a fight against the Pani, Palani.

But two who often had led had not even watched the party go; Olepi had found reason for staying inside the tipi and Ahbleza had kept at his drawing. And so Napewaśte had sought a comforting shade outside the lodge, the standing-people offering coolness and calm to this woman who wanted to cry and knew that she dared not drop a tear.

The warriors had returned and danced their victories until the thinly frozen edges of the stream signaled that the people had used up the summer; let the hoop break and move.

Tabloka had bellowed out something, and soon the bands had started out, the four moving in the same direction. But on reaching rapid creek, certain villages had headed downstream toward the good river, where, according to the newscarriers, a whiteman known as Red Lake had set up a trading post.

The Mahto villages, choosing a different direction, soon traveled alone. Following the blacktails and the pronghorns, they walked the eastern side of the sacred trail that surrounds the black hills, a path familiar to every moving thing. Warm, clear weather had accompanied these Mahto, but then, suddenly, they walked in rain, the days chilly and dark. And so Olepi had advised that they locate their winter villages on the creek they had chosen to follow.

The snow came during the fourth night in camp, the lodges awakening to a white morning, a day made for hunting the antlered meat. And so the women dared to arouse the sleeping husband and push him out in the cold, a certain gaiety going along with this chase.

The men returned, meat on their backs, enough fresh meat for eighty-and-five lodges, enough fresh meat for the next twenty days. Gladly now they welcomed the cold.

Warm, content, the people began the telling of those stories that usually go on until the snow melts, each story tied on to the one before, a winterlong string of words.

XII

ONE GLISTENING night halfway through the winter, Tonweya and his little son walked along the edge of the frozen stream, the snow squeaking underfoot and the trees snapping overhead. The two stopped before Ahbleza's lodge, the child glancing at his father, seeking—and receiving—permission to scratch on the tipi cover.

Instantly Ahbleza called out a welcome; he had recognized a child's fingers on the hide and knew who stood at the flap.

Perhaps certain persons considered a boy of three winters as someone too young for night-talk in a Shirtman's lodge but not Tonweya; whenever will big words injure small ears, he had asked the boy's mother, and certainly Mahtola never will hear any gossip in the Shirtman's tipi.

And now the child sat at the back of this lodge, his shoulder touching against the scout's knee, his eyes, big in awe, staring at Ahbleza.

The Shirtman smiled and pointed toward the top of the tipi: "My little son, from where you sit the smoke hole seems a far distance up. But as you grow, the tipi will seem not nearly so tall. And the same thing with certain words you will hear this night. Even when the talk goes over your head, listen closely. For you will grow up and remember and understand."

Looking into the fire, Ahbleza spoke most softly: "Some things, little son, always will seem far-off even when you stand tall, things like the tops of trees and birds flying and the sky above the clouds."

The child, knowing the Shirtman as his second-father and calling Ahbleza 'ahte' as his mother had taught him, now made answer: "If I find two big wings I will have a way for getting to the sky. I will fly with Wambli . . . like this. . . ." The boy stood and, bending his body slightly forward, moved his arms in a soaring manner.

The eyes of the brother-friends met briefly, in memory of their vision, and then Ahbleza spoke: "Perhaps you will fly with the great wingflapper. But I know a different way for getting to the sky."

The Shirtman pulled a container from between the backrests and took out a wingbone, breath-feathers quilled onto the tip. "I not yet find any wings big enough to carry you," he told the child, "but this wingbone will carry your voice. When you breathe here—at this mouthpiece—the soaring birds hear you and perhaps one will answer and tell you the way to the high places."

The boy accepted the gift. Then, after turning the bone carefully and blowing gently on the fluff, he smiled shyly. "Pila maye," he said, expressing thanks as his mother, as any woman, spoke her thanks, this child not yet of age to use the man's phrase for appreciation. But he had begun a little song about flying with 'ñuya,' with all sorts of big birds who flap across the sky.

The night shadows lengthened but neither Olepi nor Napewaśte came into the lodge. The old woman who kept up the fire brought bowls of meat for the two men and the child, but after a while she, also, went out somewhere into the dark.

The three ate without talk and when their bowls sat empty, Ahbleza began to cut the mixings for a smoke. And now Tonweya wondered whether the presence of the child accounted for the changes in procedure this night. Always he and Ahbleza had smoked the pipe within moments of sitting together and always they spoke of the white pte before they talked of anything different.

But glancing suddenly at his son, Tonweya had not resisted a smile; the boy slept, cuddled on the robe like a puppy.

The men smoked and then Ahbleza brought out the hide that he recently had painted. "Misun," he said quietly, "view this picture. And tell me if you understand."

The scout looked down without moving his head; he looked for a long while. He gazed upon a drawing of the vision that had made a dreaming-pair of these two.

And now he lifted his eyes, ready to speak. But something stopped him.

Ahbleza sat leaning forward, his head bent for listening but not for anything Tonweya intended to say. Instead, his posture revealed that he strained to catch some far-distant sound, something that hinted danger.

But why, Tonweya puzzled, will his own ears, sharp as the true-dog's hearing, pick up nothing unfamiliar? Will the brother-friend make contact with some mystery?

He saw that Ahbleza stood, the man's eyes staring at the tipi flap. Next thing, the Shirtman had gone, the quickly fading crunching sounds telling only that he hurried.

After a little wait, the scout also went out of the lodge, the sleeping child over his shoulder.

Ahbleza had walked down the long line of tipi to an open space beyond the trees where he stood looking across the moon-bright snow, his palms bending forward his ears, his posture once again that of a man who listened tensely.

The night sat still, everything quiet but those wandering-dogs who yapped at their relatives on the moon. And now, as if confused at finding himself in this place, Ahbleza looked back at the lodges. He saw that the cover of the sacred-lodge glowed softly red; perhaps Wanaǵi sat awake at his fire.

The wakanĥca had not appeared surprised on seeing Ahbleza stoop in the entrance before he had scratched on the tipi, on hearing Ahbleza speak abruptly, neglecting the formal term of respect.

"My father's voice calls out to me. Yet I know that he visits certain Śahiela who winter north of the shell. He goes alone to this camp, across old-woman creek and two days' travel beyond."

Ahbleza paused; he waited for the wakanĥca to say something, to tell him whether he imagined the voice or whether a very real call of distress had reached his ears.

Wanaǵi sat as if deaf.

And now a shame swept over the Shirtman. Coming out of his daze, he stood aware of his rudeness; he had acted in the manner of a boy improperly reared. But as he started to back out and take himself away, he observed that Wanaǵi's hands, moving slightly, uncovered four small stones.

"My son, you come here seeking something." The sacred-man's voice sounded calm, factual.

"I seek advice from my father-friend," Ahbleza answered evenly. "Tell me, shall I get up a search party and hunt for my father or shall I go out alone and look for him?"

When Wanaǧi had not answered at once, Ahbleza spoke again: "Or perhaps I misunderstand that which occurs."

The wakanhca's face, shadowy in the red embers, suddenly glowed with mysterious brilliance: "I stay, my son, at this tipi fire but you shall find a knoll. In separate places I and you will listen. Perhaps you will receive the message. Go quickly."

Ahbleza, hurrying away, had not seen the sadness that crept into the sacred-man's eyes.

Uttering soft birdcalls as he moved swiftly over hard-packed snow, the Shirtman identified himself to any scouts who watched out from brush clumps back of the lodges.

Now, atop a hummock beyond the edge of camp, he dropped off his robe and so exposed his skin to any invisible touch. But he also sniffed the night and tasted the air with his tongue. And certainly he listened.

In the same instant he heard and saw movement; something dark hovered slightly above the white earth, something in the near distance. He waited for a more certain sound, a more certain view of whatever moved.

The next moment he came sliding down the little hill, rushing onto the white crust, his feet making deep holes in the untrampled snow. He had perceived the shape of a lone horse and the form of a man slumped over the creature's back.

The horse walked slowly along a furrow, the trail hard where the high ground had prevented drifts.

But long before Ahbleza recognized either the horse or the collapsed body across the horse, he understood who came. And that, truly, he had heard his father's call whether from this or some invisible realm.

Approaching the horse, Ahbleza made the calming 'shuhs' and then, sensing that help followed him here, he gave a little sign, something to tell whoever came that they had nothing to fear. And now he threw his robe onto the ground.

The son's arms reached for the wounded father; gently he lowered the man onto the robe. Yet more gently he spoke to the Mahto: "My father, your son holds on to you. Tell me where they wound you."

Suddenly viewing the wound, the Shirtman marveled that the man's heart yet beat. "My father," he said quickly, "hear your son's plea. Name this enemy who hurts you."

Holding his breath and leaning in close, Ahbleza willed that his father's eyes open, willed that the dying warrior speak.

And so the eyes opened; and so the son heard himself recognized, his request understood. The lips moved; Olepi named the enemy.

The next moment the half-moon shone down on a still face, on unseeing eyes and an open mouth. And on a son who slowly bowed his head, his long black hair softly covering his father's cheeks and breast.

After a while the Shirtman closed the staring eyes and composed the good, the strong, the handsome face. Then, putting his arms under the body to lift the dead man, he noticed that many hands reached out to help. But the one who stood most close: the brother-friend.

And so Tonweya lifted the Mahto's shoulders while different ones came alongside the body, each one carrying gently, crying softly.

Ahbleza led the procession back to the village, to a place outside the sacred-lodge where Wanaǧi waited, the sacred-man singing a death-song for Olepi, a song he had composed at sunrise this same day.

Napewaśte knew, awakening in Kehala's lodge to tugs on the tipi flap, that the news she had dreaded all the seasons of her life as Olepi's wife awaited her outside this lodge. And so a wail of despair escaped her before ever she saw Ahbleza's wet eyes.

Then, in one wide glance, she viewed the horse without rider and the crowd who stood weeping nearby the sacred-lodge. And so she dropped to her knees on the frozen ground, her body swaying back and forth, her howls most pathetic. And now, bowing over herself, she became a huddled moaning thing.

Kehala leaned down, her slim arms covering the woman in a gesture of protection, her wails mingling with the

944

moans. And so these two grieved outside the lodge until relatives lifted each one back inside, where embers from a dying fire acted to reflect their weeping hearts.

Throughout the night and into the dawn old Eyanpaha walked the cold ground singing sadly. And only children slept.

When next Ahbleza saw his mother, she shuffled along back of the red death-bundle, a woman suddenly stooped and old, her hair pulled out or broken, her skin slashed wherever, indifferently, she had swung her knife. Never before had the Shirtman observed so tremendous a change in any one person, a change that had occurred overnight.

Ahbleza had stayed the night in the sacred-man's lodge, where he had helped Wanaǧi prepare a spirit-bundle, these two wrapping a strand of Olepi's hair in soft skin, the wakanḣca proposing that Heḣloǧeca's wife quill a pattern onto this blacktail-hide, a design meaningful to the wakanḣca and the dead leader.

Soon after dawn Cankuna and her relatives had begun bundling the body. Tonweya had brought the Mahto's pipe, which they had placed in the cold hands, but shield, arrows, and paint sacks the scout had hung on two of the four poles that supported the death-platform. Whoever had attacked the leader had taken bow and pipe-sack, these things missing when the son discovered his father.

During the ceremony at the death-rack the Shirtman fought his rising anger against the enemy who had killed his father; again and again he recalled the vow they had demanded of him when he accepted the Shirt. And so he knew that he dared say nothing to anyone concerning Olepi's killer. Perhaps, he told himself, he dared not risk speaking at all for three, four days.

But seeing that they had tied two fine horses to the death-rack poles and then suddenly realizing that they intended to kill these creatures with a gun, he felt himself compelled to speak.

"My friends, not the shooting-stick. The bone knife or the strangling cord on these horses but not the firestick," he called out. Not only had he remembered his father's aversion to anything the whiteman had brought to the Lakotah but he had known, from the look of the wound, that this weapon of the wašicun had killed Olepi.

And so the bereaved son, having spoken his one request, grew silent. He walked back alone from the death-rack, the people aware that he had cut his hair short to the jawline, that he had painted the black streaks of man-grief on his face, and that he had not talked with anyone, not even with Wanaġi.

And yet this same night Ahbleza stood inside the sacred-man's lodge and put forth his claim. The Mahto people, he said, now belong to him as a band. He shall lead.

"The one they wrap in the red robe already sits at the campfire-of-souls." On his way to Wanaġi's lodge he had seen the long cloud streamers that flickered and dimmed, then flashed bright again. "I, his son, will fill the empty place he leaves here. I am fit. I am of the rank for leading this band. But I need someone speaking out for me in the center lodge. And who but you, the one who really knows me. Who but you, my father-through-choice. Who but you, a seer who keeps proving himself most wise, a wakanlica with a voice in the council.

"You, a Tatanka-man, a member of the Pta-lodge, and one of seven itancan. Here sits the power.

"When the strangers bring their peace-leaf, the Mahto names you as the one to represent this band. So will not the advisers, the councilors, the principal ones in these villages and in this tribe see wisdom and aptness in your speaking out for the son of . . . of this man . . . not here?"

Wanaġi, sucking on his pipe, had not signed that he heard.

And so Ahbleza spoke again, audibly inhaling his breath as if he smoked a ceremonial pipe, something Wanaġi had not yet offered him: "Once I have two fathers. Now I have one."

The full reality of his loss had not struck Ahbleza until this moment, and now water suddenly ran out of his eyes and over his cheeks, his tears splashing upon the memory of an old sorrow, grief effecting grief.

The mist cleared, and Ahbleza, having regained his calm, saw that Wanaġi stood, the wakanlica's gaze full upon him and without empathy.

The sacred-man wore his hair tied up in a thin, round topknot, and for an instant Ahbleza marveled the frosty look to this hair and the aging skin at the man's neck. But the voice that demanded his attention came forth as strong and firm as ever.

"My son knows that with or without my support he will lead the people when he so chooses. He wears the Shirt; he owns the people. They observe him closely and never find him wanting. He earns the respect of the Mahto band; they will accept him as leader. I am the one who will not accept him."

The skin beneath the Shirtman's eyes quivered and his cheek muscles throbbed as he strove for control.

Wanaġi spoke on, unrelenting: "I also refuse Ahbleza the second request he intends to make of me. I will not circle his head with a strip of white pte-hide; I will not decorate him with the ptesan headband whether or not he procures this strip of white hide.

"Three, they say, only three ptesan—three white pte—ever roam the grasses. Ten ten-hundred Lakotah but only three ptesan. And but one Ptesanwin, pipe-bringer.

"The white pte, they say, belong to the people even as Ptesanwin, Pte-woman, belong to the people. So who will dare request this headband, this symbol? Who among these many, many Lakotah on the plain yet accepts the true meaning of Ptesanwin and dares say so? Who yet accepts Pte-woman as something more than pipe-bringer and so dares to demonstrate?"

The Shirtman had pulled himself tall, and Wanaġi, aware of the arrogant posture and haughty eyes, remembered far back to a certain inipi and a face unlike this one, back to the day when Olepi had demanded that he, the seer, instantly purify a pipe for war. And so he heard without surprise the Shirtman's response.

"This thing I decide," Ahbleza said, his tone cold as ice.

"This thing I recognize," Wanaġi agreed coolly.

For a moment the two stared at each other. And now, before any visible sign betrays in what manner this meeting affects him, Ahbleza turned and went out of the lodge.

XIII

TONWEYA HAD decided that he understood why Ahbleza closed his ears to those voices who protested his refusal to name Olepi's killer, but the scout yet puzzled why the Shirtman withheld this information from him. Will not their bond, he had asked himself, permit Ahbleza to share this secret with his brother-friend?

Apparently not. Ahbleza remained indifferent toward all, looking through persons who passed his lodge as if he saw nothing but their shadows. Even Napewaśte, staring out from her grief, had met with eyes that said that she, the same as anyone, sat as an obstacle in the way of her son's strange new sight.

Then, four days after Olepi's dying, the Iyuptala and Tatanka lodges, working together, raised a spirit-lodge for the deceased leader, a gathering place for relatives and friends who sought spirit-contact, who chose to keep alive the warrior-spirit and so draw upon whatever strength the invisible will lend.

This old, old custom of raising a spirit-lodge, a practice they had neglected. True, each family will take hairs from the head of a deceased, something they wrap, something they call soul-bundle and keep inside the lodge for a winter or more. But Wanaǵi, remembering that which happens to the camp—and to himself—when Peta, father to Olepi and to this band, dies, had talked with persons among the Pta, that lodge which makes him an honorary member; he had spoken for the raising of a soul-lodge, a spirit-keeping place, a place to keep Olepi's spirit.

Icabu, an itancan, had accepted the request of his lodge-brothers—Pta and Iyuptala—to act as keeper-of-the-spirit for the next two winters, and eight more lodgemen had agreed to assist him in this restricting work. For whoever became caretaker of a spirit-lodge occupied himself at this one thing. He dared neither take hold of weapons nor run nor swim nor move violently. He denied himself many different foods, and whether or not he lived with his family, he kept away from his wife's robes.

Hinhan had cut the three crotched-sticks and fastened together the shoulder-tall rack on which Wanaǧi hung the soul-bundle, the rack placed inside the spirit-lodge and directly back of mellowed earth. Icabu had made the fire circle in front of the mellow-earth, the itancan and his helpers instructed to maintain a constant flame and to use only a birdwing fan at this fire.

"But more important," Wanaǧi had said, "observe whoever speaks in here. Let none mention war or make quarrelsone talk."

Next, the sacred-man had given Icabu personal instructions. He told the caretaker to remember himself these next two winters as wholly the peaceman. Meaning that Icabu shall cancel any grudges he perhaps holds. And that not only shall he refrain from war and hunting but he shall disregard a pipe in the hands of anyone who carries enmity toward another person.

"These requirements compel peace in your thoughts and acts; they set you aside while you care for this lodge and the spirit in contact with this lodge." Wanaǧi had spoken firmly.

Napewaśte and Kehala had begun working on a gift pile, these two already looking toward the day, two winters distant, when they shall release the warrior's spirit, a ceremonial of gifting. Let the people remember, Wanaǧi had said, that spirit-keeping and family-giving go together.

And now, the spirit-lodge in use, the people waited for the son to honor his father's memory; let the band hear Ahbleza name the enemy; let the warriors know against whom they shall move next summer.

But Ahbleza had not named this enemy. Nor had he entered the spirit-lodge. Instead, he walked the wet and sticky ground, his eyes strangely watchful, his glance skimming over faces as if each one refused to answer a question he intended never to ask.

The moon changed shape twice—bitten to round—before Ahbleza again pointed his moccasins toward the sacred-lodge, where he intended to visit someone with whom he had not talked—had not wanted talk—since the night after Olepi's dying.

The winter sun shone weakly on old snow this day, neither shadows nor glare, but Ahbleza walked hurriedly as if to escape any manner of reflection. But on seeing Wanaǧi's young helper who stood outside the sacred-lodge, the Shirtman suddenly requested the initi. Let Waglula bring water and a cover and prepare hot stones for a man who desires to renew himself.

The news that the Shirtman sat alone with the sizzling stones spread quickly. Not an inipi, the people told one another, but a cleansing bath, proof that he revives and so prepares to name his father's killer.

Perhaps he will encourage a surprise attack on the enemy's winter camp? Or so the young warriors began talk among their own while they waited for the Shirtman to emerge from the sweat lodge.

The more seasoned men also talked of an avenging, but when finally the avengers go out, these warriors agreed, they go out a cool party, none looking for wounds.

In a different tipi the old and wise smoked their long pipes and spoke of the Shirt as a desirable restraint. And so they mentioned only briefly Ahbleza's prowess but talked instead about Ahbleza's views, his attitude toward ceremony, toward custom, toward the ways of the grandfathers. And certainly each one here knew that they spoke not as persons who awaited Ahbleza's announcement but as persons who sat aware that the day approached when they needed to agree—or not agree—on the son of Olepi as the new leader of the Mahto band.

Icabu sat in the spirit-lodge this same day, host to persons who had come bringing gifts and asking for certain ceremonial acts. They also had learned that Ahbleza entered the initi and they looked for him to appear afterwards in the spirit-lodge.

The caretaker, recognizing Wanaǧi as the proper one to conduct these ceremonies, had sent for the sacred-man.

Wanaǧi came, but he neither carried rattles nor wore the grizzly-claw neckpiece. Nor had he painted his face in the manner usual with seers. But he brought a hand-drum; he had come prepared to speak and to sing.

And now the assembled group, perhaps thirty persons, listened to the wakaṅhca as he referred to the spirit as something luminous that hovers over the body until at death

950

when this light slowly fades. And then they heard him advise that they treat their hands as something wonderful, their hands and also their eyes and mouth and ears. Let each one, he said, make wonderful use of these things; let each one treat with himself as something sacred, as a power for truth.

Wanaġi had spoken in language these persons understood, and certainly they appreciated his effort to avoid the abstruse when not among his own.

And why not speak simply, Wanaġi had asked himself; why confuse someone? Will each one in this place recognize his meaning if he talks about the spirit-lodge as something that retards any spirit ready for transition? Or if he describes grief as something that the invisibles deplore? Or if he announces that all symbols—sunpole, pipe, spirit-lodge—exist as wrappings which hide the truth? And will anyone here truly understand if he, a wakanhca, suddenly discloses that Pte-woman symbolizes a power that belongs not to the woman—not to Ptesanwin—but to the people, to the one and to the whole?

Certainly these persons who sit here recall that Ptesanwin, after handing the original pipe to the Dakotah, starts to walk away. And that, turning for a second look at the people, her form changes from woman to pte. But will they recall that on her third backward glance, her pte-form changes from white to red?

The Lakotah say that a spirit-lodge memorializes the pipe-bringer's transformation. But will not Pte-woman's transformation signify that the people, watching, slowly lose a certain power? He, Wanaġi, will say so, but not here, not to this assembly.

But neither will this wakanhca mislead anyone; man truly shall renew himself through sacred use of sacred things, meaning his own hands and mouth and eyes. And the spirit, whether one imagines his spirit as luminiferous or as a body-within, shall disappear. But not until a man chooses to sever the tie between visible and invisible form.

And now, inhaling deeply, Wanaġi lifted drum and beater and so began a song, the song he had sung originally on the night they had carried Olepi's body from the plain to the sacred-lodge, a song the Mahto people intended to sing in the seasons ahead whenever a great warrior died.

951

"Olepi, nita oyate ceya glapi lo;
Ceya tiyata ani glapi."

"Olepi, your people come here crying;
Weeping, they bring you here."

The women listened, memorizing the phrases as the wakanlica repeated his song; the men listened, appreciating the message as the sacred-man began anew.

"Paha sapa he ciya ya on;
He makoce nitawa yelo."

"You rest nearby the black hills;
This earth belongs to you."

The women listened and wept; the men cried also, men always crying when a relative died. But only when a relative died.

"Olepi, nita oyate ceya glapi lo;
Ceya tiyata ani glapi."

Wanaǧi finished his song and went away. But the people stayed, waiting for the son of Olepi, looking for Ahbleza to come and sit for a smoke with his relatives.

But Ahbleza had not come to the spirit-lodge.

Alone with the voices in stone, the Shirtman realized the agonizing struggle that went on inside him, his second confrontation with that which he called his true-self.

At one moment he wanted to jump out of this place of rising, wet heat and, uttering a fierce cry, rush forth in vengeance upon his father's killers. The next moment he wanted only to slump down into the choking steam and disappear under the earth.

But whichever the impulse, he only splashed more water on the hot stones, accepting the need for a decision: to name or not to name the killer.

When finally Ahbleza came out of the initi, Waglula saw the Shirtman's tortured face, saw the man grab up moccasins and, throwing a robe violently around his body, start walking barefoot across the snow-patched ground.

And then Waglula saw that Wanaġi stood in the Shirtman's path, the sacred-man holding out a Pipe.

But the Shirtman passed, ignoring the stem and the man who held the stem.

Waglula moved from his place at the fire circle outside the initi; he took two, three steps in the sacred-man's direction, then stopped. He saw the Shirtman turning, coming back for the pipe.

The Shirtman took the pipe from the outstretched hand; he started out again, not toward the spirit-lodge but facing instead the ancient mound they called pahasapa, the black hills.

And now Waglula found himself trembling, but for what reason Waglula had not known.

XIV

THE PEOPLE say that the giant Waziya lives far to the north and on an empty plain where the sun never gets through the clouds to warm anything. And that this hairy white creature occasionally plays tricks, leaping over a big hill to spread snow on new red grass and freeze the budding trees.

And the people say that in the same whimsical manner the wakinyan who flash and roar in the summer sky occasionally rumble over a Lakotah snow camp. And that their noisy mysterious-flight on a cold winter day acts to frighten even the heyoka whose pipes and songs usually propitiate these off-earth visitors.

Two nights, three days Ahbleza walked, a certain ledge within the black hills his objective. If hunger and weariness attended him, he had managed to ignore their presence. And neither thinning moccasins nor the dampness that crept into his bones seemed to concern him. Somewhere on the high ledge, he had told himself, he shall find sheltering stones, and here he will seek a second vision, something that will answer his terrible uncertainty.

Then, suddenly, scarcely remembering his climb, he stood on his ledge sniffing and listening. He had discovered a cave, but he intended to make certain that none among the winter sleepers drowsed inside the big dark hollow.

Now satisfied that nothing dangerous awaited him here, he sat down wearily. Almost at once he heard a growl. But not from the hollow.

He looked up and saw that great black cloudlike shapes came swooping into the darkening old-winter sky. He listened for echoing rumbles and he watched for flashing light. But he refused to identify such noise with the flight of wingflappers and such flashes with the blinking of strange yellow eyes. The strokes and rumble, he told himself, relate neither to bird nor to a big stone rolling over the sky nor to strange little forms beating a drum nor to . . .

He stopped, remembering back to his boy-seasons, to the day when Ogle asked that he identify certain tracks. He had named all those creatures who will not make such tracks instead of naming the one who will. And so why review that which they say about the streaks and crashes? Why mislead himself? Until a man knows something, he uses one word: mystery. And mystery means mystery, not something he shall personify.

Recognize, the grandfathers had said, that nothing unnatural exists. And that when man knows the truth, the whole truth, he gives name to that which he once calls mystery. And that when a man needs to know something, a teacher appears. And now he, a Shirtman, needed to know something.

Rising, Ahbleza threw off his robe. Moving to the front of the ledge, pipe in hand, he lifted his head to the sudden fall of rain, living water from an unstable sky.

The next moment, gusting divergent winds came flying over the slopes and a shredding cloudtop hurled down icy seeds. The air had overturned and the sky began to crack.

Naked and defiant, Ahbleza faced the violence. The hail stung his breast and the wind sneaked around to lash his bareness, to cut across his back like a whip, and the crashing noise roared painfully in his ears.

Suddenly glaring upward, he shrieked a vow to avenge his father's killing in the one way that the Shirt permitted; here, in the midst of nature's violence he will demand to know the path to peace.

And now he flung back at the cloud all the fury that this sky-power hurled at him. His eyes followed the zig-zagging light and toward the most brilliant flashes he stood unflinching. A whistling streak split the tree above his ledge and, seeing the branches that fell down around him, he laughed.

Instantly something above hissed at him. Throwing back his head, he stared at a white ball of fire, a ball that hurtled from the cloud toward the earth, something that suddenly seemed to hang suspended above him, something that he now dared look upon even as he remembered that which he dared. For, gazing at this ball of living light, he, Ahbleza, dares an unobstructed view of śkan, the permeating force. And so he, Ahbleza, dares to probe the ultimate depths of the fiery energy. And so he, Ahbleza, dares a second look into the far-distant reaches of his soul.

Emitting a harsh cry, he challenged not mystery but that which he and all who move on this earth know as the life-force, visible and invisible.

Why Ptesanwin, he shouted; why this Pte-woman, this one who brings a pipe and a demand for peace?

Who Ptesanwin, this one who relates as sister to the tribe and who demands only good in her hoop? Who Pte-woman, this one who influences until I, Shirtwearer, become as woman, as peace-keeper?

I, warrior and son of a warrior, feel my father's influence, and so I will tell who kills the Mahto leader. But I will tell only this warring sky.

And I will say that I never shall know whether the enemy kills my father out of loathing or self-defense or fear or mischief. Or perhaps something different.

I, Ahbleza, own a Shirt and so I vow good. I see nothing good in revenge and so I will not start warring with a new people. But truly I shall defend my own if ever my father's enemy approaches camp.

Again Ahbleza made the challenging cry; again he demanded that the sky hear him.

Who Ptesanwin? Who invites this woman? Who brings her to the people? Why will she come?

But the sky had not shouted back; the cloud, having spread, moved away dying.

Instead, the answer came softly, the familiar-voice speaking, telling who and why.

THREE HUNDRED WINTERS IN THE PAST THE DAKOTAH DISCOVER A CRITICAL NEED FOR SOMETHING THAT SHALL COMPEL TRUTH. AND SO THEY COME TOGETHER AS ONE BODY, ONE THOUGHT.

FOUR OLD WAKANĤCA WHO EVERYONE KNOWS INSTRUCT THE PEOPLE. AND SO THE DAKOTAH—NOT ONE DISSENTING VOICE, NONE OF DIFFERENT HEART—WATCH THE ROUND MOON LIGHT THE FACES OF EIGHT PURE YOUNG WOMEN, PERSONS TENDER AND RECEPTIVE WHOSE PRESENCE WILL ATTRACT AND PERMIT INFLUENCE.

AND NOW THE DAKOTAH, MAKING CONSCIOUS USE OF SKAN, COMMAND THE APPEARANCE OF SOMETHING GOOD.

AND THE INVISIBLE GRANDFATHERS, RECOGNIZING AN URGENCY FOR WISDOM AND A NEED FOR HELP DIRECTLY FROM THE SOURCE, EXERT A MATCHING STRENGTH.

NOW PTESANWIN EMERGES, THE LIFE-FORCE IN THE SHAPE OF A GOODLOOKING YOUNG WOMAN, SOMEONE WHO ANNOUNCES HERSELF AS VISIBLE BREATH.

FOR SO LONG AS THE POWER ENDURES—POWER FROM VISIBLE AND INVISIBLE SUSTAINING HER AS WOMAN-BODY—PTESANWIN INSTRUCTS IN CEREMONY AND PRESENTS THE PIPE. BUT WHEN THE PEOPLE START LETTING GO, THIS WOMAN WALKS AWAY. THEN, SITTING DOWN, SHE BECOMES PTE, THE RELIABLE FOUR-LEGGED THROUGH WHOM THE UNSEEN ANCIENTS OFTEN SEND MESSAGES.

BUT WHEN THE POWER FOR HOLDING ON TRULY WANES, THE PTE-FORM ALSO DISAPPEARS; ONLY THE STONE PIPE ENDURES.

AND SO THE PEOPLE KEEP THE PIPE AS A SYMBOL OF

THAT WHICH THEY ASK FOR, A SYMBOL THEY WILL USE IN ALL CEREMONIES, A SYMBOL THAT WILL COMPEL TRUTH.

BUT OF WHAT IMPORTANCE PTESANWIN OR ANY DIFFERENT MESSENGER WHO EVER COMES IN ANSWER TO A PEOPLE'S COMMAND FOR HELP?

RECOGNIZE THE MESSAGE AS THE ONLY IMPORTANCE. MESSAGE, NOT MESSENGER; MESSAGE, NOT MESSENGER, NOT PIPE OR ANY DIFFERENT SYMBOL; RECOGNIZE THE MESSAGE AS THE ONLY IMPORTANCE.

AND NOW RECOGNIZE WOMAN AS THE ONE MOST CLOSE TO THOSE SPIRITS WHO SEEK COMMUNICATION AND YOU WILL UNDERSTAND WHY THE GRANDFATHERS DEMAND THAT THE SHIRTMAN—THE SPIRIT-BODY IMAGE FOR THE PEOPLE—SHALL BECOME AS WOMAN.

WOMAN, SECURE OF POSITION AND PURE OF BLOOD; WOMAN, KEEPER OF THE MORALITY AND PERSONIFICATION OF SPIRITUAL STRENGTH. WOMAN, REAL AND UNPRETENTIOUS AND ON A DEFINITE PATH.

AND SO LET THE SHIRTMAN UNDERSTAND IN WHAT MANNER HE BECOMES AS WOMAN.

Quiet had returned all around, the sunset sky, gently red, spread out to cover the plain, and the new grass, wet and shining, reflected the color overhead.

"Red earth," Ahbleza whispered; "red earth and red sky. And I, red man." Shivering, he put his arms across his breast. Now, glancing toward the cave, he saw that the winds had tossed his robe inside the stone hollow.

Bending slightly, he entered the cave; he spread his robe evenly and lay down on the soft hair. Again he felt cold and so, rolling onto his side, he pulled the robe over his chilled body. He sighed wearily; perhaps he will imagine this robe a red robe, his body a death-bundle but his spirit alive and soaring. Then perhaps more true-understanding will come, much, much more understanding.

Ahbleza woke to an earth the weathers had transformed; a glittering skin of ice covered every branch and twig and the split tree on the ledge above had become an exciting creature-shape. And the sun, beaming out from a

957

fresh sky, flashed points of color everywhere, colors for which the man neither knew nor wanted to know names.

Looking beyond his ledge, Ahbleza gazed upon the great plain, not red with new grass as he remembered but now a sparkling white.

Viewing this snow scene, the man accepted the sudden splendor as the naturalness of earth. And in appreciation he lifted his face to the sun, to the power that sustains earth for man's personal enjoyment. At once something awakened a memory of Heyatawin, not a remembrance related to the sungazing but a strange flash of recognition that seemed relative to snow, to this sudden snow.

After a while he pulled his robe slowly around him and, climbing down from the ledge, began his walk back to the Mahto camp.

Toward evening this same day he came upon the tracks of a lone pte. He looked for signs of a companion but he saw marks of only the one, her hoofs throwing snow on the thinly covered patches of ground. And then her tracks disappeared abruptly, the snow ahead untrampled.

The sun, now a great red ball, touched down on earth, and the traveling Lakotah recognized that he needed to stop his search for the pte and hunt something small enough to kill with stick, stone, or hands; either he finds something that hops or that runs on short legs or he will need to ease his gnawing belly with pods from the old reliable stem, such pods usually in sight.

Again glancing toward the red sun, he noticed that a swirl of fine snow skipped lightly over bare ground and that back of this blur—a boulderlike form.

Walking slowly forward, Ahbleza perceived a big, curly head, the head lifted as if sniffing the wind. And yet the form had not moved. Perhaps he looked upon another creature-form born of split wood or split stone and covered with frost? Or perhaps he truly comes upon pte, a creature with ice clinging to her hair, a pte who freezes, who dies in the sudden cold?

Getting close, he saw that he had discovered a pte but that nothing covered or clung to her hairs, her naturally white hairs; he stood looking at ptesan, the sacred white pte.

But her gauntness startled him; he wondered whether

she had the strength to move. But then he saw the cracked horns and recognized her thinness as age. Perhaps this one approached his age, thirty-and-five winters, old age for pte if not for a man.

And now he remembered. And remembering, he understood—or imagined that he understood. Here, the ptesan of his boy-hunt, the white one whose tail he touches, one who awaits this day before she offers herself to his bow, gives her hide for the white-pte ceremony.

But he, Ahbleza, walked as a vision-seeker during this traveling; he carried neither bow nor knife. And so he approached only to marvel and perhaps to touch.

For a long while he looked into the eyes—the color of pale summer sky—but when finally he reached out his hand, she moved; turning abruptly, she pounded off toward the south.

Wistfully, Ahbleza watched the disappearing form. South, he told himself, to the place of the ever-flowing stick from whence comes the original man; south, to the place where each person finishes his journey, returns his breath.

Why these thoughts? Walking here alone, he comes upon his prize. Or will he regret that neither Tonweya nor Wanaǧi share this moment with him? But will not man always come upon his most wonderful discoveries when he sits alone, walks alone? On lonely ledges and to lonely hearts the answers come.

Then perhaps he regrets that he finds the ptesan? Or that this white one, eluding his touch, heads south, perhaps signaling a sudden change in his own direction?

Or will the overwhelming picture that moves before his eyes while he drowses in the cave fix his thoughts along but one path?

A party of Mahto met Ahbleza a half-day out from camp. Wanaǧi had advised the akicita that the Shirtman walked alone, and certain ones, not wanting an enemy to chance upon the lonely tracks, had come looking for him. The father of this man, who now lay bundled in red, also traveled alone; why risk, they had said, losing the son.

The Shirtman spoke nothing of his experiences to anyone in the party, and, on entering camp, he went directly to the sacred-lodge. He held the pipe as when he had gone out six, seven days previously, but, sitting down alongside Wanaġi, he neither offered nor accepted a smoke.

"My father," he began, "I recognize the pipe as one more symbol that covers up truth. I now see the ceremonial smoking as something between two persons who will not trust one another."

Wanaġi sat quietly, waiting for Ahbleza to recognize something much more important, wanting Ahbleza to understand all ceremony, all ritual, as something for a person who not yet trusts himself.

But Ahbleza went on: "I overcome loathing. I rise above vengeance. I will not permit revenge as the force that motivates me. I never yet find joy in killing, in killing anything.

"But that which moves different persons, they decide and not I. Each man owns a reasoning power and so he dares to choose and to act, dares to use the life-force as he sees fit.

"Nevermore shall I try to influence in any direction. I only harm those persons whom I desire to protect if I interfere with their power for identifying truth, making a choice. I will not keep any man or ask that any man keep me. For this reason I prefer not to appear wearing the Shirt.

"And so, my father-friend, I will not try to restrain the warriors from killing or the people from their acts of revenge. But I, Ahbleza, will walk before the Lakotah as a man who enjoys living without these things."

Wanaġi glanced at the speaker; something more than Olepi's dying, he told himself, makes this change in a man who eight, ten moons past endeavors to sway the people toward a peace among tribes and an active resistance wherever white tradesmen appear.

But when finally the wakanlica spoke, he used a demanding tone: "You say that you accept this manner of living, that henceforth you become as woman. You know the meaning of this phrase, become-as-woman?"

Ahbleza answered easily: "I know that to become-as-woman means that I become as a certain woman instructs. I shall possess those traits that Ptesanwin sets forth."

Remembering something, the wakanlica again looked directly at his visitor: "Certain ones will speak against you

960

and cover your name with filth when you refuse to tell which enemy kills your father. Prepare to answer these noisy tongues with a silent heart that stays clean. Rare as the white pte, the man who knows himself imperturbable."

But now Wanaġi had heard enough to accept Ahbleza's demand that he speak for him as leader of the Mahto. And, more important, he shall begin arrangements that make of Ahbleza the first man on the plain to perform the ptesan, the white-pte ceremony.

"Two winters hence, my son, on the day that you release your father's spirit from the spirit-lodge, my hands shall place a band around your head, a thong wide as my palm and cut from the hide of the white pte. And the people shall recognize this white headband—something that neither Lakotah nor any man who lives on the mixed grasses yet wears—as the mark of a true peaceman, a man who recognizes the ptesan.

"Certainly the people who demand symbols as a way of remembering rarely hold on to the true meaning; they lose or change the important thing. But in the generations ahead perhaps someone who listens to the legend of Ahbleza will ask about the white-pte headband. Perhaps someone somewhere will seek until he finds the truth. And so the young generation, hearing, will remember their grandfathers proudly."

And now Ahbleza became the one to sit quietly, the Shirtman marveling the wakanlica's speech even as he sensed a desire to tell of his second vision, a vision he shares with none but himself. Instead he waited a little while, then held out the pipe. "You lend me this stem and bowl," he said, "when I walk out of the initi and start for the hills. Gladly I will smoke now—as an act of joy."

Wanaġi lifted his hand but not to take the stem: "I and you will smoke when next you come here. But understand that the pipe belongs to you. I make this stem on the day that you and the brother-friend return as a dreaming-pair. I carve this bowl remembering that a pronghorn enters your vision, that the creature stands at the top of your climb and so reveals your altitude. I say altitude meaning that you get above the level of your emotions.

"But I will ask that before this winter camp breaks, you show me something. I want to see whether you recognize in what manner a people travel spiritually, in what manner they climb, level to level."

"And I want to hear you tell the true-reason why the people make three attempts before they enact a ceremony."

Ahbleza lifted his eyes from the pipe. "I know the true-reason," he said quietly.

"So remember your own power, my son; remember that which occurs when you dance gazing-at-the-sun. Your vision reveals that you own tremendous power, most great power. . . ." Wanaǧi spoke these thoughts quickly, as if something or someone urged that he hurry.

Or, Ahbleza wondered, will this wakanĥca recognize that I experience a second vision; will Wanaǧi hint that I have more to say? "True, my father-friend," he said aloud, "I am not telling something . . . not yet. I lack the words. . . . "

And now, gazing into the fire, Ahbleza spoke his thanks for the pipe and his understanding of the sacred-man's request; certainly he will return to this lodge within the next two, three moons, and then he will show that he comprehends the spiraling trail each generation travels. And perhaps he shall find words to describe those scenes that pass before his eyes while he waits in the cave, find words to relate those messages that a familiar-voice transmits while he stands on the ledge and afterwards.

Stepping out of the sacred-lodge, Ahbleza started toward the tipi wherein he looked to find Tonweya. He had not visited with the brother-friend since the night of the Mahto's dying, and the scout had not accompanied the party that greeted the returning Shirtman. But suddenly he changed his direction; he had nothing to tell Tonweya until he, Ahbleza, truly understood his strange meeting with the white pte.

He moved toward the spirit-lodge but again he stopped; he had not intended to walk this path. "Not yet," he murmured.

But where will he go? Among warriors who will look wonderingly at him, waiting for him to name his father's killer? Or among the principal men who have yet to call him leader? Perhaps he will enter but one lodge comfortably, his mother's lodge.

But walking this direction, he remembered that his things hung at the back where his father's things had hung. But that, unlike the father's weapons, the son's arrows had use only when the band hunted. He felt a sting in his heart and an uneasiness grabbed him; will his body ache for an avenging whenever he recalls his father's interceptors?

Again changing paths, he headed for the far edge of camp; certainly he needed to regain that which Wanaǧi had called altitude; certainly he needed to reflect those answers that had come in response to his demand on the fiery ledge.

Reaching an open space, nothing between his gaze and the setting sun, he stood remembering those Dakotah who had come together perhaps ten generations in the past—a people with an urgent desire to compel good. They had made three attempts before an all-powerful contact with the invisibles had permitted the manifestation of Ptesanwin; Pte-woman had appeared on their fourth effort.

And Wambli-woman, the sharp-eyed birdwoman from the wingflapper family who came originally in response to a demand for a caretaker in the black hills, had appeared only after an old stone-dreamer had sung his powerful song twice and then once again. And once again.

Ahbleza stopped himself. But will Wanaǧi, he marveled, identify my power with that of a stone-dreamer? Will he imagine that I effect something? Will Wanaǧi imagine the white pte as something I . . .

Thoughts in picture form crowded his head but without order or arrangement. True, he not yet understood through whose power he had heard his father's voice calling across the snow on the tragic night. And most certainly he not yet comprehended his powerful experience on the ledge or the vision that had come during his night's stay in the cave. Or even his experience as one of a dreaming-pair. He knew only that his dance at the sunpole had taken him to-the-center where he had recognized Heyatawin, his wife's joyful laughter and her ascertaining message something that had renewed his heart.

But why these things happening to him? Why will a second vision carry a meaning perhaps too powerful to describe? He will not choose to become wapiya or wakanlica. He becomes Shirtman, but the Shirt will not endow him with the power to manifest a white pte ... if truly this white pte emerges as his own creation.

He went back over the encounter, trying to recall any flash of uncertainty, any point at which he had hesitated to accept the reality of this ptesan. Perhaps when he had reached out his hand to touch ...

But the thought-picture that now came in most vividly concerned Wambli-woman, who guards the sacred hill, not the white pte. The people never shall let go this great mound of ancient stone, she had told the stone-dreamer, for on these ledges man dares consciously absorb śkan, dares accumulate enough of the life-force to propel him along his path as far as he chooses to go.

He, Ahbleza, had stood on that ancient stone while the powers on earth and in the sky and from four directions had compounded in a demonstration of the ultimate consciousness; certainly he, Ahbleza, had accumulated enough of the power to ...

To ... what? To recreate the white pte of his boy-hunt, a white pte that not one other person sees—neither on that hunting-day twenty-five winters in the past nor on the slopes of the black hills three, four days back?

Starting on, walking again toward his mother's lodge, Ahbleza suddenly recalled that he had not mentioned the white pte to Wanaġi; instead the sacred-man had brought the creature into his talk. Perhaps Wanaġi knows everything about ledge and cave and the ptesan?

Even so, Ahbleza answered himself, when I return to the sacred-lodge, I shall go not as a youth to ask meanings but to tell meanings; I shall go as a man ready to demonstrate the truth of my vision.

He looked at the pipe-bowl in his palm, the stem resting against his arm. And now he marveled, as if he had not really seen this pipe until now, the beauty that Wanaġi had given to a small piece of redstone carved in the likeness of a pronghorn head.

XV

The snow had disappeared and the cold had given way to clear days and cloudy, to the moon of changeable weather.

On the clear days Napewaśte, quillwork in hand, wandered out to sit alongside the tall rack that supported Olepi's remains. She had raised a new, unpainted tipi cover over the platform, and, after pegging the cover tight to the ground, she had closed the smoke flaps and fastened the entrance permanently. But finding more comfort out here alone than inside the spirit-lodge where Icabu kept watch, she had begun to frequent this place. And usually she brought along easy work, like moccasins for the gift pile that awaited the release of Olepi's spirit.

She had come this morning, again bringing a sack of quills to arrange in accordance with her dream pattern. But before the day reached middle, she had grown uncomfortably sensitive to the shouting on the playground. She knew that a group of Mahto and their Sicangu visitors joined in a contest of pole-and-hoop and that the noise signaled their excitement whenever someone scored. The game had begun with sunrise and only the most skilled joined in play; even so she looked up apprehensively on hearing the yells or, as now, on noticing a strange quiet.

Over on the gaming-ground the judges had stopped the contest; they had needed to council. Twice the same player had declared his hoop misused and so made unfit for play, meaning that the contestants had rubbed out their scores and begun again. But on hearing this player's third complaint, the judges had turned to the old men among the spectators and asked their advice. When these aged ones had refused to agree, the judges had called for a break in the game while they met to deliberate. Considerable betting had taken place and they wanted to see someone winning before night interrupted. But winning honorably.

Originally Peśla had put up a trifling bet, but seeing that luck attended the player on whom he gambled—a player called Wośkate—the warrior had increased his stakes from arrows to robes to horses. And certainly Wośkate had thrown his two pairs of slender sticks at the rolling hoop in a most skillful manner.

Lowansa, deciding to join the spectators, arrived on the playground as the game resumed, scores unchanged. And so she watched for one of those remarkable plays they talk about—the double-sticks either over or under a certain color on the hoop's rim when the hoop falls—but the break in action had brought about a change in Woskate's composure. His next throws counted nothing.

Pesla, observing this sudden negligence, looked around for something or someone who perhaps had effected this change in Woskate's game. Noticing that Lowansa now stood among the women spectators, the warrior called out a new bet; he will wager the family tipi on Woskate's next throw.

Lowansa, hearing that the husband had bet her lodge, struggled to hide her concern. Losing a tipi cover will not distress her but she had imagined him saying next that he will toss in his wife with the lodge. Instead she heard Woze matching Pesla's bet, the heyoka calling to the crowd that he will meet the warrior's offer; he will gamble his wife against Pesla's lodge. And Pesla's woman.

For an instant Lowansa stood frozen; she had not understood the quick laughter, not until she recalled that Woze never had taken a wife. And not until she had recognized that the heyoka intended his humor as something to ease the growing tension. Even so, she had not smiled; one never knew about Pesla.

But while different ones carried on the joking, the Sicangu contestant came within one point of Woskate's score. Let the gamblers remember, someone had shouted, that either contestant perhaps wins the game in a single play, whatever his score now.

The next moment Pesla shouted out a new wager, something to make hearts tremble: "I will make one more bet. I will bet my own person."

Hands popped over mouths, the startled people listened for any takers. But those persons most quick to accept a wager stood silent.

Disdainfully Pesla viewed those men whose arrows, bows, moccasins, and robes made up the big pile of bets. Then, letting his robe drop to his waist, he walked toward the clubman who stood guard over the pile. But someone came in ahead of him.

None had noticed Osóta as the good-natured Canoni warrior moved toward the mound of pledges, but here he stood, plump and firm, arms folded across his breast, eyes squinted almost closed.

Heads turned and more than one throat grunted surprise that this jocular man who had brought his tiyóspaye to the Mahto camp after Isná's death chose to meet such a challenge.

"My friend," Osóta said quietly, his words for the guard, "I accept the warrior's bet. Tell the Mahto that I pledge to make meat for him during all the seasons I live . . . if his player scores the winning point."

Pesla's eyes glared contempt: "Tell the Canoni that I trust he has the strong arm of a hunter. I am a big eater."

Hearing an appreciative laugh, Pesla glanced toward a group of his friends, then back at Osóta. "Answer the Canoni that I live my child-winters in the lodge of a hunter whom none surpasses and that my own bow provides for me and my family generously."

Osóta smiled: "I, also like a full belly, but if my arm lacks push or my eyes dim, I pledge to eat sparingly while my companion stuffs. But truly, I intend that the Mahto warrior shall grow a belly as fat as mine for all the seasons I hunt for him."

Pesla came back quickly, his tone ridiculing: "The Canoni counts his pte before his arrows stick in the meat."

"Say to the Mahto that I am not counting pte here, I count only the notches on top of the double-sticks. Or will the daring warrior refuse to consider that a player will make a point in my favor?" The smile had gone from Osóta's face.

None laughed now and certain Iyuptala, seeing Pesla's eyes, carried pipes toward the two men; the gaming-ground, they said, never shall become the scene of any unpleasantness.

But before the pipes reached these two, Woze had jumped forward in an antic so vulgar and yet so funny that even the most modest young women giggled. And the next moment the judges signaled that the game begin again; push-out-the-hoop and throw sticks.

The sun climbed down to touch the earth and not yet a

winning score. And then the unusual happened; slowly the hoop settled down on sticks belonging to the Sicaŋgu. His play—colors and notches on hoop and sticks matching— gained him ten points and decided the game.

Peśla had not asked that the old men on the sidelines give an opinion nor had he glanced at the matching marks which meant his life. He turned, instead, toward Ośota and in a contemptuous manner offered his breast to the Canoni's knife.

The crowd made a restraining cry even as they cheered the bold gesture. But that which many persons now stood admiring as bravery, as courage, the wise ones recognized as something different. They saw at once that Peśla relied not upon his own honor in this moment of facing truth but upon the integrity of the one to whom he had lost his bet.

"Back away, my friend. I ask nothing of you that I will not ask of myself. And so I say hunt for me. I will send for meat when I starve."

But walking off, Ośota had wondered to himself which of two persons Peśla now despised the more: the contestant who had brought about the warrior's loss or the man who had won the bet.

While the bettors gathered around the pile to claim their winnings, Peśla stood with friends making fun over his losing wager. He flexed his bow-arm and, posturing in the manner of a child, mimicked the clumsy and the inexperienced. He soon had everyone around him laughing, and from all the joking going on for the next little while, Ośota will seem the loser.

Napewaśte had returned to her lodge before the finish of the game but she had not welcomed the two, three old gossips who came at sundown to tell her about the contest. Her anxieties had persisted and she had wanted to hear nothing about that which had occurred on the gaming-ground. Not now, not ever, she had said and in a voice that had sent the old women scurrying away.

After the game the grandfathers had gathered for talk concerning Peśla's bet, a wager that had related neither to bravery nor to foolish impulse. The Mahto warrior—many youthful eyes watching—had dismissed his life as nothing more than an item to throw down on the betting robes along with hair ornaments, leg-covers, and other replaceables; he had demonstrated an abuse of the life-force in front of ones too young to recognize guile. Will any Mahto, they asked, truly desire as war leader of the band a man who depreciates life? And if Pešla only pretends this depreciation, then he enacts a betrayal to self and tribe.

These wise ones had accepted Ahbleza as leader of the Mahto but the people demanded a war leader also, someone to sit alongside Ahbleza, one man the most in peace and one man the most in war. Certainly none among the Mahto underestimated Pešla's prowess, but these grandfathers remembered that any abuse of škan means a misdirection of power, a bent toward lust instead of control, a tendency toward destruction instead of creation, toward trickery instead of truth. Will Pešla inspire acts of courage, they wondered, or will he incite rashness and cunning? Will he sustain the warrior-image that this band demands in their war leaders? And will Pešla understand war—war—as an act against but one thing: whoever, whatever interferes with generating life. Certainly Pešla recognizes as enemy an intruder who comes to cut off meat and warmth, who comes to injure the camp. But will Pešla understand that whoever interferes with circulating good becomes the enemy even if he call himself Lakotah?

Pešla had brought friends to his lodge after the contest, the warrior in good temper and asking that his woman feed these guests as on a feast occasion; his wife shall warm the meat in berry juice, he said, and make soup using dried tipsila and maize.

Lowansa had hurried to Cankuna's lodge to borrow bowls and to hint that the hunter's wife help with the preparations. She needed more berries for the sauce and more dried maize.

Cankuna went quickly, the woman pleased to lend and glad to help. And she stayed on, wiping, stacking empty bowls and filling little food sacs with leftovers. Then, understanding that Pešla and his guests intended to smoke and talk half the night, she invited the warrior's wife and little son to sleep in the hunter's lodge. But as the two women and the boy started out, Pešla called back his son.

Regretfully Lowansa saw the child staying as Peśla demanded. The man will use his son as messenger boy, she told herself, and the child, who seems to fear his father, will go wherever Peśla sends him, day or night.

Cankuna dared say nothing, but she knew that Lowansa wanted her son in contact with his grandfather, the proper companion for a boy age six, a patient man and a good teacher. But Peśla, determined that his son become a warrior, insisted on instructing the boy in all things. Nor will he accept that his harshness affected the child unfavorably as the grandmother had hinted more than once.

After the women had gone, Peśla again joked about his loss on the playground and now, none aware exactly when the talk began, his guests sat listening to a commentary on Ahbleza.

"I and you accept this son of the Mahto as the man to follow," Peśla said, "and certainly the Mahto people will demonstrate this choice when the band moves off this winter campsite. And yet I listen to persons who deliberate the wisdom of a man, Shirtwearer or not, who refuses to name his father's enemy."

The warrior spoke boldly but not without a reason to look for acceptance of his speech; he had seen the unrest in the eyes of his companions and knew the distance he dared go.

"I and you remember," he went on, "that a Shirtman will not strike the man who kills his relative, but his pledge will not demand silence of him. So why will this Shirtman deny the young a chance at counting honors and the true fighters a chance at revenge?

"I am not your war leader and yet I stand to inflame you. This band suffers enough insult from among all Titonwan who regard these Mahto villages as a dumping ground for undesirables.

"For one, I refer to a fine-looking woman who agrees to accept a Kiyuksa and so please those Mahto who fear a strain on relations between Tabloka's following and the Mahto band.

"For another, I refer to a Canoni who wanders in among the Mahto to raise four, five little lodges, a Canoni who on this day I humor and so avert a need for pipes on

970

the playground. But where sits Ahbleza on these occasions? True, he will not play games until he releases his father's spirit, but the wakanhca will not restrain him from looking in on his people. Icabu protects the spirit-lodge; who protects the living camp?

"Certainly I am not your war leader—your new leader has yet to name his principal clubman—but I and my akicita-lodge intend to watch over this camp until the villages move out near the hills . . . or wherever Tabloka decides the summer encampment."

Peśla had risked his life for this night of talk, for a chance at discovering where the power sat among the Mahto—he knew where the tribal power sat—and what importance the band really gave him. For if the Mahto will not raise his rank to war leader, he had told himself, he shall separate from this people and find an influential woman among the Kiyuksa. He will throw away Lowansa and live with his new wife's band. And become a principal man.

But his true choice: a high place among his own. He saw Ahbleza as someone who had decided to settle for peaceman at thirty-and-five, but he saw the band—providing the people want to survive as a band—as a group of villages who needed someone vigorous, someone unafraid of implementing whatever acts will make the Mahto appear as the most powerful Titonwan band.

And who this someone, Peśla now hinted to his listeners, if not himself?

Ahbleza knew that much talk went on about him, more resentful talk than favorable, but he had imagined all words spoken in the tones of the perplexed. And so in answer to the puzzled, the questing, the demanding eyes, he had kept silent. For so he understood the Shirtman's oath. But on this day, a day of many rumors, the day after the sticks-hoop contest, he walked toward Tonweya's lodge, his own the most perplexed heart in the tribe.

Graciously, modestly, Anpagli received her husband's friend. But the small son of her lodge hovered near while Ahbleza ate from the bowl set before him, the child's eyes on the Shirtman's face whenever he imagined himself unnoticed. After a while the boy told that his father had gone out to look for meat. And so the Shirtman went away; the pipe he had wanted to put in Tonweya's hands had not left his own.

The evening of this same day Anpagli filled soup bowls for those Mahto women who called her relative. One by one her guests had arrived, each person looking for a comfort in the lodge of this woman that they will not find in their own.

Kipanna came hinting for an invitation to sleep here, the tipi that shelters herself and three old women a most depressing place. And Lowansa had come seeking release from an anxiety that concerned her young son. And Cankuna, following along that same trail, had found herself in Anpagli's lodge.

Seeing the bright blaze in this place, Winu had imagined that friends gathered for a seed-toss game. And, wanting to sit in on some plays, she also had come.

Suddenly Anpagli sent her young son to the adjoining tipi with a message that invited Tacincala to join the group of visitors. Let Tacincala not only see who all seek the warmth of her lodge, but let Tacincala understand that her presence will mean more than all the others put together; Tacincala, the one friend to the Psa-woman from the day of their meeting.

One more person scratched on this same tipi cover during the evening. Napewaśte, weary of gloom-bearers and old wags, came yearning for the sound of young laughing voices, for the sight of long braids and shining hair.

And so these women visitors acted to raise Napewaśte's heart, each one here willing to lend of her new-found comfort, even as each one here had borrowed from the gladness and contentment within Anpagli's lodge.

At sunrise the next day, Tonweya came in to report a small herd of pte grazing near the camp. Eyanpaha sang the scout's news and soon afterwards Ahbleza advised that the band not organize as for a big hunt but that two akicita accompany any group of men awake and eager to chase, cut, and pack meat.

Ten, twelve old hunters had gone out, the party returning before most young men had rolled off their sleeping robes. The group brought in meat from seven; their eighth

972

kill they had not touched. The clubmen had stayed to guard this one, the hunters insisting that Wanaǵi visit the site before anyone handled the meat; certainly, they had told one another, the wakanĥca will treat differently with a white pta, a white pta with short curled horns.

Ahbleza had known before the hunters went out that a white pta stood center of the small herd; Tonweya had brought the exciting news directly to the Shirtman. But to the scout's amazement Ahbleza had shown little interest. True, he had looked for a white pte during the long search, a herd-mother and not a herd-father, but the discovery of either one called for ceremony and celebration. Yet Ahbleza acted indifferent toward the whole thing; he had smoked with Tonweya as on any occasion, as if the scout had reported nothing unusual. And after the hunt, the Shirtman had stayed in camp; he had not ridden out with the wakanĥca to view this rare, perhaps portentous, mystery.

But many things about Ahbleza now puzzled Tonweya, puzzled the Mahto people; certainly their Shirtman seemed to drift into legend before he had used up his place in the sun.

Almost everyone in the band had accompanied Wanaǵi to the scene of the kill. And so Ahbleza, sitting alone, pondered this white mystery who had wandered toward the Mahto villages, who had offered his hide to the Mahto hunters. Next winter—or whenever they release Olepi's spirit—Wanaǵi will need strips of white hide for the head-band ceremony. But will the spirit-lodge attract the white one they kill this morning? Or will Wanaǵi, sending out his stones, bring the creature close to camp?

"Or," Ahbleza murmured aloud, "will my power, a power I not yet recognize, draw the white mystery here? If truly I manifest the white pte in the snow, perhaps I also bring in this one.

"But if I entertain such thoughts, what keeps me from going with the people to view the one they kill? Will I fear that I shall discover something?"

The next instant the Shirtman understood why he had waited back in camp: the day had come for him to visit his father's spirit-lodge. Perhaps the answer to all that perplexed him hovered over this place; perhaps the lodge stood

973

empty but for his father's spirit, whose influence he never will deny.

On entering the spirit-lodge, Ahbleza saw two persons: Icabu sat on and a woman stood looking at the gift pile. Anpagli, remembering that the Psa tribe avoid contact with white pte, had sought this sanctum where none dared disagree with her or embarrass her or speak unkindly.

The Shirtman had not known why the wife of his brother-friend had come to the spirit-lodge on this day nor will he wonder why; he knew only that she belonged here—here in the spirit-lodge—on the same day that he made his visit to this place, this lodge where Olepi's influence yet dominates.

XVI

THE WARM sun and budding trees pulled the Mahto out of their lodges, the winter fires left to die. Children and parents, frisky as any four-legged, romped over the fresh grass.

Someone had heard the tiblo-bird calling to all Lakotah, advising that the bands assemble. Someone different had reported a personal conversation with the bird-of-two-voices, this winged advising that he comb his hair and start moving out for the summer camp. But the newscarriers had not yet arrived with proposals as to a campground.

Even so, the women made preparation. Each one had hung the sleeping robes on outside racks where the wind took hold, cleaning and removing any smell. Some wives laid their winter garments over the little sandpiles and then invited those tiny shortnecks, those specks who live in sand, to carry off the season's accumulation of grease and soil. And all the while Woze and two heyoka companions kept an eye on the sky. The south wind frequently blew in a mischievous cloud to dampen robes and hides put out to sun, but not when a heyoka stood ready to drive off the chance of rain.

Out on the playground on this certain day a group of men suddenly stopped their fun to appraise a party of horsebacks who came riding the sign that identified their camps—Kiyuksa and Oglalahca—whirling their horses atop the near rise.

"Here comes the answer to the summer campsite," Sluka called out. And certainly these visitors approached in the manner of an inviting-party. But instead the group had come prepared for games.

They felt in the mood for a ball game, they told, and had ridden a day and a half to contend against such experts as Woskate and Sunktanka.

"And to make use of this wide stretch of level, bare ground," one of the Oglalahca laughed; "so what will you say to a game of knocking-the-ball?"

Agreeable. But on foot, not horseback. Why risk a horse falling on this soggy earth?

Quickly, now, they decided the distance between goals and the space between goal markers. The visitors had brought along their own curved sticks but the Mahto shall provide a quilled ball, two, three balls in the event players damage or lose the original.

Sluka had hurried back among the Mahto lodges shouting for players. And so Pesla along with fifteen, twenty more Mahto headed for the playground. The rough and dangerous game appealed to these warriors, especially Pesla. True, the judges often called Pesla on a play—improper use of hands or interference—but he played a bold game and he often scored.

Soon the players had stripped to loin-covers and moccasins, painted their arms and legs, and tied up their hair. And now they lined up, forty-five Mahto against thirty Kiyuksa-Oglalahca, this unevenness of players not a concern in a game where deftness decides victory.

Sunktanka took an outside position, Woskate going far out on the opposite side. But now Pesla, standing next to the center man, suddenly left his place, moving out alongside Woskate.

975

"I will knock the ball when you miss," he said coldly "perhaps the Mahto need not lose their moccasins and horses this day."

Wośkate, a great gameman but without rank as warrior, had not answered. Instead he watched the ball, tossed up from the center and now striking the ground, instantly someone swinging, the ball flying over heads, falling, everyone running. . . .

The Mahto team scored at the start, Wośkate knocking the ball most of the way, then passing to those men near the goal.

The second score went to the Kiyuksa-Oglalaĥca but not before many daring plays and much confusion, players tramping over the ball, falling over one another, and rapping one another on the shins.

A big crowd had gathered to watch the contest, big and noisy, everyone aware that the next goal decides the winners.

But now a party of Śiyo rode in, the men claiming that they had heard the shouting all the way across the valley and over a ridge. And so the judges announced a break in the game to permit these kinsmen to make bets, to tie their wagers onto whatever items lacked a taker.

Again the teams formed two lines halfway between goals and again Peśla growled at Wośkate: "Stay out of my way. I will run this ball."

The surprised player made a grunting sound; none shall give him orders on the playground.

The ball went into play and persons who watched for any misuse of hands or any kicking had difficulty following the action, the contest suddenly violent, as many sticks swinging in the air as on the ground.

Suddenly a yell went up. And now everyone—watchers, winners, losers—began cheering. The Mahto team had scored and won. And when the men untangled at the goal, they agreed that Peśla had made the winning point.

But now a murmuring began among the spectators. A man had crumpled, a player who had not pulled himself up: Wośkate, face down in the mud, one leg twitching.

The peźuta Huhupiye examined the injured man where he lay, then motioned for a robe. He wanted Wośkate carried to the peźuta-lodge for a second look at the damage;

certainly the man's wounds called for more than warm water and a song.

Ahbleza, hearing the change from cheers to a wail, came quickly to the playground, where he helped with the robe on which they moved Woskate. Seeing the deep cuts in the man's knees and the place where bone pushed through skin, the Shirtman recognized the importance of a competent bone-setter if Woskate ever intends to run again, or even walk.

Relatives of the hurt man walked alongside the robe-carriers, their faces anxious. And so the Shirtman hunted something that will ease these hearts. But what thing shall he say?

The truth, his familiar-voice had answered; say only that the boneman's knowing hands and Woskate's own spirit-power shall decide whether or not the gameman uses his legs again. And so Ahbleza had spoken.

After looking in on Woskate, the Oglalahca and Siyo visitors rode off at dawn the next day but the Kiyuksa players stayed on another day and night. And so they saw many persons making gifts in Woskate's name.

Huhupiye, after straightening the gameman's leg, had said that Woskate will hobble around but that he will require a strong branch under his arm to help him.

Pesla, hearing, had sent two horses to Huhupiye's lodge, one for the healer and one for the gameman.

Promptly someone had made a song about Pesla, something for the crier to sing the length of camp, a song that told of a warrior who never bore a grudge, who always respected the brave. And then the Kiyuksa visitors heard many persons praising this warrior's name, certain Mahto speaking of Pesla as the one man they approve for war leader. The difference in temperament between Pesla and the Shirtman, they said, will balance the camp; one man will lean toward war, one man toward peace. And the voice of the council shall decide which way.

But these Kiyuksa, coming for the ball game and now ready to go back, suddenly projected into the Mahto camp something that interested everyone far more than Pesla's bid for head warrior.

Whoever waits for Tabloka to propose a site for this summer's encampment, they told, get ready to meet with

977

surprise. Tabloka already had moved his villages up the good river to Red Lake's place; he had wanted to see the new post before the trader closed for the summer. And here the powerful leader intended to stay whether or not the other Titonwan bands joined him.

The ball-players also told of two, three Oglalahca families who had camped close by Red Lake's lodge this past winter and who had reported a most unusual collection of trade items.

Mnisa's people also had visited Red Lake and they, like the Oglalahca, had found many new and pleasing things at the post. Or so these Kiyuksa told.

Listening to the ball-players speak, Ahbleza found himself remembering Miyaca, his Sahiela friend who had taken his band south in answer to the people's request for campsites on the fat-meat earth and nearby Little Whiteman's big mud fort.

The wasicun raise their trading places everywhere, the gamemen went on to say; even now Mnikooźu and Canoni stay close to the forks of the good river, where the traders scheme a second post for the convenience of these bands.

But who invites these whitemen, someone had asked.

Who knows, someone had answered. But will not most persons welcome something new and amusing during the cold winter moons?

Amusing like crazy-walk and crazy-eyes, someone had murmured, someone who had remembered the brawls on the muddy river.

And now Ahbleza recognized 'Oglala post'—or so they named this trading place where those Oglalahca families had visited, where the Kiyuksa chose to camp—as something he will not avoid in the manner his father had avoided contact with those traders on the muddy-water. A prohibiting dream had kept Olepi from taking his people to the big river. And as a defense against the fiery drink, guns, and disease, Olepi had performed the sungazing. But these new seasons bring the traders to the Lakotah and so the Mahto either live on lonely campgrounds or they accept the presence of these intruders.

Intruders? But if intruders, Ahbleza told himself, why

978

these many eyes brightening to the talk of more rapidly firing guns and at the mention of a new trap for catching 'beaver'? And what about these throats that make the wistful sound on learning that the whitemen gladly will trade cloth and beads and 'tobacco' for tallow and hides, for things plentiful in most Mahto lodges?

The ball-players rode off to join Tabloka, their leader, and soon Ahbleza saw his own people gathering in little groups, sitting to deliberate that which the Kiyuksa visitors had told.

And now, before dark, certain warriors scratched on the Shirtman's lodge; they came as a group they said, to speak their decision after considerable talk with the principals in each warrior-lodge. They ask that the Shirtman lead the band to Oglala post. But if on arrival the Mahto leader judges this place undesirable as a campsite, the people shall wait at a different site until all Titonwan come together. Certainly this Red Lake, like all traders, will go away before midsummer, before the ceremonial sungathering of the Lakotah.

Quietly Ahbleza accepted the wisdom in that which they proposed, but he knew that whatever his decision, certain ones will go on to the post.

Soon after this delegation, Ośota stood at the same lodge flap. He came, the Canoni told, to reveal the voice of the many, more than half the Mahto expressing fear that the band shall break in two.

"I shall not try to displace any man," Ośota said firmly, "through straight talk or hints. But I will sit here and report that the Shirtman embarrasses his warriors. His men tell that they suffer an insult when the Kiyuksa ball-players offer to get up an avenging party in the name of the Mahto.

"Many persons in this band now agree that they find the roaring personality of a Tabloka more pleasing to their disposition than the silent lips of a leader who refuses his warriors a war. Warriors without a war, these persons say, will cease to feel like warriors. And a band without warriors will not hold together.

"I am a Canoni who proudly chooses to live among the Mahto, who desires to see his children growing up in this

979

camp. I will not choose to see this important band break and scatter. For this reason I dare come here and speak bluntly."

Ahbleza heard Ośota's earnest appeal with the same outward calm he had shown toward all who came to see him, a calm born of but one thought: a Shirtman remembers the good of the tribe. And what good will he, Ahbleza, bring his people if—telling who kills Olepi—he throws his band and eventually all Lakotah into a war they will not win, into a war they will not survive.

Yet who will understand him if he attempts to describe such a war? Who but Tonweya sees the picture, originally as a vision they share in their youth and again on a piece of hide, something that he, Ahbleza, paints to stir the scout's memory. And yet he will not tell the scout or any man about the second vision, his stone-shelter vision. And so only he, Ahbleza, knows that those two visions form one picture, one terrifying picture.

Or will Wanaǵi know? Perhaps the wakaṅlica sees the whole picture even before Ahbleza sees? And so Wanaǵi knows that the news about Oglala post and Tabloka's indifference to a summer hoop give startling reality to this war picture. But certainly Wanaǵi knows; Wanaǵi, all his life a seer and now a stone-dreamer, most certainly he knows ... everything. And so he, Ahbleza, dares not delay his visit with Wanaǵi another day. At sunrise he shall return the pronghorn pipe to the sacred-man and Wanaǵi will understand why he returns this stem and bowl. Truly the day comes for Shirtman and seer to begin their talk concerning the spiral path, the path of vision.

During the long pause, Ośota had caught fragments of Ahbleza's thoughts, enough to understand that the Mahto leader intended to hear each one who approached his lodge flap but not to make answer. And now, watching Ahbleza empty the pipe, he wondered whether he had told the Shirtman anything of importance.

Walking back to his own lodge, Ośota reflected on the differences among men and before he reached his own fire his face had set in anger. The unfamiliar expression had surprised his wife, nor had the woman understood when suddenly he called to his adopted son, sending the youth to Peśla's tipi with a demand for meat: "Tell the warrior that

Ośóta starves. Say that Ośóta wants meat, much meat. And that he wants this meat now."

Staring at the full bowl she had set before him, his wife raised her eyes in astonishment. Then looking away quickly, she murmured that the boy shall go at once.

This same evening one more person had expressed a desire to visit the Oglala post. Speaking through an old one who visited her lodge, Napewaśte let the son know that she wanted to see Red Lake's place. The trading posts, she hinted, become familiar ground to everyone in the tribe but herself.

Ahbleza had answered gently: "Tell my mother that I am uneasy about making this move. But when I council with the camp leaders next day, I and they shall count robes and dry meat and containers of fat. Soon I will know whether or not this band owns enough for trade without neglecting the have-nots among the Mahto. For I choose never to see someone starving or cold or afoot while meat and robes and horses go out in exchange for danger and disaster."

Listening to the answer, Napewaśte imagined that she had heard his father speak. But during the long silence that followed she closed her eyes, ashamed of her request.

Ahbleza had not intended the silence as reproof. Instead the Shirtman, remembering that he had begun his life in this woman's lodge, sat wondering whether he will finish his life, his visible life, here. But now he saw a hand reaching out, grasping on to the pipe that rested in a little rack at his side, the pipe that Wanaġi had presented him. The next instant he recognized the hand for his own, the pipe compelling him to rise, to go out of the lodge. And so he understood that for some reason the visit with the sacred-man dared not wait for dawn.

Wanaġi sat at his lodge-fire while the day turned into dusk. Alongside him lay the piece of white hide from which he intended to cut a headband for Ahbleza. Four pure young women had treated this piece, these four the only ones to handle the rare pta since the hunt. And so he had sensed a desire to renew himself ceremonially before he cut the circular strip.

But a strange weariness intercepted his desire. He sat on, reflecting for a while this day's experiences even as the tipi cover reflected dusk fading into dark.

At midday he had sat with a blind man. Tunkaśila, grandfather to Ahbleza, lived on in the scout-lodge where, his ears and touch as keen as ever, he kept count of the days each man stayed out. And in return for this work, the scouts fed and sheltered him. Napewaśte had urged her father to stay in her tipi but Tunkaśila had wanted a place where he sat useful. Then this morning, while wandering alone outside the scout-lodge, the old man had slipped and fallen, twisting his leg and skinning his forehead. He had refused everyone's help but he had welcomed a visit with Wanaǧi. Soon afterwards, the scouts had noticed Tunkaśila getting onto his feet without assistance and that his forehead showed neither cuts nor a bruise. The story had spread, and while none in the band had asked Tunkaśila concerning this mystery, certain ones had paused to marvel and to fear. Will not a stone-dreamer, they murmured, who instantly closes wounds also derive a power that destroys? Will not this remarkable wakanlica, whatever his good intentions, even yet trifle with power beyond his control? Then will he not create something crude that pulses with desire for harm? What of limunǧa, they whispered; limunǧa, control of another man's soul. But these murmurs and whispers had fallen to the ground when someone told that he had seen the stone-dreamer throw away his sacred stones.

True, Wanaǧi had let go his stones. On the way back to his lodge he had walked slowly along the edge of the stream, stopping at the place where the running waters rested in a quiet pool. Here he had stood marveling his own reflection. After a while he had opened his hand, dropping two shell-like stones into the still water. "Return to the source," he had said softly, watching the stones settle into the watery sand before he moved on.

Whatever he will not need, he had told himself, he shall not keep. But he had not imagined himself beyond the need for sacred stones until the day of Olepi's dying. True, his stability had evolved into something more than ordinary perception before that day, but he had not demonstrated his permanent contact with the true-companion, with the familiar-voice of all these seasons, with the presence he had begun to feel wherever he walked, wherever he sat or slept. And certainly he had not dared ask twice to meet his soul; not until his eternal self had taken over completely dared he seek again to view his soul, the heart of his spiritual body. He had made frequent excursions to that indefinite border between visible and invisible realms, experiencing discomfort only on his original visit and before he had learned to move and breathe on that different level. But only through a most careful disassociation with his flesh-body had he gradually acquired the strength that permitted him to approach and grow into certain conditions in the spiritual realm. Even so, the invisibles always had sent him back; go, they had told him, and in the seasons ahead someone will call your name.

Then on the night that he transmitted Olepi's song of defiance to the dying leader's son, he had seen proof of his power as something independent of the sacred stones. But he had demanded of his invisible self a second demonstration. And so neither sending out his spiral-shaped stones nor using any other stone, he had brought a small herd close to camp, the white pta standing center.

And now on this day he learned that he had strengthened Tunkaśila. Returning to the sacred-lodge, he had heard Waglula, his young assistant, speak of the old man's astounding recovery. Instantly he had sensed a need to review his vision of seasons past, not the grizzly-dream which had conformed to the pattern for a wapiya but his secret vision, something he never had revealed to anyone but about which he once had hinted to Olepi. Within Ahbleza, he had told the father, sat the power to keep a piece of the people on whatever day the Lakotah began their death-walk.

He remembered the picture he had seen back on the day the enemy killed Peta, a vision of the tribe breaking, each band limping off, then splitting into pieces. He had recognized the destroyer only as something terrifying set into motion, something silent and invisible, unnoticeable yet powerful enough to disintegrate a people. But he had understood the message: he, a tribal seer, shall act to help prepare each Lakotah for this inevitable happening so as to keep alive the spirit on whatever day the destroyer comes to shred the body.

Accepting this work as his responsibility, he had not

wavered. Habitually he had overlapped visible and spiritual realms, entering this high level of consciousness in an effort to promote the growth of careful reporting and so avoid definitions that limit, concepts that obstruct. And certainly he had sought to perceive those truths which the invisible grandfathers tried to communicate, truths for enhancing life among the visibles. On the day he had heard the dreaming-pair recite their vision, he had recognized Ahbleza as a force for preservation but as a preserver who needed to confront resistance at every turn; what different way, he had asked himself, to strengthen such power and so prepare Ahbleza for the season when he shall face alone a resisting force that threatens to overwhelm the whole tribe. Ahbleza the pre-server, the vision had revealed, and Tonweya the truthbear-er, the example of that which Ahbleza shall choose to preserve.

But he had watched Ahbleza go out again, the Shirt-man seeking a vision of peace, hunting an answer to proud survival without war. He had welcomed Ahbleza's return, knowing that the Shirtman had witnessed fighting wherever he had looked—clouds battling in the sky, man and creature battling in the valley—but that out of the great understand-ing and above the noise, a voice had reached Ahbleza. And so Ahbleza had understood more than he had seen, more than he had words for: something incomparable. Now the night had come for talk concerning this second vision, the vision that confirmed the youth-dream, that answered at the mature level all that had perplexed Ahbleza; the night had come for a full understanding, for the help of a true-seer wherever something yet puzzles the new leader of the Mahto band. And if Ahbleza neglects to come to the sacred-lodge before midnight, he, Wanaġi, intends to compel the Shirtman's appearance.

Compel? Wanaġi sat shocked at his own thought; what nature of seer compels another person's acts? Will the cer-tainty of his true-power suddenly drive him toward such abuse? Will this same certainty effect an irresistible impulse to use his power for controlling another man's soul? Then truly his own soul suffers defects.

During the next moments he reflected on those risks he had taken when he had demanded the stone-vision. But he had not experienced the calamitous dream that exacted a life of contrary behavior. And for all his contact with pebbles and boulders, he never had seen the giant stone that some persons reported, a flying mystery that whirled down noisily and flashed red around the edge, that sat on the bare plain like a round, shivering white bird but a bird without wings or beak or feathers, a bird that left tracks in the shape of four zigzag furrows. Nor had he any memory of a previous existence such as many seers claimed, these persons hinting at a life in the clouds and in contact with the apprehensible force, with the makers of the startling forked-light. And certainly he never had contemplated the destructive use of stone-power; he never had tried to cut off someone's resistance, never had arranged for someone to die. And yet this very night he had considered using the same power to bring Ahbleza to the sacred-lodge that he had used to bring the white pta close to camp.

Reaching forward an unsteady hand, he grasped his pipe; carefully he filled the bowl with cuttings he had prepared on his return to the lodge. Then, using a short forked stick, he lifted an ember onto the bowl. He drew in his breath, and smoke came thinly from his nose. He felt a chill in his legs and, staring at the fire circle, he saw that the flame had disappeared and that the blinking wood slowly faded into ashes. Dry sticks lay within his reach, but he neither moved his hand toward the pile nor touched the robe that had slipped off his knees. He will not need legs for this night's journey, he told himself; he will feel neither cold nor warmth on approaching the realm of the invisibles.

Drawing once again on the pipestem, he sensed an urgency to start on his journey and to extend the boundary on this visit, an urgency to view his soul and recognize his imperfection. "I am a creation, an image of the creative force," he murmured; "I go now to claim my heritage." The hand that held the pipe dropped to his side and in the same instant he knew the exaltation of a spirit in flight, a spirit joyous and without restraints.

Walking through the soft, dark night, Ahbleza looked forward to the sweetgrass comfort of the sacred-lodge and to the strengthening silences between talk whenever he and Wanaġi met. For during the quiet he always felt lifted, not as if his heart soared but as if someone, something, pulled him up onto a bright new level. Occasionally he had entered the sacred-lodge bearing antagonism and then the father-friend had known to say nothing until the distracting force had dissipated. Virtue, Wanaġi had said, never enters a place where mischief lurks, nor will truth flow into him who refuses to prepare for truth. But to this meeting with Wanaġi, he brought a clean heart. He had decided to talk with the sacred-man concerning his vision in the cave; he wanted to make certain that Wanaġi understood why he brought back the pipe. But he intended to speak in a manner entirely different from a youth who seeks an interpretation. He had interpreted his own vision but for one unknown. And that one mystery he had not tried to understand. For on the day a man discovers that he knows the unknowable, he belongs to a different realm; Wanaġi had said so.

And now, approaching the sacred-lodge, Ahbleza suddenly realized that he and the father-friend already had answered all the things that they had considered truly important.

Not a visitor but a spirit coming to stay, to live ever-more in the realm of the grandfathers, all the grandfathers back to the beginning.

"You demand your heritage but will you recognize your demand?"

A voice had answered Wanaġi, a sound neither familiar nor unfamiliar.

"I, Wanaġi, desire to view my soul, to see my self born. I am here in spirit and on this realm to see my soul. I recognize certain deficiencies. I know my soul as imperfect, as something I choose to improve."

"You choose to improve your soul, but will you recognize the meaning in your choice?"

Wanaġi sensed impatience. On previous visits he had felt movement around him whenever a voice spoke and he had heard encouragement. Now he pulsed through a strange darkness, aware only of a glow in the distance.

"I choose to perfect my soul. Let me out."

The distant glow became a brightness that moved toward him. Or perhaps he moved toward the brightness.

"Wanaġi."

Someone called his name.

"Wanaǧi, know your self."

The bareness he had experienced when first he had overlapped these realms and seen his spiritual self in infancy seemed as nothing to the bareness he knew now. Something had happened to the spiritual covering to which he had become accustomed.

"Wanaǧi, you know your soul as your constant companion. Now you become your soul. In this manner and only in this manner will you improve."

His soul, then, will require a new covering, a different cover?

"Wanaǧi. Stay."

He makes the transfer? Always before they say 'go'; now they say 'stay.'

He heard crying. But who will want to cry? He saw brightness in many places and some of this brightness began to look familiar. Suddenly he knew; he had entered into the realm of the grandfathers. And he wanted to stay. He had made the choice: a good day to die.

The entrance flap to the sacred-lodge hung loose, and Ahbleza, calling gently, lifted the covering and stepped inside.

Wanaǧi sat before a dead fire; he sat unmoving and a little slumped. His pipe, the ashes warm, lay on the earth. And next to the pipe, a piece of hide from the white pta.

Ahbleza gazed a long while upon the still form before he reached out his hand; he had heard the cry in his heart and had sensed the feel of cool, loose skin and undeniable limpness. But now he let himself down alongside the dead, his arms folding around the shoulders of this father-friend. And so Wanaǧi's body fell forward, the head touching against Ahbleza's breast, one hand falling onto the piece of white hide.

After a while Ahbleza laid out the empty form, wrapping the body as if for a winter's sleep. And then, stepping outside, he crossed two long sticks in front of the tipi flap. Why ask the crier to announce the death in the middle of the night? Wanaǧi leaves none who carry his blood and this one who calls him father-friend already knows and takes care. Why not, instead, let Winkte's wonderful voice awaken the camp at sunrise. Winkte's song telling the people that a sacred-man among the Mahto walks the spirit-trail.

But moving away from the sacred-lodge, Ahbleza felt the seer's presence, almost as if Wanaǧi walked alongside him. Twice he stopped, holding his breath to listen. But he heard nothing; as he had told himself, he and the father-friend had answered whatever had seemed important to answer.

I, WANAǦI, TELL YOU SOMETHING. TRY TO HEAR.

ONE CONSCIOUSNESS, ONE INSEPARABLE, INDIVISIBLE CONSCIOUSNESS: SPIRITUAL CONSCIOUSNESS. ONE SELF, ONE ETERNAL SELF: YOU, YOUR SOUL; YOU, THE ONENESS OF THE WHOLE.

ONE FORCE, THE CREATIVE FORCE. ONE POWER, THE REASONING POWER. ONE SACREDNESS: TRUTH.

RECOGNIZE THE SPIRAL PATH UPON WHICH YOU MOVE LEVEL TO NEXT HIGH LEVEL, A SPIRITUAL PATH UPON WHICH YOU EVOLVE TOWARD THE WHOLENESS OF THE ONE. YOU LIVE ON ONE EARTH, ONE EARTH WITH MANY, MANY PLANES. THE SAME INVARIABLES—THE ABSOLUTES—EXTEND ONTO EACH PLANE, BUT YOU ENCOUNTER MORE SPIRITUAL INFUSION AT EACH LEVEL.

RECOGNIZE YOUR TRUE PARENTS: SUN AND EARTH. DEMAND YOUR TRUE HERITAGE: TO INHERIT THE WHOLE.

I, WANAǦI, KNOW. I RETURN TO THE SOURCE, TO THE BIRTHPLACE OF CONSCIOUSNESS.

XVII

OBSERVING A clear sky and warm sun, Ahbleza asked that someone raise the sides of the center lodge for a council meeting open to everyone in camp. The meeting concerned the band's next move and the Shirtman wanted each one to have a voice in the decision.

At dawn the people had heard Winkte sing of the seer's dying. Then, mid-morning, they had listened to old Eyanpa-ha, mouth for the Shirtman, calling together the principal ones in the village, also inviting any man or woman who desired to hear these leaders in council or who wished to speak a thought.

And so they came, someone from every lodge, from eighty-five Mahto lodges. Leaders and clubmen took places inside the big tipi, more than sixty men sitting in two circles. And outside, twice as many men and even more women.

Ahbleza sat at the back, to one side of the place of honor. And now the people waited to see who will sit next to the Shirtman, everyone knowing that whoever took this empty place recognized himself as Ahbleza's choice for war leader of the Mahto.

But Ahbleza had yet to indicate a preference. Certainly he wanted someone competent, someone vigorous yet un-bending, but he sat aware of the importance of selecting a man popular with the warrior-lodges. The war leader headed all clubmen; he walked in a position to hold together or to scatter the band. Occasionally a band had but one leader, a man adept at war and adequate in peace; Olepi, such a man. But Olepi never had worn the Shirt. The Shirt made a man something more than warrior, something more than leader, but with restraints in either direction.

So who for war leader, a man the council will confirm? Pesla? Never Pesla.

Looking again at the front circle, he suddenly fancied his Mahto as a band of retired warriors who had followed his father in their young-man seasons. His glance rested a moment on Icabu and Cetan, these two fifty or more win-ters, two wise middle-aged men. And sitting next, Iku and

Żola, Catka and Śunktanka, somewhere in their forties. And then those really old ones; Wambli Okiye, who used a stick to help him walk and Tunkaśila who rarely walked at all. And Heħaka, into his eighties but sturdy-legged and strong-armed and certainly clear-headed.

His eyes moved on around the circle, noticing Ħoka, who sat next to Pasu, and at the far edge of the arc, Ogle and Hinhan, boy-companions to his father, these four approaching or passing sixty.

Viewing the second circle, he looked upon the young members of Tokala, Iyuptala, Iħoka, three warrior-lodges that grew strong within the Mahto camp. Here sat perhaps fifty young men, each one striving for war honors. Six in this group already had achieved that which the council required of a war leader: leading out four separate war parties and returning, the party all horseback and unhurt. But the council also demanded firmness and stability in such leaders.

But why, with fifty eager young clubmen and twenty, thirty mature warriors will he envision the Mahto as a band that has seen the last of the great warriors? Will he come to the place in body and spirit where he loses his intensity?

He saw the pipe returning, the stem now in Yuza's hands. At one point he had considered Yuza for the rank, a man his same age and husband to his adopted sister, Kehala. The people will not remember Yuza as someone born Psa, he had told himself, but they will look upon the appointment as an imbalance; only in Tabloka's band will leader and war leader come from the same family.

Whom, then, will the people want as head-of-war? Whom will the council accept? Whom, if not Ośota?

True, Ośota had arrived only recently among the Mahto, among any Titonwan. Yet many persons spoke this Canoni's name, his good nature and big heart as famous as his war exploits.

Why not Ośota, a proficient warrior and a good father, a man who had taken into his lodge the orphaned sons and daughters of Iśna and wife; Ośota, who had adopted all five children.

Ośota born four winters before Ahbleza; Ośota, a man who had lost none of his vigor; Ośota, the man who had defied Peśla on the playground. Perhaps Peśla will resent this one as head warrior but whom will Peśla not resent?

Receiving back the pipe, Ahbleza used the stem to gesture Ośota forward and into the place next to him.

And now the council meeting began, Ahbleza standing and speaking of Wanaǵi. He asked that they honor his request and stake down the sacred-lodge; that they tie shut the flaps and leave the seer's body under the cover where he had stayed alone these many winters, these many lonesome winters. He asked that Śunihanble and Huhupiye perform this act. "And let the youth Waglula accompany the two healers to the sacred-lodge," he said evenly, "but neither he nor they shall remove anything." And so he had answered firmly his crying heart: the white pta hide stays where he had placed the piece, alongside the father-friend.

The Shirtman talked next of breaking camp, of traveling north to the fork in old-woman creek, up the fork to a new campsite, to a place west of the black hills, south and west. But now he intended to hear the people speak, to hear his people saying that which they desire.

And so many persons made known their choice, asking for a move in the opposite direction, asking for a campsite at Oglala post.

"And if the whiteman makes trouble," one speaker said, "the Mahto need not stay. They shall await the Oglalahca and Kiyuksa at split-toe creek or at the water hole, wherever they decide."

Or return to Oglala post, the next speaker advised, after this Red Lake goes, the trader certain to start out as soon as the big river rises to a swift flow.

"Perhaps Red Lake will trade fairly," another person said, "and so Mahto along with Oglalahca and Kiyuksa shall own the iron traps that catch 'beaver.' They say that the traders want 'beaver' skins, not 'buffler' hides this summer."

Certain ones smiled back of their palms, not so much at the speaker's use of whiteman words but at his effort to mimic the unfamiliar *r* sound. Even so, everyone had caught the meaning.

But Ahbleza had not smiled, either at words or hint. Will these persons eager to trade for traps, he mused, ever try out this method? Perhaps swims-with-stick already discovers a way to open the trap or to turn the thing upside down. Old Ištakpe claims that this wise little creature whose grandfathers stood perhaps tall as the grizzly, once lived like a man, reasoning and perceiving like a man. But if this creature lacks the cunning to escape the trap, will the Lakotah trade those skins for yet more traps until all four-legged live or die at the whiteman's whim?

The councilors sat until sundown but Ahbleza had said nothing more. Instead he had listened closely, foreseeing the final decision before all the spoken words had made that decision obvious to everyone.

And now Eyanpaha made his rounds, calling for all tipi down at dawn. Before sunrise the Mahto band starts moving toward Oglala post, campsite of the Titonwan this summer. The people speak, telling their desire. The people decide.

The people? But I am the people, Ahbleza whispered to himself, and I will not desire this move. I grieve this move.

Stepping out of his mother's lodge, he walked under the red evening sky to the horse enclosure. Choosing two of his own, he led the creatures close by the spirit-lodge.

Icabu, already returned, came outside in answer to Ahbleza's gentle call.

"My friend"—Ahbleza slipped the horses' cord into Icabu's hand—"clip their tails and shave their sides. These horses drag the spirit-lodge on the trail to Oglala post." He walked away remembering that he had seen his father-friend dead this morning, his blood-father dead four moons previously, that one soul-lodge stays here, one soul-lodge goes to Oglala post. And that he had sensed a separation within himself, his body soon leading the Mahto band to Red Lake's trading place but his spirit going in a different direction.

He shuddered. Who dares even imagine such a division between body and spirit? Certainly not a man with a great vision, a Shirtman who, dancing at the sunpole, had glimpsed the light of his own soul.

XVIII

THEIR FOURTH night on the trail, the Mahto camped on ground not far from the ledge of Ahbleza's second vision. They had met with Hinyete's village of Siyo, the two bands raising lodges in a hoop for this overnight camp. These Siyo also traveled toward Oglala post, the Kiyuksa influencing their move even as they had influenced the Mahto. And now, while the sun climbed down, the people sat in little circles, coming together for talk and gossip, for quiet laughter and a peaceful smoke.

But Tonweya had not joined any one of these groups and so Ahbleza found the scout staking his horse nearby his lodge but within reach of deep grass.

"Mount, my brother," Ahbleza said smiling, "and ride with me to the near-distant ledge. I will tell you something."

The Shirtman had not spoken to the brother-friend of his second vision, but now, on the ledge and in front of the cave, he turned his face to Tonweya: "Misun, I am not a stranger to this ledge, this cave. In the recent past I stand here, I dream here."

Feeling Ahbleza's hand touch gently on his shoulder, the scout looked upon this man whose youth-vision he had shared. He saw those rays from the fiery ball in the west that danced on Ahbleza's breast and suddenly he knew that in some different way he shared this second dream even as he had shared the sungazing experience.

Ahbleza spoke on: "I remember hail striking this ledge, rattling and bouncing crazily. And a wind that tried to sweep me away. I recall the sky streaking and roaring, summer and winter clashing overhead.

"Afterwards, in the quiet of the cave, a most amazing picture moves before my eyes. I ponder carrying this picture to him who gives meaning to the vision I and you share; I lack words for describing all that I see. But, on the night before I lead the people onto this trail, I go to his lodge to speak of that which I understand, to describe as much of the vision as I now comprehend. But the ears in the sacred-lodge hear nothing."

The full meaning of his loss had reached Ahbleza. He removed his hand from Tonweya's shoulder and his body shook. "Who ever will sit in his place," he cried; "who ever will understand me?"

After a moment his calm returned; he went on, speaking evenly: "Misun, a similar vision ties together my existence and yours and so reveals that something depends upon I and you, not as one but as a pair.

"I intend now that you see me demonstrate my second vision. Perhaps the whole truth will unfold for me and for you as I enact the picture. Listen closely."

In strong, clear tones Ahbleza recited the story of his vision, his hands making the sweeping gestures and the delicate signs that put each important phrase into motion.

"I again stand on the hill as in the youth-vision. You again try to climb up to me with the pipe in your hand but you fall back down the hill. I look and see where you fall.

"Below me spreads a wide valley. A lake fills the valley and a great battle fills the lake. All the people join in the fight, Lakotah and Dakotah.

"This war goes on against a strange people, but I see that many creatures fight here also, creatures I recognize but for whom I hear unfamiliar names.

"I look across the lake, far to the opposite side. And I see a second hill, tall as the one where I stand. And on top of that hill I observe a man, someone who stands as I stand. But he resembles the strangers who fight below me.

"Many persons cling to the sides of each hill, mine and the one across the lake. And I notice that certain ones try to hold back their relatives, try to prevent their kinsmen from rushing into battle or falling into the lake. But those persons who struggle to get into the fight, pull away and enter the contest.

"Different ones—persons whose emotions influence their acts—lose their balance and drop into the lake. And I observe that the water, now impure, slowly turns red.

"I look more closely into this red lake and so I see that which I never before see. The Lakotah, Dakotah fight not only the strangers; they fight their own. They act like blind persons without a way for telling who, the relative and who, the stranger. But this same thing holds true for the strangers; they also, fight their own.

"And something more. All these persons fight with the creatures in the same way and so the whole lake becomes a noisy, terrifying battle, man-yells and creature-yells, all fighting and none hunting thought for whom they kill. Or why they kill.

"A great fear clouds over me and I shout to the Lakotah to come away. But they will not hear me.

"I look again at the top of the far-distant hill where the stranger stands. I look under my palm and with strong eyes until I see him clearly. And suddenly my heart sits still. I find my own. I am he.

"He calls to me but the distance and all the yelling from the contest below makes hearing difficult. Yet I call back in a powerful voice, and so I and this one whom I recognize as my self keep trying to hear above the terrible cries of war.

"All at once the contest ceases, the valley empty and quiet. The picture disappears. And yet I am not awakening in the cave on this ledge. Instead I stand on the hill as before. And you, my brother, stand calm and straight in front of me. And in your hand, the pipe."

Ahbleza had finished speaking, but for a moment the two stood looking across the valley as if the vision echoed in their ears. Then slowly they turned, the wonder of prophecy shutting off their breath until a flood of tears broke the tie with mystery and splashing onto the stone at their feet gently washed the ancient face of earth.

Arriving back in camp, the brother-friends heard the laughter of an amused people. Two, three mimics among the Siyo entertained in a manner to shake the giggles out of women and to wreathe the faces of men into smiles. Children also laughed, not at the entertainers but in imitation of the grownups. And even the dogs ran around making little squeals of pleasure until someone threw sticks at the pup who got too noisy.

And now, the impersonators going on to mimic the wašicun, the laughter mounted. One funny man, flinging his long hair over the front of his face, pantomimed a whiteman combing his beard. And a different actor, clasping some old scalps to his breast, mocked the paleskins' hairiness and their awkward walk, their rears like a wagging tail.

Ahbleza, sitting alongside the scout, made evident his amusement, his eyes and lips smiling as these Siyo clowned yet more whiteman traits: the mouths that talk too much and too loud, the long arm and extended finger that commands or threatens, and the shriveling shoulders of an entreating captive.

But as the show came to a finish, Ahbleza sat aware of one omission in all this acting: none of the actors had mimicked the effect of firewater on a Lakotah who accepts the burning-danger. Why, he wondered, will anyone avoid ridiculing this fool's drink?

When the people moved on at sunrise, the Shirtman and Hinyete walked front, the heads of Mahto and Siyo families directly back of these two. The line advanced twice as fast as on the previous day, the people aware that they approached the mouth of rapid creek and eager to reach the Oglala post before evening.

The sun had climbed to middle when finally they saw the tops of poles. And soon afterwards a party of young men and women had appeared, the group riding slowly and singing a welcome song.

Ahbleza, astonished, gazed upon the encampment; he had not pictured the lodges clustered so close to the trading-place. Truly, he had looked a long while before locating the rough-wood post. Any more tipi, he told himself, and a dog will not have space to lift a leg.

The women of the two newly arrived bands had seen nothing that indicated an orderly hoop and so they had chosen places on the edge of camp, setting up their poles and pulling on their lodge covers while the principal men among Mahto and Siyo sat smoking, each one pondering the wise procedure at this irregular campsite.

And while they smoked, Tasúnkekokipapi—Shirtman and now leader of a small wandering band of Kuya—came to welcome Mahto and Siyo. He appeared glad that Ahbleza and Hinyete had brought their people, but he avoided comment on the post. He told only that four whitemen managed the trades.

Suddenly Ahbleza determined to throw away his apprehension, to raise the big tipi and feast this man Red Lake and his three helpers. He will invite the traders to come this evening and he shall permit nothing that embarrasses either Lakotah or paleskins while these four visit the center lodge. He shall ask that all principal Mahto attend, also Tasunkekokipapi; perhaps the Shirtman, once a member of Isna's band, remembers some of the whiteman's words.

And he will invite Hinyete along with Pta Isna, the Siyo's head clubman, who had said that Red Lake once kept a Siyo woman as wife. And he will have Tonweya sit with this group for meat and smoke, the scout's eyes and ears quick at reason for alarm. Throwing out apprehension will not mean sitting unprepared for danger; the whole point of this gathering—to meet Red Lake, to know whether the Mahto more wisely go or stay.

And so Ahbleza, announcing his intention and hearing approval from these persons with whom he smoked, sent a messenger to the post, inviting the whitemen to come when the sun lengthened shadows.

Kehala, Anpagli, and many more women helped Napewaste raise the big cover, helped her spread the ground under this cover with mint. Then they went out asking for a loan of bowls and ladles.

The Mahto camp had plenty of fresh meat, six branched-horns killed on next to the final day of travel, but many women brought berries and sauces and flavoring to Napewaste's lodge. And so the Mahto prepared for a feast even before all Kiyuksa and Oglalahca had heard that this band had arrived.

But before the meat had cooked, long before the shadows had lengthened, the whitemen-guests had come, a boy running up to tell Ahbleza that the traders approached.

Glancing at the tree shadows, the Shirtman raised the back of his hand; he signaled to the Siyo breed who came along to interpret that these guests shall wait. The leaders not yet come to sit in their places; the fragrant herb not yet permeates the big lodge.

Somewhere, then, these whitemen had waited, perhaps impatiently.

The Mahto leader had looked for four wasicun, the four whites from the post, but he saw that only two stepped into the center lodge. And one of these two—a black wasicun, a black whiteman.

Red Lake had not come. In his place he had sent his new man, someone called Watts. And accompanying Watts, a big sad-eyed blackman, a Negro brought to the post for heavy work.

Watts, never before on the plains and mostly unfamiliar with Lakotah customs, had entered the lodge in a hardy manner, his flushed face and clumsy effort to appear congenial evoking a soft murmur of surprise from members of the Mahto band.

Then before Ahbleza had so much as reached for the pipe-bowl, something he intended to fill in a ceremonial way, Watts began to speak, telling that the other two men stayed back at the post to get things ready for the trade. But certain ones noticed that he winked at his black companion.

The translator, not looking up, told only that Red Lake looked for the new arrivals to visit the post next day. But now this Siyo son of an anonymous trader on the Missouri quietly advised Watts that talk here will not begin until after the ceremonial smoke and feast.

Affecting apology with a finger placed across his lips, Watts now crossed his legs, his foot shoving against the little pipe rack Ahbleza had placed to the front of himself and guests.

Many Lakotah eyes narrowed, but the Shirtman, unnoticing, reached for the bundle of smoke-leaves alongside the rack.

Presently, the bowl filled and glowing, Ahbleza passed the pipe to the Siyo breed, who, after puffing twice, offered the bowl to Watts.

Watts examined the spiral stem curiously. Then, as if suddenly recalling instructions, he put the stem to his lips. Exhaling, he reached across the blackman to hand the bowl to the next Mahto. Next, he leaned toward the interpreter, whispering a request: find out if the headman's got another pipe like this one.

At this moment someone lifted the lodge flap; the women had come with soup and meat. And now they handed in their offering to the two youths whom Ahbleza had appointed his helpers.

Watts, curious about those floating pieces, sniffed the soup; he glanced at the interpreter but the breed appeared not to notice.

After a while, most bowls twice filled and emptied, Ahbleza sent around a second pipe. And now, awaiting the pipe's return, he reflected upon those strange dead leaves that had come to him during his boy-seasons, those dry leaves on which a whiteman had pictured not only horses but creatures unlike any four-legs he, Ahbleza, ever sees.

And so rising to welcome his guests, the Mahto leader invited these persons to tell about the place from which they come, to speak concerning the different four-legged and winged with whom they share their dwelling places.

But even as Ahbleza stood speaking, Watts again leaned toward the translator, again whispered that the breed find out his chances of getting hold of the spiral-stem pipe. Or one like it.

Unfamiliar with the rudeness of an interruption, Ahbleza stopped and waited. And so carefully, most carefully, the Siyo translated the whiteman's wish in terms of appreciation; the wašicun, he told, expresses much interest in Lakotah pipes.

Responding, the Shirtman spoke about the soft redstone from which they shape many pipe-bowls. And about the great mystery that had visited canumpa oke, the scene of many pipe-digs. Here, from out the midst, a voice had called saying that all tribes shall meet as friends at the redstone ledge.

"The Lakotah remember this mystery," Ahbleza said softly, "in the peace-smoke of the pipestone bowl."

The blackman had followed Ahbleza's gestures and the translator's words with wide, rolling eyes and affirming murmurs. And so the Mahto, sitting again, listened for the black-wašicun to speak, to describe his place in the east, the place of the red-and-white banner with stars.

Instead Watts spoke. Pushing back his slouch hat and clearing his throat, he talked not only about 'Kaintuck,' his birthplace, and 'Saint Louie,' his home, but about places he'd never seen, people he'd never known. And he managed easily to enlarge upon whatever he mentioned.

• • • •

The Śiyo translator struggled to stay abreast, hunting phrases that will identify things he scarcely understood himself. Until this day his interpreting had consisted of those words that answered to the number of hides wanted for gun or knife, for trade-cloth or a cup of whiskey. But now he needed phrases for describing the white population, so many whites that they raise tipi on top of tipi until they touch the clouds. Or so he interpreted Watts's description of whitemen as numerous as grass-stems and living in tipi 'sky high.'

And he needed phrases for explaining 'the-president,' the leader of all these whites, someone who dares speak of himself as hunka-father to his red children, someone who, Watts tells, wants all these red children living out on the mixed grasses where he more easily will protect the whole.

And certainly he needed a phrase for describing the whiteman's 'deadly weapon'—the cannon—and Watts's boast about these cannons.

Many logs-that-belch-fire-and-spit-out-an-egg, the interpreter told now, and not only many cannon but more white soldiers than any 'Injin' knows to count.

Watts's gutsy boldness had impressed some of his listeners but not all. Ahbleza had remembered himself back on the muddy river during those whiteman peace-talks, the whites one day feeding the Titonwan meat from six pte, the next day displaying manpower and gunpower. And on the third day requesting that the Titonwan touch-the-stick, make the peace mark. Twice the rolling-gun had flashed and boomed, before and after the Titonwan had signed the whiteman's peace-leaf. They celebrated, those whites had told, a great event in the lives of their people, something most important that had occurred perhaps fifty years past, something that had put an enduring pride in those white-eyes.

And now Ahbleza wondered whether the war story Watts sat telling related back to the commemorating flash-and-boom, to the winning of some great contest. Nothing similar to the running fights of the Lakotah, Ahbleza understood, but instead a fight that went on for many moons, neither side stopping when night came. But the noisy Watts apparently describes more than one such fight; perhaps these whitemen fight in many big contests? So who, their enemies?

The Shirtman reflected on the black-whiteman sitting here, this one perhaps a war captive? Someone whom Watts adopts? He remembered something he had heard as a boy, a story about Hasapa, a blackskin who had come onto the muddy river in company with a red-haired man; Hasapa, the people said, someone Red Hair protects.

Watts had stopped talking, and so Ahbleza understood that the man, now twisting the edges of his hat, signaled the finish of his long speech, the horse the only creature to which he had referred.

But Watts had not finished; he now instructed the Síyo breed to let him know what more the headman wants to hear.

Ahbleza wanted to hear the blackman speak.

At once, Watts had begun explaining a difference between whites and blacks, naming the blackman 'nigger' and speaking of him as 'slave' and 'run-away' but also praising the blackman's strength and willingness.

When Ahbleza appeared puzzled, Watts looked disgustedly at the translator: "The blacks ain't war captives, tell him. They're slaves or call them hands, field hands. You don't capture them, you buy them. See, it's like this: a whiteman owns land for growin' cotton. . . . "

Watts waited for the breed to catch up with his translation, but the Síyo had not even begun; he sat lost for words or gestures that signify owning earth in the sense a whiteman owns earth, owns land.

But whatever this Síyo interpreter's gain or loss through a whiteman-father, he had maintained the perceptiveness of his mother's people. Now, in an instant of sudden enlightenment, he saw that even as the Lakotah perhaps always experience difficulty understanding what 'own' and 'lend' mean to the whiteman, so shall the whiteman experience difficulty recognizing what the Lakotah means when he speaks of a Shirtman as 'owner of the people,' when he speaks saying that wherever a man sits or walks, for a moment or for a day or forever, this place he calls the center and this place belongs to him.

Will real understanding ever come for two peoples

whose language reveals so great a difference in nature and conduct?

Watts's sudden movement distracted the breed. He saw the whiteman reaching into the bag he had brought with him, pulling out a handful of trade items, extending his palm in Ahbleza's direction. And now he heard Watts speaking a request but not in whispers.

"Find out what more he wants for that pipe."

Unwilling to translate, the breed kept silent.

"Go ahead, Joe, ask him." Watts pushed back his hat once again; he stroked his short, curly beard and squinted his eyes in an attempt to look shrewd.

Ahbleza regarded the interpreter sternly. "I will know what he desires."

The breed stumbled through the offending proposal, but even before he finished, Ahbleza had lifted the pipe from the little rack.

He offered the stem-and-bowl with a steady hand. Glancing at the Siyo, he spoke: "Say that the pipe belongs to the whiteman, also the leg-covers that hang on the pole back of me. Say that I offer the black-whiteman the backrest against which he sits, also those robes that hang over the backrest."

The vow he had taken as Shirtman will compel this gifting as truly as the pipe compels truth; a man who pledges neither revenge nor loathing whatever happens dares not permit himself loss of composure in the presence of a fool.

Watts, his face reddening, pushed the gilt buttons, small mirror, hanks of beads, everything back into the bag. He looked up, glancing around; the group seemed mild enough.

He told the breed to thank everybody for the feed. And to say that he'd have sweet 'black soup' hot and ready to pour when they arrive at the post next day. He winked and patted the pipestem.

Getting to his feet, he rubbed his stiff knees. Suddenly remembering the gift of leggings, he ordered the blackman to take the pair from the pole and follow him outside.

And now, passing between the fire circle and his hosts—a discourtesy of which he was unaware—Watts left the big lodge.

The blackman accepted robes and backrest with a bow, his eyes wet with gratitude for the good thing coming to him. Walking to the back of the seated circle, he moved quietly out of the tipi. Nor had he so much as glanced at the pole where the leggings hung.

The Lakotah sat on, their faces still, not an eye flickering, not a gesture of any sort to show that they had noticed the departure of their guests. They knew only that the feast had come to a finish and that not a man in the tipi had heart for the coming day.

XIX

THE NEXT morning Peśla and three companions stood gazing at a bateau that crept upriver. Two men rode in the boat, two whitemen who waved their arms at the observers. But Peśla and these three from Mniśa's camp had not returned the wave, and when the boatmen came near the water's edge, the warriors dropped out of sight.

Concealed back of trees, the four watched the blackman carry many loads from the bateau to the post. The pale young man who helped him, the Mniśa told Peśla, worked at counting robes and hides and pte-tongues at the post. And the one who had talked and talked to the boatmen before the unloading began, who had kept turning his head from side to side in the whiteman's denying motion, this one: Red Lake.

The Mahto painted carefully; they had decided to wear their most decorated gowns, moccasins, leg-covers. For when they saw the sun bending toward the west, they intended to move as a band to the trading post. Here they shall meet Red Lake, who, judging their appearance, will know that the Mahto band lives proudly. Seeing their women in clean, colorful gowns, the whiteman will recognize the Mahto as a band of competent hunters; seeing each person head up, face calm, tongue silent, he will recognize the Mahto as a band of durable, perceptive people.

They had chosen to approach the post horseback, children and women also mounted. The scheme called for the Mahto leader and his principals to dash toward the post, then quietly wait horseback while the villagers, bearing one hundred choice robes, rode up slowly in an orderly line. And so Red Lake, observing, will know that these proud Mahto come looking for an honorable trade. And nothing more.

Ahbleza had put aside all signs of sorrow for his father nor had he raised his father's spirit-lodge on this campground. And the Mahto people, accepting Ahbleza as the one they now followed, had rubbed out or covered up their grief-marks. Even so, certain persons had wondered aloud why the Shirtman had not waited until after the release of his father's spirit before dismissing this sorrow.

Alone in his mother's lodge, preparing for the short ride to the traders, Ahbleza found other things more difficult to answer. He sat on this campground, he told himself, for the reason that his people had chosen to come here. He had walked front leading the people to this place but he had belonged at the rear, a follower. But he had come and so he intended to take a second look at the wašicun, at the whiteman.

He will wear the Shirt to the trading post, he decided now, and a single spotted feather at the back of his hair. But he will not wear paint, either on his face or body. The horses he rides, white, with ears and mane and tail red, and he will carry the summer robe on which he paints the graceful pronghorn of his youth's vision.

The people, seeing their Shirtman ride up in front of the Mahto council lodge, likened him to the sun; so the Lakotah compare a man handsome and whole.

And now they watched the leaders of the four Mahto tiyóśpaye line up, Catka and Iku riding to one side of Ahbleza, Cetan and Icabu taking the opposite side.

A second line formed back of these leaders, Ośota and

Peśla each on a side, two clubmen between, each man on a spotted horse and carrying a feathered lance.

Many Oglalahca and Kiyuksa had gathered outside their lodges to see these Mahto make the fast ride, even Tabloka looking on respectfully. And all th᠁ Śiyo who had traveled with the Mahto stood in the crowd of proud observers. But Ahbleza felt surprise on seeing Mniśa and many of his warriors among the onlookers. The wily old leader had managed to stay outside any tribal affiliation, to enter the hoop each summer as a guest and so to hold on to his edge.

Suddenly aware that a silence spread out in every direction, the Shirtman turned to look upon his own, the whole band now assembled and prepared to ride, four hundred and forty Mahto who waited for his signal. But as he looked, he sensed the eyes of all these people upon him, something mysterious and yet familiar about this moment.

He puzzled the scene, the strange silence and attentive faces not unlike something he had experienced before. And then he remembered: the people had looked at him in this same manner on the day he had raced out alone and routed the Psa.

I encounter a more dangerous enemy this day, he whispered to himself. Yet I dare not speak until I truly comprehend this danger. And for this same reason I dare not name my father's killer.

Now, moving a little forward of the riders to either side, he suddenly kicked his horse. "Hanta yo," he shouted, and led off the dash to the deadwood lodge, to the place a whiteman, out of ignorance, had called Oglala post.

Until yesterday the branch manager at Oglala post had been pleased about many things. A glance at those square log cribs where Watts and the Negro had piled and pressed hides told that he'd had a good season: one hundred packs, ten big hides to a pack. And he'd done well in beaver, tallow, and tongues too. According to reports he'd done better than Chardon at the 'forks' and probably better than Pilon over on Little Bend, Pilon's Shiennes trading down on the Arkansas this year.

Until yesterday he, Thomas L.—known as Red Lake, even his colleagues picking up this Indien mistranslation of his French family name—had felt good about seeing his place almost bare of trade goods. He was clearing out within the next three days, his season's returns all set for hauling to the Missouri, he and his help—Watts, his clerk, and the blackman—ready to go their separate ways. Not likely would he see the Negro again and he had no intention of rehiring Watts, a case of mistaken identity in the first place. The John Watts he'd contracted for spoke Sioux like a native; the John Watts who had turned up late in the season spoke neither Sioux nor French and exhibited a gaucheness that made him unattractive to the Indiens. For this reason he, Red Lake, had seen to it that Watts attended no tribal functions, not until yesterday when Watts had asked to do the welcoming at the Mahto camp. And had promised to bring back important information, something that might affect the trades. Yesterday, the day that had brought two more Titon bands to Oglala post and changed things all around.

Today Red Lake had reason to worry about that lack of trade goods. And reason for an even bigger worry: this same morning he let an old renegade boatman talk him into trading ten packs of hides for alcohol.

He always opposed the use of alcohol in making trades. One of a French family of traders out of St. Louis, he prided himself on securing the Indien trade through humoring and fair dealing. He saw nothing permanent about a trade in liquor, irrespective of the prediction made by the head of the Upper Missouri Outfit who believed that without a liquor traffic the U.M.O. could not endure. And yet this chance arrival of a bateau carrying raw alcohol on a day when new bands showed up at a depleted post had seemed opportune.

Now, waiting for those bands, he cursed himself for this imprudence. Could be that these Sioux had come only for tobacco and ammunition and would be flitting off the next day. And even should their presence mean twenty more packs, it hardly seemed worth the risk in illegal liquor trade. He knew about those brawls on the Big Muddy during the trade wars. And those two killings during a recent frolic at Papin's.

He poured himself a cup of coffee and noted items yet on hand: some Northwest fusils, flint and lead and a fifty-pound keg of powder; three dozen knives, a few square axes and a few more half-axes. And one new bright-metal musket for trade only in an emergency.

He shifted his eyes to the dry goods: two three-point blankets, a dozen blue strouds but a fair supply of scarlet. Lacking tin kettles and traps, the trade-cloth might prove a saving factor.

He had some tobacco and plenty of coffee besides boxes of those combs and mirrors always in demand. And he had overstocked on Iroquois beads. Many tribes prized these little shell tubes as hair ornament, but the Sioux had ignored this adornment so far. But perhaps these hair-pipes, as the trade had begun to call them, would divert the newcomers' attention from the fact that he had no elk teeth, no walnut bows, nor barrel staves, and damn little vermilion.

He glanced disdainfully at the yellow paper the boatman had tossed on the counter, a 'receipt' for 'loosening up the young bucks and old squaws for the trade.' To each quart of alcohol, it read, add red pepper and black chewing tobacco boiled together, some black molasses, some ginger or the musk gland of beaver. River water as needed.

"Sacré!" Red Lake tore up the paper as Watts walked into the room.

"I've already boiled what it tells," Watts announced. But he would wait awhile before diluting the 'likker' with this mixture. And he might throw in a rattler's head, like the boatman said.

Watts saw the look of disgust in his employer's eyes, but before Red Lake said anything, he began talking about the measures. Three three-gill cups, the boatman had said, was the amount commonly given for one robe. But the boatman had shown Watts how to save a gill on each cup. And he'd also told about putting tallow in the bottom of the cups. And a trick with the fingers.

Red Lake pushed back his chair and stood; he pulled himself as tall as his short legs permitted: "I am a trader among the Indiens ten years, since 1822, and my father before me. My brother, John B., is a partner in the Company, but I never . . ."

A whoop beyond the door and the thud of horses' hoofs sent the branch manager hurrying outside, his speech unfinished. He wanted to be standing in clear view of these Sioux, applauding their mock charge, their fast ponies. And all the while he will be hoping that this Titon leader they call Ahbleza possesses a more agreeable personality than the overbearing loudmouth they call Tabloka.

Ahbleza waited horseback while his people rode up, formed a great arc.

Now, everyone here and everything quiet, he heard Red Lake speaking Lakotah, welcoming the Mahto band, inviting leaders and principals inside the log post. Then quickly but courteously he heard the same voice telling that the trading-place accommodates not more than fifteen persons; perhaps ten among the principals and five women in the first group to come inside?

Approaching the deadwood lodge, Ahbleza noticed that the blackman who had visited the Mahto stood alongside the entrance, his eyes looking down, not a sign of recognition either on the black one's face or in his manner. But even as he puzzled this thing, Red Lake, with an eloquent sweep of his arm, offered the fascinations of the trade-room to Ahbleza and those eight men, four women who accompanied their leader to the door.

Stepping into the trade-room, Ahbleza saw that Watts stood back of the counter and that he thrust out his hand.

And so the Shirtman moved forward to enact the whiteman's greeting-sign, a touching-of-fingers. Certainly the Lakotah never raises this hand—the knife-hand—in the presence of relative or friend, but Ahbleza will not offend a whiteman who extends a welcome in this manner.

Red Lake had come up quickly, the man's eyes warning his employee. He suspected Watts of making some kind of a blunder in the Mahto camp. When he had questioned the man about his meeting with the Mahto, Watts had shrugged indifferently. But later he had heard Watts curse the Negro for 'not getting those leggins.' He regretted having to use Watts at the counter this afternoon but who else? He needed the clerk for receiving at the stock table and he wanted the big black guarding the door. As for himself, he would stay outside for the most part; four hundred Indiens milling around, impatiently awaiting their turn inside, could create a considerable problem.

Ahbleza had observed the warning look but almost at

once the manager had left the room, going back out among the Mahto, perhaps announcing his readiness for the next group.

And now Watts, knocking on the counter to signal Ahbleza's attention, poured something out of a battered pot into a small container. He pushed the container toward the Shirtman.

For an instant Ahbleza wondered whether Watts offered him the 'burning' cup. But now he saw that this cup held something black and steaming; this drink, the white-man's tastes-sweet drink?

The man behind the counter winked: "Wash-stay?" He rubbed his stomach. Here was sign language anybody oughta understand. Why bother pointin' to the tongue or movin' a hand across the breast? Tom L. had showed him these ways of sign talk but stomach-rubbin' made more sense. "Tastes good? Black soup wash-stay?"

Waśte; the black drink tastes good. Ahbleza drank slowly, relishing the heavily sweetened coffee.

Those Mahto who had come inside with Ahbleza stood a long while looking. At their own trade fairs they had known the exchanges. Here, perhaps one offends the trader if he offers a braid of pte-hair or a thong of pte-hide in exchange for looking-glass or knife or paint. Yet those Titonwan who camp here before the Mahto arrive say never offer robes at the beginning. Trade your robes, they say, for the big things: guns and powder, blankets and tobacco.

Ahbleza finished his drink and turned over the empty cup; he moved away from the counter. But now he felt a pull on his shoulder; Watts, leaning over the counter, had tugged on his Shirt.

"Don't go. I . . . " Seeing Ahbleza's eyes, the trader instantly took his hand off the Shirt.

He began again: "First cup I give you. Next cup, too."

Ahbleza turned away but the Siyo interpreter, answering Watts's call, came to the counter and stood alongside the Mahto. He translated as Watts instructed: "The trader gifts you with this cup. He will fill the cup twice if you want more drink."

The Shirtman, looking from Watts to the tin cup, picked up the empty vessel and so he will not offend. Again he started away.

Watts shook his head emphatically and the translator spoke quickly: "The whiteman's gift, not the cup but the drink he puts in the cup."

Ahbleza watched the trader refill the cup but this one not steaming, not black. So the whiteman gives him firewater?

The Śiyo breed translated the Shirtman's courteous refusal, and Watts, glimpsing the leader's face, decided against any urging. In fact he decided against several things, like asking about the leggins offered him in the teepee or mentioning the headman's buckskin shirt.

But on seeing Ahbleza walk toward the door, Watts spoke quickly to the Śiyo. He wanted the breed circulating certain information among the warriors, something that will get them hurrying up to the counter, unloading those robes.

Persons who had tasted two drinks held out their cups for a third. But now the man back of the counter wanted a robe before he again filled the cup. And so the Mahto pushed their way out of the door to the robe-holders, some persons going out and staying out. But for each one who had gone out, two had come in.

Peśla had traded five robes for a musket and some powder; now he joined friends at the counter to watch whatever went on here. But almost at once he heard the familiar bellow that always announced Tabloka; the Kiyuksa had demanded that they admit him to the trading-room. Curious, Peśla turned to see what influence this man held over the waśicun.

Red Lake, back inside the trade-room, also recognized the voice; he cursed his misfortune. Why did this arrogant, fat Sioux and his sneaky-eyed war chiefs have to show up now? But he will let the Śiyo breed do the explaining, telling that the room is full, that Tabloka already trades and now he gives his friends a chance. Tomorrow Tabloka comes; today, the newcomers.

But Tabloka took little interest in what happens 'tomorrow'; he comes and so he trades. Now.

1010

Many heads turned, many eyes focused on the Kiyuksa, who stood suddenly silent, the man more of a threat now than when he bellowed.

But Watts used these moments to bend under the counter, to add much, much water to the mixing that already diluted the alcohol.

Ahbleza, remembering himself as 'observer,' stood aside in the crowded room, a man who listened and watched.

He had heard the dangerous muttering when three of his warriors, discovering a gun with bright metal finish, determined to hold on. Defying the interpreter who told that 'this U.S. flintlock not something Red Lake wants to trade,' they refused to let go. Ahbleza saw the breed walk away but he noticed that the pale young clerk who counted robes watched anxiously while these warriors haggled over the firestick as before.

Now hearing unnaturally loud voices in another direction, Ahbleza glanced toward the men who crowded against the counter. Observing that certain of his warriors lacked either the fringed leg-covers or the brightly quilled shirts they had worn on arrival, he wondered for which of the whiteman's commodities they had traded these fine garments.

Suddenly a man pushed out from this crowd and came zigzagging toward the door, near the place Ahbleza stood. And then, amidst yells and unfamiliar laughter, something thudded to the ground. When arguing voices replaced those unreal laughs, the Shirtman looked around for a pipe-carrier. But he saw neither peacemen nor pipes. He saw, instead, that a second man came swaying from the counter.

He, Ahbleza, their leader, had brought his people where they had desired to come; he dared not interfere.

He turned to where the women stood fingering buttons and beads and looking-glasses; he saw that they appeared as always, a reassuring sight. And yet, glimpsing his mother—Napewaśte stood with a little group of women who gazed curiously at a stack of tin pans—he felt strangely disturbed.

Now he saw that Peśla's wife held up a colorful strip of her quillwork and that she fixed her gaze on the one remaining piece of red cloth. But Red Lake apparently ignored her offer and so she turned away, hurrying out the door, a woman humbled, angry. And then Ahbleza saw that Red Lake had stepped back only to return with more of the red cloth; certainly the trader will wonder at this Mahto woman's rude disappearance.

But the scout's wife obviously experienced something most pleasant in her contact with the trader, the Shirtman a witness to this incident also. He had seen the manager smilingly fill Anpagli's hands with the hair-pipes in exchange for the tallow she shyly offered him.

And Ahbleza quickly saw that any woman with a robe to trade found Red Lake a most agreeable man.

The warriors had opened a path for Tabloka, the man heading for the counter where Watts filled cups, where the clerk at the far side took in robes. And now, crowding in tight again, some of the warriors jostled Peśla, who, in turn, bumped against Tabloka. But instead of showing annoyance, the important Kiyuksa made space for the Mahto, his eyes cooly taking count of Peśla's feathers and paint, of each war honor. Then, turning neither head nor eyes toward the counter, Tabloka slapped the wood and demanded that Watts fill a cup for Peśla. Next season, he bellowed, the waśicun will get a robe in trade for these cups; next season, in the manner of trades on the muddy-water.

And so Peśla stood alongside the principal one in the Kiyuksa band, the Mahto warrior laughing whenever Tabloka laughed. And certainly Tabloka found the wobbly Mahto braves a most amusing sight, Tabloka who had treated with the flaming-cup on the big river.

Suddenly the Kiyuksa stopped his unnatural laughter; he began to talk about the enemy south—the Pani. He and Peśla and perhaps four of his Kiyuksa warriors will go out after Pani horses and bring back hundreds—he made the big arc with the hand that held the cup—hundreds and hundreds, ten hundreds. And Peśla, draining his cup, showed a face that agreed to any party Tabloka chose to lead.

But now the Kiyuksa looked around back of Peśla; something displeasing had caught his eye. He saw that two of his warriors to whom Red Lake had granted entrance stood begging for a fight, one man already pulling his knife.

Reaching out, Tabloka grabbed each man's neck; he

smacked their heads together, then threw the two aside. Moving back as if nothing had occurred, he lifted his cup from the counter. "Damn-fine," he said; "damn-fine." For so he understood the name these whites give to the water that feels like flame in the mouth, like embers in the belly.

Peśla drank from his second cup, never glancing at the two whom Tabloka had separated so roughly. But now he spoke out, his loud voice intended for the ears of any Mahto warrior within hearing: "The Kiyuksa follow a leader who never shrinks back from anything. He dares name an enemy. And if ever a Kiyuksa relative lies bleeding at his feet, he will wrap a pipe and go out after the killer."

The next instant Peśla felt Tabloka's breath hot on his cheek and heard as grim a voice as ever entered his ears.

"Perhaps this Kiyuksa," Tabloka said clearly, "will live in a manner that permits nothing regrettable if ever a great honor hangs on his shoulders. But this Kiyuksa owns neither the Shirt . . . nor a woman's undergown."

The phrases stung Peśla like a plunge into icy water, the Mahto instantly awake to the injury he had enacted against himself. His strangely loose tongue had lost him his image as someone the Kiyuksa leader desired as a pipeman in his next war party, as a relative in his band. Tabloka had not approved disrespect for a Shirtman and certainly he had remembered Peśla's boastful song during the sungazing one summer . . . and the woman of whom Peśla had boasted.

Will he not recall that I am brother to his wife Cuwe; I am his relative whether or not he likes this tie. Holding back a growl, Peśla finished his drink. But now a sense of shame swept over him, anger edging the shame; he glared at the man back of the counter.

Watts had begun pouring whiskey into jugs and sacs for certain ones who demanded their portion in a container they dared carry outside, these persons choosing to share their drinks with relatives who awaited Red Lake's invitation to enter the post. And now Peśla, striking the counter in the manner of Tabloka, pointed his chin at the jug Watts had started to refill.

Watts pointed his chin at the clerk; Peśla drinks when he hands over a robe to the pale young man.

The Mahto's eyes narrowed; why not trade back his

gun, get the robe, bring the robe to this counter. . . . Suddenly he remembered something. Walking toward the women's table, where he had glimpsed his wife, Lowansa, he demanded that she present him with all her items for trade.

The woman, whom Anpagli had persuaded to return to the trading-room, gave a little cry. But she handed over the big folder, her quillwork inside.

The folder and contents proved not enough; Watts asked for the warrior's leg-covers too. "Tell him to go buy another wife, one who sews," he yelled at the interpreter; "then he can have lotsa leggins." He laughed foolishly at his own remark; he had been dramming a little on the side.

Peśla had not understood the meaning in all these words but he knew a ridiculing laugh when he heard one. He dropped his leg-covers as abruptly as a stalking hunter who comes within an arrow of the branched-horn; snarling, he threw the pair across the shop table.

Watts poured the contents of a cup into a little sac, Peśla all the while staring fiercely at a big jug on the counter. When the man stopped pouring, the warrior jerked the sac up against his breast and walked crookedly toward the door. At the entrance he met Ośota.

The sight of this man to whom Peśla lived bound to provide meat, fanned the anger that Tabloka's rebuke and Watts's ridicule had left smoldering.

"Perhaps my friend wants drink instead of meat." Peśla spoke thickly and his eyes warned danger.

Ośota accepted a swallow. He wanted none of the firewater but neither will he want trouble with Peśla. He had come only to advise Ahbleza of the lamentable situation outside this place.

The next instant Peśla jerked the sac from the Canoni's lips and rushed crazily out the door.

Ośota turned now to Ahbleza, to this man whose power never had waned when he rode as warrior, to this man whose spirit had made contact with the vital force and from whose strength the whole people had chosen to draw. Until now. Now a burning, yellow mystery in a whiteman's cup provided most of the Mahto warriors and many women and children with a crazy, unreal strength.

And so, his manner conveying urgency, Ośota reported the coarseness outside this door.

On the ground that surrounded the post, a whooping mob of Mahto danced and drank, women and men looking eagerly toward anyone coming from the trade-room. Almost everyone wanted a drink and those persons taking more than a taste kept on asking for more tastes, more swallows.

One group had made up a game, the people sitting opposite as if they engaged in a contest, one side filling their mouths with the fool's water while the second side waited like gaping birds for someone to spit whiskey into their open throats.

In some places men lay stretched out as if dead; in different places wives, their eyes frightened, sat alongside husbands who slumped or grinned foolishly or looked out from sullen faces.

On a pile of dry grass lay a young woman for whom they once had made the puberty ceremony, her body and spirit numb, a stinking jug nearby and empty. Someone had brought a healer who danced indifferently over her body; his rattles without meaning for himself or the woman.

Peśla sat away from everyone, the warrior looking at his bare legs and muttering. Two, three of his usual companions had rambled past him, their eyes round and glazed, the feathers that had marked their honors gone from their hair. And like Peśla, they wore only loin-cover and moccasins.

Hungry babies whimpered for a breast, and little children, taught never to cry, blinked back tears and swallowed sobs. Now and then a grandfather came looking for these small ones, folding his arms over their heads, a grandfather who sought to hide the eyes and ears of the young from this distressing scene.

A woman's howl alarmed Napewaśte and brought her hurriedly from the trade-room. But the sight beyond the door filled her with instant terror. She recognized nothing familiar, not until another terrifying howl drew her eyes to the healer who performed a stumbling dance over a woman's body. And so she saw the peźuta they call Huhupiye drop to his knees, straddling the limp form in strange manner, then lifting the top of the woman's gown to expose her breast.

Suddenly Napewaśte's fear turned into strength; she had identified the howling shape that huddled close by this

1015

vulgar enactment: her friend Cankuna. And now, running out to comfort the hunter's wife, she recognized the young woman on the ground as Peśla's daughter, born of the mother who had hung herself.

The healer pulled lustfully at the young woman's breasts and now Napewaśte heard why the grandmother howled: Huhupiye drinks something and turns crazy. Huhupiye loses his power as healer and so Wipatawin, in her sixteenth winter, shall die. A grandmother says so, says so.

Looking around Napewaśte saw where Peśla wandered, the warrior trying now to locate his horse. She had started in his direction when Cankuna's cries stopped her.

"They tell my son but he knows not his own relatives, neither mother nor father nor his own daughter." The woman finished with another howl.

Napewaśte walked on but now she looked for Winu.

Not all the Mahto band had remained at the post. Iku, Icabu, and most of the old men had returned to camp, these wise ones leading away children and women who trembled at the frightful din.

But Cetan, along with two, three warriors, had chosen to stand guard outside the trading-house. Refusing any offers from the jug, they waited for Ahbleza to come out and mount his horse; until they saw the Shirtman unharmed and on his way back to camp, they intended to stay.

Napewaśte had not found Winu, but now she saw Ogle, the hunter coming from the trade-room, the Shirtman and Waglula alongside him, these three walking straight, not zigzag like so many persons who came out this same door. Stopping to watch, she saw that the hunter hurried toward Cankuna and the vulgarity that evoked his wife's cries. Next thing, Ogle had grabbled the healer and sent him spinning across the stony ground.

Ahbleza came forward now with Waglula, the young seer who had learned from a stone-dreamer but his powers yet unproved. Kneeling alongside the stricken woman, Waglula sprayed a mouthful of water on her forehead; next, he turned her body gently, his hands pressing slightly on each side. At a certain place on her neck, he laid a small, dark stone, a soft feather attached.

1016

After a while he looked up sadly. Perhaps a different wapiya, a more experienced healer, will know a way to overcome the firewater disease. Perhaps someone will know of root or stem or bloom that will help where his stone will not help.

And so Ogle went looking for any man who ever had dreamed of the grizzly, who knew something about the healing grasses, and who will treat the hunter's granddaughter without requesting a dog-feast ceremony before he acts. But Ahbleza, looking down on the prostrate form, had known that neither stone nor grass nor drum nor rattle will renew this young woman.

Napewaśte pulled firmly on Cankuna's gown; once again she urged the distraught woman to come with her, to return to camp. But Cankuna sat reluctant; who will watch over her granddaughter, she wept; who will wait until the young woman returns to herself?

The next moment the women heard a gunshot inside the post; they saw a man come staggering out the door, his face bloody.

Cankuna jumped to her feet, not looking to see what happened next or who went where. And so the two women headed for camp, the setting sun making long, amusing shadows of their scampering forms. For in their haste they had left behind the horses they had ridden here; they had remembered only that when an enemy attacks, women and children run for their lives.

Ogle located one grizzly-dreamer, a peźuta who clawed the ground around the post, who growled and chased people in the manner these dreamers performed when they painted their bodies red and wore claws and grizzly hides. But the man Ogle had found scarcely demonstrated his powers as a healer; to the contrary, he demonstrated the overwhelming power of the whiteman's cup.

And so the hunter returned to where the young woman lay, Cankuna gone now but Ośota standing watch, the warrior's knife-hand open, ready to pull out his knife.

Ahbleza rode back to camp telling himself that he dared not dwell in the memory of this day; why remember

1017

his people on a day when they become insensitive to the life-force, when they lose consciousness and fall away from all the good they experience through grandfather-contact.

True, he brings the people to rapid creek; he answers their request for a campsite among relatives. They grant him the rank of leader, someone who will lead the band safely in whatever direction they desire to move. And so they arrive unhurt at this campground whereon they now make tragedy.

But they also grant him a Shirt, a rank that makes him protector of all Lakotah, hunka-relative to the one and the whole.

For an instant Ahbleza's hands covered his ears; he wished desperately to shut out the shrieks and whoops that followed him back to camp. And now he remembered Cetan, who had returned the Shirt when the people disregarded his warning. But those persons whom Cetan had confronted, whether or not they reasoned wisely, had retained their senses; they had not lost the gift of ears.

Riding in front of Eyanpaha's lodge, Ahbleza suddenly decided to call a council, to ask that the old crier announce a meeting of grandfathers and fathers, of family leaders. A group, he told himself, that will sit—sit throughout the night, if necessary—until the substance of their thought permeates the campsite, until good attracts good and those men who wander without a direction feel a pull toward their lodges, toward wives and sisters and mothers who wait, each one trying to conceal her apprehension. And he shall ask that Eyanpaha make his round twice while this council sits, the crier saying that at dawn all Mahto tipi come down, that the band moves out.

Dismounting, Ahbleza scratched on the crier's tipi, but neither Eyanpaha nor any member of his family gave answer. And so the Shirtman went looking for someone who yet owned the power of legs and voice, someone who will run calling out the Mahto leader's request for a council, this meeting to take place at once. At once.

Not many persons had appeared in the council lodge, certain ones preferring not to show their faces, different ones remaining at the post where they joined those groups who disturbed the night with loud singing and coarse laughter, their fuzzy tongues desecrating the brave-heart songs.

And so, lifting an ember to the pipe, Ahbleza saw but ten reliable men around him. True, these ten showed dark faces—they, also, dreaded a killing or a crippling on this campground—but these same ones also recognized that they had nothing to regain through dread; instead, each man needed to make demands upon his spirit, to call for close identification with the life-force as his personal power.

But before half of this council had puffed smoke, someone rudely jerked aside the entrance flap and stumbled into the meeting. Mocking his own awkwardness, he limped toward his place in this group of responsible men.

None glanced his way but three, four of the councilors, unwilling to view Catka in his shame, raised a robe to their eyes. Even so, they heard the man's laugh as he fell across someone's knees.

Presently two persons arose; they led Catka away, the man unacceptable, the incident regrettable.

Outside, Catka pulled back from his supporters; he demanded that they take their hands off him. And so, dropping his arms, they let him slip to the ground. Turning, the two stepped back inside the lodge but without heart for the council.

Catka lay sprawled on the ground but not for long. Whooping relatives swept him up, taking him horseback—but in the manner they carry the wounded—to the post, to more of the whiteman's 'damn-fine' drink.

The councilors sat on, none giving sign that he heard the whiskey-crazed at their furious play, none—yet—giving sign that he saw this counciling—ten men and their leader—as so many feathers in a whirlwind. For certainly each one recognized that something more dangerous than yellow mystery-water worked injury at this campsite. Somewhere, they knew, someone had abandoned that for which he stood responsible, the substance of his neglect now running loose, moving without a control and gaining power, a power for destruction that perhaps nothing shall deflect.

The morning broke cold, as cold as the dead fires in the many empty lodges. At dawn Ahbleza had walked among

1019

the tipi; he had moved similar to a man who views a fighting ground whereon lay bodies, dead and dying. And so he saw those persons who slept where they had dropped, knife cuts and club bruises marking their skin, more than half his Mahto band indisposed and unfit for travel.

When the sun began to climb, he went for his horse. Approaching the enclosure, he observed the smallness of the herd as compared with the previous day. And he noticed that two horses lay dead, the deep gashes of a stabbing at their necks.

He made the ride to the post remembering in what different manner he had traveled this little distance the day before. Now he followed a trail of broken arrows and bows, of torn leg-covers and ripped moccasins. He heard the sorrowing sounds of the old women who ran along the path, who gathered up these scattered possessions. And he saw the one who sat crying softly, a robe over her head and her man sprawled alongside, his body bare but for the torn piece of loin-cover she had laid over his manliness.

Outside the trader's place Ahbleza observed much more clutter. And here he saw more persons than he dared count either in like-dead sleep or squatting gloomily, the signs of retching nearby. He glanced toward certain ones who stirred, but their dull eyes looked around indifferently.

He saw where the young woman had lain, this place now empty; Peśla's daughter lay back in camp, her body wrapped in a red robe, tragedy twice rubbing out the woman-name Wipatawin.

But one person he had not seen; apparently Tonweya had shunned this abasement.

And now a noise inside the deadwood lodge attracted Ahbleza's attention. He saw the door flung open, Watts and the black-whiteman dragging out a warrior. Holding on to the man's arms and legs, they threw him onto the ground. Then they hurried back inside, but Watts stood squinting through an opening in the door.

Two, three persons on the outside looked up dazedly but one man got to his feet; he lurched toward the lodge, a gun in his hand; never before had he felt this killing-hate.

Recognizing this man, Ahbleza sounded a warning. But Catka ignored the Shirtman's voice. Shooting at the door, he ran up and pushed inside.

Watts, standing ready, struck him on the head.

Red Lake, hearing this new disturbance, jumped from his bed. He dressed quickly, enough clothes to make himself presentable before the sobering Titons.

Certain warriors tightened their bowstrings at his appearance, but they saw this man neither flinching nor retreating.

And now Ahbleza heard Red Lake calling out, saying that he will give a horse to the struck man, that he acknowledges his employee's act as foolish and unfortunate.

Those persons whose senses had returned awaited Ahbleza's response. But their murmurs warned that this whiteman shall give two horses in Catka's name and one horse to the warrior whom Watts drags out this morning. Truly, why not demand that the wasicun give one horse for each man he tosses out of the deadwood lodge during the night?

Red Lake spoke again, repeating his offer, using hand-signs for emphasis, the fingers of his right hand astride the left. He will give a horse, one horse.

When finally the Shirtman spoke, he directed his answer to his people: "Perhaps, my kinsmen, I and you show wisdom in accepting the one horse. Remember that these whitemen invite the Mahto band to trade at this place, not to sleep here."

After a while the muttering subsided and the Mahto people, gathering up their things, began wandering off.

Not Ahbleza. He stayed, watching the manager assist the stunned man to his feet, hearing him tell Catka—in Lakotah— to take whatever horse he desires from the Company's stock. But he noticed that Red Lake sent the blackman to the horse 'pen' along with Catka.

Upon his return to camp, Ahbleza had not given the order to strike lodges; the people needed a day to regain their composure and locate missing property. As for himself, he had decided to sit in his lodge available to whoever desired smoking with him.

But the sun reached middle and not one had come for a smoke with Ahbleza; not one. Only once before will he remember sitting as lonely as now. But on that long-past day when the band had seemed turned against him, he had remembered his bond with Tonweya, the brother-friend.

And now? Where goes this brother-friend that he will not come here? And why this terrible longing for those two he remembers as his fathers? Two fathers—the warrior through blood, the seer through choice; two fathers and one true-grandfather: Tunkaśila.

Tunkaśila, living in the old-scout tipi, living out his life as scout, this same Tunkaśila who once guides a boy's footsteps onto a new trail; Tunkaśila, old but not aged, not someone to whom they toss soft meat and ladle out warm soup in return for a legend; Tunkaśila, a remarkable old man, perhaps in touch with many familiar-voices now, voices that identify the danger that lurks here, upsetting this camp, despoiling this campground.

And now Ahbleza moved out of the tipi on his way to a visit with Tunkaśila. And in his hand, the pronghorn pipe that none had come to smoke.

But before the Shirtman had taken many steps, Osóta approached. Red Lake, he told, invites back the band for an orderly trade, the 'door' to close at sundown. But bring robes, the trader had said, bring many robes.

Turning from Osóta, the Shirtman looked toward the trail that led to the post. And so he saw that more women than men walked this direction, women whose husbands had slept through midday, who not yet awakened. Fastening drags onto their dogs, these wives carried robes to the traders while they yet owned a robe to trade.

But the Shirtman saw neither his mother nor his sister Kehala nor Tonweya's wife; certainly these three understand to stay back in camp and inside their lodges.

"Tunkaśila, grandfather, you hear my voice and so you know that I, Ahbleza, sit at your fire. I come here remembering the day you let me sleep while you go ahead along a trail, a path that you will have me travel alone, learning as I walk.

"I find my way on that day . . . nor am I lost now. But I perceive great danger in the direction I and this band—this band and all Lakotah—now face. I speak of a danger not yet visible. And I will not mean the cold and hunger that gnaws on bones and belly but which man endures. Nor will I refer to changes in thought, those slow changes that keep strong roots in tribal custom yet permit new growth within the hoop.

"I refer, instead, to thoughts that come from outside this hoop, this circle; I refer to thoughts that threaten, injure, perhaps destroy the Lakotah way of life. And I mean thoughts that the Lakotah invite and encourage, the people agreeable to walking blind.

"My grandfather, you live always as scout, as truth-bearer. You listen and so you find your way, light or dark; you listen and so you hear everything. Will you hear crying?

"I am a Shirtman. They say that I shall own the people in the manner a protecting father owns his children. But who among fathers ever commands that his children turn about?

"I am a man with a great vision. I see danger here and on the path ahead. Yet I own not the power to stop even one man."

Ahbleza had spoken, and now Tunkaśila, reaching out his hand, lifted his own pipe off the little rack nearby; unfalteringly he used the fire-stick to lay an ember on the bowl. He puffed twice, the smoke coming thinly through his nose.

He handed the stem to Ahbleza. "Taǵoza, grandson," he said quietly, "you own the power to stop the people, to turn the people. But whether or not you use the power, you alone decide.

"My grandson, you own the consuming power. Hear me: you own the consuming power. But whether you use this perilous power as warrior or peaceman, you alone decide.

"You speak of danger here; you, my grandson, bring this danger. You come here, a warrior on the warpath, a man out for revenge.

"You wear the Shirt and will not name your father's killer, yet you dash toward the trading post, your fighting men on their war horses and the echo of your lonely ride against the Psa in your ears. My grandson's power never wanes while he rides as warrior, something that he and his people remember. And so these Mahto ride to the post remembering their leader as someone responsible for their safety; they feel secure.

"Instead, they meet something dangerous, something that you, my grandson, put into motion on the day you agree to this campground.

"True, many persons not yet comprehend that which happens here; they relate their difficulties to the compelling drink. But those wise ones who council with you through the night know that something more than a mysterious water sits back of these foul demonstrations. They know that a warrior's heart beats under your Shirt and they see that you cling to your father's spirit. But they also remember that before a man receives the Shirt, someone recognizes the otancan in him, recognizes him as the most, the very most.

"True, I hear crying in my sleep. But for whom those tears I know not. I know only that danger attracts danger. And yet more danger."

Ahbleza touched Tunkaśila's pipe to his lips, then replaced the stem in the old man's hand: "My grandfather, I hear you and so I go. I ride now to the post. Here I shall wait and see whether or not someone again will recognize me as otancan, as the most."

The Shirtman stepped out of the scout tipi aware that not even Tunkaśila had smoked the pipe he brought here. But mounting his horse, he remembered that, once before, the people had tried him for endurance; they had found him not lacking that day and they will find him not lacking now.

More than half of those Mahto who had traded for liquor the previous day came again to the post, appearing between midday and evening. They came pretending to search for their wives but seeking instead to get back the robes their women had taken out of the lodges.

Soon many men stood outside, holding up robes and demanding entry. And not only Mahto stood in this crowd; Siyo, Oglalaĥica, Kiyuksa, and Mnikoóźu had joined the group, two hundred persons in all. And perhaps twelve managed to squeeze inside whenever the blackman opened the door for someone to go out.

The whitemen had appeared unalarmed, even when the fighting began; apparently they looked for these easily excited temperaments to turn against their own as had happened on the day before, as had happened back on the 'Big Muddy' ten winters past.

So who will hear the warrior who mutters that someone replaces him as rattle-bearer in his warrior-lodge, some impostor who claims this rank while he, the true rattleman, sleeps his strange sleep? So who will hear the Mnikooźu who mutters that someone he calls 'hunka' now carries away three of his five robes, robes for trading here?

Certain Titonwan had heard. But everyone knows that akicita elect their rattle-bearers and that hunka-relatives share robes, everything. Even so, someone spoke saying that he sees the Mnikooźu carrying only three robes, three fine robes which he already trades for the makes-crazy drink.

And now the group who had stood within hearing took sides; eyes flashed and knives appeared. And three men stood bleeding from cuts before they heard Red Lake vow to close the trade if their quarreling persists.

For a while things stayed quiet. But then two Kiyuksa began the unfriendly grunts, this disagreement over a woman. At the insistence of their own clubmen they took their bitterness outside, the perpetrator of this quarrel biting off the tip of his rival's nose. Next, someone hinted that the howling victim resembled an indiscreet wife among the Sinteȟla. Hearing this ridicule, relatives of the disfigured man threw arrows at the agitator's legs. And now the women who yet remained around the post began to run, scuttling back to camp, escaping from their own as from an enemy.

Riding toward the trader's lodge, Ahbleza passed the fleeing women, each one of these persons pulling a robe over one side of her face. But they need not have hidden their eyes; the Shirtman rode unnoticing of anyone. He came not to recognize but to discover whether anyone will recognize him.

Ośota sat outside the post, his usually friendly, laughing mouth tightly closed, his eyes a dark squint. During the night his young wife had run away. But not until now—certain ones bringing him the news—had he learned that she ran off with Peśla.

A man of consequence appears indifferent to such loss, Ośota had told himself, and so he shall treat his wife's choice to separate from him as something he barely notices. He will want none of the appeasing gifts, neither pipe nor horses. And he will keep a good heart toward wife and abductor, perhaps even joke about the whole thing; most certainly he, Osóta, shall sustain his loss. Only one thing will seem irreconcilable: what manner of woman ever will choose Peśla to himself?

Peśla turned on his sleeping robe, shaking off the child who tugged at his moccasins. Opening his eyes, he blinked at the flickering shadows; apparently he had slept through a day. He put a hand to his head, marveling that which had struck him to bring this dullness. And then he remembered.

He sneaked a look around the tipi; when had he returned to Lowansa's lodge? And where had he left the Canoni's wife, the woman he had persuaded to go off with him? Hearing someone approach the entrance, he rolled over on his side; he pretended sleep.

Lowansa entered quietly. Speaking softly to the child, she sent him out to play, then laid her sticks on the fire. She stirred the soup which had begun to simmer. And now she glanced in Peśla's direction.

Sensing her look the man got up; he hurried outside to relieve himself and to see whether he or someone had staked his horse nearby the lodge.

Returning, he demanded in an angry voice that the woman tell him where she had tied the horse.

Lowansa looked up surprised. She knew nothing about his horse; he had returned to the lodge after sunrise and walking.

Even so Peśla managed a reproach. Why will not Lowansa emulate his brother's wife? Anpagli waits outside the lodge for her husband, wipes off his horse, brings the man fresh moccasins, sees to his comfort. "My wife neither waits nor observes whether I ride or walk. Any different man will strike the drum and throw off one like you." He gave the woman a warning glare and again went outside the tipi.

Lowansa heard the man and saw his look but she sat uncaring. She had lived with his threats fourteen winters and his cruelness now lacked the power to pain her. She had told herself that she never will throw out his things, but more than once she had wished that he enact his words and throw her away.

The soup, seasoned to Peśla's liking, now bubbled noisily, and so she remembered that the boy had waited to eat with his father. But before calling her son into the man's presence she had waited to determine Peśla's mood; on more than one occasion recently he had treated with the child most roughly.

Now looking out the tipi, she saw that the man had disappeared; Peśla had gone, neither touching the soup nor asking for his son. Something truly will upset him.

She hurried outside, looking for the boy, relieved when she found him in his grandmother's lodge, his young belly already full.

For a little while Lowansa considered staying the night with Cankuna, she and her child more at ease in this tipi than in their own. Yet why, she asked herself, stay away and perhaps provoke Peśla into a yet more disagreeable temper? The warrior-father disapproves the influence of a hunter's lodge, whether the boy's grandfather or any different hunter. And so after a little visiting—Lowansa not once mentioning her difficulties—mother and son reluctantly returned to their own tipi. And Ogle, watching these two go, felt an ache in his heart for all grandsons on this campground, all grandsons and granddaughters.

The young-summer evening held off darkness to make this day a long one. But not long enough for Peśla to locate his favorite mount or find the woman he had taken away from Ośota. The war horse stood neither in camp nor with the herd on the edge of camp. And he had not recalled where he put down the young woman after he had satisfied himself.

Now, hearing the sound of drum and war-dance songs in the direction of the traders, he jumped on a different horse and raced toward the post. Striking viciously at his mount, he released those blows intended for Lowansa. His woman, he hissed at the wind, a fool who lets him sleep all day, who deprives him of a trade; certainly those strutting Kiyuksa will empty the hollow-wood before ever he arrives. But then he remembered that he had nothing to trade; he had used up his shirt, leg-covers, robes. And all of his wife's quillwork.

Why not a horse? He yet owns horses, he told himself, and so he will trade a horse. But not the one he rides now or the war horse whom he certainly will find wandering somewhere. Instead, he will lead a second horse to the post. And not only a horse . . .

In response to a pound on the head, Peśla's mount whirled, carrying the rider back to the Mahto village.

Lowansa and the boy had returned to the lodge only moments before the woman heard a sound at the flap, then saw her husband crouched in the entrance. "Come," he said. And Lowansa glimpsing his face, got up promptly.

Riding her horse close behind Peśla, the woman suddenly understood why he demanded that she accompany him to the post; he had nothing left to trade but a wife. A little moan escaped her.

On their arrival, he pushed inside the trading-room, pulling her in after him. Forcing his way past the liquor-excited warriors, he reached the counter. And now, jerking Lowansa forward, he called to the Śiyo breed for a translation: "Let the trader fill my cup until he empties the hollow-wood and he shall have a woman for use on this night and the next. And the next."

Even as Lowansa heard herself offered, she saw Watts looking her over speculatively.

Red Lake had come hurriedly to the counter and now the trembling woman imagined herself as someone required to satisfy two different men. Stories of Sicaṅgu women flashed into her head, women ordered to lie with whitemen and so gain favors for the husband. And, always brutal, the waśicun often destroyed a woman's usefulness in one night.

And yet Lowansa knew that any gesture of withdrawal, any sign of her unwillingness, implied a disrespect for Peśla. And so, feeling his hand on her arm, she waited for him to pull off her gown if for nothing more than to prove her submissive.

But Peśla, wanting only to make certain that Watts understood his offer, pushed his wife's arm between her legs. Now, will the whitemen fully understand?

Suddenly Peśla's eyes narrowed. He saw that Watts whispered something to Red Lake and that Red Lake shook his head, the whiteman's negating gesture. So these two refuse a husband's generous trade-offer? Peśla looked around for the interpreter but the breed had slipped away.

Watts made a sign or two but Peśla, seeing only that they will not desire his wife, strode off. And Lowansa, covering her head, followed her husband out the door.

Peśla had not intended to stay away. He came back without the woman but he carried a small stick, one tip black. Pointing to the keg with his chin, the warrior extended the hand that held the stick, the wood that signified Lowansa's horse.

Red Lake nodded and the clerk accepted the stick.

Not all the firewater in the keg, Watts signaled Peśla now, but many cups, as many as the warrior's belly and brain will hold.

Certain Titonwan knew at exactly what moment Watts and his paleskin helper began to pour out of the tallow-bottom measures, but they had chosen not to mention their discovery. Instead they schemed to convey the message with their eyes, but not until they had ascertained that someone truly intended to trick the people. Perhaps the traders only try out a little magic, they had told each other; perhaps the whitemen enjoy playing a joke on the Titonwan, a foolish little joke, something they look for the Titonwan to discover quickly.

And so two clubmen, wearing similar paint, now stood guard, neither man offering or accepting anything across the counter. They stood, instead, eyes fixed on the pudgy white fingers that shortened each measure, cup after cup after cup after cup. Even so, their glances told, not yet; wait.

But as always, the hot bloods will not wait.

The boisterous and the sullen, the wobbly and the steady—everyone had looked up at the fierce yell. And so they saw the measures grabbed out of the fat white hands of one man, the thin white hands of a second man.

Red Lake had jumped toward the trouble, but not fast enough, not before a small circle of warriors had closed in on him. And now a knife lay on Watts's throat and a lance pricked the clerk's bottom. The blackman, the only one not molested.

The two similarly painted clubmen began to pour out of the keg, cup matched against cup, the untrue measures held up for everyone's viewing.

And now the unnatural quiet gave way to a murmur and the murmur expanded into a noisy scramble for bows and lances, for any weapon in that stack outside the door.

Red Lake held on to one hope: the Mahto who sat horseback outside the post. When Ahbleza sees his warriors grabbing up their weapons, perhaps this leader who wears the peace-shirt . . .

Suddenly the trader heard certain words, recognized certain signs: these Titon intend to see how bravely Watts will die!

Peśla had decided on an ordeal by fire, Peśla and four, five drunk Tokala warriors. But certain clubmen in control of the Mahto camp had grunted disapprovingly; Lakotah never burn anyone.

Perhaps not before this day, Peśla had dared to answer.

Confident of their hold on the whitemen, the warriors either clustered around the open diluted keg or climbed over the counter to drag out the hidden, undiluted kegs. Tugging on these little casks, they hunted an opening into the alcohol.

Now someone pushed Watts forward, the warriors pressing close to watch his cleverness with the spigot.

But some eyes kept turning in the direction of the clerk and so they saw the start of his attempt to dart across the room and out the door.

Three lances brought him down, their owners arguing over whose lance made the kill even before the clerk's body had stopped twitching.

And so those men who originally had intercepted Red Lake, again encircled the trader. But now they demanded that someone roll over a keg; they wanted their drinks within easy reach. And those persons who took to guarding Watts once again sat clamoring for refills.

Peśla stood at the counter preparing a firebrand. For a while he had wondered about using the tallow-sticks to which he had seen Red Lake put flame. But then he had decided on the firebrand, on something familiar. And now he sensed a need for hurry, to get at the whiteman before someone went looking for Ahbleza, the Shirtman perhaps coming in with pipe-bearers and persuasive harangue. True, some persons prefer to see these whites run off instead of a killing. But not he, Pešla. All his difficulties on this campground relate to these wašicun.

The burning wood now ready, Pešla glanced toward his Tokala friends; he smiled inside his mouth. Let the Mahto leader arrive with ten peacemen and as many pipes; nothing will stop these warriors.

Two Tokala, suddenly bending down, cut the tendons in the man's wrists and feet. And then these same two stood back while Pešla instructed the Siyo breed to tell Watts that they permit him to get up and run. But if he will not go soon, they understand that he agrees to whatever ridicule his trickery earns him.

Pešla, waving the firebrand, approached and Watts toppled from his sitting position, his wrists without muscle to support him. Pešla touched the fire to the hair on Watts's chest.

Certain warriors held their nose against the disagreeable smell of burning hair and flesh but they stayed to watch Pešla lay the brand on all the hairy places. Afterwards they lost interest; what excitement in watching a man who yells through his torture? Watts stinks and makes noise and spoils the show.

Pešla handed the firebrand to his friend Sluka. But he had one more performance before he finished with the wašicun. Bending over the writhing body, he cut off three fingers, one for each trick-cup. Next, his Tokala friends helping, he pushed the bloody pieces down the man's throat. Pressing his moccasin on the whiteman's mouth, he balanced for an instant on one foot. So now, he growled, Pešla leaves this choking fool to the knives and arrows and laughter of young braves.

The group surrounding Red Lake kicked aside the dripping keg; whooping and posturing, they danced toward the counter. One man, glancing back, saw that Red Lake stared at the clerk's mutilated body. Not likely, he told himself, will the little trader try sneaking out the door.

But Red Lake had managed to reach the blackman, who stood near the door; he intended sending the Negro with a message for Ahbleza. And now someone blocked his path. Tabloka, his arms folded, stood looking at him.

"The Kiyuksa have use for a whiteman in the band," Tabloka said abruptly. "True, he shall live as an old woman who covers over where the people squat and he shall eat with the camp-dogs until he speaks something more than a trader's Lakotah. But when I need understanding of the little black talking-signs, this whiteman shall sit in my lodge as friend. The Psa keep two, three whitemen as captives and so the Psa learn many clever things. Why not the Lakotah?"

Tabloka turned to Tatekahomni, his principal clubman; tie this Red Lake, he told, arms and legs. And stake him back of the counter. "I take him with me when the bands travel."

The Kiyuksa pushed his way into the crowded room; he moved toward the pack of robes. He intended to return these items—all items his people bring here—to their owners.

Peśla, leaning against the counter, tried to straighten out events from the previous day. He remembered that he had offered a stick—a horse—in trade for a cup this evening and so he most likely had acted in similar manner the day before. And now he understood what had happened to his war horse; the creature stood in the big enclosure back of the post where Red Lake had tied all those horses traded for the firewater.

The warrior helped himself to another cup; the drink seemed to confirm his reasoning. He left the counter, heading for the place they had confined his mount. Perhaps he will find the misplaced woman standing alongside his horse.

Sluka, never one to miss a chance to enact the humorous, had hurried back to camp, where he pantomimed the capture of the whitemen and the attack on Watts. His presentation had aroused even those persons most reticent about returning to the post. Why not return, someone had said, but go as to a dance; why not sing and celebrate? They say that the people get back their possessions, that the band soon leaves this place for clean grass and a true-hoop. Perhaps the Mahto leader, sitting horseback at the post, awaits his band.

And so many persons again painted, again moved toward the post. And among these Mahto walking in that direction: Tonweya.

The scout had returned to his village after a day and night of watching from the knolls, of guarding a campground that had sounded crazy, the noise spreading as far as the scout's nest. Sensing a sudden concern for Anpagli, he had run back to camp, arriving after sunrise but finding many persons yet asleep.

Not his woman; she sat contentedly at work on binders for the scout's hair, making her gift out of the beads and little pipes she had acquired during her one brief visit to the post.

"Next, I make you a string of beads with armbands to match," she told him, her eyes smiling welcome. But she spoke also of the strange noises during the night and of her uneasiness when she saw what happened to each one who tried the whiteman's cup.

Pulling the woman's head against his breast, Tonweya caressed her cheek with his finger. "I sit alongside my wife until the Mahto travel again," he said quietly. He had not asked about Ahbleza nor gone looking for the brother-friend.

But after hearing Sluka report that the kegs had dried up, that the traders lay dead or tied, and that the people dared to reclaim their robes, bows, horses, he had decided to view the deadwood lodge, his curiosity not different from any other man.

On arrival, Tonweya saw that not all containers stood empty; the warriors had found something new, a white mystery-water that seemed different from anything Watts had poured. But none had known to dilute this barrel, to diminish the strength.

"Try this new cup," certain Mahto shouted to the scout, these persons standing outside and passing around drinks.

Tonweya glanced toward Ahbleza, but the Shirtman sat unmoving, recognizing none of his people, not even this one who calls him brother-friend. And so the scout took the cup Pasu offered him. Why not? This uncle had named him; certainly he will not look for anything dangerous from Pasu's hands.

Before the dancing began, someone had compared the post with an enemy village. Why not a mock raid, he had yelled; let each one—woman and children also—seize whatever things excite or interest. And so the people rushed inside to attack the shelves, the robe packs, the dried meat, and tallow.

And whoever had happened to look in the Shirtman's direction, affected not to see him. For certainly the Shirtman affected not to see his people.

Red Lake, hearing the warriors at his carefully packaged returns, raised himself as high as the staking-thong permitted. Even if they see him looking over the counter, who will dare attack Tabloka's captive.

He slumped back down shaking, not at the sight of those scattered supplies but at the sight of an Indien bringing a firebrand to light the candle that sat on the far end of the counter. And directly below, a fifty-pound powder keg.

Curious, the man with the firebrand moved his hand slowly toward the wax. He fingered the wick. Then touching the brand to the wick, he stepped back quickly to watch. "Peta-o-żan-żan," he murmured softly; "peti-żanżan," he said, naming the candle, something that brightens the lodge. When the flame burned steadily, he pushed two more candles the length of the counter and close against the burning one. He lighted these wicks with the same firebrand, but before he moved away, he blew gently on these flames, delighting in their flicker.

The candle glow brightened the evening-dark room and two old women, grabbing on to the clerk's remains, began cutting up the man's hide, handing over skin and flesh to their attentive young granddaughters. The girls, tying these pieces onto sticks, took turns jostling the wood up and down in the manner of a wife who dances the scalps.

XX

Tašunkekokipapi, sitting in a tightly closed lodge with wife and son, reconsidered his intention to become a steady summer resident of the Titonwan hoop; perhaps he, like Mniša, will stand off yet another season. One family from among his band of thirty lodges joins in the confusion at the post, persons he now regards as outside his following. But whether different ones visit Red Lake this day, he will not know. A Shirtman shall act as their example, they say, so let the people notice where he keeps himself while certain ones despoil this campground.

As for the Kiyuksa, only Tabloka and his head clubmen had appeared at the post this day, those two staying long enough to stake Red Lake back of the counter and to gather up robes and different trade items that belonged to Kiyuksa lodges.

But Tanažin, never one to own his Oglalahca through threat and force, had seen more of his warriors head for the deadwood lodge than he had wanted to count. And in their footsteps the Šiyo, a people who seemed more like a small family of hangers-on than a true band.

Wanapin, noticeably absent from this campground, had opposed the move to Oglala post. He had watched the band go out; a people, he had told himself, who choose to walk blind.

Crossed sticks in front of one big lodge in the Mahto village shut out even the children who knew this tipi as their shelter; Ošota and his young wife sat alone. The woman's head hung low, her shoulders humbled, as she awaited whatever treatment the husband intended to mete out for her offensive behavior the night before.

The young woman had returned to the lodge at the old wife's request—these two, sisters—the one pleading that they let nothing occur to dishonor the family name. The true-wife, learning that her young sister had run in shame and fear to a relative's tipi, had asked that she return. The good woman had seen many forms of trouble poured out of the trader's keg and she knew that her sister had swallowed some of the fool's water. But she blamed herself; she had not noticed when the young woman disappeared from the tipi. True, everything had seemed mixed up the previous day, everything different from Lakotah ways. Never until now had a good woman walked anywhere alone; never until now had parents acted so disgracefully in front of their children. She had seen strong, reliable men performing acts usually attributed to rash young braves and she had seen old men on whom the people called for wisdom acting like heyoka.

Tactfully, then, the mother of Ośota's first son had approached the husband, asking that he remember under what conditions his young wife had misbehaved, asking that he receive back the errant woman with never a whisper against her family. Gratefully she had heard the man agree. But Ośota had demanded that upon the young wife's return she come to him at once, that she sit with him awhile, these two the only ones in the lodge.

And so they now sat, the woman made to reflect on her foolishness while Ośota, leaning against his backrest, tried not to remember who had dared to dishonor his wife.

Suddenly the man requested that she come close to him and that she bring her knife.

The woman's eyes flew to the husband's face; will he cut her tongue, her nose, or perhaps only her hair? Remembering her offense, she dared not look for compassion. Trembling, she crawled over to sit alongside the man.

Ośota took the knife from her hand and, holding a clump of her hair, pulled back her head. Coolly, he pressed the tip into her cheekbone and cut down her face, a deep gash running from near the corner of the eye to the chin, a cut that will heal but as a shameful scar.

He released her and she fell forward with a wail, her hands catching the drops that fell like red rain. The punishment, truly mild, but her humiliation, next to unbearable.

Letting the knife slip from his fingers, the man went out of the tipi, his moccasins pointed toward the post.

On his arrival, Ośota heard the noisy disagreements, viewed the lurching forms, the unfamiliar stares, and foolish grins. But he dared not look up at the straight back, the clear eyes and calm face of his leader. For he had not come here to show himself as an example of orderly conduct; he had come here looking for Peśla.

He had acted most leniently toward the man who had become his meat-maker, he told himself, but his easygoing nature never yet had permitted an insult. If Peśla imagined to improve his status in the tribe by taking the wife of a man whose high position required that he not notice the act, then he, Osóta, acknowledged a warrior's privilege to try such a thing. And a wife's privilege to change mates if she so desired. But for a warrior—any warrior—to take a wife for one night as an act against the woman's husband, this thing neither he nor any different man will ignore. Not that he, Osóta, desires killing Peśla—more important men than Peśla injure their image these past two days—but that he needs to warn Peśla, to let Peśla know that he will not tolerate a second grievance against his lodge, his tiyóśpaye.

Outside the trading post dogs played with the dead clerk's bowels; inside, they licked at scents and whined softly. But Osóta saw neither the blood patches nor scattered goods; his eyes focused directly on Peśla, who stood arguing with an Oglalahca over the possession of a gun.

"I trade a robe for this firestick," the Mahto warrior muttered disagreeably.

"A robe for a firestick, perhaps, but not for this one." The accosted man had answered hotly.

Peśla's glare demanded that the man remove his hands from the musket, but the Oglalahca refused to let go.

Osóta stepped forward. "Talk about this thing in the morning," he said firmly. "The sun provides a bright light and you more easily will identify the shooting-stick."

Hearing this voice, Peśla braced himself; certainly Osóta had come here to kill him. But when nothing happened, Peśla flashed the intervening clubman a hostile glance. One quick stab, he told himself, and this man for whom he hunts will not need any more meat.

The next instant he had his knife out and raised. But the weapon never fell. Someone grabbed Peśla's arm, the two struggling briefly, Peśla slipping, falling.

Even so the knife had spoken; the man who had stopped the attack stood looking at his fingers, at the two fingers that hung on a thin string of skin. Catka, suffering the loss of two fingers from his bow hand; Catka, unlikely ever to use his arrows again. . . .

And now Huśte, hunka-son to the injured man, rushed toward Peśla, swinging at the warrior with a club.

But Ośota bent over Peśla, risking his own head to stay the dangerous stone. "Hear me," he shouted. "This Mahto warrior makes meat for me at the summer hunts, but I will make meat summer and winter for the good man who loses his bow fingers, who protects my life."

Huśte dropped the war club; Ośota had averted the sort of trouble that divided a band. But certain persons, staring at Peśla, muttered something about not wanting this warrior in the Mahto camp. None cared to see the akicita driving out a brave man but twice this day Peśla's knife had cut off fingers, this second cutting against one of his own band.

The next moment they saw a heyoka coming up. Some clear-headed Mahto had sent for Woze, someone who looked for the contrary's amusing antics to divert Peśla, perhaps lure the warrior from the deadwood lodge before his lust for blood spread through the post.

Three, four persons, hearing a warning cry, peered over the counter at Red Lake. But these same ones will suspect the trader's motive for wanting the flickering light put out. Who here will scheme a burning fire while the people sit laughing, so many amusing things happening?

Outside the trading post Woze had run into difficulty keeping Peśla entertained. The warrior, suddenly catching sight of his missing war horse, demanded to know who dares ride his property to this place; who stakes his horse nearby the entrance to the post?

Running backwards into the trading-room, the heyoka hunted for someone from Catka's lodge to tell Peśla that this horse belongs to a different man now. And why.

But the contrary's maneuvers, translatable among sensible men, appeared as nonsense to those warriors who long since had lost touch with tact and restraint. They chose, instead, to call upon Woze for a performance. And so the heyoka, whose vision compelled him to respond, remained inside this place of dangerous mischief, the drunk and near drunk cheering his ludicrous exhibition. Perhaps only Sluka, his eyes ever open and looking for news, had perceived Woze's message.

And now the news actor, standing alongside Peśla, revealed in what manner Red Lake had made good the bump on Catka's head.

"The whiteman gives away my war horse?"

Sluka stepped back but the warrior's eyes demanded an answer.

So Peśla will not remember that he trades this same horse for . . .

"The trade means nothing now. The Lakotah receive back everything."

Hearing Peśla's angry shout, two Ihoka clubmen hurried up to their lodge-brother. True, they told Peśla, the people had taken back from the tricky whites, but Catka had not tricked anyone; Catka had received a short cup for his robes and a blow on the head. Let this Mahto kinsman keep the war horse and these two Ihoka—each one—shall give Peśla a horse, Peśla choosing these horses.

But the warrior recalled only that Catka had interfered when he struck at Ośota. Refusing this offer of two horses for one, Peśla stalked back inside the trading-room.

The Ihoka had not repeated their persuasions. While they not yet knew that Peśla's knife had severed two of Catka's fingers, they remembered that Peśla, irritated, often acted in a manner that led to big trouble. And so they returned to their places at the drum, the singers about to begin a victory-dance song.

Wandering around alone, Tatewin, the old weatherwoman, had found some nearly empty jugs but containing enough swallows to prompt something most disgraceful.

The woman, hearing the drum as a voice that called her onto the dance-ground, now leapt among the dancers. Grabbing hold of a warrior's arm, she jumped and kicked similar to a Sahiela wrestling contest. But before the man had overcome her, before he had shaken off Tatewin, three more women had rushed forward, each one taking hold on a man dancer.

And now something strange happened: these men neither threw off the women nor stopped dancing. Instead, one warrior reached an arm around the woman's shoulder, his hand clasping her breast. And a second man took a handful of woman, his actions encouraging more women to enter this unbecoming dance.

Never before had man and woman danced together, but who cared about 'never before' on an exciting night like this one.

I care, I who am Ahbleza, I care. I care the most.

Why, why, the Shirtman had heard his heart cry out, will none here recognize me? I am Ahbleza, he who throws off symbols and uncovers the real. I am he who acts to elevate himself above the reach of change and decay. Why, why will they not recognize this thing? But even as his heart cried out again, he had begun to answer himself.

Perhaps some persons wonder whether Ahbleza ever uncovers the real Ahbleza. Or whether he hides, instead, under the Shirt. Will not Ahbleza secretly look for that which happens here to happen? Will he not sense satisfaction when he learns that his warriors kill two whitemen yet he keeps his vow not to tell who kills Olepi? Ahbleza asks that his people see him as their protector, but they see that he protects only the Shirt. They experience nothing good on this campground; instead they observe a consuming power, something put into motion and now moving without director or direction. They see craziness and killing; they see dogs sniffing man-blood and man-bones. They see kinsman injuring kinsman; they see tiny red lakes that come of dripping wounds. They recognize a camp without a stonedreamer influence and without a true war leader. They see many good persons who suspend their reason, who run blind and fall down. And now they imagine that which legend calls Iya, the Camp Eater; Iya, a mouth that appears everywhere at once, a terrifying mouth that devours the camp, crunching bones and drinking the blood of women, men, children. And, unstable and irrational, they imagine Ahbleza in some way responsible for the Camp Eater's appearance here.

Who, then, will recognize a protector—or even a symbol of protection—in the man who sits horseback outside the deadwood lodge this night? Who will recognize Ahbleza as otancan?

Peśla re-entered the trading-room, a warrior on the trail of his enemy. For any man who takes a horse from one in his own tribe becomes the same as enemy.

Persons who had glimpsed Peśla's face as the warrior searched the room, turned again to Woze as a way of distraction. But the heyoka sat propped against the wall, his head rolling side to side, his companions uncertain whether he had drunk too frequently from the cup or whether he only pretended this wobbliness. Either way, they now commanded him to wakefulness, ordering a performance.

Two wapiti dreamers pulled the contrary to his feet. "Leap, big-voice, leap," they demanded and let go his arms.

Woze slumped to the ground, a little grin on his face.

One of the dreamers knelt and, grasping Woze's hair, repeated the command to leap.

The heyoka's grin widened into a smile. He put out his feet to each side but he lacked the power to rise. His head flopped and his eyes rolled back.

The curious, gathering around, demanded loudly that the man enact his heyoka dream or suffer the consequences. Then someone spit a mouthful of liquor at his face.

At once an Oglalaĥca, remembering a jug he had hidden under a pile of trade-cloth, dug for the container. But before he poured anything down Woze's throat, every man standing nearby took a gulp.

The heyoka tried to pull away but his tormentors held his nose, forcing open his mouth, laughing when the firewater backed up. True to his dream—or so they imagined— Woze drinks 'whee-skee' in his contrary way, his writhing and spewing more entertaining than the leaps he had made famous. And so they held on to his nose and poured, laughing at his contortions until they noticed something more amusing.

A dog had lifted his leg against an old woman who sat eyes closed, perhaps asleep. But feeling the wetness on her face, she had opened her mouth to receive more of this 'firewater'; the people play the new game again and so they squirt a drink into her throat?

The woman's husband came to see what had brought on such loud laughter. And seeing, he used his bow to strike the head of the man most near him. And now the people took sides, affinities ignored and kinsman-rule unremembered, most of these Mahto barely aware of their surroundings.

And so none of the quarreling persons inside the lodge had noticed Peśla's disappearance; none knew that Peśla, taking back his war horse, returned to the village, his anger directed at Lowansa, the one he saw now as responsible for all his difficulties.

Peśla approached his tipi, knife in hand. He slashed at the flap, jerked loose the cover. Pulling out pegs, he lunged inside. Instantly he demanded to know why his wife slept instead of waiting up to care for his sweating horse.

Lowansa had pretended not to hear, but when he kicked at her robes, she cried out in hurt and alarm. Snarling, he grabbed her legs; he dragged her close to the fire circle.

And now she saw that he held a thick stick in one hand, a knife in the other hand. But she knew not with which weapon he struck the first blow.

Catka, warned about Peśla, crouched behind a partition to the rear of the trading area; he will wait until Peśla's ears again will hear and until he, Catka, dares trust himself to speak calmly into those ears. And now he reflected briefly on Red Lake.

Crawling toward this place, he had passed back of the counter where Red Lake, gesturing frantically and gasping Lakotah, forewarned a terrible occurrence, something that will happen if the tallow melts into the barrel, if Catka neglects to put out the flame.

So, Catka and Red Lake will blow up? Catka who loses two fingers, someone for whom hereafter they need to make meat? Catka who already considers this day as a good day to die—but not at Peśla's hands, not someone whose act will bring on more killing.

And now Huśte, keeping a secret watch over his hunka-father, sneaked into Catka's hiding place. He reported the post almost empty of Mahto, the drunk giving up their search for any more kegs and the quarrelsome going outside. Even so, he advised that the wounded man stay back of the partition. Tonweya appears outside, he told, the scout full of firewater and acting strangely. And so the son of Ogle perhaps comes here as Peśla's brother, perhaps comes to stab Catka.

But Catka suddenly will see as if with new eyes; he will not blame his own for all his quarreling and wounding. Who concocts the burning-drink? Who demands this trade in 'whee-skee' that makes a fool of Catka and loses him his high standing . . . and his two fingers? So why not he, Catka, destroying the trader Red Lake, whose fiery drink brings on this humiliation?

Rising, pushing past the hunka-son, Catka limped back into the disarray of the trading area. He moved slowly, quietly, around the counter; he wondered whether Red Lake sat tied as before. If so, he will throw his knife, a weapon quick and silent. Not likely will anyone in this half-dark place know who kills the trader. Perhaps eight, ten Mahto linger inside, some of these persons on the ground, the sleep sounds gurgling in their throats. And what manner of Mahto ever will report to a Kiyuksa—any Kiyuksa—that Catka tricks Tabloka out of a captive? Will they not say instead that the captive tricks Catka out of a horse?

Suddenly the lame man saw Red Lake in the candle's glow, the trader looking at him, gesturing differently now, moving his hand from forehead across breast as if he signed susweca, the double-wing swift-fly, symbol for long life.

And now Catka leaned across the counter, his knife in a hand unfamiliar to weapons, his injured hand—swollen and unfeeling—dragging on the countertop, pushing a burning candle to the edge. And over.

The explosion shook the ground but the silent man on the tall white horse heard the roar with a sense of relief. The force he had qualified for devastation—and to which the people had loaned impetus—had crashed against the trader's post, had materialized as flame, as a consuming power; his long watch over tragedy had come to a finish.

But now the burning deadwood brightened the night, exposing a shameful scene: kinsman chasing kinsman, women yelling at children, horses pawing and rearing and breaking loose.

A gun boomed twice, the whistle of arrows close on the sound of these shots. And then the shouts of relatives who berated relatives, all these unnatural noises mingling with the crash of wood, deadwood and living trees.

Flames licked the sky, and for an instant Ahbleza wondered whether this fire, all fire, originated in the clouds, perhaps traveling to earth on the wings of mysterious-flight or crashing into earth on the tail of a noisy star.

But whatever the origin, he understood that this blaze and these puffs of black smoke come of a great hoop burning, a way of life that disappears in the flame of a consuming power.

And that the next generation of Lakotah shall grow up on this plain never knowing about those songs back at the beginning, never hearing the true parent-tongue, never glimpsing the real Dakotah heart.

Ahbleza closed his eyes; he wanted to tell himself that he only dreams this fire and destruction, he only dreams this day when not a man looks up to him or even looks toward him.

A gust of warm air fanned his cheek and disquieted his horse. He stroked the creature's neck, but his hand lacked the comforting power; the horse, stamping and quivering, had lost touch with the man.

But suddenly the smell and taste of the great smoke-cloud acted most strongly upon the Shirtman; he sensed his memory aroused and startled, his heart responding with a rapid beat. And then he knew, knew everything he needed to know.

Moments before he had wanted to tell himself that he only dreamed this destruction. Now his familiar-voice had spoken, telling him that he had dreamed—twice dreamed—this same scene, twenty winters past and again this winter. For that which occurred here at Oglala post: the reality of his vision.

Here, the war in the valley wherein his people not only fought each other most fiercely but ran in fear from their relatives and from their horses and even from their dogs.

Here, the red lake and the hillsides, the scene wherein kinsman violated kinsman, abuse arising from within, the Lakotah the founders and the destroyers of their own scheme for living, a tribe who dies by suicide.

And now remembering himself naked on a ledge, remembering that he had challenged the zigzag fire that streaked out from the cloud and had demanded a vivid picture of his youth-vision, Ahbleza knew that he shall wait here for Tonweya. The scout will come to him here, pipe in hand as in the vision. They will smoke together—he and Tonweya—before the scout goes out to look for a clean new trail, for a path upon which one small group shall travel, one small group who choose to perpetuate the voice of the grandfathers.

He leaned forward on his horse; he had heard something familiar, a certain shout. And now he saw what he looked for: Tonweya came, the scout riding out from the sky of flame and smoke, quirting his mount through the stumbling crowd, hurrying through this chaos to reach Ahbleza.

True, the scout came, someone rushing horseback through frightened huddles of women and children, his furious whoops scattering whatever groups stood in his way. But he neither looked for nor remembered Ahbleza; he hunted a Siyo warrior who had run off with a sac containing the flaming-drink, a sac Tonweya wanted for himself.

The scout, having sipped from many sacs outside the deadwood lodge, had entered the trading-room, where he had looked under the shop tables for any kegs not yet empty. Then, noticing a Siyo who sneaked out of the room with a sac in his hand, he had started out after the man. The Siyo had reached his horse before the scout caught up with him but at the same moment that the warrior mounted, a terrible noise had frightened the horse, knocked down the man. Tonweya had grabbed for the sac but the Siyo had held on. Then, seeing the flames that brightened the sky, the scout had looked upward. And the Siyo had disappeared. Angrily Tonweya had gone looking for his own horse; once mounted, he easily will find the Siyo with the sac. Or so he had told himself.

A loud, commanding voice stopped Tonweya. Whirling his horse, the scout approached the Shirtman. He jumped down from his mount in the usual way, ready to run three, four steps as his feet touched ground. Instead he fell. He got up laughing. And he kept on laughing even as he bumped against the Shirtman's horse.

The next instant Ahbleza quirted his mount and dashed away.

Tonweya stood watching, an absurd smile on his lips.

1045

Suddenly he flung himself around but the movement had made him dizzy; he fell backwards trying to climb onto his horse.

He made a second attempt to mount, jumping high, almost catching hold before he went off the opposite side. This thing also seemed funny, something to whoop about. He regretted only that Ahbleza had ridden off and so missed seeing these amusing acts. Then, recalling the stern eyes, he wondered whether Ahbleza ever saw anything as funny any more. Why not go and cheer up the brother-friend?

When none responded to Tonweya's loud cough outside the Shirtman's lodge, the scout had dared to pull aside the flap and stoop in the entrance.

Ahbleza, bare of paint and cover, sat near the tall rack that supported his smoking-sack and the Shirt. But seeing who came, he reached for a robe; he covered himself, feet to eyes.

The intruder smiled mischievously at this sign of rejection. "Drop the robe to your shoulders, my brother. I am your scout, not the enemy."

"I am unaware of any scout in this lodge." The robe muffled Ahbleza's voice but the scout heard.

"So look more carefully. I will go out in any direction you send me."

Ahbleza let go the robe; he regarded Tonweya coldly: "This band moves out before sunrise. I lead whoever will follow me. I travel toward pahamni ridge. I look for a scout who will ride front and advise a new trail. I see none here competent for this work." The speaker again drew up the robe.

Tonweya's eyes flared defiance; his smile had gone. "The Mahto leader will not remember to whom he speaks. I am someone, his most important scout. I am he who seeks the herd and finds the big one. I am he who discovers the enemy's moccasin and locates his camp. I am he who fights when they need another person in the fight. I am he . . ." his body swayed as he spoke on, "the most important scout in this camp, in any camp." Hearing a small sound back of him, he spun around.

Anpagli came creeping through the entrance. The husband's loudness had reached her tipi and, alarmed at the strangeness in his tone, she sought knowing.

Waiting outside the brother-friend's lodge, she had heard Tonweya's boasts. Fearful and saddened, then, she crept into the tipi; perhaps the terrible noise at the post and the red in the sky answered why her husband shouted, spoke unnaturally?

Now, seeing the scout's face, she gave a sorrowful wail.

Instantly Tonweya demanded that she stop her crying. "My wife says she never wails, she never demonstrates sorrow with tears and sound. So why these sounds now?"

The woman broke into more wailing. And Tonweya, lunging toward her, shoved roughly. Anpagli fell backwards.

"You shall not hurt the woman." Ahbleza spoke quietly but he had spoken; he had chosen to remember himself this once as the distant-husband.

"I decide concerning this woman." Tonweya struck at Anpagli but she dodged his assault; his hand struck, instead, the three-stick rack on which hung the pipe-sack and the Shirt. The pronghorn pipe-bowl dropped from the container onto the ground.

Anpagli gave a loud cry. An echoing cry came from behind the backrest where Napewaśte sat hidden.

His attention diverted, his reasoning unsettled, the scout stepped forward on unsteady feet. Suddenly, as if he lost balance, his moccasin shoved the pipe-bowl against a stone in the fire circle; the bowl cracked in two places.

Anpagli crawled backwards out of the lodge, her frightened eyes on the broken pipe. Behind her cover, Napewaśte sat in a silent darkness.

And now Tonweya, the mischief shaken out of him, knelt trembling alongside the thing he had destroyed. He touched the broken pieces gently; he lifted his face to Ahbleza, his eyes pleading an understanding of his distress.

But the brother-friend looked neither at scout nor pipe. Gazing beyond the lodge cover, Ahbleza recognized yet another truth: the exploding roar at the post had not brought to a finish his long watch over tragedy. The force he had qualified for destruction when he brought the people here had disintegrated. And yet each piece retained enough power to demolish wherever a collision occurred. But what nature of man dares destroy that which he lacks the power—the knowing—for putting back together?

The scout raced his horse across the moon-white plain, his face twisted in self-despising; he wished for something to reach out and destroy him.

And the horse, responding to the thumping heels, the urging knees and hands, seemed to sense the rider's desire to exhaust himself and his mount, to let the people find a crazy man and a crazy horse wandering on the grasses.

When drops of moisture appeared on the scout's forehead, he wondered whether this sweat purified him as in an initi; perhaps this dizzy run through the darkness cleansed blood mixed with firewater; perhaps he approached his finish without shame.

But now his frothing mount breathed noisily and slowed to a lope. And the scout, glancing over his shoulder, viewed the wide space of earth he had put between himself and the camp. Even so, the red sky reached out like a stalking danger, something to keep a man running. And so he again quirted the horse.

But neither the horse nor the scout possessed the energy for another exhausting run. The creature stayed at a slow walk and the man, his body gently curving forward, dozed. And finally slept.

For a while the horse kept the rider from falling but when this thing proved difficult, the creature dropped the man softly onto the grass, then stood watch.

Certain persons had heard a woman's pleading cry and the painful moans and wails that followed this cry. But these same ones, carrying supplies from the post to their own lodges, remembered that none interferes between husband and wife. And that a quarreling pair usually resent help from outside the tipi. Yet nothing about this night seemed usual and so someone, recalling Peśla's vicious appearance at the post, went looking for Lowansa's relatives.

Soon Lowansa's father appeared at the tipi flap, the old man asking that Peśla put down his stick, put away his knife; let this whipping stop, he said, before the woman suffers a real injury.

The warrior answered rudely but coherently, his drinking not evident: "When a woman will not learn respect in her parents' lodge, a husband needs to teach this lesson."

The Sicaṅgu father, looking upon his daughter's bleeding shoulder and arm and at the cut on her cheek, wondered what disrespect she had shown the husband. Even so, he made a second plea: "Remember her as the mother of your son."

In response, Peśla struck his wife another blow. And Lowansa fell to her knees.

"They speak of you as a man who will not deserve a wife."

The Sicaṅgu had shouted his insult, and those persons outside the tipi, hearing, now stood hands at mouth, their concern more than their surprise. For suddenly they had recognized Peśla as a power for destroying woman, not only this woman Lowansa but any woman with whom he came in close contact. They remembered the wife who had killed herself and the daughter of that same wife, a young woman who had died here. They recalled his treatment of Winu and that he had shamed one woman with his song about her undergown and a second woman through his acts. And that he had tried to mate his sister with a Kiyuksa whom she disliked.

Peśla had ignored the old man's taunt, but suddenly aware of a murmuring outside his lodge, he lifted his hand—the one that held the knife—over the woman's bowed head.

But now the woman's father grabbed the warrior's arm, twisting the knife point toward Peśla's breast.

Taken by surprise, the warrior slipped on the bloody ground under his feet. He fell backwards, the old man stumbling down on top of him, the knife entering Peśla's heart.

Lowansa began to howl.

And now certain ones on the outside cut down the entrance flap. They saw Peśla's head turned to the side, his eyes open and staring. And they saw his attacker, the pockmarks of an old disease vivid on the Sicaṅgu's face as he crawled off the body.

Most witnesses remained outside, the women crying softly, the men making sounds of amazement and regret. If the dead warrior's relatives demand an ordeal before the council, they told each other, the old man never will survive.

1049

And instant reprisal will bring on more killings, the band breaking and scattering, the Mahto name soon disappearing from the plain.

But even as these thoughts hung over the crowd, they saw the Sicangu fling himself down on the warrior's body. Crying to the onlookers, he begged that they finish him here; he will walk the spirit-trail next to his daughter's husband.

But who will want more blood flowing? Six from the Mahto camp already lay dead on this campground and six more suffer serious wounds; iy-i-i, the women truly have reason to wail.

Slowly the people moved away, the old Sicangu left clinging to the dead warrior, the knife yet in Pesla's breast, a little blood oozing from the edge. But someone had remembered that a boy in his eighth winter huddled in this tragic tipi, a youth who will find comfort in Tacincala's lodge. A favored daughter in the hunter's lodge and now wife to Tawitko, she seemed the proper relative with whom to place the youth this night, a woman competent and willing to give of her understanding to a son whose father dies and whose mother bleeds, the same knife wounding, killing.

And each one had known not to talk with Lowansa but to let the woman seek comfort in whatever direction she chose. Let her decide whether to wait alongside her father, they had said, or to go to her brothers or to visit Cankuna's lodge. She will know, they had said, that a welcome awaits her in every tipi.

The night passed middle but none in Cankuna's lodge looked for any sleep; they sat, instead, as a family of wounded hearts, antagonistic hearts.

Ogle had heard many voices speaking in this lodge, but most of the talk had bounced off his ears. He knew that firewater had wet some of these tongues, the burning-drink yet in the blood, perhaps staying in the blood for many days, and so he had chosen not to consider the schemes these persons had proposed concerning Pesla's killer.

Different persons had mentioned the killer's willingness to die but these same ones talked for letting the old man live; let him live, they had said, but as a wanderer, as a man without a camp among the Lakotah. They had urged that

Ogle make a ceremony of driving out the murderer and his sons, of sending a worn-out horse to drag their scanty possessions.

But now, while many of his relatives awaited their turn to speak, Ogle became aware of a need to understand that which had led up to this grief and so to comprehend what really had happened this day. This day? Reflecting on the manner in which he had used the morning, the evening, the hunter suddenly wondered whether he had overlooked something, neglected something, that made him in any way responsible for the tragedy.

Midmorning he had visited Tacincala's lodge, where he had discovered that the daughter and her husband shared his view concerning the danger in any alliances with persons on this campground. Remembering that a relative once had abused him, Tawitko had said quickly that he never again wanted to get mixed up in any family intrigue and that most certainly he intended to avoid any kinsman who caroused at the post. He and his wife and the young in their lodge had chosen to stay inside, sticks crossed in front of the tipi.

Stepping out Tacincala's lodge, he recalled that he had sensed much relief. A meeting between Tawitko and Tabloka seemed unlikely, and while he, Ogle, yearned to see his daughter Cuwe and her children, he recognized the danger in any contact between Peśla's relatives and the Kiyuksa.

He had walked on, not stopping at Lowansa's lodge. He had seen the woman on her way to the stream and he had noticed the absence of Peśla's war horse, an almost certain sign that the warrior-son had gone somewhere horseback. Nor had he seen anything to hint that Lowansa's son played nearby.

Returning, then, to his own tipi, he had tied down the front, Cankuna and Winu made to understand that they neither go out nor permit visitors. And so he had not known that those distress cries and subsequent commotion concerned his family, not until Pasu had scratched at the cover, the scout identifying himself as a relative on an urgent errand.

Truly, truly, he Ogle will not neglect anyone this day, but what about those thirty-and-eight winters he knows Peśla as his son, his first-born son? Peśla, whom they call

Cicila and then Gnuśka; Peśla, whom he calls his warrior-son. But whatever the name, will not Peśla—child, youth, warrior—always go out looking for trouble? Will not Peśla always look for any shortcuts to power? Will not he push for favors, using the warrior-lodges, using women, using his extraordinary boldness? Using and abusing, Peśla's way.

But for all his boldness, for all his renown as a warrior, had any man in camp ever looked up to Peśla? They said that Sluka admired Peśla. Sluka? A waunca, an imitator; who ever regards an imitator seriously?

Peśla and Tonweya, two sons born of the same parents, each one with eyes to see for himself, ears to hear for himself, and a reasoning power to decide for himself. But one of those sons born with a different heart, an angry heart. And so Wośkate, once a gameman, walks with a crooked foot and Ośota's young wife sits with a scarred face, and Lowansa, they say, hides a darkly bruised body and face. And Wipatawin, fifteen winters in the past, hangs herself before any of these things happen to her.

Ogle rested his head between his palms; truly, wherever, whenever Peśla had gone out, to fight or to dance, he had gone out daring someone to kill him. But who will know why the old Sicanǵu becomes that one?

And now the hunter heard a foreboding mutter; the young men hinted that they had sat long enough, perhaps too long; if neither Ogle nor his brother Hinhan nor Pasu choose to speak, they grumbled, let the sons and nephews of these men decide the murderer's punishment.

But Ogle had chosen to speak: "My brothers, my sons, you have reason for vengeance and truly these women have reason for weeping. The warrior-son dies in his own lodge, his wife's father the murderer; little wonder your hearts catch fire. A Lakotah spills Lakotah blood in this village, and so why not kill or drive out this murderer before blackness sprouts in many more hearts."

The hunter paused: "And yet, my relatives, I see a different way."

Slowly, clearly Ogle described this different way: "I and you recognize one another as persons of high standing; the people observe in what manner each member of this hunter's family acts. And so I ask that each one brings to this lodge something he prizes, something I shall present to the Sicaṅgu who deeply hurts this family. These gifts shall make him a hunka-relative to each member of this tiyo-śpaye; I and you will choose him to take the place of the warrior who dies. And so certain ones here shall call the Sicaṅgu 'my uncle' and different ones here will speak saying 'grandfather.' I intend to make him my brother, his winters near to mine."

Most of Ogle's listeners clasped a hand over their mouth; will the hunter truly mean that which he says? That they shall make the murderer a relative-through-choice?

Ogle had spoken truly. He wanted to see the Sicaṅgu going out and coming into camp without fear for his life. "I will take him to the center lodge, where the people shall hear that this Sicaṅgu becomes hunka to each one in the hunter's big-family ... providing my kinspeople, that you agree." Ogle's gesture included the women and the children; he sought approval from each one.

Iku began the agreeing sounds. Pasu next. Why not act as Ogle proposes, their murmurs said; why not hold together a family if not a band? And a band if not a hoop, if not a tribe?

But not all thirty in this gathering voiced assent, not even when they knew that the saddened father and mother of the dead warrior awaited their sanction.

And so Iku began a speech in which he asked that they reflect on the fighting among relatives at the post, the shameful and dangerous quarreling, the deaths and near-deaths. "Suspicion replaces sense; out come knives and someone gets hurt, someone dies. Yet these persons who injure or kill on this day, on this night, will not scheme violence. They suffer shock the same as I and you. And so I extend to the Sicaṅgu my true-sympathy, something that recognizes neither regret nor truth but, instead, the same sympathy I extend to myself and to you, relatives all."

A deep silence followed Iku's speech, but after a while Ogle heard each one present agree to that which he desires to offer the Sicaṅgu. Even so, the hunter wondered about those two missing voices; will anyone know, he asked himself, where Tonweya stays this night? Or why Anpagli sits weeping, the woman alone in her tipi?

XXI

OLD EYANPAHA awakened the Mahto lodges. As usual, the far-distant light of the eastern sky had signaled the start of his song, but he sang a strangely different message, unlike anything he previously had sung. Mouth for Ahbleza, he announced the leader's intention to lead out the Mahto people before the rim of the rising sun touched the plain. The band shall return to the campground of Ahbleza's youth, to the ridge and stream they once name 'pahamni,' to the hill with a view, to slender trees along a narrow creek, to the bird who sings with two different voices, to those mixed grasses that bloom red and turn yellow. Here, beneath a hill black from old signal fires and on a flat circled with old lodge sites, the Mahto shall make their own summer hoop, even if none but ten lodges form this circle.

Here, at pahamni, the Mahto shall live the old customs, the old scheme of life; here, at pahamni, they shall live the truth of the grandfathers. For Ahbleza never again shall lead his people in any different direction.

And let whoever takes down his lodge now remember this thing; let him understand where he goes. And why.

Napewaśte's tipi cover fluttered to the ground as Eyanpaha finished his rounds. And now Kehala's young son, the boy's eyes sparkling his pride, brought front the horse Ahbleza had chosen to ride, an ordinary horse, the one from his horse-catching adventure with Miyaca.

Mounting instantly, Ahbleza rode to a center place. Here he intended to wait until all persons who chose to go with him had gathered close by. He had not painted and he had not put on the Shirt; a single feather flat at the back of his head distinguished him as leader, this one feather decoration enough.

None had remembered him as Shirtwearer, none had recognized him as otancan on the day before; perhaps none shall notice him as leader on this day. But once again, he will wait and see, wait until the sun's rim rose into view.

Icabu came first, the good man taking care of the spirit-lodge as before, everything intact. And then Icabu's family, four lodges, a tiyóspaye certain to lend strength to the band.

Next, Ahbleza's own, his mother walking alongside the two horses who pack her belongings, drag her tipi poles. And back of Napewaśte, Kehala and her daughter, the young one thirteen winters and awaiting the puberty ceremony. Yuza, the husband-father, sat mounted and ready to ride, his young son on a little spotted horse alongside him.

And now Catka's wife joined Napewaśte's group, the fringe cut off her gown, her long braids missing. But close by, watching over this grieving woman: Huśte, the hunka-son.

The old men of the band assembled in their customary manner, Wambli Okiye and Hehaka in this group along with seven more who kept their thoughts active if not their bodies. They sat together now, smoking, waiting.

The people gathered quietly, scarcely any talking, but soon a murmur passed through the crowd; they saw that Ogle approached. And at the hunter's side, they saw the old man who had pushed the knife into the heart of the warrior-son.

Ogle walked a little ahead of his big family, his robe in shreds, his hair cut above the ears. His Sicangu companion presented a similar appearance, but Hinhan, Pasu, Iku who came next, had not cut their hair this short, not to the point of looking bald. Lowansa's brothers followed closely and then the women who belonged to all these men, wives who came leading horses, each horse packing either bundles or lodge covers, one horse dragging the poles that supported an aching Lowansa.

Tacincala and her husband rode side by side at the rear of the line, Lowansa's boy proudly up back of Tawitko. None from this lodge, at Tacincala's request, displayed any sign of grief; Peśla's son had endured enough, she had said quietly, and as for herself, she refused to pretend anything. And Tawitko, understanding, had agreed. Certainly Tacincala had chosen wisely when she accepted Tawitko for husband, the lightskin woman and the darkskin Kiyuksa not only a handsome pair but a most congenial wife and husband.

Now, Ogle's tiyošpaye approaching the place those wise old ones sat smoking, the hunter called out loudly, his message for all ears: "Lakotah, hear. The man alongside me becomes something to each one in this family. I am calling him 'my brother'; I and mine make him a relative."

At once Eyanpaha began a song, the crier telling that the hunter gives a horse to whoever loses a relative in the fire and that Hinhan, the hunter's brother, presents a horse to each of the severely hurt.

And so the people gathered, not yet forty lodges, but Ahbleza, watching the tipi go down, marveled that anyone chose to follow him, each one knowing that he leaves to memory the black hills, the heart-shape ancient mound they call sacred earth; the black hills, the true-image of spiritual vitality.

Sunihanble and his relatives walked up now, but the lodge that sheltered a different pezúta remained standing, the flap tight, everyone closed out; Huhupiye had not risked a meeting with anyone. True, Huhupiye had heard the message; he knew that the hunter had made the Sicangu his relative. But will not a father regard an old man who kills an aberrant son much differently than a healer who molests his granddaughter? Huhupiye intended to raise his lodge among the Oglalahca from this day forward.

But Ahbleza rejoiced on seeing that Waglula stayed with the Mahto; the young seer whom Wanaĝi had entrusted with something most meaningful chooses to raise a tipi at pahamni.

And certainly Ahbleza sensed comfort on viewing Cetan and his relatives in the gathering; Cetan, who had pulled off the Shirt when none respected his advice, Cetan who truly will understand why the Mahto leader never again will wear the Shirt.

"Nor ever again will any one man wear the Shirt more courageously than the one to whom I now speak."

Ahbleza turned, marveling the sound of Tašunkekokipapi's voice in his ear yet scarcely aware of that which the handsome Kuya had said. And certainly he had not realized until now that his friend came bringing thirty lodges, all these persons choosing to travel with the Mahto.

The Kuya's hand touched briefly on Ahbleza's shoulder; then he spoke again: "Perhaps I hear your thoughts; I remember that I and you often look upon things as through one pair of eyes."

The man's horse shifted slightly, his leg touching against Ahbleza's leg in the manner of boy-companions. But the Kuya knew that a man spoke here, not a boy. "You recognize, my friend," he went on, "that twice the Titonwan present a Shirt, then shun the example of him who wears the Shirt. I speak of you and Cetan, but this thing happens also to me. And yet I neither turn in nor lay aside the Shirt. I choose to remember that this Shirt represents man's privilege to accept or reject something. And until I see the people living without this privilege—and this responsibility—I will not discard the Shirt. I see the Shirt as that which symbolizes the privilege of choice. And I look upon the man who wears the Shirt as the one who chooses truth."

Tasunkekokipapi sat waiting in the event Ahbleza will decide to reply. But the Mahto had accepted this moment as something above the reach of words.

And so the Kuya turned his horse, riding to meet his people, all lodges packed, everyone prepared to travel alongside these Mahto.

Ośota and his relatives, slow at packing, saw the procession form and start to move before they had collected everything and stood ready to join the movers. And so certain ones had counted the lodges that made up this moving band. Seventy-and-seven lodges, they told, as they hurried to take their place in the line, seventy-seven lodges including Ośota's camp, seventy-and-seven lodges starting out together, traveling in the direction of the red rim on the edge of the plain, a rising red ball that will climb the sky this day, perhaps every day for so long as the Lakotah live.

Seventy-and-seven lodges, Ahbleza told himself, but thirty of these families in Tasunkekokipapi's following, not mine.

He had invited the Kuya leader to ride alongside him, and so they rode now, two Shirted leaders, one man wearing his Shirt, one man not.

Desiring to show yet more respect for the Tasunkekokipapi band, the Mahto had assigned certain ones among the Kuya's clubmen to help keep the procession orderly. And now these clubmen—they called their warrior-lodge 'Wiciska'—began a song, a song not unfamiliar to the Ihoka-lodge.

But none among the Mahto yet had the heart for singing. A certain Ihoka member lay dead, the gift of a red robe from his own, and neither father nor any different relative telling where they had left the body of this warrior-son. Why sing lodge-songs when women, men, even horses plod along dispiritedly, the people remembering that half the Mahto lodges choose not to accompany their relatives. True, a song lifts a people but what song ever mends a band?

At the resting places the headmen smoked in a silent little circle, the hunters and healers and bow-makers all sitting in their own quiet groups, each one perhaps wondering whether he had decided wisely, each man perhaps remembering the Mahto strength as something cut in half. Or will someone remember that two Shirtmen walk here? Two Shirtmen, true, but who will count the warriors?

Reaching the top of the high rise beyond the river—the same ridge from which Tonweya had viewed the glowing sky—the travelers had stopped to look back into the hazy distance. And so they saw the long, long line of people who moved hugging the black hills, following up the good river. And so they understood that Tabloka led the Titonwan camps to a new location, the Oglalaca, the Siyo, and many Mahto going gladly wherever the Kiyuksa pointed.

And now will someone with the Mahto leader suddenly sense regret? Wish himself going in the opposite direction, following Tabloka instead of Ahbleza? Perhaps not yet, not yet.

Many persons showing weariness, the band made an overnight camp soon after the sun had passed middle. But the women kept up their sorrowful wails until dark.

Ahbleza heard these mourners as from a distant knoll, but a different crying came from a nearby lodge; Anpagli sat weeping, this woman who had said that she never cried. And so the leader approached, calling her 'sister' and disclosing his plan to ride out and find Tonweya. Once he saw his people calmly underway again, he intended to go out looking for the scout. And so let Tonweya's wife cease her wails.

Anpagli dropped the robe covering her face; in a breaking voice she spoke saying that she cried at the memory of someone who had abused the pipe, who had lost touch with his brother-friend.

Sternly Ahbleza gave answer: "The scout abuses nothing, my sister, nor will he ever lose touch. I, Ahbleza, break the pipe on the day that I lead the people to Oglala post. I, Ahbleza, lose contact with that which demands constant attendance. And so why shall I, Ahbleza, look for the scout to recognize a brother-friend where none exists? Why shall I, Ahbleza, imagine that any Lakotah sees me as hunka, as Shirtman?

"The scout of whom I and you speak, my sister, drinks of the mystery-water, but for a different reason he denies Ahbleza."

The woman again pulled the robe to her face, hiding the fright in her eyes and smothering a wail.

But the leader spoke on: "Certainly I respect the tears of woman but not these tears, not the tears of a wife who weeps when she remembers Tonweya."

Ahbleza had spoken and now he walked away, the woman gazing after him.

The song of the crier again awakened the band before sunrise. The Mahto Shirtman, he announced, rides out after the scout who goes ahead to prepare a new path. Those family-leaders who walk front, keep front. The people, in good hands. And now, down with tipi. Break camp; the Mahto travel.

But as the people rose up from their sleeping robes, they heard a different song, most persons knowing that only Winkte owned such a wonderful voice. And so they came out from their lodges to appreciate the birdlike tones, to see the singer standing on a hummock and looking in the direction where a man, horseback, grew small on the plain. Listening to Winkte's song of Ahbleza, they, also, watched the Shirtman disappear across the grasses, the sunrise lighting his way.

Soon afterwards the camp moved on, Taśunkekokipapi

at the head of the line, Ośota alongside him and sitting close, those Mahto and Kuya who had fathered the great-families within these bands.

Tonweya awakened in his customary manner, his eyes opening to the joy of a new sun. Then remembering, he arose slowly, his breast paining as from a fresh wound.

The horse waited close by and so, mounting, he rode on, the sweetness of morning and the sense of aloneness easing his heart. He will not cringe remembering that he broke a certain pipe, he told himself; instead he shall recognize this event as something that awakens him to the importance of his youth-vision.

He rode slowly, striving to relate to the mystery that bound him to the Shirtman, his thoughts shaping into pictures. But the pictures seemed to blur before he had managed a true-look.

The sun climbed high, sending beams to dance on the plain. And the scout, gazing at the indistinct shapes that loomed ahead, puzzled his uncertainty; even as these distant watery forms appear and disappear, will he confuse dream and reality? Perhaps an imaginary pipe breaks, not the real one. Yet he need only glance down at his hand to see the pieces of redstone bowl.

Pondering now the summer-snow vision Ahbleza had described, he recalled that in this vision he had carried the pipe. But that he also had fallen back down the cliff. Ruefully he reviewed the incident at the post; he had fallen but not down any cliff. He tried to remember exactly what the brother-friend had told about the scene in the valley where the people fought, Ahbleza shouting over their heads to a man who stood on a hill.

But even as he considered these things, Tonweya neglected nothing along the trail, the edges of his eyes alert to each moving thing: bird, cloud, grass, shadow. Whatever the importance of the vision, he knew that nothing sat above his importance as a scout, as the eyes and ears and nose of the people.

More than once he had wet his nostrils, sniffed the air, as he rode along but now he came to an abrupt stop. Jumping to the ground, he pressed an ear against the earth. He mounted again, but he rode uneasily, keeping to the gullies. Suddenly he knew himself as a man afraid, this realization more startling than his fear.

He looked from under his palm toward the ridges but he saw nothing hostile. He waited, looked again. And now he caught a glimpse of two robes flapping.

Someone signaled someone that three hundred and fifty Titonwan moved along this trail.

The scout's eyes searched the nearby ledges for brush, for a boulder that he dared use as a shield while he looked back over the plain, locating his band. And he needed to discover who, this enemy and where they waited.

He staked his horse and began to maneuver himself out of the gully and toward an overhang of stone. Upon reaching the ledge, he lifted his head cautiously; he saw neither a traveling people nor a grazing herd of pte. Yet enemy scouts swung their robes as before. Someone, somewhere watched.

The danger, then, waited beyond the next ridge. But to see in that direction required that he climb a tree on the ledge above him, the branches thinly leafed and offering scant protection. He took a moment to examine the risk. He recognized that one thing favored him: the signaling scouts had come on foot and for one observation; not likely will they discover his horse or look for a Titonwan scout so far in advance of his people.

And one thing he dared consider: that these two robe-flappers signaled a small party of hunters, not a war party. But until he managed a view over the far ridge, he lacked a way to appraise the extent of the danger.

He waited until the signalers climbed down from their lookout. Then, pulling himself up onto the near ledge, he crept toward the lone tree. He jumped for the one strong branch and chinned himself high enough for a look.

The sight froze his grasp: Pani on the move, perhaps seven hundred lodges, more than three thousand people.

But he had perceived the situation almost at once. These red-roach people come out from their earth lodges to hunt, he remembered, once during the cool moons and once during the warm. They arrived now for the summer hunt. And they made three lines moving evenly in one direction, all these lodges not a half-day's walk from where he clung to this branch.

Turning only his eyes, he looked back along the trail he

had ridden. A dimly rising dust hinted that the Mahto people moved toward this same place. And if the paths of these two tribes cross? The Mahto not likely will survive the encounter; not eighty lodges—if, truly, the Mahto band counts eighty lodges now—against seven hundred.

Here, the danger he had sensed, his sudden, unfamiliar fear.

But that fear had fallen to the ground; he held on to a single thought: the people's lives depend on his warning.

He let himself drop off the branch. He heard a pebble roll from ledge into brush; touching ground, he had loosened a stone. And if enemy ears had heard, enemy eyes now watched. He dared not try signaling the Mahto.

And so what way but to reach his horse and ride back over the trail, swift-travel his weapon, and the space between the two tribes his shield.

XXII

BEFORE THE approaching horseback ever rode the sign of the Titonwan, the scout had recognized Ahbleza. Who will ride with such superb bearing and who but the brother-friend will come out alone looking for Tonweya?

Rushing toward their meeting, the scout reached Ahbleza quickly. He jumped down with a yell, running along the ground in his familiar way. But suddenly he dropped onto one knee, posing the same as when he brought news to leaders and deciders in a camp circle. He lifted his face to Ahbleza, the broken pipe-bowl in his hand. "This scout lacks a pipe for vowing truth before he reports. But he will hold up these two pieces and say that he never speaks an untrue word to his brother-friend. Nor to anyone."

Then, before the moment became unbearable for either man, Tonweya began his account. Using his thumb to gesture, he emphasized the great strength of the Pani. And the enemy's nearness to the Mahto band.

Ahbleza, replying only to the scout's news, answered formally. The Mahto band, as Tonweya foresees, walks directly onto the path of the enemy. And certainly Pani warriors, receiving their scouts' message, prepare an attacking party. Perhaps they ride out knowing that Titonwan travel on open ground and without a chance to change direction.

"And so I will make the Pani change their path." Tonweya jumped on his horse, instantly away.

Ahbleza had not dared to protest. He had seen in the scout's eyes a desperate wish to gain back the honor he imagined lost to him. Even so, he waited awhile before turning his horse for a fast run back to the people.

Suddenly he heard Tonweya's challenging shout; enemy scouts pursuing Tonweya had come up close. And now an answering yell echoed from the valley; the whole Pani tribe rode alerted.

The Shirtman quirted his mount and the horse leapt forward. "Never will I live for you, my brother-friend, but die for you I will."

Ahbleza's words had fallen softly on the sand, but his chilling whoop as he rushed toward the danger echoed off the cliff.

Tonweya, approaching the top of the ridge, heard the whoop and yet he had not looked for Ahbleza to ride up alongside him this quickly.

But Ahbleza had come. And his face wore a boylike smile as if he and the scout shared a wondrous secret. "Why not lead this bunch a puzzling chase," he said; "none will know that they pursue two Titonwan instead of one. I and you will play a game that keeps their scouts guessing. Hiyu wo, my young brother." He lifted his face in a youthful laugh.

The next moment Ahbleza dashed out along the ridge, plunging instantly into a contest of elusive tactics. He knew himself competent to lose the enemy scouts among the gullies of the surrounding earth, but suddenly he had decided to make the pursuit as interesting for the Mahto scout as for the Pani, to match his cunning against Tonweya's aptness.

"A good day to die," he shouted, the words surprising his lips. "A good day for dying," he called out again, marveling that his thoughts traveled back to Tunkaśila.

But now he heard the sound of more than one horse. Riding slowly forward to a view point, he saw that a group of Pani warriors, rushing ahead of the big party, moved toward the rise; apparently they intended to distract the Mahto scout while the true Pani war party maneuvered for a surround.

Knowing almost exactly where Tonweya now rode, Ahbleza encountered little difficulty circling back to the brother-friend. On his approach, he had called out quickly, asking that Tonweya follow him into a narrow ravine, enough space for hiding two men, two horses, also a way of escape.

Soon the two stood close together in the ravine, each man with a hand on his horse, ready to mount at any instant.

Gazing into the scout's face, Ahbleza spoke as if he gave a most simple direction: "I stay, my brother, and mislead the enemy." His hand touched on Tonweya's shoulder: "You, my scout, will lead the people along a safe path to the rises of pahamni."

Tonweya's mouth curved in a gentle smile; he had sensed in the hand that clasped his shoulder and in the serene eyes, the choice Ahbleza had made. Together they had outwitted the Pani scouts but now a party of warriors pursued. And one man needed to stay and divert the attackers while the second man raced back to warn the Mahto people.

But Tonweya intended to stay: "If one dies here, my brother, I am this one."

From the moment Tonweya had met Ahbleza on the trail, he never had considered anything different. He had ridden out as a scout, as a man who confronts whatever danger, visible or invisible, sits along the path a people travel.

Ahbleza had withdrawn his hand but the memory of the touch held on, giving comfort to the scout while he listened to whatever more his brother-friend chose to say.

"I know you, misun, and so I never wonder about your courage, neither this day nor any day that you live. I know also the need of my people." Ahbleza spoke firmly: "They need the voice of a truthbearer as never before."

After a pause Ahbleza spoke on, his phrases unhurried, almost as if these two sat together on a knoll and under a clear, warm sky, the day lent for their pleasure and theirs alone.

"Will my brother-friend truly understand his place among the people? Certainly he lives as the ears and eyes of the tribe but will he recognize himself as the one man truly out in front? Tell me, whose moccasins make the original man-track on new ground, moving across grass where none but the grizzly roams, pushing through brush where none but the grizzly naps? Who in the tribe sneaks up on danger and returns with a factual report?

"Tell me, who discovers the plentiful earth where a man shall make meat and see his horses graze? Who but the scout dares say, 'I know where the path leads, for my feet touch upon all this earth, from where the flowering stick blooms to where the hills rise up?'

"Who walks alone under sun and moon and so feeds and shelters himself, defends and heals himself?"

Tonweya had listened as if to a story about someone he wanted very much to meet.

"Each man chooses, misun, the place he will take in the scheme of things . . . I and you talk concerning this truth in those youth-seasons . . . and so I dare wonder: will my brother-friend recognize the place he takes . . . and keeps?"

"I point the way," the scout answered slowly, a certain awe gathering in his eyes: "I make . . . the path."

And so Tonweya accepted the truth Ahbleza had named: he, a scout, the proper one to ride back and warn the people about the danger on the trail.

But he also shall return to the Mahto camps carrying a message; who, a more proper messenger, Ahbleza had said, than a truthbearer.

"Certain answers to my second vision suddenly come clear," Ahbleza told now. "I understand why the stranger on the hill across the valley—the one to whom I call and who calls back to me—resembles myself. And this understanding reveals a great importance for man, for man as something peopling the earth, whatever his look, whatever his custom.

1065

"I and the stranger look alike for the reason that I am looking into his heart and seeing my own. Even from a far distance and with many people fighting between us—red and not-red, white and not-white—I know him and he knows me. And so I and this one call to each other.

"To the Mahto people, my brother, give this message: that not all whitemen act alike; not all wašicun desire to eat up the earth. In those seasons that stand ahead many whitemen shall visit the Lakotah, certain ones holding the same good heart toward the Lakotah that I and you hold toward one another."

Ahbleza spoke his next thoughts most softly, as if he whispered a secret that he wanted to shout: "Misun, the youth-vision I and you share reveals the way to know these good persons when they come. For these persons, whatever the difference in language or symbols, identify with the spirit-consciousness; they also recognize the absolutes that make and keep man. They will see the good in Lakotah ways and honor Lakotah precept and custom, even those customs that appear strange.

"And so speak as my mouth at the council fire. Speak saying that the Lakotah will recognize these good persons for the reason that these good persons will recognize the Lakotah."

Hearing a whinny in the near distance, each man grabbed his horse's nose against an answering neigh. But Ahbleza also made the detaining gesture: "Before you go, one request: I ask for those pieces of the pipe."

Tonweya pulled the broken bowl from the sack at his waist; averting his eyes, he dropped the redstone into Ahbleza's hand.

"Hold open your palm," Ahbleza ordered. Then, loosening his hand from the horse's nose, he reached for a small bundle tied to the creature's mane. He lifted out a pipe-bowl identical with the broken one.

"The true-pipe remains whole," Ahbleza said smiling. "On the day that I and you return as a dreaming-pair, he to whom I tell the vision makes two pipes with the peace-creature's head, look-alike pipes. One he gives me as I walk out seeking a second vision. And one—this one—he puts in Waglula's care to await . . . ."

Tonweya, glancing up, wished never to see anything more wonderful than this look on Ahbleza's face.

"I remember you, misun," Ahbleza went on, "as the one who carries the pipe back to the village after the youth-vision. And so take back to the Mahto people this true one.

"In my second vision you appear, my brother, exactly as you stand here now, a man straight and firm and holding the pipe. During the winters ahead, you shall understand why I see you so."

Tonweya's eyes lingered yet another moment on Ahble-za, the scout marveling that for an instant he had imagined that he looked upon Olepi; never before had he seen so strong a resemblance to the father of this man.

Now, jumping horseback, Tonweya prepared to go out the escape path.

Ahbleza also mounted, but before turning to ride in the opposite direction, he moved up close to the scout. And so the brother-friends, smiling, touched legs as in their youth-seasons whenever they rode together.

The next instant they had separated, each man going his way.

Ahbleza climbed cautiously to the top of the ridge. Looking back, he saw that Tonweya rode beyond reach of the enemy. And so, his eyes shining, he gave breath to a great feeling. "Hanta yo, hanta yo," he cried, his voice sent to sky and earth and four directions. "Clear the way, in a sacred manner I come." His shout echoed along the ridge and down the gully and out onto the plain.

He sensed the power flowing back into him, the same power he had used many seasons in the past. And now, once again, he schemed to use this glorious force to keep some-thing whole. But in a different manner, in a more wondrous way.

"Hanta yo," he sang to the winds, his heart without a burden.

He saw nothing difficult about leading astray the trav-eling lines of Pani, but he intended to protect the Mahto and the Kuya through a more certain maneuver. When next he rides atop the ridge, he told himself, he will stop and reveal his identity as a leader among the Titonwan. He will let the

1067

enemy recognize the single feather that slants into his hair and they shall see him pulling out a bundle, waving the Shirt. And so the Pani shall know him for a Shirtman among the Lakotah.

And once these Pani discover whom they pursue, each one will try to touch him. For certainly the interception of an otancan will bring far more reward than the wiping out of a Titonwan band; even the Pani know enough to demonstrate selectiveness. Taking him, they will let the people go.

He rode down from the top and began again those antics that permitted the Pani to glimpse him appearing, disappearing, and reappearing as he made use of hill, gully, ridge, ravine.

Climbing out of one gully, he saw the enemy lines breaking, their clubmen losing control, the warriors dashing forward in little groups; apparently everyone had become interested in this unusual game.

But he had lost view of the original party who started out after him; perhaps they waited, hidden in the neck of a nearby ravine. Even so, he need not concern himself about an arrow in the back; not a man on the plain, whatever his tribe, risks his honor on such an act.

Looking up at the ledges now, he saw one high point, the one place on the rise to stop his horse and wave the Shirt and so make certain that the Pani recognize their prize.

But as he rode in this direction, the whoops grew dim and before he had reached the top a quiet prevailed, not a sound anywhere. Will the Pani decide that they chase either a fool or a decoy and so they abandon pursuit?

"To the top, friend." Ahbleza spoke firmly to his horse: "Step high and these tumbling stones will not injure your feet." He dared not let the silence distract either himself or the horse. "Hanta yo, hanta yo," he whooped, to the cloud and the ridge and the mystery that encircled him.

A remarkable surge of power carried horse and rider to the summit.

Ahbleza halted. Quickly he untied the bundle and pulled out the Shirt. He touched the feather at the back of his head. Then looking across the plain—Tonweya riding somewhere on that vastness—he lifted the hand that held the broken pipe-bowl. At the same moment the welcoming tones of the bird-with-two-voices floated up onto the ridge.

I am man, Ahbleza heard himself saying, but I, also, own two voices. But now I hear only my familiar-voice, my spirit's voice.

Shall I hear now that I put back together that which I break even as I see the pipe whole and in the hand of my brother-friend?

The bird whistled again and somewhere a woman sang.

Shall I hear now that I bring Heyatawin to the sunpole and the white pte onto the snow, yet these two fade before I touch either one for reason that I never own the power to go all the way? For certainly I never truly own the power for the white-pte ceremony. Perhaps only once man will own this power. And that once, when Ptesanwin appears, the woman-messenger who comes bringing truth, carrying a pipe.

I come, in a sacred manner I come. Wambli-woman sends me a wing and so I let go my horse and ride on the feathers of the warrior bird, the winged who flies me through this dark gully and toward a soft light. My grandfather, you say so.

Two Pani arrows, straight and swift, had pierced the Shirtman's breast, one point entering his heart.

The shouting faces of the enemy warriors wore a look of victory; they had struck down the Titonwan. True, neither lance nor club nor hand had touched the Shirtman, but even an arrow-striking carries honor when the people see whose heart this arrow strikes.

And so the excited cries brought the whole of the warriors running to the high place. But suddenly this onrushing crowd stopped, their whooping silenced. For a moment they stood as a people turned to stone, a moment during which they experienced the mystery and the power that once dismayed and routed a Psa war party.

For a wound in the heart had not changed the face of the Mahto; his, the face of true victory. Poised on his horse, he seemed to gaze upon the enemy, his whole countenance a thing of honor, his body beyond the injury of arrows, his spirit absorbing the whole.

And only now the body of the killed Shirtman fell

slowly forward. And from his hand dropped the pieces of broken pipe, the redstone falling onto the earth as if to signal a finish to the awesome stillness.

At once the enemy resumed attack, their exulting cries as they surrounded their prey something to echo along the ridge and down the gullies and out onto the plain.

XXIII

ONCE AGAIN Heȟaka spread out the painted robe that remembered the importance of each Lakotah winter; once again he asked himself which event out of this recent season truly belonged on the Mahto memory-robe.

Certainly none in this band ever will need a picture to remember Ahbleza; the voices of the people will remember him from generation to generation. And within the same story the people will tell that Tonweya led the Mahto safely along a new trail to pahamni ridge, the Kuya band staying on, the Mahto and the Kuya making a summer circle of their own.

Looking back on pictures of winters past, Heȟaka saw where his line drawings told of many-pte, not-many-pte, but in what manner will his pointed stick tell that many Titonwan hunters never saw even one pte during these past ten, twelve moons?

Truly the bands see changes and changing, he told himself; for example, what about this renaming of the people, calling all four bands 'Oglala'? Newscarriers reported that Tabloka had pushed aside Hinyete and that Tanaźin's people also recognized the Kiyuksa's roar as the ruling voice. And that in return for such favor Tabloka had approved the name-changing.

Oglala? Why not, he had agreed; why not a name that recalls the reluctance of a Kiyuksa woman to receive seeds from the loins of an Isanyati? Who wants a tie with a Dakotah band only thirty lodges now? Why not Oglala? Tabloka decides for all two hundred and forty lodges whether his following call their villages Oglala or Kiyuksa or something different.

But the Mahto had rejected the name; they chose to remember that they belonged to the great Dakotah family whether they spoke with a *d* or an *l*. And so they held on to one more good reason not to join the tribal circle this approaching summer ... not that anyone in the big hoop waited for the Mahto.

Changes and things changing, Heȟaka repeated to himself. Now, suddenly, he knew what to record.

During the moon of falling-leaves, the Mahto had watched the stars changing in the sky—stars floating everywhere overhead—and they had accepted the wondrous sight as a demonstration of their own tribal changes.

But as Heȟaka drew the star-picture, he imagined something different; perhaps these stars reveal that all the truly great warriors—Dakotah, Lakotah—now sit at one big campfire above the clouds. Icabu had released Olepi's spirit from the spirit-lodge, and the son of Olepi had walked the spirit-trail. And so these two join Peta, the grandfather. Three generations, each one truly a warrior; will not the stars say so?

XXIV

HESAPA, THE black mountain; pahasapa, the black hills. Either name, sacred earth.

Pahasapa, 'meat pack'; here, the source of body strength.

But they also call these hills 'vision-pipe ledge'; here the source of spirit-power, spiritual vitality.

Pahasapa, the black hills, sacred earth.

Old-woman hill: here, Wambli-woman sits guard over hoof and wing, all creatures knowing these slopes as a meeting place for the four-legged and the feathered and the tiny people of the air.

Dancer hill: here, Lakotah women, hoop in hand, dance the power these hills release, energy from the ancient stone that forms this great earth-heart, this heart-shape mound they call 'black hills.'

A path circles these sacred hills and the true Lakotah knows why this path—not a lodge trail, not a way for travelers, not a legend—here, instead, a hoop of śkan, the life-force, that which makes life, keeps life; taku śkanśkan, something in movement, circling, protecting, this great heart of the Lakotah tribe.

Pahasapa, the black hills, sacred earth.

Hesapa, pahasapa, unchanging, the one true comfort during these seasons of change; what band, then, will resist forever the urge to raise a winter camp within view of the black mountain, the black hills?

One winter had passed since the night of floating stars, the Mahto band staying on at pahamni, warm moons and cold.

But awakening to frost one morning, certain persons had sat aware of true lonesomeness for the grizzly-lodge butte, and so they had asked that someone lead the band once again across the mixed grasses to the old campsite.

The Mahto had leaders but not any one great leader as in those seasons when Peta led, Olepi led. Instead the people looked upon Ośota and Taśunkekokipapi—Tonweya also—as persons competent to guide their moccasins when they sought guidance. And certainly they looked to the Tokala and Ihoka lodges for protection within and beyond their camp.

During this past winter, the Mahto had lost two families to the Sicangu hoop—Makatożanżan had brought his Sicangu into an orderly circle. Even so, the band raised thirty lodges, thirty more when they counted Taśunkekokipapi's people. Six, eight of the young women—Iku's daughter for one—had mated, bringing new warrior-blood into

1072

the Mahto villages, these young wives living with their families now but soon to raise lodges of their own.

But now almost everyone talked of growing lonesome for grizzly butte and the black hills. And so Ośota and Taśunkekokipapi called to the people to pack their bundles; the bands travel.

Gentle weather had accompanied the travelers—night and dawn frosty but mostly sunny days—and they had found meat plentiful along the way. And so, hearts soaring, they approached the butte and those many relatives they had not seen since the tragic experience at burned-post.

But before any real visiting had begun, a different group of persons had arrived. Whitemen appeared in each village. They came, they told, to invite all Titonwan to travel a far distance south of the butte, onto the prickly earth where meat awaited their arrows. And then they spoke of a big trading-place, a log stockade they called Fort William. They had raised this fort, they said, for the Titonwan's pleasure, and each day—all seasons, all moons—great herds of pte grazed within view of the stockade. These whitemen had called the pte 'buffalo' but the interpreter had understood.

The Oglala had shown distant faces; these waśicun, they murmured, shall not lure their camps to drink and shame as in previous seasons. Enough pte graze here at the butte to feed three, four hundred lodges; the Oglala stay.

But the whitemen persisted. The big herd grazes near the butte, they answered, provided the winter remains mild; a blizzard snow will change the story.

In the Kiyuksa village the whitemen heard Tabloka agree about the snow. Perhaps, the leader had said, he will call a council of all bands and they will talk concerning the invitation.

Before ever the counciling began, most persons knew Tabloka's desire. And so they had agreed at the close of the meeting to prepare for travel, to go south to this new wintering place.

But the decision of this council—mostly a gathering of war leaders—had displeased many persons. And so the heads of families, aware that the Kiyuksa's booming tones often intimidated his listeners, called a different meeting.

1073

Let each man make his decision at his own village campfire, they said, this changing of a winter camp not a little thing.

And so the leaders now discovered that the Oglala sat as a divided people, half the tribe agreeable to camping near the fort on the swimming-bird river—Laramie, the whitemen had said but the interpreter had understood—and half choosing to stay at the butte.

Taṅkekokipapi's people along with the Mahto and some of Ośota's relatives never even considered the whitemen's invitation; they had seen at once that these strangers who came to the butte came neither to understand nor to honor Lakotah ways.

But for a while the many different villages at the butte had not known who goes, who stays.

One hundred lodges followed Tabloka to the new post on the fork of the Laramie.

Some stay-backs, watching their relatives go, had worn wistful faces, Cankuna among these persons. Not that the hunter's wife wished to accompany these people but that, seeing her daughter Cuwe in the procession, she had sensed a true sadness; most likely she never will see this woman again. Nor ever see the grandchild Cuwe grows under her gown.

As for Ogle, he regretted seeing old Iśtakpe go; everyone respected this peaceman who wore the eye patch. Even with one eye out, Iśtakpe had appeared to see more clearly than certain ones among his Kiyuksa relatives who had the use of two. Or so Ogle often told himself.

Before the old-winter snows had melted, travelers brought news concerning the tribal-half who wintered south. Tabloka, pleased with the trades his people had made at the fort, schemed a big hunt along the river shell once he saw that the warm moons approached. Moon of geese, he had said, but the people had understood.

And now many persons talked of joining Tabloka for this hunt . . . but only for this one hunt, they said.

The winter moons died and one hundred more lodges went out from the butte to follow along the trail south to the river shell.

Thirty lodges—the Taśunkekokipapi people—took a

different path; they traveled north of the butte. This strong leader, sensing the unrest among his own, recalled those many, many seasons they had camped alone. And so, until his people really knew in which direction their pleasure sat, he intended to keep away from all Titonwan bands ... whatever his personal desire, whatever his sense of closeness to the Mahto.

Forty indecisive lodges wandered off quarreling, the group splitting before they had gone beyond the second ridge, some families looking for the Sicaŋgu hoop, different ones hurrying to catch up with those villages who headed toward Fort William.

Only the Mahto traveled east. And as before, Tonweya stayed front, clearing the way. And so they moved, thirty lodges, thirty contented, confident families, across the red and mixed grasses, up and down the rolling hills and alongside the running waters; and so they moved, these Mahto, over sand and clay and stone, thirty families headed for the welcoming ridge that had become as familiar as their own faces.

But one who saw this place of memories looked out from eyes forever dull and dry. Nothing ever will make her cry again; she, Napewaśte, had used up all her tears.

XXV

TONWEYA LIFTED a glad face to the sky; he knew that never again will he leave this ridge—pahamni ridge—for any different campsite. "I stay," he announced to himself and laughed for the joy in laughing.

The band had returned from the butte seven days previously, seven wonderful days back on the ridge but none more wonderful than this one. The sun painted the young summer morning a brilliant yellow, and the whole earth throbbed with new life. Even the sticky gumbo bloomed white-stars, the gentle flower whose life drains out of a cut stem.

For an instant the flower brought forth a memory of the brother-friend whose blood had drained out on some distant knoll. "But whose spirit lives here with mine . . ."

Suddenly he found himself wondering who among the youths in this camp will lead the new generation of Mahto. Leaning back against the side of his tipi, he watched a group of boys who played with grass lances and blunt arrows.

He called two of these young persons 'my son': Mahtola, his own boy, and Lowansa's son, age ten, this one staying on in Tacincala's lodge when his mother returned to the Sicanġu camp. But even as his experienced eyes observed their play, he pondered the need for a great leader. They followed Ośota this season and perhaps they will follow this good man for many seasons . . . and certainly Ośota raised sons, one of his dead sister's sons a most clever youth . . . but . . .

He saw that Mahtola helped one of the boys mend a broken toy-arrow. And now, watching and listening closely, he heard his own son speak, the boy's words revealing whom he quoted.

"Someone I once know," Mahtola said slowly, "tells me that if I will see nothing but the mark I want my arrow to pierce, I never shall miss the target. But that if I see something different, I hit something different."

Tonweya rose, his heart full to overflowing. He untied his horse and led the creature away from the tipi stake. Perhaps a ride along the ridge, he had told himself, a ride and a moment alone to reflect again the youth-vision, to wonder again as so often before, whether he and the one he once calls brother-friend live as one man in this son Mahtola.

Atop the ridge, the scout paused as always at the one place that provided him an unobstructed view of the wide plain. And now the laughter of children and the chattering of women at work in the village drifted up to him. He heard also the joyful shout of one who had scored a point on the gaming-ground, someone who had won a contest or almost won.

Then, looking down in the direction of scolding tones, he saw where a dog jumped at the meat rack. But he saw also those two good men who worked together, smiling and talking their memories as they painted a new tipi cover.

Again he looked out upon the plain. And wondered many things.

After a while he heard the sound of hoofs climbing the slope and so he had known when to turn and see his son riding eagerly toward him. And his ears had told him that Anpagli came also, his wife walking and not far behind the young rider.

The woman, a bundle of firewood on her back, walked proudly forward to greet the man, but Mahtola suddenly restrained his eagerness to join his father. Acting in the manner of a scout, he advanced cautiously, his keen eyes darting toward the far horizon.

But now Mahtola's gaze suddenly held at one place.

Following the boy's eyes, Tonweya saw that a lone person rode the plain.

Jumping down from his horse, the father walked toward the boy. "Will my son say who rides on the grass?"

Tonweya had spoken calmly, and the boy, shielding his eyes, puzzled the horseback.

After a moment the scout spoke again, his voice as before. "A whiteman rides. See the way he holds his body and carries a firestick. These things tell me at once that a whiteman comes."

Mahtola turned startled eyes toward his father; he lifted his quirt. But Tonweya placed a restraining hand on the horse's neck; he gestured that the boy dismount.

Anpagli had concealed her concern; she waited to hear the husband speak. But Tonweya only motioned that she stay while he walked to the edge for a more certain view.

And now the scout observed that the man in the distance neither came nor showed any sign of coming toward the Mahto camp.

But, everything silent around him, Tonweya had stood on, listening to the memory of a voice.

IN THE SEASONS AHEAD MANY, MANY WHITEMEN

WILL VISIT THIS TRIBE. CERTAIN ONES WILL HOLD THE SAME GOOD HEART TOWARD THE LAKOTAH THAT I AND YOU HOLD TOWARD ONE ANOTHER. THEY SHALL SEE THE GOOD LAKOTAH WAYS AND HONOR THE LAKOTAH PRE-CEPT AND CUSTOM.

THE LAKOTAH WILL RECOGNIZE THESE GOOD PER-SONS FOR THE REASON THAT THESE GOOD PERSONS WILL RECOGNIZE THE LAKOTAH.

The scout moved back to his wife and son. He smiled at the boy: "You need not send for warriors. Let the man go his way or let him come yours. If he comes here, the people will know in what manner to receive him."

The boy, looking shyly into his father's eyes, saw the sunshine dancing on the man's face. But Anpagli turned away, a mist filling her eyes.

But now the woman felt the husband's hands on her cheeks; gently he lifted her face to his, his eyes asking that she share in this moment of pure and wondrous affection.

Then silently he took her load of wood, bundling the sticks on each side of Mahtola's horse.

"Fear not," Tonweya told the boy, "one load will not turn this fine old war horse into a pack-bearer. For all her winters—perhaps twenty-and-five—Tatezi walks proudly whatever she carries."

Laughing, he lifted his wife onto the yellow's back, then waited, his sudden thought something he wanted her to hear.

"I am glad that you pick up these sticks along the trail. I look for a long-burning fire this night for I intend to tell my son the legend of Ahbleza."

While his father stood speaking, Mahtola had stepped back for a run and jump onto Tatezi's rear. And so he came now, leaping up back of his mother. But in one quick turn, he spun around grabbing Tatezi's tail and ready to ride backwards.

Tonweya smiled at the boy's stunt. But he spoke his words to Anpagli: "One day I shall give this son Ahbleza's name. . . ."

He moved toward his own horse but not to ride. He sent the boy and his mother on down the slope, saying only that he chose to stay on the ridge for a little while.

He wanted to look again upon the plain and to send a

voice to whatever above or below or in any direction now listened, to send a voice telling that on the day he gives his son Ahbleza's name, he also shall give his son the prong-horn pipe, the true-pipe of a dreaming-pair.

Idiomatic Phrases

*English equivalents of Lakotah terms
for geographical features, animals, and plants*

THE WATERS AND THE HILLS
(Rivers and Streams, Hills and Buttes)
In South Dakota unless otherwise specified

arrow creek: Pryor Creek, Montana

baby-place: sandstone rim above Pryor Creek, Montana

berry creek: Cherry Creek, tributary of the Cheyenne River

big bend: Big Bend of the Missouri River, loop in the Missouri between the mouths of the Bad and White rivers

big butte: Bear Butte

big river, big muddy river: Missouri River (also called mud-water, muddy-water)

big-stones river: Cedar Creek, south fork of the Cannonball River

black hill, black hills, black mountain: Black Hills

black lake, briny lake: near the head of Sand Creek in east-central Colorado

brackish lakes: Spirit Lake, Iowa branched-horn river: Yellowstone River, Wyoming/Montana

bunch-of-timbers creek: Smoky Hill River, Colorado/Kansas

dakotah river: James River

dust (their-hoofs-raise-dust) river: Powder River, Wyoming/Montana

earth-lodge creek: in the Fort Yates area, North Dakota

earth mother: Black Hills

earth-of-the-sitting-down-pte: area in eastern Colorado from the Arkansas River north to the South Platte earth-smoke river: White River

fat-grass river: Little Bighorn River, Wyoming/Montana

fat-meat earth: area from the Arkansas River to the South Platte, Colorado

fat-meat river: South Platte River, Colorado/Nebraska

fatty-foam river: Missouri River (also called greasy-foam river)

feather river: Arkansas River, Colorado/Kansas

fine-hair river: Arkansas River, Colorado/Kansas (also called river of fur, river of pelts)

flat-water river: North Platte River, Colorado/Wyoming/Nebraska

flying-mystery butte: Thunder Butte

good river: Cheyenne River

grass-lodge creek: White River, high up the river (location of Pierre Papin's small trading hut)

greasy-foam river: Missouri River

greasy-grass river: Little Bighorn River, Wyoming/Montana

great bend: Big Bend of the Missouri

great butte: Bear Butte

great lakes: the five Great Lakes

great river: Mississippi River (also called river of canoes)

grizzly butte, grizzly hill: Bear Butte

hanging-woman creek: in the Turtle Butte area of the Keya Paha river

hill-in-the-woods: Cache Butte, near the headwaters of the White River

kills-himself creek: on the edge of the Black Hills

lone-woman creek: on the eastern side of the Black Hills, north of Elk Creek

lodgepole hills: Black Hills

many-lakes river: Minnesota River, Minnesota

mischievous river: Bad River (also called tricky river)

muddy creek: Lame Deer River, Montana

muddy river, muddy-water river, mud-water: Missouri River

mystery lake: Spirit Lake, Iowa

old-woman creek: south of the Black Hills, flowing into a tributary of the south fork of the Cheyenne River

old-woman hill: near old-woman creek

pahamni ridge: in the upper Willow Creek area

palani river: Grand River

pani river: Loup River, Nebraska

pelt river: Arkansas River, Colorado/Kansas

powder river: Powder River, Wyoming/Montana (also called dust river, shifting-sands river)

pte-jump-over-edge river: Stillwater River, Montana

pte-tongue river: Tongue River, Montana/Wyoming

quill creek: in the Fort Yates area, North Dakota

rapid creek: Rapid Creek

red-shield river, red river: Republican River, Colorado/Nebraska/ Kansas

redstone-ledge: quarries near Pipestone, Minnesota

redstone river: Des Moines River, Iowa

river of canoes: Mississippi River

river of hides, river of pelts: Arkansas River, Colorado/Kansas

river of pronghorn pits: Little Missouri River, North Dakota

river of water-worn stones: Cannonball River, North Dakota

running-water river: Niobrara River, Nebraska (also called spreading-water river)

sacred hills: Black Hills

sand creek, sandy creek: tributary of the Arkansas River, Colorado

sandhills: eastern Colorado and Nebraska

scout creek: Kiowa Creek, tributary of the Arkansas River, eastern Colorado

shell river, shell-on-the-neck river: North Platte River, Nebraska (after 1835 the South Platte was also called shell river)

shifting-sands river: Powder River, Wyoming/Montana

short-timber creek: Wild Horse Creek, Colorado

sits-with-young-one butte: near the headwaters of the Belle Fourche River, Wyoming

slender butte, slim butte: in the little badlands, Harding County

snow hills, snowy hills: Big Horn Mountains, Wyoming

split-toe-creek: in the Black Hills, an eastern tributary of the Cheyenne River

spreading-water river: Niobrara River, Nebraska (also called running-water river)

swimming-bird river: Laramie River, Colorado/Wyoming

teaching hill: Bear Butte

thickwoods river: Belle Fourche River, north branch of the Cheyenne River

titon river, Teton river: Bad River renamed

tree-covered island: Cedar Island, in the Missouri River, near Pierre

tricky river: Bad River (also called mischievous river)

white cliffs: near the head of the White River, at Crawford, Nebraska

white hills: Bighorn Mountains

white-paint creek: White Clay Creek, near Butte Cache

windy river, wind river: Wind River, Wyoming

yellowish-whitewood river: James River

THE FOUR-LEGGED (Animals)

antlered creatures: plains deer (blacktail), timber deer (whitetail)

big-dog: horse (original name)

big female: six-year-old buffalo cow

bighorn: bighorn sheep (occasionally, mountain goat)

black dog: mystical wolf

black-forehead-stripe: black-footed ferret

blacktail: western blacktail deer

blunt-horns: two-year-old buffalo (also called two-teeth)

branched horn: elk

camp-dog: gentled, camp-bred coyote

chipmungk: chipmunk, striped prairie ground squirrel

cracked-horn, herd father, grandfather: old buffalo bull

crawling people: all legless creatures

creature: any animal

curly-horn, curled-horn: bighorn sheep (also called bighorn)

curly horse: colt

curved-horn: three-year-old buffalo

digs-with-mouth: badger (also called flat-face, chunky striped-face, striped-face)

dominant-tail: leader among wolves

fine-haired creatures: any animal with furry, fine hairs

flat-faced one: badger (also called digs-with-mouth; striped-face) fluffed-hair: buffalo yearling

fork-horn, forked-horn: deer (also called true-meat)

four-legged warrior: grizzly bear

four-teeth (best for robes): four-year-old buffalo

great long-horned pte: long-horned prehistoric bison

hair-on-lip: hare

jumps-and-splashes: frog (also called big-voice)

little black-legged dog: red fox (also called reddish-yellow little-dog, red-dog-with-black-feet)

little yellow-hair (robes for children): buffalo calf under one year old

little yappers who burrow on the plain: prairie dogs

long-claws: grizzly bear

longhorn pte, long-horned pte: prehistoric bison

narrow pte: buffalo cow with remarkably narrow body

ordinary horse: bay

pronghorn: antelope (also called sandy-belly, little bighorn)

quill: porcupine

reddish-yellow little-dog: fox, kit fox

red horse: sorrel

sandy-belly: pronghorn antelope

scorched horse: roan

seed-horse: stallion

shell: turtle

shell (shell-on-the-neck): clam

short-forehairs pte: a buffalo cow with hair growing short in front and around the horns, making it resemble a woman who cuts her hair short as an act of mourning

small-head: small-headed short-horned female buffalo, of ordinary size

snow-skin: ermine (also called winter-skin)

soft-nose: moose

spike-horns: fat young buffalo

spotted horse: painted horse

sticky-mouth: black bear

striped-face: badger

swims-carrying-stick, swims-stick-in-mouth: beaver

tall-ears: whitetail jack rabbit, or cottontail

traveling-dog: coyote, prairie wolf, brush wolf

true-dog: wolf (also called mountain-dog, different-dog, white-dog)

tuft-ears: bobcat

two-teeth: two-year-old buffalo (also called blunt-horns)

wandering-dog: coyote (also called traveling-dog)

wapiti: elk

white-chin: mink

whitefoot: mouse

whitetail: whitetail deer

winter-skin: ermine

big black-bird who soars on flat wings: raven

bird who calls out certain colors: lark bunting

bird who carries mud in mouth: swallow

bird who chews the fat of the big gut: western meadowlark (this bird's call after nesting sounded to the Lakotah like gut popping)

bird who comes at dusk and splashes in the air: nighthawk

bird who knocks on wood: woodpeckers, including common (downy), redheaded, and big redheaded (pileated) woodpeckers

bird who rides back of enemy yelling: kingbird

birds who sing in flight: vesper sparrow; meadowlark; horned lark; lark bunting

bird who sits smiling at excrement: magpie (also called noisy winged)

bird who speaks Lakotah: meadowlark

bird with grease-spotted breast: western meadowlark

bird with long curved-down nose: prairie curlew

bird with two different voices: meadowlark

chattering bird who foretells snow (chattering in the evening): tree sparrow

child of Iktomi who hunts at night: wolf spider

cloud bird: eagle

courageous bird who stays north: raven

double-wing: dragonfly

fighter-bird, warrior bird: hawk; falcon; eagle

fluttering-wing: butterfly

fork-tails: swallows

flapping black-bird: raven

friend, I bundle smoke-leaves: meadowlark

grass-bird, ground-bird: prairie grouse, sharptail

grows-a-horn: great horned owl

hoo-hoo: great horned owl

hummer, bird who vexes: hummingbird

hushed-wing: owl

little old grandmother who scolds but not unkindly: crow

little wing who rides back of enemy yelling: kingbird

longnecks: geese

lump-raiser, stab-and-raise-a-lump: mosquito

night-birds: owls (screech, short-eared, long-eared, great horned, large great horned, saw-whet, snowy; the burrowing owl is a day/night owl)

noisy winged: magpie

painted-fly, painted-wing: butterfly (also called fluttering-wing)

points out pte, tells about pte: a large wingless grasshopper with wide upper legs (erroneously called black prairie cricket; not to be confused with the 'dung roller')

quiet-woman bird: lark bunting (also known as the bird who calls out certain colors)

rain-bird, rain/snow slides off feathers: owl

red-dawning-coming: sharptail grouse (so named from its call)

red-shoulders: redwing blackbird

red wingfeather: red-shafted flicker

shivery bird: screech owl (so named because its call sounds like the voice of someone shivering with cold)

shortneck, shortneck bug: large ant

sits in a row: kingbird (also called bird who rides back of enemy yelling)

snowbird: horned lark; snowbird (flutters up a snowstorm when taking a snow bath)

swift bird: nighthawk

swift-fly: dragonfly (also called whirlwind fly)

tiblo-bird: killdeer (so named from its call)

tiny shortneck: small ant

water-birds: goose; duck; coot; crane; loon; white swan

whirlwind fly: dragonfly

whitewing who perches on brush: lark bunting

winged warrior: prairie falcon

wingflapper: golden eagle; bald eagle

THE STANDING-PEOPLE (Trees, Grasses, Blooms, Berries, Roots)

TREES

arrow-wood: any of various woods used for arrow shafts—currant, ash, juneberry, dogwood, chokecherry, gooseberry

attracts ants, crawling up and looking for sweet juice: box elder bark water: bark of various trees boiled to make healing drinks or applications

bow-wood: any wood used for making bows—osage orange (Lakotah secured through trade), ash, cedar, rock elm, dogwood, willow, cherry saplings, etc.

cooking wood: small cottonwoods, no smoke to taint food

counting-stick stalks: sumac

good-for-nothing wood: box elder

initi tree: willow

lodgepoles: pine, ponderosa, slender white spruce (found in the Black Hills)

pipestem wood: ash, sumac

pse-wood: ash; pse-htin, green ash (strong wood)

robe-paint tree: cottonwood (Cheyenne idiom)

rustling tree: cottonwood

scabby-leaf tree: red cedar (juniper)

shaggy-leaf: pines

shelter tree: red cedar shrub (juniper)

small twisted trees: red cedar (juniper or hillside cedar growing close to the ground)

snow-moccasin tree: water ash

snow tree: cottonwood

squatting trees: mountain juniper (hollow evergreens growing on the high hillsides)

sticky wood: box elder (also called tree with ants, sweet juice; the knots are used for bowls)

sunpole tree: cottonwood

trembling tree: cottonwood, poplar

tree with old-wood smell: ash

weapon-wood: ash (used for bows); also the variety of woods used for making arrows

white wood: elm, the white elm; the slippery elm

yellow-wood: sumac

GRASSES

bunch grass: buffalo grass, sedge grass, mesquite grass

ceremonial grass: sweetgrass, sage (wormwood); fragrant grasses clubgrass: cattail

curly grass: buffalo grass (stubs-big-toe-against-grass-clumps-and-stumbles)

drumbeater stalk: cattail

everlasting grass: sage

flat grass: blue grass

grasses children use in their play: slough grass (boys); rush grass (girls)

mixed grasses: buffalo grass, Indian grass, sedge, cactus, grama, beard grass, June grass, marsh grass, sage

never ages, never dies: sweetgrass (never withers)

prickly-leaf: cactus

quill grass: porcupine grass (also called spear grass, stab grass)

red grass: beard grass; blue-stem; Indian grass

red-stems, red-stemmed grass: Indian grass (grass-that-buffalo-never-eat)

sharp grass: slough grass, reeds, rush

short grass: plains grasses contrasted to tall prairie grasses

sinew-grass: wire grass (twisting-into-thread grass); rush grass (large stems for use as sinew)

smoke-leaves: kinnikinnick (mixture); whatever bark and leaves are smoked—red osier dogwood, red willow bark, red sumac leaves, bearberry, pulverized calamus root—usually with tobacco added

smoky grass: sage

stiff grass, suds grass: yucca, soapweed

stub-your-toe grass: buffalo grass

sweet-smelling grass: sage, sweetgrass, mint

thorny grass: spiny, brambly grass

water-grasses: marsh (tough); calamus (mild)

yellow grass: summer grass (sun-burned grass of the plain)

BLOOMS (Flowers)

bright flower on prickly stalk: shrub cinquefoil

ever-flowering stick: stems, branches

that bloom year-round; plants that flourish in a warm climate, in the south

flower that brightens quills
to resemble summer
sky: blue-flowered
spiderwort; also provides
a blue paint
life pours out of cut
stem: gumbo lily
night-blooming
stems: evening
primrose, rain lily (this
prairie lily blooms at
night only)

pods off a reliable
stem: rosehip, wild
primrose
tall, yellow hollow-stem
flower: sunflower
white flower: white-
flowered beardtongue
white-stars: gumbo lily
(butte primrose)

BERRIES (Fruits)

berry: chokecherry
berry stones: plum seeds
(large seeds used in a
game)
berrywood: chokecherry
wood
big berry: plum
fat-moon
berry: Juneberry, early
berry, serviceberry
pte-berry, red and tart
berry: buffalo-berry,
rabbit nose, stinkwood
(smoke unpleasant)

small berry: chokecherry,
sandberry (ground
cherry)
stems of saskatoon: June
berry, serviceberry
sweet berry: plum
tart berry: chokecherry,
buffalo-berry
ten-seed berry: Juneberry,
serviceberry
thirst-relieving
berry: grape,
strawberry, black
raspberry

ROOTS (as cures, as food)

black root: narrow-leaf
purple coneflower with
long slender black root;
called snakeroot in some
localities (used for the
relief of aches in general;

especially in a concoction
for bellyaches, and chewed
or used in powdered form
for distress related to the
mouth—including teeth,
throat, swellings)

borage, to quicken
   life: borage family, red-
   root, hairy gromwell,
   mertensia (used to relieve
   itching, swelling, measles,
   smallpox)
fat root with yellow
   skin: yucca, soapweed
   (used for childbirth,
   stomach disorders; also
   for hair and skin care)
healing roots: all roots (as
   the life source of the
   plant) possess healing
   power; among those
   commonly in use:
   coneflower, milkweed,
   locoweed, ragweed,
   soapweed, dock, mint,
   broomweed, bird's-root,
   sages, meadow rue,
   beardtongue, alum,
   fleabane, bush morning-
   glory, hairy puccoon,
   calamus
heyoka-root: prairie
   mallow, red false mallow
little ears that attach to
   wood: pore fungus,
   mushroom
prairie root, the
   root: prairie turnip
   (used as food and
   appetizer)
ripe, bulbous root: prairie
   turnip (seedpods mature
   in June)
roots helpful in
   childbirth: soapweed,
   yucca, ragweed,
   wormwood (*Artemisia*

canadensis) for difficulty
   in delivering child; dock
   (afterbirth), tender
   milkweed, red baneberry
   (used to hurry the flow
   of milk)
root to relieve
   thirst: purple cone plant
root to relieve
   weariness: calamus,
   sweet flag
root that scents breath and
   scares off invisible
   tricksters: calamus,
   sweet flag
sinkpe-root: calamus
   (eaten by muskrats)
swamp root: calamus,
   sweet flag (used
   medicinally,
   psychosomatically)
sweet root scalded in greasy
   water: red baneberry
   (used to hurry the flow
   of mother's milk)
tastes-bitter root: calamus
   (*Acorus calamus*), sweet
   flag (chewed or rubbed
   on skin for any
   discomfort)
tastes-dry root: alum root
   (pulverized for use on
   sores, swellings)
white-stalk: gromwell
   (*Lithospermum ruderale*;
   used for birth control)
young man's
   food: artichoke
   (bachelor's food)

Glossary of Lakotah Words

Meaning and pronunciation of Lakotah words used in
Hanta Yo
(Prepared by Chunksa Yuha with James E. Ricketson)

To FACILITATE pronunciation of the Dakotah/Lakotah words, the sounds are indicated as nearly as possible by phonetic respellings in parentheses in each entry.

In general the vowels in Dakotah/Lakotah have their continental values—that is, roughly: 'a' as in English *far* or *arm*, 'e' as in *obey* or *bet*, 'i' as in *machine* or *pit*, 'o' as in *hope*, 'u' as in *rule* or *put*.

When the vowels 'a,' 'i,' 'o,' and 'u' are followed by 'n' in the same syllable, the 'n' is not sounded but the vowel is nasalized—that is, pronounced through the nose (like the nasal vowels in French). The nasal 'o' is pronounced like the nasal 'u.' In the phonetic respelling this nasalization is indicated by ñ (nasal 'a' is shown as ahñ or uñ, nasal 'i' as eeñ or iñ, nasal 'o' and 'u' as ooñ).

An obscure vowel sound may be heard in the middle of certain combinations of consonants beginning a syllable. This is indicated by an apostrophe in the respelling—e.g., Mniśa (m'nee-SHAH).

The consonants 'b,' 'd,' 'h,' 'k', 'l,' 'm,' 'n' (before a vowel), 'p,' 's,' 't,' 'w,' 'y,' and 'z' have approximately the same sounds as in English. The letter 'g' is always hard, as in English *go*.

The letter 'c' is pronounced like English *ch*. The character 'ś' represents the sound of English *sh*; and 'ż' represents a *zh* sound, like the *s* in plea*s*ure.

The character 'ḣ' represents a voiceless guttural "throat-clearing" sound like German or Scottish *ch*; this is shown as kh in the phonetic respelling. The character 'g'

1093

represents a "gargling" voiced guttural sound, approximately like 'ḣ' but with the vocal cords vibrating, shown as gh in the respelling.

The character 'c̣' indicates an emphatic or explosive *ch* sound, formed by pronouncing the *ch* with a strong pressure of the organs, followed by a sudden expulsion of the breath. The character 'k' indicates an emphatic "clicking" sound with approximately the same relationship to the sound of *k* as 'c̣' has to *ch*; the letter 'q' represents a similar but somewhat softer sound. The character 'p' likewise indicates an explosive *p* sound; and 't' indicates an explosive *t* sound. These emphatic sounds are indicated by a dot after the consonant in the respelling—e.g., wakiċun (wah-KEE-ch•ooñ); Wanapin (wah-NAH-p•eeñ).

The suffix '-win' (a contraction of 'winyan,' woman) makes a word or phrase feminine—e.g., Napewaśtewin, "good-hands *woman*." The suffix '-pi' makes a word or phrase plural—Olepi, "*they* seek him."

The prefix 'o-' indicates the chief or principal example of anything—Odakotah, "the real Dakotah," the parent tribe; otancan, "the most."

Absa (ahb-SAH) *contraction of* Absaroka, *the name of the* Crow tribe *in their own language*

ah-ah (ah-ah) *child's term for* sh! listen

Ahbleza (ah-BLAY-zah) observer, *literally perceives*

ahboo (AH-boo) *child's term for* sleep

ahpe (ah-PAY) wait

ahte (ah-TAY) father

a-i-i-i (AH-ee-ee-ee) *an expression of anxiety*

ake iyayapi (ah-KAY ee-YAH-yah-pee) again they go

akicita (ah-KEE-chee-tah) "clubmen," watchmen for the hunts, camps, and traveling bands; police

akita mani yo (ah-KEE-tah MAH-nee yo) observe everything as you walk

amonmonla (ah-MOOÑ-mooñ-lah) *child's word for* doll

anhe (ahñ-HAY) *exclamation of self-satisfaction*

Anpagliwin (ahñ-PAH-GLEE-weeñ) returns-at-dawn woman

anpetuwi (ahñ-PAY-too-wee) the sun, *literally* day-sun

blotahunka (blo-TAH-hooñ-KAH) advisers to a large war party

bo-ton-ton (bo-TOOÑ-tooñ) confusion

Cankuna (chuñ-KOO-nah) little path

cannakpa (chuñ-NAH-k'pah) a mushroom growing on trees, *literally* tree-ears

Canoni (chuñ-OH-nee) wanderers-in-the-woods, *certain Dakotah families who eventually come onto the plain*

canoźake (chuñ-OH-zhah-kay) fork in a tree

canpahmiyan (chuñ-PAH-h'mee-YAHÑ) wagon, *literally* rolling-wood

canpaza (chuñ-PAH-zah) wood pointing toward the sky, *ancient term for* tree

Cante Ṭinza (chuñ-TAY-T·EEÑ-zah) brave heart, *used as name of a warrior society*

canumpa (chuñ-OOM-pah) pipe

canumpa o'ke (chuñ-OOM-pah o'-K·AY) pipe-dig, pipestone quarry (Pipestone, Minnesota)

capa (cha-PAH) beaver, *contraction of* canyapaniwan, *literally* swims-stick-in-mouth

Catka (chah-T'KAH) left hand

catkuta (chah-T'KOO-tah) seat of honor

catkuta iyaya yo (chah-T'KOO-tah ee-YAH-yah yo) go to the back, the place of honor

ce (chay) penis

ceazin (chay-AH-zeeñ) oral copulation

cekpa (chay-K'PAH) navel, umbilical cord; a twin

Cetan (chay-TAHÑ) hawk, small falcon

ceźi (chay-ZHEE) tongue

ceźin (chay-ZHEEÑ) erect penis

Cicila (chee-CHEE-lah) *child's term for* a small bug

cin (cheeñ) desire, want

cinye (cheeñ-YAY) *man's term for* older brother

cokata hiyupo (cho-KAH-tah hee-YOO-po) come to the center

Cuwe (choo-WAY) *woman's term for* older sister

Dakotah (dah-KO-tah) the allied ones, *true name of the* Sioux tribe ece (ay-CHAY) *connotes uncertainty*

e-i-i-i (AY-ee-ee-ee) *connotes regret*

Eyanpaha (ah-YAHÑ-pah-hah) camp crier, a herald

Gnuśka (G'NOO-shkah) *contraction of* gnugnuśka, grasshopper

Hahatonwan (khah-khah-TOOÑ-wahñ) Ojibwa (Chippewa) tribe

hai (hah-EEE) *startled sound*

hakamya upo (hah-KAHM-yah oo-PO) come, follow closely

hanhepi wakan (hahñ-HAY-pee wah-KAHÑ) mysterious night, aurora borealis

hankaśi (hahñ-KAH-shee) *man's term for* sister-in-law

hanpa ahpe (hanñ-PAH ah-PAY) strike the moccasin, a game

hanta yo (hahñ-TAH-yo) clear the way

Hapstin (hap-P'STEEN) *name for a third daughter*

hasapa (hah-SAH-pah) black-skin

hau (hah-OO) I am attentive

haun-nn (hah-OOÑ-n-n) *cry of a dying man*

hecitu yelo, *or* welo (hay-CHEE-too yay-LO, way-LO) that is true

Hehaka (hay-KHAH-kah) branched-horn, elk

Hehakapa (hay-KHAH-kah-PAH) elk's head

Hehilogeca (hay-KHLO-ghay-chah) hollow horn

hekinskayapi (hay-KIÑ-skah-yah-pee) bighorn sheep

hesapa (khay-sah-PAH) black mountain, black hills

Hewanźi (hay-WAHÑ-zhee) one-horn

Heyatawin (khay-YAH-tah-weeñ) woman-on-the-ridge

heyoka (hay-YO-kah) clown, a contrary

Hinhan (heeñ-HAHÑ) owl, *contraction of* hinhanska, white owl or young owl

hinu, hinu (hee-NOO, hee-NOO) *woman's term of astonishment*

Hinyete (hiñ-YEH-tay) shoulder

Hinziwin (hiñ-ZEE-weeñ) yellow-hair woman

hiye aheye hibu (hee-YAY-ah-HAY-yay hee-BOO) a returning visitor suddenly appears

hiye haya (hee-YAY hah-YAH) *vocables*

hiye-hey-i-i (hee-YAY-hay-EE-EE) *meaningful vocable*

1096

hiye pila maya (hee-YAY-pee-LAH-mah-yah) *ceremonial thanks*

hiyupo (hee-YOO-po) come forward (plural)

hiyu wo (hee-YOO wo) come forward (singular)

ĥmunġa (KH'MOOÑ-ghah) a mystery to be dreaded

ho (ho) *expression of readiness*

hoĥ (hokh) *expression of wonder, used by men only*

Hohe (ho-HAY) Assiniboine tribe

ho iyaya yo (ho ee-YAH-yah yo) ready forward!

Hoka (kho-KAH) badger

hoye (ho-YAY) *expression of assent, agreement*

huhukaĥniġapi (hoo-hoo-KAH-kh'nee-ghah-pee) voting stick

Huhupiye (hoo-hoo-PEE-yay) bone-setter

hu iĥpeya wicayapo (hoo ee-KH'PAY-yah wee-CHAH-yah-po) *an expression used by warriors calling for total defeat of an enemy, with the implication that the enemy will be forced to submit to sodomy*

huka (hu-KAH) I am not afraid

huka hey (hu-KAH hay) *war cry, obscene term for attack*

hunhunhe (hooñ-hooñ-HAY) *man's expression of sorrow, astonishment, or apprehension*

hunhunhe panġeca (hooñ-hooñ-HAY pahñ-GHAY-chah) outstanding performance

hunka (hooñ-KAH) relative by choice

hunkaġapi (hooñ-KAH-GHAH-pee) *contraction of* hunkakaġapi, previously made a relative

hunkapi (hooñ-KAH-pee) everyone's relative (without need of ceremony)

hunkayapi (hooñ-KAH-yah-pee) everyone's relative (with ceremony)

hunku (hooñ-KOO) someone else's mother (blood relative)

hunumpa (hoo-NOOM-pah) biped, *ancient term for* grizzly bear

Huśte (hoo-SHTAY) lame

ĥuya (khoo-YAH) winged, bird

Icabu (ee-CHAH-boo) drum-beater

Icamani (ee-CHAH-mah-nee) walks alongside

icamani iyapi (ee-CHAH-mah-nee ee-YAH-pee) they travel

ie wakan lake (ee-AY wah-KAHÑ lah-KAY) precocious

1097

ihambleiçiyapi (ee-HAHM-blay-ee-ch•ee-YAH-pee) *contracted to* ihamblecya, vision-quest, *literally* they go beyond

Ihanktonwan (ee-HAHÑ-k'tooñ-WAHÑ) Yankton tribe of the Dakotah

iho (ee-HO) *term to get attention*

Ihoka (ee-KHO-kah) badger, *used as name for a warrior society*

ihomniya (ee-HO-m'nee-YAH) circulating

iktomi (ee-KTO-mee) spider, trickster (legendary practical jokester)

Iku (ee-KOO) chin

ikusan (ee-KOO-sahñ) mink, *literally* yellowish white chin

ina (ee-NAH) mother

inahma śkatapi (ee-nah-KH'MAH shkah-TAH-pee) hide-and-seek

inipi (ee-NEE-pee) sweat-lodge ceremony, renewing ceremony

initi (ee-NEE-tee) sweat lodge, steam bath

inyan (eeñ-YAHÑ) pebble

Isanyati (ee-SAHÑ-yah-tee) Santee tribe, parent-stock of the Dakotah

Iśna (ee-SHNAH) alone

iśnati (ee-SHNAH-tee) menstruating

iśnatipi (ee-SHNAH-tee-pee) tipi for isolation of women during menstruation

Iśtahota (ee-SHTAH-kho-TAH) grey-eyes

Iśtakpe (ee-SHTAH-k'pay) one-eye-out

iśtima (ee-SHTEE-mah) sleep

itancan (ee-TAHÑ-chuñ) leader of any kind of group

Itazipicola (ee-TAH-zee-pee-CHO-lah) without-bows, Sans Arc subtribe of the Dakotah

iteopta sapa (ee-TAY-oh-p'tah SAH-pah) black-footed ferret, *literally* black stripe across the face

iwicahupi (ee-wee-CHAH-hoo-pee) forced copulation between men

Iya (ee-YAH) camp eater (legendary character)

iyotanyapi (ee-YO-tahñ-yah-pee) honorable

Iyuptala (ee-yoo-P'TAH-lah) together, *used as name of a warrior society*

kakiśniyapi (ka-KEE-shnee-yah-pee) they torment you

Kangi (kahñ-GHEE) raven, *Dakotah name of the* Crow tribe

Kangi Yuha (kahñ-GHEE yoo-HAH) raven-owners, *name of a warrior society* kanta su (kahñ-TAH soo) plumstone

kaonspe (kah-OOÑ-spay) teaching-with-force

Kehala (kay-HAH-lah) small turtle shell

Kipanna (kee-PAHÑ-nah) a little call, *as in calling to a child*

kiwani (kee-WAH-nee) awakening

kiwani owapi (kee-WAH-nee oh-WAH-pee) *literally* awakening of earth, *the Dakotah calendar, calculated from springtime to springtime, popularly called* winter count

Kiyuksa (kee-YOO-k'sah) break-their-own-customs

ku-hu-hu (koo-HOO-HOO) *vocables uttered by children when an elk is brought into camp*

Kuya Wicaśa (koo-YAH wee-CHAH-shah) Lower Brulé, a Sicanġu band, *literally* lower man, *so called from their original location downstream from the other Sicanġu*

Lakotah (lah-KO-tah) *Teton pronunciation of the word* Dakotah, *used especially in reference to the* Teton tribe

Lekśi (leh-k'SHEE) *woman's term for* uncle

Lowansa (lo-WAHÑ-sah) singer

Maḣpiya-luta (mah-KHPEE-yah-loo-TAH) colored cloud

maḣpiyato (mah-KHPEE-yah-TOH) cloud, sky, Arapaho tribe

Mahto (mah-TOH) grizzly bear

Mahtociqala (mah-TOH-CHEE-q-ah-lah) small bear

Mahtola (mah-TOH-lah) bear cub

Mahtowin (mah-TOH-weeñ) bear woman

maka (mah-KAH) earth

maka (mah-KAH) skunk

maka kin le, mítawa ca (mah-KAH keeñ lay, mee-TAH-wah chah) I own the earth

makamnaya (mah-KAH-m'nah-YAH) they go smelling like a skunk

Makatoźanźan (mah-KAH-toh-ZHAHN-ZHAHN) clear blue earth

maśtincala (mah-SHTEEN-chah-lah) little rabbit

micante (mee-CHUÑ-tay) *contraction of* mitacante, my heart

micinkśi (mee-CHEEÑ-k'shee) my son

micunkśi (mee-CHOOÑ-k'shee) my daughter

mihigna (mee-HEEG-nah) my husband

mihunka (mee-HOOÑ-kah) my relative through choice

Minikayawoźupi (mi-NEE-kah-yah-WO-ZHOO-pee) they-plant-alongside-the-water, the Miniconjou band of Dakotah

miniśupekaźo (mi-NEE-shoo-PAY-kah-zho) loosening of the bowels, diarrhea

Miniwatu (mi-nee-WAH-too) legendary water-creature

misun (mee-SOOÑ) *man's term for* younger brother

mitakoźa (mee-TAH-ko-zhah) my grandson, my grandchildren

mitaoyate (mee-TAH-oh-yah-tay) my relatives

mitaśunke (mee-TAH-shooñ-kay) my horse

mitawaśicun he omakiyake (mee-TAH-wah-SHEE-chooñ hay oh-mah-KEE-yah-kay) my familiar-voice (messenger) tells me so

mitawicu (mee-TAH-wee-choo) I take this woman for wife

mitawin (mee-TAH-weeñ) my woman, wife

Miwatani (mee-WAH-tah-nee) Mandan tribe; *also a Dakotah fraternal society*

Miyaca (mee-YAH-chah) prairie wolf, coyote

Mnikooźu (m'nee-KOO-zhoo) *contraction of* Minikayawoźupi, the Miniconjou band

Mniśa (m'nee-SHAH) *contraction of* minisala, red water

naġi napeyapi (nah-GHEE nah-PAY-yah-pee) psychic shock, *literally* they make the spirit flee

nakpa cikcika (nah-K'PAH chee-k'chee-kah) very small ears (*of an animal*)

Napewaśtewin (nah-PAY-wah-SHTAY-weeñ) good-hands woman

nitaśunke (nee-TAH-shooñ-kay) your horse

niteiyapehe (nee-TAY-ee-YAH-pay-hay) apron used in sungazing dance

nitohompi (nee-TOH-home-pee) underskirt

Nuġe (NOO-ghay) ear

oglala (oh-GLAH-lah) throwing small particles into something of one's own

1100

oglala, śan oglala (oh-GLAH-lah, shuñ oh-GLAH-lah) she throws dust into her vagina

Oglalaḣca (oh-GLAH-lah-kh'chah) true Oglala, a Lakotah band

Ogle (oh-GLAY) shirt

ogleśa (oh-GLAY-sha) red shirt

Okandada (oh-KAHÑ-dah-dah) asking for a place

o'ko wayelo (O'K-O wah-yay-LO) I talk nonsense

Olepi (oh-LAY-pee) they seek him

onśimaya (OOÑ-shee-mah-yah) I command recognition (*esoteric word*)

onze nihupi kte lo (ooñ-ZAY nee-HOO-pee K'TAY lo) they will use your anus, unnatural copulation

onze wicahupo (ooñ-ZAY wee-CHAH-hoo-po) already violated, sodomy

onze wicawahu (ooñ-ZAY wee-CHAH-wah-hoo) sodomy

Ooweśica (oh-oh-WAY-shee-CHAH) bad wound

Ośota (oh-SHO-tah) smoky

otancan (oh-TAHÑ-chuñ) the principal leader, the most

owanyake waśte (oh-WAHÑ-yah-kay wah-SHTAY) good-looking, handsome

oyate nimkte wacin yelo (oh-YAH-tay nim-K'TAY wah-CHEEÑ yay-lo) I want the people to live (spiritually)

Oyatenumpa (oh-YAH-tay-noom-PAH) two-circle people, Omaha tribe

Oyateyamni (oh-YAH-tay-yah-M'NEE) three-circle people, Ponca tribe

oźu (oh-ZHOO) to plant or put in the ground

Padani (pah-DAH-nee) *original Santee Dakotah form of* Palani

Paḣaḣa (pah-KHAH-KHAH) curly-hair

pahamni (pah-HAH-m'nee) hill and spring water near a ridge

pahasapa (pah-HAH-sah-PAH) black hills, the hills

Palani (pah-LAH-nee) *Lakotah name for the* Arikara (Ree) tribe

pangeca (PAHÑ-ghay-chah) *colloquial term for* person with unusual talents

pangiciya wo (pahñ-GHEE-ch•ee-yah wo) *colloquial expression for* live it up

Pani (pah-NEE) *Dakotah name for the* Pawnee tribe

Pasu (pah-SOO) nose

pasu śkopa (pah-SOO shko-PAH) curved-down nose, prairie curlew

paza (pah-ZAH) *archaic word for* tree

Peśla (pay-SHLAH) baldhead, *contracted from* peyuślaślapi, pluck out hair

Peta (pay-TAH) fire

Petala (pay-TAH-lah) little fire

peta-o-żan-żan, *or* peti-żan-żan (pay-TAH-oh-ZHAHÑ-ZHAHÑ, pay-TEE-ZHAHÑ-ZHAHÑ) brightens-the-lodge, candle

Peźi (pay-ZHEE) mature grass

peźuta (pay-ZHOO-tah) grass roots; healer

peźuta-wicaśa (pay-ZHOO-tah-wee-CHAH-shah) healer

pila maye (pee-LAH mah-YAY) thank you

pinspinza (peeñs-peeñ-ZAH) prairie dog

piśko (pi-SHKO) the night hawk

Po (p.o) fog

poġeĥli (po-GHAY-khlee) snotty-nose, *child's interpretation of the call of the red-winged blackbird*

popotka (po-PO-t'kah) *child's term for a* little owl

Psa (p'sah) *Dakotah pronunciation of* Absa, *name of the* Crow tribe

psatoka (P'SAH-toh-KAH) Crow tribe as enemy

pseĥtin (p'say-KH'TEEÑ) showshoe tree, water ash

pta (p'tah) male buffalo, a herd-father

ptaġica (P'TAH-GHEE-chah) any animal with a hump, buffalo

ptasapa (P'TAH-sah-PAH) black male buffalo

pta-tanka wapahaun okolakiciyapi (P'TAH-tahñ-KAH wah-PAH-hah-ooñ oh-KO-lah-kee-CH.EE-yah-pee) wearers of the buffalo-bull headdress, a governing society of headmen

pte (p'tay) buffalo cow; *also* herd

ptepazo, *or* pte woyaka (P'TAY-pah–ZO, P'TAY wo-YAH-kah) points-in-direction-of-the-herd, a large wingless grasshopper

ptesan (P'TAY-sahñ) yellowish white buffalo cow

Ptesanwin (P'TAY-sahñ-weeñ) white (yellowish white) buffalo-cow woman (messenger who brought the Dakotah their moral code)

1102

ptewinkte (P'TAY weeñ-K'TAY) hermaphrodite buffalo

putehin (poo-TAY-heeñ) hair-on-upper-lip, rabbit *or* hare

Śahiela (shah-HEE-ay-lah) they-come-red, Cheyenne tribe

Śaiela (shah-EE-ay-lah) they-talk-red, Cheyenne language

śakehanska (śha-KAY-hahñ-SKAH) long-claws, the grizzly bear

śan (shahñ) vagina

śanke (shahñ-KAY) one's father's other wife

śica (shee-CHAH) distasteful, tricky, mischievous

Sicanġu (see-CHUÑ-ghoo) burnt thigh, the Brulé subtribe of the Lakotah

śice (shee-CHAY) a woman's brother-in-law

Śinagleglega (shee-NAH-glay-glay-ghah) striped-robe people, the Navaho

Śinaska (shee-NAH-skah) white-robe

sinkpe (siñ-K'PAY) muskrat

Sinte (siñ-TAY) tail

Sintehla Wicaśa (siñ-TAY-khlah wee-CHAH-shah) rattle-tail (rattlesnake) man, Comanche tribe

Sioux (soo) *French*

contraction of the Ojibwa word Naduesiu, *meaning* little snake *or* enemy, *used as a name for the* Dakotah

Śiyo (shee-YO) sharptail grouse, a Lakotah band

śkan, taku
śkanśkan (SHKAHÑ, tah-KOO SHKAHÑ–SHKAHÑ) something in movement, spiritual vitality

Sluka (sloo-KAH) foreskin-pushed-back, adult penis

Slukila (sloo-KEE-lah) child's penis

Suhtai *Cheyenne term meaning* on the ridge

śuktanka (shook-TAHÑ-kah) horse

śungcincala (shuñg-CHEEÑ-chah-lah) foal

śungila (shooñ-GHEE-lah) fox

śungwiyela (shooñg-WEE-yay-lah) mare, mother of foal

Śunihanble (shooñ-EE-hahñ-blay) fox dreamer

śunka-tanka (shooñ-KAH-tahñ-KAH) big-dog, horse

śunka-wakan (shooñ-KAH-wah-KAHÑ) mysterious-dog, horse

Śunktanka (shooñk–TAHN–kah) horse

susweca (soo-SWAY-chah) dragonfly

1103

Tabloka (tah-BLO-kah) bull moose, male grizzly, buffalo bull, male mountain goat (*the word* ta *originally specified animals with a hump— e.g., moose, mountain goat, buffalo, grizzly— later becoming a generic term for all ruminating animals;* bloka *signifies* bull)

tacanśina (tah-CHUÑ-shee-nah) corpse-carrier, the Big Dipper

tacante canku (tah-CHUÑ-tay chuñ-KOO) heart-shaped path, the spiritual hoop encircling the Black Hills

Tacincala (tah-CHEEÑ-chah-lah) fawn

tagoźa (tah-GHO-zhah) grandchild

tahanśi (tah-HAHÑ-shee) *man's term for* cousin

tahca (tah-KH'CHA) deer

tahin (tah-HEEÑ) his hair

takpe (tah-K'PAY) attack, *meaning* kill

taku śkan *see* śkan, taku śkanśkan

Tanaźin (tah-NAH-zheeñ) *contraction of* tatanka naźin, standing bull

tanka (tahñ-KAH) *woman's term for* younger sister

tanka (TAHÑ-kah) big

tankala (TAHÑ-kah-lah) little-big, *a derogatory term meaning* too big for one's boots

tanke (tahñ-KAY) *man's term for* older sister

Taśa (tah-SHAH) *contraction* of tatanka śa, red buffalo

tasiha unpi (tah-SEE-hah OON—pee) deer-bone game (played with four ankle bones of deer or pronghorn)

Taśunkekokipapi (tah-SHOOÑ-kay-ko-kee-PAH-pee) they-fear-his-horse (*misinterpreted as* owner-afraid-of-his-horse)

ta ta iciya wo (t.ah t.ah ee-CH.EE-yah wo) make-yourself-as-if-dead, relax

tatanka (tah-TAHÑ-kah) big-hump creature— moose (*wood and lakes*), mountain goat (*high hills*), grizzly bear *and* buffalo (*plains*); *commonly signifies* buffalo bull; *used as a name for the headmen's lodge*

Tatanka Naźin (tah-TAHÑ-kah nah-ZHEEÑ) standing bull

Tatekohomni (tah-TAY-kah-HO-m'nee) whirlwind

Tatewin (tah-TAY-weeñ) wind-woman, weather forecaster

Tatezi (tah-TAY-zee) yellow wind

tatokala (tah-TOH-kah-lah) pronghorn, antelope

tawaiciyapi (tah-WAH-ee-ch•ee-yah-pee) they belong to themselves, free of other men

tawamiciya (tah-WAH-mee-ch•ee-yah) to belong to one's self, free of other men

tawicu (tah-WEE-choo) wife

Tawitko (tah-WEE-t'koh) a foolish buffalo

tawiyela (tah-WEE-yay-lah) doe, female deer

Tayaźo (tah-YAH-zho) flute player

tażuśka (tah-ZHOO-shkah) short-necks, ants

teciħila (tay-CHEE-khee-lah) I love you

teya (tay-YAH) *term of relationship between two wives of one husband*

Tezi (tay-ZEE) belly

tiblo (tee-BLO) *woman's term for* older brother; *also the call of the killdeer*

tikaħpa (tee-KAH-kh'pah) tipi-down, strike camp

tinmaśtinca (teeñ-MAH-shteeñ-chah) white-tail rabbit found on the plains (hare)

tipi (tee-pee) a dwelling place, moveable lodge

tipsila (TEE-p'see-lah) turnip

Tiśayaota (tee-SHAH-yah-OH-tah) many red-top lodges, Red Top band of the Brulé subtribe

Titonwan (tee-TOOÑ-wahñ) they-roam-the-plains, Titon/Teton bands of the Lakotah

Tiyataonwan (tee-YAH-tah-ooñ–wahñ) they-stay-in-their-camp, *original name of the* Oglala

tiyośpaye (tee-YO-shpah-yay) big family, blood and affinal relatives

toka (toh-KAH) enemy

tokaħca (toh-KAH-kh'chah) real enemy

tokahe (toh-KAH-hay) the first

Tokala (toh-KAH-lah) kit fox, *name of a warrior lodge*

tokata (toh-KAH-tah) forward, *meaning* in the future

tokeca (toh-KAY-chah) different

Tonweya (tooñ-WAY-yah) scout

tunkan (tooñ-KAHÑ) stone

Tunkaśila (tooñ-KAH-shee-lah) grandfather

tuwe miye he (too-WAY mee-YAY hay) Who am I?

Unci (ooñ–CHEE) grandmother

uncisicala (ooñ-CHEE-shee-chah-lah) little grandmother; *also* the crow

unkce (ooñ-K'CHAY) excrement

unpongapi kilo (ooñ-POOÑ-ghah-pee kee-lo) an extremely joyful surprise

usi maya ye (OO-SHEE MAH-yah yay) I command attention

Wacape (wah-CHAH-pay) stabber

Waglula (wah-GLOO-lah) worm

Wagmiza (wahg-MEE-zah) maize

wahanksica (wah-KHAHÑ-k'see-chah) arrogant and overpowering; grizzly bear

Wahcawin (wah-KH'CHAH-weeñ) flower woman

wahinhan (WAH-heeñ-hahñ) snowing

Wahin-numpa (wah-HEEÑ–noom-pah) two-arrows

wahn,
wan (wahñ) *man's term of surprise*

Wahosi (wah-HO-shee) messenger

wahpani iciya wo (wah-KH'PAH-nee ee-CH•EE-yah wo) give away everything

wahupa (wah-HOO-pah) realization of the ultimate, enlightenment

wahupa (wah-KHOO-pah) all birds

wakan (wah-KAHÑ) mystery, an unknown

wakanhca (wah-KAHÑ-kh'chah) a true seer, a philosopher

wakanka (wah-KAHÑ-kah) contraction of wankanyanka, one-who-sits-above-all, wife

wakantanka (wah-KAHÑ-tahñ-kah) any big mystery, undiscovered law

wakanya hibu yelo (wah-KAHÑ-yah hee-BOO yay-LO) in a mysterious manner I come

wakicun, wakicunsa (wah-KEE-ch•ooñ, wah-KEE-ch•ooñ-sah) decider, deciders

wakinyan (wah-KEEÑ-yahñ) *contraction of* wakankinyan, mysterious flight, lightning

wakinyan hoton (wah-KEEÑ-yahñ ho-tooñ) lightning-gives-birth-to-sound, thunder

wambli (wahm-BLEE) eagle, a wingflapper

wambli gleska (wahm-BLEE glay-shkah) spotted eagle, immature golden eagle

Wambli Okiye (wahm-BLEE oh-KEE-yay) eagle-helps-him

Wanaǧi (wah-NAH-ghee) spiritual self

wanaǧi yuha (wah-NAH-ghee yoo-HAH) spirit-owner

Wanapin (wah-NAH-p·eeñ) fur neckpiece

wanasa (wah-NAH-sah) make meat

wanasapi (wah-NAH-sah-pee) buffalo hunt, surround

wanisugna (wah-NEE-soo-gnah) *contraction of* owani wasu ognaka, life-within-the-seed *or* seed-within-the-shell, creative-force

wankanl yanka (wahñ-KAHÑL yahñ-KAH) to reckon as a mystery, wife

wanyaka, tuwena icunśni (wahñ-YAH-kah, too-WAY-nah ee-CHOON-shnee) look, no one acts in this manner

waonspekiye (wah-OOÑ-spay-KEE-yay) teaching with patience

Wapaśa (WAH-pah-shah) *contraction of* wapaha śa un, wears-the-red-headdress, historical leader of the Dakotah

wapiya (wah-PEE-yah) a seer, sacred man, healer

waśicun (wah-SHEE-chooñ) *contraction of* wahośi icun, messenger-delivers-a-message to an individual, whiteman *(originally referring to the French clergy)*

wasna (wah-SNAH) pemmican

waśte, waśteśte (wah-SHTAY, wah-SHTAY-SHTAY) good, very good

Wasu (wah-SOO) snow-seeds, hail

Wasuhula (wah-soo-hoo-lah) Iroquois tribe

waunca (wah-OOÑ-chah) imitator

Waźaźa (wah-ZHAH-ZHAH) Osage tribe (originally Lakotah)

waziya (wah-ZEE-yah) *contraction of* waziyata, toward-snow-and-pine-trees, north; the north wind; legendary white giant

weh weh (way way) *sound used by women for calling dogs*

wicaĥca (wee-CHAH-kh'chah) the true husband

wicaśa (wee-CHAH-shah) man

wicaśa iyotanyapi (wee-CHAH-shah ee-yo-TAHÑ-yah-pee) man of honor

wicaśa okinihan (wee-CHAH-shah oh-KEE-nee-hahñ) an honorable and respected individual

wicaśaśni (wee-CHAH-shah-shnee) not man, deceitful

Wiciska (wee-CHEE-skah) *name of a fraternity, whose members use white markings*

Wiciyela (wee-CHEE-yay-lah) Yankton tribe of the Dakotah

Winkte (weeñ-K'TAY) *contraction of* winyanktelica, wants-to-be-woman, hermaphrodite

Winu (wee-NOO) captive woman

Wipatawin (wee-PAH-TAH-weeñ) quill-worker woman

wiśahibu (wee-SHAH-HEE-boo) red-sun coming, *song of the sharptail grouse*

Witanhantahipi (wee-TAHN-HAHÑ-tah-HEE-pee) they-come-from-the-place-of-sunrise, *Santee Dakotah name for the* Teton

Witantanpi (wee-TAHÑ-TAHÑ-pee) false pride, *Santee Dakotah name for the* Teton

Witapaha (WEE-tah-PAH-tah) island butte, *Dakotah name for the* Kiowa tribe

wiwanyag wacipi (wee-WAHÑ-yahg wah-CHEE-pee) sungazing, the sundance

Wiyaka (WEE-yah-kah) eagle's tail feather

Wiyanna (wee-YAHÑ-nah) girl child

wiyokeze paha (wee-YO-kay-zay PAH-hah) Bijou Hills (near Pierre, South Dakota), *so called from stones found here which are used to make zigzag lines on arrows*

Wiyukcan Mani (wee-yoo-K'CHUÑ–mah–NEE) ponders-as-she-walks

wocinpi (wo-CHEEÑ-pee) starve, beg

woksapa (wo-K'SAH-pah) wisdom

Wośkate (wo-SHKAH-tay) tribal fair; game man

wotawe (wo-TAH-way) whatever token is relied upon in war

Woze (wo-ZAY) take something (such as meat) out-of-boiling-water

yugmi oyucayuspapi na, cankpe un poge nawicaźuźu po (yoog-mee oh-YOO-chah-yoo-spah-pee nah, chuñ-K'PAY ooñ po-ghay nah-WEE-chah-zhoo-zhoo po) attack-upset-smash-smash-nose, kick-and-swing game

yuwakan (yoo-WAH-kahñ) to set apart, consecrate

Yuza (yoo-ZAH) to take hold of, catch, hold; to take a wife

Zitkala (zee-TʼKAH-
  lah) small bird
Źola (ZHO-lah) whistle
zuya (ZOO-YAH) going
  to war

Zuzueca (ZOO-ZOO-ay-
  chah) common striped
  ground snake

BOOKS OF DISTINCTION
by **THEODORE H. WHITE**

__AMERICA IN SEARCH OF ITSELF

(l37-559, $8.95, U.S.A.)
(l37-560, $10.75, Canada)

This is the climax of White's famous series, THE MAKING OF A PRESIDENT. The author illuminates the story of Reagan's election, the explosion of events in Iran and their impact on Carter's election race. White also deals with the last quarter of a century: how television took over the political process, how the Great Inflation came into being and how it came to undermine all American life. Finally, White addresses several demanding questions: What kind of people are we? Who leads us? Where are we now? Where are we going?

__IN SEARCH OF HISTORY

(l30-814, $4.95, U.S.A.)
(l30-815, $6.25, Canada)

This is a book about the people who, making history, have changed your life—and about a great correspondent who listened to their stories for forty years. Now he has woven all those stories into this splendid tale of his own. **"In Search Of History** is the most fascinating and most useful personal memoir of this generation." —*William Safire*

Excellent Fiction by *Joyce Carol Oates*

__A BLOODSMOOR ROMANCE

(A30-825, $3.95, U.S.A.)
(A30-826, $4.95, Canada)

So it begins . . . one beauteous autumn day in 1879, a sinister black balloon swooped from the skies and abducted Miss Deirdre Zinn as her four sisters gaped, mute and terror-struck. For their family nothing was ever the same again . . .

__ANGEL OF LIGHT

(A30-189, $3.95)

In this book, Joyce Carol Oates explores our political heritage and gives us a novel of mounting drama with all the import of Greek tragedy. It is a story of loyalty, betrayal, revenge, and finally, forgiveness. Oates weaves a strand of history throughout—the quest for justice against those in power begins with America's founding—but dominating the novel is the story of this highly placed family whose private lives are played out in a public arena.

__BELLEFLEUR

(A30-732, $4.50)

Travel through a "dark, chaotic, unfathomable pool of time" with Joyce Carol Oates as she explores the Bellefleur curse. Your journey begins one dark and stormy night when Mahalaleel arrives at the 64-room castle and everything begins to happen. Back and forth you pass through six generations of the Bellefleur family, enchanted by a novel "rich, extravagant, varied" filled with "the magic of pure storytelling."
—*Chicago Sun Times*

OUTSTANDING READING
FROM
WARNER BOOKS

__THE EXECUTIONER'S SONG
by Norman Mailer (A36-353, $4.95, U.S.A.)
(A30-646, $5.95, Canada)

The execution is what the public remembers: on January 17, 1977, a firing squad at Utah State Prison put an end to the life of convicted murderer Gary Gilmore. But by then the real story was over—the true tale of violence and fear, jealousy and loss, of a love that was defiant even in death. Winner of the Pulitzer Prize. "The big book no one but Mailer could have dared . . . an absolutely astonishing book."—Joan Didion, *New York Times Book Review.*

To order, use the coupon below. If you prefer to use your own stationery, please include complete title as well as book number and price. Allow 4 weeks for delivery.

WARNER BOOKS
P.O. Box 690
New York, N.Y. 10019

Please send me the books I have checked. I enclose a check or money order (not cash), plus 50¢ per order and 50¢ per copy to cover postage and handling.*

_____ Please send me your free mail order catalog.
(If ordering only the catalog, include a large self-addressed, stamped envelope.)

Name _____

Address _____

City _____

State _____ Zip _____

*N.Y. State and California residents add applicable sales tax.